A Dictionary of Irregular
Russian Verb Forms

A DICTIONARY OF IRREGULAR
RUSSIAN VERB FORMS

D. B. POWERS

John Wiley & Sons, Inc.
New York · London · Sydney · Toronto

Library of Congress Catalog Card Number: 68-31648
SBN 471 69595 5
Printed in the United States of America

PREFACE

Objective. The purpose of this work is to provide both students and translators of Russian with a means of determining the infinitives, and consequently the meanings of Russian verbs, from the irregular finite forms. In a large number of cases, because of vowel insertions or deletions, consonant insertions, and mutations or alternations, which are characteristic of the Russian language, such conjugated forms are rendered unrecognizable as derivatives of their related infinitives. As I know from personal experience, observation in the classroom, and discussion with numerous academic personnel, translators, and students, much time is lost in futile search in standard dictionaries for the infinitive and/or meaning of an irregular finite form.

Included herein are a number of verbs that are not strictly speaking considered irregular and can in many instances be regarded as conforming to a certain pattern of conjugation. When a chance of confusion exists (e.g., in the case of the verbs сгла́дить and сгла́зить in which the first person singular is сгла́жу and the past passive participle is сгла́женный), these verbs have been included. The finite form is given as a separate entry for each of the infinitives to which it is related.

Because this book is designed to facilitate translation of not only modern Russian literature but also the works of early classical Russian authors, many verbs as well as definitions now considered archaic or obsolete are contained in it. Technical usages are also listed to assist the translator of scientific material. Although it is impractical in a dictionary of this kind to incorporate all the definitions and usages found in an unabridged dictionary, such as *The Dictionary of the Russian Language*, published by the Academy of Sciences of the U.S.S.R., an effort has been made to supply definitions that suggest the widest possible range of the verb meanings.

Although this dictionary is designed primarily for the reader and translator, it will prove useful as well to the student engaged in composition. Once acquainted with the format and contents, the user will be able to find the conjugated form of the verb he requires. The native speaker should also find it a useful reference, much as I have found it necessary from time to time to refer to an English dictionary.

Organization. The entry words, which are the irregular finite forms of the Russian verbs, occur as first and second persons singular and

v

occasionally third person plural in present or future tense, as past tense forms (preterites), as imperatives, as past passive, past active, and present passive participles, and as adverbial past and present participles (gerunds). Usually only the masculine singular of the past tense appears as an entry word, followed by the feminine singular, for they are the key to the formation of the neuter and plural forms (e.g., **грести́,** past, **грёб, гребла́,** the neuter and plural forms, of course, being **гребло́** and **гребли́**). When, however, the stress on the past neuter and plural forms differs from that of the feminine past, all four forms are shown. Also, when the mobile vowel disappears in the formation of the feminine past, as in the verb **жечь,** (namely, **жёг, жгла**), the feminine past appears as an entry word, followed by the neuter and plural past forms (namely, **жгла, жгло, жгли**). The entries are presented in strict alphabetical order.

Because this is a dictionary of irregular finite forms of verbs, infinitives have not been listed as entry words in the main body of the work but appear in alphabetical order in the appendix. There, following each infinitive, are its finite forms which appear as entries in the body of the dictionary. Thus the appendix provides not only a concise list of the verbs represented in the work but also a key to the conjugation of the verb in that the finite forms following each infinitive include those from which the remaining parts of the verb may be constructed. This feature should prove to be particularly useful when the infinitive is known and a specific conjugated form of the verb is required. The arrangement of the appendix is discussed further under *Appendix*.

The inclusion of infinitives as main entries in the body of the dictionary with other entries referred to them was considered, but because the verb in its finite form is far more often encountered it was felt that the dictionary in its present form would prove more useful, that is, with finite forms as main entries and the infinitives, which can be found in any standard dictionary, included as entry items only in the appendix.

Reflexive or passive forms have not been used unless the verb appears only or principally in one or the other of these forms, for its conjugation is unaffected by the reflexive suffix.

Similarly, verbs ending in **—овать** or **—евать** are not listed, for their infinitive forms are readily recognized from their conjugated endings, **—ую, —уешь,** etc., for **—овать** verbs, **—юю, —юешь,** etc., for **—евать** verbs (except, of course, after sibilants, in which **—юю** becomes **—ую,** as with **ночева́ть,—ночу́ю** and not **ночю́ю**), the suffixes **—ова** and **—ева** dropping out. The verb **дуть** and its compounds (e.g., **поду́ть**) which conjugate as **ду́ю** and **ду́ешь,** are included to avoid confusion with the **—овать** verbs. Verbs with the **—ну** suffix, that is, the **—нуть** ending, which are of the first conjugation, are not present. When, however, the past tense is formed irregularly, these entries appear.

vi

Verbs ending in —ти, —чь, for example, бере́чь (conjugated forms—берегу́, бережёшь, берегу́т; past, берёг, etc.), течь (conjugated forms—теку́, течёшь, теку́т; past тёк, etc.), грести́ (гребу́, гребёшь; past, грёб, etc.), вести́ (веду́, ведёшь; past, вёл, etc.), везти́ (везу́, везёшь; past, вёз, etc.), and verbs of special conjugations are included for obvious reasons.

It was not considered practicable to have in this dictionary all prefixed forms of verbs in the Russian language. The user should, however, be able to determine the prefixed infinitive by consulting the relevant entry of the basic verb.

Main Entries. The normal procedure has been to regard the irregular first person singular (present or future) form as a main entry and to give full information about the verb (e.g., its infinitives and definitions). When irregularities occur in conjugated forms of the verb other than the first person singular (present or future), those forms appear as entries and are cross-referred to the first person singular main entry (e.g., бережёшь—see берегу́) for the full coverage. (Usually the third person singular and the first, second, and third persons plural do not appear as entries, for these forms are normally determined by the conjugation pattern indicated by the first and second person singular.) When, however, some other form of the verb is the only irregularity in or exception to the usual pattern of conjugation (as in the case of ки́снуть, in which the masculine singular of the past tense may appear as кис and the feminine singular as ки́сла instead of the expected ки́снул, ки́снула), the first form, кис, is treated as a main entry, and the related infinitives and definitions are given.

Further, although most cross references are to entries on the same or adjacent page, some are to relatively distant locations in the book (e.g., when the first person singular сожгу́ of the verb сжечь is a number of pages removed from the masculine past tense сжёг). Then complete information on the verb is given in both locations, in contrast to customary lexicographical practice; that is, each is treated as a main entry.

Order of Items in the Main Entries. The normal order of items in main entries, then, is as follows: if the first person singular of the present or future tense is the main entry word, it is followed by the second person singular, which usually provides the user, who, it is assumed, has an elementary knowledge of Russian grammar, with the key to the conjugation of the verb. When the conjugation does not follow the general rule, the third person plural is entered (e.g., бегу́, бежи́шь, бегу́т, of the infinitive, бежа́ть); or, when necessary, all irregular forms are given, as in the case of the infinitive, дать and its compounds. (See дам ,etc.).

The infinitive in Russian is the next item. If the main entry is in the perfective aspect, the perfective infinitive immediately follows, with the imperfective infinitive appearing second. Conversely, if the main entry word is in the imperfective aspect, the imperfective infinitive follows, with the perfective infinitive appearing second. It should also be noted that the aspect of the infinitive(s) is indicated by the uppercase letter immediately preceding, namely, P. for perfective and I. for imperfective. When there is more than one imperfective or perfective infinitive, the P. or I. precedes only the first of the series (e.g., see **настелю** in text). When the verb takes a special case or preposition in all its meanings, that case or preposition immediately follows the first infinitive. When the verb takes different cases or prepositions for the different meanings, the meanings are given with the proper case or preposition following each meaning. The third and final item in the main entry is the definition.

Definitions. The user should note that all the meanings listed for a main entry may not apply to both perfective and imperfective forms of the verb. When such differences exist, the meanings to which the subsequent listed infinitives apply are indicated numerically in parentheses immediately after the affected infinitive, e.g., P. **посветить** (mean. 2), which appears under the main entry **свечу.** To conserve space homonyms are seldom listed separately.

In phrasing definitions, constructions in English that duplicate insofar as possible the Russian constructions have been given, a practice that often sacrifices grace for the greater grammatical benefit. In addition, some verbs have no precise English equivalent and the result is rather involved and sometimes seemingly awkward definitions. It is felt, however, that the system employed will best assist the user in both translation and composition. Finally, for those verbs that take different cases or prepositions for different meanings, as stated above, those cases or prepositions are supplied here.

It should also be noted that to reduce the chances of error on the part of the user all Russian words are spelled out; endings only are not employed except in the short forms of the past passive participles.

Imperatives. Because the formation of the imperative has always proved a stumbling block for students of Russian, the imperative forms of verbs appearing in this book have been included (1) when these forms are irregular (e.g., for the infinitive **бить;** imperative, **бей**), (2) when they end in a soft sign (e.g., for the infinitive **ограбить;** imperative, **ограбь**), (3) when the imperative cannot be recognized as a derivative of its infinitive (e.g., for the infinitive, **отмести;** imperative, **отмети**), or (4) when a shift in accentuation can cause confusion. With few exceptions, only the singular form of the imperative is given, for the plural is formed by adding —те to the singular or, in the case of a reflexive verb, by dropping the reflexive ending from the singular form and adding —тесь (e.g., **смейся, смейтесь**).

Participles. Past passive particles are generally listed under the masculine long form, separated by a semicolon from the four short forms in the following manner: for the infinitive, **отвинти́ть: отви́нченный, отви́нчсн, —а, —о, —ы,** which indicates that the stress remains on the second syllable throughout; i.e., the short forms are **отви́нчен, отви́нчена, отви́нчено, отви́нчены.** If the stress shifts, as in the case of the verb **отли́ть,** e.g., **отли́тый; отли́т, —а́, —о, —ы,** the absence of a stress mark over the **—о** and **—ы** indicates that the stress on the forms bearing these endings shifts back to the second syllable, the short forms being **отли́т, отлита́, отли́то, отли́ты.** If the stress remains on the neuter and plural endings, these endings will carry a stress mark. Only the masculine singular of the long form past passive participle is given, for it declines in number and gender as an adjective. The same is true of past active participles as well as of present passive participles in the few cases in which the latter are shown. Irregularities in the formation of present passive participles are rare.

Adverbial past participles are shown only when they are not formed in the customary manner from the masculine singular of the past tense (e.g., for the verb **понести́**), when the modern form of the adverbial past participle appears as **понеся́** and not **понёсши,** and for the verb **стере́ть** when the adverbial past participle appears as **стерёв** instead of **стёрши.**

Appendix. As previously mentioned, all infinitives whose finite forms appear in the main body of the dictionary are listed in the appendix in alphabetical order. (The infinitives appear also in the main body of the dictionary as one of the items under the related main entries, as previously stated in the paragraph entitled, *order of items in main entries.*) Immediately following each infinitive are its finite main entry forms, succeeded by such other forms appearing in the body of the work that will provide a key to the conjugation of the verb; e.g., the appendix entry for **потере́ть** appears as follows: **потере́ть Р.; потру́, потрёшь; потри́; потёр; потёртый; потерёв** and **потёрши;** i.e., following the infinitive, which is designated as the perfective form by the letter P., are the first and second persons singular of the future tense (which provide the key to the conjugation of the verb in the future tense), the singular imperative, the masculine singular of the past tense, the past passive participle in its masculine long form, and the two forms of the adverbial past participle (past gerund).

For all infinitives the irregular finite forms that appear as entries in the main body appear in the appendix, as stated above. The appendix thus provides a compact source of information when the infinitive is known and a particular conjugated form of the verb is sought.

If the less experienced student is unable to construct the form required from the information provided in the appendix, a cross reference to the pertinent entry in the body of the work will provide the word sought; e.g., if the feminine short form of the past passive participle of the verb, удивйть, is wanted and the student is unable to construct it from the masculine singular long form удивлённый, given in the appendix, he need only turn to the entry удивлённый in the body of the dictionary to find удивлена́, the word he is looking for.

The order in which the pertinent finite forms appear after the infinitive is given at the beginning of the appendix.

Stress. Because stress is indicative of aspect, meaning, and pronunciation, the user is cautioned to pay particular attention to stress as shown. For the benefit of the student in particular, stress has been indicated on all Russian words.

Abbreviations. A list of abbreviations employed in this work appears on page xiii.

This reference work is not intended to take the place of a standard dictionary but to be a ready source of the much needed information that, to date, has been omitted from our best dictionaries. As an aid to the student, reader, and translator of Russian, it should be a valuable time saver.

I wish to express my sincere appreciation for the constructive criticism I have received from Dr. Rolf Ekmanis, Russian Department, Arizona State University, during the period in which this book was in preparation. I am also very much indebted to Charles G. Higgins and Charles Tichy for their valued and loyal assistance in the formulation and preparation of the manuscript, as I am to Margaret Powers Hall who has been so generous of her time and skills.

D. B. Powers

Tempe, Arizona
July 10, 1968

Russian Alphabet

Upper and Lower Case		Upper and Lower Case	
А	а	Р	р
Б	б	С	с
В	в	Т	т
Г	г	У	у
Д	д	Ф	ф
Е	е	Х	х
Ё	ё	Ц	ц
Ж	ж	Ч	ч
З	з	Ш	ш
И	и	Щ	щ
Й	й	Ъ	ъ
К	к	Ы	ы
Л	л	Ь	ь
М	м	Э	э
Н	н	Ю	ю
О	о	Я	я
П	п		

Bibliography

Академия наук СССР, Институт русского языка, *Грамматика русского языка*. В двух томах. Москва, 1960.

Академия наук СССР, Институт языкознания, *Словарь русского языка*. В четырех томах. Москва, 1957–1961.

Р. И. Аванесов и С. И. Ожегов, *Русское литературное произношение и ударение*. Москва, 1960.

С. И. Ожегов, *Словарь русского языка*. Москва, 1961.

Русско-латышский словарь, Латвийское государственное издательство. Рига, 1959.

L. I. Callaham, *Russian-English Chemical and Polytechnical Dictionary*, 2nd. ed. New York: Wiley, 1962.

V. K. Müller, *English-Russian Dictionary*, 6th ed. New York: Dutton, 1959.

A. I. Smirnitsky, *Russian-English Dictionary*, 3rd. ed., rev. New York: Dutton, 1959.

B. O. Unbegaun, *Russian Grammar*. Oxford: Oxford University Press, 1962.

Webster's New International Dictionary of the English Language, 3rd. ed., unabridged. Springfield, Mass.: G. and C. Merriam, 1964.

Abbreviations

a	active
acc.	accusative
adv.	adverbial
adv. past part.	adverbial past participle (past gerund)
adv. pres. part.	adverbial present participle (present gerund)
agr.	agriculture
amt.	amount
arch.	archaic
bot.	botanical
chem.	chemical
dat.	dative
e.g.	*exempli gratia* (for example)
elec.	electrical
fig.	figurative
gen.	genitive
geom.	geometry
gram.	grammar
I.	imperfective infinitive
i.e.	*id est* (that is)
imp.	imperative
impers.	impersonal
inst.	instrumental
intr.	intransitive (Does not take accusative case; when other cases are required, they are so indicated.)
ling.	linguistics
lit.	literal
math.	mathematics
mech.	mechanics
med.	medicine
mil.	military
min.	mining, minerology
naut.	nautical terminology
o.s.	oneself
P.	perfective infinitive
pap	past active participle
ppp	past passive participle

ABBREVIATIONS

part.	participle
past	past tense (preterite)
pers.	person
philos.	philosophy
photo.	photography
phys.	physics
pl.	plural
prep.	prepositional
pres.	present
pres. a.p.	present active participle
pres. pp	present passive participle
R.R.	railroad
sing.	singular
s.o.	someone
s.p.	someplace
s.t.	something
s.w.	somewhere
tech.	technical
typ.	typography

A

АЛКА́Й, and а́лчи (imp.), see а́лчу.
АЛКА́Я (adv. pres. part.), see а́лчу.
А́ЛЧА (adv. pres. part.), see а́лчу.
А́ЛЧЕШЬ, see а́лчу.
А́ЛЧИ, and алка́й (imp.), see а́лчу.

А́ЛЧУ, а́лчешь (also алка́ю, алка́ешь). I. Алка́ть. Р. Взалка́ть. 1. To be hungry (intr.). 2. To crave, hunger for (gen.).

B

БА́ЕШЬ, see ба́ю.
БАЙ (imp.), see ба́ю.
БАЛАМУ́ТЬ (imp.), see баламу́чу.
БАЛАМУ́ЧУ, баламу́тишь. I. Баламу́тить (acc.). Р. Взбаламу́тить. 1. To agitate (as water). 2. (fig.) To agitate, disturb.
БА́Ю, ба́ешь. I. Ба́ять (arch.) (acc.) or (intr.). To say, speak.
БЕГИ́ (imp.), see бегу́.
БЕГУ́, бежи́шь, бегу́т. I. Бежа́ть (intr.). 1. To run, hurry. 2. To flee, escape from (от/из + gen.). 3. (fig.) To fly (as time). 4. To boil over (e.g., milk).
БЕЖИ́ШЬ, see бегу́.
БЕЗОБРА́ЖУ, безобра́зишь. I. Безобра́зить. Р. Обезобра́зить (mean. 1). 1. To disfigure, mutilate (acc.). 2. To behave disgracefully (intr.).
БЕЗОБРА́ЗЬ (imp.), see безобра́жу.
БЕЙ (imp.). I. Бить. Р. Поби́ть (mean. 1), проби́ть (mean. 7 and 8), разби́ть (mean. 4). 1. To beat (acc.). 2. To strike (acc.). 3. To kill, slaughter (acc.). 4. To break (as dishes) (acc.). 5. To gush (as a spring) (inst.). 6. To shoot (acc.). 7. To strike (of a clock) (intr.) or (acc.). 8. To sound (as an alarm, retreat, etc.) (acc.). (Also see БЬЮ.)
БЕРЁГ, берегла́ (past), see берегу́.
БЕРЕГИ́ (imp.), see берегу́.
БЕРЕГУ́, бережёшь, берегу́т. I. Бере́чь. Р. Сбере́чь. 1. To take care of (acc.). 2. To preserve, protect against (acc. + от + gen.).

БЕРЕЖЁШЬ, see берегу́.
БЕРЕЖУ́, береди́шь. I. Береди́ть (acc.). Р. Разбереди́ть. 1. (lit. and fig.) To irritate. 2. To rouse, stir up.
БЕРЁШЬ, see беру́.
БЕРИ́ (imp.), see беру́.
БЕРУ́, берёшь. I. Брать (acc.). Р. Взять. 1. To take. 2. To obtain. 3. To employ, hire. 4. To arrest. (For numerous lit. and fig. meanings, see unabridged dictionary.)
БЕСЧЕ́СТИ (imp.), see бесче́щу.
БЕСЧЕ́ЩУ, бесче́стишь. I. Бесче́стить (acc.). Р. Обесче́стить. To disgrace, dishonor.
БЕШУ́, бе́сишь. I. Беси́ть (acc.). Р. Взбеси́ть. To enrage, infuriate.
БИ́ТЫЙ; би́т, —а, —о, —ы (ppp), see бей, and бью.
БЛА́ГОВЕСТИ (imp.), see бла́говещу.
БЛА́ГОВЕЩУ, бла́говестишь. I. Бла́говестить (intr.). Р. Отбла́говестить (mean. 1). 1. To ring the bell for church. 2. To publish, noise abroad (о + prep.).
БЛАГОСЛОВЛЮ́, благослови́шь. Р. Благослови́ть (acc.). I. Благословля́ть. 1. To bless. 2. To give one's blessings to.
БЛЕ́ЕТ, бле́ют (3rd pers. only). I. Бле́ять (intr.). To bleat.
БЛЕЙ (imp.), see бле́ет.
БЛЁК, блёкла (past). I. Блёкнуть (intr.). Р. Поблёкнуть. 1. To fade, wither (of plants). 2. To grow dim (of stars, etc.).

1

БЛЕСТИ́ (imp.), see блещу́¹.
БЛЕСТИ́ШЬ, see блещу́¹.
БЛЕСТЯ́Т, see блещу́¹.
БЛЕ́ЩЕШЬ, see блещу́².
БЛЕЩИ́ (imp.), see блещу́².
БЛЕЩУ́¹, блести́шь. I. Блесте́ть (intr.). To shine, glitter.
БЛЕЩУ́², бле́щешь. I. Блесте́ть (intr.). To shine, glitter.
БЛЕ́ЮТ, see бле́ет.
БЛУЖУ́¹, блуди́шь. I. Блуди́ть (intr.). To lead a dissolute life.
БЛУЖУ́², блу́дишь. I. Блуди́ть (intr.). To roam.
БЛЮДЁШЬ, see блюду́.
БЛЮДИ́ (imp.), see блюду́.
БЛЮДУ́, блюдёшь. I. Блюсти́ (acc.). Р. Соблюсти́. 1. To preserve, keep, protect (as order, interests of the government, etc.). 2. To look at, observe.
БЛЮ́ДШИЙ (pap), see блюду́.
БЛЮЛ, блюла́ (past), see блюду́.
БО́ЙШЬСЯ, see бою́сь.
БО́ЙСЯ (imp.), see бою́сь.
БОЛЕ́Ю, боле́ешь. I. Боле́ть (intr.). 1. To be ill (with s.t.) (inst.). 2. (fig.) To suffer (for s.o. or s.t.) (за + acc.), (о + prep.). 3. To feel keenly (e.g., success, failure, etc.) (за + acc.), (о + prep.).
БОЛИ́Т, боля́т (3rd pers. only). I. Боле́ть (intr.). To pain, hurt.
БОЛЯ́Т (3rd pers. pl.), see боли́т.
БО́РЕШЬСЯ, see борю́сь.
БОРИ́СЬ (imp.), see борю́сь.
БОРМО́ЧЕШЬ, see бормочу́.
БОРМОЧИ́ (imp.), see бормочу́.
БОРМОЧУ́, бормо́чешь. I. Бормота́ть (acc.) or (intr.). Р. Пробормота́ть. To mutter, mumble.
БОРОЗЖУ́, борозди́шь. I. Борозди́ть (acc.). Р. Взборозди́ть (mean. 1), избороздѝть. 1. To furrow, plow. 2. (fig.) To furrow (as wrinkles furrow one's face).
БОРЮ́СЬ, бо́решься. I. Боро́ться (intr.). 1. To fight (with) (с + inst.). 2. To fight (for) (за + acc.). 3. To fight against (про́тив + gen.).
БОЮ́СЬ, бои́шься. I. Боя́ться (gen.) To fear; to dread.
БРЕДЁШЬ, see бреду́.
БРЕДИ́ (imp.), see бреду́.
БРЕДУ́, бредёшь. I. Брести́ (intr.).

1. To make one's way with difficulty.
2. To stroll.
БРЕ́ДШИЙ (pap), see бреду́.
БРЕДЬ (imp.), see бре́жу.
БРЕ́ЕШЬ, see бре́ю.
БРЕ́ЖУ, бре́дишь. I. Бре́дить (intr.). 1. To be delirious, rave. 2. To be infatuated with, rave about (inst.).
БРЕЙ (imp.), see бре́ю.
БРЁЛ, брела́ (past), see бреду́.
БРЕНЧА́Т, see бренчу́.
БРЕНЧИ́ (imp.), see бренчу́.
БРЕНЧИ́ШЬ, see бренчу́.
БРЕНЧУ́, бренчи́шь. I. Бренча́ть (intr.). 1. To jingle (as one's keys) (inst.). 2. To strum on a musical instrument (на + prep.).
БРЕ́ШЕШЬ, see Брешу́.
БРЕШИ́ (imp.), see брешу́.
БРЕШУ́, бре́шешь. I. Бреха́ть (intr.). Р. Брехну́ть. 1. To bark, yelp. 2. To lie (tell lies). 3. To talk nonsense.
БРЕ́Ю, бре́ешь. I. Брить (acc.). Р. Побри́ть. To shave.
БРИ́ТЫЙ; брит, —а, —о, —ы (ppp), see бре́ю.
БРОЖУ́, бро́дишь. I. Броди́ть (intr.). 1. To roam, wander. 2. To ferment.
БРОСЬ (imp.), see бро́шу.
БРО́ШЕННЫЙ; бро́шен, —а, —о, —ы (ppp), see бро́шу.
БРО́ШУ, бро́сишь. Р. Бро́сить. I. Броса́ть. 1. To throw, hurl (acc./inst.). 2. To give up, abandon, quit (as a habit, etc.) (acc.) or (+ inf.). 3. To give up, desert (as friends) (acc.). 4. (fig.) To fling, throw, hurl, cast (acc.).
БРЫ́ЗЖЕШЬ, see бры́зжу.
БРЫ́ЗЖИ (imp.), see бры́зжу.
БРЫ́ЗЖУ, бры́зжешь. I. Бры́згать (intr.). Р. Бры́знуть. To splash, spatter, sprinkle (s.o. or s.t. with s.t.) (на + acc. + inst.).
БРЮЗЖА́Т, see брюзжу́.
БРЮЗЖИ́ (imp.), see брюзжу́.
БРЮЗЖИ́ШЬ, see брюзжу́.
БРЮЗЖУ́, брюзжи́шь. I. Брюзжа́ть (intr.). To grumble.
БУ́ДУ, бу́дешь. I. Быть (intr.). To be.
БУ́ДУЧИ (adv. pres. part.), see бу́ду.
БУДЬ (imp.), see бу́ду.

БУЖУ́, бу́дишь. I. Буди́ть (acc.).
Р. Разбуди́ть (mean. 1), пробуди́ть.
1. To awaken. 2. (fig.) To arouse,
excite.

БУРА́ВЛЮ, бура́вишь. I. Бура́вить
(acc.). To drill, bore (as a piece of
metal).

БУРА́ВЬ (imp.), see бура́влю.

БУРЧА́Т, see бурчу́.

БУРЧИ́ШЬ, see бурчу́.

БУРЧИ́ (imp.), see бурчу́.

БУРЧУ́, бурчи́шь. I. Бурча́ть. Р.
Пробурча́ть. 1. To mumble, mutter,
grumble (intr./acc.). 2. To rumble
(of one's stomach) (intr.) (impers.).

БУХ, бу́хла (past). I. Бу́хнуть (intr.).
To swell (from moisture).

БУ́ХНУЛ, бу́хнула (past). Р. Бу́хнуть.
I. Бу́хать. 1. To make a dull, thudd-
ing sound, thump (intr.). 2. To
thunder (as a cannon) (intr.). 3. To
blurt out (acc.).

БУЧУ́, бути́шь. I. Бути́ть (acc.). Р.
Забути́ть. To construct or fill with
rubble masonry.

БЬЁШЬ, see бью.

БЬЮ, бьёшь. I. Бить. Р. Поби́ть
(mean. 1), проби́ть (mean. 7, 8),
разби́ть (mean. 4). 1. To beat (acc.).
2. To strike (acc.). 3. To kill, slaughter
(acc.). 4. To break (as dishes) (acc.).
5. To gush (as a spring) (inst.). 6. To
shoot (acc.). 7. To strike (of a clock)
(intr.) or (acc.). 8. To sound (as an
alarm, retreat, etc.) (acc.). (For other
meanings see unabridged dictionary.)

В

ВА́КСИ (imp.), see ва́кшу.

ВА́КШУ, ва́ксишь. I. Ва́ксить (acc.). Р. Нава́ксить. To polish with blacking (as shoes).

ВБЕГИ́ (imp.), see вбегу́.

ВБЕГУ́, вбежи́шь, вбегу́т. Р. Вбежа́ть (intr.). I. Вбега́ть. To enter running; to come running in.

ВБЕЖИ́ШЬ, see вбегу́.

ВБЕЙ (imp.). Р. Вбить (acc.). I. Вбива́ть. (lit. and fig.) To drive in, hammer in (also see вобью́).

ВБЕРЁШЬ, see вберу́.

ВБЕРИ́ (imp.), see вберу́.

ВБЕРУ́, вберёщь. Р. Вобра́ть (acc.). I. Вбира́ть. 1. To absorb. 2. To suck in, drink in. 3. To inhale.

ВБИ́ТЫЙ; вбит, —а, —о, —ы (ppp), see вбей and вобью́.

ВБРОСЬ (imp.), see вбро́шу.

ВБРО́ШЕННЫЙ; вбро́шен, —а, —о, —ы (ppp), see вбро́шу.

ВБРО́ШУ, вбро́сишь. Р. Вбро́сить (acc.). I. Вбра́сывать. To throw (s.t.) in (as a ball).

ВВЕДЁННЫЙ; введён, —а́, —о́, —ы́ (ppp), see введу́.

ВВЕДЁШЬ, see введу́.

ВВЕДИ́ (imp.), see введу́.

ВВЕДУ́, введёшь. Р. Ввести́ (acc. + в + acc.). I. Вводи́ть. 1. To bring in, introduce into (as new ideas, troops, etc.). 2. To lead (s.o. into s.t.) (as expense, trouble, etc.). 3. To put (s.t.) into effect, operation (as a law, piece of equipment. 4. To acquaint (s.o.) with (s.t.).

ВВЕ́ДШИЙ (pap), see введу́.

ВВЁЗ, ввезла́ (past), see ввезу́.

ВВЕЗЁННЫЙ; ввезён, —а́, —о́, —ы́ (ppp), see ввезу́.

ВВЕЗЁШЬ, see ввезу́.

ВВЕЗИ́ (imp.), see ввезу́.

ВВЕЗУ́, ввезёшь. Р. Ввезти́ (acc.). I. Ввози́ть. 1. To carry in. 2. To import.

ВВЕЙ (imp.), Р. Ввить (acc.). I.

Ввива́ть. To plait, interlace, intertwine (also see вовью́).

ВВЁЛ, ввела́ (past), see введу́.

ВВЕРГ, вве́ргла (past). Р. Вве́ргнуть (acc. + в + acc.). I. Вверга́ть. 1. To fling, throw (s.t. or s.o. into s.t.). 2. (fig.) To throw (as s.o. into despair).

ВВИ́НЧЕННЫЙ; вви́нчен, —а, —о, —ы (ppp), see ввинчу́.

ВВИНЧУ́, ввинти́шь. Р. Ввинти́ть (acc. + в + acc.). I. Вви́нчивать. To screw into (e.g., a screw into a wall).

ВВИ́ТЫЙ; ввит, —а́, —о, —ы (ppp), see ввей (also see вовью́).

ВВОЖУ́[1], вво́дишь. Р. Вводи́ть (acc. + в + acc.). Р. Ввести́. 1. To bring in, introduce into (as new ideas, troops, etc.). 2. To lead (s.o. into s.t.) (as expense, trouble, etc.). 3. To put (s.t.) into effect, operation (as a law, piece of equipment). 4. To acquaint (s.o.) with (s.t.).

ВВОЖУ́[2], вво́зишь. I. Ввози́ть (acc.). Р. Ввезти́. 1. To carry in. 2. To import.

ВВЯ́ЖЕШЬ, see ввяжу́.

ВВЯЖИ́ (imp.), see ввяжу́.

ВВЯЖУ́, ввя́жешь. Р. Ввяза́ть (acc.). I. Ввя́зывать. 1. To knit in (as a stripe), 2. (fig.) To involve (as s.o. in s.t.).

ВВЯ́ЗАННЫЙ; ввя́зан, —а, —о, —ы (ppp), see ввяжу́.

ВГЛЯДИ́СЬ (imp.), see вгляжу́сь.

ВГЛЯДИ́ШЬСЯ, see вгляжу́сь.

ВГЛЯДЯ́ТСЯ, see вгляжу́сь.

ВГЛЯЖУ́СЬ, вгляди́шься. Р. Вгляде́ться (intr.) (в + acc.) I. Вгля́дываться. 1. To look intently, closely at. 2. To peer into (s.t.).

ВГОНИ́ (imp.), see вгоню́.

ВГО́НИШЬ, see вгоню́.

ВГОНЮ́, вго́нишь. Р. Вогна́ть (acc. + в + acc.). I. Вгоня́ть. 1. To drive (s.t. or s.o. into s.t.) (as cattle into a pen). 2. To drive (s.t. into s.t.) (as a

4

nail into a board). 3. To bring (s.o.) to an emotional state (as to tears).

ВГРЫЗЁШСЯ, see вгрызу́сь.

ВГРЫЗЙСЬ (imp.), see вгрызу́сь.

ВГРЫЗСЯ, вгры́злась (past), see вгрызу́сь.

ВГРЫЗУ́СЬ, вгрызёшься. Р. Вгры́зться (в + acc.). I. Вгрыза́ться. 1. To seize firmly with the teeth. 2. To bite into.

ВДАВА́ЙСЯ (imp.), see вдаю́сь.

ВДАВА́ЯСЬ (adv. pres. part.), see вдаю́сь.

ВДА́ВЛЕННЫЙ; вда́влен, —а, —о, —ы (ppp), see вдавлю́.

ВДАВЛЮ́, вда́вишь. Р. Вдави́ть (acc.) I. Вда́вливать. 1. To press in (as a cork in a bottle). 2. To bend or sag (as a load bends a beam).

ВДАДЙМСЯ, вдади́тесь, вдаду́тся (pl. forms), see вда́мся.

ВДАЁШЬСЯ, see вдаю́сь.

ВДА́ЙСЯ (imp.), see вда́мся.

ВДА́МСЯ, вда́шься, вда́стся (sing. forms). Р. Вда́ться (intr.). I. Вдава́ться. 1. To jut out (into) (в + acc.). 2. (fig.) To go into detail (on some subject) (в + acc.).

ВДА́СТСЯ (3rd pers. sing.), see вда́мся.

ВДА́ШЬСЯ (2nd pers. sing.), see вда́мся.

ВДАЮ́СЬ, вдаёшься. I. Вдава́ться (intr.). Р. Вда́ться. 1. To jut out (into) (в + acc.). 2. (fig.) To go into detail on some subject (в + acc.).

ВДЕ́НЕШЬ, see вде́ну.

ВДЕ́НУ, вде́нешь. Р. Вдеть (acc. + в + acc.). I. Вдева́ть. To pass s.t. through s.t. (as thread through a needle).

ВДЕНЬ (imp.), see вде́ну.

ВДЕ́ТЫЙ; вдет, —а, —о, —ы (ppp), see вде́ну.

ВДОЛБЛЁННЫЙ; вдолблён, —а́, —о́, —ы́ (ppp), see вдолблю́.

ВДОЛБЛЮ́, вдолби́шь. Р. Вдолби́ть (acc. + в + acc.) or (acc. + dat.) I. Вда́лбливать. 1. To drive or hammer (s.t.) in. 2. (fig.) To din (s.t.) into (s.o.).

ВДОХНОВЛЁННЫЙ, вдохновлён, —а́, —о́, —ы́ (ppp), see вдохновлю́.

ВДОХНОВЛЮ́, вдохнови́шь. Р. Вдохнови́ть (acc.). I. Вдохновля́ть. 1. To inspire (e.g., the people). 2. To inspire,

induce, incite (e.g., s.o. to some action) (acc. + на + acc.).

ВДУ́ЕШЬ, see вду́ю.

ВДУ́Й (imp.), see вду́ю.

ВДУ́ТЫЙ; вду́т, —а, —о, —ы (ppp), see вду́ю.

ВДУ́Ю, вду́ешь. Р. Вдуть (acc. + в + acc.). I. Вдува́ть. To blow (s.t.) into (s.t.) (as air into a football).

ВЕДЁШЬ, see веду́.

ВЕДЙ (imp.), see веду́.

ВЕДО́МЫЙ (pres. pp), see веду́.

ВЕДУ́, ведёшь. I. Вести́. Р. Повести́ (mean. 1 thru 5). 1. To take, conduct (as s.o.) (acc.). 2. To accompany (as s.o.) (acc.). 3. To drive, steer (as a car, a boat) (acc.). 4. To construct (as a road to somewhere) (acc.). 5. To conduct (as a law suit, scientific work, etc.) (acc.). 6. To lead (as a road leads somewhere) (intr.).

ВЕ́ДШИЙ (pap), see веду́.

ВЕ́ЕШЬ, see ве́ю.

ВЁЗ, везла́ (past), see везу́.

ВЕЗЁТ (3rd pers. only). I. Везти́. Р. Повезти́ and подвезти́. To be lucky (dat.) (impers.) (as ему́ везёт—he is lucky).

ВЕЗЁШЬ, see везу́.

ВЕЗЙ (imp.), see везу́.

ВЕЗУ́, везёшь. I. Везти́ (acc.). Р. Повезти́. To convey, carry (as by vehicle, horse, etc.).

ВЕЙ[1] (imp.), see ве́ю.

ВЕЙ[2] (imp.). I. Вить (acc.). Р. Свить. 1. To twist (as a thread, a rope, etc.). 2. To weave (as a wreath, a nest, etc.). 3. To wind, coil. (Also see вью.)

ВЕЛ, вела́ (past), see веду́.

ВЕЛЙ (imp.), see велю́.

ВЕЛЙШЬ, see велю́.

ВЕЛЮ́, вели́шь. I. and Р. Веле́ть (dat. + inf.). To order (as s.o. to do s.t.).

ВЕЛЯ́Т, see велю́.

ВЕРЕЖУ́, вереди́шь. I. Вереди́ть (acc.). Р. Развереди́ть. (lit. and fig.) To irritate.

ВЕРЕЩА́Т, see верещу́.

ВЕРЕЩЙ (imp.), see верещу́.

ВЕРЕЩЙШЬ, see верещу́.

ВЕРЕЩУ́, вереши́шь. I. Вереща́ть (intr.). To chirp or squeak.

ВЕРТЙ (imp.), see верчу́.

ВЕ́РТИШЬ, see верчу́.

ВЕ́РТЯТ, see верчу́.

ВЕРХОВОЖУ́, верховóдишь. I.Верхо-
водѝть. 1. To boss (s.o. or s.t.) (inst.).
2. To lord it over (s.o. or s.t.)
(inst.).

ВÉРЧЕННЫЙ; вéрчен, —а, —о, —ы
(ppp), see верчу́.

ВЕРЧУ́, вéртишь. I. Вертéть. 1. To
turn, spin (acc.). 2. To twirl (acc./
inst.). 3. To roll (as a cigarette) (acc.).
4. To manage (s.o. or s.t.) as one
likes (inst.).

ВЕСЬ (imp.), see вéшу.

ВÉШУ, вéсишь. I. Вéсить. 1. (lit. and
fig.) To weigh (intr.). 2. To weigh
(acc.). 3. (fig.) To carry weight (e.g.,
one's words) (intr.).

ВÉЮ, вéешь. I. Вéять. P. Провéять
(mean. 3). 1. To blow (of the wind)
(intr.). 2. To fly (of a banner) (intr.).
3. To winnow (acc.).

ВÉЯННЫЙ; вéян,—а,—о,—ы (ppp),
see вéю.

ВЖИВЁШЬСЯ, see вживу́сь.

ВЖИВИ́СЬ (imp.), see вживу́сь.

ВЖИВУ́СЬ, вживёшься. P. Вжи́ться
(intr.). I. Вживáться. To get used to,
accustom oneself to (в + acc.).

ВЗБАЛАМУ́ТЬ (imp.), see взбала-
му́чу.

ВЗБАЛАМУ́ЧУ, взбаламу́тишь. P.
Взбаламу́тить (acc.). I. Баламу́тить.
1. To agitate (as water). 2. (fig.) To
agitate, disturb.

ВЗБАЛАМУ́ЧЕННЫЙ; взбаламу́чен,
—а,—о,—ы (ppp), see взбаламу́чу.

ВЗБЕГИ́ (imp.), see взбегу́.

ВЗБЕГУ́, взбежи́шь, взбегу́т. P. Взбе-
жáть (intr.). I. Взбегáть. To run up
(as a hill).

ВЗБЕЖИ́ШЬ, see взбегу́.

ВЗБЕЙ (imp.). P. Взбить (acc.). I.
Взбивáть. 1. To shake up, fluff up (as
a pillow, etc.). 2. To whip up (as
cream). (Also see взобью́.)

ВЗБЕШЁННЫЙ; взбешён, —á, —ó,
—ы́ (ppp), see взбешу́.

ВЗБЕШУ́, взбéсишь. P. Взбеси́ть
(acc.). I. Беси́ть. To enrage, infuriate.

ВЗБИ́ТЫЙ; взбит, —а, —о, —ы
(ppp), see взбей and взобью́.

ВЗБОРОЖДЁННЫЙ; взборождён,
—á, —ó, —ы́ (ppp), see взборозжу́.

ВЗБОРОЗЖУ́, взборозди́шь. P. Взбо-
розди́ть (acc.). I. Борозди́ть. 1. To

furrow, plow. 2. (fig.) To furrow (as
wrinkles furrow one's face).

ВЗБРЕДЁШЬ, see взбреду́.

ВЗБРЕДИ́ (imp.), see взбреду́.

ВЗБРЕДУ́, взбредёшь. P. Взбрести́
(intr.). I. Взбредáть. 1. To make
one's way up with difficulty (as up a
hill) (на + acc.). 2. (fig.) To occur to
one, come into one's head (в + acc.
of head or mind).

ВЗБРÉДШИЙ (pap), see взбреду́.

ВЗБРЁЛ, взбрелá (past), see взбреду́.

ВЗБУХ, взбу́хла (past). P. Взбу́хнуть
(intr.). I. Взбухáть. To swell (out).

ВЗВЕДЁННЫЙ; взведён, —á, —ó,
—ы́ (ppp), see взведу́.

ВЗВЕДЁШЬ, see взведу́.

ВЗВЕДИ́ (imp.), see взведу́.

ВЗВЕДУ́, взведёшь. P. Взвести́ (acc.).
I. Взводи́ть. 1. To cock (as a gun).
2. To impute, attribute (s.t. to s.o.)
(acc. + на + acc.).

ВЗВÉДШИЙ (pap), see взведу́.

ВЗВЕЙ (imp.). P. Взвить (acc.). I.
Взвивáть. To raise and whirl (of the
wind) (also see взовью́).

ВЗВЁЛ, взвелá (past), see взведу́.

ВЗВЕСЬ (imp.), see взвéшу.

ВЗВÉШЕННЫЙ; взвéшен, —а, —о,
—ы (ppp), see взвéшу.

ВЗВÉШУ, взвéсишь. P. Взвéсить
(acc.). I. Взвéшивать. 1. To weigh,
weigh out. 2. (fig.) To weigh. 3.
(phys.) (ppp only) To be in suspen-
sion.

ВЗВИ́НЧЕННЫЙ; взви́нчен,—а,—о,
—ы (ppp), see взвинчу́.

ВЗВИНЧУ́, взвинти́шь. P. Взвинти́ть
(acc.). I. Взви́нчивать. To excite,
work up.

ВЗВИ́ТЫЙ; взвит, —á, —о, —ы
(ppp), see взвей and взовью́.

ВЗВОЁШЬ, see взвою́.

ВЗВОЖУ́, взвóдишь. I. Взводи́ть
(acc.). P. Взвести́. 1. To cock (as a
gun). 2. To impute (s.t. to s.o.) (acc.
+ на + acc.).

ВЗВОЙ (imp.), see взвою́.

ВЗВОЮ́, взвоёшь. P. Взвыть (intr.).
To set up a howl, start to howl.

ВЗГРОМОЖДЁННЫЙ; взгромождён,
—á, —ó, —ы́ (ppp), see взгромозжу́.

ВЗГРОМОЗЖУ́, взгромозди́шь. P.
Взгромозди́ть (acc.). I. Взгромож-
дáть. To pile up.

ВЗДЕ́НЕШЬ, see вздену.

ВЗДЕ́НУ, взде́нешь. Р. Вздеть (acc.). I. Вздева́ть. 1. To put on (as glasses). 2. To raise (as one's arm). 3. To pierce, impale.

ВЗДЕНЬ (imp.), see вздену.

ВЗДЕ́ТЫЙ; вздет, —а, —о, —ы (ppp), see вздену.

ВЗДУ́ЕШЬ, see вздую.

ВЗДУ́Й (imp.), see вздую.

ВЗДУ́ТЫЙ; вздут, —а, —о, —ы (ppp), see вздую.

ВЗДУ́Ю, вздуешь. Р. Вздуть (acc.). I. Вздува́ть (mean. 1 thru 4). 1. To blow up (as dust). 2. To kindle (as a fire). 3. To inflate. 4. (fig.) To raise (as the price). 5. To thrash, beat.

ВЗДЫ́БЛЕННЫЙ; взды́блен, —а, —о, —ы (ppp), see вздыблю.

ВЗДЫ́БЛЮ, вздыбишь. Р. Вздыбить (acc.). I. Вады́бливать. To cause to rear (as a horse).

ВЗДЫБЬ (imp.), see вздыблю.

ВЗЛЕЛЕ́ЕШЬ, see взлелею.

ВЗЛЕЛЕ́Й (imp.), see взлелею.

ВЗЛЕЛЕ́Ю, взлеле́ешь. Р. Взлеле́ять (acc.). 1. To cherish (as a thought). 2. To cherish (as a person).

ВЗЛЕЛЕ́ЯННЫЙ; взлеле́ян, —а, —о, —ы (ppp), see взлелею.

ВЗЛЕТИ́ (imp.), see взлечу.

ВЗЛЕТИ́ШЬ, see взлечу.

ВЗЛЕТЯ́Т, see взлечу.

ВЗЛЕЧУ́, взлети́шь. Р. Взлете́ть (intr.). I. Взлета́ть. To fly up.

ВЗЛОХМА́ТЬ (imp.), see взлохмачу.

ВЗЛОХМА́ЧЕННЫЙ; взлохма́чен, —а, —о, —ы (ppp), see взлохмачу.

ВЗЛОХМА́ЧУ, взлохма́тишь. Р. Взлохма́тить (acc.). I. Взлохма́чивать, лохма́тить. To tousle, rumple, dishevel.

ВЗМЁЛ, взмела́ (past), see взмету.

ВЗМЁТАННЫЙ; взмётан, —а, —о, —ы (ppp), see взмечу.

ВЗМЕТЁННЫЙ; взметён, —а́, —о́, —ы́ (ppp), see взмету.

ВЗМЕТЁШЬ, see взмету.

ВЗМЕТИ́ (imp.), see взмету.

ВЗМЕТУ́, взметёшь. Р. Взмести́ (acc.). To fling up, toss up.

ВЗМЁТШИЙ (pap), see взмету.

ВЗМЕТЯ́ (adv. past part.), see взмету.

ВЗМЕ́ЧЕШЬ, see взмечу.

ВЗМЕЧИ́ (imp.), see взмечу.

ВЗМЕЧУ́, взме́чешь. Р. Взмета́ть (acc.). I. Взмётывать. To fling up, toss up.

ВЗМО́ЕШЬ, see взмою.

ВЗМОЙ (imp.), see взмою.

ВЗМОЩУ́СЬ, взмости́шься. Р. Взмости́ться (intr.) (на + acc.). To perch on.

ВЗМО́Ю, взмоешь. Р. Взмыть (intr.). I. Взмыва́ть. To soar up.

ВЗМУ́ЧЕННЫЙ; взму́чен, —а, —о, —ы (ppp), see взмучу.

ВЗМУЧУ́, взмути́шь (or взму́тишь). Р. Взмути́ть (acc.). I. Мути́ть. To stir up, agitate (as a liquid).

ВЗОБЬЁШЬ, see взобью.

ВЗОБЬЮ́, взобьёшь. Р. Взбить (acc.). I. Взбива́ть. 1. To shake up, fluff up (as a pillow, etc.). 2. To whip up (as cream).

ВЗОВЬЁШЬ, see взовью.

ВЗОВЬЮ́, взовьёшь. Р. Взвить (acc.). I. Взвива́ть. To raise and whirl (of the wind.)

ВЗОЙДЁШЬ, see взойду.

ВЗОЙДИ́ (imp.), see взойду.

ВЗОЙДУ́, взойдёшь. Р. Взойти́ (intr.). I. Всходи́ть, восходи́ть (mean. 1 and 2). 1. To ascend, mount (на + acc.). 2. To rise, ascend (of the sun, etc.). 3. To come up, sprout (of plants from seeds). 4. (arch.) To enter (e.g., a room) (в + acc.). 5. To rise (of dough).

ВЗОЙДЯ́ (adv. past part.), see взойду.

ВЗО́РВАННЫЙ; взорван, —а, —о, —ы (ppp), see взорву.

ВЗОРВЁШЬ, see взорву.

ВЗОРВИ́ (imp.), see взорву.

ВЗОРВУ́, взорвёшь. Р. Взорва́ть (acc.). I. Взрыва́ть (mean. 1). 1. To blow up. 2. To exasperate, anger.

ВЗОШЕ́ДШИЙ (pap), see взойду.

ВЗОШЁЛ, взошла́ (past), see взойду.

ВЗРАЩЁННЫЙ; взращён, —а́, —о́, —ы́ (ppp), see взращу.

ВЗРАЩУ́, взрасти́шь. Р. Взрасти́ть (acc.). I. Взра́щивать. 1. To cultivate. 2. To bring up, nurture.

ВЗРЕВЁШЬ, see взреву.

ВЗРЕВИ́ (imp.), see взреву.

ВЗРЕВУ́, взревёшь. Р. Взреве́ть (intr.). To utter a roar.

ВЗРЕ́ЖЕШЬ, see взрежу.

ВЗРЕ́ЖУ, взре́жешь. Р. Взре́зать (acc.). I. Взреза́ть, взре́зывать. 1.

To cut (make an incision). 2. To cut open.

ВЗРЕЖЬ (imp.), see взрѐжу.

ВЗРЕ́ЗАННЫЙ; взре́зан, —а, —о, —ы (ppp), see взре́жу.

ВЗРО́ЕШЬ, see взро́ю.

ВЗРОЙ (imp.), see взро́ю.

ВЗРО́Ю, взро́ешь. Р. Взрыть (acc.). I. Взрыва́ть. To plow up, dig up.

ВЗРЫ́ТЫЙ; взры́т, —а, —о, —ы (ppp), see взро́ю.

ВЗ'ЕДИ́МСЯ, вз'еди́тесь, вз'едя́тся (pl. forms), see вз'ѐмся.

ВЗ'Е́ЛСЯ, вз'е́лась (past), see вз'ѐмся.

ВЗ'Е́МСЯ, вз'е́шься, вз'е́стся (sing. forms). Р. Вз'е́сться (на + acc.). I. Вз'еда́ться. To scold, pitch into.

ВЗ'Е́СТСЯ, see вз'ѐмся.

ВЗ'Е́ШЬСЯ[1] (2nd pers. sing.), see вз'ѐмся.

ВЗ'Е́ШЬСЯ[2] (imp.), see вз'ѐмся.

ВЗЫ́СКАННЫЙ; взы́скан, —а, —о, —ы (ppp), see взыщу́.

ВЗЫ́ЩЕШЬ, see взыщу́.

ВЗЫЩИ́ (imp.), see взыщу́.

ВЗЫЩУ́, взы́щешь. Р. Взыска́ть. I. Взы́скивать. 1. To exact (s.t. from s.o.) (acc. + с + gen.). 2. To recover (e.g. a debt) (acc.). 3. To make (s.o.) answer for (s.t.) (с + gen. + за + acc.). 4. To reward (arch.) (acc.).

ВЗЯ́ТЫЙ; взя́т, —а́, —о, —ы (ppp). Р. Взять (acc.). I. Брать. 1. To take. 2. To obtain. 3. To employ, hire. 4. To arrest. (Also see возьму́.) (For numerous lit. and fig. meanings, see unabridged dictionary.)

ВИ́ДЕННЫЙ; ви́ден, —а, —о, —ы (ppp), see ви́жу.

ВИ́ДИШЬ, see ви́жу.

ВИ́ДИШЬСЯ, see ви́жусь.

ВИ́ДЯТ, see ви́жу.

ВИ́ДЯТСЯ, see ви́жусь.

ВИ́ЖУ, ви́дишь. I. Ви́деть. Р. Уви́деть (mean. 2, 3). 1. To see (intr.). 2. To see (s.o. or s.t.) (acc.). 3. To understand.

ВИ́ЖУСЬ, ви́дишься. I. Ви́деться (intr.). Р. Приви́детсья (mean. 2), сви́деться (mean. 1), уви́деться (mean. 1). 1. To see each other (meet). 2. (lit. and fig.) To dream (dat. of person + impers. + во + сне) or (dat. of person + сон).

ВИЗЖА́Т, see визжу́.

ВИЗЖИ́ (imp.), see визжу́.

ВИЗЖИ́ШЬ, see визжу́.

ВИЗЖУ́, визжи́шь. I. Визжа́ть (intr.). To squeal, whine, yelp.

ВИНЧУ́, винти́шь. I. Винти́ть. 1. To screw up (acc.). 2. To play vint (a card game) (intr.).

ВИС (and ви́снул), ви́сла (past). I. Ви́снуть (intr.). Р. Пови́снуть. 1. To hang (on) (на + prep.) 2. (fig.) To cling to, hang on (as to hang on s.o.'s neck) (на + prep.).

ВИСИ́ (imp.), see вишу́.

ВИСИ́ШЬ, see вишу́.

ВИСЯ́Т, see вишу́.

ВИ́ТЫЙ; ви́т, —а́, —о, —ы (ppp). I. Вить (acc.). Р. Свить. 1. To twist. 2. To weave. (Also see вью.)

ВИШУ́, виси́шь. I. Висе́ть (intr.). To be suspended, to hang (over: над + inst.), (under: под + inst.), (on: на + prep.).

ВКА́ЧЕННЫЙ; вка́чен, —а, —о, —ы (ppp), see вкачу́.

ВКАЧУ́, вка́тишь. Р. Вкати́ть. I. Вка́тывать. 1. To roll or wheel in (acc. + в + acc.). 2. To do (s.t.) unpleasant (to s.o.) (as give a reprimand) (acc. + dat.). 3. To roll in (of vehicles, waves, etc.) (intr.).

ВКО́ЛЕШЬ, see вколю́.

ВКОЛИ́ (imp.), see вколю́.

ВКО́ЛОТЫЙ; вко́лот, —а, —о, —ы (ppp), see вколю́.

ВКОЛО́ЧЕННЫЙ; вколо́чен, —а, —о, —ы (ppp), see вколочу́.

ВКОЛОЧУ́, вколо́тишь. Р. Вколоти́ть (acc. + в + acc.). I. Вкола́чивать. (lit. and fig.) To drive in, hammer in (e.g., a nail, a thought, etc.).

ВКОЛЮ́, вко́лешь. Р. Вколо́ть (acc. + в + acc.). I. Вка́лывать. To stick (in/into) (as a pin into s.t.).

ВКРАДЁШЬСЯ, see вкраду́сь.

ВКРАДИ́СЬ (imp.), see вкраду́сь.

ВКРАДУ́СЬ, вкрадёшься. Р. Вкра́сться (intr.). I. Вкра́дываться. (lit. and fig.) To creep in, steal in (unnoticed).

ВКРА́ЛСЯ, вкра́лась (past), see вкраду́сь.

ВКРА́ПЛЕННЫЙ; вкра́плен, —а, —о, —ы (ppp), see вкра́плю.

ВКРАПЛЁННЫЙ; вкраплён, —а́, —о́, —ы́ (ppp), see вкраплю́.

ВКРА́ПЛЮ, вкра́пишь. Р. Вкра́пить

(acc.). I. **Вкрапля́ть, вкра́пливать.**
1. To sprinkle, speckle. 2. (fig.) To intersperse with (as a speech with clever remarks).

ВКРАПЛЮ, вкрапи́шь. Р. **Вкрапи́ть**
(acc.). I. **Вкрапля́ть, вкра́пливать.**
1. To sprinkle, speckle. 2. (fig.) To intersperse with (as a speech with clever remarks).

ВКРАПЬ (imp.), see вкра́плю.

ВКРУ́ЧЕННЫЙ; вкру́чен, —а, —о, —ы (ppp), see вкручу́.

ВКРУЧУ́, вкру́тишь. Р. **Вкрути́ть**
(acc. + в + acc.). I. **Вкру́чивать.**
To screw into, in (e.g., a lamp into a socket).

ВКУШЁННЫЙ; вкушён, —а́, —о́, —ы́ (ppp), see вкушу́.

ВКУШУ́, вку́сишь. Р. **Вкуси́ть** (acc./gen.). I. **Вкуша́ть.** 1. (fig.) To taste (as success). 2. To partake of.

ВЛЁГ, влегла́ (past), see вля́гу.

ВЛЕЗ, вле́зла (past), see вле́зу.

ВЛЕ́ЗЕШЬ, see вле́зу.

ВЛЕ́ЗУ, вле́зешь. Р. **Влезть** (intr.).
I. **Влеза́ть.** 1. To get into (в + acc.).
2. To climb (up) (на + acc.). 3. To go in (as books go in a box) (в + acc.). 4. To fit (of clothes, etc.).

ВЛЕЗЬ (imp.), see вле́зу.

ВЛЕЙ (imp.). Р. **Влить** (acc.). I.
Влива́ть. 1. (lit. and fig.) To pour (s.t. into s.t.) (acc. + в + acc.).
2. To bring in (as replacements). (Also see волью́.)

ВЛЁК, влекла́ (past), see влеку́.

ВЛЕКИ́ (imp.), see влеку́.

ВЛЕКО́МЫЙ (pres. pp), see влеку́.

ВЛЕКУ́, влечёшь, влеку́т. I. **Влечь[1]**
(acc.). 1. To draw, drag, carry. 2. To attract. 3. To be attracted (to s.t.) (impers.) (acc. of person + к + dat.).

ВЛЕ́ПЛЕННЫЙ; вле́плен, —а, —о, —ы (ppp), see влеплю́.

ВЛЕПЛЮ́, вле́пишь. Р. **Влепи́ть**
(acc.). I. **Влепля́ть.** 1. To stick, place (s.t. into an adhesive material) (as tile in a mosaic, etc.) (acc. + в + acc.). 2. To give (s.o. a blow, slap, reprimand, etc.) (acc. + dat. of person). 3. To put (a bullet into s.o.) (acc. + в + acc.).

ВЛЕТИ́ (imp.), see влечу́.

ВЛЕТИ́ШЬ, see влечу́.

ВЛЕТЯ́Т, see влечу́.

ВЛЕЧЁШЬ, see влеку́.

ВЛЕЧУ́, влети́шь. Р. **Влете́ть** (intr.).
I. **Влета́ть.** 1. To fly in (в + acc.).
2. To dash in (в + acc.). 3. To be punished, "catch it" (impers. + dat.).

ВЛИ́ТЫЙ; влит, —а́, —о, —ы (ppp), see влей and волью́.

ВЛОМЛЮ́СЬ, вло́мишься. Р. **Вло-ми́ться** (intr.). I. **Вла́мываться.** To break into, burst into (e.g., a room) (в + acc.).

ВЛЮБЛЮ́, влю́бишь. Р. **Влюби́ть**
(acc. + в + acc.). I. **Влюбля́ть.** To make fall in love with.

ВЛЯГ (imp.), see вля́гу.

ВЛЯ́ГУ, вля́жешь, вля́гут. Р. **Влечь[2]**
(intr.). To wedge (as oneself into s.t.) (в + acc.).

ВЛЯ́ЖЕШЬ, see вля́гу.

ВМА́ЖЕШЬ, see вма́жу.

ВМА́ЖУ, вма́жешь. Р. **Вма́зать** (acc.).
I. **Вма́зывать.** To mortar, cement, or putty (as bricks into a wall, etc.) (acc. + в + acc.).

ВМАЖЬ (imp.), see вма́жу.

ВМА́ЗАННЫЙ; вма́зан, —а, —о, —ы (ppp), see вма́жу.

ВМЁЛ, вмела́ (past), see вмету́.

ВМЁРЗ, вмёрзла (past). Р. **Вмёрзнуть**
(intr.). I. **Вмерза́ть.** To become frozen in position (as a ship in the ice, etc.).

ВМЕТЁННЫЙ; вметён, —а́, —о́, —ы́ (ppp), see вмету́.

ВМЕТЁШЬ, see вмету́.

ВМЕТИ́ (imp.), see вмету́.

ВМЕТУ́, вметёшь. Р. **Вмести́** (acc.). To sweep (s.t. somewhere or into s.t.).

ВМЁТШИЙ (pap), see вмету́.

ВМЕ́ШЕННЫЙ; вме́шен, —а, —о, —ы (ppp), see вмешу́.

ВМЕШУ́, вме́сишь. Р. **Вмеси́ть** (acc.).
I. **Вме́шивать.** To add (s.t.) while kneading (as nuts to dough) (acc. + в + acc.).

ВМЕЩЁННЫЙ; вмещён, —а́, —о́, —ы́ (ppp), see вмещу́.

ВМЕЩУ́, вмести́шь. Р. **Вмести́ть**
(acc.). I. **Вмеща́ть.** 1. To contain, hold (of a container, a room, etc.) (3rd pers. only). 2. To find room for, place (s.t. in s.t.) (as one's clothes in a trunk).

ВМЯ́ТЫЙ; вмят, —а, —о, —ы (ppp).

Р. **Вмять** (acc.). I. **Вмина́ть.** 1. To press in (as a cork into a bottle) (acc. + в + acc.). 2. To dent. (Also see **вомну́.**)

ВНЕ́МЛЕШЬ, see **вне́млю.**

ВНЕМЛИ́ and **вне́мли** (imp.), see **вне́млю.**

ВНЕ́МЛЮ, вне́млешь (archaic and poetic conjugation shown). I. **Внима́ть** (dat.). Р. **Внять.** To listen to, hark to, heed.

ВНЁС, внесла́ (past), see **внесу́.**

ВНЕСЁННЫЙ; внесён, —а́, —о́, —ы́ (ppp), see **внесу́.**

ВНЕСЁШЬ, see **внесу́.**

ВНЕСИ́ (imp.), see **внесу́.**

ВНЕСУ́, внесёшь. Р. **Внести́** (acc.). I. **Вноси́ть.** 1. To bring in, carry in. 2. To pay (as fees). 3. To insert, enter, add (as a name in a list). 4. To introduce, put (as fertilizer into soil). 5. (fig.) To introduce (as a resolution).

ВНИК, вни́кла (past). Р. **Вни́кнуть** (в + acc.). I. **Вника́ть.** To penetrate the meaning of (s.t.), think over and understand.

ВНОШУ́, вно́сишь. I. **Вноси́ть** (acc.). Р. **Внести́.** 1. To bring in, carry in. 2. To pay (as fees). 3. To insert, enter, add (as a name in a list) (acc. + в + acc.). 4. To introduce, put (as fertilizer into soil) (acc. + в + acc.). 5. (fig.) To introduce (as a resolution).

ВО́БРАННЫЙ; во́бран, —а, —о, —ы (ppp). Р. **Вобра́ть** (acc.). I. **Вбира́ть.** 1. To absorb. 2. To suck in, drink in. 3. To inhale (also see **вберу́**).

ВОБЬЁШЬ, see **вобью́.**

ВОБЬЮ́, вобьёшь. Р. **Вбить** (acc.). I. **Вбива́ть.** (lit. and fig.) To drive in; to hammer in (e.g., a nail into ·s.t., a thought into s.o.'s head).

ВОВЛЁК, вовлекла́ (past), see **вовлеку́.**

ВОВЛЕКИ́ (imp.), see **вовлеку́.**

ВОВЛЕКУ́, вовлечёшь, вовлеку́т. Р. **Вовле́чь** (acc. + в + acc.). I. **Вовле-ка́ть.** 1. To involve (as s.o. in s.t.). 2. To draw or drag (s.o. or s.t. into s.t.).

ВОВЛЕЧЁННЫЙ; вовлечён, —а́, —о́, —ы́ (ppp), see **вовлеку́.**

ВОВЛЕЧЁШЬ, see **вовлеку́.**

ВОВЬЁШЬ, see **вовью́.**

ВОВЬЮ́, вовьёшь. Р. **Ввить** (acc.).

I. **Ввива́ть.** To plait, interlace, inter-twine.

ВО́ГНАННЫЙ; во́гнан, —а, —о, —ы (ppp). Р. **Вогна́ть** (acc. + в + acc.). I. **Вгоня́ть.** 1. To drive (s.t. or s.o. into s.t.) (as cattle into a pen). 2. To drive (s.t. into s.t.) (as a nail into a board). 3. (fig.) To bring (s.o.) to an emotional state (as to tears). (Also see **вгоню́.**)

ВОДРУЖЁННЫЙ; водружён, —а́, —о́, —ы́ (ppp), see **водружу́.**

ВОДРУЖУ́, водрузи́шь. Р. **Водрузи́ть** (acc.). I. **Водружа́ть.** 1. To erect, mount (e.g. equipment, etc.). 2. To raise, hoist (as a flag).

ВО́ЕШЬ. I. **Выть** (intr.). To howl or wail (also see **во́ю**).

ВОЖУ́[1], во́дишь. I. **Води́ть.** 1. To take, conduct, lead (as s.o. or s.t.) (acc.). 2. accompany (as s.o.) (acc.). 3. To drive, steer (as a car, a boat) (acc.). 4. To maintain (as a friendship with s.o.) (acc. + с + inst.). 5. To pass (s.t.) over the surface (of s.t.) (e.g., pass one's hand over one's face) (inst. of hand + по + dat.).

ВОЖУ́[2], во́зишь. I. **Вози́ть.** 1. To carry, convey (by vehicle, etc., s.o. or s.t.) (acc.). 2. To draw, drag (as one's foot along the floor) (inst. of foot + по + dat.). 3. To pull, draw (of horses, etc.) (acc.). 4. To beat, strike (s.o. or s.t. with s.t.) (acc. + inst.).

ВОЗБУЖДЁННЫЙ; возбуждён, —а́, —о́, —ы́ (ppp), see **возбужу́.**

ВОЗБУЖУ́, возбуди́шь. Р. **Возбуди́ть** (acc.). 1. **Возбужда́ть.** 1. To excite, arouse, rouse. 2. To incite, stir up. 3. To raise (as a question). 4. To institute (as proceedings).

ВОЗВЕДЁННЫЙ; возведён, —а́, —о́, —ы́ (ppp), see **возведу́.**

ВОЗВЕДЁШЬ, see **возведу́.**

ВОЗВЕДИ́ (imp.), see **возведу́.**

ВОЗВЕДУ́, возведёшь. Р. **Возвести́** (acc.). I. **Возводи́ть.** 1. (lit. and fig.) To raise, elevate. 2. To erect (as a building). 3. To raise mathematically to a given power (acc. + в + acc.). 4. To trace/attribute to (as one's behavior to one's religious beliefs) (acc. of behavior + к + dat. of religious beliefs). 5. To attribute (s.t. to s.o.), charge (s.o. with s.t.) (e.g., slander) (acc. of slander + **на** + acc. of s.o.).

ВОЗВЕ́ДШИЙ (pap), see **возведу́.**

ВОЗВЁЛ, возвела́ (past), see **возведу́.**

ВОЗВЕЩЁННЫЙ; возвещён, —а́, —о́, —ы́ (ppp), see **возвещу́.**

ВОЗВЕЩУ́, возвести́шь. P. **Возвести́ть** (acc.). I. **Возвеща́ть.** To announce, proclaim.

ВОЗВОЖУ́, возво́дишь. I. **Возводи́ть** (acc.). P. **Возвести́.** 1. (lit. and fig.) To raise, elevate. 2. To erect (as a building). 3. (fig.) To raise mathematically to a given power (acc. + **в** | acc.). 4. To trace/attribute to (as one's behavior to one's religious beliefs) (acc. of behavior + **к** + dat. of religious beliefs). 5. To attribute (s.t. to s.o.), charge (s.o. with s.t.), (e.g., slander) (acc. of slander + **на** + acc. of s.o.).

ВОЗВРАЩЁННЫЙ; возвращён, —а́, —о́, —ы́ (ppp), see **возвращу́.**

ВОЗВРАЩУ́, возврати́шь. P. **Возврати́ть** (acc.). I. **Возвраща́ть.** To return, give back.

ВОЗВЫ́СЬ (imp.), see **возвы́шу.**

ВОЗВЫ́ШЕННЫЙ; возвы́шен, —а, —о, —ы (ppp), see **возвы́шу.**

ВОЗВЫ́ШУ, возвы́сишь. P. **Возвы́сить** (acc.). I. **Возвыша́ть.** 1. (arch.) To raise, make higher (as a fence). 2. (arch.) To raise (as price). 3. To raise (as one's voice). 4. (fig.) To enhance (as one's image).

ВОЗГЛА́ВЛЕННЫЙ; возгла́влен, —а, —о, —ы (ppp), see **возгла́влю.**

ВОЗГЛА́ВЛЮ, возгла́вишь. P. **Возгла́вить** (acc.) (mean. 1). I. **Возглавля́ть** (mean. 2). 1. To put oneself at the head (of s.t.) 2. To head (s.t.), be at the head of (as an organization).

ВОЗГЛА́ВЬ (imp.), see **возгла́влю.**

ВОЗГЛАШЁННЫЙ; возглашён, —а́, —о́, —ы́ (ppp), see **возглашу́.**

ВОЗГЛАШУ́, возгласи́шь. P. **Возгласи́ть** (acc.). I. **Возглаша́ть.** To proclaim.

ВОЗГОРЖУ́СЬ, возгорди́шься. P. **Возгорди́ться** (inst.). To pride oneself, be conceited (about s.t.).

ВОЗГОРИ́СЬ (imp.), see **возгорю́сь.**

ВОЗГОРИ́ШЬСЯ, see **возгорю́сь.**

ВОЗГОРЮ́СЬ, возгори́шься. P. **Возгоре́ться** (intr.). I. **Возгора́ться.** 1. To flare up (as a flame). 2. (fig.)

To flare up. 3. (fig.) To flame (with s.t.) (as anger) (inst.).

ВОЗГОРЯ́ТСЯ, see **возгорю́сь.**

ВОЗДАВА́Й (imp.), see **воздаю́.**

ВОЗДАВА́Я (adv. pres. part.), see **воздаю́.**

ВОЗДАДИ́М, воздади́те, воздаду́т (pl. forms), see **возда́м.**

ВОЗДАЁШЬ, see **воздаю́.**

ВОЗДА́Й (imp.), see **возда́м.**

ВОЗДА́М, возда́шь, возда́ст (sing. forms). P. **Возда́ть.** I. **Воздава́ть.** 1. To render (to s.o.) what is due (him) (as homage) (acc. + dat.). 2. (fig.) To pay back, return (as good for evil) (inst. of good + **за** + acc. of evil).

ВО́ЗДАННЫЙ; во́здан, —а́, —о, —ы (ppp), see **возда́м.**

ВОЗДА́СТ, see **возда́м.**

ВОЗДА́ШЬ, see **возда́м.**

ВОЗДАЮ́, воздаёшь. I. **Воздава́ть.** P. **Возда́ть.** 1. To render (to s.o.) what is due (him) (as homage) (acc. + dat.). 2. (fig.) To pay back, return (as good for evil) (inst. of good + **за** + acc. of evil).

ВОЗДВИ́Г, воздви́гла (past). P. **Воздви́гнуть** (acc.). I. **Воздвига́ть.** To erect, build.

ВОЗДЕ́НЕШЬ, see **возде́ну.**

ВОЗДЕ́НУ, возде́нешь. P. **Возде́ть** (acc.). I. **Воздева́ть.** To lift (as one's hands to heaven) (acc. + **к** + dat.).

ВОЗДЕ́НЬ (imp.), see **возде́ну.**

ВОЗДЕ́РЖАТСЯ, see **воздержу́сь.**

ВОЗДЕРЖИ́СЬ (imp.), see **воздержу́сь.**

ВОЗДЕ́РЖИШЬСЯ, see **воздержу́сь.**

ВОЗДЕРЖУ́СЬ, возде́ржишься. P. **Воздержа́ться** (intr.). I. **Возде́рживаться.** 1. To refrain or abstain (from) (**от** + gen.). 2. To decline (to do s.t.) (+ inf.).

ВОЗДЕ́ТЫЙ; возде́т, —а, —о, —ы (ppp), see **возде́ну.**

ВОЗЖГИ́ (imp.), see **возжгу́.**

ВОЗЖГЛА́, возжгло́, возжгли́ (past), see **возжгу́** and **возжёг.**

ВОЗЖГУ́, возжжёшь, возжгу́т. P. **Возже́чь** (acc.) (arch.). I. **Возжига́ть.** 1. To light; to set fire, ignite. 2. To inspire, kindle.

ВОЗЖЁГ, возжгла́ (past), see **возжгу́.**

ВОЗЖЖЁННЫЙ; возжжён, —а́, —о́, —ы́ (ppp), see **возжгу́.**

ВОЗЖЖЁШЬ, see возжгу́.

ВОЗЗОВЁШЬ, see воззову́.

ВОЗЗОВИ́ (imp.), see воззову́.

ВОЗЗОВУ́, воззовёшь. Р. Воззва́ть (intr.). I. Взыва́ть. To call (as to s.o. for s.t.) (e.g., for help) (к + dat. + о + prep.).

ВОЗЛЁГ, возлегла́ (past), see возля́гу.

ВОЗЛЕЖА́Т, see возлежу́.

ВОЗЛЕЖИ́ (imp.), see возлежу́.

ВОЗЛЕЖИ́ШЬ, see возлежу́.

ВОЗЛЕЖУ́, возлежи́шь. I. Возлежа́ть (intr.). To recline (on s.t.) (на + prep.).

ВЗОЛЮ́БЛЕННЫЙ; возлю́блен, —а, —о, —ы (ppp), see возлюблю́.

ВОЗЛЮБЛЮ́, возлю́бишь. Р. Возлюби́ть (arch.) (acc.). 1. To grow fond of. 2. To come to love, fall in love with.

ВОЗЛЯ́Г (imp.), see возля́гу.

ВОЗЛЯ́ГУ, возля́жешь, возля́гут. Р. Возле́чь (intr.). To recline, lie (на + acc.).

ВОЗЛЯ́ЖЕШЬ, see возля́гу.

ВОЗМЕЩЁННЫЙ; возмещён, —а́, —о́, —ы́ (ppp) see возмещу́.

ВОЗМЕЩУ́, возмести́шь. Р. Возмести́ть (acc. + dat.). I. Возмеща́ть. To refund (as money to s.o.). 2. To compensate (s.o. for s.t.).

ВОЗМУЩЁННЫЙ; возмущён, —а́, —о́, —ы́ (ppp), see возмущу́.

ВОЗМУЩУ́, возмути́шь. Р. Возмути́ть (acc.). I. Возмуща́ть. 1. To fill with indignation. 2. (arch.) To incite to rebellion. 3. To disturb, agitate.

ВОЗНАГРАЖДЁННЫЙ; вознаграждён, —а́, —о́, —ы́ (ppp), see вознагражу́.

ВОЗНАГРАЖУ́, вознагради́шь. Р. Вознагради́ть (acc.). I. Вознагражда́ть. To reward (s.o. for s.t.) (acc. + за + acc.).

ВОЗНЕНАВИ́ДИШЬ, see возненави́жу.

ВОЗНЕНАВИ́ДЬ (imp.), see возненави́жу.

ВОЗНЕНАВИ́ДЯТ, see возненави́жу.

ВОЗНЕНАВИ́ЖУ, возненави́дишь. Р. Возненави́деть (acc.). To come to hate.

ВОЗНЁС, вознесла́ (past), see вознесу́.

ВОЗНЕЁНСНЫЙ; вознесён, —а́, —о́, —ы́ (ppp), see воснесу́.

ВОЗНЕСЁШЬ, see вознесу́.

ВОЗНЕСИ́ (imp.), see вознесу́.

ВОЗНЕСУ́, вознесёшь. Р. Вознести́ (acc.). I. Возноси́ть. (lit. and fig.) To raise, lift.

ВОЗНИ́К, возни́кла (past). Р. Возни́кнуть (intr.). I. Возника́ть. To arise, appear.

ВОЗНОШУ́, возно́сишь. I. Возноси́ть (acc.). Р. Вознести́. (lit. and fig.) To raise, lift.

ВОЗОБНОВЛЁННЫЙ; возобновлён, —а́, —о́, —ы́ (ppp), see возобновлю́.

ВОЗОБНОВЛЮ́, возобнови́шь. Р. Возобнови́ть (acc.). I. Возобновля́ть. 1. To begin again, resume. 2. To revive (as a play). 3. To renew, renovate.

ВОЗОПИЁШЬ, see возопию́.

ВОЗОПИЙ (imp.), see возопию́.

ВОЗОПИЮ́, возопиёшь. Р. Возопия́ть (arch.) (intr.). To begin to call loudly.

ВОЗОПЛЮ́, возопи́шь. Р. Возопи́ть (intr.). To begin to howl, shout.

ВОЗРАЖУ́, возрази́шь. Р. Возрази́ть (intr.). I. Возража́ть. 1. To object (to) (на + acc.) or (про́тив + gen.). 2. To reply (to) (dat.).

ВОЗРАСТЁШЬ, see возрасту́.

ВОЗРАСТИ́ (imp.), see возрасту́.

ВОЗРАСТУ́, возрастёшь. Р. Возрасти́ (intr.). I. Возраста́ть. 1. (arch.) To grow (of people). 2. To increase (in size, strength, volume).

ВОЗРОЖДЁННЫЙ; возрождён, —а́, —о́, —ы́ (ppp), see возрожу́.

ВОЗРОЖУ́, возроди́шь. Р. Возроди́ть (acc.). I. Возрожда́ть. 1. To revive, reestablish. 2. To revitalize.

ВОЗРО́ПЩЕШЬ, see возропщу́.

ВОЗРОПЩИ́ (imp.), see возропщу́.

ВОЗРОПЩУ́, возро́пщешь. Р. Возропта́ть (arch.) (intr.). To murmur, grumble.

ВОЗРО́С, возросла́ (past), see возрасту́.

ВОЗЬМЁШЬ, see возьму́.

ВОЗЬМИ́ (imp.), see возьму́.

ВОЗЬМУ́, возьмёшь. Р. Взять (acc.). I. Брать (mean. 1 thru 3). 1. To take. 2. To obtain. 3. To employ, hire. 4. To arrest (For numerous lit. and fig. meanings see unabridged dictionary.)

ВОЙ (imp.). I. Выть (intr.). To howl or wail. (Also see во́ю.)

ВОЙДЁШЬ, see **войду́.**

ВОЙДИ́ (imp.), see **войду́.**

ВОЙДУ́, войдёшь. Р. Войти́ (intr.).
I. **Входи́ть.** 1. To enter, enter into
(в + асс.). 2. To become (as a member of s.t.) (в + асс.). 3. To go in, fit
in (as clothes in a drawer) (в + асс.).
4. To come in (as to fashion, use, etc.)
(в + асс.).

ВОЙДЯ́ (adv. past part.), see **войду́.**

ВОЛО́К, волокла́ (past), see **волоку́.**

ВОЛОКИ́ (imp.), see **волоку́.**

ВОЛОКУ́, волочёшь, волоку́т. I. **Во-
ло́чь** (асс.). To drag.

ВОЛОЧА́ (adv. pres. part.), see **волоку́.**

ВОЛОЧЁШЬ, see **волоку́.**

ВОЛЬЁШЬ, see **волью́.**

ВОЛЬЮ́, вольёшь. Р. Влить (асс.).
I. **Влива́ть.** 1. (lit. and fig.) To pour
(s.t. into s.t.) (асс. + в + асс.). 2.
To bring in (as replacements).

ВОМНЁШЬ, see **вомну́.**

ВОМНИ́ (imp.), see **вомну́.**

ВОМНУ́, вомнёшь. Р. Вмять (асс.).
I. **Вмина́ть.** 1. To press in (as a cork
into a bottle (асс. + в + асс.). 2. To
dent.

ВОМЧА́ТСЯ, see **вомчу́сь.**

ВОМЧИ́СЬ (imp.), see **вомчу́сь.**

ВОМЧИ́ШЬСЯ, see **вомчу́сь.**

ВОМЧУ́СЬ, вомчи́шься. Р. Вомча́ться
(intr.). To rush, dash (into).

ВОНЖУ́, вонзи́шь. Р. Вонзи́ть (асс.).
I. **Вонза́ть.** 1. To thrust, plunge (as
a dagger into s.t.). 2. To direct one's
glance (at s.t. or s.o.) (в + асс.).

ВОНЗЁННЫЙ; вонзён, —а́, —о́, —ы́
(ррр), see **вонжу́.**

**ВООБРАЖЁННЫЙ; воображён, —а́,
—о́, —ы́** (ррр), see **воображу́.**

**ВООБРАЖУ́, вообрази́шь. Р. Во-
образи́ть** (асс.). I. **Вообража́ть.** 1.
To imagine, fancy (frequently—to
o.s.: себе́). 2. To suppose, assume,
consider (that: что) or (s.o. or s.t. to
be s.t.) (асс. + inst.).

**ВООДУШЕВЛЁННЫЙ; воодушев-
лён, —а́, —о́, —ы́** (ррр), see **вооду-
шевлю́.**

**ВООДУШЕВЛЮ́, воодушеви́шь. Р.
Воодушеви́ть** (асс.). I. **Воодушев-
ля́ть.** To inspire, fill with enthusiasm.

ВОПИЁШЬ, see **вопию́.**

ВОПИ́Й (imp.), see **вопию́.**

ВОПИЮ́, вопиёшь. I. **Вопия́ть** (arch.)
(intr.). To cry out.

**ВОПЛОЩЁННЫЙ; воплощён, —а́,
—о́, —ы́** (ррр), see **воплощу́.**

**ВОПЛОЩУ́, воплоти́шь. Р. Вопло-
ти́ть** (асс.). I. **Воплоща́ть.** To per-
sonify, embody, incarnate.

ВОПЛЮ́, вопи́шь. I. **Вопи́ть** (intr.).
To howl, wail.

**ВОПРОШЁННЫЙ; вопрошён, —а́,
—о́, —ы́** (ррр), see **вопрошу́.**

ВОПРОШУ́, вопроси́шь. Р. Вопроси́ть
(arch.) (асс.). I. **Вопроша́ть.** To
question, inquire (of s.o.).

ВОПЬЁШЬСЯ, see **вопью́сь.**

ВОПЬЮ́СЬ, вопьёшься. Р. Впи́ться
(intr.). I. **Впива́ться.** 1. To pierce,
penetrate, stick into (в + асс.). 2. To
cling to (в + асс.). 3. To fix one's
eyes on (в + асс.). 4. To accustom
oneself to drink.

ВОРВЁШЬСЯ, see **ворву́сь.**

ВОРВИ́СЬ (imp.), see **ворву́сь.**

ВОРВУ́СЬ, ворвёшься. Р. Ворва́ться
(intr.). I. **Врыва́ться.** To burst into
(as a room) (e.g., of people, sounds,
etc.) (в + асс.).

ВОРОЧУ́[1], воро́тишь. Р. Вороти́ть
(асс.). 1. To return (s.t.). 2. To make
(s.o.) return (e.g., home). 3. To get
back (e.g., s.t. stolen).

ВОРОЧУ́[2], воро́тишь. I. **Вороти́ть.**
1. To turn (s.o. or s.t.) (асс.). 2. (fig.)
To turn (one's nose up at s.t. or s.o.)
(асс. + от + gen.). 3. To manage,
boss (inst.).

ВОРЧА́Т, see **ворчу́.**

ВОРЧИ́ (imp.), see **ворчу́.**

ВОРЧИ́ШЬ, see **ворчу́.**

ВОРЧУ́, ворчи́шь. I. **Ворча́ть** (intr.)
1. To grumble, growl (of a person).
2. To growl (of a dog).

ВОСКРЕ́С, воскре́сла (past). Р. **Воск-
ре́снуть** (intr.). I. **Воскреса́ть.** 1. To
come to life, rise from the dead.
2. (fig.) To revive.

**ВОСКРЕШЁННЫЙ; воскрешён, —а́,
—о́, —ы́** (ррр), see **воскрешу́.**

**ВОСКРЕШУ́, воскреси́шь. Р. Вос-
креси́ть** (асс.). I. **Воскреша́ть.** 1. To
resurrect. 2. (fig.) To revive.

ВОСПЕ́ТЫЙ; воспе́т, —а, —о, —ы
(ррр), see **воспою́.**

ВОСПОЁШЬ, see **воспою́.**

ВОСПОЙ (imp.), see воспою.

ВОСПОЮ, воспоёшь. Р. Воспеть (acc.). I. Воспевать. 1. To eulogize. 2. To praise, sing the praises of (in song or poem).

ВОСПРЕЩЁННЫЙ; воспрещён, —а, —о, —ы (ppp), see воспрещу.

ВОСПРЕЩУ, воспретишь. Р. Воспретить (acc.). I. Воспрещать. To prohibit (e.g., s.t. to s.o.) (acc. of s.t. + dat. of s.o.).

ВОСПРИМЕШЬ, see восприму.

ВОСПРИМИ (imp.), see восприму.

ВОСПРИМУ, воспримешь. Р. Воспринять (acc.). I. Воспринимать. 1. To apprehend, perceive, grasp. 2. To receive.

ВОСПРИНЯТЫЙ; воспринят, —а, —о, —ы (ppp), see восприму.

ВОСПРОИЗВЕДЁННЫЙ; воспроизведён, —а, —о, —ы (ppp), see воспроизведу.

ВОСПРОИЗВЕДЁШЬ, see воспроизведу.

ВОСПРОИЗВЕДИ (imp.), see воспроизведу.

ВОСПРОИЗВЕДУ, воспроизведёшь. Р. Воспроизвести (acc.). I. Воспроизводить. 1. To reproduce. 2. To copy, re-create. 3. To recall (to mind) (в + памяти).

ВОСПРОИЗВЕ́ДШИ and воспроизведя́ (adv. past. part), see воспроизведу.

ВОСПРОИЗВЕ́ДШИЙ (pap), see воспроизведу.

ВОСПРОИЗВЕДЯ́ and воспроизве́дши (adv. past part.), see воспроизведу.

ВОСПРОИЗВЁЛ, воспроизвела́ (past), see воспроизведу.

ВОСПРОИЗВОЖУ́, воспроизво́дишь. I. Воспроизводить (acc.). Р. Воспроизвести. 1. To reproduce. 2. To copy, recreate. 3. To recall (to mind) (в + памяти).

ВОСПРОТИ́ВЛЮСЬ, воспроти́вишься. Р. Воспроти́виться (dat.). I. Проти́виться. To oppose, object to.

ВОСПРОТИ́ВЬСЯ (imp.), see воспроти́влюсь.

ВОССЕ́Л, воссе́ла (past), see восся́ду.

ВОССЛА́ВЛЕННЫЙ; воссла́влен,—а —о, —ы (ppp), see воссла́влю.

ВОССЛА́ВЛЮ, воссла́вишь. Р. Восславить (acc.). I. Восславля́ть. 1. To glorify. 2. To praise, extol.

ВОССЛА́ВЬ (imp.), see воссла́влю.

ВОССОЗДАВА́Й (imp.), see воссоздаю́.

ВОССОЗДАВА́Я (adv. pres. part.), see воссоздаю́.

ВОССОЗДАДИ́М, воссоздади́те, воссоздаду́т (pl. forms) see воссозда́м.

ВОССОЗДАЁШЬ, see воссоздаю́.

ВОССОЗДА́Й (imp.), see воссозда́м.

ВОССОЗДА́М, воссозда́шь, воссозда́ст (sing. forms). Р. Воссозда́ть (acc.). I. Воссоздава́ть. (lit. and fig.) To re-create, reconstruct.

ВОССО́ЗДАННЫЙ; воссо́здан, —а́ (or —а) —о, —ы (ppp), see воссоздам.

ВОССОЗДА́СТ, see воссозда́м.

ВОССОЗДА́ШЬ, see воссозда́м.

ВОССОЗДАЮ́, воссоздаёшь. I. Воссоздава́ть (acc.). Р. Воссозда́ть. (lit. and fig.) To re-create, reconstruct.

ВОССТАВА́Й (imp.), see восстаю́.

ВОССТАВА́Я (adv. pres. part.), see восстаю́.

ВОССТА́ВЛЕННЫЙ; восста́влен, —а, —о, —ы (ppp), see восста́влю.

ВОССТА́ВЛЮ, восста́вишь. Р. Восста́вить (acc.). I. Восставля́ть. (math.) To raise (a perpendicular to s.t.) (acc. + к + dat.).

ВОССТА́ВЬ (imp.), see восста́влю.

ВОССТАЁШЬ, see восстаю́.

ВОССТА́НЕШЬ, see восста́ну.

ВОССТАНО́ВЛЕННЫЙ; восстано́влен, —а, —о, —ы (ppp), see восстановлю́.

ВОССТАНОВЛЮ́, восстано́вишь. Р. Восстанови́ть (acc.). I. Восстана́вливать. 1. To reestablish, restore. 2. (tech.) To reduce, regenerate, reclaim. 3. To incite (against) (acc. + про́тив + gen.). 4. To recall (to mind) (acc. + в + памяти).

ВОССТА́НУ, восста́нешь. Р. Восста́ть (intr.). I. Восстава́ть. 1. To get up, rise (e.g., early). 2. (fig.) To arise, rise. 3. To rebel, take up arms (against) (про́тив + gen.).

ВОССТА́НЬ (imp.), see восста́ну.

ВОССТАЮ́, восстаёшь. I. Восстава́ть (intr.). Р. Восста́ть. 1. (arch.) To get up, rise. 2. (fig.) To arise, rise. 3. To rebel, take up arms (against) (про́тив + gen.).

ВОССЯ́ДЕШЬ, see восся́ду.

ВОССЯ́ДУ, восся́дешь. Р. Воссе́сть (intr.) (ironical and arch.). To sit down solemnly.

ВОССЯ́ДЬ (imp.), see восся́ду.

ВОСХИ́ТЬ (imp.), see восхи́щу.

ВОСХИ́ЩЕННЫЙ; восхи́щен, —а, —о, —ы (ppp), see восхи́щу.

ВОСХИЩЁННЫЙ; восхищён, —а́, —о́, —ы́ (ppp), see восхищу́.

ВОСХИ́ЩУ, восхи́тишь. Р. Восхи́тить (arch., poetic, acc.). I. Восхища́ть. To carry up (e.g., to Mount Olympus).

ВОСХИЩУ́, восхити́шь. Р. Восхити́ть (acc.). I. Восхища́ть. To delight, enrapture.

ВОСХОЖУ́, восхо́дишь. I. Восходи́ть (intr.). Р. Взойти́ (mean. 1 and 2). 1. To ascend, mount (на + acc.). 2. To rise, ascend (of the sun, etc.). 3. To go back to, date back to (as to the 2nd century (к + dat.).

ВО́ТКАННЫЙ; во́ткан, —а, —о, —ы (ppp), see воткý.

ВОТКЁШЬ, see воткý.

ВОТКИ́ (imp.), see воткý.

ВОТКУ́, воткёшь. Р. Воткáть (acc.). To weave in (a design), interweave.

ВОТРЁШЬ, see вотрý.

ВОТРИ́ (imp.), see вотрý.

ВОТРУ́, вотрёшь. Р. Втерéть (acc.). I. Втирáть. 1. To rub (s.t. into s.t.) (as ointment into one's arm) (acc. + в + acc.). 2. To deceive (очки́ + dat. of person).

ВОШÉДШИЙ (pap), see вошёл.

ВОШЁЛ, вошлá (past). Р. Войти́ (intr.). I. Входи́ть. 1. To enter, enter into (в + acc.). 2. To become (as a member of s.t.) (в + acc.). 3. To go in, fit in (as clothes in a drawer (в + acc.). 4. To come in (as to fashion, use, etc.) (в + acc.).

ВОШЬЁШЬ, see вошью́.

ВОШЬЮ́, вошьёшь. Р. Вшить (acc.). I. Вшивáть. To sew (in) (acc. + в + acc.).

ВО́Ю, вóешь. I. Выть (intr.). To howl or wail.

ВОЮ́ЕШЬ, see воюю.

ВОЮ́Й (imp.), see воюю.

ВОЮЮ́, воюешь. I. Воевáть (с +

inst.). 1. To wage war (with). 2. To quarrel (with).

ВПАДЁШЬ, see впадý.

ВПАДИ́ (imp.), see впадý.

ВПАДУ́, впадёшь. Р. Впасть (intr.). I. Впадáть. 1. To become sunken (of one's cheeks, etc.). 2. (fig.) To fall (into despair, thought, disgrace, etc.) (в + acc.).

ВПАЛ, впáла (past), see лладý.

ВПЕ́ЙСЯ (imp.). Р. Впи́ться (intr.). I. Впивáться. 1. To pierce, penetrate deeply, stick into (в + acc.). 2. To cling to (в + acc.). 3. To fix one's eyes on (в + acc.). 4. To accustom oneself to drink. (Also see вопью́сь.)

ВПИ́САННЫЙ; впи́сан, —а, —о, —ы (ppp), see впишý.

ВПИ́ШЕШЬ, see впишý.

ВПИШИ́ (imp.), see впишý.

ВПИШУ́, впи́шешь. Р. Вписáть (acc.). I. Впи́сывать. 1. To insert, enter (as s.t. in a list) (в + acc.). 2. To inscribe (as one figure within another).

ВПЛЁЛ, вплелá (past), see вплетý.

ВПЛЕТЁННЫЙ; вплетён, —á, —ó, —ы́ (ppp), see вплетý.

ВПЛЕТЁШЬ, see вплетý.

ВПЛЕТИ́ (imp.), see вплетý.

ВПЛЕТУ́, вплетёшь. Р. Вплести́ (acc. + в + acc.). I. Вплетáть. 1. To intertwine, plait. 2. To intersperse (as one's conversation with oaths).

ВПЛЁТШИЙ (pap), see вплетý.

ВПЛЫВЁШЬ, see вплырý.

ВПЛЫВИ́ (imp.), see вплывý.

ВПЛЫВУ́, вплывёшь. Р. Вплыть (intr.) (в + acc.). I. Вплывáть. 1. To swim in; to float in. 2. (fig.) To float in.

ВПОЛЗ, вползлá (past), see вползý.

ВПОЛЗЁШЬ, see вползý.

ВПОЛЗИ́ (imp.), see вползý.

ВПОЛЗУ́, вползёшь. Р. Вползти́ (intr.). I. Вползáть. To crawl into, in (в + acc.); on, up (на + acc.).

ВПРÁВЛЕННЫЙ; впрáвлен, —а, —о, —ы (ppp), see впрáллю.

ВПРÁВЛЮ, впрáвишь. Р. Впрáвить (acc.). I. Вправля́ть. 1. To set (as a broken or dislocated bone). 2. To adjust.

ВПРАВЬ (imp.), see впрáвлю.

ВПРЯГ, впрягла́ (past), see впрягу́.

ВПРЯГИ́ (imp.), see впрягу́.

ВПРЯГУ́, впряжёшь, впрягу́т. Р. Впрячь (acc.). I. Впряга́ть. To harness (s.t. to s.t.) (acc. + в + acc.).

ВПРЯЖЁННЫЙ; впряжён, —а́, —о́, —ы́ (ppp), see впрягу́.

ВПРЯЖЁШЬ, see впрягу́.

ВПУ́ЩЕННЫЙ; впу́щен, —а, —о, —ы (ppp), see впущу́.

ВПУЩУ́, впу́стишь. Р. Впусти́ть (acc.). I. Впуска́ть. 1. To admit, let in. 2. To stick in, thrust in.

ВРАЗУМЛЁННЫЙ; вразумлён, —а́, —о́, —ы́ (ppp), see вразумлю́.

ВРАЗУМЛЮ́, вразуми́шь. Р. Вразуми́ть (acc.). I. Вразумля́ть. 1. To convince, make understand. 2. To admonish.

ВРАСТЁТ, расту́т (3rd pers. only). Р. Врасти́ (intr.). I. Враста́ть. 1. To grow into (в + acc.). 2. (fig.) To settle into (of a stone in the ground, a house into its surroundings, etc.) (в + acc.).

ВРАСТУ́Т (3rd pers. pl.), see врастёт.

ВРЕ́ЖЕШЬ, see вре́жу.

ВРЕЖУ́, вреди́шь. I. Вреди́ть (dat.). Р. Повреди́ть. To injure, harm, hurt, damage (e.g., s.o., s.o.'s health, interests, etc.).

ВРЕ́ЖУ, вре́жешь. Р. Вре́зать (acc.). I. Вреза́ть. 1. To fit (as a lock in a door) (acc. + в + acc.). 2. To cut in, carve. 3. (fig.) To engrave (as s.t. on one's memory) (acc. + в + acc.).

ВРЕЖЬ (imp.), see вре́жу.

ВРЕ́ЗАННЫЙ; вре́зан, —а, —о, —ы (ppp), see вре́жу.

ВРЁШЬ, see вру́.

ВРИ́ (imp.), see вру́.

ВРОЕШЬ, see врою.

ВРОЙ (imp.), see врою.

ВРОС, вросла́ (past). Р. Врасти́ (intr.). I. Враста́ть. 1. To grow into (в + acc.). 2. (fig.) To settle into (of a stone in the ground, a house into its surroundings, etc.) (в + acc.). (Also see врастёт.)

ВРО́Ю, вро́ешь. Р. Врыть (acc.). I. Врыва́ть. To implant, set securely in the ground (acc. + в + acc.).

ВРУ́, врёшь. I. Врать (intr.). Р. Навра́ть, совра́ть. 1. To lie, tell lies.

2. To chatter, talk nonsense. 3. To make mistakes (in s.t.) (в + prep.).

ВРУ́БЛЕННЫЙ; вру́блен, —а, —о, —ы (ppp), see врублю́.

ВРУБЛЮ́, вру́бишь. Р. Вруби́ть (acc.). I. Вруба́ть. To cut (s.t. into s.t.) (e.g., a door, into a wall (acc. + в + acc.).

ВРЫ́ТЫЙ; врыт, —а, —о, —ы (ppp), see врою.

ВСА́ЖЕННЫЙ; вса́жен, —а, —о, —ы (ppp), see всажу́.

ВСАЖУ́, вса́дишь. Р. Всади́ть (acc.). I. Вса́живать. 1. To plunge (into), stick (into), imbed (in) (acc. + в + acc.). 2. To spend or lay out (as a lot of money) (acc.).

ВСКИПИ́ (imp.), see вскиплю́.

ВСКИПИ́ШЬ, see вскиплю́.

ВСКИПЛЮ́, вскипи́шь. Р. Вскипе́ть (intr.). I. Вскипа́ть (mean. 1). 1. To boil (of a kettle, water, etc.). 2. To become exasperated, flare up.

ВСКИПЯ́Т, see вскиплю́.

ВСКИПЯЧЁННЫЙ; вскипячён, —а́, —о́, —ы́ (ppp), see вскипячу́.

ВСКИПЯЧУ́, вскипяти́шь. Р. Вскипяти́ть (acc.). I. Кипяти́ть. To boil.

ВСКО́РМЛЕННЫЙ; вско́рмлен, —а, —о, —ы (ppp), see вскормлю́.

ВСКОРМЛЁННЫЙ; вскормлён, —а́, —о́, —ы́ (arch.) (ppp), see вскормлю́.

ВСКОРМЛЮ́, вско́рмишь. Р. Вскорми́ть (acc.). I. Вска́рмливать. 1. To rear, bring up (as children). 2. To raise, breed (animals).

ВСКРИЧА́Т, see вскричу́.

ВСКРИЧИ́ (imp.), see вскричу́.

ВСКРИЧИ́ШЬ, see вскричу́.

ВСКРИЧУ́, вскричи́шь. Р. Вскрича́ть. 1. To exclaim (intr.) or (acc.). 2. To call, call out (intr.). 3. (arch.) To call (s.o.) (acc.).

ВСКРО́ЕШЬ, see вскро́ю.

ВСКРОЙ (imp.), see вскро́ю.

ВСКРО́Ю, вскро́ешь. Р. Вскрыть (acc.). I. Вскрыва́ть. 1. To open, unseal. 2. To reveal. 3. To dissect. 4. To cut, lance.

ВСКРЫ́ТЫЙ; вскрыт, —а, —о, —ы (ppp), see вскро́ю.

ВСМОТРИ́СЬ (imp.), see всмотрю́сь.

ВСМО́ТРИШЬСЯ, see всмотрю́сь.

ВСМОТРЮ́СЬ, всмо́тришься. Р. Всмотре́ться (intr.). I. Всма́триваться.

To scrutinize, observe closely (в + acc.).

ВСМОТРЯТСЯ, see всмотрюсь.

ВСО́САННЫЙ; всо́сан, —а, —о, —ы (ppp), see всосу́.

ВСОСЁШЬ, see всосу́.

ВСОСИ́ (imp.), see всосу́.

ВСОСУ́, всосёшь. Р. Всоса́ть (acc.). I. Вса́сывать. 1. To suck. 2. To absorb. 3. To soak up.

ВСПА́ХАННЫЙ; вспа́хан, —а, —о, —ы (ppp), see вспашу́.

ВСПА́ШЕШЬ, see вспашу́.

ВСПАШИ́ (imp.), see вспашу́.

ВСПАШУ́, вспа́шешь. Р. Вспаха́ть (acc.). I. Вспа́хивать, паха́ть. To plow, till.

ВСПЛЫВЁШЬ, see всплыву́.

ВСПЛЫВИ́ (imp.), see всплыву́.

ВСПЛЫВУ́, всплывёшь. Р. Всплыть (intr.). I. Всплыва́ть. 1. To come, swim, to the surface. 2. (fig.) To come to light, come to the surface, crop up.

ВСПО́РЕШЬ, see вспорю́.

ВСПОРИ́ (imp.), see вспорю́.

ВСПО́РОТЫЙ; вспо́рот, —а, —о, —ы (ppp), see вспорю́.

ВСПОРЮ́, вспо́решь. Р. Вспоро́ть (acc.). I. Вспа́рывать. To rip open.

ВСПУХ, вспу́хла (past). Р. Вспу́хнуть (intr.), I. Вспуха́ть, пу́хнуть. To swell.

ВСТАВА́Й (imp.), see встаю́.

ВСТАВА́Я (adv. pres. part.), see встаю́.

ВСТА́ВЛЕННЫЙ; вста́влен, —а, —о, —ы (ppp), see вста́влю.

ВСТА́ВЛЮ, вста́вишь. Р. Вста́вить (acc. + в + acc.). I. Вставля́ть. 1. To put (s.o. or s.t.) into (s.t.). 2. To insert, introduce (e.g., a remark, etc.). 3. To mount (e.g., a picture, a gem).

ВСТАВЬ (imp.), see вста́влю.

ВСТАЁШЬ, see встаю́.

ВСТА́НЕШЬ, see вста́ну.

ВСТА́НУ, вста́нешь. Р. Встать (intr.). I. Встава́ть. 1. To get up, rise (e.g., people, sun, etc.). 2. To stand (of an object or person). 3. To stand up for, defend (s.o.), (на защи́ту + gen.). 4. (fig.) To arise (as problems). 5. To stop (e.g., a clock, motor, etc.).

ВСТАНЬ (imp.), see вста́ну.

ВСТАЮ́, встаёшь. I. Встава́ть (intr.). Р. Встать. 1. To get up, rise (e.g., people, the sun). 2. To stand (of an object or person). 3. To stand up for, defend, (s.o.) (на защи́ту + gen.). 4. To arise (as problems). 5. To stop (e.g., a clock, motor, etc.).

ВСТРЕТЬ (imp.), see встре́чу.

ВСТРЕ́ЧЕННЫЙ; встре́чен, —а, —о, —ы (ppp), see встре́чу.

ВСТРЕ́ЧУ, встре́тишь. Р. Встре́тить (acc.). I. Встреча́ть. 1. (lit. and fig.) To meet. 2. To greet.

ВСТРЯ́НЕШЬ, see встря́ну.

ВСТРЯ́НУ, встря́нешь. Р. Встрять (intr.) (в + acc.). To meddle, become involved, interfere in s.t.).

ВСТРЯНЬ (imp.), see встря́ну.

ВСТУПЛЮ́, всту́пишь. Р. Вступи́ть (intr.). I. Вступа́ть. 1. To enter (as a university) (в + acc.). 2. To join (as a party) (в + acc.). 3. To enter into (e.g., correspondence) (в + acc.). 4. To join, start an argument (в + acc.). 5. To step on/in (на/в + acc.).

ВСХОЖУ́, вхо́дишь. I. Входи́ть (intr.). Р. Взойти́. 1. To ascend, mount (на + acc.). 2. To rise, ascend (of the sun, etc.). 3. To come up, sprout (of plants) (from seeds). 4. (arch.) To enter (e.g., a room) (в + acc.). 5. To rise (of dough).

ВСЫ́ПАННЫЙ; всы́пан, —а, о, —ы (ppp), see всы́плю.

ВСЫ́ПЛЕШЬ, see всы́плю.

ВСЫ́ПЛЮ, всы́плешь. Р. Всы́пать. I. Всыпа́ть. 1. To pour (s.t. into s.t.) e.g., grain into a bin (acc. + в + acc.). 2. To give (s.o.) a thrashing (verbal or physical) (dat.).

ВСЫПЬ (imp.), see всы́плю.

ВТЁК, втекла́ (past), see втечёт.

ВТЕКУ́Т, see втечёт.

ВТЁР, втёрла (past). Р. Втере́ть (acc.). I. Втира́ть. 1. To rub (s.t. into s.t.) (as ointment into one's arm) (acc. + в + acc.). 2. To deceive (очки́ + dat. of person). (Also see вотру́.)

ВТЕРЁВ and втёрши (adv. past part.), see втёр and вотру́.

ВТЁРТЫЙ; втёрт, —а, —о, —ы (ppp), see втёр.

ВТЁРШИ and втере́в (adv. past part.), see втёр and вотру́.

ВТЕЧЁТ, втеку́т (3rd pers. only). Р. **Втечь** (intr.) (в + acc.). I. **Втека́ть.** To flow into.

ВТЕ́ШЕШЬСЯ, see втешу́сь.

ВТЕШИ́СЬ (imp.), see втешу́сь.

ВТЕШУ́СЬ, вте́шешься. Р. **Втеса́ться** (intr.) (в + acc.). I. **Втёсываться.** To push one's way in somewhere brazenly.

ВТО́ПТАННЫЙ; вто́птан, —а, —о, —ы (ppp), see втопчу́.

ВТО́ПЧЕШЬ, see втопчу́.

ВТОПЧИ́ (imp.), see втопчу́.

ВТОПЧУ́, вто́пчешь. Р. **Втопта́ть** (acc.). I. **Вта́птывать.** To trample down.

ВТРА́ВЛЕННЫЙ; втра́влен, —а, —о, —ы (ppp), see втравлю́.

ВТАРАВЛЮ, втра́вишь. Р. **Втрави́ть** (acc.). I. **Втра́вливать.** 1. To train to hunt (as a dog). 2. To involve (s.o.) in s.t.), draw (s.o. into s.t.) (e.g., a card game) (acc. + в + acc.).

ВХОЖУ́, вхо́дишь. I. **Входи́ть** (intr.). Р. **Войти́.** 1. To enter, enter into (в + acc.). 2. To become (as a member of s.t.) (в + acc.). 3. To go in, fit in (as clothes in a drawer) (в + acc.). 4. To come in (as to fashion, use, etc.) (в + acc.).

ВЦЕПЛЮ́СЬ, вце́пишься. Р. **Вцепи́ться.** I. **Вцепля́ться.** To seize (as s.o. by the hair) (dat. of person + в + acc. of hair).

ВШЕЙ (imp.). Р. **Вшить** (acc.). I. **Вшива́ть.** To sew in (acc. + в + acc.). (Also see вошью́.)

ВШИ́ТЫЙ; вшит, —а, —о, —ы (ppp), see вшей.

В'Е́ДЕШЬ, see в'е́ду.

В'ЕДИ́МСЯ, в'еди́тесь, в'едя́тся (pl. forms), see в'е́мся.

В'Е́ДУ, в'е́дешь. Р. **В'е́хать** (intr.). I. **В'езжа́ть.** 1. To drive into (в + acc.). 2. To drive up, go up (as a mountain) (на + acc.). 3. To move into (as a new apartment) (в + acc.). 4. To strike (e.g., s.o. on the arm) (dat. of pers. + в + acc. of arm).

В'ЕЗЖА́Й (imp.), see в'е́ду.

В'Е́ЛСЯ, в'е́лась (past), see в'е́мся.

В'Е́МСЯ, в'е́шься, в'е́стся (sing. forms). Р. **В'е́сться** (intr.) (в + acc.). I. **В'еда́ться.** 1. To eat into

corrode (3rd pers. only). 2. To penetrate with force (of the blade of an axe, etc.) (3rd pers. only). 3. To become accustomed to, be used to (as foods) (of men and animals).

В'Е́СТСЯ, see в'е́мся.

В'Е́ШЬСЯ[1] (2nd pers. sing.), see в'е́мся.

В'Е́ШЬСЯ[2] (imp.), see в'е́мся.

ВЫ́БЕГИ (imp.), see вы́бегу.

ВЫ́БЕГУ, вы́бежишь, вы́бегут. Р. **Вы́бежать** (intr.). I. **Выбега́ть.** 1. To run out (of) (из + gen.). 2. To run out on (as the street) (на + acc.).

ВЫ́БЕЖИШЬ, see вы́бегу.

ВЫ́БЕЙ (imp.). Р. **Вы́бить** (acc.). I. **Выбива́ть.** 1. To knock out, kick out, beat out, beat down. 2. To mark, stamp. (Also see вы́бью.)

ВЫ́БЕРЕШЬ, see вы́беру.

ВЫ́БЕРИ (imp.), see вы́беру.

ВЫ́БЕРУ, вы́берешь. Р. **Вы́брать** (acc.). I. **Выбира́ть.** 1. To select, choose. 2. To elect. 3. To obtain, take out (as a patent). 4. To take everything out, away. 5. To haul in (as an anchor).

ВЫ́БИТЫЙ; вы́бит, —а, —о, —ы (ppp), see вы́бей and вы́бью.

ВЫ́БРАННЫЙ; вы́бран, —а, —о, —ы (ppp), see вы́беру.

ВЫ́БРЕДЕШЬ, see вы́бреду.

ВЫ́БРЕДИ (imp.), see вы́бреду.

ВЫ́БРЕДУ, вы́бредешь. Р. **Вы́брести** (intr.). To make one's way out (of someplace).

ВЫ́БРЕДШИЙ (pap), see вы́бреду.

ВЫ́БРЕЕШЬ, see выбрею.

ВЫ́БРЕЙ (imp.), see вы́брею.

ВЫ́БРЕЛ, вы́брела (past), see вы́бреду.

ВЫ́БРЕЮ, вы́бреешь. Р. **Вы́брить** (acc.). I. **Выбрива́ть.** To shave off.

ВЫ́БРИТЫЙ; вы́брит, —а, —о, —ы (ppp), see вы́брею.

ВЫ́БРОСЬ and вы́броси (imp.), see вы́брошу.

ВЫ́БРОШЕННЫЙ; вы́брошен, —а, —о, —ы (ppp), see вы́брошу.

ВЫ́БРОШУ, вы́бросишь. Р. **Вы́бросить** (acc.). I. **Выбра́сывать.** 1. To throw out. 2. To reject, discard. 3. To throw (as goods on the market) (acc. + на + acc.). 4. To put out (shoots) (of plants, etc.). 5. (fig.) To squander, waste.

ВЫ́БУДЕШЬ, see вы́буду.

ВЫ́БУДУ, вы́будешь. Р. Вы́быть (intr.) (из + gen.). I. Выбыва́ть. 1. To leave (as a location). 2. To quit (as a member of an organization).

ВЫ́БУДЬ (imp.), see вы́буду.

ВЫ́БЬЕШЬ, see вы́бью.

ВЫ́БЬЮ, вы́бьешь. Р. Вы́бить (acc.). I. Выбива́ть. 1. To knock out, kick out, beat out, beat down. 2. To mark, stamp.

ВЫ́ВЕДЕШЬ, see вы́веду.

ВЫ́ВЕДЕННЫЙ; вы́веден, а, о, —ы (ppp), see вы́веду.

ВЫ́ВЕДИ (imp.), see вы́веду.

ВЫ́ВЕДУ, вы́ведешь. Р. Вы́вести (acc.). I. Выводи́ть. 1. To lead out, lead away, withdraw. 2. To exclude or force out (as from a club). 3. To remove (as a spot). 4. To exterminate. 5. To conclude, infer, deduce. 6. To raise (as cattle, plants, etc.). 7. To construct. 8. To portray.

ВЫ́ВЕДШИЙ (pap), see вы́веду.

ВЫ́ВЕЗ, вы́везла (past), see вы́везу.

ВЫ́ВЕЗЕННЫЙ; вы́везен, —а, —о, —ы (ppp), see вы́везу.

ВЫ́ВЕЗЕШЬ, see вы́везу.

ВЫ́ВЕЗИ (imp.), see вы́везу.

ВЫ́ВЕЗУ, вы́везешь. Р. Вы́везти (acc.). I. Вывози́ть. 1. To take away, out; to remove. 2. To bring (from someplace). 3. To save or rescue.

ВЫ́ВЕЛ, вы́вела (past), see вы́веду.

ВЫ́ВЕРТИ (imp.), see вы́верчу.

ВЫ́ВЕРТИШЬ, see вы́верчу.

ВЫ́ВЕРТЯТ, see вы́верчу.

ВЫ́ВЕРЧЕННЫЙ; вы́верчен, —а, —о, —ы (ppp), see вы́верчу.

ВЫ́ВЕРЧУ, вы́вертишь. Р. Вы́вертеть. (acc.). I. Вывёртыватв. To unscrew.

ВЫ́ВЕСИ (imp.), see вы́вешу.

ВЫ́ВЕСЬ (imp.), see вы́вешу.

ВЫ́ВЕШЕННЫЙ; вы́вешен, —а, —о, —ы (ppp), see вы́вешу.

ВЫ́ВЕШУ, вы́весишь. Р. Вы́весить (acc.). I. Выве́шивать. 1. To post (e.g., a notice). 2. To hang out (e.g., a flag, laundry, etc.). 3. To weigh (e.g., a package).

ВЫ́ВИНЧЕННЫЙ; вы́винчен, —а, —о, —ы (ppp), see вы́винчу.

ВЫ́ВИНЧУ, вы́винтишь. Р. Вы́винтить (acc.). I. Выви́нчивать. To unscrew.

ВЫ́ВОЖЕННЫЙ; вы́вожен, —а, —о, —ы (ppp), see вы́вожу[1] and [3].

ВЫ́ВОЖУ[1], вы́водишь. Р. Вы́водить (acc.). I. Выва́живать. 1. To lead, conduct (through various places) (as to conduct s.o. through the various rooms of a house). 2. To cool off (e.g., a race horse) by leading around, walking.

ВЫВОЖУ́[1], выво́дишь. I. Выводи́ть (acc.). Р. Вы́вести. 1. To lead out, lead away, withdraw. 2. To exclude or force out (as from a club). 3. To remove (as a spot). 4. To exterminate. 5. To conclude, infer, deduce. 6. To raise (as cattle, plants, etc.). 7. To construct. 8. To portray.

ВЫ́ВОЖУ[2], вы́возишь. Р. Вы́возить (acc.). To soil, dirty (e.g., a dress).

ВЫВОЖУ́[2], выво́зишь. I. Вывози́ть (acc.). Р. Вы́везти. 1. To take away, out; to remove. 2. To bring (from someplace). 3. To save or rescue.

ВЫ́ВОЛОК, вы́волокла (past), see вы́волоку.

ВЫ́ВОЛОКИ (imp.), see вы́волоку.

ВЫ́ВОЛОКУ, вы́волочешь, вы́волокут. Р. Вы́волочь (acc.). I. Выво́лакивать. To drag out.

ВЫ́ВОЛОЧЕННЫЙ; вы́волочен, —а, —о, —ы (ppp), see вы́волоку.

ВЫ́ВОЛОЧЕШЬ, see вы́волоку.

ВЫ́ВОРОЧЕННЫЙ; вы́ворочен, —а, —о, —ы (ppp), see вы́ворочу.

ВЫ́ВОРОЧУ, вы́воротишь. Р. Вы́воротить (acc.). I. Вывора́чивать. 1. To unscrew. 2. To wrench, twist, turn. 3. To turn inside out.

ВЫ́ВЯЖЕШЬ, see вы́вяжу.

ВЫ́ВЯЖИ (imp.), see вы́вяжу.

ВЫ́ВЯЖУ, вы́вяжешь. Р. Вы́вязать (acc.). I. Выв я́зывать. To knit, crochet.

ВЫ́ВЯЗАННЫЙ; вы́вязан, —а, —о, —ы (ppp), see вы́вяжу.

ВЫ́ГЛАДЬ rimp.), see вы́глажу.

ВЫ́ГЛАЖЕННЫЙ; вы́глажен, —а, —о, —ы (ppp), see вы́глажу.

ВЫ́ГЛАЖУ, вы́гладишь. Р. Вы́гладить (acc.). I. Гла́дить. 1. To iron, press. 2. To smooth.

ВЫ́ГЛЯДИ (imp.), see вы́гляжу[1] and [2].

ВЫ́ГЛЯДИШЬ, see вы́гляжу[1] and [2].

ВЫ́ГЛЯДЯТ, see **вы́гляжу**[1] and [2].

ВЫ́ГЛЯЖУ[1], **вы́глядишь**. I. Выгля-деть (intr.). To look, appear, seem (e.g., young, old, well) (inst.) or (+ adverb).

ВЫ́ГЛЯЖУ[2], **вы́глядишь**. Р. Выгля-деть (acc.). I. Выгля́дывать. 1. To find, discover. 2. To see.

ВЫ́ГНАННЫЙ; **вы́гнан**, —а, —о, —ы (ppp), see **вы́гоню**.

ВЫ́ГНИЕТ, **вы́гниют** (3rd pers. only). Р. Вы́гнить (intr.). I. Выгнива́ть. To rot, decay from within, decay completely.

ВЫ́ГНИЮТ (3rd pers. pl.), see **вы́гниет**.

ВЫ́ГОНИ (imp.), see **вы́гоню**.

ВЫ́ГОНИШЬ, see **вы́гоню**.

ВЫ́ГОНЮ, **вы́гонишь**. Р. Вы́гнать (acc.). I. Выгоня́ть. 1. To drive out, turn out (as people, cattle). 2. To exterminate. 3. To force (as plants). 4. To fire, discharge, expel. 5. To distill. 6. To produce (usually by one's efforts).

ВЫ́ГОРИТ, **вы́горят** (3rd pers. only). Р. Вы́гореть (intr.). I. Выгора́ть. 1. To turn out well, be a success. 2. To burn down, burn out, burn up. 3. To fade (in the sun) (of cloth, etc.).

ВЫ́ГОРОЖЕННЫЙ; **вы́горожен**,—а, —о, —ы (ppp), see **вы́горожу**.

ВЫ́ГОРОЖУ, **вы́городишь**. Р. Вы́го-родить (acc.). I. Выгора́живать. 1. To fence off. 2. (fig.) To shield (s.o.).

ВЫ́ГОРЯТ (3rd pers. pl.), see **вы́го-рит**.

ВЫ́ГРЕБ, **вы́гребла** (past), see **вы́-гребу**.

ВЫ́ГРЕБЕННЫЙ; **вы́гребен**, —а, —о, —ы (ppp), see **вы́гребу**.

ВЫ́ГРЕБЕШЬ, see **вы́гребу**.

ВЫ́ГРЕБИ (imp.), see **вы́гребу**.

ВЫ́ГРЕБУ, **вы́гребешь**. Р. Вы́грести. I. Выгреба́ть. 1. To rake out, clean out (acc.). 2. To row away from (от + gen.), toward (к + dat.), against (про́тив + gen.).

ВЫ́ГРУЖЕННЫЙ; **вы́гружен**, —а, —о, —ы (ppp), see **вы́гружу**.

ВЫ́ГРУЖУ, **вы́грузишь**. Р. Вы́гру-зить (acc.). I. Выгружа́ть. To un-load, discharge.

ВЫ́ГРЫЗ, **вы́грызла** (past), see **вы́-грызу**.

ВЫ́ГРЫЗЕННЫЙ; **вы́грызен**; —а, —о, —ы (ppp), see **вы́грызу**.

ВЫ́ГРЫЗЕШЬ, see **вы́грызу**.

ВЫ́ГРЫЗИ (imp.), see **вы́грызу**.

ВЫ́ГРЫЗУ, **вы́грызешь**. Р. Вы́грызть (acc.). I. Выгрыза́ть. To gnaw out (as a hole in a sack).

ВЫДАВА́Й (imp.), see **выдаю́**.

ВЫДАВА́Я (adv. pres. part.), see **выдаю́**.

ВЫ́ДАВЛЕННЫЙ; **вы́давлен**, —а, —о, —ы (ppp), see **вы́давлю**.

ВЫ́ДАВЛЮ, **вы́давишь**. Р. Вы́давить (acc.). I. Выда́вливать. 1. To squeeze out (e.g., juice, etc.). 2. To extrude (e.g., metal). 3. (fig.) To force or squeeze out (as a word). 4. To stamp, impress, imprint. 5. To break in (as a window).

ВЫ́ДАДИМ, **вы́дадите**, **вы́дадут** (pl. forms), see **вы́дам**.

ВЫДАЁШЬ, see **выдаю́**.

ВЫ́ДАЙ (imp.), see **вы́дам**.

ВЫ́ДАМ, **вы́дашь**, **вы́даст** (sing. forms). Р. Вы́дать (acc.). I. Выд-ава́ть. 1. To give; to distribute. 2. To give up, hand over. 3. To betray. 4. To represent (s.o. or s.t. as s.o. or s.t. else) (acc. + за + acc.). 5. To turn out, produce (e.g., a product).

ВЫ́ДАННЫЙ; **вы́дан**, —а, —о, —ы (ppp), see **вы́дам**.

ВЫ́ДАСТ, see **вы́дам**.

ВЫ́ДАШЬ, see **вы́дам**.

ВЫДАЮ́, **выдаёшь**. I. Выдава́ть (acc.). Р. Вы́дать. 1. To give; to distribute. 2. To give up, hand over. 3. To betray. 4. To represent (s.o. or s.t. as s.o. or s.t. else) (acc. + за + acc.). 5. To publish. 6. To turn out, produce (e.g., a product).

ВЫ́ДЕРЕШЬ, see **вы́деру**.

ВЫ́ДЕРЖАННЫЙ; **вы́держан**, —а, —о, —ы (ppp), see **вы́держу**.

ВЫ́ДЕРЖАТ, see **вы́держу**.

ВЫ́ДЕРЖИ (imp.), see **вы́держу**.

ВЫ́ДЕРЖИШЬ, see **вы́держу**.

ВЫ́ДЕРЖУ, **вы́держишь**. Р. Вы́дер-жать. I. Выде́рживать. 1. To sup-port, bear, sustain (acc.). 2. To endure, stand (acc.). 3. To pass (as an examination) (acc.). 4. To con-tain, restrain oneself (intr.). 5. To observe, adhere to (as rules, etc.) (acc.). 6. To keep for a period of time (acc.). 7. To undergo several publications (of a book) (acc. of several publications).

ВЫДЕРИ (imp.), see вы́деру.

ВЫДЕРУ, вы́дерешь. Р. Вы́драть (acc.). I. Драть (mean. 1), выдира́ть (mean. 2). 1. To flog, beat. 2. To tear out.

ВЫ́ДОЛБЛЕННЫЙ; вы́долблен, —а, —о, —ы (ppp), see вы́долблю.

ВЫ́ДОЛБЛЮ, вы́долбишь. Р. Вы́долбить (acc.). I. Выда́лбливать. 1. To hollow out. 2. To learn by heart.

ВЫ́ДРАННЫЙ; вы́дран, —а, —о, —ы (ppp), see вы́деру.

ВЫ́ДУБЛЕННЫЙ; вы́дублен, —а, —о, —ы (ppp), see вы́дублю.

ВЫ́ДУБЛЮ, вы́дубишь. Р. Вы́дубить (acc.). I. Дуби́ть. To tan (as hides, leather).

ВЫ́ДУЕШЬ, see вы́дую.

ВЫ́ДУЙ (imp.), see вы́дую.

ВЫ́ДУТЫЙ; вы́дут, —а, —о, —ы (ppp), see вы́дую.

ВЫ́ДУЮ, вы́дуешь. Р. Вы́дуть (acc.). I. Выдува́ть, дуть (mean. 3 and 4). 1. To blow (s.t. out of s.t.). 2. To cool by blowing (often impers.). 3. To blow (as glass). 4. To drink much of (s.t.).

ВЫ́ЕДЕННЫЙ; вы́еден, —а, —о, —ы (ppp), see вы́ем.

ВЫ́ЕДЕШЬ, see вы́еду.

ВЫ́ЕДИМ, вы́едите, вы́едят (pl. forms), see вы́ем.

ВЫ́ЕДУ, вы́едешь. Р. Вы́ехать (intr.). I. Выезжа́ть. 1. To leave (из/с + gen.). 2. To go (to). 3. To move (as from a house) (из + gen.). 4. To make use of, exploit (s.o. or s.t.) (на + prep.).

ВЫЕЗЖА́Й (imp.), see вы́еду.

ВЫ́ЕЗЖЕННЫЙ; вы́езжен, —а, —о, —ы (ppp), see вы́езжу.

ВЫ́ЕЗЖУ, вы́ездишь. Р. Вы́ездить (acc.). I. Выезжа́ть. 1. To break or train (a horse). 2. To earn (money) as a drayman. 3. To travel all over (e.g., the country).

ВЫ́ЕЛ, вы́ела (past), see вы́ем.

ВЫ́ЕМ, вы́ешь, вы́ест (sing. forms). Р. Вы́есть (acc.). I. Выеда́ть. 1. To eat out the inner part (of s.t.) (as a roll). 2. To corrode, eat away.

ВЫ́ЕСТ, see вы́ем.

ВЫ́ЕШЬ[1] (2nd pers. sing.), see вы́ем.

ВЫ́ЕШЬ[2] (imp.), see вы́ем.

ВЫ́ЖАТЫЙ[1]; вы́жат, —а, —о, —ы (ppp), see вы́жму.

ВЫ́ЖАТЫЙ[2]; вы́жат, —а, —о, —ы (ppp), see вы́жну.

ВЫ́ЖГИ (imp.), see вы́жгу.

ВЫ́ЖГЛА, вы́жгло, вы́жгли (past), see вы́жгу.

ВЫ́ЖГУ, вы́жжешь, вы́жгут. Р. Вы́жечь (acc.). I. Выжига́ть. 1. To burn out, burn down. 2. (tech.) To calcine. 3. To cauterize. 4. To burn (as a hole; a brand on cattle, etc.).

ВЫ́ЖДАННЫЙ; вы́ждан, —а, —о, —ы (ppp), see вы́жду.

ВЫ́ЖДЕШЬ, see вы́жду.

ВЫ́ЖДИ (imp.), see вы́жду.

ВЫ́ЖДУ, вы́ждешь. Р. Вы́ждать. I. Выжида́ть. 1. To wait for (as an opportunity) (acc./gen.). 2. To wait, bide one's time (intr.).

ВЫ́ЖЕГ, вы́жгла (past), see вы́жгу.

ВЫ́ЖЖЕННЫЙ; вы́жжен, —а, —о, —ы (ppp), see вы́жгу.

ВЫ́ЖЖЕШЬ, see вы́жгу.

ВЫ́ЖИВЕШЬ, see вы́живу.

ВЫ́ЖИВИ (imp.), see вы́живу.

ВЫ́ЖИВУ, вы́живешь. Р. Вы́жить. I. Выжива́ть. 1. To survive (intr.) or (acc.). 2. To live through, endure (acc.). 3. To live (somewhere for a period of time). 4. To drive out (as s.o.) (acc.).

ВЫ́ЖИТЫЙ; вы́жит, —а, —о, —ы (ppp), see вы́живу.

ВЫ́ЖМЕШЬ, see вы́жму.

ВЫ́ЖМИ (imp.), see вы́жму.

ВЫ́ЖМУ, вы́жмешь. Р. Вы́жать (acc.). I. Выжима́ть. 1. To squeeze out, press out (as juice from an orange) (из + gen.). 2. To wring out (as laundry). 3. To press (in weight lifting). 4. (fig.) To squeeze, wring out.

ВЫ́ЖНЕШЬ, see вы́жну.

ВЫ́ЖНИ (imp.), see вы́жну.

ВЫ́ЖНУ, вы́жнешь. Р. Вы́жать (acc.). I. Выжина́ть. 1. To reap (as a large area of wheat, etc.). 2. To reap (a quantity of).

ВЫ́ЗВАННЫЙ; вы́зван, —а, —о, —ы (ppp), see вы́зову.

ВЫ́ЗОВЕШЬ, see вы́зову.

ВЫ́ЗОВИ (imp.), see вы́зову.

ВЫ́ЗОВУ, вы́зовешь. Р. Вы́звать (acc.). I. Вызыва́ть. 1. To call out, send for. 2. To challenge (as to a duel, contest) (acc. + на + acc.). 3. To challenge (as s.o. to fight) (acc. + inf.). 4. To cause, provoke (as anger).

ВЫ́ЗОЛОЧЕННЫЙ; вы́золочен, —а, —о, —ы (ppp), see вы́золочу.

ВЫ́ЗОЛОЧУ, вы́золотишь. Р. Вы́золотить (acc.). I. Золоти́ть. To gild.

ВЫ́ЗЯБ, вы́зябла (past). Р. Вы́зябнуть (intr.). I. Вызяба́ть. To be killed by frost.

ВЫ́ИСКАННЫЙ; вы́искан, —а, —о, —ы (ppp), see вы́ищу.

ВЫ́ИЩЕШЬ, see вы́ищу.

ВЫ́ИЩИ (imp.), see вы́ищу.

ВЫ́ИЩУ, вы́ищешь. Р. Вы́искать (acc.). I. Вы́искивать. To hunt up, to find.

ВЫ́ЙДЕШЬ, see вы́йду.

ВЫ́ЙДИ (imp.), see вы́йду.

ВЫ́ЙДУ, вы́йдешь. Р. Вы́йти (intr.). I. Выходи́ть. 1. To go out, alight, get out. 2. To be published. 3. To come out, turn out. 4. To run out, be spent (as money, time, etc.). 5. To leave. 6. To be by origin, originate from (из + gen.). 7. To become a wife of (s.o.) (за + acc.). 8. To become (s.t. or s.o.) (inst.). (For other idiomatic uses, see unabridged dictionary.)

ВЫ́ЙДЯ (adv. past part.), see вы́йду.

ВЫ́КАЖЕШЬ, see вы́кажу.

ВЫ́КАЖИ (imp.), see вы́кажу.

ВЫ́КАЖУ, вы́кажешь. Р. Вы́казать (acc.). I. Выка́зывать. To show, display, manifest.

ВЫ́КАЗАННЫЙ; вы́казан, —а, —о, —ы (ppp), see вы́кажу.

ВЫ́КАЧЕННЫЙ; вы́качен, —а, —о, —ы (ppp), see вы́качу.

ВЫ́КАЧУ, вы́катишь. Р. Вы́катить. I. Вы́ка́тывать. 1. To roll out (as a barrel, carriage, etc.) (acc.). 2. To roll or ride out rapidly (of a cyclist, vehicle, etc.) (intr.). 3. To "goggle" (acc. of eyes).

ВЫ́КИПИТ, вы́кипят (3rd pers. only). Р. Вы́кипеть (intr.). I. Вы́кипа́ть. To boil away.

ВЫ́КИПЯТ (3rd pers. pl.), see вы́кипит.

ВЫ́КИПЯЧЕННЫЙ; вы́кипячен, —а, —о, —ы (ppp), see вы́кипячу.

ВЫ́КИПЯЧУ, вы́кипятишь. Р. Вы́кипятить (acc.). To boil out (e.g., laundry).

ВЫ́КИС, вы́кисла (past). Р. Вы́киснуть (intr.). I. Выкиса́ть. To ferment, become leavened (of dough) (3rd pers. only).

ВЫ́КОЛЕШЬ, see вы́колю.

ВЫ́КОЛИ (imp.), see вы́колю.

ВЫ́КОЛОТЫЙ; вы́колот, —а, —о, —ы (ppp), see вы́колю.

ВЫ́КОЛОЧЕННЫЙ; вы́колочен, —а, —о, —ы (ppp), see вы́колочу.

ВЫ́КОЛОЧУ, вы́колотишь. Р. Вы́колотить (acc.). I. Выкола́чивать. 1. To beat out (as dust from a carpet). 2. To beat (as a carpet). 3. To knock out (as nails from a board). 4. To extract (e.g., as payments from s.o.). 5. To obtain, earn with much effort. 6. To work (as leather).

ВЫ́КОЛЮ, вы́колешь. Р. Вы́колоть (acc.). I. Выка́лывать. 1. To prick (a design). 2. To put out (as eyes). 3. To chop (e.g., a hole in the ice).

ВЫ́КОРМЛЕННЫЙ; вы́кормлен, —а, —о, —ы (ppp), see вы́кормлю.

ВЫ́КОРМЛЮ, вы́кормишь. Р. Вы́кормить (acc.). I. Выка́рмливать. 1. To bring up, rear. 2. To feed to satiety (of horses).

ВЫ́КОШЕННЫЙ; вы́кошен, —а, —о, —ы (ppp), see вы́кошу.

ВЫ́КОШУ, вы́косишь. Р. Вы́косить (acc.). I. Выка́шивать. 1. To mow, cut (e.g., all the grain in a field). 2. (fig.) To mow down, cut down (e.g., the enemy).

ВЫ́КРАДЕННЫЙ; вы́краден, —а, —о, —ы (ppp), see вы́краду.

ВЫ́КРАДЕШЬ, see вы́краду.

ВЫ́КРАДИ (imp.), see вы́краду.

ВЫ́КРАДУ, вы́крадешь. Р. Вы́красть (acc.). I. Выкра́дывать. To steal.

ВЫ́КРАЛ, вы́крала (past), see вы́краду.

ВЫ́КРАСЬ (imp.), see вы́крашу.

ВЫ́КРАШЕННЫЙ; вы́крашен, —а, —о, —ы (ppp), see вы́крашу.

ВЫ́КРАШУ, вы́красишь. Р. Вы́красить (acc.). I. Кра́сить. To color, dye, paint.

ВЫ́КРУЧЕННЫЙ; вы́кручен, —а, —о, —ы (ppp), see вы́кручу.

ВЫ́КРУЧУ, вы́крутишь. Р. Вы́крутить (acc.). I. Выкру́чивать. 1. To

unscrew. 2. To twist (e.g., a rope).
3. To wring out (as laundry).

**ВЫКУПЛЕННЫЙ; выкуплен, —а,
—о, —ы** (ppp), see **выкуплю.**

ВЫКУПЛЮ, выкупишь. Р. **Вы-
купить** (acc.). I. **Выкупать.** 1. To
redeem. 2. To ransom. 3. To buy up.

ВЫЛЕЖАТ, see **вылежу.**

ВЫЛЕЖИ (imp.), see **вылежу.**

ВЫЛЕЖИШЬ, see **вылежу.**

ВЫЛЕЖУ, вылежишь. Р. **Вылежать**
(intr.). To remain in bed (e.g.,
because of illness).

ВЫЛЕЗ, вылезла (past), see **вылезу.**

ВЫЛЕЗЕШЬ, see **вылезу.**

ВЫЛЕЗИ (imp.), see **вылезу** and
вылезь.

ВЫЛЕЗУ, вылезешь. Р. **Вылезть** and
вылезти (intr.). I. **Вылезать.** 1. To
climb out, crawl out. 2. To get out
(as of a car). 3. To fall out, come out
(of hair, fur, etc.).

ВЫЛЕЗЬ (imp.), see **вылезу** and
вылези.

ВЫЛЕЙ (imp.), see **вылью.**

**ВЫЛЕПЛЕННЫЙ; вылеплен, —а,
—о, —ы** (ppp), see **вылеплю.**

ВЫЛЕПЛЮ, вылепишь. Р. **Выле-
пить** (acc.). I. **Лепить.** To model,
sculpture.

ВЫЛЕТИ (imp.), see **вылечу.**

ВЫЛЕТИШЬ, see **вылечу.**

ВЫЛЕТЯТ, see **вылечу.**

ВЫЛЕЧУ, вылетишь. Р. **Вылететь**
(intr.). I. **Вылетать.** 1. (lit. and fig.)
To fly out, take off. 2. (fig.) To be
discharged, expelled.

ВЫЛИЖЕШЬ, see **вылижу.**

ВЫЛИЖИ (imp.), see **вылижу.**

ВЫЛИЖУ, вылижешь. Р. **Вылизать**
(acc.). I. **Вылизывать.** 1. To lick (as
a plate). 2. To lick clean.

**ВЫЛИЗАННЫЙ; вылизан, —а, —о,
—ы** (ppp), see **вылижу.**

ВЫЛИТЫЙ; вылит, —а, —о, —ы
(ppp), see **вылью.**

**ВЫЛОВЛЕННЫЙ; выловлен, —а,
—о, —ы** (ppp), see **выловлю.**

ВЫЛОВЛЮ, выловишь. Р. **Выловить**
(acc.). I. **Вылавливать.** 1. To catch
and remove (as logs from the water).
2. To catch all (e.g., the fish in a
pond, etc.).

**ВЫЛУЖЕННЫЙ; вылужен, —а, —о,
—ы** (ppp), see **вылужу.**

ВЫЛУЖУ, рылудишь. Р. **Вылудить**
(acc.). I. **Лудить.** To tin (cover with).

**ВЫЛУПЛЕННЫЙ; вылуплен, —а,
—о, —ы** (ppp), see **вылуплю.**

ВЫЛУПЛЮ, вылупишь. Р. **Вы-
лупить** (acc.). I. **Вылуплять.** 1. To
shell (as nuts). 2. To open wide (as
one's eyes).

ВЫЛЬЕШЬ, see **вылью.**

ВЫЛЬЮ, вольешь. Р. **Вылить** (acc.).
I. **Выливать.** 1. (lit. and fig.) To
pour out, empty. 2. To cast, mould.

ВЫМАЖЕШЬ, see **вымажу.**

ВЫМАЖИ (imp.), see **вымажу** and
вымажь.

ВЫМАЖУ, вымажешь. Р. **Вымазать.**
I. **Вымазывать.** 1. To smear (s.t.
with s.t.) (acc. + inst.). 2. To dirty,
to smear (acc.).

ВЫМАЖЬ (imp.), see **вымажу** and
вымажи.

**ВЫМАЗАННЫЙ; вымазан, —а, —о,
—ы,** (ppp), see **вымажу.**

ВЫМЕЛ, вымела (past), see **вымету.**

ВЫМЕР, вымерла (past), see **вымрет.**

ВЫМЕРЗ, вымерзла (past), Р. **Вы-
мерзнуть** (intr.). I. **Вымерзать.** 1. To
be killed by frost. 2. To freeze (e.g.,
a pond).

**ВЫМЕТЕННЫЙ; выметен, —а, —о,
—ы** (ppp), see **вымету.**

ВЫМЕТЕШЬ, see **вымету.**

ВЫМЕТИ (imp.), see **вымету.**

ВЫМЕТУ, выметешь. Р. **Вымести**
(acc.). I. **Выметать.** 1. To sweep
(e.g., a room). 2. To sweep out,
sweep up (e.g., dust).

ВЫМЕТШИЙ (pap), see **вымету.**

ВЫМЕТЬ (imp.), see **вымечу².**

ВЫМЕТЯ (adv. past part.), see
вымету.

**ВЫМЕЧЕННЫЙ; вымечен, —а, —о,
—ы** (ppp), see **вымечу¹** and **².**

ВЫМЕЧЕШЬ, see **вымечу¹.**

ВЫМЕЧИ (imp.), see **вымечу¹.**

ВЫМЕЧУ¹, вымечешь. Р. **Выметать**
(acc.). I. **Метать** (mean. 2 and 3).
1. To fling out (as a fish net, seine).
2. To spawn (of fish). 3. To bear (of
animals). 4. To put out (as sprouts,
etc.) (of plants).

ВЫМЕЧУ², выметишь. Р. **Выметить**
(acc.). To mark all (of s.t.) (as one's
clothing).

**ВЫМЕШЕННЫЙ; вымешен, —а, —о,
—ы** (ppp), see **вымешу.**

ВЫ́МЕШУ, вы́месишь. Р. Вы́месить (acc.). I. Выме́шивать. To knead.

ВЫ́МЕЩЕННЫЙ; вы́мещен,—а,—о, —ы (ppp), see вы́мешу.

ВЫ́МЕЩУ, вы́местишь. Р. Вы́местить. I. Вымеща́ть. 1. To wreak (as one's anger on s.o.) (acc. + на + prep.). 2. To pay back (e.g., s.o. for an insult) (dat. of pers. + acc. of insult) or (dat. of pers. + за + acc.).

ВЫ́МОЕШЬ, see вы́мою.

ВЫ́МОЙ (imp.), see вы́мою.

ВЫ́МОК, вы́мокла (past). Р. Вы́мокнуть (intr.). I. Вымока́ть. 1. To be steeped, soaked (in s.t.). 2. To be soaked, wet through.

ВЫ́МОЛВИ (imp.), see вы́молвлю.

ВЫ́МОЛВЛЕННЫЙ; вы́молвлен, —а, —о, —ы (ppp), see вы́молвлю.

ВЫ́МОЛВЛЮ, вы́молвишь. Р. Вы́молвить (acc.). To utter, say.

ВЫ́МОРОЖЕННЫЙ; вы́морожен, —а, —о, —ы (ppp), see вы́морожу.

ВЫ́МОРОЖУ, вы́морозишь. Р. Вы́морозить (acc.). I. Вымора́живать. 1. To freeze out, make cold (as a house). 2. To freeze, kill by frost.

ВЫ́МОРОЗЬ (imp.), see вы́морожу.

ВЫ́МОЩЕННЫЙ; вы́мощен, —а, —о, —ы (ppp), see вы́мощу.

ВЫ́МОЩУ, вы́мостишь. Р. Вы́мостить (acc.). I. Мости́ть. To pave.

ВЫ́МОЮ, вы́моешь. Р. Вы́мыть (acc.). I. Мыть (mean. 1). 1. To wash. 2. To wash out, wash away (as earth).

ВЫ́МРЕТ, вы́мрут (1st and 2nd pers. sing. not used). Р. Вы́мереть (intr.). I. Вымира́ть. 1. To die out, become extinct. 2. To become desolate, depopulated.

ВЫ́МРИ (imp.), see вы́мрет.

ВЫ́МРУТ, see вы́мрет.

ВЫ́МЫТЫЙ; вы́мыт, —а, —о, —ы (ppp), see вы́мою.

ВЫ́НЕС, вы́несла (past), see Вы́несу.

ВЫ́НЕСЕННЫЙ; вы́несен, —а, —о, —ы (ppp), see вы́несу.

ВЫ́НЕСЕШЬ, see вы́несу.

ВЫ́НЕСИ (imp.), see вы́несу.

ВЫ́НЕСУ, вы́несешь. Р. Вы́нести (acc.). I. Выноси́ть. 1. To carry out, bring out. 2. To endure, stand, bear. 3. To submit (as a resolution to a conference). 4. To pass (as a resolution, sentence, etc.). 5. To obtain,

derive (e.g., s.t. from experience) (acc. + из + gen.).

ВЫ́НОШЕННЫЙ; вы́ношен, —а, —о, —ы (ppp), see вы́ношу.

ВЫ́НОШУ, вы́носишь. Р. Вы́носить (acc.). I. Вына́шивать. 1. To bear (as a mother a child). 2. (fig.) To nurture (as a thought). 3. To wear out (as clothing).

ВЫНОШУ́, выно́сишь. I. Выноси́ть (acc.). Р. Вы́нести. 1. To carry out, bring out. 2. To endure, stand, bear. 3. To submit (as a resolution to a conference). 4. To pass (as a resolution, sentence, etc.). 5. To obtain, derive (e.g., s.t. from experience) (acc. + из + gen.).

ВЫ́НУЖДЕННЫЙ; вы́нужден, —а, —о, —ы (ppp), see вы́нужу.

ВЫ́НУЖУ, вы́нудишь. Р. Вы́нудить (acc.). I. вынужда́ть. 1. To compel, oblige, force (as s.o. to do s.t.) (acc. + inf.) or (acc. + к + dat.). 2. To obtain by force (as information from s.o.) (acc. + от/у + gen.).

ВЫ́НУТЫЙ; вы́нут, —а, —о, —ы (ppp), see вынь.

ВЫНЬ (imp.). Р. Вы́нуть (acc.). I. Вынима́ть. 1. To take out. 2. To draw out (as money). 3. To extract.

ВЫ́ПАДЕШЬ, see вы́паду.

ВЫ́ПАДИ (imp.), see вы́паду.

ВЫ́ПАДУ, вы́паешь. Р. Вы́пасть (intr.). I. Выпада́ть. 1. To fall out, come out. 2. To fall (as rain). 3. (fig.) To fall (as luck, to s.o.) (dat.). 4. To occur, happen.

ВЫ́ПАЛ, вы́пала (past), see вы́паду.

ВЫ́ПЕЙ (imp.). Р. Вы́пить (acc.). I. Пить. To drink.(also see вы́пью).

ВЫ́ПЕК, вы́пекла (past), see Вы́пеку.

ВЫ́ПЕКИ (imp.), see вы́пеку.

ВЫ́ПЕКУ, вы́печешь, вы́пекут. Р. Вы́печь (acc.). I. Выпека́ть. 1. To bake. 2. To bake completely, properly.

ВЫ́ПЕР, вы́перла (past). Р. Вы́переть. I. Выпира́ть. 1. To bulge, protrude (intr.). 2. To push out (acc.). 3. To throw out, drive out (as s.o.) (acc.). (Also see вы́пру.)

ВЫ́ПЕРТЫЙ; вы́перт, —а, —о, —ы (ppp), see вы́пер and вы́пру.

ВЫ́ПЕТЫЙ; вы́пет, —а, —о, —ы (ppp), see вы́пою.

ВЫ́ПЕЧЕННЫЙ; вы́печен, —а, —о, —ы (ppp), see вы́пеку.

ВЫ́ПЕЧЕШЬ, see вы́пеку.

ВЫ́ПИСАННЫЙ; вы́писан, —а, —о, —ы (ppp), see вы́пишу.

ВЫ́ПИТЫЙ; вы́пит, —а, —о, —ы (ppp), see вы́пей and вы́пью.

ВЫ́ПИШЕШЬ, see вы́пишу.

ВЫ́ПИШИ (imp.), see вы́пишу.

ВЫ́ПИШУ, вы́пишешь. Р. Вы́писать (acc.). I. Выпи́сывать. 1. To write out, copy out. 2. To order, send for. 3. To subscribe to. 4. To strike from a list, discharge from (e.g., a hospital) (acc. + из + gen.).

ВЫ́ПЛАВИ and вы́плавь (imp.), see вы́плавлю.

ВЫ́ПЛАВЛЕННЫЙ; вы́плавлен, —а, —о, —ы (ppp), see вы́плавлю.

ВЫ́ПЛАВЛЮ, вы́плавишь. Р. Вы́плавить (acc.). I. Выплавля́ть. To smelt (as metal).

ВЫ́ПЛАВЬ and вы́плави (imp.), see вы́плавлю.

ВЫ́ПЛАКАННЫЙ; вы́плакан, —а, —о, —ы (ppp), see вы́плачу[1].

ВЫ́ПЛАЧЕННЫЙ; вы́плачен, —а, —о, —ы (ppp), see вы́плачу[2].

ВЫ́ПЛАЧЕШЬ, see вы́плачу[1].

ВЫ́ПЛАЧУ[1], вы́плачешь. Р. Вы́плакать (acc.). I. Выпла́кивать. 1. To sob out (as one's grief). 2. To obtain by crying.

ВЫ́ПЛАЧУ[2], вы́платишь. Р. Вы́платить (acc.). I. Выпла́чивать. To pay, pay off, pay in full (as a debt).

ВЫ́ПЛАЧЬ (imp.), see вы́плачу[1].

ВЫ́ПЛЕЛ, вы́плела (past), see вы́плету.

ВЫ́ПЛЕСКАННЫЙ; вы́плескан, —а, —о, —ы (ppp), see вы́плещу.

ВЫ́ПЛЕТЕННЫЙ; вы́плетен, —а, —о, —ы (ppp), see вы́плету.

ВЫ́ПЛЕТЕШЬ, see вы́плету.

ВЫ́ПЛЕТИ (imp.), see вы́плету.

ВЫ́ПЛЕТУ, вы́плетешь. Р. Вы́плести (acc.). I. Выплета́ть. 1. To weave, braid. 2. To unbraid and remove (as a ribbon from a braid) (acc. + из + gen.).

ВЫ́ПЛЕТШИЙ (pap), see вы́плету.

ВЫ́ПЛЕТЯ (adv. past part.), see вы́плету.

ВЫ́ПЛЕЩЕШЬ, see вы́плещу.

ВЫ́ПЛЕЩИ (imp.), see вы́плещу.

ВЫ́ПЛЕЩУ, вы́плещешь. Р. Вы́плескать (acc.). I. Выплёскивать. To splash out (as water out of a basin).

ВЫ́ПЛЫВЕШЬ, see вы́плыву.

ВЫ́ПЛЫВИ (imp.), see вы́плыву.

ВЫ́ПЛЫВУ, вы́плывешь. Р. Вы́плыть (intr.). I. Выплыва́ть. 1. (lit. and fig.) To swim out, float out, sail out. 2. To come, swim, to the surface. 3. (fig.) To come up, crop up (as a question, an idea, etc.).

ВЫ́ПОЕШЬ, see вы́пою.

ВЫ́ПОЙ (imp.), see вы́пою.

ВЫ́ПОЛЕШЬ, see вы́полю.

ВЫ́ПОЛЗ, вы́ползла (past), see вы́ползу.

ВЫ́ПОЛЗЕШЬ, see вы́ползу.

ВЫ́ПОЛЗИ (imp.), see вы́ползу.

ВЫ́ПОЛЗУ, вы́ползешь. Р. Вы́ползти (intr.). I. выполза́ть. 1. To crawl out. 2. (fig.) To drag oneself out, come out with difficulty.

ВЫ́ПОЛИ (imp.), see вы́полю.

ВЫ́ПОЛОСКАННЫЙ; вы́полоскан, —а, —о, —ы (ppp), see вы́полощу.

ВЫ́ПОЛОТЫЙ; вы́полот, —а, —о, —ы (ppp), see вы́полю.

ВЫ́ПОЛОЩЕШЬ, see вы́полощу.

ВЫ́ПОЛОЩИ (imp.), see вы́полощу.

ВЫ́ПОЛОЩУ, вы́полощешь. Р. Вы́полоскать (acc.). I. Полоска́ть. 1. To rinse (as laundry, one's mouth, etc.). 2. To gargle (one's throat).

ВЫ́ПОЛЮ, вы́полешь. Р. Вы́полоть (acc.). I. Выпа́лывать, поло́ть. 1. To weed (as a garden). 2. To weed out, pull out (as weeds, grass, etc.).

ВЫ́ПОРЕШЬ, see вы́порю[1] and [2].

ВЫ́ПОРИ (imp.), see вы́порю[1] and [2].

ВЫ́ПОРОТЫЙ; вы́порот, —а, —о, —ы (ppp), see вы́порю[1] and [2].

ВЫ́ПОРЮ[1], вы́порешь. Р. Вы́пороть (acc.). I. Выпа́рывать. To rip out.

ВЫ́ПОРЮ[2], вы́порешь. Р. Вы́пороть (acc.). I. Поро́ть. To beat, switch, flog.

ВЫ́ПОЮ, вы́поешь. Р. Вы́петь. I. Выпева́ть. 1. To sing clearly, distinctly (as a song) (acc.). 2. To speak bluntly (intr.).

ВЫ́ПРАВЛЕННЫЙ; вы́правлен, —а, —о, —ы (ppp), see вы́правлю.

ВЫ́ПРАВЛЮ, вы́правишь. Р. вы́править (acc.). I. Выправля́ть. 1. To straighten out (as s.t. crooked.)

2. To correct. 3. To improve or remedy (as a situation). 4. To obtain (as a ticket).

ВЫ́ПРАВЬ (imp.), see вы́правлю.

ВЫ́ПРЕШЬ, see вы́пру.

ВЫ́ПРИ (imp.), see вы́пру.

ВЫ́ПРОВОЖЕННЫЙ; вы́провожен, —а, —о, —ы (ppp), see вы́провожу.

ВЫ́ПРОВОЖУ, вы́проводишь. Р. Вы́проводить (acc.). I. Выпрова́живать. To escort off the premises, throw (s.o.) out.

ВЫ́ПРОШЕННЫЙ; вы́прошен, —а, —о, —ы (ppp), see вы́прошу.

ВЫ́ПРОШУ, вы́просишь. Р. Вы́просить (acc./gen.). I. Выпра́шивать. To get (s.t.) by asking.

ВЫ́ПРУ, вы́прешь. Р. Вы́переть. I. Выпира́ть. 1. To bulge, protrude (intr.). 2. To push out (acc.). 3. To throw out, drive out (as s.o.) (acc.).

ВЫ́ПРЯГ, вы́прягла (past), see вы́прягу.

ВЫ́ПРЯГИ (imp.), see вы́прягу.

ВЫ́ПРЯГУ, вы́пряжешь, вы́прягут. Р. Вы́прячь (acc.). I. Выпряга́ть. To unharness.

ВЫ́ПРЯЖЕННЫЙ; вы́пряжен, —а, —о, —ы (ppp), see вы́прягу.

ВЫ́ПРЯЖЕШЬ, see вы́прягу.

ВЫ́ПРЯМЛЕННЫЙ; вы́прямлен, —а, —о, —ы (ppp), see вы́прямлю.

ВЫ́ПРЯМЛЮ, вы́прямишь. Р. Вы́прямить (acc.). I. Выпрямля́ть. 1. To straighten out, straighten up. 2. To rectify (alternating electric current).

ВЫ́ПУЩЕННЫЙ; вы́пущен, —а, —о, —ы (ppp), see вы́пущу.

ВЫ́ПУЩУ, вы́пустишь. Р. Вы́пустить (acc.). I. Выпуска́ть. 1. To release. 2. To let out (e.g., a seam). 3. To graduate (a student). 4. To issue (as supplies, books, etc.). 5. To publish. 6. To produce, put out (as goods). 7. To omit.

ВЫ́ПЬЕШЬ, see вы́пью.

ВЫ́ПЬЮ, вы́пьешь. Р. Вы́пить (acc.). I. Пить. To drink.

ВЫ́ПЯТИ and вы́пять (imp.), see вы́пячу.

ВЫ́ПЯЧЕННЫЙ; вы́пячен, —а, —о, —ы (ppp), see вы́пячу.

ВЫ́ПЯЧУ, вы́пятишь. Р. Вы́пятить (acc.). I. Выпя́чивать. 1. To thrust out. 2. To overemphasize.

ВЫ́РАЖЕННЫЙ; вы́ражен, —а, —о, —ы (ppp), see вы́ражу.

ВЫ́РАЖУ, вы́разишь. Р. Вы́разить (acc.). I. Выража́ть. To express (as an idea, desire).

ВЫ́РАСТЕШЬ, see вы́расту.

ВЫ́РАСТИ (imp.), see вы́расту and вы́рацу.

ВЫ́РАСТУ, вы́растешь. Р. Вы́расти (intr.). I. Расти́ (mean. 1, 2, 4, 5), вырастать. 1. To grow. 2. To grow up (of a child). 3. To grow out of (из + gen.). 4. (fig.) to increase, grow. 5. (Fig.) to mature, improve (as an artist). 6. (fig.) To appear, grow (as hills in the distance). 7. (fig.) To develop into (в + acc.).

ВЫ́РАЩЕННЫЙ; вы́ращен, —а, —о, —ы (ppp), see вы́ращу.

ВЫ́РАЩУ, вы́растишь. Р. Вы́растить (acc.). I. Выра́щивать. 1. To rear (as a child). 2. To raise, cultivate (as flowers). 3. To raise, breed (as animals). 4. (mil.) To train (as a cadre).

ВЫ́РВАННЫЙ; вы́рван, —а, —о, —ы (ppp), see вы́рву.

ВЫ́РВЕШЬ, see вы́рву.

ВЫ́РВИ (imp.), see вы́рву.

ВЫ́РВУ, вы́рвешь. Р. Вы́рвать (acc.). I. Вырыва́ть (mean 1 and 2), рвать (mean. 1 and 3). 1. To pull out, extract. 2. To extort (from) (acc. + y + gen.). 3. To vomit (impers.) (acc.).

ВЫ́РЕЖЕШЬ, see вы́режу.

ВЫ́РЕЖИ and вы́режь (imp.), see вы́режу.

ВЫ́РЕЖУ, вы́режешь. Р. Вы́резать (acc.). I. Выреза́ть. 1. To cut out. 2. To engrave, carve. 3. To massacre, butcher.

ВЫ́РЕЖЬ and вы́режи (imp.), see вы́режу.

ВЫ́РЕЗАННЫЙ; вы́резан, —а, —о, —ы (ppp), see вы́режу.

ВЫ́РОЕШЬ, see вы́рою.

ВЫ́РОЙ (imp.), see вы́рою.

ВЫ́РОС, вы́росла (past), see вы́расту.

ВЫ́РОЮ, вы́роешь. Р. Вы́рыть (acc.). I. Вырыва́ть, рыть (mean. 1 thru 3). 1. To dig. 2. To dig out, up. 3. To excavate. 4. To exhume.

ВЫ́РУБЛЕННЫЙ; вы́рублен, —а, —о, —ы (ppp), see вы́рублю.

ВЫ́РУБЛЮ, вы́рубишь. Р. Вы́рубить

(acc.). I. **Выруба́ть.** 1. To cut down (as a grove). 2. To cut out (as a part of s.t.). 3. To cut, carve, make (as a notch, figure in s.t.).

ВЫ́РЫТЫЙ; вы́рыт, —а, —о, —ы (ppp), see **вы́рою.**

ВЫ́РЯЖЕННЫЙ; вы́ряжен, —а, —о, —ы (ppp), see **вы́ряжу.**

ВЫ́РЯЖУ, вы́рядишь. Р. Вы́рядить (acc.). I. **Выряжа́ть.** To dress up.

ВЫ́САЖЕННЫЙ; вы́сажен, —а, —о, —ы (ppp), see **вы́сажу.**

ВЫ́САЖУ, вы́садишь. Р. Вы́садить (acc.). I. **Выса́живать.** 1. To disembark, put ashore, put down (e.g., passengers from a vehicle, etc.). 2. To transplant. 3. To break or smash in (as a door).

ВЫ́СВОБОЖДЕННЫЙ; вы́свобожден, —а, —о, —ы (ppp), see **вы́свобожу.**

ВЫ́СВОБОЖУ, вы́свободишь. Р. Вы́свободить (acc.). I. **Высвобожда́ть.** 1. To free, let out, disengage. 2. To release (as funds).

ВЫ́СЕЕШЬ, see **вы́сею.**

ВЫ́СЕЙ (imp.), see **вы́сею.**

ВЫ́СЕК, вы́секла (past), see **вы́секу.**

ВЫ́СЕКИ (imp.), see **вы́секу.**

ВЫ́СЕКУ, вы́сечешь, вы́секут. Р. Вы́сечь (acc.). I. **Высека́ть** (mean. 1 thru 3), **сечь** (mean. 4). 1. To carve. 2. To sculpture. 3. To strike (a fire). 4. To whip, flog.

ВЫ́СЕЧЕННЫЙ; вы́сечен, —а, —о, —ы (ppp), see **вы́секу.**

ВЫ́СЕЧЕШЬ, see **вы́секу.**

ВЫ́СЕЮ, вы́сеешь. Р. Вы́сеять (acc.). I. **Высева́ть.** To sow (all or a given quantity of grain, etc.).

ВЫ́СЕЯННЫЙ; вы́сеян, —а, —о, —ы (ppp), see **вы́сею.**

ВЫ́СИДИ (imp.), see **вы́сижу.**

ВЫ́СИДИШЬ, see **вы́сижу.**

ВЫ́СИДЯТ, see **вы́сижу.**

ВЫ́СИЖЕННЫЙ; вы́сижен, —а, —о, —ы (ppp), see **вы́сижу.**

ВЫ́СИЖУ, вы́сидишь. Р. Вы́сидеть. I. **Выси́живать.** 1. To remain, stay (for a period of time) (intr.). 2. To incubate, hatch (acc.). 3. To think up (s.t.) (acc.).

ВЫ́СКАЖЕШЬ, see **вы́скажу.**

ВЫ́СКАЖИ (imp.), see **вы́скажу.**

ВЫ́СКАЖУ, вы́скажешь. Р. Выска-

зать (acc.). I. **Выска́зывать.** 1. To express, say, state. 2. (arch.) To disclose, reveal (as a secret).

ВЫ́СКАЗАННЫЙ; вы́сказан, —а, —о, —ы (ppp), see **вы́скажу.**

ВЫ́СКРЕБ, вы́скребла (past), see **вы́скребу.**

ВЫ́СКРЕБЕННЫЙ; вы́скребен, —а, —о, —ы (ppp), see **вы́скребу.**

ВЫ́СКРЕБЕШЬ, see **вы́скребу.**

ВЫ́СКРЕБИ (imp.), see **вы́скребу.**

ВЫ́СКРЕБУ, вы́скребешь. Р. Вы́скрести (acc.). I. **Выскреба́ть.** 1. To scrape off, out. 2. To rake (as a yard).

ВЫ́СЛАННЫЙ; вы́слан, —а, —о, —ы (ppp). Р. **Вы́слать** (acc.). I. **Высыла́ть.** 1. To send, send out, ship out, dispatch. 2. To exile, banish, deport (also see **Вы́шлю**).

ВЫ́СЛЕЖЕННЫЙ; вы́слежен, —а, —о, —ы (ppp), see **вы́слежу.**

ВЫ́СЛЕЖУ, вы́следишь. Р. Вы́следить (acc.). I. **Выслеживать.** To track, trace, shadow.

ВЫ́СМЕЕШЬ, see **вы́смею.**

ВЫ́СМЕЙ (imp.), see **вы́смею.**

ВЫ́СМЕЮ, вы́смеешь. Р. Вы́смеять (acc.). I. **Высме́ивать.** To ridicule, make fun (of).

ВЫ́СМЕЯННЫЙ; вы́смеян, —а, —о, —ы (ppp), see **вы́смею.**

ВЫ́СМОТРЕННЫЙ; вы́смотрен, —а, —о, —ы (ppp), see **вы́смотрю.**

ВЫ́СМОТРИ (imp.), see **вы́смотрю.**

ВЫ́СМОТРИШЬ, see **вы́смотрю.**

ВЫ́СМОТРЮ, вы́смотришь. Р. Вы́смотреть (acc.). I. **Высма́тривать.** 1. To look out for, spy out. 2. To examine/observe closely.

ВЫ́СМОТРЯТ, see **вы́смотрю.**

ВЫ́СОСАННЫЙ; вы́сосан, —а, —о, —ы (ppp), see **вы́сосу.**

ВЫ́СОСЕШЬ, see **вы́сосу.**

ВЫ́СОСИ (imp.), see **вы́сосу.**

ВЫ́СОСУ, вы́сосешь. Р. Вы́сосать (acc.). I. **Выса́сывать.** 1. (lit. and fig.) To suck out, exhaust, extract. 2. (fig.) To fabricate, make up (as a story) (acc. + из + па́льца).

ВЫ́СОХ, вы́сохла (past). Р. **Вы́сохнуть** (intr.). I. **Со́хнуть.** 1. To dry, become dry. 2. To wither (of plants). 3. To waste away (of people).

ВЫ́СПИСЬ (imp.), see **вы́сплюсь.**

ВЫ́СПИШЬСЯ, see **вы́сплюсь.**

ВЫСПЛЮСЬ, вы́спишься. Р. Вы́-спаться (intr.). I. Высыпа́ться. To have a good, or enough, sleep.

ВЫСПРОШЕННЫЙ; вы́спрошен, —а, —о, —ы (ppp), see вы́спрошу.

ВЫСПРОШУ, вы́спросишь. Р. Вы́-спросить (acc.). I. Выспра́шивать. To find out (s.t.) by questioning (s.o.) (acc. of s.t. + у + gen. of s.o.).

ВЫСПЯТСЯ, see вы́сплюсь.

ВЫСТАВЛЕННЫЙ; вы́ставлен, —а, —о, —ы (ppp), see вы́ставлю.

ВЫСТАВЛЮ, вы́ставишь. Р. Вы́-ставить (acc.). I. Выставля́ть. 1. To move (s.t.) forward, out, etc. 2. To run (s.o.) out. 3. To exhibit, display. 4. To propose (as a candidate). 5. To put forward, adduce (as strong arguments). 6. To post, place (as a guard). 7. To write down, post (as a grade). 8. (fig.) To show, expose (e.g., s.o. as bright, stupid, etc.) (acc. + inst.). 9. To remove (e.g., storm windows).

ВЫСТАВЬ (imp.), see вы́ставлю.

ВЫСТЕЛЕШЬ, see вы́стелю.

ВЫСТЕЛИ (imp.), see вы́стелю.

ВЫСТЕЛЮ, вы́стелешь. Р. Вы́стлать and вы́стелить (acc.). I. Выстила́ть. 1. To cover (as a floor). 2. To line. 3. To pave.

ВЫСТЛАННЫЙ; вы́стлан, —а, —о, —ы (ppp), see вы́стелю.

ВЫСТОИ and вы́стой (imp.), see вы́стою.

ВЫСТОИШЬ, see вы́стою.

ВЫСТОЮ, вы́стоишь. Р. Вы́стоять (intr.). I. Выста́ивать. 1. To remain standing, stand. 2. To withstand, stand up against (про́тив + gen.), under (под + inst.).

ВЫСТРИГ, вы́стригла (past), see вы́стригу.

ВЫСТРИГИ (imp.), see вы́стригу.

ВЫСТРИГУ, вы́стрижешь, вы́стригут. Р. Вы́стричь (acc.). I. Выстрига́ть. 1. To cut off, shear, clip (e.g., hair). 2. To shear (e.g., s.o.'s head).

ВЫСТРИЖЕННЫЙ; вы́стрижен, —а, —о, —ы (ppp), see вы́стригу.

ВЫСТРИЖЕШЬ, see вы́стригу.

ВЫСТУЖЕННЫЙ; вы́стужен, —а, —о, —ы (ppp), see вы́стужу.

ВЫСТУЖУ, вы́студишь. Р. Вы́сту-дить (acc.). I. Высту́живать. To chill, cool.

ВЫСТУПЛЮ, вы́ступишь. Р. Вы́-ступить (intr.). I. Выступа́ть. 1. To move or step forward. 2. To start out. 3. To appear, speak (as at a meeting). 4. To come out, express an opinion (in favor of: за + acc., against: про́тив + gen.). 5. To appear (as perspiration on one's face). 6. (fig.) To stand out.

ВЫСУЖЕННЫЙ; вы́сужен, —а, —о, —ы (ppp), see вы́сужу.

ВЫСУЖУ, вы́судишь. Р. Вы́судить (acc.). I. Высу́живать. To obtain through court of law.

ВЫСЫПАННЫЙ; вы́сыпан —а, —о, —ы (ppp), see вы́сыплю.

ВЫСЫПИ and вы́сыпь (imp.), see вы́сыплю.

ВЫСЫПЛЕШЬ, see вы́сыплю.

ВЫСЫПЛЮ, вы́сыплешь. Р. Вы́-сыпать. I. Высыпа́ть. 1. To pour out (as sugar from a sack) (acc.). 2. To break out (of a rash) (intr.) (impers.). 3. To pour out (of a crowd) (intr.). 4. To appear in large numbers (of stars, etc.) (intr.).

ВЫСЫПЬ and вы́сыпи, see вы́сыплю.

ВЫТВЕРЖЕННЫЙ; вы́твержен, —а, —о, —ы (ppp), see вы́твержу.

ВЫТВЕРЖУ, вы́твердишь. Р. Вы́-твердить (acc.). I. Тверди́ть. To learn by heart (by repetition).

ВЫТЕК, вы́текла (past), see вы́течет.

ВЫТЕКИ (imp.), see вы́течет.

ВЫТЕКУТ, see вы́течет.

ВЫТЕР, вы́терла (past), see вы́тру.

ВЫТЕРЕБЛЕННЫЙ; вы́тереблен, —а, —о, —ы (ppp), see вы́тереблю.

ВЫТЕРЕБЛЮ, вы́теребишь. Р. Вы́-теребить (acc.). I. Тереби́ть. (agr.) To pull (flax).

ВЫТЕРЕВ and вы́терши (adv. past part.), see вы́тру.

ВЫТЕРПИ (imp.), see вы́терплю.

ВЫТЕРПИШЬ, see вы́терплю.

ВЫТЕРПЛЮ, вы́терпишь. Р. Вы́-терпеть (acc.). To endure, suffer, bear.

ВЫТЕРПЯТ, see вы́терплю.

ВЫТЕРТЫЙ; вы́терт, —а, —о, —ы (ppp), see вы́тру.

ВЫТЕРШИ and вы́терев (adv. past part.), see вы́тру.

ВЫ́ТЕСАННЫЙ; вы́тесан, —а, —о, —ы (ppp), see вы́тешу.

ВЫ́ТЕЧЕТ, вы́текут (3rd pers. only). Р. Вы́течь (intr.). I. Вытека́ть. To run out, flow out, escape (of fluids).

ВЫ́ТЕШЕШЬ, see вы́тешу.

ВЫ́ТЕШИ (imp.), see вы́тешу.

ВЫ́ТЕШУ, вы́тешешь. Р. Вы́тесать (acc.). I. Вы́тёсывать. 1. To hew, hew out. 2. To trim.

ВЫ́ТКАННЫЙ; вы́ткан, —а, —о, —ы (ppp), see вы́тку.

ВЫ́ТКЕШЬ, see вы́тку.

ВЫ́ТКИ (imp.), see вы́тку.

ВЫ́ТКУ, вы́ткешь. Р. Вы́ткать (acc.). 1. To weave (e.g., a rug). 2. To weave (a design).

ВЫ́ТОПЛЕННЫЙ; вы́топлен, —а, —о, —ы (ppp), see вы́топлю.

ВЫ́ТОПЛЮ, вы́топишь. Р. Вы́топить (acc.). I. Вытáпливать. 1. To heat. 2. To render (as lard).

ВЫ́ТОПТАННЫЙ; вы́топтан, —а, —о, —ы (ppp), see вы́топчу.

ВЫ́ТОПЧЕШЬ, see вы́топчу.

ВЫ́ТОПЧИ (imp.), see вы́топчу.

ВЫ́ТОПЧУ, вы́твпчешь. Р. Вы́топтать (acc.). I. Вытáптывать. 1. To trample (as grass). 2. To dirty (as a floor) by walking.

ВЫ́ТРАВЛЕННЫЙ; вы́травлен, —а, —о, —ы (ppp), see вы́травлю.

ВЫ́ТРАВЛЮ, вы́травишь. Р. Вы́травить (acc.). I. Вытравля́ть, вы́трáвливать, трави́ть (mean. 1, 3, 4, 5, 6), 1. To exterminate. 2. (lit. and fig.) To remove, erase (e.g., stains, s.t. from one's memory, etc.). 3. To etch. 4. To trample down. 5. To hunt down. 6. (naut.) To slacken off, ease off.

ВЫ́ТРЕЗВЛЕННЫЙ; вы́трезвлен, —а, —о, —ы (ppp), see вы́трезвлю.

ВЫ́ТРЕЗВЛЮ, вы́трезвишь. Р. Вы́трезвить (acc.). I. Вытрезвля́ть. To sober.

ВЫ́ТРЕШЬ, see вы́тру.

ВЫ́ТРИ (imp.), see вы́тру.

ВЫ́ТРУ, вы́трешь. Р. Вы́тереть (acc.). I. Вытирáть. 1. To wipe, wipe dry. 2. To wear threadbare.

ВЫ́ТРУШЕННЫЙ; вы́трушен, —а, —о, —ы (ppp), see вы́трушу.

ВЫ́ТРУШУ, вы́трусишь. Р. Вы́трусить (acc.). To shake out (as flour from a sack).

ВЫ́ТРЯС, вы́трясла (past), see вы́трясу.

ВЫ́ТРЯСЕННЫЙ; вы́трясен, —а, —о, —ы (ppp), see вы́трясу.

ВЫ́ТРЯСЕШЬ, see вы́трясу.

ВЫ́ТРЯСИ (imp.), see вы́трясу.

ВЫ́ТРЯСУ, вы́трясешь. Р. Вы́трясти (acc.). I. Вытряся́ть, трясти́. To shake out (as a rug, flour from a sack).

ВЫ́УЖЕННЫЙ; вы́ужен, —а, —о, —ы (ppp), see вы́ужу.

ВЫ́УЖУ, вы́удишь. Р. Вы́удить (acc.). I. Выу́живать. 1. To catch (as fish). 2. To obtain (s.t.) by guile (from s.o.) (acc. + y + gen.). 3. (fig.) To fish out.

ВЫ́ХВАЧЕННЫЙ; вы́хвачен, —а, —о, —ы (ppp), see вы́хвачу.

ВЫ́ХВАЧУ, вы́хватишь. Р. Вы́хватить (acc.). I. Выхвáтывать. 1. To snatch (s.t. out of s.t.). 2. To cut out (too much, or a large piece).

ВЫ́ХЛОПОТАННЫЙ; вы́хлопотан, —а, —о, —ы (ppp), see вы́хлопочу.

ВЫ́ХЛОПОЧЕШЬ, see вы́хлопочу.

ВЫ́ХЛОПОЧИ (imp.), see вы́хлопочу.

ВЫ́ХЛОПОЧУ, вы́хлопочешь. Р. Вы́хлопотать (acc.). I. Выхлопáтывать.

ВЫ́ХЛОПОЧУ, вы́хлопочешь. Р. Вы́хлопотать (acc.). I. Выхлопáтывать. To get, obtain (after much trouble).

ВЫ́ХОЖЕННЫЙ; вы́хожен, —а, —о, —ы (ppp), see вы́хожу.

ВЫХОЖУ́, выхóдишь. I. Выходи́ть (intr.). Р. Вы́йти (mean. 1 thru 8). 1. To go out, alight, get out. 2. To be published. 3. To come out, turn out. 4. To run out, be spent (as money, time, etc.). 5. To leave. 6. To be by origin, originate from (из + gen.). 7. To become a wife (of s.o.) (за + acc.). 8. To become (s.t. or s.o.) (inst.). 9. To face (as a house faces a street) (на + acc.). (For other idiomatic uses see unabridged dictionary.)

ВЫ́ХОЖУ, вы́ходишь. Р. Вы́ходить (acc.). I. Выхáживать. 1. To nurse (as a patient). 2. To raise, (as animals). 3. To bring up (as a child). 4. To travel around, visit (several places).

ВЫ́ХОЛОЩЕННЫЙ; вы́холощен, —а, —о, —ы (ppp), see вы́холощу.

ВЫХОЛОЩУ, вы́хопостшь. Р. вы́холостить (асс.). I. Выхола́щивать, холости́ть (mean. 1). 1. To emasculate, castrate. 2. (fig.) To impoverish, emasculate.

ВЫ́ЦВЕЛ, вы́цвела (past), see вы́цветет.

ВЫ́ЦВЕТЕТ, вы́цветут (3rd pers. only). Р. Вы́цвести (intr.). I. Выцвета́ть. To fade.

ВЫ́ЦВЕТИ (imp.), see вы́цветет.

ВЫ́ЦВЕТУТ, see вы́цветет.

ВЫ́ЦВЕТШИЙ (pap), see вы́цветет.

ВЫ́ЦЕЖЕННЫЙ; вы́цежен, —а, —о, —ы (ppp), see вы́цежу.

ВЫ́ЦЕЖУ, вы́цедишь. Р. Вы́цедить (асс.). I. Выце́живать. 1. To strain (to strain while pouring, etc.). 2. To drink slowly. 3. (fig.) To strain (words through one's teeth).

ВЫ́ЧЕЛ, вы́чла (past), see вы́чту.

ВЫ́ЧЕРЧЕННЫЙ; вы́черчен, —а, —о, —ы (ppp), see вы́черчу.

ВЫ́ЧЕРЧУ, вы́чертишь. Р. Вы́чертить (асс.). I. Выче́рчивать. To draw, trace.

ВЫ́ЧЕСАННЫЙ; вы́чесан, —а, —о, —ы (ppp), see вы́чешу.

ВЫ́ЧЕТШИЙ (pap), see вы́чту.

ВЫ́ЧЕШЕШЬ, see вы́чешу.

ВЫ́ЧЕШИ (imp.), see вы́чешу.

ВЫ́ЧЕШУ, вы́чешешь. Р. Вы́чесать (асс.). I. Вычёсывать. To comb out.

ВЫ́ЧИСТИ (imp.), see вы́чищу.

ВЫ́ЧИСТЬ (imp.), see вы́чищу.

ВЫ́ЧИЩЕННЫЙ; вы́чищен, —а, —о, —ы (ppp), see вы́чищу.

ВЫ́ЧИЩУ, вы́чистишь. Р. Вы́чистить (асс.). I. Вычища́ть, чи́стить (mean. 1). 1. To clean (as a surface). 2. To clean out (as a room).

ВЫ́ЧЛА, вы́чло, вы́чли (past), see вы́чту and вы́чел.

ВЫ́ЧТЕННЫЙ; вы́чтен, —а, —о, —ы (ppp), see вы́чту.

ВЫ́ЧТЕШЬ, see вы́чту.

ВЫ́ЧТИ (imp.), see вы́чту.

ВЫ́ЧТУ, вы́чтешь. Р. Вы́честь (асс.). I. Вычита́ть. 1. To deduct. 2. (math.) To subtract.

ВЫ́ЧТЯ (adv. past part.), see вы́чту.

ВЫ́ШЕДШИЙ (pap), see вы́шел.

ВЫ́ШЕЙ (imp.), see вы́шью.

ВЫ́ШЕЛ, вы́шла (past). Р. Вы́йти (intr.). I. Выходи́ть. 1. To go out, alight, get out. 2. To be published. 3. To come out, turn out. 4. To run out, be spent (as money, time, etc.). 5. To leave. 6. To be by origin, originate from (из + gen.). 7. To become a wife (of s.o.) (за + acc.). 8. To become (s.t. or s.o.) (inst.) (also see вы́йду). (For other idiomatic usages, see unabriged dictionary.)

ВЫ́ШИБ, вы́шибла (past), see вы́шибу.

ВЫ́ШИБЕШЬ, see вы́шибу.

ВЫ́ШИБИ (imp.), see вы́шибу.

ВЫ́ШИБЛЕННЫЙ; вы́шиблен, —а, —о, —ы (ppp), see вы́шибу.

ВЫ́ШИБУ, вы́шибешь. Р. Вы́шибить (асс.). I. Вышиба́ть. 1. To knock (s.t. or s.o.) out, down. 2. To break (s.t.) in (as a door). 3. To throw (s.o.) out, expel. 4. (fig.) To discharge (s.o.).

ВЫ́ШИТЫЙ; вы́шит, —а, —о, —ы (ppp), see вы́шью.

ВЫ́ШЛА, вы́шло, вы́шли (past), see вы́шел and вы́йду.

ВЫ́ШЛЕШЬ, see вы́шлю.

ВЫ́ШЛИ¹, see вы́шел and вы́йду.

ВЫ́ШЛИ² (imp.), see вы́шлю.

ВЫ́ШЛЮ, вы́шлешь. Р. Вы́слать (асс.). I. Высыла́ть. 1. To send, send out, ship out, dispatch. 2. To exile, banish, deport.

ВЫ́ШУЧЕННЫЙ; вы́шучен, —а, —о, —ы (ppp), see вы́шучу.

ВЫ́ШУЧУ, вы́шутишь. Р. Вы́шутить (асс.). I. Вышу́чивать. To ridicule, make fun (of).

ВЫ́ШЬЕШЬ, see вы́шью.

ВЫ́ШЬЮ, вы́шьешь. Р. Вы́шить (асс.). I. Вышива́ть, шить. To embroider (e.g., a towel, a design).

ВЫ́ЩЕРБЛЕННЫЙ; вы́щерблен, —а, —о, —ы (ppp), see вы́щерблю.

ВЫ́ЩЕРБЛЮ, вы́щербишь. Р. Вы́щербить (асс.). I. Выщербля́ть. To spoil or damage by chipping.

ВЫ́ЩИПАННЫЙ; вы́щипан, —а, —о, —ы (ppp), see вы́щиплю.

ВЫ́ЩИПЛЕШЬ, see вы́щиплю.

ВЫ́ЩИПЛИ (imp.), see вы́щиплю.

ВЫ́ЩИПЛЮ, вы́щиплешь. Р. Вы́щипать (асс.). I. Выщи́пывать. To pluck, pull out.

ВЫ́ЯВЛЕННЫЙ; вы́явлен, —а, —о, —ы (ppp), see вы́явлю.

ВЫ́ЯВЛЮ, вы́явишь. Р. Вы́явить (асс.). I. Выявля́ть. 1. To expose. 2. To reveal. 3. To bring out (make known).

ВЬЁШЬ, see вью.

ВЬЮ, вьёшь. I. Вить (асс.). Р. Свить. 1. To twist (as a thread, a rope, etc.). 2. To weave (as a wreath, a nest, etc.). 3. To wind, coil.

ВЯ́ЖЕШЬ, see вяжу́.

ВЯЖИ́ (imp.), see вяжу́.

ВЯЖУ́, вя́жешь. I. Вяза́ть. Р. Связа́ть (mean. 1. and 2). 1. To bind, tie up (асс.). 2. To knit, crochet (асс.). 3. To have an astringent effect (intr.) or (асс.).

ВЯЗ, вя́зла (past), I. Вя́знуть (intr.) (в + prep.). Р. Завя́знуть (mean. 1), увя́знуть (mean. 1). 1. To sink into and become stuck (in) (as mud). 2. To stick (as food to one's teeth).

ВЯ́ЗАННЫЙ; вя́зан, —а, —о, —ы (ppp), see вяжу́.

ВЯЛ, вя́ла (past) (also вя́нул, вя́нула). I. Вя́нуть (intr.). Р. Завя́нуть, увя́нуть. (lit. and fig.) To fade, wither, droop (of plants and people).

ВЯ́НУВШИЙ (pap), see вял.

Г

ГАДЬ (imp.), see **гáжу**.

ГÁЖУ, гáдишь. I. **Гáдить**. P. **Нагá-**
дить (mean. 3 and 4). 1. To foul,
soil (acc.). 2. To spoil. 3. To defecate
(of animals) (intr.). 4. To play a
mean trick (on s.o.) (dat.).

ГАЛДИ́ (imp.), see **галди́шь**.

ГАЛДИ́ШЬ, галдя́т (1st pers. sing.
not used). I. **Галде́ть** (intr.). To
make an uproar, yell, etc.

ГАЛДЯ́Т, see **галди́шь**.

ГАС, гáсла (past). I. **Гáснуть** (intr.).
P. **Загáснуть** (mean. 1 and 2),
погáснуть, угáснуть (mean. 1 and
2). 1. To go out (as a flame, light,
etc.). 2. (lit. and fig.) To grow dim,
fade, die out. 3. (fig.) To grow weak,
wither (of a person).

ГАЧУ́, гати́шь. I. **Гати́ть** (acc.). P.
Загати́ть. To corduroy (as a road)
(to make a road of logs).

ГАШУ́, гáсишь. I. **Гаси́ть** (acc.). P.
Погаси́ть, загаси́ть (mean. 1). 1. To
extinguish, put out (as a fire). 2.
To liquidate (as a debt). 3. (tech.)
To quench, damp. 4. To cancel (as a
stamp, a debt, etc.). 5. (fig.) To
extinguish.

ГИБ, ги́бла (past). I. **Ги́бнуть** (intr.).
P. **Погибнуть**. 1. To perish. 2. To
suffer destruction. 3. To disappear.

ГЛАДЬ (imp.), see **глáжу**.

ГЛÁЖЕННЫЙ; глáжен, —а, —о,
—ы (ppp), see **глáжу**.

ГЛÁЖУ, глáдишь. I. **Глáдить** (acc.).
P. **Поглáдить, Вы́гладить** (mean. 1).
1. To iron out, to press. 2. To stroke,
caress.

ГЛАШУ́, гласи́шь. I. **Гласи́ть** (acc.)
or (intr.).1. To say, go, run (e.g., the
saying goes, the proverb says, etc.).
2. (arch.) to proclaim.

ГЛÓДАННЫЙ; глóдан, —а, —о, —ы
(ppp), see **гложу́**.

ГЛОЖÁ and глодáя (adv. pres. part.)
see **гложу́**.

ГЛÓЖЕШЬ, see **гложу́**.

ГЛОЖИ́ (imp.), see **гложу́**.

ГЛОЖУ́, глóжешь. I. **Глодáть** (acc.).
(lit. and fig.) To gnaw.

ГЛОХ, глóхла (past). I. **Глóхнуть**
(intr.). P. **Оглóхнуть** (mean. 1),
заглóхнуть (mean. 2 and 3). 1. To
become deaf. 2. To die out, subside
(of noise, fire, etc.). 3. To become
overgrown through neglect (of a
garden, etc.).

ГЛУПЛЮ́, глупи́шь. I. **Глупи́ть**
(intr.). P. **Сглупи́ть**. To act foolishly.

ГЛЯДИ́ (imp.), see **гляжу́**.

ГЛЯДИ́ШЬ, see **гляжу́**.

ГЛЯДЮЧИ (poetic and dial.) (adv.
pres. part.), see **гляжу́**.

ГЛЯ́ДЯ and глядя́ (adv. pres. part.),
see **гляжу́**.

ГЛЯДЯ́Т, see **гляжу́**.

ГЛЯЖУ́, гляди́шь. I. **Гляде́ть** (intr.).
P. **Погляде́ть** (mean. 1, 4, 6). 1. To
look at, stare at (на + acc.). 2. To
face (as a house faces a street)
(на + acc.). 3. To look like (inst.).
4. To look after, care for (за + inst.).
5. To be seen, show (as a shirt from
under a coat). 6. To consider (s.t.)
(на + acc.).

ГНЕВЛЮ́, гневи́шь. I. **Гневи́ть** (arch.)
(acc.). P. **Прогневи́ть**. To anger.

ГНЕТЁШЬ, see **гнету́**.

ГНЕТИ́ (imp.), see **гнету́**.

ГНЕТУ́, гнетёшь (past tense not used).
I. **Гнести́** (acc.). 1. To press, squeeze.
2. (fig.) To depress, torment. 3. To
oppress.

ГНИЁШЬ, see **гнию́**.

ГНИЮ́, гниёшь. I. **Гнить** (intr.) (no
imp.). P. **Погни́ть** (3rd pers. only),
сгнить. (lit. and fig.) To decay,
decompose.

ГНУСÁВЛЮ, гнусáвишь. I. **Гнусá-**
вить (intr.). To speak with a nasal
tone, talk through the nose.

ГНУСÁВЬ (imp.), see **гнусáвлю**.

ГНУШУ́, гнуси́шь. I. Гнуси́ть (intr.). To speak with a nasal tone, talk through the nose.

ГОГО́ЧЕШЬ, see гогочу́.

ГОГОЧИ́ (imp.), see гогочу́.

ГОГОЧУ́, гого́чешь. I. Гогота́ть (intr.). 1. To cackle (as geese). 2. To roar with laughter.

ГОДИ́СЬ (imp.), see гожу́сь.

ГОЖУ́СЬ, годи́шься. I. Годи́ться (intr.). 1. To serve as, be fit for/to **(на** + acc.), **(в** + acc.), **(для** + gen.), (+ inf.). 2. To be proper (3rd pers. only).

ГОЛОШУ́, голоси́шь. I. Голоси́ть. 1. To wail (intr.). 2. To cry (as a merchant his wares) (acc.).

ГОЛУ́БЛЮ, голу́бишь. I. Голу́бить (acc.). 1. To cherish, take care of. 2. To caress.

ГОЛУ́БЬ (imp.), see голу́блю.

ГОНИ́ (imp.), see гоню́.

ГО́НИШЬ, see гоню́.

ГОНЮ́, го́нишь. I. Гнать. 1. To drive, turn out (as a herd) (acc.). 2. To urge on (acc.). 3. To rush, drive, or ride rapidly (intr.). 4. To pursue, chase (acc.). 5. To persecute, oppress (acc.). 6. To distill (as liquor) (acc.).

ГО́НЯТ, see гоню́.

ГО́РБИ and горбь (imp.), see го́рблю.

ГО́РБЛЮ, го́рбишь. I. Го́рбить (acc.). Р. **Сго́рбить.** To hunch, arch, bend (as one's back).

ГО́РБЬ and го́рби (imp.), see го́рблю.

ГОРЖУ́СЬ, горди́шься. I. Горди́ться. 1. To be proud (of) (inst.). 2. To put on airs (intr.).

ГОРИ́ (imp.), see горю́.

ГОРИ́ШЬ, see горю́.

ГОРК, го́ркла (past). I. **Го́ркнуть** (intr.). Р. **Прого́ркнуть.** To turn bitter, rancid (of foods).

ГОРОЖУ́, горо́дишь (and городи́шь). I. **Городи́ть** (acc.). 1. To fence (as a garden). 2. To talk nonsense **(городи́ть, чепуху́, вздор,** etc.).

ГОРЮ́, гори́шь. I. Горе́ть (intr.). Р. **Сгоре́ть** (mean. 1, 4, 5, 6). 1. To burn. 2. (fig.) To burn (of one's cheeks, a wound, etc.). 3. (fig.) To shine (of eyes, etc.). 4. (fig.) To burn (from emotion, fever, shame, etc.). 5. To rot (of damp hay, etc.). 6. To wear out (of shoes, etc.).

ГОРЯ́Т, see горю́.

ГОТО́ВЛЮ, гото́вишь. I. Гото́вить (acc.). Р. **Пригото́вить.**1. To prepare. 2. To prepare for (acc. + к + dat.). 3. To cook. 4. To store up, lay in (as supplies).

ГОТО́ВЬ (imp.), see гото́влю.

ГОЩУ́, гости́шь. I. Гости́ть (intr.) **(у** + gen). To stay with, visit.

ГРА́БЛЮ, гра́бишь. I. Гра́бить (acc.). Р. **Огра́бить** (mean. 1 and 2). 1. (lit. and fig.) To rob. 2. To sack, pillage. 3. To rake (as hay).

ГРАБЬ (imp.), see гра́блю.

ГРАФЛЁННЫЙ; графлён, —а́, —о́, —ы́ (ppp), see графлю́.   i

ГРАФЛЮ́, графи́шь. I. Графи́ть (acc.). Р. **Разграфи́ть.** To rule (with lines).

ГРЁБ, гребла́ (past), see гребу́.

ГРЕБЁШЬ, see гребу́.

ГРЕБИ́ (imp.), see гребу́.

ГРЕБУ́, гребёшь. I. Грести́. 1. To rake (acc.). 2. To row (with oars) (inst.).

ГРЁЖУ, грёзишь. I. Грёзить (intr.). 1. To dream. 2. To dream about (о + prep.).

ГРЕЗЬ (imp.), see грёжу.

ГРЕМИ́ (imp.), see гремлю́.

ГРЕМИ́ШЬ, see гремлю́.

ГРЕМЛЮ́, греми́шь. I. Греме́ть (intr.). 1. To thunder (of thunder). 2. To roar (of a cannon, people, etc.). 3. To ring out (of shots, etc.). 4. To clatter, clank (as dishes, chains, etc.) (inst.). 5. (fig.) To resound.

ГРЕМЯ́Т, see гремлю́.

ГРОЖУ́, грози́шь. I. Грози́ть. Р. **Погрози́ть** (mean. 1), **пригрози́ть** (mean. 1 and 2). 1. To threaten (s.o. with a gesture) (dat. + inst.). 2. To threaten (s.o. with s.t.) (dat. + inst.). 3. To threaten (as death threatens) (intr.). 4. To threaten (to do s.t.) (+ inf.). 5. To threaten (as a cliff threatens to fall) (inst. of fall).

ГРОМЛЮ́, громи́шь. I. Громи́ть (acc.). Р. **Разгроми́ть.** 1. To raid, sack. 2. To rout, shatter, destroy. 3. To inveigh against.

ГРОМОЗЖУ́, громозди́шь. I. Громозди́ть (acc.). Р. **Нагромозди́ть.** (lit. and fig.) To pile up, heap up.

ГРОХО́ЧЕШЬ, see грохочу́.[1]

ГРОХОЧИ́ (imp.), see грохочу́.[1]

ГРОХОЧУ́[1], грохо́чешь. I. Грохота́ть (intr.). 1. To crash, peal, roar (as thunder). 2. To roar (with laughter).

ГРОХОЧУ́², грохоти́шь. I. Грохоти́ть (acc.). P. Прогрохоти́ть. To sift, screen, riddle, sieve.

ГРУБЛЮ́, груби́шь. I. Груби́ть (dat.). P. Нагруби́ть. To be rude to, speak rudely to s.o.

ГРУ́ЖЕННЫЙ; гру́жен, —а, —о, —ы (ppp), see гружу́.

ГРУЖЁННЫЙ; гружён, —а́, —о́, —ы́ (ppp), see гружу́.

ГРУЖУ́, гру́зишь (also грузи́шь). I. Грузи́ть (acc.). P. Зргрузи́ть (mean. 1), нагрузи́ть, погрузи́ть. 1. To load (s.t. with s.t.) (as a truck with produce) (acc. + inst.). 2. To load (s.t. on s.t.) (acc. + на + acc.).

ГРУЩУ́, грусти́шь. I. Грусти́ть (intr.). 1. To be sad or melancholy. 2. To long for, mourn (o + prep.) or (по + dat.).

ГРЫЗ, гры́зла (past), see грызу́.

ГРЫЗЁШЬ, see грызу́.

ГРЫЗИ́ (imp.), see грызу́.

ГРЫЗУ́, грызёшь. I. Грызть (acc.). P. Разгры́зть (mean. 1). 1. To gnaw, nibble. 2. (fig.) To torment, gnaw.

ГРЯДЁШЬ, see гряду́.

ГРЯДИ́ (imp.), see гряду́.

ГРЯДУ́, грядёшь (inf. and past not used, 1st pers. seldom used). I. Грясти́ (arch. and bookish) (intr.). To approach, come (usually said of a period of time as "the hour is coming when . . ."").

ГУБЛЮ́, гу́бишь. I. Губи́ть (acc.). P. Погуби́ть. 1. (lit. and fig.) To ruin, destroy. 2. (lit and fig.) To spoil. 3. To kill.

ГУДИ́ (imp.), see гужу́.

ГУДИ́ШЬ, see гужу́.

ГУДЯ́Т, see гужу́.

ГУЖУ́, гуди́шь. I. Гуде́ть (intr.). 1. To drone, buzz. 2. To hoot. 3. To ache (as one's legs).

Д

ДАВА́Й (imp.), see даю́.

ДАВА́Я (adv. pres. part.), see даю́.

ДА́ВЛЕННЫЙ; да́влен, —а, —о, —ы (ppp), see давлю́.

ДАВЛЮ́, да́вишь. I. Дави́ть (acc.). P. Задави́ть (mean. 4, 5, 6), разда́вить (mean. 4 and 6), удави́ть (mean. 5). 1. To press, lie heavy (as snow on a roof). 2. To squeeze, press, pinch (of shoes, etc.). 3. To squeeze (as a lemon). 4. (lit. and fig.) To crush. 5. To strangle (s.o. or s.t.). 6. To run over, knock down and injure or kill. 7. To oppress, suppress.

ДАВЛЮ́СЬ, да́вишься. I. Дави́ться. P. Подави́ться (mean. 1 and 3), удави́ться (mean. 4). 1. To choke (with s.t.) (inst.). 2. To choke down (s.t.) (inst.). 3. To choke from (as laughter) (от + gen.). 4. To hang oneself.

ДАДИ́М, дади́те, даду́т (pl. forms), see дам.

ДАЁШЬ, see даю́.

ДАЙ (imp.), see дам.

ДАМ, дашь, даст (sing. forms). P. Дать. I. Дава́ть. 1. To give (acc.). 2. To produce (acc.). 3. To permit, allow, let (s.o. do s.t.) (dat. + inf.). (For various other meanings and idiomatic usages see unabridged dictionary.)

ДА́ННЫЙ; дан, —а́, —о́, —ы́ (ppp), see дам.

ДАСТ, see дам.

ДАШЬ, see дам.

ДАЮ́, даёшь. I. Дава́ть. P. Дать (mean. 1, 2, 3). 1. To give, present (acc.). 2. To produce (acc.). 3. To permit, allow, let (s.o. do s.t.) (dat. + inf.). 4. (imp.) Let('s) (дава́й/ дава́йте + 1st pers. indicative). (For other meanings and idiomatic usages see unabridged dictionary.)

ДВИ́ГАЙ (imp.), see дви́жу.

ДВИ́ГАЯ (adv. pres. part.), see дви́жу.

ДВИ́ЖЕШЬ, see дви́жу.

ДВИ́ЖИМЫЙ (pres. p.p.), see дви́жу.

ДВИ́ЖУ, дви́жешь (also дви́гаю, дви́гаешь). I. Дви́гать. P. Дви́нуть. 1. To move (as furniture) (acc.). 2. To move (part of one's body) (as shoulders, lips, etc.) (inst.). 3. To advance, promote (as science, etc.) (acc.).

ДЕ́ЕТСЯ (3rd pers. only). I. Де́яться (intr.). To happen, occur.

ДЕ́НЕШЬ, see де́ну.

ДЕ́НУ, де́нешь. P. Деть (acc.). I. Дева́ть. To put, to do with, dispose of (e.g., things, money, time, etc.) (+ куда́) or (+ не́куда) (куда́ дел де́ньги).

ДЕНЬ (imp.), see де́ну.

ДЕРЁШЬ, see деру́.

ДЕРЁШЬСЯ, see деру́сь.

ДЕ́РЖАННЫЙ; де́ржан, —а, —о, —ы (ppp), see держу́.

ДЕРЖИ́ (imp.), see держу́.

ДЕ́РЖИШЬ, see держу́.

ДЕРЖУ́, де́ржишь. I. Держа́ть (acc.). 1. To hold. 2. To support (as a roof). 3. To keep. 4. (imp.) Stop! 5. When used in conjunction with a noun, indicates action of noun, e.g., держа́ть экза́мен—to take an examination. (For other idiomatic usages see unabridged dictionary.)

ДЕРИ́ (imp.), see деру́.

ДЕРИ́СЬ (imp.), see деру́сь.

ДЕРУ́, дерёшь. I. Драть (acc.). P. Вы́драть (mean. 5), задра́ть (mean. 6), содра́ть (mean. 2, 3, 7). 1. To tear to bits. 2. To strip, to bark. 3. (fig.) To fleece (s.o.). 4. (fig.) To irritate. 5. To flog, beat. 6. To kill, tear to pieces. 7. To skin, flay.

ДЕРУ́СЬ, дерёшься. I. Дра́ться (intr.). P. Подра́ться (mean. 2). 1. To fight (with) (с + inst.). 2. To fight. 3. (fig.) To fight (for) (за + acc.).

ДИВЛЮ́, диви́шь. I. Диви́ть (acc.). To astound, astonish (s.o.).

35

ДОБА́ВЛЕННЫЙ; доба́влен, —а, —о, —ы (ppp), see доба́влю.

ДОБА́ВЛЮ, доба́вишь. Р. Доба́вить (acc.). I. Добавля́ть. To add (to) (acc. + к + dat.).

ДОБА́ВЬ (imp.), see доба́влю.

ДОБЕГИ́ (imp.), see добегу́.

ДОБЕГУ́, добежи́шь, добегу́т. Р. Добежа́ть (intr.). I. Добега́ть. 1. To run as far as (до + gen.). 2. (fig.) To reach rapidly (as sound reaches one's ears) (до + gen.).

ДОБЕЖИ́ШЬ, see добегу́.

ДОБЕ́Й (imp.), see добью́.

ДОБЕРЁШЬ, see деберу́.

ДОБЕРЁШЬСЯ, see деберу́сь.

ДОБЕРИ́ (imp.), see деберу́.

ДОБЕРИ́СЬ (imp.), see деберу́сь.

ДОБЕРУ́, дебрёшь. Р. Добра́ть (acc./ gen.). I. Добира́ть. 1. To finish gathering, collecting. 2. To collect, gather (an additional number, quantity). 3. (typ.) To finish setting type.

ДОБЕРУ́СЬ, деберёшься. Р. Добра́ться (до + gen.). I. Добира́ться. 1. To reach, get to (s.o. or some place) after some effort. 2. (fig.) To take (s.o.) in hand. 3. (fig.) To arrive at (e.g., a decision).

ДОБИ́ТЫЙ; доби́т, —а, —о, —ы (ppp), see добью́.

ДО́БРАННЫЙ; добран, —а́, (or —а), —о, —ы (ppp), see деберу́.

ДОБРЕДЁШЬ, see дебреду́.

ДОБРЕДИ́ (imp.), see дебреду́.

ДОБРЕДУ́, дебредёшь. Р. Добрести́ (intr.). To reach (a place) on foot slowly, with difficulty (до + gen.).

ДОБРЕ́ДШИЙ (pap), see дебреду́.

ДОБРЕДЯ́ (adv. past part.), see дебреду́.

ДОБРЁЛ, добрела́ (past), see дебреду́.

ДОБРО́СЬ (imp.), see добро́шу.

ДОБРО́ШЕННЫЙ; добро́шен, —а, —о, —ы (ppp), see добро́шу.

ДОБРО́ШУ, добро́сишь. Р. Добро́сить (acc.). I. Добра́сывать. 1. To throw so far. 2. To throw as far as (acc. + до + gen.).

ДОБУ́ДЕШЬ, see добу́ду.

ДОБУ́ДУ, добу́дешь. Р. Добы́ть (acc.). I. Добыва́ть. 1. To obtain. 2. To mine, extract.

ДОБУ́ДЬ (imp.), see добу́ду.

ДОБУЖУ́СЬ, добу́дишься. Р. Добу-

ди́ться (gen.). To succeed in waking (s.o.).

ДО́БЫЛ or добы́л, добыла́, до́было or добы́ло, до́были or добы́ли (past), see добу́ду.

ДОБЫ́ТЫЙ; до́быт, —а́, —о, —ы or добы́т, —а, —о, —ы (ppp), see добу́ду.

ДОБЬЁШЬ, see добью́.

ДОБЬЮ́, добьёшь. Р. Доби́ть (acc.). I. Добива́ть. 1. To kill, finish off. 2. (lit. and fig.) To smash. 3. To beat (e.g., to death) (acc. + до + gen.). 4. To finish striking (e.g., the hour, of a clock, etc.).

ДОВЕДЁННЫЙ; доведён, —а́, —о, —ы́ (ppp), see доведу́.

ДОВЕДЁШЬ, see доведу́.

ДОВЕДИ́ (imp.), see доведу́.

ДОВЕДУ́, доведёшь. Р. Довести́ (acc. + до + gen.). I. Доводи́ть. 1. To lead, bring (s.o. or s.t.) to. 2. To continue (s.t.) to (as a road to someplace, studies to completion, etc.). 3. To lead or bring (s.o.) to some emotional state (as tears). 4. To communicate (s.t. to s.o.).

ДОВЕ́ДШИЙ (pap), see доведу́.

ДОВЕДЯ́ and доведши (adv. past part.), see доведу́.

ДОВЁЗ, довезла́ (past), see довезу́.

ДОВЕЗЁННЫЙ; довезён, —а́, —о, —ы́ (ppp), see довезу́.

ДОВЕЗЁШЬ, see довезу́.

ДОВЕЗИ́ (imp.), see довезу́.

ДОВЕЗУ́, довезёшь. Р. Довезти́ (acc.). I. Довози́ть. 1. To take or carry (s.o. or s.t.) there (by vehicle, etc.). 2. To take or carry (s.o. or s.t. to someplace by vehicle, etc.) (acc. + до + gen.).

ДОВЕЗЯ́ and довёзши (adv. past part.), see довезу́.

ДОВЁЛ, довела́ (past), see доведу́.

ДОВОЖУ́¹, дово́зишь. I. Довози́ть (acc.). Р. Довезти́. 1. To take or carry (s.o. or s.t.) there. 2. To take or carry (s.o. or s.t. to someplace by vehicle, etc.) (acc. + до + gen.).

ДОВОЖУ́², дово́дишь. I. Доводи́ть (acc. + до + gen.). Р. Довести́. 1. To lead, bring (s.o. or s.t.) to (as a place). 2. To continue (s.t.) to (as a road to someplace, studies to completion, etc.). 3. To lead or bring (s.o.)

to some emotional state (as tears).
4. To communicate (s.t. to s.o.).

ДОВОЛО́К, доволокла́ (past), see доволоку́.

ДОВОЛОКИ́ (imp.), see доволоку́.

ДОВОЛОКУ́, доволочёшь, доволоку́т. Р. Доволо́чь (acc.). 1. To drag there. 2. To drag to (acc. + до + gen.).

ДОВОЛОЧЁШЬ, see доволоку́.

ДОГЛЯДИ́ (imp.), see догляжу́.

ДОГЛЯДИ́ШЬ, see догляжу́.

ДОГЛЯДЯ́Т, see догляжу́.

ДОГЛЯЖУ́, доглядишь. Р. Догляде́ть. 1. To watch or see to the end (as a play) (acc.). 2. To look after, watch (за + inst.).

ДО́ГНАННЫЙ; до́гнан, —а, —о, —ы (ppp), see догоню́.

ДОГОНИ́ (imp.), see догоню́.

ДОГО́НИШЬ, see догоню́.

ДОГОНЮ́, дого́нишь. Р. Догна́ть. I. Догоня́ть. 1. (lit. and fig.) To catch up with, overtake (acc.). 2. To drive as far as (acc. + до + gen.). 3. To exceed (as a given goal) (до + gen.).

ДОГО́НЯТ, see догоню́.

ДОГОРИ́ (imp.), see догорю́.

ДОГОРИ́ШЬ, see догорю́.

ДОГОРЮ́, догори́шь. Р. Догоре́ть (intr.). I. Догора́ть. 1. To burn out (as a camp fire, a candle, etc.). 2. (fig.) To burn out, fade (of a sunset).

ДОГОРЯ́Т, see догорю́.

ДОГРЁБ, догребла́ (past), see догребу́.

ДОГРЕБЁННЫЙ; догребён, —а́, —о́, —ы́ (ppp), see догребу́.

ДОГРЕБЁШЬ, see догребу́.

ДОГРЕБИ́ (imp.), see догребу́.

ДОГРЕБУ́, догребёшь. Р. Догрести́. I. Догреба́ть. 1. To row (e.g., there) (туда́) (intr.). 2. To row to, or as far as (intr.) (до + gen.). 3. To finish raking (e.g., grass) (acc.).

ДОГРУ́ЖЕННЫЙ; догру́жен, —а, —о, —ы (ppp), see догружу́.

ДОГРУЖЁННЫЙ; догружён, —а́, —о́, —ы́ (ppp), see догружу́.

ДОГРУЖУ́, догру́зишь (and догрузи́шь). Р. Догрузи́ть. I. Догружа́ть. 1. To finish loading (as a truck (acc.). 2. To add (s.t.) to a load (acc./gen.).

ДОДАВА́Й (imp.), see додаю́.

ДОДАВА́Я (adv. pres. part.), see додаю́.

ДОДА́ВШИЙ (pap), see дода́м.

ДОДАДИ́М, додади́те, додаду́т (pl. forms), see дода́м.

ДОДАЁШЬ, see додаю́.

ДОДА́Й (imp.), see дода́м.

ДОДА́М, дода́шь, дода́ст (sing. forms). Р. Дода́ть (acc.). I. Додава́ть. To give the remainder, the rest (as the rest of what is owed).

ДО́ДАННЫЙ; до́дан, —á (or —а), —о, —ы (ppp), see дода́м.

ДОДА́СТ, see дода́м.

ДОДА́ШЬ, see дода́м.

ДОДАЮ́, додаёшь. I. Додава́ть (acc.). Р. Дода́ть. To give the remainder, the rest (as the rest of what is owed).

ДОЕ́ВШИЙ (pap), see доем.

ДОЕ́ДЕННЫЙ; доеден, —а, —о, —ы (ppp), see доем.

ДОЕ́ДЕШЬ, see дое́ду.

ДОЕДИ́М, доеди́те, доедя́т (pl. forms), see доем.

ДОЕ́ДУ, дое́дешь. Р. Дое́хать. I. Доезжа́ть. 1. To arrive at or reach someplace (до + gen.) or (туда́, сюда́). 2. (fig.) To exhaust, wear out (as s.o.) (acc.).

ДОЕЗЖА́Й (imp.), see дое́ду.

ДОЕ́Л, дое́ла (past), see доем.

ДОЕ́М, дое́шь, дое́ст (sing. forms). Р. Дое́сть (acc.). I. Доеда́ть. 1. To eat up. 2. To finish eating.

ДОЕ́СТ, see доем.

ДОЕ́ШЬ[1] (2nd pers. sing.), see доем.

ДОЕ́ШЬ[2] (imp.), see доем.

ДОЖДЁШЬСЯ, see дождусь.

ДОЖДИ́СЬ (imp.), see дождусь.

ДОЖДУ́СЬ, дождёшься. Р. Дожда́ться (gen.). To await (s.t. or s.o. expected).

ДОЖИВЁШЬ, see доживу́.

ДОЖИВИ́ (imp.), see доживу́.

ДОЖИВУ́, доживёшь. Р. Дожи́ть. I. Дожива́ть. 1. To live until (as Christmas) (до + gen.). 2. To spend, stay, the remainder of a period of time (as the rest of the winter) (acc. of winter). 3. To spend (e.g., one's last dollar), (acc.).

ДО́ЖИТЫЙ; до́жит, —á, —о, —ы (ppp), see доживу́.

ДОЗОВЁШЬСЯ, see дозовусь.

ДОЗОВИ́СЬ (imp.), see дозовусь.

ДОЗОВУ́СЬ, дозовёшься. Р. Дозва́ться (gen.). To get an answer or response from (s.o. or s.t.) in response to a call.

ДОЙЩЕШЬСЯ, see доищусь.

ДОИЩИ́СЬ (imp.), see доищу́сь.

ДОИЩУ́СЬ, доищешься. Р. Доиска́ться (gen.). I. Дойскиваться. 1. To search for and find. 2. To find out, discover, determine.

ДОЙДЁШЬ, see дойду́.

ДОЙДИ́ (imp.), see дойду́.

ДОЙДУ́, дойдёшь. Р. Дойти́ (intr.). 1. Доходи́ть. 1. To reach (someplace) on foot (до + gen.). 2. To reach (as sound, a letter, etc., reaches s.o.) (до + gen.). 3. (fig.) To reach or attain (a certain condition or objective, etc.) (до + gen.). 4. To amount to (до + gen.). 5. To be done (as bread). 6. To ripen (as fruit). 7. (fig.) To touch or move (e.g., an audience (до + gen.).

ДОЙДЯ́ and дошéдши (adv. past part.), see дойду́.

ДОЙМЁШЬ, see дойму́.

ДОЙМИ́ (imp.), see дойму́.

ДОЙМУ́, доймёшь. Р. Доня́ть (acc.). I. Донима́ть. To weary, exasperate.

ДОКА́ЖЕШЬ, see докажу́.

ДОКАЖИ́ (imp.), see докажу́.

ДОКАЖУ́, дока́жешь. Р. Доказа́ть. I. Дока́зывать. 1. To prove (acc.). 2. To inform on, denounce (s.o.) (на + acc.).

ДОКА́ЗАННЫЙ; дока́зан, —а, —о, —ы (ppp), see докажу́.

ДОКА́ЧЕННЫЙ; дока́чен, —а, —о, —ы (ppp), see докачу́.

ДОКАЧУ́, дока́тишь. Р. Докати́ть. I. Дока́тывать. 1. To roll (s.t. to someplace) (acc. + до + gen.). 2. To reach (someplace) quickly by conveyance (до + gen.).

ДОКРИЧА́ТСЯ, see докричу́сь.

ДОКРИЧИ́СЬ (imp.), see докричу́сь.

ДОКРИЧИ́ШЬСЯ, see докричу́сь.

ДОКРИЧУ́СЬ, докричи́шься. Р. Докрича́ться. 1. To shout (to s.o. or s.t.) until one is heard (gen.). 2. To shout oneself into some condition (as hoarse, tired, etc.) (intr.) (до + gen. of hoarse).

ДОЛБЛЁННЫЙ; долблён, —á, —ó, —ы́ (ppp), see долблю́.

ДОЛБЛЮ́, долби́шь. I. Долби́ть (acc.). Р. Продолби́ть (mean. 1). 1. To hollow, gouge. 2. To learn by heart. 3. To repeat over and over.

ДОЛЕЙ́ (imp.), see долью́.

ДОЛЕТИ́ (imp.), see долечу́.

ДОЛЕТИ́ШЬ, see долечу́.

ДОЛЕТЯ́Т, see долечу́.

ДОЛЕЧУ́, долети́шь. Р. Долете́ть (intr.). I. Долета́ть. 1. To fly to, as far as (до + gen.). 2. (fig.) To reach (as sound reaches one) (до + gen.).

ДО́ЛИТЫЙ; до́лит, —á, —о, —ы (ppp), see долью́.

ДО́ЛИТЫЙ; доли́т, —á, —о, —ы (ppp), see долью́.

ДОЛЬЁШЬ, see долью́.

ДОЛЬЮ́, дольёшь. Р. Доли́ть. I. Долива́ть (mean. 1 and 2). 1. To pour some more, add (as water) (gen.). 2. To fill (as a tea kettle) (acc.). 3. (arch.) To overcome, overpower (acc.).

ДОМЕ́ЛЕШЬ, see домелю́.

ДОМЕЛИ́ (imp.), see домелю́.

ДОМЕЛЮ́, доме́лешь. Р. Домоло́ть (acc.). I. Дома́лывать. To finish grinding.

ДОМО́ЛОТЫЙ; домо́лот, —а, —о, —ы (ppp), see домелю́.

ДОМОЛО́ЧЕННЫЙ; домоло́чен, —а, —о, —ы (ppp), see домолочу́.

ДОМОЛОЧУ́, домоло́тишь. Р. Домолоти́ть (acc.). I. Домола́чивать. To finish threshing.

ДОМЧА́Т, see домчу́.

ДОМЧИ́ (imp.), see домчу́.

ДОМЧИ́ШЬ, see домчу́.

ДОМЧУ́, домчи́шь. Р. Домча́ть. 1. To bring quickly (acc.). 2. To reach someplace quickly, rapidly (intr.).

ДОНЁС, донесла́ (past), see донесу́.

ДОНЕСЁННЫЙ; донесён, —á, —ó, —ы́ (ppp), see донесу́.

ДОНЕСЁШЬ, see донесу́.

ДОНЕСИ́ (imp.), see донесу́.

ДОНЕСУ́, донесёшь. Р. Донести́. I. Доноси́ть. 1. To take, carry (s.t. to someplace) (acc. + до + gen.). 2. To carry, bring (as the wind brings a sound, an odor) (acc.). 3. To report on (s.o. or s.t. to s.o.) (dat. + о + prep.). 4. To denounce, inform against (s.o. to s.o.) (на + acc. + dat.).

ДОНЕСЯ́ and ДОНЁСШИ (adv. past part.), see донесу́.

ДОНО́ШЕННЫЙ; доно́шен, —а, —о, —ы (ppp), see доношу́[2].

ДОНОШУ́[1], доно́сишь. I. Доноси́ть. Р. Донести́. 1. To take, carry (s.t. to someplace) (acc. + до + gen.). 2.

To carry, bring (as the wind brings a sound, an odor (acc.). 3. To report on (s.o. or s.t. to s.o.) (dat. + о + prep.). 4. To denounce, inform against (s.o. to s.o.) (на + acc. + dat.).

ДОНОШУ́², доно́сишь. Р. Доноси́ть (acc.). I. Дона́шивать. 1. To wear out (completely—as clothes). 2. To be delivered of child at proper time. 3. To finish carrying (s.t. somewhere).

ДО́НЯТЫЙ; до́нят, —а́, —о, —ы (ppp), see дойму́.

ДОПЕ́Й (imp.), see допью́.

ДОПЁК, допекла́ (past), see допеку́.

ДОПЕКИ́ (imp.), see допеку́.

ДОПЕКУ́, допечёшь, допеку́т. Р. Допе́чь. I. Допека́ть. 1. To bake until done (acc.). 2. To weary, exasperate (acc.). 3. To bake more (of) (gen.).

ДОПЕЧЁННЫЙ; допечён, —а́, —о́, —ы́ (ppp), see допеку́.

ДОПЕЧЁШЬ, see допеку́.

ДОПИ́САННЫЙ; допи́сан, —а, —о, —ы (ppp), see допишу́.

ДОПИ́ТЫЙ; допи́т, —а́, —о, —ы (ppp), see допью́.

ДОПИ́ШЕШЬ, see допишу́.

ДОПИШИ́ (imp.), see допишу́.

ДОПИШУ́, допи́шешь. Р. Дописа́ть. I. Допи́сывать. 1. To finish writing (e.g., a letter) (acc.). 2. To finish writing (intr.). 3. To write to (e.g., the middle of a page) (intr.) (до + gen.). 4. To add by writing (e.g., a line) (acc.).

ДОПЛА́ЧЕННЫЙ; допла́чен, —а, —о, —ы (ppp), see доплачу́.

ДОПЛАЧУ́, допла́тишь. Р. Допла-ти́ть (acc.). I. Допла́чивать. 1. To pay the remainder (e.g., $5.00). 2. To pay in addition (e.g., $5.00).

ДОПЛЁЛСЯ, доплела́сь (past), see доплету́сь.

ДОПЛЕТЁШЬСЯ, see доплету́сь.

ДОПЛЕТИ́СЬ (imp.), see доплету́сь.

ДОПЛЕТУ́СЬ, доплетёшься. Р. До-плести́сь (intr.). I. Доплета́ться. To drag oneself to (до + gen.).

ДОПЛЁТШИЙСЯ (pap), see допле-ту́сь.

ДОПЛЫВЁШЬ, see доплыву́.

ДОПЛЫВИ́ (imp.), see доплыву́.

ДОПЛЫВУ́, доплывёшь. Р. Доплы́ть (intr.). I. Доплыва́ть. To swim, sail,

float as far as (to), or (up to) (до + gen.).

ДОПРО́ШЕННЫЙ; допро́шен, —а, —о, —ы (ppp), see допрошу́.

ДОПРОШУ́, допро́сишь. Р. Допроси́ть (acc.). I. Допра́шивать. To interrogate, question.

ДОПУ́ЩЕННЫЙ; допу́щен, —а, —о, —ы (ppp), see допущу́.

ДОПУЩУ́, допу́стишь. Р. Допусти́ть (acc.). I. Допуска́ть. 1. To admit (as s.o. to s.t.) (acc. + до + gen.) or (acc. + к + dat.). 2. To permit (s.t.). 3. To assume (s.t.).

ДОПЬЁШЬ, see допью́.

ДОПЬЮ́, допьёшь. Р. Допи́ть (acc.). I. Допива́ть. To drink up, finish drinking.

ДОРАСТЁШЬ, see дорасту́.

ДОРАСТИ́ (imp.), see дорасту́.

ДОРАСТУ́, дорастёшь. Р. Дорасти́ (intr.). I. Дораста́ть. 1. To grow to, up to (as a given height) (до + gen.). 2. To attain a certain age (до + gen.). 3. To be old enough. 4. (fig.) To attain a certain level of physical or mental development (до + gen.).

ДО́РВАННЫЙ; до́рван, —а, (—а́), —о, —ы (ppp), see дорву́.

ДОРВЁШЬ, see дорву́.

ДОРВЁШЬСЯ, see дорву́сь.

ДОРВИ́ (imp.), see дорву́.

ДОРВИ́СЬ (imp.), see дорву́сь.

ДОРВУ́, дорвёшь. Р. Дорва́ть (acc.). I. Дорыва́ть. 1. To finish plucking, picking (as flowers). 2. To wear out completely (as one's shoes).

ДОРВУ́СЬ, дорвёшься. Р. Дорва́ться (intr.). I. Дорыва́ться (mean. 2). 1. To fall greedily upon, "take to" avidly (до + gen.). 2. To wear out completely (of clothing).

ДОРЕ́ЖЕШЬ, see доре́жу.

ДОРЕ́ЖУ, доре́жешь. Р. Доре́зать (acc.). I. Дореза́ть. To finish cutting.

ДОРЕ́ЖЬ (imp.), see доре́жу.

ДОРЕ́ЗАННЫЙ; доре́зан, —а, —о, —ы (ppp), see доре́жу.

ДОРО́С, доросла́ (past) see дорасту́.

ДОСА́ЖЕННЫЙ; доса́жен, —а, —о, —ы (ppp), see досажу́².

ДОСАЖУ́¹, досади́шь. Р. Досади́ть (dat.). I. Досажда́ть. To annoy, irritate, vex.

ДОСАЖУ́², доса́дишь. Р. Досади́ть

(acc.). I. Доса́живать. 1. To finish planting. 2. To plant additional.

ДОСКА́ЖЕШЬ, see доскажу́.

ДОСКАЖИ́ (imp.), see доскажу́.

ДОСКАЖУ́, доска́жешь. Р. Досказа́ть (acc.). I. Доска́зывать. 1. To finish telling, finish (e.g., a story). 2. To tell a part of (a story) (e.g., half) (acc. + до + середи́ны).

ДОСКА́ЗАННЫЙ; доска́зан, —а, —о, —ы (ppp), see доскажу́.

ДОСКА́ЧЕШЬ, see доскачу́.

ДОСКАЧИ́ (imp.), see доскачу́.

ДОСКАЧУ́, доска́чешь. Р. Доскака́ть (intr.). I. Доска́кивать. 1. To hop as far as, to (до + gen.). 2. To gallop to (до + gen.).

ДО́СЛАННЫЙ; до́слан, —а, —о, —ы (ppp), see дошлю́.

ДОСМО́ТРЕННЫЙ; досмо́трен, —а, —о, —ы (ppp), see досмотрю́.

ДОСМОТРИ́ (imp.), see досмотрю́.

ДОСМО́ТРИШЬ, see досмотрю́.

ДОСМОТРЮ́, досмо́тришь. Р. Досмотре́ть (acc.). I. Досма́тривать. 1. To look through (as a book). 2. To see, watch partway through (e.g., a play up to the 3rd act) (acc. + до + gen.). 3. To examine (e.g., goods in customs).

ДОСМО́ТРЯТ, see досмотрю́.

ДОСПИ́ (imp.), see досплю́.

ДОСПИ́ШЬ, see досплю́.

ДОСПЛЮ́, доспи́шь. Р. Доспа́ть. I. Досыпа́ть. 1. To sleep until (as morning) (до + gen.). 2. To sleep through (as the night) (acc.).

ДОСПЯ́Т, see досплю́.

ДОСТАВА́Й (imp.), see достаю́.

ДОСТАВА́Я (adv. pres. part.), see достаю́.

ДОСТА́ВЛЕННЫЙ; доста́влен, —а, —о, —ы (ppp), see доста́влю.

ДОСТА́ВЛЮ, доста́вишь. Р. Доста́вить (acc.). I. Доставля́ть. 1. To supply, furnish (as s.t. to s.o.) (acc. + dat.). 2. To deliver. 3. To convey, take (e.g., s.t. home). 4. To cause, give (as happiness, trouble, etc.) (acc. + dat.).

ДОСТА́ВЬ (imp.), see доста́влю.

ДОСТАЁШЬ, see достаю́.

ДОСТА́НЕШЬ, see доста́ну.

ДОСТА́НУ, доста́нешь. Р. Доста́ть. I. Доставать. 1. To obtain, get (acc./gen.). 2. To reach for and take (acc.).

3. To touch (gen.) or (до + gen.). 4. To suffice (impers. + gen.).

ДОСТА́НЬ (imp.), see доста́ну.

ДОСТАЮ́, достаёшь. I. Достава́ть. Р. Доста́ть. 1. To obtain, get (acc./gen.). 2. To reach for and take (acc.). 3. To touch (gen.) or (до + gen.). 4. To suffice (impers. + gen.).

ДОСТИ́Г, дости́гла (past). Р. Дости́гнуть and дости́чь. I. Достига́ть. 1. To reach (as a place) (gen.). 2. To reach, attain (as old age, full growth, a certain level, etc.) (gen.). 3. To achieve (as an objective) (gen.). 4. (arch.) To overtake (acc.).

ДОСТИ́ГНУТЫЙ; дости́гнут, —а, —о, —ы (ppp), see дости́г.

ДОСТУЧА́ТСЯ, see достучу́сь.

ДОСТУЧИ́СЬ (imp.), see достучу́сь.

ДОСТУЧИ́ШЬСЯ, see достучу́сь.

ДОСТУЧУ́СЬ, достучи́шься. Р. Достуча́ться (intr.). To knock until one is heard (as at a door) (в + acc.).

ДОСЫ́ПАННЫЙ; досы́пан, —а, —о, —ы (ppp), see досы́плю.

ДОСЫ́ПЛЕШЬ, see досы́плю.

ДОСЫ́ПЛЮ, досы́плешь. Р. Досы́пать. I. Досыпа́ть. 1. To add (pour) some more (e.g., grain, sugar, etc.) (acc./gen.). 2. To fill (acc.).

ДОСЫ́ПЬ (imp.), see досы́плю.

ДОХ, до́хла (past). I. До́хнуть (intr.). Р. Издо́хнуть, подо́хнуть, сдо́хнуть. To die (of animals).

ДОХОЖУ́, дохо́дишь. I. Доходи́ть (intr.). Р. Дойти́. 1. To reach someplace on foot (до + gen.). 2. To reach (as sound, a letter, etc. reaches one) (до + gen.). 3. (fig.) To reach or attain (a certain condition or objective, etc.) (до + gen.). 4. To amount to (до + gen.). 5. To be done (as bread). 6. To ripen (as fruit). 7. (fig.) To touch or move (e.g., an audience) (до + gen.).

ДОЧИ́СТИ (imp.), see дочи́щу.

ДОЧИ́СТЬ (imp.), see дочи́щу.

ДОЧИ́ЩЕННЫЙ; дочи́щен, —а, —о, —ы (ppp), see дочи́щу.

ДОЧИ́ЩУ, дочи́стишь. Р. Дочи́стить (acc.). 1. To finish cleaning. 2. To clean until (e.g., s.t. has lustre) (acc. + до + gen. of lustre).

ДОШЕ́ДШИЙ (pap), see дошёл and дойду́.

ДОШЁЛ, дошла́ (past). Р. Дойти́

(intr.). I. Доходи́ть. 1. To reach someplace on foot (до + gen.). 2. To reach (as sound, a letter, etc., reaches one) (до + gen.). 3. (fig.) To reach or attain (a certain condition or objective, etc.) (до + gen.). 4. To amount to (до + gen.). 5. To be done (as bread). 6. To ripen (of fruit). 7. (fig.) To touch or move (e.g., an audience) (до + gen.).

ДОШЛА́, дошло́, дошли́ (past), see дошёл and дойду́.

ДОШЛЁШЬ, see дошлю́.

ДОШЛИ́[1] (past), see дошёл and дойду́.

ДОШЛИ́[2] (imp.), see дошлю́.

ДОШЛЮ́, дошлёшь. Р. Досла́ть (acc.). I. Досыла́ть. 1. To send in addition, or the remainder. 2. To "ram home" (a cartridge, a charge of powder, etc.).

ДРЕБЕЗЖА́Т, see дребезжи́т.

ДРЕБЕЗЖИ́ (imp.), see дребезжи́т.

ДРЕБЕЗЖИ́Т, дребезжа́т (3rd pers. only). I. Дребезжа́ть (intr.). 1. To rattle. 2. To tinkle, jingle.

ДРЕ́ЙФЛЮ, дре́йфишь. I. Дре́йфить (intr.). Р. Сдре́йфить. 1. To be afraid, cowardly. 2. To lose courage, heart.

ДРЕ́ЙФЬ (imp.), see дре́йфлю.

ДРЕ́МЛЕШЬ, see дремлю́.

ДРЕМЛИ́ (imp.), see дремлю́.

ДРЕМЛЮ́, дре́млешь. I. Дрема́ть (intr.). 1. (lit. and fig.) To doze. 2. To dally.

ДРОБЛЁННЫЙ; дроблён, —а́, —о́, —ы́ (ppp), see дроблю́.

ДРОБЛЮ́, дроби́шь. I. Дроби́ть. Р. Раздроби́ть (mean. 1 and 2). 1. To splinter, crush, break to pieces (acc.). 2. To divide up, split up, break down (acc.). 3. To beat (intermittently) (as rain beats on the roof, leaves, etc.) (intr.) (по + dat.).

ДРОГ, дро́гла (past). I. Дро́гнуть (intr.). To shiver (as from cold).

ДРО́ГНУЛ, дро́гнула (past). Р. Дро́гнуть (intr.). 1. To flicker (as a flame). 2. To shake, quiver (of one's hand, body, etc.). 3. To pound (as one's heart, pulse, etc.).

ДРОЖА́Т, see дрожу́.

ДРОЖИ́ (imp.), see дрожу́.

ДРОЖУ́, дрожи́шь. I. Дрожа́ть (intr.). 1. To quiver, tremble, shake. 2. (fig.) To tremble, fear (for s.o. or s.t.) (за + acc.). 3. To fear (s.t. or s.o.) (пе́ред + inst.). 4. To begrudge (s.t.) (над + inst.). 5. To thrill, shake (e.g., from joy) (от + gen.).

ДРЫХ (and дры́хнул), дры́хла (past). I. Дры́хнуть (intr.). To sleep.

ДУБА́СЬ (imp.), see дуба́шу.

ДУБА́ШУ, дуба́сишь. I. Дуба́сить. Р. Отдуба́сить (mean. 1). 1. To beat severely (acc.). 2. To knock, bang, strike (as on a door, etc.) (в + acc.) or (по + dat.).

ДУ́БЛЕННЫЙ; ду́блен, —а, —о, —ы (ppp), see дублю́.

ДУБЛЮ́, дуби́шь. I. Дуби́ть (acc.). Р. Вы́дубить. To tan (as hides, leather).

ДУДИ́ (imp.), see дуди́шь.

ДУДИ́ШЬ (1st pers. sing. not used). I. Дуде́ть (intr.). 1. To play the fife. 2. (fig.) To repeat to the point of boredom.

ДУДЯ́Т, see дуди́шь.

ДУ́ЕШЬ, see ду́ю.

ДУ́Й (imp.), see ду́ю.

ДУ́Ю, ду́ешь. I. Дуть. Р. Вы́дуть (mean. 3 and 4) ду́нуть (mean. 1, 2, 5) поду́ть (mean. 1 and 2). 1. To blow (of the wind) (intr.). 2. To blow (of a person—on/into s.t.) (intr.) (в/на + acc.). 3. To blow (as glass) (acc.). 4. To drink much of (s.t.) (acc.). 5. To do (s.t.) rapidly (acc.) or (intr.) (на + prep.) (meaning is dependent on noun—e.g., to beat a man with a club, to play on the piano, etc.). 6. To run rapidly, rush (intr.).

ДЫМЛЮ́, дыми́шь. I. Дыми́ть (intr.). Р. Надыми́ть. 1. To smoke, emit smoke (as a stove). 2. To smoke (as a pipe) (inst.).

ДЫ́ШАТ, see дышу́.

ДЫШИ́ (imp.), see дышу́.

ДЫ́ШИШЬ, see дышу́.

ДЫШУ́, ды́шишь. I. Дыша́ть (intr.). 1. To breathe. 2. (fig.) To be absorbed, wrapped up in (as one's child) (inst.). 3. (fig.) To be imbued with, breathe (as confidence) (inst.).

E

ЕГОЖУ́, егози́шь. I. **Егози́ть** (intr.).
1. To fidget, bustle, be restless. 2. (fig.)
To fawn upon (s.o.) (**пе́ред** + inst.).

Е́ДЕШЬ, see **е́ду.**

ЕДИ́М, еди́те, едя́т (pl. forms), see **ем.**

Е́ДУ, е́дешь. I. **Е́хать** (intr.). 1. To go
other than on foot, ride, drive. 2. To
slip (as one's feet on ice, etc.).

Е́ДУЧИ (arch.) (adv. pres. part.), see
е́ду.

ЕЗЖА́Й (imp.), see **е́ду** and **пое́ду.**

Е́ЗЖУ, е́здишь. I. **Е́здить** (intr.). 1. To
go other than on foot, ride, drive. 2.
To slip (as one's feet on ice, etc.).

ЕЛ, е́ла (past), see **ем.**

ЕЛО́ЖУ, ело́зишь. I. **Ело́зить** (intr.).
To crawl.

ЕЛО́ЗЬ (imp.), see **ело́жу.**

ЕМ, ешь, ест (sing. forms). I. **Есть**
(acc.). P. **С'есть.** 1. To eat. 2. To
corrode (of chemical action). 3.
To sting or burn (as one's eyes). 4.
To torment, exasperate, abuse, reproach.

Е́МЛЕШЬ, see **Е́МЛЮ.**

Е́МЛИ (imp.), see **е́млю.**

Е́МЛЮ, е́млешь (arch.) (also **има́ю,
има́ешь**). I. **Има́ть** (acc.). 1. To take.
2. To seize. 3. To catch.

ЕСТ, see **ем.**

ЕСТЬ (3rd pers. sing.). I. **Быть** (intr.).
To be.

ЕШЬ[1] (2nd pers. sing.), see **ем.**

ЕШЬ[2] (imp.), see **ем.**

42

Ж

ЖА́ЖДАЙ and жа́жди (imp.), see
жажду.

ЖА́ЖДЕШЬ, see жа́жду.

ЖА́ЖДИ and жа́ждай (imp.), see
жа́жду.

ЖА́ЖДУ, жа́ждешь. I. Жа́ждать
(intr.). 1. To be thirsty, thirst. 2.
(fig.) To crave, thirst for/to (gen.) or
(+ inf.).

ЖА́ТЫЙ; жа́т, —а, —о, —ы (ppp),
see жму and жну.

ЖГИ (imp.), see жгу.

ЖГЛА, жгло, жгли (past), see жёг and
жгу.

ЖГУ, жжёшь, жгут. I. Жечь. Р.
Сжечь (mean. 1 and 2). 1. To burn,
burn up (acc.). 2. To burn (of the
sun, etc.) (acc.). 3. To burn (of the
sun, etc.) (intr.). 4. (fig.) To worry,
torment (acc.) or (intr.). 5. To produce a burning or stinging sensation
(intr.).

ЖДЁШЬ, see жду.

ЖДИ (imp.), see жду.

ЖДУ, ждёшь. I. Ждать (gen./acc.).
To wait (for), expect.

ЖЁВАННЫЙ; жёван, —а, —о, —ы
(ppp), see жую.

ЖЁГ, жгла (past), see жгу.

ЖЕЛЧУ́, желти́шь. I. Желти́ть (acc.)·
Р. Зажелти́ть. To make yellow.

ЖЖЁШЬ, see жгу.

ЖИВЁШЬ, see живу́.

ЖИВИ́ (imp.), see живу́ and живлю́.

ЖИВЛЮ́, живи́шь. I. Живи́ть (acc.).
To invigorate, stimulate, revive.

ЖИВОПИСУ́ЕШЬ, see живопису́ю.

ЖИВОПИСУ́Й (imp.), see живопису́ю.

ЖИВОПИСУ́Ю, живопису́ешь. I. and
Р. Живописа́ть (arch.) (acc.:. To
describe, portray clearly, graphically.

ЖИВУ́, живёшь. I. Жить (intr.). To
live. (For various lit. and fig. usages
see unabridged dictionary.)

ЖМЁШЬ, see жму.

ЖМИ (imp.), see жму.

ЖМУ, жмёшь. I. Жать. 1. To squeeze,
press (acc.). 2. To pinch (of a shoe)
(acc.) or (intr.). 3. (fig.) To press (in
weight lifting) (acc.). 4. To urge on,
press forward (intr.).

ЖНЁШЬ, see жну.

ЖНИ (imp.), see жну.

ЖНУ, жнёшь. I. Жать (acc.). Р.
Сжать. To reap, cut.

ЖРЁШЬ, see жру.

ЖРИ (imp.), see жру.

ЖРУ, жрёшь. I. Жрать (acc.) and
(intr.). Р. Сожра́ть. To eat greedily,
gorge, devour.

ЖУЁШЬ, see жую.

ЖУЖЖА́Т, see жужжу́.

ЖУЖЖИ́ (imp.), see жужжу́.

ЖУЖЖИ́ШЬ, see жужжу́.

ЖУЖЖУ́, жужжи́шь. I. Жужжа́ть
(intr.). To buzz, hum, drone.

ЖУЙ (imp.), see жую.

ЖУРЧА́Т, see журчи́т.

ЖУРЧИ́ (imp.), see журчи́т.

ЖУРЧИ́Т, журча́т (3rd pers. only).
I. Журча́ть (intr.). To murmur,
babble (as a brook).

ЖУЮ́, жуёшь. I. Жева́ть (acc.). 1. To
chew, masticate. 2. (fig.) To chew
over, rehash, talk over repeatedly.

З

ЗАБА́ВЛЮ, заба́вишь. I. and P. Заба́вить (arch.) (acc.). To amuse.

ЗАБА́ВЬ (imp.), see заба́влю.

ЗАБЕГИ́ (imp.), see забегу́.

ЗАБЕГУ́, забежи́шь, забегу́т. Р. Забежа́ть (intr.). I. Забега́ть. 1. To call on/drop in on (s.o.) (к + dat.). 2. To run in. 3. To run away. 4. To outrun.

ЗАБЕЖИ́ШЬ, see забегу́.

ЗАБЕ́Й (imp.). Р. Заби́ть (acc.). I. Забива́ть. 1. To hammer, drive in. 2. To drive in (e.g., a run in a ball game). 3. To cram full of, with (acc. + inst.). 4. To close up/obstruct (with) (acc. + inst.). 5. To outdo, excel, beat. 6. To choke (out) (as weeds choke out flowers). 7. To kill, slaughter. 8. (lit. and fig.) To beat to death. (Also see забью́.)

ЗАБЕРЁШЬ, see заберу́.

ЗАБЕРИ́ (imp.), see заберу́.

ЗАБЕРУ́, заберёшь. Р. Забра́ть. I. Забира́ть. 1. To take (acc.). 2. To capture, seize (acc.). 3. (fig.) To seize (as fear seizes one) (acc.). 4. To take in (as a seam) (acc.). 5. To take to, turn (e.g., to the right) (intr.). 6. To close up, block (as a door with boards) (acc. + inst.). 7. To seize, catch (of an anchor) (intr.).

ЗАБИ́ТЫЙ; заби́т, —а, —о, —ы (ppp), see забью́ and забе́й.

ЗАБЛЕСТИ́ (imp.), see заблещу́[1].

ЗАБЛЕСТИ́ШЬ, see заблещу́[1].

ЗАБЛЕСТЯ́Т, see заблещу́[1].

ЗАБЛЕ́ЩЕШЬ, see заблещу́[2].

ЗАБЛЕЩИ́ (imp.), see заблещу́[2].

ЗАБЛЕЩУ́[1], заблести́шь. Р. Заблесте́ть (intr.). 1. To become shiny. 2. To begin to sparkle, glitter.

ЗАБЛЕЩУ́[2], заблещешь. Р. Заблесте́ть (intr.). 1. To become shiny. 2. To begin to sparkle, glitter.

ЗАБЛУЖУ́СЬ, заблу́дишься. Р. Заблуди́ться (intr.). To lose one's way.

ЗАБОЛЕ́Й (imp.), see заболе́ю.

ЗАБОЛЕ́Ю, заболе́ешь. Р. Заболе́ть (intr.). I. Заболева́ть. To become ill.

ЗАБОЛИ́Т, заболя́т (3rd pers. only). Р. Заболе́ть (intr.). To begin to ache.

ЗАБОЛЯ́Т, see заболи́т.

ЗАБО́ТЬ (imp.), see забо́чу.

ЗАБО́ЧУ, забо́тишь. I. Забо́тить (acc.). Р. Озабо́тить. To worry (s.o.).

ЗА́БРАННЫЙ; за́бран, —а́ (and —а), —о, —ы (ppp), see заберу́.

ЗАБРЕДЁШЬ, see забреду́.

ЗАБРЕДИ́ (imp.), see забреду́.

ЗАБРЕДУ́, забредёшь. Р. Забрести́ (intr.). I. Забреда́ть. 1. To wander, stray. 2. To drop in, wander in.

ЗАБРЕ́ДШИЙ (pap), see забреду́.

ЗАБРЕ́ДЬ (imp.), see забре́жу.

ЗАБРЕДЯ́ and забре́дши (adv. past part.), see забреду́.

ЗАБРЕ́ЕШЬ, see забре́ю. ·

ЗАБРЕ́ЖУ, забре́дишь. Р. Забре́дить (intr.). To become delirious.

ЗАБРЕ́Й (imp.), see забре́ю.

ЗАБРЁЛ, забрела́ (past), see забреду́.

ЗАБРЕ́Ю, забре́ешь. Р. Забри́ть (arch.) (acc.). I. Забрива́ть. To recruit (s.o.).

ЗАБРИ́ТЫЙ; забри́т, —а, —о, —ы (ppp), see забре́ю.

ЗАБРО́СЬ (imp.), see забро́шу.

ЗАБРО́ШЕННЫЙ; забро́шен, —а, —о, —ы (ppp), see забро́шу.

ЗАБРО́ШУ, забро́сишь. Р. Забро́сить (acc.). I. Забра́сывать (mean. 1 thru 4). 1. To throw far. 2. To throw back (as one's head). 3. (fig.) To abandon, give up, (as one's studies). 4. To supply, bring, deliver (acc. + dat.). 5. To throw away.

ЗАБРЫ́ЗЖЕШЬ, see забры́зжу.

ЗАБРЫ́ЗЖИ (imp.), see забры́зжу.

ЗАБРЫ́ЗЖУ, забры́зжешь (also забры́згаю, забры́згаешь, etc.). Р. Забры́згать. 1. To begin to sprinkle, spatter, spray, scatter (of rain, sparks, etc.) (intr.). 2. To begin to sprinkle, spatter, spray (s.o. or s.t. with s.t.) (acc. + inst.).

ЗАБУ́ДЕШЬ, see забу́ду.

ЗАБУ́ДУ, забу́дешь. Р. Забы́ть. I. Забыва́ть. 1. To forget (acc.). 2. To forget (to do s.t.) (+ inf.). 3. To forget (about s.t. or s.o.) (o + prep.).

ЗАБУ́ДЬ (imp.), see забу́ду.

ЗАБУ́ЧЕННЫЙ; забу́чен, —а, —о, —ы (ppp), see забучу́.

ЗАБУЧУ́, забути́шь. Р. Забути́ть (acc.). I. Бути́ть. To construct or fill with rubble masonry.

ЗАБУ́Х, забу́хла (past). Р. забу́хнуть (intr.). To swell (from moisture).

ЗАБЫ́ТЫЙ, забы́т, —а, —о, —ы (ppp), see забу́ду.

ЗАБЬЁШЬ, see забью́.

ЗАБЬЮ́, забьёшь. Р. Заби́ть (acc.). I. Забива́ть. 1. To hammer, drive in. 2. To drive in (as a ball, a run in a game). 3. To cram (s.t.) full (of/with s.t.) (acc. + inst.). 4. To close up (s.t. with s.t.) (acc. + inst.). 5. To outdo, excel, beat. 6. To choke (out) (as weeds choke out flowers). 7. To kill, slaughter. 8. (lit. and fig.) To beat to death.

ЗАВЕДЁННЫЙ; заведён, —а́, —о́, —ы (ppp), see заведу́.

ЗАВЕДЁШЬ, see заведу́.

ЗАВЕДИ́ (imp.), see заведу́.

ЗАВЕДУ́, заведёшь. Р. завести́ (acc.). I. Заводи́ть. 1. To lead, take, conduct, bring. 2. To acquire. 3. To wind (as a watch). 4. To start (as a motor). 5. To establish (as a business).

ЗАВЕ́ДШИЙ (pap), see заведу́.

ЗАВЕДЯ́ (adv. past part.), see заведу́.

ЗАВЁЗ, завезла́ (past), see завезу́.

ЗАВЕЗЁННЫЙ; завезён, —а́, —о́, —ы (ppp), see завезу́.

ЗАВЕЗЁШЬ, see завезу́.

ЗАВЕЗИ́ (imp.), see завезу́.

ЗАВЕЗУ́, завезёшь. Р. завезти́ (acc.). I. Завози́ть. 1. To bring. 2. To deliver. 3. To supply.

ЗАВЕЗЯ́ and завёзши (adv. past part.), see завезу́.

ЗАВЕ́Й[1] (imp.), see заве́ю.

ЗАВЕ́Й[2] (imp.), Р. Зави́ть (acc.). I. Завива́ть. 1. To wave, curl, twist, crimp. 2. To weave. 3. To entwine. (Also see завью́.)

ЗАВЁЛ, завела́ (past), see заведу́.

ЗАВЕРТИ́ (imp.), see заверчу́.

ЗАВЕ́РТИШЬ, see заверчу́.

ЗАВЕ́РТЯТ, see заверчу́.

ЗАВЕ́РЧЕННЫЙ; заве́рчен, —а, —о, —ы (ppp), see заверчу́.

ЗАВЕРЧУ́, заве́ртишь. Р. Заверте́ть (acc.). 1. To begin to whirl, twirl. 2. (fig.) To turn s.o.'s head (acc. of s.o.).

ЗАВЕ́СЬ (imp.), see заве́шу.

ЗАВЕ́ШЕННЫЙ; заве́шен, —а, —о, —ы (ppp), see заве́шу.

ЗАВЕ́ШУ, заве́сишь. Р. Заве́сить (acc.). I. Заве́шивать. To curtain (off).

ЗАВЕ́Ю, заве́ешь. Р. Заве́ять. I. Завева́ть (mean. 1 and 2). 1. To cover, bury (as a blizzard covers a trail) (3rd pers. only), (acc.). 2. To blow away (3rd pers. only) (acc.). 3. To begin to blow, winnow, etc. (see ве́ю) (intr.) or (acc.).

ЗАВЕ́ЯННЫЙ; заве́ян, —а, —о, —ы (ppp), see заве́ю.

ЗАВИ́ДЕВШИ and зави́дя (adv. past part.), see зави́жу.

ЗАВИ́ДИШЬ, see зави́жу.

ЗАВИ́ДЯ and зави́девши (adv. past part.), see зави́жу.

ЗАВИ́ДЯТ, see зави́жу.

ЗАВИ́ЖУ, зави́дишь. Р. Зави́деть (acc.). To catch sight of, see.

ЗАВИ́НЧЕННЫЙ; зави́нчен, —а, —о, —ы (ppp), see завинчу́.

ЗАВИНЧУ́, завинти́шь. Р. Завинти́ть (acc.). I. Зави́нчивать. To screw up.

ЗАВИ́СИШЬ, see зави́шу.

ЗАВИ́СЯТ, see зави́шу.

ЗАВИ́ТЫЙ; зави́т, —а́, —о, —ы (ppp), see завью́.

ЗАВИ́ШУ, зави́сишь. I. Зави́сеть (от + gen.). To depend on.

ЗАВЛЁК, завлекла́ (past), see завлеку́.

ЗАВЛЕКИ́ (imp.), see завлеку́.

ЗАВЛЕКУ́, завлечёшь, завлеку́т. Р. Завле́чь (acc.). I. Завлека́ть. 1. To lure, entice. 2. To seduce.

ЗАВЛЕЧЁННЫЙ; завлечён, —а́, —о́, —ы (ppp), see завлеку́.

ЗАВЛЕЧЁШЬ, see завлеку́.

ЗАВОЁШЬ, see заво́ю.

ЗАВО́ЖЕННЫЙ; заво́жен, —а, —о, —ы (ppp), see завожу́[3].

ЗАВОЖУ́[1], заво́дишь. I. Заводи́ть (acc.). Р. Завести́. 1. To lead, take, conduct, bring. 2. To acquire. 3.

To wind (as a watch). 4. To start (as a motor). 5. To establish (as a business).

ЗАВОЖУ́[2], завóзишь. I. Завозѝть (acc.). Р. **Завезтѝ.** 1. To bring. 2. To deliver. 3. To supply.

ЗАВОЖУ́[3], завóзишь. Р. Завозѝть (acc.). To dirty (as one's clothes).

ЗАВÓЙ (imp.), see **завóю.**

ЗАВОЛÓК, заволоклá (past), see **заволоку́.**

ЗАВОЛОКЍ (imp.), see **заволочу́.**

ЗАВОЛОКУ́, заволочёшь, заволоку́т. Р. Заволóчь (acc.). I. **Заволáкивать.** 1. To cloud. 2. To pull, drag, port (s.t. somewhere).

ЗАВОЛОЧЁННЫЙ; заволочён, —á, —ó, —ы́ (ppp), see **заволоку́.**

ЗАВОЛОЧЁШЬ, see **заволоку́.**

ЗАВОПЛЮ́, завопѝшь. Р. Завопѝть (intr.). To begin to yell, howl, wail.

ЗАВОРÓЧЕННЫЙ; завóрочен, —а, —о, —ы (ppp), see **заворочу́.**

ЗАВОРОЧУ́, заворóтишь. Р. заворотѝть. I. заворáчивать. 1. To turn (as aside) (intr.). 2. To turn (s.t. or s.o. aside) (acc.). 3. To roll up, turn up (as one's sleeves) (acc.).

ЗАВÓЮ, завóешь. Р. Завы́ть (intr.). To begin to howl.

ЗАВРЁШЬСЯ, see **заврýсь.**

ЗАВРИ́СЬ (imp.), see **заврýсь.**

ЗАВРУ́СЬ, заврёшься. Р. Заврáться (intr.). I. **Завирáться** (mean. 2). 1. To become an inveterate liar. 2. To talk nonsense, "talk through one's hat."

ЗАВЫ́СЬ (imp.), see **завы́шу.**

ЗАВЫ́ШЕННЫЙ; завы́шен, —а, —о, —ы (ppp), see **завы́шу.**

ЗАВЫ́ШУ, завы́сишь. Р. Завы́сить (acc.). I. **Завышáть.** 1. To raise, make, or mark too high (as a price, a grade, etc.). 2. To overestimate, overstate.

ЗАВЬЁШЬ, see **завью́.**

ЗАВЬЮ́, завьёшь. Р. Завѝть (acc.) or (intr.). I. **Завивáть.** 1. To wave, curl, twist, crimp. 2. To weave. 3. To entwine.

ЗАВЯ́ДШИЙ (also **завя́нувший**) (pap), see **завя́л.**

ЗАВЯ́ЖЕШЬ, see **завяжу́.**

ЗАВЯЖИ́ (imp.), see **завяжу́.**

ЗАВЯЖУ́, завя́жешь. Р. Завязáть (acc.). I. **Завя́зывать.** 1. To tie up,

bind (e.g., a bundle, one's hand, etc.). 2. To knot (e.g., a necktie, shoelace, etc.). 3. To start (as a conversation). 4. To initiate (as a relationship). 5. To form (as fruit) (acc. of fruit).

ЗАВЯ́З, завя́зла (past). Р. **Завя́знуть** (intr.). I. **Завязáть, вя́знуть** (mean. 1). 1. To become stuck (in) as mud (в + prep.). 2. (fig.) To become entangled (in) mired in, stuck in (as debt, some undesirable job, etc.) (в + prep.).

ЗАВЯ́ЗАННЫЙ; завя́зан, —а, —о, —ы (ppp), see **завяжу́.**

ЗАВЯ́ЗНУВ (adv. past part.), see **завя́з.**

ЗАВЯ́ЗНУВШИЙ (pap), see **завя́з.**

ЗАВЯ́Л, завя́ла. Р. Завя́нуть (intr.). I. **Вя́нуть.** (lit. and fig.) To droop, fade, wither.

ЗАГА́ДЬ (imp.), see **загá́жу.**

ЗАГА́ЖЕННЫЙ; загá́жен, —а, —о, —ы (ppp), see **загá́жу.**

ЗАГА́ЖУ, загá́дишь. Р. Загá́дить (acc.). I. **Загá́живать.** 1. To dirty, make filthy. 2. To defame, profane, defile.

ЗАГА́С, загá́сла (past). Р. **Загá́снуть** (intr.). I. **Загасáть, гá́снуть.** 1. To go out (of a light, fire, etc.). 2. (lit. and fig.) To grow dim, fade, die out.

ЗАГА́ЧЕННЫЙ; загá́чен, —а, —о, —ы (ppp), see **загачу́.**

ЗАГАЧУ́, загатѝшь. Р. Загатѝть (acc.). I. **Гатѝть.** To corduroy (as a road) (to make a road of logs).

ЗАГА́ШЕННЫЙ; загá́шен, —а, —о, —ы (ppp), see **загашу́.**

ЗАГАШУ́, загá́сишь. Р. Загасѝть (acc.). I. **Гасѝть.** To put out (as a fire, a light, a cigarette, etc.).

ЗАГЛА́ДЬ (imp.), see **заглá́жу.**

ЗАГЛА́ЖЕННЫЙ; заглá́жен, —а, —о, —ы (ppp), see **заглá́жу.**

ЗАГЛА́ЖУ, заглá́дишь. Р. Заглá́дить (acc.). I. **Заглá́живать.** 1. To smooth over, down. 2. To make amends for.

ЗАГЛÓХ, заглóхла (past). Р. **Заглóхнуть** (intr.). I. **Глóхнуть.** 1. To die out, subside (of noise, fire, etc.). 2. To become overgrown through neglect (of a garden, etc.).

ЗАГЛЯДИ́СЬ (imp.), see **загляжу́сь.**

ЗАГЛЯДИ́ШЬСЯ, see **загляжу́сь.**

ЗАГЛЯДЯ́ТСЯ, see **загляжу́сь.**

ЗАГЛЯЖУ́СЬ, загляди́шься. Р. Загляде́ться (на + acc.). I. Загля́дываться. To stare at.

ЗА́ГНАННЫЙ; за́гнан, —а, —о, —ы (ppp), see загоню́.

ЗАГНИЁШЬ, see загнию́.

ЗАГНИЮ́, загниёшь. Р. Загни́ть (intr.). I. Загнива́ть. 1. To begin to rot, decay. 2. (fig.) To decay, become decadent.

ЗАГОНИ́ (imp.), see загоню́.

ЗАГО́НИШЬ, see загоню́.

ЗАГОНЮ́, заго́нишь. Р. Загна́ть (acc.). I. Загоня́ть. 1. To drive (in) (e.g., cattle). 2. To drive (in) (e.g., a ball, make a goal) (acc. + в + acc.). 3. To drive away. 4. To exhaust, tire out. 5. To sell, get rid of.

ЗАГО́НЯТ, see загоню́.

ЗАГОРЖУ́СЬ, загорди́шься. Р. Загорди́ться (intr.). 1. To become proud, haughty, arrogant. 2. To put on airs.

ЗАГОРИ́ (imp.), see загорю́.

ЗАГОРИ́ШЬ, see загорю́.

ЗАГОРО́ЖЕННЫЙ; загоро́жен, —а, —о, —ы (ppp), see загорожу́.

ЗАГОРОЖУ́, загоро́дишь (and загороди́шь). Р. Загороди́ть (acc.). I. Загора́живать. 1. To fence in, enclose. 2. To obstruct, bar, block.

ЗАГОРЮ́, загори́шь. Р. Загоре́ть (intr.). I. Загора́ть. To become tanned, sunburned.

ЗАГОРЯ́Т, see загорю́.

ЗАГОТО́ВЛЕННЫЙ; загото́влен, —а, —о, —ы (ppp), see загото́влю.

ЗАГОТО́ВЛЮ, загото́вишь. Р. Загото́вить (acc.). I. Заготовля́ть, загота́вливать. 1. To lay in a stock, store up. 2. To prepare in advance.

ЗАГОТО́ВЬ (imp.), see загото́влю.

ЗАГОЩУ́СЬ, загости́шься. Р. Загости́ться (intr.). To overstay one's welcome.

ЗАГРАЖДЁННЫЙ; загражде́н, —а́, —о́, —ы́ (ppp), see загражу́.

ЗАГРАЖУ́, загради́шь. Р. Загради́ть (acc.). I. Загражда́ть. 1. To fence in. 2. To block, obstruct.

ЗАГРЁБ, загребла́ (past), see загребу́.

ЗАГРЕБЁННЫЙ; загребён, —а́, —о́, —ы́ (ppp), see загребу́.

ЗАГРЕБЁШЬ, see загребу́.

ЗАГРЕБИ́ (imp.), see загребу́.

ЗАГРЕБУ́, загребёшь. Р. Загрести́. I. Загреба́ть (mean. 1, 2, 3). 1. To rake up, rake together (acc.). 2. (fig.) To rake in (e.g., money) (acc.). 3. To change direction rowing (intr.). 4. To begin to row (intr.). 5. To begin to rake (acc.).

ЗАГРЕМИ́ (imp.), see загремлю́.

ЗАГРЕМИ́ШЬ, see загремлю́.

ЗАГРЕМЛЮ́, загреми́шь. Р. Загреме́ть (intr.). 1. To begin to thunder. 2. To fall with a crash.

ЗАГРЕМЯ́Т, see загремлю́.

ЗАГРОМОЖДЁННЫЙ; загроможде́н, —а́, —о́, —ы́ (ppp), see загромозжу́.

ЗАГРОМОЗЖУ́, загромозди́шь. Р. Загромозди́ть (acc.). I. Загроможда́ть. 1. To encumber (e.g., a room with furniture). 2. To block up, clog (e.g., a street with cars). 3. (fig.) To overload (as with details) (acc. + inst.).

ЗАГРУ́ЖЕННЫЙ; загру́жен, —а, —о, —ы (ppp), see загружу́.

ЗАГРУЖЁННЫЙ; загруже́н, —а́, —о́, —ы́ (ppp), see загружу́.

ЗАГРУЖУ́, загру́зишь (and загрузи́шь). Р. Загрузи́ть (acc.). I. Загружа́ть, грузи́ть (mean. 1). 1. To load (s.t. with s.t.) (acc. + inst.). 2. (fig.) To load up (s.o.) (as with work) (acc. + inst.). 3. To feed (as fuel into a furnace).

ЗАГРУЩУ́, загрусти́шь. Р. Загрусти́ть (intr.). To become sad.

ЗАГРЫ́З, загры́зла (past), see загрызу́.

ЗАГРЫ́ЗЕННЫЙ; загры́зен, —а, —о, —ы (ppp), see загрызу́.

ЗАГРЫЗЁШЬ, see загрызу́.

ЗАГРЫЗИ́ (imp.), see загрызу́.

ЗАГРЫЗУ́, загрызёшь. Р. Загры́зть (acc.). I. Загрыза́ть. 1. To tear to pieces, kill by biting. 2. (fig.) to worry to death, torment, exhaust.

ЗАГУ́БЛЕННЫЙ; загу́блен, —а, —о, —ы (ppp), see загублю́.

ЗАГУБЛЮ́, загу́бишь. Р. Загуби́ть (acc.). 1. To ruin (e.g., s.o., s.o.'s life). 2. To waste.

ЗАГУЩЁННЫЙ; загуще́н, —а́, —о́, —ы́ (ppp), see загущу́.

ЗАГУЩУ́, загусти́шь. Р. Загусти́ть (acc.). To make thick, thicken.

ЗАДАВА́Й (imp.), see задаю́.

ЗАДАВА́Я (adv. pres. part.), see задаю́.

ЗАДА́ВЛЕННЫЙ; зада́влен,—а,—о, —ы (ppp), see задавлю́.

ЗАДАВЛЮ́, зада́вишь. Р. Задави́ть (acc.). I. Зада́вливать, дави́ть (mean. 1, 2, 3). 1. To crush. 2. To run over, knock down and injure or kill. 3. To strangle (s.o. or s.t.). 4. To suppress (as one's anger).

ЗАДАДИ́М, задади́те, зададу́т (pl. forms), see зада́м.

ЗАДАЁШЬ, see задаю́.

ЗАДА́Й (imp.), see зада́м.

ЗАДА́М, зада́шь, зада́ст (sing. forms). Р. Зада́ть (acc.). I. Задава́ть. 1. To give or assign (as work to s.o.). 2. To set, indicate (as the course of a ship, tone, etc.). 3. To arrange, organize (as a festival); give (as a dinner, a party). 4. To ask (as a question of s.o.) (acc. + dat.).

ЗА́ДАННЫЙ; за́дан, —а́, —о, —ы (ppp), see зада́м.

ЗАДА́СТ, see зада́м.

ЗАДА́ШЬ, see зада́м.

ЗАДАЮ́, задаёшь. I. Задава́ть (acc.). Р. Зада́ть. 1. To give or assign (as work to s.o.). 2. To set, indicate (as the course of a ship, tone, etc.). 3. To arrange, organize (as a festival); give (as a dinner, a party). 4. To ask (as a question of s.o.) (acc. + dat.).

ЗАДЕ́НЕШЬ, see заде́ну.

ЗАДЕ́НУ, заде́нешь. Р. Заде́ть (acc.). I. Задева́ть. 1. To touch, come against (acc.). 2. To catch on (as a nail) (за + acc.). 3. (fig.) To upset, offend (s.o.) (acc.).

ЗАДЕ́НЬ (imp.), see заде́ну.

ЗАДЕРЁШЬ, see задеру́.

ЗАДЕ́РЖАННЫЙ; заде́ржан, —а, —о,—ы (ppp), see задержу́.

ЗАДЕ́РЖАТ, see задержу́.

ЗАДЕРЖИ́ (imp.), see задержу́.

ЗАДЕ́РЖИШЬ, see задержу́.

ЗАДЕРЖУ́, заде́ржишь. Р. Задержа́ть (acc.). I. Заде́рживать. 1. To detain, delay. 2. To hold back, withhold. 3. To slow down. 4. To arrest (as a culprit).

ЗАДЕРИ́ (imp.), see задеру́.

ЗАДЕРУ́, задерёшь. Р. Задра́ть (acc.). I. Задира́ть, драть (mean. 1.). 1. To tear to pieces, kill. 2. To break, split. 3. To lift up, turn up, turn

back, throw back. 4. To beat, lash, flog (to death).

ЗАДЕ́ТЫЙ; заде́т,—а,—о,—ы (ppp), see заде́ну.

ЗА́ДРАННЫЙ; за́дран, —а (and —а́), —о, —ы (ppp), see задеру́.

ЗАДРЕ́МЛЕШЬ, see задремлю́.

ЗАДРЕМЛИ́ (imp.), see задремлю́.

ЗАДРЕМЛЮ́, задре́млешь. Р. Задрема́ть (intr.). I. Задрёмывать. To doze off.

ЗАДУ́ЕШЬ, see заду́ю.

ЗАДУ́Й (imp.), see заду́ю.

ЗАДУ́ТЫЙ; заду́т, —а, —о, —ы (ppp), see заду́ю.

ЗАДУ́Ю, заду́ешь. Р. Заду́ть. I. Задува́ть. 1. To blow out (as a candle) (acc.). 2. To blow in, fire up (as a blast furnace) (acc.). 3. To begin to blow (of the wind, etc.) (intr.).

ЗАДЫМЛЁННЫЙ; задымлён, —а́, —б, —ы́ (ppp), see задымлю́.

ЗАДЫМЛЮ́, задыми́шь. Р. Задыми́ть. I. Задымля́ть (mean. 1). 1. (mil.) To screen with smoke (acc.). 2. To smoke (blacken with smoke) (acc.). 3. To begin to smoke (intr.).

ЗАЕ́ДЕННЫЙ; зае́ден, —а, —о, —ы (ppp), see заём.

ЗАЕ́ДЕШЬ, see зае́ду.

ЗАЕДИ́М, заеди́те, заедя́т (pl. forms), see заём.

ЗАЕ́ДУ, зае́дешь. Р. Зае́хать (intr.). I. Заезжа́ть. 1. To call (on s.o.) en route (к + dat.). 2. To reach (someplace) (в + acc.). 3. To drop by for (s.o.) (за + inst.). 4. To go around (e.g., a corner) (за + acc.). 5. To strike (s.o.) (as in the face) (dat. of s.o. + в + acc. of face).

ЗАЕ́ЗДИ (imp.), see зае́зжу.

ЗАЕЗЖА́Й (imp.), see зае́ду.

ЗАЕ́ЗЖЕННЫЙ; зае́зжен, —а, —о, —ы (ppp), see зае́зжу.

ЗАЕ́ЗЖУ, зае́здишь. Р. Зае́здить (acc.). 1. To work too hard (s.o. or s.t.). 2. (fig.) To wear or tire out (s.o. or s.t.).

ЗАЕ́Л, зае́ла (past), see заём.

ЗАЁМ, заёшь, зае́ст (sing. forms). Р. Зае́сть (acc.). I. Заеда́ть. 1. To eat, kill by eating (as a wolf kills and eats a sheep). 2. (fig.) To eat (as insects eat one). 3. To take (eat or drink) (s.t. with s.t.) (as medicine with sugar) (acc. + inst.). 4. To become jammed, catch (as a cable) (impers. + acc.). 5. To worry, wear out, prey on (s.o.).

ЗАЕ́СТ, see заём.

ЗАЕ́ШЬ[1], see заём.

ЗАЕ́ШЬ[2] (imp.), see заём.

ЗАЖА́ТЫЙ; зажа́т, —а, —о, —ы (ppp), see зажму́.

ЗАЖГИ́ (imp.), see зажгу́.

ЗАЖГЛА́, зажгло́, зажгли́ (past), see зажгу́ and зажёг.

ЗАЖГУ́, зажжёшь, зажгу́т. Р. Заже́чь (acc.). I. Зажига́ть. 1. To set fire to. 2. To light (as a lamp, etc.). 3. (fig.) To kindle, inspire (s.t. in s.o.) (acc. + в + prep.) (s.o. with s.t.) (acc. + inst.).

ЗАЖДЁШЬСЯ, see зажду́сь.

ЗАЖДИ́СЬ (imp.), see зажду́сь.

ЗАЖДУ́СЬ, зажждёшься. Р. Зажда́ться (gen.). 1. To be tired of waiting (for s.o. or s.t.). 2. To wait a long while (for s.o. or s.t.).

ЗАЖЁГ, зажгла́ (past), see зажгу́.

ЗАЖЕЛЧЁННЫЙ; зажелчён, —а́, —о́, —ы́ (ppp), see зажелчу́.

ЗАЖЕЛЧУ́, зажелти́шь. Р. Зажелти́ть (acc.). I. Желти́ть. To make yellow.

ЗАЖЖЁННЫЙ; зажжён, —а́, —о́, —ы́ (ppp), see зажгу́.

ЗАЖЖЁШЬ, see зажгу́.

ЗАЖИВЁШЬ, see заживу́[1] and [2].

ЗАЖИВИ́ (imp.), see заживу́[1], and [2] and заживлю́.

ЗАЖИВЛЁННЫЙ; заживлён, —а́, —о́, —ы́ (ppp), see заживлю́.

ЗАЖИВЛЮ́, заживи́шь. Р. Заживи́ть (acc.). I. Заживля́ть. To heal (e.g., a wound, an injured leg, etc.).

ЗАЖИВУ́[1], заживёшь. Р. Зажи́ть (intr.). To begin to live (a new life etc.) (inst.).

ЗАЖИВУ́[2], заживёшь. Р. Зажи́ть. I. Зажива́ть. 1. To heal (of a wound) (3rd pers.) (intr.). 2. To earn (money, a salary) as a worker, servant (acc.). 3. To work off (as money paid in advance) (acc.).

ЗАЖМЁШЬ, see зажму́.

ЗАЖМИ́ (imp.), see зажму́.

ЗАЖМУ́, зажмёшь. Р. Зажа́ть (acc.). I. Зажима́ть. 1. To clutch, squeeze. 2. To stop up (e.g., a hole, one's

ears, etc.). 3. (fig.) To suppress (e.g., criticism).

ЗА́ЗВАННЫЙ; за́зван, —а́, —о, —ы (ppp), see зазову́.

ЗАЗВЕНИ́ (imp.), see зазвени́т.

ЗАЗВЕНИ́Т, зазвеня́т (3rd pers.) (1st and 2nd pers. seldom used). Р. Зазвене́ть (intr.). To begin to ring, jingle, clink.

ЗАЗВЕНЯ́Т, see зазвени́т.

ЗАЗНАВА́ЙСЯ (imp.), see зазнаю́сь.

ЗАЗНАВА́ЯСЬ (adv. pres. part.), see зазнаю́сь.

ЗАЗНАЁШЬСЯ, see зазнаю́сь.

ЗАЗНАЮ́СЬ, зазнаёшься. I. Зазнава́ться (intr.). Р. Зазна́ться. To think too highly of oneself, be conceited.

ЗАЗОВЁШЬ, see зазову́.

ЗАЗОВИ́ (imp.), see зазову́.

ЗАЗОВУ́, зазовёшь. Р. Зазва́ть (acc.). I. Зазыва́ть. To urge to come in, call in (insistently).

ЗАЙДЁШЬ, see зайду́.

ЗАЙДИ́ (imp.), see зайду́.

ЗАЙДУ́, зайдёшь. Р. Зайти́ (intr.). I. Заходи́ть, заха́живать (mean. 1 and 2). 1. To drop in at, call on (в + acc.), (к + dat.). 2. To call for, come after (s.o. or s.t.) (за + inst.). 3. To go beyond, behind, around (за + acc.). 4. To arrive (someplace) in a roundabout way (в + acc.). 5. To set (of the sun). 6. To turn on, come up about (s.t.) (of a conversation) (о + prep.).

ЗАЙДЯ́ (adv. past part.), see зайду́.

ЗАЙМЁШЬ, see займу́.

ЗАЙМЁШЬ, see займу́.

ЗАЙМИ́ (imp.), see займу́.

ЗАЙМУ́, займёшь. Р. Заня́ть (acc.). I. Занима́ть. 1. To borrow. 2. To occupy. 3. To interest, entertain. 4. To engage, hold, secure (as a seat, etc.). 5. To employ.

ЗАКА́ЖЕШЬ, see закажу́.

ЗАКАЖИ́ (imp.), see закажу́.

ЗАКАЖУ́, зака́жешь. Р. Заказа́ть (acc.). I. Зака́зывать. 1. To order (s.t.). 2. To forbid (s.t. to s.o.) (arch.) (acc. + dat.) or (s.o. to do s.t.) (dat. + inf.).

ЗАКА́ЗАННЫЙ; зака́зан, —а, —о, —ы (ppp), see закажу́.

ЗАКА́ЧЕННЫЙ; зака́чен, —а, —о, —ы (ppp), see закачу́.

ЗАКАЧУ́, зака́тишь. Р. Закати́ть. I. Зака́тывать. 1. To roll (move by rolling) (acc.). 2. To create, cause (acc.). 3. To strike (e.g., s.o. in the face) (acc. + в + acc.). 4. To go away (intr.).

ЗАКВА́СЬ (imp.), see заква́шу.

ЗАКВА́ШЕННЫЙ; заква́шен, —а, —о, —ы (ppp) see заква́шу.

ЗАКВА́ШУ, заква́сишь. Р. Заква́сить (acc.). I. Заква́шивать, ква́сить. 1. To sour, ferment. 2. To leaven (as dough).

ЗАКИПИ́ (imp.), see закиплю́.

ЗАКИПИ́ШЬ, see закиплю́.

ЗАКИПЛЮ́, закипи́шь. Р. Закипе́ть (intr.). I. Закипа́ть. 1. To start to boil, simmer. 2. (fig.) To start to boil, start to seethe.

ЗАКИПЯ́Т, see закиплю́.

ЗАКИ́С, заки́сла (past). Р. Заки́снуть (intr.). I. Закиса́ть. 1. To sour, turn sour. 2. (fig.) To lose interest, taste for life; become indifferent, despondent.

ЗАКЛЕЙМЁННЫЙ; заклеймён, —а́, —о́, —ы́ (ppp), See заклеймлю́.

ЗАКЛЕЙМЛЮ́, заклейми́шь. Р. Заклейми́ть (acc.). I. Клейми́ть. 1. To stamp, brand. 2. (fig.) To stigmatize, brand.

ЗАКЛЯ́ЛСЯ, закля́ла́сь, закля́ло́сь, закля́лись (past), see заклян́ус.

ЗАКЛЯНЁШЬСЯ, see заклян́ус.

ЗАКЛЯНИ́СЬ (imp.), see заклян́ус.

ЗАКЛЯНУ́СЬ, заклянёшься. Р. Закля́сться (intr.). To pledge, promise, vow not to do (s.t.) (+ inf.).

ЗАКО́ЛЕШЬ, see заколю́.

ЗАКОЛИ́ (imp.), see заколю́.

ЗАКО́ЛОТЫЙ; зако́лот, —а, —о, —ы (ppp), see заколю́.

ЗАКОЛО́ЧЕННЫЙ; заколо́чен, —а, —о, —ы (ppp), see заколочу́.

ЗАКОЛОЧУ́, заколо́тишь. Р. Заколоти́ть (acc.). I. Закола́чивать (mean. 1 thru 3). 1. To board, nail up. 2. To drive in (as a nail). 3. To beat to death, beat senseless. 4. To begin to beat, strike, etc.

ЗАКОЛЮ́, зако́лешь. Р. Заколо́ть. I. Коло́ть (mean. 1), зака́лывать (mean. 2). 1. To stab, kill, slaughter (acc.). 2. To fasten or pin up (acc.). 3. To begin to stick, prick (impers.).

ЗАКОНОПА́ТЬ (imp.), see законопа́чу.

ЗАКОНОПА́ЧЕННЫЙ; законопа́чен, —а, —о, —ы (ppp), see законопа́чу.

ЗАКОНОПА́ЧУ, законопа́тишь. Р. Законопа́тить (acc.). I. Конопа́тить. 1. To caulk. 2. To banish, send off, place (as in prison).

ЗАКО́НЧЕННЫЙ; зако́нчен, —а, —о, —ы (ppp), see зако́нчу.

ЗАКО́НЧИ (imp.), see зако́нчу.

ЗАКО́НЧУ, зако́нчишь. Р. Зако́нчить (acc.). I. Зака́нчивать. To finish, complete.

ЗАКОПТИ́ (imp.), see закопти́т and закопчу́.

ЗАКОПТИ́Т, закоптя́т (3rd pers. only). Р. Закопте́ть (intr.). I. Копте́ть. To become covered with smoke, soot.

ЗАКОПТЯ́Т, see закопти́т.

ЗАКОПЧЁННЫЙ; закопчён, —а́, —о́, —ы́ (ppp), see закопчу́.

ЗАКОПЧУ́, закопти́шь. Р. Закопти́ть (acc.). I. Копти́ть. 1. To cure in smoke (as a ham). 2. To blacken with smoke.

ЗАКО́РМЛЕННЫЙ; зако́рмлен, —а, —о, —ы (ppp), see закормлю́.

ЗАКОРМЛЮ́, зако́рмишь. Р. Закорми́ть (acc.). I. Зака́рмливать. To overfeed.

ЗАКО́ШЕННЫЙ; зако́шен, —а, —о, —ы (ppp), see закошу́.

ЗАКОШУ́, зако́сишь. Р. Закоси́ть (acc.). I. Зака́шивать (mean. 1). 1. To mow beyond given boundaries (as another's grain). 2. (lit. and fig.) To begin to cut, mow, mow down.

ЗАКРАДЁШЬСЯ, see закраду́сь.

ЗАКРА́ЙСЬ (imp.), see закраду́сь.

ЗАКРАДУ́СЬ, закрадёшься. Р. Закра́сться (intr.). I. Закра́дываться. 1. To steal in, enter stealthily. 2. (fig.) To creep in (as suspicion) (3rd pers. only).

ЗАКРА́ЛСЯ, закра́лась (past), see закраду́сь.

ЗАКРА́СЬ (imp.), see закра́шу.

ЗАКРА́ШЕННЫЙ; закра́шен, —а, —о, —ы (ppp), see закра́шу.

ЗАКРА́ШУ, закра́сишь. Р. Закра́сить (acc.). I. Закра́шивать. To paint over, cover with paint.

ЗАКРЕПЛЁННЫЙ; закреплён, —а́, —о́, —ы́ (ppp), see закреплю́.

ЗАКРЕПЛЮ́, закрепи́шь. Р. Закрепи́ть (acc.). I. Закрепля́ть. 1. To secure, fix, fasten (s.t.). 2. To allot (s.t. to s.o. or s.t.) (acc. + за + inst.). 3. To fix (photographic film). 4. To consolidate (as gains). 5. To assure, ensure (as success). 6. To be constipated (acc. + impers.).

ЗАКРЕПОЩЁННЫЙ; закрепощён, —а́, —о́, —ы́ (ppp), see закрепощу́.

ЗАКРЕПОЩУ́, закрепости́шь. Р. Закрепости́ть (acc.). I. Закрепоща́ть. (lit. and fig.) To enslave.

ЗАКРИЧА́Т, see закричу́.

ЗАКРИЧИ́ (imp.), see закричу́.

ЗАКРИЧИ́ШЬ, see закричу́.

ЗАКРИЧУ́, закричи́шь. Р. Закрича́ть (intr.). I. Крича́ть (mean. 2). 1. To begin to shout. 2. To give a shout, scream.

ЗАКРО́ЕШЬ, see закро́ю.

ЗАКРО́Й (imp.), see закро́ю.

ЗАКРО́Ю, закро́ешь. Р. Закры́ть (acc.). I. Закрыва́ть. 1. To shut, close. 2. To turn off (as a faucet). 3. To cover (acc. + inst.). 4. To shut down (as a factory, etc.). 5. To suppress (as a publication).

ЗАКРУ́ЧЕННЫЙ; закру́чен, —а, —о, —ы (ppp), see закручу́.

ЗАКРУЧУ́, закру́тишь. Р. Закрути́ть (acc.). I. Закру́чивать (mean. 1 thru 4). 1. To twist. 2. To roll (as a cigarette). 3. To wind (s.t. around s.t.) (acc. + на + acc.). 4. To say or relate (s.t.) in a witty or pointed manner. 5. To begin to turn, twirl, etc.

ЗАКРЫ́ТЫЙ; закры́т, —а, —о, —ы (ppp), see закро́ю.

ЗАКУ́ПЛЕННЫЙ; заку́плен, —а, —о, —ы (ppp), see закуплю́.

ЗАКУПЛЮ́, заку́пишь. Р. Закупи́ть (acc.). I. Закупа́ть. 1. To buy up, lay in a stock of. 2. To purchase. 3. To bribe.

ЗАКУ́ШЕННЫЙ; заку́шен, —а, —о, —ы (ppp), see закушу́.

ЗАКУШУ́, заку́сишь. Р. Закуси́ть. I. Заку́сывать. 1. To bite (as one's lips) (acc.). 2. To have a snack (intr.). 3. To eat a little (of s.t.) (inst.). 4. To take (eat or drink) (s.t. with s.t.) (acc. + inst.).

ЗАЛА́ДЬ (imp.), see залажу.

ЗАЛА́ЕШЬ, see залаю.

ЗАЛА́ЖЕННЫЙ; зала́жен, —а, —о, —ы (ppp), see зала́жу.

ЗАЛА́ЖУ, зала́дишь. Р. Зада́дить. 1. To repeat (acc.). 2. To begin to do (s.t.) persistently (as "the wind began to blow without letting up") (inf.). 3. To acquire the habit of, take to doing (s.t.) (+ inf.).

ЗАЛА́Й (imp.), see залаю.

ЗАЛА́Ю, зала́ешь. Р. Зала́ять (intr.). To begin to bark.

ЗАЛЁГ, залегла́ (past), see заля́гу.

ЗАЛЕЖА́ТСЯ, see залежу́сь.

ЗАЛЕЖИ́СЬ (imp.), see залежу́сь.

ЗАЛЕЖИ́ШЬСЯ, see залежу́сь.

ЗАЛЕЖУ́СЬ, залежи́шься. Р. Залежа́ться (intr.). I. Залёживаться. 1. To lie too long. 2. To spoil from lying too long, to become stale (e.g., fruit, food, etc.).

ЗАЛЕ́З, зале́зла (past), see зале́зу.

ЗАЛЕ́ЗЕШЬ, see зале́зу.

ЗАЛЕ́ЗУ, зале́зешь. Р. Зале́зть (intr.). I. Залеза́ть. 1. To climb (up) (на + acc.). 2. To climb (into) (в + acc.). 3. To creep or steal (into) (в + acc.). 4. To get (into) (e.g., a coat, pocket, etc.) (в + acc.).

ЗАЛЕ́ЗЬ (imp.), see зале́зу.

ЗАЛЕ́Й (imp.), see залью́.

ЗАЛЕ́ПЛЕННЫЙ; зале́плен, —а, —о, —ы (ppp), see залеплю́.

ЗАЛЕПЛЮ́, зале́пишь. Р. Залепи́ть (acc.). I. Залепля́ть. 1. To glue up, paste over (s.t.). 2. To close up (as a hole in a roof). 3. To give (e.g., s.o. a slap, blow in the face) (dat. + acc.) (кому́ пощёчину).

ЗАЛЕТИ́ (imp.), see залечу́.

ЗАЛЕТИ́ШЬ, see залечу́.

ЗАЛЕТЯ́Т, see залечу́.

ЗАЛЕЧУ́, залети́шь. Р. Залете́ть (intr.). I. Залета́ть. 1. To fly into (в + acc.). 2. To fly beyond (за + acc.). 3. To land somewhere en route (в + acc.) or (на + acc.). 4. To drop in (on s.o.) for a short time (к + dat.).

ЗАЛИ́ЖЕШЬ, see залижу́.

ЗАЛИЖИ́ (imp.), see залижу́.

ЗАЛИЖУ́, зали́жешь. Р. Зализа́ть (acc.). I. Зали́зывать. 1. To slick down (as one's hair). 2. To lick (as a wound). 3. To embellish excessively.

ЗАЛИ́ЗАННЫЙ; зали́зан, —а, —о, —ы (ppp), see залижу́.

ЗА́ЛИТЫЙ; за́лит, —а́, —о, —ы (ppp), see залью́.

ЗАЛИ́ТЫЙ; зали́т, —а́, —о, —ы (ррр), see залью́.

ЗАЛО́МЛЕННЫЙ; зало́млен, —а, —о, —ы (ррр), see заломлю́.

ЗАЛОМЛЮ́, зало́мишь. Р. Заломи́ть (асс.). I. Зала́мывать (mean. 1 and 2). 1. To ask too high a price (асс. of price). 2. To bend and break (e.g., a branch). 3. To begin to break.

ЗАЛЬЁШЬ, see залью́.

ЗАЛЬЮ́, зальёшь. Р. Зали́ть. I. Залива́ть. 1. (lit. and fig.) To flood (асс.). 2. To pour, spill (as soup on one's shirt) (асс. of shirt + inst. of soup). 3. (lit. and fig.) To fill (s.t. with s.t.) (асс. + inst.). 4. To put out, extinguish (as fire) (асс.).

ЗАЛЯ́Г (imp.), see заля́гу.

ЗАЛЯ́ГУ, заля́жешь, заля́гут. Р. Зале́чь (intr.). I. Залега́ть. 1. To lie (as on a bed, in a trench, etc.). 2. To lie, be located (of a town, etc.). 3. To lie, be deposited (or ore, etc.). 4. To appear, form (as furrows on one's forehead) (на лбу́).

ЗАЛЯ́ЖЕШЬ, see заля́гу.

ЗАМА́ЕШЬСЯ, see зама́юсь.

ЗАМА́ЖЕШЬ, see зама́жу.

ЗАМА́ЖУ, зама́жешь. Р. Зама́зать (асс.). I. Зама́зывать. 1. To paint over. 2. To putty (seal with putty); plaster. 3. To daub, smear. 4. (fig.) To slur over, intentionally conceal (as facts).

ЗАМА́ЖЬ (imp.), see зама́жу.

ЗАМА́ЗАННЫЙ; зама́зан, —а, —о, —ы (ррр), see зама́жу.

ЗАМА́ЙСЯ (imp.), see зама́юсь.

ЗАМА́ШЕШЬ, see замашу́.

ЗАМАШИ́ (imp.), see замашу́.

ЗАМАШУ́, зама́шешь (and замаха́ю, etc.). Р. Замаха́ть (intr.). 1. To start waving (as one's hand) (inst.). 2. To start to flap (as wings) (inst.).

ЗАМА́ЮСЬ, зама́ешься. Р. Зама́яться (intr.). To be exhausted, very tired.

ЗАМЕ́Л, замела́ (past), see замету́.

ЗА́МЕР, замерла́, за́мерло, за́мерли (past), see замру́.

ЗАМЁРЗ, замёрзла (past). Р. Замёрзнуть (intr.). I. Замерза́ть, мёрзнуть. 1. (lit. and fig.) to freeze. 2. To become frostbitten. 3. To freeze to death.

ЗАМЕТЁННЫЙ; заметён, —а́, —о́, —ы́ (ррр), see замету́.

ЗАМЕТЁШЬ, see замету́.

ЗАМЕТИ́ (imp.), see замету́.

ЗАМЕТУ́, заметёшь. Р. Замести́ (асс.). I. Замета́ть. 1. To sweep (up). 2. To cover (as with snow) (асс. + inst.); to become covered (e.g., with snow), (impers. + асс. + inst. of snow).

ЗАМЕ́ТШИЙ (рар), see замету́.

ЗАМЕ́ТЬ (imp.), see заме́чу.

ЗАМЕТЯ́ (adv. past part.), see замету́.

ЗАМЕ́ЧЕННЫЙ; заме́чен, —а, —о, —ы (ррр), see заме́чу.

ЗАМЕ́ЧЕШЬСЯ, see замечу́сь.

ЗАМЕЧИ́СЬ (imp.), see замечу́сь.

ЗАМЕ́ЧУ, заме́тишь. Р. Заме́тить. I. Замеча́ть. 1. To notice, observe (асс.). 2. To note, make note of (асс.). 3. To remark (intr.) or (асс.).

ЗАМЕЧУ́СЬ, заме́чешься. Р. Замета́ться (intr.). 1. To begin to bustle, rush about. 2. To begin to toss about (in bed).

ЗАМЕ́ШЕННЫЙ; заме́шен, —а, —о, —ы (ррр), see замешу́.

ЗАМЕШУ́, заме́сишь. Р. Замеси́ть (асс.). I. Заме́шивать. To mix, knead (as dough).

ЗАМЕЩЁННЫЙ; замещён, —а́, —о́, —ы́ (ррр), see замещу́.

ЗАМЕЩУ́, замести́шь. Р. Замести́ть (асс.). I. Замеща́ть. 1. To replace (s.o. or s.t. with s.o. or s.t.) (асс. + inst.). 2. To fill a vacancy (with s.o.) (асс. + inst.).

ЗАМНЁШЬ, see замну́.

ЗАМНИ́ (imp.), see замну́.

ЗАМНУ́, замнёшь. Р. Замя́ть (асс.). I. Замина́ть. 1. To hush up, suppress (as a conversation, an affair, etc.) 2. To snuff out, crush out (e.g., A cigarette).

ЗАМО́ЕШЬ, see замо́ю.

ЗАМО́Й (imp.), see замо́ю.

ЗАМО́К, замо́кпа (past). Р. Замо́кнуть (intr.). I. Замока́ть. To become damp or wet through absorption of moisture.

ЗАМО́ЛВИ (imp.), see замо́лвлю.

ЗАМО́ЛВЛЮ, замо́лвишь. Р. Замо́лвить (асс.) (arch.). To speak (used in expression "to put in a word for" (сло́во + за + асс.) or (сло́во + о + prep.).

ЗАМО́ЛК, замо́лкла (past). Р. Замо́лкнуть (intr.). I. Замолка́ть. 1. To fall or become silent. 2. To cease speaking. 3. To cease (of sound, conversation, etc.).

ЗАМОЛЧА́Т, see замолчу́[1] and [2].

ЗАМОЛЧИ́ (imp.), see замолчу́[1] and [2].

ЗАМОЛЧИ́ШЬ, see замолчу́[1] and [2].

ЗАМОЛЧУ́[1], замолчи́шь. Р. За-молча́ть (intr.). I. **Замолка́ть.** 1. To fall or become silent. 2. To cease speaking. 3. To cease (of sound, conversation, etc.).

ЗАМОЛЧУ́[2], замолчи́шь. Р. За-молча́ть (acc.). I. **Зама́лчивать.** 1. To ignore. 2. To keep silent (about).

ЗАМОРО́ЖЕННЫЙ; заморо́жен, —а, —о, —ы (ppp), see заморо́жу.

ЗАМОРО́ЖУ, заморо́зишь. Р. За-моро́зить (acc.). I. **Замора́живать.** 1. To freeze. 2. To chill (as wine). 3. To anaesthetize by freezing. 4. (fig.) To freeze (as wages).

ЗАМОРО́ЗЬ (imp.), see заморо́жу.

ЗАМОЩЁННЫЙ; замощён, —а́, —о́, —ы́ (ppp), see замощу́.

ЗАМОЩУ́, замости́шь. Р. Замости́ть (acc.). I. **Мости́ть, зама́щивать.** To pave.

ЗАМО́Ю, замо́ешь. Р. Замы́ть (acc.). I. **Замыва́ть.** To wash off, wash away.

ЗАМРЁШЬ, see замру́.

ЗАМРИ́ (imp.), see замру́.

ЗАМРУ́, замрёшь. Р. Замере́ть (intr.). I. **Замира́ть.** 1. To stand stock-still. 2. (fig.) To die out, away, stop (of sound, movement, etc.).

ЗАМУТНЁННЫЙ; замутнён, —а́, —о́, —ы́ (ppp), see замучу́.

ЗАМУЧУ́, замути́шь (and заму́тишь). Р. **Замути́ть** (acc.). I. **Мути́ть** (mean. 1 and 2). 1. To stir up, make turbid (as a liquid). 2. (fig.) To stir up (as populace). 3. To begin to stir up, etc.

ЗАМЫ́ТЫЙ; замы́т, —а, —о, —ы (ppp), see замо́ю.

ЗАМЯ́ТЫЙ; замя́т, —а, —о, —ы (ppp), see замну́.

ЗАНАВЕ́СЬ (imp.), see занаве́шу.

ЗАНАВЕ́ШЕННЫЙ; занаве́шен, —а, —о, —ы (ppp), see занаве́шу.

ЗАНАВЕ́ШУ, занаве́сишь. Р. За-наве́сить (acc.). I. **Занаве́шивать.** To curtain, screen, cover (as a window).

ЗАНЕМО́Г, занемогла́ (past), see занемогу́.

ЗАНЕМОГИ́ (imp.), see занемогу́.

ЗАНЕМОГУ́, занемо́жешь, занемо́гут. Р. Занемо́чь (intr.). To fall ill.

ЗАНЕМО́ЖЕШЬ, see занемогу́.

ЗАНЁС, занесла́ (past), see занесу́.

ЗАНЕСЁННЫЙ; занесён, —а́, —о́, —ы́ (ppp), see занесу́.

ЗАНЕСЁШЬ, see занесу́.

ЗАНЕСИ́ (imp.), see занесу́.

ЗАНЕСУ́, занесёшь. Р. Занести́ (acc.). I. **Заноси́ть.** 1. To drop in (on one's way) and bring (s.t.). 2. To bring, carry. 3. To note down, enter (as in a register, notebook, etc.) (acc. + в + acc.). 4. To raise (as one's arm). 5. To cover or strew with (acc. + inst.) or (impers. + acc. + inst.). 6. To skid, swerve (of a car) (impers. + acc.).

ЗАНЕСЯ́ and **занёсши** (adv. past part.), see занесу́.

ЗАНИ́ЖЕННЫЙ; зани́жен, —а, —о, -ы (ppp), see зани́жу.

ЗАНИ́ЖУ, зани́зишь. Р. Зани́зить (acc.). I. **Занижа́ть.** 1. To underestimate. 2. To understate.

ЗАНИ́ЗЬ (imp.), see зани́жу.

ЗАНО́ЕШЬ, see заною́.

ЗАНОЖУ́, занози́шь. Р. Занози́ть (acc.). To get a splinter (as in the hand) (acc. of hand).

ЗАНО́Й (imp.), see заною́.

ЗАНО́ШЕННЫЙ; зано́шен, —а, —о, —ы (ppp), see зчношу́[2].

ЗАНОШУ́[1], зано́сишь. I. Заноси́ть (acc.). Р. **Занести́.** 1. To drop in on one's way and bring (s.t.). 2. To bring, carry. 3. To note down, enter (as in a register, notebook, etc.) (acc. + в + acc.). 4. To raise (as one's arm). 5. To cover or strew with (acc. + inst.) or (impers. + acc. + inst.). 6. To skid or swerve (of a car) (impers. + acc.).

ЗАНОШУ́[2], зано́сишь. Р. Заноси́ть (acc.). I. **Зана́шивать.** 1. To wear out. 2. To wear too long (till dirty, etc.).

ЗАНО́Ю, зано́ешь. Р. Заны́ть (intr.). 1. To begin to ache. 2. To begin to complain, whimper, whine.

ЗА́НЯТЫЙ; за́нят, —а́, —о, —ы (ppp). Р. **Заня́ть** (acc.). I. **Занима́ть.** 1. To borrow. 2. To occupy. 3. To interest, entertain. 4. To engage, hold, secure (as a seat, etc.). 5. To employ. (Also see займу́.)

ЗАПАДЁТ, западу́т (3rd pers. only). Р. Запа́сть (intr.). I. Запада́ть. 1. To sink, become sunken (of one's cheeks, etc.). 2. To fall through, or in (as a hole). 3. (fig.) To make an impression (as on one's memory, heart) (в + acc.) or (на + acc.).

ЗАПАДИ́ (imp.), see западёт.

ЗАПАДУ́Т, see западёт.

ЗАПА́КОСТИ (imp.), see запа́кощу.

ЗАПА́КОЩЕННЫЙ; запа́кощен, —а, —о, —ы (ррр), see запа́кощу.

ЗАПА́КОЩУ, запа́костишь. Р. Запа́костить (acc.). I. Па́костить. To soil.

ЗАПА́Л, запа́ла (past), see западёт.

ЗАПА́С, запасла́ (past). see запасу́.

ЗАПАСЁННЫЙ; запасён, —а́, —о́, —ы́ (ррр), see запасу́.

ЗАПАСЁШЬ, see запасу́.

ЗАПАСИ́ (imp.), see запасу́.

ЗАПАСУ́, запасёшь. Р. Запасти́ (acc./gen.). I. Запаса́ть. To store, stock, lay in a stock.

ЗАПА́ХАННЫЙ; запа́хан, —а, —о, —ы (ррр), see запашу́.

ЗАПА́ШЕШЬ, see запашу́.

ЗАПАШИ́ (imp.), see запашу́.

ЗАПАШУ́, запа́шешь. Р. Запаха́ть (acc.). I. Запа́хивать. 1. To plow (as a field). 2. To plow in (as manure).

ЗАПЕ́Й (imp.), Р. Запи́ть. I. Запива́ть. 1. To take (wash down) (s.t. with a drink) (as a pill with water) (acc. + inst.). 2. To go on a drunk (intr.). (Also see запью́.)

ЗАПЁК, запекпа́ (past), see запеку́.

ЗАПЕКИ́ (imp.), see запеку́.

ЗАПЕКУ́, запечёшь, запеу́т. Т. Запе́чь (acc.). I. Запека́ть. 1. To bake (until brown crust is formed). 2. To bake (s.t. wrapped in dough) (acc. + в + acc.).

ЗА́ПЕР, заперла́, за́перло (past). Р. Запере́ть (acc.). I. Запира́ть. 1. To lock, bolt (as a door). 2. To lock up (as the dog). 3. To bar, block up, block, cut off (also see запру́).

ЗАПЕРЁВ (or за́перши) (adv. past part.), see за́пер and запру́.

ЗА́ПЕРТЫЙ; за́перт, —а́, —о, —ы (ррр), see за́пер and запру́.

ЗАПЕ́ТЫЙ; запе́т, —а, —о, —ы (ррр), see запою́.

ЗАПЕЧЁННЫЙ; запечён, —а́, —о́, —ы́ (ррр), see запеку́.

ЗАПЕЧЁШЬ, see запеку́.

ЗАПИ́САННЫЙ; запи́сан, —а, —о, —ы (ррр), see запишу́.

ЗАПИ́ТЫЙ; запи́т, —а́ or —а, —о, —ы (ррр), see запе́й and запью́.

ЗАПИ́ШЕШЬ, see запишу́.

ЗАПИШИ́ (imp.), see запишу́.

ЗАПИШУ́, запи́шешь. Р. Записа́ть (acc.). I. Запи́сывать. 1. To write down. 2. To record (as on tape). 3. To enter (as in the minutes, on a list, etc.). 4. To deed, transfer (s.t. to s.o.).

ЗАПЛА́ЧЕННЫЙ; запла́чен, —а, —о, —ы (ррр), see заплачу́.

ЗАПЛАЧУ́, запла́тишь. Р. Заплати́ть. I. Плати́ть. 1. To pay (as a debt) (acc.). 2. To pay (for s.t.) (за + acc.). 3. (lit. and fig.) To repay (s.o. with s.t.) (dat. + inst.).

ЗАПЛЁЛ, заплела́ (past), see заплету́.

ЗАПЛЕСКА́Й and заплещи́ (imp.), see заплещу́.

ЗАПЛЁСКАННЫЙ; заплёскан, —а, —о, —ы (ррр), see заплещу́.

ЗАПЛЕТЁННЫЙ; заплетён, —а́, —о́, —ы́ (ррр), see заплету́.

ЗАПЛТЁШЬ, see заплету́.

ЗАПЛЕТИ́ (imp.), see заплету́.

ЗАПЛЕТУ́, заплетёшь. Р. Заплести́ (acc.). I. Заплета́ть (mean. 1 and 2). 1. To braid, plait, weave. 2. To entwine. 3. To begin to braid, etc.

ЗАПЛЁТШИЙ (рар), see заплету́.

ЗАПЛЕТЯ́ (adv. past part.), see заплету́.

ЗАПЛЁЩЕШЬ, see заплещу́.

ЗАПЛЕЩИ́ and заплеска́й (imp.), see заплещу́.

ЗАПЛЕЩУ́, запле́щешь (also заплеска́ю, etc.). Р. Заплеска́ть (acc.). I. Заплёскивать (mean. 1). 1. To splash or spatter (as with water) (acc. + inst.). 2. To begin to splash, etc.

ЗАПЛЫВЁШЬ, see заплыву́.

ЗАПЛЫВИ́ (imp.), see заплыву́.

ЗАПЛЫВУ́, заплывёшь. Р. Заплы́ть (intr.). I. Заплыва́ть. 1. To float, sail, or swim somewhere. 2. To become covered with (as a pond with

slime, a candle with wax) (inst.). 3. To become fat with bloated, (inst.).
ЗАПОЁШЬ, see запою́.
ЗАПО́Й (imp.), see запою́.
ЗАПО́ЛЗ, заползла́ (past), see заползу́.
ЗАПОЛЗЁШЬ, see заползу́.
ЗАПОЛЗИ́ (imp.), see заползу́.
ЗАПОЛЗУ́, заползёшь. Р. Заползти́ (intr.). I. Заполза́ть. To creep or crawl somewhere (as under a bed, etc.).
ЗАПО́РЕШЬ, see запорю́.
ЗАПОРИ́ (imp.), see запорю́.
ЗАПО́РОТЫЙ; запо́рот, —а, —о, —ы (ppp), see запорю́.
ЗАПОРЮ́, запо́решь. Р. Запоро́ть (acc.). I. Запа́рывать. 1. To flog to death. 2. To rip open, kill. 3. To ruin or spoil by careless, unskillful work.
ЗАПОЮ́, запоёшь. Р. Запе́ть (intr.) or (acc.). I. Запева́ть. To begin to sing.
ЗАПРА́ВЛЕННЫЙ; запра́влен, —а, —о, —ы (ppp), see запра́влю.
ЗАПРА́ВЛЮ, запра́вишь. Р. Запра́вить (acc.). I. Заправля́ть. 1. To tuck in (s.t. into s.t.). 2. To season. 3. To service, fuel (e.g., an auto with gasoline) (acc. + inst.).
ЗАПРА́ВЬ (imp.), see запра́влю.
ЗАПРЁШЬ, see запру́.
ЗАПРЕЩЁННЫЙ; запрещён, —а́, —о́, —ы́ (ppp), see запрещу́.
ЗАПРЕЩУ́, запрети́шь, Р. Запрети́ть (acc.). I. Запреща́ть. To forbid, prohibit, suppress.
ЗАПРИ́ (imp.), see запру́.
ЗАПРИМЕ́ТЬ (imp.), see запримечу.
ЗАПРИМЕ́ЧЕННЫЙ; заприме́чен, —а, —о, —ы (ppp), see заприме́чу.
ЗАПРИМЕ́ЧУ, заприме́тишь. Р. Заприме́тить (acc.). To notice, spot.
ЗАПРОДАВА́Й (imp.), see запродаю́.
ЗАПРОДАВА́Я (adv. pres. part.), see запродаю́.
ЗАПРОДАДИ́М, запродади́те, запродаду́т (pl. forms), see запрода́м.
ЗАПРОДАЁШЬ, see запродаю́.
ЗАПРОДА́Й (imp.), see запрода́м.
ЗАПРОДА́М, запрода́шь, запрода́ст (sing. forms). Р. Запрода́ть (acc.). I. Запродава́ть. To agree to sell (at a specific price, under specific conditions, etc.).
ЗАПРО́ДАННЫЙ; запро́дан, —а, —о, —ы (ppp), see запрода́м.

ЗАПРОДА́СТ, see запрода́м.
ЗАПРОДА́ШЬ, see запрода́м.
ЗАПРОДАЮ́, запродаёшь. I. Запродава́ть (acc.). Р. Запрода́ть. To agree to sell (at a specific price, under specific conditions, etc.).
ЗАПРОПАДЁШЬ, see запропаду́.
ЗАПРОПАДИ́ (imp.), see запропаду́.
ЗАПРОПАДУ́, запропадёшь. Р. Запропа́сть (intr.). To get lost, disappear.
ЗАПРОПА́Л, запропа́ла (past), see запропаду́.
ЗАПРОПАЩУ́СЬ, запропасти́шься, Р. Запропасти́ться (intr.). To get lost, disappear.
ЗАПРО́ШЕННЫЙ; запро́шен, —а, —о, —ы (ppp), see запрошу́.
ЗАПРОШУ́, запро́сишь. Р. Запроси́ть. I. Запра́шивать. 1. To request (s.o. or s.t.) (acc./gen.). 2. To inquire about (o + prep.). 3. To ask (an exhorbitant price) (acc.).
ЗАПРУ́, запрёшь. Р. Запере́ть (acc.). I. Запира́ть. 1. To lock, bolt (as a door). 2. To lock up (as the dog). 3. To bar, block up, block, cut off.
ЗАПРУ́ЖЕННЫЙ; запру́жен, —а, —о, —ы (ppp), see запружу́.
ЗАПРУЖЁННЫЙ; запружён, —а́, —о́, —ы́ (ppp), see запружу́.
ЗАПРУЖУ́, запру́дишь (and запруди́шь). Р. Запруди́ть (acc.). I. Запру́живать, пруди́ть (mean. 1). 1. To dam (as a stream). 2. (fig.) To fill completely (as, a crowd fills a hall).
ЗАПРЯ́Г, запрягла́ (past), see запрягу́.
ЗАПРЯГИ́ (imp.), see запрягу́.
ЗАПРЯГУ́, запряжёшь, запрягу́т. Р. Запря́чь (acc.), запре́чь (arch.). I. Запряга́ть. 1. To harness (to) (acc. + в + acc.). 2. (fig.) To load (s.o.) with work.
ЗАПРЯЖЁННЫЙ; запряжён, —а́, —о́, —ы́ (ppp), see запрягу́.
ЗАПРЯЖЁШЬ, see запрягу́.
ЗАПРЯ́ТАННЫЙ; запря́тан, —а, —о, —ы (ppp), see запря́чу.
ЗАПРЯ́ЧЕШЬ, see запря́чу.
ЗАПРЯ́ЧУ, запря́чешь. Р. Запря́тать (acc.). I. Запря́тывать. To conceal, hide.
ЗАПРЯ́ЧЬ (imp.), see запря́чу.

ЗАПУ́ЩЕННЫЙ; запу́щен, —а, —о,
—ы (ppp), see запущу́.
ЗАПУЩУ́, запу́стишь. Р. Запусти́ть.
I. Запуска́ть. 1. To fling (as a stone)
(acc./inst.). 2. To thrust (as hand
into pocket) (acc.). 3. To launch (as
a rocket (acc.). 4. To start (as a
motor) (acc.). 5. To release (acc.).
6. To neglect (as one's duties) (acc.).
7. To permit to develop (as an
illness) (acc.).
ЗАПЫХТИ́ (imp.), see запыхчу́.
ЗАПЫХТИ́ШЬ, see запыхчу́.
ЗАПЫХТЯ́Т, see запыхчу́.
ЗАПЫХЧУ́, запыхти́шь. Р. Запых-
те́ть (intr.). To begin to puff, pant.
ЗАПЬЁШЬ, see запью́.
ЗАПЬЮ́, запьёшь. Р. Запи́ть. I.
Запива́ть. 1. To take (wash down)
(s.t. with a drink) (as a pill with
water) (acc. + inst.). 2. To go on a
drunk (intr.).
ЗАРАЖЁННЫЙ; заражён, —а́, —о́,
—ы́ (ppp), see заражу́.
ЗАРАЖУ́, зарази́шь. Р. Зарази́ть
(acc.). I. Заража́ть. 1. To infect,
contaminate. 2. (fig.) To infect (as s.o.
with one's enthusiasm) (acc. + inst.).
ЗАРАСТЁШЬ, see зарасту́.
ЗАРАСТИ́ (imp.), see зарасту́.
ЗАРАСТУ́, зарастёшь. Р. Зарасти́
(intr.). I. Зараста́ть. 1. To be overgrown with (inst.). 2. To heal (of a
wound).
ЗАРВЁШЬСЯ, see зарву́сь.
ЗАРВИ́СЬ (imp.), see зарву́сь.
ЗАРВУ́СЬ, зарвёшься. Р. Зарва́ться
(intr.). I. Зарыва́ться. To go to
extremes, too far.
ЗАРЕВЁШЬ, see зареву́.
ЗАРЕВИ́ (imp.), see зареву́.
ЗАРЕВУ́, заревёшь. Р. Зареве́ть
(intr.). 1. To start to roar. 2. To
start to cry loudly, howl.
ЗАРЕ́ЖЕШЬ, see заре́жу.
ЗАРЕ́ЖУ, заре́жешь. Р. Заре́зать
(acc.). I. Ре́зать (mean. 1 and 3).
1. To kill, slaughter (as cattle). 2.
To exhaust by fast driving (as
horses). 3. To ruin, spoil (s.o. or s.t.).
ЗАРЕ́ЖЬ (imp.), see заре́жу.
ЗАРЕ́ЗАННЫЙ; заре́зан, —а, —о,
—ы (ppp), see заре́жу.
ЗАРЕКИ́СЬ (imp.), see зареку́сь.
ЗАРЁКСЯ, зарекла́сь (past), see за-
реку́сь.

ЗАРЕКУ́СЬ, заречёшься, зареку́тся.
Р. Заре́чься (intr.). I. Зарека́ться.
1. To renounce (s.t.) (от + gen.). 2.
To promise, vow not (to do s.t.)
(+ inf.).
ЗАРЕЧЁШЬСЯ, see зареку́сь.
ЗАРО́ЕШЬ, see заро́ю.
ЗАРОЖДЁННЫЙ; зарождён, —а́,
—о́, —ы́ (ppp), see зарожу́.
ЗАРОЖУ́, зароди́шь. Р. Зароди́ть
(acc.). I. Зарожда́ть. 1. To arouse,
engender (as s.t. in s.o.) (acc. + в +
prep.). 2. To beget, give birth to
(arch.).
ЗАРО́Й (imp.), see заро́ю.
ЗАРО́С, заросла́ (past), see зарасту́.
ЗАРО́Ю, заро́ешь. Р. Зары́ть (acc.). I.
Зарыва́ть. (lit. and fig.) To bury.
ЗАРУ́БЛЕННЫЙ; зару́блен, —а, —о,
—ы (ppp), see зарублю́.
ЗАРУБЛЮ́, зару́бишь. Р. Заруби́ть
(acc.). I. Заруба́ть. 1. To slash to
death. 2. To groove, cut a notch (in
s.t.) (в + prep.). 3. To expose the
surface (of a layer of some mineral)
(as a stratum of coal).
ЗАРЫ́ТЫЙ; зары́т, —а, —о, —ы
(ppp), see заро́ю.
ЗАРЫЧА́Т, see зарычу́.
ЗАРЫЧИ́ (imp.), see зарычу́.
ЗАРЫЧИ́ШЬ, see зарычу́.
ЗАРЫЧУ́, зарычи́шь. Р. Зарыча́ть
(intr.). To begin to growl, snarl.
ЗАРЯ́ЖЕННЫЙ; заря́жен, —а, —о,
—ы (ppp), see заряжу́.
ЗАРЯЖЁННЫЙ; заряжён, —а́, —о́,
—ы́ (ppp), see заряжу́.
ЗАРЯЖУ́, заряди́шь (and заря́дишь).
Р. Заряди́ть. I. Заряжа́ть (mean. 1
thru 3). 1. To load (as a camera,
gun, etc.) (acc.). 2. To charge (as a
battery, fire extinguisher, etc.) (acc.).
3. To inspire (s.o. with s.t.) (acc. +
inst.). 4. To repeat over and over
(acc.). 5. To continue without letup
(as rain) (intr.).
ЗАСА́ЖЕННЫЙ; заса́жен, —а, —о,
—ы (ppp), see засажу́.
ЗАСАЖУ́, заса́дишь. Р. Засади́ть
(acc.). I. Заса́живать. 1. To plant
(as a field with grain) (acc. + inst.).
2. To shut in, put in (as in a cage,
prison, etc.) (acc. + в + acc.). 3.
To set (s.o. to s.t.) (as to work)
(acc. + за + acc.) or (acc. + inf.).
4. To sink, plant, drive (as an

axe, spike in a log) (acc. + в + acc.).

ЗАСВÉЧЕННЫЙ; засвéчен, —а, —о, —ы (ppp), see засвечý.

ЗАСВЕЧУ́, засвéтишь. Р. Засветить (acc.). 1. To light (as a candle). 2. To spoil, expose to light (as a film).

ЗАСÉК, засеклá (past), see засекý.

ЗАСЕКИ́ (imp.), see засекý.

ЗАСЕКРÉТЬ (imp.), see засекрéчу.

ЗАСЕКРÉЧЕННЫЙ; засекрéчен, —а, —о, —ы (ppp), see засекрéчу.

ЗАСЕКРÉЧУ, засекрéтишь. Р. Засекрéтить (acc.). I. Засекрéчивать. 1. To make secret, restrict (as a document). 2. To admit (s.o.) to secret, classified work.

ЗАСЕКУ́, засечёшь, засекýт. Р. Засéчь (acc.). I. Засекáть. 1. To get a bearing (on s.t.) determine location by intersection. 2. To notch. 3. To cut (as a horse cuts his hind legs). 4. To note, mark (as time). 5. To flog (to death).

ЗАСÉЛ, засéла (past). Р. Засéсть (intr.). I. Засáживаться. 1. To stay (as at home). 2. To sit down to, set to (as work) (за + acc.) or (+ inf.). 3. To settle oneself (as in a chair) (в + prep.). 4. To lodge, become embedded (as a bullet in the wall) (в + prep.). (Also see засяду.)

ЗАСЕЧЁННЫЙ; засечён, —á, —ó, —ы́ (ppp), see засекý (mean. 1 thru 4).

ЗАСÉЧЕННЫЙ; засéчеи, —а, —о, —ы (ppp), see засекý (mean. 5 only).

ЗАСЕЧÉШЬ, see засекý.

ЗАСИДИ́ (imp.), see засидит.

ЗАСИДИ́СЬ (imp.), see засижýсь.

ЗАСИДИ́Т, засидя́т (3rd pers. only). Р. Засидéть (acc.). I. Засиживать. To spot, soil (of flies, birds, etc.).

ЗАСИДИ́ШЬСЯ, see засижýсь.

ЗАСИДЯ́Т, see засидит.

ЗАСИДЯ́ТСЯ, see засижýсь.

ЗАСИ́ЖЕННЫЙ; засижен, —а, —о, —ы (ppp), see засидит.

ЗАСИЖУ́СЬ, засиди́шься. Р. Засидéться (intr.). I. Засиживаться. To sit or stay too long.

ЗАСКАЧЕШЬ, see заскачý.

ЗАСКАЧИ́ (imp.), see заскачý.

ЗАСКАЧУ́, заскáчешь. Р. Заскакáть (intr.). 1. To start, begin to gallop. 2. To start, begin to jump, hop, skip.

ЗАСКОРУ́З, заскорýзла (past). Р. Заскорýзнуть (intr.). 1. To become hardened (of hands, etc.). 2. To become stiff. 3. (fig.) To stagnate.

ЗАСКРЕЖÉЩЕШЬ, see заскрежещý.

ЗАСКРЕЖЕЩИ́ (imp.), see заскрежещý.

ЗАСКРЕЖЕЩУ́, заскрежéщешь. Р. Заскрежетáть (intr.). I. Скрежетáть (mean. 2.). 1. To begin to gnash, grind one's teeth (inst. of teeth). 2. To grit, grind, or gnash one's teeth (inst. of teeth).

ЗÁСЛАННЫЙ; зáслан, —а, —о, —ы (ppp). Р. Заслáть (acc.). I. Засылáть. 1. To send far away or to wrong address. 2. To send (as spies). (Also see зашлю́.)

ЗАСЛÉЖЕННЫЙ; заслéжен, —а, —о, —ы (ppp), see заслежý.

ЗАСЛЕЖУ́, заследи́шь. Р. Заследи́ть (acc.). I. Заслéживать. To soil with one's feet, track.

ЗАСЛЫ́ШАННЫЙ; заслы́шан, —а, —о, —ы (ppp), see заслы́шу.

ЗАСЛЫ́ШАТ, see заслы́шу.

ЗАСЛЫ́ШИШЬ, see заслы́шу.

ЗАСЛЫ́ШУ, заслы́шишь. Р. Заслы́шать. 1. To hear, catch a sound (acc.). 2. To scent, catch a scent, smell (acc.). 3. To hear about (о + prep.).

ЗАСЛЫ́ШЬ (imp.), see заслы́шу.

ЗАСМЕЁШЬ, see засмею́.

ЗАСМÉЙ (imp.), see засмею́.

ЗАСМЕЮ́, засмеёшь. Р. Засмея́ть (acc.). I. Засмéивать. To ridicule.

ЗАСМÉЯННЫЙ; засмéян, —а, —о, —ы (ppp), see засмею́.

ЗАСМОТРИ́СЬ (imp.), see засмотрю́сь.

ЗАСМОТРИ́ШЬСЯ, see засмотрю́сь.

ЗАСМОТРЮ́СЬ, засмóтришься. Р. Засмотрéться (intr.). I. Засмáтриваться. To be lost in contemplation of (на + acc.).

ЗАСМÓТРЯТСЯ, see засмотрю́сь.

ЗАСНИ́МЕШЬ, see заснимý.

ЗАСНИМИ́ (imp.), see заснимý.

ЗАСНИМУ́, сними́мешь. Р. Засня́ть (acc.). To photograph.

ЗАСНЯ́ТЫЙ; засня́т, —á, —о, —ы (ppp), see заснимý.

ЗАСÓВЕЩУСЬ, засóвестишься. Р. Засóвеститься (intr.). 1. To be ashamed (of) (gen.). 2. To be ashamed (to) (+ inf.).

ЗАСОСАННЫЙ; засосан, —а, —о, —ы (ppp), see засосу́.

ЗАСОСЁШЬ, see засосу́.

ЗАСОСИ (imp.), see засосу́.

ЗАСОСУ́, засосёшь. P. Засоса́ть (acc.). I. Заса́сывать (mean. 1 and 2). 1. To suck in. 2. (fig.) To swallow, suck in (of quicksand, a crowd, etc.). 3. To begin to suck, etc.

ЗАСО́Х, засо́хла (past). P. Засо́хнуть (intr.). I. Со́хнуть. 1. To dry, become dry. 2. To waste away (of people). 3. To wither (of flowers).

ЗА́СПАННЫЙ; за́спан, —а, —о, —ы (ppp), see засплю́.

ЗАСПИ́ (imp.), see засплю́.

ЗАСПИ́СЬ (imp.), see засплю́сь.

ЗАСПИ́ШЬ, see засплю́.

ЗАСПИ́ШЬСЯ, see засплю́сь.

ЗАСПЛЮ́, заспи́шь. P. Заспа́ть (acc.). I. Засыпа́ть. 1. To forget about (s.t.) after sleeping. 2. To smother (as a child) while sleeping.

ЗАСПЛЮ́СЬ, заспи́шься. P. Заспа́ться (intr.). To oversleep.

ЗАСПЯ́Т, see засплю́.

ЗАСПЯ́ТСЯ, see засплю́сь.

ЗАСРАМЛЁННЫЙ; засрамлён, —а́, —о́, —ы́ (ppp), see засрамлю́.

ЗАСРАМЛЮ́, засрами́шь. P. Засрами́ть (acc.). To shame.

ЗАСТАВА́Й (imp.), see застаю́.

ЗАСТАВА́Я (adv. pres. part.), see застаю́.

ЗАСТА́ВЛЕННЫЙ; заста́влен, —а, —о, —ы (ppp), see заста́влю.

ЗАСТА́ВЛЮ, заста́вишь. P. Заста́вить (acc.). I. Заставля́ть. 1. To force, compel. 2. To cram, fill. 3. To block, obstruct. 4. To put (s.t. in the wrong place).

ЗАСТА́ВЬ (imp.), see заста́влю.

ЗАСТАЁШЬ, see застаю́.

ЗАСТА́НЕШЬ, see заста́ну.

ЗАСТА́НУ, заста́нешь. P. Заста́ть (acc.). I. Застава́ть. To find (as s.o. at home).

ЗАСТА́НЬ (imp.), see заста́ну.

ЗАСТАЮ́, застаёшь. I. Застава́ть (acc.). P. Заста́ть. To find (as s.o. at home).

ЗАСТЕ́ЛЕННЫЙ; засте́лен, —а, —о, —ы (ppp), see застелю́.

ЗАСТЕ́ЛЕШЬ, see застелю́.

ЗАСТЕЛИ́ (imp.), see застелю́.

ЗАСТЕЛЮ́, засте́лешь. P. Застла́ть (acc.), застели́ть (mean. 1). I. Застила́ть. 1. To cover (as with a spread, carpet, etc.). 2. To screen, hide from view.

ЗА́СТИ and засть (imp.), I. За́стить (acc.) or (intr.). To screen, shield, obstruct (as light) (also see за́шу).

ЗАСТИ́Г, засти́гла (past), see засти́гну.

ЗАСТИ́ГНИ (imp.), see засти́гну.

ЗАСТИ́ГНУ, засти́гнешь. P. Засти́чь and засти́гнуть (acc.). I. Застига́ть. To take unawares, surprise.

ЗАСТИ́ГНУТЫЙ; засти́гнут, —а, —о, —ы (ppp), see засти́гну.

ЗА́СТЛАННЫЙ; за́стлан, —а, —о, —ы (ppp), see застелю́.

ЗАСТОИ́ШЬСЯ, see застою́сь.

ЗАСТО́ЙСЯ (imp.), see застою́сь.

ЗАСТОЮ́СЬ, застои́шься. P. Застоя́ться (intr.). I. Заста́иваться. 1. To stand too long. 2. To become stale, stagnant. 3. To linger.

ЗАСТРИ́Г, застри́гла (past), see застригу́.

ЗАСТРИГИ́ (imp.), see застригу́.

ЗАСТРИГУ́, застрижёшь, застригу́т. P. Застри́чь (acc.). I. Застрига́ть (mean. 1). 1. To cut too close or short. 2. To begin to cut, etc.

ЗАСТРИ́ЖЕННЫЙ; застри́жен, —а, —о, —ы (ppp), see застригу́ (mean. 1).

ЗАСТРИЖЁШЬ, see застригу́.

ЗАСТРЯ́НЕШЬ, see застря́ну.

ЗАСТРЯ́НУ, застря́нешь. P. Застря́ть (intr.). I. Застрева́ть. 1. To stick (as in the mud). 2. (fig.) To stick (be stuck) somewhere.

ЗАСТРЯ́НЬ (imp.), see застря́ну.

ЗАСТУ́ЖЕННЫЙ; засту́жен, —а, —о, —ы (ppp), see застужу́.

ЗАСТУЖУ́, засту́дишь. P. Застуди́ть (acc.). I. Засту́живать. 1. To chill. 2. To cause a cold by chilling.

ЗАСТУПЛЮ́, засту́пишь. P. Заступи́ть. I. Заступа́ть. 1. To take the place of (s.o., s.t.), replace (as a father, etc.) (acc.). 2. To replace s.o. (at work), take over (a job) (на + acc. of work, job, etc.). 3. To step on (acc.). 4. To go in, enter (arch.) (intr.). 5. To defend, protect (arch.) (acc.).

ЗАСТУПЛЮСЬ, заступишься. Р. Заступиться (за + acc.). I. Заступаться. To stand up (for), defend.

ЗАСТЫЖЁННЫЙ; застыжён, —á, —ó, —ы́ (ppp), see застыжу́.

ЗАСТЫЖУ́, застыди́шь. Р. Застыди́ть (acc.). To shame (s.o.), make ashamed.

ЗАСТЫНЕШЬ, see застыну.

ЗАСТЫНУ, застынешь. Р. Застыть (intr.). I. Застывать. 1. To thicken, congeal, solidify, set. 2. To freeze slightly. 3. To become numb with cold. 4. (fig.) To freeze (of a smile, person, etc.).

ЗАСТЫНЬ (imp.), see застыну.

ЗАСТЬ and за́сти (imp.), see за́щу.

ЗАСУ́ЖЕННЫЙ; засу́жен, —а, —о, —ы (ppp), see засужу́.

ЗАСУЖУ́, засу́дишь. Р. Засуди́ть (acc.). To condemn.

ЗАСЫ́ПАННЫЙ; засы́пан, —а, —о, —ы (ppp), see засы́плю.

ЗАСЫ́ПЛЕШЬ, see засы́плю.

ЗАСЫ́ПЛЮ, засы́плешь. Р. Засы́пать (acc.). I. Засыпа́ть. 1. To fill (s.t. with s.t.) (acc. + inst.). 2. To cover (s.t. with s.t.) (acc. + inst.). 3. To strew (s.t. with s.t.) (acc. + inst.). 4. To pour (as grain, salt) (acc.).

ЗАСЫ́ПЬ (imp.), see засы́плю.

ЗАСЯ́ДЕШЬ, see зася́ду.

ЗАСЯ́ДУ, зася́дешь. Р. Засе́сть (intr.). I. Заса́живаться. 1. To stay (as at home). 2. To sit down to, set to (as work) (за + acc.) or (inf.). 3. To settle oneself (as in a chair) (в + prep.). 4. To lodge, become embedded (as a bullet in a wall) (в + prep.).

ЗАСЯ́ДЬ (imp.), see зася́ду.

ЗАТВЕРЖЁННЫЙ; затвержён, —á, —ó, —ы́ (ppp), see затвержу́.

ЗАТВЕ́РЖЕННЫЙ; затве́ржен, —а, —о, —ы (ppp), see затвержу́.

ЗАТВЕРЖУ́, затверди́шь. Р. Затверди́ть (acc.). I. Тверди́ть (mean. 1). 1. To learn by heart (by repetition). 2. To begin to repeat or learn by heart.

ЗАТЕ́ЕШЬ, see зате́ю.

ЗАТЕ́Й (imp.), see зате́ю.

ЗАТЁК, затекла́ (past), see затечёт.

ЗАТЕКУ́Т, see затечёт.

ЗАТЁР, затёрла (past), see затру́.

ЗАТЕРЁВ and затёрши (adv. past part.), see затру́.

ЗАТЁРТЫЙ; затёрт, —а, —о, —ы (ppp), see затру́.

ЗАТЁРШИ and затерёв, see затру́.

ЗАТЁСАННЫЙ; затёсан, —а, —о, —ы (ppp), see затешу́.

ЗАТЕЧЁТ, затеку́т (3rd pers. only). Р. Зате́чь (intr.). I. Затека́ть. 1. To flow, leak (into) (в + acc.), behind (за + acc.). 2. To become numb (of one's legs, etc.). 3. To become swollen (of eyes, etc.).

ЗАТЕ́ШЕШЬ, see затешу́.

ЗАТЕШИ́ (imp.), see затешу́.

ЗАТЕШУ́, зате́шешь. Р. Затеса́ть (acc.). I. Затёсывать. 1. To hew. 2. To notch.

ЗАТЕ́Ю, зате́ешь. Р. Зате́ять (acc.). I. Затева́ть. To undertake, venture, begin to do (s.t.).

ЗАТЕ́ЯННЫЙ; зате́ян, —а, —о, —ы (ppp), see зате́ю.

ЗА́ТКАННЫЙ; за́ткан, —а, —о, —ы (ppp), see затку́.

ЗАТКЁШЬ, see затку́.

ЗАТКИ́ (imp.), see затку́.

ЗАТКУ́, заткёшь. Р. Заткáть (acc.). To interweave (with) (acc. + inst.).

ЗАТО́ПЛЕННЫЙ; зато́плен, —а, —о, —ы (ppp), see затоплю́[1] and [2].

ЗАТОПЛЮ́[1], зато́пишь. Р. Затопи́ть (acc.). I. Зата́пливать, light a fire, fire up (as a stove).

ЗАТОПЛЮ́[2], зато́пишь. Р. Затопи́ть (acc.). I. Затопля́ть. 1. To inundate, flood, submerge. 2. To scuttle, sink (as a ship).

ЗАТО́ПТАННЫЙ; зато́птан, —а, —о, —ы (ppp), see затопчу́.

ЗАТО́ПЧЕШЬ, see затопчу́.

ЗАТОПЧИ́ (imp.), see затопчу́.

ЗАТОПЧУ́, зато́пчешь. Р. Затопта́ть (acc.). I. Зата́птывать. 1. To trample underfoot. 2. To soil, dirty (as the floor).

ЗАТОРМОЖЁННЫЙ; заторможён, —á, —ó, —ы́ (ppp), see заторможу́.

ЗАТОРМОЖУ́, затормози́шь. Р. Затормози́ть. I. Тормози́ть. 1. To brake (as an auto) (acc.). 2. To put on the brakes, slow down (intr.). 3. To inhibit, impede, hamper (acc.).

ЗАТОРОПЛЮ́СЬ, заторо́пишься. Р. Заторопи́ться (intr.). 1. To begin to hurry (to do s.t.). 2. To begin to hurry (somewhere).

ЗАТРА́ВЛЕННЫЙ; затра́влен, —а, —о, —ы (ppp), see затравлю́.

ЗАТРАВЛЮ́, затра́вишь. Р. Затрави́т (acc.). I. Тва́вить. 1. To hunt down. 2. To persecute.

ЗАТРА́ТЬ (imp.), see затра́чу.

ЗАТРА́ЧЕННЫЙ; затра́чен, —а, —о, —ы (ppp), see затра́чу.

ЗАТРА́ЧУ, затра́тишь. Р. Затра́тить (acc.). I. Затра́чивать. 1. To spend, use (as money, time, etc.). 2. To waste (one's money, time, etc.).

ЗАТРЁПАННЫЙ; затрёпан, —а, —о, —ы (ppp), see затреплю́.

ЗАТРЕПЕ́ЩЕШЬ, see затрепещу́.

ЗАТРЕПЕЩИ́ (imp.), see затрепищу́.

ЗАТРЕПЕЩУ́, затрепе́щешь. Р. Затрепета́ть (intr.). 1. To begin to tremble. 2. To begin to palpitate. 3. To begin to flicker (as a flame).

ЗАТРЕ́ПЛЕШЬ, see затреплю́.

ЗАТРЕПЛИ́ (imp.), see затреплю́.

ЗАТРЕПЛЮ́, затре́плешь. Р. Затрепа́ть (acc.). (lit. and fig.) To wear out.

ЗАТРЁШЬ, see затру́.

ЗАТРИ́ (imp.), see затру́.

ЗАТРУ́, затрёшь. Р. Затере́ть (acc.). I. Затира́ть. 1. To rub over, rub out. 2. To press, squeeze, jam. 3. To soil, dirty. 4. To give (s.o.) no chance. 5. To prepare (s.t.) by grinding.

ЗАТРЯ́С, затрясла́ (past), see затрясу́.

ЗАТРЯСЁШЬ, see затрясу́.

ЗАТРЯСИ́ (imp.), see затрясу́.

ЗАТРЯСУ́, затрясёшь. Р. Затрясти́. 1. To begin to shake (as a tree, s.o.'s hand, etc.) (acc.). 2. To begin to shake (as one's leg, head) (inst.). 3. To begin to shake, rock (as a car) (intr.). 4. To begin to tremble (intr.).

ЗАТУ́ПЛЕННЫЙ; зату́плен, —а, —о, —ы (ppp), see затуплю́.

ЗАТУПЛЮ́, зату́пишь. Р. Затупи́ть (acc.). I. Тупи́ть. To dull, blunt.

ЗАТУ́Х, зату́хла (past). Р. Зату́хнуть (intr.). I. Затуха́ть. 1. To die out, down (of sound, fire, etc.). 2. To fade, attenuate (of radio waves, etc.).

ЗАХА́ЕШЬ, see заха́ю.

ЗАХА́Й (imp.), see заха́ю.

ЗАХА́Ю, заха́ешь. Р. Заха́ять (acc.). I. Заха́ивать. To disgrace, defame, discredit.

ЗАХА́ЯННЫЙ; заха́ян, —а, —о, —ы (ppp), see заха́ю.

ЗАХВА́ЧЕНЫЙ; захва́чен, —а, —о, —ы (ppp), захвачу́.

ЗАХВАЧУ́, захва́тишь. Р. Захвати́ть (acc.). I. Захва́тывать. 1. To take. 2. To seize, capture. 3. To catch. 4. To catch in time (as a fire). 5. To occupy, fill (as sun fills a garden). 6. To captivate, thrill.

ЗАХЛЁСТАННЫЙ; захлёстан, —а, —о, —ы (ppp), see захлещу́.

ЗАХЛЕ́ЩЕШЬ, see захлещу́.

ЗАХЛЕЩИ́ (imp.), see захлещу́.

ЗАХЛЕЩУ́, захле́щешь. Р. Захлеста́ть. I. Захлёстывать (mean. 1). 1. To whip, lash, beat unmercifully (acc.). 2. To begin to lash, beat, gush, pour, splash, etc. (see хлещу́) (acc.) or (intr.).

ЗАХЛОПО́ЧЕШЬСЯ, see захлопочу́сь.

ЗАХЛОПОЧИ́СЬ (imp.), see захлопочу́сь.

ЗАХЛОПОЧУ́СЬ, захлопо́чешься. Р. Захлопота́ться (intr.). To become tired from hurrying about.

ЗАХОЖУ́[1], захо́дишь. Р. Заходи́ть (intr.). To start to walk, pace (as up and down a room).

ЗАХОЖУ́[2], захо́дишь. I. Заходи́ть (intr.). Р. Зайти́. 1. To drop in at, call on (в + acc.), (к + dat.). 2. To call, for come after (s.o. or s.t.) (за + instr.). 3. To go beyond, behind, around (за + acc.). 4. To arrive (someplace) in a roundabout way (в + acc.). 5. To set (of the sun). 6. To turn on, come up about (s.t.) (of a conversation) (о + prep.).

ЗАХОТИ́М, захоти́те, захотя́т (pl. forms), see захочу́.

ЗАХОТЯ́Т, see захочу́, захоти́м.

ЗАХО́ЧЕШЬ, see захочу́.

ЗАХОЧУ́, захо́чешь, захо́чет (sing. forms). Р. Захоте́ть (acc./gen.) or (inf.). I. Хоте́ть. To want, wish, like, desire.

ЗАЦВЁЛ, зацвела́ (past), see зацвету́.

ЗАЦВЕТЁШЬ, see зацвету́.

ЗАЦВЕТИ́ (imp.), see зацвету́.

ЗАЦВЕТУ́, зацветёшь. Р. Зацвести́ (intr.). I. Зацвета́ть. 1. To burst into bloom, to blossom. 2. To effloresce. 3. To become mouldy.

ЗАЦВЕ́ТШИЙ (pap), see зацвету́.

ЗАЦЕ́ПЛЕННЫЙ; заце́плен, —а, —о, —ы (ppp), see зацеплю́.

ЗАЦЕПЛЮ́, заце́пишь. P. Зацепи́ть. I. Зацепля́ть. 1. To hook (acc.). 2. To catch (as s.t. on s.t.) (acc. + за + acc.) or (inst. + за + acc.). 3. To engage, mesh (acc.). 4. (fig.) To engage, catch (as s.o.'s interest) (acc.).

ЗАЧА́ТЫЙ; зача́т, —а́, —о, —ы (ppp), see зачну́ (mean. 1 and 2).

ЗАЧА́Х, зача́хла (past). P. Зача́хнуть (intr.). I. Ча́хнуть. 1. To wither (of plants). 2. To pine (of people).

ЗАЧАЩУ́, зачасти́шь. P. Зачасти́ть. 1. To take to doing (s.t.) often (+ inf.). 2. To begin to play or say (s.t.) rapidly (acc.). 3. To start to visit (s.o.) regularly (к + dat.). 4. To increase in frequency or intensity) (e.g., rain, wind, artillery fire, etc.) (intr.).

ЗАЧЁЛ, зачла́ (past), see зачту́.

ЗАЧЁРЧЕННЫЙ; заче́рчен, —а, —о, —ы (ppp), see зачерчу́.

ЗАЧЕРЧУ́, заче́ртишь. P. Зачерти́ть. I. Заче́рчивать (mean. 1 and 2). 1. To cover with sketches, lines (acc.). 2. To sketch (acc.). 3. To begin to draw (acc.) or (intr.).

ЗАЧЁСАННЫЙ; зачёсан, —а, —о, —ы (ppp), see зачешу́.

ЗАЧЁТШИЙ (pap), see зачту́.

ЗАЧЕ́ШЕШЬ, see зачешу́.

ЗАЧЕШИ́ (imp.), see зачешу́.

ЗАЧЕШУ́, заче́шешь. P. Зачеса́ть. I. Зачёсывать (mean. 1). 1. To comb (acc.). 2. To begin to comb, scratch (acc.) or (intr.).

ЗАЧИ́СТИ (imp.), see зачи́щу.

ЗАЧИ́СТЬ (imp.), see зачи́щу.

ЗАЧИ́ЩЕННЫЙ; зачи́щен, —а, —о, —ы (ppp), see зачи́щу.

ЗАЧИ́ЩУ, зачи́стишь. P. Зачи́стить (acc.). I. Зачища́ть. To clean and smooth (as a surface, electrical contact).

ЗАЧЛА́, зачло́, зачли́ (past), see зачту́ and зачёл.

ЗАЧНИ́ (imp.), see зачну́.

ЗАЧНЁШЬ, see зачну́.

ЗАЧНУ́, зачнёшь. P. Зача́ть. 1. To conceive (acc.). 2. To become pregnant (intr.). 3. To begin (acc.) or (inf.).

ЗАЧТЁННЫЙ; зачтён, —а́, —о́, —ы́ (ppp), see зачту́.

ЗАЧТЁШЬ, see зачту́.

ЗАЧТИ́ (imp.), see зачту́.

ЗАЧТУ́, зачтёшь. P. Заче́сть (acc.). I. Зачи́тывать. 1. To accept (s.t.) on account (acc. + в + acc.). 2. To accept (as school homework, etc.) (acc.).

ЗАЧТЯ́ (adv. past part.), see зачту́.

ЗАЧУ́ЕШЬ, see зачу́ю.

ЗАЧУ́Й (imp.), see зачу́ю.

ЗАЧУ́Ю, зачу́ешь. P. Зачу́ять (acc.). 1. To smell, scent. 2. (fig.) To sense, feel.

ЗАЧУ́ЯННЫЙ; зачу́ян, —а, —о, —ы (ppp), see зачу́ю.

ЗАШЕ́ДШИЙ (pap), see зашёл and зайду́.

ЗАШЕ́Й (imp.), see зашью́.

ЗАШЁЛ, зашла́ (past). P. Зайти́ (intr.). I. Заходи́ть, заха́живать (mean. 1 and 2). 1. To drop in at, call on (в + acc.), (к + dat.). 2. To call for, come after (s.o. or s.t.) (за + inst.). 3. To go beyond, behind, around (за + acc.). 4. To arrive (someplace) in a roundabout way (в + acc.). 5. To set (of the sun). 6. To turn on/to (as conversation turns on/to a different topic) (о + prep. of topic). (Also see зайду́.)

ЗАШИ́Б, зашиби́ла (past), see зашибу́.

ЗАШИБЁШЬ, see зашибу́.

ЗАШИБИ́ (imp.), see зашибу́.

ЗАШИ́БЛЕННЫЙ; заши́блен, —а, —о, —ы (ppp), see зашибу́.

ЗАШИБУ́, зашибёшь. P. Зашиби́ть (acc.). I. Зашиба́ть. 1. To hurt, bruise. 2. To earn (as money).

ЗАШИ́ТЫЙ; заши́т, —а, —о, —ы (ppp), see зашью́.

ЗАШЛА́, зашло́, зашли́ (past), see зашёл.

ЗАШЛЁШЬ, see зашлю́.

ЗАШЛИ́[1] (imp.), see зашлю́.

ЗАШЛИ́[2] (past), see зашёл and зашла́.

ЗАШЛЮ́, зашлёшь. P. Засла́ть (acc.). I. Засыла́ть. 1. To send far away or to the wrong address. 2. To send (as spies).

ЗАШУРША́Т, see зашуршу́.

ЗАШУРШИ́ (imp), see зашуршу́.

ЗАШУРШИ́ШЬ, see зашуршу́.

ЗАШУРШУ́, зашурши́шь. P. Зашурша́ть (intr.). 1. To begin to rustle (of leaves, etc.). 2. To begin to rustle (as one rustles the pages of a book) (inst. of pages).

ЗАШЬЁШЬ, see зашью.

ЗАШЬЮ, зашьёшь. Р. Зашить (acc.). I. Зашивать. 1. To mend. 2. To sew up. 3. To board up.

ЗАЩЕКОЧЕННЫЙ; защекочен, —а, —о, —ы (ppp), see защекочу.

ЗАЩЕКОЧЕШЬ, see защекочу.

ЗАЩЕКОЧИ (imp.), see защикочу.

ЗАЩЕКОЧУ́, защекочешь. Р. Защекотать. I. Щекотать (mean. 1). 1. To tickle (acc.). 2. To begin to tickle (acc.) or (intr.).

ЗАЩЕМЛЁННЫЙ; защемлён, —а́, —о́, —ы́ (ppp), see защемлю́.

ЗАЩЕМЛЮ́, защеми́шь. Р. Защеми́ть. I. Защемля́ть (mean. 1, 2, 3). 1. To pinch, squeeze (acc.). 2. To jam (acc.). 3. To feel a pang (impers. + acc. of heart) or (impers. + на + acc. of heart). 4. To begin to feel a pang, etc. (same construction as mean. 3).

ЗАЩИ́ПАННЫЙ; защи́пан, —а, —о, —ы (ppp), see защиплю́.

ЗАЩИ́ПЛЕШЬ, see защиплю́.

ЗАЩИПЛИ́ (imp.), see защиплю́.

ЗАЩИПЛЮ́, защи́плешь. Р. Защипа́ть (acc.). 1. To torment by pinching or tweaking. 2. To crimp.

ЗАЩИЩЁННЫЙ, защищён, —а́, —о́, —ы́ (ppp), see защищу́.

ЗАЩИЩУ́, защити́шь. Р. Защити́ть (acc.). I. Защища́ть. 1. To defend, protect, shield (physically). 2. To defend, support (verbally).

ЗА́ЩУ, за́стишь. I. За́стить (acc.) or (intr.). To screen, shield, obstruct (as light).

ЗАЯ́ВЛЕННЫЙ, зая́влен, —а, —о, —ы (ppp), see заявлю́.

ЗАЯВЛЮ́, зая́вишь. Р. Заяви́ть. I. Заявля́ть. 1. To declare, announce (acc.). 2. To reveal, show, manifest (acc.). 3. To testify, make a statement (about) (о + prep.). 4. To witness (as a document) (arch.) (acc.).

ЗВА́ННЫЙ; зва́н, —а́, —о, —ы (ppp), see зову́.

ЗВЕНИ́, see звеню́.

ЗВЕНИ́ШЬ, see звеню́.

ЗВЕНЮ́, звени́шь. I. Звене́ть (intr.).

1. To ring, jingle, clink. 2. To jingle (as money) (inst.).

ЗВЕНЯ́Т, see звеню́.

ЗВУЧА́Т, see звучу́.

ЗВУЧИ́ (imp.), see звучу́.

ЗВУЧИ́ШЬ, see звучу́.

ЗВУЧУ́, звучи́шь. I. Звуча́ть (intr.). 1. To sound (make a sound). 2. To be heard (as a voice). 3. (fig.) To sound (as strange).

ЗИ́ЖДЕТСЯ, зи́ждутся (3rd pers. only). I. Зи́ждиться (intr.) (на + prep.). To be founded, based on.

ЗИ́ЖДУТСЯ, see зи́ждется.

ЗЛОБ́ЛЮСЬ, зло́бишься. I. Зло́биться (intr.). To be angry, irritated (at s.t.) (на + acc.).

ЗЛО́БЬСЯ (imp.), see зло́блюсь.

ЗЛОСЛО́ВЛЮ, злосло́вишь. I. Злосло́вить (intr.). To talk scandal.

ЗЛОСЛО́ВЬ (imp.), see злосло́влю.

ЗЛОУПОТРЕБЛЮ́, злоупотреби́шь. Р. Злоупотреби́ть (inst.). I. Злоупотребля́ть. To abuse, misuse (as power).

ЗНАКО́МЛЮ, знако́мишь. I. Знако́мить (acc. + с + inst.). Р. Познако́мить, Ознако́мить (mean. 1). 1. To acquaint (s.o. with s.t.). 2. To introduce (s.o. to s.o.).

ЗНАКО́МЬ (imp.), see знако́млю.

ЗОВЁШЬ, see зову́.

ЗОВИ́ (imp.), see зову́.

ЗОВУ́, зовёшь. I. Звать. Р. Позва́ть (mean. 1 and 2). 1. To call (s.o. or s.t.) (acc.). 2. To invite, ask (acc.). 3. To call, name (acc. + inst.).

ЗОЛОЧЁННЫЙ; золочён, —а́, —о́, —ы́, (ppp), see золочу́.

ЗОЛОЧУ́, золоти́шь. I. Золоти́ть (acc.). Р. Вы́золотить (mean. 1), позолоти́ть (mean. 1 and 2). 1. To gild. 2. To illuminate with a golden light.

ЗРИ́МЫЙ (pres. pp), see зрю.

ЗРИШЬ, see зрю.

ЗРЮ, зришь. I. Зреть (arch., poetic). Р. Узре́ть (mean. 1). 1. To see, behold (acc.). 2. To look at (на + acc.).

ЗРЯТ, see зрю.

ЗУДИ́ (imp.), see зужу́ and зуди́т.

ЗУДИ́Т, зудя́т (3rs pers. only). I. Зуде́ть and зуди́ть (intr.). 1. To itch (physically). 2. (fig.) To itch (to do s.t.) (of one's hands).

ЗУДИШЬ, see зужу́.

ЗУДЯ́Т[1], see зужу́.

ЗУДЯ́Т[2], see зуди́т.

ЗУЖУ́, зуди́шь. I. **Зуде́ть** and **зуди́ть.**
1. To emit a monotonous humming or twanging sound (of bees, stringed instruments, etc.) (intr.). 2. (fig.) To nag (acc.) or (intr.).

ЗЫ́БЛЕТСЯ, зы́блются (3rd pers. only). I. **Зы́биться** (intr.). To swell, ripple (as waves).

ЗЫ́БЛЮТСЯ, see зы́блется.

ЗЯБ, зя́бла (past). I. **Зя́бнуть** (intr.). P. **Озя́бнуть.** 1. To suffer from cold, feel cold. 2. To freeze (of plants).

И

ИДЁШЬ, see иду́.

ИДИ́ (imp.), see иду́.

ИДУ́, идёшь. I. Идти́ (intr.). 1. To go (of a person, on foot). 2. To go (of a vehicle). 3. To start, leave (of a train, etc.). 4. To go, lead (of a road). 5. To take place, occur (of rain, snow, etc.). 6. To go on, proceed (of classes, discussions, etc.). 7. To play (as a motion picture, etc.). 8. To elapse, pass (of time). 9. To function (of a watch, etc.). 10. To become, to suit (s.o.) (of clothes) (dat.). (For other lit. and fig. uses see an unabridged dictionary.)

И́ДУЧИ and ИДЯ́ (adv. pres. part.), see ИДУ́.

ИДЯ́ and И́ДУЧИ (adv. pres. part.), see ИДУ́.

ИЗБА́ВЛЕННЫЙ; изба́влен, —а, —о, —ы (ppp), see изба́влю.

ИЗБА́ВЛЮ, изба́вишь. Р. Изба́вить (acc. + от + gen.). I. Избавля́ть. 1. To save from, deliver (from). 2. To release, free (from).

ИЗБА́ВЬ (imp.), see изба́влю.

ИЗБЁГ (and arch. избе́гнул), избе́гла (past). Р. Избе́гнуть (gen.). To avoid, evade.

ИЗБЕГИ́ (imp.), see избегу́.

ИЗБЕГУ́, избежи́шь, избегу́т. Р. Избежа́ть (gen.). I. Избега́ть. To avoid, evade.

ИЗБЕЖИ́ШЬ, see избегу́.

ИЗБЕ́Й (imp.). Р. Изби́ть (acc.). I. Избива́ть. 1. To beat cruelly, unmercifully. 2. To kill, destroy. 3. To smash, beat to pieces. 4. To wear out (of clothes, etc.) (also see изобью́).

ИЗБЕРЁШЬ, see изберу́.

ИЗБЕРИ́ (imp.), see изберу́.

ИЗБЕРУ́, изберёшь. Р. Избра́ть (acc.). I. Избира́ть. 1. To choose, select. 2. To elect (s.o. as s.t.) (acc. + inst.).

ИЗБИ́ТЫЙ; изби́т, —а, —о, —ы (ppp), see избе́й and изобью́.

ИЗБОРОЖДЁННЫЙ; изборождён, —а́, —о́, —ы́ (ppp), see изборозжу́.

ИЗБОРОЗДИ́ШЬ, see изборозжу́.

ИЗБОРОЗЖУ́, изборозди́шь. Р. Избороздить (acc.). I. Борозди́ть (mean. 1 and 2). 1. To furrow, plow. 2. (fig.) To furrow (as wrinkles furrow one's face). 3. To travel all over.

И́ЗБРАННЫЙ; И́ЗБРАН, —а, —о, —ы (ppp), see изберу́.

ИЗБУ́ДЕШЬ, see избу́ду.

ИЗБУ́ДУ, избу́дешь. Р. Избы́ть (arch.) (acc.). I. Избыва́ть. To get rid of, free oneself from (as grief, habit, etc.).

ИЗБУ́ДЬ (imp.), see избу́ду.

ИЗБЫ́ТЫЙ; избы́т, —а, —о, —ы, (ppp), see избу́ду.

ИЗВЕДЁННЫЙ; изведён, —а́, —о́, —ы́ (ppp), see изведу́.

ИЗВЕДЁШЬ, see изведу́.

ИЗВЕДИ́ (imp.), see изведу́.

ИЗВЕДУ́, изведёшь. Р. Известѝ (acc.). I. Изводи́ть. 1. To use up, spend. 2. To exhaust. 3. To torment, exasperate. 4. To exterminate.

ИЗВЕ́ДШИЙ (pap), see изведу́.

ИЗВЕДЯ́ and изве́дши (adv. past part.), see изведу́.

ИЗВЕ́Й (imp.). Р. Изви́ть (acc.). I. Извива́ть. To wind, twist, coil. (Also see изовью́.)

ИЗВЁЛ, извела́ (past), see изведу́.

ИЗВЕ́РГ, изве́ргла (past). Р. Изве́ргнуть (acc.). I. Изверга́ть. 1. To throw out, eject, expel. 2. To excrete. 3. To vomit.

ИЗВЕ́РЖЕННЫЙ; изве́ржен, —а, —о, —ы (also изве́ргнутый, etc.) (ppp), see изве́рг.

ИЗВЕЩЁННЫЙ; извещён, —а́, —о́, —ы́ (ppp), see извещу́.

ИЗВЕЩУ́, извести́шь. Р. Извести́ть (acc.). I. Извеща́ть. To inform, notify, advise (as s.o. of s.t.) (acc. + о + prep.).

ИЗВИ́ТЫЙ; изви́т, —а́, —о, —ы (ppp), see изве́й and изовью́.

ИЗВЛЁК, извлекла́ (past), see извлеку́.

ИЗВЛЕКИ́ (imp.), see извлеку́.

ИЗВЛЕКУ́, извлечёшь, извлеку́т. Р. Извле́чь (acc.). I. Извлека́ть. 1. To extract (from) (acc. + из + gen.). 2. (math.) To extract, derive. 3. To elicit, evoke (from) (acc. + из + gen.). 4. To derive (e.g., benefit).

ИЗВЛЕЧЁННЫЙ; извлечён, —а́, —о́, —ы́ (ppp), see извлеку́.

ИЗВЛЕЧЁШЬ, see извлеку́.

ИЗВО́ЖЕННЫЙ; изво́жен, —а, —о, —ы (ppp), see извожу́².

ИЗВОЖУ́¹, изво́дишь. I. Изводи́ть (acc.). Р. Извести́. 1. To use up, spend. 2. To exhaust. 3. To torment, exasperate. 4. To exterminate.

ИЗВОЖУ́², изво́зишь. Р. Извози́ть (acc.). To dirty or fray by dragging (as the hem of a skirt).

ИЗВРАЩЁННЫЙ; извращён, —а́, —о́, —ы́ (ppp), see извращу́.

ИЗВРАЩУ́, изврати́шь. Р. Изврати́ть (acc.). I. Извраща́ть. 1. To misinterpret, misconstrue. 2. To pervert.

ИЗГА́ДЬ (imp.), see изга́жу.

ИЗГА́ЖЕННЫЙ; изга́жен, —а, —о, —ы (ppp), see изга́жу.

ИЗГА́ЖУ, изга́дишь. Р. Изга́дить (acc.). I. Изга́живать. To soil, spoil.

ИЗГЛА́ДЬ (imp.), see изгла́жу.

ИЗГЛА́ЖЕННЫЙ; изгла́жен, —а, —о, —ы (ppp), see изгла́жу.

ИЗГЛА́ЖУ, изгла́дишь. Р. Изгла́дить (acc.). I. Изгла́живать. (lit. and fig.) To efface, erase, obliterate.

И́ЗГНАННЫЙ; и́згнан, —а, —о, —ы (ppp), see изгоню́.

ИЗГОНИ́ (imp.), see изгоню́.

ИЗГО́НИШЬ, see изгоню́.

ИЗГОНЮ́, изго́нишь. Р. Изгна́ть (acc.). I. Изгоня́ть. 1. To banish, expel, exile, drive out. 2. To ban.

ИЗГОТО́ВЛЕННЫЙ; изгото́влен, —а, —о, —ы (ppp), see изгото́влю.

ИЗГОТО́ВЛЮ, изгото́вишь. Р. Изгото́вить (acc.). I. Изготовля́ть, изгота́вливать. 1. To manufacture, to make, produce. 2. To prepare (arch.).

ИЗГОТО́ВЬ (imp.), see изгото́влю.

ИЗГРЫ́З, изгры́зла (past), see изгрызу́.

ИЗГРЫ́ЗЕННЫЙ; изгры́зен, —а, —о, —ы (ppp), see изгрызу́.

ИЗГРЫЗЁШЬ, see изгрызу́.

ИЗГРЫЗИ́ (imp.), see изгрызу́.

ИЗГРЫЗУ́, изгрызёшь. Р. Изгры́зть (acc.). I. Изгрыза́ть. To spoil or ruin by gnawing.

ИЗДАВА́Й (imp.), see издаю́.

ИЗДАВА́Я (adv. pres. part.), see издаю́.

ИЗДАДИ́М, издади́те, издаду́т (pl. forms), see изда́м.

ИЗДАЁШЬ, see издаю́.

ИЗДА́Й (imp.), see издаю́.

ИЗДА́М, изда́шь, изда́ст (sing. forms). Р. Изда́ть (acc.). I. Издава́ть. 1. To publish (as a book). 2. To issue, promulgate (a decree, etc.). 3. To utter.

И́ЗДАННЫЙ; И́ЗДАН, —а́, —о, —ы (ppp), see изда́м.

ИЗДА́СТ, see изда́м.

ИЗДА́ШЬ, see изда́м.

ИЗДАЮ́, издаёшь. I. Издава́ть (acc.). Р. Изда́ть. 1. To publish (as a book). 2. To issue, promulgate (as a decree). 3. To utter.

ИЗДЕРЁШЬ, see издеру́.

ИЗДЕ́РЖАННЫЙ; изде́ржан, —а, —о, —ы (ppp), see издержу́.

ИЗДЕ́РЖАТ, see издержу́.

ИЗДЕРЖИ́ (imp.), see издержу́.

ИЗДЕ́РЖИШЬ, see издержу́.

ИЗДЕРЖУ́, изде́ржишь. Р. Издержа́ть (acc.). I. Изде́рживать. 1. To spend, expend. 2. To consume.

ИЗДЕРИ́ (imp.), see издеру́.

ИЗДЕРУ́, издерёшь. Р. Изодра́ть (acc.). 1. To lacerate. 2. To tear to pieces, to wear out (as clothing).

ИЗДО́Х, издо́хла (past). Р. Издо́хнуть (intr.). I. До́хнуть. To die (of animals).

ИЗЖИВЁШЬ, see изживу́.

ИЗЖИВИ́ (imp.), see изживу́.

ИЗЖИВУ́, изживёшь. Р. Изжи́ть (acc.). I. Изжива́ть. 1. To get rid of, overcome (as troubles, deficiencies, etc.). 2. To outlive. 3. To live through.

ИЗЖИ́ТЫЙ; изжи́т, —а́, —о, —ы (ppp), see изживу́.

ИЗЗЯ́Б, иззя́бла (past). Р. Иззя́бнуть (intr.). To become chilled to the bone.

ИЗЛА́ДЬ (imp.), see изла́жу¹.

ИЗЛА́ЕШЬ, see изла́ю.

ИЗЛА́ЖЕННЫЙ; изла́жен, —а, —о, —ы (ppp), see изла́жу¹ and ².

ИЗЛА́ЖУ¹, изла́дишь. Р. Изла́дить (acc.). 1. To make. 2. To prepare.

ИЗЛА́ЖУ², изла́зишь. Р. Изла́зить (acc.). To clamber or climb around.

ИЗЛА́ЗЬ (imp.), see изла́жу².

ИЗЛА́Й (imp.), see изла́ю.

ИЗЛА́Ю, изла́ешь. Р. Изла́ять (асс.). To revile, abuse, attack.

ИЗЛА́ЯННЫЙ; изла́ян, —а, —о, —ы (ppp), see изла́ю.

ИЗЛЕ́Й (imp.). Р. Изли́ть (асс.). I. Излива́ть. 1. To pour (out). 2. (fig.) To pour out, give vent to (e.g., one's thoughts, grief, etc.). (Also see изолью́.)

ИЗЛИ́ТЫЙ; изли́т, —а́, —о, —ы (ppp), see изле́й and изолью́.

ИЗЛО́ВЛЕННЫЙ; изло́влен, —а, —о, —ы (ppp), see изловлю́.

ИЗЛОВЛЮ́, изло́вишь. Р. Излови́ть (асс.). 1. To catch, trap (as a wild animal). 2. (fig.) To catch (e.g., s.o. in a lie) (асс. + на + prep.).

ИЗМА́ЕШЬ, see изма́ю.

ИЗМА́ЖЕШЬ, see изма́жу.

ИЗМА́ЖУ, изма́жешь. Р. Изма́зать (асс.). I. Изма́зывать, ма́зать (mean. 1.). 1. To soil, smear. 2. To use up (as ointment, grease).

ИЗМА́ЖЬ (imp.), see изма́жу.

ИЗМА́ЗАННЫЙ; изма́зан, —а, —о, —ы (ppp), see изма́жу.

ИЗМА́Й (imp.), see изма́ю.

ИЗМА́Ю, изма́ешь. Р. Изма́ять (асс.). To exhaust, to weary greatly.

ИЗМА́ЯННЫЙ; изма́ян, —а, —о, —ы (ppp), see изма́ю.

ИЗМО́К, измо́кла (past). Р. Измо́кнуть (intr.). To get thoroughly wet, to become soaked.

ИЗМЯ́ТЫЙ; измя́т, —а, —о, —ы (ppp). Р. Измя́ть (асс.). I. Мять (mean. 1 and 2). 1. To rumple, crumple. 2. To trample. 3. To demoralize (also see изомну́).

ИЗНЕМО́Г, изнемогла́ (past), see изнемогу́.

ИЗНЕМОГИ́ (imp.), see изнемогу́.

ИЗНЕМОГУ́, изнемо́жешь, изнемо́гут Р. Изнемо́чь (intr.). I. Изнемога́ть. To become exhausted.

ИЗНЕМО́ЖЕШЬ, see изнемогу́.

ИЗНО́ЕШЬ, see изно́ю.

ИЗНО́Й (imp.), see изно́ю.

ИЗНО́ШЕННЫЙ; изно́шен, —а, —о, —ы (ppp), see изношу́.

ИЗНОШУ́, изно́сишь. Р. Износи́ть (асс.). I. Изна́шивать. 1. To wear out, away. 2. To fray. 3. To erode.

ИЗНО́Ю, изно́ешь. Р. Изны́ть (intr.). I. Изныва́ть. 1. To pine away. 2. To

be weary, exhausted (from s.t.) (от + gen.).

ИЗОБИ́ДИШЬ, see изоби́жу.

ИЗОБИ́ДЬ (imp.), see изоби́жу.

ИЗОБИ́ДЯТ, see изоби́жу.

ИЗОБИ́ЖЕННЫЙ; изоби́жен, —а, —о, —ы (ppp), see изоби́жу.

ИЗОБИ́ЖУ, изоби́дишь. Р. Изоби́деть (асс.). To grossly offend, insult.

ИЗОБРАЖЁННЫЙ; изображён, —а́, —о́, —ы́ (ppp), see изображу́.

ИЗОБРАЖУ́, изобрази́шь. Р. Изобрази́ть (асс.). I. Изобража́ть. 1. To portray, represent, express (in art form or words). 2. To design.

ИЗОБРЁЛ, изобрела́ (past), see изобрету́.

ИЗОБРЕТЁННЫЙ; изобретён, —а́, —о́, —ы́ (ppp), see изобрету́.

ИЗОБРЕТЁШЬ, see изобрету́.

ИЗОБРЕТИ́ (imp.), see изобрету́.

ИЗОБРЕТУ́, изобретёшь. Р. Изобрести́ (асс.). I. Изобрета́ть. To invent, contrive, devise.

ИЗОБРЁТШИЙ (pap), see изобрету́.

ИЗОБРЕТЯ́ (adv. past part.), see изобрету́.

ИЗОБЬЁШЬ, see изобью́.

ИЗОБЬЮ́, изобьёшь. Р. Изби́ть (асс.). I. Избива́ть. 1. To beat cruelly, unmercifully. 2. To kill, destroy. 3. To smash, beat to pieces. 4. To wear out (of clothes, etc.).

ИЗОВРЁШЬСЯ, see изовру́сь.

ИЗОВРИ́СЬ (imp.), see изовру́сь.

ИЗОВРУ́СЬ, изоврёшься. Р. Изовра́ться (intr.). To become an inveterate liar.

ИЗОВЬЁШЬ, see изовью́.

ИЗОВЬЮ́, изовьёшь. Р. Изви́ть (асс.). I. Извива́ть. To wind, twist, coil.

ИЗО́ДРАННЫЙ; изо́дран, —а, —о, —ы (ppp). Р. Изодра́ть (асс.). 1. To lacerate. 2. To tear to pieces, wear out (of clothing). (Also see издеру́.)

ИЗОЙДЁШЬ, see изойду́.

ИЗОЙДИ́ (imp.), see изойду́.

ИЗОЙДУ́, изойдёшь. Р. Изойти́. I. Исходи́ть (mean. 1). 1. To grow weak from loss (of s.t.) (e.g., blood, tears, etc.) (inst.). 2. To be used up, spent (intr.). 3. To travel around (e.g., the country) (асс.).

ИЗОЙДЯ́ (adv. past part.), see изойду́.

ИЗОЛГИ́СЬ (imp.), see изолгу́сь.

ИЗОЛГУ́СЬ, изолжёшься, изолгу́тся. Р. Изолга́ться (intr.). To become an inveterate liar.

ИЗОЛЖЁШЬСЯ, see изолгу́сь.

ИЗОЛЬЕШЬ, see изолью́.

ИЗОЛЬЮ́, изольёшь. Р. Изли́ть (acc.). I. Излива́ть. 1. To pour out. 2. (fig.) To pour out, give vent to (e.g., one's thoughts, grief, etc.).

ИЗОМНЁШЬ, see изомну́.

ИЗОМНИ́ (imp.), see изомну́.

ИЗОМНУ́, изомнёшь. Р. Измя́ть (acc.). I. Мять (mean. 1). 1. To rumple, crumple. 2. To trample. 3. To demoralize.

ИЗОПЬЁШЬ, see изопью́.

ИЗОПЬЮ́, изопьёшь. Р. Испи́ть. 1. To sip (gen.). 2. To drink up (acc.). 3. (fig.) To experience in full (as "to drink the cup of life," etc.) (acc.).

ИЗО́РВАННЫЙ; изо́рван, —а, —о, —ы (ppp), see изорву́.

ИЗОРВЁШЬ, see изорву́.

ИЗОРВИ́ (imp.), see изорву́.

ИЗОРВУ́, изорвёшь. Р. Изорва́ть (acc.). To tear to pieces, rend.

ИЗОТРЁШЬ, see изотру́.

ИЗОТРИ́ (imp.), see изотру́.

ИЗОТРУ́, изотрёшь. Р. Истере́ть (acc.). I. Истира́ть. 1. To grate. 2. To wear out, down, by rubbing (as an eraser, clothing, etc.). 3. To erode (arch.).

ИЗОШЕ́ДШИЙ (pap), see изойду́.

ИЗОШЁЛ, изошла́ (past), see изойду́.

ИЗОШЛА́, изошло́, изошли́ (past), see изошёл and изойду́.

ИЗРЕ́ЖЕШЬ, see изре́жу.

ИЗРЕ́ЖУ, изре́жешь. Р. Изре́зать (acc.). I. Изре́зывать. 1. To cut up, cut to pieces. 2. To dissect. 3. (fig.) To cut up (as roads cut up a piece of land, etc.).

ИЗРЕ́ЖЬ (imp.), see изре́жу.

ИЗРЕ́ЗАННЫЙ; изре́зан, —а, —о, —ы (ppp), see изре́жу.

ИЗРЁК (arch. изре́к), изрекла́ (past), see изреку́.

ИЗРЕКИ́ (imp.), see изреку́.

ИЗРЕКУ́, изречёшь, изреку́т. Р. Изре́чь (acc.). I. Изрека́ть. 1. To utter. 2. To announce, pronounce.

ИЗРЕ́КШИЙ (pap), see изреку́.

ИЗРЕЧЁННЫЙ; изречён, —а́, —о́, —ы́ (ppp), see изреку́.

ИЗРЕЧЁННЫЙ; изречён, —а́, —о́, —ы́ (ppp), (arch.), see изреку́.

ИЗРЕЧЁШЬ, see изреку́.

ИЗРЕШЕЧЁННЫЙ; изрешечён, —а́, —о́, —ы́ (ppp), see изрешечу́.

ИЗРЕШЁЧЕННЫЙ; изрешёчен, —а, —о, —ы (ppp), see изрешечу́.

ИЗРЕШЕЧУ́, изрешети́шь. Р. Изрешети́ть (acc.). I. Изреше́чивать. To riddle, pierce with holes.

ИЗРО́ЕШЬ, see изро́ю.

ИЗРО́Й (imp.), see изро́ю.

ИЗРО́Ю, изро́ешь. Р. Изры́ть (acc.). I. Изрыва́ть. 1. To dig up. 2. To pit.

ИЗРУ́БЛЕННЫЙ; изру́блен, —а, —о, —ы (ppp), see изрублю́.

ИЗРУБЛЮ́, изру́бишь. Р. Изруби́ть (acc.). I. Изруба́ть. 1. To chop up, hack up, mince. 2. To slaughter.

ИЗРЫ́ТЫЙ; изры́т, —а, —о, —ы (ppp), see изро́ю.

ИЗУКРА́СЬ (imp.), see изукра́шу.

ИЗУКРА́ШЕННЫЙ; изукра́шен, —а, —о, —ы (ppp), see изукра́шу.

ИЗУКРА́ШУ, изукра́сишь. Р. Изукра́сить (acc.). I. Изукра́шивать. (lit. and ironically) to adorn.

ИЗУМЛЁННЫЙ; изумлён, —а́, —о́, —ы́ (ppp), see изумлю́.

ИЗУМЛЮ́, изуми́шь. Р. Изуми́ть (acc.). I. Изумля́ть. To astound, amaze.

ИЗ'Е́ДЕННЫЙ; из'е́ден, —а, —о, —ы (ppp), see из'е́ст.

ИЗ'ЕДЯ́Т, see из'е́ст.

ИЗ'Е́ЗДИ (imp.), see из'е́зжу.

ИЗ'Е́ЗЖЕННЫЙ; из'е́зжен, —а, —о, —ы (ppp), see из'е́зжу.

ИЗ'Е́ЗЖУ, из'е́здишь. Р. Из'е́здить (acc.). 1. To travel all over (someplace). 2. To spoil by creating ruts (as wheels rut a field).

ИЗ'Е́Л, из'е́ла (past), see из'е́ст.

ИЗ'Е́МЛЕШЬ, see из'е́млю.

ИЗ'Е́МЛИ (imp.) (arch.), see из'е́млю.

ИЗ'Е́МЛЮ, из'е́млешь (arch.) (also изыма́ю, изыма́ешь). I. Изыма́ть (acc.). Р. Из'я́ть. 1. To exclude, remove, withdraw. 2. To confiscate.

ИЗ'Е́СТ, из'едя́т (3rd pers. only). Р. Из'е́сть (acc.). I. Из'еда́ть. 1. To spoil by gnawing. 2. To corrode.

ИЗ'Я́ВЛЕННЫЙ; из'я́влен, —а, —о, —ы (ppp), see из'явлю́.

ИЗ'ЯВЛЮ́, из'я́вишь. Р. Из'яви́ть

(acc.). I. Из'являть. To express, state.

ИЗ'ЯЗВЛЁННЫЙ; из'язвлён, —á, —б, —ы (ppp), see из'язвлю.

ИЗ'ЯЗВЛЮ, из'язвишь. Р. Из'язвить (acc.). I. Из'являть. To ulcerate.

ИЗ'ЯТЫЙ; из'ят, —а, —о, —ы (ppp), see изыму.

ИЗЫМЕШЬ, see изыму.

ИЗЫМИ (imp.), see изыму.

ИЗЫМУ, изымешь. Р. Из'ять (acc.). I. Изымать. 1. To exclude, remove, withdraw. 2. To confiscate.

ИЗЫСКАННЫЙ; изыскан, —а, —о, —ы (ppp), see изыщу.

ИЗЫЩЕШЬ, see изыщу.

ИЗЫЩИ (imp.), see изыщу.

ИЗЫЩУ, изыщешь. Р. Изыскáть (acc.). I. Изыскивать. To find, procure (as a result of diligent effort).

ИСКАЖЁННЫЙ; искажён, —á, —б, —ы (ppp), see искажу.

ИСКАЖУ, исказишь. Р. Исказить (acc.). I. Искажáть. 1. To misrepresent. 2. To distort (as one's features).

ЙСКАННЫЙ; йскан, —а, —о, —ы (ppp), see искóмый and ищу.

ИСКОЛЕШЁННЫЙ; исколешён, —á, —б, —ы (ppp), see исколешу.

ИСКОЛЕШУ, исколесишь. Р. Исколесить (acc.). To travel all over (someplace).

ИСКОЛЕШЬ, see исколю.

ИСКОЛИ (imp.), see исколю.

ИСКÓЛОТЫЙ; искóлот, —а, —о, —ы (ppp), see исколю.

ИСКОЛÓЧЕННЫЙ; исколóчен, —а, —о, —ы (ppp), see исколочу.

ИСКОЛОЧУ, исколóтишь. Р. Исколотить (acc.). I. Исколáчивать. 1. To beat severely (as a person). 2. To ruin by hammering, pounding (as a table top).

ИСКОЛЮ, исколешь. Р. Исколóть (acc.). I. Искáлывать. 1. To prick all over. 2. To stab many times.

ИСКÓМЫЙ (pres. pp). I. Искáть. 1. To look for (acc.). 2. To seek (acc./gen.). 3. To curry favor (with s.o.) (arch.) (в + prep.) or (у + gen.). 4. To try, strive to do (+ inf.). (Also see ищу.)

ИСКРИВЛЁННЫЙ; искривлён, —á, —б, —ы (ppp), see искривлю.

ИСКРИВЛЮ, искривишь. Р. Искривить (acc.). I. Искривлять. 1. To bend. 2. (fig.) To distort, twist.

ИСКУ́ПЛЕННЫЙ; искýплен, —а, —о, —ы (ppp), see искуплю.

ИСКУПЛЮ, искýпишь. Р. Искупить (acc.). I. Искупáть. 1. To atone for, expiate (s.t. with s.t.) (acc. + inst.). 2. To compensate for (as for a deficiency with s.t.) (acc. + inst.).

ИСКУШЁННЫЙ; искушён, —á, —б, —ы (ppp), see искушу.

ИСКУКШУ, искусишь. Р. Искусить (acc.). I. Искушáть. To tempt, seduce.

ИСПÁКОСТИ (imp.), see испáкошу.

ИСПÁКОЩЕННЫЙ; испáкощен, а, —о, —ы (ppp), see испáкошу.

ИСПÁКОЩУ, испáкостишь. Р. Испáкостить (acc.). I. Пáкостить. 1. To spoil (as by poor work). 2. To soil.

ИСПЕЙ (imp.). Р. Испить. 1. To sip (gen.). 2. To drink up (acc.). 3. To experience in full (as "To drink the cup of life," etc.) (acc.). (Also see изопью.)

ИСПЁК, испеклá (past), see испеку.

ИСПЕКИ (imp.), see испеку.

ИСПЕКУ, испечёшь, испекут. Р. Испéчь (acc.). I. Печь. To bake.

ИСПЕЧЁННЫЙ; испечён, —á, —б, —ы (ppp), see испеку.

ИСПЕЧЁШЬ, see испеку.

ИСПИСАННЫЙ; исписан, —а, —о, —ы (ppp), see испишу.

ИСПИТЫЙ; испит, —á, —о, —ы (ppp), see испей and изопью.

ИСПИШЕШЬ, see испишу.

ИСПИШИ (imp.), see испишу.

ИСПИШУ, испишешь. Р. Исписáть (acc.). I. Исписывать. 1. To use up by writing (as paper, pencils, etc.). 2. To cover with writing.

ИСПÓРТИ (imp.), see испóрчу.

ИСПÓРТЬ (imp.), see испóрчу.

ИСПÓРЧЕННЫЙ; испóрчен, —а, —о, —ы (ppp), see испóрчу.

ИСПÓРЧУ, испóртишь. Р. Испóртить (acc.). I. Пóртить. 1. To spoil, damage. 2. To corrupt.

ИСПОХÁБЛЕННЫЙ; испохáблен, —а, —о, —ы (ppp), see испохáблю.

ИСПОХÁБЛЮ, испохáбишь. Р. Испохáбить (acc.). To degrade.

ИСПОХÁБЬ (imp.), see испохáблю.

ИСПРА́ВЛЕННЫЙ; испра́влен, —а, —о, —ы (ppp), see испра́влю.

ИСПРА́ВЛЮ, испра́вишь. Р. Испра́вить (acc.). I. Исправля́ть. 1. To correct, rectify. 2. To mend, repair.

ИСПРА́ВЬ (imp.), see испра́влю.

ИСПРО́ШЕННЫЙ; испро́шен, —а, —о, —ы (ppp), see испрошу́.

ИСПРОШУ́, испро́сишь. Р. Испроси́ть (acc.). I. Испра́шивать. To obtain by asking, begging, petition, etc.

ИСПУ́ЩЕННЫЙ; испу́щен, —а, —о, —ы (ppp), see испущу́.

ИСПУЩУ́, испу́стишь. Р. Испусти́ть (acc.). I. Испуска́ть. 1. To emit, give off. 2. To utter. 3. To exhale.

ИССЕ́К, иссекла́ (past), see иссеку́.

ИССЕКИ́ (imp.), see иссеку́.

ИССЕКУ́, иссечёшь, иссеку́т. Р. Иссе́чь (acc.). I. Иссека́ть. 1. To slash, cut to pieces. 2. To carve, chisel. 3. (med.) To excise, cut out. 4. To beat, whip unmercifully.

ИССЕЧЁННЫЙ; иссечён, —а́, —о́, —ы́ (ppp), see иссеку́ (mean. 2 and 3).

ИССЕ́ЧЕННЫЙ; иссе́чен, —а, —о, —ы (ppp), see иссеку́ (mean. 1 and 4).

ИССЕЧЁШЬ, see иссеку́.

ИССЛЕ́ЖЕННЫЙ; иссле́жен, —а, —о, —ы (ppp), see исслежу́.

ИССЛЕЖУ́, исследи́шь. Р. Исследи́ть (acc.). I. Иссле́живать. To track up (to make dirty with tracks.)

ИССО́Х, иссо́хла (past). Р. Иссо́хнуть (intr.). I. Иссыха́ть. 1. To dry up (as a stream). 2. To become thin, emaciated.

ИСТА́ЕШЬ, see иста́ю.

ИСТА́Й (imp.), see иста́ю.

ИСТА́Ю, иста́ешь. Р. Иста́ять (intr.). 1. To melt, thaw. 2. (fig.) To melt away, wane, dwindle (e.g., one's energy, strength, money, etc.).

ИСТЁК, истекла́ (past), see истеку́.

ИСТЕКИ́ (imp.), see истеку́.

ИСТЕКУ́, истечёшь, истеку́т. Р. Исте́чь (intr.). I. Истека́ть. 1. To flow out (of fluids). 2. To elapse (of time). 3. (fig.) To flow from (as from one's soul). 4. To grow weak from loss of blood, etc. (inst.).

ИСТЁР, истёрла (past). Р. Истере́ть (acc.). I. Истира́ть. 1. To grate. 2. To wear out, wear down by rubbing (e.g., an eraser, clothing, etc.). 3. To erode (arch.). (Also see изотру́.)

ИСТЕРЕ́В (also истёрши) (adv. past part.). see истёр and изотру́.

ИСТЁРТЫЙ; истёрт, —а, —о, —ы (ppp), see истёр and изотру́.

ИСТЁРШИ (also истере́в) (adv. past part.). see истёр and изотру́.

ИСТЕЧЁШЬ, see истеку́.

ИСТОЛКИ́ (imp.), see истолку́.

ИСТОЛКЛА́, see истоло́к and истолку́.

ИСТОЛКУ́, истолчёшь, истолку́т. Р. Истоло́чь (acc.). I. Толо́чь. 1. To pound, crush. 2. To grind. 3. To pulverize.

ИСТОЛО́К, истолкла́ (past), see истолку́.

ИСТОЛЧЁННЫЙ; истолчён, —а́, —о́, —ы́ (ppp), see истолку́.

ИСТОЛЧЁШЬ, see истолку́.

ИСТОМЛЁННЫЙ; истомлён, —а́, —о́, —ы́ (ppp), see истомлю́.

ИСТОМЛЮ́, истоми́шь. Р. Истоми́ть (acc.). I. Томи́ть. 1. To weary, wear out, exhaust. 2. To torment.

ИСТО́ПЛЕННЫЙ; исто́плен, —а, —о, —ы (ppp), see истоплю́.

ИСТОПЛЮ́, исто́пишь. Р. Истопи́ть (acc.). I. Иста́пливать. 1. To heat. 2. To burn up (as fuel). 3. To melt.

ИСТО́ПТАННЫЙ; исто́птан, —а, —о, —ы (ppp), see истопчу́.

ИСТО́ПЧЕШЬ, see истопчу́.

ИСТОПЧИ́ (imp.), see истопчу́.

ИСТОПЧУ́, исто́пчешь. Р. Истопта́ть (acc.). I. Иста́птывать. 1. To trample. 2. To wear out. 3. To track up (as a floor). 4. To walk, stroll about (someplace).

ИСТО́РГ, исто́ргла (past). Р. Исто́ргнуть (acc.). I. Исторга́ть. 1. To throw out. 2. To expel, exclude. 3. To tear out, pull out. 4. To extort, extract.

ИСТО́РЖЕННЫЙ; исто́ржен, —а, —о, —ы (also исто́ргнутый, etc.) (ppp), see исто́рг.

ИСТРА́ТЬ (imp.), see истра́чу.

ИСТРА́ЧЕННЫЙ; истра́чен, —а, —о, —ы (ppp), see истра́чу.

ИСТРА́ЧУ, истра́тишь. Р. Истра́тить (acc.). I. Тра́тить. 1. To spend, expend. 2. To waste.

ИСТРЕБЛЁННЫЙ; истреблён, —а́, —о́, —ы́ (ppp), see истреблю́.

ИСТРЕБЛЮ, истреби́шь. Р. Истреби́ть (асс.). I. **Истребля́ть**. To destroy, annihilate, exterminate.

ИСТРЁПАННЫЙ; истрёпан, —а, —о, —ы (ppp), see истреплю́.

ИСТРЕПЛЕШЬ, see истреплю́.

ИСТРЕПЛИ (imp.), see истреплю́.

ИСТРЕПЛЮ́, истре́плешь. Р. Истрепа́ть (асс.). I. Истрёпывать, трепа́ть (mean. 1.). 1. To wear out, abuse (as clothing, books, etc.). 2. (fig.) To wear out, exhaust (as a person).

ИСТУ́ПЛЕННЫЙ; исту́плен, —а, —о, —ы (ppp), see иступлю́.

ИСТУПЛЮ́, исту́пишь. Р. Иступи́ть (асс.). I. **Тупи́ть**. To dull, blunt.

ИСХИ́ТЬ (imp.), see исхи́щу.

ИСХИ́ЩЕННЫЙ; исхи́щен, —а, —о, —ы (ppp), see исхи́щу.

ИСХИ́ЩУ, исхи́тишь. Р. Исхи́тить (arch.) (асс.). I. Исхища́ть. (lit. and fig.) To take or tear away, tear out, snatch.

ИСХЛЁСТАННЫЙ; исхлёстан, —а, —о, —ы (ppp), see исхлещу́.

ИСХЛЕ́ЩЕШЬ, see исхлещу́.

ИСХЛЕЩИ́ (imp.', see исхлещу́.

ИСХЛЕЩУ́, исхлё́щешь. Р. Исхлеста́ть (асс.). I. Исхлёстывать. 1. To wear out (as a whip) while beating. 2. To flog, lash cruelly.

ИСХЛОПО́ТАННЫЙ; исхлопо́тан, —а, —о, —ы (ppp), see исхлопочу́.

ИСХЛОПО́ЧЕШЬ, see исхлопочу́.

ИСХЛОПОЧИ́ (imp.), see исхлопочу́.

ИСХЛОПОЧУ́, исхлопо́чешь. Р. Исхлопота́ть (асс.). I. Исхлопа́тывать. To obtain after considerable trouble.

ИСХО́ЖЕННЫЙ; исхо́жен, —а, —о, —ы (ppp), see исхожу́[1].

ИСХОЖУ́[1], исхо́дишь. Р. Исходи́ть (асс.). To stroll, walk all over (someplace).

ИСХОЖУ́[2], исхо́дишь. I. Исходи́ть (intr.). Р. Изойти́ (mean. 1). 1. To grow weak from loss of (s.t.) (as blood, tears, etc.). 2. To pass, run out (of time).

ИСХОЖУ́[3], исхо́дишь. I. Исходи́ть (intr.). 1. To originate, come from (от + gen. of person or thing—кого́, чего́), (из + gen. of thing—чего́). 2. To proceed (from) (as an assumption) (из + gen. of thing—чего́).

ИСЧА́Х, исча́хла (past). Р. Исча́хнуть (intr.). To become sickly, waste away.

ИСЧЁРЧЕННЫЙ; исчёрчен, —а, —о, —ы (ppp), see исчерчу́.

ИСЧЕРЧУ́, исче́ртишь. Р. Исчерти́ть (асс.). I. Исче́рчивать. 1. To cover with lines, drawings, etc. 2. To use up while drawing (as paper, pencil, etc.).

ЙЩЕШЬ, see ищу́.

ИЩИ́ (imp.), see **ИЩУ́**.

ИЩУ́, и́щешь. I. Иска́ть. 1. To look for (асс.). 2. To seek (acc./gen.). 3. To curry favor (with s.o.) (arch.) (в + prep.) or (у + gen.). 4. To try, strive to do (s.t.) (+ inf.).

К

КА́ВЕРЖУ, ка́верзишь. I. Ка́верзить (dat.). P. **Нака́верзить.** To trick, deceive.

КА́ВЕРЗИ (imp.), see **ка́вержу.**

КА́ЕШЬСЯ, see **ка́юсь.**

КА́ЖЕШЬ, see **кажу́².**

КАЖИ́ (imp.), see **кажу́².**

КАЖУ́¹, кади́шь. I. Кади́ть (intr.). 1. To spread incense. 2. (fig.) To flatter (dat.).

КАЖУ́², ка́жешь. I. Каза́ть (acc.). To show.

КА́ЙСЯ (imp.), see **ка́юсь.**

КА́ПАЙ (imp.), see **ка́плю.**

КА́ПАЯ (adv. pres. part.), see **ка́плю.**

КА́ПЛЕШЬ, see **ка́плю.**

КА́ПЛЮ, ка́плешь (arch.) (modern forms: ка́паю, ка́паешь) .I. **Ка́пать.** P. **Нака́пать** (mean. 2 and 3). 1. To drip, drop, trickle, dribble (intr.). 2. To pour out by drops (as medicine) (acc./gen.). 3. To spill, spot (s.t. with s.t.) (**на** + acc. + inst.).

КАРТА́ВЬ (imp.), see **карта́влю.**

КАРТА́ВЛЮ, карта́вишь. I. Карта́вить (intr.). To pronounce or speak with a burr.

КАЧУ́, ка́тишь. I. Кати́ть. P. **Покати́ть** (mean. 1). 1. To roll (s.t.) (acc.). 2. To drive (as a vehicle) (acc.). 3. To go rapidly (as in a car, a boat) (intr.).

КА́ЮСЬ, ка́ешься. I. Ка́яться (intr.). P. **Пока́яться.** 1. To repent (s.t.) (**в** + prep.). 2. To confess (s.t.) (**в** + prep.).

КВАСЬ (imp.), see **ква́шу.**

КВА́ШЕННЫЙ; ква́шен, —а, —о, —ы (ppp), see **ква́шу.**

КВА́ШУ, ква́сишь. I. Ква́сить (acc.). P. **Заква́сить.** 1. To sour, ferment. 2. To leaven (as dough).

КВО́ХЧЕТ, кво́хчут (3rd pers. only). I. **Квохта́ть** (intr.). To cluck (of hens).

КВОХЧИ́ (imp.), see **кво́хчет.**

КВО́ХЧУТ, see **кво́хчет.**

КИПИ́ (imp.), see **киплю́.**

КИПИ́ШЬ, see **киплю́.**

КИПЛЮ́, кипи́шь. I. Кипе́ть (intr.). P. **Вскипе́ть.** 1. To boil (of water, etc.). 2. (fig.) To boil, seethe.

КИПЯ́Т, see **киплю́.**

КИПЯЧЁННЫЙ; кипячён, —а́, —о́, —ы́ (ppp), see **кипячу́.**

КИПЯЧУ́, кипяти́шь. I. Кипяти́ть (acc.). P. **Вскипяти́ть.** To boil.

КИС, ки́сла (and **ки́снул**) (past). I. **Ки́снуть** (intr.). P. **Проки́снуть** (mean. 1). 1. To turn sour, to become acid. 2. (fig.) To be despondent.

КИША́Т, see **киши́т.**

КИШИ́, (imp.), see **киши́т.**

КИШИ́Т, киша́т (3rd pers. only) I. **Кише́ть** (intr.). 1. To swarm. 2. To teem or swarm with (inst.).

КЛАДЁШЬ, see **кладу́.**

КЛАДИ́ (imp.), see **кладу́.**

КЛАДУ́, кладёшь. I. Класть (acc.). P. **Положи́ть** (mean. 1, 2, and 4). 1. To lay, put, set, or place (s.t.) 2. To apply (as paint). 3. To lay (as bricks). 4. To assign (as time, effort, money, a beginning, etc. to s.t.) (acc. + **на** + acc.). (For other lit. and fig. meanings see unabridged dictionary.)

КЛАЛ, кла́ла (past), see **кладу́.**

КЛЕВЕ́ЩЕШЬ, see **клевещу́.**

КЛЕВЕЩИ́ (imp.), see **клевещу́.**

КЛЕВЕЩУ́, клеве́щешь. I. Клевета́ть (**на** + acc.). P. **Наклевета́ть.** To slander.

КЛЕЙМЁННЫЙ; клеймён, —а, —о, —ы (ppp), see **клеймлю́.**

КЛЕЙМЛЮ́, клейми́шь. I. Клейми́ть (acc.). P. **Заклейми́ть.** 1. To stamp, brand. 2. (fig.) To stigmatize.

КЛЕКО́ЧЕТ, клеко́чут (3rd pers. only). I. **Клекота́ть** (intr.). To scream (of certain birds of prey, eagles, etc.).

КЛЕКО́ЧУТ, see **клеко́чет.**

КЛЕПА́Й and **клепли́** (imp.), see **клеплю́².**

КЛЁПАННЫЙ; клёпан, —а, —о,
—ы (ppp), see клеплю².

КЛЕ́ПЛЕШЬ, see клеплю¹ and ².

КЛЕПЛЙ (imp.), see клеплю¹ and ².

КЛЕПЛЮ¹, кле́плешь. I. Клепа́ть
(на + acc.). P. Наклепа́ть. To
slander.

КЛЕПЛЮ², кле́плешь (also клепа́ю,
клепа́ешь). I. Клепа́ть (acc.). To
rivet (s.t.).

КЛИ́ЧЕШЬ, see кли́чу.

КЛИ́ЧУ, кли́чешь. I. Кли́кать. P.
Кли́кнуть (mean. 1 and 3). 1. To
call loudly (as a person, dog, etc.)
(acc.). 2. To call (as s.o. by a name)
(acc. and inst.). 3. To call, shout,
scream (intr.).

КЛИ́ЧЬ (imp.), see кли́чу.

КЛОКО́ЧЕШЬ, see клокочу́.

КЛОКОЧЙ (imp.), see клокочу́.

КЛОКОЧУ́, клоко́чешь (generally in
3rd person). I. Клокота́ть (intr.).
(lit. and fig.) To boil, bubble.

КЛО́ХЧЕШЬ, see клохчу́.

КЛОХЧЙ (imp.), see клохчу́.

КЛОХЧУ́, кло́хчешь. I. Клохта́ть
(intr.). To cluck (as a hen).

КЛЯЛ, кляла́, кля́ло, кля́ли (past),
see кляну́.

КЛЯ́ЛСЯ, кляа́сь, кляло́сь, кляли́сь
(past), see кляну́сь.

КЛЯНЁШЬ, see кляну́.

КЛЯНЁШЬСЯ, see кляну́сь.

КЛЯНЙ (imp.), see кляну́.

КЛЯНЙСЬ (imp.), see кляну́сь.

КЛЯНУ́, клянёшь. I. Клясть (acc.).
To curse, damn.

КЛЯНУ́СЬ, клянёшься. I. Кля́сться
(intr.). P. Покля́сться. 1. To vow,
swear (as friendship) (в + prep.).
2. To vow, swear to do (s.t.) (+
inf.).

КЛЯ́ТЫЙ; кля́т, —а́, —о, —ы (ppp),
see кляну́.

КОЛЕ́БЛЕМЫЙ (pres. pp), see
коле́блю.

КОЛЕ́БЛЕШЬ, see коле́блю.

КОЛЕ́БЛИ (imp.), see коле́блю.

КОЛЕ́БЛЮ, коле́блешь. I. Колеба́ть
(acc.). P. Поколеба́ть. 1. To shake,
oscillate. 2. (fig.) To shake (as one's
confidence).

КОЛЕШУ́, колеси́шь. I. Колеси́ть
(по + dat.). 1. To go in a roundabout
way, wander. 2. To travel all over.

КО́ЛЕШЬ, see колю́.

КОЛЙ (imp.), see колю́.

КО́ЛОТЫЙ; ко́лот, —а, —о, —ы
(ppp), see колю́.

КОЛОЧУ́, коло́тишь. I. Колоти́ть.
P. Поколоти́ть (mean. 3, 5). 1. To
strike (as a table) (по + dat.). 2. To
beat on (as a door) (в + acc.). 3. To
beat (a person, a thing) (acc.). 4. To
thresh (as grain) (acc.). 5. To break
(s.t. fragile, as dishes) (acc.). 6. To
shake (as fever shakes one) (3rd pers.)
(acc.).

КОЛЮ́, ко́лешь. I. Коло́ть (acc.).
P. Заколо́ть (mean. 3 and 4),
расколо́ть (mean. 1 and 2), кольну́ть
(mean. 5 and 6). 1. To chop, split,
break. 2. To crack. 3. To stab (kill).
4. To slaughter. 5. To prick. 6. (fig.)
To reproach.

КОЛЫХА́Й (imp.), see колы́шу.

КОЛЫХА́Я (adv. pres. part.), see
колы́шу.

КОЛЫ́ША (adv. pres. part.), see
колы́шу.

КОЛЫ́ШЕШЬ, see колы́шу.

КОЛЫ́ШУ, колы́шешь (also колыха́ю,
колыха́ешь). I. Колыха́ть (acc.).
P. Колыхну́ть. To sway, rock,
flutter.

КОНОВО́ДЬ (imp.), see коново́жу.

КОНОВО́ЖУ, коново́дишь. I. Коно-
во́дить (intr.). 1. To be a ring leader.
2. To be a horse-holder, groom.

КОНОПА́ТЬ (imp.), see конопа́чу.

КОНОПА́ЧЕННЫЙ; конопа́чен, —а,
—о, —ы (ppp), see конопа́чу.

КОНОПА́ЧУ, конопа́тишь. I. Коно-
па́тить (acc.). P. Законопа́тить,
проконопа́тить. To caulk.

КОНТУ́ЖЕННЫЙ; конту́жен, —а,
—о, —ы (ppp), see конту́жу.

КОНТУ́ЖУ, конту́зишь. P. Конту́-
зить (acc.). To contuse, bruise.

КОНТУ́ЗЬ (imp.), see конту́жу.

КОНФУ́ЖУ, конфу́зишь. I. Конфу́-
зить (acc.). P. Сконфу́зить. To disconcert, fluster.

КОНФУ́ЗЬ (imp), see конфу́жу.

КО́НЧЕННЫЙ; ко́нчен, —а, —о, —ы
(ppp), see ко́нчу.

КО́НЧИ (imp.), see ко́нчу.

КО́НЧУ, ко́нчишь. P. Ко́нчить (acc.).
I. Конча́ть. 1. To finish (as a job,
school, studies, etc.). 2. To kill.

КОПЛЮ́, ко́пишь. I. Копи́ть (acc.).
P. Накопи́ть. 1. To accumulate, lay

in a supply. 2. To save up, lay away (as money). 3. (fig.) To store up (as memories etc.).

КОПТЙ (imp.), see копчу́[1] and [2] and коптйт.

КОПТЙТ, коптя́т (3rd pers. only). I. Коптѣ́ть (intr.). Р. Закоптѣ́ть (mean. 2). 1. To smoke (of a stove). 2. To become covered with smoke, soot.

КОПТЙШЬ, see копчу́[1] and [2].

КОПТЯ́Т, see коптйт and копчу́[1] and [2].

КОПЧУ́[1], коптйшь. I. Коптѣ́ть (intr.). 1. To live in obscurity, vegetate. 2. To work hard at, pour over (as one's studies) (над + inst.).

КОПЧУ́[2], коптйшь. I. Коптйть. Р. Закоптйть (mean. 1 and 2). накоптйть (mean. 1 thru 3). 1. To cure in smoke (as a ham) (acc.). 2. To blacken with smoke (acc.). 3. To smoke (as a stove) (intr.).

КО́РМЛЕННЫЙ; ко́рмлен, —а, —о, —ы (ppp), see кормлю́.

КОРМЛЮ́, ко́рмишь. I. Кормѝть (acc.). Р. Накормѝть (mean. 1 and 2), покормѝть (mean. 1 and 2). 1. To feed. 2. To nurse (as an infant). 3. (fig.) To support (as one's family).

КОРО́БЬ (imp.), see коро́блю.

КОРО́БЛЮ, коро́бишь. I. Коро́бить. Р. Покоро́бить. 1. To warp, distort, deform (acc.). 2. To be warped, warp (impers. + acc.). 3. To create a bad impression (on), to disturb (acc.). 4. To have a bad impression created on one (by s.t.), be disturbed (by s.t.) (impers. + acc. + от + gen. of s.t.).

КОРПЙ (imp.), see корплю́.

КОРПЙШЬ, see корплю́.

КОРПЛЮ́, корпѝшь. I. Корпѣ́ть (intr.). To pore over, sweat over (as one's studies, books, etc.) (над + inst.).

КОРПЯ́Т, see корплю́.

КОСМА́ТЬ (imp.), see космачу́.

КОСМАЧУ́, косма́тишь. I. Косма́тить (acc.). To rumple, dishevel.

КО́ШЕННЫЙ; ко́шен, —а, —о, —ы (ppp), see кошу́[2].

КОШУ́[1], косѝшь. I. Косѝть. Р. Скосѝть (mean. 1 and 3), покосѝть (mean. 1 and 3). 1. To cock, make crooked, slope, bevel, slant (acc.). 2. To slant, be crooked (intr.). 3. To squint, cock (one's eyes) (acc./inst.).

КОШУ́[2], ко́сишь. I. Косѝть (acc.). Р. Скосѝть. 1. To mow, cut (as hay, etc.). 2. (fig.) To mow down, cut down, kill.

КОШУ́СЬ, косѝшься. I. Косѝться. Р. Покосѝться (mean. 1 and 2). 1. To slant, slope, settle unevenly (intr.). 2. To squint (at) look sideways at (на + acc.). 3. To look askance (at) (на + acc.).

КОШУ́, костѝшь. I. Костѝть (acc.). To scold, abuse, nag.

КРА́ДЕННЫЙ; кра́ден, —а, —о, —ы (ppp), see краду́.

КРАДЁШЬ, see краду́.

КРАДЙ (imp.), see краду́.

КРАДУ́, крадёшь. I. Красть (acc.). Р. Укра́сть. To steal.

КРА́Л, кра́ла (past), see краду́.

КРА́ПАЙ and кра́пли (imp.), see кра́плю.

КРА́ПЛЕННЫЙ; кра́плен, —а, —о, —ы (ppp), see кра́плю.

КРА́ПЛЕШЬ, see кра́плю.

КРА́ПЛИ and кра́пай (imp.), see кра́плю.

КРА́ПЛЕННЫЙ; кра́плен, —а, —о, —ы (ppp), see кра́плю.

КРА́ПЛЮ, кра́плешь (also кра́паю, кра́паешь), I. Кра́пать. 1. To sprinkle spit (of rain) (3rd pers.) (intr.). 2. To spray, speckle (acc.).

КРАСЬ (imp.), see кра́шу.

КРА́ШЕННЫЙ; кра́шен, —а, —о, —ы (ppp), see кра́сить.

КРА́ШУ, кра́сишь. I. Кра́сить (acc.). Р. Вы́красить (mean. 1), окра́сить (mean. 1), покра́сить (mean. 1). 1. To color, dye, paint. 2. (fig.) To color (as events). 3. (fig.) To adorn, beautify.

КРЕП (and кре́пнул), кре́пла (past). I. Кре́пнуть (intr.). Р. Окре́пнуть. 1. (lit. and fig.) To become strong or stronger. 2. (fig.) To become firmly established.

КРЕПЛЁННЫЙ; креплён, —а́, —о́, —ы́ (ppp), see креплю́.

КРЕПЛЮ́, крепѝшь. I. Крепѝть (acc.) 1. To timber, shore up, brace, prop. 2. To fasten. 3. (naut.) To make fast. 4. (lit. and fig.) To strengthen. 5. To constipate (med.).

КРЕЩЁННЫЙ; крещён, —а́, —о́, —ы́ (ppp), see крещу́[1] and [2].

КРЕЩУ́[1], крестѝшь. I. Крестѝть (acc.). Р. Окрестѝть (mean. 1). 1. To baptize, christen. 2. To be a god-father or godmother (to s.o.). 3. (arch.) To cross out.

КРЕЩУ́², кре́стишь. I. Крести́ть (acc.). Р. Перекрести́ть. To cross (make the sign of the cross over s.o.).

КРИВЛЮ́, криви́шь. I. Криви́ть. Р. Покриви́ть, скриви́ть. 1. To distort (as one's features), (e.g., one's mouth by sneering) (acc.). 2. To bend, twist, curve (acc.). 3. (fig.) To act hypocritically (intr.) (inst. of "soul": душо́й).

КРИЧА́Т, see кричу́.

КРИЧИ́ (imp.), see кричу́.

КРИЧИ́ШЬ, see кричу́.

КРИЧУ́, кричи́шь. I. Крича́ть. Р. Закрича́ть (mean. 1), кри́кнуть. 1. To shout, yell (intr.). 2. To shout at (на + acc.). 3. To call loudly (as s.o.) (acc.), or (to s.o.) (dat.). 4. To shout (s.t.) (acc.) or about (s.t.) (о + prep.).

КРО́ЕШЬ, see кро́ю.

КРОЙ (imp.), see кро́ю.

КРОПЛЮ́, кропи́шь. I. Кропи́ть. Р. Окропи́ть (mean. 1). 1. To sprinkle (s.t. with s.t.) (acc. + inst.). 2. To sprinkle (of rain) (intr.).

КРО́Ю, кро́ешь. I. Крыть. Р. Покры́ть. 1. To cover, coat, plate. 2. To roof. 3. To conceal. 4. To cover, trump (as a card). 5. To abuse, scold, rail at.

КРУ́ЧЕННЫЙ; кру́чен, —а, —о, —ы (ppp), see кручу́.

КРУЧУ́, кру́тишь. I. Крути́ть (acc.). Р. Скрути́ть (mean. 2, 3, 4). 1. To turn, twirl. 2. To twist. 3. To roll (as a cigarette). 4. To bind, pinion (as one's arms). 5. To manage, command (inst.). 6. To evade (intr.) or (acc.). 7. To court (e.g., girls) (с + inst.).

КРЫ́ТЫЙ; крыт, —а, —о, —ы (ppp), see кро́ю.

КРЯХТИ́ (imp.), see кряхчу́.

КРЯХТИ́ШЬ, see кряхчу́.

КРЯХТЯ́Т, see кряхчу́.

КРЯХЧУ́, кряхти́шь. I. Кряхте́ть (intr.). To groan.

КУДА́ХЧЕШЬ, see куда́хчу.

КУДА́ХЧИ (imp.), see куда́хчу.

КУДА́ХЧУ, куда́хчешь. I. Куда́хтать (intr.). To cackle.

КУ́КСИСЬ (imp.), see ку́кшусь.

КУ́КШУСЬ, ку́ксишься. I. Ку́кситься (intr.). 1. To sulk, be in a bad mood. 2. To be indisposed.

КУМЛЮ́СЬ, куми́шься. I. Куми́ться (intr.). Р. Покуми́ться. To become a godparent.

КУ́ПЛЕННЫЙ; ку́плен, —а, —о, —ы (ppp), see куплю́.

КУПЛЮ́, ку́пишь. Р. Купи́ть (acc.). I. Покупа́ть. 1. (lit. and fig.) To buy. 2. To bribe, suborn.

КУЧУ́, ку́тишь. I. Кути́ть (intr.). Р. Кутну́ть. To be on a spree, carouse.

Л

ЛАДЬ (imp.), see **ЛА́ЖУ¹.**

ЛА́ЕШЬ, see **ЛА́Ю.**

ЛА́ЖУ¹, ла́дишь. I. Ла́дить. 1. To get along, agree (with s.o. or s.t.) (с + inst.). **2.** To prepare; construct (acc.). **3.** To intend (to do s.t.) (+ inf.). **4.** To repeat endlessly, harp on (acc.).

ЛА́ЖУ², ла́зишь. I. Ла́зить (intr.). **1.** To climb or clamber on (на + acc.), into (в + acc.). **2.** To reach into (as one's pocket) (в + acc.).

ЛАЗЬ (imp.), see **ла́жу².**

ЛАЙ (imp.), see **ла́ю.**

ЛА́КОМИ and **ла́комь** (imp.), see **ла́комлю.**

ЛА́КОМИСЬ and **ла́комься** (imp.), see **ла́комлюсь.**

ЛА́КОМЛЮ, ла́комишь. I. Ла́комить (acc.) (arch.). **Р. Пола́комить.** To feed sumptuously, to provide with gourmet meals.

ЛА́КОМЛЮСЬ, ла́комишься. I. Ла́комиться (inst.). **Р. Пола́комиться.** To feast (on).

ЛА́КОМЬ and **ла́коми** (imp.), see **ла́комлю.**

ЛА́КОМЬСЯ and **ла́комись** (imp.), see **ла́комлюсь.**

ЛА́Ю, ла́ешь. I. Ла́ять. 1. To bark or bay (at) (на + acc.). **2.** (fig.) (arch.) To bark at, scold, abuse (acc.).

ЛГИ (imp.), see **лгу.**

ЛГУ, лжёшь, лгут. I. Лгать. Р. Солга́ть. 1. To lie, tell lies (intr.). **2.** (arch.) To slander (на + acc.).

ЛЕБЕЖУ́, лебези́шь. I. Лебези́ть (intr.). To fawn (upon), cringe (before) (пе́ред + inst.).

ЛЁГ, легла́ (past). **Р. Лечь** (intr.). **I. Ложи́ться. 1.** To lie, lie down. **2.** To lie on, cover (as snow covers the ground) (на + acc.). **3.** (fig.) To lie (on) (as guilt lies on one's conscience) (на + acc.). **4.** (naut.) To lie (of a ship, etc.). (Also see **ля́гу.**)

ЛЁЖА (adv. prcs. part.), see **лежу́.**

ЛЕЖА́Т, see **лежу́.**

ЛЕЖИ́ (imp.), see **лежу́.**

ЛЕЖИ́ШЬ, see **лежу́.**

ЛЕЖУ́, лежи́шь. I. Лежа́ть (intr.). **1.** To lie in a horizontal position. **2.** To lie or be ill with (as a fever) (в + prep.). **3.** To be located somewhere (of an object, a city, etc.). **4.** (fig.) To be the responsibility of (s.o.) (на + prep.). **5.** (fig.) To lie (as at the root of the matter, etc.) (в + prep.).

ЛЕЗ, ле́зла (past), see **ле́зу.**

ЛЕ́ЗЕШЬ, see **ле́зу.**

ЛЕ́ЗУ, ле́зешь. I. Лезть (intr.). **Р. Поле́зть. 1.** To get into (в + acc.). **2.** To thrust o.s. (upon s.o.) (к + dat.). **3.** To climb (as a tree) (на + acc.). **4.** To fall out (as hair) (intr.). **5.** To ravel (as cloth) (intr.). **6.** To fit (as shoes fit s.o.) (dat.) or (to fit s.o.'s feet) (dat. + на + acc.). **7.** To reach into (as one's pocket) (в + acc.). (For other meanings see an unabridged dictionary.)

ЛЕЗЬ (imp.), see **ле́зу.**

ЛЕЙ (imp.), see **лью.**

ЛЕЛЕ́ЕШЬ, see **леле́ю.**

ЛЕЛЕ́Й (imp.), see **леле́ю.**

ЛЕЛЕ́Ю, леле́ешь. I. Леле́ять (acc.). **1.** To cherish. **2.** To charm, delight.

ЛЕЛЕ́ЯННЫЙ; леле́ян, —а, —о, —ы (ppp), see **леле́ю.**

ЛЕПЕ́ЧЕШЬ, see **лепечу́.**

ЛЕПЕЧИ́ (imp.), see **лепечу́.**

ЛЕПЕЧУ́, лепе́чешь. I. Лепета́ть (acc.) or (intr.). (lit. and fig.) To babble, prattle.

ЛЕПЛЮ́, ле́пишь. I. Лепи́ть. Р. Вы́лепить (mean. 1), **слепи́ть** (mean. 1, 2), **налепи́ть** (mean. 2). **1.** To model, sculpture (acc.). **2.** To stick (s.t. to s.t.), make adhere (acc.). **3.** To cover, bury, spatter (of snow, a storm, wind, etc.) (intr.), (в + acc.), (в + acc. + inst. of snow, etc.), or (impers. + в + acc. + inst. of snow).

ЛЕТИ́ (imp.), see лечу́.
ЛЕТИ́ШЬ, see лечу́.
ЛЕТЯ́Т, see лечу́.
ЛЕЧУ́, лети́шь. I. Лете́ть (intr.). P. Полете́ть. (lit. and fig.) To fly.
ЛЖЁШЬ, see лгу.
ЛИ́ЖЕШЬ, see лижу́.
ЛИЖИ́ (imp.), see лижу́.
ЛИЖУ́, ли́жешь. I. Лиза́ть (acc.). P. Лизну́ть. (lit. and fig.) To lick.
ЛИП (and ли́пнул), ли́пла (past). I. Ли́пнуть (intr.). 1. (lit. and fig.) To stick to, cling to (к + dat.). 2. To close (of one's eyes).
ЛИ́ТЫЙ; ли́т, —а́, —о, —ы (ppp), see лью.
ЛИЦЕЗРИ́ (imp.), see лицезрю́.
ЛИЦЕЗРИ́ШЬ, see лицезрю́.
ЛИЦЕЗРЮ́, лицезри́шь. I. Лицезре́ть (arch.) (acc.). P. Улицезре́ть. To contemplate, to see (s.o.) with one's own eyes.
ЛИЦЕЗРЯ́Т, see лицезрю́.
ЛО́ВЛЕННЫЙ; ло́влен, —а, —о, —ы (ppp), see ловлю́.
ЛОВЛЮ́, ло́вишь. I. Лови́ть (acc.). P. Пойма́ть. 1. To catch (as fish). 2. (fig.) To catch (as a word, s.o. in a lie, etc.).
ЛОМЛЮ́, ло́мишь. I. Ломи́ть. 1. To break (s.t.) (acc.). 2. To break through (of an army) (intr.). 3. To ache (as one's leg) (impers.) or (impers. + acc.). 4. To ask too high a price (acc. of price).
ЛОПА́ТЬ (imp.), see лопа́чу.
ЛОПА́ЧЕННЫЙ; лопа́чен, —а, —о, —ы (ppp), see лопа́чу.
ЛОПА́ЧУ, лопа́тишь. I. Лопа́тить (acc.). To shovel, spade.
ЛОПО́ЧЕШЬ, see лопочу́.
ЛОПОЧИ́ (imp.), see лопочу́.
ЛОПОЧУ́, лопо́чешь. I. Лопота́ть (intr.). 1. To mutter, speak unclearly. 2. To rustle.

ЛОХМА́ТЬ (imp.), see лохма́чу.
ЛОХМА́ЧУ, лохма́тишь. I. Лохма́тить (acc.). P. Взлохма́тить. To tousle, rumple, dishevel.
ЛУЖЁННЫЙ; лужён, —а́, —о́, —ы́ (ppp), see лужу́.
ЛУЖУ́, лу́дишь. I. Луди́ть (acc.). P. Вы́лудить, полуди́ть. To tin (plate with tin).
ЛУКА́ВЛЮ, лука́вишь. I. Лука́вить (intr.). To be cunning, crafty.
ЛУКА́ВЬ (imp.), see лука́влю.
ЛУ́ПЛЕННЫЙ; лу́плен, —а, —о, —ы (ppp), see луплю́.
ЛУПЛЮ́, лу́пишь. I. Лупи́ть (acc.). P. Облупи́ть (mean. 1 and 2), слупи́ть (mean. 1 and 2), отлупи́ть (mean. 1 and 3). 1. To peel, strip, pare, bark. 2. To overcharge, cheat. 3. To thrash, flog, beat. 4. (Used in place of another verb to indicate energetic action, e.g., "to tear along the street," лупи́ть по шоссе́).
ЛЬЁШЬ, see лью.
ЛЬЩУ, льсти́шь. I. Льсти́ть (dat.). P. Польсти́ть. 1. To flatter (s.o.). 2. To please (s.o.).
ЛЬЮ, льёшь. I. Лить. 1. To pour (as a liquid) (acc.). 2. To pour, flow, run (of water, rain, etc.) (intr.). 3. To mound, found, cast (acc.).
ЛЮБЛЮ́, лю́бишь. I. Люби́ть (acc.). 1. To love. 2. To like, be fond of. 3. To thrive on or in, require (as plants thrive in sunlight, require water, etc.).
ЛЯГ (imp.), see ля́гу.
ЛЯ́ГУ, ля́жешь, ля́гут. P. Лечь (intr.). I. Ложи́ться. 1. To lie, lie down. 2. To lie on, cover (as snow covers the ground) (на + acc.). 3. (fig.) To lie (on) (as guilt lies on one's conscience) (на + acc.). 4. (naut.) To lie (of a ship).
ЛЯ́ЖЕШЬ, see ля́гу.

M

МА́ЕШЬСЯ, see ма́юсь.

МА́ЖЕШЬ, see ма́жу[1] and [2].

МА́ЖУ[1], ма́жешь. I. Ма́зать. Р. Вы́-мазать (mean. 1, 2), зама́зать (mean. 2), изма́зать (mean. 2), нама́зать (mean. 1, 3, 4, 5), пома́зать (mean. 1 and 3). 1. To grease, lubricate (acc.). 2. To soil, smear (acc.). 3. To spread with (as bread with butter) (acc. + inst.). 4. To apply (as make-up to one's face) (acc. of face + inst. of makeup). 5. To daub (as a poor painter) (intr.).

МА́ЖУ[2], ма́жешь. I. Ма́зать (intr.). Р. Прома́зать. To miss (as a shot).

МАЖЬ (imp.), see ма́жу[1] and [2].

МА́ЗАННЫЙ; ма́зан, —а, —о, —ы (ppp), see ма́жу[1].

МА́ЙСЯ (imp.), see ма́юсь.

МАХА́Я (occasionally маша́) (adv. pres. part.), see машу́.

МА́ШЕШЬ, see машу́.

МАШИ́ (imp.), see машу́.

МАШУ́, ма́шешь (also маха́ю, маха́ешь, etc.). I. Маха́ть. Р. Мах-ну́ть. 1. To wave (as one's hand, etc.) (inst.). 2. To wave (to s.o.) (dat.). 3. To flap (as wings) (inst.). 4. (fig.) To give up (s.t.) as hopeless (inst. of hand + на + acc.). 5. To go a dis-tance (acc. of distance).

МА́ЮСЬ, ма́ешься. I. Ма́яться (intr.). 1. To languish, worry, suffer. 2. To suffer (from an illness) (inst.). 3. To toil.

МЁЛ, мела́ (past), see мету́.

МЕ́ЛЕШЬ, see мелю́.

МЕЛИ́ (imp.), see мелю́.

МЕЛЮ́, ме́лешь. I. Моло́ть. Р. Смо-ло́ть. 1. To grind (as grain, etc.) (acc.). 2. (fig.) To babble, talk non-sense (intr.) or (acc.).

МЁР, мёрла (past), see мрёт.

МЁРЗ (and мёрзнул), мёрзла (past). I. Мёрзнуть (intr.). Р. Замёрзнуть. 1. (lit. and fig.) To freeze. 2. To become frostbitten. 3. To freeze to death.

МЕРК (and ме́ркнул), ме́ркла (past). I. Ме́ркнуть (intr.). Р. Поме́ркнуть. 1. To grow dim, fade (of stars, etc.). 2. (fig.) To dim, fade.

МЕРТВЛЮ́, мертви́шь. I. Мертви́ть (acc.). 1. To deprive of vitality, cheerfulness, etc., depress. 2. To kill.

МЕТЁННЫЙ; метён, —а́, —о́, —ы́ (ppp), see мету́.

МЕТЁШЬ, see мету́.

МЕТУ́, метёшь. I. Мести́ (acc.). 1. To sweep (acc.). 2. To snow hard (impers.).

МЕТЬ (imp.), see мечу́[1] and [2].

МЁТШИЙ (pap), see мету́.

МЕ́ЧЕННЫЙ; ме́чен, —а, —о, —ы (ppp), see мечу́[1].

МЕ́ЧЕШЬ, see мечу́.

МЕЧИ́ (imp.), see мечу́.

МЕЧУ́, ме́чешь. I. Мета́ть (acc.). Р. Вы́метать (mean. 2 and 3), метну́ть (mean. 1). 1. To throw, cast, fling. 2. To spawn. 3. To bear (of animals).

МЕ́ЧУ[1], ме́тишь. I. Ме́тить (acc.). Р. Наме́тить, поме́тить. To mark (as a page, clothing, etc.).

МЕ́ЧУ[2], ме́тить. I. Ме́тить. Р. Наме́-тить (mean. 1). 1. To aim at (в + acc.). 2. To aspire to (as a position) (в + acc.). 3. (fig.) To mean, hint at, allude to (в/на + acc.). 4. (fig.) (arch.) To intend (intr.), intend to (+ inf.).

МЕ́ШЕННЫЙ; ме́шен, —а, —о, —ы (ppp), see мешу́.

МЕШУ́, ме́сишь. I. Меси́ть (acc.). Р. Смеси́ть. 1. To knead (as dough). 2. To work up, puddle (as clay).

МНЁШЬ, see мну.

МНИ (imp.), see мну.

МНУ, мнёшь. I. Мять (acc.). Р. Измя́ть (mean. 1), размя́ть (mean. 3), смять (mean. 1, 2, 3). 1. To crumple, rumple. 2. To trample. 3. To knead, work up (as clay, leather, etc.). 4. To brake (as hemp, flax). 5. To throttle (as steam).

МОГ, могла́ (past), see **могу́.**

МОГУ́, мо́жешь, мо́гут. I. **Мочь** (intr.). P. **Смочь.** To be able (to do s.t.) (+ inf.).

МО́ЕШЬ, see **мо́ю.**

МО́ЖЕШЬ, see **могу́.**

МОЙ (imp.), see **мо́ю.**

МОК (and **мо́кнул**), **мо́кла** (past). I. **Мо́кнуть** (intr.). 1. To become wet, soaked. 2. To soak, steep.

МО́ЛВИ (imp.), see **мо́лвлю.**

МО́ЛВЛЮ, мо́лвишь. P. **Мо́лвить** (arch.) (acc.). To say.

МОЛОЖУ́, молоди́шь. I. **Молоди́ть** (acc.). 1. To make (look) young. 2. To rejuvenate.

МО́ЛОТЫЙ; мо́лот, —а, —о, —ы (ppp), see **мелю́.**

МОЛО́ЧЕННЫЙ; моло́чен, —а, —о, —ы (ppp), see **молочу́.**

МОЛОЧУ́, моло́тишь. I. **Молоти́ть.** P. **Смолоти́ть.** 1. To thresh (acc.) or (intr.). 2. To thrash, beat (e.g., a person) (acc.). 3. To beat on (e.g., on a door) (в + acc.), (e.g., on one's back) (по + dat.).

МОЛЧА́Т, see **молчу́.**

МОЛЧИ́ (imp.), see **молчу́.**

МОЛЧИ́ШЬ, see **молчу́.**

МОЛЧУ́, молчи́шь. I. **Молча́ть** (intr.). 1. To keep silent, refuse to speak. 2. To keep silent (about s.t.) (о + prep.).

МОРО́ЖЕННЫЙ; моро́жен, —а, —о, —ы (ppp), see **моро́жу.**

МОРО́ЖУ, моро́зишь. I. **Моро́зить.** 1. To freeze (acc.). 2. To become frosty, freeze (impers.) (intr.).

МОРО́ЗЬ (imp.), see **моро́жу.**

МОЩЁННЫЙ; мощён, —а́, —о́, —ы́ (ppp), see **мощу́.**

МОЩУ́, мости́шь. I. **Мости́ть** (acc.) P. **Вы́мостить** (mean. 1), **замости́ть** (mean. 1), **намости́ть** (mean. 1 and 2). 1. To pave (with a hard surface material). 2. To pave or lay (with planks, logs, etc.).

МО́Ю, мо́ешь. I. **мыть.** P. **Вы́мыть** (mean. 1), **помы́ть** (mean. 1). 1. To

wash. 2. (fig.) To wash (as waves wash the shore).

МРЁТ, мрут (3rd pers. only). I. **Мере́ть** (intr.). 1. To die (in quantities, as people of a plague, etc.). 2. To stop (of one's breathing, heartbeat, etc.).

МРИ (imp.), see **мрёт.**

МРУТ (3rd pers. pl.), see **мрёт.**

МУРА́ВЛЕННЫЙ; муравлен, —а, —о, —ы (ppp), see **мура́влю.**

МУРА́ВЛЮ, мура́вишь. I. **Мура́вить** (acc.). To glaze (as tile, pottery, etc.).

МУРА́ВЬ (imp.), see **мура́влю.**

МУЧУ́, мути́шь (also **му́тишь**). I. **Мути́ть** (acc.). P. **Взмути́ть** (mean. 1), **замути́ть** (mean. 1 and 3), **помути́ть** (mean. 1 and 2). 1. To stir up, make turbid (as a liquid). 2. (fig.) To dull (as alcohol dulls one's senses). 3. (fig.) To stir up (as the populace). 4. To feel sick to one's stomach (impers. + acc.).

МЧАТ, see **мчу.**

МЧИ (imp.), see **мчу.**

МЧИШЬ, see **мчу.**

МЧУ, мчишь. I. **Мчать.** 1. To rush, speed along, hurry, etc. (as a taxi hurries one to the station, etc.) (acc.). 2. To rush, speed along, hurry, etc. (as a car speeds along the highway) (intr.).

МЩУ, мстишь. I. **Мстить.** P. **Отомсти́ть, отмсти́ть.** 1. To take vengeance on (dat.). 2. To take vengeance, revenge (on s.o. for s.t.) (dat. + за + acc.).

МЫ́ТЫЙ; мыт, —а, —о, —ы (ppp), see **мо́ю.**

МЫЧА́Т, see **мычу́.**

МЫЧИ́ (imp.), see **мычу́.**

МЫЧИ́ШЬ, see **мычу́.**

МЫЧУ́, мычи́шь. I. **Мыча́ть** (intr.). 1. To bellow, moo (of cattle). 2. To mumble, hem, and haw.

МЯТЕ́ШЬСЯ, see **мяту́сь.**

МЯТИ́СЬ (imp.), see **мяту́сь.**

МЯТУ́СЬ, мяте́шься. I. **Мясти́сь** (intr.) (past tense not used). 1. To rebel, mutiny. 2. (fig.) To be restless. 3. To mill about.

МЯ́ТЫЙ; мя́т, —а, —о, —ы (ppp), see **мну.**

Н

НАБÁВЛЕННЫЙ; набáвлен, —а, —о, —ы (ppp), see набáвлю.

НАБÁВЛЮ, набáвишь. P. Набáвить (acc.). I. Набавля́ть. 1. To add (s.t. to s.t.) (acc./gen. | на + acc.). 2. To increase (as price, speed, etc.) (acc./gen.).

НАБÁВЬ (imp.), see набáвлю.

НАБАЛАМУ́ТЬ (imp.), see набаламу́чу.

НАБАЛАМУ́ЧЕННЫЙ; набаламу́чен, —а, —о, —ы (ppp), see набаламу́чу.

НАБАЛАМУ́ЧУ, набаламу́тишь. P. Набаламу́тить (acc.) or (intr.). To thoughtlessly and pointlessly disturb or agitate (s.o.).

НАБЕГИ́ (imp.), see набегу́.

НАБЕГУ́, набежи́шь, набегу́т. P. Набежа́ть (intr.). I. Набега́ть. 1. To run against (на + acc.). 2. To come running, hurriedly assemble. 3. To collect, accumulate (of water, money, interest, etc.). 4. To rise, suddenly appear (of wind, people, etc.).

НАБЕЖИ́ШЬ, see набегу́.

НАБЕЙ (imp.), see набью́.

НАБЕРЁШЬ, see наберу́.

НАБЕРИ́ (imp.), see наберу́.

НАБЕРУ́, наберёшь. P. Набра́ть. I. Набира́ть. 1. To collect, gather (gen./acc.). 2. (typ.) To compose (acc.). 3. To recruit (acc.). 4. To dial (a telephone number) (acc.). 5. To count (e.g., 100 tanks) (acc.). 6. (fig.) To attain (as speed, height) (acc.).

НАБИ́ТЫЙ; наби́т, —а, —о, —ы (ppp), see набью́.

НАБЛЮДЁННЫЙ; наблюдён, —á, —ó, —ы́ (ppp), see наблюду́.

НАБЛЮДЁШЬ, see наблюду́.

НАБЛЮДИ́ (imp.), see наблюду́.

НАБЛЮДУ́, наблюдёшь. P., Наблюсти́ (acc.) or (intr.). To supervise, observe, watch.

НАБЛЮ́ДШИЙ (pap), see наблюду́.

НАБЛЮЛ, наблюла́ (past), see наблюду́.

НАБОРМО́ЧЕШЬ, see набормочу́.

НАБОРМОЧИ́ (imp.), see набормочу́.

НАБОРМОЧУ́, набормо́чешь. P. Набормота́ть (acc./gen.). To mutter a lot (of nonsense).

НÁБРАННЫЙ; нáбран, —á (or —a), —о, —ы (ppp), see наберу́.

НАБРЕДЁШЬ, see набреду́.

НАБРЕДИ́ (imp.), see набреду́.

НАБРЕДУ́, набредёшь. P. Набрести́. I. Набреда́ть. 1. (lit. and fig.) To happen upon, run across (на + acc.). 2. To collect in one place (as a number of people) (impers. + gen.).

НАБРЕ́ДШИЙ (pap), see набреду́.

НАБРЁЛ, набрела́ (past), see набреду́.

НАБРО́СЬ (imp.), see набро́шу.

НАБРО́ШЕННЫЙ; набро́шен, —а, —о, —ы (ppp), see набро́шу.

НАБРО́ШУ, набро́сишь. P. Набро́сить (acc.). I. Набра́сывать. 1. To throw, cast (s.t.) on or over (s.o. or s.t.) (acc. + на + acc.). 2. To sketch rapidly; write hurriedly.

НАБУ́Х, набу́хла (past). P. Набу́хнуть (intr.). I. Набуха́ть. To swell.

НАБЬЁШЬ, see набью́.

НАБЬЮ́, набьёшь. P. Наби́ть. I. Набива́ть. 1. To stuff, fill (with s.t.) (acc. + inst.). 2. To stuff, cram (s.t. into s.t.) (acc./gen. + в + acc.). 3. To nail (e.g., a sign to a door) (acc. + на + acc.). 4. To pound, drive on (as a hoop on a cask) (acc. + на + acc.). 5. To print (as cloth) (acc.). 6. To break a quantity of (as dishes) (gen.). 7. To shoot a quantity of (as pheasants) (gen.). 8. To trample down (acc.). 9. To raise (a price) (acc. of price). (For other meanings, see an unabridged dictionary.)

НАВÁКСИ (imp.), see накáкшу.

НАВА́КШЕННЫЙ; нава́кшен, —а, —о, —ы (ppp), see нава́кшу.

НАВА́КШУ, нава́ксишь. Р. Нава́-ксить (acc.). I. Ва́ксить. То polish with blacking (as shoes).

НАБЕДЁННЫЙ; наведён, —а́, —о́, —ы́ (ppp), see наведу́.

НАВЕДЁШЬ, see наведу́.

НАВЕДИ́ (imp.), see наведу́.

НАВЕДУ́, наведёшь. Р. Навести́ (acc.). I. Наводи́ть. 1. To direct, aim (s.t. at s.t.) (acc. + на/в + acc.). 2. To build, construct (as a road) (acc.). 3. To suggest (as an idea to s.o.) (i.e., lead s.o. to an idea, thought, etc.) (acc. of s.o. + на + acc. of idea, etc.). 4. To arouse (fear, horror, etc., in s.o.) (acc. of fear + на + acc. of s.o.). 5. To bring, introduce (e.g., order). 6. To bring in a quantity of (acc./gen.). 7. (lit. and fig.) To apply (as polish, gloss, etc. to s.t.) (acc. + на + acc.).

НАВЕ́ДШИЙ (pap), see наведу́.

НАВЕДЯ́ (adv. past part.), see наведу́.

НАВЕ́ЕШЬ, see наве́ю.

НАВЁЗ, навезла́ (past), see навезу́.

НАВЕЗЁННЫЙ; навезён, —а́, —о́, —ы́ (ppp), see навезу́.

НАВЕЗЁШЬ, see навезу́.

НАВЕЗИ́ (imp.), see навезу́.

НАВЕЗУ́, навезёшь. Р. Навезти́. I. Навози́ть. 1. To drive against (acc. + на + acc.). 2. To bring in a quantity of, by vehicle (gen./acc.).

НАВЕ́Й[1] (imp.), see наве́ю.

НАВЕ́Й[2] (imp.), see навью́.

НАВЁЛ, навела́ (past), see наведу́.

НАВЕРТИ́ (imp.), see наверчу́.

НАВЕ́РТИШЬ, see наверчу́.

НАВЕ́РТЯТ, see наверчу́.

НАВЕ́РЧЕННЫЙ; наве́рчен, —а, —о, —ы (ppp), see наверчу́.

НАВЕРЧУ́, наве́ртишь. Р. Наверте́ть. I. Навёртывать (mean. 1), навёрчивать (mean. 2 and 3). 1. To wind, twist (as s.t. around s.t.) (acc. + на + acc.). 2. To drill a quantity of (as holes) (gen.). 3. To make (by twisting s.t.) (as artificial flowers, etc.) (acc./gen.).

НАВЕ́СЬ (imp.), see наве́шу.

НАВЕ́ШЕННЫЙ; наве́шен, —а, —о, —ы (ppp), see наве́шу.

НАВЕ́ШУ, наве́сишь. Р. Наве́сить (acc.). I. Наве́шивать. 1. To hang, suspend (s.t.). 2. To hang (as a door).

НАВЕЩЁННЫЙ; навещён, —а́, —о́, —ы́ (ppp), see навещу́.

НАВЕЩУ́, навести́шь. Р. Навести́ть (acc.). I. Навеща́ть. To visit, call upon.

НАВЕ́Ю, наве́ешь. Р. Наве́ять. I. Навева́ть, наве́ивать. 1. To blow, to bring by blowing (of the wind (acc.) or (impers. + acc.). 2. To arouse (a feeling in s.o.) (as sadness) (acc. + на + acc. of s.o.). 3. To winnow a quantity of (as grain) (gen.).

НАВЕ́ЯННЫЙ; наве́яни, —а, —о, —ы (ppp), see наве́ю.

НАВИ́НЧЕННЫЙ; нави́нчен, —а, —о, —ы (ppp), see навинчу́.

НАВИНЧУ́, навинти́шь. Р. Навинти́ть. I. Нави́нчивать. To screw on (as a nut on s.t.) (acc. + на + acc.).

НАВИ́С, нави́сла (past). Р. Нави́снуть (intr.). I. Нависа́ть. 1. To hang over (s.t.) (на + acc.). 2. To overhang (s.t.) (над + inst.). 3. (fig.) To threaten, to hang over one (as danger) (над + inst.).

НАВИ́ТЫЙ; нави́т, —а́, —о, —ы (ppp), see навью́.

НАВЛЁК, навлекла́ (past), see навлеку́.

НАВЛЕКУ́, навлечёшь, навлеку́т. Р. Навле́чь (acc. + на + acc.). I. Навлека́ть. 1. To bring on, cause (as disgrace, etc. to s.o.). 2. To incur (as displeasure, etc.) (acc. + на + себя́).

НАВЛЕКИ́ (imp.), see навлеку́.

НАВЛЕЧЁННЫЙ; навлечён, —а́, —о́, —ы́ (ppp), see навлеку́.

НАВЛЕЧЁШЬ, see навлеку́.

НАВО́ЖЕННЫЙ; наво́жен, —а, —о, —ы (ppp), see наво́жу and навожу́[2].

НАВОЖУ́[1], наво́дишь. I. Наводи́ть. Р. Навести́. 1. To direct, aim (s.t. at s.t.) (acc. + в/на + acc.). 2. To build, construct (as a road) (acc.). 3. To suggest (as an idea to s.o.) (i.e., lead s.o. to an idea, thought, etc.). (acc. of s.o. + на + acc. of idea, etc.). 4. To arouse (fear, horror etc. in s.o.) (acc. of fear + на + acc. of s.o.). 5. To bring, introduce (e.g., order) (acc.). 6. To bring in a quantity of (acc./gen.). 7. (lit. and fig.) To apply (as polish, gloss etc. to s.t.) (acc. + на + acc.).

НАВОЖУ́², наво́зишь. Р. Навози́ть (gen./acc.). To bring in a quantity of (by vehicle).

НАВОЖУ́³, наво́зишь. I. Навози́ть. Р. Навезти́. 1. To drive against (acc. + на + acc.). 2. To bring in a quantity of, by vehicle (gen./acc.).

НАВОЖУ́, наво́зишь. I. Наво́зить (acc.). Р. Унаво́зить. To fertilize, manure.

НАВО́З (imp.), see наво́жу.

НАВОЛО́К, наволокла́ (past), see наволоку́.

НАВОЛОКИ́ (imp.), see наволоку́.

НАВОЛОКУ́, наволоко́шь, наволоку́т. Р. Наволо́чь. I. Наволáкивать. 1. To bring, drag in a quantity of (acc./gen.). 2. To cloud over (impers.) (intr.) or (gen.).

НАВОЛОЧЁННЫЙ; наволочён, —á, —ó, —ы́ (ppp), see наволоку́.

НАВОЛОЧЁШЬ, see наволоку́.

НАВОРО́ЧЕННЫЙ; наворо́чен, —а, —о, —ы (ppp), see наворочу́.

НАВОРОЧУ́, наворо́тишь. Р. Навороти́ть (acc./gen.). I. Наворáчивать. (lit. and fig.) To pile up, heap up.

НАВОРЧА́Т, see наворчу́.

НАВОРЧИ́ (imp.), see наворчу́.

НАВОРЧИ́ШЬ, see наворчу́.

НАВОРЧУ́, наворчи́шь. Р. Наворчáть (на + acc.). To grumble at, scold.

НÁВРАННЫЙ; нáвран, —á, —о, —ы (ppp), see навру́.

НАВРЕЖУ́, навреди́шь. Р. Навреди́ть (dat.). To do much harm (to s.o./s.t. by s.t.) (dat. + inst.).

НАВРЁШЬ, see навру́.

НАВРИ́ (imp.), see навру́.

НАВРУ́, наврёшь. Р. Наврáть. I. Врать (mean. 1, 2, 4). 1. To lie, tell lies (intr.) or (acc./gen.). 2. To talk nonsense (intr.) or (acc./gen.). 3. To slander (s.o.) (на + acc.). 4. To make mistakes (in s.t.) (в + prep.).

НАВЫ́К, навы́кла (past). Р. Навы́кнуть (intr.) I. Навыкáть. To acquire a habit (к + dat.) or (dat.) or (+ inf.).

НАВЬЁШЬ, see навью́.

НАВЬЮ́, навьёшь. Р. Нави́ть (acc.). I. Навивáть. 1. To wind (as thread on a spool) (acc. + на + acc.). 2. To twist, make (as a rope, thread, etc.). 3. To pile, load, pitch (as hay on a wagon). 4. To drift, pile (as wind drifts snow).

НАВЯ́ЖЕШЬ, see навяжу́.

НАВЯЖИ́ (imp.), see навяжу́.

НАВЯЖУ́, навя́жешь. Р. Навязáть. I. Навя́зывать. 1. To tie, fasten (s.t. to s.t.) (acc. + на + acc.). 2. To knit (acc./gen.). 3. (fig.) To thrust or impose (s.t. on s.o. or s.t.) (e.g., an object, an idea) (acc. + dat.).

НАВЯ́З, навя́зла (past). Р. Навя́знуть (intr.). I. Навязáть. 1. To stick to (на + prep.). 2. To stick in (в + prep.).

НАВЯ́ЗАННЫЙ; навя́зан, —а, —о, —ы (ppp), see навяжу́.

НАГА́ДЬ (imp.), see нагáжу.

НАГА́ЖЕННЫЙ; нагáжен, —а, —о, —ы (past), see нагáжу.

НАГА́ЖУ, нагáдишь. Р. Нагáдить. I. Гáдить. 1. To defecate (of animals) (intr.). 2. To play a mean trick (on s.o.) (dat.).

НАГЛА́ДЬ (imp.), see наглáжу.

НАГЛА́ЖЕННЫЙ; наглáжен, —а, —о, —ы (ppp), see наглáжу.

НАГЛА́ЖУ, наглáдишь. Р. Наглáдить. I. Наглáживать. 1. To iron (as one's laundry) (acc./gen.). 2. To press (as a suit) (acc.).

НАГЛЯДИ́СЬ (imp.), see нагляжу́сь.

НАГЛЯДИ́ШЬСЯ, see нагляжу́сь.

НАГЛЯДЯ́ТСЯ, see нагляжу́сь.

НАГЛЯЖУ́СЬ, нагляди́шься. Р. Наглядéться (на + acc.). To see enough (of s.o., s.t.).

НÁГНАННЫЙ; нáгнан, —а, —о, —ы (ppp), see нагоню́.

НАГНЕТЁННЫЙ; нагнетён, —á, —ó, —ы́ (ppp), see нагнету́.

НАГНЕТЁШЬ, see нагнету́.

НАГНЕТИ́ (imp.), see нагнету́.

НАГНЕТУ́, нагнетёшь. I. Нагнести́ (acc.) (past tense not used). Р. Нагнетáть. To force, pump (as water, air, etc.).

НАГНЕТЯ́ (adv. past part.), see нагнету́.

НАГОНЙ (imp.), see нагоню́.
НАГО́НИШЬ, see нагоню́.
НАГОНЮ́, наго́нишь. Р. Нагна́ть (acc.). I. Нагоня́ть. 1. (lit. and fig.) To overtake, catch up with. 2. To make up for (s.t.) (as work not done.). 3. To make up (time). 4. To drive (in) (as cattle) (acc./gen.). 5. To distill (acc./gen.). 6. (fig.) To arouse, instill (as fear in s.o.) (acc./gen. + на + acc.). 7. To raise sharply (e.g., pressure, price, etc.).
НАГО́НЯТ, see нагоню́.
НАГОРИ́Т, нагоря́т (3rd pers. only). Р. Нагоре́ть. I. Нагора́ть. 1. To char (of a wick, etc.) (intr.). 2. To be used up, expend (as fuel) (impers. + gen.). 3. (fig.) To befall one, to "catch it" for s.t. (as "he caught it for . . .") (impers. + dat. of person + за + acc.).
НАГОРО́ЖЕННЫЙ; нагоро́жен, —а, —о, —ы (ppp), see нагорожу́.
НАГОРОЖУ́, нагоро́дишь (and нагороди́шь). Р. Нагороди́ть (acc./gen.). I. Нагора́живать. 1. To build (as a fence). 2. To pile up (as trash). 3. (fig.) To talk, write a lot (of nonsense).
НАГОРЯ́Т, see нагори́т.
НАГОТО́ВЛЕННЫЙ; нагото́влен, —а, —о, —ы (ppp), see нагото́влю.
НАГОТО́ВЛЮ, нагото́вишь. Р. Наготовить (acc./gen.). I. Нагота́вливать. 1. To lay in a store of (s.t.). 2. To prepare, cook a quantity of (s.t.).
НАГОТО́ВЬ (imp.), see наготовлю.
НАГРА́БЛЕННЫЙ; награ́блен, —а, —о, —ы (ppp), see награ́блю.
НАГРА́БЛЮ, награ́бишь. Р. Награбить (gen./acc.). 1. To rob, steal a lot of (s.t.). 2. To rake up a quantity of (s.t.).
НАГРА́БЬ (imp.), see награ́блю.
НАГРАЖДЁННЫЙ; награждён, —а́, —о́, —ы́ (ppp), see награжу́.
НАГРАЖУ́, награди́шь. Р. Награди́ть (acc. + inst.). I. Награжда́ть. 1. To reward, recompense (s.o. with s.t.). 2. To decorate (as a soldier with a medal). 3. (fig.) To endow (s.o. with s.t.) (as nature endows one with intelligence, etc.).
НАГРАФЛЁННЫЙ; награфлён, —а́, —о́, —ы́ (ppp), see награфлю́.

НАГРАФЛЮ́, награфи́шь. Р. Награфи́ть (acc.). To rule, mark with a number of parallel lines.
НАГРЁБ, награбла́ (past), see нагребу́.
НАГРЕБЁННЫЙ; нагребён, —а́, —о́, —ы́ (ppp), see нагребу́.
НАГРЕБЁШЬ, see нагребу́.
НАГРЕБИ́ (imp.), see нагребу́.
НАГРЕБУ́, нагребёшь. Р. Нагрести́ (gen./acc.). I. Нагреба́ть. To rake up a quantity of (s.t.).
НАГРЕМИ́ (imp.), see нагремлю́.
НАГРЕМИ́ШЬ, see нагремлю́.
НАГРЕМЛЮ́, нагреми́шь. Р. Нагреме́ть (intr.). 1. To make, cause a noise, din (with s.t.) (inst.). 2. (fig.) To cause a sensation (with s.t.) (inst.).
НАГРЕМЯ́Т, see нагремлю́.
НАГРОМОЖДЁННЫЙ; нагромождён, —а́, —о́, —ы́ (ppp), see нагромозжу́.
НАГРОМОЗЖУ́, нагромозди́шь. Р. Нагромозди́ть (acc./gen.). I. Громозди́ть, нагроможда́ть. (lit. and fig.) To pile up, heap up.
НАГРУБЛЮ́, нагруби́шь. Р. Нагруби́ть (dat.). I. Груби́ть. To be rude (to), speak rudely (to s.o.).
НАГРУ́ЖЕННЫЙ; нагру́жен, —а, —о, —ы (ppp), see нагружу́.
НАГРУЖЁННЫЙ; нагружён, —а́, —о́, —ы́ (ppp), see нагружу́.
НАГРУЖУ́, нагру́зишь (also нагрузи́шь). Р. Нагрузи́ть (acc.). I. Нагружа́ть, грузи́ть (mean. 1, 2). 1. To load (s.t. with s.t.) (acc. + inst.). 2. To load (s.t. on s.t.) (acc. + на + acc.). 3. (fig.) To burden (s.o. with s.t.) (as with work) (acc. + inst.).
НАГРЫ́З, нагры́зла (past), see нагрызу́.
НАГРЫ́ЗЕННЫЙ; нагры́зен, —а, —о, —ы (ppp), see нагрызу́.
НАГРЫЗЁШЬ, see нагрызу́.
НАГРЫЗИ́ (imp.), see нагрызу́.
НАГРЫЗУ́, нагрызёшь. Р. Нагры́зть (acc.). I. Нагрыза́ть. 1. To crack a quantity of (as nuts). 2. To nibble, eat, gnaw a quantity of.
НАДА́ВЛЕННЫЙ; нада́влен, —а, —о, —ы (ppp), see надавлю́.
НАДАВЛЮ́, нада́вишь. Р. Надави́ть. I. Нада́вливать. 1. To press (acc.) or (на + acc.). 2. To squeeze or

press out (as juice from berries) (acc./gen.). 3. To mash (as potatoes) (acc./gen.). 4. To kill (mash, squash) (as bugs) (acc./gen.).

НАДБА́ВЛЕННЫЙ; надба́влен, —а, —о, —ы (ppp), see надба́влю.

НАДБА́ВЛЮ, надба́вишь. Р. Надба́вить. I. Надбавля́ть. 1. To add (s.t. to s.t.) (acc./gen. + на + acc.). 2. To increase (as price, speed, etc.) (acc./gen.).

НАДБА́ВЬ (imp.), see надба́влю.

НАДБЕ́Й (imp.), see надобью́.

НАДБИ́ТЫЙ; надби́т, —а, —о, —ы (ppp), see надобью́.

НАДВЯ́ЖЕШЬ, see надвяжу́.

НАДВЯЖИ́ (imp.), see надвяжу́.

НАДВЯЖУ́, надвя́жешь. Р. Надвяза́ть (acc.). I. Надвя́зывать. 1. To knit (a foot in a sock, etc.). 2. To enlarge or lengthen (s.t.) by knitting. 3. To lengthen, add a length (as of rope) (acc. of rope).

НАДВЯ́ЗАННЫЙ; надвя́зан, —а, —о, —ы (ppp), see надвяжу́.

НАДДАВА́Й (imp.), see наддаю́.

НАДДАВА́Я (adv. pres. part.), see наддаю́.

НАДДАДИ́М, наддади́те, наддаду́т (pl. forms), see надда́м.

НАДДА́Й (imp.), see надда́м.

НАДДА́М, надда́шь, надда́ст (sing. forms). Р. Надда́ть (acc./gen.). I. Наддава́ть. To add, increase.

НА́ДДАННЫЙ; на́ддан, —а́, —о, —ы (ppp), see надда́м.

НАДДА́СТ, see надда́м.

НАДДА́ШЬ, see надда́м.

НАДДАЮ́, наддаёшь. I. Наддава́ть (gen./acc.). Р. Надда́ть. To add, increase.

НАДЕ́ЕШЬСЯ, see наде́юсь.

НАДЕ́ЙСЯ (imp.), see наде́юсь.

НАДЕ́НЕШЬ, see наде́ну.

НАДЕ́НУ, наде́нешь. Р. Наде́ть (acc.). I. Надева́ть. To put on (as clothes, glasses, etc.).

НАДЕ́НЬ (imp.), see наде́ну.

НАДЕРЁШЬ, see надеру́.

НАДЕРИ́ (imp.), see надеру́.

НАДЕРУ́, надерёшь. Р. Надра́ть (gen./acc.). I. Надира́ть. To tear, strip a quantity of.

НАДЕ́ТЫЙ; наде́т, —а, —о, —ы (ppp), see наде́ну.

НАДЕ́ЮСЬ, наде́ешься. I. Наде́яться

(intr.). Р. Понаде́яться. 1. To hope (for s.t.) (на + acc.). 2. To hope (to do s.t.) (inf.). 3. To rely on (s.o. or s.t.), have confidence in (на + acc.).

НАДИВЛЮ́СЬ, надиви́шься. Р. Надиви́ться (intr.). To wonder greatly (at something) (на + acc.) or (dat.).

НАДКО́ЛЕШЬ, see надколю́.

НАДКОЛИ́ (imp.), see надколю́.

НАДКО́ЛОТЫЙ; надко́лот, —а, —о, —ы (ppp), see надколю́.

НАДКОЛЮ́, надко́лешь. Р. Надколо́ть (acc.). I. Надка́лывать. 1. To split slightly. 2. To pierce slightly, prick.

НАДКУ́ШЕННЫЙ; надку́шен, —а, —о, —ы (ppp), see надкушу́.

НАДКУШУ́, надку́сишь. Р. Надкуси́ть (acc.). I. Надку́сывать. To bite, nibble at.

НАДЛЕЖА́ЛО (past), see надлежи́т.

НАДЛЕЖИ́Т. I. Надлежа́ть (inf. not used). "It is necessary" (as "it was necessary for him to do s.t.") (ему́ надлежа́ло сде́лать что́-то) (impers. + dat. + inf.).

НАДЛО́МЛЕННЫЙ; надло́млен, —а, —о, —ы (ppp), see надломлю́.

НАДЛОМЛЮ́, надло́мишь. Р. Надломи́ть (acc.). I. Надла́мывать. 1. To fracture, crack. 2. (fig.) To overtax (as one's strength).

НАДОБЬЁШЬ, see надобью́.

НАДОБЬЮ́, надобьёшь. Р. Надби́ть (acc.). I. Надбива́ть. To crack, chip (as dishes).

НАДОЕДИ́М, надоеди́те, надоедя́т (pl. forms), see надоем.

НАДОЕ́Л, надое́ла (past), see надоем.

НАДОЕ́М, надое́шь, надое́ст (sing. forms). Р. Надое́сть (no imperative). I. Надоеда́ть. 1. To bore or pester (s.o.) (dat.). 2. To bore (s.o. with s.t.) (dat. + inst.). 3. To be tired of, sick of, bored with (doing s.t.) (dat. + impers. form of надое́сть + inf.).

НАДОЕ́СТ, see надоем.

НАДОЕ́ШЬ (2nd pers. sing.), see надоем.

НАДО́РВАННЫЙ; надо́рван, —а, —о, —ы (ppp), see надорву́.

НАДОРВЁШЬ, see надорву́.

НАДОРВИ́ (imp.), see надорву́.

НАДОРВУ́, надорвёшь. Р. Надорва́ть

(acc.). I. **Надрыва́ть**. 1. To tear slightly. 2. (fig.) To overstrain, overtax (as one's strength).

НАДОШЬЁШЬ, see надошью́.

НАДОШЬЮ́, надошьёшь. Р. **Надши́ть** (acc.). I. **Надшива́ть**. 1. To lengthen. 2. To sew on (s.t. to s.t. to lengthen) (acc. + к + dat.).

НАДПИ́САННЫЙ; надпи́сан, —а, —о, —ы (ppp), see надпишу́.

НАДПИ́ШЕШЬ, see надпишу́.

НАДПИШИ́ (imp.), see надпшу́.

НАДПИШУ́, надпи́шешь. Р. **Надписа́ть** (acc.). I. **Надпи́сывать**. 1. To inscribe, superscribe. 2. To address (as an envelope). 3. To dedicate (as a book).

НАДПО́РЕШЬ, see надпорю́.

НАДПОРИ́ (imp.), see надпорю́.

НАДПО́РОТЫЙ; надпо́рот, —а, —о, —ы (ppp), see надпорю́.

НАДПОРЮ́, надпо́решь. Р. **Надпоро́ть** (acc.). I. **Надпа́рывать**. To rip open slightly.

НА́ДРАННЫЙ; на́дран, —а, —о, —ы (ppp), see надеру́.

НАДРЕ́ЖЕШЬ, see надре́жу.

НАДРЕ́ЖУ, надре́жешь. Р. **Надре́зать** (acc.). I. **Надре́зывать**, **надреза́ть**. 1. To make an incision (on). 2. To cut slightly.

НАДРЕ́ЖЬ (imp.), see надре́жу.

НАДРЕ́ЗАННЫЙ; надре́зан, —а, —о, —ы (ppp), see надре́жу.

НАДРУ́БЛЕННЫЙ; надру́блен, —а, —о, —ы (ppp), see надрублю́.

НАДРУБЛЮ́, надру́бишь. Р. **Надруби́ть** (acc.). I. **Надруба́ть**. To notch (as a tree).

НАДСА́ЖЕННЫЙ; надса́жен, —а, —о, —ы (ppp), see надсажу́.

НАДСАЖУ́, надса́дишь. Р. **Надсади́ть** (acc.). I. **Надса́живать**. To strain (as one's voice, a muscle, etc.).

НАДСЕ́К, надсекла́ (past), see надсеку́.

НАДСЕКИ́ (imp.), see надсеку́.

НАДСЕКУ́, надсечёшь, надсеку́т. Р. **Надсе́чь** (acc.). I. **Надсека́ть**. 1. To notch, gash. 2. To make incisions, incise.

НАДСЕЧЁННЫЙ; надсечён, —а́, —о́, —ы́ (ppp), see надсеку́.

НАДСЕЧЕ́ШЬ, see надсеку́.

НАДСТА́ВЛЕННЫЙ; надста́влен, —а, —о, —ы (ppp), see надста́влю.

НАДСТА́ВЛЮ, надста́вишь. Р. **Надста́вить** (acc.). I. **Надставля́ть**. 1. To lengthen (as a sleeve, etc.). 2. To sew on (s.t. to s.t. to lengthen) (acc. + к + dat.).

НАДСТА́ВЬ (imp.), see надста́влю.

НАДУ́ЕШЬ, see наду́ю.

НАДУ́Й (imp.), see наду́ю.

НАДУ́ТЫЙ; наду́т, —а, —о, —ы (ppp), see наду́ю.

НАДУ́Ю, наду́ешь. Р. **Наду́ть** (acc.). I. **Надува́ть** (mean. 1 and 2). 1. To inflate. 2. To swindle, cheat (s.o.). 3. To blow (impers.) and (impers. + acc.).

НАДШЕ́Й (imp.), see надошью́.

НАДШИ́ТЫЙ; надши́т, —а, —о, —ы (ppp), see надошью́.

НАДЫМЛЮ́, надыми́шь. Р. **Надыми́ть**. I. **Дыми́ть**. 1. To smoke, emit smoke (as a stove) (intr.). 2. smoke (as a pipe) (inst.).

НАДЫ́ШАТ, see надышу́.

НАДЫШИ́ (imp.), see надышу́.

НАДЫ́ШИШЬ, see надышу́.

НАДЫШУ́, нады́шишь. Р. **Надыша́ть**. 1. To make the air stuffy or warm with breathing (as in a room, etc.) (в + prep.). 2. To fog with one's breath (as a mirror) (на + acc.).

НАЕ́ДЕННЫЙ; нае́ден, —а, —о, —ы (ppp), see наем.

НАЕ́ДЕШЬ, see нае́ду.

НАЕДИ́М, наеди́те, наедя́т (pl. forms), see наем.

НАЕ́ДУ, нае́дешь. Р. **Нае́хать** (intr.). I. **Наезжа́ть**. 1. To run into (s.o. or s.t.) en route (на + acc.). 2. To arrive (come) in numbers. 3. To arrive unexpectedly, suddenly.

НАЕ́ЗДИ (imp.), see нае́зжу.

НАЕЗЖА́Й (imp.), see нае́ду.

НАЕ́ЗЖЕННЫЙ; нае́зжен, —а, —о, —ы (ppp), see нае́зжу.

НАЕ́ЗЖУ, нае́здишь. Р. **Нае́здить** (acc.). I. **Наезжа́ть** (mean. 1, 2, and 4), **нае́зживать** (mean. 2, 3 and 4). 1. To cover a certain amount of ground in a given time, riding. 2. To pack, smooth (of traffic) (as traffic packs a road). 3. To earn (money) by traveling (of a conductor, etc.). 4. To break a horse.

НАЕ́Л, нае́ла (past), see наем.

НАЕ́М, нае́шь, нае́ст. Р. **Нае́сть**. I.

Наеда́ть. 1. To eat a quantity or given amount of (acc./gen.). 2. (fig.) To acquire from overeating (as, fat, paunch, etc.) (acc.).

НАЕ́СТ, see **нае́м.**

НАЕ́ШЬ[1] (2nd pers. sing.), see **нае́м.**

НАЕ́ШЬ[2] (imp.), see **нае́м.**

НАЖА́ТЫЙ; нажа́т, —а, —о, —ы (ppp), see **нажму́** and **нажну́.**

НАЖГИ́ (imp.), see **нажгу́.**

НАЖГЛА́, нажгло́, нажгли́ (past), see **нажгу́** and **нажёг.**

НАЖГУ́, нажжёшь, нажгу́т. Р. **На-жéчь.** I. **Нажига́ть.** 1. To burn a quantity of (acc./gen.). 2. To burn (as the sun burns the grass, etc.) (acc.). 3. To burn (as a brand) (acc.). 4. To swindle or cheat (s.o.) (acc.).

НАЖЁГ, нажгла́ (past), see **нажгу́.**

НАЖЖЁННЫЙ; нажжён, —а́, —о́, —ы́ (ppp), see **нажгу́.**

НАЖЖЁШЬ, see **кажгу́.**

НАЖИВЁШЬ, see **наживу́.**

НАЖИВИ́ (imp.), see **наживу́** and **наживлю́.**

НАЖИВЛЁННЫЙ; наживлён, —а́, —о́, —ы́ (ppp), see **наживлю́.**

НАЖИВЛЮ́, наживи́шь. Р. **Нажи-ви́ть** (acc.). I. **Наживля́ть.** To bait (as a hook, or a trap).

НАЖИВУ́, наживёшь. Р. **Нажи́ть** (acc.). I. **Нажива́ть.** 1. To acquire, make (e.g., one's growth, money, etc.). 2. (fig.) To contract (as a disease). 3. To live (someplace) for a period of time (intr.).

НА́ЖИТЫЙ; на́жит, —а́, —о, —ы (ppp), see **наживу́.**

НАЖИ́ТЫЙ; нажи́т, —а́, —о, —ы (ppp), see **наживу́.**

НАЖМЁШЬ, see **нажму́.**

НАЖМИ́ (imp.), see **нажму́.**

НАЖМУ́, нажмёшь. Р. **Нажа́ть.** I. **Нажима́ть.** 1. To press, push (acc.). 2. To press on, push on (на + acc.). 3. To squeeze (as juice) (acc./gen.). 4. (fig.) To put pressure on (as s.o., s.t.) (на + acc.). 5. To exert influence (intr.).

НАЖНЁШЬ, see **нажну́.**

НАЖНИ́ (imp.), see **нажну́.**

НАЖНУ́, нажнёшь. Р. **Нажа́ть** (gen./acc.). I. **Нажина́ть.** To reap, harvest a quantity (of s.t.).

НА́ЗВАННЫЙ; на́зван, —а́, —о, —ы (ppp), see **назову́.** ·

НАЗОВЁШЬ, see **назову́.**

НАЗОВИ́ (imp.), see **назову́.**

НАЗОВУ́, назовёшь. Р. **Назва́ть.** I. **Называ́ть.** 1. To name or call (s.o. or s.t.) by a name (acc. + inst.). 2. To name or designate (s.o. or s.t.) (acc.). 3. To invite a number of (as guests) (acc./gen.).

НА́ЙДЕННЫЙ; на́йден, —а, —о, —ы (ppp), see **найду́.**

НАЙДЁШЬ, see **найду́.**

НАЙДИ́ (imp.), see **найду́.**

НАЙДУ́, найдёшь. Р. **Найти́.** I. **Находи́ть.** 1. To find, discover (acc.). 2. To consider (come to a conclusion) (e.g., to consider s.o. healthy) (acc. + inst.). 3. To cover (as clouds cover the sky) (на + acc.). 4. To assemble, come (intr.). 5. To run into (s.o. or s.t.) (на + acc.). 6. (fig.) To come over (s.o.) (as a feeling comes over one) (на + acc.). (For additional meanings see unabridged dictionary.)

НАЙДЯ́ and **наше́дши** (adv. past part.), see **найду́.**

НАЙМЁШЬ, see **найму́.**

НАЙМИ́ (imp.), see **найму́.**

НАЙМУ́, наймёшь. Р. **Наня́ть** (acc.). I. **Нанима́ть.** 1. To hire, employ. 2. To rent.

НАКА́ВЕРЖУ, нака́верзишь. Р. **На-ка́верзить** (dat.). I. **Ка́верзить,** ка́верзничать. To trick, deceive.

НАКА́ВЕРЗИ (imp.), see **нака́верржу.**

НАКА́ЖЕШЬ, see **накажу́.**

НАКАЖИ́ (imp.), see **накажу́.**

НАКАЖУ́, нака́жешь. Р. **Наказа́ть.** I. **Нака́зывать.** 1. To punish (acc.). 2. (arch.) To order (s.o. to do s.t.) (dat. + что́бы + past tense) or (dat. + inf.).

НАКА́ЗАННЫЙ; нака́зан, —а, —о, —ы (ppp), see **накажу́.**

НАКА́ПАЙ (imp.), see **нака́плю.**

НАКА́ПАННЫЙ; нака́пан, —а, —о, —ы (ppp), see **нака́плю.**

НАКА́ПЛЕШЬ, see **нака́плю.**

НАКА́ПЛЮ, нака́плешь (arch. forms) (modern forms: нака́паю, нака́паешь). Р. **Нака́пать.** I. **Ка́пать,** нака́пывать. 1. To pour out by drops (as medicine) (acc./gen.). 2. To spill, spot (s.t. with s.t.) (на + acc. + inst.).

НАКÁЧЕННЫЙ; накáчен, —а, —о, —ы (ppp), see накачу́.
НАКАЧУ́, накáтишь. Р. Накати́ть. I. Накáтывать (mean. 1 thru 6). 1. To roll (s.t. somewhere) (acc.). 2. To roll a quantity of (s.t. somewhere) (acc./gen.). 3. To arrive in numbers (of guests, etc.) (intr.). 4. To strike (as waves strike the shore) (на + acc.). 5. (fig.) To occur, arise (intr.). 6. (fig.) To seize, possess (s.o.) (на + acc.). 7. To make drunk (acc.).
НАКВÁСЬ (imp.), see наквáшу.
НАКВÁШЕННЫЙ; наквáшен, —а, —о, —ы (ppp), see наквáшу.
НАКВÁШУ, наквáсишь. Р. Наквáсить (acc./gen.) I. Наквáщи вать. 1. To prepare a quantity of a fermented food (as sauerkraut). 2. To leaven a quantity of (dough).
НАКИПЍТ, накипя́т (3rd pers. only). Р. Накипéть (intr.). I. Накипáть. 1. To form a scum or scale. 2. (fig.) To seethe, smoulder (as anger seethes in one).
НАКИПЯ́Т, see накипи́т.
НАКИПЯЧЁННЫЙ; накипячён, —á, —ó, —ы́ (ppp), see накипячу́.
НАКИПЯЧУ́, накипяти́шь. Р. Накипяти́ть (acc./gen.). To boil a quantity of.
НАКЛЕВÉЩЕШЬ, see наклевещу́.
НАКЛЕВЕЩЍ (imp.), see наклевещу́.
НАКЛЕВЕЩУ́, наклевéщешь. Р. Наклеветáть (на + acc.). I. Клеветáть. To slander.
НАКЛЁПАННЫЙ; наклёпан, —а, —о, —ы (ppp), see наклеплю́[2].
НАКЛЁПЛЕШЬ, see наклеплю́[1] and [2].
НАКЛЕПЛЍ (imp.), see наклеплю́[1] and [2].
НАКЛЕПЛЮ́[1], наклéплешь. Р. Наклепáть (на + acc.). I. Клепáть. To slander.
НАКЛЕПЛЮ́[2], наклéплешь. (also наклепáю, наклепáешь). Р. Наклепáть. I. Наклёпывать. 1. To rivet (s.t.) (acc.). 2. To rivet a quantity of (acc./gen.).
НАКЛЍКАННЫЙ; накли́кан, —а, —о, —ы (ppp), see накли́чу.
НАКЛЍЧЕШЬ, see накли́чу.
НАКЛЍЧУ, накли́кать (acc.). I. Накликáть. To court, call down (e.g., disaster).

НАКЛЍЧЬ (imp.), see накли́чу.
НАКÓЛЕШЬ, see наколю́.
НАКОЛЍ (imp.), see наколю́.
НАКÓЛОТЫЙ; накóлот, —а, —о, —ы (ppp), see наколю́.
НАКОЛÓЧЕННЫЙ; наколóчен, —а, —о, —ы (ppp), see наколочу́.
НАКОЛОЧУ́, наколóтишь. Р. Наколоти́ть. I. Накалáчивать. 1. To knock (s.t. on s.t.) (as a hoop on barrel) (acc. + на + acc.). 2. To nail (as a board to a fence) (acc.). 3. To drive in a quantity of (as nails in a board) (acc./gen. + в + acc.). 4. To break a quantity of (as dishes) (acc./gen.). 5. To shoot a number of (as ducks, etc.) (acc./gen.). 6. To beat, thrash (s.o., s.t.) (acc.). 7. To accumulate, scrape together (as money) (acc./gen.).
НАКОЛЮ́, накóлешь. Р. Наколóть. I. Накáлывать. 1. To break a quantity of (as sugar loafs) (acc./gen.). 2. To chop a quantity of (as wood) (acc./gen.). 3. To kill, slaughter, stab a quantity of (as cattle) (acc./gen.). 4. To pin, fasten with a pin (acc.). 5. To prick (as one's finger (acc.). 6. To stick a number of (s.t. in s.t.) (as pins in a pincushion) (acc./gen.).
НАКÓПЛЕННЫЙ; накóплен, —а, —о, —ы (ppp), see накоплю́.
НАКОПЛЮ́, накóпишь. Р. Накопи́ть (acc./gen.). I. Копи́ть (acc.). 1. To accumulate, lay in a supply. 2. To save up, lay away (as money). 3. (fig.) To store up (as memories).
НАКОПЧЁННЫЙ; накопчён, —á, —ó, —ы́ (ppp), see накопчу́.
НАКОПЧУ́, накопти́шь. Р. Накопти́ть. I. Копти́ть (mean. 1, 2) (acc.), (mean. 3) (intr.), накáпчивать (mean. 1 and 2). 1. To blacken with smoke (acc./gen.). 2. To cure in smoke (as a quantity of hams) (acc./gen.). 3. To smoke (of a stove, etc.) (intr.).
НАКÓРМЛЕННЫЙ; накóрмлен, —а, —о, —ы (ppp), see накормлю́.
НАКОРМЛЮ́, накóрмишь. Р. Накорми́ть (acc.). I. Корми́ть. 1. To feed. 2. To nurse (as an infant).
НАКÓШЕННЫЙ; накóшен, —а, —о, —ы (ppp), see накошу́.
НАКОШУ́, накóсишь. Р. Накоси́ть

(acc./gen.). To mow a quantity of.

НАКРÁВ and **накрадя́** (adv. past part.), see **накраду́**.

НАКРÁДЕННЫЙ; накрáден, —а, —о, —ы (ppp), see **накраду́**.

НАКРÁДЕШЬ, see **накраду́**.

НАКРАДИ́ (imp.), see **накраду́**.

НАКРАДУ́, накрадёшь. Р. **Накрáсть** (gen./acc.). I. **Накрáдывать**. To steal a quantity of.

НАКРАДЯ́ and **накрáв** (adv. past part.), see **накраду́**.

НАКРÁЛ, накрáла (past), see **накраду́**.

НАКРÁСЬ (imp.), see **накрáшу**.

НАКРÁШЕННЫЙ; накрáшен, —а, —о, —ы (ppp), see **накрáшу**.

НАКРÁШУ, накрáсишь. Р. **Накрáсить**. I. **Накрáшивать**. 1. To make up (one's face, eyebrows, etc.) (acc.). 2. To paint or dye a quantity of (acc./gen.).

НАКРИЧÁТ, see **накричу́**.

НАКРИЧИ́ (imp.), see **накричу́**.

НАКРИЧИ́ШЬ, see **накричу́**.

НАКРИЧУ́, накричи́шь. Р. **Накричáть**. 1. To shout (intr.). 2. To reprimand (s.o.) sharply, in a loud voice (на + acc.). 3. To talk a lot about (о + prep.).

НАКРÓЕШЬ, see **накрóю**.

НАКРÓЙ (imp.), see **накрóю**.

НАКРÓЮ, накрóешь. Р. **Накры́ть** (acc.). I. **Накрывáть**. 1. To cover (with) (acc. + inst.). 2. To catch in the act (as a criminal in the act).

НАКРУ́ЧЕННЫЙ; накрýчен, —а, о, —ы (ppp), see **накручу́**.

НАКРУЧУ́, накру́тишь. Р. **Накрути́ть**. I. **Накру́чивать**. 1. To wind (as wire on a spool) (acc.). 2. To screw (as a nut on a bolt) (acc. + на + acc.). 3. To twist, make (as rope) (acc./gen.). 4. To put on too much (jewelry, clothes, etc.) (acc./gen.). 5. (fig.) To say, do, "dream up" (s.t. complex and unusual) (acc./gen.).

НАКРЫ́ТЫЙ; накры́т, —а, —о, —ы (ppp), see **накрóю**.

НАКУ́ПЛЕННЫЙ; накýплен, —а, —о, —ы (ppp), see **накуплю́**.

НАКУПЛЮ́, накýпишь. Р. **Накупи́ть** (acc./gen.). I. **Накупáть**. To buy a quantity of, a lot of.

НАЛÁДЬ (imp.), see **налáжу**.

НАЛÁЖЕННЫЙ; налáжен, —а, —о, —ы (ppp), see **налáжу**.

НАЛÁЖУ, налáдишь. Р. **Налáдить** ге-(acc.). I. **Налáживать**. 1. To mend, pair. 2. To adjust (as a machine). 3. To arrange, organize (as production, etc.). 4. To tune (as a piano). 5. (fig.) To reconcile, to attune. 6. (arch.) To send. 7. To start repeating the same thing over and over (intr.) or (acc.).

НАЛГИ́ (imp.), see **налгу́**.

НАЛГУ́, налжёшь, налгýт. Р. **Налгáть**. 1. To lie, tell lies (intr.) 2. To slander (на + acc.).

НАЛЁГ, налеглá (past), see **наля́гу**.

НАЛЁЖАННЫЙ; налёжан, —а, —о, —ы (ppp), see **належу́**.

НАЛЕЖÁТ, see **належу́**.

НАЛЕЖИ́ (imp.), see **належу́**.

НАЛЕЖИ́ШЬ, see **належу́**.

НАЛЕЖУ́, належи́шь. Р. **Належáть** (acc.). I. **Налёживать**. To cause a sore spot on a part of the body by lying on it too long (as a sore on one's hip) (acc. of sore).

НАЛЁЗ, налéзла (past), see **налéзет**.

НАЛЁЗЕТ, налéзут (3rd pers. only). Р. **Налéзть** (intr.). I. **Налезáть**. 1. To collect, accumulate (of flies, people, etc.) (intr.). 2. To fit (of clothing, etc.) (as shoes fit one's foot) (на + acc.). 3. To slide or climb up or down (as a hat slides down one's forehead) (на + acc.). 4. To climb up (as up a ladder) (на + acc.).

НАЛÉЗУТ (3rd pers. pl.), see **налéзет**.

НАЛÉЙ (imp.), see **налью́**.

НАЛÉПЛЕННЫЙ; налéплен, —а, —о, —ы (ppp), see **налеплю́**.

НАЛЕПЛЮ́, налéпишь. Р. **Налепи́ть** (acc.). I. **Лепи́ть** (mean. 2). 1. To model, sculpture a quantity of. 2. To stick (s.t. to s.t.), make adhere.

НАЛЕТИ́ (imp.), see **налечу́**.

НАЛЕТИ́ШЬ, see **налечу́**.

НАЛЕТЯ́Т, see **налечу́**.

НАЛЕЧУ́, налети́шь. Р. **Налетéть**. I. **Налетáть**. 1. To fly into (s.t.) (на/в + acc.). 2. To swoop down on, attack (of birds, planes, cavalry, etc.) (на + acc.). 3. To come flying in (in large numbers) (of flies, locusts, planes, etc.) (intr.). 4. To bump into (на + acc.). 5. To attack (as in a speech) (на + acc.). 6. To come suddenly, appear (of squalls, wind, storms, etc.) (intr.). 7. To accumulate (e.g., dust, leaves) (intr.).

НАЛЖЁШЬ, see налгу́.

НАЛИ́ЖЕШЬСЯ, see налижу́сь.

НАЛИЖИ́СЬ (imp.), see налижу́сь.

НАЛИЖУ́СЬ, нали́жешься. Р. Нализа́ться (intr.). I. Нали́зываться. 1. To lick (s.t.) to one's hearts content (gen.). 2. To get drunk (intr.).

НА́ЛИТЫЙ; на́лит, —а́, —о, —ы (ppp), see налью́.

НАЛИ́ТЫЙ; нали́т, —а́, —о, —ы (ppp), see налью́.

НАЛО́ВЛЕННЫЙ; нало́влен, —а, —о, —ы (ppp), see наловлю́.

НАЛОВЛЮ́, нало́вишь. Р. Налови́ть (acc./gen.). I. Нала́вливать. To catch a quantity of (as fish).

НАЛЬЁШЬ, see налью́.

НАЛЬЮ́, нальёшь. Р. Нали́ть. I. Налива́ть. 1. To pour (as a cup of tea) (acc. + gen.). 2. To pour (as tea into a cup) (gen. + в + acc.). 3. To fill (as the cup with tea) (acc. + inst.). 4. To spill (as tea on the table) (acc. + на + acc.).

НАЛЯ́Г (imp.), see наля́гу.

НАЛЯ́ГУ, наля́жешь, наля́гут. Р. Нале́чь (intr.) (на + acc.). I. Налега́ть. 1. To lean on. 2. To overlie (as one stratum overlies another). 3. To exert influence on. 4. To apply o.s. (as to one's studies, etc.). 5. (fig.) To lie on (as on one's conscience).

НАЛЯ́ЖЕШЬ, see наля́гу.

НАМАГНИ́ТЬ (imp.), see намагни́чу.

НАМАГНИ́ЧЕННЫЙ; намагни́чен, —а, —о, —ы (ppp), see намагни́чу.

НАМАГНИ́ЧУ, намагни́тишь. Р. Намагни́тить (acc.). I. Намагни́чивать. To magnetize.

НАМА́ЕШЬСЯ, see нама́юсь.

НАМА́ЖЕШЬ, see нама́жу.

НАМА́ЖУ, нама́жешь. Р. Нама́зать. I. Ма́зать (mean. 1 thru 3), нама́зывать (mean. 1 thru 3). 1. To grease, lubricate (with) (acc. + inst.). 2. To butter, spread with butter (acc.) or (acc. + inst.). 3. To apply (as makeup to one's face) (acc. of face + inst. of makeup). 4. To soil (на + acc.). 5. To write poorly, paint poorly (intr.) or (acc./gen.).

НАМА́ЖЬ (imp.), see нама́жу.

НАМА́ЗАННЫЙ; нама́зан, —а, —о, —ы (ppp), see нама́жу.

НАМА́ЙСЯ (imp.), see нама́юсь.

НАМА́ЮСЬ, нама́ешься. Р. Нама́яться (intr.). (lit. and fig.) To become exhausted, worn out.

НАМЁЛ, намела́ (past), see намету́.

НАМЕ́ЛЕШЬ, see наме́лю.

НАМЕЛИ́ (imp.), see наме́лю.

НАМЕ́ЛЮ, наме́лешь. Р. Намоло́ть (acc./gen.). I. Нама́лывать (mean. 1). 1. To mill or grind a quantity of. 2. (fig.) To talk a lot (of nonsense).

НАМЁРЗ, намёрзла (past). Р. Намёрзнуть (intr.). I. Намерза́ть. 1. To freeze on the surface of (s.t.) (as ice, snow freezes on a window, etc.) (на + prep.). 2. To become very cold (of one's hands, etc.).

НАМЁТАННЫЙ; намётан, —а, —о, —ы (ppp), see намечу́.

НАМЕТЁННЫЙ; наметён, —а́, —о́, —ы́ (ppp), see намету́.

НАМЕТЁШЬ, see намету́.

НАМЕТИ́ (imp.), see намету́.

НАМЕТУ́, наметёшь. Р. Намести́ (gen./acc.). I. Намета́ть. 1. To sweep together (a quantity of). 2. To drift (a quantity of) (as wind drifts snow).

НАМЁТШИЙ (pap), see намету́.

НАМЁТЬ (imp.), see намечу́.

НАМЕТЯ́ (adv. past part.), see намету́.

НАМЕ́ЧЕННЫЙ; наме́чен, —а, —о, —ы (ppp), see наме́чу.

НАМЕ́ЧЕШЬ, see наме́чу.

НАМЕЧИ́ (imp.), see наме́чу.

НАМЕ́ЧУ, наме́тишь. Р. Наме́тить. I. Намеча́ть (mean. 3, 5, 6), ме́тить (mean. 1, 4). 1. To aim at (в + acc.). 2. To aim (e.g., a gun at s.t.) (acc. + на + acc.). 3. To nominate (acc.). 4. To mark (as a page, clothing, etc.) (acc.). 5. To outline, plan (acc.). 6. To determine, fix (acc.).

НАМЕЧУ́, наме́чешь. Р. Намета́ть. I. Намётывать. 1. To pile (up) (as hay) (acc./gen.). 2. To spawn (acc./gen.). 3. To acquire (a skill in) (acc. of "hand" + на + prep.). 4. To acquire (an eye for) (acc. of eye + на + prep.).

НАМЕ́ШЕННЫЙ; наме́шен, —а, —о, —ы (ppp), see намешу́.

НАМЕШУ́, наме́сишь. Р. Намеси́ть

(acc./gen.). I. Наме́шивать. To knead a quantity of (as dough, clay, etc.).

НАМНЁШЬ, see намну́.

НАМНИ́ (imp.), see намну́.

НАМНУ́, намнёшь. Р. Намя́ть. I. Намина́ть. 1. To knead (as bread, clay, etc.) (acc./gen.). 2. To trample down (as grass) (acc./gen.). 3. To rub, pinch (as shows pinch feet) (acc.).

НАМО́ЕШЬ, see намо́ю.

НАМО́Й (imp.), see намо́ю.

НАМО́К, намо́кла (past). Р. Намо́кнуть (intr.). I. Намока́ть. To become wet.

НАМО́ЛОТЫЙ; намо́лот, —а, —о, —ы (ppp), see намелю́.

НАМОЛО́ЧЕННЫЙ; намоло́чен, —а, —о, —ы (ppp), see намолочу́.

НАМОЛОЧУ́, намоло́тишь. Р. Намолоти́ть (gen./acc.). I. Намола́чивать. To thresh a quantity of.

НАМОЩЁННЫЙ; намощён, —а́, —о́, —ы́ (ppp), see намощу́.

НАМОЩУ́, намости́шь. Р. Намости́ть (acc.). I. Мости́ть. 1. To pave (with a hard surface material). 2. To pave or lay (with planks, logs, etc.).

НАМО́Ю, намо́ешь. Р. Намы́ть (acc./gen.). I. Намыва́ть. 1. To wash a quantity of (as dishes). 2. To wash, pan (gold dust). 3. To construct by hydraulic means (as hydraulic fill, etc.).

НАМУЧУ́, намути́шь (and наму́тишь). Р. Намути́ть. 1. To make turbid (e.g., water) (acc.). 2. To cause alarm, turmoil, anxiety, etc. (intr.).

НАМЫ́ТЫЙ; намы́т, —а, —о, —ы (ppp), see намо́ю.

НАМЯ́ТЫЙ; намя́т, —а, —о, —ы (ppp), see намну́.

НАНЁС, нанесла́ (past), see нанесу́.

НАНЕСЁННЫЙ; нанесён, —а́, —о́, —ы́ (ppp), see нанесу́.

НАНЕСЁШЬ, see нанесу́.

НАНЕСИ́ (imp.), see нанесу́.

НАНЕСУ́, нанесёшь. Р. Нанести́. I. Наноси́ть (mean. 1 thru 7). 1. To bring quantities of (s.t.) (acc./gen.). 2. To drift (as wind drifts snow against s.t.) (acc. + на + acc.). 3. To dash, carry (as wind dashes a ship

on the rocks) (acc. + на + acc.) or (a ship is dashed against the rocks) (impers. + acc. of ship + на + acc.). 4. To reach (s.o.) (as the odor of tobacco reaches one) (impers. + acc. of odor + на + acc.). 5. To mark or note (s.t.) (as on a map) (acc. + на + acc.). 6. To cover the surface (of s.t. with a layer of s.t.) (e.g., to put oil on a gun) (acc. of oil + на + acc. of gun). 7. To cause, inflict (s.t. on s.o.) (as an insult) (acc. + dat. of s.o.). 8. To lay (eggs) in quantities (acc./gen.). (For other meanings see unabridged dictionary.)

НАНЕСЯ́ (adv. past part.), see нанесу́.

НАНИ́ЖЕШЬ, see нанижу́.

НАНИЖИ́ (imp.), see нанижу́.

НАНИЖУ́, нани́жешь. Р. Наниза́ть (acc.). I. Низа́ть, нани́зывать. To string, thread (e.g., beads).

НАНИ́ЗАННЫЙ; нани́зан, —а, —о, —ы (ppp), see нанижу́.

НАНО́ШЕННЫЙ; нано́шен, —а, —о, —ы (ppp), see наношу́².

НАНОШУ́¹, нано́сишь. I. Наноси́ть. Р. Нанести́. 1. To bring quantities of (s.t.) (acc./gen.). 2. To drift (as wind drifts snow against s.t.) (acc. + на + acc.). 3. To dash; carry (as wind dashes a ship on the rocks) (acc. + на + acc.) or (a ship is dashed against the rocks) (impers. + acc. of ship + на + acc.). 4. To reach (s.o.) (as the odor of tobacco reaches one) (impers. + acc. of odor + на + acc.). 5. To mark or note (s.t.) (as on a map) (acc. + на + acc.). 6. To cover the surface (of s.t. with a layer of s.t.) (e.g., to put oil on a gun) (acc. of oil + на + acc. of gun). 7. To cause, inflict (s.t. on s.o.) (as an insult) (acc. + dat. of s.o.). (For other meanings see unabridged dictionary.)

НАНОШУ́², нано́сишь. Р. Наноси́ть (acc./gen.). I. Нана́шивать. To bring (a quantity of).

НА́НЯТЫЙ; на́нят, —а́, —о, —ы (ppp). Р. Наня́ть (acc.). I. Нанима́ть. 1. To hire, employ. 2. To rent (also see найму́).

НАОРЁШЬ, see наору́.

НАОРИ́ (imp.), see наору́.

НАОРУ́, наорёшь. Р. Наора́ть. 1. To

shout (intr.). 2. To shout at, berate
(на + acc.).
НАПАДЁШЬ, see нападу́.
НАПАДИ́ (imp.), see нападу́.
НАПАДУ́, нападёшь. Р. Напа́сть
(на + acc.). I. Напада́ть. 1. (lit.
and fig.) To attack, fall upon. 2. To
come upon, discover. 3. To come
over (s.o.) (as a feeling). 4. To fall
(3rd pers. only) (as snow).
НАПА́КОСТИ (imp.), see напа́кощу.
НАПА́КОЩЕННЫЙ; напа́кощен,
—а, —о, —ы (ppp), see напа́кощу.
НАПА́КОЩУ, напа́костишь. Р. На-
па́костить. I. Па́костить. 1. To soil,
dirty (acc.). 2. To play a mean
trick (on s.o.) (dat.).
НАПА́Л, напа́ла (past), see нападу́.
НАПА́С, напасла́ (past), see напасу́.
НАПАСЁННЫЙ; напасён, —а́, —о́,
—ы́ (ppp), see напасу́.
НАПАСЁШЬ, see напасу́.
НАПАСИ́ (imp.), see напасу́.
НАПАСУ́, напасёшь. Р. Напасти́
(acc./gen.). I. Напаса́ть. To lay in a
stock (of s.t.).
НАПА́ХАННЫЙ; напа́хан, —а, —о,
—ы (ppp), see напашу́.
НАПА́ШЕШЬ, see напашу́.
НАПАШИ́ (imp.), see напашу́.
НАПАШУ́, напа́шешь. Р. Напаха́ть
(acc./gen.). I. Напа́хивать. To plow
(a large area, a number of acres,
etc.).
НАПЕ́ЙСЯ (imp.). Р. Напи́ться. I.
Напива́ться. 1. To quench one's
thirst, to have (s.t.) to drink (gen.)
or (intr.). 2. To get drunk (intr.).
(Also see напью́сь.)
НАПЁК, напекла́ (past), see напеку́.
НАПЕКИ́ (imp.), see напеку́.
НАПЕКУ́, напечёшь, напеку́т. Р.
Напе́чь. I. Напека́ть. 1. To bake a
quantity of (acc./gen.). 2. To over-
heat (of the sun) (as one becomes
overheated in the sun) (impers. +
acc.).
НАПЁР, напёрла (past), see напру́.
НАПЕРЁВ (adv. past part.), see
напру́.
НАПЁРШИ (adv. past part.), see
напру́.
НАПЕ́ТЫЙ; напе́т, —а, —о, —ы
(ppp), see напою́.
НАПЕЧЁННЫЙ; напечён, —а́, —о́,
—ы́ (ppp), see напеку́.

НАПЕЧЁШЬ, see напеку́.
НАПИ́САННЫЙ; напи́сан, —а, —о,
—ы (ppp), see напишу́.
НАПИ́ШЕШЬ, see напишу́.
НАПИШИ́ (imp.), see напишу́.
НАПИШУ́, напи́шешь. Р. Написа́ть
(intr.) or (acc.). I. Писа́ть. 1. To
write. 2. To paint (as an artist).
НАПЛА́КАННЫЙ; напла́кан, —а,
—о, —ы (ppp), see напла́чу.
НАПЛА́ЧЕШЬ, see напла́чу.
НАПЛА́ЧУ, напла́чешь. Р. Напла́-
кать. 1. To become red-eyed from
crying (acc. of eyes). 2. To shed a
lot of tears (acc./gen.) or (intr.).
НАПЛА́ЧЬ (imp.), see напла́чу.
НАПЛЁЛ, наплела́ (past), see на-
плету́.
НАПЛЁСКАННЫЙ; наплёскан, —а,
—о, —ы (ppp), see наплещу́.
НАПЛЕТЁННЫЙ; наплетён, —а́,
—о́, —ы́ (ppp), see наплету́.
НАПЛЕТЁШЬ, see наплету́.
НАПЛЕТИ́ (imp.), see наплету́.
НАПЛЕТУ́, наплетёшь. Р. Наплести́.
I. Наплета́ть. 1. To weave, make
(as baskets, lace, etc.) (gen./acc.).
2. To slander, gossip (about s.o.)
(на + acc.). 3. To talk a lot (of
nonsense) (acc./gen.) or (intr.).
НАПЛЁТШИЙ (pap), see наплету́.
НАПЛЕТЯ́ (adv. past part.), see
наплету́.
НАПЛЁЩЕШЬ, see наплещу́.
НАПЛЕЩИ́ (imp.), see наплещу́.
НАПЛЕЩУ́, наплё́щешь. Р. На-
плеска́ть (acc./gen.). I. Наплёски-
вать. To spill (as water).
НАПЛОЖЁННЫЙ; напложён, —а́,
—о́, —ы́ (ppp), see напложу́.
НАПЛОЖУ́, наплоди́шь. Р. На-
ПЛОДИ́ТЬ (acc./gen.). To give
birth to, bear, breed a number of
(as animals, insects, etc.).
НАПЛЫВЁШЬ, see наплыву́.
НАПЛЫВИ́ (imp.), see наплыву́.
НАПЛЫВУ́, наплывёшь. Р. На-
плы́ть (intr.). I. Наплыва́ть. 1.
To strike against (s.t.) (swimming,
drifting, or floating) (на + acc.). 2.
To drift over (as clouds drift over
the sun) (на + acc.). 3. To drift (of
sound, odor, etc.). 4. To accumulate
(as scum).
НАПОЁШЬ, see напою́.
НАПОЙ (imp.), see напою́.

НАПÓЛЗ, наползá (past), see наползý.
НАПОЛЗЁШЬ, see наползý.
НАПОЛЗЙ (imp.), see ноползý.
НАПОЛЗУ́, наползёшь. Р. Наползти́
(intr.). I. Наползáть. 1. To crawl,
creep across, against, over, etc.
(of clouds, animals, etc.) (на +
acc.). 2. To come crawling in large
numbers (of insects, etc.) (3rd pers.
only).
НАПОМÁДЬ (imp.), see напомáжу.
НАПОМÁЖЕННЫЙ; напомáжен,
—а, —о, —ы (ppp), see напомáжу.
НАПОМÁЖУ, напомáдишь. Р. На-
помáдить (acc.). I. Помáдить. To
apply pomade (to one's hair).
НАПÓРЕШЬ, see напорю́.
НАПОРЙ (imp.), see напорю́.
НАПÓРОТЫЙ; напóрот, —а, —о,
—ы (ppp), see напорю́.
НАПÓРТИ (imp.), see напóрчу.
НАПÓРТЬ (imp.), see напóрчу.
НАПÓРЧЕННЫЙ; напóрчен, —а,
—о, —ы (ppp), see напóрчу.
НАПÓРЧУ, напóртишь. Р. Напóр-
тить. 1. To spoil (a quantity of s.t.)
(acc./gen.). 2. To bungle, wreck
(as plans, work, etc.) (dat.). 3. To
do (s.o.) much harm (dat.).
НАПОРЮ́, напóрешь. Р. Напорóть.
I. Напáрывать (mean. 1 and 2).
1. To rip (as one's clothes) (acc./gen.).
2. To injure (o.s. on s.t. sharp) (as
one's leg on a nail, splinter, etc.)
(acc. + на + acc.). 3. To talk a lot
(of nonsense) (acc. of nonsense).
НАПОЮ́, напоёшь. Р. Напéть. I.
Напевáть. 1. To sing (as songs,
arias, etc.) (acc./gen.). 2. To record
(as one's voice on tape) (acc. +
на + acc.). 3. To make a record
(acc. of record). 4. To gossip (intr.);
To relate as gossip (acc./gen.).
НАПРÁВЛЕННЫЙ; напрáвлен, —а,
—о, —ы (ppp), see напрáвлю.
НАПРÁВЛЮ, напрáвишь. Р. На-
прáвить (acc.). I. Направля́ть. 1. To
direct (s.t. at s.o. or s.t.) (acc. +
на + acc.). 2. (fig.) To direct, refer
(s.o. to s.o. or s.t.) (acc. + к +
dat.). 3. To send (s.o. or s.t. to s.o.
or someplace) (acc. + к + dat.) or
(acc. + в/на + acc.). 4. To sharpen
(as a razor). 5. To put in order,

organize, set right (as work, an
affair).
НАПРÁВЬ (imp.), see напрáвлю.
НАПРЁШЬ, see напру́.
НАПРЙ (imp.), see напру́.
НАПРОКÁЖУ, напрокáзишь. Р. На-
прокáзить (intr.). I. Прокáзить. To
play pranks, be naughty.
НАПРОКÁЗЬ (imp.), see напрокáжу.
НАПРОШУ́СЬ, напрóсишься. Р. На-
проси́ться. I. Напрáшиваться. 1.
To invite o.s. (e.g., to dinner)
(на + acc.), (for a visit) (в +
гóсти). 2. To invite (as a compliment) (на + acc.). 3. To expend
time and effort in requesting (s.t.)
(gen. of s.t.). 4. To expend time and
effort in obtaining (a high price for
s.t.) (gen. of price).
НАПРУ́, напрёшь. Р. Наперéть (на
+ acc.). I. Напирáть. 1. To press
(on s.t. or s.o.). 2. (fig.) To put
pressure on (s.o.).
НАПРЯ́Г, напрягла́ (past), see на-
прягу́.
НАПРЯГЙ (imp.), see напрягу́.
НАПРЯГУ́, напряжёшь, напрягу́т.
Р. Напря́чь (acc.). I. Напрягáть.
1. (lit. and fig.) To strain, exert. 2. To
stretch, flex.
НАПРЯЖЁННЫЙ; напряжён, —á,
—ó, —ы́ (ppp), see напрягу́.
НАПРЯЖЁШЬ, see напрягу́.
НАПУ́ЩЕННЫЙ; напу́щен, а, о,
—ы (ppp), see напущу́.
НАПУЩУ́, напу́стишь. Р. Напусти́ть.
I. Напускáть. 1. To let in, admit, fill
(with) (as people, water, etc.) (acc./
gen.). 2. To affect (as indifference)
(acc. + на + себя́). 3. To let loose
(on) (as dogs on people) (acc. +
на + acc.). 4. To terrify (s.o.) (acc.
of fear + на + acc. of s.o.) (страх
на кого́).
НАПЬЁШЬСЯ, see напьюсь.
НАПЬЮ́СЬ, напьёшься. Р. Напи́ться.
I. Напивáться. 1. To quench one's
thirst; to have (s.t.) to drink (gen.)
or (intr.). 2. To get drunk
(intr.).
НАРАСТЁТ, нарасту́т (3rd pers. only).
Р. Нарасти́ (intr.). I. Нарастáть. 1.
To grow (on the surface of s.t.) (на +
prep.). 2. To grow in quantity (of
trees in a forest, etc.). 3. To accumulate, increase (of interest, debts, etc.).

4. To grow, intensify, increase (as noise, etc.).

НАРАСТУ́Т, see нарастёт.

НАРАЩЁННЫЙ; наращён, —а́, —о́, —ы́ (ppp), see наращу́.

НАРАЩУ́, нарасти́шь. Р. Нарасти́ть. I. Нара́щивать. 1. To grow a quantity of (as vegetables) (acc./gen.). 2. To build up, develop (as muscles, etc.) (acc.). 3. To increase, lengthen (e.g., a pipe, cable) (acc.). 4. To add (e.g., 10 feet to a cable) (acc.). 5. To accumulate (as interest, debts, etc.) (acc.).

НА́РВАННЫЙ; на́рван, —а, —о, —ы (ppp), see нарву́.

НАРВЁТ, нарву́т (3rd pers. only). Р. Нарва́ть (intr.). I. Нарыва́ть. To swell and fester.

НАРВЁШЬ, see нарву́.

НАРВИ́ (imp.), see нарву́.

НАРВУ́, нарвёшь. Р. Нарва́ть (acc./gen.). 1. To pick (as flowers). 2. To tear to pieces a quantity of (s.t.). 3. To obtain by blasting (as ore).

НАРВУ́Т, see нарвёт and нарву́.

НАРЕ́ЖЕШЬ, see наре́жу.

НАРЕ́ЖУ, наре́жешь. Р. Наре́зать (acc./gen.). I. Нареза́ть, наре́зывать. 1. To cut into pieces. 2. To slice, carve. 3. To cut thread(s) (as on screws, etc.). 4. To subdivide (as land). 5. To kill (as chickens, etc.). 6. To cut or slice a quantity of. 7. (fig.) To cut (as a strap cuts one's shoulder).

НАРЕ́ЖЬ (imp.), see наре́жу.

НАРЕ́ЗАННЫЙ; наре́зан, —а, —о, —ы (ppp), see наре́жу.

НАРЕ́К, нарекла́ (past), see нареку́.

НАРЕКИ́ (imp.), see нареку́.

НАРЕКУ́, наречёшь, нареку́т. Р. Наре́чь. I. Нарека́ть. To name (e.g., S. O. John) (acc. of s.o. + inst. of John) or (dat. of s.o. + acc. of name, John, i.e., кому + и́мя + Ива́н).

НАРЕЧЁННЫЙ; наречён, —а́, —о́, —ы́ (ppp), see нареку́.

НАРЕЧЁННЫЙ; наречён, —а́, —о́, —ы́ (ppp), see нареку́.

НАРЕЧЁШЬ, see нареку́.

НАРО́ЕШЬ, see наро́ю.

НАРОЖДЁННЫЙ; нарождён, —а́, —о́, —ы́ (ppp), see нарожу́.

НАРОЖУ́, народи́шь. Р. Народи́ть (acc./gen.). To give birth (to a number of).

НАРО́Й (imp.), see наро́ю.

НАРО́С, наросла́ (past), see нарастёт.

НАРО́Ю, наро́ешь. Р. Нары́ть (acc./gen.). I. Нарыва́ть. 1. To dig (as trenches). 2. To dig a quantity of (as potatoes).

НАРУ́БЛЕННЫЙ; нару́блен, —а, —о, —ы (ppp), see нарублю́.

НАРУБЛЮ́, нару́бишь. Р. Наруби́ть (acc./gen.). I. Наруба́ть. 1. To chop a quantity of. 2. To chop down, fell a quantity.

НАРЫ́ТЫЙ; нары́т, —а, —о, —ы (ppp), see наро́ю.

НАРЯ́ЖЕННЫЙ; наря́жен, —а, —о, —ы (ppp), see наряжу́[1].

НАРЯЖЁННЫЙ; наряжён, —а́, —о́, —ы́ (ppp), see наряжу́[2].

НАРЯЖУ́[1], наря́дишь (and наряди́шь). Р. Наряди́ть. I. Наряжа́ть. 1. To dress up (s.o.) (acc.). 2. To dress (s.o. as s.t. or s.o.) (acc. + inst.). 3. To dress, array (s.o. in s.t.) (acc. + в + acc.).

НАРЯЖУ́[2], наряди́шь. Р. Наряди́ть (acc.). I. Наряжа́ть. 1. To detail (s.o. to some duty) (acc. + в + acc.). 2. To order (e.g., s.o. to do s.t.) (acc. + inf.). 3. To order (as an investigation, trial, etc.) (acc.). 4. To send (e.g., s.o. somewhere) (acc.).

НАСА́ЖЕННЫЙ; наса́жен, —а, —о, —ы (ppp), see насажу́.

НАСАЖУ́, наса́дишь. Р. Насади́ть. I. Наса́живать (mean. 1 thru 6), насажда́ть (mean. 7 and 8). 1. To seat a number of people (acc./gen.). 2. To plant a quantity (as flowers, etc.) (acc./gen.). 3. To plant (as an area with flowers) (acc. of area + inst. of flowers). 4. To stick, impale (as on a hook, spit) (acc. + на + acc.). 5. To haft (as an axe) (acc. of axe head + на + acc. of handle). 6. To put on (e.g., one's glasses on one's nose) (acc. + на + acc.). 7. To disseminate (as ideas) (acc.). 8. To inculcate (e.g., s.t. in s.o.), (acc. + в + acc.).

НАСЕ́ЕШЬ, see насе́ю.

НАСЕ́Й (imp.), see насе́ю.

НАСЕ́К, насекла́ (past), see насеку́.

НАСЕКИ́ (imp.), see насеку́.

НАСЕКУ́, насечёшь, насеку́т. Р.

Насе́чь. I. Насека́ть. 1. To incise, groove (e.g., metal, a file, etc.) (acc.). 2. To hatch, frost (acc.). 3. To notch (acc.). 4. To carve (e.g., one's initials on the surface of s.t.) (acc./gen. + на + acc.). 5. To damascene (acc.). 6. To cut into small pieces (e.g., cabbage) (acc./gen.).

НАСЁЛ, насе́ла (past). Р. Насе́сть (intr.). I. Населда́ть (mean. 1, 2, 3), насла́живаться (mean. 4). 1. To settle, collect (of dust, etc.). 2. To lean all one's weight on (на + acc.). 3. (fig.) To press (e.g., s.o. with questions) (на + acc.). 4. To sit, take seats, in large numbers (в/на + acc.). (Also see нася́ду.)

НАСЕЧЁННЫЙ; насечён, —а́, —о́, —ы́ (ppp), see насеку́.

НАСЕЧЁШЬ, see насеку́.

НАСЕ́Ю, насе́ешь. Р. Насе́ять (acc./gen.). I. Насева́ть, насе́ивать. 1. To sow a quantity of (as grain). 2. To sift, screen, a quantity of (as flour).

НАСЕ́ЯННЫЙ; насе́ян, —а, —о, —ы (ppp), see насе́ю.

НАСИДИ́ (imp.), see насижу́.

НАСИ́ЖЕННЫЙ; наси́жен, —а, —о, —ы (ppp) see насижу́.

НАСИЖУ́, насиди́шь. Р. Насиде́ть (acc.). I. Наси́живать. 1. To hatch (eggs). 2. To warm (as a seat from sitting). 3. To cause, from too much sitting (e.g., some illness or discomfort, as hemorrhoids).

НАСКА́ЖЕШЬ, see наскажу́.

НАСКАЖИ́ (imp.), see наскажу́.

НАСКАЖУ́, наска́жешь. Р. Наска-за́ть. I. Наска́зывать. 1. To tell, relate a lot of (as news, gossip, etc.) (acc./gen.). 2. To gossip about, slander (s.o.) (на + acc.).

НАСКА́ЗАННЫЙ; наска́зан, —а, —о, —ы (ppp), see наскажу́.

НАСКА́ЧЕШЬ, see наскачу́.

НАСКАЧИ́ (imp.), see наскачу́.

НАСКАЧУ́, наска́чешь. Р. Наскака́ть (intr.). I. Наска́кивать. 1. To run into, collide with, strike (s.t.) (на + acc.). 2. To arrive in numbers at a gallop.

НАСКРЁБ, наскребла́ (past), see наскребу́.

НАСКРЕБЁННЫЙ; наскребён, —а́, —о́, —ы́ (ppp) see наскребу́.

НАСКРЕБЁШЬ, see наскребу́.

НАСКРЕБИ́ (imp.), see наскребу́.

НАСКРЕБУ́, наскребёшь. Р. Наскрести́ (acc./gen.). I. Наскреба́ть. (lit. and fig.) To scrape up, scrape together.

НАСЛАЖУ́СЬ, наслади́шься. Р. Насла-ди́ться (intr.). I. Наслажда́ться. To enjoy, take pleasure (in) (inst.).

НА́СЛАННЫЙ; на́слан, —а, —о, —ы (ppp). Р. Насла́ть. I. Насыла́ть. 1. To send a number of (acc./gen.). 2. (fig.) To send, call down (as a plague, misfortune, etc.) (acc.). (Also see нашлю́.)

НАСЛАЩЁННЫЙ; наслащён, —а́, —о́, —ы́ (ppp), see наслащу́.

НАСЛАЩУ́, насласти́шь. Р. Насласти́ть (acc.). To make very sweet.

НАСЛЁЖЕННЫЙ; наслёжен, —а, —о, —ы (ppp), see наслежу́.

НАСЛЕЖУ́, наследи́шь. Р. Наследи́ть (intr.). I. Следи́ть. To leave dirty tracks (as on a floor with one's boots) (на + prep. of floor + inst. of boots).

НАСМЕЁШЬСЯ, see насмею́сь.

НАСМЕ́ЙСЯ (imp.) see насмею́сь.

НАСМЕЮ́СЬ, насмеёшься. Р. На-сме́яться (intr.). 1. To have a good laugh (intr. + вдо́воль or до́сыта). 2. To laugh at, deride (e.g., s.o.) (над + inst. of s.o.).

НАСМО́ТРЕННЫЙ; насмо́трен, —а, —о, —ы (ppp), see насмотрю́.

НАСМОТРИ́ (imp.), see насмотрю́.

НАСМО́ТРИШЬ, see насмотрю́.

НАСМОТРЮ́, насмо́тришь. Р. На-смотре́ть. To see, discern (acc.).

НАСМО́ТРЯТ, see насмотрю́.

НАСО́САННЫЙ; насо́сан, —а, —о, —ы (ppp), see насосу́.

НАСОСЁШЬ, see насосу́.

НАСОСИ́ (imp.), see насосу́.

НАСОСУ́, насосёшь. Р. Насоса́ть. I. Наса́сывать. 1. To pump a quantity of (as water) (acc./gen.). 2. To suck a quantity of (as milk) (acc./gen.). 3. To injure by sucking (as a breast) (acc.).

НАСТАВА́Й (imp.), see настаёт.

НАСТА́ВЛЕННЫЙ; наста́влен, —а, —о, —ы (ppp), see наста́влю.

НАСТА́ВЛЮ, наста́вишь. Р. На-ста́вить. I. Наставля́ть (mean. 2 thru 6). 1. To place a quantity of (s.t.) (as dishes on a table) (acc./gen.).

2. To lengthen (as a dress) (acc.). 3. To add to lengthen (as material to a dress) (acc. + к + dat.). 4. To aim (s.t. at s.t.) (acc. + на + acc.). 5. To instruct, direct (s.o. in s.t.) (acc. + в + acc.), or (s.o. how to do s.t.) (acc. + как + inf.). 6. To exhort (s.o. to s.t.) (acc. + на + acc.). 7. To give (as black eyes to s.o.) (gen. of black eyes).

НАСТА́ВЬ (imp.), see наста́влю.

НАСТАЁТ, настаю́т (3rd pers. only). I. Наставáть (intr.). P. Настáть. To come, arrive, begin (of time, etc.).

НАСТА́НЕТ, настáнут (3rd pers. only). P. Настáть (intr.). I. Наставáть. To come, arrive, begin (of time, etc.).

НАСТА́НУТ, see настáнет.

НАСТА́НЬ (imp.), see настáнет.

НАСТАЮ́Т, see настаёт.

НАСТЕ́ЛЕННЫЙ; настéлен, —а, —о, —ы (ppp), see настелю́ (mean. 1).

НАСТЕ́ЛЕШЬ, see настелю́.

НАСТЕЛИ́ (imp.), see настелю́.

НАСТЕЛЮ́, настéлешь. P. Настлáть (acc./gen.), настели́ть (mean. 1). I. Настилáть. 1. To spread, lay (as a rug, a layer of straw, etc.). 2. To lay (as tile, planks, etc.). 3. To pave (as a road).

НАСТИ́Г (and насти́гнул), насти́гла (past), see насти́гну.

НАСТИ́ГНЕШЬ, see насти́гну.

НАСТИ́ГНИ (imp.), see насти́гну.

НАСТИ́ГНУ, насти́гнешь. P. Насти́чь (acc.), насти́гнуть. I. Настигáть. 1. To overtake. 2. (fig.) To strike.

НАСТИ́ГНУТЫЙ; насти́гнут, —а, —о, —ы (ppp), see насти́гну.

НА́СТЛАННЫЙ; нáстлан, —а, —о, —ы (ppp), see настелю́.

НАСТО́ЙШЬ, see настою́.

НАСТО́Й (imp.), see настою́.

НАСТОЮ́, настои́шь. P. Настоя́ть. I. Настáивать. 1. To insist on (intr.) (на + prep.). 2. To prepare an infusion (of s.t.) (acc./gen.). 3. To infuse (as tea in hot water) (acc. of water + на + prep. of tea).

НАСТО́ЯННЫЙ; настóян, —а, —о, —ы (ppp), see настою́ (mean. 2 and 3).

НАСТРИ́Г, настри́гла (past), see настригу́.

НАСТРИГИ́ (imp.), see настригу́.

НАСТРИГУ́, настрижёшь, настригу́т. P. Настри́чь (acc./gen.). I. Настригáть. 1. To shear a quantity of. 2. To cut a quantity of (s.t.) into small pieces.

НАСТРИ́ЖЕННЫЙ; настри́жен, —а, —о, —ы (ppp), see настригу́.

НАСТРИЖЁШЬ, see настригу́.

НАСТУ́ЖЕННЫЙ; настýжен, —а, —о, —ы (ppp), see настужу́.

НАСТУЖУ́, настýдишь. P. Настуди́ть (acc.). I. Настýживать. To chill, cool off (as a room) by letting in cold air.

НАСТУПЛЮ́, настýпишь. P. Наступи́ть (intr.). I. Наступáть. 1. (lit. and fig.) To step on, tread on (на + acc.).[1] 2. To come, arrive, ensue (of time, etc.) (e.g., "night came") (3rd pers. only).

НАСТЫ́Л, насты́ла (past), see насты́ну.

НАСТЫ́НЕШЬ, see насты́ну.

НАСТЫ́НУ, насты́нешь. P. Насты́ть (intr.), насты́нуть. I. Настывáть. 1. To become cold. 2. To freeze to the surface (of s.t.) (e.g., ice to the pavement) (на + prep.) (3rd pers.).

НАСТЫ́НЬ (imp.), see насты́ну.

НАСУ́ПЛЕННЫЙ; насýплен, —а, —о, —ы (ppp), see насýплю.

НАСУ́ПЛЮ, насýпишь. P. Насýпить (acc.). I. Сýпить. To frown, knit one's brow (acc. of brow).

НАСУ́ПЬ (imp.), see насýплю.

НАСУРЬМЛЁННЫЙ; насурьмлён, —á, —ó, —ы́ (ppp), see насурьмлю́.

НАСУРЬМЛЮ́, насурьми́шь. P. Насурьми́ть (acc.). I. Сурьми́ть. To decorate, cover with antimony (used as a cosmetic and in pigments).

НАСЫ́ПАННЫЙ; насы́пан, —а, —о, —ы (ppp), see насы́плю.

НАСЫ́ПЛЕШЬ, see насы́плю.

НАСЫ́ПЛЮ, насы́плешь. P. Насы́пать. I. Насыпáть. 1. To pour (s.t. into s.t.) (acc./gen. + в + acc.). 2. To spread (as sand, etc. on s.t.) (acc./gen. + на + acc.). 3. To fill (as a sack) (with s.t.) (acc. + inst.). 4. To build a mound (of sand, grain, etc.) (acc. of sand, etc.).

НАСЫ́ПЬ (imp.), see насы́плю.

НАСЫ́ТЬ (imp.), see насы́щу.

НАСЫ́ЩЕННЫЙ; насы́щен, —а, —о, —ы (ppp), see насы́щу.

НАСЫ́ЩУ, насы́тишь. Р. Насы́тить (acc. + inst.). I. Насыща́ть. 1. To satiate, sate, satisfy (with). 2. (lit. and fig.) To saturate, impregnate (with).

НАСЯ́ДЕШЬ, see нася́ду.

НАСЯ́ДУ, нася́дешь. Р. Насе́сть (intr.). I. Насела́ть (mean. 1, 2, 3), наса́живаться (mean. 4). 1. To settle, collect (of dust, etc.). 2. To lean all one's weight on (на + acc.). 3. (fig.) To press (e.g., s.o. with questions) (на + acc.). 4. To sit, take seats, in large numbers (в/на + acc.).

НАСЯ́ДЬ (imp.), see нася́ду.

НАТА́ЕШЬ, see ната́ю.

НАТА́Й (imp.), see ната́ю.

НАТА́Ю, ната́ешь. Р. Ната́ять. I. Ната́ивать. 1. To melt a quantity of (as snow) (acc./gen.). 2. To melt, thaw (of snow, etc.) (intr.).

НАТА́ЯННЫЙ; ната́ян, —а, —о, —ы (ppp), see ната́ю.

НАТЁК, натекла́ (past), see натечёт.

НАТЕКУ́Т, see натечёт.

НАТЁР, натёрла (past), see натру́.

НАТЕРЕБЛЁННЫЙ; натереблён, —а́, —о́, —ы́ (ppp), see натерблю́.

НАТЕРЕБЛЮ́, натереби́шь. Р. Натереби́ть (acc./gen.). To pull a quantity of (as flax).

НАТЕРЁВ and натёрши (adv. past part.), see натру́.

НАТЕРПИ́СЬ (imp.), see натерплю́сь.

НАТЕ́РПИШЬСЯ, see натерплю́сь.

НАТЕРПЛЮ́СЬ, натерпишься. Р. Натерпе́ться (gen.). To experience much which is unpleasant, suffer (as freight, hardship, etc.).

НАТЕ́РПЯТСЯ, see натерплю́сь.

НАТЁРТЫЙ; натёрт, —а, —о, —ы (ppp), see натру́.

НАТЁРШИ and натерёв (adv. past part.), see натру́.

НАТЁСАННЫЙ; натёсан, —а, —о, —ы (ppp), see натешу́.

НАТЕЧЁТ, натеку́т (3rd pers. only). Р. Нате́чь (intr.). I. Натека́ть. To accumulate, collect seepage or leakage, etc. (of a liquid).

НАТЕ́ШЕШЬ, see натешу́.

НАТЕШИ́ (imp.), see натешу́.

НАТЕШУ́, нате́шешь. Р. Натеса́ть (acc./gen.). I. Натёсывать. To hew (as boards from a log, etc.).

НА́ТКАННЫЙ; на́ткан, —а, —о, —ы (ppp), see натку́.

НАТКЁШЬ, see натку́.

НАТКИ́ (imp.), see натку́.

НАТКУ́, наткёшь. Р. Натка́ть (gen./ acc.). To weave a quantity of (cloth, etc.).

НАТОЛКИ́ (imp.), see натолку́.

НАТОЛКУ́, натолчёшь, натолку́т. Р. Натоло́чь (gen./acc.). To crush or crack a quantity of.

НАТОЛО́К, натолкла́ (past), see натолку́.

НАТОЛЧЁННЫЙ; натолчён, —а́, —о́, —ы́ (ppp), see натолку́.

НАТОЛЧЁШЬ, see натолку́.

НАТО́ПЛЕННЫЙ; нато́плен, —а, —о, —ы (ppp), see натоплю́.

НАТОПЛЮ́, нато́пишь. Р. Натопи́ть. I. Ната́пливать. 1. To heat well (as a room) (acc.). 2. To prepare a quantity of (s.t.) by heating or melting (acc./gen.).

НАТО́ПТАННЫЙ; нато́птан, —а, —о, —ы (ppp), see натопчу́.

НАТО́ПЧЕШЬ, see натопчу́.

НАТОПЧИ́ (imp.), see натопчу́.

НАТОПЧУ́, нато́пчешь. Р. Натоптáть. I. Ната́птывать. 1. To leave dirty foot marks on (s.t.) (на + acc.). 2. To wear, blaze (as a path, road, etc.) (acc.).

НАТРА́ВЛЕННЫЙ; натра́влен, —а, —о, —ы (ppp), see натравлю́.

НАТРАВЛЮ́, натра́вишь. Р. Натрави́ть. I. Натра́вливать, натравля́ть. 1. To set on (as dogs on a fox) (acc. + на + acc.). 2. (fig.) To set (s.o.) against (s.o.) (acc. + на + acc.). 3. To exterminate (as vermin) (acc./gen.). 4. To etch (as a design) (acc./gen.).

НАТРЁШЬ, see натру́.

НАТРИ́ (imp.), see натру́.

НАТРУ́, натрёшь. Р. Натере́ть (acc.). I. Натира́ть. 1. To rub (s.t. with s.t.) (acc. + inst.). 2. To rub sore (as one's heel). 3. To rub, polish (as a table). 4. To grate (as radishes, etc.) (acc./gen.).

НАТРУБЛЮ́, натруби́шь. Р. Натруби́ть (intr.). 1. To proclaim, spread (as news, etc.) (o + prep.).

2. To din into (s.o.'s ear) (dat. of
s.o. + в + acc. of ear).

НАТРУ́ЖЕННЫЙ; натру́жен, —а,
—о, —ы (ppp), see натружу́.

НАТРУЖЁННЫЙ; натружён, —а́,
—о́, —ы́ (ppp), see натружу́.

НАТРУЖУ́, натруди́шь (and на-
тру́дишь). Г. Натруди́ть (acc.).
I. Натру́живать. To tire out (as
one's arms, legs, etc.).

НАТРУ́ШЕННЫЙ; натру́шен, —а,
—о, —ы (ppp), see натрушу́.

НАТРУШУ́, натруси́шь. Р. Натру-
си́ть (acc./gen.). I. Труси́ть. To
scatter while shaking (as grain from
a bag).

НАТРЯ́С, натрясла́ (past), see на-
трясу́.

НАТРЯСЁННЫЙ; натрясён, —а́,
—о́, —ы́ (ppp), see натрясу́.

НАТРЯСЁШЬ, see натрясу́.

НАТРЯСИ́ (imp.), see натрясу́.

НАТРЯСУ́, натрясёшь. Р. Натрясти́
(acc./gen.). 1. To pour out a quantity
(of s.t.) by shaking (as sugar from a
bag, etc.). 2. To shake down or out a
quantity (of s.t.) (as apples from a
tree).

НАУ́ЖЕННЫЙ; нау́жен, —а, —о,
—ы (ppp), see наужу́.

НАУЖУ́, нау́дишь. Р. Нау́дить (acc./
gen.). I. Нау́живать. To catch a
quantity of (with a fishing rod).

НАУЩЁННЫЙ; наущён, —а́, —о́,
—ы́ (ppp), see наущу́.

НАУЩУ́, наусти́шь. Р. Наусти́ть
(arch.) (acc.). I. Наущáть. To
incite (s.o.) to an evil deed.

НАХАМЛЮ́, нахами́шь. Р. Наха-
ми́ть (intr.). To be rude or caddish
(to s.o.) (dat.).

НАХЛЁСТАННЫЙ; нахлёстан, —а,
—о, —ы (ppp), see нахлещу́.

НАХЛЕ́ЩЕШЬ, see нахлещу́.

НАХЛЕЩИ́ (imp.), see нахлещу́.

НАХЛЕЩУ́, нахлё́щешь. Р. На-
хлеста́ть (acc.). I. Нахлёстывать.
To whip, lash severely.

НАХОЖУ́, нахо́дишь. I. Находи́ть.
Р. Найти́. 1. To find, discover
(acc.). 2. To consider (come to a
conclusion) (e.g., to consider s.o.
healthy) (acc. + inst.). 3. To cover
(as clouds cover the sky) (на + acc.).
4. To assemble, come (intr.). 5. To
run into (s.o. or s.t.) (на + acc.).

6. (fig.) To come over (s.o.) (as a
feeling comes over one) (на + acc.).
(For other meanings see unabridged
dictionary.)

НАХОЛОЖЁННЫЙ; нахоложён,
—а́, —о́, —ы́ (ppp), see наоложу́.

НАХОЛОЖУ́, наолоди́шь. Р. Нахо-
лоди́ть (acc.). I. Холоди́ть. 1. To
cool (as a room). 2. To chill (e.g.,
wine, water).

НАХОХО́ЧЕШЬСЯ, see нахохочу́сь.

НАХОХОЧИ́СЬ (imp.), see нахохо-
чу́сь.

НАХОХОЧУ́СЬ, нахохо́чешься. Р.
Нахохотáться (intr.). To laugh a
great deal, have a good laugh.

НАЦЕ́ЖЕННЫЙ; наце́жен, —а, —о,
—ы (ppp) see нацежу́.

НАЦЕЖУ́, нацедишь. Р. Нацеди́ть
(acc./gen.). I. Наце́живать. To decant or strain off a quantity.

НАЦЕ́ПЛЕННЫЙ; наце́плен, —а,
—о, —ы (ppp), see нацеплю́.

НАЦЕПЛЮ́, наце́пишь. Р. Нацепи́ть
(acc.). I. Нацепля́ть. 1. To hang (as
on a hook) (acc. + на + acc.). 2.
To pin or fasten on (as a badge). 3.
To put on (as a hat).

НАЧАЖУ́, начади́шь. Р. Начади́ть
(intr.). I. Чади́ть. 1. To smoke (of
a stove, etc.). 2. To smoke (as
tobacco) (inst.).

НА́ЧАТЫЙ; на́чат, —á, —о, —ы
(ppp), see начну́.

НАЧЁЛ, начла́ (past), see начту́.

НАЧЁРЧЕННЫЙ; начёрчен, —а,
—о, —ы (ppp), see начерчу́.

НАЧЕРЧУ́, начéртишь. Р. Начер-
ти́ть. I. Начéрчивать, черти́ть
(mean. 1). 1. To draw, sketch,
design, etc. (acc./gen.). 2. (arch.) To
inscribe, write.

НАЧЁСАННЫЙ; начёсан, —а, —о,
—ы (ppp), see начешу́.

НАЧЁТШИЙ (pap), see начту́.

НАЧЕ́ШЕШЬ, see начешу́.

НАЧЕШИ́ (imp.), see начешу́.

НАЧЕШУ́, начéшешь. Р. Начесáть.
I. Начёсывать. 1. To comb or card
a quantity of (as hemp, hair, etc.)
(acc./gen.). 2. To injure, scratch
while combing (as one's hand) (acc.).

НАЧИ́СТИ (imp.), see начи́щу.

НАЧИ́СТЬ (imp.), see начи́щу.

НАЧИ́ЩЕННЫЙ; начи́щен, —а, —о,
—ы (ppp), see начи́щу.

НАЧИЩУ, начи́стишь. Р. Начи́стить. I. Начища́ть. 1. To clean thoroughly (e.g., pots, shoes, etc.) (acc.). 2. To clean, or peel a quantity of (as vegetables) (acc./gen.).

НАЧЛА́, начло́, начли́ (past), see начту́ and начёл.

НАЧНЁШЬ, see начну́.

НАЧНИ́ (imp.), see начну́.

НАЧНУ́, начнёшь. Р. Нача́ть. I. Начина́ть. 1. To begin, start, commence (s.t.) (acc.). 2. To begin to (inf.). 3. To begin with (c + gen.) or (acc. + c + gen.) or (acc. | inst.).

НАЧТЁННЫЙ; начтён, —а́, —о́, —ы́ (ppp), see начту́.

НАЧТЁШЬ, see начту́.

НАЧТИ́ (imp.), see начту́.

НАЧТУ́, начтёшь. Р. Наче́сть (acc.). I. Начи́тывать. To add up, reckon (as an account).

НАШЕ́ДШИ and найдя́ (adv. past part.), see нашёл and найду́.

НАШЕ́ДШИЙ (pap), see нашёл and найду́.

НАШЕ́Й (imp.), see нашью́.

НАШЁЛ, нашла́ (past). Р. Найти́. I. Находи́ть. 1. To find, discover (acc.). 2. To consider (come to a conclusion) (e.g., to consider s.o. healthy) (acc. + inst.). 3. To cover (as clouds cover the sky) (на + acc.). 4. To assemble, come (intr.). 5. To run into (s.o. or s.t.) (на + acc.). 6. (fig.) To come over (s.o.) (as a feeling comes over one) (на + acc.). (Also see найду́.)

НАШЁПТАННЫЙ; нашёптан, —а, —о, —ы (ppp), see нашепчу́.

НАШЕ́ПЧЕШЬ, see нашепчу́.

НАШЕ́ПЧИ (imp), see нашепчу́.

НАШЕ́ПЧУ́, нашё́пчешь. Р. Нашепта́ть. I. Нашёптывать. 1. To whisper (s.t. to s.o.) (usually pejorative) (acc./gen. + dat.). 2. To whisper (intr.) (usually pejoratively). 3. To pronounce an incantation (over s.o. or s.t.) (intr.) (на + acc.).

НАШИ́ТЫЙ; наши́т, —а, —о, —ы (ppp), see нашью́.

НАШЛА́, нашло́, нашли́ (past), see нашёл and найду́.

НАШЛЁШЬ, see нашлю́.

НАШЛИ́¹ (imp. of насла́ть), see нашлю́.

НАШЛИ́² (past of найти́), see нашёл and найду́.

НАШЛЮ́, нашлёшь. Р. Насла́ть (acc.). I. Насыла́ть. 1. To send a number of (acc./gen.). 2. (fig.) To send, call down (as a plague, misfortune, etc.) (acc.).

НАШУМИ́ (imp.), see нашумлю́.

НАШУМИ́ШЬ, see нашумлю́.

НАШУМЛЮ́, нашуми́шь. Р. Нашуме́ть (intr.). 1. To make much noise. 2. To cause a sensation, attract attention.

НАШУМЯ́Т, see нашумлю́.

НАШЬЁШЬ, see нашью́.

НАШЬЮ́, нашьёшь. Р. Наши́ть. I. Нашива́ть. 1. To sew (s.t.) on (acc.). 2. To sew a quantity of (acc./gen.).

НАЩЕ́ПАННЫЙ; наще́пан, —а, —о, —ы (ppp), see нащеплю́.

НАЩЕ́ПЛЕШЬ, see нащеплю́.

НАЩЕПЛИ́ (imp.), see нащеплю́.

НАЩЕПЛЮ́, наще́плешь. Р. Нащепа́ть (acc./gen.). To chop a quantity of (chips, splinters, etc.).

НАЩИ́ПАННЫЙ; нащи́пан, —а, —о, —ы (ppp), see нащиплю́.

НАЩИ́ПЛЕШЬ, see нащиплю́.

НАЩИПЛИ́ (imp.), see нащиплю́.

НАЩИПЛЮ́, нащи́плешь. Р. Нащипа́ть. 1. To pick, pluck a quantity of (gen./acc.). 2. To pinch (as one's hand) (acc.).

НАЗКОНО́МЛЕННЫЙ; назконо́млен, —а, —о, —ы (ppp), see наэконо́млю.

НАЭКОНО́МЛЮ, наэконо́мишь. Р. Наэконо́мить (gen./acc.). To save by economizing.

НАЭКОНО́МЬ (imp.), see наэконо́млю.

НЕБРЁГ, небрегла́ (past), see небрегу́.

НЕБРЕГИ́ (imp.), see небрегу́.

НЕБРЕГЛА́, небрегло́, небрегли́ (past), see небрегу́ and небрёг.

НЕБРЕГУ́, небрежёшь, небрегу́т. I. Небре́чь (arch.) (inst.) or (о + prep.). 1. To neglect. 2. To disregard.

НЕБРЕЖЁШЬ, see небрегу́.

НЕВЗВИ́ДИШЬ, see невзви́жу.

НЕВЗВИ́ДЯТ, see невзви́жу.

НЕВЗВИ́ЖУ, невзви́дишь. Р. Невзви́деть (gen.). To experience a strong sensation, due to fear, pain, anger, etc. (used in the expression: невзви́деть све́та/дня).

НЕВЗЛЮБЛЮ, невзлюбишь. Р. Невзлюбить (acc.). To take a strong dislike to, feel hostility towards.

НЕДОБЕРЁШЬ, see недоберу.

НЕДОБЕРИ (imp.), see недоберу.

НЕДОБЕРУ, недоберёшь. Р. Недобрать (acc./gen.). I. Недобирать. 1. To gather, collect less than the proper amount. 2. To recruit, fewer than required.

НЕДОБРАННЫЙ; недобран, —а, —о, —ы (ppp), see недоберу.

НЕДОВЕСЬ (imp.), see недовешу.

НЕДОВЕШЕННЫЙ; недовешен, —а, —о, —ы (ppp), see недовешу.

НЕДОВЕШУ, недовесишь. Р. Недовесить (acc./gen.). I. Недовешивать. To give short weight, short-weight (s.t. or a certain amount).

НЕДОГЛЯДИ (imp.), see недогляжу.

НЕДОГЛЯДИШЬ, see недогляжу.

НЕДОГЛЯДЯТ, see недогляжу.

НЕДОГЛЯЖУ, недоглядишь. Р. Недоглядеть. 1. To overlook, miss (acc./gen.). 2. Not to take proper care of, neglect (за + inst.).

НЕДОПЛАЧЕННЫЙ; недоплачен, —а, —о, —ы (ppp), see недоплачу.

НЕДОПЛАЧУ, недоплатишь. Р. Недоплатить. I. Недоплачивать. To underpay (by a certain amount for s.t.) (acc./gen. + за + acc.).

НЕДОСКАЖЕШЬ, see недоскажу.

НЕДОСКАЖИ (imp.), see недоскажу.

НЕДОСКАЖУ, недоскажешь. Р. Недосказать (acc./gen.) or (intr.). I. Недосказывать. To leave (s.t.) unsaid.

НЕДОСКАЗАННЫЙ; недосказан, —а, —о, —ы (ppp), see недоскажу.

НЕДОСЛАННЫЙ; недослан, —а, —о, —ы (ppp), see недошлю.

НЕДОСЛЫШАННЫЙ; недослышан, —а, —о, —ы (ppp), see недослышу.

НЕДОСЛЫШАТ, see недослышу.

НЕДОСЛЫШИШЬ, see недослышу.

НЕДОСЛЫШУ, недослышишь. Р. Недослышать. 1. To fail to hear, catch (acc./gen.). 2. To be somewhat hard of hearing (intr.).

НЕДОСМОТРЕННЫЙ; недосмотрен, —а, —о, —ы (ppp), see недосмотрю.

НЕДОСМОТРИ (imp.), see недосмотрю.

НЕДОСМОТРИШЬ, see недосмотрю.

НЕДОСМОТРЮ, недосмотришь. Р.
Недосмотреть. 1. To overlook, miss (acc./gen.). 2. Not to take sufficient care of, neglect (за + inst.).

НЕДОСМОТРЯТ, see недосмотрю.

НЕДОСПИ (imp.), see недосплю.

НЕДОСПИШЬ, see недосплю.

НЕДОСПЛЮ, недоспишь. Р. Недоспать (intr.). I. Недосыпать. Not to get enough sleep.

НЕДОСПЯТ, see недосплю.

НЕДОСТАЁТ (3rd pers. only). I. Недоставать (impers. + gen.). Р. Недостать (mean. 1). 1. To be insufficient, lacking (as funds, etc.). 2. To be missing (of a person or thing). 3. To be needed (of a person or thing).

НЕДОСТАНЕТ (3rd pers. only). Р. Недостать (impers. + gen.). I. Недоставать. To be insufficient, lacking (as funds, etc.).

НЕДОШЛЁШЬ, see недошлю.

НЕДОШЛИ (imp.), see недошлю.

НЕДОШЛЮ, недошлёшь. Р. Недослать (acc./gen.). I. Недосылать. To send too little, too few, an insufficiency (as money, books, etc.).

НЕЙДУ, нейдёшь. I. Нейти (arch.) (intr.). Used in place of не идти.

НЕНАВИДИШЬ, see ненавижу.

НЕНАВИДЬ (imp.), see ненавижу.

НЕНАВИДЯТ, see ненавижу.

НЕНАВИЖУ, ненавидишь. I. Ненавидеть (acc.). To hate.

НЁС, несла (past), see несу.

НЕСЁШЬ, see несу.

НЕСИ (imp.), see несу.

НЕСОМЫЙ (pres. pp) see несу.

НЕСУ, несёшь. I. Нести. Р. Понести (mean. 1, 6, 7, 8), снести (mean. 9). 1. (lit. and fig.) To carry (acc.). 2. To wear (acc.). 3. To incur (acc.). 4. To bear (as weight) (acc.). 5. To cause, bring (as illness) (acc.). 6. To bear, endure, suffer (acc.). 7. To smell of (impers. + inst.). 8. To blow (cold, warm, etc.) (impers. + inst.). 9. To lay (as an egg) (acc.). 10. To perform, fulfill (duties) (acc.). (For other usages see unabridged dictionary.)

НИЖЕШЬ, see нижу.

НИЖИ (imp.), see **НИЖУ.**

НИЖУ, нижешь. I. Низать. Р. Нанизать. 1. To string, thread (e.g. beads, etc.) (acc.). 2. (fig.) To string (acc.). 3. (arch.) To penetrate, pierce (as the sun pierces a cloud with its rays) (intr.) (**сквозь** + acc. of cloud + inst. of rays). 4. (fig.) To pierce (s.o. with one's eyes) (acc. of s.o. + inst. of eyes).

НИЗВЕДЁННЫЙ; низведён, —а́, —о, —ы́ (ppp), see **низведу́**.

НИЗВЕДЁШЬ, see **низведу́**.

НИЗВЕДИ́ (imp.), see **низведу́**.

НИЗВЕДУ́, низведёшь. P. Низвести́ (acc.). I. Низводи́ть. 1. To bring down. 2. To reduce, degrade (s.o. or s.t.).

НИЗВЕ́ДШИЙ (pap), see **низведу́**.

НИЗВЕДЯ́ and низве́дши (adv. past part.), see **низведу́**.

НИЗВЁЛ, низвела́ (past), see **низведу́**.

НИЗВОЖУ́, низво́дишь. I. Низводи́ть (acc.). P. Низвести́. 1. To bring down. 2. To reduce, degrade (s.o. or s.t.).

НИЗОЙДЁШЬ, see **низойду́**.

НИЗОЙДИ́ (imp.), see **низойду́**.

НИЗОЙДУ́, низойдёшь. P. Низойти (arch., poetic) (intr.). I. Нисходи́ть. To descend.

НИЗОЙДЯ́ and нисше́дши (adv. past part.), see **низойду́**.

НИЗОШЛА́, низошло́, низошли́ (past), see **низойду́** and **нисшёл**.

НИК, ни́кла (past). I. Ни́кнуть (intr.). P. Пони́кнуть, сни́кнуть. 1. (lit. and fig.) To droop, wilt. 2. (lit. and fig.) To weaken.

НИСПАДЁТ, ниспаду́т (3rd pers.). P. Ниспа́сть (arch., poetic) (intr.). I. Ниспада́ть. To fall, fall down (on s.t.) (as leaves fall on the lawn) (**на** + acc.).

НИСПАДИ́ (imp.), see **ниспадёт**.

НИСПАДУ́Т, see **ниспадёт**.

НИСПА́Л, ниспа́ла (past), see **ниспадёт**.

НИСПО́СЛАННЫЙ; ниспо́слан, —а, —о, —ы (ppp), see **ниспошлю́**.

НИСПОШЛЁШЬ, see **ниспошлю́**.

НИСПОШЛИ́ (imp.), see **ниспошлю́**.

НИСПОШЛЮ́, ниспошлёшь. P. Нис-

послать (arch.) (acc.). I. Ниспосыла́ть. 1. To grant. 2. To send down (as from heaven).

НИСПРОВЕ́РГ (and ниспрове́ргнул), ниспрове́ргла (past). P. Ниспрове́ргнуть (acc.). I. Ниспроверга́ть. 1. To throw down, overturn. 2. (fig.) To overthrow, subvert.

НИСПРОВЕ́РГНУТЫЙ; ниспрове́ргнут, —а, —о, —ы (ppp), see **ниспрове́рг**.

НИСПРОВЕ́РЖЕННЫЙ; ниспрове́ржен, —а, —о, —ы (ppp), see **ниспрове́рг**.

НИСХОЖУ́, нисхо́дишь. I. Нисходи́ть (arch., poetic) (intr.). P. Низойти́. To descend.

НИСШЕ́ДШИ and низойдя́ (adv. past part.), see **низойду́**.

НИСШЕ́ДШИЙ (pap), see **низойду́**.

НИСШЁЛ, низошла́ (past), see **низойду́**.

НИШКНИ́ (imp.), P. Нишкну́ть (intr.). To keep silent, shut up (used only in the imperative).

НО́ЕШЬ, see **но́ю**.

НОЙ (imp.), see **но́ю**.

НОРОВЛЮ́, норови́шь. I. Норови́ть. To strive to, to aim at (+ inf.).

НО́ШЕННЫЙ; но́шен, —а, —о, —ы (ppp), see **ношу́**.

НОШУ́, но́сишь. I. Носи́ть. 1. (lit. and fig.) To carry (acc.). 2. To be carried along, driven (impers. + acc.). 3. To wear (as clothes) (acc.). 4. To be pregnant (carry a child) (intr.) or (acc.).

НО́Ю, но́ешь. I. Ныть (intr.). 1. To ache (of a leg, head, etc.). 2. To complain, whine. 3. To make a plaintive sound (of a violin, etc.).

НРА́ВЛЮСЬ, нра́вишься. I. Нра́виться (intr.). P. Понра́виться. To please (dat.).

НРА́ВЬСЯ (imp.), see **нра́влюсь**.

НУДЬ (imp.), see **ну́жу**.

НУ́ЖУ, ну́дишь. I. Ну́дить (arch.) (acc.). 1. To force, coerce. 2. To tire, wear out.

O

ОБАНКРО́ТЬСЯ (imp.), see **обанкро́-чусь.**

ОБАНКРО́ЧУСЬ, обанкро́тишся. Р. Обанкро́титься (intr.). (lit. and fig.) To become bankrupt.

ОБАНКРУ́ТЬСЯ (imp.), see **обанкру́-чусь.**

ОБАНКРУ́ЧУСЬ, обанкру́тишься. Р. Обанкру́титься (intr.). (arch.). (lit. and fig.) To become bankrupt.

ОБВЕДЁННЫЙ; обведён, —а́, —о́, —ы́ (ppp), see **обведу́.**

ОБВЕДЁШЬ, see **обведу́.**

ОБВЕДИ́ (imp.), see **обведу́.**

ОБВЕДУ́, обведёшь. Р. Обвести́. I. Обводи́ть. 1. To lead (s.o.) around (acc.). **2.** To encircle (s.t. with s.t.) (acc. + inst.). **3.** To outline, border (s.t. with s.t.) (acc. + inst.). **4.** To look around (e.g., a room) (acc. of room + inst. of eyes). **5.** To deceive (s.o.) (acc.).

ОБВЕ́ДШИ and **обведя́** (adv. past part.), see **обведу́.**

ОБВЕ́ДШИЙ (pap), see **обведу́.**

ОБВЕДЯ́ and **обве́дши** (adv. past part.), see **обведу́.**

ОБВЕ́ЕШЬ, see **обве́ю.**

ОБВЕ́Й[1] (imp.). **Р. Обви́ть** (acc.). **I. Обвива́ть. 1.** To wind (s.t. around s.t.) (acc. + вокру́г + gen.). **2.** To wind (s.t. with s.t.) (acc. + inst.). **3.** To wind around, entwine (s.t.) (as ivy winds around a tree). **4.** To embrace (as s.o.'s waist). (Also see **обовью́.**)

ОБВЕ́Й[2] (imp.), see **обве́ю.**

ОБВЁЛ, обвела́ (past), see **обведу́.**

ОБВЕРТИ́ (imp.), see **обверчу́.**

ОБВЕ́РТИШЬ, see **обверчу́.**

ОБВЕ́РТЯТ, see **обверчу́.**

ОБВЕ́РЧЕННЫЙ; обве́рчен, —а, —о, —ы (ppp), see **обверчу́.**

ОБВЕРЧУ́, обве́ртишь. Р. Обверте́ть (acc.). **I. Обвёртывать. 1.** To wrap (up) (as one's neck in a scarf) (acc. + inst. of scarf). **2.** To wrap (s.t.

around s.t.) (acc. + Вокру́г + gen.). **3.** To deceive (s.o.). **4.** (arch.) To marry (s.o.).

ОБВЕ́СЬ (imp.), see **обве́шу.**

ОБВЕ́ШЕННЫЙ; обве́шен, —а, —о, —ы (ppp), see **обве́шу.**

ОБВЕ́ШУ, обве́сишь. Р. Обве́сить. I. Обве́шивать. 1. To give false weight, cheat (s.o.) in weighing (acc.). **2.** To hang (s.t. with s.t.) (as a tree with ornaments) (acc. + inst.).

ОБВЕ́Ю, обве́ешь. Р. Обве́ять (acc.). **I. Обвева́ть. 1.** To winnow (as grain). **2.** (lit. and fig.) To fan (with) (e.g., cool air, enthusiasm, etc.) (acc. + inst.).

ОБВЕ́ЯННЫЙ; обве́ян, —а, —о, —ы (ppp), see **обве́ю.**

ОБВИ́С, обви́сла (past). **Р. Обви́снуть** (intr.). **I. Обвиса́ть.** To hang, droop.

ОБВИ́ТЫЙ; обви́т, —а́, —о, —ы (ppp), see **обве́й**[1] and **обовью́.**

ОБВОЖУ́, обво́дишь. I. Обводи́ть. Р. Обвести́. 1. To lead (s.o.) around (acc.). **2.** To encircle (s.t. with s.t.) (acc. + inst.). **3.** To outline, border (s.t. with s.t.) (acc. + inst.). **4.** To look around (e.g., a room) (acc. of room + inst. of eyes). **5.** To deceive (s.o.) (acc.).

ОБВОЛО́К, обволокла́ (past), see **обволочёт.**

ОБВОЛОКИ́ (imp.), see **обволочёт.**

ОБВОЛОКУ́Т, see **обволочёт.**

ОБВОЛОЧЁННЫЙ; обволочён, —а́, —о́, —ы́ (ppp), see **обволочёт.**

ОБВОЛОЧЁТ, обволоку́т (3rd pers. only). **Р. Обволо́чь** (acc.). **I. Обво-ла́кивать.** To cover, envelope (of clouds, etc.).

ОБВЫ́К, обвы́кла (past). **Р. Обвы́-кнуть** (intr.). **I. Обвыка́ть.** To become accustomed (to) (с + inst.).

ОБВЯ́ЖЕШЬ, see **обвяжу́.**

ОБВЯЖИ́ (imp.), see **обвяжу́.**

ОБВЯЖУ́, обвя́жешь. Р. Обвяза́ть (acc.). **I. Обвя́зывать. 1.** To tie or wind (s.t. with s.t.) (as one's neck with a kerchief, etc.) (acc. + inst.). 2. To edge or stitch (s.t. with s.t.) (acc. + inst.). 3. To knit everything necessary (for s.o.) (acc. of s.o.).

ОБВЯ́ЗАННЫЙ; обвя́зан, —а, —о, —ы (ppp), see обвяжу́.

ОБГЛО́ДАННЫЙ; обгло́дан, —а,—о, —ы (ppp) see обгложу́.

ОБГЛО́ЖЕШЬ, see обгложу́.

ОБГЛОЖИ́ (imp.), see обгложу́.

ОБГЛОЖУ́, обгло́жешь. Р. Обглода́ть (acc.). I. Обгла́дывать. To gnaw around (as a bone).

ОБГОНИ́ (imp.), see обгоню́.

ОБГО́НИШЬ, see обгоню́.

ОБГОНЮ́, обго́нишь. Р. Обогна́ть (acc.). I. Обгоня́ть. (lit. and fig.) To outrun, outdistance, outstrip.

ОБГОРИ́ (imp.), see обгорю́.

ОБГОРИ́ШЬ, see обгорю́.

ОБГОРЮ́, обгори́шь. Р. Обгоре́ть (intr.). I. Обгора́ть. 1. To char, become scorched. 2. To become sunburned.

ОБГОРЯ́Т, see обгорю́.

ОБГРЫ́З, обгры́зла (past), see обгрызу́.

ОБГРЫ́ЗЕННЫЙ; обгры́зен, —а, —о, —ы (ppp), see обгрызу́.

ОБГРЫЗЁШЬ, see обгрызу́.

ОБГРЫЗИ́ (imp.), see обгрызу́.

ОБГРЫЗУ́, обгрызёшь. Р. Обгры́зть (acc.). I. Обгрыза́ть. To gnaw around (as an apple).

ОБДАВА́Й (imp.), see обдаю́.

ОБДАВА́Я (adv. pres. part.). see обдаю́.

ОБДАДИ́М, обдади́те, обдаду́т (pl. forms), see обда́м.

ОБДАЁШЬ, see обдаю́.

ОБДА́Й (imp.), see обда́м.

ОБДА́М, обда́шь, обда́ст (sing. forms). Р. Обда́ть. I. Обдава́ть. 1. To pour (e.g., water) over (s.o. or s.t.) (acc. of s.t. + inst. of water). 2. To splash (s.o. or s.t.) (as with mud) (acc. + inst.). 3. (fig.) To come over, seize (s.o.) (as a feeling) (impers. + acc. + inst. of feeling).

О́БДАННЫЙ; о́бдан, —а́, —о, —ы (ppp), see обда́м.

ОБДА́СТ, see обда́м.

ОБДА́ШЬ, see обда́м.

ОБДАЮ́, обдаёшь. I. Обдава́ть (acc.). Р. Обда́ть. 1. To pour (e.g., water)

over (s.o. or s.t.) (acc. of s.t. + inst. of water). 2. To splash (s.o. or s.t.) (as with mud) (acc. + inst.). 3. (fig.) To come over, seize (s.o.) (as a feeling) (impers. + acc. + inst. of feeling).

ОБДЕРЁШЬ, see обдеру́.

ОБДЕРИ́ (imp.), see обдеру́.

ОБДЕРУ́, обдерёшь. Р. Ободра́ть (acc.). I. Обдира́ть. 1. To flay (as a carcass). 2. To bark (as a tree). 3. To fray, wear to tatters (as clothing, etc.). 4. (fig.) To fleece (as a person).

ОБДУ́ЕШЬ, see обду́ю.

ОБДУ́Й (imp.), see обду́ю.

ОБДУ́ТЫЙ; обду́т, —а, —о, —ы (ppp), see обду́ю.

ОБДУ́Ю, обду́ешь. Р. Обду́ть (acc.). I. Обдува́ть. 1. To blow on or around (s.o. or s.t.). 2. (fig.) to dupe, cheat.

ОБЕГИ́ (imp.), see обегу́.

ОБЕГУ́, обежи́шь, обегу́т. Р. Обежа́ть (acc.). I. Обега́ть. 1. To run around (s.t. or s.o.). 2. To run around (to a number of places), visit (a number of people), etc. 3. To outrun (in sports).

ОБЕЖИ́ШЬ, see обегу́.

ОБЕЗВО́ДЬ (imp.), see обезво́жу.

ОБЕЗВО́ЖЕННЫЙ; обезво́жен, —а, —о, —ы (ppp), see обезво́жу.

ОБЕЗВО́ЖУ, обезво́дишь. Р. Обезво́дить (acc.). I. Обезво́живать. To dehydrate.

ОБЕЗВРЕ́ДЬ (imp.), see обезвре́жу.

ОБЕЗВРЕ́ЖЕННЫЙ; обезвре́жен, —а, —о, —ы (ppp), see обезвре́жу.

ОБЕЗВРЕ́ЖУ, обезвре́дишь. Р. Обезвре́дить (acc.). I. Обезвре́живать. To render harmless.

ОБЕЗГЛА́ВЛЕННЫЙ; обезгла́влен, —а, —о, —ы (ppp), see обезгла́влю.

ОБЕЗГЛА́ВЛЮ, обезгла́вишь. Р. Обезгла́вить (acc.). I. Обезгла́вливать. 1. To behead, decapitate. 2. To deprive of leadership (as a party, etc.).

ОБЕЗГЛА́ВЬ (imp.), see обезгла́влю.

ОБЕЗЗАРА́ЖЕННЫЙ; обеззара́жен, —а, —о, —ы (ppp), see обеззара́жу.

ОБЕЗЗАРА́ЖУ, обеззара́зишь. Р. Обеззара́зить (acc.). I. Обеззара́живать. To disinfect, sterilize, decontaminate.

ОБЕЗЗАРА́ЗЬ (imp.), see обеззара́жу.

ОБЕЗОБРА́ЖЕННЫЙ; обезобра́жен, —а, —о, —ы (ppp), see обезобра́жу.

ОБЕЗОБРÁЖУ, обезобрáзишь. Р. Обезобрáзить (асс.). I. Обезобрáживать, безобрáзить (mean. 1). 1. To disfigure, mutilate. 2. (fig.) To mutilate.

ОБЕЗОБРÁЗЬ (imp.), see обезобрáжу.

ОБЕЗОПÁСЕННЫЙ; обезопáсен, —а, —о, —ы (ppp), see обезопáшу.

ОБЕЗОПÁСЬ (imp.), see обезопáшу.

ОБЕЗОПÁШУ, обезопáсишь. Р.Обезопáсить (асс.). 1. To secure, protect, guard. 2. To secure, etc. against (асс. + от + gen.).

ОБÉЙ (imp.). Р. Обúть (асс.). I. Обивáть. 1. To cover, upholster. 2. To bind (e.g., a cask with iron) (асс. + inst.). 3. To knock off (as snow from a roof, etc.). 4. To injure or damage (the surface or edge of s.t.). (Also see обобью.)

ОБЕРЁГ, обереглá (past), see оберегу́.

ОБЕРЕГИ́ (imp.), see оберегу́.

ОБЕРЕГУ́, обережёшь, оберегу́т Р. Оберéчь (асс.). I. Оберегáть. To guard or protect (against) (асс. + от + gen.).

ОБЕРЕЖЁННЫЙ; обережён, —á, —ó, —ы́ (ppp), see оберегу́.

ОБЕРЕЖЁШЬ, see оберегу́.

ОБЕРЁШЬ, see оберу́.

ОБЕРИ́ (imp.), see оберу́.

ОБЕРУ́, оберёшь. Р. Обобрáть (асс.). I. Обирáть. 1. To pick or gather (as berries, etc.). 2. To rob or fleece.

ОБЕСКРÓВЛЕННЫЙ; обескрóвлен, —а, —о, —ы (ppp), see обескрóвлю.

ОБЕСКРÓВЛЮ, обескрóвишь. Р. Обескрóвить (асс.). I. Обескрóвливать. (lit. and fig.) To bleed (s.o. or s.t.).

ОБЕСКРÓВЬ (imp.), see обескрóвлю.

ОБЕСПЛÓДЬ (imp.), see обесплóжу.

ОБЕСПЛÓЖЕННЫЙ; обесплóжен, —а, —о, —ы (ppp), see обесплóжу.

ОБЕСПЛÓЖУ, обесплóдишь. Р. Обесплóдить (асс.). I. Обесплóживать. To render barren, sterilize.

ОБЕССЛÁВЛЕННЫЙ; обесслáвлен, —а, —о, —ы (ppp), see обесслáвлю.

ОБЕССЛÁВЛЮ, обесслáвишь. Р. Обесслáвить (асс.). I. Обесслáвливать. To defame.

ОБЕССЛÁВЬ (imp.), see обесслáвлю.

ОБЕССМÉРТЬ (imp.), see обессмéрчу.

ОБЕССМÉРЧЕННЫЙ; обессмéрчен, —а, —о, —ы (ppp), see обессмéрчу.

ОБЕССМÉРЧУ, обессмéртишь. Р. Обессмéртить (асс.). To immortalize.

ОБЕССУ́ДЬ, обессу́дьте (imp.). Р. Обессу́дить (arch.). Used in expression, не обессу́дь ("don't judge too harshly").

ОБЕСЦВÉТЬ (imp.), see обесцвéчу.

ОБЕСЦВÉЧЕННЫЙ; обесцвéчсп, —а, —о, —ы (ppp), see обесцвéчу.

ОБЕСЦВÉЧУ, обесцвéтишь. Р. Обесцвéтить (асс.). I. Обесцвéчивать. 1. To fade (as sun fades color). 2. (fig.) To make insipid, colorless.

ОБЕСЧÉСТИ (imp.), see обесчéщу.

ОБЕСЧÉЩЕННЫЙ; обесчéщен, —а, —о, —ы (ppp), see обесчéщу.

ОБЕСЧÉЩУ, обесчéстишь. Р. Обесчéстить (асс.). I. Бесчéстить. To disgrace, dishonor.

ОБЖÁТЫЙ¹; обжáт, —а, —о, —ы (ppp). Р. Обжáть (асс.). To wring out (as wet laundry) (also see обожму́).

ОБЖÁТЫЙ²; обжáт, —а, —о, —ы (ppp). Р. Обжáть (асс.). To reap; reap around (s.t.) (also see обожну́).

ОБЖЁГ, обожглá (past). Р. Обжéчь (асс.). I. Обжигáть. 1. To burn, char, scorch. 2. To burn (as one's hand). 3. To bake (as bricks). (Also see обожгу́.)

ОБЖИВЁШЬ, see обживу́.

ОБЖИВИ́ (imp.), see обживу́.

ОБЖИВУ́, обживёшь. Р. Обжúть (асс.). I. Обживáть. To make (a site or new dwelling) livable.

ОБЖИТÓЙ; óбжит, —á, —о, —ы (ppp), see обживу́.

ОБЖИ́ТЫЙ; обжи́т, —á, —о, —ы (ppp), see обживу́.

ОБЗАВЕДЁШЬ, see обзаведу́.

ОБЗАВЕДИ́ (imp.), see обзаведу́.

ОБЗАВЕДУ́, обзаведёшь. Р. Обзавести́ (асс. + inst.). I. Обзаводи́ть. To supply (s.o.) with some necessity.

ОБЗАВÉДШИЙ (pap), see обзаведу́.

ОБЗАВЕДЯ́ (adv. past part.), see обзаведу́.

ОБЗАВЁЛ, обзавелá (past), see обзаведу́.

ОБЗАВОЖУ́, обзаводишь. I. Обзаводи́ть (асс. + inst.). Р. Обзавести́. To supply (s.o.) with some necessity.

ОБЗОВЁШЬ, see обзову́.

ОБЗОВИ́ (imp.), see обзову́.

ОБЗОВУ́, обзовёшь. Р. Обозва́ть (acc. + inst.). I. Обзыва́ть. 1. To call (s.o.) by an insulting name (as "fool") 2. (arch.) To call (s.o.) by an endearing name (as "angel").

ОБИ́ДИШЬ, see оби́жу.

ОБИ́ДЬ (imp.), see оби́жу.

ОБИ́ДЯТ, see оби́жу.

ОБИ́ЖЕННЫЙ; оби́жен, —а, —о, —ы (ppp), see оби́жу.

ОБИ́ЖУ, оби́дишь. Р. Оби́деть (acc.). I. Обижа́ть. 1. To offend (s.o.). 2. To treat (s.o.) badly.

ОБИ́ТЫЙ; оби́т, —а, —о, —ы (ppp), see обе́й and обобью́.

ОБКО́ЛЕШЬ, see обколю́.

ОБКОЛИ́ (imp.), see обколю́.

ОБКО́ЛОТЫЙ; обко́лот, —а, —о, —ы (ppp), see обколю́.

ОБКОЛЮ́, обко́лешь. Р. Обколо́ть (acc.). I. Обка́лывать. 1. To prick (as one's hand on barbed wire) (acc. + inst.). 2. To split off, chop off (as ice from a ship's deck).

ОБКО́РМЛЕННЫЙ; обко́рмлен, —а, —о, —ы (ppp), see обкормлю́.

ОБКОРМЛЮ́, обко́рмишь. Р. Обкорми́ть (acc.). I. Обка́рмливать. To overfeed.

ОБКО́ШЕННЫЙ; обко́шен, —а, —о, —ы (ppp), see обкошу́.

ОБКОШУ́, обко́сишь. Р. Обкоси́ть (acc.). I. Обка́шивать. 1. To mow around (s.t.). 2. To mow (e.g., a quantity of, a field). 3. To outmow. 4. To "break in" (condition for use) (a scythe).

ОБКРА́ДЕННЫЙ; обкра́ден, —а, —о, —ы (ppp), see обкраду́.

ОБКРАДЁШЬ, see обкраду́.

ОБКРАДИ́ (imp.), see обкраду́.

ОБКРАДУ́, обкрадёшь. Р. Обокра́сть (acc.). I. Обкра́дывать. 1. To rob (a person). 2. To burglarize (a house).

ОБЛАГОРО́ДЬ (imp.), see облагоро́жу.

ОБЛАГОРО́ЖЕННЫЙ; облагоро́жен, —а, —о, —ы (ppp), see облагоро́жу.

ОБЛАГОРО́ЖУ, облагоро́дишь. Р. Облагоро́дить (acc.). I. Облагора́живать. 1. (lit. and fig.) To ennoble (a person, etc.). 2. To improve (as a species, strain, etc.).

ОБЛА́ДЬ (imp.), see обла́жу¹.

ОБЛА́ЕШЬ, see обла́ю.

ОБЛА́ЖЕННЫЙ; обла́жен, —а, —о, —ы (ppp), see обла́жу¹.

ОБЛА́ЖУ¹, обла́дишь. Р. Обла́дить (acc.). I. Обла́живать. 1. To put in order. 2. To arrange, organize.

ОБЛА́ЖУ², обла́зишь. Р. Обла́зить (acc.). To clamber all over (s.t. or someplace).

ОБЛА́ЗЬ (imp.), see обла́жу².

ОБЛА́Й (imp.), see обла́ю.

ОБЛА́ПЛЕННЫЙ; обла́плен, —а, —о, —ы (ppp), see обла́плю.

ОБЛА́ПЛЮ, обла́пишь. Р. Обла́пить (acc.). I. Обла́пливать. 1. To give a rough embrace, a bear hug. 2. To embrace with paws (of a bear, etc.).

ОБЛА́ПЬ (imp.), see обла́плю.

ОБЛА́Ю, обла́ешь. Р. Обла́ять (acc.). I. Обла́ивать. 1. To bark at (of a dog). 2. (fig.) To bark at, scold, fly at (of a person).

ОБЛА́ЯННЫЙ; обла́ян, —а, —о, —ы (ppp), see обла́ю.

ОБЛЁГ, облегла́ (past), see обля́жет

ОБЛЕ́З, облезла (past), see обле́зет and обле́зу.

ОБЛЕ́ЗЕТ, обле́зут (3rd pers. only). Р. Обле́зть (intr.). I. Облеза́ть. 1. To fall out (of hair, fur, feathers, etc.). 2. To become or wear bare (through loss of hair, fur, etc.). 3. To peel (of paint, walls, etc.).

ОБЛЕ́ЗУ, обле́зешь. Р. Обле́зть (acc.). I. Облеза́ть. To crawl around (s.t.).

ОБЛЕ́ЗУТ, see обле́зет and обле́зу.

ОБЛЕ́ЗЬ (imp.), see обле́зу and обле́зет.

ОБЛЕ́Й (imp.). Р. Обли́ть. I. Облива́ть. 1. (lit. and fig.) To pour or spill (s.t.) (inst.) on or over (s.t.) (acc.). 2. To glaze (s.t. with s.t.) (acc. + inst.). (Also see оболью́.)

ОБЛЁК, облекла́ (past), see облеку́.

ОБЛЕКИ́ (imp.), see облеку́.

ОБЛЕКУ́, облечёшь, облеку́т. Р. Обле́чь (acc.). I. Облека́ть. 1. To clothe (s.o. in s.t.) (acc. + в + acc.). 2. (lit. and fig.) To cover, envelope. 3. (fig.) To present, express, embody in some form (as an idea in a story) (acc. + в + acc.). 4. (fig.) To invest (s.o. or s.t. with s.t.) (as a person with authority) (acc. + inst.).

ОБЛЕ́ПЛЕННЫЙ; обле́плен, —а, —о, —ы (ppp), see облеплю́.

ОБЛЕПЛЮ́, обле́пишь. Р. Облепи́ть. I. Облепля́ть. 1. To cling or stick to (as mud clings to shoes, a dog to its quarry, etc.) (acc.). 2. To cover by pasting, etc. (as a wall with bills) (acc. + inst.).

ОБЛЕТИ (imp.), see облечу.

ОБЛЕТИШЬ, see облечу.

ОБЛЕТЯТ, see облечу.

ОБЛЕЧЁННЫЙ; облечён, —а, —о, —ы (ppp), see облеку.

ОБЛЕЧЁШЬ, see облеку.

ОБЛЕЧУ, облетишь. Р. **Облететь**. I. **Облетать**. 1. To fly around or about (as a lake, country, etc.) (acc.) or (**вокруг** + gen.). 2. (fig.) To fly about, spread (as rumors spread over the city) (acc. of city). 3. To fall (of leaves) (intr.).

ОБЛИЖЕШЬ, see оближу.

ОБЛИЖИ (imp.), see оближу.

ОБЛИЖУ, оближешь. Р. **Облизать** (acc.). I. **Облизывать**. To lick.

ОБЛИЗАННЫЙ; облизан, —а, —о, —ы (ppp), see оближу.

ОБЛИП, облипла (past). Р. **Облипнуть** (intr.). I. **Облипать**. 1. To be covered all over with s.t. that adheres, clings (as shoes are covered with mud) (intr. + inst.). 2. To cling.

ОБЛИТОЙ; облит, —а, —о, —ы (ppp) see облей and обольью.

ОБЛИТЫЙ; облит, —а, —о, —ы (ppp), see облей and обольью.

ОБЛИТЫЙ; облит, —а, —о, —ы (ppp), see облей and обольью.

ОБЛОКОЧЕННЫЙ; облокочен, —а, —о, —ы (ppp), see облокочу.

ОБЛОКОЧУ, облокотишь (and облокотишь). Р. **Облокотить**. I. **Облокачивать**. To lean (one's arm/elbow) (on s.t.) (acc. of arm + на + acc. of s.t.).

ОБЛОМЛЕННЫЙ; обломлен, —а, —о, —ы (ppp), see обломлю.

ОБЛОМЛЮ, обломишь. Р. **Обломить** (acc.). I. **Обламывать**. To break off (as a branch).

ОБЛУПЛЕННЫЙ; облуплен, —а, —о, —ы (ppp), see облуплю.

ОБЛУПЛЮ, облупишь. Р. **Облупить** (acc.). I. **Лупить**. 1. To peel, bark, strip, pare. 2. To overcharge, cheat.

ОБЛЯГУТ, see обляжет.

ОБЛЯЖЕТ, облягут (3rd pers. only). Р. **Облечь** (acc.). I. **Облегать**. 1. To cover (of clouds, etc.). 2. To fit closely (of a dress, etc.). 3. (arch.) To surround (of an army, etc.).

ОБМАЖЕШЬ, see обмажу.

ОБМАЖУ, обмажешь. Р. **Обмазать** (acc. + inst.). I. **Обмазывать**. 1. To coat (with s.t.). 2. To smear (with s.t.).

ОБМАЖЬ (imp.), see обмажу.

ОБМАЗАННЫЙ; обмазан, —а, —о, —ы (ppp), see обмажу.

ОБМЁЛ, обмела (past), see обмету.

ОБМЕР, обмерла, обмерло, обмерли (past). Р. **Обмереть** (intr.). I. **Обмирать**. 1. To faint. 2. (fig.) To "freeze" (as from fright, etc.) (от + gen.). (Also see обомру.)

ОБМЕРЕВ (adv. past part.), see обмер and обомру.

ОБМЁРЗ, обмёрзла (past). Р. **Обмёрзнуть** (intr.). I. **Обмерзать**. 1. To become covered with frost or ice. 2. To become numb with cold.

ОБМЁТАННЫЙ; обмётан, —а, —о, —ы (ppp), see обмечу.

ОБМЕТЁННЫЙ; обметён, —а, —о, —ы (ppp), see обмету.

ОБМЕТЁШЬ, see обмету.

ОБМЕТИ (imp.), see обмету.

ОБМЕТУ, обметёшь. Р. **Обмести** (acc.). I. **Обметать**. 1. To sweep (off) (as walls, etc.). 2. To sweep away (as dust, etc.). 3. To dust (e.g., a table).

ОБМЁТШИЙ (pap), see обмету.

ОБМЕТЯ (adv. past part.), see обмету.

ОБМЕЧЕШЬ, see обмечу.

ОБМЕЧИ (imp.), see обмечу.

ОБМЕЧУ, обмечешь. Р. **Обметать** (acc.). I. **Обмётывать**. 1. To whip-stitch, overcast (as a hem). 2. To become chapped (as one's lips), have sores (impers.).

ОБМОЕШЬ, see обмою.

ОБМОЙ (imp.), see обмою.

ОБМОЛВИСЬ and обмолвься (imp.), see обмолвлюсь.

ОБМОЛВЛЮСЬ, обмолвишься. Р. **Обмолвиться** (intr.). 1. To mention in passing, casually. 2. To make a mistake or slip in speaking.

ОБМОЛОЧЕННЫЙ; обмолочен, —а, —о, —ы (ppp), see обмолочу.

ОБМОЛОЧУ, обмолотишь. Р. **Обмолотить** (acc.). I. **Обмолачивать**. To thresh.

ОБМОРОЖЕННЫЙ; обморожен, —а, —о, —ы (ppp), see обморожу.

ОБМОРÓЖУ, обморóзишь. Р. Обморóзить (acc.). I. Обморáживать. To freeze or get frostbitten (as one's ears, hands, etc.).

ОБМОРÓЗЬ (imp.), see обморóжу.

ОБМÓЮ, обмóешь. Р. Обмыть (acc.). I. Обмывáть. 1. To bathe. 2. To do all the washing or laundry for (as one's family) (acc. of family).

ОБМЫТЫЙ; обмыт, —а, —о, —ы (ppp), see обмóю.

ОБМЯК, обмякла (past). Р. Обмякнуть (intr.). I. Обмякáть. (lit. and fig.) To become soft.

ОБМЯТЫЙ; обмят, —а, —о, —ы (ppp). Р. Обмять (acc.). I. Обминáть. 1. To press down. 2. To trample down. (Also see обомну.)

ОБНЁС, обнеслá (past), see обнесу.

ОБНЕСЁННЫЙ; обнесён, —á, —ó, —ы (ppp), see обнесу.

ОБНЕСЁШЬ, see обнесу.

ОБНЕСИ (imp.), see обнесу.

ОБНЕСУ, обнесёшь. Р. Обнести (acc.). I. Обносить. 1. To enclose (as a garden with a wall) (acc. + inst.). 2. To serve everyone (with s.t.) (acc. + inst.). 3. To pass up (s.o.) while serving (s.t.) (acc. + inst.). 4. To carry (s.o. or s.t.) around (s.t.) (acc. + вокруг/кругóм + gen.). 5. (arch.) To slander (acc.).

ОБНЕСЯ and обнёсши (adv. past part.), see обнесу.

ОБНИМЕШЬ, see обниму.

ОБНИМИ (imp.), see обниму.

ОБНИМУ, обнимешь. Р. Обнять (acc.). I. Обнимáть. 1. To embrace. 2. To come over, seize (as terror seizes one). 3. To envelope (of flames). 4. (fig.) To grasp (as an idea, etc.). (Also see обойму.)

ОБНОВЛЁННЫЙ; обновлён, —á, —ó, —ы (ppp), see обновлю.

ОБНОВЛЮ, обновишь. Р. Обновить (acc.). I. Обновлять. 1. To renovate, renew. 2. To replace (s.t. with s.t. new). 3. To use (s.t.) for the first time. 4. To revive.

ОБНÓШЕННЫЙ; обнóшен, —а, —о, —ы (ppp), see обношу[2].

ОБНОШУ[1], обнóсишь. I. Обносить (acc.). Р. Обнести. 1. To enclose (as a garden with a wall) (acc. + inst.). 2. To serve everyone (with s.t.) (acc. + inst.). 3. To pass up (s.o.) while serving (s.t.) (acc. + inst.). 4. To carry (s.o. or s.t.) around (s.t.) (acc. + вокруг/кругóм + gen.). 5. (arch.) To slander (acc.).

ОБНОШУ[2], обнóсишь. Р. Обносить (acc.). I. Обнáшивать. To "break in" by wearing (as new shoes).

ÓБНЯТЫЙ; óбнят, —á, —о, —ы (ppp), see обниму and обойму.

ОБÓБРАННЫЙ; обóбран, —а, (or —á), —о, —ы. Р. Обобрáть (acc.). I. Обирáть. 1. To pick or gather (as berries, etc.). 2. To rob or fleece. (Also see оберу.)

ОБОБЩЕСТВЛЁННЫЙ; обобществлён, —á, —ó, —ы (ppp), see обобществлю.

ОБОБЩЕСТВЛЮ, обобществишь. Р. Обобществить (acc.). I. Обобществлять. 1. To socialize. 2. To collectivize.

ОБОБЬЁШЬ, see обобью.

ОБОБЬЮ, обобьёшь. Р. Обить (acc.). I. Обивáть. 1. To cover, upholster. 2. To bind (e.g., a cask with iron) (acc. + inst.). 3. To knock off (as snow from a roof, etc.). 4. To injure or damage (the surface or edge of s.t.).

ОБОВЬЁШЬ, see обовью.

ОБОВЬЮ, обовьёшь. Р. Обвить (acc.). I. Обвивáть. 1. To wind (s.t. around s.t.) (acc. + вокруг + gen.). 2. To wind (s.t. with s.t.) (acc. + inst.). 3. To wind around, entwine s.t. (as ivy winds around a tree). 4. To embrace (as s.o.'s waist).

ОБОГАЩЁННЫЙ; обогащён, —á, —ó, —ы (ppp), see обогащу.

ОБОГАЩУ, обогатишь. Р. Обогатить (acc.). I. Обогащáть. (lit. and fig.) To enrich.

ОБÓГНАННЫЙ; обóгнан, —а, —о, —ы (ppp). Р. Обогнáть (acc.). I. Обгонять. (lit. and fig.) To outrun, outdistance, outstrip (also see обгоню).

ОБÓДРАННЫЙ; обóдран, —а, —о, —ы (ppp). Р. Ободрáть (acc.). I. Обдирáть. 1. To flay (as a carcass). 2. To bark (as a tree). 3. To fray, wear to tatters (as clothes, etc.). 4. (fig.) To fleece (as a person). (Also see обдеру.)

ОБОЖГИ (imp.), see обожгу.

ОБОЖГЛÁ, обожглó, обожгли (past), see обожгу and обжёг.

ОБОЖГУ, обожжёшь, обожгут. Р. **Обжечь** (acc.). I. **Обжигать**. 1. To burn, char, scorch. 2. To burn (as one's hand). 3. To bake (as bricks).

ОБОЖДЁШЬ, see обожду.

ОБОЖДИ (imp.), see обожду.

ОБОЖДУ, обождёшь. Р. **Обождать**. 1. To wait for a while (intr.). 2. To wait for (acc.).

ОБОЖЕСТВЛЁННЫЙ; обожествлён, —á, —ó, —ы́ (ppp), see обожествлю.

ОБОЖЕСТВЛЮ, обожествишь. Р. **Обожествить** (acc.). I. **Обожествлять**. To apotheosize, deify.

ОБОЖЖЁННЫЙ; обожжён, —á, —ó, —ы́ (ppp), see обожгу.

ОБОЖЖЁШЬ, see обожгу.

ОБОЖМЁШЬ, see обожму.

ОБОЖМИ (imp.), see обожму.

ОБОЖМУ, обожмёшь. Р. **Обжать** (acc.). I. **Обжимать**. To wring out (as wet laundry).

ОБОЖНЁШЬ, see обожну.

ОБОЖНИ (imp.), see обожну.

ОБОЖНУ, обожнёшь. Р. **Обжать** (acc.). I. **Обжинать**. To reap; to reap around (s.t.).

ОБОЗВАННЫЙ; обóзван, —а, —о, —ы (ppp). Р. **Обозвать** (acc. + inst.). I. **Обзывать**. 1. To call (s.o.) by an insulting name (as "fool"). 2. (arch.) To call (s.o.) by an endearing name (as "angel"). (Also see обзову.)

ОБОЗНАВАЙСЯ (imp.), see обознаюсь.

ОБОЗНАВАЯСЬ (adv. pres. part.), see обознаюсь.

ОБОЗНАЕШЬСЯ, see обознаюсь.

ОБОЗНАЮСЬ, обознаёшься. I. **Обознаваться** (intr.). Р. **Обознаться**. To be mistaken in s.o.'s identity.

ОБОЗРИ (imp.), see обозрю.

ОБОЗРИШЬ, see обозрю.

ОБОЗРЮ, обозришь. Р. **Обозреть** (acc.). I. **Обозревать**. 1. To look over, examine, survey (as the landscape, etc.). 2. To review, examine (as an editorial, etc.).

ОБОЗРЯТ, see обозрю.

ОБОЙДЁННЫЙ; обойдён, —á, —ó, —ы́ (ppp), see обойду.

ОБОЙДЁШЬ, see обойду.

ОБОЙДИ (imp.), see обойду.

ОБОЙДУ, обойдёшь. Р. **Обойти** (acc.). I. **Обходить**. 1. To circle, go around,

skirt. 2. To bypass. 3. To make the rounds, visit a number of places, people. 4. To outstrip (as in a race). 5. To evade, circumvent, avoid. 6. To deceive. 7. To spread over (as news spreads over the city).

ОБОЙДЯ and обошéдши (adv. past part.), see обойду.

ОБОЙМЁШЬ, see обойму.

ОБОЙМИ (imp.), see обойму.

ОБОЙМУ, обоймёшь. Р. **Обнять** (acc.), об'ять. I. **Обнимать**. 1. To embrace. 2. To come over, seize (as terror seizes one). 3. To envelope (of flames). 4. (fig.) To grasp (as an idea). (Also see обниму.)

ОБОКРАДЕННЫЙ; обокрáден, —а, —о, —ы (ppp), see обокрáл and обкраду.

ОБОКРАЛ, обокрáла (past). Р. **Обокрасть** (acc.). I. **Обкрáдывать**. 1. To rob (s.o.). 2. To burglarize (e.g., a house). (Also see обкраду.)

ОБОЛГАННЫЙ; обóлган, —а, —о, —ы (ppp), see оболгу.

ОБОЛГИ (imp.), see оболгу.

ОБОЛГУ, оболжёшь, оболгут. Р. **Оболгать** (acc.). To slander.

ОБОЛЖЁШЬ, see оболгу.

ОБОЛЬЁШЬ, see оболью.

ОБОЛЬЩЁННЫЙ; обольщён, —á, —ó, —ы́ (ppp), see обольщу.

ОБОЛЬЩУ, обольстишь. Р. **Обольстить** (acc.). I. **Обольщать**. 1. To tempt, allure. 2. To seduce.

ОБОЛЬЮ, обольёшь. Р. **Облить**. I. **Обливать**. 1. (lit. and fig.) To pour or spill (s.t.) (inst.) on or over (s.t.) (acc.). 2. To glaze (s.t. with s.t.) (acc. + inst.).

ОБОМНЁШЬ, see обомну.

ОБОМНИ (imp.), see обомну.

ОБОМНУ, обомнёшь. Р. **Обмять** (acc.). I. **Обминать**. 1. To press down. 2. To trample down.

ОБОМРЁШЬ, see обомру.

ОБОМРИ (imp.), see обомру.

ОБОМРУ, обомрёшь. Р. **Обмереть** (intr.). I. **Обмирать**. 1. To faint. 2. (fig.) To freeze (as from fright, etc.) (от + gen.).

ОБОПРЁШЬ, see обопру.

ОБОПРИ (imp.), see обопру.

ОБОПРУ, обопрёшь. Р. **Опереть** (acc.). I. **Опирать**. To rest, lean, brace (s.t. on or against s.t.).

ОБОПЬЁШЬ, see **обопью.**

ОБОПЬЮ́, обопьёшь. Р. **Опи́ть** (acc.). I. **Опива́ть.** To drink (s.o.) "out of house and home" (to drink much at the expense of someone else).

ОБО́РВАННЫЙ; обо́рван, —а, —о, —ы (ppp), see **оборву́.**

ОБОРВЁШЬ, see **оборву́.**

ОБОРВИ́ (imp.), see **оборву́.**

ОБОРВУ́, оборвёшь. Р. **Оборва́ть** (acc.). I. **Обрыва́ть.** 1. To pluck, pick (as flowers). 2. To break (as a cord, thread, etc.). 3. To break off. 4. (fig.) To cut short (as a speech). 5. (fig.) To cut (s.o.) off (as with a rude remark).

ОБОРО́ЧЕННЫЙ; оборо́чен, —а, —о, —ы (ppp), see **оборочу́.**

ОБОРОЧУ́, оборо́тишь. Р. **Оборотить** (acc.). I. **Обора́чивать.** 1. To turn (as one's face toward s.t.) (acc. + к + dat.). 2. To overturn (as a glass). 3. (myth.) To turn (e.g., s.o. into a monster) (acc. + в + acc.) or (acc. + inst.).

ОБОСО́БЛЕННЫЙ; обосо́блен, —а, —о, —ы (ppp), see **обосо́блю.**

ОБОСО́БЛЮ, обосо́бишь. Р. **Обосо́бить** (acc.). I. **Обособля́ть.** To isolate.

ОБОСО́БЬ (imp.), see **обосо́блю.**

ОБОТРЁШЬ, see **оботру́.**

ОБОТРИ́ (imp.), see **оботру́.**

ОБОТРУ́, оботрёшь. Р. **Обтере́ть** (acc.). I. **Обтира́ть.** 1. To wipe, wipe dry, wipe away. 2. To rub. 3. To wear threadbare. 4. To polish, abrade.

ОБОЧЛА́, обочло́, обочли́ (past), see **обочту́ and обчёл.**

ОБОЧТЁШЬ, see **обочту́.**

ОБОЧТИ́ (imp.), see **обочту́.**

ОБОЧТУ́, обочтёшь. Р. **Обче́сть** (acc.). To cheat by intentionally miscalculating (as s.o. out of a dollar) (acc. + на + acc. of dollar).

ОБОЧТЯ́ (adv. past part.), see **обочту́.**

ОБОШЕ́ДШИ and обойдя́ (adv. past part.), see **обойду́.**

ОБОШЕ́ДШИЙ (pap), see **обойду́.**

ОБОШЁЛ, обошла́ (past), see **обойду́.**

ОБОШЬЁШЬ, see **обошью́.**

ОБОШЬЮ́, обошьёшь. Р. **Обши́ть** (acc.). I. **Обшива́ть.** 1. To edge, border, bind. 2. To revet, sheathe (as with planks, etc.) (acc. + inst.). 3. To sew up (as a bale of goods). 4. To

make the necessary clothes (as for a family).

ОБРАЗУ́МЛЕННЫЙ; образу́млен, —а, —о, —ы (ppp), see **образу́млю.**

ОБРАЗУ́МЛЮ, образу́мишь. Р. **Образу́мить** (acc.). I. **Образу́мливать.** To bring (s.o.) to reason, bring (s.o.) to his senses.

ОБРАЗУ́МЬ (imp.), see **образу́млю.**

ОБРА́МЛЕННЫЙ; обра́млен, —а, —о, —ы (ppp), see **обра́млю.**

ОБРАМЛЁННЫЙ; обрамлён, —а́, —о́, —ы́ (ppp), see **обрамлю́.**

ОБРА́МЛЮ, обра́мишь. Р. **Обра́мить** (acc.). I. **Обрамля́ть.** To frame, place in a frame (as a picture).

ОБРАМЛЮ́, обрами́шь. Р. **Обрами́ть** (acc./gen.). I. **Обрамля́ть.** To surround, border, frame (e.g., a garden with shrubbery) (acc. + inst.).

ОБРА́МЬ (imp.), see **обра́млю.**

ОБРАСТЁШЬ, see **обрасту́.**

ОБРАСТИ́ (imp.), see **обрасту́.**

ОБРАСТУ́, обрастёшь. Р. **Обрасти́.** I. **Обраста́ть.** 1. To become or be overgrown with (inst.). 2. (fig.) To accumulate, acquire (as dirt, a large population, etc.) (inst.). 3. (arch.) To grow over (as a beard over a face) (acc. of face).

ОБРАЩЁННЫЙ; обращён, —а́, —о́, —ы́ (ppp), see **обращу́.**

ОБРАЩУ́, обрати́шь. Р. **Обрати́ть.** I. **Обраща́ть.** 1. To turn (s.t.) toward s.t.) (in some direction, as one's head, a cannon, etc.) (acc. + к + dat.) or (acc. + в/на + acc.). 2. To direct (as one's gaze, eyes, etc., at s.o. or s.t.) (acc. + к + dat.) or (acc. + на + acc.). 3. (fig.) To direct, turn (as one's attention, affection, conversation, etc., to s.o. or s.t.) (acc. + к + dat.) or (acc. + на + acc.). 4. To convert (s.t. into s.t.) (as gas into a liquid) (acc. + в + acc.).

ОБРЕ́ЕШЬ, see **обре́ю.**

ОБРЕ́ЖЕШЬ, see **обре́жу.**

ОБРЕ́ЖУ, обре́жешь. Р. **Обре́зать** (acc.). I. **Обреза́ть, обре́зывать.** 1. To cut off, trim. 2. To cut (as one's finger). 3. (fig.) To cut (s.o.) off (while speaking). 4. To circumcise.

ОБРЕ́ЖЬ (imp.), see **обре́жу.**

ОБРЕ́ЗАННЫЙ; обре́зан, —а, —о, —ы (ppp), see **обре́жу.**

ОБРЕ́Й (imp.), see **обре́ю.**

ОБРЁК, обрекла́ (past), see обреку́.

ОБРЕКИ́ (imp.), see обреку́.

ОБРЕКУ́, обречёшь, обреку́т. Р. Обре́чь (acc.). I. Обрека́ть. To destine, condemn, doom (to) (acc. + на + acc.).

ОБРЁЛ, обрела́ (past), see обрету́.

ОБРЕМИ́ЖУ, обреми́зишь. Р. Обреми́зить (acc.). I. Реми́зить. 1. To set (as in the game of bridge). 2. (arch.) (fig.) To set (s.o.) back, put in a disadvantageous position.

ОБРЕМИ́ЗЕННЫЙ; обреми́зен, —а, —о, —ы (ppp), see обреми́жу.

ОБРЕМИ́ЗЬ (imp.), see обреми́жу.

ОБРЕТЁННЫЙ; обретён, —а́, —о́, —ы́ (ppp), see обрету́.

ОБРЕТЁШЬ, see обрету́.

ОБРЕТИ́ (imp.), see обрету́.

ОБРЕТУ́, обретёшь. Р. Обрести́ (acc.). I. Обрета́ть. To find, obtain after some effort.

ОБРЕ́ТШИ and обретя́ (adv. past part.), see обрету́.

ОБРЕ́ТШИЙ (pap), see обрету́.

ОБРЕТЯ́ and обре́тши (adv. past part.), see обрету́.

ОБРЕЧЁННЫЙ; обречён, —а́, —о́, —ы́ (ppp), see обреку́.

ОБРЕЧЁШЬ, see обреку́.

ОБРЕШЁТЬ (imp.), see обрешéчу.

ОБРЕШЁЧЕННЫЙ; обрешéчен, —а, —о, —ы (ppp), see обрешéчу.

ОБРЕШЁЧУ, обрешéтишь. Р. Обрешéтить (acc.). I. Обрешéчивать. To cover with laths, to lath.

ОБРЕ́Ю, обре́ешь. Р. Обри́ть (acc.). I. Обрива́ть. 1. To shave (as one's head). 2. To shave off (as one's beard).

ОБРИ́ТЫЙ; обри́т, —а, —о, —ы (ppp), see обре́ю.

ОБРО́С, обросла́ (past) see обрасту́.

ОБРУ́БЛЕННЫЙ; обру́блен, —а, —о, —ы (ppp), see обрублю́.

ОБРУБЛЮ́, обру́бишь. Р. Обруби́ть (acc.). I. Обруба́ть. 1. To lop off, cut off. 2. To hem (as a handkerchief).

ОБРЮ́ЗГ, обрю́згла (past). Р. Обрю́згнуть (intr.). To become fat and flabby.

ОБРЯ́ЖЕННЫЙ; обря́жен, —а, —о, —ы (ppp), see обряжу́.

ОБРЯЖУ́, обря́дишь (or обряди́шь). Р. Обряди́ть (acc.). I. Обряжа́ть. 1. To dress up (s.o. in s.t.) (acc. + в

+ acc.). 2. To take care of, look after (as one's horse).

ОБСА́ЖЕННЫЙ; обса́жен, —а, —о, —ы (ppp), see обсажу́.

ОБСАЖУ́, обса́дишь. Р. Обсади́ть (acc. + inst.). I. Обса́живать. To circle or line with planting (as a square, a street with trees, etc.).

ОБСЕ́К, обсекла́ (past), see обсеку́.

ОБСЕКИ́ (imp.), see обсеку́.

ОБСЕКУ́, обсечёшь, обсеку́т. Р. Обсе́чь (acc.). I. Обсека́ть. 1. To cut off. 2. To hew.

ОБСЕ́Л, обсе́ла (past), see обси́дет.

ОБСЕЧЁННЫЙ; обсечён, —а́, —о́, —ы́ (ppp), see обсеку́.

ОБСЕЧЁШЬ, see обсеку́.

ОБСКА́КАННЫЙ; обска́кан, —а, —о, —ы (ppp), see обскачу́.

ОБСКА́ЧЕШЬ, see обскачу́.

ОБСКАЧИ́ (imp.), see обскачу́.

ОБСКАЧУ́, обска́чешь. Р. Обскака́ть (acc.). I. Обска́кивать. 1. To gallop around (s.t.). 2. To outgallop. 3. To surpass, outstrip.

ОБСМО́ТРЕННЫЙ; обсмо́трен, —а, —о, —ы (ppp), see обсмотрю́.

ОБСМОТРИ́ (imp.), see обсмотрю́.

ОБСМО́ТРИШЬ, see обсмотрю́.

ОБСМОТРЮ́, обсмо́тришь. Р. Обсмотре́ть (acc.). I. Обсма́тривать. To inspect, examine.

ОБСМО́ТРЯТ, see обсмотрю́.

ОБСО́САННЫЙ; обсо́сан, —а, —о, —ы (ppp), see обсосу́.

ОБСОСЁШЬ, see обсосу́.

ОБСОСИ́ (imp.), see обсосу́.

ОБСОСУ́, обсосёшь. Р. Обсоса́ть (acc.). I. Обса́сывать. 1. To lick around, suck at (as a piece of candy, a bone, etc.). 2. To examine, study in detail.

ОБСО́Х, обсо́хла (past). Р. Обсо́хнуть (intr.). I. Обсыха́ть. To become dry.

ОБСТА́ВЛЕННЫЙ; обста́влен, —а, —о, —ы (ppp), see обста́влю.

ОБСТА́ВЛЮ, обста́вишь. Р. Обста́вить (acc.). I. Оьставля́ть. 1. To encircle, surround, etc. (s.o. with s.t.) (acc. + inst.). 2. To furnish (as an apartment). 3. To organize, arrange. 4. To cheat, trick. 5. To outstrip (s.o.). 6. To beat (s.o.) (in a game) (acc. + в + acc.).

ОБСТА́ВЬ (imp.), see обста́влю.

ОБСТРИ́Г, обстри́гла (past), see об-
стригу́.

ОБСТРИГИ́ (imp.), see обстригу́.

ОБСТРИГУ́, оьстрижёшь, обстригу́т.
Р. **Обстри́чь** (acc.). I. **Стричь**. 1. To
cut, clip, shear. 2. To give (s.o.) a
haircut (acc. of person).

ОБСТРИ́ЖЕННЫЙ; обстри́жен, —а,
—о, —ы (ppp), see обстригу́.

ОБСТРИЖЁШЬ, see обстригу́.

ОБСТУ́ПЛЕННЫЙ; обсту́плен, —а,
—о, —ы (ppp), see обступлю́.

ОБСТУПЛЮ́, обсту́пишь. Р. **Обсту-
пи́ть** (acc.). 1. **Обступа́ть**. 1. To
surround, crowd around (s.o. or s.t.).
2. (fig.) To envelope (e.g., as memories, thoughts, envelope one).

ОБСУЖДЁННЫЙ; обсуждён, —а́,
—о́, —ы́ (ppp), see обсужу́.

ОБСУЖУ́, обсу́дишь. Р. **Обсуди́ть**
(acc.). I. **Обсужда́ть**. To discuss.

ОБСЫ́ПАННЫЙ; обсы́пан, —а, —о,
—ы (ppp), see обсы́плю.

ОБСЫ́ПЛЕШЬ, see обсы́плю.

ОБСЫ́ПЛЮ, обсы́плешь. Р. **Обсы́-
пать** (acc.). I. **Обсыпа́ть**. 1. To
strew. 2. To sprinkle (with) (acc. +
inst.). 3. To break out in a rash
(impers. + acc.).

ОБСЫ́ПЬ (imp.), see обсы́плю.

ОБСЯ́ДЕТ, обся́дем, обся́дете, обся́дут
(1st and 2nd pers. sing. not used).
Р. **Обсе́сть** (acc.). 1. To sit around
(s.o. or s.t.). 2. To sit all over (s.t.)
(as birds sit all over the branches of
a tree).

ОБСЯ́ДУТ (3rd pers. pl.), see обся́дет.

ОБСЯ́ДЬТЕ (imp.), see обся́дет.

ОБТА́ЕТ, обта́ют (3rd pers. only).
Р. **Обта́ять** (intr.). I. **Обта́ивать**.
To melt away, thaw (on the surface,
edges, etc.).

ОБТА́Й (imp.), see обта́ет.

ОБТА́ЮТ, see обта́ет.

ОБТЁК, обтекла́ (past), see обтечёт.

ОБТЕКИ́ (imp.), see обтечёт.

ОБТЕКУ́Т, see обтечёт.

ОБТЁР, обтёрла (past). Р. **Обтере́ть**
(acc.). I. **Обтира́ть**. 1. To wipe, wipe
dry, wipe away. 2. To rub. 3. To
wear threadbare. 4. To polish, abrade.
(Also see оботру́.)

ОБТЕРЁВ and обтёрши (adv. past
part.), see обтёр and оботру́.

ОБТЕРПИ́СЬ (imp.), see обтерплю́сь.

ОБТЕ́РПИШЬСЯ, see обтерплю́сь.

ОБТЕРПЛЮ́СЬ, обтёрпишься. Р.
Обтерпе́ться (intr.). To become
accustomed to, endure (as conditions)
(в + prep.).

ОБТЕ́РПЯТСЯ, see обтерплю́сь.

ОБТЁРТЫЙ; обтёрт, —а, —о, —ы
(ppp), see обтёр and оботру́.

ОБТЁРШИ and обтерёв (adv. past
part.), see обтёр and оботру́.

ОБТЁСАННЫЙ; обтёсан, —а, —о,
—ы (ppp), see обтешу́.

ОБТЕЧЁТ, обтеку́т (3rd pers. only).
Р. **Обте́чь** (acc.) or (вокру́г + gen).
I. **Обтека́ть**. (lit. and fig.) To flow
around.

ОБТЕ́ШЕШЬ, see обтешу́.

ОБТЕШИ́ (imp.), see обтешу́.

ОБТЕШУ́, обте́шешь. Р. **Обтеса́ть**
(acc.). I. **Обтёсывать**. 1. To hew
smooth. 2. (fig.) To polish, inculcate
(s.o.) with savoir faire.

ОБТРЁПАННЫЙ; обтрёпан, —а,
—о, —ы (ppp), see обтреплю́.

ОБТРЕ́ПЛЕШЬ, see обтреплю́.

ОБТРЕПЛИ́ (imp.), see обтреплю́.

ОБТРЕПЛЮ́, обтре́плешь. Р. **Обтре-
па́ть** (acc.). To fray (through wear)
(as cuff of trousers, etc.).

ОБУ́ЕШЬ, see обу́ю.

ОБУ́ЖЕННЫЙ; обу́жен, —а, —о,
—ы (ppp), see обу́жу.

ОБУ́ЖУ, обу́зишь. Р. **Обу́зить** (acc.).
I. **Обу́живать**. To make too tight or
too narrow (as a sleeve, etc.).

ОБУ́ЗЬ (imp.), see обу́жу.

ОБУ́Й (imp.), see обу́ю.

ОБУ́ТЫЙ; обу́т, —а, —о, —ы (ppp),
see обу́ю.

ОБУ́Ю, обу́ешь. Р. **Обу́ть** (acc.). I.
Обува́ть. 1. To put shoes on (s.o.)
(acc. of s.o.). 2. To put on shoes,
slippers, etc. (acc. of shoes, etc.).
3. To supply (s.o.) with shoes (acc.
of s.o.). 4. To swindle, deceive (acc.).

ОБХВА́ЧЕННЫЙ; обхва́чен, —а,
—о, —ы (ppp), see обхвачу́.

ОБХВАЧУ́, обхва́тишь. Р. **Обхвати́ть**
(acc.). I. **Обхва́тывать**. 1. To embrace. 2. To clasp. 3. (lit. and fig.)
To envelope, engulf, surround.

ОБХО́ЖЕННЫЙ; обхо́жен, —а, —о,
—ы (ppp), see обхожу́[1].

ОБХОЖУ́[1], обхо́дишь. Р. **Обходи́ть**
(acc.). To go all around (as a city),
visit everywhere.

ОБХОЖУ́[2], обхо́дишь. I. **Обходи́ть**

(acc.). Р. **Обойти́**. 1. To circle, go around, skirt. 2. To bypass. 3. To make the rounds, visit a number of people, places. 4. To outstrip (as in a race). 5. To spread over (as news spreads over a city). 6. To evade, circumvent, avoid. 7. To deceive.

ОБХОХО́ЧЕШЬСЯ, see обхохочу́сь.

ОБХОХОЧИ́СЬ (imp.), see обхохочу́сь.

ОБХОХОЧУ́СЬ, обхохо́чешься. Р. **Обхохота́ться** (intr.). I. **Обхоха́тываться**. To laugh until exhausted.

ОБЧЁЛ, обочла́ (past). Р. **Обче́сть** (acc.). To cheat through intentional miscalculation (as s.o. out of some change) (acc. + на + acc.). (Also see обочту́.)

ОБЧИ́СТИ (imp.), see обчи́щу.

ОБЧИ́СТЬ (imp.), see обчи́щу.

ОБЧИ́ЩЕННЫЙ; обчи́щен, —а, —о, —ы (ppp), see обчи́щу.

ОБЧИ́ЩУ, обчи́стишь. Р. **Обчи́стить** (acc.). I. **Обчища́ть**. 1. To clean (off). 2. To brush. 3. To rob, clean out.

ОБШЕ́Й (imp.). Р. **Обши́ть** (acc.). I. **Обшива́ть**. 1. To edge, border, bind. 2. To revet, sheathe (as with planks, etc.) (acc. + inst.). 3. To sew up (as a bale of goods). 4. To make the necessary clothes for (as a family). (Also see обошью́.)

ОБШИ́ТЫЙ; обши́т, —а, —о, —ы (ppp), see обше́й and обошью́.

ОБЩИ́ПАННЫЙ; общи́пан, —а, —о, —ы (ppp), see общиплю́.

ОБЩИ́ПЛЕШЬ, see общиплю́.

ОБЩИПЛИ́ (imp.), see общиплю́.

ОБЩИПЛЮ́, общи́плешь. Р. **Общипа́ть** (acc.). I. **Общи́пывать**. To pluck (petals, grass, feathers, etc.).

ОБ'Е́ДЕННЫЙ; об'е́ден, —а, —о, —ы (ppp), see об'е́м.

ОБ'Е́ДЕШЬ, see об'е́ду.

ОБ'ЕДИ́М, об'еди́те, об'едя́т (pl. forms), see об'е́м.

ОБ'Е́ДУ, об'е́дешь. Р. **Об'е́хать**. I. **Об'езжа́ть**. 1. To travel over, all over (acc.) or (intr.). 2. To detour, go around (acc.). 3. To overtake, pass (acc.). 4. To deceive (acc.).

ОБ'Е́ЗДИ (imp.), see об'е́зжу.

ОБ'ЕЗЖА́Й (imp.), see об'е́ду.

ОБ'Е́ЗЖЕННЫЙ; об'е́зжен, —а, —о, —ы (ppp), see об'е́зжу.

ОБ'Е́ЗЖУ, об'е́здишь. Р. **Об'е́здить** (acc.). I. **Об'езжа́ть**. 1. To break (as a horse). 2. To travel all over (as Europe, a city, etc.).

ОБ'Е́Л, об'е́ла (past), see об'е́м.

ОБ'Е́М, об'е́шь, об'е́ст (sing. forms). Р. **Об'е́сть** (acc.). I. **Об'еда́ть**. 1. To gnaw around. 2. To "eat s.o. out of house and home," be a burden (to s.o.). 3. To eat away, corrode (of acid, alkali).

ОБ'Е́МЛИ (imp.), see об'е́млю.

ОБ'Е́МЛЮ, об'е́млешь (arch. and bookish forms); (обыма́ю, обыма́ешь —modern forms). I. **Обыма́ть** (acc.). Р. **Об'я́ть**. 1. To embrace, grasp. 2. To come over, seize (as terror seizes one). 3. To envelope (of flames). 4. (fig.) To grasp (as an idea).

ОБ'Е́СТ, see об'е́м.

ОБ'Е́ШЬ[1] (2nd pers. sing.), see об'е́м.

ОБ'Е́ШЬ[2] (imp.), see об'е́м.

ОБ'Я́ВЛЕННЫЙ; об'я́влен, —а, —о, —ы (ppp), see об'явлю́.

ОБ'ЯВЛЮ́, об'я́вишь. Р. **Об'яви́ть** (acc.). I. **Об'явля́ть**. To declare, publish, announce, proclaim.

ОБ'Я́ТЫЙ; об'я́т, —а —о —ы (ppp), see обыму́.

ОБЫ́К, обы́кла (past). Р. **Обы́кнуть** (intr.). I. **Обыка́ть**. To become accustomed (to) (+ inf.) or (к + dat.).

ОБЫ́МЕШЬ, see обыму́.

ОБЫМИ́ (imp.), see обыму́.

ОБЫМУ́, обы́мешь (arch. forms). Р. **Об'я́ть** (acc.). I. **Обыма́ть**. 1. To embrace. 2. To come over, seize (as terror seizes one). 3. To envelope (as flames envelope s.t.). 4. To grasp, comprehend.

ОБЫ́СКАННЫЙ; обы́скан, —а, —о, —ы (ppp), see обыщу́.

ОБЫ́ЩЕШЬ, see обыщу́.

ОБЫЩИ́ (imp.), see обыщу́.

ОБЫЩУ́, обы́щешь. Р. **Обыска́ть** (acc.). I. **Обы́скивать**. To search.

ОБЮРОКРА́ТЬ (imp.), see обюрокра́чу.

ОБЮРОКРА́ЧЕННЫЙ; обюрокра́чен, —а, —о, —ы (ppp), see обюрокра́чу.

ОБЮРОКРА́ЧУ, обюрокра́тишь. Р. **Обюрокра́тить** (acc.). I. **Обюрокра́чивать**. To make (s.o.) a bureaucrat or bureaucratic.

ОБЯ́ЖЕШЬ, see обяжу́.

ОБЯЖИ́ (imp.), see обяжу́.

ОБЯЖУ́, обя́жешь. Р. **Обяза́ть** (acc.). I. **Обя́зывать**. 1. To oblige, require (as s.o. to do s.t.) (acc. + inf.). 2. To oblige (s.o.), do (s.o.) a favor (acc. of s.o.).

ОВЕ́ЕШЬ, see **ове́ю**.

ОВЕ́Й (imp.), see **ове́ю**.

ОВЕЩЕСТВЛЁННЫЙ; овеществлён, —а́, —о́, —ы́ (ppp), see **овеществлю́**.

ОВЕЩЕСТВЛЮ́, овеществи́шь. Р. Овеществи́ть (acc.). I. Овеществля́ть. To express, represent in a material form (as labor is expressed in productivity) (acc. + в + prep.).

ОВЕ́Ю, ове́ешь. Р. Ове́ять (acc. + inst.). I. Овева́ть. 1. To fan (as s.o. with cool air). 2. (fig.) To fan (as with enthusiasm). 3. (fig.) To cover (as with glory, fame, etc.).

ОВЕ́ЯННЫЙ; ове́ян, —а, —о, —ы (ppp), see **ове́ю**.

ОГЛА́ДЬ (imp.), see **огла́жу**.

ОГЛА́ЖЕННЫЙ; огла́жен, —а, —о, —ы (ppp), see **огла́жу**.

ОГЛА́ЖУ, огла́дишь. Р. Огла́дить (acc.). I. Огла́живать. 1. To smooth, stroke (as a beard). 2. To soothe by stroking (as a horse).

ОГЛАШЁННЫЙ; оглашён, —а́, —о́, —ы́ (ppp), see **оглашу́**.

ОГЛАШУ́, огласи́шь. Р. Огласи́ть (acc.). I. Оглаша́ть. 1. To announce, proclaim. 2. (arch.) To make public. 3. To fill with sound (as the house with song, etc.).

ОГЛО́Х, огло́хла (past). Р. Огло́хнуть (intr.). I. Гло́хнуть. To become deaf.

ОГЛУПЛЁННЫЙ; оглуплён, —а́, —о́, —ы́ (ppp), see **оглуплю́**.

ОГЛУПЛЮ́, оглупи́шь. Р. Оглупи́ть (acc.). I. Оглупля́ть. To make stupid, foolish, silly.

ОГЛЯДИ́ (imp.), see **огляжу́**.

ОГЛЯДИ́ШЬ, see **огляжу́**.

ОГЛЯДЯ́Т, see **огляжу́**.

ОГЛЯЖУ́, огляди́шь. Р. Огляде́ть (acc.). I. Огля́дывать. To examine, look over, inspect.

ОГОРО́ЖЕННЫЙ; огоро́жен, —а, —о, —ы (ppp), see **огорожу́**.

ОГОРОЖУ́, огоро́дишь (and огоро-ди́шь). Р. Огороди́ть (acc.). I. Огора́живать. To fence in, enclose.

ОГРА́БЛЕННЫЙ; огра́блен, —а, —о, —ы (ppp), see **огра́блю**.

ОГРА́БЛЮ, огра́бишь. Р. Огра́бить (acc.). I. Гра́бить. 1. (lit. and fig.) To rob. 2. To sack, pillage.

ОГРА́БЬ (imp.), see **огра́блю**.

ОГРАЖДЁННЫЙ; ограждён, —а́, —о́, —ы́ (ppp), see **огражу́**.

ОГРАЖУ́, огради́шь. Р. Огради́ть (acc.). I. Огражда́ть. 1. To guard, protect (s.o. or s.t.) (acc.) or (acc. + от + gen.). 2. (arch.) To fence in, enclose (acc.) or (acc. + inst.).

ОГРЁБ, огребла́ (past), see **огребу́**.

ОГРЕБЁННЫЙ; огребён, —а́, —о́, —ы́ (ppp), see **огребу́**.

ОГРЕБЁШЬ, see **огребу́**.

ОГРЕБИ́ (imp.), see **огребу́**.

ОГРЕБУ́, огребёшь. Р. Огрести́ (acc.). I. Огреба́ть. 1. To rake up. 2. (fig.) To rake in (as money).

ОГРУ́З, огру́зла (past). Р. Огру́знуть (intr.). To become too heavy, fat, corpulent.

ОДЕ́НЕШЬ, see **оде́ну**.

ОДЕ́НУ, оде́нешь. Р. Оде́ть (acc.). I. Одева́ть. 1. To dress or clothe (a person, etc.). 2. To cover (as with a blanket). 3. (fig.) To dress, clothe, cover (e.g., trees are dressed in white, etc.).

ОДЕ́НЬ (imp.), see **оде́ну**.

ОДЕ́РЖАННЫЙ; оде́ржан, —а, —о, —ы (ppp), see **одержу́**.

ОДЕ́РЖАТ, see **одержу́**.

ОДЕ́РЖИ (imp.), see **одержу́**.

ОДЕ́РЖИШЬ, see **одержу́**.

ОДЕРЖУ́, оде́ржишь. Р. Одержа́ть (acc.). I. Оде́рживать. To gain, win (as a victory, the upper hand over s.o., etc.) (acc. of victory + над + inst. of s.o.).

ОДЕ́ТЫЙ; оде́т, —а, —о, —ы (ppp), see **оде́ну**.

ОДУШЕВЛЁННЫЙ; одушевлён, —а́, —о́, —ы́ (ppp), see **одушевлю́**.

ОДУШЕВЛЮ́, одушеви́шь. Р. Одушеви́ть (acc.). I. Одушевля́ть. 1. To animate, inspire. 2. to attribute animistic qualities to things.

ОЖГИ́ (imp.), see **ожгу́**.

ОЖГЛА́, ожгло́, ожгли́ (past), see **ожгу́** and **ожёг**.

ОЖГУ́, ожжёшь, ожгу́т. Р. ожéчь. (acc.). I. Ожига́ть. 1. To burn, scorch. 2. To bake (as bricks). 3. To strike, whip.

ОЖЁГ, ожгла́ (past), see **ожгу́**.

ОЖЖЁННЫЙ; ожжён, —а́, —о́, —ы́ (ppp), see **ожгу́**.

ОЖЖЁШЬ, see **ожгу́**.

ОЖИВЁШЬ, see оживу́.

ОЖИВИ́ (imp.), see оживу́ and оживлю́.

ОЖИВЛЁННЫЙ; оживлён, —а́, —о́, —ы́ (ppp), see оживлю́.

ОЖИВЛЮ́, оживи́шь. Р. Оживи́ть (acc.). I. Оживля́ть. 1. To revive. 2. To enliven. 3. To revitalize. 4. To brighten (as colors).

ОЖИВУ́, оживёшь. Р. Ожи́ть (intr.). I. Ожива́ть. (lit. and fig.) To come to life, revive.

ОЗАБО́ТЬ (imp.), see озабо́чу.

ОЗАБО́ЧЕННЫЙ; озабо́чен, —а, —о, —ы (ppp), see озабо́чу.

ОЗАБО́ЧУ, озабо́тишь. Р. Озабо́тить (acc.). I. Забо́тить, озабо́чивать. To worry (s.o.), cause (s.o.) anxiety, trouble, etc.

ОЗАГЛА́ВЛЕННЫЙ; озагла́влен, —а, —о, —ы (ppp), see озагла́влю.

ОЗАГЛА́ВЛЮ, озагла́вишь. Р. Озагла́вить (acc.). I. Озагла́вливать. To entitle (as a book).

ОЗАГЛА́ВЬ (imp.), see озагла́влю.

ОЗДОРОВЛЁННЫЙ; оздоровлён, —а́ —о́, —ы́ (ppp), see оздоровлю́.

ОЗДОРОВЛЮ́, оздорови́шь. Р. Оздорови́ть (acc.). I. Оздоровля́ть. 1. To improve the state of health (of s.o.). 2. To make more conductive to health (as working conditions). 3. (fig.) To improve, make healthy (as the finances of a corporation).

ОЗЛО́БЛЕННЫЙ; озло́блен, —а, —о, —ы (ppp), see озло́блю.

ОЗЛО́БЛЮ, озло́бишь. Р. Озло́бить (acc.). I. Озлобля́ть. To embitter.

ОЗЛО́БЬ (imp.), see озло́блю.

ОЗНАКО́МЛЕННЫЙ; ознако́млен, —а, —о, —ы (ppp), see ознако́млю.

ОЗНАКО́МЛЮ, ознако́мишь. Р. Ознако́мить (acc. + с + inst.). I. Знако́мить, ознакомля́ть. To acquaint with (as s.o. with the rules).

ОЗНАКО́МЬ (imp.), see ознако́млю.

ОЗНОБЛЁННЫЙ; озноблён, —а́, —о́, —ы́ (ppp), see озноблю́.

ОЗНОБЛЮ́, озноби́шь. Р. Озноби́ть (acc.). I. Ознобля́ть. To get (s.t.) slightly frostbitten (as one's hands).

ОЗОЛОЧЁННЫЙ; озолочён, —а́, —о́, —ы́ (ppp), see озолочу́.

ОЗОЛОЧУ́, озолоти́шь. Р. Озолоти́ть (acc.). 1. To make rich, endow, give money generously (to s.o.). 2. (fig.) To gild (as the sun gilds a dome).

ОЗЯ́Б, озя́бла (past). Р. Озя́бнуть (intr.). I. Зя́бнуть. 1. To suffer from cold, feel cold. 2. To freeze (of plants).

ОКА́ЖЕШЬ, see окажу́.

ОКАЖИ́ (imp.), see окажу́.

ОКАЖУ́, ока́жешь. Р. Оказа́ть (acc.). I. Ока́зывать. 1. To display, show (as willingness, etc.). 2. To exert (as influence, pressure). 3. To render, give (as aid, service).

ОКА́ЗАННЫЙ; ока́зан, —а, —о, —ы (ppp), see окажу́.

ОКАЙМЛЁННЫЙ; окаймлён, —а́, —о́, —ы́ (ppp), see окаймлю́.

ОКАЙМЛЮ́, окайми́шь. Р. Окайми́ть (acc. + inst.). I. Окаймля́ть. To edge, border, outline (with).

ОКА́ЧЕННЫЙ; ока́чен, —а, —о, —ы (ppp), see окачу́.

ОКАЧУ́, ока́тишь. Р. Окати́ть (acc.). I. Ока́чивать. To douse, drench, pour over (as with water) (acc. + inst.).

ОКО́ЛЕШЬ, see околю́.

ОКОЛИ́ (imp.), see околю́.

ОКО́ЛОТЫЙ; око́лот, —а, —о, —ы (ppp), see околю́.

ОКОЛО́ЧЕННЫЙ; около́чен, —а, —о, —ы (ppp), see околочу́.

ОКОЛОЧУ́, около́тишь. Р. Околоти́ть (acc.). I. Окола́чивать. 1. To knock off (as snow from one's coat). 2. To strike, beat.

ОКОЛЮ́, око́лешь. Р. Около́ть (acc.). I. Ока́лывать. To break off, chop off (as ice from a ship's deck).

ОКОНФУ́ЖЕННЫЙ; оконфу́жен, —а, —о, —ы (ppp), see оконфу́жу.

ОКОНФУ́ЖУ, оконфу́зишь. Р. Оконфу́зить (acc.). To embarass.

ОКОНФУ́ЗЬ (imp.), see оконфу́жу.

ОКО́РМЛЕННЫЙ; око́рмлен, —а, —о, —ы (ppp), see окормлю́.

ОКОРМЛЮ́, око́рмишь. Р. Окорми́ть (acc.). I. Ока́рмливать. 1. To overfeed. 2. To poison with poisoned food (as gophers, wolves, etc.).

ОКОРО́ЧЕННЫЙ; окоро́чен, —а, —о, —ы (ppp), see окорочу́.

ОКОРОЧУ́, окороти́шь. Р. Окороти́ть (acc.). I. Окора́чивать. 1. To make too short. 2. To curtail, crop.

ОКÓШЕННЫЙ; окóшен, —а, —о, —ы (ppp), see окошý.

ОКОШУ́, окóсишь. Р. Окосѝть (acc.). I. Окáшивать. To mow around (s.t.).

ОКРÁСЬ (imp.), see окрáшу.

ОКРÁШЕННЫЙ; окрáшен, —а, —о, —ы (ppp), see окрáшу.

ОКРÁШУ, окрáсишь. Р. Окрáсить (acc.). I. Крáсить, окрáшивать. 1. To dye, paint, color. 2. (fig.) To color (e.g., one's life, impressions, etc.).

ОКРÉП, окрéпла (past). Р. Окрéпнуть (intr.). I. Крéпнуть. 1. (lit. and fig.) To become strong or stronger. 2. (fig.) To become firmly established. 3. To become healthier.

ОКРЕЩЁННЫЙ; окрещён, —á, —ó, —ы́ (ppp), see окрещý.

ОКРЕЩУ́, окрéстишь. Р. Окрестѝть (acc.). I. Крестѝть (mean. 1). 1. To christen, baptize. 2. To nickname, name, call by a name (acc. + inst.).

ОКРОВÁВЛЕННЫЙ; окровáвлен, —а, —о, —ы (ppp), see окровáвлю.

ОКРОВÁВЛЮ, окровáвишь. Р. Окровáвить (acc.). I. Окровáвливать. To stain with blood.

ОКРОВÁВЬ (imp.), see окровáвлю.

ОКРОПЛЁННЫЙ; окроплён, —á, —ó, —ы́ (ppp), see окроплю́.

ОКРОПЛЮ́, окропѝшь. Р. Окропѝть (acc.). I. Кропѝть. To sprinkle (s.t. or s.o. with s.t.) (acc. + inst.).

ОКРУ́ЧЕННЫЙ; окрýчен, —а, о, —ы (ppp), see окручý.

ОКРУЧУ́, окрýтишь. Р. Окрутѝть (acc.). I. Окрýчивать (mean. 1). 1. To bind or wind around (s.t. with s.t.) (acc. + inst.). 2. (arch.) To marry (s.o.) (perform the ceremony).

ОКУ́ПЛЕННЫЙ; окýплен, —а, —о, —ы (ppp), see окуплю́.

ОКУПЛЮ́, окýпишь. Р. Окупѝть (acc.). I. Окупáть. 1. To repay (as expenditures for s.t. to s.o.), compensate (acc. + dat.). 2. To make amends for, atone for (s.t.).

ОКУРГУ́ЖЕННЫЙ; окургýжен, —а, —о, —ы (ppp), see окургýжу.

ОКУРГУ́ЖУ, окургýзишь. Р. Окургýзить (acc.). To make too short/ tight (as a dress, etc.).

ОКУРГУ́ЗЬ (imp.), see окургýжу.

ОМЕРТВЛЁННЫЙ; омертвлён, —á, —ó, —ы́ (ppp), see омертвлю́.

ОМЕРТВЛЮ́, омертвѝшь. Р. Омерт-

вѝть (acc.). I. Омертвля́ть. 1. To immobilize (as capital). 2. (fig.) To make lifeless (as cloth). 3. To necrotize.

ОМÓЕШЬ, see омóю.

ОМÓЙ (imp.), see омóю.

ОМОЛОЖЁННЫЙ; омоложён, —á, —ó, —ы́ (ppp), see омоложý.

ОМОЛОЖУ́, омолодѝшь. Р. Омолодѝть (acc.). I. Омолáживать. (lit. and fig.) To rejuvenate.

ОМÓЮ, омóешь. Р. Омы́ть (acc.). I. Омывáть. 1. To bathe. 2. (lit. and fig.) To wash, wash away.

ОМЫ́ТЫЙ; омы́т, —а, —о, —ы (ppp), see омóю.

ОПАДЁШЬ, see опадý.

ОПАДЍ (imp.), see опадý.

ОПАДУ́, опадёшь. Р. Опáсть (intr.). I. Опадáть. 1. To fall (of leaves, etc.). 2. To subside (of wind, a swelling, etc.). 3. To grow thinner, lose weight (of a person, etc.). 4. To lose leaves (intr.).

ОПÁЛ, опáла (past), see опадý.

ОПÁЛУБЛЕННЫЙ; опáлублен, —а, —о, —ы (ppp), see опáлублю.

ОПÁЛУБЛЮ, опáлубишь. Р. Опáлубить (acc.). To cover (as a structure with planking, sheet iron, etc.).

ОПÁЛУБЬ (imp.), see опáлублю.

ОПÁХАННЫЙ; опáхан, —а, —о, —ы (ppp), see опашý.

ОПÁШЕШЬ, see опашý.

ОПАШЍ (imp.), see опашý.

ОПАШУ́, опáшешь. Р. Опахáть (acc.). I. Опáхивать. To plow or till around (s.t.).

ОПЕЙ (imp.). Р. Опѝть (acc.). I. Опивáть. To drink (s.o.) "out of house and home" (to drink much at the expense of s.o. else.), (see обопью́).

ОПЁР, оперлá (and опёрла), оперлó, оперлѝ (past). Р. Оперéть (acc.). I. Опирáть. To rest, lean, brace (s.t. on or against s.t.) (also see обопрý).

ОПЕРЁВ and опёрши (adv. past part.), see опёр and обопрý.

ОПЕРЕЖЁННЫЙ; опережён, —á, —ó, —ы́ (ppp), see опережý.

ОПЕРЕЖУ́, опередѝшь. Р. Опередѝть (acc.). I. Опережáть. 1. To overtake and pass. 2. To outstrip. 3. To anticipate.

ОПЁРТЫЙ; опёрт, —á, —о, —ы (ppp), see опёр and обопрý.

ОПЁРШИ and опере́в (adv. past part.), see опёр and обопру́.

ОПИ́САННЫЙ; опи́сан, —а, —о, —ы (ppp), see опишу́.

ОПИ́ШЕШЬ, see опишу́.

ОПИ́ШИ (imp.), see опишу́.

ОПИШУ́, опи́шешь. Р. Описа́ть (acc.). I. Опи́сывать. 1. To describe. 2. To inventory. 3. (math.) To describe, circumscribe.

ОПЛА́КАННЫЙ; опла́кан, —а, —о, —ы (ppp), see опла́чу.

ОПЛА́ЧЕННЫЙ; опла́чен, —а, —о, —ы (ppp), see оплачу́.

ОПЛА́ЧЕШЬ, see опла́чу.

ОПЛА́ЧУ, опла́чешь. Р. Опла́кать (acc.). I. Опла́кивать. To mourn (s.o., s.t.).

ОПЛАЧУ́, опла́тишь. Р. Оплати́ть (acc.). I. Опла́чивать. 1. To pay for (s.t.). 2. To pay (e.g., an account, expenses, etc.).

ОПЛА́ЧЬ (imp.), see опла́чу.

ОПЛЁЛ, оплела́ (past), see оплету́.

ОПЛЕТЁННЫЙ; оплетён, —а́, —о́, —ы́ (ppp), see оплету́.

ОПЛЕТЁШЬ, see оплету́.

ОПЛЕТИ́ (imp.), see оплету́.

ОПЛЕТУ́, оплетёшь. Р. Оплести́ (acc.). I. Оплета́ть. 1. To braid,. weave (s.t. with s.t.), to cover (s.t.) with braided material) (acc. + inst.). 2. To entwine, wind around (as roots wind around rocks, etc.). 3. To swindle, cheat.

ОПЛЁТШИ and оплетя́ (adv. past part.), see оплету́.

ОПЛЁТШИЙ (pap), see оплету́.

ОПЛЕТЯ́ and оплётши (adv. past. part.), see оплету́.

ОПЛЫВЁШЬ, see оплыву́.

ОПЛЫВИ́ (imp.), see оплыву́.

ОПЛЫВУ́, оплывёшь. Р. Оплы́ть. I. Оплыва́ть. 1. To swim, float, sail around (s.t.) (acc.). 2. To become swollen, bloated, fat (intr.). 3. To gutter (of a candle) (intr.). 4. To slide (of land, landslide) (intr.).

ОПЛЫ́ТЫЙ; оплы́т, —а, —о, —ы (ppp), see оплыву́.

ОПОВЕЩЁННЫЙ; оповещён, —а́, —о́, —ы́ (ppp), see оповещу́.

ОПОВЕЩУ́, оповести́шь. Р. Оповести́ть (acc.). I. Оповеща́ть. To notify, inform.

ОПОЗНАВА́Й (imp.), see опознаю́.

ОПОЗНАВА́Я (adv. pres. part.), see опознаю́.

ОПОЗНАЁШЬ, see опознаю́.

ОПОЗНАЮ́, опознаёшь. I. Опознава́ть (acc.). Р. Опозна́ть. To identify.

ОПО́ЛЗ, оползла́ (past), see оползу́.

ОПОЛЗЁШЬ, see оползу́.

ОПОЛЗИ́ (imp.), see оползу́.

ОПОЛЗУ́, оползёшь. Р. Оползти́. I. Оползать. 1. To crawl around (as a snake around a tree) (acc.). 2. To slip, settle (of a foundation of a building, etc.) (intr.).

ОПОЛО́СКАННЫЙ; ополо́скан, —а, —о, —ы (ppp), see ополощу́.

ОПОЛО́ЩЕШЬ, see ополощу́.

ОПОЛОЩИ́ (imp.), see ополощу́.

ОПОЛОЩУ́, ополо́щешь. Р. Ополоска́ть (acc.). I. Опола́скивать. To rinse, wash.

ОПОСТЫ́НЕШЬ, see опосты́ну.

ОПОСТЫ́НУ, опосты́нешь. Р. Опосты́ть and опосты́нуть (dat.). 1. To bore (s.o.) exceedingly. 2. To become repellent, hateful (to s.o.).

ОПОСТЫ́НЬ (imp.), see опосты́ну.

ОПОЧИ́ЕШЬ, see опочи́ю.

ОПОЧИ́Й (imp.), see опочи́ю.

ОПОЧИ́Ю, опочи́ешь. Р. Опочи́ть (arch.) (intr.). 1. To fall asleep. 2. To pass away, die.

ОПОЯ́САННЫЙ; опоя́сан, —а, —о, —ы (ppp), see опоя́шу.

ОПОЯ́ШЕШЬ, see опоя́шу.

ОПОЯ́ШУ, опоя́шешь. Р. Опоя́сать (acc.). I. Опоя́сывать. 1. To gird, girdle. 2. To surround (as a city).

ОПОЯ́ШЬ (imp.), see опоя́шу.

ОПРА́ВЛЕННЫЙ; опра́влен, —а, —о, —ы (ppp), see опра́влю.

ОПРА́ВЛЮ, опра́вишь. Р. Опра́вить (acc.). I. Оправля́ть. 1. To put in order, proper position, to set right (as one's hair, tablecloth, etc.). 2. (arch.) To justify (e.g., s.o.'s action). 3. To mount, set (as a gem, picture, etc.).

ОПРА́ВЬ (imp.), see опра́влю.

ОПРО́ШЕННЫЙ; опро́шен, —а, —о, —ы (ppp), see опрошу́.

ОПРОШУ́, опро́сишь. Р. Опроси́ть (acc.). I. Опра́шивать. To interrogate, question.

ОПРОЩУСЬ, опростишься. Р. Опроститься (intr.). I. Опрощаться. To adopt a more simple standard of living.

ОПУХ, опухла (past). Р. Опухнуть (intr.). I. Опухать, пухнуть. To swell.

ОПУЩЕННЫЙ; опущен, —а, —о, —ы (ppp), see опущу.

ОПУЩУ, опустишь. Р. Опустить (acc.). I. Опускать. 1. To lower. 2. To let down, pull down. 3. To drop (as a letter in a postbox). 4. To turn down (as one's collar). 5. To loosen (as a belt, girth). 6. To omit.

ОРАННЫЙ; оран, —а, —о, —ы (ppp), see орю and ору (mean. 5).

ОРЕШЬ, see орю.

ОРЁШЬ, see ору.

ОРИ (imp.), see ору and орю.

ОРОШЁННЫЙ; орошён, —á, —ó, —ы (ppp), see орошу.

ОРОШУ, оросишь. Р. Оросить (acc.). I. Орошать. 1. To irrigate. 2. To water.

ОРУ, орёшь. I. Орать. 1. To yell (intr.); yell at (на + acc.). 2. To talk too loudly (intr.). 3. To cry loudly (intr.). 4. To sing loudly (intr.) or (acc.). 5. To plow (acc.).

ОРЮ, орёшь. I. Орать (arch.) (acc.). To plow.

ОСАЖДЁННЫЙ; осаждён, —á, —ó, —ы (ppp), see осажу[1] and [2].

ОСАЖЕННЫЙ; осажен, —а, —о, —ы (ppp), see осажу[3].

ОСАЖУ[1], осадишь. Р. Осадить (acc.). I. Осаждать. 1. To beseige (as a fort). 2. (fig.) To beseige (as with questions) (acc. + inst.).

ОСАЖУ[2], осадишь. Р. Осадить (acc.). I. Осаждать (mean. 1), осаживать (mean. 2). 1. (chem.) To precipitate, deposit. 2. To drive, seat (as piling).

ОСАЖУ[3], осадишь. Р. Осадить (acc.). I. Осаживать. 1. To rein in (as a horse). 2. To cause to back, backstep (as a horse). 3. To rebuff, check.

ОСВЕДОМЛЁННЫЙ; осведомлён, —á, —ó, —ы (ppp), see осведомлю.

ОСВЕДОМЛЮ, осведомишь. Р. Осведомить (acc.). I. Осведомлять. To inform (s.o. about s.t.) (acc. + о + prep.).

ОСВЕДОМЬ (imp.), see осведомлю.

ОСВЕЩЁННЫЙ; освещён, —á, —ó, —ы (ppp), see освещу.

ОСВЕЩУ, осветишь. Р. Осветить (acc.). I. Освещать. 1. (lit. and fig.) To light up, illuminate. 2. To elucidate, explain.

ОСВИСТАННЫЙ; освистан, —а, —о, —ы (ppp), see освищу.

ОСВИЩЕШЬ, see освищу.

ОСВИЩИ (imp.), see освищу.

ОСВИЩУ, освищешь. Р. Освистать (acc.). I. Освистывать. To hiss, catcall (e.g., to hiss an actor).

ОСВОБОЖДЁННЫЙ; освобождён, —á, —ó, —ы (ppp), see освобожу.

ОСВОБОЖУ, освободишь. Р. Освободить (acc.). I. Освобождать. 1. To liberate, free. 2. To release, let go. 3. To empty, clear, release (as a book shelf, an apartment, etc.). 4. (fig.) To free (as a period of time).

ОСВЯЩЁННЫЙ; освящён, —á, —ó, —ы (ppp), see освящу.

ОСВЯЩУ, освятишь. Р. Освятить (acc.). I. Освящать. (lit. and fig.) To consecrate, sanctify.

ОСЕКИСЬ (imp.), see осекусь.

ОСЕКСЯ, осеклась (past), see осекусь.

ОСЕКУСЬ, осечёшься, осекутся. Р. Осечься (intr.). I. Осекаться. 1. (lit. and fig.) To misfire. 2. To stop short while speaking.

ОСЕЛ, осела (past). Р. Осесть (intr.). I. Оседать. 1. To settle, sink (of a building, ground, etc.). 2. To sit down slowly. 3. To settle (as dust settles, etc.). 4. To settle down, take up residence. (Also see осяду.)

ОСЕРЖУСЬ, осердишься. Р. Осердиться (intr.). To become angry (at) (на + acc.).

ОСЕЧЁШЬСЯ, see осекусь.

ОСИП, осипла (past). Р. Осипнуть (intr.). I. Сипнуть. To become hoarse.

ОСКЛАБЛЮСЬ, осклабишься. Р. Осклабиться (intr.). To grin.

ОСКЛАБЬСЯ (imp.), see осклабнюсь.

ОСКОПЛЁННЫЙ; оскоплён, —á, —ó, —ы (ppp), see оскоплю.

ОСКОПЛЮ, оскопишь. Р. Оскопить (acc.). I. Оскоплять. To emasculate.

ОСКОРБЛЁННЫЙ; оскорблён, —á, —ó, —ы (ppp), see оскорблю.

ОСКОРБЛЮ, оскорбишь. Р. Оскорбить (acc.). I. Оскорблять. 1. To insult, offend. 2. To defile, profane.

ОСКОРОМЛЮСЬ, оскоромишься. Р.

Оскоро́миться (intr.). I. **Скоро́миться**. To eat meat on days of fast (during Lent, etc.).

ОСКОРО́МЬСЯ, see **оскоро́млюсь**.

ОСЛА́Б, осла́бла (past). P. **Осла́бнуть** (intr.). I. **Ослабева́ть, сла́бнуть**. 1. To weaken, grow weak. 2. To relax, slacken (of tension, attention, etc.).

ОСЛА́БЛЕННЫЙ; осла́блен, —а, —о, —ы (ppp), see **осла́блю**.

ОСЛА́БЛЮ, осла́бишь. P. **Осла́бить** (acc.). I. **Ослабля́ть**. 1. To weaken (as disease weakens one, etc.). 2. To loosen (as belt, rope, etc.). 3. To relax, slacken (as tension, attention, etc.).

ОСЛА́БЬ (imp.), see **осла́блю**.

ОСЛА́ВЛЕННЫЙ; осла́влен, —а, —о, —ы (ppp), see **осла́влю**.

ОСЛА́ВЛЮ, осла́вишь. P. **Осла́вить** (acc.). I. **Ославля́ть, сла́вить**. 1. To defame, give a bad name. 2. To spread rumors (about s.o.).

ОСЛА́ВЬ (imp.), see **осла́влю**.

ОСЛЕ́П, осле́пла (past). P. **Осле́пнуть** (intr.). I. **Сле́пнуть**. (lit. and fig.) To become blind.

ОСЛЕПЛЁННЫЙ; ослеплён, —а́, —о́, —ы́ (ppp), see **ослеплю́**.

ОСЛЕПЛЮ́, ослепи́шь. P. **Ослепи́ть** (acc.). I. **Ослепля́ть**. 1. (lit. and fig.) To blind. 2. To dazzle.

ОСЛИ́З, осли́зла (past). P. **Осли́знуть** (intr.). To become slippery or covered with slime.

ОСЛЫ́ШАТСЯ, see **ослы́шусь**.

ОСЛЫ́ШИШЬСЯ, see ослы́шусь.

ОСЛЫ́ШУСЬ, ослы́шишься. P. **Ослы́шаться** (intr.). To hear incorrectly.

ОСМЕЁШЬ, see осмею́.

ОСМЕ́Й (imp.), see осмею́.

ОСМЕЮ́, осмеёшь. P. **Осмея́ть** (acc.). I. **Осме́ивать**. To ridicule, deride.

ОСМЕ́ЯННЫЙ; осме́ян, —а, —о, —ы (ppp), see осмею́.

ОСМО́ТРЕННЫЙ; осмо́трен, —а, —о, —ы (ppp), see **осмотрю́**.

ОСМОТРИ́ (imp.), see **осмотрю́**.

ОСМО́ТРИШЬ, see осмотрю́.

ОСМОТРЮ́, осмо́тришь. P. **Осмотре́ть** (acc.). I. **Осма́тривать**. To examine, inspect.

ОСМО́ТРЯТ, see осмотрю́.

ОСНАЩЁННЫЙ; оснащён, —а́, —о́, —ы́ (ppp), see оснащу́.

ОСНАЩУ́, оснасти́шь. P. **Оснасти́ть**

(acc.). I. **Оснаща́ть**. 1. To equip, outfit. 2. To rig (as a ship).

ОСОЗНАВА́Й (imp.), see осознаю́.

ОСОЗНАВА́Я (adv. pres. part.), see осознаю́.

ОСОЗНАЁШЬ, see осознаю́.

ОСОЗНАЮ́, осознаёшь. I. **Осознава́ть** (acc.). P. **Осозна́ть**. To realize, perceive.

ОСРАМЛЁННЫЙ; осрамлён, —а́, —о́, —ы́ (ppp), see осрамлю́.

ОСРАМЛЮ́, осрами́шь. P. **Осрами́ть** (acc.). I. **Срами́ть**. To put to shame, shame.

ОСТАВА́ЙСЯ (imp.), see остаю́сь.

ОСТАВА́ЯСЬ (adv. pres. part.), see остаю́сь.

ОСТА́ВЛЕННЫЙ; оста́влен, —а, —о, —ы (ppp), see оста́влю.

ОСТА́ВЛЮ, оста́вишь. P. **Оста́вить** (acc.). I. **Оставля́ть**. 1. To leave. 2. To abandon. 3. To retain, reserve (acc. + за + собо́й). 4. To preserve. 5. To cease. 6. To give up (as hope, etc.). (For other uses see unabridged dictionary.)

ОСТА́ВЬ (imp.), see оста́влю.

ОСТАЁШЬСЯ, see остаю́сь.

ОСТА́НЕШЬСЯ, see оста́нусь.

ОСТАНО́ВЛЕННЫЙ; остано́влен, —а, —о, —ы (ppp), see остановлю́.

ОСТАНОВЛЮ́, остано́вишь. P. **Останови́ть** (acc.). I. **Остана́вливать**. 1. To stop, halt. 2. (fig.) To direct/rest (as one's gaze, attention at/on s.o. or s.t.) (acc. + на + prep.).

ОСТА́НУСЬ, оста́нешься. P. **Оста́ться** (intr.). I. **Остава́ться**. 1. To remain. 2. To stay. 3. To be left. (For idiomatic usages, see unabridged dictionary.)

ОСТА́НЬСЯ (imp.), see оста́нусь.

ОСТАЮ́СЬ, остаёшься. I. **Остаьа́ться** (intr.). P. **Оста́ться**. 1. To remain. 2. To stay. 3. To be left. (For idiomatic uses see unabridged dictionary.)

ОСТЕРЁГ, остерегла́ (past), see остерегу́.

ОСТЕРЕГИ́ (imp.), see остерегу́.

ОСТЕРЕГУ́, остережёшь, остерегу́т. P. **Остере́чь** (acc.). I. **Остерега́ть**. To warn, caution.

ОСТЕРЕЖЁННЫЙ; остережён, —а́, —о́, —ы́ (ppp), see остерегу́.

ОСТЕРЕЖЁШЬ, see остерегу́.

ОСТРИ́Г, острига́ла (past), see остригу́.

ОСТРИГИ́ (imp.), see остригу́.

ОСТРИГУ́, острижёшь, остригу́т. Р. Остри́чь (acc.). I. Стричь. 1. To cut, clip, shear. 2. To give (s.o.) a haircut (acc. of person).

ОСТРИ́ЖЕННЫЙ; остри́жен, —а, —о, —ы (ppp), see остригу́.

ОСТРИЖЁШЬ, see остригу́.

ОСТРОСЛО́ВЛЮ, остросло́вишь. I. Острословить (intr.). To make jokes, witty remarks.

ОСТРОСЛО́ВЬ (imp.), see острословлю.

ОСТУ́ЖЕННЫЙ; осту́жен, —а, —о, —ы (ppp), see остужу́.

ОСТУЖУ́, осту́дишь. Р. Остуди́ть (acc.). I. Студи́ть. 1. To cool. 2. To chill.

ОСТУПЛЮ́СЬ, осту́пишься. Р. Оступи́ться (intr.). I. Оступа́ться. (lit. and fig.) To stumble.

ОСТЫ́Л, остыла (past), see остыну.

ОСТЫ́НЕШЬ, see остыну.

ОСТЫ́НУ, осты́нешь. Р. Осты́ть and осты́нуть (intr.). I. Остыва́ть, стыть. 1. To become cool, cool off. 2. (fig.) To cool (down) (as of one's interest, ardor, animation, etc.).

ОСТЫ́НЬ (imp.), see остыну.

ОСУЖДЁННЫЙ; осуждён, —а́, —о́, —ы́ (ppp), see осужу́.

ОСУЖУ́, осу́дишь. Р. Осуди́ть (acc.). I. Осужда́ть. 1. To blame, censure, condemn. 2. To convict. 3. To condemn (as to imprisonment) (acc. + на + acc.). 4. (fig.) To condem, doom (as to failure) (acc. + на + acc.) or (to do s.t.) (+ inf.).

ОСУЩЕСТВЛЁННЫЙ; осуществлён, —а́, —о́, —ы́ (ppp), see остществлю́.

ОСУЩЕСТВЛЮ́, осуществи́шь. Р. Осуществи́ть (acc.). I. Осуществля́ть. 1. To accomplish, carry out, realize. 2. To put into practice.

ОСЧАСТЛИ́ВЛЕННЫЙ; осчастли́влен, —а, —о, —ы (ppp), see осчастли́влю.

ОСЧАСТЛИ́ВЛЮ, осчастли́вишь. Р. Осчастли́вить (acc.). I. Осчастли́вливать. To make happy.

ОСЧАСТЛИ́ВЬ (imp.), see осчастли́влю.

ОСЫ́ПАННЫЙ; осы́пан, —а, —о, —ы (ppp), see осы́плю.

ОСЫ́ПЛЕШЬ, see осы́плю.

ОСЫ́ПЛЮ, осы́плешь. Р. Осы́пать (acc.). I. Осыпа́ть. 1. To strew (with) (acc. + inst.). 2. To scatter (acc.). 3. (fig.) To heap on, shower with (as gifts) (acc. + inst.).

ОСЫ́ПЬ (imp.), see осы́плю.

ОСЯ́ДЕШЬ, see ося́ду.

ОСЯ́ДУ, ося́дешь. Р. Осе́сть (intr.). I. Оседа́ть. 1. To settle, sink (of a building, ground, etc.). 2. To sit down slowly. 3. To settle (as dust settles, etc.). 4. To settle down, take up residence.

ОСЯ́ДЬ (imp.), see ося́ду.

ОТБА́ВЛЕННЫЙ; отба́влен, —а, —о, —ы (ppp), see отба́влю.

ОТБА́ВЛЮ, отба́вишь. Р. Отба́вить (acc./gen.). I. Отбавля́ть. 1. To take away (as a part of s.t.). 2. To pour off.

ОТБА́ВЬ (imp.), see отба́влю.

ОТБЕГИ́ (imp.), see отбегу́.

ОТБЕГУ́, отбежи́шь, отбегу́т. Р. Отбежа́ть (intr.). I. Отбега́ть. To run off, run away (e.g., a distance).

ОТБЕЖИ́ШЬ, see отбегу́.

ОТБЕ́Й (imp.), Р. Отби́ть (acc.). I. Отбива́ть. 1. To repel, beat off. 2. To take or retake (as a city in a battle). 3. To break off (as a handle). 4. To sharpen (as a blade). 5. To beat (as a metronome beats time, etc.). 6. To discourage or eliminate. 7. To take away (as s.t. from s.o.). 8. To injure, damage (as by repeated blows). (Also see отобью.) (For other usages see unabridged dictionary.)

ОТБЕРЁШЬ, see отберу́.

ОТБЕРИ́ (imp.), see отберу́.

ОТБЕРУ́, отберёшь. Р. Отобра́ть (acc.). I. Отбира́ть. 1. To take away. 2. To take back. 3. To choose, select. 4. To take or obtain by means of an interrogatory (as information, opinion, etc.).

ОТБИ́ТЫЙ; отби́т, —а, —о, —ы (ppp), see отбе́й and отобью.

ОТБЛА́ГОВЕСТИ (imp.), see отбла́говещу.

ОТБЛА́ГОВЕЩУ, отбла́говестишь. Р. Отбла́говестить (intr.). I. Благовестить. To ring the bell for church.

ОТБОМБЛЮСЬ, отбомби́шься. Р. **Отбомби́ться** (intr.). To finish bombing.

ОТБРЕ́ЕШЬ, see отбре́ю.

ОТБРЕ́Й (imp.), see отбре́ю.

ОТБРЕ́Ю, отбре́ешь. Р. **Отбри́ть** (acc.). I. **Отбрива́ть**. 1. To rebuff. 2. To rebuke. 3. To finish shaving (as one's beard).

ОТБРИ́ТЫЙ; отбри́т, —а, —о, —ы (ppp), see отбре́ю.

ОТБРО́СЬ (imp.), see отбро́шу.

ОТБРО́ШЕННЫЙ; отбро́шен, —а, —о, —ы (ppp), see отбро́шу.

ОТБРО́ШУ, отбро́сишь. Р. **Отбро́сить** (acc.). I. **Отбра́сывать**. 1. To throw off, away, aside. 2. To cast (as a shadow). 3. To repel, throw back (as an attack). 4. (fig.) To reject, dismiss.

ОТБУ́ДЕШЬ, see отбу́ду.

ОТБУ́ДУ, отбу́дешь. Р. **Отбы́ть**. I. **Отбыва́ть**. 1. To depart, go away (intr.). 2. To serve (as a sentence) (acc.). 3. To serve (e.g., a period of time as a soldier) (intr.) (в + prep. of soldier). 4. (arch.) To avoid (as death, etc.) (acc.).

ОТБУ́ДЬ (imp.), see отбу́ду.

ОТВА́ДЬ (imp.), see отва́жу.

ОТВА́ЖЕННЫЙ; отва́жен, —а, —о, —ы (ppp), see отва́жу.

ОТВА́ЖУ, отва́дишь. Р. **Отва́дить** (acc.). I. **Отва́живать**. 1. To break (s.o.) of the habit (of s.t.) (acc. + от + gen.). 2. To drive away (as unwanted guests) (acc.).

ОТВЕДЁННЫЙ; отведён, —а́, —о́, —ы́ (ppp), see отведу́.

ОТВЕДЁШЬ, see отведу́.

ОТВЕДИ́ (imp.), see отведу́.

ОТВЕДУ́, отведёшь. Р. **Отвести́** (acc.). I. **Отводи́ть**. 1. To lead, take away, remove. 2. To extract, draw off (as liquid, etc.). 3. To parry, deflect, divert. 4. (elec.) To shunt. 5. To reject, challenge (e.g., a juror). 6. To allot.

ОТВЕ́ДШИЙ (pap), see отведу́.

ОТВЕДЯ́ (adv. past part.), see отведу́.

ОТВЁЗ, отвезла́ (past), see отвезу́.

ОТВЕЗЁННЫЙ; отвезён, —а́, —о́, —ы́ (ppp), see отвезу́.

ОТВЕЗЁШЬ, see отвезу́.

ОТВЕЗИ́ (imp.), see отвезу́.

ОТВЕЗУ́, отвезёшь. Р. **Отвезти́** (acc.). I. **Отвози́ть**. 1. To take, drive, deliver (s.o. or s.t. to someplace). 2. To take (s.o. or s.t.) away (from someplace).

ОТВЕЗЯ́ (adv. past part.), see отвезу́.

ОТВЁЛ, отвела́ (past), see отведу́.

ОТВЕ́РГ, отве́ргла (past). Р. **Отве́ргнуть** (acc.). I. **Отверга́ть**. To reject, repudiate.

ОТВЕ́РГНУЛ, отве́ргнула (arch.) (past), see отве́рг.

ОТВЕ́РГНУТЫЙ; отве́ргнут, —а, —о, —ы (ppp), see отве́рг.

ОТВЕ́РЖЕННЫЙ; отве́ржен, —а, —о, —ы (arch.) (ppp), see отве́рг.

ОТВЕРТИ́ (imp.), see отверчу́.

ОТВЕ́РТИШЬ, see отверчу́.

ОТВЕ́РТЯТ, see отверчу́.

ОТВЕ́РЧЕННЫЙ; отве́рчен, —а, —о, —ы (ppp), see отверчу́.

ОТВЕРЧУ́, отве́ртишь. Р. **Отверте́ть** (acc.). I. **Отвёртывать**. 1. To unscrew. 2. To twist off (as a button from a coat).

ОТВЕ́СЬ (imp.), see отве́шу.

ОТВЕТВЛЁННЫЙ; ответвлён, —а́, —о́, —ы́ (ppp), see ответвлю́.

ОТВЕТВЛЮ́, ответви́шь. Р. **Ответви́ть** (acc.). I. **Ответвля́ть**. 1. To make a branch (as of a canal, a railroad). 2. To tap (as a water line). 3. (elec.) To shunt.

ОТВЕ́ТЬ (imp.), see отве́чу.

ОТВЕ́ЧЕННЫЙ; отве́чен, —а, —о, —ы (ppp), see отве́чу.

ОТВЕ́ЧУ, отве́тишь. Р. **Отве́тить**. I. **Отвеча́ть**. 1. To answer, reply to (as a letter, question) (на + acc.). 2. To answer or respond (to s.t. with s.t.) (as with a gesture) (на + acc. + inst.). 3. To answer for or be responsible for (за + acc.).

ОТВЕ́ШЕННЫЙ; отве́шен, —а, —о, —ы (ppp), see отве́шу.

ОТВЕ́ШУ, отве́сишь. Р. **Отве́сить**. I. **Отве́шивать**. 1. To weigh out (acc./gen.). 2. To give (as a blow to s.o.) (acc. of blow + dat. of s.o.).

ОТВИ́НЧЕННЫЙ; отви́нчен, —а, —о, —ы (ppp), see отвинчу́.

ОТВИНЧУ́, отви́нтишь. Р. **Отвинти́ть** (acc.). I. **Отви́нчивать**. To unscrew.

ОТВИ́С, отви́сла (past). Р. **Отви́снуть** (intr.). I. **Отвиса́ть**. To hang; sag.

ОТВИ́СИТСЯ, отви́сятся (3rd pers.

only). Р. **Отвисе́ться** (intr.). To hang out (to lose wrinkles through hanging, as do clothes).

ОТВИСЯ́ТСЯ, see **отвиси́тся.**

ОТВЛЁК, отвлекла́ (past), see **отвлеку́.**

ОТВЛЕКИ́ (imp.), see **отвлеку́.**

ОТВЛЕКУ́, отвлечёшь, отвлеку́т. Р. **Отвле́чь** (acc.). I. **Отвлека́ть.** 1. To divert. 2. To distort. 3. (philos.) To abstract. 4. To segregate. 5. To draw off.

ОТВЛЕЧЁННЫЙ; отвлечён, —а́, —о́, —ы́ (ppp), see **отвлеку́.**

ОТВЛЕЧЁЬ, see **отвлеку́.**

ОТВО́ЖЕННЫЙ; отво́жен, —а, —о, —ы (ppp), see **отвожу́³.**

ОТВОЖУ́¹, отво́дишь. I. **Отводи́ть** (acc.). Р. **Отвести́.** 1. To lead, take away, remove. 2. To extract, draw off (as a liquid, etc.). 3. To parry, deflect, divert. 4. (elec.) To shunt. 5. To reject, challenge (e.g., a juror). 6. To allot.

ОТВОЖУ́², отво́зишь. I. **Отвози́ть** (acc.). Р. **Отвезти́.** 1. To take, drive, deliver (s.o. or s.t. to someplace). 2. To take (s.t. or s.o.) away (from someplace).

ОТВОЖУ́³, отво́зишь. Р. **Отвози́ть.** 1. To finish taking away, delivering, etc. (acc.) or (intr.). 2. To beat, whip (acc.). 3. To soil (e.g., a shirt) (acc.).

ОТВОЛО́К, отволокла́ (past), see **отволоку́.**

ОТВОЛОКИ́ (imp.), see **отволоку́.**

ОТВОЛОКУ́, отволочёшь, отволоку́т. Р. **Отволо́чь** (acc.). I. **Отвола́кивать.** To drag away.

ОТВОЛОЧЁННЫЙ; отволочён, —а́, —о́, —ы́ (ppp), see **отволоку́.**

ОТВОЛОЧЁШЬ, see **отволоку́.**

ОТВОРО́ЧЕННЫЙ; отворо́чен, —а, —о, —ы (ppp), see **отворочу́.**

ОТВОРОЧУ́, отворо́тишь. Р. **Отворотить** (acc.). I. **Отвора́чивать.** 1. To move (s.t.) to one side, remove. 2. To turn aside (e.g., one's head, etc.). 3. To turn back (as one's cuffs).

ОТВРАЩЁННЫЙ; отвращён, —а́, —о́, —ы́ (ppp), see **отвращу́.**

ОТВРАЩУ́, отврати́шь. Р. **Отврати́ть** (acc.). I. **Отвраща́ть.** 1. To avert. 2. (arch.) To prevent, restrain (s.o. from s.t.) (acc. + **от** + gen.). 3. To disgust (s.o.).

ОТВЫ́К, отвы́кла (past). Р. **Отвы́кнуть** (intr.). I. **Отвыка́ть.** 1. To get out of or break oneself of a habit (**от** + gen.) or (+ inf.). 2. To become accustomed to being away from, forget about (as one's family, home, etc.) (**от** + gen.).

ОТВЯ́ЖЕШЬ, see **отвяжу́.**

ОТВЯЖИ́ (imp.), see **отвяжу́.**

ОТВЯЖУ́, отвя́жешь. Р. **Отвяза́ть** (acc.). I. **Отвя́зывать.** To untie, unfasten, untether.

ОТВЯ́ЗАННЫЙ; отвя́зан, —а, —о, —ы (ppp), see **отвяжу́.**

ОТГЛА́ДЬ (imp.), see **отглажу.**

ОТГЛА́ЖЕННЫЙ; отгла́жен, —а, —о, —ы (ppp), see **отгла́жу.**

ОТГЛА́ЖУ, отгла́дишь. Р. **Отгла́дить.** I. **Отгла́живать** (mean. 1). 1. To iron out, press (acc.). 2. To finish ironing, pressing (acc.) or (intr.).

ОТГНИЁТ, отгнию́т (3rd pers. only). Р. **Отгни́ть** (intr.). I. **Отгнива́ть.** To rot off.

ОТГНИЮ́Т, see **отгниёт.**

ОТГОНИ́ (imp.), see **отгоню́.**

ОТГО́НИШЬ, see **отгоню́.**

ОТГОНЮ́, отго́нишь. Р. **Отогна́ть** (acc.). I. **Отгоня́ть.** 1. To drive, drive away (as cattle to pasture). 2. (lit. and fig.) To drive away, fight off, repel. 3. To distill.

ОТГОРИ́ (imp.), see **отгори́т.**

ОТГОРИ́Т, отгоря́т (3rd pers. only). Р. **Отгоре́ть** (intr.). 1. To burn out. 2. To burn off (as a branch of a tree).

ОТГОРО́ЖЕННЫЙ; отгоро́жен, —а, —о, —ы (ppp), see **отгорожу́.**

ОТГОРОЖУ́, отгоро́дишь (and **отгороди́шь**). Р. **Отгороди́ть** (acc.). I. **Отгора́живать.** 1. To fence off, partition off. 2. (fig.) To shield, protect (e.g., s.o. from s.t.) (acc. + **от** + gen.).

ОТГОРЯ́Т, see **отгори́т.**

ОТГОЩУ́, отгости́шь. Р. **Отгости́ть** (intr.). 1. To stay as a guest, visit. 2. To complete, finish, a visit.

ОТГРЁБ, отгребла́ (past), see **отгребу́.**

ОТГРЕБЁННЫЙ; отгребён, —а́, —о́, —ы́ (ppp), see **отгребу́.**

ОТГРЕБЁШЬ, see **отгребу́.**

ОТГРЕБИ́ (imp.), see **отгребу́.**

ОТГРЕБУ́, отгребёшь. Р. **Отгрести́.**

I. **Отгреба́ть.** 1. To rake away (to one side) (acc.). 2. To row away (intr.).

ОТГРЕБЯ́ (adv. past part.), see отгребу́.

ОТГРЕМИ́ (imp.), see отгреми́т.

ОТГРЕМИ́Т, отгремя́т (3rd pers. only). P. **Отгреме́ть** (intr.). To cease to thunder, resound, etc. (of thunder, applause, cannon, etc.).

ОТГРЕМЯ́Т, see отгреми́т.

ОТГРУ́ЖЕННЫЙ; отгру́жен, —а, —о, —ы (ppp), see отгружу́.

ОТГРУЖЁННЫЙ; отгружён, —а́, —о́, —ы́ (ppp), see отгружу́.

ОТГРУЖУ́, отгру́зишь (and отгрузи́шь). P. **Отгрузи́ть** (acc.). I. **Отгружа́ть.** 1. To dispatch. 2. To ship. 3. To unload.

ОТГРЫ́З, отгры́зла (past), see отгрызу́.

ОТГРЫ́ЗЕННЫЙ; отгры́зен, —а, —о, —ы (ppp), see отгрызу́.

ОТГРЫЗЁШЬ, see отгрызу́.

ОТГРЫЗИ́ (imp.), see отгрызу́.

ОТГРЫЗУ́, отгрызёшь. P. **Отгры́зть** (acc.). I. **Отгрыза́ть.** To gnaw off (as meat from a bone).

ОТДАВА́Й (imp.), see отдаю́.

ОТДАВА́Я (adv. pres. part.), see отдаю́.

ОТДА́ВЛЕННЫЙ; отда́влен, —а, —о, —Ы (ppp), see отдавлю́.

ОТДАВЛЮ́, отда́вишь. P. **Отдави́ть** (acc.). I. **Отда́вливать.** To squeeze, crush.

ОТДАДИ́М, отдади́те, отдаду́т (pl. forms), see отда́м.

ОТДАЁШЬ, see отдаю́.

ОТДА́Й (imp.), see отда́м.

ОТДА́М, отда́шь, отда́ст (sing. forms). P. **Отда́ть.** I. **Отдава́ть.** 1. To give back, return (acc.). 2. To give up, hand over, yield (acc.). 3. To donate, devote, sacrifice (acc.). 4. To recoil (e.g., a rifle) (intr.). 5. To send (as a child to school) (acc.). 6. (naut.) To loosen, slacken, pay out (acc.). 7. To give (as an order etc.) (acc.). (For other usages, see unabridged dictionary.)

О́ТДАННЫЙ; о́тдан, —а́, —о, —ы (ppp), see отда́м.

ОТДА́СТ, see отда́м.

ОТДА́ШЬ, see отда́м.

ОТДАЮ́, отдаёшь. I. **Отдава́ть.** P. **Отда́ть** (mean. 1 thru 7). 1. To give back, return (acc.). 2. To give up, hand over, yield (acc.). 3. To donate, devote, sacrifice (acc.). 4. To recoil (e.g., a rifle) (intr.). 5. To send (as a child to school) (acc.). 6. (naut.) To loosen, slacken, pay out (acc.). 7. To give (as an order, etc.) (acc.). 8. (lit. and fig.) To smell or taste (of s.t.) (3rd pers. only) (intr.) (inst.). (For other usages, see unabridged dictionary.)

ОТДЕРЁШЬ, see отдеру́.

ОТДЕРИ́ (imp.), see отдеру́.

ОТДЕРУ́, отдерёшь. P. **Отодра́ть** (acc.). I. **Отдира́ть.** 1. To tear off. 2. To pull (e.g., s.o. by the ears) (acc. + за + acc.). 3. To flog.

ОТДУБА́СЬ (imp.), see отдуба́шу.

ОТДУБА́ШЕННЫЙ; отдуба́шен, —а, —о, —ы (ppp), see отдуба́шу.

ОТДУБА́ШУ, отдуба́сишь. P. **Отдуба́сить** (acc.). I. **Дуба́сить.** To beat severely.

ОТДУ́ЕШЬ, see отду́ю.

ОТДУ́Й (imp.), see отду́ю.

ОТДУ́ТЫЙ; отду́т, —а, —о, —ы (ppp), see отду́ю.

ОТДУ́Ю, отду́ешь. P. **Отду́ть** (acc.). I. **Отдува́ть** (mean. 3). 1. To beat severely. 2. To run, race, cover (a long distance). 3. To blow (s.t.) away.

ОТДЫ́ШАТСЯ, see отдышу́сь.

ОТДЫШИ́СЬ (imp.), see отдышу́сь.

ОТДЫ́ШИШЬСЯ, see отдышу́сь.

ОТДЫШУ́СЬ, отды́шишься. P. **Отдыша́ться** (intr.). 1. To recover one's breath. 2. To recover one's health.

ОТЁК, отекла́ (past), see отеку́.

ОТЕКИ́ (imp.), see отеку́.

ОТЕКУ́, отечёшь, отеку́т. P. **Оте́чь** (intr.). I. **Отека́ть.** 1. To swell, become swollen. 2. To gutter (said of candle).

ОТЁР, отёрла (past). P. **Отере́ть** (acc.). I. **Отира́ть.** 1. To wipe, wipe dry, wipe away. 2. To rub (also see отру́).

ОТЕРЁВ and отёрши (adv. past part.), see отёр and отру́.

ОТЁРТЫЙ; отёрт, —а, —о, —ы (ppp), see отёр and отру́.

ОТЁРШИ and отерёв (adv. past part.), see отёр and отру́.

ОТЁСАННЫЙ; отёсан, —а, —о, —ы (ppp), see отешу́.

ОТЕЧЁШЬ, see отеку́.

ОТЁШЕШЬ, see отешу́.

ОТЕШИ́ (imp.), see отешу́.

ОТЕШУ́, отёшешь. Р. Отеса́ть (acc.). I. Отёсывать. 1. To hew smooth. 2. (fig.) To polish, inculcate (s.o.) with savoir faire.

ОТЖА́ТЫЙ[1]; отжа́т, —а, —о, —ы (ppp). Р. Отжа́ть (acc.). I. Отжима́ть. 1. To wring out (as laundry). 2. To force out, squeeze out, press out (also see отожму́).

ОТЖА́ТЫЙ[2], отжа́т, —а, —о, —ы (ppp). Р. Отжа́ть (acc.) or (intr.). I. Отжина́ть. To finish harvesting. (Also see отожну́.)

ОТЖЁГ, отожгла́ (past). Р. Отжéчь (acc.). I. Отжига́ть. To anneal (also see отожгу́).

ОТЖИВЁШЬ, see отживу́.

ОТЖИВИ́ (imp.), see отживу́.

ОТЖИВУ́, отживёшь. Р. Отжи́ть. I. Отжива́ть. 1. To outlive (as one's age or day) (to have had one's day) (acc.). 2. To become antiquated, obsolete (intr.). 3. To live out (as a period of time) (acc.). 4. To die, live one's life out (intr.). 5. (arch.) To experience, survive (s.t.) (acc.). 6. To come to life, revive (intr.).

О́ТЖИТЫЙ; о́тжит, —а́, —о, —ы (ppp), see отживу́.

ОТЖИ́ТЫЙ; отжи́т, —а́, —о, —ы (ppp), see отживу́.

ОТЗОВЁШЬ, see отзову́.

ОТЗОВИ́ (imp.), see отзову́.

ОТЗОВУ́, отзовёшь. Р. Отозва́ть (acc.). I. Отзыва́ть. 1. To call away, call aside, take aside. 2. To recall (as an ambassador).

ОТКА́ЗАННЫЙ; отка́зан, —а, —о, —ы (ppp), see откажу́.

ОТКА́ЖЕШЬ, see откажу́.

ОТКАЖИ́ (imp.), see откажу́.

ОТКАЖУ́, отка́жешь. Р. Отказа́ть. I. Отка́зывать. 1. To refuse or deny (as a request) (в + prep.). 2. To refuse or deny (s.t. to s.o.) (в + prep. + dat.). 3. To discharge (s.o.) (dat.) from a job (dat. + от + gen.). 4. To cease to function (e.g., a motor) (intr.). 5. (arch.) To will (as one's property) (acc.).

ОТКА́ЧЕННЫЙ; отка́чен, —а, —о, —ы (ppp), see откачу́.

ОТКАЧУ́, отка́тишь. Р. Откати́ть. I. Отка́тывать. 1. To roll away, aside (acc.). 2. To haul away (acc.). 3. To drive away rapidly (in a vehicle) (intr.).

ОТКО́ЛЕШЬ, see отколю́.

ОТКОЛИ́ (imp.), see отколю́.

ОТКО́ЛОТЫЙ; отко́лот, —а, —о, —ы (ppp), see отколю́.

ОТКОЛО́ЧЕННЫЙ; отколо́чен, —а, —о, —ы (ppp), see отколочу́.

ОТКОЛОЧУ́, отколо́тишь. Р. Отколоти́ть (acc.). I. Откола́чивать. 1. To break or knock off. 2. To beat severely.

ОТКОЛЮ́, отко́лешь. Р. Отколо́ть (acc.). I. Отка́лывать. 1. To chop or break off. 2. (fig.) To cut off, cut out (as a cow from a herd). 3. To unpin. 4. To perform (a dance) skillfully (acc. of dance). 5. To say or do (s.t.) unexpected or inappropriate. 6. To force (s.o.) to break off with (s.o. or s.t.) (acc. + от + gen.).

ОТКО́РМЛЕННЫЙ; отко́рмлен, —а, —о, —ы (ppp), see откормлю́.

ОТКОРМЛЮ́, отко́рмишь. Р. Откорми́ть (acc.). I. Отка́рмливать. To fatten.

ОТКРЕПЛЁННЫЙ; откреплён, —а́, —о́, —ы́ (ppp), see откреплю́.

ОТКРЕПЛЮ́, открепи́шь. Р. Открепи́ть (acc.). I. Открепля́ть. 1. To unfasten, detach. 2. To strike from or cross off of a register; detach (as a soldier).

ОТКРО́ЕШЬ, see откро́ю.

ОТКРО́Й (imp.), see откро́ю.

ОТКРО́Ю, откро́ешь. Р. Откры́ть (acc.). I. Открыва́ть. 1. To open (as a window, umbrella, meeting, etc.). 2. To clear (as a road). 3. To bare (as one's chest). 4. To discover. 5. To reveal. 6. To unveil. 7. To open up (as a vein of coal). 8. To open (as fire on the enemy) (acc. + в + acc.) or (acc. + по + dat.). 9. To turn on (e.g., water, gas).

ОТКРУ́ЧЕННЫЙ; откру́чен, —а, —о, —ы (ppp), see откручу́.

ОТКРУЧУ́, откру́тишь. Р. Открути́ть (acc.). I. Откру́чивать. 1. To open (as a faucet). 2. To unscrew. 3. To unwind (as a rope).

ОТКРЫ́ТЫЙ; откры́т, —а, —о, —ы (ppp), see откро́ю.

ОТКУ́ПЛЕННЫЙ; отку́плен, —а, —о, —ы (ppp), see откуплю́.

ОТКУПЛЮ́, отку́пишь. Р. **Откупи́ть** (acc.). I. **Откупа́ть**. 1. To buy up, to corner. 2. To rent, take on lease, lease (as a piece of land). 3. To ransom.

ОТКУ́ШЕННЫЙ; отку́шен, —а, —о, —ы (ppp), see **откушу́**.

ОТКУШУ́, отку́сишь. Р. **Откуси́ть** (acc./gen.). I. **Отку́сывать**. 1. To bite off. 2. To cut off (as a piece of wire).

ОТЛЁГ, отлегла́ (past), see **отля́гу**.

ОТЛЁЖАННЫЙ; отлёжан, —а, —о, —ы (ppp), see **отлежу́**.

ОТЛЕЖА́Т, see **отлежу́**.

ОТЛЕЖИ́ (imp.), see **отлежу́**.

ОТЛЕЖУ́, отлежи́шь. Р. **Отлежа́ть**. I. **Отлёживать**. 1. To numb (as an arm or leg by lying on it) (acc.). 2. To lie in bed for a period of time (intr.).

ОТЛЕ́Й (imp.). Р. **Отли́ть**. I. **Отлива́ть**. 1. To pour out or off (as liquid) (acc./gen.). 2. To bail or pump out (as water) (acc.). 3. To cast, found (as a statue) (acc.). 4. To rush or flow away from (as blood from one's head) (intr.) (от + gen.). (Also see **отолью́**.)

ОТЛЕ́ПЛЕННЫЙ; отле́плен, —а, —о, —ы (ppp), see **отлеплю́**.

ОТЛЕПЛЮ́, отле́пишь. Р. **Отлепи́ть** (acc.). I. **Отлепля́ть**. 1. To unstick, unglue. 2. To take off.

ОТЛЕТИ́ (imp.), see **отлечу́**.

ОТЛЕТИ́ШЬ, see **отлечу́**.

ОТЛЕТЯ́Т, see **отлечу́**.

ОТЛЕЧУ́, отлети́шь. Р. **Отлете́ть** (intr.). I. **Отлета́ть**. 1. To fly away, off, take off. 2. To come off, fly off (as a button). 3. (fig.) To fly away, disappear (as one's youth).

ОТЛИ́П, отли́пла (past). Р. **Отли́пнуть** (intr.). I. **Отлипа́ть**. To come off, come unstuck.

ОТЛИ́ТЫЙ; о́тлит, —а́, —о, —ы (ppp), see **отле́й** and **отолью́**.

ОТЛИ́ТЫЙ; отли́т, —а́, —о, —ы (ppp), see **отле́й** and **отолью́**.

ОТЛО́ВЛЕННЫЙ; отло́влен, —а, —о, —ы (ppp), see **отловлю́**.

ОТЛОВЛЮ́, отло́вишь. Р. **Отлови́ть** (acc.). I. **Отла́вливать** (mean. 2). 1. To finish catching. 2. To fish out, catch.

ОТЛО́МЛЕННЫЙ; отло́млен, —а, —о, —ы (ppp), see **отломлю́**.

ОТЛОМЛЮ́, отло́мишь. Р. **Отломи́ть** (acc.). I. **Отла́мывать**. To break off.

ОТЛУ́ПЛЕННЫЙ; отлу́плен, —а, —о, —ы (ppp), see **отлуплю́**.

ОТЛУПЛЮ́, отлу́пишь. Р. **Отлупи́ть** (acc.). I. **лупи́ть**. 1. To thrash, to flog, beat. 2. To peel, strip, pare, bark.

ОТЛЯ́Г (imp.), see **отля́гу**.

ОТЛЯ́ГУ, отля́жешь, отля́гут. Р. **Отле́чь** (intr.). To cease to oppress, disturb (usually used with **от се́рдца, от души́**, and often used impersonally, e.g., **у него́ от се́рдца отлегло́**).

ОТЛЯ́ЖЕШЬ, see **отля́гу**.

ОТМАХА́Й and **отмаши́** (imp.), see **отмашу́**.

ОТМА́ХАННЫЙ; отма́хан, —а, —о, —ы (ppp), see **отмашу́**.

ОТМА́ШЕШЬ, see **отмашу́**.

ОТМАШИ́ and **отмаха́й** (imp.), see **отмашу́**.

ОТМАШУ́, отма́шешь (also **отмаха́ю, отмаха́ешь**, etc.). Р. **Отмаха́ть** (acc.). I. **Отма́хивать**. 1. To signal (by waving) (intr.). 2. To signal (an answer, a message, by waving) (acc. of answer). 3. To use (as a scythe, a flail, etc.) for a period of time (inst. of scythe) (**отмаха́ю**, etc., only). 4. To tire (as one's arm by flailing, etc.) (acc.). 5. To go, travel, cover (a distance) rapidly (**отмаха́ю**, etc., only). 6. To do (s.t.) rapidly (e.g., read several pages of a book) (**отмаха́ю**, etc., only).

ОТМЁЛ, отмела́ (past), see **отмету́**.

ОТМЕ́ЛЕШЬ, see **отмелю́**.

ОТМЕЛИ́ (imp.), see **отмелю́**.

ОТМЕЛЮ́, отме́лешь. Р. **Отмоло́ть**. 1. To mill, grind, for a period of time (intr.). 2. To finish milling, grinding (acc.) or (intr.).

О́ТМЕР, отмерла́, о́тмерло, о́тмерли (past). Р. **Отмере́ть** (intr.). I. **Отмира́ть**. 1. To die off. 2. (fig.) To cease to exist (as old customs, etc.). (Also see **отомрёт**.)

ОТМЕРЁВ and **отмёрши** (adv. past part.), see **о́тмер** and **отомрёт**.

ОТМЁРЗ, отмёрзла (past). Р. **Отмёрзнуть** (intr.). I. **Отмерза́ть**. 1. To freeze (as shoots, twigs, etc.). 2. To

freeze, become numb from cold (as
one's ears, hands, etc.).
ОТМЕ́РШИ and **отмере́в** (adv. past
part.), see **о́тмер** and **отомрёт**.
ОТМЕТЁННЫЙ; отметён, —а́, —о́,
—ы́ (ppp), see **отмету́**.
ОТМЕТЁШЬ, see **отмету́**.
ОТМЕТИ́ (imp.), see **отмету́**.
ОТМЕТУ́, отметёшь. Р. **Отмести́**
(acc.). I. **Отмета́ть**. 1. To sweep
away, aside, off. 2. To reject,
repudiate.
ОТМЕ́ТШИЙ (pap), see **отмету́**.
ОТМЕ́ТЬ (imp.), see **отме́чу**.
ОТМЕТЯ́ (adv. past part.), see **отмету́**.
ОТМЕ́ЧЕННЫЙ; отме́чен, —а, —о,
—ы (ppp), see **отме́чу**.
ОТМЕ́ЧУ, отме́тишь. Р. **Отме́тить**
(acc.). I. **Отмеча́ть**. 1. To mark
(as a page in a book). 2. To note,
observe. 3. To mark down, record.
4. To mention. 5. To register the
departure of (e.g., s.o.) (acc. of s.o.).
ОТМО́ЕШЬ, see **отмо́ю**.
ОТМО́Й (imp.), see **отмо́ю**.
ОТМО́К, отмо́кла (past). Р. **Отмо́к-**
нуть (intr.). I. **Отмока́ть**. 1. To get
wet and come off, soak off. 2. To
become soaked.
ОТМО́ЛОТЫЙ; отмо́лот, —а, —о,
—ы (ppp), see **отмелю́**.
ОТМОЛО́ЧЕННЫЙ; отмоло́чен, —а,
—о, — ы (ppp), see **отмолочу́**.
ОТМОЛОЧУ́, отмоло́тишь. Р. **От-**
молоти́ть. I. **Отмола́чивать** (mean.
1). 1. To thresh for a period of time
(intr.). 2. To finish threshing (acc.)
or (intr.).
ОТМОЛЧА́ТСЯ, see **отмолчу́сь**.
ОТМОЛЧИ́СЬ (imp.), see **отмолчу́сь**.
ОТМОЛЧИ́ШЬСЯ, see **отмолчу́сь**.
ОТМОЛЧУ́СЬ, отмолчи́шься. Р. **От-**
молча́ться (intr.). I. **Отма́лчиваться**.
To keep silent, avoid answering.
ОТМОРО́ЖЕННЫЙ; отморо́жен, —а,
—о, —ы (ppp), see **отморо́жу**.
ОТМОРО́ЖУ, отморо́зишь. Р. **От-**
моро́зить (acc.). I. **Отмора́живать**.
To get (a part of the body) frost-
bitten.
ОТМОРО́ЗЬ (imp.), see **отморо́жу**.
ОТМО́Ю, отмо́ешь. Р. **Отмы́ть** (acc.).
I. **Отмыва́ть**. 1. To wash off, wash
away (as dirt). 2. To wash, clean
(as one's hands). 3. To erode (as a
river erodes or washes its banks).

ОТМЩЁННЫЙ; отмщён, —а́, —о́,
—ы́ (ppp), see **отмщу́**.
ОТМЩУ́, отмсти́шь. Р. **Отмсти́ть**
(dat.). I. **Мстить**. 1. To take
vengence on (dat.). 2. To take
vengeance, revenge (on s.o. for s.t.)
(dat. + за + acc.).
ОТМЫ́ТЫЙ; отмы́т, —а, —о, —ы
(ppp), see **отмо́ю**.
ОТМЯ́К, отмя́кла (past). Р. **От-**
мя́кнуть (intr.). I. **Отмяка́ть**. (lit.
and fig.) To become soft, to soften.
ОТНЁС, отнесла́ (past), see **отнесу́**.
ОТНЕСЁННЫЙ; отнесён, —а́, —о́,
—ы́ (ppp), see **отнесу́**.
ОТНЕСЁШЬ, see **отнесу́**.
ОТНЕСИ́ (imp.), see **отнесу́**.
ОТНЕСУ́, отнесёшь. Р. **Отнести́** (acc.).
I. **Относи́ть**. 1. To carry away. 2. To
take, deliver, put (somewhere). 3.
To put off (as a trip until spring)
(acc. + на + acc.). 4. To cut off.
5. To attribute (s.t. to s.o. or s.t.)
(acc. + к + dat.).
ОТНЕСЯ́ (adv. past part.), see
отнесу́.
ОТНИ́МЕШЬ, see **отниму́**.
ОТНИМИ́ (imp.), see **отниму́**.
ОТНИМУ́, отни́мешь. Р. **Отня́ть**
(acc.). I. **Отнима́ть**. 1. To take
away. 2. To take, require (as time
of s.o.). 3. To subtract (from) (acc.
+ от + gen.). 4. To amputate, take
off.
ОТНО́ШЕННЫЙ; отно́шен, —а, —о,
—ы (ppp), see **отношу́**[1].
ОТНОШУ́[1], отно́сишь. Р. **Относи́ть**
(acc.). To stop wearing (e.g., a hat).
ОТНОШУ́[2], отно́сишь. I. **Относи́ть**
(acc.). Р. **Отнести́**. 1. To carry away.
2. To take or put somewhere. 3. To
put off (as a trip until spring)
(acc. + на + acc.). 4. To cut off.
5. To attribute (s.t. to s.o. or s.t.)
(acc. + к + dat.).
О́ТНЯТЫЙ; о́тнят, —а́, —о, —ы
(ppp), see **отниму́** and **отыму́**.
ОТОБРАЖЁННЫЙ; отображён, —а́,
—о́, —ы́ (ppp), see **отображу́**.
ОТОБРАЖУ́, отобрази́шь. Р. **От-**
образи́ть (acc.). I. **Отобража́ть**. To
represent, reflect, embody.
ОТО́БРАННЫЙ; ото́бран, —а, —о,
—ы (ppp). Р. **Отобра́ть** (acc.). I.
Отбира́ть. 1. To take away. 2. To

take back. 3. To choose, select. 4. To take or obtain by means of an interrogatory (as information, opinion, etc.). (Also see **отберу́**.)

ОТОБЬЁШЬ, see **отобью́**.

ОТОБЬЮ́, отобьёшь. Р. Отби́ть (acc.). I. **Отбива́ть.** 1. To repel, beat off. 2. To take or retake (as a city in a battle). 3. To break off (as a handle). 4. To sharpen (as a blade). 5. To beat (as a metronome beats time, etc.). 6. To discourage or eliminate (as an odor, desire, etc.). 7. To take away (as s.t. from s.o.). 8. To injure, damage (as by repeated blows). (For other usages see unabridged dictionary.)

ОТО́ГНАННЫЙ; ото́гнан, —а, —о, —ы (ppp). Р. **Отогна́ть** (acc.). I. **Отгоня́ть.** 1. To drive, drive away (as cattle to a pasture). 2. (lit. and fig.) To drive away, fight off, repel. 3. To distill. (Also see **отгоню́**.)

ОТО́ДРАННЫЙ; ото́дран, —а, —о, —ы (ppp). Р. **Отодра́ть** (acc.). I. **Отдира́ть.** 1. To tear off. 2. To pull (as s.o. by the ears) (acc. + **за** + acc.). 3. To flog (also see **отдеру́**).

ОТОЖГИ́ (imp.), see **отожгу́**.

ОТОЖГЛА́. отожгло́, отожгли́ (past), see **отожгу́** and **отжёг**.

ОТОЖГУ́, отожжёшь, отожгу́т. Р. **Отжечь** (acc.). I. **Отжига́ть.** To anneal.

ОТОЖДЕСТВЛЁННЫЙ; отождест- влён, —а́, —о́, —ы́ (ppp), see **отождествлю́**.

ОТОЖДЕСТВЛЮ́, отождестви́шь. Р. **Отождестви́ть** (acc.). I. **Отождеств- ля́ть.** To identify.

ОТОЖЕСТВЛЁННЫЙ; отожествлён, —а́, —о́, —ы́ (ppp), see **отожествлю́**.

ОТОЖЕСТВЛЮ́, отожестви́шь. Р. **Отожестви́ть** (acc.). I. **Отожеств- ля́ть.** To identify.

ОТОЖЖЁНЫЙ; отожжён, —а́, —о́, —ы́ (ppp), see **отожгу́**.

ОТОЖЖЁШЬ, see **отожгу́**.

ОТОЖМЁШЬ, see **отожму́**.

ОТОЖМИ́ (imp.), see **отожму́**.

ОТОЖМУ́, отожмёшь. Р. Отжа́ть (acc.). I. **Отжима́ть.** 1. To wring out (as laundry). 2. To force out, squeeze out, press out.

ОТОЖНЁШЬ, see **отожну́**.

ОТОЖНИ́ (imp.), see **отожну́**.

ОТОЖНУ́, отожнёшь. Р. Отжа́ть (acc.) or (intr.). I. **Отжина́ть.** To finish harvesting.

ОТО́ЗВАННЫЙ; ото́зван, —а, —о, —ы (ppp). Р. **Отозва́ть** (acc.). I. **Отзыва́ть.** 1. To call away, call aside, take aside. 2. To recall (as an ambassador). (Also see **отзову́**.)

ОТОЙДЁШЬ, see **отойду́**.

ОТОЙДИ́ (imp.), see **отойду́**.

ОТОЙДУ́, отойдёшь. Р. Отойти́ (intr.). I. **Отходи́ть.** 1. To depart, go away, leave. 2. To withdraw, fall back, fall away, retreat (from), deviate (from). 3. To come off (as wallpaper). 4. To disappear (as spots). 5. To recover from (as an illness) (**от** + gen.). 6. To come to an end (as a church service). 7. To pass (of holidays). 8. To pass into possession of (**к** + dat.) or (dat.).

ОТОЙДЯ́ (adv. past part.), see **отойду́**.

ОТОЛЬЁШЬ, see **отолью́**.

ОТОЛЬЮ́, отольёшь. Р. Отли́ть. I. **Отлива́ть.** 1. To pour out or off (as liquid) (acc./gen.). 2. To bail or pump out (as water) (acc.). 3. To cast, found (as a statue, etc) (acc.). 4. To rush or flood away from (as blood from one's head) (intr.).

ОТОМРЁТ, отомру́т (3rd pers. only). Р. **Отмере́ть** (intr.). I. **Отмира́ть.** 1. To die off. 2. (fig.) To cease to exist (as old customs, etc.).

ОТОМРИ́ (imp.), see **отомрёт.**

ОТОМРУ́Т, see **отомрёт.**

ОТОМЩЁННЫЙ; отомщён, —а́, —о́, —ы́ (ppp), see **отомщу́**.

ОТОМЩУ́, отомсти́шь. Р. Отомсти́ть. I. **Мстить.** 1. To take vengeance on (dat.). 2. To take vengeance, revenge (on s.o. for s.t.) (dat. + **за** + acc.).

ОТО́ПЛЕННЫЙ; ото́плен, —а, —о, —ы (ppp), see **отоплю́**.

ОТОПЛЮ́, ото́пишь. Р. Отопи́ть (acc.). I. **Ота́пливать.** To heat (as a room, house, etc.).

ОТОПРЁШЬ, see **отопру́**.

ОТОПРИ́ (imp.), see **отопру́**.

ОТОПРУ́, отопрёшь. Р. Отпере́ть (acc.). I. **Отпира́ть.** 1. To unlock, unfasten. 2. To open (having unlocked, etc.).

ОТОПЬЁШЬ, see **отопью́**.

ОТОПЬЮ́, отопьёшь. Р. Отпи́ть. I.

Отпива́ть. 1. To sip, take a sip (acc./gen.). 2. To drink off, finish drinking (acc./gen.) or (intr.).

ОТО́РВАННЫЙ; ото́рван, —а, —о, —ы (ppp), see оторву́.

ОТОРВЁШЬ, see оторву́.

ОТОРВИ́ (imp.), see оторву́.

ОТОРВУ́, оторвёшь. Р. Оторва́ть (acc.). I. Отрыва́ть. 1. (lit. and fig.) To tear away. 2. To remove, detach. 3. To distract, divert, interrupt.

ОТО́СЛАННЫЙ; ото́слан, —а, —о, —ы (ppp), see отошлю́.

ОТОСПИ́СЬ (acc.), see отосплю́сь.

ОТОСПИ́ШЬСЯ, see отосплю́сь.

ОТОСПЛЮ́СЬ, отоспи́шься. Р. Отоспа́ться (intr.). I. Отсыпа́ться. 1. To have a long sleep. 2. To make up for lost sleep.

ОТОСПЯ́ТСЯ, see отосплю́сь.

ОТОТРЁШЬ, see ототру́.

ОТОТРИ́ (imp.), see ототру́.

ОТОТРУ́, ототрёшь. Р. Оттере́ть (acc.). I. Оттира́ть. 1. To rub off, away. 2. To warm by rubbing (as one's arm with snow) (acc. + inst.). 3. To force out, push aside.

ОТОШЕ́ДШИЙ (pap), see отойду́.

ОТОШЁЛ, отошла́ (past), see отойду́.

ОТОШЛА́, отошло́, отошли́ (past), see отошёл and отойду́.

ОТОШЛЁШЬ, see отошлю́.

ОТОШЛИ́¹ (past), see отошёл and отойду́.

ОТОШЛИ́² (imp.), see отошлю́.

ОТОШЛЮ́, отошлёшь. Р. Отосла́ть (acc.). I. Отсыла́ть. 1. To send away, off. 2. To send back. 3. To refer (as s.o. to s.o. or s.t.) (acc. + к + dat.).

ОТОШЬЁШЬ, see отошью́.

ОТОШЬЮ́, отошьёшь. Р. Отши́ть. I. Отшива́ть (mean. 1 and 2). 1. To rip off (as boards from a building) (acc.). 2. To snub, rebuff (acc.). 3. To finish sewing (acc.) or (intr.).

ОТПА́ВШИЙ (pap), see отпаду́ and отпа́дший.

ОТПАДЁШЬ, see отпаду́.

ОТПАДИ́ (imp.), see отпаду́.

ОТПАДУ́, отпадёшь. Р. Отпа́сть (intr.). I. Отпада́ть. (lit. and fig.) To fall off, away.

ОТПА́ДШИЙ (arch.) (pap), see отпаду́ and отпа́вший.

ОТПА́Л, отпа́ла (past), see отпаду́.

ОТПА́ХАННЫЙ; отпа́хан, —а, —о, —ы (ppp), see отпашу́.

ОТПА́ШЕШЬ, see отпашу́.

ОТПАШИ́ (imp.), see отпашу́.

ОТПАШУ́, отпа́шешь. Р. Отпаха́ть. 1. To finish plowing (acc.) or (intr.). 2. To spend some time plowing (intr.).

ОТПЕ́Й (imp.). Р. Отпи́ть. I. Отпива́ть. 1. To sip, take a sip of (acc./gen.). 2. To drink off, finish drinking (acc./gen.) or (intr.). (Also see отопью́.)

О́ТПЕР, отперла́, о́тперло, о́тперли (past). Р. Отпере́ть (acc.). I. Отпира́ть. 1. To unlock, unfasten. 2. To open (having unlocked) (also see отопру́).

ОТПЕРЁВ and отпёрши (adv. past part.), see о́тпер and отопру́.

О́ТПЕРТЫЙ; о́тперт, —а́, —о, —ы (ppp), see о́тпер and отопру́.

ОТПЁРШИ and отпере́в (adv. past part.), see о́тпер and отопру́.

ОТПЕ́ТЫЙ; отпе́т, —а, —о, —ы (ppp), see отпою́.

ОТПИ́САННЫЙ; отпи́сан, —а, —о, —ы (ppp), see отпишу́.

ОТПИ́ТЫЙ; о́тпит, —а́, —о, —ы (ppp), see отпе́й and отопью́.

ОТПИ́ТЫЙ; отпи́т, —а́, —о, —ы (ppp), see отпе́й and отопью́.

ОТПИШУ́, отпи́шешь. Р. Отписа́ть. 1. Отпи́сывать (mean. 1 thru 4). 1. To will, bequeath (acc.). 2. To confiscate (acc.). 3. To answer, inform (s.o.) by letter (intr.) (dat. of s.o.). 4. To transfer (e.g., soldiers) (acc.). 5. To finish writing (acc.) or (intr.).

ОТПЛА́ЧЕННЫЙ; отпла́чен, —а, —о, —ы (ppp), see отплачу́.

ОТПЛАЧУ́, отпла́тишь. Р. Отплати́ть (dat.). I. Отпла́чивать. (lit. and fig.) To pay back, repay (s.o. for s.t.) (dat. of s.o. + за + acc.).

ОТПЛЁЛ, отплела́ (past), see отплету́.

ОТПЛЕТЁННЫЙ; отплетён, —а́, —о́, —ы́ (ppp), see отплету́.

ОТПЛЕТЁШЬ, see отплету́.

ОТПЛЕТИ́ (imp.), see отплету́.

ОТПЛЕТУ́, отплетёшь. Р. Отплести́ (acc.). I. Отплета́ть (mean. 1). 1. To separate or detach by untwining, unbraiding, unraveling. 2. To finish braiding, weaving, etc.

ОТПЛЁТШИ and **отплетя** (adv. past part.), see **отплету́**.

ОТПЛЁТШИЙ (pap), see **отплету́**.

ОТПЛЕТЯ and **отплётши** (adv. past part.), see **отплету́**.

ОТПЛЫВЁШЬ, see **отплыву́**.

ОТПЛЫВИ́ (imp.), see **отплыву́**.

ОТПЛЫВУ́, отплывёшь. Р. Отплы́ть (intr.). I. **Отплыва́ть**. 1. To swim, sail, or float off, out. 2. To go swimming, sailing.

ОТПЛЫВЯ (adv. past part.), see **отплыву́**.

ОТПЛЯСАННЫЙ; отпля́сан, —а, —о, —ы (ppp), see **отпляшу́**.

ОТПЛЯШЕШЬ, see **отпляшу́**.

ОТПЛЯШИ́ (imp.), see **отпляшу́**.

ОТПЛЯШУ́, отпля́шешь. Р. Отпляса́ть. I. **Отпля́сывать** (mean. 1 and 2). 1. To perform a dance (acc.). 2. To tire by dancing (as one's legs) (acc.). 3. To finish dancing (intr.).

ОТПОЛЗ, отползла́ (past), see **отползу́**.

ОТПОЛЗЁШЬ, see **отползу́**.

ОТПОЛЗИ́ (imp.), see **отползу́**.

ОТПОЛЗУ́, отползёшь. Р. Отползти́ (intr.). I. **Отполза́ть**. To crawl away.

ОТПОЁШЬ, see **отпою́**.

ОТПОЙ (imp.), see **отпою́**.

ОТПО́РЕШЬ, see **отпорю́**.

ОТПОРИ́ (imp.), see **отпорю́**.

ОТПО́РОТЫЙ; отпо́рот, —а, —о, —ы (ppp), see **отпорю́**.

ОТПОРЮ́, отпо́решь. Р. Отпоро́ть (acc.). I. **Отпа́рывать** (mean. 1). 1. To rip off. 2. To flog.

ОТПОЮ́, отпоёшь. Р. Отпе́ть. I. **Отпева́ть** (mean. 1). 1. To perform a funeral service (over s.o.) (acc.). 2. To sing (e.g., a song) (acc.). 3. To finish singing (intr.).

ОТПРА́ВЛЕННЫЙ; отпра́влен, —а, —о, —ы (ppp), see **отпра́влю**.

ОТПРА́ВЛЮ, отпра́вишь. Р. Отпра́вить (acc.). I. **Отправля́ть**. 1. To send, forward, dispatch. 2. To ship, consign. 3. (arch.) To fulfill (e.g., duties).

ОТПРА́ВЬ (imp.), see **отпра́влю**.

ОТПРОШУ́СЬ, отпро́сишься. Р. Отпроси́ться (intr.). I. **Отпра́шиваться**. To obtain leave through a request.

ОТПРЯГ, отпрягла́ (past), see **отпрягу́**.

ОТПРЯГИ́ (imp.), see **отпрягу́**.

ОТПРЯГУ́, отпряжёшь, отпрягу́т. Р. Отпря́чь. I. **Отпряга́ть**. To unharness.

ОТПРЯЖЁННЫЙ); отпряжён, —а́, —о́, —ы́ (ppp, see **отпрягу́**.

ОТПРЯЖЁШЬ, see **отпрягу́**.

ОТПУ́ЩЕННЫЙ; отпу́щен, —а, —о, —ы (ppp), see **отпущу́**.

ОТПУЩУ́, отпу́стишь. Р. Отпусти́ть (acc.). I. **Отпуска́ть**. 1. To let go, release. 2. To supply (as goods to a customer) (acc. of goods). 3. To let grow (as one's beard). 4. To loosen (as one's belt). 5. To make (as a joke), pay (as a compliment). 6. To temper (as steel). 7. To forgive (e.g., an insult) (acc. + dat.: кому). 8. To grant, allot.

ОТРА́ВЛЕННЫЙ; отра́влен, —а, —о, —ы (ppp), see **отравлю́**.

ОТРАВЛЮ́, отра́вишь. Р. Отрави́ть (acc.). I. **Отравля́ть**. 1. To poison (as a rat, water, etc.). 2. (fig.) To envenom. 3. (fig.) To poison, ruin, spoil.

ОТРАЖЁННЫЙ; отражён, —а́, —о́, —ы́ (ppp), see **отражу́**.

ОТРАЖУ́, отрази́шь. Р. Отрази́ть (acc.). I. **Отража́ть**. 1. (lit. and fig.) To reflect. 2. To repel, repulse, ward off, deflect.

ОТРАСТЁТ, отрасту́т (3rd pers. only). Р. **Отрасти́** (intr.). I. **Отраста́ть**. To grow out (of horns, nails, plants, etc.).

ОТРАСТИ́ (imp. and inf.), see **отрастёт**.

ОТРАСТУ́Т, see **отрастёт**.

ОТРАЩЁННЫЙ; отращён, —а́, —о́, —ы́ (ppp), see **отращу́**.

ОТРАЩУ́, отрасти́шь. Р. Отрасти́ть (acc.). I. **Отра́щивать**. To allow to grow (as a beard).

ОТРЕ́ЖЕШЬ, see **отре́жу**.

ОТРЕ́ЖУ, отре́жешь. Р. Отре́зать. I. **Отреза́ть, отре́зывать**. 1. To cut off (as a piece of s.t.) (acc.). 2. To bar, cut off (as a route, retreat) (acc.). 3. (fig.) To cut (s.o.) off (acc.). 4. To reply sharply (intr.).

ОТРЕ́ЖЬ (imp.), see **отре́жу**.

ОТРЕ́ЗАННЫЙ; отре́зан, —а, —о, —ы (ppp), see **отре́жу**.

ОТРЕЗВЛЁННЫЙ; отрезвлён, —а́, —о́, —ы́ (ppp), see отрезвлю́.

ОТРЕЗВЛЮ́, отрезви́шь. Р. Отрезви́ть (acc.). I. Отрезвля́ть. (lit. and fig.) To sober.

ОТРЁКСЯ, отрекла́сь (past), see отреку́сь.

ОТРЕКИ́СЬ (imp.), see отреку́сь.

ОТРЕКУ́СЬ, отречёшься, отреку́тся. Р. Отре́чься (от + gen.). I. Отрека́ться. 1. To repudiate, disavow (as one's friends, words). 2. To renounce, give up (as a throne, etc.).

ОТРЁПАННЫЙ; отрёпан, —а, —о, —ы (ppp), see отреплю́.

ОТРЕ́ПЛЕШЬ, see отреплю́.

ОТРЕПЛИ́ (imp.), see отреплю́.

ОТРЕПЛЮ́, отре́плешь. Р. Отрепа́ть. To fray (through wear) (as cuffs of trousers, etc.).

ОТРЕЧЁШЬСЯ, see отреку́сь.

ОТРЁШЬ, see отру́.

ОТРИ́ (imp.), see отру́.

ОТРО́ЕШЬ, see отро́ю.

ОТРО́Й (imp.), see отро́ю.

ОТРО́С, отросла́ (past), see отрастёт.

ОТРО́Ю, отро́ешь. Р. Отры́ть (acc.). I. Отрыва́ть, рыть (mean. 1 and 2). 1. To dig out. 2. To excavate. 3. (fig.) To unearth, dig out.

ОТРУ́, отрёшь. Р. Отере́ть (acc.). I. Отира́ть. 1. To wipe, wipe dry, wipe away. 2. To rub.

ОТРУ́БЛЕННЫЙ; отру́блен, —а, —о, —ы (ppp), see отрублю́.

ОТРУБЛЮ́, отру́бишь. Р. Отруби́ть. I. Отруба́ть (mean. 1). 1. To chop off, cut off (acc.). 2. To answer (s.o.) sharply (acc.) or (intr.).

ОТРЫ́ТЫЙ; отры́т, —а, —о, —ы (ppp), see отро́ю.

ОТРЯЖЁННЫЙ; отряжён, —а́, —о́, —ы́ (ppp), see отряжу́.

ОТРЯЖУ́, отряди́шь. Р. Отряди́ть (acc.). I. Отряжа́ть. 1. To detach (as soldiers from an organization). 2. To appoint or order (e.g., s.o. to do s.t.).

ОТРЯ́С, отрясла́ (past), see отрясу́.

ОТРЯСЁННЫЙ; отрясён, —а́, —о́, —ы́ (ppp), see отрясу́.

ОТРЯСЁШЬ, see отрясу́.

ОТРЯСИ́ (imp.), see отрясу́.

ОТРЯСУ́, отрясёшь. Р. Отрясти́ (acc.). I. Отряса́ть. To shake off.

ОТСА́ЖЕННЫЙ; отса́жен, —а, —о, —ы (ppp), see отсажу́.

ОТСАЖУ́, отса́дишь. Р. Отсади́ть (acc.). I. Отса́живать. 1. To seat apart; to separate. 2. To transplant (as a bush). 3. (min.) To jig. 4. To cut off.

ОТСЕ́ЕЬ, see отсе́ю.

ОТСЕ́Й (imp.), see отсе́ю.

ОТСЕ́К, отсекла́ (past), see отсеку́.

ОТСЕКИ́ (imp.), see отсеку́.

ОТСЕКУ́, отсечёшь, отсеку́т. Р. Отсе́чь (acc.). I. Отсека́ть. 1. To cut off, chop off. 2. (fig.) To cut off (as reinforcements, etc.).

ОТСЁЛ, отсе́ла (past), see отся́ду.

ОТСЕЧЁННЫЙ; отсечён, —а́, —о́, —ы́ (ppp), see отсеку́.

ОТСЕЧЁШЬ, see отсеку́.

ОТСЕ́Ю, отсе́ешь. Р. Отсе́ять (acc.) I. Отсе́ивать (mean. 1.). 1. (lit. and fig.) To screen, sift. 2. To finish sowing.

ОТСЕ́ЯННЫЙ; отсе́ян, —а, —о, —ы (ppp), see отсе́ю.

ОТСИДИ́ (imp.), see отсижу́.

ОТСИДИ́ШЬ, see отсижу́.

ОТСИДЯ́Т, see отсижу́.

ОТСИ́ЖЕННЫЙ; отси́жен, —а, —о, —ы (ppp), see отсижу́.

ОТСИЖУ́, отсиди́шь. Р. Отсиде́ть (acc.). I. Отси́живать. 1. To spend time, serve time, stay (as in prison) (acc. of time). 2. To sit through (as a play). 3. To numb from sitting (as a leg).

ОТСКА́ЧЕШЬ, see отскачу́.

ОТСКАЧИ́ (imp.), see отскачу́.

ОТСКАЧУ́, отска́чешь. Р. Отскака́ть. I. Отска́кивать (mean. 1). 1. To gallop off (intr.). 2. To cover (a distance) at a gallop (acc.). 3. To finish galloping (intr.).

ОТСКРЁБ, отскребла́ (past), see отскребу́.

ОТСКРЕБЁННЫЙ; отскребён, —а́, —о́, —ы́ (ppp), see отскребу́.

ОТСКРЕБЁШЬ, see отскребу́.

ОТСКРЕБИ́ (imp.), see отскребу́.

ОТСКРЕБУ́, отскребёшь. Р. Отскрести́ (acc.). I. Отскреба́ть. To scrape off, scratch off.

ОТСО́САННЫЙ; отсо́сан, —а, —о, —ы (ppp), see отсосу́.

ОТСОСЁШЬ, see отсосу́.

ОТСОСИ́ (imp.), see отсосу́.

ОТСОСУ́, отсосёшь. Р. Отсоса́ть (acc.). I. Отса́сывать (mean. 1 and 2). 1. To draw off (with suction), suck. 2. To exhaust. 3. To finish drawing off, exhausting, etc.

ОТСО́Х, отсо́хла (past). Р. Отсо́хнуть (intr.). I. Отсыха́ть. 1. To wither (as a part of the body). 2. To dry up, wither (as leaves, etc.).

ОТСТАВА́Й (imp.), see отстаю́.

ОТСТАВА́Я (adv. pres. part.), see отстаю́.

ОТСТА́ВЛЕННЫЙ; отста́влен, —а, —о, —ы (ppp), see отста́влю.

ОТСТА́ВЛЮ, отста́вишь. Р. Отста́вить (acc.). I. Отставля́ть (mean. 1 and 2). 1. To put, move aside. 2. (arch.) To dismiss, discharge. 3. As a command in infinitive form— "as you were."

ОТСТА́ВЬ (imp.), see отста́влю.

ОТСТАЁШЬ, see отстаю́.

ОТСТА́НЕШЬ, see отста́ну.

ОТСТА́НУ, отста́нешь. Р. Отста́ть (intr.). I. Отстава́ть. 1. To fall behind, lag behind (от + gen.). 2. (fig.) To be backward, lag behind (as in one's studies) (в + prep.). 3. (fig.) To lose contact with (as old friends) (от + gen.). 4. To miss, fail to catch (as a train) (от + gen.). 5. To fall or come off (as wallpaper) (от + gen.). 6. To be slow (as a clock) (на + acc.). 7. To let alone, leave alone (as s.o.) (от + gen.). 8. (arch.) To quit (s.t.) (от + gen.).

ОТСТА́НЬ (imp.), see отста́ну.

ОТСТАЮ́, отстаёшь. I. Отстава́ть (intr.). Р. Отста́ть. 1. To fall behind, lag behind (от + gen.). 2. (fig.) To be backward, lag behind (as in studies) (в + prep.). 3. (fig.) To lose contact with (as old friends) (от + gen.). 4. To miss, fail to catch (as a train) (от + gen.). 5. To fall or come off (as wallpaper) (от + gen.). 6. To be slow (as a clock) (на + acc.). 7. To let alone, leave alone (as s.o.) (от + gen.). 8. (arch.) To quit (s.t.) (от + gen.).

ОТСТО́ИШЬ, see отстою́[1] and[2].

ОТСТО́Й (imp.), see отстою́[1].

ОТСТОЮ́[1], отстои́шь. Р. Отстоя́ть (acc.). I. Отста́ивать (mean. 1 thru 3). 1. To defend (as one's country,

freedom, etc.). 2. To uphold, defend (as one's point of view, principles, etc.). 3. To stand for a period of time (e.g., to stand a watch, to stand through a service). 4. To tire by standing (as one's feet).

ОТСТОЮ́[2], отстои́шь. I. Отстоя́ть (intr.). To be located at a distance (e.g., a city lies/stands 100 miles from the coast) (от + gen.).

ОТСТО́ЯННЫЙ; отсто́ян, —а, —о, —ы (ppp), see отстою́[1].

ОТСТОЯ́Т, see отстою́[1] and [2].

ОТСТРИ́Г, отстри́гла (past), see отстригу́.

ОТСТРИГИ́ (imp.), see отстригу́.

ОТСТРИГУ́, отстрижёшь, отстригу́т. Р. Отстри́чь (acc.). I. Отстрига́ть. To cut off (with shears, scissors).

ОТСТРИ́ЖЕННЫЙ; отстри́жен, —а, —о, —ы (ppp), see отстригу́.

ОТСТРИЖЁШЬ, see отстригу́.

ОТСТУПИ́В and ОТСТУПЯ́ (adv. past. part.), see отступлю́.

ОТСТУПЛЮ́, отсту́пишь. Р. Отступи́ть (intr.). I. Отступа́ть. 1. To step back. 2. To retreat, fall back. 3. To deviate from (от + gen.). 4. To digress from (от + gen.). 5. (fig.) To recede (as a shore line, timber line, etc.). 6. To make or leave space (as at the bottom of a page) (от + gen.).

ОТСТУПЯ́ and отступи́в (adv. past part.), see отступлю́.

ОТСУ́ЖЕННЫЙ; отсу́жен, —а, —о, —ы (ppp), see отсужу́.

ОТСУЖУ́, отсу́дишь. Р. Отсуди́ть (acc.). I. Отсу́живать. To obtain by court action (as money, a judgement, etc.).

ОТСЫ́ПАННЫЙ; отсы́пан, —а, —о, —ы (ppp), see отсы́плю.

ОТСЫ́ПЛЕШЬ, see отсы́плю.

ОТСЫ́ПЛЮ, отсы́плешь. Р. Отсы́пать (acc./gen.). I. Отсыпа́ть. 1. To pour out (e.g., grain, etc.). 2. To measure out (e.g., grain, etc.). 3. To give generously.

ОТСЫ́ПЬ (imp.), see отсы́плю.

ОТСЯ́ДЕШЬ, see отся́ду.

ОТСЯ́ДУ, отся́дешь. Р. Отсе́сть (intr.). I. Отса́живаться. To seat oneself apart, or away from (s.t. or s.o.) (от + gen.).

ОТСЯ́ДЬ (imp.), see отся́ду.

ОТТА́ЕШЬ, see отта́ю.

ОТТА́Й (imp.), see отта́ю.

ОТТА́Ю, отта́ешь. Р. Отта́ять. I. Отта́ивать. 1. To thaw out (intr.) or (acc.). 2. (fig.) To thaw (of people) (intr.). 3. (fig.) To thaw (e.g., s.o.'s heart) (acc. of heart).

ОТТА́ЯННЫЙ; отта́ян, —а, —о, —ы (ppp), see отта́ю.

ОТТЁК, оттекла́ (past), see оттечёт.

ОТТЕКУ́Т, see оттечёт.

ОТТЁР, оттёрла (past). Р. Оттере́ть (acc.). I. Оттира́ть. 1. To rub off, away. 2. To warm by rubbing. 3. To force out, push aside. (Also see ототру́.)

ОТТЕРЁВ and оттёрши (adv. past part.), see оттёр and ототру́.

ОТТЁРТЫЙ; оттёрт, —а, —о, —ы (ppp), see оттёр and ототру́.

ОТТЁРШИ and оттере́в (adv. past part.), see оттёр and ототру́.

ОТТЁСАННЫЙ; оттёсан, —а, —о, —ы (ppp), see оттешу́.

ОТТЕЧЁТ, оттекут (3rd pers. only). Р. Отте́чь (acc.). I. Оттека́ть. To flow away, off, down.

ОТТЕ́ШЕШЬ, see оттешу́.

ОТТЕШИ́ (imp.), see оттешу́.

ОТТЕШУ́, отте́шешь. Р. Оттеса́ть. I. Оттёсывать (mean. 1). 1. To hew off, trim off (as with an axe) (acc.). 2. To finish hewing off (acc.) or (intr.).

ОТТО́ПТАННЫЙ; отто́птан, —а, —о, —ы (ppp), see оттопчу́.

ОТТО́ПЧЕШЬ, see оттопчу́.

ОТТОПЧИ́ (imp.), see оттопчу́.

ОТТОПЧУ́, отто́пчешь. Р. Оттопта́ть (acc.). I. Отта́птывать. 1. To trample on (s.t.). 2. To injure or tire by walking (as one's feet).

ОТТО́РГ, отто́ргла (past). Р. Отто́ргнуть (acc.). I. Отторга́ть. To tear away, to forcibly take away.

ОТТО́РГНУТЫЙ; отто́ргнут, —а, —о, —ы (ppp), see отто́рг.

ОТТО́РЖЕННЫЙ; отто́ржен, —а, —о, —ы (arch. form) (ppp), see отто́рг.

ОТТРЕ́ПАННЫЙ; оттрёпан, —а, —о, —ы (ppp), see оттреплю́.

ОТТРЕ́ПЛЕШЬ, see оттреплю́.

ОТТРЕПЛИ́ (imp.), see оттреплю́.

ОТТРЕПЛЮ́, оттре́плешь. Р. Оттрепа́ть. I. Оттрёпывать (mean. 1). 1. To scutch (as flax fibre) (acc.). 2. To punish by thrashing, shaking, pulling (as by the ears, hair, etc.) (acc.). 3. To finish scutching (acc.) or (intr.).

ОТТРЯ́С, оттрясла́ (past), see оттрясу́.

ОТТРЯСЁННЫЙ; оттрясён, —а́, —о́, —ы́ (ppp), see оттрясу́.

ОТТРЯСЁШЬ, see оттрясу́.

ОТТРЯСИ́ (imp.), see оттрясу́.

ОТТРЯСУ́, оттрясёшь. Р. Оттрясти́ (acc.). I. Оттряса́ть. 1. To shake off (as dust). 2. To damage by shaking or jolting.

ОТТУЖУ́, оттузи́шь. Р. Оттузи́ть (acc.). I. Тузи́ть. To pommel, thrash (as with one's fists).

ОТХЛЁСТАННЫЙ; отхлёстан, —а, —о, —ы (ppp), see отхлещу́.

ОТХЛЕЩИ́ (imp.), see отхлещу́.

ОТХЛЕЩУ́, отхле́щешь. Р. Отхлеста́ть (acc.). I. Отхлёстывать. 1. To whip, lash. 2. To scold, "bawl out."

ОТХО́ЖЕННЫЙ; отхо́жен, —а, —о, —ы (ppp), see отхожу́².

ОТХОЖУ́¹, отхо́дишь. I. Отходи́ть (intr.). Р. Отойти́. 1. To depart, go away, leave. 2. To withdraw, fall back, fall away, retreat (from). 3. To come off (as wallpaper). 4. To disappear (as spots). 5. To recover from (as an illness) (от + gen.). 6. To come to an end (as a church service). 7. To pass (of holidays, etc.). 8. To pass into possession of (к + dat.) or (dat.).

ОТХОЖУ́², отхо́дишь. Р. Отходи́ть. I. Отха́живать (mean. 1, 2, 4). 1. To cure, heal (s.o.) (acc.). 2. To injure walking (as one's foot) (acc.). 3. To spend some time (e.g., as a soldier) (inst.). 4. To beat severely (acc.). 5. To finish walking (intr.).

ОТЦВЁЛ, отцвела́ (past), see отцвету́.

ОТЦВЕТЁШЬ, see отцвету́.

ОТЦВЕТИ́ (imp.), see отцвету́.

ОТЦВЕТУ́, отцветёшь. Р. Отцвести́ (intr.). I. Отцвета́ть. 1. To finish blooming. 2. (lit. and fig.) To fade.

ОТЦВЕ́ТШИЙ (pap), see отцвету́.

ОТЦВЕТЯ́ (adv. past part.), see отцвету́.

ОТЦЕ́ЖЕННЫЙ; отце́жен, —а, —о, —ы (ppp), see отцежу́.

ОТЦЕЖУ́, отце́дишь. Р. **Отцеди́ть** (acc.). I. **Отце́живать**. To strain off, filter.

ОТЦЕ́ПЛЕННЫЙ; отце́плен, —а, —о, —ы (ppp), see отцеплю́.

ОТЦЕПЛЮ́, отце́пишь. Р. **Отцепи́ть** (acc.). I. **Отцепля́ть**. To unhook, uncouple, unfasten, disengage, release.

ОТЧА́ЕШЬСЯ, see отча́юсь.

ОТЧА́ЙСЯ (imp.), see отча́юсь.

ОТЧА́ЮСЬ, отча́ешься. Р. **Отча́яться**. I. **Отча́иваться**. 1. To despair (intr.). 2. To dispair of (s.t.) (в + prep.). 3. To despair of doing (s.t.) (+ inf.). 4. To dare, venture (s.t.) (на + acc.).

ОТЧИ́СТИ (imp.), see отчи́щу.

ОТЧИ́СТЬ (imp.), see отчи́щу.

ОТЧИ́ЩЕННЫЙ; отчи́щен, —а, —о, —ы (ppp), see отчи́щу.

ОТЧИ́ЩУ, отчи́стишь. Р. **Отчи́стить** (acc.). I. **Отчища́ть**. 1. To clean (off). 2. To brush off.

ОТЧУЖДЁННЫЙ; отчуждён, —а́, —о́, —ы́ (ppp), see отчужу́.

ОТЧУЖУ́, отчуди́шь. Р. **Отчуди́ть** (arch.) (acc.). I. **Отчужда́ть**. 1. To alienate (as property). 2. To alienate (as a person).

ОТШЕ́Й (imp.). Р. **Отши́ть**. I. **Отшива́ть** (mean. 1 and 2). 1. To rip off (as boards from a building) (acc.). 2. To snub, rebuff (acc.). 3. To finish sewing (acc.) or (intr.). (Also see отошью́.)

ОТШИ́Б, отши́бла (past), see отшибу́.

ОТШИБЁШЬ, see отшибу́.

ОТШИБИ́ (imp.), see отшибу́.

ОТШИ́БЛЕННЫЙ; отши́блен, —а, —о, —ы (ppp), see отшибу́.

ОТШИБУ́, отшибёшь. Р. **Отшиби́ть** (acc.). I. **Отшиба́ть**. 1. To knock off (as a handle). 2. To hurt or injure (as with a blow). 3. To fling, throw, hit back (as a ball). 4. To cause to disappear, to lose (as one's memory, appetite) (often impers. + acc.) (e.g., ему́ отши́бло аппети́т).

ОТШИ́ТЫЙ; отши́т, —а, —о, —ы (ppp), see отше́й and отошью́.

ОТШУМИ́ (imp.), see отшумлю́.

ОТШУМИ́ШЬ, see отшумлю́.

ОТШУМЛЮ́, отшуми́шь. Р. **Отшуме́ть** (intr.). 1. To cease making noise. 2. (fig.) To cease, die out (e.g., fame).

ОТШУМЯ́Т, see отшумлю́.

ОТШУЧУ́СЬ, отшу́тишься. Р. **Отшути́ться** (intr.). I. **Отшу́чиваться**. To reply to s.t. serious with a joke, to "laugh it off."

ОТЩЕПЛЁННЫЙ; отщеплён, —а́, —о́, —ы́ (ppp), see отщеплю́.

ОТЩЕПЛЮ́, отщепи́шь. Р. **Отщепи́ть** (acc.). I. **Отщепля́ть**. To chip off.

ОТЩИ́ПАННЫЙ; отщи́пан, —а, —о, —ы (ppp), see отщиплю́.

ОТЩИ́ПЛЕШЬ, see отщиплю́.

ОТЩИПЛИ́ (imp.), see отщиплю́.

ОТЩИПЛЮ́, отщи́плешь (also отщипа́ю, etc.). Р. **Отщипа́ть** (acc.). I. **Отщи́пывать**. To nip off, pinch off.

ОТ'Е́ДЕННЫЙ; от'е́ден, —а, —о, —ы (ppp), see от'е́м.

ОТ'Е́ДЕШЬ, see от'е́ду.

ОТ'ЕДИ́М, от'еди́те, от'едя́т (pl. forms), see от'е́м.

ОТ'Е́ДУ, от'е́дешь. Р. **От'е́хать** (intr.) (от + gen.). I. **От'езжа́ть**. 1. To drive off, depart, leave. 2. To depart from a normal position (as a shelf, fixture, etc. comes away from the wall).

ОТ'Е́ЗДИ (imp.), see от'е́зжу.

ОТ'ЕЗЖА́Й (imp.), see от'е́ду.

ОТ'Е́ЗЖУ, от'е́здишь. Р. **От'е́здить** (intr.). 1. To spend some time riding, driving. 2. To finish or stop riding, driving (somewhere).

ОТ'Е́Л, от'е́ла (past), see от'е́м.

ОТ'Е́М, от'е́шь, от'е́ст (sing. forms). Р. **От'е́сть**. I. **От'еда́ть** (mean. 1 and 2). 1. To eat off, gnaw off (acc.). 2. To take out, remove (as stains) (acc.). 3. To finish eating (acc.) or (intr.).

ОТ'Е́СТ, see от'е́м.

ОТ'Е́ШЬ¹, see от'е́м.

ОТ'Е́ШЬ² (imp.), see от'е́м.

ОТ'Я́ТЫЙ; от'я́т, —а, —о, —ы (ppp), see отыму́.

ОТЫ́МЕШЬ, see отыму́.

ОТЫМИ́ (imp.), see отыму́.

ОТЫМУ́, оты́мешь. Р. **От'я́ть** (acc.),

отня́ть. I. **Отнима́ть.** 1. To take away. 2. To take, require (as time of s.o.). 3. To subtract (from) (acc. | от + gen.). 4. To amputate, take off. (Also see **отниму́, отни́мешь.**)

ОТЫ́СКАННЫЙ; оты́скан, —а, —о, —ы (ppp), see **отыщу́.**

ОТЫ́ЩЕШЬ, see **отыщу́.**

ОТЫЩИ́ (imp.), see **отыщу́.**

ОТЫЩУ́, оты́щешь. Р. **Отыска́ть** (acc.). I. **Оты́скивать.** 1. To look for and find. 2. (fig.) To run to earth, track down.

ОТЯГОЩЁННЫЙ; отягощён, —а́, —о́, —ы́ (ppp), see **отягощу́.**

ОТЯГОЩУ́, отяготи́шь. Р. **Отяготи́ть** (acc.). I. **Отягоща́ть.** (lit. and fig.) To burden (as s.o. or s.t. with s.t.) (acc. + inst.).

ОФО́РМИ (imp.), see **офо́рмлю.**

ОФО́РМЛЕННЫЙ; офо́рмлен, —а, —о, —ы (ppp), see **офо́рмлю.**

ОФО́РМЛЮ, офо́рмишь. Р. **Офо́рмить** (acc.). I. **Оформля́ть.** 1. To put in proper form, shape, etc. 2. make official, formalize. 3. To register, enroll (as a member of an organization, staff, etc.).

ОХА́ЕШЬ, see **оха́ю.**

ОХА́Й (imp.), see **оха́ю.**

ОХА́Ю, оха́ешь. Р. **Оха́ять** (acc.). I. **Ха́ять,** оха́ивать. To find fault with, abuse, run down.

ОХА́ЯННЫЙ; оха́ян, —а, —о, —ы (ppp), see **оха́ю.**

ОХВА́ЧЕННЫЙ; охва́чен, —а, —о, —ы (ppp), see **охвачу́.**

ОХВАЧУ́, охва́тишь. Г. **Охвати́ть** (acc.). I. **Охва́тывать.** 1. (lit. and fig.) To seize, grip. 2. To envelope (as flames). 3. To embrace, include. 4. To comprehend, grasp. 5. To outflank, envelope (as an enemy).

ОХЛАЖДЁННЫЙ; охлаждён, —а́, —о́, —ы́ (ppp), see **охлажу́.**

ОХЛАЖУ́, охлади́шь. Р. **Охлади́ть** (acc.). I. **Охлажда́ть.** (lit. and fig.) To cool, cool off, chill.

ОХОЛОЖУ́, охолоди́шь. Р. **Охолоди́ть** (arch.) (acc.). (lit. and fig.) To cool, cool off, chill.

ОХОЛОЩЁННЫЙ; охолощён, —а́, —о́, —ы́ (ppp), see **охолощу́.**

ОХОЛОЩУ́, охолости́шь. Р. **Ох-олости́ть** (acc.). I. **Холости́ть.** 1.

To castrate, emasculate. 2. To geld.

ОХО́ТЬСЯ (imp.), see **охо́чусь.**

ОХО́ЧУСЬ, охо́тишься. I. **Охо́титься.** 1. (lit. and fig.) To hunt, hunt for (на + acc.) or (за + inst.). 2. To strive, desire (to do s.t.) (+ inf.).

ОХРИ́П, охри́пла (past). Р. **Охри́пнуть** (intr.). I. **Хри́пнуть.** To grow/ become hoarse.

ОЦЕ́ПЛЕННЫЙ; оце́плен, —а, —о, —ы (ppp), see **оцеплю́.**

ОЦЕПЛЮ́, оце́пишь. Р. **Оцепи́ть** (acc.). I. **Оцепля́ть.** 1. To surround. 2. To cordon off.

ОЧЕ́РЧЕННЫЙ; оче́рчен, —а, —о, —ы (ppp), see **очерчу́.**

ОЧЕРЧУ́, оче́ртить. Р. **Очерти́ть** (acc.). I. **Оче́рчивать.** 1. To outline (draw a line around). 2. To outline (as a figure in a sketch). 3. To outline, describe (as an event).

ОЧЁСАНЫЙ; очёсан, —а, —о, —ы (ppp), see **очешу́.**

ОЧЁШЕШЬ, see **очешу́.**

ОЧЕШИ́ (imp.), see **очешу́.**

ОЧЕШУ́, очё́шешь. Р. **Очеса́ть** (acc.). I. **Очёсывать.** To comb out, to clean by combing/carding (as flax).

ОЧИ́СТИ (imp.), see **очи́щу.**

ОЧИ́СТЬ (imp.), see **очи́щу.**

ОЧИ́ЩЕННЫЙ; очи́щен, —а, —о, —ы (ppp), see **очи́щу.**

ОЧИ́ЩУ, очи́стишь. Р. **Очи́стить** (acc.). I. **Очища́ть, чи́стить** (mean. 1, 4, 5, 6). 1. To clean. 2. To purify, refine. 3. To clean out (as a room). 4. (fig.) To clean out. 5. To rob. 6. To peel, shell. 7. To evacuate (as one's bowels).

ОШЕЛОМЛЁННЫЙ; ошеломлён, —а́, —о́, —ы́ (ppp), see **ошеломлю́.**

ОШЕЛОМЛЮ́, ошеломи́шь. Р. **Оше-ломи́ть** (acc.). I. **Ошеломля́ть.** To astound, shock, stun.

ОШИБЁШЬСЯ, see **ошибу́сь.**

ОШИБИ́СЬ, see **ошибу́сь.**

ОШИ́БСЯ, оши́блась (past), see **ошибу́сь.**

ОШИБУ́СЬ, ошибёшься. Р. **Оши-би́ться** (intr.). I. **Ошиба́ться.** 1. To make mistake(s), be mistaken. 2. To be mistaken (in s.t. or s.o.) (в + prep.).

ОЩИ́ПАННЫЙ; ощи́пан, —а, —о, —ы (ppp), see **ощиплю́.**

ОЩИ́ПЛЕШЬ, see ощиплю́.

ОШИПЛИ́ (imp.). see ошиплю́.

ОЩИПЛЮ́, ощи́плешь. Р. **Ощипа́ть** (acc.). I. **Щипа́ть.** To pluck (as petals, grass, feathers, etc.).

ОЩУЩЁННЫЙ; ощущён, —а́, —о́, —ы́ (ppp), see ощущу́.

ОЩУЩУ́, ощути́шь. Р. **Ощути́ть** (acc.). I. **Ощуща́ть.** 1. To sense, to feel (through the senses) (e.g., to feel a desire to do s.t.; to sense impending disaster, etc.). 2. To become aware of (as the odor of gas; a hand on one's shoulder, etc.).

П

ПА́ВШИЙ and па́дший (arch.) (pap), see паду́.

ПАДЕ́ШЬ, see паду́.

ПАДИ́ (imp.), see паду́.

ПАДУ́, падёшь. P. Пасть (intr.). I. Па́дать. 1. To fall, drop. 2. To sink. 3. To fall on (на + acc.). 4. To die (of animals). (For numerous lit. and fig. usages see unabridged dictionary.)

ПА́ДШИЙ (arch.) and па́вший (pap), see паду́.

ПА́КОСТИ (imp.), see па́кощу.

ПА́КОЩУ, па́костишь. I. Па́костить. P. Запа́костить (mean. 1), испа́костить (mean. 1 and 2), напа́костить (mean. 1 and 3). 1. To soil (acc.). 2. To spoil (acc.). 3. To play a mean trick (intr.) on s.o. (dat.).

ПАЛ, па́ла (past), see паду́.

ПАС, пасла́ (past), see пасу́.

ПАСЁШЬ, see пасу́.

ПАСИ́ (imp.), see пасу́.

ПАСКУ́ДЬ (imp.), see паску́жу.

ПАСКУ́ЖУ, паску́дишь. I. Паску́дить (acc.). 1. To spoil. 2. To soil, dirty.

ПАСУ́, пасёшь. I. Пасти́ (acc.). 1. To graze, pasture (as cattle). 2. To shepherd.

ПАХ, ПА́ХЛА (past). I. Па́хнуть (intr.). 1. To smell, reek (intr.). 2. (lit. and fig.) To smell, reek, savor (of s.t.) (inst.).

ПА́ХАННЫЙ; па́хан, —а, —о, —ы (ppp), see пашу́.

ПА́ШЕШЬ, see пашу́.

ПАШИ́ (imp.), see пашу́.

ПАШУ́, па́шешь. I. Паха́ть (acc.) or (intr.). P. Вспаха́ть. To plow, till.

ПЕЙ (imp.). I. Пить (acc.) or (intr.). P. Вы́пить. To drink (also see пью).

ПЁК, пекла́ (past), see пеку́.

ПЕКИ́ (imp.), see пеку́.

ПЕКУ́, печёшь, пеку́т. I. Печь. P. Испе́чь (mean. 1). 1. To bake (acc.). 2. To be hot (intr.) (3rd pers.).

3. To burn (of the sun) (intr.) or (acc.) or (в + acc.).

ПЁР, пёрла (past). I. Пере́ть. 1. To go on, push on, press on (intr.). 2. To press against (as one's back) (в + acc.). 3. To carry, drag, pull (acc.). 4. (lit. and fig.) To become apparent, stick out, appear (3rd pers. only) (intr.). 5. To steal, pilfer (acc.) or (intr.). (Also see пру.)

ПЕРЕБЕГИ́ (imp.), see перебегу́.

ПЕРЕБЕГУ́, перебежи́шь, перебегу́т. P. Перебежа́ть. I. Перебега́ть. 1. To run across (as a street) (acc.) or (че́рез + acc.). 2. To run (someplace) (intr.). 3. To desert (to) (as to the enemy), (к + dat.) (to the side of the enemy) (на + acc. of side). 4. To look over, pass one's eyes/gaze over (s.t.) (acc. of s.t. + inst. of gaze).

ПЕРЕБЕЖИ́ШЬ, see перебегу́.

ПЕРЕБЕ́Й (imp.), see перебью́.

ПЕРЕБЕРЁШЬ, see переберу́.

ПЕРЕБЕРИ́ (imp.), see переберу́.

ПЕРЕБЕРУ́, переберёшь. P. Перебра́ть. I. Перебира́ть. 1. To sort out, look over (acc.). 2. To finger (as keys on a piano, etc.) (acc.). 3. To take a large number of (acc./gen.). 4. To take apart and reassemble (acc.). 5. To recall, turn over (in one's mind), touch upon, bring up (acc.). 6. (typ.) To reset (acc.).

ПЕРЕБЕШУ́СЬ, перебе́сишься. P. Перебеси́ться (intr.). 1. To go mad (of a number of animals). 2. To fly into a rage (of a number of people). 3. To finish sowing one's wild oats, become discrete, soberminded.

ПЕРЕБИ́ТЫЙ; перебИ́т, —а, —о, —ы (ppp), see перебью́.

ПЕРЕБОЛИ́Т, переболя́т (3rd pers. only). P. Переболе́ть (intr.). To experience great pain (usually fig.— of one's soul, spirits, heart).

ПЕРЕБОЛЯ́Т, see переболи́т.

ПЕРЕБО́РЕШЬ, see переборю́.

ПЕРЕБОРЙ 134 ПЕРЕВОЖУ́

ПЕРЕБОРЙ (imp.), see переборю́.

ПЕРЕБОРЮ́, перебо́решь. Р. Переборо́ть (acc.). 1. (lit. and fig.) To overcome, conquer. 2. To master (as oneself).

ПЕРЕ́БРАННЫЙ; пере́бран, —а, —о, —ы (ppp), see переберу́.

ПЕРЕБРО́СЬ (imp.), see переброшу́.

ПЕРЕБРО́ШЕННЫЙ; переброшен, —а, —о, —ы (ppp), see перебро́шу.

ПЕРЕБРО́ШУ, перебро́сишь. Р. Перебро́сить (acc.). I. Перебра́сывать. 1. To throw over (as a coat over one's shoulders) (acc. + че́рез + acc.). 2. To construct across (as a bridge across a river) (acc. + че́рез + acc.). 3. To move, send, transfer (as an army into a new position). 4. To throw, etc., too far.

ПЕРЕБЬЁШЬ, see перебью́.

ПЕРЕБЬЮ́, перебьёшь. Р. Переби́ть (acc.). I. Перебива́ть. 1. To kill (many), slaughter. 2. To break (as dishes, etc.). 3. To reupholster. 4. To shake up or fluff up (e.g., a pillow). 5. To interrupt (s.o. speaking). 6. To smother (as a stronger odor conceals a milder). 7. To outbid (s.o.) (as at an auction) (acc. of s.o.). 8. To buy (s.t.) at an auction (acc. of s.t.). 9. To nail (s.t.) somewhere else.

ПЕРЕВЕДЁННЫЙ; переведён, —а́, —о́, —ы́ (ppp), see переведу́.

ПЕРЕВЕДЁШЬ, see переведу́.

ПЕРЕВЕДИ́ (imp.), see переведу́.

ПЕРЕВЕДУ́, переведёшь. Р. Перевести́ (acc.). I. Переводи́ть. 1. To transfer, move. 2. To promote. 3. To take, conduct across (acc. + че́рез + acc.). 4. To translate (as a book from one language into another) (acc. + с + gen. + на + acc.). 5. To send (as money by wire). 6. To expend completely (as one's money). 7. To set (as a clock up or back). 8. To transfer (as a pattern or design). 9. To transfer (as property). 10. To exterminate, eliminate. 11. To convert (as meters to yards) (acc. + в + acc.). 12. To shift (as one's gaze to s.o.) (acc. + на + acc.).

ПЕРЕВЕ́ДШИ and переведя́ (adv. past part.), see переведу́.

ПЕРЕВЕ́ДШИЙ (pap), see переведу́.

ПЕРЕВЕДЯ́ and переве́дши (adv. past part.), see переведу́.

ПЕРЕВЁЗ, перевезла́ (past), see перевезу́.

ПЕРЕВЕЗЁННЫЙ; перевезён, —а́, —о́, —ы́ (ppp), see перевезу́.

ПЕРЕВЕЗЁШЬ, see перевезу́.

ПЕРЕВЕЗИ́ (imp.), see перевезу́.

ПЕРЕВЕЗУ́, перевезёшь. Р. Перевезти́ (acc.). I. Перевози́ть. To transport, take, carry (from one place to another, or across s.t.).

ПЕРЕВЕЗЯ́ (adv. past part), see перевезу́.

ПЕРЕВЕЙ (imp.). Р. Переви́ть (acc.). I. Перевива́ть. 1. To interweave, intertwine. 2. To wind (s.t.) around (s.t.) (acc. + вокру́г + gen.). 3. To reweave, retwist. (Also see перевью́.)

ПЕРЕВЁЛ, перевела́ (past), see переведу́.

ПЕРЕВЕРТИ́ (imp.), see переверчу́.

ПЕРЕВЁРТИШЬ, see переверчу́.

ПЕРЕВЁРТЯТ, see переверчу́.

ПЕРЕВЁРЧЕННЫЙ; переве́рчен, —а, —о, —ы (ppp), see переверчу́.

ПЕРЕВЕРЧУ́, переве́ртишь. Р. Перевертеть (acc.). I. Перевёртывать. 1. To screw up again, retighten (e.g., a bolt). 2. To overwind.

ПЕРЕВЕ́СЬ (imp.), see переве́шу.

ПЕРЕВЕ́ШЕННЫЙ; переве́шен, —а, —о, —ы (ppp), see переве́шу.

ПЕРЕВЕ́ШУ, переве́сишь. Р. Переве́сить (acc.). I. Переве́шивать. 1. To hang in another place. 2. To weigh again, reweigh. 3. (lit. and fig.) To overbalance, outweigh.

ПЕРЕВИ́НЧЕННЫЙ; переви́нчен, —а, —о, —ы (ppp), see перевинчу́.

ПЕРЕВИНЧУ́, перевинти́шь. Р. Перевинти́ть (acc.). I. Переви́нчивать. 1. To screw up (into) again. 2. To screw up too tight.

ПЕРЕВИ́ТЫЙ (and перевито́й) —а́, —о, —ы (ppp), see переве́й and перевью́.

ПЕРЕВОЖУ́[1], перево́дишь. I. Переводи́ть (acc.). Р. Перевести́. 1. To transfer, move. 2. To take, conduct across (acc. + че́рез + acc.). 3. To translate (as a book from one language into another (acc. + с + gen. + на + acc.). 4. To send (as money by wire). 5. To expend completely (as one's money). 6. To set (as a clock up or back). 7. To promote,advance (s.o.). 8. To transfer (as a pattern or design). 9. To transfer (as property). 10. To exterminate, eliminate. 11. To convert (as meters to yards) (acc. + в + acc.). 12. To shift (as one's gaze to s.o.) (acc. + на + acc.).

ПЕРЕВОЖУ́², перево́зишь. I. Перевози́ть (acc.). P. Перевезти́. To transport, take, carry (from one place to another, or across s.t.).

ПЕРЕВОЛО́К, переволокла́ (past), see переволоку́.

ПЕРЕВОЛОКИ́ (imp.), see переволоку́.

ПЕРЕВОЛОКУ́, переволочёшь, переволркут. P. Переволо́чь (acc.). I. Переволáкивать. To port, carry across (e.g., a canoe).

ПЕРЕВОЛО́КШИ and переволочá (adv. past part.), see переволоку́.

ПЕРЕВОЛОЧА́ and переволо́кши (adv. past part.), see переволоку́.

ПЕРЕВОЛО́ЧЕННЫЙ; переволо́чен, —а, —о, —ы (ppp), see переволоку́.

ПЕРЕВОЛОЧЁННЫЙ; переволочён, —á, —ó, —ы́ (ppp), see переволоку́.

ПЕРЕВОЛО́ЧЁШЬ, see переволоку́.

ПЕРЕВОПЛОЩЁННЫЙ; перевоплощён, —á, —ó, —ы́ (ppp), see перевоплощу́.

ПЕРЕВОПЛОЩУ́, перевоплоти́шь. P. Перевоплоти́ть (acc.). I. Перевоплощáть. 1. To incarnate, embody, incorporate. 2. To reincarnate, re-embody, reincorporate.

ПЕРЕВОРО́ЧЕННЫЙ; переворо́чен, —а, —о, —ы (ppp), see переворочу́.

ПЕРЕВОРОЧУ́, переворо́тишь. P. Переворотúть (acc.). I. Переворáчивать. 1. To turn, turn over. 2. To overturn, turn upside down (create disorder).

ПЕРЕ́ВРАННЫЙ; перéвран,—а, —о, —ы (ppp), see перевру́.

ПЕРЕВРЁШЬ, see перевру́.

ПЕРЕВРИ́ (imp.), see перевру́.

ПЕРЕВРУ́, перевршь. P. Переврáть (acc.). I. Перевирáть. 1. To distort (in relating, intentionally or otherwise). 2. To garble (intentionally or otherwise). 3. To excel (s.o.) in lying.

ПЕРЕВЫ́БЕРЕШЬ, see перевы́беру.

ПЕРЕВЫ́БЕРИ (imp.), see перевы́беру.

ПЕРЕВЫ́БЕРУ, перевы́берешь. P. Перевы́брать (acc.). I. Перевыбирáть. To re-elect.

ПЕРЕВЫ́БРАННЫЙ; перевы́бран, —а, —о, —ы (ppp), see перевы́беру.

ПЕРЕВЬЁШЬ, see перевью.

ПЕРЕВЬЮ, перевьёшь. P. Переви́ть (acc.). I. Перевивáть. 1. To interweave, intertwine. 2. To wind (s.t.) around (s.t.) (acc. + вокру́г + gen.). 3. To reweave, retwist.

ПЕРЕВЯ́ЖЕШЬ, see перевяжу́.

ПЕРЕВЯЖИ́ (imp.), see перевяжу́.

ПЕРЕВЯЖУ́, перевя́жешь. P. Перевязáть (acc.). I. Перевя́зывать. 1. To bandage, dress (as a wound). 2. To rebandage, redress. 3. To tie up. 4. To retie. 5. To reknit (as a scarf, etc.).

ПЕРЕВЯ́ЗАННЫЙ; перевя́зан, —а, —о, —ы (ppp), see перевяжу́.

ПЕРЕГЛА́ДЬ (imp.), see переглáжу.

ПЕРЕГЛА́ЖЕННЫЙ; переглáжен, —а, —о, —ы (ppp), see переглáжу.

ПЕРЕГЛА́ЖУ, переглáдишь. P. Переглáдить (acc.). I. Переглáживать. 1. To iron again. 2. To iron everything (as the whole laundry).

ПЕРЕГЛЯДИ́ (imp.), see перегляжу́.

ПЕРЕГЛЯДИ́ШЬ, see перегляжу́.

ПЕРЕГЛЯДИ́Т, see перегляжу́.

ПЕРЕГЛЯЖУ́, переглядúшь. P. Переглядéть (acc.). I. Перегля́дывать. 1. To look through, look over (again). 2. To look through a large number (as books, etc.).

ПЕРЕ́ГНАННЫЙ; перéгнан, —а, —о, —ы (ppp), see перегоню́.

ПЕРЕГНИЁТ, перегниют (3rd pers. only). P. Перегни́ть (intr.). I. Перегнивáть. 1. To decay, rot completely. 2. To rot through (as a rope).

ПЕРЕГНИЮ́Т (3rd pers. pl.), see перегниёт.

ПЕРЕГОЖУ́, перегодúшь. P. Перегоди́ть (acc.). To wait out (to wait till s.t. is over) (as a storm).

ПЕРЕГОНИ́ (imp.), see перегоню́.

ПЕРЕГО́НИШЬ, see перегоню́.

ПЕРЕГОНЮ́, перего́нишь. P. Перегнáть (acc.). I. Перегоня́ть. 1. (lit. and fig.) To outdistance, leave behind. 2. To drive (from one place to another) (as cattle). 3. To drive too hard, exhaust (as horses). 4. To distill.

ПЕРЕГÓНЯТ, see **перегоню́**.

ПЕРЕГОРИ́ (imp.), see **перегори́т**.

ПЕРЕГОРИ́Т, **перегоря́т** (3rd pers. only). Р. **Перегоре́ть** (intr.). I. **Перегора́ть**. 1. To burn out (as a lamp). 2. To burn up, burn to ashes. 3. (fig). To burn out (as one's ambition, desire, etc.). 4. To decay completely (as manure).

ПЕРЕГОРÓЖЕННЫЙ; перегорÓжен, —а, —о, —ы (ppp), see **перегорожу́**.

ПЕРЕГОРОЖУ́, перегорÓдишь (and **перегороди́шь**). Р. **Перегороди́ть** (acc.). I. **Перегора́живать**. 1. To partition off. 2. To block, obstruct.

ПЕРЕГОРЯ́Т (3rd pers. pl.), see **перегори́т**.

ПЕРЕГРУ́ЖЕННЫЙ; перегру́жен, —а, —о, —ы (ppp), see **перегружу́**.

ПЕРЕГРУЖЁННЫЙ; перегружён, —á, —ó, —ы́ (ppp), see **перегружу́**.

ПЕРЕГРУЖУ́, перегру́зишь (and **перегрузи́шь**). Р. **Перегрузи́ть** (acc.). I. **Перегружа́ть**. 1. To transfer a load. 2. To overload. 3. (fig.) To overload, (e.g., a person with work, an article with detail, etc.).

ПЕРЕГРЫ́З, перегры́зла (past), see **перегрызу́**.

ПЕРЕГРЫ́ЗЕННЫЙ; перегры́зен, —а, —о, —ы (ppp), see **перегрызу́**.

ПЕРЕГРЫЗЁШЬ, see **перегрызу́**.

ПЕРЕГРЫЗИ́ (imp.), see **перегрызу́**.

ПЕРЕГРЫЗУ́ перегрызёшь. Р. Перегры́зть (acc.). I. **Перегрыза́ть**. 1. To gnaw, bite, in two, through. 2. To bite tó death, tear to pieces, kill a number of. (e.g., sheep). 3. To crack, chew up a quantity of (e.g., nuts).

ПЕРЕДАВА́Й (imp.), see **передаю́**.

ПЕРЕДАВА́Я (adv. pres. part.), see **передаю́**.

ПЕРЕДАДИ́М, передади́те, передаду́т (pl. forms), see **переда́м**.

ПЕРЕДАЁШЬ, see **передаю́**.

ПЕРЕДА́Й (imp.), see **переда́м**.

ПЕРЕДА́М, переда́шь, переда́ст (sing. forms). Р. **Переда́ть**. I. **Передава́ть**. 1. To communicate, impart, tell (acc.). 2. To broadcast (as by radio) (acc.). 3. To give, transfer (acc.). 4. To transmit (characteristics) (acc.).

5. To reproduce, recreate (acc.). 6. To give/pay more than necessary (acc./gen.) or (intr.). 7. To send (as a letter) (acc.).

ПÉРЕДАННЫЙ; пéредан, —á, —о, —ы (ppp), see **переда́м**.

ПЕРЕДА́СТ, see **переда́м**.

ПЕРЕДА́ШЬ, see **переда́м**.

ПЕРЕДАЮ́, передаёшь. I. Передава́ть. Р. Переда́ть. 1. To communicate, impart, tell (acc.). 2. To broadcast (as by radio) (acc.). 3. To give, transfer (acc.). 4. To transmit (characteristics, etc.) (acc.) 5. To reproduce, recreate (acc.). 6. To give/pay more than necessary (acc./ gen.) or (intr.). 7. To send (as a letter) (acc.).

ПЕРЕДЕРЁШЬ, see **передеру́**.

ПЕРЕДЕРЁШЬСЯ, see **передеру́сь**.

ПЕРЕДÉРЖАННЫЙ; передéржан, —а, —о, —ы (ppp), see **передержу́**.

ПЕРЕДÉРЖАТ, see **передержу́**.

ПЕРЕДÉРЖИ (imp.), see **передержу́**.

ПЕРЕДÉРЖИШЬ, see **передержу́**.

ПЕРЕДЕРЖУ́, передéржишь. Р. Передержа́ть (acc.). I. **Передéрживать**. 1. To hold, keep too long. 2. To overcook, overdo. 3. To overexpose (photo).

ПЕРЕДЕРИ́ (imp.), see **передеру́**.

ПЕРЕДЕРИ́СЬ (imp.), see **передеру́сь**.

ПЕРЕДЕРУ́, передерёшь. Р. Передра́ть (acc.). I. **Передира́ть**. 1. To wear out a number of (as all of one's socks). 2. To kill, tear to pieces (as a wolf kills sheep, etc.). 3. To beat (all or many).

ПЕРЕДЕРУ́СЬ, передерёшься. Р. Передра́ться (intr.). To fight (with) (с + inst.).

ПЕРЕДОПРÓШЕННЫЙ; передопрÓшен, —а, —о, —ы (ppp), see **передопрошу́**.

ПЕРЕДОПРОШУ́, передопрÓсишь. Р. Передопроси́ть (acc.). I. **Передопра́шивать**. 1. To requestion, reinterrogate. 2. To question, interrogate (all, many).

ПЕРЕДÓХ, передÓхла (past). Р. **ПередÓхнуть** (intr.). To die (as a number of animals).

ПЕРÉДРАННЫЙ; перéдран, —а, —о, —ы (ppp), see **передеру́**.

ПЕРЕДРÉМЛЕШЬ, see **передремлю́**.

ПЕРЕДРЕМЛЙ (imp.), see **пере-дремлю.**
ПЕРЕДРЕМЛЮ, передрéмлешь. Р. Передремáть (acc.). To dawdle, loiter, linger a period of time.
ПЕРЕЕ́ДЕННЫЙ; переéден, —а, —о, —ы (ppp), see **переéм.**
ПЕРЕЕ́ДЕШЬ, see **переéду.**
ПЕРЕЕДИ́М, переедúте, переедя́т (pl. forms), see **переéм.**
ПЕРЕЕ́ДУ, переéдешь. Р. Переéхать. I. Переезжáть. 1. To cross (acc.) or (чéрез + acc.). 2. To run over (as s.o.) (acc.). 3. To move (as to another city, apartment, etc.) (intr.).
ПЕРЕЕЗЖА́Й (imp.), see **переéду.**
ПЕРЕЕ́Л, переéла (past), see **переéм.**
ПЕРЕЕ́М, переéшь, переéст (sing. forms). Р. Переéсть. I. Переедáть. 1. To overeat, eat too much (intr.) or (gen.). 2. To eat everything, a great deal (acc.). 3. (chem.) To corrode, eat away, eat through (acc.).
ПЕРЕЕ́СТ, see **переéм.**
ПЕРЕЕ́ШЬ[1], (imp.), see **переéм.**
ПЕРЕЕ́ШЬ[2], (2nd pers. sing.), see **переéм.**
ПЕРЕЖГИ́ (imp.), see **пережгу́.**
ПЕРЕЖГЛА́, пережгло́, пережгли́ (past), see **пережгу́** and **пережёг.**
ПЕРЕЖГУ́, пережжёшь, пережгу́т. Р. Пережéчь (acc.). I. Пережигáть. 1. To burn out (as a lamp, a fuse, etc.). 2. To burn through (by fire, acid, etc.). 3. To burn an excessive amount of (as fuel). 4. (tech.) To calcine. 5. To spoil by burning (e.g., food).
ПЕРЕЖДЁШЬ, see **переждý.**
ПЕРЕЖДИ́ (imp.), see **переждý.**
ПЕРЕЖДУ́, переждёшь. Р. Переждáть. I. Пережидáть. 1. To wait until s.t. is over, wait out (as a storm); to wait (e.g., a minute) (acc.). 2. To wait (intr.).
ПЕРЕЖЁГ, пережгла́ (past), see **пережгу́.**
ПЕРЕЖЖЁННЫЙ; пережжён, —á, —ó, —ы́ (ppp), see **пережгу́.**
ПЕРЕЖЖЁШЬ, see **пережгу́.**
ПЕРЕЖИВЁШЬ, see **переживу́.**
ПЕРЕЖИВИ́ (imp.), see **переживу́.**
ПЕРЕЖИВУ́, переживёшь. Р. Пережи́ть (acc.). I. Переживáть. 1. To live through (s.t.), survive (as an

illness). 2. To experience (s.t.). 3. To outline (s.o. or s.t.).
ПЕ́РЕЖИТЫЙ; пе́режит, —á, —о, —ы (ppp), see **переживу́.**
ПЕРЕЖИ́ТЫЙ; пережи́т, —á, —о, —ы (ppp), see **переживу́.**
ПЕРЕЗАБУ́ДЕШЬ, see **перезабу́ду.**
ПЕРЕЗАБУ́ДУ, перезабу́дешь. Р. Перезабы́ть (acc.). To forget (much,/ everything/everyone, etc.).
ПЕРЕЗАБУ́ДЬ (imp.), see **перезабу́ду.**
ПЕРЕЗАБЫ́ТЫЙ; перезабы́т, —а, —о, —ы (ppp), see **перезабу́ду.**
ПЕРЕЗАРАЖЁННЫЙ; перезаражён, —á, —ó, —ы́ (ppp), see **перезаражу́.**
ПЕРЕЗАРАЖУ́, перезарази́шь. Р. Перезарази́ть (acc.). To infect all, many.
ПЕРЕЗАРЯ́ЖЕННЫЙ; перезаря́жен, —а, —о, —ы (ppp), see **перезаряжу́.**
ПЕРЕЗАРЯЖЁННЫЙ; перезаряжён, —á, —ó, —ы́ (ppp), see **перезаряжу́.**
ПЕРЕЗАРЯЖУ́, перезаряди́шь (and перезаря́дишь). Р. Перезаряди́ть (acc.). I. Перезаряжáть. To reload, recharge (e.g., a camera, gun, battery, etc.).
ПЕРЕЗНАКÓМЛЕННЫЙ; перезнакóмлен, —а, —о, —ы (ppp), see **перезнакóмлю.**
ПЕРЕЗНАКÓМЛЮ, перезнакóмишь. Р. Перезнакóмить (acc. + с + inst.). To acquaint (as one or more persons with a number of people).
ПЕРЕЗНАКÓМЬ (imp.), see **перезнакóмлю.**
ПЕРЕЗЯ́Б, перезя́бла (past). Р. Перезя́бнуть (intr.). To become chilled, frostbitten.
ПЕРЕИЗБЕРЁШЬ, see **переизберу́.**
ПЕРЕИЗБЕРИ́ (imp.), see **переизберу́.**
ПЕРЕИЗБЕРУ́, переизберёшь. Р. Переизбрáть (acc.). I. Переизбирáть. To re-elect.
ПЕРЕИ́ЗБРАННЫЙ; переи́збран, —а, —о, —ы (ppp), see **переизберу́.**
ПЕРЕИЗДАВА́Й (imp.), see **переиздаю́.**
ПЕРЕИЗДАВА́Я (adv. pres. part.), see **переиздаю́.**
ПЕРЕИЗДАДИ́М, переиздади́те, переиздаду́т (pl. forms), see **переиздáм.**
ПЕРЕИЗДАЁШЬ, see **переиздаю́.**
ПЕРЕИЗДА́Й (imp.), see **иереиздáм.**
ПЕРЕИЗДА́М, переиздáшь, переиздáст

(sing. forms). Р. Переиздать (acc.).
I. Переиздавать. To republish, reprint, reissue.

ПЕРЕЙЗДАННЫЙ; переиздан, —á,
—о, —ы (ppp), see переиздáм.

ПЕРЕИЗДА́СТ, see переиздáм.

ПЕРЕИЗДА́ШЬ, see переиздáм.

ПЕРЕИЗДАЮ, переиздаёшь. I. Переиздавáть (acc.). Р. Переиздáть. To republish, reprint, reissue.

ПЕРЕЙДЁННЫЙ; перейдён, —á,
—ó, —ы́ (ppp), see перейду́.

ПЕРЕЙДЁШЬ, see перейду́.

ПЕРЕЙДИ́ (imp.), see перейду́.

ПЕРЕЙДУ́, перейдёшь. Р. Перейти́.
I. Переходи́ть. 1. To cross (as a street (acc.) or (чéрез + acc.). 2. To move from one place to another (intr.). 3. To go over (as to the enemy) (к + dat.); (to the enemy's side) (на + acc. of side). 4. To pass to (as property passes to s.o.) (к + dat.). 5. To change to (as a new job) (на + acc.); (a new school) (в + acc.). 6. To pass on to, turn to (as a subject) (к + dat.). 7. To turn into (s.t. else) (as love into hate) (в + acc.). 8. To pass, change (as from defense to attack) (от + gen. + к + dat.). 9. To exceed (as the cost exceeds a dollar, the flight lasted more than an hour) (за + acc.). 10. To cease, stop (of rain, etc.) (intr.).

ПЕРЕЙДЯ́ (adv. past part.), see перейду́.

ПЕРЕЙМЁШЬ, see перейму́.

ПЕРЕЙМИ́ (imp.), see перейму́.

ПЕРЕЙМУ́, переймёшь. Р. Переня́ть (acc.). I. Перенимáть. 1. To adopt (as an idea), imitate. 2. To intercept. 3. To borrow (for a short while).

ПЕРЕКА́ЧЕННЫЙ; перекáчен, —а,
—о, —ы (ppp), see перекачу́.

ПЕРЕКАЧУ́, перекáтишь. Р. Перекати́ть (acc.). I. Перекáтывать. To roll, move by rolling (as a hoop, vehicle, etc.).

ПЕРЕКИПИ́ (imp.), see перекиплю́.

ПЕРЕКИПИ́ШЬ, see перекиплю́.

ПЕРЕКИПЛЮ́, перекипи́шь. Р. Перекипéть (intr.). I. Перекипáть. 1. To boil too long. 2. To calm down (of people).

ПЕРЕКИПЯ́Т, see перекиплю́.

ПЕРЕКИПЯЧЁННЫЙ; перекипячён, —á, —ó, —ы́ (ppp), see перекипячу́.

ПЕРЕКИПЯЧУ́, перекипяти́шь. Р. Перекипяти́ть (acc.). To boil again.

ПЕРЕКО́ЛЕШЬ, see переколю́.

ПЕРЕКОЛИ́ (imp.), see переколю́.

ПЕРЕКО́ЛОТЫЙ; перекóлот, —а, —о, —ы (ppp), see переколю́.

ПЕРЕКОЛО́ЧЕННЫЙ; переколóчен, —а, —о, —ы (ppp), see переколочу́.

ПЕРЕКОЛОЧУ́, переколóтишь. Р. Переколоти́ть (acc.). I. Переколáчивать. 1. To nail in another place (after moving). 2. To break all or a quantity of (as dishes). 3. To beat all or many (as people, animals, etc.).

ПЕРЕКОЛЮ́, перекóлешь. Р. Переколóть (acc.). I. Перекáлывать (mean. 1 thru 3). 1. To pin (s.t.) somewhere else or differently. 2. To prick all over (as one's hands with thorns). 3. To kill, slaughter. 4. To chop (as wood, trees, etc.). 5. To crack (e.g., nuts).

ПЕРЕКО́РМЛЕННЫЙ; перекóрмлен, —а, —о, —ы (ppp), see перекормлю́.

ПЕРЕКОРМЛЮ́, перекóрмишь. Р. Перекорми́ть (acc.). I. Перекáрмливать. To overfeed, surfeit.

ПЕРЕКО́ШЕННЫЙ; перекóшен, —а, —о, —ы (ppp), see перекошу́[1] and [2].

ПЕРЕКОШЁННЫЙ; перекошён, —á, —ó, —ы́ (ppp), see перекошу́[1].

ПЕРЕКОШУ́[1], перекоси́шь. Р. Перекоси́ть. I. Перекáшивать. 1. To make crooked, slant, cant, warp (acc.). 2. To warp (impers. + acc.). 3. To distort, become distorted (of one's features, etc.) (impers. + acc.).

ПЕРЕКОШУ́[2], перекóсишь. Р. Перекоси́ть (acc.). I. Перекáшивать. 1. To mow (as all the grass). 2. (fig.) To mow or cut down, kill (as all the enemy).

ПЕРЕКРА́СЬ (imp.), see перекрáшу.

ПЕРЕКРА́ШЕННЫЙ; перекрéашен, —а, —о, —ы (ppp), see перекрáшу.

ПЕРЕКРА́ШУ, перекрáсишь. Р. Перекрáсить (acc.). I. Перекрáшиват. 1. To repaint. 2. To paint a number of. 3. To re-dye. 4. To re-dye a quantity of.

ПЕРЕКРЕЩЁННЫЙ; перекрещён, —а́, —о́, —ы́ (ppp), see перекрещу́.

ПЕРЕКРЕЩУ́, перекре́стишь. P. Перекрести́ть (acc.). I. Перекре́щиват, крести́ть (mean. 1). 1. To cross (make sign of, over s.o.) (acc. of s.o.). 2. To re-christen. 3. To rename or nickname. 4. To criss-cross (as straps, etc.).

ПЕРЕКРИЧА́Т, see перекричу́.

ПЕРЕКРИЧИ́ (imp.), see перекричу́.

ПЕРЕКРИЧИ́ШЬ, see перекричу́.

ПЕРЕКРИЧУ́, перекричи́шь. P. Перекрича́ть (acc.). I. Перекри́кивать. To outshout, drown out (another), with one's voice.

ПЕРЕКРО́ЕШЬ, see перекро́ю.

ПЕРЕКРО́Й (imp.), see перекро́ю.

ПЕРЕКРО́Ю, перекро́ешь. P. Перекры́ть (acc.). I. Перекрыва́ть. 1. To re-cover, re-roof, etc. 2. To block (as a road, movement of troops, etc.). 3. To dam (as a stream). 4. To shut off (as a valve). 5. To exceed, excel. 6. To compensate for (a deficiency). 7. To overlap, lap (e.g., shingles), superimpose. 8. To span. 9. To trump (as a card). 10. To cover a number of.

ПЕРЕКРУ́ЧЕННЫЙ; перекру́чен, —а, —о, —ы (ppp), see перекручу́.

ПЕРЕКРУЧУ́, перекру́тишь. P. Перекрути́ть (acc.). I. Перекру́чивать. 1. To wind (as a cord). 2. To wind (s.t. with s.t.) (as a package with a cord) (acc. + inst.). 3. To turn (as a key). 4. To overwind (as a spring).

ПЕРЕКРЫ́ТЫЙ; перекры́т, —а, —о, —ы (ppp), see перекро́ю.

ПЕРЕКУ́ПЛЕННЫЙ; перекуплен, —а, —о, —ы (ppp), see перекуплю́.

ПЕРЕКУПЛЮ́, переку́пишь. P. Перекупи́ть (acc.). I. Перекупа́ть. 1. To outbid (s.o.) 2. To buy back. 3. To buy all or a quantity of.

ПЕРЕКУ́ШЕННЫЙ; переку́шен, —а, —о, —ы (ppp), see перекушу́.

ПЕРЕКУШУ́, переку́сишь. P. Перекуси́ть. I. Переку́сывать. 1. To bite in two (acc.). 2. To have a bite, snack (gen.) or (intr.).

ПЕРЕЛЁГ, перелегла́ (past), see переля́гу.

ПЕРЕЛЕЖА́Т, see перележу́.

ПЕРЕЛЕЖИ́ (imp.), see перележу́.

ПЕРЕЛЕЖИ́ШЬ, see перележу́.

ПЕРЕЛЕЖУ́, перележи́шь. P. Перележа́ть. 1. To lie too long (e.g., as a person in the sun, fruit on the ground, etc.) (intr.). 2. To lie longer (than s.o. else) (acc.). 3. To wait out (s.t.) while lying (e.g., to lie in a shelter until bombardment stops) (acc.) or (intr. + до + конца́ + gen.). 4. To injure, numb (s.t.) by lying on it (as one's arm) (acc.).

ПЕРЕЛЕ́З, переле́зла (past), see переле́зу.

ПЕРЕЛЕ́ЗЕШЬ, see переле́зу.

ПЕРЕЛЕ́ЗУ, переле́зешь. P. Переле́зть. I. Перелеза́ть. 1. To clamber, crawl, climb through or over (acc.) or (че́рез + acc.). 2. To clamber, crawl, climb (onto) (на + acc.); (into) (в + acc.).

ПЕРЕЛЕ́ЗЬ (imp.), see переле́зу.

ПЕРЕЛЕ́Й (imp.), see перелью́.

ПЕРЕЛЕТИ́ (imp.), see перелечу́.

ПЕРЕЛЕТИ́ШЬ, see перелечу́.

ПЕРЕЛЕТЯ́Т, see перелечу́.

ПЕРЕЛЕЧУ́, перелети́шь. P. Перелете́ть. I. Перелета́ть. 1. To fly over, across (as the ocean, etc.) (acc.) or (че́рез + acc.). 2. (fig.) To fly over, across, through (acc.) or (че́рез + acc.). 3. To fly from one place to another (intr.) (+ proper Preposition). 4. To fly too far (of a plane, artillery shell, etc.) (intr.).

ПЕРЕЛИ́ТЫЙ; перели́т, —а́, —о, —ы (ppp), see перелью́.

ПЕРЕЛО́ВЛЕННЫЙ; перело́влен, —а, —о, —ы (ppp), see переловлю́.

ПЕРЕЛОВЛЮ́, перело́вишь. P. Перелови́ть (acc.). I. Перела́вливать. To catch all, many (as fish, fowl, fugitives, etc.).

ПЕРЕЛО́МЛЕННЫЙ; перело́млен, —а, —о, —ы (ppp), see переломлю́.

ПЕРЕЛОМЛЮ́, перело́мишь. P. Переломи́ть (acc.). I. Перела́мывать. 1. To break (s.t.) in two. 2. To fracture. 3. (fig.) To break, overcome (as a habit, a weakness, etc.).

ПЕРЕЛОПА́ТЬ (imp.), see перелопа́чу.

ПЕРЕЛОПА́ЧЕННЫЙ; перелопа́чен, —а, —о, —ы (ppp), see перелопа́чу.

ПЕРЕЛОПА́ЧУ, перелопа́тишь. P. Перелопа́тить (acc.). I. Перелопа́чивать. To shovel from one place to another (to avoid rotting—as grain, potatoes, etc.).

ПЕРЕЛЬЁШЬ, see перелью́.

ПЕРЕЛЬЮ́, перельёшь. Р. Перели́ть.
I. Перелива́ть. 1. To pour (s.t.) from
one container into another (acc.).
2. To transfuse (as blood) (acc.).
3. (fig.) To transfuse, transmit (as
one's enthusiasm to s.o.) (acc. + в
+ acc.). 4. To pour too much (acc.).
5. To recast (as a bronze bell) (acc.).
6. To overflow (of water, etc.) (intr.).

ПЕРЕЛЯ́Г (imp.), see переля́гу.

ПЕРЕЛЯ́ГУ, переля́жешь, переля́гут.
Р. Переле́чь (intr.). 1. To lie somewhere else. 2. To shift one's position
while lying.

ПЕРЕЛЯ́ЖЕШЬ, see переля́гу.

ПЕРЕМА́ЖУ, перема́жешь. Р. Пере-
ма́зать (acc.). I. Перема́зывать.
1. To soil, dirty (s.t.) completely
(with s.t.) (acc. + inst.). 2. To recoat
(s.t. with s.t.—as wax, grease, etc.)
(acc. + inst.).

ПЕРЕМА́ЖЬ (imp.), see перема́жу.

ПЕРЕМА́ЗАННЫЙ; перема́зан, —а,
—о, —ы (ppp), see перема́жу.

ПЕРЕМЁЛ, перемела́ (past), see пере-
мету́.

ПЕРЕМЕ́ЛЕШЬ, see перемелю́.

ПЕРЕМЕЛИ́ (imp.), see перемелю́.

ПЕРЕМЕЛЮ́, переме́лешь. Р. Пере-
моло́ть (acc.). I. Перема́лывать.
1. To mill, grind all, a quantity of.
2. To grind again, regrind. 3. To
destroy (e.g., the enemy's forces).

ПЕ́РЕМЕР, перемерла́, пе́ремерло,
пе́ремерли (past), see перемрёт.

ПЕРЕМЁРЗ, перемёрзла (past). Р.
перемёрзнуть (intr.). 1. To be frostbitten, frozen, killed by frost (of
plants, etc.) (all or many). 2. To
become frostbitten, chilled (of people)
3. To freeze completely (of bodies of
water).

ПЕРЕМЕТЁННЫЙ; переметён, —а́,
—о́, —ы́ (ppp), see перемету́.

ПЕРЕМЕТЁШЬ, see перемету́.

ПЕРЕМЕТИ́ (imp.), see перемету́.

ПЕРЕМЕТУ́, переметёшь. Р. Пере-
мести́ (acc.). 1. To sweep away. 2. To
re-sweep. 3. To sweep everywhere,
a whole area (as a room). 4. To
become covered with snow (as a road,
etc.) (impers. + acc. of road).

ПЕРЕМЕ́ТШИЙ (pap), see пере-
мету́.

ПЕРЕМЕ́ТЬ (imp.), see переме́чу.

ПЕРЕМЕТЯ́ (adv. past part.), see
перемету́.

ПЕРЕМЕ́ЧЕННЫЙ; переме́чен, —а,
—о, —ы (ppp), see переме́чу.

ПЕРЕМЕ́ЧУ, переме́тишь. Р. Пере-
ме́тить (acc.). I. Перемеча́ть. 1. To
mark all or a quantity of (as linen).
2. To mark again or change the mark
(as on linen, etc.).

ПЕРЕМЕ́ШЕННЫЙ; переме́шен, —а,
—о, —ы (ppp), see перемешу́.

ПЕРЕМЕШУ́, переме́сишь. Р. Пере-
меси́ть (acc.). I. Переме́шивать.
1. To convert into a homogeneous
mass by stirring, kneading, etc. 2. To
reknead, knead again.

ПЕРЕМЕЩЁННЫЙ; перемещён, —а́,
—о́, —ы́ (ppp), see перемещу́.

ПЕРЕМЕЩУ́, перемести́шь. Р. Пере-
мести́ть (acc.). I. Перемеща́ть. 1. To
move (s.o. or s.t.) from one place
to another. 2. To transfer (s.o.)
to another assignment.

ПЕРЕМО́Г, перемогла́ (past), see
перемогу́.

ПЕРЕМОГИ́ (imp.), see перемогу́.

ПЕРЕМОГУ́, перемо́жешь, перемо́гут.
Р. Перемо́чь (acc.). I. Перемога́ть.
To overcome.

ПЕРЕМО́ЕШЬ, see перемо́ю.

ПЕРЕМО́ЖЕШЬ, see перемогу́.

ПЕРЕМО́Й, see перемо́ю.

ПЕРЕМО́ЛВИ (imp.), see перемо́лвлю.

ПЕРЕМО́ЛВЛЕННЫЙ; перемо́лвлен,
—а, —о, —ы (ppp), see перемо́лвлю.

ПЕРЕМО́ЛВЛЮ, перемо́лвишь. Р.
Перемо́лвить (acc.). To exchange
words (with s.o.) (usually employed
with acc. of сло́во + с + inst.).

ПЕРЕМО́ЛОТЫЙ; перемо́лот, —а,
—о, —ы (ppp), see перемелю́.

ПЕРЕМОРО́ЖЕННЫЙ; переморо́-
жен, —а, —о, —ы (ppp), see перемо-
ро́жу.

ПЕРЕМОРО́ЖУ, переморо́зишь. Р.
Перемороз́ить (acc.). I. Перемора́-
живать. To allow to freeze, allow to
become frostbitten (e.g., vegetables,
flowers, etc.).

ПЕРЕМОРО́ЗЬ (imp.), see переморо́жу.

ПЕРЕМОЩЁННЫЙ; перемощён, —а́,
—о́, —ы́ (ppp), see перемощу́.

ПЕРЕМОЩУ́, перемости́шь. Р. Пере-
мости́ть (acc.). 1. To repave. 2. To
pave all or many (e.g., streets, etc.).

ПЕРЕМО́Ю, перемо́ешь. Р. Перемы́ть (acc.). I **Перемыва́ть.** 1. To wash again. 2. To wash all, or a quantity of (as dishes).

ПЕРЕМРЁМ, перемрёте, перемру́т (pl. forms), see **перемрёт.**

ПЕРЕМРЁТ (3rd pers. sing.) (1st and 2nd pers. sing. not used). Р. **Перемере́ть** (intr.). I. **Перемира́ть.** To die (said of all or many).

ПЕРЕМРИ́ (imp.), see **перемрёт.**

ПЕРЕМРУ́Т (3rd pers. pl.), see **перемрёт** and **перемрём.**

ПЕРЕМЫ́ТЫЙ; перемы́т, —а, —о, —ы (ppp), see **перемо́ю.**

ПЕРЕНАПРЯ́Г, перенапрягла́ (past), see **перенапрягу́.**

ПЕРЕНАПРЯГИ́ (imp.), see **перенапрягу́.**

ПЕРЕНАПРЯГУ́, перенапряжёшь, перенапрягу́т. Р. **Перенапря́чь** (acc.). I. **Перенапряга́ть.** To overstrain.

ПЕРЕНАПРЯЖЁННЫЙ; перенапряжён, —а́, —о́, —ы́ (ppp), see **перенапрягу́.**

ПЕРЕНАПРЯЖЁШЬ, see **перенапрягу́.**

ПЕРЕНАСЫ́ТЬ (imp.), see **перенасы́щу.**

ПЕРЕНАСЫ́ЩЕННЫЙ; перенасы́щен, —а, —о, —ы (ppp), see **перенасы́щу.**

ПЕРЕНАСЫ́ЩУ, перенасы́тишь. Р. **Перенасы́тить** (acc.). I. **Перенасыща́ть.** (chem.) To supersaturate.

ПЕРЕНЁС, перенесла́ (past), see **перенесу́.**

ПЕРЕНЕСЁННЫЙ; перенесён, —а́, —о́, —ы́ (ppp), see **перенесу́.**

ПЕРЕНЕСЁШЬ, see **перенесу́.**

ПЕРЕНЕСИ́ (imp.), see **перенесу́.**

ПЕРЕНЕСУ́, перенесёшь. Р. **Перенести́** (acc.). I. **Переноси́ть.** 1. To carry, convey, take to another place. 2. To transfer, switch (s.o. or s.t. to another place or position). 3. To reschedule (as a meeting). 4. To postpone, put off. 5. To endure, bear. 6. To undergo. 7. (math.) To transpose.

ПЕРЕНЕСЯ́ (adv. past part.), see **перенесу́.**

ПЕРЕНО́ШЕННЫЙ; перено́шен, —а, —о, —ы (ppp), see **переношу́[2].**

ПЕРЕНОШУ́[1], перено́сишь. I. **Переноси́ть** (acc.). Р. **Перенести́.** 1. To carry, convey, take to another. 2. To transfer, switch (s.o. or s.t.) to another place or position. 3. To reschedule (as a meeting). 4. To postpone, put off. 5. To endure, bear. 6. To undergo. 7. (math.) To transpose.

ПЕРЕНОШУ́[2], перено́сишь. Р. **Переноси́ть** (acc.). I. **Перена́шивать.** 1. To bring, carry, carry away (in several trips). 2. To wear out all, a number of (as socks). 3. To carry a child more than normal length of time (said of pregnancy).

ПЕ́РЕНЯТЫЙ; пе́ренят, —á, —о, —ы (ppp). Р. **Переня́ть** (acc.). I. **Перенима́ть.** 1. To adopt (as an idea), imitate. 2. To intercept. 3. To borrow (for a short while). (Also see **перейму́.**)

ПЕРЕОБУ́ЕШЬ, see **переобу́ю.**

ПЕРЕОБУ́Й (imp.), see **переобу́ю.**

ПЕРЕОБУ́ТЫЙ; переобу́т, —а, —о, —ы (ppp), see **переобу́ю.**

ПЕРЕОБУ́Ю, переобу́ешь. Р. **Переобу́ть** (acc.). I. **Переобува́ть.** 1. To change s.o.'s shoes (acc. of pers.). 2. To change one's own shoes (acc. of shoes).

ПЕРЕОДЕ́НЕШЬ, see **переоде́ну.**

ПЕРЕОДЕ́НУ, переоде́нешь. Р. **Переоде́ть** (acc.). I. **Переодева́ть.** 1. To change (s.o.'s) clothes (acc. of person). 2. To change clothes (one's own) (acc. of clothes). 3. To disguise (s.o. as s.o. else) by changing his clothes (acc. + inst.).

ПЕРЕОДЕ́НЬ (imp.), see **переоде́ну.**

ПЕРЕОДЕ́ТЫЙ; переоде́т, —а, —о, —ы (ppp), see **переоде́ну.**

ПЕРЕОСНАЩЁННЫЙ; переоснащён, —á, —о́, —ы́ (ppp), see **переоснащу́.**

ПЕРЕОСНАЩУ́, переоснасти́шь. Р. **Переоснасти́ть** (acc.). I. **Переоснаща́ть.** To reequip, rerig.

ПЕРЕПАДЁТ, перепаду́т (3rd pers. only). Р. **Перепа́сть** (intr.). I. **Перепада́ть.** 1. To occur intermittently (of rain, etc.). 2. To fall to one's lot, come one's way (impers. + dat.). 3. To pass (of time). 4. To grow thin, emaciated.

ПЕРЕПАДУ́Т (3rd pers. pl.), see **перепадёт.**

ПЕРЕПА́КОСТИ (imp.), see перепа́кощу.

ПЕРЕПА́КОЩЕННЫЙ; перепа́кощен, —а, —о, —ы (ppp), see перепа́кощу.

ПЕРЕПА́КОЩУ, перепа́костишь. Р. Перепа́костить (acc.). 1. To soil completely, all, a number of. 2. To spoil completely, all, a quantity of.

ПЕРЕПА́Л, перепа́ла (past), see перепадёт.

ПЕРЕПА́ХАННЫЙ; перепа́хан, —а, —о, —ы (ppp), see перепашу́.

ПЕРЕПА́ШЕШЬ, see перепашу́.

ПЕРЕПАШИ́ (imp.), see перепашу́.

ПЕРЕПАШУ́, перепа́шешь. Р. Перепаха́ть (acc.). I. Перепа́хивать. 1. To plow again. 2. To plow a whole area. 3. To cross-plow.

ПЕРЕПЕ́Й (imp.), see перепью́.

ПЕРЕПЁК, перепекла́, see перепеку́.

ПЕРЕПЕКИ́ (imp.), see перепеку́.

ПЕРЕПЕКУ́, перепечёшь, перепеку́т. Р. Перепе́чь (acc.). I. Перепека́ть. 1. To overbake. 2. To bake all, much.

ПЕРЕПЕЧЁННЫЙ; перепечён, —а́, —о́, —ы́ (ppp), see перепеку́.

ПЕРЕПЕЧЁШЬ, see перепеку́.

ПЕРЕПИ́САННЫЙ; перепи́сан, —а, —о, —ы (ppp), see перепишу́.

ПЕРЕПИ́ШЕШЬ, see перепишу́.

ПЕРЕПИШИ́ (imp.), see перепишу́.

ПЕРЕПИШУ́, перепи́шешь. Р. Переписа́ть (acc.). I. Перепи́сывать. 1. To rewrite, copy, transcribe. 2. To make a list (of), inventory, etc. 3. To transfer (s.o.) (as a man from one branch of the military service to another) (acc. + в + acc.). 4. To transfer (as property to s.o.) (acc. + на + acc.).

ПЕРЕПЛА́ВЛЕННЫЙ; перепла́влен, —а, —о, —ы (ppp), see перепла́влю.

ПЕРЕПЛА́ВЛЮ, перепла́вишь. Р. Перепла́вить (acc.). I. Переплавля́ть. 1. To smelt all or a quantity of. 2. To remelt, refound, recast (s.t. into s.t.) (acc. + в + acc.). 3. To float (as logs on or across a river, etc.).

ПЕРЕПЛА́ВЬ (imp.), see перепла́влю.

ПЕРЕПЛА́ЧЕННЫЙ; перепла́чен, —а, —о, —ы (ppp), see переплачу́.

ПЕРЕПЛАЧУ́, перепла́тишь. Р. Переплати́ть (acc.). I. Перепла́чивать. 1. To overpay, pay too much.

2. To spend or pay much (for s.t.) (in a series of payments) (acc. + за + acc.).

ПЕРЕПЛЁЛ, переплела́ (past), see переплету́.

ПЕРЕПЛЕТЁННЫЙ; переплетён, —а́, —о́, —ы́ (ppp), see переплету́.

ПЕРЕПЛЕТЁШЬ, see переплету́.

ПЕРЕПЛЕТИ́ (imp.), see переплету́.

ПЕРЕПЛЕТУ́, переплетёшь. Р. Переплести́ (acc.). I. Переплета́ть. 1. To interlace, interknit, intertwine (s.t. with s.t.) (acc. + inst.). 2. To bind (as a book). 3. To rebraid, reweave.

ПЕРЕПЛЁТШИЙ (pap), see переплету́.

ПЕРЕПЛЕТЯ́ (adv. past part.), see переплету́.

ПЕРЕПЛЫВЁШЬ, see переплыву́.

ПЕРЕПЛЫВИ́ (imp.), see переплыву́.

ПЕРЕПЛЫВУ́, переплывёшь. Р. Переплы́ть (acc.) or (че́рез + acc.) or (intr.). I. Переплыва́ть. To swim, float, sail, row across.

ПЕРЕПО́ЛЕШЬ, see переполю́.

ПЕРЕПО́ЛЗ, переползла́ (past), see переползу́.

ПЕРЕПОЛЗЁШЬ see переползу́.

ПЕРЕПОЛЗИ́ (imp.), see переползу́.

ПЕРЕПОЛЗУ́, переползёшь. Р. Переползти́ (intr.). I. Переполза́ть. 1. To crawl over, across (че́рез + acc.). 2. To crawl somewhere.

ПЕРЕПОЛИ́ (imp.), see переполю́.

ПЕРЕПО́ЛОТЫЙ; перепо́лот —а —о —ы (ppp), see переполю́.

ПЕРЕПОЛЮ́, перепо́лешь. Р. Переполо́ть (acc.). I. Перепа́лывать. 1. To weed out again, re-weed (as a garden). 2. To weed a whole area.

ПЕРЕПОРТИ́ (imp.), see перепо́рчу.

ПЕРЕПО́РТЬ (imp.), see перепо́рчу.

ПЕРЕПО́РЧЕННЫЙ; перепо́рчен, —а, —о, —ы (ppp), see перепо́рчу.

ПЕРЕПО́РЧУ; перепо́ртишь. Р. Перепо́ртить (acc.). 1. To spoil completely. 2. To spoil all or many.

ПЕРЕПОЯ́САННЫЙ; перепоя́сан, —а, —о, —,ы (ppp), see перепояшу́.

ПЕРЕПОЯ́ШЕШЬ, see перепояшу́.

ПЕРЕПОЯ́ШУ, перепоя́шешь. Р. Перепоя́сать (acc.). I. Перепоя́сывать. 1. To gird, belt (e.g., s.t. with s.t.) (acc. + inst.). 2. To lash, whip. 3. To regird, rebelt.

ПЕРЕПОЯ́ШЬ (imp.), see перепояшу́.

ПЕРЕПРА́ВЛЕННЫЙ; перепра́влен, —а, —о, —ы (ppp), see перепра́влю.

ПЕРЕПРА́ВЛЮ, перепра́вишь. Р. Перепра́вить (acc.). I. Переправля́ть. 1. To convey across. 2. To forward (as a letter). 3. To correct.

ПЕРЕПРА́ВЬ (imp.), see перепра́влю.

ПЕРЕПРОДАВА́Й (imp.), see перепродаю́.

ПЕРЕПРОДАВА́Я (adv. pres. part.), see перепродаю́.

ПЕРЕПРОДАДИ́М, перепродади́те, перепродаду́т (pl. forms), see перепрода́м.

ПЕРЕПРОДАЁШЬ, see перепродаю́.

ПЕРЕПРОДА́Й (imp.), see перепрода́м.

ПЕРЕПРОДА́М, перепрода́шь, перепрода́ст (sing. forms). Р. Перепрода́ть (acc.). I. Перепродава́ть. To resell.

ПЕРЕПРО́ДАННЫЙ; перепро́дан, —а, —о, —ы (ppp), see перепрода́м.

ПЕРЕПРОДА́СТ, see перепрода́м.

ПЕРЕПРОДА́ШЬ, see перепрода́м.

ПЕРЕПРОДАЮ́, перепродаёшь. I. Перепродава́ть (acc.). Р. Перепрода́ть. To resell.

ПЕРЕПРУ́ЖЕННЫЙ; перепру́жен, —а, —о, —ы (ppp), see перепружу́.

ПЕРЕПРУЖУ́, перепру́дишь. Р. Перепруди́ть (acc.). I. Перепру́живать. To dam (as a river).

ПЕРЕПРЯ́Г, перепрягла́ (past), see перепрягу́.

ПЕРЕПРЯГИ́ (imp.), see перепрягу́.

ПЕРЕПРЯГУ́, перепряжёшь, перепрягу́т. Р. Перепря́чь (acc.). I. Перепряга́ть. To reharness.

ПЕРЕПРЯЖЁННЫЙ; перепряжён, —а́, —о́, —ы́ (ppp), see перепрягу́.

ПЕРЕПРЯЖЁШЬ, see перепрягу́.

ПЕРЕПЬЁШЬ, see перепью́.

ПЕРЕПЬЮ́, перепьёшь. Р. Перепи́ть. I. Перепива́ть. 1. To drink too much (intr.) or (gen.). 2. To outdrink (s.o.) (acc.).

ПЕРЕРАСТЁШЬ, see перерасту́.

ПЕРЕРАСТИ́ (imp.), see перерасту́.

ПЕРЕРАСТУ́, перерастёшь. Р. Перерасти́. I. Перераста́ть. 1. (lit. and fig.) To outgrow (acc.). 2. To overgrow (acc.). 3. (fig.) To develop into, turn into (as admiration into love, etc.) (intr.) (в + acc.).

ПЕРЕ́РВАННЫЙ; пере́рван, —а, —о, —ы (ppp), see перерву́.

ПЕРЕРВЁШЬ, see перерву́.

ПЕРЕРВИ́ (imp.), see перерву́.

ПЕРЕРВУ́, перервёшь. Р. Перерва́ть (acc.). I. Перерыва́ть. 1. To tear apart, break to pieces. 2. To tear up all, or a quantity of. 3. To break, sever, suspend, interrupt (as communications, conversations, relations etc.).

ПЕРЕРЕ́ЖЕШЬ, see перере́жу.

ПЕРЕРЕ́ЖУ, переpе́жешь. Р. Переpе́зать (acc.). I. Перерезать, переpе́зывать. 1. To cut in two or to pieces. 2. To cross (as streams cross a plain). 3. (fig.) To cut (as the route of escape, etc.). 4. To cut in many places or cut a quantity of. 5. To slaughter, kill many.

ПЕРЕРЕ́ЖЬ (imp.), see переpе́жу.

ПЕРЕРЕ́ЗАННЫЙ; переpе́зан, —а, —о, —ы (ppp), see переpе́жу.

ПЕРЕРО́ЕШЬ, see переро́ю.

ПЕРЕРОЖДЁННЫЙ; перерождён, —а́, —о́, —ы́ (ppp), see перерожу́.

ПЕРЕРОЖУ́, перероди́шь. Р. Перероди́ть (acc.). I. Перерожда́ть. To regenerate, revive, make a new person of.

ПЕРЕРО́Й (imp.), see переро́ю.

ПЕРЕРО́С, переросла́ (past), see перерасту́.

ПЕРЕРО́Ю, переро́ешь. Р. Перерыть (acc.). I. Перерыва́ть. 1. To dig up (as a whole area). 2. To dig across (as a road). 3. To rummage, look (in or through s.t.). 4. To redig.

ПЕРЕРУ́БЛЕННЫЙ; переру́блен, —а, —о, —ы (ppp), see перерублю́.

ПЕРЕРУБЛЮ́, переру́бишь. Р. Переруби́ть (acc.). I. Переруба́ть. 1. To chop in two, to pieces. 2. To chop up a quantity of (as cabbage). 3. To kill (as with a sabre) all/many.

ПЕРЕРЫ́ТЫЙ; переры́т, —а, —о, —ы (ppp), see переро́ю.

ПЕРЕРЯ́ЖЕННЫЙ; переря́жен, —а, —о, —ы (ppp), see переряжу́.

ПЕРЕРЯЖУ́, переря́дишь (and переря́дишь). Р. Переряди́ть (acc.). I. Переряжа́ть. 1. To dress, disguise (s.o. as s.o.) (acc. + inst.). 2. To dress, disguise (s.o. in s.t.) (acc. + в + acc.).

ПЕРЕСА́ЖЕННЫЙ; переса́жен, —а, —о, —ы (ppp), see пересажу́.

ПЕРЕСАЖУ́, переса́дишь. Р. Пересади́ть (acc.). I. Переса́живать. 1. To reseat (s.o.) (change s.o.'s seat). 2. To transplant. 3. (med.) To transplant, graft. 4. To transfer, move. 5. To change (as s.o. from one diet to another, etc.) (acc. + от + gen. + на + acc.). 6. To rehaft (as an axe).

ПЕРЕСДАВА́Й (imp.), see пересдаю́.

ПЕРЕСДАВА́Я (adv. pres. part.), see пересдаю́.

ПЕРЕСДАДИ́М, пересдади́те, пересдаду́т (pl. forms), see пересда́м.

ПЕРЕСДАЁШЬ, see пересдаю́.

ПЕРЕСДА́Й (imp.), see пересда́м.

ПЕРЕСДА́М, пересда́шь, пересда́ст (sing. forms). Р. Пересда́ть (acc.). I. Пересдава́ть. 1. To transfer, turn over (s.t. to s.o.). 2. To retake (as an examination). 3. To deal (cards) around again.

ПЕРЕСДА́ННЫЙ; пересда́н, —а́, —о́, —ы́ (ppp), see пересда́м.

ПЕРЕСДА́СТ, see пересда́м.

ПЕРЕСДА́ШЬ, see пересда́м.

ПЕРЕСДАЮ́, пересдаёшь. I. Пересдава́ть (acc.). Р. Пересда́ть. 1. To transfer, turn over (s.t. to s.o.). 2. To retake (as an examination). 3. To deal (cards) around again.

ПЕРЕСЕ́К, пересекла́ (past), see пересеку́.

ПЕРЕСЕКИ́ (imp.), see пересеку́.

ПЕРЕСЕКУ́, пересечёшь, пересеку́т. Р. Пересе́чь (acc.). I. Пересека́ть (mean. 1 thru 4). 1. To cut in two, cut to pieces. 2. To cross (as a street). 3. To intersect. 4. To block, cut off (as a road, retreat). 5. To flog, whip, all or many.

ПЕРЕСЕ́Л, пересе́ла (past). Р. Пересе́сть (intr.). I. Переса́живать. 1. To change seats. 2. To change trains, carriages, etc. (Also see переся́ду.)

ПЕРЕСЕЧЁННЫЙ; пересечён, —а́, —о́, —ы́ (ppp), see пересеку́ (mean. 1 thru 4).

ПЕРЕСЕ́ЧЕННЫЙ; пересе́чен, —а, —о, —ы (ppp), see пересеку́ (mean. 5).

ПЕРЕСЕЧЁШЬ, see пересеку́.

ПЕРЕСИДИ́ (imp.), see пересижу́.

ПЕРЕСИДИ́ШЬ, see пересижу́.

ПЕРЕСИДЯ́Т, see пересижу́.

ПЕРЕСИ́ЖЕННЫЙ; переси́жен, —а, —о, —ы (ppp), see пересижу́.

ПЕРЕСИЖУ́, пересиди́шь. Р. Пересиде́ть. I. Переси́живать. 1. To outstay, outsit, remain longer than (s.o.) (acc.). 2. To sit, stay too long (intr.). 3. To sit, stay through (as a performance) (acc.), or (to the end: до конца́) (intr.). 4. To cause to grow numb by prolonged sitting (as one's leg) (acc.).

ПЕРЕСКА́ЖЕШЬ, see перескажу́.

ПЕРЕСКАЖИ́ (imp.), see перескажу́.

ПЕРЕСКАЖУ́, переска́жешь. Р. Пересказа́ть (acc.). I. Переска́зывать. 1. To relate. 2. To tell all (in detail).

ПЕРЕСКА́ЗАННЫЙ; переска́зан, —а, —о, —ы (ppp), see перескажу́.

ПЕРЕ́СЛАННЫЙ; пере́слан, —а, —о, —ы (ppp). Р. Пересла́ть (acc.). I. Пересыла́ть. 1. To send. 2. To remit (as money). 3. To forward. (Also see перешлю́.)

ПЕРЕСЛАЩЁННЫЙ; переслащён, —а́, —о́, —ы́ (ppp), see переслащу́.

ПЕРЕСЛАЩУ́, пересласти́шь. Р. Переласти́ть (acc.). I. Пересла́щивать. To make too sweet, oversweeten.

ПЕРЕСМО́ТРЕННЫЙ; пересмо́трен, —а, —о, —ы (ppp), see пересмотрю́.

ПЕРЕСМОТРИ́ (imp.), see пересмотрю́.

ПЕРЕСМО́ТРИШЬ, see пересмотрю́.

ПЕРЕСМОТРЮ́, пересмо́тришь. Р. Пересмотре́ть (acc.). I. Пересма́тривать. 1. To go over again, reexamine, review. 2. To revise. 3. To look over, (e.g., a number of books).

ПЕРЕСМО́ТРЯТ, see пересмотрю́.

ПЕРЕСНИ́МЕШЬ, see пересниму́.

ПЕРЕСНИМИ́ (imp.), see пересниму́.

ПЕРЕСНИМУ́, пересни́мешь. Р. Пересня́ть (acc.). I. Переснима́ть. 1. To make a copy (of s.t.). 2. To take another photograph (of s.t.). 3. To resurvey (a plot of land). 4. To cut again (playing cards).

ПЕРЕСНЯ́ТЫЙ; пересня́т, —а́, —о, —ы (ppp), see пересниму́.

ПЕРЕСОЗДАВА́Й (imp.), see пересоздаю́.

ПЕРЕСОЗДАВА́Я (adv. pres. part.), see пересоздаю́.

ПЕРЕСОЗДАДИ́М, пересоздади́те, пересоздаду́т (pl. forms), see пересозда́м.

ПЕРЕСОЗДАЁШЬ, see пересоздаю́.

ПЕРЕСОЗДА́Й (imp.), see пересозда́м.

ПЕРЕСОЗДА́М, пересозда́шь, пересозда́ст (sing. forms). P. Пересозда́ть (acc.). I. Пересоздава́ть. To re-create, reestablish.

ПЕРЕСО́ЗДАННЫЙ; пересо́здан, —а́, —о, —ы (ppp), see пересозда́м.

ПЕРЕСОЗДА́СТ, see пересозда́м.

ПЕРЕСОЗДА́ШЬ, see пересозда́м.

ПЕРЕСОЗДАЮ́, пересоздаёшь. I. Пересоздава́ть (acc.). P. Пересозда́ть. To re-create, reestablish.

ПЕРЕСО́Х, пересо́хла (past). P. Пересо́хнуть (intr.). I. Пересыха́ть. To become completely dry, dry up.

ПЕРЕ́СПАННЫЙ; пере́спан, —а, —о, —ы (ppp), see пересплю́.

ПЕРЕСПИ́ (imp.), see пересплю́.

ПЕРЕСПИ́ШЬ, see пересплю́.

ПЕРЕСПЛЮ́, переспи́шь. P. Переспа́ть. 1. To oversleep (intr.). 2. To sleep through (as the morning) (acc.). 3. To spend the night (intr.).

ПЕРЕСПРО́ШЕННЫЙ; переспро́шен, —а, —о, —ы (ppp), see переспрошу́.

ПЕРЕСПРОШУ́, переспро́сишь. P. Переспроси́ть. I. Переспра́шивать. 1. To ask again (acc.) or (intr.). 2. To ask (s.o.) to repeat (acc.). 3. To ask, interrogate everyone or many (acc.). 4. To ask about (everything) (acc.).

ПЕРЕСПЯ́Т, see пересплю́.

ПЕРЕСТАВА́Й (imp.), see перестаю́.

ПЕРЕСТАВА́Я (adv. pres. part.), see перестаю́.

ПЕРЕСТА́ВЛЕННЫЙ; переста́влен, —а, —о, —ы (ppp), see переста́влю.

ПЕРЕСТА́ВЛЮ, переста́вишь. P. Переста́вить (acc.). I. Переставля́ть. 1. To move, shift. 2. To rearrange. 3. To transpose.

ПЕРЕСТА́ВЬ (imp.), see переста́влю.

ПЕРЕСТАЁШЬ see перестаю́.

ПЕРЕСТА́НЕШЬ see переста́ну.

ПЕРЕСТА́НУ переста́нешь. P. Переста́ть. I. Переставать. 1. To stop, cease (as smoking) (inf.). 2. To stop, cease (as "the rain stopped") (intr.).

ПЕРЕСТА́НЬ (imp.), see переста́ну.

ПЕРЕСТАЮ́ перестаёшь. I. Переставать. P. Переста́ть. 1. To stop, cease (as smoking) (+ inf.). 2. To stop, cease (as "the rain stopped") (intr.).

ПЕРЕСТЕ́ЛЕННЫЙ; перестéлен, —а, —о, —ы (ppp), see перестелю́.

ПЕРЕСТЕ́ЛЕШЬ, see перестелю́.

ПЕРЕСТЕЛИ́ (imp.), see перестелю́.

ПЕРЕСТЕЛЮ́, перестéлешь. P. Перестла́ть and перестели́ть (acc.). I. Перестила́ть. 1. To remake, respread (as a bed). 2. To recover (as a floor).

ПЕРЕ́СТЛАННЫЙ; пере́стлан, —а, —о, —ы (ppp), see перестелю́.

ПЕРЕСТОИ́ШЬ, see перестою́.

ПЕРЕСТОЙ (imp.), see перестою́.

ПЕРЕСТОЮ́, перестои́шь. P. Перестоя́ть. I. Перестáивать. 1. To stand too long (so as to spoil—as milk, crops, etc.) (intr.). 2. To wait out (as a rain storm, etc.) (acc.).

ПЕРЕСТУ́ПЛЕННЫЙ; переступ́лен, —а, —о, —ы (ppp), see переступлю́.

ПЕРЕСТУПЛЮ́, пересту́пишь. P. Переступи́ть. I. Переступа́ть. 1. To step over, across (as a threshold) (acc.). 2. To move, step (intr.). 3. (fig.) To overstep, transgress (as the bounds of decorum) (acc.). 4. To shift (from one foot to the other) (с ноги́ на́ ногу) (intr.).

ПЕРЕСЫ́ПАННЫЙ; пересы́пан, —а, —о, —ы (ppp), see пересы́плю.

ПЕРЕСЫ́ПЛЕШЬ, see пересы́плю.

ПЕРЕСЫ́ПЛЮ, пересы́плешь. P. Пересы́пать. I. Пересыпа́ть. 1. To pour (s.t.) from one place (in)to another (as from one container into another) (acc.). 2. To pour too much (of s.t.) (acc./gen.). 3. To sprinkle (s.t. with s.t.) (acc. + inst.). 4. (fig.) To intersperse (as one's talk with jokes) (acc. + inst.).

ПЕРЕСЫ́ПЬ (imp.), see пересы́плю.

ПЕРЕСЫ́ТЬ (imp.), see пересы́щу.

ПЕРЕСЫ́ЩЕННЫЙ; пересы́щен, —а, —о, —ы (ppp), see пересы́щу.

ПЕРЕСЫ́ЩУ, пересы́тишь. P. Пересы́тить (acc.). I. Пересыща́ть. (chem.) To supersaturate.

ПЕРЕСЯ́ДЕШЬ, see переся́ду.

ПЕРЕСЯ́ДУ, переся́дешь. P. Пересе́сть (intr.). I. Переса́живаться. 1. To change seats. 2. To change trains, carriages, etc.

ПЕРЕСЯ́ДЬ (imp.), see переся́ду.

ПЕРЕТЁР, перетёрла (past), see перетру́.

ПЕРЕТЕРЕ́В and перетёрши (adv. past part.), see перетру́.

ПЕРЕТЕРПИ́ (imp.), see перетерплю́.

ПЕРЕТЕ́РПИШЬ, see перетерплю́.

ПЕРЕТЕРПЛЮ́, перете́рпишь. Р. Перетерпе́ть (acc.). 1. To suffer or endure much. 2. To overcome (as an illness, adversity, etc.).

ПЕРЕТЕ́РПЯТ, see перетерплю́.

ПЕРЕТЁРТЫЙ; перетёрт, —а, —о, —ы (ppp), see перетру́.

ПЕРЕТЁРШИ and перетере́в (adv. past part.), see перетру́.

ПЕРЕТО́ПЛЕННЫЙ; перето́плен, —а, —о, —ы (ppp), see перетоплю́[1,2,3].

ПЕРЕТОПЛЮ́[1], перето́пишь. Р. Перетопи́ть (acc.). I. Перета́пливать. 1. To melt. 2. To melt all, a quantity of.

ПЕРЕТОПЛЮ́[2], перето́пишь. Р. Перетопи́ть (acc.). I. Перета́пливать. 1. To heat all or many (as kilns, furnaces, etc.). 2. To re-heat. 3. To use up all or much (fuel) in heating.

ПЕРЕТОПЛЮ́[3], перето́пишь. Р. Перетопи́ть (acc.). 1. To drown all or many (as cats). 2. To sink all or many (as ships).

ПЕРЕТРЁШЬ, see перетру́.

ПЕРЕТРИ́ (imp.), see перетру́.

ПЕРЕТРУ́, перетрёшь. Р. Перетере́ть (acc.). I. Перетира́ть. 1. To wear out (as a rope, cord). 2. To grind, grate (as radishes). 3. To dry or wipe all of (s.t.) (as dishes).

ПЕРЕТРУ́СЬ (imp.), see перетру́шу.

ПЕРЕТРУ́ШЕННЫЙ; перетру́шен, —а, —о, —ы (ppp), see перетрушу́.

ПЕРЕТРУШУ́, перетруси́шь. Р. Перетруси́ть (acc.). To shake and turn over (e.g., hay, etc.).

ПЕРЕТРУ́ШУ, перетру́сишь. Р. Перетру́сить (intr.). To be badly frightened.

ПЕРЕТРЯ́С, перетрясла́ (past), see перетрясу́.

ПЕРЕТРЯСЁННЫЙ; перетрясён, —а́, —о́, —ы́ (ppp), see перетрясу́.

ПЕРЕТРЯСЁШЬ, see перетрясу́.

ПЕРЕТРЯСИ́ (imp.), see перетрясу́.

ПЕРЕТРЯСУ́, перетрясёшь. Р. Перетрясти́ (acc.). 1. To shake out a number of (as clothes, rugs, etc.). 2. To shake out or up (as the contents of a bag in search of s.t.).

ПЕРЕУПРЯ́МЛЮ, переупря́мишь. Р. Переупря́мить (acc.). To force (s.o.) to agree, change opinion or action through persistence (indicates stubbornness on the part of both people).

ПЕРЕУПРЯ́МЬ (imp.), see переупря́млю.

ПЕРЕУСТУ́ПЛЕННЫЙ; переусту́плен, —а, —о, —ы (ppp), see переуступлю́.

ПЕРЕУСТУПЛЮ́, переусту́пишь. Р. Переуступи́ть (acc.). I. Переуступа́ть. 1. To give up (s.t. to s.o.). 1. To cede (s.t. to s.o.).

ПЕРЕУТОМЛЁННЫЙ; переутомлён, —а́, —о́, —ы́ (ppp), see переутомлю́.

ПЕРЕУТОМЛЮ́, переутоми́шь. Р. Переутоми́ть (acc.). I. Переутомля́ть. 1. To overtire, exhaust. 2. To overwork.

ПЕРЕУЧЁЛ, переучла́ (past), see переучту́.

ПЕРЕУЧЁТШИЙ (pap), see переучту́.

ПЕРЕУЧЛА́, переучло́, переучли́ (past), see переучту́ and переучёл.

ПЕРЕУЧТЁННЫЙ; переучтён, —а́, —о́, —ы́ (ppp), see переучту́.

ПЕРЕУЧТЁШЬ, see переучту́.

ПЕРЕУЧТИ́ (imp.), see переучту́.

ПЕРЕУЧТУ́, переучтёшь. Р. Переуче́сть (acc.). I. Переучи́тывать. To take stock (of s.t.) again, reinventory.

ПЕРЕУЧТЯ́ (adv. past part.), see переучту́.

ПЕРЕХВА́ЧЕННЫЙ; перехва́чен, —а, —о, —ы (ppp), see перехвачу́.

ПЕРЕХВАЧУ́, перехва́тишь. Р. Перехвати́ть (acc.). I. Перехва́тывать. 1. To intercept. 2. (lit. and fig.) To seize. 3. To clasp. 4. To take, "grab" a bite to eat, snack. 5. To borrow for a short while. (For other lit. and fig. meanings see unabridged dictionary.).

ПЕРЕХОЖУ́, перехо́дишь. I. Переходи́ть. Р. Перейти́. 1. To cross (as a street) (acc.) or (че́рез + acc.). 2. To move from one place to another (intr.) 3. To go over to (as the enemy) (к + dat.), (to the enemy's side) (на + acc. of side). 4. To pass to (as property passes to s.o.) (к + dat.). 5. To change to (as a new job) (на + acc.), (a new school) (в + acc.). 6. To pass on to, turn to (as a new subject) (к + dat.). 7. To turn into (s.t. else) (as love into hate) (в + acc.). 8. To pass, change (as from defense to attack) (от + gen. + к + dat.). 9. To exceed (as the cost exceeds a dollar, the fight lasted more than an hour) (за + acc.). 10. To cease, stop (of rain, etc.) (intr.).

ПЕРЕЧЁЛ, перечла́ (past), see **пере-чту́**[1] and [2].

ПЕРЕЧЁРЧЕНЫЙ; перечёрчен, —а, —о, —ы (ppp), see **перечерчу́**.

ПЕРЕЧЕРЧУ́, перечёртишь. Р. Пере-черти́ть (acc.). I. **Перечёрчивать.** 1. To redraw. 2. To copy, trace (as a drawing, a plan, etc.). 3. To draw all or many.

ПЕРЕЧЁСАННЫЙ; перечёсан, —а, —о, —ы (ppp), see **перечешу́**.

ПЕРЕЧЁТШИЙ (pap), see **перечту́**[1] and [2].

ПЕРЕЧЁШЕШЬ, see **перечешу́**.

ПЕРЕЧЕШИ (imp.), see **перечешу́**.

ПЕРЕЧЕШУ́, перечёшешь. Р. Пере-чеса́ть (acc.). I. **Перечёсывать.** 1. To do (s.o.'s) hair over, brush, or dress (s.o.'s) hair again (acc. of person/hair). 2. To do the hair of a number of people. 3. To comb all or much (as wool, etc.).

ПЕРЕЧЛА́, перечло́, перечли́ (past), see **перечту́**[1] and [2] and **перечёл.**

ПЕРЕЧТЁННЫЙ; перечтён, —а́, —о́, —ы́ (ppp), see **перечту́**[1] and [2].

ПЕРЕЧТЁШЬ, see **перечту́**[1] and [2].

ПЕРЕЧТИ (imp.), see **перечту́**[1] and [2].

ПЕРЕЧТУ́[1]**, перечтёшь. Р. Перечёсть** (acc.). I. **Пересчи́тывать.** 1. To count again, recalculate. 2. To convert (as production units into dollars) (acc. + в + prep.). 3. To count all of (as change in one's pocket).

ПЕРЕЧТУ́[2]**, перечтёшь. Р. Перечёсть** (acc.). I. **Перечи́тывать.** 1. To reread. 2. To read all, many, much.

ПЕРЕЧТЯ (adv. past part.), see **перечту́**[1] and [2].

ПЕРЕШЁДШИЙ (pap), see **перешёл** and **перейду́.**

ПЕРЕШЕЙ (imp.), see **перешью́.**

ПЕРЕШЁЛ, перешла́ (past). Р. Перей-ти́. I. **Переходи́ть.** 1. To cross (as a street) (acc.) or (че́рез + acc.). 2. To move from one place to another (intr.). 3. To go over to (as the enemy) (к + dat.) (to the enemy's side) (на + acc. of side). 4. To pass to (as property passes to s.o.) (к + dat.). 5. To change to (as to a new job) (на + acc.) (a new school) (в + acc.). 6. To pass on to, turn to (as a new subject) (к + dat.). 7. To turn into (s.t. else) (as love turns into hate) (в + acc.). 8. To pass, change (as from defense to attack) (от + gen. + к + dat.). 9. To exceed (as the cost exceeds a dollar, the fight lasted more than an hour) (за + acc.). 10. To cease, stop (of rain, etc.) (intr.). (Also see **перейду́.**)

ПЕРЕШИ́Б, переши́бла (past), see **перешибу́.**

ПЕРЕШИБЁШЬ, see **перешибу́.**

ПЕРЕШИБИ (imp.), see **перешибу́.**

ПЕРЕШИ́БЛЕННЫЙ; переши́блен, —а, —о, —ы (ppp), see **перешибу́.**

ПЕРЕШИБУ́, перешибёшь. Р. Пере-шиби́ть (acc.). I. **Перешиба́ть.** 1. To break, fracture. 2. To break in two. 3. (fig.) To excel (s.o.).

ПЕРЕШИ́ТЫЙ; переши́т, —а, —о, —ы (ppp), see **перешью́.**

ПЕРЕШЛА́, перешло́, перешли́ (past), see **перешёл** and **перейду́.**

ПЕРЕШЛЁШЬ, see **перешлю́.**

ПЕРЕШЛИ́[1] (past), see **перешёл** and **перейду́.**

ПЕРЕШЛИ́[2] (imp.), see **перешлю́.**

ПЕРЕШЛЮ́, перешлёшь. Р. Пере-сла́ть (acc.). I. **Пересыла́ть.** 1. To send. 2. To remit (as money). 3. To forward.

ПЕРЕШЬЁШЬ, see **перешью́.**

ПЕРЕШЬЮ́, перешьёшь. Р. Пере-ши́ть (acc.). I. **Перешива́ть.** 1. To resew, alter (as a garment). 2. To replank, revet again. 3. To sew all, many.

ПЕСТРИ (imp.), see **пестри́т.**

ПЕСТРИ́Т, пестря́т (3rd pers. only). I. **Пестре́ть** (intr.). 1. To be colorful (as flags in a breeze). 2. To abound in, be gay with s.t., colorful (inst.). 3. To be too colorful.

ПЕСТРЯ́Т (3rd pers. pl.), see пестри́т.

ПЕ́ТЫЙ; пе́т, —а, —о, —ы (ppp), I. **Петь.** Р. **Пропе́ть** (mean. 1 and 2), **спеть** (mean. 1 and 2). 1. To sing (intr.). 2. To sing a song, a part, etc. (acc.). 3. (fig.) To sing (as one's love), to glorify, celebrate (acc.). 4. To talk a lot (about), repeat (intr. + о + prep.). (Also see пою́.)

ПЕЧЁННЫЙ; печён, —а́, —о́, —ы́ (ppp), see пече́шь and пеку́.

ПЕЧЁШЬ (2nd pers. sing.). I. **Печь.** Р. **Испе́чь** (mean. 1). 1. To bake (acc.) 2. To be hot (3rd pers.) (intr.). 3. To burn (of the sun) (intr.) or (acc.) or (в + acc.). (Also see пеку́.)

ПИ́САННЫЙ; пи́сан, —а, —о, —ы (ppp), see пишу́.

ПИ́ТЫЙ; пи́т, —а́, —о, —ы (ppp). I. **Пить** (acc.) or (intr.). Р. **Вы́пить.** To drink (also see пей and пью).

ПИ́ШЕШЬ, see пишу́.

ПИШИ́ (imp.), see пишу́.

ПИШУ́, пи́шешь. I. **Писа́ть** (acc.) or (intr.). Р. **Написа́ть.** 1. To write. 2. To paint (as pictures).

ПИЩА́Т, see пищу́.

ПИЩИ́ (imp.), see пищу́.

ПИЩИ́ШЬ, see пищу́.

ПИЩУ́, пищи́шь. I. **Пища́ть.** Р. **Пропища́ть.** 1. To peep, chirp (intr.). 2. To squeak (intr.). 3. To whine (intr.). 4. To speak, say in a squeaky voice (intr.) or (acc.).

ПЛА́ВЛЕННЫЙ; пла́влен, —а, —о, —ы (ppp), see пла́влю.

ПЛА́ВЛЮ, пла́вишь. I. **Пла́вить** (acc.). Р. **Распла́вить** (mean. 1). 1. To melt, fuse. 2. To smelt. 3. To raft, float (as logs).

ПЛАВЬ (imp.), see пла́влю.

ПЛА́ЧЕННЫЙ; пла́чен, —а, —о, —ы (ppp), see плачу́.

ПЛА́ЧЕШЬ, see пла́чу.

ПЛАЧУ́, пла́тишь. I. **Плати́ть.** Р. **Заплати́ть, уплати́ть** (mean. 1 and 2). 1. To pay (as a debt) (acc.). 2. To pay for (s.t. with s.t.) (за + acc. + inst.). 3. (lit. and fig.) To repay (s.o. with s.t.) (dat. of s.o. + inst. of s.t.).

ПЛА́ЧУ, пла́чешь. I. **Пла́кать** (intr.).

(lit. and fig.) To cry, weep (of people and things).

ПЛАЧЬ (imp.), see пла́чу.

ПЛЁЛ, плела́ (past), see плету́.

ПЛЁЛСЯ, плела́сь (past), see плету́сь.

ПЛЕСКА́Я and **ПЛЕЩА́** (adv. pres. part.), see плещу́.

ПЛЕТЁННЫЙ; плетён, —а́, —о́, —ы́ (ppp), see плету́.

ПЛЕТЁШЬ, see плету́.

ПЛЕТЁШЬСЯ, see плету́сь.

ПЛЕТИ́ (imp.), see плету́.

ПЛЕТИ́СЬ (imp.), see плету́сь.

ПЛЕТУ́, плетёшь. I. **Плести́** (acc.). Р. **Сплести́** (mean. 1 thru 3). 1. To braid, plait. 2. To weave (as a basket, etc.). 3. (fig.) To weave, concoct (plot) (as intrigue). 4. To talk nonsense.

ПЛЕТУ́СЬ, плетёшься. I. **Плести́сь** (intr.). To plod along.

ПЛЁТШИЙ (pap), see плету́.

ПЛЁТШИЙСЯ (pap), see плету́сь.

ПЛЕЩА́ and **плеска́я** (adv. pres. part.) see плещу́.

ПЛЕ́ЩЕШЬ, see плещу́.

ПЛЕЩИ́ (imp.), see плещу́.

ПЛЕЩУ́, пле́щешь. I. **Плеска́ть.** Р. **Плесну́ть** (mean. 1 thru 3). 1. To splash (intr.). 2. To splash (s.o. with s.t.) (на + acc. + inst.). 3. To splash (pour) (as water on the floor) (acc. + на + acc.). 4. (fig.) To flutter (of a sail, flag, etc.) (intr.). 5. (arch.) To applaud (intr.) or (dat.).

ПЛОЖУ́, плоди́шь. I. **Плоди́ть** (acc.). Р. **Расплоди́ть.** 1. To breed (aise as cattle, crops, etc.). 2. To procreate. 3. (fig.) To create, engender, give rise to, produce.

ПЛЫВЁШЬ, see плыву́.

ПЛЫВИ́ (imp.), see плыву́.

ПЛЫВУ́, плывёшь. I. **Плыть** (intr.). 1. (lit. and fig.) To float, drift, sail. 2. (lit. and fig.) To swim.

ПЛЯ́ШЕШЬ, see пляшу́.

ПЛЯШИ́ (imp.), see пляшу́.

ПЛЯШУ́, пля́шешь. I. **Пляса́ть** (acc.). or (intr.). Р. **Спляса́ть.** (lit. and fig.) To dance.

ПОБЕГИ́ (imp.), see побегу́.

ПОБЕГУ́, побежи́шь, побегу́т. Р. **Побежа́ть** (intr.). 1. To break into a run. 2. To begin to move rapidly (of fog, sound, ships, etc.). 3. To begin to

flow (of water, blood, etc.). 4. (fig.)
To begin to flow, pass rapidly (of
time, life, etc.).

ПОБЕЖИШЬ, see побегу́.

ПОБЕ́Й (imp.). P. Поби́ть (acc.).
I. Бить (mean. 1). 1. To beat (as a
horse, etc.). 2. To slaughter, kill all,
many. 3. To defeat (as an enemy,
competitor). 4. To break all, many
(as dishes). 5. To injure, damage (s.o.
or s.t.). 6. To lay, beat down (as rain,
wind, hail beats down grain, etc.).
7. To nip (as frost nips buds, etc.).
(Also see побью́.)

ПОБЕРЁГ, побе́регла́ (past), see по-
берегу́.

ПОБЕРЕГИ́ (imp.), see поберегу́.

ПОБЕРЕГУ́, побережёшь, поберегу́т.
P. Побере́чь (acc.). 1. To keep,
preserve. 2. To look after, take care
of (as a sick person, child, etc.).

ПОБЕРЕЖЁННЫЙ; побережён, —á,
—б, —ы́ (ppp), see поберегу́.

ПОБЕРЕЖЁШЬ, see поберегу́.

ПОБЕРЁШЬ, see поберу́.

ПОБЕРИ́ (imp.), see поберу́.

ПОБЕРУ́, поберёшь. P. Побра́ть
(acc.). To collect, take (a quantity
of).

ПОБИ́ТЫЙ; поби́т, —а, —о, —ы
(ppp), see побе́й and побью́.

ПОБЛЁК, поблёкла (past). P. Поблёкнуть (intr.). I. Блёкнуть. 1. To
fade, wither (of plants). 2. To grow
dim (of stars, etc.). 3. To grow pale
(of people).

ПОБОИ́ШЬСЯ, see побою́сь.

ПОБОЙ́СЯ (imp.), see побою́сь.

ПОБО́РЕШЬ, see поборю́.

ПОБОРИ́ (imp.), see поборю́.

ПОБОРЮ́, побо́решь. P. Поборо́ть
(acc.). To overcome (as an enemy,
one's feelings, etc.).

ПОБОЮ́СЬ, побои́шься. P. Побоя́ть-
ся. 1. To fear (s.t.) (gen.). 2. To be
afraid (to do s.t.) (+ inf.).

ПО́БРАННЫЙ; по́бран, —а, —о, —ы
(ppp), see поберу́.

ПОБРЕДЁШЬ, see побреду́.

ПОБРЕДИ́ (imp.), see побреду́.

ПОБРЕДУ́, побредёшь. P. Побрести́
(intr.). 1. To wander. 2. To trudge.

ПОБРЕ́ДШИЙ (pap), see побреду́.

ПОБРЕ́Й (imp.), see побре́ю.

ПОБРЁЛ, побрела́ (past), see побреду́.

ПОБРЕ́Ю, побре́ешь. P. Побри́ть
(acc.). I. Брить. To shave (as one's
face).

ПОБРИ́ТЫЙ; побри́т, —а, —о, —ы
(ppp), see побре́ю.

ПОБРОЖУ́, побро́дишь. P. Побро-
ди́ть (intr.). 1. To stroll a while. 2.
To ferment a while (3rd pers. only).

ПОБУ́ДЕШЬ, see побу́ду.

ПОБУ́ДУ, побу́дешь. P. Побы́ть
(intr.). To spend some time (somewhere).

ПОБУ́ДЬ (imp.), see побу́ду.

ПОБУЖДЁННЫЙ; побуждён, —á,
—б, —ы́ (ppp), see побужу́[2].

ПОБУ́ЖЕННЫЙ; побу́жен, —а, —о,
—ы (ppp), see побужу́[1].

ПОБУЖУ́[1], побу́дишь. P. Побуди́ть
(acc.). 1. To awaken (s.o. or s.t.).
2. To awaken all, or many.

ПОБУЖУ́[2], побуди́шь (and по-
бу́дишь.) P. Побуди́ть (acc.). I.
Побужда́ть. 1. To induce (s.o. to do
s.t.) (acc. + inf.). 2. To persuade,
incline (s.o. toward s.t.) (acc. + к +
dat.).

ПОБЬЁШЬ, see побью.

ПОБЬЮ́, побьёшь. P. Поби́ть (acc.).
I. Бить (mean. 1). 1. To beat (as a
horse, etc.). 2. To slaughter, kill
many, all. 3. To defeat (as an enemy,
competition). 4. To break all, many
(as dishes). 5. To injure, damage
(s.o. or s.t.). 6. To lay, beat down
(as rain, wind, hail, beats down
grain, etc.). 7. To nip (as frost nips
buds, etc.).

ПОВА́ДЬСЯ (imp.), see пова́жусь.

ПОВА́ЖУСЬ, пова́дишься. P. По-
ва́диться (intr.). To fall into the
habit of (doing s.t.) (+ inf.).

ПОВЕДЁННЫЙ; поведён, —á, —б,
—ы́ (ppp), see поведу́[1].

ПОВЕДЁШЬ, see поведу́[1] and [2].

ПОВЕДИ́ (imp.), see поведу́[1] and [2].

ПОВЕДУ́[1], поведёшь. P. Повести́. I.
Вести́. 1. To take, conduct (s.o.)
(acc.). 2. To accompany (s.o.) (acc.).
3. To drive, steer (as a car, a boat
(acc.). 4. To construct (as a road
somewhere) (acc.). 5. To conduct (as
a lawsuit, a meeting, scientific work,
etc.) (acc.). 6. To draw (as a bow
across a violin string) (inst. of bow +
по + dat.).

ПОВЕДУ́², поведёшь. Р. Повести́ (inst.). I. Поводи́ть. To move, lift (as one's eyebrows), shrug (as one's shoulders) (inst.).

ПОВЕ́ДШИЙ (pap), see поведу́¹ and ².

ПОВЕ́ДЯ (adv. past part.), see поведу́¹ and ².

ПОВЕ́ЕТ, пове́ют (3rd pers. only). Р. Пове́ять. I. Ве́ять. 1. To begin to blow (of a breeze) (intr.). 2. To begin to blow (cool, fresh, warm, etc.) (of a breeze) (impers. + inst.). 3. To winnow for a period of time (acc.) or (intr.).

ПОВЁЗ, повезла́ (past), see повезу́.

ПОВЕЗЁННЫЙ; повезён, —а́, —о́, —ы́ (ppp), see повезу́.

ПОВЕЗЁШЬ, see повезу́.

ПОВЕЗИ́ (imp.), see повезу́.

ПОВЕЗУ́, повезёшь. Р. Повезти́. I. Везти́. 1. To carry, take (by vehicle, etc.) (acc.). 2. To be lucky (impers. + dat.).

ПОВЕЗЯ́ (adv. past part.), see повезу́.

ПОВЕ́Й (imp.), see пове́ет.

ПОВЁЛ, повела́ (past), see поведу́¹ and ².

ПОВЕ́РГ (and пове́ргнул), пове́ргла (past). Р. Пове́ргнуть (acc.) . I. Поверга́ть. 1. (arch.) To overturn, upset, throw down. 2. To subdue, defeat. 3. To bring (s.t.) to some state or condition, to plunge (e.g., s.o. into sorrow, etc.) (acc. + в + acc.).

ПОВЕ́РГНТУЫЙ; пове́ргнут, —а, —о, —ы (ppp), see пове́рг.

ПОВЕ́РЖЕННЫЙ; пове́ржен, —а, —о, —ы (ppp), see пове́рг.

ПОВЕ́СЬ (imp.), see пове́шу.

ПОВЕ́ШЕННЫЙ; пове́шен, —а, —о, —ы (ppp), see пове́шу.

ПОВЕ́ШУ, пове́сишь. Р. Пове́сить (acc.). I. Веша́ть. 1. To hang (up) (as a picture). 2. To hang (execute) (as a convict).

ПОВЕ́ЮТ (3rd pers. pl.), see пове́ет.

ПОВИ́С (and пови́снул), пови́сла (past). Р. Пови́снуть (intr.). I. Ви́снуть, повиса́ть. 1. To hang (on) (на + prep.). 2. To hang (down), hang/droop (over) (над + inst.). 3. (fig.) To cling to, hang on (as to hang on s.o.'s neck) (на + prep.).

ПОВИ́СИ (imp.), see повишу́.

ПОВИСИ́ШЬ, see повишу́.

ПОВИСЯ́Т, see повишу́.

ПОВИШУ́, повиси́шь. Р. повисе́ть (intr.). To be suspended, hang for a while.

ПОВЛЁК, повлекла́ (past), see повлеку́.

ПОВЛЕКИ́ (imp.), see повлеку́.

ПОВЛЕКУ́, повлечёшь, повлкут. Р. повле́чь (acc.). 1. To entail, necessitate (as hardship, consequences, etc.) (acc. + за + собо́й). 2. To drag, pull (s.t. or s.o. after oneself) (acc. of s.t. or s.o.).

ПОВЛЕЧЁННЫЙ; повлечён, —а́, —о́, —ы́ (ppp), see повлеку́.

ПОВЛЕЧЁШЬ, see повлеку́.

ПОВО́ЖЕННЫЙ; пово́жен, —а, —о, —ы (ppp), see повожу́² and³.

ПОВОЖУ́¹, пово́дишь. I. Поводи́ть (inst.). Р. Повести́. To move, lift (as one's eyebrows), shrug (as one's shoulder) (inst.).

ПОВОЖУ́², пово́дишь. Р. Поводи́ть. 1. To walk (as a horse) (acc.). 2. To draw, pass (as a bow across a violin string, etc.) (inst. + по + dat.).

ПОВОЖУ́³, пово́зишь. Р. Повози́ть (acc.). To drive, convey for a while (s.o. or s.t.).

ПОВОЛО́К, поволокла́ (past), see поволоку́.

ПОВОЛОКИ́ (imp.), see поволоку́.

ПОВОЛОКУ́, поволочёшь, поволоку́т. Р. Поволо́чь (acc.). 1. To drag. 2. To begin to drag.

ПОВОЛОЧЁННЫЙ; поволочён, —а́, —о́, —ы́ (ppp), see поволоку́.

ПОВОЛОЧЁШЬ, see поволоку́.

ПОВОРО́ЧЕННЫЙ; пово́рочен, —а, —о, —ы (ppp), see поворочу́.

ПОРОЧУ́, поворо́тишь. Р. Повороти́ть. I. Повора́чивать, повёртывать. 1. To turn (s.o. or s.t.) (acc.). 2. To turn (e.g., to the right, left, etc.) (intr.). 3. (fig.) To turn, change (as the subject to s.t. else) (acc. + к + dat.).

ПОВРЕЖДЁННЫЙ; повреждён, —а́, —о́, —ы́ (ppp), see повр ежу́.

ПОВРЕЖУ́, повреди́шь. Р. Повреди́ть. I. Поврежда́ть, вреди́ть (mean. 2). 1. To damage, injure, wound (acc.). 2. To injure, hurt, harm (e.g., s.o., one's health, interests, etc.) (dat.).

ПОВЫ́СЬ (imp.), see повы́шу.

ПОВЫ́ШЕННЫЙ; повы́шен, —а, —о, —ы (ppp), see повы́шу.

ПОВЫ́ШУ, повы́сишь. P. Повы́сить (acc.). I. Повыша́ть. 1. To raise, increase (as a water level, pressure, demands, etc.). 2. To improve, better. 3. To advance, promote. 4. To enhance.

ПОВЯ́ДШИЙ and повя́нувший (pap), see повя́л.

ПОВЯ́ЖЕШЬ, see повяжу́.

ПОВЯЖИ́ (imp.), see повяжу́.

ПОВЯЖУ́, повя́жешь. P. Повяза́ть (acc.). I. Повя́зывать. 1. To tie (as a kerchief, necktie, etc.). 2. To knit, crochet, weave, etc., for a while.

ПОВЯ́ЗАННЫЙ; повя́зан, —а. —о, —ы (ppp), see повяжу́.

ПОВЯ́Л, повя́ла (past). P. Повя́нуть (intr.). To wither, fade.

ПОВЯ́НУВШИЙ and повя́дший (pap), see повя́л.

ПОГА́С, пога́сла (past). P. Пога́снуть (intr.). I. Погаса́ть, га́снуть (mean. 1 thru 3). 1. To go out (as a flame, light, etc.). 2. (lit. and fig.) To fade, grow dim, die out. 3. (fig.) To wither (of a person). 4. To die (of a person).

ПОГА́ШЕННЫЙ; пога́шен, —а, —о, —ы (ppp), see погашу́.

ПОГАШУ́, пога́сишь. P. Погаси́ть (acc.). I. Гаси́ть. 1. To extinguish (as a fire). 2. To liquidate (as a debt). 3. To cancel (e.g., a stamp, note, etc.). 4. (tech.) To quench, dampen. 5. (fig.) To extinguish.

ПОГИ́Б, поги́бла (past). P. Поги́бнуть (intr.). 1. Погиба́ть, ги́бнуть. 1. (lit. and fig.) To perish (of people, dreams, etc.). 2. To suffer destruction.

ПОГЛА́ДЬ (imp.), see погла́жу.

ПОГЛА́ЖЕННЫЙ; погла́жен, —а, —о, —ы (ppp), see погла́жу.

ПОГЛА́ЖУ, погла́дишь. P. Погла́дить (acc.). I. Гла́дить. 1. To iron out, press. 2. To stroke (caress).

ПОГЛОЩЁННЫЙ; поглощён, —а, —о, —ы (ppp), see поглощу́.

ПОГЛОЩУ́, погло́тишь. P. Поглоти́ть (acc.). I. Поглоща́ть. 1. (lit. and fig.) To absorb. 2. To swallow,

engulf. 3. (fig.) To devour (as reading matter, etc.). 4. (fig.) To demand, consume, take (as time, energy, etc.).

ПОГЛЯДИ́ (imp.), see погляжу́.

ПОГЛЯДИ́ШЬ, see погляжу́.

ПОГЛЯДЯ́Т, see погляжу́.

ПОГЛЯЖУ́, погляди́шь. P. Погляде́ть (intr.). I. Гляде́ть. 1. To look at, stare at (на + acc.). 2. To look after (за + inst.). 3. To consider (s.t.) (на + acc.).

ПО́ГНАННЫЙ; по́гнан, —а, —о, —ы (ppp), see погоню́.

ПОГНИЁТ, погниют (3rd pers. only). P. Погни́ть (intr.). To rot, decompose (of all or a quantity).

ПОГНИЮ́Т (3rd pers. pl.), see погниёт.

ПОГОЖУ́, погоди́шь. P. Погоди́ть (intr.). To wait a little.

ПОГОНИ́ (imp.), see погоню́.

ПОГО́НИШЬ, see погоню́.

ПОГОНЮ́, пого́нишь. P. Погна́ть (acc.). 1. To drive/begin to drive, turn out (as cattle). 2. To urge on/ begin to urge on. 3. To pursue, chase/ begin to pursue, chase. 4. To persecute/begin to persecute.

ПОГОРИ́ (imp.), see погорю́.

ПОГОРИ́ШЬ, see погорю́.

ПОГОРЮ́, погори́шь. P. Погоре́ть (intr.). I. Погора́ть. 1. To be burnt out (i.e., to have one's house destroyed by fire). 2. (lit. and fig.) To burn up (e.g., a house, a person with fever, crops from heat, etc.). 3. To burn a while. 4. To experience failure (intr.), (in s.t.) (на + prep.). 5. To rot completely (e.g., damp hay).

ПОГОРЯ́Т, see погорю́.

ПОГРЕ́Б, погребла́ (past), see погребу́.

ПОГРЕБЁННЫЙ; погребён, —а́, —о́, —ы́ (ppp), see погребу́.

ПОГРЕБЁШЬ, see погребу́.

ПОГРЕБИ́ (imp.), see погребу́.

ПОГРЕБУ́, погребёшь. P. Погрести́. I. Погреба́ть (mean. 1). 1. To bury (acc.). 2. To row a while (intr.). 3. To rake a while (intr.) or (acc.).

ПОГРОЖУ́, погрози́шь. P. Погрози́ть. I. Грози́ть. To threaten (s.o.) with a gesture (dat. + inst.).

ПОГРУ́ЖЕННЫЙ   152   ПОДБЕРУ́

ПОГРУ́ЖЕННЫЙ; погру́жен, —а,
—о, —ы (ppp), see погружу́[1].
ПОГРУЖЁННЫЙ; погружён, —а́,
—о́, —ы́ (ppp), see погружу́[1] and [2].
ПОГРУЖУ́[1], погру́зишь (and по-
грузи́шь). Р. Погрузи́ть (acc.). I.
Грузи́ть. 1. To load (s.t. with s.t.)
(as a truck with produce) (acc. +
inst.). 2. To load (s.t. on s.t.)
(acc. + на + acc.).
ПОГРУЖУ́[2], погрузи́шь. Р. Погру-
зи́ть (acc.). I. Погружа́ть. (lit. and
fig.) To submerge, immerse, plunge
(s.t. or s.o. in s.t.) (acc. + в + acc.).
ПОГРЯ́З, погря́зла (past). Р. По-
гря́знуть (intr.). I. Погряза́ть. 1.
(lit. and fig.) To wallow (in) (в +
prep.). 2. (lit. and fig.) To be mired
(in) (в + prep.).
ПОГУ́БЛЕННЫЙ; погу́блен, —а,
—о, —ы (ppp), see погублю́.
ПОГУБЛЮ́, погу́бишь. Р. Погуби́ть.
I. Губи́ть. 1. (lit. and fig.) To ruin,
destroy. 2. (lit. and fig.) To spoil.
3. To kill.
ПОДАВА́Й (inp.), see подаю́.
ПОДАВА́Я (adv. pres. part.), see
подаю́.
ПОДА́ВЛЕННЫЙ; пода́влен, —а,
—о, —ы (ppp), see подавлю́.
ПОДАВЛЮ́, пода́вишь. Р. Подави́ть
(acc.). I. Подавля́ть (mean 1 thru
5). 1. To suppress (e.g., a rebellion,
etc.). 2. To annihilate, destroy. 3.
(lit. and fig.) To overwhelm, crush.
4. (fig.) To depress, suppress, restrain. (e.g., a smile). 5. To oppress,
depress. 6. To crush, squash all,
many (as insects). 7. To subject to
pressure, to depress (e.g., a spring)
for a while.
ПОДАВЛЮ́СЬ, пода́вишься. Р. По-
дави́ться (intr.). I. Дави́ться. 1. To
choke (on s.t.) (inst.). 2. To choke
from (as from laughter) (от + gen.).
ПОДАДИ́М, подади́те, подаду́т (pl.
forms), see пода́м.
ПОДАЁШЬ, see подаю́.
ПОДА́Й (imp.), see пода́м.
ПОДА́М, пода́шь, пода́ст (sing. forms).
Р. Пода́ть (acc.). I. Подава́ть. 1. To
give. 2. To serve (as dinner). 3. To
drive (as a vehicle) up to (as the
entrance) (3rd pers. pl. + acc. of
vehicle). 4. To come in (as a train
to a platform) (3rd pers. pl. + acc.

of "train" + к + dat.). 5. (sport)
To serve (as a tennis ball). 6. To
submit (as a petition, resignation).
7. To send (as a telegram). 8. To
move (as a chair). 9. To represent,
portray (as a character). 10. (tech.)
To feed. (For other usages see
unabridged dictionary.)
ПО́ДАННЫЙ; по́дан, —а́, (or —а)
—о, —ы (ppp), see пода́м.
ПОДА́СТ, see пода́м.
ПОДА́ШЬ, see пода́м.
ПОДАЮ́, подаёшь. I. Подава́ть (acc.).
Р. Пода́ть. 1. To give. 2. To serve
(as dinner). 3. To drive (as a vehicle)
up to (as the entrance) (3rd pers.
pl. + acc. of vehicle). 4. To come in
(as a train to a platform) (3rd pers.
pl. + acc. of "train" + к + dat.).
5. (sport) To serve (as tennis balls).
6. To submit (as a petition, resignation). 7. To send (as a telegram). 8.
To present, portray (as a character).
9. To move (as a chair). 10. (tech.)
To feed. (For other usages see unabridged dictionary.)
ПОДБА́ВЛЕННЫЙ; подба́влен, —а,
—о, —ы (ppp), see подба́влю.
ПОДБА́ВЛЮ, подба́вишь. Р. Под-
ба́вить (acc./gen.). I. Подбавля́ть.
To add (a little).
ПОДБА́ВЬ (imp.), see подба́влю.
ПОДБЕГИ́ (imp.), see подбегу́.
ПОДБЕГУ́, подбежи́шь, подбегу́т. Р.
Подбежа́ть (intr.). I. Подбега́ть.
1. To run up to (к + dat.). 2. To run
under (под + acc.).
ПОДБЕЖИ́ШЬ, see подбегу́.
ПОДБЕ́Й (imp.). Р. Подби́ть (acc.). I.
Подбива́ть. 1. To line (as a garment
with s.t.) (acc. + inst.). 2. To resole
(as a shoe). 3. To knock down, put
out of action (as a plane). 4. To
strike, injure. 5. To force, pound
(s.t.) under (s.t.) (acc. + под +
acc.). 6. To persuade, incite (s.o.
to s.t.) (acc. + на + acc.) or (acc. +
inf.). (Also see подобью́.)
ПОДБЕРЁШЬ, see подберу́.
ПОДБЕРИ́ (imp.), see подберу́.
ПОДБЕРУ́, подберёшь. Р. Подобра́ть
(acc.). I. Подбира́ть. 1. To pick up.
2. To select, sort out. 3. To tuck up
(as hair under a hat) (acc. + под +
acc.). 4. To take up the slack (as in a

line, reins, etc.). 5. To match (as a tie in color) (acc. + под свет). 6. To fit (as a key to a lock) (acc. + к + dat.).

ПОДБИ́ТЫЙ; подби́т, —а, —о, —ы (ppp), see подбе́й and подобью́.

ПОДБРЕ́ЕШЬ, see подбре́ю.

ПОДБРЕ́Й (imp.), see подбре́ю.

ПОДБРЕ́Ю, подбре́ешь. P. Подбри́ть (acc.). I. Подбрива́ть. To shave along the edges, along the sides.

ПОДБРИ́ТЫЙ; подбри́т, —а, —о, —ы (ppp), see подбре́ю.

ПОДБРОСЬ (imp.), see подбро́шу.

ПОДБРО́ШЕННЫЙ; подбро́шен, —а, —о, —ы (ppp), see подбро́шу.

ПОДБРО́ШУ, подбро́сишь. P. Подбро́сить. I. Подбра́сывать. 1. To toss (up), throw up (acc.). 2. To add, throw on (as wood on a fire) (acc./gen.). 3. To throw in (as reserve troops) (acc.). 4. To secretly place (s.t. somewhere) (acc.). 5. To abandon (as a shild) (acc.). 6. To throw under (acc. + под + acc.). 7. To rake, drive (s.o. somewhere) (acc.).

ПОДВЕДЁННЫЙ; подведён, —а́, —о́, —ы́ (ppp), see подведу́.

ПОДВЕДЁШЬ, see подведу́.

ПОДВЕДИ́ (imp.), see подведу́.

ПОДВЕДУ́, подведёшь. P. Подвести́ (acc.). I. Подводи́ть. 1. To bring, lead up (to) (acc. + к + dat.). 2. To place under (acc. + под + acc.). 3. (lit. and fig.) To sum up. 4. (fig.) To let (s.o.) down, do (s.o.) an ill turn. 5. To color (make up with cosmetics) (as eyes, cheeks, etc.). 6. To make thin (impers. + acc.). (For other usages see unabridged dictionary.)

ПОДВЕ́ДШИЙ (pap), подведу́.

ПОДВЕДЯ́ (adv. past part.), see подведу́.

ПОДВЁЗ, подвезла́, подвезло́, подвезли́ (past), see подвезу́.

ПОДВЕЗЁННЫЙ; подвезён, —а́, —о́, —ы́ (ppp), see подвезу́.

ПОДВЕЗЁШЬ, see подвезу́.

ПОДВЕЗИ́ (imp.), see подвезу́.

ПОДВЕЗУ́, подвезёшь. P. Подвезти́. I. Подвози́ть (mean. 1 and 2), везти́ (mean. 3). 1. To bring, transport (people, things) (acc./gen.). 2. To give (s.o.) a lift (e.g., to take s.o. in one's vehicle) (acc.). 3. To be lucky (impers. + dat.).

ПОДВЕЗЯ́ (adv. past part.), see подвезу́.

ПОДВЕ́Й (imp.). P. Подви́ть (acc.). I. Подвива́ть. To curl slightly (also see подовью́)

ПОДВЁЛ, подвела́ (past), see подведу́.

ПОДВЕ́РГ (and arch. подве́ргнул), подве́ргла (past). P. Подве́ргнуть (acc. + dat.). I. Подверга́ть. To subject, expose (s.t. or s.o. to s.t.) (as to criticism).

ПОДВЕ́РГНУТЫЙ; подве́ргнут, —а, —о, —ы (ppp), see подве́рг.

ПОДВЕ́РЖЕННЫЙ; подве́ржен, —а, —о, —ы (arch.) (ppp), see подве́рг.

ПОДВЕ́СЬ (imp.), see подве́шу.

ПОДВЕ́ШЕННЫЙ; подве́шен, —а, —о, —ы (ppp), see подве́шу.

ПОДВЕ́ШУ, подве́сишь. P. Подве́сить (acc.). I. Подве́шивать. To suspend, hang up.

ПОДВИ́НЧЕННЫЙ; подви́нчен, —а, —о, —ы (ppp), see подвинчу́.

ПОДВИНЧУ́, подвинти́шь. P. Подвинти́ть (acc.). I. Подви́нчивать. 1. To screw up, tighten. 2. (fig.) To tighten up (on s.o.).

ПОДВИ́ТЫЙ; подви́т, —а, —о, —ы (ppp), see подве́й and подовью́.

ПОДВОЖУ́[1], подво́дишь. I. Подводи́ть (acc.). P. Подвести́. 1. To bring, lead up (to) (acc. + к + dat.). 2. To place under (acc. + под + acc.). 3. (lit. and fig.) To sum up. 4. (fig.) To let (s.o.) down, do (s.o.) an ill turn. 5. To color (make up with cosmetics) (as eyes, cheeks, etc.). 6. To make thin (impers. + acc.). (For other usages see unabridged dictionary.)

ПОДВОЖУ́[2], подво́зишь. I. Подвози́ть. P. Подвезти́. 1. To bring, transport (people, things) (acc./gen.). 2. To give (s.o.) a lift (e.g., to take s.o. in one's vehicle) (acc.).

ПОДВЫ́ПЕЙ (imp.), see подвы́пью.

ПОДВЫ́ПЬЕШЬ, see подвы́пью.

ПОДВЫ́ПЬЮ, подвы́пьешь. P. Подвы́пить. 1. To become slightly drunk (intr.). 2. To drink a little (liquor) (gen.).

ПОДВЯ́ЖЕШЬ, see подвяжу́.

ПОДВЯЖИ́ (imp.), see подвяжу́.

ПОДВЯЖУ́, подвя́жешь. P. Подвяза́ть (acc.). I. Подвя́зывать. 1. To tie up, bind (s.t.). 2. To tie (s.t. to s.t.) (acc. + к + dat.). 3. To add to, lengthen by knitting, crocheting.

ПОДВЯ́ЗАННЫЙ; подвя́зан, —а, —о, —ы (ppp), see подвяжу́.

ПОДГА́ДЬ (imp.), see подга́жу.

ПОДГА́ЖУ, подга́дишь. Р. Подга́дить. I. Подга́живать. 1. To play a mean trick (on s.o.) (dat.). 2. To spoil, harm (dat.). 3. To spoil an effect (intr.).

ПОДГЛЯДИ́ (imp.), see подгляжу́.

ПОДГЛЯДИ́ШЬ, see подгляжу́.

ПОДГЛЯДЯ́Т, see подгляжу́.

ПОДГЛЯЖУ́, подгляди́шь. Р. Подгляде́ть. I.II огля́дывать. 1. To spy on (за + inst.). 2. To peep through (as a crack) (в + acc.). 3. To see inadvertently (acc.).

ПОДГНИЁТ, подгнию́т (3rd pers. only). Р. Подгни́ть (intr.). I. Подгнива́ть. 1. To rot (on the bottom). 2. To rot slightly.

ПОДГНИЮ́Т (3rd pers. pl.), see подниёт.

ПОДГОНИ́ (imp.), see подгоню́.

ПОДГО́НИШЬ, see подгоню́.

ПОДГОНЮ́, подго́нишь. Р. Подогна́ть (acc.). I. Подгоня́ть. 1. To drive (to) (as cattle, etc.) (acc. + к + dat.). 2. To drive under (acc. + под + acc.). 3. To hurry (s.o. or s.t.) (acc.). 4. To fit, adjust (s.t. to s.t.) (as components of a machine to each other) (acc. + к + dat.). 5. To time (s.t. to s.t.) (as one's arrival to s.o.'s convenience) (acc. + к + dat.).

ПОДГО́НЯТ, see подгоню́.

ПОДГОРИ́ (imp.), see подгори́т.

ПОДГОРИ́Т, подгоря́т (3rd pers. only). Р. Подгоре́ть (intr.). I. Подгора́ть. 1. To scorch, burn, become overdone (of foods, etc.). 2. To burn (on the bottom or base) (as a post, etc.).

ПОДГОРЯ́Т, see подгори́т.

ПОДГОТО́ВЛЕННЫЙ; подгото́влен, —а, —о, —ы (ppp), see подгото́влю.

ПОДГОТО́ВЛЮ, подгото́вишь. Р. Подгото́вить (acc.). I. Подгота́вливать, подготовля́ть. 1. To prepare (as material for a job, etc.) (acc. + для + gen.). 2. To prepare (as a lecture, etc.) (acc.). 3. To prepare (as s.o. for an examination) (acc. + к + dat.). 4. (fig.) To prepare (as

s.o. for bad news) (acc. + к + dat.). 5. (tech.) To prime (as an engine). 6. To train (as a cadre).

ПОДГОТО́ВЬ (imp.), see подгото́влю.

ПОДГРЁБ, подгребла́ (past), see подгребу́.

ПОДГРЕБЁННЫ; подгребён, —а́, —о́, —ы́ (ppp), see подгребу́ (mean. 1 and 2).

ПОДГРЕБЁШЬ, see подгребу́.

ПОДГРЕБИ́ (imp.), see подгребу́.

ПОДГРЕБУ́, подгребёшь. Р. Подгрести́. I. Подгреба́ть. 1. To rake up, scrape up (acc.). 2. To rake (s.t.) under (acc. + под + acc.). 3. To row toward (intr.) (к + dat.).

ПОДГРУ́ЖЕННЫЙ; подгру́жен, —а, —о, —ы (ppp), see подгружу́.

ПОДГРУЖЁННЫЙ; подгружён, —а́, —о́, —ы́ (ppp), see подгружу́.

ПОДГРУЖУ́, подгру́зишь (and подгрузи́шь). Р. Подгрузи́ть. I. Подгружа́ть. 1. To load more (of s.t.) (gen.). 2. To load more heavily (as a truck) (acc.).

ПОДДАВА́Й (imp.), see поддаю́.

ПОДДАВА́Я (adv. pres. part.), see поддаю́.

ПОДДАДИ́М, поддати́те, поддаду́т (pl. forms), see подда́м.

ПОДДАЁШЬ, see поддаю́.

ПОДДА́Й (imp.), see подда́м.

ПОДДА́М, подда́шь, подда́ст (sing. forms). Р. Подда́ть. I. Поддава́ть. 1. To strike or kick (as a ball) (acc.). 2. To strike (s.o.) (dat.). 3. To offer, give away (as men in chess) (acc.). 4. To add, increase (as fuel, steam pressure, etc.) (gen.). 5. (fig.) To stimulate (as pride in s.o.) (gen. + dat.). 6. (fig.) To give (as sincerity to one's tone) (gen. + dat.).

ПО́ДДАННЫЙ; по́ддан, —а́, —о, —ы (ppp), see подда́м.

ПОДДА́СТ, see подда́м.

ПОДДА́ШЬ, see подда́м.

ПОДДАЮ́, поддаёшь. I. Поддава́ть. Р. Подда́ть. 1. To strike or kick (as a ball) (acc.). 2. To strike (s.o.) (dat.). 3. To offer, give away (as men in a chess game) (acc.). 4. To add, increase (e.g., fuel, steam pressure, etc.) (gen.). 5. To stimulate (e.g., pride in s.o.) (gen. + dat.). 6. (fig.) To give (as sincerity to one's tone) (gen. + dat.).

ПОДДЕ́НЕШЬ, see поддѣ́ну.

ПОДДЕ́НУ, поддѣ́нешь. Р. Поддѣ́ть (acc.). I. Поддева́ть. 1. To put on under, wear under (acc. + под + acc.). 2. To pick up (as with a hook, pitch fork, etc.) (acc. + inst.). 3. To bait, tease (s.o.). 4. To cheat, deceive (s.o.). 5. To obtain, get.

ПОДДЕ́НЬ (imp.), see поддѣ́ну.

ПОДДЕ́РЖАННЫЙ; поддѣ́ржан, —а, —о, —ы (ppp), see поддержу́.

ПОДДЕ́РЖАТ, see поддержу́.

ПОДДЕРЖИ́ (imp.), see поддержу́.

ПОДДЕ́РЖИШЬ, see поддержу́.

ПОДДЕРЖУ́, поддѣ́ржишь. Р. Поддержа́ть (acc.). I. Поддѣ́рживать. 1. To support (s.o. or s.t. physically). 2. (fig.) To support, back up (as a resolution, a person, etc.). 3. To maintain, keep up, feed (as a fire, a family, etc.). 4. To maintain (as a correspondence, conversation, etc.).

ПОДДЕ́ТЫЙ; поддѣ́т, —а, —о, —ы (ppp), see поддѣ́ну.

ПОДЕРЕ́ШЬСЯ, see подеру́сь.

ПОДЕ́РЖАННЫЙ; подѣ́ржан, —а, —о, —ы (ppp), see подержу́.

ПОДЕ́РЖАТ, see подержу́.

ПОДЕРЖИ́ (imp.), see подержу́.

ПОДЕ́РЖИШЬ, see подержу́.

ПОДЕРЖУ́, подѣ́ржишь. Р. Подержа́ть (acc.). To hold or keep for a while.

ПОДЕРИ́СЬ (imp.), see подеру́сь.

ПОДЕРУ́СЬ, подерѣ́шься. Р. Подра́ться (intr.). I. Дра́ться. To fight.

ПОДЖА́ТЫЙ; поджа́т, —а, —о, —ы (ppp). Р. Поджа́ть (acc.). I. Поджима́ть. 1. To purse (one's lips) (acc. of lips). 2. To cross (one's legs) (acc. of legs). 3. (lit. and fig.) To put (tuck one's tail between one's legs) (acc. of tail). 4. To draw in, tighten, press. (Also see подожму́.)

ПОДЖЁГ, подожгла́ (past). Р. Подже́чь (acc.). I. Поджига́ть. 1. To light, kindle (as logs). 2. To set on fire (in committing arson) (as a building). 3. To let burn (as a pie). 4. (fig.) To inflame, incite. (Also see подожгу́.)

ПОДЖИВЁТ, поживу́т (3rd pers. only). Р. Пожи́ть (intr.). I. Пожива́ть. To heal a little (of a wound).

ПОДЖИВИ́ (imp.), see подживёт.

ПОДЖИВУ́Т (3rd pers. pl.), see подживёт.

ПОДЗАБУ́ДЕШЬ, see подзабу́ду.

ПОДЗАБУ́ДУ, подзабу́дешь. Р. Подзабы́ть (acc.). To forget partly, not retain fully in one's memory (as a poem).

ПОДЗАБУ́ДЬ (imp.), see подзабу́ду.

ПОДЗАБЫ́ТЫЙ; подзабы́т, —а, —о, —ы (ppp), see подзабу́ду.

ПОДЗАКУШУ́, подзаку́сишь. Р. Подзакуси́ть (intr.). To have a little snack.

ПОДЗОВЁШЬ, see подзову́.

ПОДЗОВИ́ (imp.), see подзову́.

ПОДЗОВУ́, подзовёшь. Р. Подозва́ть (acc.). I. Подзыва́ть. To call up or over (e.g., s.o. to one's desk) (acc. + к + dat.).

ПОДЗУ́ЖЕННЫЙ; подзу́жен, —а, —о, —ы (ppp), see подзужу́.

ПОДЗУЖУ́, подзу́дишь. Р. Подзуди́ть (acc.). I. Подзу́живать. To incite, urge, induce.

ПОДИВЛЮ́, подиви́шь. Р. Подиви́ть (acc.). To astound, amaze s.o.

ПОДКА́ЧЕННЫЙ; подка́чен, —а, —о, —ы (ppp), see подкачу́.

ПОДКАЧУ́, подка́тишь. Р. Подкати́ть. I. Подка́тывать. 1. To roll (s.t.) up to (acc. + к + dat.). 2. To drive up to, roll up to (intr.) (к + dat.). 3. (Used impersonally or in 3rd person in reference to a pain— e.g., "a lump arose in his throat," к + dat.).

ПОДКО́ЛЕШЬ, see подколю́.

ПОДКОЛИ́ (imp.), see подколю́.

ПОДКО́ЛОТЫЙ; подко́лот, —а, —о, —ы (ppp), see подколю́.

ПОДКОЛЮ́, подко́лешь. Р. Подколо́ть. I. Подка́лывать. 1. To pin up, pin to (acc.). 2. To wound (acc.). 3. (fig.) To bait (acc.). 4. To chop some more (as kindling) (acc./gen.).

ПОДКО́РМЛЕННЫЙ; подко́рмлен, —а, —о, —ы (ppp), see подкормлю́.

ПОДКОРМЛЮ́, подко́рмишь. Р. Подкорми́ть (acc.). I. Подка́рмливать. 1. To feed. 2. To feed up, fatten. 3. To fertilize, feed (the soil).

ПОДКО́ШЕННЫЙ; подко́шен, —а, —о, —ы (ppp), see подкошу́.

ПОДКОШУ́, подко́сишь. Р. Подкоси́ть (acc.). I. Подка́шивать. 1. To mow (as grass) (acc.). 2. (fig.) To mow down (e.g., the enemy with gun fire) (acc.). 3. (fig.) To stun, knock (s.o.) off his feet (as with bad news) (acc.). 4. To mow a little more (acc./gen.).

ПОДКРАДЁШЬСЯ, see подкрадусь.

ПОДКРАДИСЬ (imp.), see подкрадусь.

ПОДКРАДУСЬ, подкрадёшься. Р. Подкрасться (intr.). I. Подкрадываться. 1. To sneak up to, steal up to (к + dat.). 2. (fig.) To steal in, sneak up (e.g., of death, darkness, etc.).

ПОДКРАЛСЯ, подкралась (past), see подкрадусь.

ПОДКРАСЬ (imp.), see подкрашу.

ПОДКРАШЕННЫЙ; подкрашен, —а, —о, —ы (ppp), see подкрашу.

ПОДКРАШУ, подкрасишь. Р. Подкрасить (acc.). I. Подкрашивать. 1. To tint, color. 2. To touch up (with color). 3. (fig.) To touch up (improve).

ПОДКРЕПЛЁННЫЙ; подкреплён, —а, —о, —ы (ppp), see подкреплю.

ПОДКРЕПЛЮ, подкрепишь. Р. Подкрепить (acc.). I. Подкреплять. 1. To strengthen, reinforce (s.t.). 2. To reinforce (as troops). 3. To confirm, support, corroborate (as an opinion). 4. To refresh (with food) (acc. + inst.).

ПОДКУЗЬМЛЮ, подкузьмишь. Р. Подкузьмить (acc.). To let (s.o.) down, do (s.o.) an ill turn.

ПОДКУПЛЕННЫЙ; подкуплен, —а, —о, —ы (ppp), see подкуплю.

ПОДКУПЛЮ, подкупишь. Р. Подкупить. I. Подкупать. 1. To bribe, suborn (acc.). 2. To win over (as s.o. by kindness) (acc. + inst.). 3. To buy a little more of (acc./gen.).

ПОДЛАДЬ (imp.), see подлажу.

ПОДЛАДЬСЯ (imp.), see подлажусь.

ПОДЛАЖЕННЫЙ; подлажен, —а, —о, —ы (ppp), see подлажу.

ПОДЛАЖУ, подладишь. Р. Подладить. I. Подлаживать. 1. To tune (as a violin to a piano) (acc. + + под + acc.). 2. To adapt, adjust (as one's conduct to a situation) (acc. + под + acc.). 3. To fit, adjust (s.t. under s.t.) (as legs to a table) (acc. + к + dat.).

ПОДЛАЖУСЬ, подладишься. Р. Подладиться. I. Подлаживаться. 1.

To adapt o.s. (to s.o. or s.t.) (к + dat.). 2. (fig.) To make up (to s.o.) (к + dat.). 3. To find room (somewhere) (or o.s.) (intr.).

ПОДЛЕЖАТ, see подлежу.

ПОДЛЕЖИ (imp.), see подлежу.

ПОДЛЕЖИШЬ, see подлежу.

ПОДЛЕЖУ, подлежишь. I. Подлежать (dat.). 1. To be subject (to), liable (to). 2. To depend (on). 3. To be under the jurisdiction or authority (of).

ПОДЛЕЗ, подлезла (past), see подлезу.

ПОДЛЕЗЕШЬ, see подлезу.

ПОДЛЕЗУ, подлезешь. Р. Подлезть (intr.). I. Подлезать. To creep under (под + acc.).

ПОДЛЕЗЬ (imp.), see подлезу.

ПОДЛЕЙ (imp.). Р. Подлить (acc./gen.). I. Подливать. To pour out, add some more (as cream to one's coffee, etc.) (of liquids) (also see подолью).

ПОДЛЕТИ (imp.), see подлечу.

ПОДЛЕТИШЬ, see подлечу.

ПОДЛЕЧУ, подлетишь. Р. Подлететь (intr.). I. Подлетать. 1. (lit. and fig.) To fly up (to) (к + dat.) or (до + gen.). 2. To rush up to (к + dat.).

ПОДЛЕТЯТ, see подлечу.

ПОДЛИЖЕШЬ, see подлижу.

ПОДЛИЖЕШЬСЯ, see подлижусь.

ПОДЛИЖИ (imp.), see подлижу.

ПОДЛИЖИСЬ (imp.), see подлижусь.

ПОДЛИЖУ, подлижешь. Р. Подлизать (acc.). I. Подлизывать. To lick up.

ПОДЛИЖУСЬ, подлижешься. Р. Подлизаться (intr.). I. Подлизываться. To ingratiate o.s. (with s.o.) by flattery and obsequiousness (to lick s.o.'s boots) (к + dat. of s.o.).

ПОДЛИЗАННЫЙ; подлизан, —а, —о, —ы (ppp), see подлижу.

ПОДЛИТЫЙ; подлит, —а, —о, —ы (ppp), see подлей and подолью.

ПÓДЛИТЫЙ; пóдлит, —а, —о, —ы (ppp), see подлей and подолью.

ПОДЛОМЛЕННЫЙ; подломлен, —а, —о, —ы (ppp), see подломлю.

ПОДЛОМЛЮ, подломишь. Р. Подломить (acc.). I. Подламывать. To break, fracture the under part (of s.t.) (as a branch).

ПОДМА́ЖЕШЬ, see подма́жу.

ПОДМА́ЖУ, подма́жешь. Р. Под-
ма́зать (acc.). I. Подма́зывать. 1.
To grease, oil (a little) or (from
underneath). 2. To bribe.

ПОДМА́ЖЬ (imp.), see подма́жу.

ПОДМА́ЗАННЫЙ; подма́зан, —а,
—о, —ы (ppp), see подма́жу.

ПОДМЁЛ, подмела́ (past), see под-
мету́.

ПОДМЁРЗ, подмёрзла (past). Р. Подмёрзнуть (intr.). I. Подмерза́ть.
To freeze slightly.

ПОДМЕТЁННЫЙ; подметён, —а́,
—о́, —ы́ (ppp), see подмету́.

ПОДМЕТЁШЬ, see подмету́.

ПОДМЕТИ́ (imp.), see подмету́.

ПОДМЕТУ́, подметёшь. Р. Под-
мести́ (acc.). I. Подмета́ть. To
sweep, sweep up.

ПОДМЁТШИЙ (pap), see подмету́.

ПОДМЕ́ТЬ (imp.), see подме́чу.

ПОДМЕТЯ́ (adv. past part.), see
подмету́.

ПОДМЕ́ЧЕННЫЙ; подме́чен, —а,
—о, —ы (ppp), see подме́чу.

ПОДМЕ́ЧУ, подме́тишь. Р. Подме́-
тить (acc.). I. Подмеча́ть. To
notice, observe (s.t. not immediately
evident).

ПОДМЕ́ШЕННЫЙ; подме́шен, —а,
—о, —ы (ppp), see подмешу́.

ПОДМЕШУ́, подме́сишь. Р. Подме-
си́ть (acc./gen.). I. Подме́шивать.
To add a little while kneading (as
flour).

ПОДМО́ЕШЬ, see подмо́ю.

ПОДМО́Й (imp.), see подмо́ю.

ПОДМО́К, подмо́кла (past). Р. Под-
мо́кнуть (intr.). I. Подмока́ть. To
get slightly wet (on the bottom, as
shoes).

ПОДМО́Ю, подмо́ешь. Р. Подмы́ть
(acc.). I. Подмыва́ть. 1. To wash
away. 2. To undermine (as a river
its banks). 3. To wash (under) (as
one's arms). 4. To wash hastily (as
a floor).

ПОДМЫ́ТЫЙ; подмы́т, —а, —о, —ы
(ppp), see подмо́ю.

ПОДМЯ́ТЫЙ; подмя́т, —а, —о, —ы
(ppp), see подомну́.

ПОДНАЖМЁШЬ, see поднажму́.

ПОДНАЖМИ́ (imp.), see поднажму́.

ПОДНАЖМУ́, поднажмёшь. Р. Под-
нажа́ть. I. Поднажима́ть. 1. (fig.)

To push (s.o. to do s.t.), exert
influence (on s.o.) (на + acc.). 2.
(fig.) To attack forcefully, put
pressure (on) (as a problem, project,
etc.) (на + acc.). 3. (lit. and fig.) To
press or push harder (intr.) (on s.t.)
(acc.) or (на + acc.).

ПОДНЁС, поднесла́ (past), see под-
несу́.

ПОДНЕСЁННЫЙ; поднесён, —а́,
—о́, —ы́ (ppp), see поднесу́.

ПОДНЕСЁШЬ, see поднесу́.

ПОДНЕСИ́ (imp.), see поднесу́.

ПОДНЕСУ́, поднесёшь. Р. Поднести́
(acc.). I. Подноси́ть. 1. To bring,
carry (to) (acc. + к + dat.). 2. To
present (s.t. to s.o.), (acc. + dat.).
3. To offer (s.t. to s.o.), to treat (e.g.,
give s.o. a glass of wine) (acc. + dat.).

ПОДНЕСЯ́ (adv. past part.), see
поднесу́.

ПОДНИ́МЕШЬ, see подниму́.

ПОДНИМИ́ (imp.), see подниму́.

ПОДНИМУ́, подни́мешь. Р. Подня́ть
(acc.). I. Поднима́ть. 1. To lift,
raise, hoist. 2. To pick up. 3. To
incite, stir up, rouse. 4. (fig.) To
raise. 5. (tech.) To step up, increase
(as pressure, voltage, etc.). 6. To
plow (as new land). (For other
usages see unabridged dictionary.)

ПОДНОВЛЁННЫЙ; подновлён, —а́,
—о́, —ы́ (ppp), see подновлю́.

ПОДНОВЛЮ́, поднови́шь. Р. Под-
нови́ть (acc.). I. Подновля́ть. To
renew, renovate, refresh, repair.

ПОДНОШУ́, подно́сишь. I. Подно-
си́ть (acc.). Р. Поднести́. 1. To
bring, carry (to) (acc. + к + dat.).
2. To present (s.t. to s.o.) (acc. +
dat.). 3. To offer (s.t. to s.o.), to
treat (e.g., to give s.o. a glass of
wine) (acc. + dat.).

ПО́ДНЯТЫЙ; по́днят, —а́, —о, —ы
(ppp), see подниму́.

ПОДО́БРАННЫЙ; подо́бран, —а
(and —а́), —о, —ы (ppp). Р. По-
добра́ть (acc.). I. Подбира́ть. 1. To
pick up. 2. To select, sort out. 3. To
tuck up (as hair under a hat, etc.)
(acc. + под + acc.). 4. To take up
the slack (as in a line, reins, etc.).
5. To match (e.g., a tie in color)
(acc. + под + свет). 6. To fit (as a
key to a lock) (acc. + к + dat.). (Also
see подберу́.)

ПОДОБЬЁШЬ, see подобью́.
ПОДОБЬЮ́, подобьёшь. Р. Подби́ть (acc.). I. Подбива́ть. 1. To line (as a garment with s.t.) (acc. + inst.). 2. To resole (as a shoe). 3. To knock down, put out of action (as a plane). 4. To strike, injure. 5. To force, pound (s.t.) under (s.t.) (acc. + под + acc.). 6. To persuade, incite (s.o. to s.t.) (acc. + на + acc.) or (acc. + inf.).
ПОДОВЬЁШЬ, see подовью́.
ПОДОВЬЮ́, подовьёшь. Р. Подви́ть (acc.). I. Подвива́ть. To curl slightly (as hair).
ПОДО́ГНАННЫЙ; подо́гнан, —а, —о, —ы) (ppp). Р. Подогна́ть (acc.). I. Подгоня́ть. 1. To drive (to) (as cattle, etc.) (acc + к + dat.). 2. To drive under (acc. + под + acc.). 3. To hurry (s.o. or s.t.) (acc.). 4. To fit, adjust (s.t. to s.t.) (as components of a machine to each other) (acc. + к + dat.). 5. To time (s.t. to s.t.) (as one's arrival to s.o.'s convenience) (acc. + к + dat.). (Also see подгоню́.)
ПОДОЖГИ́ (imp.), see подожгу́.
ПОДОЖГЛА́, подожгло́, подожгли́ (past), see подожгу́ and поджёг.
ПОДОЖГУ́, подожжёшь, подожгу́т. Р. Подже́чь (acc.). I. Поджига́ть. 1. To light, kindle (as logs). 2. To set on fire (in committing arson) (as a building). 3. To let burn (as a pie). 4. (fig.) To incite, inflame.
ПОДОЖДЁШЬ, see подожду́.
ПОДОЖДИ́ (imp.), see подожду́.
ПОДОЖДУ́, подождёшь. Р. Подожда́ть. 1. To wait for (acc./gen.). 2. To wait (intr.).
ПОДОЖЖЁННЫЙ; подожжён, —а́, —о́, —ы́ (ppp), see подожгу́.
ПОДОЖЖЁШЬ, see подожгу́.
ПОДОЖМЁШЬ, see подожму́.
ПОДОЖМИ́ (imp.), see подожму́.
ПОДОЖМУ́, подожмёшь. Р. Поджа́ть (acc.). I. Поджима́ть. 1. To purse (one's lips). 2. To cross (one's legs). 3. (lit. and fig.) To put one's tail between one's legs (acc. of tail). 4. To draw in, tighten, press.
ПОДО́ЗВАННЫЙ; подо́зван, —а, (and —а́) —о, —ы) (ppp). Р. Подозва́ть (acc.). I. Подзыва́ть. To call up or over (e.g., s.o. to one's

desk) (acc. + к + dat.). (Also see подзову́.)
ПОДОЙДЁШЬ, see подойду́.
ПОДОЙДИ́ (imp.), see подойду́.
ПОДОЙДУ́, подойдёшь. Р. Подойти́ (intr.). I. Подходи́ть. 1. To approach (s.t. or s.o.) (к + dat.). 2. (fig.) To approach (of time). 3. To start, proceed (to) (e.g., to study) (к + dat.). 4. To approach (as a question, etc.) (к + dat.). 5. To fit, suit, become (s.o.) (as clothes) (dat.).
ПОДОЙДЯ́ (adv. past part.), see подойду́.
ПОДОЛЬЁШЬ, see подолью́.
ПОДОЛЬЩУ́СЬ, подольсти́шься. Р. Подольсти́ться (intr.). I. Подольща́ться. To work one's way into someone's good graces (through flattery) (к + dat. of s.o.).
ПОДОЛЬЮ́, подольёшь. Р. Подли́ть (acc./gen.). I. Подлива́ть. To pour out, add some more (as cream to one's coffee, etc.) (of liquids).
ПОДОМНЁШЬ, see подомну́.
ПОДОМНИ́ (imp.), see подомну́.
ПОДОМНУ́, подомнёшь. Р. Подмя́ть (acc.). I. Подмина́ть. 1. To crush, press down. 2. (fig.) To crush (as one's enemy).
ПОДОПРЁШЬ, see подопру́.
ПОДОПРИ́ (imp.), see подопру́.
ПОДОПРУ́, подопрёшь. Р. Подпере́ть (acc.). I. Подпира́ть. To prop up.
ПОДО́РВАННЫЙ; подо́рван, —а, —о, —ы) (ppp), see подорву́.
ПОДОРВЁШЬ, see подорву́.
ПОДОРВИ́ (imp.), see подорву́.
ПОДОРВУ́, подорвёшь. Р. Подорва́ть (acc.). I. Подрыва́ть. 1. To undermine, sap, blow up (as a bridge abutment). 2. (fig.) To undermine, shake (as one's health, s.o.'s confidence, etc.).
ПОДО́СЛАННЫЙ; подо́слан, —а, —о, —ы) (ppp), see подошлю́.
ПОДО́СТЛАННЫЙ; подо́стлан, —а, —о, —ы) (ppp). Р. Подостла́ть (acc. + под + acc.). I. Подстила́ть. To lay (s.t.) under (s.o., s.t.) (e.g., a bed sheet, etc.). (Also see подстелю́.)
ПОДОТРЁШЬ, see подотру́.
ПОДОТРИ́ (imp.), see подотру́.
ПОДОТРУ́, подотрёшь. Р. Подтере́ть (acc.). I. Подтира́ть. To wipe (up) (as the floor).

ПОДОХ, подохла (past). P. По-дохнуть (intr.). I. Дохнуть. To die (of animals).

ПОДОШЕ́ДШИЙ (pap), see подойду́.

ПОДОШЁЛ, подошла́ (past), see подойду́.

ПОДОШЛА́, подошло́, подошли́ (past), see подойду́ and подошёл.

ПОДОШЛЁШЬ, see подошлю́.

ПОДОШЛИ́[1] (past), see подойду́ and подошёл.

ПОДОШЛИ́[2] (imp.), see подошлю́.

ПОДОШЛЮ́, подошлёшь. P. Подо-сла́ть. I. Подсыла́ть. 1. To send (with secret purpose, e.g., as a spy) (acc.). 2. To send (s.t. in addition) (acc./gen.).

ПОДОШЬЁШЬ, see подошью́.

ПОДОШЬЮ́, подошьёшь. P. Подши́ть (acc.). I. Подшива́ть. 1. To sew (s.t.) underneath. 2. To line (as a coat with s.t.) (acc. + inst.). 3. To hem. 4. To sole (as a shoe). 5. To nail underneath (as sub-flooring). 6. To file (as correspondence).

ПОДПАДЁШЬ, see подпаду́.

ПОДПАДИ́ (imp.), see подпаду́.

ПОДПАДУ́, попадёшь. P. Подпа́сть (intr.). I. Подпада́ть. To fall under (as influence of s.o.) (под + acc.).

ПОДПА́Л, подпа́ла (past), see под-паду́.

ПОДПЁР, подёрла (past), see по-допру́.

ПОДПЕРЁВ and подпёрши (adv. past part.), see подопру́.

ПОДПЁРТЫЙ; подпёрт, —а, —о, —ы (ppp), see подопру́.

ПОДПЁРШИ and подперёв (adv. past part.), see подопру́.

ПОДПИ́САННЫЙ; подпи́сан, —а, —о, —ы (ppp), see подпишу́.

ПОДПИ́ШЕШЬ, see подпишу́.

ПОДПИШИ́ (imp.), see подпишу́.

ПОДПИШУ́, подпи́шешь. P. Под-писа́ть. I. Подпи́сывать. 1. To sign (s.t.) (acc.). 2. To add (s.t. to s.t. already written) (as several lines to a poem) (acc. + к + dat.). 3. To sign, enroll (as s.o. as a subscriber to s.t.) (acc. + на + acc.).

ПОДПЛЫВЁШЬ, see подплыву́.

ПОДПЛЫЙ (imp.), see подплыву́.

ПОДПЛЫВУ́, подплывёшь. P. По-дплы́ть (intr.). I. Подплыва́ть. 1.

To swim, sail, row, float, etc. up (to) (к + dat.). 2. To swim, etc., under (под + acc.). 3. (fig.) To float, sail, up (to) (к + dat.).

ПОДПО́ЛЗ, подползла́ (past), see подползу́.

ПОДПЛЗЁШЬ, see подползу́.

ПОДПО́ЛЗИ (inp.), see подползу́.

ПОДПОЛЗУ́, подползёшь. P. Под-ползти́ (intr.). I. Подполза́ть. 1. To creep or crawl up to (к + dat.). 2. To creep or crawl under (под + acc.).

ПОДПО́РЕШЬ, see подпорю́.

ПОДПОРИ́ (imp.), see подпорю́.

ПОДПО́РОТЫЙ; подпо́рот, —а, —о, —ы (ppp), see подпорю́.

ПОДПОРЮ́, подпо́решь. P. Подпо-ро́ть (acc.). I. Подпа́рывать. 1. To rip (up) or unstitch from underneath. 2. To rip (up) or unstitch a little.

ПОДПОЯ́САННЫЙ; подпоя́сан, —а, —о, —ы (ppp), see подпоя́шу.

ПОДПОЯ́ШЕШЬ, see подпоя́шу.

ПОДПОЯ́ШУ, подпоя́шешь. P. Под-поя́сать (acc.). I. Подпоя́сывать. To belt or girdle.

ПОДПОЯ́ШЬ (imp.), see подпоя́шу.

ПОДПРА́ВЛЕННЫЙ; подпра́влен, —а, —о, —ы (ppp), see подпра́влю.

ПОДПРА́ВЛЮ, подпра́вишь. P. Под-пра́вить (acc.). I. Подправля́ть. 1. To correct, rectify, to put in order. 2. To repair, mend. 3. To touch up, retouch. 4. To treat, make healthier.

ПОДПРА́ВЬ (imp.), see подпра́влю.

ПОДПУ́ЩЕННЫЙ; подпу́щен, —а, —о, —ы (ppp), see подпущу́.

ПОДПУЩУ́, подпу́стишь. P. Под-пусти́ть. I. Подпуска́ть. 1. To allow to approach (acc. + к + dat.). 2. To add (as a liquid to s.t.) (acc./gen.). 3. (fig.) To add (as a comment, remark, a "dirty dig") (acc.).

ПОДРАСТЁШЬ, see подрасту́.

ПОДРАСТИ́ (imp.), see подрасту́.

ПОДРАСТУ́, подрастёшь. P. Под-расти́ (intr.). I. Подраста́ть. To grow up.

ПОДРАЩЁННЫЙ; подращён, —а́, —о́, —ы́ (ppp), see подрасти́ть.

ПОДРАЩУ́, подрасти́шь. P. Подрас-ти́ть (acc.). I. Подра́щивать. To raise (as flowers, children, etc.).

ПОДРЕ́ЖЕШЬ, see подре́жу.

ПОДРЕ́ЖУ, подре́жешь. Р. Подре́-зать. I. Подреза́ть, подре́зывать. 1. To cut, trim, clip, prune (as shrubbery, etc.) (acc.). 2. To cut, trim (e.g., hair, cloth) (acc.). 3. To cut an additional amount (as more bread) (gen.). 4. (lit. and fig.) To undercut (acc.).

ПОДРЕ́ЖЬ (imp.), see подре́жу.

ПОДРЕ́ЗАННЫЙ; подре́зан, —а, —о, —ы (ppp), see подре́жу.

ПОДРЕ́МЛЕШЬ, see подремлю́.

ПОДРЕМЛИ́ (imp.), see подремлю́.

ПОДРЕМЛЮ́, подре́млешь. Р. Подрема́ть (intr.). To take a nap, sleep a little while.

ПОДРО́ЕШЬ, see подро́ю.

ПОДРО́Й (imp.), see подро́ю.

ПОДРО́С, подросла́ (past), see подрасту́.

ПОДРО́Ю, подро́ешь. Р. Подры́ть (acc.). I. Подрыва́ть. 1. To dig up the earth under (s.t.) (acc. of s.t.). 2. To undermine, sap (acc.). 3. To dig a little more (e.g., earth) (acc./gen.).

ПОДРУ́БЛЕННЫЙ; подру́блен, —а, —о, —ы (ppp), see подрублю́.

ПОДРУБЛЮ́, подру́бишь. Р. Подруби́ть. I. Подруба́ть. 1. To hew (acc.). 2. To cut down (as a tree) (acc.). 3. To cut off (as a table leg) (acc.). 4. To chop an additional amount (as kindling (acc./gen.). 5. To mine (as coal) (acc./gen.). 6. To hem (as a handkerchief) (acc.).

ПОДРЫ́ТЫЙ; подры́т, —а, —о, —ы (ppp), see подро́ю.

ПОДРЯЖЁННЫЙ; подряжён, —а́, —о́, —ы́ (ppp), see подряжу́.

ПОДРЯ́ЖЕННЫЙ; подря́жен, —а, —о, —ы (ppp), see подряжу́.

ПОДРЯЖУ́, подряди́шь. Р. Подряди́ть (acc.). I. Подряжа́ть. To hire.

ПОДСА́ЖЕННЫЙ; подса́жен, —а, —о, —ы (ppp), see подсажу́.

ПОДСАЖУ́, подса́дишь. Р. Подсади́ть. I. Подса́живать. 1. To help (s.o.) to a seat (acc.); help (s.o.) mount (a horse, etc.) (acc. + на + acc.). 2. To seat or place (s.o. or s.t.) near or next to (s.o. or s.t.) (acc. + к + dat.). 3. To plant an additional amount (as flowers) (acc./gen.).

ПОДСВЕ́ЧЕННЫЙ; подсве́чен, —а, —о, —ы (ppp), see подсвечу́.

ПОДСВЕЧУ́, подсве́тишь. Р. Под-свети́ть (acc.). I. Подсве́чивать. To light from underneath (as the setting sun lights the clouds).

ПОДСЕ́ЕШЬ, see подсе́ю.

ПОДСЕ́Й (imp.), see подсе́ю.

ПОДСЕ́К, подсекла́ (past), see подсеку́.

ПОДСЕКИ́ (imp.), see подсеку́.

ПОДСЕКУ́, подсечёшь, подсеку́т. Р. Подсе́чь (acc.). I. Подсека́ть. 1. To cut or hew off from underneath. 2. To cut short (as a life). 3. To hook, strike (a fish).

ПОДСЕ́Л, подсе́ла (past). Р. Подсе́сть (intr.). I. Подса́живаться. To sit down next to or take a seat near (s.o. or s.t.) (к + dat.) (also see подся́ду).

ПОДСЕЧЁННЫЙ; подсечён, —а́, —о́, —ы́ (ppp), see подсеку́.

ПОДСЕЧЁШЬ, see подсеку́.

ПОДСЕ́Ю, подсе́ешь. Р. Подсе́ять (acc./gen.). I. Подсева́ть, подсе́ивать. 1. To show an additional amount. 2. To sow (s.t.) between crop rows (e.g., clover among corn, etc.) (gen. of clover + по + dat. of corn).

ПОДСЕ́ЯННЫЙ; подсе́ян, —а, —о, —ы (ppp), see подсе́ю.

ПОДСИДИ́ (imp.), see подсижу́.

ПОДСИДИ́ШЬ, see подсижу́.

ПОДСИДЯ́Т, see подсижу́.

ПОДСИ́ЖЕННЫЙ; подси́жен, —а, —о, —ы (ppp), see подсижу́.

ПОДСИЖУ́, подсиди́шь. Р. Подсиде́ть (acc.). I. Подси́живать. 1. To scheme, intrigue against (s.o.). 2. To be on watch for, lie in wait for (s.o. or s.t.) (e.g., game, etc.).

ПОДСКА́ЖЕШЬ, see подскажу́.

ПОДСКАЖИ́ (imp.), see подскажу́.

ПОДСКАЖУ́, подска́жешь. Р. Подсказа́ть. I. Подска́зывать. 1. (lit. and fig.) To suggest (as s.t. to s.o.) (acc. + dat.). 2. To prompt (acc. + dat.) (что + кому).

ПОДСКА́ЗАННЫЙ; подска́зан, —а, —о, —ы (ppp), see подскажу́.

ПОДСКА́ЧЕШЬ, see подскачу́.

ПОДСКАЧИ́ (imp.), see подскачу́.

ПОДСКАЧУ́, подска́чешь. Р. Подскака́ть (intr.). I. Подска́кивать. To gallop up to (к + dat.).

ПОДСКО́БЛЕННЫЙ; подско́блен, —а, —о, —ы (ppp), see подскоблю́.

ПОДСКОБЛЮ, подско́блишь (or под-
скобли́шь). Р. Подскобли́ть (acc.).
I. Подска́бливать. To scrape off,
erase (e.g., a mark on a paper).

ПОДСКРЁБ, подскребла́ (past), see
подскребу́.

ПОДСКРЕБЁННЫЙ; подскребён,
—а́, —о́, —ы́ (ppp), see подскребу́.

ПОДСКРЕБЁШЬ, see подскребу́.

ПОДСКРЕБИ́ (imp.), see подскребу́.

ПОДСКРЕБУ́, подскребёшь. Р. Под-
скрести́ (acc.). I. Подскреба́ть. 1.
To scrape up or out (as food from a
pan). 2. To scrape (as a pan, etc.).

ПОДСЛАЩЁННЫЙ; подслащён, —а́,
—о́, —ы́ (ppp), see подслащу́.

ПОДСЛАЩУ́, подласти́шь. Р. Под-
ласти́ть (acc.). I. Подсла́щивать.
(lit. and fig.) To sweeten.

ПОДСМО́ТРЕННЫЙ; подсмо́трен,
—а, —о, —ы (ppp), see подсмотрю́.

ПОДСМОТРИ́ (imp.), see подсмотрю́.

ПОДСМО́ТРИШЬ, see подсмотрю́.

ПОДСМОТРЮ́, подсмо́тришь. Р. Под-
смотре́ть. I. Подсма́тривать. 1.
To spy (on) (за + inst.). 2. To see or
notice unexpectedly (acc.).

ПОДСМО́ТРЯТ, see подсмотрю́.

ПОДСОБЛЮ́, подсоби́шь. Р. Под-
соби́ть (dat.). I. Подсобля́ть. To
help.

ПОДСО́Х, подсо́хла (past). Р. Под-
со́хнуть (intr.). I. Подсыха́ть, To
become drier, dry out somewhat.

ПОДСТА́ВЛЕННЫЙ; подста́влен,
—а, —о, —ы (ppp), see подста́влю.

ПОДСТА́ВЛЮ, подста́вишь. Р. Под-
ста́вить. I. Подставля́ть. 1. To put
(s.o. or s.t.) under (s.t.) (acc. +
под + acc.). 2. To substitute (as
s.t. in another equation) (acc. + в +
acc.) or (s.t. in place of s.t.) (acc. +
вме́сто + gen.). 3. To move or hold
(s.t.) up to or against (s.o. or s.t.)
(acc. + dat.). 4. To offer or expose
(s.t. to s.o. or s.t.) (e.g., one's face
to the sun, one's flank to attack)
(acc. + dat.).

ПОДСТА́ВЬ (imp.), see подста́влю.

ПОДСТЕ́ЛЕННЫЙ; подсте́лен, —а,
—о, —ы (ppp), see подстелю́.

ПОДСТЕ́ЛЕШЬ, see подстелю́.

ПОДСТЕЛИ́ (imp.), see подстелю́.

ПОДСТЕЛЮ́, подсте́лешь. Р. По-
достла́ть and подстели́ть (acc. +
под + acc.). I. Подстила́ть. To lay

(s.t. under s.t. or s.o.) (as a bed
sheet).

ПОДСТЕРЁГ, подстерегла́ (past), see
подстерегу́.

ПОДСТЕРЕГУ́, подстережёшь, под-
стерегу́т. Р. Подстере́чь (acc.).
I. Подстерега́ть. 1. To lie in wait
for, be on the watch for (s.t. or s.o.).
2. (fig.) To catch.

ПОДСТЕРЕЖЁННЫЙ; подстережён,
—а́, —о́, —ы́ (ppp), see подстерегу́.

ПОДСТЕРЕЖЁШЬ, see подстерегу́.

ПОДСТРИ́Г, подстри́гла (past), see
подстригу́.

ПОДСТРИГИ́ (imp.), see подстригу́.

ПОДСТРИГУ́, подстрижёшь, под-
стригу́т. Р. Подстри́чь (acc.). I.
Подстрига́ть. 1. To cut, clip, trim
(as hair). 2. To prune, trim (as
shrubbery). 3. To cut s.o.'s hair (as
a man's hair) (acc. of man).

ПОДСТРИ́ЖЕННЫЙ; подстри́жен,
—а, —о, —ы (ppp), see подстригу́.

ПОДСТРИЖЁШЬ, see подстригу́.

ПОДСТУПЛЮ́, подсту́пишь. Р. Под-
ступи́ть (intr.). I. Подступа́ть. 1.
(lit. and fig.) To approach, come (to)
(к + dat.). 2. (fig.) To appear (3rd
pers. only) (as a lump in one's
throat) (к + dat.) or (as a pain in or
under one's heart) (к + dat.) or
(под + acc.), (tears in one's eyes)
(к + dat.).

ПОДСЫ́ПАННЫЙ; подсы́пан, —а,
—о, —ы (ppp), see подсы́плю.

ПОДСЫ́ПЛЕШЬ, see подсы́плю.

ПОДСЫ́ПЛЮ, подсы́плешь. Р. Под-
сы́пать (acc./gen.). 1. Подсыпа́ть.
To add by pouring (as salt, sugar,
sand, etc.).

ПОДСЫ́ПЬ (imp.), see подсы́плю.

ПОДСЯ́ДЕШЬ, see подся́ду.

ПОДСЯ́ДУ, подся́дешь. Р. Подсе́сть
(intr.). I. Подса́живаться. To sit
down next or take a seat near (s.o.
or s.t.) (к + dat.).

ПОДСЯ́ДЬ (imp.), see подся́ду.

ПОДТА́ЕТ, подта́ют (3rd pers. only).
Р. Подта́ять (intr.). I. Подта́ивать.
To thaw or melt a little.

ПОДТА́ЮТ (3rd pers. pl.), see по-
дта́ет.

ПОДТВЕРЖДЁННЫЙ; подтверж-
дён, —а́, —о́, —ы́ (ppp), see
подтвержу́.

ПОДТВЕРЖУ́, подтверди́шь. Р. Подтверди́ть (acc.). I. Подтвержда́ть. 1. To confirm, corroborate. 2. To acknowledge.

ПОДТЁК, подтекла́ (past), see подтечёт.

ПОДТЕКИ́ (imp.), see подтечёт.

ПОДТЕКУ́Т (3rd pers. pl.), see подтечёт.

ПОДТЁР, подтёрла (past).Р. Подтере́ть (acc.). I. Подтира́ть. To wipe (up) (as the floor) (also see подотру́).

ПОДТЕРЁВ and подтёрши (adv. past part.), see подтёр and подотру́.

ПОДТЁРТЫЙ; подтёрт, —а, —о, —ы (ppp), see подтёр and подотру́.

ПОДТЁРШИ and подтерёв (adv. past part.), see подтёр and подотру́.

ПОДТЕЧЁТ, подтеку́т (3rd pers. only). Р. Подте́чь (intr.). I. Подтека́ть (mean. 1 and 2). 1. To flow or run under (as a liquid) (под + acc.). 2. To leak a little. 3. To swell (as one's eye from a blow, etc.).

ПОДТО́ПЛЕННЫЙ; прдто́плен, —а, —о, —ы (ppp), see подтоплю́.

ПОДТОПЛЮ́, подто́пишь. Р. Подтопи́ть (acc.). I. Подта́пливать (mean. 1 and 2). 1. To heat a little. 2. To heat a little more (e.g., water) (acc./gen.). 3. To flood, inundate partially (acc.).

ПОДУ́ЕШЬ, see поду́ю.

ПОДУ́Й (imp.), see поду́ю.

ПОДУ́Ю, поду́ешь. Р. Поду́ть (intr.). I. Ду́ть (mean. 2). 1. To begin to blow (of the wind). 2. To blow (of the wind) or (of a person). 3. To blow for a while.

ПОДХВА́ЧЕННЫЙ; подхва́чен, —а, —о, —ы (ppp), see подхвачу́.

ПОДВХАЧУ́, подхва́тишь. Р. Подхвати́ть (acc.). I. Подхва́тывать. 1. To pick up, snatch up, catch up (s.o. or s.t.). 2. (fig.) To pick up, acquire (e.g., habit, cold, thought, tune, etc.).

ПОДХОЖУ́, подхо́дишь. I. Подходи́ть (intr.). Р. Подойти́. 1. To approach (s.t. or s.o.) (к + dat.). 2. (fig.) To approach (of time). 3. To start, proceed (to) (e.g., to study) (к + dat.). 4. To approach (as a question), (к + dat.). 5. To fit, suit, become (s.o.) (of clothes) (dat.).

ПОДЦЕ́ПЛЕННЫЙ; подце́плен, —а, —о, —ы (ppp), see подцеплю́.

ПОДЦЕПЛЮ́, подце́пишь. Р. Подцепи́ть (acc.). I. Подцепля́ть. 1. To pick up, snatch up (as a load). 2. To hook, hook up (as onto r.r. car). 3. (fig.) To pick up, catch (as a cold). 4. (fig.) To snatch (e.g., steal).

ПОДЧИ́СТИ (imp.), see подчи́щу.

ПОДЧИ́СТЬ (imp.), see подчи́щу.

ПОДЧИ́ЩЕННЫЙ; подчи́щен, —а, —о, —ы (ppp), see подчи́щу.

ПОДЧИ́ЩУ, подчи́стишь. Р. Подчи́стить. I. Подчища́ть. 1. To make cleaner, clean (acc.). 2. To erase (as an error) (acc.). 3. To clean some more (as vegetables) (gen.). 4. To eat up (everything, all of) (acc.).

ПОДШЕ́Й (imp.). Р. Подши́ть (acc.). I. Подшива́ть. 1. To sew (s.t.) underneath. 2. To line (as a coat with s.t.) (acc. + inst.). 3. To hem. 4. To sole (as a shoe). 5. To nail underneath (as sub-flooring). 6. To file (as correspondence). (Also see подошью́.)

ПОДШИ́Б, подши́бла (past), see подшибу́.

ПОДШИБЁШЬ, see подшибу́.

ПОДШИБИ́ (imp.), see подшибу́.

ПОДШИ́БЛЕННЫЙ; подши́блен, —а, —о, —ы (ppp), see подшибу́.

ПОДШИБУ́, подшибёшь. Р. Подшиби́ть (acc.). I. Подшиба́ть. 1. To knock down (as with a blow or shot). 2. To cause damage by striking (as to bruise one's cheek or eye with a blow).

ПОДШИ́ТЫЙ; подши́т, —а, —о, —ы (ppp), see подше́й and подошью́.

ПОДШУЧУ́, подшу́тишь. Р. Подшути́ть (intr.) (над + inst.). I. Подшу́чивать. 1. To play a trick or joke on. 2. To banter.

ПОД'Е́ДЕННЫЙ; под'е́ден, —а, —о, —ы (ppp), see под'е́м.

ПОД'Е́ДЕШЬ, see под'е́ду.

ПОД'ЕДИ́М, под'еди́те, под'едя́т (pl. forms), see под'е́м.

ПОД'Е́ДУ, под'е́дешь. Р. Под'е́хать (intr.). I. Под'езжа́ть. 1. To drive up to, approach (к + dat.); drive under (под + acc.). 2. To drop in (come, arrive). 3. (fig.) To get on the right side of (s.o.) (к + dat.).

ПОД'ЕЗЖА́Й (imp.), see под'е́ду.

ПОД'ÉЛ, под'éла (past), see под'éм.

ПОД'ÉМ, под'éшь, под'éст (sing. forms). Р. Под'éсть. I. Под'едáть. 1. To gnaw the lower part of s.t. (acc.). 2. To eat up, to finish (as food) (acc.). 3. To eat well, (intr.).

ПОД'ÉМЛЕШЬ, see под'éмлю.

ПОД'ÉМЛИ (imp.), see под'éмлю.

ПОД'ÉМЛЮ, под'éмлешь (arch. forms) (also подымáю, подымáешь). I. Подымáть (acc.). Р. Под'я́ть. 1. To lift, raise, hoist. 2. To pick up. 3. To incite, stir up, rouse. 4. (fig.) To raise. 5. To plow (as new land). (For other usages see unabridged dictionary.)

ПОД'ÉСТ, see под'éм.

ПОД'ÉШЬ¹ (2nd pers. sing.), see под'éм.

ПОД'ÉШЬ² (imp.), see под'éм.

ПОД'Я́ТЫЙ; под'я́т, —á, —о, —ы (ppp), see подыму́.

ПОДЫ́МЕШЬ, see подыму́.

ПОДЫМИ́ (imp.), see подыму́.

ПОДЫМУ́, подьíмешь. Р. Под'я́ть (acc.). I. Подымáть. 1. To lift, raise, hoist. 2. To pick up. 3. To incite, stir up, rouse. 4. (fig.) To raise. 5. To plow (as new land). (For other usages see unabridged dictionary.)

ПОДЫ́СКАННЫЙ; подьíскан, —а, —о, —ы (ppp), see подыщу́.

ПОДЫ́ШАТ, see подышу́.

ПОДЫ́ШИЙ (imp.), see подышу́.

ПОДЫ́ШИШЬ, see подышу́.

ПОДЫШУ́, подьíшишь. Р. Подышáть (intr.). To breathe (s.t.) for a while (as fresh air) (inst.).

ПОДЫ́ЩЕШЬ, see подыщу́.

ПОДЫЩИ́ (imp.), see подыщу́.

ПОДЫЩУ́, подьíщешь. Р. Подыскáть (acc.). I. Подьíскивать. To seek out and find.

ПОÉДЕННЫЙ; поéден, —а, —о, —ы (ppp), see поéм.

ПОÉДЕШЬ, see поéду.

ПОЕДИ́М, поедúте, поедя́т (pl. forms), see поéм.

ПОÉДУ, поéдешь. Р. Поéхать (intr.). 1. To go (by vehicle), ride. 2. To set out, depart. 3. To slip or slide (e.g., to one side on a slippery surface). 4. To speak tiresomely, annoyingly.

ПОÉЗДИ (imp.), see поéзжу.

ПОЕЗЖÁЙ (imp.), see поéду and éду.

ПОÉЗЖУ, поéздишь. Р. Поéздить (intr.). To travel about, do some traveling.

ПОÉЛ, поéла (past), see поéм.

ПОÉМ, поéшь, поéст (sing. forms). Р. Поéсть. I. Поедáть. 1. To eat a little, have a snack (acc./gen.). 2. To eat up (all of s.t.) (acc.). 3. To spoil by gnawing, nibbling (acc.).

ПОÉСТ, see поéм.

ПОÉШЬ¹ (2nd pers. sing.), see поéм.

ПОÉШЬ² (imp.), see поéм.

ПОÉШЬ (2nd pers. sing.). I. Петь. Р. Пропéть (mean. 1 and 2), спеть (mean. 1 and 2). 1. (lit. and fig.) To sing (intr.). 2. To sing (a song, a part, etc.) (acc.). 3. (fig.) To sing of (as one's love, etc.), to glorify, celebrate (acc.). 4. To talk a lot (about), repeat (intr.) (о + prep.). (Also see пою́.)

ПОЖÁТЫЙ; пожáт, —а, —о, —ы (ppp), see пожму́ and пожну́.

ПОЖГИ́ (imp.), see пожгу́.

ПОЖГЛА́, пожгло́, пожгли́ (past), see пожгу́ and пожёг.

ПОЖГУ́, пожжёшь, пожгу́т. Р. Пожéчь (acc.). I. Пожигáть. 1. To burn up (s.t.). 2. To destroy (as heat, drought, etc., destroys crops). 3. To burn (s.t.) for a while.

ПОЖДЁШЬ, see пожду́.

ПОЖДИ́ (imp.), see пожду́.

ПОЖДУ́, пождёшь. Р. Пождáть. 1. To wait a while (intr.). 2. To wait a while (for s.o. or s.t.) (acc./gen.).

ПОЖЁГ, пожгла́ (past), see пожгу́.

ПОЖЖЁННЫЙ; пожжён, —á, —ó, —ы́ (ppp), see пожгу́.

ПОЖЖЁШЬ, see пожгу́.

ПОЖИВЁШЬ, see поживу́.

ПОЖИВИ́ (imp.), see поживу́.

ПОЖИВЛЮ́СЬ, поживи́шься. Р. Поживи́ться (intr.). 1. To profit (by s.t.) (as s.o.'s kindness) (inst.). 2. To profit (at the expense of s.o.) (за + счёт + gen.). 3. To make use of (s.t.) (inst.).

ПОЖИВУ́, поживёшь. Р. Пожи́ть (intr.). 1. To live a while. 2. To live (in the sense of enjoying and seeing life).

ПОЖМЁШЬ, see пожму́.

ПОЖМИ́ (imp.), see пожму́.

ПОЖМУ́, пожмёшь. Р. Пожáть. I. Пожимáть. 1. To squeeze or press (acc.). 2. To shake hands (acc. of hands). 3. To shrug (as one's shoulders) (inst.). 4. To squeeze or press for a while (acc.).

ПОЖНЁШЬ, see пожну́.

ПОЖНИ́ (imp.), see пожну́.

ПОЖНУ́, пожнёшь. Р. Пожа́ть (acc.). I. Пожина́ть. 1. To finish reaping. 2. (fig.) To reap (as reward, praise, etc.).

ПО́ЖРАННЫЙ; по́жран, —а, —о, —ы (ppp), see пожру́.

ПОЖРЁШЬ, see пожру́.

ПОЖРИ́ (imp.), see пожру́.

ПОЖРУ́, пожрёшь. Р. Пожра́ть. I. Пожира́ть (mean. 1). 1. (lit. and fig.) To devour, eat greedily (acc.). 2. To have a bite, snack (acc./gen.) or (intr.).

ПОЗАБА́ВЛЕННЫЙ; позаба́влен, —а, —о, —ы (ppp), see позаба́влю.

ПОЗАБА́ВЛЮ, позаба́вишь. Р. Позаба́вить (acc.). To divert, amuse.

ПОЗАБА́ВЬ (imp.), see позаба́влю.

ПОЗАБУ́ДЕШЬ, see позабу́ду.

ПОЗАБУ́ДУ, позабу́дешь. Р. Позабы́ть. I. Позабыва́ть. 1. To forget (s.o. or s.t.) (acc.). 2. To forget (about s.o. or s.t.) (о + prep.). 3. To forget (to do s.t.) (+ inf.).

ПОЗАБУ́ДЬ (imp.), see позабу́ду.

ПОЗАБЫ́ТЫЙ; позабы́т, —а, —о, —ы (ppp), see позабу́ду.

ПО́ЗВАННЫЙ; по́зван, —а́, —о, —ы (ppp), see позову́.

ПОЗДРА́ВЛЕННЫЙ; поздра́влен, —а, —о, —ы (ppp), see поздра́влю.

ПОЗДРА́ВЛЮ, поздра́вишь. Р. Поздра́вить (acc.). I. Поздравля́ть. To congratulate (s.o. on the occasion of s.t.) (acc. + с + inst.).

ПОЗДРА́ВЬ (imp.), see поздра́влю.

ПОЗЛАЩЁННЫЙ; позлащён, —а́, —о́, —ы́ (ppp), see позлащу́.

ПОЗЛАЩУ́, позлати́шь. Р. Позлати́ть (arch., poetic) (acc.). I. Позлаща́ть. (lit. and fig.) To gild.

ПОЗНАВА́Й (imp.), see познаю́.

ПОЗНАВА́Я (adv. pres. part.), see познаю́.

ПОЗНАЁШЬ, see познаю́.

ПОЗНАКО́МЛЕННЫЙ; познако́млен, —а, —о, —ы (ppp), see познако́млю.

ПОЗНАКО́МЛЮ, познако́мишь. Р. Познако́мить (acc. + с + inst.). I. Знако́мить. 1. To acquaint (s.o.

with s.t.). 2. To introduce (s.o. to s.o.).

ПОЗНАКО́МЬ (imp.), see познако́млю.

ПОЗНАЮ́, познаёшь. I. Познава́ть (acc.). Р. Позна́ть. 1. To comprehend. 2. To get to know. 3. To experience (s.t.).

ПОЗОВЁШЬ, see позову́.

ПОЗОВИ́ (imp.), see позову́.

ПОЗОВУ́, позовёшь. Р. Позва́ть (acc.). I. Звать. 1. To call (s.o. or s.t.). 2. To invite, ask.

ПОЗОЛО́ЧЕННЫЙ; позоло́чен, —а, —о, —ы (ppp), see позолочу́.

ПОЗОЛОЧУ́, позолоти́шь. Р. Позолоти́ть (acc.). I. Золоти́ть. (lit. and fig.) To gild.

ПОИ́ЩЕШЬ, see поищу́.

ПОИЩИ́ (imp.), see поищу́.

ПОИЩУ́, пои́щешь. Р. Поиска́ть (acc.). To look for (for a while).

ПОЙ (imp.). I. Петь. Р. Пропе́ть (mean. 1 and 2), спеть (mean. 1 and 2). 1. (lit. and fig.) To sing (intr.). 2. To sing (a song, a part, etc.) (acc.). 3. (fig.) To sing of (as one's love, etc.), to glorify, celebrate (acc.). 4. To talk a lot (about), repeat (intr.) (о + prep.). (Also see пою́.)

ПОЙДЁШЬ, see пойду́.

ПОЙДИ́ (imp.), see пойду́.

ПОЙДУ́, пойдёшь. Р. Пойти́ (intr.). 1. To go; to come. 2. To start, leave (of a train, person, etc.). 3. To enter (as the army, a school, etc.) (в + acc.). 4. To begin or start (to do s.t.) (+ inf.). 5. To take after (as one's father) (в + acc.). (For multiple lit. and fig. meanings, see unabridged dictionary.)

ПОЙДЯ́ and поше́дши (adv. past part.), see пойду́.

ПОЙМЁШЬ, see пойму́.

ПОЙМИ́ (imp.), see пойму́.

ПОЙМУ́, поймёшь. Р. Поня́ть (acc.). I. Понима́ть. 1. To understand, comprehend. 2. To recognize, realize.

ПОКА́ЕШЬСЯ, see пока́юсь.

ПОКА́ЖЕШЬ, see покажу́.

ПОКАЖИ́ (imp.), see покажу́.

ПОКАЖУ́, пока́жешь. Р. Показа́ть. I. Пока́зывать (mean. 1 thru 7). 1. To show (s.t. to s.o.) (acc. + dat.). 2. To show (s.o. how to do s.t.) (dat. + как + inf.). 3. To point at, to (на + acc.). 4. To display (as knowledge, etc.) (acc.). 5. To indicate, register (e.g., temperature) (acc.). 6. To give evidence, testify (e.g., against) (на + acc.). 7. To show (that) (used with что). 8. To show (s.o.) (in expressions, e.g., "I'll show him") (dat.).

ПОКА́ЗАННЫЙ; пока́зан, —а, —о, —ы (ppp), see покажу́.

ПОКА́ЙСЯ (imp.), see пока́юсь.

ПОКА́ЧЕННЫЙ; пока́чен, —а, —о, —ы (ppp), see покачу́.

ПОКАЧУ́, пока́тишь. Р. Покати́ть. I. Кати́ть (mean. 1). 1. To roll (s.t.) (acc.). 2. To start to go rapidly (as in a car, boat, etc.) (intr.).

ПОКА́ЮСЬ, пока́ешься. Р. Пока́яться (intr.). I. Ка́яться. 1. To repent (of s.t.) (в + prep.). 2. To confess (s.t.) (в + prep.).

ПОКЛИ́ЧЕШЬ, see покли́чу.

ПОКЛИ́ЧУ, покли́чешь. Р. Покли́кать. 1. To call (s.o.) (in a loud voice) (acc.). 2. To call (in a loud voice) (intr.).

ПОКЛИ́ЧЬ (imp.), see покли́чу.

ПОКЛЯ́ЛСЯ, покляла́сь (past), see поклянусь.

ПОКЛЯНЁШЬСЯ, see поклянусь.

ПОКЛЯНИ́СЬ (imp.), see поклянусь.

ПОКЛЯНУ́СЬ, поклянёшься. Р. Покля́сться (intr.). I. Кля́сться. 1. To vow, swear (as friendship) (в + prep.). 2. To vow, swear (to do s.t.) (+ inf.).

ПОКОЛЕ́БЛЕННЫЙ; поколе́блен, —а, —о, —ы (ppp), see поколе́блю.

ПОКОЛЕ́БЛЕШЬ, see поколе́блю.

ПОКОЛЕ́БЛИ (imp.), see поколе́блю.

ПОКОЛЕ́БЛЮ, поколе́блешь. Р. Поколеба́ть (acc.). I. Колеба́ть. 1. To shake, oscillate. 2. (fig.) To shake (as one's confidence).

ПОКОЛО́ЧЕННЫЙ; поколо́чен, —а, —о, —ы (ppp), see поколочу́.

ПОКОЛОЧУ́, поколо́тишь. Р. Поколоти́ть. I. Колоти́ть (mean. 1 and 2). 1. To beat, (as a person, thing) (acc.). 2. To break (s.t. fragile, as dishes) (acc.). 3. To kill a number (as ducks) (acc.). 4. To pound, strike, beat a while (acc.). or (intr.) or (в + acc.) or (по + dat.).

ПОКОРМЛЕННЫЙ; поко́рмлен, —а, —о, —ы (ppp), see покормлю́.

ПОКОРМЛЮ́, поко́рмишь. Р. По-

кормить (acc.). I. Корми́ть. 1. To feed. 2. To nurse (as an infant).

ПОКОРО́БЛЕННЫЙ; покоро́блен, —а, —о, —ы (ppp), see покоро́блю.

ПОКОРО́БЛЮ, покоро́бишь. Р. Покоро́бить. I. Коро́бить. 1. To warp, distort, deform (acc.). 2. To be warped, warp (impers. + acc.). 3. To create a bad impression on, to disturb (acc.). 4. To have a bad impression created on one (by s.t.), be disturbed (by s.t.) (impers. + acc. + от + gen. of s.t.).

ПОКОРО́БЬ (imp.), see покоро́блю.

ПОКО́ШЕННЫЙ; поко́шен, —а, —о, —ы (ppp), see покошу́[1] and [2].

ПОКОШУ́[1], покоси́шь. Р. Покоси́ть. I. Коси́ть (mean. 1 and 2). 1. To cock, make crooked, slant (acc.). 2. To squint, cock (one's eyes) (acc./inst.). 3. To cock, slant (impers. + acc.).

ПОКОШУ́[2], покоси́шь. Р. Покоси́ть. 1. (lit. and fig.) To mow (down) (acc.). 2. To mow for a period of time (acc.) or (intr.).

ПОКОШУ́СЬ, покоси́шься. Р. Покоси́ться. I. Коси́ться (mean. 1 and 2). 1. To slant, slope, settle unevenly (intr.). 2. To squint (at), look sideways (at) (на + acc.). 3. To look askance for a while (at) (на + acc.).

ПОКРА́ДЕШШЫЙ; покра́ден, —а, —о, —ы (ppp), see покраду́.

ПОКРАДЁШЬ, see покраду́.

ПОКРАДИ́ (imp.), see покраду́.

ПОКРАДУ́, покрадёшь. Р. Покра́сть (acc.). To steal all or many.

ПОКРА́Л, покра́ла (past), see покраду́.

ПОКРА́ПАЙ and покра́пли (imp.), see покра́плю.

ПОКРА́ПЛЕШЬ, see покра́плю.

ПОКРА́ПЛИ and покра́пай (imp.), see покра́плю.

ПОКРА́ПЛЮ, покра́плешь (also покра́паю, покра́паешь). Р. Покра́пать. 1. To sprinkle for a while (of rain) (intr.). 2. To sprinkle, spray for a while (acc.).

ПОКРА́СЬ (imp.), see покра́шу.

ПОКРА́ШЕННЫЙ; покра́шен, —а, —о, —ы (ppp), see покра́шу.

ПОКРА́ШУ, покра́сишь. Р. Покра́сить (acc.). I. Кра́сить. 1. To color, dye, paint. 2. To spend a while painting, coloring, etc. (acc.) or (intr.).

ПОКРИВЛЁННЫЙ; покривлён, —а́, —о́, —ы́ (ppp), see покривлю́.

ПОКРИВЛЮ́, покриви́шь. Р. Покриви́ть (mean. 1 and 2). 1. To distort (as one's features) (acc.). 2. To bend, twist (acc.). 3. (arch.) To act hypocritically (intr.).

ПОКРИЧА́Т, see покричу́.

ПОКРИЧИ́ (imp.), see покричу́.

ПОКРИЧИ́ШЬ, see покричу́.

ПОКРИЧУ́, покричи́шь. Р. Покрича́ть. 1. To shout for a while (intr.). 2. To scold a little (на + acc.). 3. To call loudly (acc.) or (intr.).

ПОКРО́ЕШЬ, see покро́ю.

ПОКРО́Й (imp.), see покро́ю.

ПОКРО́Ю, покро́ешь. Р. Покры́ть (acc.). I. Крыть (mean. 1 thru 4, 7). Покрыва́ть (mean. 1 thru 6). 1. To cover, coat, plate. 2. To roof. 3. To conceal. 4. (fig.) To cover, trump (as a card). 5. (fig.) To cover (debts, ground, crime, etc.). 6. To muffle, drown out (as sound). 7. To abuse, scold, rail at.

ПОКРЫ́ТЫЙ; покры́т, —а, —о, —ы (ppp), see покро́ю.

ПОКУМЛЮ́СЬ, покуми́шься. Р. Покуми́ться (intr.). I. Куми́ться. To become a godparent.

ПОКУШУ́СЬ, покуси́шься. Р. Покуси́ться. I. Покуша́ться. 1. To attempt (s.t.) (на + acc.) or (inf.). 2. To make an attempt on (as s.o.'s life) (на + acc.). 3. To infringe, encroach (as on s.o.'s rights, property) (на + acc.).

ПОЛА́ДЬ (imp.), see пола́жу[1].

ПОЛА́ЖУ[1], пола́дишь. Р. Пола́дить (intr.). To come to an agreement, mutual understanding (with s.o.: с + inst.), (on s.t.: на + prep.).

ПОЛА́ЖУ[2], пола́зишь. Р. Пола́зить. To climb/clamber (over) a while (e.g., a mountain, a roof, etc.) (по + dat.).

ПОЛА́ЗЬ (imp.), see пола́жу[2].

ПОЛА́КОМИ and пола́комь (imp.), see пола́комлю.

ПОЛА́КОМИСЬ and пола́комься (imp.), see пола́комлюсь.

ПОЛА́КОМЛЮ, пола́комишь. Р. По-

ла́комить (acc.). I. Ла́комить. To feed sumptuously, provide with gourmet meals.

ПОЛА́КОМЛЮСЬ, пола́комишься. Р. Пола́комиться (inst.). I. Ла́комиться. To feast (on).

ПОЛА́КОМЬ and пола́коми (imp.), see пола́комлю.

ПОЛА́КОМЬСЯ and пола́комись (imp.), see пола́комлюсь.

ПОЛЁГ, полегла́ (past), see поля́жет.

ПОЛЕЖА́Т, see полежу́.

ПОЛЕЖИ́ (imp.), see полежу́.

ПОЛЕЖИ́ШЬ, see полежу́.

ПОЛЕЖУ́, полежи́шь. Р. Полежа́ть (intr.). To lie down for a while.

ПОЛЕЗА́Й and поле́зь (imp.), see поле́зу.

ПОЛЁЗ, поле́зла (past), see поле́зу.

ПОЛЕ́ЗЕШЬ, see поле́зу.

ПОЛЕ́ЗУ, поле́зешь. Р. Поле́зть (intr.). 1. To start to climb (as a tree, mountain, etc.) (на + acc.). 2. To start to climb (into) (в + acc.). 3. To get into, reach into (as one's pocket) (в + acc.). 4. To begin to fall out (of hair, etc.). 5. To begin to ravel (of cloth).

ПОЛЕ́ЗЬ and полеза́й (imp.), see поле́зу.

ПОЛЕ́Й (imp.). Р. Поли́ть. I. Полива́ть (mean. 1 and 2). 1. To pour over (as a steak with sauce) (acc. + inst.). 2. To water, irrigate (s.t.) (acc. + inst. of water). 3. To begin to pour (of rain) (intr.). (Also see полью́.)

ПОЛЕТИ́ (imp.), see полечу́.

ПОЛЕТИ́ШЬ, see полечу́.

ПОЛЕТЯ́Т, see полечу́.

ПОЛЕЧУ́, полети́шь. Р. Полете́т. (intr.). I. Лете́ть (mean. 1). 1. (lit. and fig.) To fly. 2. To fall. 3. To start to fly, fly off, take off. 4. (fig.) To begin to fly (of time).

ПО́ЛЕШЬ, see полю́.

ПОЛЗ, ползла́ (past), see ползу́.

ПОЛЗЁШЬ, see ползу́.

ПОЛЗИ́ (imp.), see ползу́.

ПОЛЗУ́, ползёшь. I. Ползти́ (intr.). 1. (lit. and fig.) To creep, crawl. 2. To slip, slide (of earth, etc.). 3. To fray (of cloth). 4. (fig.) To spread (of rumors).

ПОЛИ́ (imp.), see полю́.

ПОЛИ́ЖЕШЬ, see полижу́.

ПОЛИЖИ́ (imp.), see полижу́.

ПОЛИЖУ́, поли́жешь. Р. Полиза́ть (acc.). To lick a while.

ПОЛИ́ЗАННЫЙ; поли́зан, —а, —о, —ы (ppp), see полижу́.

ПО́ЛИТЫЙ; по́лит, —а́, —о, —ы (ppp), see полей and полью́.

ПОЛИ́ТЫЙ; поли́т, —а́, —о, —ы (ppp), see полей and полью́.

ПОЛО́СКАННЫЙ; поло́скан, —а, —о, —ы (ppp), see полощу́.

ПО́ЛОТЫЙ; по́лот, —а, —о, —ы (ppp), see полю́.

ПОЛО́ЩЕШЬ, see полощу́.

ПОЛОЩИ́ (imp.), see полощу́.

ПОЛОЩУ́, поло́щешь. I. Полоска́ть (acc.). Р. Вы́полоскать (mean. 1 and 2), пропрлоска́ть (mean. 1 and 2). 1. To rinse (as laundry, one's mouth, etc.). 2. To gargle (one's throat). 3. To blow, flap (as wind blows a flag).

ПОЛУ́ЖЕННЫЙ; полу́жен, —а, —о, —ы (ppp), see полужу́.

ПОЛУЖУ́, полу́дишь. Р. Полуди́ть (acc.). I. Луди́ть (mean. 1). 1. To tin (to plate with tin). 2. To tin for a period of time.

ПОЛУЛЁГ, полулегла́ (past), see полуля́гу.

ПОЛУЛЁЖА (adv. pres. part.), see полулежу́.

ПОЛУЛЕЖА́Т, see полулежу́.

ПОЛУЛЕЖИ́ (imp.), see полулежу́.

ПОЛУЛЕЖИ́ШЬ, see полулежу́.

ПОЛУЛЕЖУ́, полулежи́шь. I. Полулежа́ть (intr.) To recline.

ПОЛУЛЯ́Г (imp.), see полуля́гу.

ПОЛУЛЯ́ГУ, полуля́жешь, полуля́гут. Р. Полуле́чь (intr.). To recline.

ПОЛУЛЯ́ЖЕШЬ, see полуля́гу.

ПОЛЬЁШЬ, see полью́.

ПОЛЬЩУ́, польсти́шь. Р. Польсти́ть (dat.). I. Льстить. 1. To flatter (s.o.). 2. To please (s.o.).

ПОЛЬЮ́, польёшь. Р. Поли́ть. I. Полива́ть (mean. 1 and 2). 1. To pour over (as steak with sauce) (acc. + inst.). 2. To water, irrigate (s.t.) (acc. + inst. of water). 3. To begin to pour (of rain) (intr.).

ПОЛЮ́, по́лешь. I. Поло́ть (acc.). Р. Вы́полоть. 1. To weed (as a garden). 2. To weed out, pull out (as weeds).

ПОЛЮБЛЮ́, полю́бишь. Р. Полюби́ть. 1. To grow fond of, come

to love (s.o.) or (doing s.t.) (acc.) or (+ inf.). 2. To fall in love (intr.). 3. To fall in love with (acc.).

ПОЛЯ́ГТЕ (pl. imp.), see поля́жет.

ПОЛЯ́ГУТ (3rd pers. pl.), see поля́жет and поля́жем.

ПОЛЯ́ЖЕМ, поля́жете, поля́гут (pl. forms), see поля́жет.

ПОЛЯ́ЖЕТ (3rd pers. sing.) (1st and 2nd pers. sing. not used). Р. Поле́чь (intr.). I. Полега́ть (mean. 3). 1. To lie down (of all or many). 2. To be killed on the battlefield. 3. To bend down (of plants, grain, etc.).

ПОМА́ДЬ (imp.), see пома́жу[1].

ПОМА́ЖЕШЬ, see пома́жу[2].

ПОМА́ЖУ[1], пома́дишь. I. Пома́дить (acc.). Р. Напома́дить. To apply pomade.

ПОМА́ЖУ[2], пома́жешь. Р. Пома́зать (acc.). I. Ма́зать (mean. 1 and 2). 1. (lit. and fig.) To grease, lubricate. 2. To smear, spread (with) (acc. + inst.). 3. To annoint.

ПОМА́ЖЬ (imp.), see пома́жу[2].

ПОМА́ЗАННЫЙ; пома́зан, —а, —о, - ы (ppp), see пома́жу[2].

ПОМА́ШЕШЬ, see помашу́.

ПОМАШИ́ (imp.), see помашу́.

ПОМАШУ́, пома́шешь. Р. Помаха́ть. 1. To wave (for a while) (as ones' hand to s.o.) (inst. + dat.). 2. To wave (intr.) (e.g., to s.o.) (dat.).

ПО́МЕР, померла́, по́мерло, по́мерли (past), see помру́.

ПОМЁРЗ, помёрзла (past). Р. Помёрзнуть (intr.). 1. To be killed by frost, be frostbitten. 2. To suffer for a period of time in the cold.

ПОМЁРК (and arch. помёркнул), помёркла (past). Р. Помёркнуть (intr.). I. Ме́ркнуть. 1. To grow dim, fade (of stars, etc.). 2. (fig.) To dim, fade.

ПОМЕ́ТЬ (imp.), see помéчу.

ПОМЕ́ЧЕННЫЙ; поме́чен, —а, —о, —ы (ppp), see поме́чу.

ПОМЕ́ЧУ, поме́тишь. Р. Поме́тить (acc.). I. Ме́тить. To mark (as a page or one's clothing).

ПОМЕЩЁННЫЙ; помещён, —а́, —о́, —ы́ (ppp), see помещу́.

ПОМЕЩУ́, помести́шь. Р. Помести́ть (acc.). I. Помеща́ть. 1. To place, locate, put. 2. To invest (as money). 3. To publish (put) (as an article in

the paper). 4. To lodge (s.o. somewhere).

ПОМНЁШЬ, see помну.

ПОМНИ (imp.), see помну.

ПОМНУ, помнёшь. Р. Помя́ть (acc.).
1. To rumple, crumple. 2. To dent.
3. To trample. 4. To injure.

ПОМÓГ, помогла́ (past), see помогу́.

ПОМОГИ (imp.), see помогу́.

ПОМОГУ́, помо́жешь, помо́гут. Р.
Помо́чь. I. Помога́ть. 1. To help,
assist (dat.). 2. To help provide a
desired result (as medicine helps,
etc.) (intr.).

ПОМÓЕШЬ, see помо́ю.

ПОМÓЖЕШЬ, see помогу́.

ПОМÓЙ (imp.), see помо́ю.

ПОМÓЛВИ (imp.), see помо́лвлю.

ПОМÓЛВЛЕННЫЙ; помо́лвлен, —а,
—о, —ы (ppp), see помо́лвлю.

ПОМÓЛВЛЮ, помо́лвишь. Р. По-
мо́лвить (acc.) (arch.). To betroth,
engage, announce the engagement of
(s.o. to s.o.) (acc. + с + inst.) or
(acc. + за + acc.).

ПОМОЛЧА́Т, see помолчу́.

ПОМОЛЧИ (imp.), see помолчу́.

ПОМОЛЧИШЬ, see помолчу́.

ПОМОЛЧУ́, помолчи́шь. Р. По-
молча́ть (intr.). To be silent for a
while.

ПОМОРÓЖЕННЫЙ; поморо́жен, —а,
—о, —ы (ppp), see поморо́жу.

ПОМОРÓЖУ, поморо́зишь. Р. По-
моро́зить (acc.). 1. To freeze (all,
a number of). 2. To chill (all, a
number of). 3. To subject to frostbite.
4. To freeze, chill, etc., for a while.

ПОМОРÓЗЬ (imp.), see поморо́жу.

ПОМÓЮ, помо́ешь. Р. Помы́ть (acc.).
I. Мыть. To wash.

ПОМРЁШЬ, see помру́.

ПОМРИ (imp.), see помру́.

ПОМРУ́, помрёшь. Р. Помере́ть
(intr.). I. Помира́ть. 1. To die. 2.
(fig.) To disappear, to die out (e.g.,
old customs).

ПОМУТНЁННЫЙ; помутнён, —а́,
—о́, —ы́ (ppp), see помучу́ (mean. 2).

ПОМУЧУ́, помути́шь (and по-
му́тишь). Р. Помути́ть (acc.). I.
Мути́ть. 1. To stir up slightly, make
somewhat turbid (as a liquid).
2. (fig.) To dull (as alcohol dulls
one's senses).

ПОМЧА́Т, see помчу́.

ПОМЧИ (imp.), see помчу́.

ПОМЧИШЬ, see помчу́.

ПОМЧУ́, помчи́шь. Р. Помча́ть. 1.
To carry rapidly, rush (s.o. or s.t.)
(acc.). 2. To speed, rush (intr.).

ПОМЫ́ТЫЙ; помы́т, —а, —о, —ы
(ppp), see помо́ю.

ПОМЯ́ТЫЙ; помя́т, —а, —о, —ы
(ppp), see помну́.

ПОНАДЕ́ЕШЬСЯ, see понаде́юсь.

ПОНАДЕ́ЙСЯ (imp.), see понаде́юсь.

ПОНАДЕ́ЮСЬ, понаде́ешься. Р. По-
наде́яться (intr.). I. Наде́яться.
1. To hope (for s.t.) (на + acc.).
2. To hope (that) (+ что). 3. To
hope (to do s.t.) (+ inf.). 4. To rely
on, have confidence in (s.o. or s.t.)
(на + acc.).

ПОНÁДОБЛЮСЬ, пона́добишься. Р.
Пона́добиться (dat.). To be, become necessary (to s.o.) (e.g., he
needed the book) (ему́ пона́до-
билась кни́га).

ПОНÁДОБИСЬ (imp.), see пона́-
доблюсь.

ПОНАЕ́ДЕМ, понае́дете, понае́дут
(pl. forms), see понае́дет.

ПОНАЕ́ДЕТ (3rd pers. sing.) (1st and
2nd pers. sing. not used). Р. По-
нае́хать. To come or arrive gradually
in large numbers.

ПОНАЕ́ДУТ, see понае́дет.

ПОНЁС, понесла́ (past), see понесу́.

ПОНЕСЁННЫЙ; понесён, —а́, —о́,
—ы́ (ppp), see понесу́.

ПОНЕСЁШЬ, see понесу́.

ПОНЕСИ (imp.), see понесу́.

ПОНЕСУ́, понесёшь. Р. Понести́. I.
Нести́ (mean. 1, 3, 4, 5). 1. (lit. and
fig.) To carry (acc.). 2. To carry
along rapidly (s.o. or s.t.) (of a
person, vehicle, wind, etc.) (acc.).
3. To blow (of the wind, cold, heat,
etc.) (intr.) (impers. + inst.). 4. To
smell (of s.t.) (impers. + inst.). 5.
To experience, undergo, bear, suffer
(e.g., loss, punishment, etc.) (acc.).
6. To carry, etc., a while (acc.). 7. To
become pregnant (intr.). 8. To bolt,
run away (of horses, etc.) (intr.).
9. To talk nonsense (intr.) or (acc.).

ПОНЕСЯ́ (adv. past part.), see понесу́.

ПОНИ́ЖЕННЫЙ; пони́жен, —а, —о,
—ы (ppp), see пони́жу.

ПОНИ́ЖУ, пони́зишь. Р. Пони́зить
(acc.). I. Понижа́ть. 1. To lower.

2. To reduce. 3. (elec.) To step down.
ПОНИЗЬ (imp.), see **понижу**.
ПОНИК, поникла (past). Р. **Поникнуть** (intr.). I. **Никнуть** (mean. 1 and 2). 1. (lit. and fig.) To droop, wilt. 2. (fig.) To weaken. 3. To bend, bow (as one's head) (inst.).
ПОНОСИ (imp.), see **поношу¹** and ².
ПОНОШЕННЫЙ; поношен, —а, —о, —ы (ppp), see **поношу¹**.
ПОНОШУ¹, поносишь. Р. **Поносить** (acc.). 1. To carry for a while. 2. To wear for a while (as a coat).
ПОНОШУ², поносишь. I. **Поносить** (acc.). To berate, revile, abuse, insult.
ПОНУДЬ (imp.), see **понужу**.
ПОНУЖДЁННЫЙ; понуждён, —á, —ó, —ы (ppp), see **понужу**.
ПОНУЖУ, понудишь. Р. **Понудить** (acc.). I. **Понуждать**. To force, compel (s.o. or s.t. to do s.t.) (acc. + inf.).
ПОНЯТЫЙ; понят, —á, —о, —ы (ppp). Р. **Понять** (acc.). I. **Понимать**. 1. To understand, comprehend. 2. To recognize, realize. (Also see **пойму**.)
ПООБЖИВЁШЬСЯ, see **пообживусь**.
ПООБЖИВИСЬ (imp.), see **пообживусь**.
ПООБЖИВУСЬ, пообживёшься. Р. **Пообжиться** (intr.). To become gradually accustomed to one's surroundings.
ПООБНОСИСЬ (imp.), see **пообношусь**.
ПООБНОШУСЬ, пообносишься. Р. **Пообноситься** (intr.). To become somewhat short of clothes, out at the elbows.
ПОПАДЁШЬ, see **попаду**.
ПОПАДИ (imp.), see **попаду**.
ПОПАДУ, попадёшь. Р. **Попасть**. I. **Попадать**. 1. To hit (as a target (в + acc.). 2. To fall on, strike (s.t.) (e.g., spray) (на + acc.). 3. To arrive, find oneself, get to (as the theatre) (в + acc.). 4. To catch (as a train) (на + acc.). 5. To get into (as trouble) (в + acc.). 6. (fig.) To "catch it," be punished (as by one's parents) (impers. + dat. + от + gen.). (For other lit. and fig. meanings see unabridged dictionary.)
ПОПАЛ, попала (past), see **попаду**.

ПОПЕЙ (imp.). Р. **Попить** (acc./gen.) or (intr.). 1. To have a drink (of s.t.). 2. To drink (s.t.) a while. (Also see **попью**.)
ПОПЁР, попёрла (past), see **попру¹**.
ПОПЁРТЫЙ; попёрт, —а, —о, —ы (ppp), see **попру¹**.
ПОПИТО (neuter ppp), see **попью**.
ПОПИШЕШЬ, see **попишу**.
ПОПИШИ (imp.), see **попишу**.
ПОПИШУ, попишешь. Р. **Пописать** (intr.) or (acc.). To write a while, write a little.
ПОПЛАТИСЬ (imp.), see **поплачусь**.
ПОПЛАЧЕШЬ, see **поплачу**.
ПОПЛАЧУ, поплачешь. Р. **Поплакать** (intr.). To cry or weep for a while.
ПОПЛАЧУСЬ, поплатишься. Р. **Поплатиться**. I. **Платиться**. 1. (fig.) To pay (intr.). 2. (fig.) To pay (for s.t. with s.t.) (as for a crime with one's life) (за + acc. + inst.).
ПОПЛАЧЬ (imp.), see **поплачу**.
ПОПЛЁЛСЯ, поплелась (past), see **поплетусь**.
ПОПЛЕТЁШЬСЯ, see **поплетусь**.
ПОПЛЕТИСЬ (imp.), see **поплетусь**.
ПОПЛЕТУСЬ, поплетёшься. Р. **Поплестись** (intr.). 1. To plod along. 2. To walk along slowly.
ПОПЛЫВЁШЬ, see **поплыву**.
ПОПЛЫВИ (imp.), see **поплыву**.
ПОПЛЫВУ, поплывёшь. Р. **Поплыть** (intr.). (lit. and fig.) To start to swim, float, drift, sail.
ПОПЛЯШЕШЬ, see **попляшу**.
ПОПЛЯШИ (imp.), see **попляшу**.
ПОПЛЯШУ, попляшешь. Р. **Поплясать**. 1. To dance a while (intr.). 2. To dance (s.t.) (acc.).
ПОПОЛЗ, поползла (past), see **поползу**.
ПОПОЛЗЁШЬ, see **поползу**.
ПОПОЛЗИ (imp.), see **поползу**.
ПОПОЛЗУ, поползёшь. Р. **Поползти** (intr.). (lit. and fig.) To begin to creep, crawl.
ПОПОЛОЩЕШЬ, see **пополощу**.
ПОПОЛОЩИ (imp.), see **пополощу**.
ПОПОЛОЩУ, пополощешь. Р. **Пополоскать** (acc.). 1. To rinse a while (as laundry, one's mouth, etc.). 2. To gargle (one's throat) a while.
ПОПРАВЛЕННЫЙ; поправлен, —а, —о, —ы (ppp), see **поправлю**.

ПОПРА́ВЛЮ, попра́вишь. Р. Попра́вить. I. Поправля́ть (mean. 1 thru 5). 1. To repair, mend (acc.). 2. To rectify, correct (as an error) (acc.). 3. To correct (as a student) (acc.). 4. To readjust, put in order (acc.). 5. To better, improve (acc.). 6. To drive a while (e.g., a horse, car, etc.) (inst.).

ПОПРА́ВЬ (imp.), see попра́влю.

ПО́ПРАННЫЙ; по́пран, —а́, —о, —ы (ppp), see попру́[2].

ПОПРЕ́ШЬ, see попру́[1] and [2].

ПОПРИ́ (imp.), see попру́[1] and [2].

ПОПРО́ШЕННЫЙ; попро́шен, —а, —о, —ы (ppp), see попрошу́.

ПОПРОШУ́, попро́сишь. Р. Попроси́ть. I. Проси́ть. 1. To ask (s.o.) (acc.) or (s.o. to do s.t.) (acc. + inf.). 2. To ask (s.o. for s.t. or s.o.) (acc. + + o + prep.). 3. To ask or request (s.t. of s.o.) (acc./gen. + у + gen.). 4. To inquire, ask (intr.). 5. To intercede (for s.o.) (за + acc.) or (with s.o. for s.o.) (acc. + за + acc.). 6. To invite (s.o.) (acc.).

ПОПРУ́[1], попрёшь. Р. Попере́ть. 1. To push on, make one's way (usually in numbers of people, cattle, etc.) (intr.). 2. To drive out, turn out (acc.). 3. To carry, drag (acc.).

ПОПРУ́[2], попрёшь. Р. Попра́ть (acc.) (arch.; future seldom used). I. Попира́ть. 1. To trample, to stand on scornfully (as a fallen adversary). 2. To violate, scorn, flout (as s.o.'s rights).

ПОПРЯ́ТАННЫЙ; попря́тан, —а, —о, —ы (ppp), see попря́чу.

ПОПРЯ́ЧЕШЬ, see попря́чу.

ПОПРЯ́ЧУ, попря́чешь. Р. Попря́тать (acc.). To hide, conceal (all or many).

ПОПРЯ́ЧЬ (imp.), see попря́чу.

ПОПУ́ЩЕННЫЙ; пипу́щен, —а, —о, —ы (ppp), see попущу́.

ПОПУЩУ́, попу́стишь. Р. Попусти́ть (arch.) (acc.). I. Попуска́ть. To permit, allow (s.t. to happen).

ПОПЬЮ́, попьёшь. Р. Попи́ть (acc./gen.) or (intr.). 1. To have a drink (of s.t.). 2. To drink (s.t.) a while.

ПОПЯ́ТЬ (imp.), see попя́чу.

ПОПЯ́ТЬСЯ (imp.), see попя́чусь.

ПОПЯ́ЧЕННЫЙ; попя́чен, —а, —о, —ы (ppp), see попя́чу.

ПОПЯ́ЧУ, попя́тишь. Р. Попя́тить (acc.). I. Пя́тить. To back (as a horse).

ПОПЯ́ЧУСЬ, попя́тишься. Р. Попя́титься (intr.). I. Пя́титься. 1. To back up, move backward. 2. (fig.) To renounce, go back on (as a promise, etc.) (от + gen.).

ПОРАБОЩЁННЫЙ; порабощён, —а́, —о́, —ы́ (ppp), see порабощу́.

ПОРАБОЩУ́, поработи́шь. Р. Поработи́ть (acc.). I. Порабоща́ть. To enslave.

ПОРАЖЁННЫЙ; поражён, —а́, —о́, —ы́ (ppp), see поражу́.

ПОРАЖУ́, порази́шь. Р. Порази́ть (acc.). I. Поража́ть, рази́ть (mean. 1 and 2). 1. To strike, hit (with weapons, etc.). 2. To defeat, crush (as an enemy). 3. To astound, startle. 4. To affect, strike (said of disease) (e.g., pneumonia affects the lungs).

ПОРАСТЁШЬ, see порасту́.

ПОРАСТИ́ (imp.), see порасту́.

ПОРАСТУ́, порастёшь. Р. Порасти́. I. Пораста́ть. 1. To grow a while (intr.). 2. To become overgrown (with s.t.) (inst.).

ПО́РВАННЫЙ; по́рван, —а, —о, —ы (ppp), see порву́.

ПОРВЁШЬ, see порву́.

ПОРВИ́ (imp.), see порву́.

ПОРВУ́, порвёшь. Р. Порва́ть. I. Порыва́ть (mean. 2). 1. To break (e.g., a cable, communications, etc.) (acc.). 2. (fig.) To break off (as relations with s.o. or s.t.) (acc. + с + inst.). 3. To tear (as one's clothes) (acc.). 4. To pick all or many (acc./gen.).

ПОРЕ́ЖЕШЬ, see поре́жу.

ПОРЕ́ЖУ, поре́жешь. Р. Поре́зать. 1. To cut, injure (as one's hand) (acc.). 2. To slice, cut a quantity of (as bread, etc.) (acc./gen.). 3. To slaughter, kill all or a quantity of (as cattle) (acc.).

ПОРЕ́ЖЬ (imp.), see поре́жу.

ПОРЕ́ЗАННЫЙ; поре́зан, —а, —о, —ы (ppp), see поре́жу.

ПО́РЕШЬ, see порю́[1] and [2].

ПОРИ́ (imp.), see порю́[1] and [2].

ПОРО́ЕШЬСЯ, see поро́юсь.

ПОРОЖДЁННЫЙ; порождён, —а́, —о́, —ы́ (ppp), see порожу́.

ПОРОЖУ́, породи́шь. Р. Породи́ть (acc.). I. Порожда́ть. 1. To beget, give birth to. 2. (fig.) To generate, breed (as rumors).

ПОРО́ЙСЯ (imp.), see поро́юсь.

ПОРО́С, поросла́ (past), see порасту́.

ПО́РОТЫЙ; по́рот, —а, —о, —ы (ppp), see порю́[1] and [2].

ПОРО́ЮСЬ, поро́ешься. Р. Поры́ться (intr.). To rummage a while (as in one's pocket) (в + prep.).

ПО́РТИ and порть (imp.), see по́рчу.

ПОРТЬ and по́рти (imp.), see по́рчу.

ПОРУ́БЛЕННЫЙ; пору́блен, —а, —о, —ы (ppp), see порублю́.

ПОРУБЛЮ́, пору́бишь. Р. Поруби́ть. 1. To fell, cut down, chop down all or a quantity of (acc.). 2. To cut, chop up, mince (as meat) (acc./gen.). 3. To slash, kill, slaughter all or many (as the enemy) (acc.). 4. To cut (as one's foot with an axe) (acc.). 5. To fell, chop, cut, etc., a while (acc.) or (intr.).

ПО́РЧЕННЫЙ; по́рчен, —а, —о, —ы (ppp), see по́рчу.

ПО́РЧУ, по́ртишь. I. По́ртить (acc.). Р. Испо́ртить. 1. To spoil, damage. 2. To corrupt.

ПОРЮ́[1], по́решь. I. Поро́ть (acc.). Р. Распоро́ть (mean. 1 and 2). 1. To rip (as a seam). 2. To rip open (e.g., with a bayonet). 3. To talk (nonsense, etc.).

ПОРЮ́[2], по́решь. I. Поро́ть (acc.). Р. Вы́пороть. To beat, switch, flog.

ПОРЯ́ЖЕННЫЙ; поря́жен, —а, —о, —ы (ppp), see поряжу́.

ПОРЯЖУ́, поряди́шь (also поря́дишь) Р. Поряди́ть (acc.). I. Ряди́ть. To hire (s.o.) (having bargained with him).

ПОРЯЖУ́СЬ, поряди́шься (and поря́дишься). Р. Поряди́ться (intr.). I. Ряди́ться. 1. To bargain (with s.o.) (с + inst.). 2. To accept a job as, assume responsibility of (в + acc. pl.)

ПОСА́ЖЕННЫЙ; поса́жен, —а, —о, —ы (ppp), see посажу́.

ПОСАЖУ́, поса́дишь. Р. Посади́ть (acc.). I. Сади́ть (mean. 1 thru 6), Сажа́ть (mean. 1 thru 6). 1. To plant (as flowers). 2. To seat (as guests). 3. To set down (as a plane on an airfield). 4. To put (as s.o. in prison). 5. To place (as bread in an oven). 6. To sew on (as a patch). 7. (arch.) To expend (e.g., time, money). (For

other uses see unabridged dictionary.)

ПОСВЕЧУ́, посве́тишь. Р. Посвети́ть (intr.). I. Свети́ть (mean. 2). 1. To shine, give off light for a while. 2. To light the way, throw light (for s.o.) (dat. of s.o.).

ПОСВИСТИ́ (imp.), see посвищу́[2].

ПОСВИСТЯ́Т, see посвищу́[2].

ПОСВИ́ЩЕШЬ, see посвищу́[1].

ПОСВИЩИ́ (imp.), see посвищу́[1].

ПОСВИЩУ́[1], посви́щешь. Р. Посвиста́ть. 1. To whistle a while, several times (intr.). 2. To call (as a dog) by whistling, whistle for (acc.).

ПОСВИЩУ́[2], посвисти́шь. Р. Посвисте́ть (intr.). To whistle a while, several times (intr.).

ПОСВЯЩЁННЫЙ; посвящён, —а́, —о́, —ы́ (ppp), see посвящу́.

ПОСВЯЩУ́, посвяти́шь. Р. Посвяти́ть (acc.). I. Посвяща́ть. 1. To devote (as one's time to politics) (acc. + dat.) or (arch: на + acc.). 2. To dedicate (as a book to s.o.) (acc. + dat.). 3. To ordain, induct, initiate (as s.o. into an order, a club, etc.) (acc. + в + acc.). 4. To admit (as s.o. to one's secret, thoughts, etc.) (acc. + в + acc.).

ПОСЕ́ЕШЬ, see посе́ю.

ПОСЕ́Й (imp.), see посе́ю.

ПОСЁК, посекла́ (arch.: посёк, посёкла, etc.) (past), see посеку́.

ПОСЕКИ́ (imp.), see посеку́.

ПОСЁКСЯ, посекла́сь (past), see посеку́сь.

ПОСЕКУ́, посечёшь, посеку́т. Р. Посе́чь (acc.). 1. (arch.) To slash, kill (as with a sabre). 2. To cut to pieces. 3. To beat or flog a little.

ПОСЕКУ́ТСЯ (3rd pers. pl.), see посечётся.

ПОСЕЧЁННЫЙ; посечён, —а́, —о́, —ы́ (ppp), see посеку́ (mean. 1, and 2).

ПОСЕ́ЧЕННЫЙ; посе́чен, —а, —о, —ы (ppp), see посеку́ (mean. 3).

ПОСЕЧЁТСЯ, посеку́тся (3rd pers. sing. and pl.) (1st and 2nd pers. not used). Р. Посе́чься (intr.). I. Се́чься. 1. To split (as hair). 2. To cut (as silk).

ПОСЕЧЁШЬ, see посеку́.

ПОСЕЩЁННЫЙ; посещён, —а́, —о́, —ы́ (ppp), see посещу́.

ПОСЕЩУ́, посети́шь. Р. Посети́ть (acc.). I. Посеща́ть. 1. To visit, call

ПОСЕЮ 172 ПОСТАВЛЮ

on. 2. To attend (as a lecture). 3. (fig.)
To visit.
ПОСЕ́Ю, посе́ешь. Р. Посе́ять (acc.).
I. Се́ять. (lit. and fig.) To sow, strew.
ПОСЕ́ЯННЫЙ; посе́ян, —а, —о, —ы
(ppp), see посе́ю.
ПОСИДИ́ (imp.), see посижу́.
ПОСИДИ́ШЬ, see посижу́.
ПОСИДЯ́Т, see посижу́.
ПОСИЖУ́, посиди́шь. Р. Посиде́ть
(intr.). To sit awhile. (For various
idiomatic usages, see unabridged
dictionary.)
ПОСКА́ЧЕШЬ, see поскачу́.
ПОСКАЧИ́ (imp.), see поскачу́.
ПОСКАЧУ́, поска́чешь. Р. Поскака́ть
(intr.). 1. To start to hop, skip, jump.
2. To gallop off, start to gallop.
3. To gallop, hop, etc., a while.
ПОСКРИПИ́ (imp.), see поскриплю́.
ПОСКРИПИ́ШЬ, see поскриплю́.
ПОСКРИПЛЮ́, поскрипи́шь. Р. По-
скрипе́ть (intr.). 1. To squeak, creak,
crunch a while. 2. To crunch, grit a
while (as one's teeth), to squeak a
while (as a door) (inst.).
ПОСКРИПЯ́Т, see поскриплю́.
ПОСКУПЛЮ́СЬ, поскупи́шься. Р.
Поскупи́ться (intr.). I. Скупи́ться
(mean. 2). 1. To be somewhat stingy,
tightfisted. 2. To stint (on s.t.), be
sparing (of) (на + acc.).
ПО́СЛАННЫЙ; по́слан, —а, —о, —ы
(ppp). Р. Посла́ть (acc.). I. Посы-
ла́ть. To send, dispatch (s.o. or s.t.)
(also see пошлю́).
ПОСЛАЩЁННЫЙ; послащён, —а́,
—о́, —ы́ (ppp), see послащу́.
ПОСЛАЩУ́, посласти́шь. Р. Послас-
ти́ть (acc.). I. Сласти́ть. To sweeten.
ПОСЛЕЖУ́, последи́шь. Р. Последи́ть
(за + inst.). 1. To look after for a
while. 2. To watch, observe, follow.
ПОСЛЫ́ШАННЫЙ; послы́шан, —а,
—о, —ы (ppp), see послы́шу.
ПОСЛЫ́ШАТ, see послы́шу.
ПОСЛЫ́ШИШЬ, see послы́шу.
ПОСЛЫ́ШУ, послы́шишь. Р. Послы́-
шать (arch.) (acc.). I. Слы́шать. To
hear.
ПОСЛЫ́ШЬ, see послы́шу.
ПОСМО́ТРЕННЫЙ; посмо́трен, —а,
—о, —ы (ppp), see посмотрю́.
ПОСМОТРИ́ (imp.), see посмотрю́.
ПОСМО́ТРИШЬ, see посмотрю́.
ПОСМОТРЮ́, посмо́тришь. Р. По-

смотре́ть. I. Смотре́ть (mean. 1 thru
6). 1. (lit. and fig.) To look (at) (на
+ acc.). 2. To look through (as a
book) (acc.). 3. To look after (as a
child) (за + inst.). 4. To examine,
look at closely (acc.). 5. To look
through, into, out (as a window) (в
+ acc.). 6. To see, watch (as a play)
(acc.). 7. (fig.) To see (e.g., "we will
see").
ПОСМО́ТРЯТ, see посмотрю́.
ПОСОБЛЮ́, пособи́шь. Р. Пособи́ть
(dat.). I. Пособля́ть. To help, assist.
ПОСО́ВЕСТИСЬ (imp.), see посо́ве-
щусь.
ПОСО́ВЕЩУСЬ, посо́вестишься. Р.
Посо́веститься (intr.). I. Со́ве-
ститься. To be ashamed (of) (gen.) or
(+ inf.).
ПОСО́Х, посо́хла (past). Р. Посо́хнуть
(intr.). 1. To wither, dry up (of
flowers, etc.). 2. (fig.) To wither, fade
(of people).
ПОСПАДЁШЬ, see поспаду́.
ПОСПАДИ́ (imp.), see поспаду́.
ПОСПАДУ́, поспадёшь. Р. Поспа́сть
(intr.). 1. To lose (weight) (с + те́ла)
(с + лица́) (в + те́ле). 2. To lose
(one's voice) (с + го́лоса). 3. To
abate, decrease, fall a little (3rd pers.)
ПОСПА́Л[1], поспа́ла (past), see по-
спаду́.
ПОСПА́Л[2], поспала́, поспа́ло, поспа́ли
(past), see посплю́.
ПОСПИ́ (imp.), see посплю́.
ПОСПИ́ШЬ, see посплю́.
ПОСПЛЮ́, поспи́шь. Р. Поспа́ть
(intr.). 1. To sleep a little while.
2. To take a nap.
ПОСПЯ́Т, see посплю́.
ПОСРАМЛЁННЫЙ; посрамлён, —а́,
—о́, —ы́ (ppp), see посрамлю́.
ПОСРАМЛЮ́, посрами́шь. Р. Посра-
ми́ть (acc.). I. Посрамля́ть. 1. To
disgrace. 2. To shame.
ПОСТА́ВЛЕННЫЙ; поста́влен, —а,
—о, —ы (ppp), see поста́влю[1] and [2].
ПОСТА́ВЛЮ[1], поста́вишь. Р. По-
ста́вить (acc.). I. Ста́вить. 1. (lit. and
fig.) To place, put, set. 2. To erect,
raise, install, mount. 3. To organize,
regulate. 4. To produce, stage, put on
(as a play). 5. To raise, ask, put (as a
question, a problem, etc.). 6. To conduct (as an experiment). 7. To regard,
value, consider (as s.t. the equal of

s.t. else, etc.). 8. To bet, stake. (For other lit. and fig. meanings see unabridged dictionary.).

ПОСТА́ВЛЮ[2], поста́вишь. Р. Поста́вить (acc. + dat.). I. Поставля́ть. To supply, deliver, furnish (e.g., s.t. to s.o.).

ПОСТА́ВЬ (imp.), see поста́влю[1] and [2].

ПОСТАНО́ВЛЕННЫЙ; постано́влен, —а, —о, —ы (ppp), see постановлю́.

ПОСТАНОВЛЮ́, постано́вишь. Р. Постанови́ть (acc.). I. Постановля́ть. To resolve, decide, decree, stipulate, establish.

ПОСТЕ́ЛЕННЫЙ; посте́лен, —а, —о, —ы (ppp), see постелю́.

ПОСТЕ́ЛЕШЬ, see постелю́.

ПОСТЕЛИ́ (imp.), see постелю́.

ПОСТЕЛЮ́, посте́лешь. Р. Постла́ть and постели́ть (acc.). I. Стлать, стели́ть. 1. To spread (as a tablecloth, a layer of s.t., etc.). 2. To make or spread (as a bed).

ПОСТИ́Г (and arch. пости́гнул), пости́гла (past), see пости́гну.

ПОСТИ́ГНЕШЬ, see пости́гну.

ПОСТИ́ГНИ (imp.), see пости́гну.

ПОСТИ́ГНУ, пости́гнешь. Р. Пости́чь (acc.), пости́гнуть. I. Постига́ть. 1. To comprehend, understand. 2. To befall, overtake (as fortune, etc., befalls one).

ПОСТИ́ГНУТЫЙ; пости́гнут, —а, —о, —ы (ppp), see пости́гну.

ПО́СТЛАННЫЙ; по́стлан, —а, —о, —ы (ppp), see постелю́.

ПОСТО́ИШЬ, see постою́.

ПОСТО́Й (imp.), see постою́.

ПОСТОЮ́, постои́шь. Р. Постоя́ть. 1. To stand or stay for a while (intr.). 2. To stand up for (as one's friend, country (за + acc.). 3. To wait a bit (intr.). 4. (With neg. particle не + постои́ть + за + inst.). Not to stint on, not to begrudge (s.t.).

ПОСТОЯ́Т, see постою́.

ПОСТРИ́Г, постри́гла (past), see постригу́.

ПОСТРИГИ́ (imp.), see постригу́.

ПОСТРИГУ́, пострижёшь, постригу́т. Р. Постри́чь (acc.). I. Острига́ть (mean. 2). 1. To cut (hair). 2. To make, consecrate (a monk).

ПОСТРИ́ЖЕННЫЙ; постри́жен, —а, —о, —ы (ppp), see постригу́.

ПОСТРИЖЁШЬ, see постригу́.

ПОСТУПЛЮ́, посту́пишь. Р. Поступи́ть. I. Поступа́ть. 1. To act, conduct or behave oneself (intr.). 2. To enroll (in), enter (as a college, army, etc.) (в + acc.). 3. To start work (as in a factory) (на + acc.), (in an office) (в + acc.). 4. To deal or treat (with s.o. or s.t.) (с + inst.). 5. To come in, be received, arrive (somewhere) (of payments, complaints, law suits, etc.) (в + acc.). 6. (tech.) To enter (as oil enters a pipeline, etc.) (в + acc.). 7. To go (as on sale, into production, etc.) (в + acc.).

ПОСТУЧА́Т, see постучу́.

ПОСТУЧИ́ (imp.), see постучу́.

ПОСТУЧИ́ШЬ, see постучу́.

ПОСТУЧУ́, постучи́шь. Р. Постуча́ть (intr.). I. Стуча́ть (mean. 2). 1. To knock, rap, tap a while. 2. To knock, rap (on a door, window, etc.) (в + acc.).

ПОСТЫЖЁННЫЙ; постыжён, —а́, —о́, —ы́ (ppp), see постыжу́.

ПОСТЫЖУ́, постыди́шь. Р. Постыди́ть (acc.). 1. To shame (s.o.) a little, make (s.o.) a little ashamed. 2. (arch.) To disgrace.

ПОСУДИ́ (imp.), see посужу́.

ПОСУЖУ́, посу́дишь. Р. Посуди́ть. 1. (arch.) To judge (intr.). 2. (imp. form) Think! Judge for yourself (intr.). 3. To consider for a while (acc.) or (о + prep.).

ПОСЫ́ПАННЫЙ; посы́пан, —а, —о, —ы (ppp), see посы́плю.

ПОСЫ́ПЛЕШЬ, see посы́плю.

ПОСЫ́ПЛЮ, посы́плешь. Р. Посыпать. I. Посыпа́ть (mean. 1 and 2). 1. To strew, sprinkle (as with salt, sand, etc.) (acc. + inst.). 2. To pour (e.g., salt in soup) (acc./gen.). 3. To begin to fall, drift down, sift down (of light snow, rain) (intr.) or (impers. + inst. of snow, etc.). 4. (fig.) To pour (as a crowd pours out of a theatre) (intr.). 5. To talk rapidly without stopping (acc./inst.).

ПОСЫ́ПЬ (imp.), see посы́плю.

ПОТЁК, потекла́ (past), see потеку́.

ПОТЕКУ́Т (3rd pers. pl.), see потечёт.

ПОТЁР, потёрла (past), see потру́.

ПОТЕРЕ́В and потёрши (adv. past part.), see потру́.

ПОТЕРПИ́ (imp.), see потерплю́.

ПОТЕ́РПИШЬ, see потерплю́.

ПОТЕРПЛЮ́, потéрпишь. Р. Потер-
пéть. 1. To be patient for a while
(intr.). 2. To bear, endure, tolerate
(acc.). 3. To suffer, experience (as a
loss) (acc.). 4. (arch.) To suffer (for
s.t.) (intr.) (за + acc.).

ПОТЕ́РПЯТ, see потерплю́.

ПОТЁРТЫЙ; потёрт, —а, —о, —ы
(ppp), see потру́.

ПОТЁРШИ and потерёв (adv. past
part.), see потру́.

ПОТЕЧЁТ, потеку́т (3rd pers. only).
Р. Потéчь (intr.). 1. To begin to flow.
2. To begin to leak.

ПОТО́ПЛЕННЫЙ; потóплен, —а,
—о, —ы (ppp), see потоплю́.

ПОТОПЛЮ́, потóпишь. Р. Потопи́ть
(acc.). I. Топи́ть (mean. 1, 2, 3, 4).
1. To sink. 2. To inundate, flood,
submerge. 3. (lit. and fig.) To drown.
4. To ruin (as a business, person, etc.).
5. To heat a while.

ПОТО́ПТАННЫЙ; потóптан, —а,
—о, —ы (ppp), see потопчу́.

ПОТО́ПЧЕШЬ, see потопчу́.

ПОТОПЧИ́ (imp.), see потопчу́.

ПОТОПЧУ́, потóпчешь. Р. Потоп-
тáть. 1. To trample all or many
(acc.). 2. To stamp a while (with feet)
(intr.) (inst.).

ПОТОРО́ПЛЕННЫЙ; поторóплен,
—а, —о, —ы (ppp), see потороплю́.

ПОТОРОПЛЮ́, поторóпишь. Р. Пото-
ропи́ть (acc.). I. Торопи́ть. To
hasten, hurry (s.o. or s.t.).

ПОТРА́ВЛЕННЫЙ; потрáвлен, —а,
—о, —ы (ppp), see потравлю́.

ПОТРАВЛЮ́, потрáвишь. Р. Потра-
ви́ть (acc.). I. Трави́ть (mean. 1).
1. To damage by trampling (as crops).
2. To poison all or many (e.g., rats).
3. To hunt for a while (as wild game,
etc.). 4. To torment, persecute for a
while.

ПОТРА́ТЬ (imp.), see потрáчу.

ПОТРА́ФЛЮ, потрáфишь. Р. Потрá-
фить (intr.). I. Потрафля́ть. To
please, give satisfaction (to) (dat.) or
(на + acc.).

ПОТРА́ФЬ (imp.), see потрáфлю.

ПОТРА́ЧЕННЫЙ; потрáчен, —а,
—о, —ы (ppp), see потрáчу.

ПОТРА́ЧУ, потрáтишь. Р. Потрáтить
(acc.). I. Трáтить. 1. To spend,
expend. 2. To waste.

ПОТРЕБЛЁННЫЙ; потреблён, —á,
—б, —ы́ (ppp), see потреблю́.

ПОТРЕБЛЮ́, потреби́шь. Р. Потре-
би́ть (acc.). I. Потребля́ть. To consume, use.

ПОТРЁПАННЫЙ; потрёпан, —а,
—о, —ы (ppp), see потреплю́.

ПОТРЕ́ПЛЕШЬ, see потреплю́.

ПОТРЕПЛИ́ (imp.), see потреплю́.

ПОТРЕПЛЮ́, потрéплешь. Р. Потре-
пáть (acc.). I. Трепáть. 1. To pull,
tug. 2. To bother, pester. 3. To wear
out, abuse (e.g., clothing). 3. To
blow/toss about (of wind, waves, etc.)
5. To pat (as s.o. on the back) (acc.
+ по + dat.).

ПОТРЁШЬ, see потру́.

ПОТРЕЩА́Т, see потрещу́.

ПОТРЕЩИ́ (imp.), see потрещу́.

ПОТРЕЩИ́ШЬ, see потрещу́.

ПОТРЕЩУ́, потрещи́шь. Р. Потре-
щáть (intr.). 1. To crackle, chatter,
chirp a while. 2. (lit. and fig.) To
chatter a while (of people, machine
guns, etc.).

ПОТРИ́ (imp.), see потру́.

ПОТРУ́, потрёшь. Р. Потерéть (acc.).
1. To rub (irritate). 2. To rub (as with
ointment) (acc. + inst.).

ПОТРУДИ́СЬ (imp.), "Be so kind as to
— — — (+ inf.)" (see потружу́сь).

ПОТРУЖУ́СЬ, потру́дишься. Р. По-
труди́ться (intr.). 1. To spend a while
working. 2. To take pains in doing
(s.t.) (+ inf.). 3. (See потруди́сь for
use of imperative form.)

ПОТРЯ́С, потряслá (past), see потрясу́

ПОТРЯСЁННЫЙ; потрясён, —á, —б,
—ы́ (ppp), see потрясу́.

ПОТРЯСЁШЬ, see потрясу́.

ПОТРЯСИ́ (imp.), see потрясу́.

ПОТРЯСУ́, потрясёшь. Р. Потрясти́.
I. Потрясáть (mean. 1, 2, and 3).
1. (lit. and fig.) To shake (acc.).
2. To brandish (e.g., a sword) (inst.).
3. (fig.) To shock, astound (acc.).
4. To shake a little, shake several
times (acc.).

ПОТУ́ПЛЕННЫЙ; поту́плен, —а,
—о, —ы (ppp), see поту́плю.

ПОТУ́ПЛЮ, поту́пишь. Р. Поту́пить
(acc.). I. Потупля́ть. To drop, lower
(as one's eyes, head, etc.).

ПОТУ́ПЬ (imp.), see поту́плю.

ПОТУ́Х, поту́хла (past). Р. Поту́хнуть
(intr.). I. Ту́хнуть. 1. To go out, die

out (as a fire). 2. (fig.) To die out, vanish.

ПОХИ́ТЬ (imp.), see похи́щу.

ПОХИ́ЩЕННЫЙ; похи́щен, —а, —о, —ы (ppp), see похи́щу.

ПОХИ́ЩУ, похи́тишь. Р. Похи́тить (acc.). I. Похища́ть. 1. To steal. 2. To kidnap, abduct.

ПОХЛОПО́ЧЕШЬ, see похлопочу́.

ПОХЛОПОЧИ́ (imp.), see похлопочу́.

ПОХЛОПОЧУ́, похлопо́чешь. Р. Похлопота́ть (intr.). I. Хлопота́ть (mean. 1, 2). 1. To solicit, seek, try to obtain (s.t.) (e.g., a position) (о + prep.) or (чтобы). 2. To intercede for, try to help (s.o.) (за + acc.) or (о + prep.). 3. To spend a while bustling about.

ПОХОЖУ́[1], похо́дишь. I. Походи́ть (intr.). To resemble (s.o. or s.t.) (на + acc.).

ПОХОЖУ́[2], похо́дишь. Р. Походи́ть (intr.). To walk for a while.

ПОХОХО́ЧЕШЬ, see похохочу́.

ПОХОХОЧИ́ (imp.), see похохочу́.

ПОХОХОЧУ́, похохо́чешь. Р. Похохота́ть (intr.). To laugh a while, a little.

ПО́ЧАТЫЙ; по́чат, —а́, —о, —ы (ppp), see почну́.

ПОЧА́ТЫЙ; поча́т, —а́, —о, —ы (ppp), see почну́.

ПОЧЁЛ, почла́ (past), see почту́[1].

ПОЧЁСАННЫЙ; почёсан, —а, —о, —ы (ppp), see почешу́.

ПОЧЁТШИЙ (pap), see почту́[1].

ПОЧЕ́ШЕШЬ, see почешу́.

ПОЧЕШИ́ (imp.), see почешу́.

ПОЧЕШУ́, поче́шешь. Р. Почеса́ть (acc.). I. Чеса́ть (mean 1 and 2). 1. To scratch (to relieve itch). 2. To comb (as hair). 3. To comb or card (as flax). 4. To scratch/comb/card a while.

ПОЧИ́ЕШЬ, see почи́ю.

ПОЧИ́Й (imp.), see почи́ю.

ПОЧИ́СТИ (imp.), see почи́щу.

ПОЧИ́СТЬ (imp.), see почи́щу.

ПОЧИ́ЩЕННЫЙ; почи́щен, —а, —о, —ы (ppp), see почи́щу.

ПОЧИ́ЩУ, почи́стишь. Р. Почи́стить. I. Чи́стить (mean. 1). 1. To clean. 2. To clean a while.

ПОЧИ́Ю, почи́ешь. Р. Почи́ть (intr.). I. Почива́ть (mean. 1 and 2). 1. To fall asleep. 2. To rest. 3. To die.

ПОЧНЁШЬ, see почну́.

ПОЧНИ́ (imp.), see почну́.

ПОЧНУ́, почнёшь. Р. Поча́ть (arch.). 1. To begin (acc.); begin to (+ inf.). 2. To start to use (to open for the first time) (as a new bottle of wine) (acc.).

ПОЧТЁННЫЙ; почтён, —а́, —о́, —ы́ (ppp), see почту́[1] and [2].

ПОЧТЁШЬ, see почту́[1].

ПОЧТИ́ (imp.), see почту́[1] and [2].

ПОЧТУ́[1], почтёшь. Р. Поче́сть (arch.). I. Почита́ть. 1. To consider (e.g., as one's enemy) (acc. + inst.) or (acc. + за + acc.). 2. To consider (e.g., as necessary to do s.t.) (inst. of necessary + inf.).

ПОЧТУ́[2], почти́шь, почту́т (and почта́т). Р. Почти́ть (acc.). To honor (s.o. with s.t.) (acc. + inst.).

ПОЧТУ́Т, see почту́[1] and [2].

ПОЧТЯ́ (adv. past part.), see почту́[1].

ПОЧТЯ́Т, see почту́[2].

ПОЧУ́ЕШЬ, see почу́ю.

ПОЧУ́Й (imp.), see почу́ю.

ПОЧУ́Ю, почу́ешь. Р. Почу́ять (acc.). I. Чу́ять. 1. To scent, smell (of an animal). 2. (fig.) To sense or feel.

ПОЧУ́ЯННЫЙ; почу́ян, —а, —о, —ы (ppp), see почу́ю.

ПОШЕ́ДШИ and пойдя́ (adv. past part.), see пошёл and пойду́.

ПОШЕ́ДШИЙ (pap), see пошёл and пойду́.

ПОШЕ́Й (imp.), see пошью́.

ПОШЁЛ, пошла́ (past). Р. Пойти́ (intr.). 1. To go; to come. 2. To start, leave (of a train, a person, etc.). 3. To enter (as the army, a school, etc.) (в + acc.). 4. To take after (as one's father) (в + acc.). 5. To begin or start (to do s.t.) (+ inf.). (For multiple lit. and fig. meanings, see unabridged dictionary). (Also see пойду́).

ПОШИ́ТЫЙ; поши́т, —а, —о, —ы (ppp), see пошью́.

ПОШЛА́, пошло́, пошли́ (past), see пошёл and пойду́.

ПОШЛЁШЬ, see пошлю́.

ПОШЛИ́[1] (past), see пошёл and пойду́.

ПОШЛИ́[2] (imp.), see пошлю́.

ПОШЛЮ́, пошлёшь. Р. Посла́ть (acc.). I. Посыла́ть. To send, dispatch (s.o. or s.t.).

ПОШУМИ́ (imp.), see пошумлю́.

ПОШУМИ́ШЬ, see пошумлю́.

ПОШУМЛЮ́, пошуми́шь. Р. Пошуме́ть (intr.). To make some noise, make noise for a while.

ПОШУМЯ́Т, see **пошумлю́.**

ПОШУЧУ́, пошу́тишь. Р. Пошути́ть (intr.). I. **Шути́ть** (mean. 1 thru 3). 1. To joke. 2. To mock, deride (s.o.) (над + inst.). 3. To trifle with,(с + inst.) or (inst.). 4. To joke a while.

ПОШЬЁШЬ, see **пошью́.**

ПОШЬЮ́, пошьёшь. Р. Поши́ть. 1. To sew a while (acc.) or (intr.). 2. To sew (make) (s.t.) (acc.).

ПОЩАЖЁННЫЙ; пощажён, —а́, —б, —ы́ (ppp), see **пощажу́.**

ПОЩАЖУ́, пощади́шь. Р. Пощади́ть (acc.). I. **Щади́ть.** 1. To show compassion, pity for (s.o.) (acc.). 2. To spare (s.o. or s.t.) (acc.). 3. To spare (s.o. or s.t. from s.t.) (acc. + от + gen.).

ПОЩЕКО́ЧЕШЬ, see **пощекочу́.**

ПОЩЕКОЧИ́ (imp.), see **пощекочу́.**

ПОЩЕКОЧУ́, пощеко́чешь. Р. Пощекота́ть. I. **Щекота́ть** (mean. 1 and 2). 1. (lit. and fig.) To tickle (acc.). 2. To have a tickling sensation (as in the throat) (impers. + в + prep.). 3. To tickle a while (acc.).

ПОЩИ́ПАННЫЙ; пощи́пан, —а, —о, —ы (ppp), see **пощиплю́.**

ПОЩИ́ПЛЕШЬ, see **пощиплю́.**

ПОЩИПЛИ́ (imp.), see **пощиплю́.**

ПОЩИПЛЮ́, пощи́плешь. Р. Пощипа́ть (acc.). 1. To nibble a while (as a horse nibbles grass). 2. To pinch. 3. To rob (used humorously). 4. To criticize, scold.

ПОЩУ́СЬ, пости́шься. I. Пости́ться (intr.). 1. To keep the fast. 2. To fast.

ПОЮ́, поёшь. I. Петь. Р. Пропе́ть (mean. 1 and 2), **спеть** (mean. 1 and 2). 1. To sing (intr.). 2. To sing (a song, a part) (acc.). 3. (fig.) To sing of (as one's love, etc.), to glorify, celebrate (acc.). 4. To talk a lot (about), repeat (intr.) (о + prep.).

ПОЯВЛЮ́СЬ, поя́вишься. Р. Появи́ться (intr.). I. **Появля́ться.** 1. To appear, show up, emerge. 2. To arise (as a problem, difficulty, etc.).

ПРА́ВЛЕННЫЙ; пра́влен, —а, —о, —ы (ppp), see **пра́влю.**

ПРА́ВЛЮ, пра́вишь. I. Пра́вить. 1. To govern, rule, direct, administer, manage (inst.). 2. To drive or steer

(as a car, horses, a boat, etc.) (inst.). 3. To make (as a bow to s.o.) (arch.) (acc.). 4. To sharpen (acc.). 5. To straighten, even, level (acc.). 6. To correct (as a mistake, galley proof, etc.) (acc.).

ПРАВЬ (imp.), see **пра́влю.**

ПРЕВЗОЙДЁННЫЙ; превзойдён, —а́, —б, —ы́ (ppp), see **превзойду́.**

ПРЕВЗОЙДЁШЬ, see **превзойду́.**

ПРЕВЗОЙДИ́ (imp.), see **превзойду́.**

ПРЕВЗОЙДУ́, превзойдёшь. Р. Превзойти́ (acc.). I. **Превосходи́ть** (mean. 1 and 2). 1. To excel, exceed (as s.o. in ability) (acc. + inst.) or (acc. + в + prep.). 2. To exceed (as expenditures, estimates, etc.). 3. To master, comprehend.

ПРЕВЗОЙДЯ́ (adv. past part.), see **превзойду́.**

ПРЕВЗОШЕ́ДШИЙ (pap), see **превзойду́.**

ПРЕВЗОШЁЛ, превзошла́ (past), see **превзойду́.**

ПРЕВОЗВЫ́СЬ (imp.), see **превозвы́шу.**

ПРЕВОЗВЫ́ШЕННЫЙ; превозвы́шен, —а, —о, —ы (ppp), see **превозвы́шу.**

ПРЕВОЗВЫ́ШУ, превозвы́сишь. Р. Превозвы́сить (arch.) (acc.). I. **Превозвыша́ть.** To exalt, extol, lavish praise (on).

ПРЕВОЗМО́Г, превозмогла́ (past), see **превозмогу́.**

ПРЕВОЗМОГИ́ (imp.), see **превозмогу́.**

ПРЕВОЗМОГУ́, превозмо́жешь, превозмо́гут. Р. Превозмо́чь (acc.). I. **Превозмога́ть.** To overcome.

ПРЕВОЗМО́ЖЕШЬ, see **превозмогу́.**

ПРЕВОЗНЁС, превознесла́ (past), see **превознесу́.**

ПРЕВОЗНЕСЁННЫЙ; превознесён, —а́, —б, —ы́ (ppp), see **превознесу́.**

ПРЕВОЗНЕСЁШЬ, see **превознесу́.**

ПРЕВОЗНЕСИ́ (imp.), see **превознесу́.**

ПРЕВОЗНЕСУ́, превознесёшь. Р. Превознести́ (acc.). I. **Превозноси́ть.** To lavish praise (on s.o. or s.t.), extol, exalt.

ПРЕВОЗНЕСЯ́ (adv. past part.), see **превознесу́.**

ПРЕВОЗНОШУ́, превозно́сишь. I. Превозноси́ть (acc.). Р. **Превознести́.** To lavish praise (on s.o. or s.t.), extol, exalt.

ПРЕВОСХОЖУ́, превосхо́дишь. I.
Превосходи́ть (acc.). P. Превзойти́.
1. To excel, exceed (as s.o. in ability)
(acc. + inst.) or (acc. + в + prep.).
2. To exceed (as expenditures, estimates, etc.).

ПРЕВРАЩЁННЫЙ; превръщён, —а́,
—ó, —ы́ (ppp), see превращу́.

ПРЕВРАЩУ́, преврати́шь. P. Превра-
ти́ть (acc.). I. Превраща́ть. To convert, turn, change (s.o. or s.t. into
s.o. or s.t.) (acc. + в + acc.).

ПРЕВЫ́СЬ (imp.), see превы́шу.

ПРЕВЫ́ШЕННЫЙ; превы́шен, —а,
—о, —ы (ppp), see превы́шу.

ПРЕВЫ́ШУ, превы́сишь. P. Превы́-
сить (acc.). I. Превыща́ть. To exceed, surpass (as expectations, etc.).

ПРЕГРАЖДЁННЫЙ; прегражден,
—а́, —ó, —ы́ (ppp), see прегражу́.

ПРЕГРАЖУ́, прегради́шь. P. Прегра-
ди́ть (acc.). I. Прегражда́ть. To
interdict, bar, block.

ПРЕДАВА́Й (imp.), see предаю́.

ПРЕДАВА́Я (adv. pres. part.), see
предаю́.

ПРЕДАДИ́М, предади́те, предаду́т
(pl. forms), see предáм.

ПРЕДАЁШЬ, see предаю́.

ПРЕДА́Й (imp.), see предáм.

ПРЕДА́М, преда́шь, преда́ст (sing.
forms). P. Преда́ть (acc.). I. Пре-
дава́ть. 1. To betray. 2. To hand
over, commit to, subject to (acc. +
dat.).

ПРЕ́ДАННЫЙ; пре́дан, —á (and —а),
—о, —ы (ppp), see предáм.

ПРЕДА́СТ, see предáм.

ПРЕДА́ШЬ, see предáм.

ПРЕДАЮ́, предаёшь. I. Предава́ть
(acc.). P. Преда́ть. 1. To betray.
2. To hand over, commit to, subject
to (acc. + dat.).

ПРЕДВИ́ДЕННЫЙ; предви́ден, —а,
—о, —ы (ppp), see предви́жу.

ПРЕДВИ́ДИШЬ, see предви́жу.

ПРЕДВИ́ДЯТ, see предви́жу.

ПРЕДВИ́ЖУ, предви́дишь. I. Пред-
ви́деть (acc.). 1. To foresee. 2. To
conclude, forecast.

ПРЕДВКУШЁННЫЙ; предвкушён,
—а́, —ó, —ы́ (ppp), see предвкушу́.

ПРЕДВКУШУ́, предвку́сишь. P.
Предвкуси́ть (acc.). I. Предвку-
ша́ть. anticipate, look forward to
(usually with pleasure).

ПРЕДВОЗВЕЩЁННЫЙ; предвоз-
вещён, —á, —ó, —ы́ (ppp), see
предвозвещу́.

ПРЕДВОЗВЕЩУ́, предвозвести́шь.
P. Предвозвести́ть (acc.). I. Пред-
возвеща́ть. To foretell, forecast,
predict.

ПРЕДВОСХИ́ЩЕННЫЙ; предвосхи́-
щен, —а, —о, —ы (ppp), see пред-
восхи́щу.

ПРЕДВОСХИ́ЩУ (and предвосхищу́),
предвосхи́тишь. P. Предвосхи́тить
(acc.). I. Предвосхища́ть. To anticipate, foresee.

ПРЕДОСТА́ВЛЕННЫЙ; предоста́в-
лен, —а, —о, —ы (ppp), see
предоста́влю.

ПРЕДОСТА́ВЛЮ, предоста́вишь. P.
Предоста́вить. I. Предоставля́ть.
1. To permit, allow (s.o. to do s.t.)
(dat. + inf.). 2. To give, grant, concede (s.t. to s.o.) (acc. + dat.).

ПРЕДОСТА́ВЬ (imp.), see предо-
ста́влю.

ПРЕДОСТЕРЁГ, предостерегла́ (past),
see предостерегу́.

ПРЕДОСТЕРЕГИ́ (imp.), see предо-
стерегу́.

ПРЕДОСТЕРЕГУ́, предостережёшь,
предостерегу́т. P. Предостере́чь
(acc.). I. Предостерега́ть. 1. To
forewarn (s.o.) (acc.). 2. To warn or
caution (s.o.) against (s.o. or s.t.)
(acc. + от + gen.).

ПРЕДОСТЕРЕЖЁННЫЙ; предо-
стережён, —á, —ó, —ы́ (ppp), see
предостерегу́.

ПРЕДОСТЕРЕЖЁШЬ, see предос-
терегу́.

ПРЕДОТВРАЩЁННЫЙ; предотвра-
щён, —á, —ó, —ы́ (ppp), see
предотвращу́.

ПРЕДОТВРАЩУ́, предотврати́шь. P.
Предотврати́ть (acc.). I. Предот-
враща́ть. To avert, prevent, ward off.

ПРЕДПИ́САННЫЙ; предпи́сан, —а,
—о, —ы (ppp), see предпишу́.

ПРЕДПИ́ШЕШЬ, see придпишу́.

ПРЕДПИШИ́ (imp.), see предпишу́.

ПРЕДПИШУ́, предпи́шешь. P. Пред-
писа́ть. I. Предпи́сывать. 1. To
order (e.g., s.o. to do s.t.) (dat. +
inf.). 2. To prescribe (e.g., a treatment
for s.o.) (dat. + acc.).

ПРЕДПО́СЛАННЫЙ; предпо́слан,
—а, —о, —ы (ppp), see предпошлю́.

ПРЕДПОЧЁЛ, предпочлá (past), see предпочту́.

ПРЕДПОЧЁТШИЙ (pap), see предпочту́.

ПРЕДПОЧТЁННЫЙ; предпочтён, —á, —ó, —ы́ (ppp), see предпочту́.

ПРЕДПОЧТЁШЬ, see предпочту́.

ПРЕДПОЧТИ́ (imp.), see предпоу́ту́.

ПРЕДПОЧТУ́, предпочтёшь. Р. Предпочéсть. I. Предпочитáть. 1. To prefer (as s.t. to s.t. else) (acc. + dat.). 2. To prefer (to do s.t.) (+ inf.).

ПРЕДПОЧТЯ́ (adv. past part.), see предпочту́.

ПРЕДПОШЛЁШЬ, see предпошлю́.

ПРЕДПОШЛИ́ (imp.), see предпошлю́

ПРЕДПОШЛЮ́, предпошлёшь. Р. Предпослáть (acc.). I. Предпосылáть. 1. To provide a preface or introduction (to s.t.) (acc. + dat.). 2. To preface (e.g., a lecture with comments) (acc. of "comments" + dat. of "lecture").

ПРЕДПРИ́МЕШЬ, see предприму́.

ПРЕДПРИМИ́ (imp.), see предприму́.

ПРЕДПРИМУ́, предпри́мешь. Р. Предпринять (acc.). I. Предпринимáть. To undertake, launch (s.t.).

ПРЕДПРИ́НЯТЫЙ; предпри́нят, —á, —о, —ы (ppp), see предприму́.

ПРЕДРЁК, предреклá (past), see предреку́.

ПРЕДРЕКИ́ (imp.), see предреку́.

ПРЕДРЕКУ́, предречёшь, предреку́т. Р. Предрéчь (acc.). I. Предрекáть. To foretell, predict.

ПРЕДРЕЧЁННЫЙ; предречён, —á, —ó, —ы́ (ppp), see предреку́.

ПРЕДРЕЧЁШЬ, see предреку́.

ПРЕДСКÁЖЕШЬ, see предскажу́.

ПРЕДСКАЖИ́ (imp.), see предскажу́.

ПРЕДСКАЖУ́, предскáжешь. Р. Предсказáть (acc.). I. Предскáзывать. 1. To predict, foretell. 2. To forecast.

ПРЕДСКÁЗАННЫЙ; предскáзан, —а, —о, —ы (ppp), see предскажу́.

ПРЕДСТАВÁЙ (imp.), see представáю.

ПРЕДСТАВÁЯ (adv. pres. part.), see представáю.

ПРЕДСТÁВЛЕННЫЙ; предстáвлен, —а, —о, —ы (ppp), see предстáвлю.

ПРЕДСТÁВЛЮ, предстáвишь. Р. Предстáвить (acc.). I. Представлять. 1. To present, offer, submit. 2. To introduce (as s.o. to s.o.) (acc.

+ dat.). 3. To imagine, conceive (s.t.) (acc. + себé). 4. To portray. 5. To recommend (as s.o. for an award) (acc. + к + dat.). (For additional usages see unabridged dictionary.)

ПРЕДСТÁВЬ (imp.), see предстáвлю.

ПРЕДСТАЁШЬ, see представáю.

ПРЕДСТÁНЕШЬ, see предстáну.

ПРЕДСТÁНУ, предстáнешь. Р. Предстáть (intr.). I. Представáть. To appear (before s.o. or s.t.) (пéред + inst.) or (arch.: dat.).

ПРЕДСТÁНЬ (imp.), see предстáну.

ПРЕДСТАЮ́, представáешь. I. Представáть (intr.). Р. Предстáть. To appear (before s.o. or s.t.) (перед + inst.) or (arch.: dat.).

ПРЕДСТОИ́ШЬ, see предстою́.

ПРЕДСТОЙ́ (imp.), see предстою́.

ПРЕДСТОЮ́, предстои́шь. I. Предстоя́ть (intr.). 1. To impend, be imminent. 2. To be faced with, face (as difficulties face one) (dat. of person). 3. (arch.) To stand before, in front of (dat.).

ПРЕДСТОЯ́Т, see предстою́.

ПРЕДУБЕДИ́ШЬ (1st pers. not used). Р. Предубеди́ть (acc.). I. Предубеждáть. To prejudice.

ПРЕДУБЕЖДЁННЫЙ, предубеждён, —á, —ó, —ы́ (ppp), see предубеди́шь.

ПРЕДУВÉДОМЛЕННЫЙ; предувéдомлен, —а, —о, —ы (ppp), see предувéдомлю.

ПРЕДУВÉДОМЛЮ, предувéдомишь. Р. Предувéдомить (acc.). I. Предуведомля́ть. To inform, advise, in advance.

ПРЕДУВÉДОМЬ (imp.), see предувéдомлю.

ПРЕДУПРЕЖДЁННЫЙ; предупреждён, —á, —ó, —ы́ (ppp), see предупрежу́.

ПРЕДУПРЕЖУ́, предупреди́шь. Р. Предупреди́ть (acc.). I. Предупреждáть. 1. To notify in advance. 2. To forewarn. 3. To avert, prevent. 4. To anticipate (forestall).

ПРЕДУСМÓТРЕННЫЙ; предусмóтрен, —а, —о, —ы (ppp), see предусмотрю́.

ПРЕДУСМОТРИ́ (imp.), see предусмотрю́.

ПРЕДУСМÓТРИШЬ, see предусмотрю́.

ПРЕДУСМОТРЮ, предусмо́тришь. Р.
Предусмотре́ть (acc.). I. Преду-
сма́тривать. 1. To foresee, envisage.
2. To make provision for, stipulate
(s.t.) (as in the terms of an agreement).
ПРЕДУСМО́ТРЯТ, see предусмотрю́.
ПРЕД’Я́ВЛЕННЫЙ; пред’я́влен, —а,
—о, —ы (ppp), see пред’явлю́.
ПРЕД’ЯВЛЮ́, пред’я́вишь. Р. Пред’я
ви́ть (acc.). I. Пред’явля́ть. 1. To
produce or show (as tickets). 2. To
institute, bring (as a charge, legal
action, claim, etc.).
ПРЕЗРЕ́ННЫЙ; презре́н, —а́, —о́,
—ы́ (ppp), see презрю́.
ПРЕ́ЗРЕННЫЙ; пре́зрен, —а, —о,
—ы (ppp), see презрю́.
ПРЕЗРИ́ (imp.), see презрю́.
ПРЕЗРИ́ШЬ, see презрю́.
ПРЕЗРЮ́, презри́шь. Р. Презре́ть
(acc.). I. Презира́ть. 1. To disdain,
hold in contempt, despise, (e.g., a
person). 2. To disdain (e.g., danger).
ПРЕЗРЯ́Т, see презрю́.
ПРЕКОСЛО́ВЛЮ, прекосло́вишь. I.
Прекосло́вить (dat.). To contradict.
ПРЕКОСЛО́ВЬ (imp.), see прекосло́в-
лю.
ПРЕКРАЩЁННЫЙ; прекращён, —а́,
—о́, —ы́ (ppp), see прекращу́.
ПРЕКРАЩУ́, прекрати́шь. Р. Пре-
крати́ть. I. Прекраща́ть. 1. To stop,
cease (s.t. or doing s.t.) (acc.) or
(+ inf.). 2. To terminate (s.t.) (acc.).
ПРЕЛОМЛЁННЫЙ; преломлён, —а́,
—о́, —ы́ (ppp), see преломлю́.
ПРЕЛОМЛЮ́, прело́мишь. Р. Пре-
ломи́ть (acc.). I. Преломля́ть. 1. To
refract (as light rays). 2. To deflect,
diffract. 3. (arch.) To break in two.
4. To interpret (e.g., thoughts, ideas,
etc.).
ПРЕЛЬЩЁННЫЙ; прельщён, —а́,
—о́, —ы́ (ppp), see прельщу́.
ПРЕЛЬЩУ́, прельсти́шь. Р. Пре-
льсти́ть (acc.). I. Прельща́ть. To
lure, entice, attract (as s.o. with s.t.)
(acc. + inst.).
ПРЕНЕБРЁГ, пренебрегла́ (past), see
пренебрегу́.
ПРЕНЕБРЕГИ́ (imp.), see пренебрегу́.
ПРЕНЕБРЕГУ́, пренебрежёшь, пре-
небрегу́т. Р. Пренебре́чь. I. Пре-
небрега́ть. 1. To neglect, ignore,

disregard (inst.); (arch.) (acc.) or
(+ inf.). 2. To disdain, scorn (inst.).
ПРЕНЕБРЕЖЁННЫЙ; пренебрежён,
—а́, —о́, —ы́ (ppp), see пренебрегу́.
ПРЕНЕБРЕЖЁШЬ, see пренебрегу́.
ПРЕОБРАЖЁННЫЙ; преображён,
—а́, —о́, —ы́ (ppp), see преображу́.
ПРЕОБРАЖУ́, преобрази́шь. Р. Пре-
образи́ть (acc.). I. Преобража́ть. To
transform, convert, change.
ПРЕПОДАВА́Й (imp.), see преподаю́.
ПРЕПОДАВА́Я (adv. pres. part.), see
преподаю́.
ПРЕПОДАДИ́М, преподади́те, препо-
даду́т (pl. forms), see препода́м.
ПРЕПОДАЁШЬ, see преподаю́.
ПРЕПОДА́Й (imp.), see препода́м.
ПРЕПОДА́М, препода́шь, препода́ст
(sing. forms). Р. Препода́ть (acc.).
I. Преподава́ть. To give (as advice,
a lesson to s.o.) (acc. of advice, etc.
+ dat.).
ПРЕПО́ДАННЫЙ; препо́дан, —а́ (and
—а), —о, —ы (ppp), see препода́м.
ПРЕПОДА́СТ, see препода́м.
ПРЕПОДА́ШЬ, see препода́м.
ПРЕПОДАЮ́, преподаёшь. I. Препо-
дава́ть. Р. Препода́ть (mean. 4 only).
1. To teach (a subject) (acc.). 2. To
teach (a subject to s.o.) (acc. + dat.).
3. To teach (intr.). 4. To give (as
advice, a lesson to s.o.) (acc. +
dat.).
ПРЕПОДНЁС, преподнесла́ (past), see
преподнесу́.
ПРЕПОДНЕСЁННЫЙ; преподнесён,
—а́, —о́, —ы́ (ppp), see преподнесу́.
ПРЕПОДНЕСЁШЬ, see преподнесу́.
ПРЕПОДНЕСИ́ (imp.), see преподнесу́
ПРЕПОДНЕСУ́, преподнесёшь. Р.
Преподнести́ (acc.). I. Препод-
носи́ть. 1. To present (s.t. to s.o.) (as
a gift). 2. To present (e.g., facts,
data, etc.). 3. To bring, bear (usually
unexpected, unpleasant news, etc.).
ПРЕПОДНЕСЯ́ (adv. past. part.), see
преподнесу́.
ПРЕПОДНОШУ́, преподно́сишь. I.
Преподноси́ть (acc.). Р. Препод-
нести́. 1. To present (s.t. to s.o.) (as
a gift). 2. To present (e.g., facts, data,
etc.). 3. To bring, bear (usually unexpected, unpleasant news, etc.).
ПРЕПОЯ́САННЫЙ; препоя́сан, —а,
—о, —ы (ppp), see препоя́шу.
ПРЕПОЯ́ШЕШЬ, see препоя́шу.

ПРЕПОЯ́ШУ, препоя́шешь. Р. Препоя́сать (arch.) (acc.). I. Препоя́сывать. To girdle, gird (s.t. with s.t.) (acc. + inst.).

ПРЕПОЯ́ШЬ (imp.), see препоя́шу.

ПРЕПРОВОЖДЁННЫЙ; препровожд̀ён, —а́, —о́, —ы́ (ppp), see препровожу́.

ПРЕПРОВОЖУ́, препрводи́шь. Р. Препроводи́ть (acc.). I. Препровожда́ть. 1. To forward, dispatch, send, convey. 2. To conduct, take. 3. (arch.) To spend (time).

ПРЕ́РВАННЫЙ; пре́рван, —а, —о, —ы (ppp), see прерву́.

ПРЕРВЁШЬ, see прерву́.

ПРЕРВИ́ (imp.), see прерву́.

ПРЕРВУ́, прервёшь. Р. Прерва́ть (acc.). I. Прерыва́ть. 1. To stop, halt, break off (as work, talks, etc.). 2. To interrupt (as s.o., s.o.'s speech, etc.).

ПРЕСЁК, пресекла́ (пресёкла) (past), see пресеку́.

ПРЕСЕКИ́ (imp.), see пресеку́.

ПРЕСЕКУ́, пресечёшь, пресеку́т. Р. Пресе́чь (acc.). I. Пресека́ть. 1. To stop (s.t.) sharply and/or forcefully, cut short, suppress. 2. To interrupt. 3. (arch.) To cut off, interdict (as a route).

ПРЕСЕЧЁННЫЙ; пресечён, —а́, —о́, —ы́ (ppp), see пресеку́.

ПРЕСЕЧЁШЬ, see пресеку́.

ПРЕСТА́ВЛЮСЬ, преста́вишься. Р. Преста́виться (intr.) (arch.). To pass away, die.

ПРЕСТА́ВЬСЯ (imp.), see преста́влюсь.

ПРЕСТУ́ПЛЕННЫЙ; престу́плен, —а, —о, —ы (ppp), see преступлю́.

ПРЕСТУПЛЮ́, престу́пишь. Р. Преступи́ть (acc.). I. Преступа́ть. 1. To transgress (e.g., boundaries). 2. To violate or break (as a law). 3. (arch.) To step across.

ПРЕСЫ́ТИТЬ (imp.), see пресы́щу.

ПРЕСЫ́ЩЕННЫЙ; пресы́щен, —а, —о, —ы (ppp), see пресы́щу.

ПРЕСЫ́ЩУ, пресы́тишь. Р. Пресы́тить (acc.). I. Пресыща́ть. 1. To satiate, surfeit (s.o. with s.t.) (acc. + inst.). 2. (tech.) To supersaturate. 3. (tech.) To surcharge.

ПРЕТЕРПЁННЫЙ; претерпён, —а́, —о́, —ы́ (ppp), see претерплю́.

ПРЕТЕ́РПЕННЫЙ; прете́рпен, —а, —о, —ы (ppp), see претерплю́.

ПРЕТЕРПИ́ (imp.), see претерплю́.

ПРЕТЕ́РПИШЬ, see претерплю́.

ПРЕТЕРПЛЮ́, прете́рпишь. Р. Претерпе́ть (acc.). I. Претерпева́ть. 1. To endure, suffer (as hardship). 2. To undergo (as change).

ПРЕТЕ́РПЯТ, see претерплю́.

ПРЁШЬ (2nd pers. sing.). I. Пере́ть. 1. To go on, push on, press on (intr.). 2. To press against (as s.o.'s back) (в + acc.). 3. To carry, drag, pull (acc.). 4. (lit. and fig.) To become apparent, stick out (3rd pers. only) (intr.). 5. To steal, pilfer (acc.) or (intr.). (Also see пру.)

ПРИ (imp.), see прёшь and пру.

ПРИБА́ВЛЕННЫЙ; приба́влен, —а, —о, —ы (ppp), see приба́влю.

ПРИБА́ВЛЮ, приба́вишь. Р. Приба́вить. I. Прибавля́ть. 1. To add (s.t.) (acc./gen.). 2. To increase (e.g., speed, pay, etc.) (gen.). 3. To make wider, longer, etc. (of clothes, e.g., in the shoulders) (в + prep.). 4. To gain (weight) (в + prep.). 5. To exaggerate (in speaking) (intr.).

ПРИБА́ВЬ (imp.), see приба́влю.

ПРИБЕ́Г (and прибе́гнул), прибе́гла (past). Р. Прибе́гнуть (intr.). I. Прибега́ть. To resort to, turn to, have recourse to (s.o. or s.t.) (к + dat.).

ПРИБЕГИ́ (imp.), see прибегу́.

ПРИБЕГУ́, прибежи́шь, прибегу́т. Р. Прибежа́ть (intr.). I. Прибега́ть. To come running.

ПРИБЕЖИ́ШЬ, see прибегу́.

ПРИБЕ́Й (imp.), see прибью́.

ПРИБЕРЁГ, приберегла́ (past), see приберегу́.

ПРИБЕРЕГИ́ (imp.), see приберегу́.

ПРИБЕРЕГУ́, прибережёшь, приберегу́т. Р. Пребере́чь (acc./gen.). I. Прибере́гать. To save up, reserve, preserve (as s.t. for some purpose).

ПРИБЕРЕЖЁННЫЙ; прибережён, —а́, —о́, —ы́ (ppp), see приберегу́.

ПРИБЕРЕЖЁШЬ, see приберегу́.

ПРИБЕРЁШЬ, see приберу́.

ПРИБЕРИ́ (imp.), see приберу́.

ПРИБЕРУ́, приберёшь. Р. Прибра́ть. I. Прибира́ть. 1. To tidy up, put in order (as a room) (intr.) or (acc.). 2. To put away (e.g., books, one's clothes, etc.) (acc.). 3. To acquire (acc.). 4. (arch.) To find (s.t. appropriate, proper, fitting, etc.) (acc.).

ПРИБЍТЫЙ; приби́т, —а, —о, —ы (ppp), see **прибью́**.

ПРИБЛИ́ЖЕННЫЙ; прибли́жен, —а, —о, —ы (ppp), see **прибли́жу**.

ПРИБЛИ́ЖУ, прибли́зишь. Р. Прибли́зить (acc.). I. Приближа́ть. 1. (lit. and fig.) To bring nearer, closer. 2. To shorten (as time of delivery.

ПРИБЛИ́ЗЬ, see **прибли́жу**.

ПРИ́БРАННЫЙ; при́бран, —а́ (and —а), —о, —ы (ppp), see **прибе́ру́**.

ПРИБРЕДЁШЬ, see **прибреду́**.

ПРИБРЕДИ́ (imp.), see **прибреду́**.

ПРИБРЕДУ́, прибредёшь. Р. Прибрести́ (intr.). To wander up, come trudging up (to some place).

ПРИБРЕ́ДШИЙ (pap), see **пребреду́**.

ПРИБРЕДЯ́ (adv. past part.), see **прибреду́**.

ПРИБРЁЛ, прибрела́ (past), see **прибреду́**.

ПРИБУ́ДЕШЬ, see **прибу́ду**.

ПРИБУ́ДУ, прибу́дешь. Р. Прибы́ть. I. Прибыва́ть. 1. To arrive (intr.). 2. To rise (e.g., water) (intr.). 3. To increase (intr.) or (impers.). 4. To wax (of the moon) (intr.).

ПРИБУ́ДЬ (imp.), see **прибу́ду**.

ПРИБЬЁШЬ, see **прибью́**.

ПРИБЬЮ́, прибьёшь. Р. Приби́ть (acc.). I. Прибива́ть (mean. 1 thru 3). 1. To nail (acc.). 2. To lay, flatten (as rain lays dust, flattens grain, etc.) (acc.). 3. To wash up, throw up (as waves wash a boat up on the shore) (often impers. + acc. of boat + inst. of waves). 4. To beat (as a child) (acc.).

ПРИБА́ДЬ (imp.), see **прива́жу**.

ПРИВА́ЖЕННЫЙ; прива́жен, —а, —о, —ы (ppp), see **прива́жу**.

ПРИВА́ЖУ, прива́дишь. Р. Прива́дить (acc.). I. Прива́живать. 1. To lure (as birds with bait). 2. To win over (s.o. or s.t.).

ПРИВЕДЁННЫЙ; приведён, —а́, —о́, —ы́ (ppp), see **приведу́**.

ПРИВЕДЁШЬ, see **приведу́**.

ПРИВЕДИ́ (imp.), see **приведу́**.

ПРИВЕДУ́, приведёшь. Р. Привести́. I. Приводи́ть. 1. To bring, lead (acc.). 2. To cite, quote (acc.). 3. (fig.) To

lead to, result in (e.g., a conclusion) (intr.) (к + dat.). 4. (fig.) To lead to (in the sense of to cause, e.g., delight, rage, etc.) (acc. + в + acc.). 5. (math.) To reduce (s.t. to s.t.) (acc. + к + dat.).

ПРИВЕ́ДШИЙ (pap), see **приведу́**.

ПРИВЕДЯ́ (adv. past part.), see **приведу́**.

ПРИВЁЗ, привезла́ (past), see **привезу́**.

ПРИВЕЗЁННЫЙ; привезён, —а́, —о́, —ы́ (ppp), see **привезу́**.

ПРИВЕЗЁШЬ, see **привезу́**.

ПРИВЕЗИ́ (imp.), see **привезу́**.

ПРИВЕЗУ́, привезёшь. Р. Привезти́ (acc.). I. Привози́ть. To bring (by conveyance).

ПРИВЕЗЯ́ (adv. past part.), see **привезу́**.

ПРИВЕ́Й (imp.), see **привью́**.

ПРИВЁЛ, привела́ (past), see **приведу́**.

ПРИВЕРТИ́ (imp.), see **приверчу́**.

ПРИВЕ́РТИШЬ, see **приверчу́**.

ПРИВЕ́РТЯТ, see **приверчу́**.

ПРИВЕ́РЧЕННЫЙ; приве́рчен, —а, —о, —ы (ppp), see **приверчу́**.

ПРИВЕРЧУ́, приве́ртишь. Р. Приверте́ть (acc.). I. Привёртывать. 1. To screw down or on, tighten. 2. To clamp.

ПРИВЕ́СЬ (imp.), see **приве́шу**.

ПРИВЕ́ШЕННЫЙ; приве́шен, —а, —о, —ы (ppp), see **приве́шу**.

ПРИВЕ́ШУ, приве́сишь. Р. Приве́сить. I. Приве́шивать. 1. To suspend, hang up (acc.). 2. To add (s.t.) to increase the weight (e.g., sugar, etc.) (acc./gen.).

ПРИВИ́ДИШЬСЯ, see **привижу́сь**.

ПРИВИ́ДЯТСЯ, see **привижу́сь**.

ПРИВИЖУ́СЬ, приви́дишься. Р. Приви́деться (intr.). I. Ви́деться (lit. and fig.) To dream (dat. of person + сон) or (dat. of person + impers. form of verb + во + сне).

ПРИВИ́НЧЕННЫЙ; приви́нчен, —а, —о, —ы (ppp), see **привинчу́**.

ПРИВИНЧУ́, привинти́шь. Р. Привинти́ть (acc.). I. Приви́нчивать. To screw (s.t.) on or to (s.t.) (acc. + к + dat.).

ПРИВИ́ТЫЙ (and привито́й), приви́т, —а́ (and —а) —о, —ы (ppp), see **привью́**.

ПРИВЛЁК

ПРИВЛЁК, привлекла́ (past), see привлеку́.
ПРИВЛЕКИ́ (imp.), see привлеку́.
ПРИВЛЕКУ́, привлечёшь, привлеку́т. Р. Привле́чь (acc.). I. Привлека́ть. 1. To draw, pull, take (by physical force). 2. To attract, draw (e.g., attention). 3. To enlist (e.g., s.o., s.o.'s help, etc.). 4. To compel (s.o.) to appear (somewhere) (e.g., bring to trial) (acc. + к + dat.)
ПРИВЛЕЧЁННЫЙ; привлечён, —а́, —о́, —ы́ (ppp), see привлеку́.
ПРИВЛЕЧЁШЬ, see привлеку́.
ПРИВНЁС, привнесла́ (past), see привнесу́.
ПРИВНЕСЁННЫЙ; привнесён, —а́, —о́, —ы́ (ppp), see привнесу́.
ПРИВНЕСЁШЬ, see привнесу́.
ПРИВНЕСИ́ (imp.), see привнесу́.
ПРИВНЕСУ́, привнесёшь. Р. Привнести́ (acc.). I. Привноси́ть. To introduce (as s.t. additional to a tale, etc.) (acc. + в + acc.).
ПРИВНЕСЯ́ (adv. past part.), see привнесу́.
ПРИВНОШУ́, приво́сишь. I. Привноси́ть (acc.). Р. Привнести́. To introduce (as s.t. additional to a tale, etc.) (acc. + в + acc.).
ПРИВОЖУ́[1], приво́зишь. I. Привози́ть (acc.). Р. Привезти́. To bring (by conveyance).
ПРИВОЖУ́[2], приво́дишь. I. Приводи́ть. Р. Привести́. 1. To bring, lead (acc.). 2. To cite, quote (acc.). 3. (fig.) To lead to, result in (e.g., a conclusion) (intr.) (к + dat.). 4. (fig.) To lead to (in the sense of to cause, e.g., delight, rage, etc.) (acc. + в + acc.). 5. (math.) To reduce (s.t. to s.t.) (acc. + к + dat.).
ПРИВОЛО́К, приволокла́ (past), see приволоку́.
ПРИВОЛОКИ́ (imp.), see приволоку́.
ПРИВОЛОКУ́, приволочёшь, приволоку́т. Р. Приволо́чь (acc.). I. привола́киватв To bring, drag (s.t. or s.o. to someplace).
ПРИВОЛОЧА́ (adv. past part.), see приволоку́.
ПРИВОЛОЧЁННЫЙ; приволочён, —а́, —о́, —ы́ (ppp), see приволоку́.
ПРИВОЛО́ЧЕННЫЙ; приволо́чен, —а, —о, —ы (ppp), see приволоку́.
ПРИВОЛОЧЁШЬ, see приволоку́.

ПРИ́ВРАННЫЙ; при́вран, —а́, (and —а) —о, —ы (ppp), see привру́.
ПРИВРЁШЬ, see привру́.
ПРИВРИ́ (imp.), see привру́.
ПРИВРУ́, приврёшь. Р. Привра́ть. I. Привира́ть. 1. To tell white lies, fib (intr.). 2. To lie or fib about, exaggerate (e.g., details, etc.) in relating (s.t.) (acc. of s.t.).
ПРИВСТАВА́Й (imp.), see привстаю́.
ПРИВСТАВА́Я (adv. pres. part.), see привстаю́.
ПРИВСТА́ЕШЬ, see привстаю́.
ПРИВСТА́НЕШЬ, see привста́ну.
ПРИВСТА́НУ, привста́нешь. Р. Привста́ть (intr.). I. Привстава́ть. To rise, stand up.
ПРИВСТА́НЬ (imp.), see привста́ну.
ПРИВСТАЮ́, привстаёшь. I. Привстава́ть (intr.). Р. Привста́ть. To rise, stand up.
ПРИВЫ́К, привы́кла (past). Р. Привы́кнуть (intr.). I. Привыка́ть. 1. To become accustomed (to s.o. or s.t.) (к + dat.). 2. To become accustomed (to doing s.t.) (+ inf.).
ПРИВЬЁШЬ, see привью.
ПРИВЬЮ, привьёшь. Р. Приви́ть (acc.). I. Привива́ть. 1. To graft (as s.t. to a plant) (acc. + на + acc.) or (acc. + к + dat.). 2. To acclimatize (as a plant) (acc.). 3. To innoculate, vaccinate (s.o. with s.t.) (dat. of s.o. + acc. of s.t.). 4. To inculcate (as habits in s.o.) (dat. of s.o. + acc. of habits). 5. To splice (as a rope).
ПРИВЯ́ЖЕШЬ, see привяжу́.
ПРИВЯЖИ́ (imp.), see прувяжу́.
ПРИВЯЖУ́, привя́жешь. Р. Привяза́ть (acc.). I. Привя́зывать. 1. (lit. and fig.) To tie, fasten, tether (to s.t.) (acc. + к + dat.). 2. To inspire (s.o.) with an affectionate regard or attachment (to s.t. or s.o.) (acc. + к + dat.). 3. To tie in, connect, correlate (e.g., a survey, data, etc., to s.t.) (acc. + к + dat.).
ПРИВЯ́ЗАННЫЙ; привя́зан, —а, —о, —ы (ppp), see привяжу́.
ПРИГВОЖДЁННЫЙ; пригвождён, —а́, —о́, —ы́ (ppp), see пригвозжу́.
ПРИГВОЗЖУ́, пригвозди́шь. Р. Пригвозди́ть. I. Пригвожда́ть. 1. To nail (s.t. to s.t.) (acc. + к + dat.) or (acc. + на + prep.). 2. (fig.) To pin,

spit, skewer (as s.o. to the wall with a dagger) (acc. + к + dat.). 3. (fig.) To pin (as troops to the ground with rifle fire) (acc. + к + dat.). 4. (fig.) To pin, freeze (as s.o. with a glance) (acc. + inst.).

ПРИГЛА́ДЬ (imp.), see пригла́жу.

ПРИГЛА́ЖЕННЫЙ; пригла́жен, —а, —о, —ы (ppp), see пригла́жу.

ПРИГЛА́ЖУ, пригла́дишь. Р. Пригла́дить (acc.). I. Пригла́живать. 1. To smooth (e.g., one's hair). 2. (fig.) To smooth out (e.g., a speech, an article, etc.).

ПРИГЛАШЁННЫЙ; приглашён, —а́, —о́, —ы́ (ppp), see приглашу́.

ПРИГЛАШУ́, пригласи́шь. Р. Пригласи́ть (acc.). I. Приглаша́ть. 1. To invite (e.g., s.o. to dinner) (acc. + на + acc.). 2. To hire (e.g., s.o. to work in a factory) (acc. + на + acc.) (in an office) (acc. + в + acc.). 3. To call (as a doctor).

ПРИГЛЯДИ́ (imp.), see пригляжу́.

ПРИГЛЯДИ́ШЬ, see пригляжу́.

ПРИГЛЯ́Т, see пригляжу́.

ПРИГЛЯЖУ́, пригляди́шь. Р. Пригляде́ть. I. Пригля́дывать. 1. To look after (e.g., children) (за + inst.). 2. To look for and find (acc.).

ПРИ́ГНАННЫЙ; при́гнан, —а, —о, —ы (ppp), see пригоню́.

ПРИГОЖУ́СЬ, пригоди́шься. Р. Пригоди́ться (intr.). To be useful, of use (to s.o. or s.t.) (dat.).

ПРИГОЛУ́БЛЕННЫЙ; приголу́блен, —а, —о, —ы (ppp), see приголу́блю.

ПРИГОЛУ́БЛЮ, приголу́бишь. Р. Приголу́бить (acc.). I. Приголу́бливать. To caress, pet.

ПРИГОЛУ́БЬ (imp.), see приголу́блю.

ПРИГОНИ́ (imp.), see пригоню́.

ПРИГО́НИШЬ, see пригоню́.

ПРИГОНЮ́, приго́нишь. Р. Пригна́ть. I. Пригоня́ть (mean. 1, 2). 1. To drive (home) (as cattle) (acc.). 2. To fit, adjust (e.g., a window to a frame) (acc. + к + dat.). 3. To drive up rapidly, rush up (intr.).

ПРИГО́НЯТ, see пригоню́.

ПРИГОРИ́ (imp.), see пригори́т.

ПРИГОРИ́Т, пригоря́т (3rd pers. only). Р. Пригоре́ть (intr.). I. Пригора́ть. 1. To scorch, burn (of food). 2. (fig.) To burn (from heat or drought, said of crops).

ПРИГОРЯ́Т (3rd pers. pl.), see пригори́т.

ПРИГОТО́ВЛЕННЫЙ; приготó́влен, —а, —о, —ы (ppp), see приготовлю́.

ПРИГОТО́ВЛЮ, приготó́вишь. Р. Приготó́вить (acc.). I. Гото́вить, приготовля́ть, приготáвливать. 1. To prepare (s.t.) (acc.). 2. To prepare (s.t. for s.o.) (acc. + dat.). 3. To prepare (s.o. or s.t. for s.t.) (acc. + к + dat.). 4. To cook.

ПРИГОТО́ВЬ (imp.), see приготó́влю.

ПРИГРЁБ, пригребла́ (past), see пригребу́.

ПРИГРЕБЁННЫЙ; пригребён, —а́, —о́, —ы́ (ppp), see пригребу́.

ПРИГРЕБЁШЬ, see пригребу́.

ПРИГРЕБИ́ (imp.), see пригребу́.

ПРИГРЕБУ́, пригребёшь. Р. Пригрести́. I. Пригреба́ть. 1. To rake up and collect (as leaves) (acc.). 2. To row toward (as toward the shore) (intr.) (к + dat.).

ПРИГРОЖУ́, пригрози́шь. Р. Пригрози́ть (dat.). I. Грози́ть. To threaten (s.o. with s.t.) (dat. + inst.).

ПРИГУ́БЛЕННЫЙ; пригу́блен, —а, —о, —ы (ppp), see пригу́блю.

ПРИГУ́БЛЮ, пригу́бишь. Р. Пригу́бить (acc./gen.) or (intr.). To taste, take a sip.

ПРИГУ́БЬ (imp.), see пригу́блю.

ПРИДАВА́Й (imp.), see придаю́.

ПРИДАВА́Я (adv. pres. part.), see придаю́.

ПРИДА́ВЛЕННЫЙ; прида́влен, —а, —о, —ы (ppp), see придавлю́.

ПРИДАВЛЮ́, прида́вишь. Р. Придави́ть (acc.). I. Прида́вливать. 1. To press against, press down. 2. To crush. 3. To depress (e.g., one's spirits). 4. To oppress (e.g., a people).

ПРИДАДИ́М, придади́те, придаду́т (pl. forms), see прида́м.

ПРИДАЁШЬ, see придаю́.

ПРИДА́Й (imp.), see прида́м.

ПРИДА́М, прида́шь, прида́ст (sing. forms). Р. Прида́ть. I. Придава́ть. 1. To add (acc.). 2. To attach (as men to a platoon) (acc. + dat.). 3. To give (e.g., courage, strength, etc. to s.o.) (gen. + dat.). 4. (fig.) To attach, attribute (as importance to s.t.) (acc. + dat.).

ПРИ́ДАННЫЙ; при́дан, —а́, —о, —ы (ppp), see прида́м.

ПРИДА́СТ, see прида́м.

ПРИДА́ШЬ, see прида́м.

ПРИДАЮ́, придаёшь. I. Придава́ть. Р. Прида́ть. 1. To add (acc.). 2. To attach (as men to a platoon) (acc. + dat.). 3. To give (e.g., courage, strength, etc. to s.o.) (gen. + dat.). 4. (fig.) To attach, attribute (as importance to s.t.) (acc. + dat.).

ПРИДЕРЁШЬСЯ, see придеру́сь.

ПРИДЕ́РЖАННЫЙ; приде́ржан, —а, —о, —ы (ppp), see придержу́.

ПРИДЕ́РЖАТ, see придержу́.

ПРИДЕРЖИ́ (imp.), see придержу́.

ПРИДЕ́РЖИШЬ, see придержу́.

ПРИДЕРЖУ́, приде́ржишь. Р. Придержа́ть (acc.). I. Приде́рживать. 1. To hold. 2. To hold back, restrain (e.g., horses). 3. To hold back, withhold.

ПРИДЕРИ́СЬ (imp.), see придеру́сь.

ПРИДЕРУ́СЬ, придерёшься. Р. Придра́ться (intr.). I. Придира́ться. 1. To cavil, find fault (intr.). 2. To cavil at, find fault with (s.o. or s.t.) (к + dat.). 3. To seize upon, take advantage of (as an opportunity, incident, etc.) (к + dat.).

ПРИДЁШЬ, see приду́.

ПРИДИ́ (imp.), see приду́.

ПРИДУ́, придёшь. Р. Прийти́ (intr.). I. Приходи́ть. 1. To come, arrive. 2. To arise, come up. 3. To become (e.g., ecstatic), to find o.s. (in some condition) (e.g., in ecstasy) (в + acc.). 4. (fig.) To arrive (as at some conclusion) (к + dat.).

ПРИДЯ́ (adv. past part.), see приду́.

ПРИЕ́ДЕННЫЙ; прие́ден, —а, —о, —ы (ppp), see прие́м.

ПРИЕ́ДЕШЬ, see прие́ду.

ПРИЕДИ́М, приеди́те, приедя́т (pl. forms), see прие́м.

ПРИЕ́ДУ, прие́дешь. Р. Прие́хать (intr.). I. Приезжа́ть. To arrive, come (by conveyance).

ПРИЕДЯ́ТСЯ (3rd pers. pl.), see прие́стся.

ПРИЕЗЖА́Й (imp.), see прие́ду.

ПРИЕ́Л, прие́ла (past), see прие́м.

ПРИЕ́ЛСЯ, прие́лась (past), see прие́стся.

ПРИЕ́М, прие́шь, прие́ст (sing. forms).

Р. Прие́сть (acc.). I. Приеда́ть. To eat up all (e.g., the food).

ПРИЕ́СТ, see прие́м.

ПРИЕ́СТСЯ, приедя́тся (3rd pers. only). Р. Прие́сться. I. Приеда́ться. 1. To pall (on s.o.) (dat.). 2. To pall (intr.).

ПРИЕ́ШЬ[1] (2nd pers. sing.), see прие́м.

ПРИЕ́ШЬ[2] (imp.), see прие́м.

ПРИЖА́ТЫЙ; прижа́т, —а, —о, —ы (ppp), see прижму́.

ПРИЖГИ́ (imp.), see прижгу́.

ПРИЖГЛА́, прижгло́, прижгли́ (past), see прижёг and прижгу́.

ПРИЖГУ́, прижжёшь, прижгу́т. Р. Приже́чь (acc.). I. Прижига́ть. 1. To cauterize. 2. To burn, scorch (e.g., bread in the oven). 3. To burn slightly (as one's finger).

ПРИЖЁГ, прижгла́ (past), see прижгу́.

ПРИЖЖЁННЫЙ; прижжён, —а́, —о́, —ы́ (ppp), see прижгу́.

ПРИЖЖЁШЬ, see прижгу́.

ПРИЖИВЁШЬ, see приживу́.

ПРИЖИВЁШЬСЯ, see приживу́сь.

ПРИЖИВИ́ (imp.), see приживу́.

ПРИЖИВИ́СЬ (imp.), see приживу́сь.

ПРИЖИВУ́, приживёшь. Р. Прижи́ть (acc.). I. Прижива́ть. To beget, bear (usually a child out of wedlock).

ПРИЖИВУ́СЬ, приживёшься. Р. Прижи́ться (intr.). I. Прижива́ться. 1. To adapt, become accustomed (to) (as climate). 2. (bot.) To take root.

ПРИЖИ́ТЫЙ (and прижито́й); прижи́т, —а́, —о, —ы (ppp), see приживу́.

ПРИ́ЖИТЫЙ; при́жит, —а́, —о, —ы (ppp), see приживу́.

ПРИЖМЁШЬ, see прижму́.

ПРИЖМИ́ (imp.), see прижму́.

ПРИЖМУ́, прижмёшь. Р. Прижа́ть (acc.). I. Прижима́ть. 1. (lit. and fig.) To press, squeeze (e.g., s.o. against s.t.) (acc. + к + dat.). 2. (fig.) To pin down (e.g. the enemy to the ground) (acc. + к + dat.). 3. (fig.) To pin down (as an evasive person). 4. To oppress.

ПРИЗАЙМЁШЬ, see призайму́.

ПРИЗАЙМИ́ (imp.), see призайму́.

ПРИЗАЙМУ́, призаймёшь. Р. Призаня́ть (acc./gen.). I. Призанима́ть. To borrow a small amount (of s.t.), borrow (s.t.) for a short time (acc./gen. of s.t.).

ПРИЗА́НЯТЫЙ; приза́нят, —а́, —о,
—ы (ppp), see призайму́.
ПРИ́ЗВАННЫЙ; при́зван, —а́ (and
—а) —о, —ы (ppp), see призову́.
ПРИЗНАВА́Й (imp.), see признаю́.
ПРИЗНАВА́Я (adv. pres. part.), see
презнаю́.
ПРИЗНАЁШЬ, see признаю́.
ПРИЗНАЮ́, признаёшь. I. При-
знава́ть (acc.). Р. Призна́ть. 1. To
recognize, know (e.g., a friend, etc.).
2. To recognize (e.g., a government,
international law, an ambassador,
state of war or other condition, etc.).
3. To admit, acknowledge (e.g.,
one's guilt); that (что). 4. To consider, acknowledge (e.g., s.o. or s.t.
as a failure) (acc. + inst.). 5. To
diagnose (e.g., a disease, etc.). 6. To
identify (e.g., s.o. or s.t. with s.o.
or s.t.) (acc. + в + prep.) or (acc. +
за + acc.) or (acc. + inst.).
ПРИЗОВЁШЬ, see призову́.
ПРИЗОВИ́ (imp.), see призову́.
ПРИЗОВУ́, призовёшь. Р. Призва́ть
(acc.). I. Призыва́ть. 1. To call,
summon. 2. To call, (s.o. to order,
etc.) (acc. + к + dat.). 3. To call
(e.g., s.o. for help, etc.) (acc. + на +
acc.). 4. To call, draft (e.g., s.o. for
military service) (acc. + на + acc.).
5. To call (s.o. to do s.t.) (acc. +
inf.). 6. (arch.) To call down (as a
curse on s.o.) (acc. + на + acc.).
ПРИ́ЗРЕННЫЙ; при́зрен, —а, —о,
—ы (ppp), see призрю́.
ПРИЗРИ́ (imp.), see призрю́.
ПРИ́ЗРИШЬ, see призрю́.
ПРИЗРЮ́, при́зришь (and призри́шь).
Р. Призре́ть (acc.). I. Призрева́ть.
To support by charity, take care of.
ПРИ́ЗРЯТ, see призрю́.
ПРИИ́СКАННЫЙ; при́искан, —а,
—о, —ы (ppp), see приищу́.
ПРИИ́ЩЕШЬ, see приищу́.
ПРИИЩИ́ (imp.), see приищу́.
ПРИИЩУ́, прии́щешь. Р. Приска́ть
(acc.). I. ПриИ́скивать. To look for
and find.
ПРИКА́ЖЕШЬ, see прикажу́.
ПРИКАЖИ́ (imp.), see прикажу́.
ПРИКАЖУ́, прика́жешь. Р. При-
каза́ть. I. Прика́зывать. 1. To
order, command (as s.o. to do s.t.)
(dat. + inf.). 2. (arch.) To entrust

(s.o. or s.t. to s.o.); to will (s.t. to
s.o.) (acc. + dat.).
ПРИКА́ЗАННЫЙ; прика́зан, —а,
—о, —ы (ppp), see прикажу́.
ПРИКА́ЧЕННЫЙ; прика́чен, —а,
—о, —ы (ppp), see прикачу́.
ПРИКАЧУ́, прика́тишь. Р. При-
кати́ть. I. Прика́тывать. 1. To roll
(s.t.) up (to) (acc. + к + dat.). 2.
To arrive (intr.).
ПРИКИПИ́ (imp.), see прикипи́т.
ПРИКИПИ́Т, прикипя́т (3rd pers.
only). Р. Прикипе́ть (intr.). To
adhere from overboiling (as boiled
milk adheres to the interior of an
utensil) (к + dat.).
ПРИКИПЯ́Т (3rd pers. pl.), see
прикипи́т.
ПРИКО́ЛЕШЬ, see приколю́.
ПРИКОЛИ́ (imp.), see приколю́.
ПРИКО́ЛОТЫЙ; прико́лот, —а, —о,
—ы (ppp), see приколю́.
ПРИКОЛО́ЧЕННЫЙ; приколо́чен,
—а, —о, —ы (ppp), see приколочу́.
ПРИКОЛОЧУ́, приколо́тишь. Р. При-
колоти́ть (acc.). I. Прикола́чивать.
1. To nail, to fasten with nails. 2. To
give (s.o.) a beating.
ПРИКОЛЮ́, прико́лешь. Р. При-
коло́ть (acc.). I. Прика́лывать. 1.
To pin, fasten with a pin. 2. To
stab to death.
ПРИКО́ПЛЕННЫЙ; прико́плен, —а,
—о, —ы (ppp), see прикоплю́.
ПРИКОПЛЮ́, прико́пишь. Р. При-
копи́ть (acc./gen.). To save, store up
(e.g., money, etc.).
ПРИКО́РМЛЕННЫЙ; прико́рмлен,
—а, —о, —ы (ppp), see прикормлю́.
ПРИКОРМЛЮ́, прико́рмишь. Р. При-
корми́ть (acc.). I. Прика́рмливать.
1. To lure with food, grain, etc. (e.g.,
pheasants, etc.). 2. To bribe, win
over.
ПРИКРА́СЬ (imp.), see прикра́шу.
ПРИКРА́ШЕННЫЙ; прикра́шен,
—а, —о, —ы (ppp), see прикра́шу.
ПРИКРА́ШУ, прикра́сишь. Р. При-
кра́сить (acc.). I. Прикра́шивать.
(fig.) To embellish, color, embroider
(as a tale).
ПРИКРЕПЛЁННЫЙ; прикреплён,
—а́, —о́, —ы́ (ppp), see прикреплю́.
ПРИКРЕПЛЮ́, прикрепи́шь. Р. При-
крепи́ть (acc.). I. Прикрепля́ть. 1.
To fasten, attach (s.t. to s.t.) (acc.

+ к dat.). 2. To transfer, attach (as troops to an organization) (acc. + к + dat.). 3. To register (s.t.) (e.g., a certificate).

ПРИКРО́ЕШЬ, see прикро́ю.

ПРИКРО́Й (imp.), see прикро́ю.

ПРИКРО́Ю, прикро́ешь. Р. Прикры́ть (acc.). I. Прикрыва́ть. 1. To cover (s.t. with s.t.) (acc. + inst.). 2. (lit. and fig.) To screen, conceal, protect. 3. To close partially, half close. 4. To liquidate (as a business). 5. (tech.) To throttle.

ПРИКРУ́ЧЕННЫЙ; прикру́чен, —а, —о, —ы (ppp), see прикручу́.

ПРИКРУЧУ́, прикру́тишь. Р. Прикрути́ть (acc.). I. Прикру́чивать. 1. To fasten, bind to (acc. + к + dat.). 2. To turn down (as the wick of a lamp) (acc.).

ПРИКРЫ́ТЫЙ; прикры́т, —а, —о, —ы (ppp), see прикро́ю.

ПРИКУ́ПЛЕННЫЙ; прику́плен, —а, —о, —ы (ppp), see прикуплю́.

ПРИКУПЛЮ́, прику́пишь. Р. Прикупи́ть (acc./gen.). I. Прикупа́ть. To buy more (of s.t.).

ПРИКУ́ШЕННЫЙ; прику́шен, —а, —о, —ы (ppp), see прикушу́.

ПРИКУШУ́, прику́сишь. Р. Прикуси́ть (acc.). I. Прику́сывать. 1. (lit. and fig.) To bite (as one's lips, tongue). 2. To eat a little.

ПРИЛА́ДЬ (imp.), see прила́жу.

ПРИЛА́ЖЕННЫЙ; прила́жен, —а, —о, —ы (ppp), see прила́жу.

ПРИЛА́ЖУ, прила́дишь. Р. Прила́дить (acc.). I. Прила́живать. To fit, adjust, adapt (s.t. to s.t.) (acc. + к + dat.).

ПРИЛЁГ, прилегла́ (past), see приля́гу.

ПРИЛЕЖА́Т, see прилежу́.

ПРИЛЕЖИ́ (imp.), see прилежу́.

ПРИЛЕЖИ́ШЬ, see прилежу́.

ПРИЛЕЖУ́, прилежи́шь. I. Прилежа́ть (intr.) (к + dat.). 1. To adjoin, lie next to (s.o.). 2. (arch.) To apply o.s. diligently (to s.t.).

ПРИЛЕ́Й (imp.), see прилью́.

ПРИЛЕ́ПЛЕННЫЙ; приле́плен, —а, —о, —ы (ppp), see прилеплю́.

ПРИЛЕПЛЮ́, приле́пишь. Р. Прилепи́ть (acc.). I. Прилепля́ть. To stick (s.t. to s.t.) (acc. + к + dat.).

ПРИЛЕТИ́ (imp.), see прилечу́.

ПРИЛЕТИ́ШЬ, see прилечу́.

ПРИЛЕТЯ́Т, see прилечу́.

ПРИЛЕЧУ́, прилети́шь. Р. Прилете́ть (intr.). I. Прилета́ть. 1. To arrive by plane, fly in. 2. (fig.) To come flying (i.e., arrive in a rush).

ПРИЛИ́ЖЕШЬ, see прилижу́.

ПРИЛИЖИ́ (imp.), see прилижу́.

ПРИЛИЖУ́, прили́жешь. Р. Прилиза́ть (acc.). I. Прили́зывать. To sleek, smooth (as fur, hair).

ПРИЛИ́ЗАННЫЙ; прили́зан, —а, —о, —ы (ppp), see прилижу́.

ПРИЛИ́П, прили́пла (past). Р. Прили́пнуть (intr.) (к + dat.). I. Прилипа́ть. (lit. and fig.) To stick or adhere (to).

ПРИЛИ́ТЫЙ; прили́т, —а́, —о, —ы (ppp), see прилью́.

ПРИЛЬЁШЬ, see прилью́.

ПРИЛЬЮ́, прильёшь. Р. Прили́ть. I. Прилива́ть. 1. To add some (liquid or fluid) (to s.t.) by pouring (acc./ gen.). 2. To flow or rush to (as blood to one's head) (intr.) (к + dat.). 3. (fig.) To flow or rush (to) (as emotion flows to one's heart) (intr.) (к + dat.).

ПРИЛЯ́Г (imp.), see приля́гу.

ПРИЛЯ́ГУ, приля́жешь, приля́гут. Р. Приле́чь (intr.). I. Прилега́ть (mean. 3). 1. To lie down, take a nap. 2. To bend down, lie flattened (as grain in a field after a rain, etc.). 3. To lie close to, cling, fit closely (e.g., as a dress clings to the figure) (к + dat.).

ПРИЛЯ́ЖЕШЬ, see приля́гу.

ПРИМА́ЖЕШЬСЯ, see прима́жусь.

ПРИМА́ЖУСЬ, прима́жешься. Р. Прима́заться (intr.). I. Прима́зываться. 1. To groom one's hair (as with hair oil) (inst.). 2. (fig.) To adhere to (e.g., an organization) (к + dat.). 3. To stay in (as in a poker game).

ПРИМА́ЖЬСЯ (imp.), see прима́жусь.

ПРИМЁРЗ, примёрзла (past). Р. Примёрзнуть (intr.) (к + dat.). I. Примерза́ть. To freeze to (s.t.).

ПРИМЕ́ТЬ (imp.), see приме́чу.

ПРИМЕ́ЧЕННЫЙ; приме́чен, —а, —о, —ы (ppp), see приме́чу.

ПРИМЕ́ЧУ, приме́тишь. Р. Приме́тить (acc.). I. Примеча́ть. To notice, observe, perceive.

ПРЍМЕШЬ, see приму́.
ПРИМЍ (imp.), see приму́.
ПРИМНЁШЬ, see примну́.
ПРИМНЍ (imp.), see примну́.
ПРИМНУ́, примнёшь. Р. Прима́ть (acc.). I. Примина́ть. 1. To trample. 2. To crush, flatten.
ПРИМО́ЛК, примо́лкла (past). Р. Примо́лкнуть (intr.). To fall silent.
ПРИМОЩЁННЫЙ; примощён, —а́, —о́, —ы́ (ppp), see примощу́.
ПРИМОЩУ́, примости́шь. Р. Примости́ть (acc.). To find room for, make room for (s.t.).
ПРИМУ́, при́мешь. Р. Приня́ть (acc.). I. Принима́ть. 1. To take (e.g., medicine, bath, precautions, part in s.t., etc.). 2. To take (as s.o. for s.o. else) (acc. + за + acc.). 3. To receive (as guests, patients, radio broadcasts, etc.). 4. To accept. 5. To assume (e.g., a command, a character, etc.). 6. To adopt (as a resolution). (For other usages, see unabridged dictionary.)
ПРИМЧА́ТСЯ, see примчу́сь.
ПРИМЧИ́СЬ (imp.), see примчу́сь.
ПРИМЧИ́ШЬСЯ, see примчу́сь.
ПРИМЧУ́СЬ, примчи́шься. Р. Примча́ться (intr.). To come rushing, rush up.
ПРИМЯ́ТЫЙ; примя́т, —а, —о, —ы (ppp), see примну́.
ПРИНАДЛЕЖА́Т, see принадлежу́.
ПРИНАДЛЕЖИ́ (imp.), see принадлежу́.
ПРИНАДЛЕЖИ́ШЬ, see принадлежу́.
ПРИНАДЛЕЖУ́, принадлежи́шь. I. Принадлежа́ть (intr.). 1. To belong to (dat.). 2. To pertain to (dat.). 3. To belong, in the sense of being a member of (к + dat.).
ПРИНАЛЁГ, приналегла́ (past), see приналя́гу.
ПРИНАЛЯ́Г (imp.), see приналя́гу.
ПРИНАЛЯ́ГУ, приналя́жешь, приналя́гут. Р. Принале́чь (на + acc.). 1. To lean on, press on, push on (s.t.) with force (e.g., oars, etc.). 2. To apply o.s. (to s.t.) with diligence (e.g., to one's work).
ПРИНАЛЯ́ЖЕШЬ, see приналя́гу.
ПРИНАРЯ́ЖЕННЫЙ; принаря́жен, —а, —о, —ы (ppp), see принаря́жу.
ПРИНАРЯЖУ́, принаря́дишь (and

принаряди́шь). Р. Принаряди́ть (acc.). I. Принаряжа́ть. To dress up (s.o. or s.t.), adorn.
ПРИНЁС, принесла́ (past), see принесу́.
ПРИНЕСЁННЫЙ; принесён, —а́, —о́, —ы́ (ppp), see принесу́.
ПРИНЕСЁШЬ, see принесу́.
ПРИНЕСИ́ (imp.), see принесу́.
ПРИНЕСУ́, принесёшь. Р. Принести́ (acc.). I. Приноси́ть. 1. To bring. 2. To give, yield (as benefits, crops, etc.). 3. To bear (as young: said of animals). 4. To express (as gratitude), to give (as a blow), etc. (meaning depends on the noun used).
ПРИНЕСЯ́ (adv. past part.), see принесу́.
ПРИНИ́ЖЕННЫЙ; прини́жен, —а, —о, —ы (ppp), see прини́жу.
ПРИНИ́ЖУ, прини́зишь. Р. Прини́зить (acc.). I. Принижа́ть. 1. To belittle, disparage. 2. To humiliate, humble.
ПРИНИ́ЗЬ (imp.), see прини́жу.
ПРИНИ́К, прини́кла (past). Р. Прини́кнуть (intr.). I. Приника́ть. 1. To press o.s. (against s.o. or s.t.) (к + dat.). 2. To press (as one's ear to the door) (inst. of ear + к + dat. of door). 3. To quiet down.
ПРИНОРО́ВЛЕННЫЙ; приноро́влен, —а, —о, —ы (ppp), see приноровлю́.
ПРИНОРОВЛЮ́, принорови́шь. Р. Принорови́ть (acc. + к + dat.). I. Принора́вливать. 1. To adjust, adapt (s.t. to s.t.). 2. To time (e.g., one's arrival to some event).
ПРИНОШУ́, прино́сишь. I. Приноси́ть (acc.). Р. Принести́. 1. To bring. 2. To give, yield (as benefits, crops, etc.). 3. To bear (as young: said of animals). 4. To express (as gratitude), to give (as a blow), etc. (meaning depends on the noun used).
ПРИНУ́ДЬ (imp.), see прину́жу.
ПРИНУЖДЁННЫЙ; принуждён, —а́, —о́, —ы́ (ppp), see прину́жу.
ПРИНУ́ЖУ, прину́дишь. Р. Прину́дить (acc.). I. Принужда́ть. To compel, force.
ПРИ́НЯТЫЙ; при́нят, —а́, —о, —ы (ppp), see приму́.
ПРИОБРЁВШИЙ and приобре́тший (pap), see приобрету́.

ПРИОБРЁЛ, приобрела (past), see приобрету.

ПРИОБРЕТЁННЫЙ; приобретён, —а, —о, —ы (ppp), see приобрету.

ПРИОБРЕТЁШЬ, see приобрету.

ПРИОБРЕТЍ (imp.), see приобрету.

ПРИОБРЕТУ́, приобретёшь. Р. Приобрести́ (acc.). I. Приобрета́ть. 1. To acquire, obtain, gain. 2. To buy.

ПРИОБРЁТШИ and приобретя́ (adv. past part.), see приобрету.

ПРИОБРЁТШИЙ and приобрёвший (pap), see приобрету.

ПРИОБРЕТЯ́ and приобрётши (adv. past part.), see преобрету.

ПРИОДЕ́НЕШЬ, see приодену.

ПРИОДЕ́НУ, приоде́нешь. Р. Приоде́ть (acc.). 1. To dress up (s.o. or s.t.). 2. To dress (s.o.) (i.e., supply with clothes).

ПРИОДЕ́НЬ (imp.), see приодену.

ПРИОДЕ́ТЫЙ; приоде́т, —а, —о, —ы (ppp), see приодену.

ПРИОСТАНО́ВЛЕННЫЙ; приостано́влен, —а, —о, —ы (ppp), see приостановлю.

ПРИОСТАНОВЛЮ́, приостано́вишь. Р. Приостанови́ть (acc.). I. Приостана́вливать. 1. To stop temporarily, to suspend, halt. 2. To reprieve.

ПРИОТКРО́ЕШЬ, see приоткрою.

ПРИОТКРО́Й (imp.), see приоткрою.

ПРИОТКРО́Ю, приоткро́ешь. Р. Приоткры́ть (acc.). I. Приоткрыва́ть. To open slightly (as a door).

ПРИОТКРЫ́ТЫЙ; приоткры́т, —а, —о, —ы (ppp), see приоткрою.

ПРИОХО́ТЬ (imp.), see приохочу.

ПРИОХО́ЧЕННЫЙ; приохо́чен, —а, —о, —ы (ppp), see приохочу.

ПРИОХО́ЧУ, приохо́тишь. Р. Приохо́тить (acc.). To inspire (s.o.) with a desire or taste (for s.t.) (acc. of s.o. + dat. of s.t.).

ПРИПА́ВШИЙ and (arch.) припа́дший (pap), see припаду.

ПРИПАДЁШЬ, see припаду.

ПРИПАДЍ (imp.), see припаду.

ПРИПАДУ́, припадёшь. Р. Припа́сть (intr.). I. Припада́ть. 1. To fall on, to (s.t.) (e.g., the ground, s.o.'s neck) (к + dat.); on or to one's knees) (на + acc.). 2. To press o.s. to or against (s.o. or s.t.) (к + dat.). 3. (arch.) To arise, appear suddenly

(e.g., a passion for s.t.) (к + dat. of s.t.).

ПРИПА́ДШИЙ (arch.) and припа́вший (pap), see припаду.

ПРИПА́Л, припа́ла (past), see припаду.

ПРИПА́С, припасла́ (past), see припасу.

ПРИПАСЁННЫЙ; припасён, —а, —о, —ы (ppp), see припасу.

ПРИПАСЁШЬ, see припасу.

ПРИПАСЍ (imp.), see припасу.

ПРИПАСУ́, припасёшь. Р. Припасти́ (acc.). I. Припаса́ть. 1. To store up, lay in (e.g., a supply). 2. To prepare (as answers, etc.).

ПРИПЁР, припёрла (past), see припру.

ПРИПЕРЁВ and припёрши (adv. past part.), see припру.

ПРИПЁРТЫЙ; припёрт, —а (and припёрта) —о, —ы (ppp), see припру.

ПРИПЁРШИ and приперёв (adv. past part.), see припру.

ПРИПЍСАННЫЙ; припи́сан, —а, —о, —ы (ppp), see припишу.

ПРИПЍШЕШЬ, see припишу.

ПРИПИШЍ (imp.), see припишу.

ПРИПИШУ́, припи́шешь. Р. Приписа́ть (acc.). I. Припи́сывать. 1. To add (e.g., a line to a letter) (acc. + к + dat.). 2. To attach (as s.o. to a regiment) (acc. + к + dat.). 3. To attribute to, impute to (e.g., s.t. to s.o.) (acc. + dat.).

ПРИПЛА́ЧЕННЫЙ; припла́чен, —а, —о, —ы (ppp), see приплачу.

ПРИПЛАЧУ́, припла́тишь. Р. Приплати́ть (acc.). I. Припла́чивать. To pay in addition (e.g., $5.00).

ПРИПЛЁЛ, приплела́ (past), see приплету.

ПРИПЛЕТЁННЫЙ; приплетён, —а, —о, —ы (ppp), see приплету.

ПРИПЛЕТЁШЬ, see приплету.

ПРИПЛЕТЍ (imp.), see приплету.

ПРИПЛЕТУ́, приплетёшь. Р. Приплести́ (acc.). I. Приплета́ть. 1. To intertwine, weave in (e.g., a ribbon in a wreath) (acc. + к + dat.). 2. To imply, "drag in," implicate.

ПРИПЛЁТШИЙ (pap), see приплету.

ПРИПЛЕТЯ́ (adv. past part.), see приплету.

ПРИПОДНЍМЕШЬ, see приподниму.

ПРИПОДНИМЙ (imp.), see приподниму́.

ПРИПОДНИМУ́, приподни́мешь. Р. Приподня́ть (acc.). I. Приподнима́ть, приподыма́ть. 1. To raise slightly. 2. (fig.) To raise (as s.o. in s.o.'s estimation, the level of a conversation, etc.). 3. (fig.) To revive, stimulate.

ПРИПО́ДНЯТЫЙ; припо́днят, —а́, —о, —ы (ppp), see приподниму́.

ПРИПОДЫ́МЕШЬ, see приподыму́.

ПРИПОДЫМЙ (imp.), see приподыму́.

ПРИПОДЫМУ́, приподы́мешь. Р. Приподня́ть (acc.). I. Приподыма́ть, приподнима́ть. 1. To raise slightly. 2. (fig.) To raise (as s.o. in s.o.'s estimation, the level of a conversation, etc.). 3. (fig.) To revive, stimulate.

ПРИПО́ЛЗ, приползла́ (past), see приползу́.

ПРИПОЛЗЁШЬ, see приползу́.

ПРИПОЛЗЙ (imp.), see приползу́.

ПРИПОЛЗУ́, приползёшь. Р. Приползти́ (intr.). I. Приполза́ть. To crawl up, creep up, come crawling.

ПРИПРА́ВЛЕННЫЙ; припра́влен, —а, —о, —ы (ppp), see припра́влю.

ПРИПРА́ВЛЮ, припра́вишь. Р. Припра́вить (acc.). I. Приправля́ть. 1. To season, flavor (s.t. with s.t.) (acc. + inst.). 2. (fig.) To flavor, spice (as one's speech with colorful language) (acc. + inst.). 3. (typ.) To make ready (to level type, etc., for printing).

ПРИПРА́ВЬ (imp.), see припра́влю.

ПРИПРЁШЬ, see припру́.

ПРИПРИ́ (imp.), see припру́.

ПРИПРО́ШЕННЫЙ; припро́шен, —а, —о, —ы (ppp), see припрошу́.

ПРИПРОШУ́, припро́сишь. Р. Припроси́ть (acc.). I. Припра́шивать. To request an additional amount (as $10 more).

ПРИПРУ́, припрёшь. Р. Припере́ть. I. Припира́ть. 1. To press (s.o. or s.t.) against (s.t.) (acc. + к + dat.). 2. To close tightly by pushing or leaning (s.t.) against (s.t.) (e.g., a chair against a door) (acc. of door + inst. of chair). 3. To close, shut (as a door) (acc.). 4. To bring (acc.). 5. To arrive (intr.).

ПРИПРЯ́Г, припрягла́ (past), see припрягу́.

ПРИПРЯГЙ (imp.), see припрягу́.

ПРИПРЯГУ́, припряжёшь, припрягу́т. Р. Припря́чь (acc.). I. Припряга́ть. To harness additional (e.g., horses to a wagon) (acc. + к + dat.).

ПРИПРЯДЁННЫЙ; припрядён, —а́, —о́, —ы́ (ppp), see припряду́.

ПРИПРЯДЁШЬ, see припряду́.

ПРИПРЯДЙ (imp.), see припряду́.

ПРИПРЯДУ́, прьпрядёшь. Р. Припря́сть (acc./gen.). To spin an additional amount of (e.g., silk).

ПРИПРЯЖЁННЫЙ; припряжён, —а́, —о́, —ы́ (ppp), see припрягу́.

ПРИПРЯЖЁШЬ, see припрягу́.

ПРИПРЯ́Л, припряла́, припря́ло, припря́ли (past), see припряду́.

ПРИПРЯ́ТАННЫЙ; припря́тан, —а, —о, —ы (ppp), see припря́чу.

ПРИПРЯ́ЧЕШЬ, see припря́чу.

ПРИПРЯ́ЧУ, припря́чешь. Р. Припря́тать (acc.). I. Припря́тывать. 1. To secrete, hide. 2. To store up, put aside.

ПРИПРЯ́ЧЬ[1] (imp.), see припря́чу.

ПРИПРЯ́ЧЬ[2] (inf.), see припрягу́.

ПРИПУ́Х, припу́хла (past). Р. Припу́хнуть (intr.). I. Припуха́ть. To swell a little, become swollen.

ПРИПУ́ЩЕННЫЙ; припу́щен, —а, —о, —ы (ppp), see припущу́.

ПРИПУЩУ́, припу́стишь. Р. Припусти́ть. I. Припуска́ть. 1. To let out (as a seam) (acc.). 2. To make go faster, let out (as a horse) (acc.). 3. To go faster, quicken one's pace (intr.). 4. To come down harder (as rain) (intr.). 5. To couple, pair, breed (as one animal to another) (acc. + к + dat.). 6. To give (s.t.) access to (s.t.), let in (as a horse to its oats, etc.) (acc. + к + dat.).

ПРИРАСТЁШЬ, see прирасту́.

ПРИРАСТЙ (imp.), see прирасту́.

ПРИРАСТУ́, прирастёшь. Р. Прирасти́ (intr.). I. Прираста́ть. 1. To adhere (to), grow fast (to) (к + dat.). 2. (fig.) To become rooted to (as one becomes "rooted to the spot") (к + dat.). 3. (fig.) To form a strong attachment to (к + dat.). 4. To increase (e.g., of one's capital) (intr.).

ПРИРЕ́ЖЕШЬ, see прире́жу.

ПРИРЕ́ЖУ, прире́жешь. Р. При-ре́зать (acc.). I. **Прирезать, при-ре́зывать.** 1. To add (as a piece of land, by means of a survey). 2. To kill by cutting the throat. 3. To slaughter (all or many) (e.g., fowl).

ПРИРЕ́ЖЬ (imp.), see **прире́жу.**

ПРИРЕ́ЗАННЫЙ; прире́зан, —а, —о, —ы (ppp), see **прире́жу.**

ПРИРО́С, приросла́ (past), see **при-расту́.**

ПРИСЕ́Л, присе́ла (past). Р. При-се́сть (intr.). I. **Приса́живаться** (mean. 1), **приседа́ть** (mean. 2 and 3). 1. To sit down. 2. To squat. 3. To curtsey. (Also see **присяду.**)

ПРИСКА́ЧЕШЬ, see **прискачу́.**

ПРИСКАЧИ́ (imp.), see **прискачу́.**

ПРИСКАЧУ́, приска́чешь. Р. При-скака́ть (intr.). I. **Приска́кивать.** 1. To come galloping. 2. To come hopping, skipping.

ПРИ́СЛАННЫЙ; при́слан, —а, —о, —ы (ppp). Р. **Присла́ть** (acc.). I. **Присыла́ть.** To send (also see **пришлю́**).

ПРИСМО́ТРЕННЫЙ; присмо́трен, —а, —о, —ы (ppp), see **присмотрю́.**

ПРИСМОТРИ́ (imp.), see **присмотрю́.**

ПРИСМО́ТРИШЬ, see **присмотрю́.**

ПРИСМОТРЮ́, присмо́тришь. Р. При-смотре́ть. I. **Присма́тривать** (mean. 1 and 2). 1. To look after (as a child), supervise (**за** + inst.). 2. To seek out. 3. To look for and find (acc.).

ПРИСМО́ТРЯТ, see **присмотрю́.**

ПРИСОВОКУПЛЁННЫЙ; присово-куплён, —а́, —о́, —ы́ (ppp), see **присовокуплю́.**

ПРИСОВОКУПЛЮ́, присовокупи́шь. Р. Присовокупи́ть (acc.). I. **При-совокупля́ть.** 1. To attach (as one document to another) (acc. + **к** + dat.). 2. To add (as a remark).

ПРИСОСЕ́ДЬСЯ (imp.), see **присо-се́жусь.**

ПРИСОСЕ́ЖУСЬ, присосе́дишься. Р. Присосе́диться (**к** + dat.). To sit down next to.

ПРИСОСЁШЬСЯ, see **присосу́сь.**

ПРИСОСИ́СЬ (imp.), see **присосу́сь.**

ПРИСОСУ́СЬ, присосёшься. Р. При-соса́ться (**к** + dat.). I. **Приса́сы-ваться.** 1. To adhere to by suction (as a leech). 2. (fig.) To attach o.s. to (as to some party, group, etc.).

ПРИСО́Х, присо́хла (past). Р. При-со́хнуть. I. **Присыха́ть.** To adhere (to) in drying, dry on (to) (**к** + dat.).

ПРИСПОСО́БЛЕННЫЙ; приспосо́-блен, —а, —о, —ы (ppp), see **приспосо́блю.**

ПРИСПОСО́БЛЮ, приспосо́бишь. Р. Приспосо́бить (acc.). I. **Приспо-са́бливать.** To accommodate, adapt (s.o. or s.t. to s.t.) (acc. + **к** + dat. or (acc. + **под** + acc.).

ПРИСПОСО́БЬ (imp.), see **приспо-со́блю.**

ПРИСПУ́ЩЕННЫЙ; приспу́щен, —а, —о, —ы (ppp), see **приспущу́.**

ПРИСПУЩУ́, приспу́стишь. Р. При-спусти́ть (acc.). I. **Приспуска́ть.** 1. To lower a little. 2. To lower (a flag) to halfmast.

ПРИСТАВА́Й (imp.), see **пристаю́.**

ПРИСТАВА́Я (adv. pres. part.), see **пристаю́.**

ПРИСТА́ВЛЕННЫЙ; приста́влен, —а, —о, —ы (ppp), see **приста́влю.**

ПРИСТА́ВЛЮ, приста́вишь. Р. При-ста́вить (acc. + **к** + dat.). I. **При-ставля́ть.** 1. To place, lean (s.t.) against (s.t.). 2. To add (s.t. to s.t.) (e.g., an addition to a structure). 3. To lengthen (s.t.) by adding (s.t.) (e.g., lengthen a sleeve). 4. To designate (s.o.) to look after (s.o.), assign (s.o. to s.o.).

ПРИСТА́ВЬ (imp.), see **приста́влю.**

ПРИСТАЁШЬ, see **пристаю́.**

ПРИСТА́НЕШЬ, see **приста́ну.**

ПРИСТА́НУ, приста́нешь. Р. При-ста́ть (intr.). I. **Приставать** (mean. 1 thru 6, and 9). 1. To adhere to (3rd pers. only) (**к** + dat.). 2. To infect, strike (s.o.) (of a disease) (**к** + dat.). 3. (naut.) To moor (intr.); to moor to put in to (**к** + dat.). 4. To stop (somewhere) a while. 5. To annoy (s.o.) (**к** + dat.). 6. To join (as s.o.) (**к** + dat.). 7. To become (s.o.) (of clothing) (dat.). 8. To be proper for (s.o.) (e.g., good speech) (dat.). 9. To tire.

ПРИСТА́НЬ (imp.), see **приста́ну.**

ПРИСТАЮ́, пристаёшь. I. Приста-ва́ть (intr.). Р. **Приста́ть.** 1. To adhere to (3rd pers. only) (**к** + dat.). 2. To strike, infect (s.o.) (of a disease) (**к** + dat.). 3. (naut.) To moor (intr.); to moor to, put in to (к + dat.). 4. To stop (somewhere) for a while. 5. To annoy (s.o.) (к + dat.). 6. To join (as s.o.) (к + dat.). 7. To tire.

ПРИСТРАЩЁННЫЙ; пристращён, —а́, —о́, —ы́ (ppp), see пристращу́.

ПРИСТРАЩУ́, пристрасти́шь. Р. Пристрасти́ть (acc. + к + dat.). I. Пристраща́ть. To inspire (s.o.) with a desire or taste for (s.t.).

ПРИСТУПЛЮ́, присту́пишь. Р. Приступи́ть (intr.). I. Приступа́ть. 1. To start, begin, set about (as one's work, studies, etc.) (к + dat.). 2. (arch.) To start toward, approach (e.g., a town) (к + dat.). 3. (arch.) To importune (s.o.) (usually with a question or request) (к + dat. + с + inst.).

ПРИСТЫЖЁННЫЙ; пристыжён, —а́, —о́, —ы́ (ppp), see пристыжу́.

ПРИСТЫЖУ́, пристыди́шь. Р. Пристыди́ть (acc.). I. Стыди́ть. To make (s.o.) ashamed of himself, shame (s.o.).

ПРИСУЖДЁННЫЙ; присуждён, —а́, —о́, —ы́ (ppp), see присужу́.

ПРИСУЖУ́, прису́дишь. Р. Присуди́ть (acc.). I. Присужда́ть. 1. To sentence, condemn (s.o. to s.t.) (acc. + к + dat.). 2. To adjudge, award (s.t. to s.o.) (acc. + dat.). 3. To confer (as a degree on s.o.) (acc. + dat.).

ПРИСЫ́ПАННЫЙ; присы́пан, —а, —о, —ы (ppp), see присы́плю.

ПРИСЫ́ПЛЕШЬ, see присы́плю.

ПРИСЫ́ПЛЮ, присы́плешь. Р. Присы́пать. I. Присыпа́ть. 1. To add by pouring (as flour) (acc./gen.). 2. To sprinkle, dust (s.t. with s.t.) (acc. + inst.). 3. To pour (s.t.) close to or against (s.t.) (as dirt against a retaining wall) (acc. + к + dat.).

ПРИСЫ́ПЬ (imp.), see присы́плю.

ПРИСЯ́ДЕШЬ, see прися́ду.

ПРИСЯ́ДУ, прися́дешь. Р. Присе́сть (intr.). I. Приса́живаться (mean. 1), присда́ть (mean. 2 and 3). 1. To sit down. 2. To squat. 3. To curtsey.

ПРИСЯ́ДЬ (imp.), see прися́ду.

ПРИТЁК, притекла́ (past), see притечёт.

ПРИТЕКУ́Т (3rd pers. pl.), see притечёт.

ПРИТЁКШИЙ and прите́кший (pap), see притечёт.

ПРИТЁР, притёрла (past), see притру́.

ПРИТЕРЕ́В and притёрши (adv. past part.), see притру́.

ПРИТЕРПИ́СЬ (imp.), see притерплю́сь.

ПРИТЕ́РПИШЬСЯ, see притерплю́сь.

ПРИТЕРПЛЮ́СЬ, прите́рпишься. Р. Притерпе́ться (к + dat.). To become accustomed (to s.t. undesirable or unpleasant).

ПРИТЕ́РПЯТСЯ, see притерплю́сь.

ПРИТЁРТЫЙ; притёрт, —а, —о, —ы (ppp), see притру́.

ПРИТЁРШИ and притере́в (adv. past part.), see притру́.

ПРИТЁСАННЫЙ; притёсан, —а, —о, —ы (ppp), see притешу́.

ПРИТЕЧЁТ, притеку́т (3rd pers. only). Р. Прите́чь (intr.). I. Притека́ть. 1. To flow (somewhere) (of liquids). 2. (fig.) To flow (in) (e.g., thoughts).

ПРИТЕ́ШЕШЬ, see притешу́.

ПРИТЕШИ́ (imp.), see притешу́.

ПРИТЕШУ́, прите́шешь. Р. Притеса́ть (acc.). I. Притёсывать. To cut to fit, adjust (e.g., a joist to a beam).

ПРИТИ́Х, прити́хла (past). Р. Прити́хнуть (intr.). I. Притиха́ть. 1. To cease to make noise, become quiet. 2. To quiet down, abate (e.g., of the wind). 3. To sing more softly.

ПРИТОМЛЁННЫЙ; притомлён, —а́, —о́, —ы́ (ppp), see притомлю́.

ПРИТОМЛЮ́, притоми́шь. Р. Притоми́ть (acc.). I. Притомля́ть. To tire, weary (s.o.).

ПРИТО́ПТАННЫЙ; прито́птан, —а, —о, —ы (ppp), see притопчу́.

ПРИТО́ПЧЕШЬ, see притопчу́.

ПРИТОПЧИ́ (imp.), see притопчу́.

ПРИТОПЧУ́, прито́пчешь. Р. Притопта́ть (acc.). I. Прита́птывать. To trample down, crush, pack down.

ПРИТОРМОЖЁННЫЙ; притоможён, —а́, —о́, —ы́ (ppp), see приторможу́.

ПРИТОРМОЖУ́, притормози́шь. Р. Притормози́ть. I. Притормá́живать. 1. To put on the brakes (intr.). 2. To brake (as a machine) (acc.).

ПРИТРЁШЬ, see притру́.

ПРИТРИ́ (imp.), see притру́.

ПРИТРУ́, притрёшь. P. Притере́ть (acc.). I. Притира́ть. 1. (mech.) To fit (as one part to another). 2. (mech.) To lap or grind.

ПРИТУ́ПЛЕННЫЙ; приту́плен, —а, —о, —ы (ppp), see притуплю́.

ПРИТУПЛЁННЫЙ; притуплён, —а́, —б, —ы́ (ppp), see притуплю́.

ПРИТУПЛЮ́, приту́пишь. P. Притупи́ть (acc.). I. Притупля́ть. 1. (lit. and fig.) To blunt, dull. 2. (tech.) To truncate (a crystal).

ПРИТУ́Х, приту́хла (past). P. Приту́хнуть (intr.). I. Притуха́ть. To become faint, fainter; to diminish (as light, fire, etc.).

ПРИУГОТО́ВЛЕННЫЙ; приугото́-влен, —а, —о, —ы (ppp), see приугото́влю.

ПРИУГОТО́ВЛЮ, приугото́вишь. P. Приугото́вить (acc.). I. Приугото-вля́ть. (arch.) To prepare.

ПРИУГОТО́ВЬ (imp.), see приугото́-влю.

ПРИУКРА́СЬ (imp.), see приукра́шу.

ПРИУКРА́ШЕННЫЙ; приукра́шен, —а, —о, —ы (ppp), see приукра́шу.

ПРИУКРА́ШУ, приукра́сишь. P. Приукра́сить (acc.). I. Приукра́ши-вать, приукраша́ть. 1. To decorate, adorn, ornament somewhat. 2. (fig.) To embellish (e.g., a story).

ПРИУМО́ЛК, приумо́лкла (past). P. Приумо́лкнуть (intr.). I. Приумо-лка́ть. To fall silent (suddenly or for a while).

ПРИУНО́ЕШЬ, see приуно́ю.

ПРИУНО́Й (imp.), see приуно́ю.

ПРИУНО́Ю, приуно́ешь (use of future form arch.). P. Приуны́ть (intr.). To become melancholy.

ПРИУСТА́НЕШЬ, see приуста́ну.

ПРИУСТА́НУ, приуста́нешь. P. Приуста́ть (intr.) To become somewhat tired, weary.

ПРИУСТА́НЬ (imp.), see приуста́ну.

ПРИУТИ́Х, приути́хла (past). P. Приути́хнуть (intr.). I. Приутиха́ть. 1. To quiet down, abate (of a storm, wind, etc.) 2. To become quiet, stop talking (of people).

ПРИХВА́ЧЕННЫЙ; прихва́чен, —а, —о, —ы (ppp), see прихвачу́.

ПРИХВАЧУ́, прихва́тишь. P. При-хвати́ть (acc.). I. Прихва́тывать.

1. To take (s.t. or s.o.) along. 2. To pinch, press, squeeze, seize. 3. To fasten. 4. To borrow, take. 5. To nip, touch (said of frost) (acc.) or (impers. + acc. + inst.). 6. To strike (of an illness).

ПРИХОЖУ́, прихо́дишь. I. Прихо-ди́ть (intr.). P. Прийти́. 1. To come, arrive. 2. To arise, come up. 3. To become (e.g., ecstatic), find o.s. in some condition (e.g., in ecstacy) (в + acc.). 4. (fig.) To arrive (as at some conclusion) (к + dat.).

ПРИЦЕ́ПЛЕННЫЙ; прице́плен, —а, —о, —ы (ppp), see прицеплю́.

ПРИЦЕПЛЮ́, прице́пишь. P. При-цепи́ть (acc.). I. Прицепля́ть. 1. To hitch (s.t.). 2. To couple, hook on (as a railroad car to a train) (acc. + к + dat.). 3. To fasten or pin (as a medal to a uniform) (acc. + к + dat.).

ПРИЧАЩЁННЫЙ; причащён, —а́, —б, —ы́ (ppp), see причащу́.

ПРИЧАЩУ́, причасти́шь. P. При-части́ть (acc.). I. Причаща́ть. 1. To give (s.o.) the eucharist, (acc. of s.o.). 2. (arch.) To make (s.o.) a participant, member, partner (in s.t.).

ПРИЧЁЛ, причла́ (past), see причту́.

ПРИЧЁСАННЫЙ; причёсан, —а, —о, —ы (ppp), see причешу́.

ПРИЧЁТШИЙ (pap), see причту́.

ПРИЧЕ́ШЕШЬ, see причешу́.

ПРИЧЕШИ́ (imp.), see причешу́.

ПРИЧЕШУ́, приче́шешь. P. При-чеса́ть (acc.). I. Причёсывать. 1. To dress, brush, comb, etc. (s.o.'s) hair (acc. of person whose hair is brushed). 2. To dress, brush, comb, etc. (hair) (acc. of hair).

ПРИЧЛА́, причло́, причли́ (past), see причёл and причту́.

ПРИЧТЁННЫЙ; причтён, —а́, —б, —ы́ (ppp), see причту́.

ПРИЧТЁШЬ, see причту́.

ПРИЧТИ́ (imp.), see причту́.

ПРИЧТУ́, причтёшь. P. Приче́сть (acc.). I. Присчи́тывать (mean. 1). 1. To add to/onto (e.g., an amount, percentage, etc. to s.t.) (acc. + к + dat.). 2. (arch.) To number, reckon among (e.g., s.o. among the dead) (acc. + к + dat.).

ПРИЧТЯ́ (adv. past part.), see причту́.

ПРИШЁДШИЙ (pap), see пришёл and приду́.

ПРИШЕЙ (imp.), see пришью́.

ПРИШЁЛ, пришла́ (past). Р. Прийти́ (intr.). I. Приходи́ть. 1. To come, arrive. 2. To arise, come up. 3. To become (e.g., ecstatic), to find o.s. in some condition (e.g., in ecstacy) (в + acc.). 4. (fig.) To arrive (as at some conclusion) (к + dat.). (Also see приду́.)

ПРИШИ́Б, приши́бла (past), see пришибу́.

ПРИШИБЁШЬ, see пришибу́.

ПРИШИБИ́ (imp.), see пришибу́.

ПРИШИ́БЛЕННЫЙ; приши́блен, —а, —о, —ы (ppp), see пришибу́.

ПРИШИБУ́, пришибёшь. Р. Пришиби́ть (acc.). I. Пришиба́ть (mean. 1 and 2). 1. To knock down or injure with a blow. 2. To kill. 3. To depress, dispirit.

ПРИШИ́ТЫЙ; приши́т, —а, —о, —ы (ppp), see пришью́.

ПРИШЛА́, пришло́, пришли́ (past), see пришёл and приду́.

ПРИШЛЁШЬ, see пришлю́.

ПРИШЛИ́¹ (past), see пришёл and приду́.

ПРИШЛИ́² (imp.), see пришлю́.

ПРИШЛЮ́, пришлёшь. Р. Присла́ть (acc.). I. Присыла́ть. To send.

ПРИШЬЁШЬ, see пришью́.

ПРИШЬЮ́, пришьёшь. Р. Приши́ть (acc.). I. Пришива́ть. 1. To sew on (as a button on a coat) (acc. + к + dat.). 2. To nail (as a flag on a mast) (acc. + на + prep.). 3. To falsely attribute (s.t. to s.o.) (acc. + dat.). 4. To kill.

ПРИЩЕМЛЁННЫЙ; прищемлён, —а́, —о́, —ы́ (ppp), see прищемлю́.

ПРИЩЕМЛЮ́, прищеми́шь. Р. Прищеми́ть (acc.). I. Прищемля́ть. To pinch, catch (as one's finger).

ПРИЩЕПЛЁННЫЙ; прищеплён, —а́, —о́, —ы́ (ppp), see прищеплю́.

ПРИЩЕПЛЮ́, прищепи́шь. Р. Прищепи́ть (acc.). I. Прищепля́ть. (bot.) To graft.

ПРИЮЧУ́, приюти́шь. Р. Приюти́ть (acc.). To shelter, give refuge to (s.o.) (acc. of s.o.).

ПРОБАШУ́, пробаси́шь. Р. Пробаси́ть (intr.) or (acc.). To speak or sing in a bass voice.

ПРОБЕГИ́ (imp.), see пробегу́.

ПРОБЕГУ́, пробежи́шь, пробегу́т. Р. Пробежа́ть. I. Пробега́ть. 1. (lit. and fig.) To run, pass, flow rapidly by, through, or along (of people, animals, wind, clouds, time etc.) (intr.) or (ми́мо + gen.), (че́рез + acc.), or (по + dat.). 2. To run, cover a distance at a run (acc.). 3. (fig.) To run over (as a shiver runs over or shakes one's body) (по + dat.). 4. (fig.) To skim, look through rapidly (as a book) (acc.). 5. (fig.) To glide (as one's fingers glide over the keys of a piano) (по + dat.).

ПРОБЕЖИ́ШЬ, see пробегу́.

ПРОБЕЙ (imp.), see пробью́.

ПРОБЕРЁШЬ, see проберу́.

ПРОБЕРИ́ (imp.), see проберу́.

ПРОБЕРУ́, проберёшь. Р. Пробра́ть (acc.). I. Пробира́ть. 1. To penetrate (of cold, etc.) (acc.) or (impers. + acc. + inst.). 2. (fig.) To seize (as fear seizes one). 3. To rebuke, scold. 4. To clean out, weed out (as a garden). 5. (arch.) To part (as one's hair).

ПРОБИ́ТЫЙ; проби́т, —а, —о, —ы (ppp), see пробью́.

ПРОБОЛЕЙ (imp.), see проболе́ю.

ПРОБОЛЕ́Ю, проболе́ешь. Р. Проболе́ть (intr.). To be ill for a while.

ПРОБОЛИ́Т, проболи́т (3rd pers. only). Р. Проболе́ть (intr.). To pain, hurt for a while (e.g., a wound, one's eye's, etc.).

ПРОБОЛЯ́Т (3rd pers. pl.), see проболи́т.

ПРОБОРМО́ЧЕШЬ, see пробормочу́.

ПРОБОРМОЧИ́ (imp.), see пробормочу́.

ПРОБОРМОЧУ́, пробормо́чешь. Р. Пробормота́ть (intr.) or (acc.). I. Бормота́ть. To mutter, mumble.

ПРО́БРАННЫЙ; про́бран, —а́ (and —а), —о, —ы (ppp), see проберу́.

ПРОБРЕ́ЕШЬ, see пробре́ю.

ПРОБРЕЙ (imp.), see пробре́ю.

ПРОБРЕ́Ю, пробре́ешь. Р. Пробри́ть (acc.). I. Пробрива́ть (mean. 1). 1. To shave (a strip) (acc.). 2. To spend a while shaving (acc.) or (intr.).

ПРОБРИ́ТЫЙ; пробри́т, —а, —о, —ы (ppp), see пробре́ю.

ПРОБРОЖУ́, пробро́дишь. Р. Пробродить (intr.). 1. To wander aimlessly for a while. 2. To complete fermentation (e.g., beer, etc.). 3. To ferment for a while.

ПРОБРО́СЬ (imp.), see проброшу.

ПРОБРО́ШЕННЫЙ; проброшен, —а, —о, —ы (ppp), see проброшу.

ПРОБРО́ШУ, пробро́сишь. Р. Пробро́сить. I. Пробра́сывать. 1. To compute, calculate (the amount on an account or bill) (acc. + на + prep. of account). 2. To overcharge (e.g., $10.00 on a bill) (acc. + на + prep. of bill). 3. To miss (as a shot in a game or one's aim) (intr.) or (acc.). 4. To screen, sift (as sand through a screen) (acc.).

ПРОБУ́ДЕШЬ, see пробуду.

ПРОБУ́ДИ́ (imp.), see пробужу́.

ПРОБУ́ДУ, пробу́дешь. Р. Пробы́ть (intr.). To stay, remain, for a period of time.

ПРОБУ́ДЬ (imp.), see пробуду.

ПРОБУЖДЁННЫЙ; пробуждён, —а, —о, —ы (ppp), see пробужу́.

ПРОБУЖУ́, пробу́дишь (and пробуди́шь). Р. Пробуди́ть (acc.). **I. Буди́ть, пробужда́ть.** (lit. and fig.) To waken, arouse.

ПРОБУРА́ВЛЕННЫЙ; пробура́влен, —а, —о, —ы (ppp), see пробура́влю.

ПРОБУРА́ВЛЮ, пробура́вишь. Р. Пробура́вить (acc.). **I. Пробура́вливать.** To bore, drill (as a hole in a piece of metal) (acc. of metal).

ПРОБУРА́ВЬ (imp.), see пробура́влю.

ПРОБУРЧА́Т, see пробурчу́.

ПРОБУРЧИ́ (imp.), see пробурчу́.

ПРОБУРЧИ́ШЬ, see пробурчу́.

ПРОБУРЧУ́, пробурчи́шь. Р. Пробурча́ть. I. Бурча́ть (mean. 1 and 2). 1. To mumble, mutter, grumble (intr.) or (acc.). 2. To rumble (of one's stomach) (intr.) (impers.). 3. To mutter, etc. for a period of time (intr.) or (acc.).

ПРОБЬЁШЬ, see пробью́.

ПРОБЬЮ́, пробьёшь. Р. Проби́ть. I. Бить (mean. 1 thru 3), **пробива́ть** (mean. 4, 5, 6). 1. To strike (of a clock) (intr.) or (acc.). 2. To sound (as an alarm) (acc.). 3. To beat (a retreat) (acc.). 4. To pierce, break a hole, break through (acc.). 5. (lit. and fig.) To clear a path or road;

to blaze (acc.). 6. To caulk (as a boat) (acc.). 7. (arch.) To attain a certain age (impers. + dat. of pers. + nominative of age). 8. To score a goal (intr.).

ПРОВЕДЁННЫЙ; проведён, —а́, —о́, —ы́ (ppp), see проведу́.

ПРОВЕДЁШЬ, see проведу́.

ПРОВЕДИ́ (imp.), see проведу́.

ПРОВЕДУ́, проведёшь. Р. Провести́. I. Проводи́ть. 1. To take, lead, conduct (acc.). 2. To construct (e.g., a road, a tunnel, etc.) (acc.). 3. To draw, trace (e.g., a line) (acc.). 4. To register officially (acc.). 5. To install (e.g., a conduit, electric wiring, etc.) (acc.). 6. To conduct, carry out (e.g., a meeting, experiment, campaign, etc.) (acc.). 7. To offer, put forward, advance (e.g., an idea, thought, etc.) (acc.). 8. To obtain, achieve acceptance of (e.g., a resolution, etc.) (acc.). 9. To pursue (e.g., a policy, course of action) (acc.). 10. To pass (s.t.) over (s.t.) (e.g., one's hand over one's face) (inst. of hand + по + dat.). 11. To spend or pass a period of time (acc.). 12. To trick, deceive, (acc.).

ПРОВЕ́ДШИЙ (pap), see проведу́.

ПРОВЕДЯ́ (adv. past part.), see проведу́.

ПРОВЕ́ЕШЬ, see прове́ю.

ПРОВЁЗ, провезла́ (past), see провезу́.

ПРОВЕЗЁННЫЙ; провезён, —а́, —о́, —ы́ (ppp), see провезу́.

ПРОВЕЗЁШЬ, see провезу́.

ПРОВЕЗИ́ (imp.) see провезу́.

ПРОВЕЗУ́, провезёшь. Р. Провезти́ (acc.). **I. Провози́ть.** 1. To transport, carry somewhere by conveyance. 2. To carry, convey past or through (e.g., a field, mountains, etc.). 3. To carry, convey (s.t.) with o.s. (as in one's luggage).

ПРОВЕЗЯ́ (adv. past part.), see провезу́.

ПРОВЕ́Й (imp.), see прове́ю.

ПРОВЁЛ, провела́ (past), see проведу́.

ПРОВЕРТИ́ (imp.), see проверчу́.

ПРОВЕ́РТИШЬ, see проверчу́.

ПРОВЕ́РТЯТ, see проверчу́.

ПРОВЕ́РЧЕННЫЙ; прове́рчен, —а, —о, —ы (ppp), see проверчу́.

ПРОВЕРЧУ́, прове́ртишь. Р. Проверте́ть (acc.). **I. Провёртывать**

(mean. 1). 1. To bore, pierce, drill (s.t.). 2. To turn, spin (s.t.) for a while.

ПРОВЕ́СЬ (imp.), see прове́шу.

ПРОВЕ́ШЕННЫЙ; прове́шен, —а, —о, —ы (ppp), see прове́шу.

ПРОВЕ́ШУ, прове́сишь. Р. Провве́сить. I. Прове́шивать. 1. To give short weight, shortweigh (s.t.) (acc./gen.). 2. To dry in the open air, dry cure (acc.). 3. To check the alignment (of a wall, a line, etc.); to plumb (acc.).

ПРОВЕ́Ю, прове́ешь. Р. Прове́ять (acc.). I. Прове́ивать, ве́ять. To winnow.

ПРОВЕ́ЯННЫЙ; прове́ян, —а, —о, —ы (ppp), see прове́ю.

ПРОВИ́ДИШЬ, see прови́жу.

ПРОВИ́ДЬ (imp.), see прови́жу.

ПРОВИ́ДЯТ, see прови́жу.

ПРОВИ́ЖУ, прови́дишь. I. Прови́деть (acc.). To foresee.

ПРОВИ́С, прови́сла (past). Р. Прови́снуть (intr.). I. Провиса́ть. To sag, deflect (of a beam, etc.).

ПРОВОЖУ́[1], прово́дишь. I. Проводи́ть. Р. Провести́. 1. To take, lead, conduct (acc.). 2. To construct (e.g., a road, tunnel) (acc.). 3. To draw, trace (e.g., a line) (acc.). 4. To register officially (acc.). 5. To install (e.g., a conduit, electric wiring, etc.) (acc.). 6. To conduct, carry out (e.g., a meeting, experiment, campaign, etc.) (acc.). 7. To offer, put forward, advance (e.g., an idea, thought, etc.) (acc.). 8. To obtain, achieve acceptance of (e.g., a resolution, etc.) (acc.). 9. To pursue (e.g., a policy, course of action) (acc.). 10. To pass (s.t.) over (s.t.) (e.g., one's hand over one's face) (inst. of hand + по + dat. of face). 11. To spend or pass a period of time (acc.). 12. To trick, deceive (acc.).

ПРОВОЖУ́[2], прово́дишь. Р. Проводи́ть (acc.). I. Провожа́ть. 1. To accompany. 2. To send off, see off (e.g., s.o.). 3. To accompany (a departing person with some expression of emotion) (e.g., with tears) (acc. + inst.). 4. To follow, observe (e.g., s.o. with one's own eyes (acc. + inst.).

ПРОВОЖУ́[3], прово́зишь. I. Про-

возить (acc.). Р. Провезти́. 1. To transport, carry somewhere by conveyance. 2. To carry, convey past or through (e.g., a field, mountains, etc.). 3. To carry, convey (s.t.) with o.s. (as in one's luggage).

ПРОВОЖУ́[4], прово́зишь. Р. Провозить (acc.). To transport, convey (s.t. or s.o.) for a period of time.

ПРОВОЗВЕЩЁННЫЙ; провозвещён, —а́, —о́, —ы́ (ppp), see провозвещу́.

ПРОВОЗВЕЩУ́, провозвести́шь. Р. Провозвести́ть (acc.). I. Провозвеща́ть. 1. To predict, foretell. 2. announce, proclaim.

ПРОВОЗГЛАШЁННЫЙ; провозглашён, —а́, —о́, —ы́ (ppp), see провозглашу́.

ПРОВОЗГЛАШУ́, провозгласи́шь. Р. Провозгласи́ть (acc.). I. Провозглаша́ть. 1. To proclaim, announce, enunciate. 2. To propose (as a toast to s.o.) (acc. of toast + за + acc. of s.o.).

ПРОВОЛО́К, проволокла́ (past), see проволоку́.

ПРОВОЛОКИ́ (imp.), see проволоку́.

ПРОВОЛОКУ́, проволочёшь, проволоку́т. Р. Проволо́чь (acc.). I. Проволакивать. To drag (e.g., s.t. along the ground).

ПРОВОЛОЧЁННЫЙ; проволочён, —а́, —о́, —ы́ (ppp), see проволоку́.

ПРОВОЛО́ЧЕННЫЙ; проволо́чен, —а, —о, —ы (ppp), see проволоку́.

ПРОВОЛОЧЁШЬ, see проволоку́.

ПРОВОРЧА́Т, see проворчу́.

ПРОВОРЧИ́ (imp.), see проворчу́.

ПРОВОРЧИ́ШЬ, see проворчу́.

ПРОВОРЧУ́, проворчи́шь. Р. Проворча́ть. 1. To grumble, mutter (acc.) or (intr.). 2. To growl (of a dog) (intr.). 3. To grumble, growl a while (intr.).

ПРОВРЁШЬСЯ, see проврусь.

ПРОВРИ́СЬ (imp.), see проврусь.

ПРОВРУ́СЬ, проврёшься. Р. Провра́ться (intr.). I. Провира́ться. 1. To betray the falseness of one's own statements, give oneself away talking. 2. To talk a lot of nonsense.

ПРОГЛА́ДЬ (imp.), see прогла́жу.

ПРОГЛА́ЖЕННЫЙ; прогла́жен, —а —о, —ы (ppp), see прогла́жу.

ПРОГЛА́ЖУ, прогла́дишь. Р. Прогла́дить. I. Прогла́живать (mean. 1). 1. To iron carefully (acc.). 2. To iron a while (intr.).

ПРОГЛО́ЧЕННЫЙ; прогло́чен, —а, —о, —ы (ppp), see проглочу́.

ПРОГЛОЧУ́, прогло́тишь. Р. Проглоти́ть (acc.). I. Прогла́тывать. 1. To swallow (as food). 2. To gulp down (as food). 3. (fig.) To swallow (as a story or insult). 4. (fig.) To swallow (words, i.e., to speak indistinctly). 5. (fig.) To devour (as a book).

ПРОГЛЯДИ́ (imp.), see прогляжу́.

ПРОГЛЯДИ́ШЬ, see прогляжу́.

ПРОГЛЯДЯ́Т, see прогляжу́.

ПРОГЛЯЖУ́, проглядишь. Р. Проглядеть (acc.). I. Прогля́дывать (mean. 1). 1. To look over, look through, to skim (as a book). 2. To overlook (as a mistake). 3. To spend some time looking (at s.t.).

ПРО́ГНАННЫЙ; про́гнан, —а, —о, —ы (ppp), see прогоню́.

ПРОГНЕВЛЁННЫЙ; прогневлён, —а́, —о́, —ы́ (ppp), see прогневлю́.

ПРОГНЕВЛЮ́, прогневишь. Р. Прогневи́ть (arch.) (acc.). I. Гневи́ть. To anger.

ПРОГНИЁТ, прогнию́т (3rd pers. only). Р. Прогни́ть (intr.). I. Прогнива́ть. To rot through.

ПРОГНИЮ́Т (3rd pers. pl.), see прогниёт.

ПРОГОНИ́ (imp.), see прогоню́.

ПРОГО́НИШЬ, see прогоню́.

ПРОГОНЮ́, прого́нишь. Р. Прогна́ть. I. Прогоня́ть. 1. To drive away, out (e.g., cattle, people, clouds, etc.) (acc.). 2. (fig.) To drive away, banish (e.g., fear, boredom, etc.) (acc.). 3. To dismiss, fire (as s.o. from a job) (acc.). 4. To go, drive rapidly (e.g., by auto, horse, etc.) (intr.). 5. To drive (as a nail through a board) (acc.).

ПРОГО́НЯТ, see прогоню́.

ПРОГОРИ́ (imp.), see прогорю́.

ПРОГОРИ́ШЬ, see прогорю́.

ПРОГО́РК, прого́ркла (past). Р. Прого́ркнуть (intr.). I. Го́ркнуть. To turn bitter or rancid (of food).

ПРОГОРЮ́, прогори́шь. Р. Прогоре́ть (intr.). I. Прогора́ть (mean. 1 thru

3). 1. To burn up (of fire wood, etc.). 2. To burn through (of an utensil, cloth, etc.). 3. To go bankrupt, fail in business, etc. 4. To burn a while (of a fire, a candle, etc.).

ПРОГОРЯ́Т, see прогорю́.

ПРОГОЩУ́, прогости́шь. Р. Прогости́ть (intr.). To spend a period of time as a guest, to stay for a time.

ПРОГРЁБ, прогребла́ (past), see прогребу́.

ПРОГРЕБЁННЫЙ; прогребён, —а́, —о́, —ы́ (ppp), see прогребу́.

ПРОГРЕБЁШЬ, see прогребу́.

ПРОГРЕБИ́ (imp.), see прогребу́.

ПРОГРЕБУ́, прогребёшь. Р. Прогрести́. I. Прогреба́ть (mean. 1, 2). 1. To rake or shovel (s.t.) away (as snow) (acc.). 2. To clear (as a path through the snow) (acc.). 3. To spend some time raking or shovelling (intr.).

ПРОГРЕМИ́ (imp.), see прогремлю́.

ПРОГРЕМИ́ШЬ, see прогремлю́.

ПРОГРЕМЛЮ́, прогреми́шь. Р. Прогреме́ть (intr.). 1. To thunder (often impers.). 2. To clatter, roar along or by (e.g., a tractor). 3. (lit. and fig.) To resound, ring out (e.g., a shot, praise, etc.). 4. (fig.) To thunder, roar (of a person). 5. To thunder, roar, for a period of time.

ПОРГРЕМЯ́Т, see прогремлю́.

ПРОГРОХО́ЧЕШЬ, see прогрохочу́[1].

ПРОГРОХОЧИ́ (imp.), see прогрохочу́[1].

ПРОГРОХОЧУ́[1], прогро́хчешь. Р. Прогрохота́ть (intr.). 1. To roar, thunder (e.g., cannon). 2. To make much noise, create a din in passing by (as with one's boots) (inst. of boots). 3. To clatter, roar along (as a street car). 4. To ring out, create much noise (e.g., explosions, shots, etc.). 5. To thunder, roar for a period of time.

ПРОГРОХОЧУ́[2], прогрохоти́шь. Р. Прогрохоти́ть (acc.). I. Грохоти́ть. To sift, screen, riddle, sieve.

ПРОГРЫ́З, прогры́зла (past), see прогрызу́.

ПРОГРЫ́ЗЕННЫЙ; прогры́зен, —а, —о, —ы (ppp), see прогрызу́.

ПРОГРЫЗЁШЬ, see прогрызу́.

ПРОГРЫЗИ́ (imp.), see прогрызу́.

ПРОГРЫЗУ́, прогрызёшь. Р. Прогры́зть (acc.). I. Прогрыза́ть (mean. 1). 1. To gnaw through. 2. To gnaw a while.

ПРОГУДИ́ (imp.), see прогужу́.

ПРОГУДИ́ШЬ, see прогужу́.

ПРОГУДЯ́Т, see прогужу́.

ПРОГУЖУ́, прогуди́шь. Р. Прогуде́ть (intr.). 1. To drone, buzz. 2. To hoot (e.g., a factory whistle). 3. To drone, buzz, hoot for a period of time.

ПРОДАВА́Й (imp.), see продаю́.

ПРОДАВА́Я (adv. pres. part.), see продаю́.

ПРОДА́ВЛЕННЫЙ; прода́влен, —а, —о, —ы (ppp), see продавлю́.

ПРОДАВЛЮ́, прода́вишь. Р. Продави́ть (acc.). I. Прода́вливать. 1. To press down, through. 2. To crush, break through (as the seat of a chair).

ПРОДАДИ́М, продади́те, продаду́т (pl. forms), see прода́м.

ПРОДАЁШЬ, see продаю́.

ПРОДА́Й (imp.), see прода́м.

ПРОДА́М, прода́шь, прода́ст (sing. forms). Р. Прода́ть (acc.). I. Продава́ть. 1. To sell. 2. To betray (sell out).

ПРО́ДАННЫЙ; про́дан, —а́, —о, —ы (ppp), see прода́м.

ПРОДА́СТ, see прода́м.

ПРОДА́ШЬ, see прода́м.

ПРОДАЮ́, продаёшь. I. Продава́ть (acc.). Р. Прода́ть. 1. To sell. 2. To betray, sell out.

ПРОДЕ́НЕШЬ, see проде́ну.

ПРОДЕ́НУ, проде́нешь. Р. Проде́ть (acc.). I. Продева́ть. To put, pass, thread (s.t.) through (s.t.) (as a rope through a ring, a thread through a needle) (acc. + в + acc.).

ПРОДЕ́НЬ (imp.), see проде́ну.

ПРОДЕРЁШЬ, see продеру́.

ПРОДЕ́РЖАННЫЙ; проде́ржан, —а, —о, —ы (ppp), see продержу́.

ПРОДЕ́РЖАТ, see продержу́.

ПРОДЕРЖИ́ (imp.), see продержу́.

ПРОДЕ́РЖИШЬ, see продержу́.

ПРОДЕРЖУ́, проде́ржишь. Р. Продержа́ть (acc.). 1. To hold for a period of time. 2. To support for a period of time (e.g., a roof).

ПРОДЕРИ́ (imp.), see продеру́.

ПРОДЕРУ́, продерёшь. Р. Продра́ть.

I. Продира́ть. 1. To wear through, out (as the elbows of a jacket) (acc.). 2. To tear holes in (e.g., a coat), (acc.). 3. To go through, along, by (intr.). 4. To reprimand (acc.). 5. To open (one's eyes) (acc. of eyes).

ПРОДЕ́ТЫЙ; проде́т, —а, —о, —ы (ppp), see проде́ну.

ПРОДЕШЕВЛЁННЫЙ; продешевлён, —а́, —о́, —ы́ (ppp), see продешевлю́.

ПРОДЕШЕВЛЮ́, продешеви́шь. Р. Продешеви́ть (acc.). I. Продешевля́ть. To sell (s.t.) too cheap.

ПРОДОЛБЛЁННЫЙ; продолблён, —а́, —о́, —ы́ (ppp), see продолблю́.

ПРОДОЛБЛЮ́, продолби́шь. Р. Продолби́ть. I. Прода́лбливать (mean. 1, 2, 3), долби́ть (mean. 1). 1. To hollow, gouge a hole, chisel through (as a cliff, a tree, etc.) (acc.). 2. (fig.) To press (for) (acc.). 3. (fig.) To press (on), persevere (intr.). 4. To chisel, etc., for a period of time (intr.) or (acc.).

ПРО́ДРАННЫЙ; про́дран, —а, —о, —ы (ppp), see продеру́.

ПРОДУ́ЕШЬ, see проду́ю.

ПРОДУ́Й (imp.), see проду́ю.

ПРОДУ́ТЫЙ; проду́т, —а, —о, —ы (ppp), see проду́ю.

ПРОДУ́Ю, проду́ешь. Р. Проду́ть (acc.). I. Продува́ть. 1. To blow through. 2. (tech.) To blow down, blow off (as a boiler). 3. (tech.) To exhaust, scavenge. 4. To catch cold in a draft (impers. + acc.). 5. To lose (as money at cards).

ПРОДЫРЯ́ВЛЕННЫЙ; продыря́влен, —а, —о, —ы (ppp), see продыря́влю.

ПРОДЫРЯ́ВЛЮ, продыря́вишь. Р. Продыря́вить (acc.). I. Продыря́вливать. 1. To pierce, perforate, punch. 2. To wear out, wear holes in (e.g., one's shoes).

ПРОДЫРЯ́ВЬ (imp.), see продыря́влю.

ПРОДЫ́ШАТ, see продышу́.

ПРОДЫ́ШАТСЯ, see продышу́сь.

ПРОДЫШИ́ (imp.), see продышу́.

ПРОДЫШИ́СЬ (imp.), see продышу́сь.

ПРОДЫ́ШИШЬ, see продышу́.

ПРОДЫ́ШИШЬСЯ, see продышу́сь.

ПРОДЫШУ́, проды́шишь. Р. Продыша́ть (intr.). 1. To live, exist for a period of time. 2. To breathe for a period of time.

ПРОДЫШУ́СЬ, продышишься. Р. Продыша́ться (intr.). To breathe deeply several times.

ПРОЕ́ДЕННЫЙ; прое́ден, —а, —о, —ы (ppp), see прое́м.

ПРОЕ́ДЕШЬ, see прое́ду.

ПРОЕДИ́М, проеди́те, проедя́т (pl. forms), see прое́м.

ПРОЕ́ДУ, прое́дешь. Р. Прое́хать. I. Проезжа́ть (mean. 1, 2, 3, 5, 6). 1. To drive, ride through (acc.) or (че́рез + acc.), or by (ми́мо + gen.). 2. To drive, ride (a distance) (acc.). 3. To drive, ride, by (intr.). 4. To drive, ride, a while (intr.). 5. To drive, ride, by (miss a stop) (acc.). 6. To drive, ride, to (к + dat.), along (a road) (по + dat.).

ПРОЕ́ЗДИ (imp.), see прое́зжу.

ПРОЕЗЖА́Й (imp.), see прое́ду.

ПРОЕ́ЗЖЕННЫЙ; прое́зжен, —а, —о, —ы (ppp), see прое́зжу.

ПРОЕ́ЗЖУ, прое́здишь. Р. Прое́здить. I. Проезжа́ть (mean. 2 and 3). 1. To drive, ride, for a period of time (intr.) or (acc.). 2. To spend (money) on travel (acc.). 3. To exercise (a horse) (acc.).

ПРОЕ́Л, прое́ла (past), see прое́м.

ПРОЕ́М, прое́шь, прое́ст (sing. forms). Р. Прое́сть. I. Проеда́ть (mean. 1 thru 3). 1. To eat through (s.t.) (as a rat eats a hole in s.t.) (acc.). 2. To corrode, eat through (as rust or acid eats through metal) (acc.). 3. To spend (money) on food (to eat up one's money) (acc. of money). 4. To eat for a period of time (intr.) or (acc.).

ПРОЕ́СТ, see прое́м.

ПРОЕ́ШЬ[1] (imp.), see прое́м.

ПРОЕ́ШЬ[2] (2nd pers. sing.), see прое́м.

ПРОЖГИ́ (imp.), see прожгу́.

ПРОЖГЛА́, прожгло́, прожгли́ (past), see прожгу́ and прожёг.

ПРОЖГУ́, прожжёшь, прожгу́т. Р. Проже́чь (acc.). I. Прожига́ть (mean. 1, 2, 4, 5). 1. To burn through (s.t.). 2. To burn out (as a flue). 3. To burn (s.t.) for a period of time (as a light). 4. (fig.) to burn (of s.o.'s touch, glance, etc.). 5. To squander (e.g., money).

ПРОЖДА́ННЫЙ; про́ждан, —а́ (and —а), —о, —ы (ppp), see прожду́.

ПРОЖДЁШЬ, see прожду́.

ПРОЖДИ́ (imp.), see прожду́.

ПРОЖДУ́, прождёшь. Р. Прожда́ть (acc./gen.). To wait for.

ПРОЖЁВАННЫЙ; прожёван, —а, —о, —ы (ppp), see прожую́.

ПРОЖЁГ, прожгла́ (past), see прожгу́.

ПРОЖЖЁННЫЙ; прожжён, —а́, —о́, —ы́ (ppp), see прожгу́.

ПРОЖЖЁШЬ, see прожгу́.

ПРОЖИВЁШЬ, see проживу́.

ПРОЖИВИ́ (imp.), see проживу́.

ПРОЖИВУ́, проживёшь. Р. Прожи́ть. I. Прожива́ть (mean. 3). 1. To live for a period of time (intr.). 2. To live somewhere and/or in some manner for a while (intr.). 3. To live up, to use up living, waste, (e.g., one's money) (acc.).

ПРО́ЖИТЫЙ; про́жит, —а́, —о, —ы (ppp), see проживу́.

ПРОЖИ́ТЫЙ; прожи́т, —а́, —о, —ы (ppp), see проживу́.

ПРОЖУЁШЬ, see прожую́.

ПРОЖУЖЖА́Т, see прожужжу́.

ПРОЖУЖЖИ́ (imp.), see прожужжу́.

ПРОЖУЖЖИ́ШЬ, see прожужжу́.

ПРОЖУЖЖУ́, прожужжи́шь. Р. Прожужжа́ть. 1. To buzz, drone, hum (of flies, bullets, etc.) (intr.). 2. To buzz, etc. for a while (intr.). 3. To tire (s.o.'s ears), to bore (acc. of ears + dat. of person).

ПРОЖУ́Й (imp.), see прожую́.

ПРОЖУЮ́, прожуёшь. Р. Прожева́ть (acc.). I. Прожёвывать. To masticate, chew well.

ПРО́ЗВАННЫЙ; про́зван, —а́, —о, —ы (ppp), see прозову́.

ПРОЗВЕНИ́ (imp.), see прозвени́т.

ПРОЗВЕНИ́Т, прозвеня́т (3rd pers. only). Р. Прозвене́ть (intr.). 1. (lit. and fig.) To ring. 2. To ring for a period of time. 3. To ring out, be heard.

ПРОЗВЕНЯ́Т (3rd pers. pl.), see прозвени́т.

ПРОЗВУЧА́Т (3rd pers. pl.), see прозвучи́т.

ПРОЗВУЧИ́ (imp.), see прозвучи́т.

ПРОЗВУЧИ́Т, прозвуча́т (3rd pers. only). Р. Прозвуча́ть (intr.). 1. To sound. 2. To ring. 3. To be heard, ring out.

ПРОЗОВЁШЬ, see прозову́.

ПРОЗОВИ́ (imp.), see прозову́.

ПРОЗОВУ́, прозовёшь. Р. Прозва́ть (acc. + inst.). I. Прозыва́ть. 1. To nickname (s.o. or s.t.). 2. To call (s.t.) by a descriptive name (e.g., "Rocky Mountains").

ПРОЗРИ́ (imp.), see прозрю́.

ПРОЗРИ́ШЬ, see прозрю́.

ПРОЗРЮ́, прозри́шь (also прозре́ю, etc.). Р. Прозре́ть. I. Прозрева́ть. 1. To recover one's sight (intr.). 2. To begin to understand, realize, see clearly (intr.) or (acc.).

ПРОЗРЯ́Т, see прозрю́.

ПРОЗЯ́Б, прозя́бла (past). Р. Прозя́бнуть (intr.). 1. To be chilled through. 2. (arch.) To sprout (of plants, etc.).

ПРОИЗВЕДЁННЫЙ; произведён, —а́, —о́, —ы́ (ppp), see произведу́.

ПРОИЗВЕДЁШЬ, see произведу́.

ПРОИЗВЕДИ́ (imp.), see произведу́.

ПРОИЗВЕДУ́, произведёшь. Р. Произвести́ (acc.). I. Производи́ть. 1. To make, carry out, effect (e.g., repairs). 2. To produce, manufacture (e.g., goods). 3. To conduct, perform (e.g., an experiment). 4. (fig.) To produce, create (e.g., an impression on s.o.) (acc. + на + acc.). 5. To bear, give birth to (s.o. or s.t.). 6. To promote (e.g., s.o. to the rank of major) (acc. + в + acc. pl. of major).

ПРОИЗВЕ́ДШИЙ (pap), see произведу́.

ПРОИЗВЕДЯ́ (adv. past part.), see произведу́.

ПРОИЗВЁЛ, произвела́ (past), see произведу́.

ПРОИЗВОЖУ́, произво́дишь. I. Производи́ть (acc.). Р. Произвести́ (mean. 1 thru 6). 1. To make, carry out, effect (e.g., repairs). 2. To produce, manufacture (e.g., goods). 3. To conduct, perform (e.g., an experiment). 4. (fig.) To produce, create (e.g., an impression on s.o.) (acc. + на + acc.). 5. To bear, give birth (to s.o. or s.t.). 6. To promote (e.g., s.o. to the rank of major) (acc. + в + acc. pl. of major). 7. (ling.) To derive (e.g., a word from the greek) (acc. + от + gen.).

ПРОИЗНЁС, произнесла́ (past), see произнесу́.

ПРОИЗНЕСЁННЫЙ; произнесён, —а́, —о́, —ы́ (ppp), see произнесу́.

ПРОИЗНЕСЁШЬ, see произнесу́.

ПРОИЗНЕСИ́ (imp.), see произнесу́.

ПРОИЗНЕСУ́, произнесёшь. Р. Произнести́ (acc.). I. Произноси́ть. 1. To utter, say. 2. To make or deliver (as a speech). 3. To articulate, pronounce. 4. To pronounce (as a judgement).

ПРОИЗНЕСЯ́ (adv. past part.), see произнесу́.

ПРОИЗНОШУ́, произно́сишь. I. Произноси́ть (acc.). Р. Произнести́. 1. To utter, say. 2. To make, deliver (as a speech). 3. To articulate, pronounce. 4. To pronounce (as a judgement).

ПРОИЗОЙДЁТ, произойду́т (3rd pers. only). Р. Произойти́ (intr.). I. Происходи́ть. 1. To occur, take place. 2. To come from, arise from (от/из-за + gen.). 3. To descend from (от + gen.) (of people).

ПРОИЗОЙДУ́Т (3rd pers. pl.), see произойдёт.

ПРОИЗОЙДЯ́ and происше́дши (adv. past part.), see произойдёт.

ПРОИЗОШЁЛ, поризошла́ (past), see произойдёт.

ПРОИЗРАСТЁТ, произрасту́т (3rd pers. only). Р. Произрасти́ (intr.). I. Произраста́ть. To grow, sprout.

ПРОИЗРАСТИ́ (imp.), see произрастёт.

ПРОИЗРАСТУ́Т (3rd pers. pl.), see произрастёт.

ПРОИЗРО́С, произросла́ (past), see произрастёт.

ПРОИСТЁК, проистекла́ (past), see проистечёт.

ПРОИСТЕКУ́Т (3rd pers. pl.), see проистечёт.

ПРОИСТЕЧЁТ, проистеку́т (3rd pers. only). Р. Происте́чь (intr.) (из/от + gen.). I. Проистека́ть. 1. To result from, spring from. 2. (arch.) To flow from.

ПРОИСХОЖУ́, происхо́дишь. I. Происходи́ть (intr.). Р. Произойти́. 1. To occur, take place. 2. To come from, arise from (от/из-за + gen.). 3. To descend from (от + gen.) (of people).

ПРОИСШЕ́ДШИ and произойдя́ (adv. past. part.), see произойдёт.

ПРОИСШЁДШИЙ (pap), see произойдёт.

ПРÓЙДЕННЫЙ; прóйден, —а, —о,
—ы (ppp), see пройду́.

ПРОЙДЁННЫЙ; пройдён, —á, —ó,
—ы́ (ppp), see пройду́.

ПРОЙДЁШЬ, see пройду́.

ПРОЙДЁШЬСЯ, see пройду́сь.

ПРОЙДИ́ (imp.), see пройду́.

ПРОЙДИ́СЬ (imp.), see пройду́сь.

ПРОЙДУ́, пройдёшь. Р. Пройти́. I.
Проходи́ть. 1. To go (intr.). 2. To
go through, pass through (e.g., a
door) (в + acc.). 3. To go or cover
a certain distance (acc.). 4. To go or
pass along (e.g., a road) (по + dat.).
5. To pass by (acc.) or (ми́мо +
gen.). 6. (fig.) To pass over (as an
expression passes over one's face)
(по + dat.). 7. To pass, elapse (of
time) (intr.). 8. To pass, be over,
cease (of an event, illness, rain, etc.)
(intr.). 9. To complete (as a course of
study) (acc.). 10. To overlook (s.t.)
(ми́мо + gen.). 11. To study (e.g., a
subject) (acc.). (For other usages
see unabridged dictionary.)

ПРОЙДУ́СЬ, пройдёшься. Р. Про-
йти́сь. I. Проха́живаться (mean. 1).
1. To stroll (intr.). 2. To dance (intr.)
or (acc.). 3. (fig.) To run over (as the
keys of a piano) (по + dat.). 4. To
pass (s.t.) over (s.t.) (e.g., one's
hand over one's face, a dustcloth
over a surface, etc.). (inst. of hand +
по + dat. of face).

ПРОЙДЯ́ (adv. past part.), see
пройду́.

ПРОЙДЯ́СЬ, (adv. past part.) see
пройду́сь.

ПРОЙМЁШЬ, see пройму́.

ПРОЙМИ́ (imp.), see пройму́.

ПРОЙМУ́, проймёшь. Р. Проня́ть
(acc.). I. Пронима́ть. 1. To penetrate, chill (of cold). 2. (fig.) "To
get at," strongly affect (s.o.).

ПРОКАЖУ́, прока́зишь. I. Про-
ка́зить (intr.). Р. Напрока́зить. To
play pranks, do mischief.

ПРОКА́ЗЬ (imp.), see прокажу́.

ПРОКА́ЧЕННЫЙ; прока́чен, —а,
—о, —ы (ppp), see прокачу́.

ПРОКАЧУ́, прока́тишь. Р. Про-
кати́ть. I. Прока́тывать. 1. To take
for a ride (acc.). 2. To roll (as a ball)
(acc.). 3. To ride by rapidly (intr.).

4. To reject (s.o.) at an election
(acc.). 5. To criticize severely (acc.).

ПРОКВА́СЬ (imp.), see проква́шу.

ПРОКВА́ШЕННЫЙ; проква́шен,
—а, —о, —ы (ppp), see проква́шу.

ПРОКВА́ШУ, проква́сишь. Р. Про-
ква́сить (acc.). I. Проква́шивать.
1. To sour. 2. To leaven (as bread).
3. To permit to sour.

ПРОКИПИ́ (imp.), see прокипи́т.

ПРОКИПИ́Т, прокипя́т (3rd pers.
only). Р. Прокипе́ть (intr.). 1. To boil
properly. 2. To boil for a period of time.

ПРОКИПЯ́Т (3rd pers. pl.), see
прокипи́т.

ПРОКИПЯЧЁННЫЙ; прокипячён,
—á, —ó, —ы́ (ppp), see прокипячу́.

ПРОКИПЯЧУ́, прокипяти́шь. Р.
Прокипяти́ть (acc.). 1. To boil the
proper length of time (as food). 2.
To boil thoroughly (e.g., surgical
instruments). 3. To boil for a period
of time.

ПРОКИ́С, проки́сла (past). Р. Про-
ки́снуть (intr.). I. Ки́снуть, проки-
са́ть. To turn sour.

ПРО́КЛЯЛ, прокляла́, про́кляло, про́-
кляли (past), see прокляну́.

ПРОКЛЯНЁШЬ, see прокляну́.

ПРОКЛЯНИ́ (imp.), see прокляну́.

ПРОКЛЯНУ́, проклянёшь. Р. Про-
кля́сть (acc.). I. Проклина́ть. To
curse, damn.

ПРО́КЛЯТЫЙ; про́клят, —á, —о,
—ы (ppp), see прокляну́.

ПРОКО́ЛЕШЬ, see проколю́.

ПРОКОЛИ́ (imp.), see проколю́.

ПРОКО́ЛОТЫЙ; проко́лот, —а, —о,
—ы (ppp), see проколю́.

ПРОКОЛЮ́, проко́лешь. Р. Про-
коло́ть (acc.). I. Прока́лывать
(mean. 1 and 2). 1. To pierce. 2. To
run through (as with a sword). 3. To
chop (as wood) for a period of time.

ПРОКОНОПА́ТЬ (imp.), see про-
конопа́чу.

ПРОКОНОПА́ЧЕННЫЙ; проконо-
па́чен, —а, —о, —ы (ppp), see
проконопа́чу.

ПРОКОНОПА́ЧУ, проконопа́тишь.
Р. Проконопа́тить. I. Проконо-
па́чивать (mean. 1). 1. To caulk completely (e.g., a boat) (acc.). 2. caulk
for a period of time (intr.) or (acc.).

ПРОКОПЧЁННЫЙ; прокопчён, —á,
—ó, —ы́ (ppp), see прокопчу́.

ПРОКОПЧУ́, прокопти́шь. Р. Прокопти́ть. I. Прока́пчивать (mean. 1 and 2). 1. To smoke (as a ham) (acc.). 2. To cover with smoke, soot (acc.). 3. To smoke (of a stove) (intr.). 4. To smoke for a period of time (intr.) or (acc.).

ПРОКО́РМЛЕННЫЙ; проко́рмлен, —а, —о, —ы (ppp), see прокормлю́.

ПРОКОРМЛЮ́, проко́рмишь. Р. Прокорми́ть (acc.). I. Прока́рмливать (mean. 1 and 2). 1. To feed (as animals, people). 2. To feed, use up for feed (e.g., hay, grain). 3. To feed for a period of time.

ПРОКО́ШЕННЫЙ; проко́шен, —а, —о, —ы (ppp), see прокошу́.

ПРОКОШУ́, проко́сишь. Р. Прокоси́ть. I. Прока́шивать (mean. 1). 1. To mow (as a strip or an area) (acc.). 2. To spend a period of time mowing (intr.) or (acc.).

ПРОКРАДЁШЬСЯ, see прокраду́сь.

ПРОКРАДИ́СЬ (imp.), see прокраду́сь.

ПРОКРАДУ́СЬ, прокрадёшься. Р. Прокра́сться (intr.). I. Прокра́дываться. 1. (lit. and fig.) To steal, creep, into (в + acc.). 2. To steal, creep, by (ми́мо + gen.). 3. To be caught stealing.

ПРОКРА́ЛСЯ, прокра́лась (past), see прокраду́сь.

ПРОКРА́СЬ (imp.), see прокра́шу.

ПРОКРА́ШЕННЫЙ; прокра́шен, —а, —о, —ы (ppp), see прокра́шу.

ПРОКРА́ШУ, прокра́сишь. Р. Прокра́сить. I. Прокра́шивать (mean. 1). 1. To paint, color, dye (acc.). 2. To paint, etc. for a period of time (intr.) or (acc.).

ПРОКРИЧА́Т, see прокричу́.

ПРОКРИЧИ́ (imp.), see прокричу́.

ПРОКРИЧИ́ШЬ, see прокричу́.

ПРОКРИЧУ́, прокричи́шь. Р. Прокрича́ть. 1. To shout, cry (acc.) or (intr.). 2. To proclaim, trumpet (s.t.) (о + prep.). 3. To spend a period of time shouting, proclaiming (acc.) or (intr.).

ПРОКУ́ЧЕННЫЙ; проку́чен, —а, —о, —ы (ppp), see прокучу́.

ПРОКУЧУ́, проку́тишь. Р. Прокути́ть. I. Проку́чивать (mean. 1 and 2). 1. To go on a spree (intr.). 2. To squander (e.g., one's money)

carousing (acc.). 3. To carouse for a period of time (e.g., the whole night) (acc.).

ПРОКУ́ШЕННЫЙ; проку́шен, —а, —о, —ы (ppp), see прокушу́.

ПРОКУШУ́, проку́сишь. Р. Прокуси́ть (acc.). I. Проку́сывать. To bite through.

ПРОЛА́Й (imp.), see прола́ю.

ПРОЛА́Ю, прола́ешь. Р. Прола́ять (intr.). 1. To give a bark. 2. To bark for a period of time (e.g., all night).

ПРОЛЁГ, пролегла́ (past), see проля́жет.

ПРОЛЁЖАННЫЙ; пролёжан, —а, —о, —ы (ppp), see пролежу́.

ПРОЛЕЖА́Т, see пролежу́.

ПРОЛЕЖИ́ (imp.), see пролежу́.

ПРОЛЕЖИ́ШЬ, see пролежу́.

ПРОЛЕЖУ́, пролежи́шь. Р. Пролежа́ть. I. Пролёживать. 1. To spend time lying down (intr.). 2. To lie unused, lie about, (as a tool) (intr.). 3. To lie on some part of the body until it is sore or asleep (acc.). 4. To wear out by lying (e.g., a couch) (acc.).

ПРОЛЕ́З, проле́зла (past), see проле́зу.

ПРОЛЕ́ЗЕШЬ, see проле́зу.

ПРОЛЕ́ЗУ, проле́зешь. Р. Проле́зть (intr.). I. Пролеза́ть. 1. To get through, into with difficulty (wiggle through, climb through etc.) (в + acc.). 2. (fig.) To work oneself into (as into s.o.'s confidence) (в + acc.).

ПРОЛЕ́ЗЬ (imp.), see проле́зу.

ПРОЛЕ́Й (imp.), see пролью́.

ПРОЛЕТИ́ (imp.), see пролечу́.

ПРОЛЕТИ́ШЬ, see пролечу́.

ПРОЛЕТЯ́Т, see пролечу́.

ПРОЛЕЧУ́, пролети́шь. Р. Пролете́ть. I. Пролета́ть. 1. (lit. and fig.) To fly, fly by (intr.). 2. (lit. and fig.) To fly by someplace (acc.) or (ми́мо + gen.). 3. To fly a certain distance (acc.). 4. (fig.) To fly by (of time) (intr.).

ПРО́ЛИТЫЙ; про́лит, —а́, —о, —ы (ppp), see пролью́.

ПРОЛИ́ТЫЙ; проли́т, —а́, —о, —ы (ppp), see пролью́.

ПРОЛО́МЛЕННЫЙ; проло́млен, —а, —о, —ы (ppp), see проломлю́.

ПРОЛОМЛЮ́, проло́мишь. Р. Проломи́ть (acc.). I. Прола́мывать. To break through, stave in, fracture.

ПРОЛЬЁШЬ, see пролью́.

ПРОЛЬЮ́, прольёшь. P. Проли́ть. I. Пролива́ть. 1. To spill (as water) (acc.). 2. (fig.) To spill (as blood) (acc.). 3. To shed (e.g., tears, light, etc.) (acc.). 4. To pour (of rain) (intr.).

ПРОЛЯ́ГУТ (3rd pers. pl.), see проля́жет.

ПРОЛЯ́ЖЕТ, проля́гут (3rd pers. only). P. Проле́чь (intr.). To extend, stretch (out), lie (of paths, roads, etc.).

ПРОМА́ЖЕШЬ, see прома́жу.

ПРОМА́ЖУ, прома́жешь. P. Прома́зать. I. Прома́зывать (mean. 1, 2, 4), ма́зать (mean. 4). 1. To coat thoroughly (as with grease, oil, etc.) (acc. + inst.). 2. To seal up (as cracks with putty) (acc. + inst.). 3. To oil, grease, etc. for a while (intr.) or (acc.). 4. To miss (as a shot) (intr.).

ПРОМА́ЖЬ (imp.), see прома́жу.

ПРОМА́ЗАННЫЙ; прома́зан, —а, —о, —ы (ppp), see прома́жу.

ПРОМЁЛ, промела́ (past), see промету́.

ПРОМЕ́ЛЕШЬ, see промелю́.

ПРОМЕЛИ́ (imp.), see промелю́.

ПРОМЕЛЮ́, проме́лешь. P. Промоло́ть. I. Прома́лывать (mean. 1). 1. To grind, mill (acc.). 2. To grind or mill for a period of time (acc.) or (intr.).

ПРОМЁРЗ, промёрзла (past). P. Промёрзнуть (intr.). I. Промерза́ть (mean. 1 and 2). 1. To freeze through. 2. To be thoroughly chilled. 3. To suffer intensely from cold for a period of time.

ПРОМЕТЁННЫЙ; прометён, —а́, —о́, —ы́ (ppp), see промету́.

ПРОМЕТЁШЬ, see промету́.

ПРОМЕТИ́ (imp.), see промету́.

ПРОМЕТУ́, прометёшь. P. Промести́. I. Промета́ть (mean. 1). 1. To sweep out (thoroughly) (acc.). 2. To sweep for a period of time (intr.) or (acc.).

ПРОМЁТШИЙ (pap), see промету́.

ПРОМЕТЯ́ (adv. past part.), see промету́.

ПРОМЕ́ШЕННЫЙ; проме́шен, —а, —о, —ы (ppp), see промешу́.

ПРОМЕШУ́, проме́сишь. P. Про-меси́ть. I. Проме́шивать (mean. 1). 1. To knead thoroughly (acc.). 2. To knead for a period of time (intr.) or (acc.).

ПРОМНЁШЬ, see промну́.

ПРОМНИ́ (imp.), see промну́.

ПРОМНУ́, промнёшь. P. Промя́ть (acc.). I. Промина́ть (mean. 1 and 2). 1. To crush (as a cushion of a chair). 2. To limber up (as a horse). 3. To spend a period of time kneading, etc.

ПРОМО́ЕШЬ, see промо́ю.

ПРОМО́Й (imp.), see промо́ю.

ПРОМО́К, промо́кла (past). P. Промо́кнуть (intr.). I. Промока́ть. To get sopping wet, get soaked, get wet clear through.

ПРОМО́ЛВИ (imp.), see промо́лвлю.

ПРОМО́ЛВЛЕННЫЙ; промо́лвлен, —а, —о, —ы (ppp), see промо́лвлю.

ПРОМО́ЛВЛЮ, промо́лвишь. P. Промо́лвить (acc.). To say, utter.

ПРОМОЛОТИ́ (imp.), see промолочу́.

ПРОМО́ЛОТЫЙ; промо́лот, —а, —о, —ы (ppp), see промелю́.

ПРОМОЛО́ЧЕННЫЙ; промоло́чен, —а, —о, —ы (ppp), see промолочу́.

ПРОМОЛОЧУ́, промоло́тишь. P. Промолоти́ть. I. Промола́чивать (mean. 1). 1. To thresh (grain, etc.) (acc.). 2. To thresh for a period of time (acc.) or (intr.).

ПРОМОЛЧА́Т, see промолчу́.

ПРОМОЛЧИ́ (imp.), see промолчу́.

ПРОМОЛЧИ́ШЬ, see промолчу́.

ПРОМОЛЧУ́, промолчи́шь. P. Промолча́ть (intr.). 1. To not reply, keep silent. 2. To remain silent for a period of time.

ПРОМОРО́ЖЕННЫЙ; проморо́жен, —а, —о, —ы (ppp), see проморо́жу.

ПРОМОРО́ЖУ, проморо́зишь. P. Проморо́зить (acc.). I. Промора́живать (mean. 1, 2, 3). 1. To freeze (as meat, etc.). 2. To freeze (as a river, the ground, etc.) (impers. + acc.). 3. To freeze out, make very cold (as a room). 4. To freeze, to keep very cold for a period of time.

ПРОМОРО́ЗЬ (imp.), see проморо́жу.

ПРОМО́Ю, промо́ешь. P. Промы́ть (acc.). I. Промыва́ть (mean. 1 thru 4). 1. To bathe, wash out (as a wound). 2. To wash out (e.g., a gully, dam, etc.). 3. (tech.) To wash (as ore, gold bearing sand, etc.). 4. To wash well. 5. To wash a while.

ПРОМЧА́ТСЯ, see промчу́сь.

ПРОМЧИ́СЬ (imp.), see промчу́сь.

ПРОМЧИ́ШЬСЯ, see промчу́сь.

ПРОМЧУ́СЬ, промчи́шься. Р. Промча́ться (intr.). 1. To speed, rush by (e.g., a car, etc.). 2. (fig.) To rush by, speed by, pass rapidly (e.g., years, days, etc.).

ПРОМЫ́ТЫЙ; промы́т, —а, —о, —ы (ppp), see промо́ю.

ПРОМЯ́ТЫЙ; промя́т, —а, —о, —ы (ppp), see промну́.

ПРОНЁС, пронесла́ (past), see пронесу́.

ПРОНЕСЁННЫЙ; пронсён, —а́, —о́, —ы́ (ppp), see пронесу́.

ПРОНЕСЁШЬ, see пронесу́.

ПРОНЕСЁШЬСЯ, see пронесу́сь.

ПРОНЕСИ́ (imp.), see пронесу́.

ПРОНЕСИ́СЬ (imp.), see пронесу́сь.

ПРОНЁССЯ, пронесла́сь (past), see пронесу́сь.

ПРОНЕСУ́, пронесёшь. Р. Пронести́. I. Проноси́ть. 1. (lit. and fig.) To carry (acc.). 2. To carry by (acc. + ми́мо + gen.), carry through (acc. + че́рез + acc.). 3. (fig.) To carry, retain (e.g., memories through one's life) (acc. + че́рез + acc.). 4. To carry away (e.g., wind carries away clouds) (acc.) or (impers. + acc.). 5. To pass, be over (e.g., danger, trouble, etc.) (impers.). 6. To have loose bowels (impers. + acc. of person).

ПРОНЕСУ́СЬ, пронесёшься. Р. Пронести́сь (intr.). I. Проноси́ться. 1. To rush past, go by rapidly (ми́мо + gen.). 2. To go rapidly, to rush. 3. (fig.) To pass rapidly (of time). 4. (fig.) To spread rapidly (of rumors). 5. To be heard (of sounds, etc.). 6. To fly by, blow over (of clouds, storms, etc.). 7. (fig.) To flit, flash (e.g., as thoughts through one's head) (в + prep. of head).

ПРОНЕСИ́ (adv. past part.), see пронесу́.

ПРОНЕСЯ́СЬ (adv. past part.), see пронесу́сь.

ПРОНЖУ́, пронзи́шь. Р. Пронзи́ть (acc.). I. Пронза́ть. 1. To pierce, run through (as with a sword) (acc. + inst.). 2. (fig.) To pierce (as with a glance) (acc. + inst.).

ПРОНЗЁННЫЙ; пронзён, —а́, —о́, —ы́ (ppp), see пронжу́.

ПРОНИ́ЖЕШЬ, see пронижу́.

ПРОНИЖИ́ (imp.), see пронижу́.

ПРОНИЖУ́, прони́жешь. Р. Пронизать (acc.). I. Прони́зывать (mean. 1, 2, 4). 1. To pierce, pass through (s.t.) (e.g., of a bullet, knife, etc.). 2. To penetrate, permeate (of cold, light, thoughts, etc.). 3. To spend a period of time stringing (as beads, etc.). 4. To cover, adorn (s.t. with beads, etc.) (acc. + inst.).

ПРОНИ́ЗАННЫЙ; прони́зан, —а, —о, —ы (ppp), see пронижу́.

ПРОНИ́К, прони́кла (past). Р. Прони́кнуть. I. Проника́ть. 1. To penetrate (в + acc.). 2. (fig.) To penetrate, (acc.) (arch.), or (в + acc.).

ПРОНО́ШЕННЫЙ; проно́шен, —а, —о, —ы (ppp), see проношу́[1].

ПРОНОШУ́[1], проно́сишь. Р. Проноси́ть (acc.). I. Пропа́шивать (mean. 3). 1. To carry about for a period of time. 2. To wear for a period of time (as a hat for five years). 3. To wear out (as clothes).

ПРОНОШУ́[2], проно́сишь. I. Проноси́ть. Р. Пронести́. 1. (lit. and fig.) To carry (acc.). 2. To carry by (acc. + ми́мо + gen.), carry through (acc. + че́рез + acc.). 3. (fig.) To carry, retain (e.g., memories through one's life) (acc. + че́рез + acc.). 4. To carry away (e.g., wind carries away clouds) (acc.) or (impers. + acc.). 5. To pass, be over (e.g., danger, trouble, etc.) (impers.). 6. To have loose bowels (impers. + acc. of person).

ПРОНОШУ́СЬ, проно́сишься. I. Проноси́ться (intr.). Р. Пронести́сь. 1. To rush past, go by rapidly (ми́мо + gen.). 2. To go rapidly, rush. 3. (fig.) To pass rapidly (of time). 4. (fig.) To spread rapidly (of rumors). 5. To be heard (of sounds, etc.). 6. To fly by, blow over (of clouds, storms, etc.). 7. (fig.) To flit, flash (e.g., as thoughts through one's head) (в + prep. of head).

ПРÓНЯТЫЙ; прóнят, —á, —о, —ы (ppp). Р. Проня́ть (асс.). I. Пронима́ть. 1. To penetrate, chill (of cold). 2. (fig.) To "get at," strongly affect (s.o.). (Also see пройму́.)

ПРОПАДЁШЬ, see пропаду́.

ПРОПАДИ́ (imp.), see пропаду́.

ПРОПАДУ́, пропадёшь. Р. Пропа́сть (intr.). I. Пропада́ть. 1. To be lost, missing. 2. To disappear. 3. To die. 4. To be wasted (e.g., a day).

ПРОПА́Л, пропа́ла (past), see пропаду́.

ПРОПА́Х, пропа́хла (past). Р. Пропа́хнуть (intr.). 1. To become permeated with an odor (of s.t.) (inst.). 2. To smell due to spoilage (e.g., fish) (intr.).

ПРОПА́ХАННЫЙ; пропа́хан, —а, —о, —ы (ppp), see пропашу́.

ПРОПА́ШЕШЬ, see пропашу́.

ПРОПАШИ́ (imp.), see пропашу́.

ПРОПАШУ́, пропа́шешь. Р. Пропаха́ть. I. Пропа́хивать (mean. 1). 1. To plow (as a furrow), cultivate (acc.). 2. To plow for a period of time (intr.) or (acc.).

ПРОПЕ́Й (imp.). Р. Пропи́ть. I. Пропива́ть (mean 1, 2, 4). 1. To squander (as money) on drink (acc.). 2. To ruin by drinking (e.g., one's voice, talent, etc.) (acc.). 3. To spend a period of time drinking (intr.) or (acc.). 4. (arch.) To seal, confirm an engagement, proposal of marriage with a drink, toast (acc. of person engaged).

ПРОПЁК, пропекла́ (past), see пропеку́.

ПРОПЕКИ́ (imp.), see пропеку́.

ПРОПЕКУ́, пропечёшь, пропеку́т. Р. Пропе́чь. I. Пропека́ть (mean. 1 thru 3). 1. To bake thoroughly (e.g., bread) (acc.). 2. To burn (as the sun burns a person's face) (acc.). 3. To exasperate (s.o.) (acc.). 4. To spend a period of time baking (intr.) or (acc.).

ПРОПЕ́ТЫЙ; пропе́т, —а, —о, —ы (ppp). Р. Пропе́ть. I. Петь (mean. 1 and 2). 1. To sing (intr.). 2. To sing (a song, a part, etc.) (acc.). 3. To speak in a sing-song voice (intr.) or (acc.). 4. To lose one's voice from singing (acc. of voice). 5. To sing for

a period of time (intr.) or (acc.). (Also see пропою́.)

ПРОПЕЧЁННЫЙ; пропечён, —á, —ó, —ы́ (ppp), see пропеку́.

ПРОПЕЧЁШЬ, see пропеку́.

ПРОПИ́САННЫЙ; пропи́сан, —а, —о, —ы (ppp), see пропишу́.

ПРÓПИТЫЙ; прóпит, —á, —о, —ы (ppp), see пропе́й and пропью́.

ПРОПИ́ТЫЙ; пропи́т, —á, —о, —ы (ppp), see пропе́й and пропью́.

ПРОПИ́ШЕШЬ, see пропишу́.

ПРОПИШИ́ (imp.), see пропишу́.

ПРОПИШУ́, пропи́шешь. Р. Прописа́ть (acc.). I. Пропи́сывать (mean. 1, 2, 4, 5, 6). 1. To prescribe (as medicine). 2. To register (officially). 3. To write for a period of time (intr.) or (acc.). 4. To write a criticism of (s.o.) (acc. of s.o.). 5. To punish (give some type of punishment to s.o.) (dat. of person + acc. of punishment). 6. (art) To sketch.

ПРОПИЩА́Т, see пропищу́.

ПРОПИЩИ́ (imp.), see пропищу́.

ПРОПИЩИ́ШЬ, see пропищу́.

ПРОПИЩУ́, пропищи́шь. Р. Пропища́ть. I. Пища́ть (mean. 1 thru 4). 1. To peep, chirp (of birds, etc.) (intr.). 2. To squeak (of mice, etc.) (intr.). 3. To whine (of dogs, etc.) (intr.). 4. To speak, say in a squeaky voice (intr.) or (acc.). 5. To peep, etc. for a period of time (intr.) or (acc.).

ПРОПЛА́ЧЕШЬ, see пропла́чу.

ПРОПЛА́ЧУ, пропла́чешь. Р. Пропла́кать. 1. To cry for a period of time (intr.). 2. To cry one's eyes out (acc. of eyes).

ПРОПЛА́ЧЬ (imp.), see пропла́чу.

ПРОПЛЁЛСЯ, проплела́сь (past), see проплету́сь.

ПРОПЛЕТЁШЬСЯ, see проплету́сь.

ПРОПЛЕТИ́СЬ (imp.), see проплету́сь.

ПРОПЛЕТУ́СЬ, проплетёшься. Р. Проплести́сь (intr.). To saunter.

ПРОПЛЕТЯ́СЬ (adv. past part.), see проплету́сь.

ПРОПЛЫВЁШЬ, see проплыву́.

ПРОПЛЫВИ́ (imp.), see проплыву́..

ПРОПЛЫВУ́, проплывёшь. Р. Проплы́ть. I. Проплыва́ть (mean. 1

and 2). 1. (lit. and fig.) To swim, float, sail, drift, by or through (acc.) or (ми́мо + gen.) or (че́рез + acc.). 2. To swim, float, etc., a certain distance (acc.). 3. To swim, float, etc. for a period of time (intr.).

ПРОПОЁШЬ, see **пропою́**.

ПРОПО́Й (imp.), see **пропою́**.

ПРОПО́ЛЕШЬ, see **прополю́**.

ПРОПО́ЛЗ, проползла́ (past), see **проползу́**.

ПРОПОЛЗЁШЬ, see **проползу́**.

ПРОПОЛЗИ́ (imp.), see **проползу́**.

ПРОПОЛЗУ́, проползёшь. Р. Проползти́. I. Прополза́ть. 1. To crawl, creep (somewhere) (intr.). 2. To crawl, creep, by or past (ми́мо + gen.), through (че́рез + acc.), along (по + dat.). 3. To crawl or creep a certain distance (acc.).

ПРОПОЛИ́ (imp.), see **прополю́**.

ПРОПОЛО́СКАННЫЙ; прополо́скан, —а, —о, —ы (ppp), see **прополощу́**.

ПРОПО́ЛОТЫЙ; пропо́лот, —а, —о, —ы (ppp), see **прополю́**.

ПРОПОЛО́ЩЕШЬ, see **прополощу́**.

ПРОПОЛОЩИ́ (imp.), see **прополощу́**.

ПРОПОЛОЩУ́, прополо́щешь. Р. Прополоска́ть. I. Полоска́ть (mean. 1 and 2), прополо́скивать (mean. 1 and 2). 1. To rinse (as laundry, one's mouth, etc.) (acc.). 2. To gargle (one's throat) (acc.). 3. To spend a period of time rinsing, etc. (intr.) or (acc.).

ПРОПОЛЮ́, пропо́лешь. Р. Прорло́ть. I. Пропа́лывать (mean. 1). 1. To weed (a certain area, or crop, etc.) (acc.). 2. To spend a period of time weeding (intr.) or (acc.).

ПРОПО́РЕШЬ, see **пропорю́**.

ПРОПОРИ́ (imp.), see **пропорю́**.

ПРОПО́РОТЫЙ; пропо́рот, —а, —о, —ы (ppp), see **пропорю́**.

ПРОПОРЮ́, пропо́решь. Р. Пропоро́ть (acc.). I. Пропа́рывать (mean. 1 and 2). 1. To tear, cut through. 2. To wound (with s.t. sharp), cut (acc. + inst.). 3. To rip (a dress, coat, etc., at the seams) for a period of time.

ПРОПОЮ́, пропоёшь. Р. Пропе́ть. I. Петь (mean. 1 and 2). 1. To sing (intr.). 2. To sing (a song, a part. etc.) (acc.). 3. To speak in a sing-song voice (intr.) or (acc.). 4. To lose

one's voice from singing (acc. of voice). 5. To sing for a period of time (intr.) or (acc.).

ПРОПУ́ЩЕННЫЙ; пропу́щен, —а, —о, —ы (ppp), see **пропущу́**.

ПРОПУЩУ́, пропу́стишь. Р. Пропусти́ть (acc.). I. Пропуска́ть. 1. To permit to pass. 2. To admit, let in. 3. To accommodate (e.g., an auditorium accommodates 1000 people). 4. To omit. 5. To miss or skip (e.g. a lecture). 6. To pass through (e.g., a thread through a needle, etc.) (acc. + сквозь + acc.). 7. To pass (as a censor passes a book). 8. To absorb, be pervious to. 9. To drink (an alcoholic beverage). (For other usages see unabridged dictionary.)

ПРОПЬЁШЬ, see **пропью́**.

ПРОПЬЮ́, пропьёшь. Р. Пропи́ть. I. Пропивать (mean. 1, 2, 4). 1. To squander (as money) on drink (acc.). 2. To ruin by drinking (e.g., one's voice, talent, etc.) (acc.). 3. To spend a period of time drinking (intr.) or (acc.). 4. (arch.) To seal, confirm an engagement, proposal of marriage with a drink, toast (acc. of person engaged).

ПРОРАСТЁТ, прорасту́т (3rd pers. only). Р. Прорасти́ (intr.). I. Прораста́ть (mean. 1, 2, 3). 1. To sprout. 2. To germinate. 3. To grow (through or between) (as grass grows between cracks in the pavement, etc.) (ме́жду + inst. of cracks). 4. To grow for a period of time.

ПРОРАСТУ́Т, see **прорастёт**.

ПРОРАЩЁННЫЙ; проращён, —а́, —о́, —ы́ (ppp), see **проращу́**.

ПРОРАЩУ́, прорасти́шь. Р. Прорасти́ть (acc.). I. Прора́щивать. To germinate.

ПРО́РВАННЫЙ; про́рван, —а, —о, —ы (ppp), see **прорву́**.

ПРОРВЁШЬ, see **прорву́**.

ПРОРВИ́ (imp.), see **прорву́**.

ПРОРВУ́, прорвёшь. Р. Прорва́ть (acc.). I. Прорыва́ть (mean. 1 thru 4). 1. To break through, tear through (e.g., material, clothing, etc.). 2. To burst through, rupture due to pressure (e.g., as water ruptures a dam). 3. To break through (as the enemy's lines). 4. To lose patience (impers. + acc. of pers. concerned). 5. To tear, etc. (s.t.) for a period of time.

ПРОРЕЖЁННЫЙ; прорежён, —а́, —о́, —ы́ (ppp), see прорежу́.

ПРОРЕ́ЖЕШЬ, see проре́жу.

ПРОРЕЖУ́, прореди́шь. Р. Проредить (acc.). I. Проре́живать. (agr.) To thin out (plants, etc.).

ПРОРЕ́ЖУ, проре́жешь. Р. Проре́зать (acc.). I. Прорезать (mean. 1 thru 3), проре́зывать (mean. 1 thru 3). 1. To cut through, slit (s.t.). 2. To cut (s.t.) through (as a door, a window, etc.). 3. To cut through, across (as a road cuts across a field). 4. To cut (s.t.) for a period of time.

ПРОРЕ́ЖЬ (imp.), see проре́жу.

ПРОРЕ́ЗАННЫЙ; проре́зан, —а, —о, —ы (ppp), see проре́жу.

ПРОРО́ЕШЬ, see проро́ю.

ПРОРО́Й (imp.), see проро́ю.

ПРОРО́С, проросла́ (past), see прорастёт.

ПРОРО́Ю, проро́ешь. Р. Проры́ть. I. Прорыва́ть (mean. 1 and 2). 1. To dig (through) (acc.). 2. To dig (as a canal) (acc.). 3. To dig (s.t.) for a period of time (acc.) or (intr.).

ПРОРУ́БЛЕННЫЙ; прору́блен, —а, —о, —ы (ppp), see прорублю́.

ПРОРУБЛЮ́, прору́бишь. Р. Прорубить. I. Проруба́ть (mean. 1 and 2). 1. To cut through (as a wall, forest, etc.) (acc.). 2. To cut, chop, hew (s.t.) through (as a road, a hole, etc.) (acc.). 3. To cut, hew, chop for a period of time (intr.) or (acc.).

ПРОРЫ́ТЫЙ; проры́т, —а, —о, —ы (ppp), see проро́ю.

ПРОРЫЧА́Т, see прорычу́.

ПРОРЫЧИ́ (imp.), see прорычу́.

ПРОРЫЧИ́ШЬ, see прорычу́.

ПРОРЫЧУ́, прорычи́шь. Р. Прорыча́ть. 1. To growl or snarl (of an animal) (intr.); (of a person) (intr.) or (acc.). 2. To growl or snarl for a period of time (intr.).

ПРОСА́ЖЕННЫЙ; проса́жен, а,— —о, —ы (ppp), see просажу́.

ПРОСАЖУ́, проса́дишь. Р. Просадить (acc.). I. Проса́живать. 1. To pierce (as one's hand with a nail 2. To squander (as money).

ПРОСВЕ́ЧЕННЫЙ; просве́чен, —а, —о, —ы (ppp), see просвечу́.

ПРОСВЕЧУ́, просве́тишь. Р. Просвети́ть. I. Просве́чивать (mean. 1 and 2). 1. To penetrate, shine through (as the sun shines through the curtains, etc.) (acc.). 2. (med.) To X-ray (acc.). 3. To shine for a period of time (intr.).

ПРОСВЕЩЁННЫЙ; просвещён, —а́, —о́, —ы́ (ppp), see просвещу́.

ПРОСВЕЩУ́, просвети́шь. Р. Просвети́ть (acc.). I. Просвеща́ть. To enlighten, educate, instruct.

ПРОСВИ́СТАННЫЙ; просви́стан, —а, —о, —ы (ppp), see просвищу́[1].

ПРОСВИСТИ́ (imp.), see просвищу́[1] and [2].

ПРОСВИСТИ́ШЬ, see просвищу́[2].

ПРОСВИ́ЩЕШЬ, see просвищу́[1].

ПРОСВИЩИ́ (imp.), see просвищу́[1].

ПРОСВИЩУ́[1], просви́щешь. Р. Просвиста́ть. I. Просви́стывать (mean. 2 and 3) .1. To whistle (intr.). 2. To whistle (e.g., a tune) (acc.). 3. To waste, squander (acc.). 4. To whistle for a period of time (intr.).

ПРОСВИЩУ́[2], просвисти́шь. Р. Просвисте́ть. I. Просви́стывать (mean. 2). 1. To whistle (intr.). 2. To whistle (a tune) (acc.). 3. To whistle for a period of time (intr.).

ПРОСЕ́ЕШЬ, see просе́ю.

ПРОСЕ́Й (imp.), see просе́ю.

ПРОСЕ́К, просекла́ (past), see просеку́.

ПРОСЕКИ́ (imp.), see просеку́.

ПРОСЕКУ́, просече́шь, просеку́т. Р. Просе́чь (acc.). I. Просека́ть. To cut, pierce, cleave, cut through.

ПРОСЕЧЁННЫЙ; просечён, —а́, —о́, —ы́ (ppp), see просеку́.

ПРОСЕЧЁШЬ, see просеку́.

ПРОСЕ́Ю, просе́ешь. Р. Просе́ять. I. Просе́ивать (mean. 1). 1. To sift, screen (as flour, sand, etc.) (acc.). 2. To sift, screen, sow for a period of time (intr.) or (acc.).

ПРОСЕ́ЯННЫЙ; просе́ян, —а, —о, —ы (ppp), see просе́ю.

ПРОСИДИ́ (imp.), see просижу́.

ПРОСИДИ́ШЬ, see просижу́.

ПРОСИДЯ́Т, see просижу́.

ПРОСИ́ЖЕННЫЙ; проси́жен, —а, —о, —ы (ppp), see просижу́.

ПРОСИЖУ́, просиди́шь. Р. Просиде́ть. I. Проси́живать. 1. To sit for a period of time (intr.). 2. To spend a period of time somewhere (e.g., in Moscow, in prison, etc.) (intr.). 3. To wear out, sit out (as the seat of one's trousers) (acc.).

ПРОСКА́ЧЕШЬ, see проскачу́.

ПРОСКАЧИ́ (imp.), see проскачу́.

ПРОСКАЧУ́, проска́чешь. Р. Проскака́ть. I. Проска́кивать (mean. 1 thru 3). 1. To gallop (by, past, through, under (intr.), (ми́мо + gen.), (че́рез + acc.) (под + acc.). 2. To gallop a certain distance (acc.). 3. To hop along (intr.). 4. To gallop for a period of time (intr.).

ПРОСКРЁБ, проскребла́ (past), see проскребу́.

ПРОСКРЕБЁННЫЙ; проскребён, —а́, —о́, —ы́ (ppp), see проскребу́.

ПРОСКРЕБЁШЬ, see проскребу́.

ПРОСКРЕБИ́ (imp.), see проскребу́.

ПРОСКРЕБУ́, проскребёшь. Р. Проскрести́. I. Проскреба́ть (mean. 1). 1. To scratch, scrape, claw a hole (in s.t.) (acc. of s.t.). 2. To spend a period of time scratching, etc. (intr.) or (acc.).

ПРОСКРИПИ́ (imp.), see проскриплю́.

ПРОСКРИПИ́ШЬ, see проскриплю́.

ПРОСКРИПЛЮ́, проскрипи́шь. Р. Проскрипе́ть. I. Скрипе́ть (mean. 1, 2, 3). 1. To squeak, creak (intr.) or (acc.). 2. To crunch, grind (e.g. snow, one's teeth) (inst.). 3. To squeak, creak for a period of time (intr.). 4. To live for a period of time (usually with difficulty) (intr.).

ПРОСКРИПЯ́Т, see проскриплю́.

ПРОСЛА́ВЛЕННЫЙ; просла́влен, а, о, ы (ppp), все просла́влю.

ПРОСЛА́ВЛЮ, просла́вишь. Р. Просла́вить (acc.). I. Прославля́ть. 1. To make famous, glorify, celebrate. 2. To defame.

ПРОСЛА́ВЬ (imp.), see просла́влю.

ПРОСЛЁЖЕННЫЙ; просле́жен, —а, —о, —ы (ppp), see прослежу́.

ПРОСЛЕЖУ́, проследи́шь. Р. Проследи́ть. I. Просле́живать. 1. To trail, track, follow (s.o. or s.t.) (acc.). 2. To observe, watch, see to (s.t.) (за + inst.). 3. To study thoroughly, trace, explore (e.g. the development of s.t.) (acc.).

ПРОСЛЕЖУ́СЬ, прослези́шься. Р. Прослези́ться (intr.). To shed a few tears (due to a surge of emotion).

ПРОСЛЫВЁШЬ, see прослыву́.

ПРОСЛЫВИ́ (imp.), see прослыву́.

ПРОСЛЫВУ́, прослывёшь. Р. Прослы́ть (intr.). I. Слыть. To have a reputation as, to be reputed to be (inst.) or (за + acc.).

ПРОСЛЫ́ШАТ, see прослы́шу.

ПРОСЛЫ́ШИШЬ, see прослы́шу.

ПРОСЛЫ́ШУ, прослы́шишь. Р. Прослы́шать (о + prep.). To hear about, find out about.

ПРОСЛЫ́ШЬ (imp.), see прослы́шу.

ПРОСМО́ТРЕННЫЙ; просмо́трен, —а, —о, —ы (ppp), see просмотрю́.

ПРОСМОТРИ́ (imp.), see просмотрю́.

ПРОСМО́ТРИШЬ, see просмотрю́.

ПРОСМОТРЮ́, просмо́тришь. Р.,Просмотре́ть. I. Просма́тривать (mean. 1, 2, 3). 1. To look over (s.t.) (acc.). 2. To skim through (as a book) (acc.). 3. To overlook (as a mistake) (acc.). 4. To spend a period of time examining, looking over (intr.) or (acc.).

ПРОСМО́ТРЯТ, see просмотрю́.

ПРОСО́САННЫЙ; просо́сан, —а, —о, —ы (ppp), see прососу́.

ПРОСОСЁШЬ, see прососу́.

ПРОСОСИ́ (imp.), see прососу́.

ПРОСОСУ́, прососёшь. Р. Прососа́ть. I. Проса́сывать (mean. 1 and 2). 1. To wash an opening or hole (as in an earth dam, said of percolating water) (acc.). 2. To filter, percolate (as through a dike) (acc.). 3. To suck for a period of time (intr.) or (acc.).

ПРОСО́Х, просо́хла (past). Р. Просо́хнуть (intr.). I. Просыха́ть, со́хнуть. To dry, become dry, dry up.

ПРОСПИ́ (imp.), see просплю́.

ПРОСПИ́ШЬ, see просплю́.

ПРОСПЛЮ́, проспи́шь. Р. Проспа́ть. I. Просыпа́ть (mean. 1 and 2). 1. To oversleep (intr.). 2. To miss (s.t.) by sleeping, sleep through (s.t.) (acc.). 3. To sleep for a period of time (intr.).

ПРОСПЯ́Т, see просплю́.

ПРОСТА́ВЛЕННЫЙ; проста́влен, —а, —о, —ы (ppp), see проста́влю.

ПРОСТА́ВЛЮ, проста́вишь. Р. Проста́вить (acc.). I. Проставля́ть. To insert, write in, fill in.

ПРОСТА́ВЬ (imp.), see проста́влю.

ПРОСТЁР, простёрла (past), see простру́.

ПРОСТЕРЕ́В and простёрши (adv. past part.), see простру́.

ПРОСТЁРТЫЙ; простёрт, —а, —о, —ы (ppp), see простру́.

ПРОСТЁРШИ and простере́в (adv. past part.), see простру́.

ПРОСТИ́, прости́те (imp.). Р. Прости́ть (acc.). I. Проща́ть. 1. To forgive, pardon, excuse. 2. To remit, forgive (e.g., a debt). 3. (imp.) Excuse me!, I beg your pardon!, etc. 4. (imp.) (arch.) Good bye!, Farewell! (Also see прощу́.)

ПРОСТОЙШЬ, see простою́.

ПРОСТОЙ (imp.), see простою́.

ПРОСТО́НЕШЬ, see простону́.

ПРОСТОНИ́ (imp.), see простону́.

ПРОСТОНУ́ (and простона́ю), просто́нешь. Р. Простона́ть. 1. To utter a groan (intr.). 2. To talk or say (s.t.) in a groaning voice (intr.) or (acc.). 3. To groan for a period of time (intr.).

ПРОСТОЮ́, простойшь. Р. Простоя́ть. I. Проста́ивать. 1. To stand or remain for a period of time (intr.). 2. To stand idle (intr.). 3. To remain/ stand well-preserved for a number of years (of a house, etc.) (intr.). 4. To damage, wear out by standing (on) (e.g., grass) (acc.).

ПРОСТОЯ́Т, see простою́.

ПРОСТРЁШЬ, see простру́.

ПРОСТРИ́ (imp.), see простру́.

ПРОСТРИ́Г, простри́гла (past), see простригу́.

ПРОСТРИГИ́ (imp.), see простригу́.

ПРОСТРИГУ́, простри жёшь, простригу́т. Р. Простри́чь. I. Прострига́ть (mean. 1). 1. To cut, shear (as a strip, a part in the hair, etc.) (acc.). 2. To cut, clip, shear for a period of time (intr.) or (acc.).

ПРОСТРИ́ЖЕННЫЙ; простри́жен, —а, —о, —ы (ppp), see простригу́.

ПРОСТРИЖЁШЬ, see простригу́.

ПРОСТРУ́, прострёшь. Р. Простере́ть (acc.). I. Простира́ть. 1. To extend, hold out (as one's hand). 2. (fig.) To extend (as influence).

ПРОСТУ́ЖЕННЫЙ; просту́жен, —а, —о, —ы (ppp), see простужу́.

ПРОСТУЖУ́, просту́дишь. Р. Про-

студи́ть (acc.). I. Простужа́ть. 1. To permit or cause to catch cold. 2. To cool (as food).

ПРОСТЫ́НЕШЬ, see просты́ну.

ПРОСТЫ́НУ, просты́нешь. Р. Просты́ть and просты́нуть (intr.). I. Простыва́ть. 1. To grow cold, cool off (of soup, people, etc.). 2. To catch cold. 3. (fig.) To get cold (of a trail). 4. (fig.) To cool down, calm down (of a person).

ПРОСТЫ́НЬ (imp.), see просты́ну.

ПРОСЫ́ПАННЫЙ; просы́пан, —а, —о, —ы (ppp), see просы́плю.

ПРОСЫ́ПЛЕШЬ, see просы́плю.

ПРОСЫ́ПЛЮ, просы́плешь. Р. Просы́пать (acc.). I. Просыпа́ть. To spill (as grain, flour, etc.).

ПРОСЫ́ПЬ (imp.), see просы́плю.

ПРОТЁК, протекла́ (past), see протечёт.

ПРОТЕКУ́Т (3rd pers. pl.), see протечёт.

ПРОТЁР, протёрла (past). Р. Протере́ть (acc.). I. Протира́ть. 1. To wear out, wear through (as clothes). 2. To grate or put through a sieve. 3. To wipe dry, wipe clean. 4. (lit. and fig.) To wake up (acc. of eyes) (also see протру́).

ПРОТЕРЕ́В and протёрши (adv. past part.), see протёр and протру́.

ПРОТЕРПИ́ (imp.), see протерплю́.

ПРОТЕ́РПИШЬ, see протерплю́.

ПРОТЕРПЛЮ́, проте́рпишь. Р. Протерпе́ть (acc.). To endure, tolerate, bear for a period of time.

ПРОТЕ́РПЯТ, see протерплю́.

ПРОТЁРТЫ; протёрт, —а, —о, —ы (ppp), see протёр and протру́.

ПРОТЁРШИ and протере́в (adv. past part.), see протёр and протру́.

ПРОТЕ́САННЫЙ; проте́сан, —а,—о, —ы (ppp), see протешу́.

ПРОТЕЧЁТ, протеку́т (3rd pers. only). Р. Проте́чь (intr.). I. Протека́ть. 1. To flow, run (of liquids). 2. To seep, leak (of liquids). 3. To leak (of a roof, boat, etc.). 4. (fig.) To go by, proceed, pass (of time, events, etc.).

ПРОТЕ́ШЕШЬ, see протешу́.

ПРОТЕШИ́ (imp.), see протешу́.

ПРОТЕШУ́, проте́шешь. Р. Протеса́ть. I. Протёсывать (mean. 1).

1. To smooth by hewing (as a log, etc.) (acc.). 2. To hew, trim for a period of time (intr.) or (acc.).

ПРОТИ́ВЛЮСЬ, проти́вишься. I. Проти́виться (dat.). **Р. Воспроти́виться.** To oppose, object to, resist.

ПРОТИВОПОСТА́ВЛЕННЫЙ; проти́вопоста́влен, —а, —о, —ы (ppp), see **противопоста́влю.**

ПРОТИВОПОСТА́ВЛЮ, противопоста́вишь. Р. Противопоста́вить (acc. + dat.). **I. Противопоставля́ть.** 1. To oppose (s.o. or s.t. to s.o. or s.t.) (i.e., set s.o. or s.t. against s.o. or s.t.). 2. To contrast (s.o. or s.t. to s.o. or s.t.).

ПРОТИВОПОСТА́ВЬ (imp.), see **противопоста́влю.**

ПРОТИВОСТОИ́ШЬ, see **противостою́.**

ПРОТИВОСТО́Й (imp.), see **противостою́.**

ПРОТИВОСТОЮ́, противостои́шь. I. Противостоя́ть (dat.). 1. To stand up against, withstand. 2. To oppose, be in opposition.

ПРОТИВОСТОЯ́Т, see **противостою́.**

ПРОТИ́ВЬСЯ (imp.), see **проти́влюсь.**

ПРО́ТКАННЫЙ; про́ткан, —а, —о, —ы (ppp), see **протку́.**

ПРОТКЁШЬ, see **протку́.**

ПРОТКИ́ (imp.), see **протку́.**

ПРОТКУ́, протокёшь. Р. Протка́ть. 1. To weave a material with a yarn or thread producing a design (acc. of material + inst. of yarn). 2. To weave for a period of time (intr.) or (acc.).

ПРОТО́ПЛЕННЫЙ; прото́плен, —а, —о, —ы (ppp), see **протоплю́.**

ПРОТОПЛЮ́, прото́пишь. Р. Протопи́ть (acc.). **I. Прота́пливать** (mean. 1). 1. To heat thoroughly. 2. To heat or melt for a period of time. 3. To melt (e.g., butter).

ПРОТО́ПТАННЫЙ; прото́птан, —а, —о, —ы (ppp), see **протопчу́.**

ПРОТО́ПЧЕШЬ, see **протопчу́.**

ПРОТОПЧИ́ (imp.), see **протопчу́.**

ПРОТОПЧУ́, прото́пчешь. Р. Протопта́ть (acc.). **I. Прота́птывать.** 1. To beat or wear by walking (as a path). 2. To wear out by walking (as one's socks, shoes, a rug, etc.).

ПРОТРА́ВЛЕННЫЙ; протра́влен, —а, —о, —ы (ppp), see **протравлю́.**

ПРОТРАВЛЮ́, протра́вишь. Р. Протрави́ть (acc.). **I. Протра́вливать** (mean. 1 thru 5), **протравля́ть** (mean. 1 thru 5). 1. To treat with a mordant (as cloth). 2. To pickle (as metal). 3. To etch. 4. To stain (wood). 5. To disinfect. 6. To let escape, get away (as wild game). 7. To spend time pickling, etching, applying a mordant, hunting (game) etc.

ПРОТРЕЗВЛЁННЫЙ; протрезвлён, —а́, —о́, —ы́ (ppp), see **протрезвлю́.**

ПРОТРЕЗВЛЮ́, протрезви́шь. Р. Протрезви́ть (acc.). **I. Протрезвля́ть.** To sober, make sober.

ПРОТРЁШЬ, see **протру́.**

ПРОТРЕЩА́Т, see **протрещу́.**

ПРОТРЕЩИ́ (imp.), see **протрещу́.**

ПРОТРЕЩИ́ШЬ, see **протрещу́.**

ПРОТРЕЩУ́, протрещи́шь. Р. Протреща́ть. I. Треща́ть (mean. 1 and 2). 1. To chirp (intr.). 2. (lit. and fig.) To chatter (acc.) or (intr.). 3. To chirp, chatter, crackle, ache, for a period of time (intr.).

ПРОТРИ́ (imp.), see **протру́.**

ПРОТРУ́, протрёшь. Р. Протере́ть (acc.). **I. Протира́ть.** 1. To wear out, wear through (as clothes). 2. To grate or put through a sieve. 3. To wipe dry, wipe clean. 4. (lit. and fig.) To wake up (acc. of eyes).

ПРОТРУБЛЮ́, протруби́шь. Р. Протруби́ть. I. Труби́ть (mean. 1 thru 5). 1. To blow (into) (as into a trumpet) (в + acc.). 2. To sound, blare (intr.). 3. To sound (e.g., retreat) (acc.). 4. To proclaim (o + prep.). 5. To work hard (intr.). 6. To blow, sound, proclaim, for a period of time (intr.) or (acc.).

ПРОТРУШУ́, протруси́шь. Р. Протруси́ть. 1. To jog along (of a horse, etc.) (intr.). 2. To scatter (along) (e.g., grain) (acc.). 3. To scatter for a period of time (acc.).

ПРОТУ́Х, проту́хла (past). **Р. Проту́хнуть** (intr.). **I. Ту́хнуть, протуха́ть.** To spoil, decay.

ПРОХВА́ЧЕННЫЙ; прохва́чен, —а, —о, —ы (ppp), see **прохвачу́.**

ПРОХВАЧУ́, прохва́тишь. Р. Прохвати́ть (acc.). **I. Прохва́тывать.**

1. To penetrate (3rd pers. only) (also impers.). 2. To chill (3rd pers. only) (also impers.). 3. To bite, chew through s.t. (3rd pers. only). 4. To criticize severely.

ПРОХЛАЖУ́СЬ, прохлади́шься. Р. Прохлади́ться (intr.). I. **Прохлажда́ться.** To refresh o.s., cool off.

ПРОХОЖУ́¹, прохо́дишь. I. Проходи́ть. Р. Пройти́. 1. To go (intr.), 2. To go through, pass through (e.g.. a door) (в + acc.). 3. To go or cover a certain distance (acc.). 4. To go or pass along (e.g., a road) (по + dat.). 5. To pass by (acc.) or (ми́мо + gen.). 6. (fig.) To pass over (as an expression passes over one's face) (по + dat.). 7. To pass, elapse (of time) (intr.). 8. To pass, be over, cease (of an illness, an event, rain, etc.) (intr.). 9. To complete (as a course of study) (acc.). 10. To study (e.g., a subject) (acc.). 11. To overlook (s.t.) (ми́мо + gen.). (Also see **пройду́**.) (For other usages see unabridged dictionary.)

ПРОХОЖУ́², прохо́дишь. Р. Проходи́ть (intr.). 1. To spend a period of time walking. 2. To go around (in s.t.) for a period of time (e.g., a coat) (в + prep.). 3. To spend a period of time (in some job or position) (в + prep.). 4. To run for a period of time e.g., a clock).

ПРОХРИПИ́ (imp.), see **прохриплю́.**

ПРОХРИПИ́ШЬ, see **прохриплю́.**

ПРОХРИПЛЮ́, прохрипи́шь. Р. Прохрипе́ть. I. Хрипе́ть (mean. 1 and 2). 1. To wheeze (intr.). 2. To speak or sing in a hoarse voice (intr.) or (acc.). 3. To remain hoarse for a period of time (intr.).

ПРОЦВЁЛ, процвела́ (past), see **процвету́.**

ПРОЦВЕТЁШЬ, see **процвету́.**

ПРОЦВЕТУ́, процветёшь. Р. Процвести́ (intr.). I. **Процвета́ть** (mean. 1.). 1. To flourish, prosper (of business). 2. (arch.) To bloom, blossom (of flowers, etc.). 3. To blossom, bloom for a period of time (of flowers, etc.).

ПРОЦВЕ́ТШИЙ (pap), see **процвету́.**

ПРОЦЕ́ЖЕННЫЙ; проце́жен, —а, —о, —ы (ppp), see **процежу́.**

ПРОЦЕЖУ́, проце́дишь. Р. Проце- ди́ть. I. **Проце́живать.** 1. To filter, strain (a liquid) (acc.). 2. To speak through one's teeth (acc.) or (intr.).

ПРОЧЁЛ, прочла́ (past), see **прочту́.**

ПРОЧЁРЧЕННЫЙ; прочёрчен, —а, —о, —ы (ppp), see **прочерчу́.**

ПРОЧЕРЧУ́, прочёртишь. Р. Прочерти́ть. I. Прочёрчивать (mean. 1). 1. To draw (a line, a sketch, etc.) (acc.). 2. To spend a period of time drawing (intr.) or (acc.).

ПРОЧЁСАННЫЙ; прочёсан, —а, —о, —ы (ppp), see **прочешу́.**

ПРОЧЁТШИЙ (pap), see **прочту́.**

ПРОЧЕ́ШЕШЬ, see **прочешу́.**

ПРОЧЕШИ́ (imp.), see **прочешу́.**

ПРОЧЕШУ́, прочёшешь. Р. Прочеса́ть. I. Прочёсывать (mean. 1 thru 3). 1. To comb out (acc.). 2. To card (as flax) (acc.). 3. (fig.) To comb thoroughly, inspect (as an area) (acc.). 4. To comb, card, or scratch for a period of time (intr.) or (acc.).

ПРОЧИ́СТИ (imp.), see **прочи́щу.**

ПРОЧИ́СТЬ (imp.), see **прочи́щу.**

ПРОЧИ́ЩЕННЫЙ; прочи́щен, —а, —о, —ы (ppp), see **прочи́щу.**

ПРОЧИ́ЩУ, прочи́стишь. Р. Прочи́стить. I. Прочища́ть (mean. 1, 2, 3). 1. To clean out (as a pipe) (acc.). 2. To clear (as a road, a field) (acc.). 3. To weed (as a field, garden, etc.) (acc.). 4. To clear, clean, etc. for a period of time (intr.) or (acc.).

ПРОЧТЁННЫЙ; прочтён, —а́, —о́, —ы́ (ppp), see **прочту́.**

ПРОЧТЁШЬ, see **прочту́.**

ПРОЧТИ́ (imp.), see **прочту́.**

ПРОЧТУ́, прочтёшь. Р. Проче́сть. I. Чита́ть. 1. (lit. and fig.) To read (acc.) or (intr.). 2. To lecture, deliver a lecture (acc.) or (intr.). 3. To give, "read" (e.g., a reprimand to s.o.) (acc. of reprimand + dat. of s.o.). 4. To recite (as a poem).

ПРОЧТЯ́ (adv. past part.), see **прочту́.**

ПРОШЕ́ДШИЙ (pap), see **прошёл** and **пройду́.**

ПРОШЕ́ДШИЙСЯ (pap), see **прошёл-ся** and **пройду́сь.**

ПРОШЁЛ, прошла́ (past). Р. **Пройти́.** I. **Проходи́ть.** 1. To go (intr.). 2. To go through, pass through (e.g., a door) (в + acc.). 3. To go or cover a certain distance (acc.). 4. To go or

pass along (e.g., a road) (по + dat.).
5. To pass by (acc.) or (мимо + gen.).
6. (fig.) To pass over (as an expression passes over one's face) (по + dat.).
7. To pass, elapse (of time) (intr.).
8. To pass, be over, cease (of an illness, an event, rain, etc.) (intr.).
9. To complete (as a course of study) (acc.). 10. To study (e.g., a subject) (acc.). 11. To overlook (s.t.) (мимо + gen.). (Also see пройду.) (For other usages see unabridged dictionary.)

ПРОШЁЛСЯ, прошлась (past). P. Пройтись. I. Прохаживаться. 1. To stroll (intr.). 2. To dance (intr.) or (acc.). 3. (fig.) To run over (as the keys of a piano (по + dat.). 4. To pass (s.t.) over (s.t.) (e.g., one's hand over one's face, a dust cloth over a surface, etc.) (inst. of hand + по + dat. of face). (Also see пройдусь.)

ПРОШЕННЫЙ; прошен, —а, —о, —ы (ppp), see прошу.

ПРОШЁПТАННЫЙ; прошёптан,—а, —о, —ы (ppp), see прошепчу.

ПРОШЁПЧЕШЬ, see прошепчу.

ПРОШЕПЧИ (imp.), see прошепчу.

ПРОШЕПЧУ, прошепчешь. P. Прошептать (intr.) or (acc.). I. Шептать (mean. 1). 1. To whisper. 2. To whisper for a period of time.

ПРОШИБ, прошибла (past), see прошибу.

ПРОШИБЁШЬ, see прошибу.

ПРОШИБИ (imp.), see прошибу.

ПРОШИБЛЕННЫЙ; прошиблен, —а, —о, —ы (ppp), see прошибу.

ПРОШИБУ, прошибёшь. P. Прошибить (acc.). I. Прошибать. 1. To break through (as a door). 2. To penetrate (of cold, wind, etc.).

ПРОШИПИ (imp.), see прошиплю.

ПРОШИПИШЬ, see прошиплю.

ПРОШИПЛЮ, прошипишь. P. Прошипеть (intr.) or (acc.). I. Шипеть (mean. 1 and 2). 1. (lit. and fig.) To hiss. 2. To speak in a low, hissing voice. 3. To hiss whisper, for a period of time.

ПРОШИПЯТ, see прошиплю.

ПРОШИТЫЙ; прошит, —а, —о, —ы (ppp), see прошью.

ПРОШЛА, прошло, прошли (past), see прошёл and пройду.

ПРОШЛАСЬ, прошлось, прошлись (past), see прошёлся and пройдусь.

ПРОШЛЯПЛЮ, прошляпишь. P. Прошляпить (acc.). To miss, overlook.

ПРОШЛЯПЬ (imp.), see прошляплю.

ПРОШТРАФЛЮСЬ, проштрафишься. P. Проштрафиться (intr.). 1. To be at fault, commit an offense (intr.). 2. To be guilty (of s.t.) (в + prep.).

ПРОШТРАФЬСЯ (imp.), see проштрафлюсь.

ПРОШУ, просишь. I. Просить. P. Попросить (mean. 1 thru 6). 1. To ask (s.o.) (acc.) or (s.o. to do s.t.) (acc. + inf.). 2. To ask (s.o. for s.t. or s.o.) (acc. + о + prep.). 3. To ask or request (s.t. of s.o.) (acc./gen. + у + gen.). 4. To inquire, ask (intr.). 5. To intercede (for s.o.) (за + acc.) or (with s.o. for s.o.) (acc. + за + acc.). 6. To invite (s.o.) (acc.). 7. To ask (a price) (acc.). 8. To sue (s.o.) (на + acc.). 9. To beg (intr.).

ПРОШУМИ (imp.), see прошумлю.

ПРОШУМИШЬ, see прошумлю.

ПРОШУМЛЮ, прошумишь. P. Прошуметь (intr.). 1. To roar, to roar by, along (as waves, a car, etc.). 2. To attract attention, become noted. 3. To roar, make noise, etc. for a period of time.

ПРОШУМЯТ, see прошумлю.

ПРОШЬЁШЬ, see прошью.

ПРОШЬЮ, прошьёшь. P. Прошить. I. Прошивать (mean. 1 thru 3). 1. To sew (as a seam) (acc.). 2. (tech.) To broach (as a piece of metal) (acc.). 3. To shoot through (s.o. or s.t.) in a number of places (acc.). 4. To sew for a period of time (intr.) or (acc.).

ПРОЩЁННЫЙ; прощён, —á, —ó, —ы́ (ppp), see прощу.

ПРОЩУ, простишь. P. Простить (acc.). I. Прощать. 1. To forgive, pardon, excuse. 2. To remit, forgive (e.g., a debt). 3. (imp.) Excuse me!, I beg your pardon! etc. 4. (imp.) (arch.) Good bye! Farewell!

ПРОЯВЛЕННЫЙ; проявлен, —а, —о, —ы (ppp), see проявлю.

ПРОЯВЛЮ, проявишь. P. Проявить (acc.). I. Проявлять. 1. To display, manifest, show. 2. To develop (as a photographic film).

ПРУ, прёшь. I. Переть. 1. To go on, push on, press on (intr.). 2. To press

against (e.g., s.o.'s back) (в + acc.).
3. To carry, drag, pull (acc.). 4. (lit.
and fig.) To become apparent, stick
out, appear (3rd pers. only) (intr.).
5. To steal, pilfer (acc.) or (intr.).

ПРУЖУ́, пру́дишь (and пруди́шь).
I. Пруди́ть (acc.). Р. Запруди́ть.
To dam (up) (as a river).

ПРЯ́ДЕННЫЙ; пря́ден, —а, —о, —ы
(ppp), see пряду́.

ПРЯДЁШЬ, see пряду́.

ПРЯДИ́ (imp.), see пряду́.

ПРЯДУ́, прядёшь. I. Прясть. Р.
Спрясть (mean. 2). 1. To spin (intr.).
2. To spin (as yarn) (acc.). 3. To
prick up (the ears) (said of a horse)
(inst. of ears).

ПРЯЛ, пряла́ (and пря́ла), пря́ло,
пря́ли (past), see пряду́.

ПРЯ́ЧЕШЬ, see пря́чу.

ПРЯ́ЧУ, пря́чешь. I. Пря́тать (acc.).
Р. Спря́тать. 1. (lit. and fig.) To
conceal, hide, secrete. 2. To put
away.

ПРЯЧЬ (imp.), see пря́чу.

ПУСТОСЛО́ВЛЮ, пустосло́вишь. I.
Пустосло́вить (intr.). To talk nonsense.

ПУСТОСЛО́ВЬ (imp.), see пустосло́в-
лю.

ПУХ (and пу́хнул), пу́хла (past). I.
Пу́хнуть (intr.). Р. Вспу́хнуть. To
swell.

ПУ́ЩЕННЫЙ; пу́щен, —а, —о, —ы
(ppp), see пущу́.

ПУЩУ́, пу́стишь. Р. Пусти́ть (acc.).
I. Пуска́ть. 1. To allow, permit. 2. To

release, let go, set free. 3. To let in.
4. To throw (as a rock). 5. To send,
mail (as a letter). 6. To put out, put
forth (as a bud, shoot, etc.). 7. To put
in motion, start (as a machine). 8. To
turn on (as water, gas, etc.). 9. To
spread, disseminate, release (as information). (For other usages see
unabridged dictionary.)

ПЫХТИ́ (imp.), see пыхчу́.

ПЫХТИ́ШЬ, see пыхчу́.

ПЫХТЯ́Т, see пыхчу́.

ПЫХЧУ́, пыхти́шь. I. Пыхте́ть (intr.)
(lit. and fig.) To pant, puff.

ПЫ́ШЕШЬ, see пы́шу.

ПЫ́ШУ, пы́шешь (also пы́хаю, пы́-
хаешь, etc.). I. Пы́хать (intr.). Р.
Пыхну́ть (mean. 1 thru 3). 1. To
glow (intr.) or (inst.). 2. To radiate
(as heat) (inst.). 3. To puff (as a
steam engine puffs steam) (inst.).
4. (fig.) To radiate, glow (with) (as
health, happiness, etc.) (inst.).

ПЫ́ШУЩИЙ (pres. a.p.), see пы́шу.

ПЫШЬ (imp.), see пы́шу.

ПЬЁШЬ, see пью.

ПЬЮ, пьёшь. I. Пить (acc.) or (intr.).
Р. Вы́пить. To drink.

ПЯТЬ (imp.), see пя́чу.

ПЯ́ТЬСЯ (imp.), see пя́чусь.

ПЯ́ЧУ, пя́тишь. I. Пя́тить (acc.). Р.
Попя́тить. To back (as a horse).

ПЯ́ЧУСЬ, пя́тишься. I. Пя́титься
(intr.). Р. Попя́титься. 1. To back
up, move backward (intr.). 2. (fig.)
To renounce, go back on (as a promise
etc.) (от + gen.).

Р

РАЖУ́, рази́шь. I. Рази́ть. Р. Пора-
зи́ть (mean. 1 and 2). 1. To strike
(with arms, as the enemy) (acc.).
2. To crush, defeat (acc.). 3. To reek,
smell (of s.t.) (as he smelled of
tobacco) (от + gen. + impers. +
inst.) (от него рази́ло табако́м) or
(intr. + inst.) (он рази́л табако́м).

РАЗБА́ВЛЕННЫЙ; разба́влен, —а,
—о, —ы (ppp), see разба́влю.

РАЗБА́ВЛЮ, разба́вишь. Р. Разба́-
вить (acc.). I. Разбавля́ть. (lit. and
fig.) To dilute.

РАЗБА́ВЬ (imp.), see разба́влю.

РАЗБЕГИ́СЬ (imp.), see разбегу́сь.

РАЗБЕГУ́СЬ, разбежи́шься, разбе-
гу́тся. Р. Разбежа́ться (intr.). I.
Разбега́ться. 1. To run up, gather
momentum (as before diving, jump-
ing, etc.). 2. (lit. and fig.) To disperse,
scatter, run in different directions.
3. To be dazzled (of eyes), to be
bewildered/confused (of thoughts).

РАЗБЕЖИ́ШЬСЯ, see разбегу́сь.

РАЗБЕ́Й (imp.). Р. Разби́ть (acc.).
I. Разбива́ть, бить (mean. 1). 1. To
break, fracture. 2. To divide, split up,
separate. 3. To mark out, lay out (as
a camp). 4. (lit. and fig.) To destroy,
damage, break, smash. 5. To conquer,
defeat. 6. To break (as a ship on the
rocks) (impers.). 7. (typ.) To space.
(Also see разобью́.) (For other usages,
see unabridged dictionary.)

РАЗБЕРЕЖЁННЫЙ; разбережён,
—а́, —о́, —ы́ (ppp), see разбережу́.

РАЗБЕРЕЖУ́, разбереди́шь. Р. Раз-
береди́ть (acc.). I. Береди́ть. 1. (lit.
and fig.) To irritate. 2. To rouse, stir
up.

РАЗБЕРЁШЬ, see разберу́.

РАЗБЕРИ́ (imp.), see разберу́.

РАЗБЕРУ́, разберёшь. Р. Разобра́ть
(acc.). I. Разбира́ть. 1. To take.
2. To take apart, dismantle (e.g., a
machine, watch, etc.). 3. To sort out,
pick out. 4. To put in order. 5. To
make out, decipher (handwriting,

etc.). 6. To analyse. 7. To investigate,
examine. 8. To buy up, acquire (as
all goods, etc.). 9. (gram.) To parse.
10. To seize (as laughter seizes
one).

РАЗБИ́ТЫЙ; разби́т, —а, —о, —ы
(ppp), see разбе́й and разобью́.

РАЗБОЛЕ́ЙСЬ (imp.), see разболе́юсь.

РАЗБОЛЕ́ЮСЬ, разболе́ешься. Р.
Разболе́ться (intr.). I. Разба́ли-
ваться. To become quite ill.

РАЗБОЛИ́ТСЯ, разболя́тся (3rd pers.
only). Р. Разболе́ться (intr.). I.
Разба́ливаться. To start to ache,
pain, intensely.

РАЗБОЛЯ́ТСЯ (3rd pers. pl.), see
разболи́тся.

РАЗБОМБЛЁННЫЙ; разбомблён,
—а́, —о́, —ы́ (ppp), see разбомблю́.

РАЗБОМБЛЮ́, разбомби́шь. Р. Раз-
бомби́ть (acc.). To destroy by
bombing.

РАЗБРЕДЁМСЯ, разбредётесь, раз-
бреду́тся (pl. forms), see разбредётся.

РАЗБРЕДЁТСЯ (3rd pers. sing.) (1st
and 2nd pers. sing. not used). Р.
Разбрести́сь (intr.). I. Разбреда́ться.
1. To straggle. 2. (lit. and fig.) To
scatter, disperse (of people, thoughts,
etc.).

РАЗБРЕДИ́ТЕСЬ (imp.), see разбредётся.

РАЗБРЕДУ́ТСЯ (3rd pers. pl.), see
разбредётся.

РАЗБРЕ́ДШИЙСЯ (pap), see разбредётся.

РАЗБРЕДЯ́СЬ (adv. past part.), see
разбредётся.

РАЗБРЁЛСЯ, разбрела́сь (past), see
разбредётся.

РАЗБРО́СЬ (imp.), see разбро́шу.

РАЗБРО́ШЕННЫЙ; разбро́шен, —а,
—о, —ы (ppp), see разбро́шу.

РАЗБРО́ШУ, разбро́сишь. Р. Расбро́-
сить (acc.). I. Разбра́сывать. 1. (lit.
and fig.) To scatter, disperse. 2. To
strew about.

РАЗБРЫ́ЗГАННЫЙ; разбры́зган, —а, —о, —ы (ppp), see разбры́зжу.
РАЗБРЫ́ЗЖЕШЬ, see разбры́зжу.
РАЗБРЫ́ЗЖИ (imp.), see разбры́зжу.
РАЗБРЫ́ЗЖУ, разбры́зжешь (also разбры́згаю, разбры́згаешь). Р. **Разбры́згать** (acc.). I. **Разбры́згивать** 1. To splash (e.g., water, etc.). 2. To spray, sprinkle (e.g., perfume, water, etc.).
РАЗБРЮЗЖА́ТСЯ, see разбрюзжу́сь.
РАЗБРЮЗЖИ́СЬ (imp.), see разбрюзжу́сь.
РАЗБРЮЗЖИ́ШЬСЯ, see разбрюзжу́сь.
РАЗБРЮЗЖУ́СЬ, разбрюзжи́шся. Р. **Расбрюзжа́ться** (intr.). To begin to grumble.
РАЗБУ́ЖЕННЫЙ; разбу́жен, —а, —о, —ы (ppp), see разбужу́.
РАЗБУЖУ́, разбу́дишь. Р. **Разбуди́ть** (acc.). I. **Буди́ть.** (lit. and fig.) To awaken.
РАЗБУ́Х, разбу́хла (past). Р. **Разбу́хнуть** (intr.). I. **Разбуха́ть.** 1. To swell, distend. 2. (fig.) To swell, expand (e.g., a staff, a report, etc.).
РАЗВЕДЁННЫЙ; разведён, —а́, —о́, —ы́ (ppp), see разведу́.
РАЗВЕДЁШЬ, see разведу́.
РАЗВЕДИ́ (imp.), see разведу́.
РАЗВЕДУ́, разведёшь. Р. **Развести́** (acc.). I. **Разводи́ть.** 1. To conduct, take (to various places). 2. (mil.) To mount (as a guard). 3. To separate (as people, things). 4. To divorce. 5. To raise, open (as a drawbridge). 6. To kindle, light (as a fire). 7. To breed, cultivate, propagate. 8. To dilute (as liquid). 9. To dissolve (as salt in water). 10. To rarefy (as gases). 11. To set (as a saw). 12. To raise (as steam in a boiler, waves on the water, etc.).
РАЗВЕ́ДШИЙ (pap), see разведу́.
РАЗВЕДЯ́ (adv. past part.), see разведу́.
РАЗВЕ́ЕШЬ, see развею.
РАЗВЁЗ, развезла́ (past), see развезу́.
РАЗВЕЗЁННЫЙ; развезён, —а́, —о́, —ы́ (ppp), see развезу́.
РАЗВЕЗЁШЬ, see развезу́.
РАЗВЕЗИ́ (imp.), see развезу́.
РАЗВЕЗУ́, развезёшь. Р. **Развезти́** (acc.). I. **Развози́ть.** 1. To transport,

deliver (to various places). 2. To weaken, become worn out (e.g., from heat) (impers. + acc. of person + от + gen. of heat). 3. To become difficult to traverse (of a muddy road) (impers. + acc. of road). 4. (fig.) To drag out (as a speech).
РАЗВЕЗЯ́ (adv. past part.), see развезу́.
РАЗВЕ́Й[1] (imp.), see разве́ю.
РАЗВЕ́Й[2] (imp.). Р. **Разви́ть** (acc.). I. **Развива́ть.** 1. To develop (e.g., industry, memory, understanding, strength, a role in a play, one's voice, activities, etc.). 2. To untwist, unwind. (Also see разовью́.)
РАЗВЁЛ, развела́ (past), see разведу́.
РАЗВЕРЕЖЁННЫЙ; развережён, —а́, —о́, —ы́ (ppp), see развережу́.
РАЗВЕРЕЖУ́, развереди́шь. Р. **Развереди́ть** (acc.). I. **Вереди́ть.** (lit. and fig.) To irritate.
РАЗВЁРЗ (and разве́рзнул), разве́рзла (past). Р. **Разве́рзнуть** (acc.). I. **Разверза́ть.** To open wide.
РАЗВЁРСТЫЙ; разве́рст, —а, —о, —ы (ppp), see разве́рз.
РАЗВЕРТИ́ (imp.), see разверчу́.
РАЗВЕ́РТИШЬ, see разверчу́.
РАЗВЕ́РТЯТ, see разверчу́.
РАЗВЁРЧЕННЫЙ; разве́рчен, —а, —о, —ы (ppp), see разверчу́.
РАЗВЕРЧУ́, разве́ртишь. Р. **Разверте́ть** (acc.). I. **Разве́рчивать.** 1. To unscrew (loosen). 2. To enlarge, ream out. 3. To spin (as a wheel).
РАЗВЕ́СЬ (imp.), see разве́шу.
РАЗВЕТВЛЁННЫЙ; разветвлён, —а́, —о́, —ы́ (ppp), see разветвлю́.
РАЗВЕТВЛЮ́, разветви́шь. Р. **Разветви́ть** (acc.). I. **Разветвля́ть.** To divide into branches (e.g., a railroad line, an organization, etc.).
РАЗВЕ́ШЕННЫЙ; разве́шен, —а, —о, —ы (ppp), see разве́шу.
РАЗВЕ́ШУ, разве́сишь. Р. **Разве́сить** (acc.). I. **Разве́шивать.** 1. To weigh out (e.g., sugar, etc.). 2. To hang (e.g., pictures, etc.). 3. To hang out (as laundry). 4. To spread (as a tree spreads its branches).
РАЗВЕ́Ю, разве́ешь. Р. **Разве́ять** (acc.). I. **Разве́ивать.** 1. To disperse, scatter. 2. (lit. and fig.) To dispel.
РАЗВЕ́ЯННЫЙ; разве́ян, —а, —о, —ы (ppp), see разве́ю.

РАЗВИ́НЧЕННЫЙ; разви́нчен, —а, —о, —ы (ppp), see **развинчу́.**

РАЗВИНЧУ́, развинти́шь. Р. Развинти́ть (acc.). I. **Развинчивать.** To unscrew, twist off.

РАЗВИ́ТЫЙ (and развито́й); разви́т, —á, —о, —ы (ppp), see **развей²** and **разовью́.**

РАЗВИ́ТЫЙ; páзвит, —á, —о, —ы (ppp), see **развей²** and **разовью́.**

РАЗВЛЁК, развлекла́ (past), see **развлеку́.**

РАЗВЛЕКИ́ (imp.), see **развлеку́.**

РАЗВЛЕКУ́, развлечёшь, развлеку́т. Р. Развле́чь (acc.). I. **Развлека́ть.** 1. To entertain, amuse. 2. To distract, divert.

РАЗВЛЕЧЁННЫЙ; развлечён, —á, —ó, —ы́ (ppp), see **развлеку́.**

РАЗВЛЕЧЁШЬ, see **развлеку́.**

РАЗВОЖУ́¹, разво́дишь. I. **Разводи́ть** (acc.). Р. **Развести́.** 1. To conduct, take (to various places). 2. (mil.) To mount (as a guard). 3. To separate (as people, things). 4. To divorce. 5. To raise, open (as a drawbridge). 6. To kindle, light, (as a fire). 7. To breed, cultivate, propagate. 8. To dilute (as liquids). 9. To dissolve (as salt in water). 10. To rarefy (as gases). 11. To set (as a saw). 12. To raise (as waves in water, steam in a boiler, etc.).

РАЗВОЖУ́², разво́зишь. I. **Разво́зить** (acc.). Р. **Развезти́.** 1. To transport, deliver, (to various places). 2. To weaken, become worn out (e.g., from heat) (impers. + acc. of person + от + gen. of heat). 3. To become difficult to traverse (as a muddy road) (impers. + acc. of road). 4. (fig.) To drag out (as a speech).

РАЗВОРО́ЧЕННЫЙ; разборо́чен, —а, —о, —ы (ppp), see **разворочу́.**

РАЗВОРОЧУ́, разворо́тишь. Р. Развороти́ть (acc.). I. **Развора́чивать.** 1. To break up, break to pieces, shatter (as a pavement). 2. To play havoc with, turn upside down.

РАЗВОРЧА́ТСЯ, see **разворчу́сь.**

РАЗВОРЧИ́СЬ (imp.), see **разворчу́сь.**

РАЗВОРЧИ́ШЬСЯ, see **разворчу́сь.**

РАЗВОРЧУ́СЬ, разворчи́шься. Р. Разворча́ться (intr.). To start to grumble incessantly.

РАЗВРАЩЁННЫЙ; развращён, —á, —б, —ы́ (ppp), see **развращу́.**

РАЗВРАЩУ́, разврати́шь. Р. Разврати́ть (acc.). I. **Развраща́ть.** 1. To corrupt, debauch. 2. To spoil by overindulgence. 3. (arch.) To rape.

РАЗВЯ́ЖЕШЬ, see **развяжу́.**

РАЗВЯЖИ́ (imp.), see **развяжу́.**

РАЗВЯЖУ́, развя́жешь. Р. Развяза́ть (acc.). I. **Развя́зывать.** 1. To untie, unbind. 2. (fig.) To unleash (as war). 3. (fig.) To free (e.g., s.o. from an obligation).

РАЗВЯ́ЗАННЫЙ; развя́зан, —а, —о, —ы (ppp), see **развяжу́.**

РАЗГЛА́ДЬ (imp.), see **разгла́жу.**

РАЗГЛА́ЖЕННЫЙ; разгла́жен, —а, —о, —ы (ppp), see **разгла́жу.**

РАЗГЛА́ЖУ, разгла́дишь. Р. Разгла́дить (acc.). I. **Разгла́живать.** 1. To smooth out. 2. To iron out.

РАЗГЛАШЁННЫЙ; разглашён, —á, —б, —ы́ (ppp), see **разглашу́.**

РАЗГЛАШУ́, разгласи́шь. Р. Разгласи́ть. I. **Разглаша́ть.** 1. To divulge (e.g., a secret) (acc.). 2. To announce, proclaim, publish (s.t.) (о + prep.).

РАЗГЛЯДИ́ (imp.), see **разгляжу́.**

РАЗГЛЯДИ́ШЬ, see **разгляжу́.**

РАЗГЛЯДЯ́Т, see **разгляжу́.**

РАЗГЛЯЖУ́, разгляди́шь. Р. Разгляде́ть (acc.). I. **Разгля́дывать** (mean. 1). 1. To examine (look at). 2. To ascertain, find out, learn, discern.

РАЗГОНИ́ (imp.), see **разгоню́.**

РАЗГО́НИШЬ, see **разгоню́.**

РАЗГОНЮ́, разго́нишь. Р. Разогна́ть. I. **Разгоня́ть.** 1. (lit. and flg.) To drive away, disperse (acc.). 2. To dispel (gloom, etc.) (acc.). 3. To accelerate (as an automobile) (acc.). 4. To drive, ride at high speed, race (intr.). 5. To send (as s.o. to do s.t.) (acc.). 6. To discharge fire (s.o.), (acc.). 7. To spread (as an action over a period of time, or, a letter over two pages, etc.) (acc. + на + acc.). 8. (typ.) To space (acc.).

РАЗГОРИ́СЬ (imp.), see **разгорю́сь.**

РАЗГОРИ́ШЬСЯ, see **разгорю́сь.**

РАЗГОРО́ЖЕННЫЙ; разгоро́жен, —а, —о, —ы (ppp), see **разгорожу́.**

РАЗГОРОЖУ́, разгоро́дишь (and разгороди́шь). Р. Разгороди́ть (acc.).

I. **Разгора́живать.** To partition (as a room).

РАЗГОРЮ́СЬ, разгори́шься. Р. **Разгоре́ться** (intr.). I. **Разгора́ться.** 1. (lit. and fig.) To flare up, begin to burn. 2. (fig.) To flare up (as a war, passions). 3. (fig.) To flush (as one's face).

РАЗГОРЯ́ТСЯ, see **разгорю́сь.**

РАЗГРА́БЛЕННЫЙ; разгра́блен, —а, —о, —ы (ppp), see **разгра́блю.**

РАЗГРА́БЛЮ, разгра́бишь. Р. **Разгра́бить** (acc.). To pillage, plunder.

РАЗГРА́БЬ (imp.), see **разгра́блю.**

РАЗГРАФЛЁННЫЙ; —а́, —о́, —ы́ (ppp), see **разграфлю́.**

РАЗГРАФЛЮ́, разграфи́шь. Р. **Разграфи́ть** (acc.). I. **Разграфля́ть, графи́ть.** To rule (with lines).

РАЗГРЁБ, разгребла́ (past), see **разгребу́.**

РАЗГРЕБЁННЫЙ; разгребён, —а́, —о́, —ы́ (ppp), see **разгребу́.**

РАЗГРЕБЁШЬ, see **разбребу́.**

РАЗГРЕБИ́ (imp.), see **разгребу́.**

РАЗГРЕБУ́, разгребёшь. Р. **Разгрести́** (acc.). I. **Разгреба́ть.** 1. To rake away (as grass). 2. To shovel away (e.g., snow).

РАЗГРО́МЛЕННЫЙ; разгро́млен, —а, —о, —ы (ppp), see **разгромлю́.**

РАЗГРОМЛЁННЫЙ; разгромлён, —а́, —о́, —ы́ (ppp), see **разгромлю́.**

РАЗГРОМЛЮ́, разгроми́шь. Р. **Громи́ть** (acc.). I. **Громи́ть.** 1. To sack, raid, devastate, loot. 2. To rout, shatter (e.g., the enemy). 3. To inveigh against.

РАЗГРУ́ЖЕННЫЙ; разгру́жен, —а, —о, —ы (ppp), see **разгружу́.**

РАЗГРУЖЁННЫЙ; разгружён, —а́, —о́, —ы́ (ppp), see **разгружу́.**

РАЗГРУЖУ́, разгру́зишь (and разгрузи́шь). Р. **Разгрузи́ть** (acc.). I. **Разгружа́ть.** 1. To unload, discharge, dump. 2. (fig.) To relieve (s.o. or s.t. of s.t.) (e.g., of details, etc.).

РАЗГРЫ́З, разгры́зла (past), see **разгрызу́.**

РАЗГРЫ́ЗЕННЫЙ; разгры́зен, —а, —о, —ы (ppp), see **разгрызу́.**

РАЗГРЫЗЁШЬ, see **разгрызу́.**

РАЗГРЫЗИ́ (imp.), see **разгрызу́.**

РАЗГРЫЗУ́, разгрызёшь. Р. **Разгры́зть** (acc.). I. **Разгрыза́ть.** 1. To gnaw, nibble. 2. To crack (e. g., nuts).

РАЗДАВА́Й (imp.), see **раздаю́.**

РАЗДАВА́Я (adv. pres. part.), see **раздаю́.**

РАЗДА́ВЛЕННЫЙ; разда́влен, —а, —о, —ы (ppp), see **раздавлю́.**

РАЗДАВЛЮ́, разда́вишь. Р. **Раздави́ть** (acc.). I. **Дави́ть** (mean. 1 thru 3), **разда́вливать.** 1. To crush, smash, squash. 2. (fig.) To crush (e.g., spirits, the enemy, etc.). 3. To run over, run down (with a vehicle, horse, etc.). 4. To drink (an alcoholic beverage).

РАЗДАДИ́М, раздади́те, раздаду́т (pl. forms), see **разда́м.**

РАЗДАЁШЬ, see **раздаю́.**

РАЗДА́Й (imp.), see **разда́м.**

РАЗДА́Л, раздала́, разда́ло, разда́ли (also ро́здал, раздала́, ро́здало, ро́здали) (past), see **разда́м.**

РАЗДА́М, разда́шь, разда́ст, (sing. forms). Р. **Разда́ть** (acc.). I. **Раздава́ть.** 1. To distribute (as supplies). 2. To stretch (as shoes), widen, expand.

РАЗДАНА́ (ppp, feminine short form), see **разда́м** and **ро́зданный.**

РАЗДА́СТ, see **разда́м.**

РАЗДА́ШЬ, see **разда́м.**

РАЗДАЮ́, раздаёшь. I. **Раздава́ть** (acc.). Р. **Разда́ть.** 1. To distribute (as supplies). 2. To stretch (as shoes), widen, expand.

РАЗДЕ́НЕШЬ, see **разде́ну.**

РАЗДЕ́НУ, разде́нешь. Р. **Разде́ть** (acc.). I. **Раздева́ть.** 1. To undress (s.o.). 2. To rob (s.o. of his clothes) (acc. of s.o.).

РАЗДЕ́НЬ (imp.), see **разде́ну.**

РАЗДЕРЁШЬ, see **раздеру́.**

РАЗДЕРИ́ (imp.), see **раздеру́.**

РАЗДЕРУ́, раздерёшь. Р. **Разодра́ть** (acc.). I. **Раздира́ть.** 1. To tear. 2. To tear to pieces, tear up.

РАЗДЕ́ТЫЙ; разде́т, —а, —о, —ы (ppp), see **разде́ну.**

РАЗДОБУ́ДЕШЬ, see **раздобу́ду.**

РАЗДОБУ́ДУ, раздобу́дешь. Р. **Раздобы́ть** (acc.). I. **Раздобыва́ть.** To get, procure, obtain (usually with effort).

РАЗДОБУ́ДЬ (imp.), see **раздобу́ду.**

РАЗДОБЫ́ТЫЙ; раздобы́т, —а, —о, —ы (ppp), see **раздобу́ду.**

РАЗДОЛБЛЁННЫЙ; раздолблён, —а́, —о́, —ы́ (ppp), see **раздолблю́.**

**РАЗДОЛБЛЮ, раздолбишь. Р. Раз-
долбить** (acc.). I. **Раздалбливать.**
1. To enlarge (by striking, gouging)
(as a hole). 2. To hollow out, groove.
3. To break, spoil by chiseling,
gouging, etc.

**РАЗДРОБЛЕННЫЙ; раздроблен,—а,
—о, —ы** (ppp), see **раздроблю.**

**РАЗДРОБЛЁННЫЙ; раздроблён,—а,
—о, —ы** (ppp), see **раздроблю.**

**РАЗДРОБЛЮ, раздробишь. Р Раз-
дробить** (acc.). I. **Раздроблять, дробить** (mean. 1 and 2). 1. To splinter,
crush, break to pieces, shatter. 2. To
dismember, split up. 3. To convert
(as feet to inches) (acc. + в +
acc.).

РАЗДУЕШЬ, see **раздую.**

РАЗДУЙ (imp.), see **раздую.**

РАЗДУТЫЙ; раздут, —а, —о, —ы
(ppp), see **раздую.**

РАЗДУЮ, раздуешь. Р. Раздуть (acc.).
I. **Раздувать.** 1. To fan or blow (a
fire) (acc.). 2. To bloat, swell up (as
one's face) (impers. + acc.). 3. To
inflate (acc.). 4. To exaggerate (acc.).
5. To scatter (as wind scatters clouds,
ashes, etc.) (acc.).

**РАЗЖАЛОБЛЕННЫЙ; разжалоб-
лен, —а, —о, —ы** (ppp), see **разжалоблю.**

**РАЗЖАЛОБЛЮ, разжалобишь. Р.
Разжалобить** (acc.). To move (s.o.)
to pity.

РАЗЖАЛОБЬ (imp.), see **разжалоблю.**

РАЗЖАТЫЙ; разжат, —а, —о, —ы
(ppp). Р. **Разжать** (acc.). I. **Разжи-
мать.** 1. To unclasp, unclench (as
one's hands, teeth, etc.). 2. To release
(s.t. under tension) (as a spring) (Also
see **разожму.**)

**РАЗЖЁВАННЫЙ; разжёван, —а,
—о, —ы** (ppp), see **разжую.**

РАЗЖЁГ, разожгла (past). Р. **Разжечь**
(acc.). I. **Разжигать.** 1. To light,
kindle (as a fire). 2. (fig.) To kindle
(rouse) (as passions). (Also see **ра-
зожгу.**)

РАЗЖИВЁШЬСЯ, see **разживусь.**

РАЗЖИВИСЬ (imp.), see **разживусь.**

**РАЗЖИВУСЬ, разживёшься. Р. Раз-
житься** (intr.). I. **Разживаться.** 1. To
make a fortune, become rich. 2. To
make, obtain, a lot (as money, etc.)
(inst.). 3. To begin to live well.

**РАЗЖИЖЁННЫЙ; разжижён, —а,
—о, —ы** (ppp), see **разжижу.**

**РАЗЖИЖУ, разжидишь. Р. Разжи-
дить** (acc.). I. **Разжижать.** To dilute,
thin.

РАЗЖУЁШЬ, see **разжую.**

РАЗЖУЙ (imp.), see **разжую.**

РАЗЖУЮ, разжуёшь. Р. Разжевать
(acc.). I. **Разжёвывать.** 1. To masticate. 2. (fig.) To chew over (discuss).

**РАЗЗНАКОМЛЕННЫЙ; раззнаком-
лен, —а, —о, —ы** (ppp), see **раззнакомлю.**

**РАЗЗНАКОМЛЮ, раззнакомишь. Р.
Раззнакомить** (acc.). I. **Раззнаком-
ливать.** To break off an acquaintance
(with s.o.) (acc. of s.o.).

РАЗЗНАКОМЬ (imp.), see **раззнакомлю.**

РАЗЗУДИСЬ (imp.), see **раззудится.**

РАЗЗУДИТСЯ, раззудятся (3rd pers.
only). Р. **Раззудеться** (intr.). I.
Раззуживаться. 1. To start to itch
violently. 2. (fig.) To itch (e.g., as
one's hands itch to do s.t.).

РАЗЗУДЯТСЯ (3rd pers. pl.), see
раззудится.

**РАЗЗУЖЕННЫЙ; раззужен,—а,—о,
—ы** (ppp), see **раззужу.**

РАЗЗУЖУ, раззудишь. Р. Раззудить
(acc.). 1. To irritate, cause to itch
(e.g., a wound). 2. To arouse a desire
(in s.o. to do s.t.) (i.e., cause s.o. to
itch to do s.t.) (acc. of s.o.).

РАЗЛАДЬ (imp.), see **разлажу.**

**РАЗЛАЖЕННЫЙ; разлажен, —а,
—о, —ы** (ppp), see **разлажу.**

РАЗЛАЖУ, разладишь. Р. Разладить.
I. **Разлаживать.** 1. To derange,
spoil (acc.). 2. To put out of order,
break (as a machine) (acc.). 3. (arch.)
To break up a friendly relationship
(intr.).

**РАЗЛАКОМЛЕННЫЙ; разлакомлен,
—а, —о, —ы** (ppp), see **разлакомлю.**

**РАЗЛАКОМЛЮ, разлакомишь. Р.
Разлакомить** (acc.). To create a
desire (in s.o. for s.t.) (make s.o.'s
mouth water for s.t.) (acc. + inst.)

РАЗЛАКОМЬ (imp.), see **разлакомлю.**

РАЗЛЁГСЯ, разлеглась (past), see
разлягусь.

РАЗЛЕЖАТСЯ, see **разлежусь.**

РАЗЛЕЖИСЬ (imp.), see **разлежусь.**

РАЗЛЕЖИШЬСЯ, see **разлежусь.**

РАЗЛЕЖУ́СЬ, разлежи́шься. Р. Разлежа́ться (intr.). I. Разлёживаться. To pamper o.s. by lying around too long.

РАЗЛЕ́ЗЕТСЯ, разле́зутся (3rd pers. only). Р. Разле́зться (intr.). I. Разлеза́ться. 1. To ravel, come apart, tear. 2. To tumble down (of a building or structure).

РАЗЛЕ́ЗСЯ, разле́злась (past), see разле́зется.

РАЗЛЕ́ЗУТСЯ (3rd pers. pl.), see разле́зется.

РАЗЛЕ́ЗЬСЯ (imp.), see разле́зется.

РАЗЛЕ́Й (imp.). Р. Разли́ть (acc.). I. Разлива́ть. 1. To pour (out). 2. To spill. 3. (fig.) To pour, spread (as the sun spreads its rays). (Also see разолью́.)

РАЗЛЕ́ПЛЕННЫЙ; разле́плен, —а, —о, —ы (ppp), see разлеплю́.

РАЗЛЕПЛЮ́, разле́пишь. Р. Разлепи́ть (acc.). I. Разлепля́ть. To separate (as pages of a book stuck together).

РАЗЛЕТИ́СЬ (imp.), see разлечу́сь.

РАЗЛЕТИ́ШЬСЯ, see разлечу́сь.

РАЗЛЕТЯ́ТСЯ, see разлечу́сь.

РАЗЛЕЧУ́СЬ, разлети́шься. Р. Разлете́ться (intr.). I. Разлета́ться. 1. To fly away (in different directions) 2. To scatter, disperse. 3. To shatter, fly to pieces. 4. To spread rapidly (as news). 5. To ·vanish. 6. (fig.) To shatter (of one's hopes, etc.). 7. To pick up speed. 8. To hurry (somewhere, or, to s.o.).

РАЗЛИ́ТЫЙ; разли́т, —а́, —о, —ы (ppp), see разле́й and разолью́.

РАЗЛО́МЛЕННЫЙ; разло́млен, —а, —о, —ы (ppp), see разломлю́.

РАЗЛОМЛЮ́, разло́мишь. Р. Разломи́ть (acc.). 1. Разла́мывать. To break into pieces. 2. To be tired out, driven to exhaustion by rheumatic pain (impers. + acc.).

РАЗЛЮ́БЛЕННЫЙ; разлю́блен, —а, —о, —ы (ppp), see разлюблю́.

РАЗЛЮБЛЮ́, разлю́бишь. Р. Разлюби́ть (acc.) or (+ inf.). To cease to like/love (s.o./s.t.) or (to do s.t.).

РАЗЛЯ́ГСЯ (imp.), see разля́гусь.

РАЗЛЯ́ГУСЬ, разля́жешься, разля́гутся. Р. Разле́чься (intr.). To sprawl (of a person, town, forest, etc.).

РАЗЛЯ́ЖЕШЬСЯ, see разля́гусь.

РАЗМА́ЕШЬ, see разма́ю.

РАЗМА́ЖЕШЬ, see разма́жу.

РАЗМА́ЖУ, разма́жешь. Р. Разма́зать. I. Разма́зывать. 1. To spread, smear (s.t. over the surface of s.t.) (as dirt) (acc.). 2. To relate, portray, in excessive detail (intr.) or (acc.).

РАЗМА́ЖЬ (imp.), see разма́жу.

РАЗМА́ЗАННЫЙ; разма́зан, —а, —о, —ы (ppp), see разма́жу.

РАЗМА́Й (imp.), see разма́ю.

РАЗМА́ШЕШЬСЯ see размашу́сь.

РАЗМАШИ́СЯ (imp.), see размашу́сь.

РАЗМАШУ́СЬ, разма́шешься (also размаха́юсь, размаха́ешься). Р. Размаха́ться (inst.). To wave, brandish (as a stick, one's arms, etc.).

РАЗМА́Ю, разма́ешь. Р. Размая́ть (acc.). I. Разма́ивать. To keep (s.o. or s.t.) awake.

РАЗМА́ЯННЫЙ; разма́ян, —а, —о, —ы (ppp), see разма́ю.

РАЗМЁЛ, размела́ (past), see размету́.

РАЗМЕ́ЛЕШЬ, see размелю́.

РАЗМЕЛИ́ (imp.), see размелю́.

РАЗМЕЛЮ́, разме́лешь. Р. Размоло́ть (acc.). I. Разма́лывать. To grind, pulverize, mill (as grain).

РАЗМЕ́ТАННЫЙ; разме́тан, —а, —о, —ы (ppp), see размечу́.

РАЗМЕТЁННЫЙ; разметён, —а́, —о́, —ы́ (ppp), see размету́.

РАЗМЕТЁШЬ, see размету́.

РАЗМЕТИ́ (imp.), see размету́.

РАЗМЕТУ́, разметёшь. Р. Размести́ (acc.). I. Размета́ть. 1. To sweep (e.g., a path). 2. To sweep away (as dust).

РАЗМЁТШИЙ (pap), see размету́.

РАЗМЕ́ТЬ (imp.), see размечу́.

РАЗМЕТЯ́ (adv. past part.), see размету́.

РАЗМЕ́ЧЕННЫЙ; разме́чен, —а, —о, —ы (ppp), see разме́чу.

РАЗМЕ́ЧЕШЬ, see размечу́.

РАЗМЕЧИ́ (imp.), see размечу́.

РАЗМЕЧУ́, разме́чешь. Р. Размета́ть (acc.). I. Размётывать. 1. (lit. and fig.) To scatter, disperse, demolish. 2. To toss about (as one's arms, legs, etc.).

РАЗМЕ́ЧУ, разме́тишь. Р. Разме́тить (acc.). I. Размеча́ть. 1. To mark, mark out, lay out. 2. To trace (e.g., boundaries, etc.). 3. To annotate. 4. To graduate (as a flask, thermometer, etc.).

РАЗМЕ́ШЕННЫЙ; разме́шен, —а, —о, —ы (ppp), see **размешу́**.

РАЗМЕШУ́, разме́сишь. Р. **Размеси́ть** (acc.). I. **Разме́шивать**. To knead.

РАЗМЕЩЁННЫЙ; размещён, —а́, —о́, —ы́ (ppp), see **размещу́**.

РАЗМЕЩУ́, размести́шь. Р. **Размести́ть** (acc.). I. **Размеща́ть**. 1. To distribute, dispose, place. 2. To quarter (as troops). 3. To invest (as capital).

РАЗМО́ЕШЬ, see **размо́ю**.

РАЗМО́Й (imp.), see **размо́ю**.

РАЗМО́К, размо́кла (past). Р. **Размо́к-нуть** (intr.). I. **Размока́ть**. To swell or become sodden from moisture.

РАЗМО́ЛОТЫЙ; размо́лот, —а, —о, —ы (ppp), see **размелю́**.

РАЗМО́Ю, размо́ешь. Р. **Размы́ть** (acc.). I. **Размыва́ть**. 1. To erode. 2. To wash away.

РАЗМЫ́ТЫЙ; размы́т, —а, —о, —ы (ppp), see **размо́ю**.

РАЗМЯ́К, размя́кла (past). Р. **Размя́к-нуть** (intr.). I. **Размяка́ть**, мя́кнуть. 1. To soften, become sodden. 2. (fig.) To weaken, to soften (of a person).

РАЗМЯ́ТЫЙ; размя́т, —а, —о, —ы (ppp). Р. **Размя́ть** (acc.). I. **Разми-на́ть**, мять (mean. 1). 1. To knead, work up (as clay, leather, etc.). 2. (fig.) To stretch (as one's legs). 3. (fig.) To walk (a horse). (Also see **разомну́**.)

РАЗНЕМОГИ́СЬ (imp.), see **разнемо-гу́сь**.

РАЗНЕМО́ГСЯ, разнемогла́сь (past), see **разнемогу́сь**.

РАЗНЕМОГУ́СЬ, разнемо́жешься, разнемо́гутся. Р. **Разнемо́чься** (intr.) To become very ill.

РАЗНЕМО́ЖЕШЬСЯ, see **разнемогу́сь**

РАЗНЁС, разнесла́ (past), see **разнесу́**.

РАЗНЕСЁННЫЙ; разнесён, —а́, —о́, —ы́ (ppp), see **разнесу́**.

РАЗНЕСЁШЬ, see **разнесу́**.

РАЗНЕСИ́ (imp.), see **разнесу́**.

РАЗНЕСУ́, разнесёшь. Р. **Разнести́** (acc.). I. **Разноси́ть**. 1. To deliver, carry, convey (to various places). 2. To serve (as tea to a number of people). 3. To scatter, disperse, spread. 4. To distribute. 5. To enter, record (as accounts in a book). 6. To smash, destroy. 7. To reprimand

severely. 8. To become swollen (e.g., one's hand) (impers. × acc.).

РАЗНЕСЯ́ (adv. past part.), see **разнесу́**.

РАЗНИ́МЕШЬ, see **разниму́**.

РАЗНИМИ́ (imp.), see **разниму́**.

РАЗНИМУ́, разни́мешь. Р. **Разня́ть** (acc.). I. **Разнима́ть**. 1. To separate, part. 2. To tear apart. 3. To take apart, dismantle. 4. To dismember.

РАЗНООБРА́ЖУ, разнообра́зишь. I. **разнообра́зить** (acc.). To diversify, vary.

РАЗНООБРА́ЗЬ (imp.), see **разно-обра́жу**.

РАЗНО́ШЕННЫЙ; разно́шен, —а, —о, —ы (ppp), see **разношу́²**.

РАЗНОШУ́¹, разно́сишь. I. **Разноси́ть** (acc.). Р. **Разнести́**. 1. To deliver, carry, convey (to various places). 2. To serve (e.g., tea to a number of people). 3. To scatter, disperse, spread. 4. To distribute. 5. To enter, record (as accounts in a book). 6. To smash, destroy. 7. To reprimand severely. 8. To become swollen (e.g., one's hand) (impers. + acc.).

РАЗНОШУ́², разно́сишь. Р. **Разноси́ть** (acc.). I. **Разна́шивать**. To break in, wear in (as a new pair of shoes).

РАЗНЯ́Л, разняла́, разня́ло, разня́ли (also ро́знял, разняла́, ро́зняло, ро́зняли) (past), see **разниму́**.

РАЗНЯ́ТЫЙ; разня́т, разнята́, раз-ня́то, разня́ты (arch. forms: ро́знят, ро́знято, ро́зняты), see **разниму́**.

РАЗОБИ́ДЬ (imp.), see **разоби́жу**.

РАЗОБИ́ДЯТ, see **разоби́жу**.

РАЗОБИ́ЖЕННЫЙ; разоби́жен, —а, —о, —ы (ppp), see **разоби́жу**.

РАЗОБИ́ЖУ, разоби́дишь. Р. **Разоби́-деть** (acc.). I. **Разобижа́ть**. To insult grossly, offend greatly.

РАЗО́БРАННЫЙ; разо́бран, —а, —о, —ы (ppp). Р. **Разобра́ть** (acc.). I. **Разбира́ть**. 1. To take. 2. To take apart, dismantle (e.g., a machine, watch, etc.). 3. To sort out, pick out. 4. To put in order. 5. To make out, decipher (e.g., handwriting). 6. To analyse. 7. To investigate, examine. 8. To buy up, acquire (as all goods, etc.). 9. (gram.) To parse. 10. To seize (as laughter, etc., seizes one). (Also see **разберу́**.)

РАЗОБЬЁШЬ, see **разобью́**.

РАЗОБЬЮ, разобьёшь. Р. Разби́ть (acc.). I. Разбива́ть, бить (mean. 1). 1. To break. 2. To divide. 3. To mark out, lay out (as a camp). 4. (lit. and fig.) To destroy, damage, break, smash. 5. To conquer, defeat. 6. To break (as a ship on the rocks (impers.) 7. (typ.) To space.

РАЗОВЬЁШЬ, see разовью́.

РАЗОВЬЮ, разовьёшь. Р. Разви́ть (acc.). I. Развива́ть. 1. To develop (e.g., industry, memory, understanding, strength, a role in a play, one's voice, activities, etc.). 2. To untwist, unwind.

РАЗО́ГНАННЫЙ; разо́гнан, —а, —о, —ы (ppp). Р. Разогна́ть. I. Разгоня́ть. 1. (lit. and fig.) To drive away, disperse (acc.). 2. To dispel (e.g., gloom) (acc.). 3. To accelerate (as an auto) (acc.). 4. To drive at high speed, race (intr.). 5. To send (as s.o. to do s.t.) (acc.). 6. To discharge, fire (s.o.) (acc.). 7. To spread (as an action over a period of time, or a letter over two pages, etc.) (acc. + на + acc.). 8. (typ.) To space (acc.). (Also see разгоню́.)

РАЗОДЕ́НЕШЬ, see разоде́ну.

РАЗОДЕ́НУ, разоде́нешь. Р. Разоде́ть (acc.). To dress up.

РАЗОДЕ́НЬ (imp.), see разоде́ну.

РАЗОДЕ́ТЫЙ; разоде́т, —а, —о, —ы (ppp), see разоде́ну.

РАЗО́ДРАННЫЙ; разо́дран, —а, —о, —ы (ppp). Р. Разодра́ть (acc.). I. Раздира́ть. 1. To tear. 2. To tear to pieces, tear up. (Also see раздеру́.)

РАЗОЖГИ́ (imp.), see разожгу́.

РАЗОЖГЛА́, разожгло́, разожгли́ (past), see разожгу́ and разжёг.

РАЗОЖГУ́, разожжёшь, разожгу́т. Р. Разже́чь (acc.). I. Разжига́ть. 1. To light, kindle (as a fire). 2. (fig.) To kindle, rouse (as passions).

РАЗОЖЖЁННЫЙ; разожжён, —а́, —о́, —ы́ (ppp), see разожгу́.

РАЗОЖЖЁШЬ, see разожгу́.

РАЗОЖМЁШЬ, see разожму́.

РАЗОЖМИ́ (imp.), see разожму́.

РАЗОЖМУ́, разожмёшь. Р. Разжа́ть (acc.). I. Разжима́ть. 1. To unclasp, unclench (as one's hands, teeth, etc.). 2. To release (s.t. under tension, as a spring).

РАЗОЙДЁШЬСЯ, see разойду́сь.

РАЗОЙДИ́СЬ (imp.), see разойду́сь.

РАЗОЙДУ́СЬ, разойдёшься. Р. Разойти́сь (intr.). I. Расходи́ться. 1. To disperse, separate. 2. To be sold out. 3. To be out of print. 4. To be spent (of money). 5. To melt; dissolve. 6. To vanish, disappear. 7. To spread (of news, etc.). 8. To discontinue a relationship (part from, get a divorce from, etc.) (с + inst.). 9. (lit. and fig.) To separate (of roads, ways, etc.). 10. To differ with (s.o. in s.t.) (с + inst. + в + prep.). 11. To pick up speed. 12. To increase in intensity (e.g., rain). 13. To surpass, outdo oneself. 14. To pass without meeting or without touching.

РАЗОЙДЯ́СЬ (adv. past part.), see разойду́сь.

РАЗОЛЬЁШЬ, see разолью́.

РАЗОЛЬЮ, разольёшь. Р. Разли́ть (acc.). I. Разлива́ть. 1. To pour (out). 2. To spill. 3. (fig.) To pour, spread (as the sun spreads its rays, etc.).

РАЗОМНЁШЬ, see разомну́.

РАЗОМНИ́ (imp.), see разомну́.

РАЗОМНУ́, разомнёшь. Р. Размя́ть (acc.). I. Размина́ть, мять (mean. 1). 1. To knead, work up (as clay, etc.). 2. (fig.) To stretch (as one's legs). 3. (fig.) To walk (as a horse).

РАЗОПРЁШЬ, see разопру́.

РАЗОПРИ́ (imp.), see разопру́.

РАЗОПРУ́, разопрёшь. Р. Распере́ть (acc.) and (impers. + acc.). I. Распира́ть. 1. To burst open, split. 2. To expand, distend.

РАЗОПЬЁШЬ, see разопью́.

РАЗОПЬЮ́, разопьёшь. Р. Распи́ть (acc.). I. Распива́ть. To drink (s.t. with s.o.) (e.g., to split or share a bottle).

РАЗО́РВАННЫЙ; разо́рван, —а, —о, —ы (ppp), see разорву́.

РАЗОРВЁШЬ, see разорву́.

РАЗОРВИ́ (imp.), see разорву́.

РАЗОРВУ́, разорвёшь. Р. Разорва́ть (acc.). I. Разрыва́ть. 1. To tear, tear to pieces. 2. To break. 3. To blow up, explode (of a cannon) (3rd pers.) (impers. + acc.). 4. (fig.) To terminate, break (as diplomatic relations).

РАЗО́СЛАННЫЙ; разо́слан, —а, —о, —ы (ppp), see разошлю́.

РАЗОСПИ́СЬ (imp.), see разосплю́сь.
РАЗОСПИ́ШЬСЯ, see разосплю́сь.
РОЗОСПЛЮ́СЬ, разоспи́шься. Р. Раз-
оспа́ться (intr.). 1. To be fast asleep.
2. To oversleep.
РАЗОСПЯ́ТСЯ, see разосплю́сь.
РАЗÓСТЛАННЫЙ; разóстлан, —а,
—о, —ы (ppp), Р. Разостла́ть (асс.),
расстели́ть. I. Растила́ть. 1. To
spread (as a carpet, tablecloth, etc.).
2. To spread, strew (as a layer of
sand). 3. (fig.) To spread (as the sun
spreads its rays). (Also see расстелю́.)
РАЗÓТКАННЫЙ; разóткан, —а, —о,
—ы (ppp), see разотку́.
РАЗОТКЁШЬ, see разотку́.
РАЗОТКИ́ (imp.), see разотку́.
РАЗОТКУ́, разоткёшь. Р. Разоткáть
(асс.). To adorn, decorate, embellish
by weaving (e.g., weave a design in
a fabric).
РАЗОТРЁШЬ, see разотру́.
РАЗОТРИ́ (imp.), see разотру́.
РАЗОТРУ́, разотрёшь. Р. Растерéть
(асс.). I. Растирáть. 1. To grind,
triturate. 2. To rub, spread (s.t.
on the surface of s.t.) (на + prep.).
3. To massage, rub (as one's arms).
РАЗОХÓТЬ (imp.), see разохóчу.
РАЗОХÓЧЕННЫЙ; разохóчен, —а,
—о, —ы (ppp), see разохóчу.
РАЗОХÓЧУ, разохóтишь. Р. Раз-
охóтить (асс. + inf.). To inspire
(s.o.) with desire or liking (to do s.t.).
РАЗОЧЛА́, разочлó, разочли́ (past),
see разочту́ and расчёл.
РАЗОЧТЁННЫЙ; разочтён, —á, —ó,
—ы́ (ppp), see разочту́.
РАЗОЧТЁШЬ, see разочту́.
РАЗОЧТИ́ (imp.), see разочту́.
РАЗОЧТУ́, разочтёшь. Р. Расчéсть
(асс.). I. Рассчи́тывать. 1. To
calculate, compute. 2. To figure out.
3. (tech.) To design. 4. To dismiss,
pay off (s.o.). (For other idiomatic
usages see unabridged dictionary.)
РАЗОЧТЯ́ (adv. past part.), see
разочту́.
РАЗОШÉДШИСЬ (arch.) (adv. past
part.), see разойду́сь.
РАЗОШÉДШИЙСЯ (pap), see раз-
ойду́сь.
РАЗОШЁЛСЯ, разошла́сь (past), see
разойду́сь.
РАЗОШЛЁШЬ, see разошлю́.
РАЗОШЛИ́ (imp.), see разошлю́.

РАЗОШЛЮ́, разошлёшь. Р. Раз-
ослáть (асс.). I. Рассылáть. 1. To
send (around to various places). 2.
To distribute.
РАЗОШЬЁШЬ, see разошью́.
РАЗОШЬЮ́, разошьёшь. Р. Расши́ть
(асс.). I. Расшивáть. 1. To rip (as a
seam), remove stitching. 2. To
embroider. 3. (tech.) To point
(smooth) (as mortared joints of
brickwork, etc.).
РАЗРАЖУ́СЬ, разрази́шься. Р. Раз-
рази́ться (intr.). I. Разражáться.
1. To break, burst out (e.g., of a
storm, thunder, lightning, etc.). 2.
(fig.) To break out, burst out (with
s.t.) (e.g., with laughter, tears) (inst.).
РАЗРАСТЁТСЯ, разрасту́тся (3rd
pers. only). Р. Разрасти́сь (intr.). I.
Разрастáться. 1. To spread out,
grow bushy (of a tree). 2. (fig.) To
spread, grow (of a city, a scandal,
etc.).
РАЗРАСТИ́СЬ (imp.), see разрастётся.
РАЗРАСТУ́ТСЯ (3rd pers. pl.), see
разрастётся.
РАЗРЕВЁШЬСЯ, see разреву́сь.
РАЗРЕВИ́СЬ (imp.), see разреву́сь.
РАЗРЕВУ́СЬ, разревёшься. Р. Раз-
ревéться (intr.). 1. To start to roar,
howl, bellow. 2. To start to cry
loudly.
РАЗРЕЖЁННЫЙ; разрежён, —á,
—ó, —ы́ (ppp), see разрежу́.
РАЗРÉЖЕШЬ, see разрéжу.
РАЗРÉЖУ, разрéжешь. Р. Разрéзать
(асс.). I. Разрезáть. 1. To cut. 2. To
cut, slice, to pieces. 3. (med.) To
lance. 4. To cut in two (as a river
cuts a field in two). 5. (fig.) To cut
(as the enemy's supply route).
РАЗРЕЖУ́, разреди́шь. Р. Разреди́ть
(асс.). I. Разрежáть. 1. To thin out,
weed out (as plants). 2. To rarefy,
evacuate, exhaust (as air).
РАЗРÉЖЬ (imp.), see разрéжу.
РАЗРÉЗАННЫЙ; разрéзан, —а, —о,
—ы (ppp), see разрéжу.
РАЗРÓЕШЬ, see разрóю.
РАЗРОЖУ́СЬ, разроди́шься. Р. Раз-
роди́ться (intr.). 1. To bear children.
2. To breed, multiply (of animals,
etc.).
РАЗРÓЙ (imp.), see разрóю.
РАЗРÓССЯ, разросла́сь (past), see
разрастётся.

РАЗРО́Ю. разро́ешь. Р. Разры́ть (acc.). I. Разрыва́ть. 1. To dig up (as the ground). 2. To turn upside down, make a mess of.

РАЗРУ́БЛЕННЫЙ; разру́блен, —а, —о, —ы (ppp), see разрублю́.

РАЗРУБЛЮ́, разру́бишь. Р. Разруби́ть (acc.). I. Разруба́ть. To cut, chop to pieces.

РАЗРЫ́ТЫЙ; разры́т, —а, —о, —ы (ppp), see разро́ю.

РАЗРЯЖЁННЫЙ; разряжён, —а́, —о́, —ы́ (ppp), see разряжу́ (mean. 2 thru 6).

РАЗРЯ́ЖЕННЫЙ; разря́жен, —а, —о, —ы (ppp), see разряжу́ (mean. 1 thru 6).

РАЗРЯЖУ́, разря́дишь (and разряди́шь). Р. Разряди́ть (acc.). I. Разряжа́ть. 1. To dress up (s.o.). 2. To unload (as a gun). 3. To fire, discharge (as gun). 4. To discharge (as an electrical charge). 5. (fig.) To relieve (as tension). 6. (typ.) To justify (a line).

РАЗУБЕЖДЁННЫЙ; разубеждён, —а́, —о́, —ы́ (ppp), see разубежу́.

РАЗУБЕЖУ́, разубеди́шь. Р. Разубеди́ть (acc.). I. Разубежда́ть. To dissuade (as s.o. from s.t.) (acc. + в + prep.) or (s.o. from doing s.t.) (acc. + inf.).

РАЗУ́ЕШЬ, see разу́ю.

РАЗУ́Й (imp.), see разу́ю.

РАЗУКРА́СЬ (imp.), see разукра́шу.

РАЗУКРА́ШЕННЫЙ; разукра́шен, —а, —о, —ы (ppp), see разукра́шу.

РАЗУКРА́ШУ, разукра́сишь. Р. Разукра́сить (acc.). I. Разукра́шивать. (lit. and fig.) To decorate, adorn, embellish.

РАЗУ́ТЫЙ; разу́т, —а, —о, —ы (ppp), see разу́ю.

РАЗУ́Ю, разу́ешь. Р. Разу́ть (acc.). I. Разува́ть. To take off (s.o.'s) shoes (acc. of s.o.).

РАЗ'Е́ДЕННЫЙ; раз'е́ден, —а, —о, —ы (ppp), see раз'е́ст.

РАЗ'Е́ДЕШЬСЯ, see раз'е́дусь.

РАЗ'ЕДИ́МСЯ, раз'еди́тесь, раз'еди́тся (pl. forms), see раз'е́мся.

РАЗ'Е́ДУСЬ, раз'е́дешься. Р. Раз'е́хаться (intr.). I. Раз'езжа́ться. 1. To depart (of guests, etc.). 2. To pass (one another) (of people, autos, etc.). 3. To miss (one another en route). 4. To separate (quit living together). 5. To slip (as one's feet, skiis, on ice). 6. To fall to pieces, fray (as one's clothes). 7. To occupy much space (as a table in a room).

РАЗ'ЕДЯ́Т (3rd pers. pl.), see раз'е́ст.

РАЗ'ЕДЯ́ТСЯ (3rd pers. pl.), see раз'е́мся.

РАЗ'Е́ЗДИ (imp.), see раз'е́зжу.

РАЗ'Е́ЗДИСЬ (imp.), see раз'е́зжусь.

РАЗ'ЕЗЖА́ЙСЯ (imp.), see раз'е́дусь.

РАЗ'Е́ЗЖЕННЫЙ; раз'е́зжен, —а, —о, —ы (ppp), see раз'е́зжу.

РАЗ'Е́ЗЖУ, раз'е́здишь. Р. Раз'е́здить (acc.). I. Раз'е́зживать. 1. To damage by travel (as a road). 2. To widen and smooth (a road) by frequent travel.

РАЗ'Е́ЗЖУСЬ, раз'е́здишься. Р. Раз'е́здиться (intr.). I. Раз'е́зживаться. To begin to travel often.

РАЗ'Е́Л, раз'е́ла (past), see раз'е́ст.

РАЗ'Е́ЛСЯ, раз'е́лась (past), see раз'е́мся.

РАЗ'Е́МСЯ, раз'е́шься, раз'е́стся (sing. forms). Р. Раз'е́сться (intr.). I. Раз'еда́ться. To grow fat from eating.

РАЗ'Е́СТ, раз'едя́т (3rd pers. only). Р. Раз'е́сть (acc.). I. Раз'еда́ть. 1. To eat away (as fleas eat a dog's ears). 2. (chem.) To corrode, eat away.

РАЗ'Е́СТСЯ, see раз'е́мся.

РАЗ'Е́ШЬСЯ[1] (2nd pers. sing.), see раз'е́мся.

РАЗ'Е́ШЬСЯ[2] (imp.), see раз'е́мся.

РАЗ'Я́Л, раз'я́ла, раз'я́ло, раз'я́ли (past) (arch.), see разыму́.

РАЗ'Я́ТЫЙ; раз'я́т, —а, —о, —ы (ppp), see разыму́.

РАЗЫ́МЕШЬ, see разыму́.

РАЗЫМИ́ (imp.), see разыму́.

РАЗЫМУ́, разы́мешь. Р. Раз'я́ть (inf. form arch.) (acc.). I. Разника́ть. 1. To separate, part. 2. To tear apart. 3. To take apart, dismantle. 4. To dismember.

РАЗЫ́СКАННЫЙ; разы́скан, —а, —о, —ы (ppp), see разыщу́.

РАЗЫ́ЩЕШЬ, see разыщу́.

РАЗЫЩИ́ (imp.), see разыщу́.

РАЗЫЩУ́, разы́щешь. Р. Разыска́ть (acc.). I. Разы́скивать. To hunt for and find.

РАСКА́ЧЕННЫЙ; раска́чен, —а, —о, —ы (ppp), see раскачу́.

РАСКАЧУ́, раска́тишь. Р. Раската́ть (acc.). I. Раска́тывать. 1. To roll (things) away (e.g., barrels) (to different locations). 2. To roll (s.t.) rapidly.

РАСКВА́СЬ (imp.), see расква́шу.

РАСКВА́ШЕННЫЙ; расква́шен, —а, —о, —ы (ppp), see расква́шу.

РАСКВА́ШУ, расква́сишь. Р. Расква́сить (acc.). I. Расква́шивать. 1. To bloody (as one's nose). 2. To make wet and viscous, swampy (as rain turns the ground, road, to mud).

РАСКИ́С, раски́сла (past). Р. Раски́снуть (intr.). I. Раскиса́ть. 1. To rise (of dough). 2. To swell (from absorption of moisture). 3. To become marshy (from rains, etc.). 4. To become limp, apathetic (of people). 5. (fig.) To become deeply moved.

РАСКО́ЛЕШЬ, see расколю́.

РАСКОЛИ́ (imp.), see расколю́.

РАСКО́ЛОТЫЙ; раско́лот, —а, —о, —ы (ppp), see расколю́.

РАСКОЛО́ЧЕННЫЙ; расколо́чен, —а, —о, —ы (ppp), see расколочу́.

РАСКОЛОЧУ́, расколо́тишь. Р. Расколоти́ть (acc.). I. Раскола́чивать. 1. To un-nail (open). 2. To break (to pieces, as a dish). 3. To flatten by beating (as shoe sole leather); to shape on a last. 4. To crush, defeat (as the enemy). 5. To hurt, injure by striking.

РАСКОЛЮ́, раско́лешь. Р. Расколо́ть (acc.). I. Коло́ть (mean. 1 and 2), раска́лывать. 1. To chop, split, break. 2. To crack. 3. To disrupt (e.g., the unity of a group, peace, etc.).

РАСКО́РМЛЕННЫЙ; раско́рмлен, —а, —о, —ы (ppp), see раскормлю́.

РАСКОРМЛЮ́, раско́рмишь. Р. Раскорми́ть (acc.). I. Раска́рмливать. To fatten by feeding.

РАСКО́ШЕННЫЙ; раско́шен, —а, —о, —ы (ppp), see раскошу́.

РАСКОШЁННЫЙ; раскошён, —а́, —б, —ы́ (ppp), see раскошу́.

РАСКОШУ́, раскоси́шь. Р. Раскоси́ть (acc.). I. Раска́шивать. 1. To squint (one's eyes). 2. To reinforce with a spreader (e.g., in construction of forms for concrete).

РАСКРА́ДЕННЫЙ; раскра́ден, —а, —о, —ы (ppp), see раскраду́.

РАСКРАДЁШЬ, see раскраду́.

РАСКРАДИ́ (imp.), see раскраду́.

РАСКРАДУ́, раскрадёшь. Р. Раскра́сть (acc.). I. Раскра́дывать. To embezzle, plunder.

РАСКРА́Л, раскра́ла (past), see раскраду́.

РАСКРА́СЬ (imp.), see раскра́шу.

РАСКРА́ШЕННЫЙ; раскра́шен, —а, —о, —ы (ppp), see раскра́шу.

РАСКРА́ШУ, раскра́сишь. Р. Раскра́сить (acc.). I. Раскра́шивать. To paint, color.

РАСКРЕПЛЁННЫЙ; раскреплён, —а́, —б, —ы́ (ppp), see раскреплю́.

РАСКРЕПЛЮ́, раскрепи́шь. Р. Раскрепи́ть (acc.). I. Раскрепля́ть. 1. To strengthen, reinforce with supports. 2. To remove bracing, etc.

РАСКРЕПОЩЁННЫЙ; раскрепощён, —а́, —б, —ы́ (ppp), see раскрепощу́.

РАСКРЕПОЩУ́, раскрепости́шь. Р. Раскрепости́ть (acc.). I. Раскрепоща́ть. (lit. and fig.) To emancipate, set free.

РАСКРИЧА́ТСЯ, see раскричу́сь.

РАСКРИЧИ́СЬ (imp.), see раскричу́сь.

РАСКРИЧИ́ШЬСЯ, see раскричу́сь.

РАСКРИЧУ́СЬ, раскричи́шься. Р. Раскрича́ться. 1. To start shouting (intr.). 2. To shout or bellow (at s.o.) (на + acc.).

РАСКРО́ЕННЫЙ; раскро́ен, —а, —о, —ы (ppp), see раскрою́.

РАСКРО́ЕШЬ, see раскрою́.

РАСКРОЙ (imp.), see раскрою́.

РАСКРО́Й (imp.), see раскрою́.

РАСКРОЮ́, раскрои́шь. Р. Раскрои́ть (acc.). I. Раскра́ивать. 1. To cut out (e.g., material for a shirt). 2. To split, cleave (as s.o.'s skull).

РАСКРО́Ю, раскро́ешь. Р. Раскры́ть (acc.). I. Раскрыва́ть. 1. To open, open wide. 2. To uncover, expose (e.g., one's chest). 3. To disclose, reveal (as a secret). 4. To uncover, discover (e.g., a plot).

РАСКРУ́ЧЕННЫЙ; раскру́чен, —а, —о, —ы (ppp), see раскручу́.

РАСКРУЧУ́, раскру́тишь. Р. Раскрути́ть (acc.). I. Раскру́чивать. 1. To unwind, disentangle, undo. 2. To turn rapidly, spin rapidly (as wheels, a generator, rotor, etc.).

РАСКРЫ́ТЫЙ; раскры́т, —а, —о, —ы (ppp), see раскро́ю.
РАСКУЧУ́СЬ, раску́тишься. Р. Раскути́ться (intr.). I. Раску́чиваться. To go on a spree.
РАСКУ́ШЕННЫЙ; раску́шен, —а, —о, —ы (ppp), see раскушу́.
РАСКУШУ́, раску́сишь. Р. Раскуси́ть (acc.). I. Раску́сывать (mean. 1). 1. To bite (into pieces) (e.g., a lump of sugar). 2. To understand well, get to the heart of the matter.
РАСПАДЁТСЯ, распаду́тся (3rd pers. only). Р. Распа́сться (intr.). I. Распада́ться. 1. To disintegrate, fall to pieces. 2. (fig.) To break up (e.g., a group of people). 3. (chem.) To break down, decompose.
РАСПАДИ́СЬ (imp.), see распадётся.
РАСПАДУ́ТСЯ (3rd pers. pl.), see распадётся.
РАСПА́ЛСЯ, распа́лась, see распадётся.
РАСПА́ХАННЫЙ; распа́хан, —а, —о, —ы (ppp), see распашу́.
РАСПА́ШЕШЬ, see распашу́.
РАСПАШИ́ (imp.), see распашу́.
РАСПАШУ́, распа́шешь. Р. Распаха́ть (acc.). I. Распа́хивать. To plough up, till.
РАСПЕ́Й (imp.). Р. Распи́ть (acc.). I. Распива́ть. To drink (s.t. with s.o.) (e.g., to split, share a bottle). (Also see разопью́.)
РАСПЁК, распекла́ (past), see распеку́.
РАСПЕКИ́ (imp.), see распеку́.
РАСПЕКУ́, распечёшь, распеку́т. Р. Распе́чь (acc.). I. Распека́ть. To reprimand severely.
РАСПЁР, распёрла (past). Р. Распере́ть (acc.) and (impers. + acc.). I. Распира́ть. 1. To burst open, split. 2. To expand, distend. (Also see разопру́.)
РАСПЁРТЫЙ; распёрт, —а, —о, —ы (ppp), see распёр and разопру́.
РАСПЕ́ТЫЙ; распе́т, —а, —о, —ы (ppp). Р. Распе́ть (acc.). I. Распева́ть. 1. To practice singing (s.t.). 2. To warm up (one's voice). (Also see распою́.)
РАСПЕЧЁННЫЙ; распечён, —а́, —о́, —ы́ (ppp), see распеку́.
РАСПЕЧЁШЬ, see распеку́.

РАСПИ́Л, распила́, распи́ло, распи́ли (also ро́спил, распила́, ро́спило, ро́спили) (past), see распе́й and разопью́.
РАСПИ́САННЫЙ; распи́сан, —а, —о, —ы (ppp), see распишу́.
РАСПИ́ТЫЙ; распи́т, —а́, —о, —ы (ppp) (also распи́тый, ро́спит, распита́, ро́спито, ро́спиты) (ppp), see распе́й and разопью́.
РАСПИ́ШЕШЬ, see распишу́.
РАСПИШИ́ (imp.), see распишу́.
РАСПИШУ́, распи́шешь. Р. Расписа́ть (acc.). I. Распи́сывать. 1. To copy down (parts of a work, play, quotations, etc.) (in several places). 2. To assign. 3. To enter (as in an account book), to book. 4. To paint (with designs, etc.). 5. (fig.) To paint (e.g., relate, describe in detail, usually with embellishment).
РАСПЛА́ВЛЕННЫЙ; распла́влен, —а, —о, —ы (ppp), see распла́влю.
РАСПЛА́ВЛЮ, распла́вишь. Р. Распла́вить (acc.). I. Расплавля́ть, пла́вить. To melt down, to fuse.
РАСПЛА́ВЬ (imp.), see распла́влю.
РАСПЛАЧУ́СЬ, распла́тишься. Р. Расплати́ться (intr.). I. Распла́чиваться. 1. To pay off (intr.). 2. (lit. and fig.) To pay off (s.o.) (с + inst.). 3. To pay off (a debt) (с + inst.). 4. (fig.) To pay for (as a mistake, sins, etc.) (за + acc.).
РАСПЛЁЛ, расплела́ (past), see расплету́.
РАСПЛЁСКАННЫЙ; расплёскан, —а, —о, —ы (ppp), see расплещу́.
РАСПЛЕТЁННЫЙ; расплетён, —а́, —о́, —ы́ (ppp), see расплету́.
РАСПЛЕТЁШЬ, see расплету́.
РАСПЛЕТИ́ (imp.), see расплету́.
РАСПЛЕТУ́, расплетёшь. Р. Расплести́ (acc.). I. Расплета́ть. 1. To untwist, untwine, unweave. 2. To unbraid.
РАСПЛЁТШИЙ (pap), see расплету́.
РАСПЛЕТЯ́ (adv. past part.), see расплету́.
РАСПЛЕ́ЩЕШЬ, see расплещу́.
РАСПЛЕЩИ́ (imp.), see расплещу́.
РАСПЛЕЩУ́, расплёщешь. Р. Расплеска́ть (acc.). I. Расплёскивать. To spill, splash.
РАСПЛОЖЁННЫЙ; распложён, —а́, —о́, —ы́ (ppp), see распложу́.

РАСПЛОЖУ́, распло́дишь. Р. Расплоди́ть (acc.). I. Плоди́ть. 1. To breed, raise (as cattle, crops, etc.). 2. To procreate. 3. (fig.) To create, engender, give rise to, produce.

РАСПЛЫВЁШЬСЯ, see расплыву́сь.

РАСПЛЫВИ́СЬ (imp.), see расплыву́сь.

РАСПЛЫВУ́СЬ, расплывёшься. Р. Расплы́ться (intr.). I. Расплыва́ться. 1. To run (as colors). 2. To spread (e.g., smoke, fog, etc.). 3. (fig.) To spread, become fatter (of one's figure). 4. To lose distinctness or sharpness of outline (as an object at a distance in the dusk). 5. (fig.) To spread (as a smile, good will, spreads over one's face) (по + dat. of face). 6. To swim away (in different directions).

РАСПНЁШЬ, see распну́.

РАСПНИ́ (imp.), see распну́.

РАСПНУ́, распнёшь. Р. Распя́ть (acc.). I. Распина́ть. To crucify.

РАСПОЁШЬ, see распою́.

РАСПО́Й (imp.), see распою́.

РАСПОЛЗЁШЬСЯ, see расползу́сь.

РАСПОЛЗИ́СЬ (imp.), see расползу́сь.

РАСПО́ЛЗСЯ, располза́сь (past), see расползу́сь.

РАСПОЛЗУ́СЬ, расползёшься. Р. Расползти́сь (intr.). I. Располза́ться. 1. To crawl away, move away slowly (in various directions) 2. To spread, run (of colors). 3. To spread (of clouds, smoke, etc.). 4. To spread, grow fatter (of a person). 5. To fall to pieces (e.g., of one's clothes, house, etc.).

РАСПО́РЕШЬ, see распорю́.

РАСПОРИ́ (imp.), see распорю́.

РАСПО́РОТЫЙ; распо́рот, —а, —о, —ы (ppp), see распорю́.

РАСПОРЮ́, распо́решь. Р. Распоро́ть (acc.). I. Распа́рывать, поро́ть (mean. 1 and 2). 1. To rip (as a seam). 2. To rip open (as a bayonet rips open a person). 3. (fig.) To break, rend (as a shot rends the silence, etc.).

РАСПОРЯДИ́СЬ (imp.), see распоряжу́сь.

РАСПОРЯЖУ́СЬ, распоряди́шься. Р. Распоряди́ться (intr.). I. Распоряжа́ться. 1. To give orders (about s.t.) (o + prep.). 2. To see to arrangements (for), application or disposal (of s.t.) (inst.). 3. To order, have (s.t.) done (+ inf.). 4. To conduct o.s., act (in relation to s.o.), deal with (c + inst.).

РАСПОЮ́, распоёшь. Р. Распе́ть (acc.). I. Распева́ть. 1. To practice singing (s.t.). 2. To warm up (one's voice).

РАСПОЯ́САННЫЙ; распоя́сан, —а, —о, —ы (ppp), see распоя́шу.

РАСПОЯ́ШЕШЬ, see распоя́шу.

РАСПОЯ́ШУ, распоя́шешь. Р. Распоя́сать (acc.). I. Распоя́сывать. To unbelt, ungird.

РАСПОЯ́ШЬ (imp.), see распоя́шу.

РАСПРА́ВЛЕННЫЙ; распра́влен, —а, —о, —ы (ppp), see распра́влю.

РАСПРА́ВЛЮ, распра́вишь. Р. Распра́вить (acc.). I. Расправля́ть. 1. To straighten, smooth out. 2. To stretch, straighten (as one's legs, shoulders, etc.).

РАСПРА́ВЛЮСЬ, распра́вишься. Р. Распра́виться (intr.). I. Расправля́ться. 1. To deal severely (with s.o.) (c + inst.). 2. To finish (with), have done (with s.t.) (c + inst.). 3. To eat up (all of s.t.), finish (as with a meal) (c + inst.). 4. To straighten out, smooth out (intr.).

РАСПРА́ВЬ (imp.), see распра́влю.

РАСПРА́ВЬСЯ (imp.), see распра́влюсь.

РАСПРОДАВА́Й (imp.), see распродаю́.

РАСПРОДАВА́Я (adv. pres. part.), see распродаю́.

РАСПРОДАДИ́М, распродади́те, распродаду́т (pl. forms), see распрода́м.

РАСПРОДАЕ́ШЬ, see распродаю́.

РАСПРОДА́Й (imp.), see распрода́м.

РАСПРОДА́М, распрода́шь, распрода́ст (sing. forms). Р. Распрода́ть (acc.). I. Распродава́ть. To sell off (out) (e.g., all tickets to a game, all one's furniture, etc.).

РАСПРО́ДАННЫЙ; распро́дан, —а, —о, —ы (ppp), see распрода́м.

РАСПРОДА́СТ, see распрода́м.

РАСПРОДА́ШЬ, see распрода́м.

РАСПРОДАЮ́, распродаёшь. I. Распродава́ть (acc.). Р. Распрода́ть. To sell off (out) (e.g., all tickets to a game, all one's furniture, etc.).

РАСПРОСТЁР, распростёрла (past), see **распрострý.**
РАСПРОСТЕРЁВ and **распростёрши** (adv. past part.), see **распрострý.**
РАСПРОСТЁРТЫЙ; распростёрт, —а, —о, —ы (ppp), see **распрострý.**
РАСПРОСТЁРШИ and **распростерёв** (adv. past part.), see **распрострý.**
РАСПРОСТРИ (imp.), see **распрострý.**
РАСПРОСТРУ́, распрострёшь (future tense seldom used). P. **Распростереть** (acc.). I. **Распростирать.** 1. To stretch out (as wings). 2. (fig.) To extend (as one's influence over s.o. or s.t.) (acc. + на + acc.).
РАСПРОЩУ́СЬ, распростишься. P. **Распроститься** (intr.). 1. To take final leave, part (intr.). 2. To take final leave of, part (from s.o.) (с + inst.). 3. (fig.) To say goodbye forever (to s.t.) (e.g., one's hopes, profession, etc.). (с + inst.).
РАСПРЯ́Г, распягла́ (past), see **распрягý.**
РАСПРЯГИ́ (imp.), see **распрягý.**
РАСПРЯГУ́, распряжёшь, распрягут. P. **Распря́чь** (acc.). I. **Распрягать.** To unharness.
РАСПРЯЖЁННЫЙ; распряжён, —а́, —о́, —ы́ (ppp), see **распрягý.**
РАСПРЯЖЁШЬ, see **распрягý.**
РАСПРЯМЛЁННЫЙ; распрямлён, —а́, —о́, —ы́ (ppp), see **распрямлю́.**
РАСПРЯМЛЮ́, распрями́шь. P. **Распрями́ть** (acc.). I. **Распрямля́ть.** To straighten (as a rod, one's back, etc.).
РАСПУ́Х, распýхла (past). P. **Распýхнуть** (intr.). I. **Распухать.** 1. To swell (up), bloat. 2. (fig.) To bulge (e.g., a notebook). 3. To grow stout.
РАСПУ́ЩЕННЫЙ; распýщен, —а, —о, —ы (ppp), see **распущý.**
РАСПУЩУ́, распýстишь. P. **Распусти́ть** (acc.). I. **Распускать.** 1. To dismiss (e.g., a class, employees, etc.). 2. To disband (e.g., an organization). 3. To untie, undo, unfurl. 4. To relax (e.g., discipline, attention, etc.). 5. To dissolve (as s.t. in a liquid). 6. To diffuse. 7. To unravel (e.g., knitting). 8. To let out, let go, let loose. 9. (fig.) To release, spread (as rumors).
РАСПЯ́ТЫЙ; распя́т, —а, —о, —ы

(ppp). P. **Распя́ть** (acc.). I. **Распина́ть.** To crucify. (Also see **распнý.**)
РАССА́ЖЕННЫЙ; расса́жен, —а, —о, —ы (ppp), see **рассажý.**
РАССАЖУ́, расса́дишь. P. **Рассади́ть** (acc.), I. **Расса́живать.** 1. To seat (people). 2. To set out, place in various locations (e.g., plants, etc.). 3. To replant, transplant (separating). 4. To break or injure by striking (s.t. or s.o.).
РАССВЕЛО́ (past), see **рассветёт.**
РАССВЕТЁТ (3rd pers. sing.). P. **Рассвести́** (intr.) (impers.). I. **Рассветать.** To dawn.
РАССЕ́ЕШЬ, see **рассею.**
РАССЕ́Й (imp.), see **рассею.**
РАССЕ́К, рассекла́, рассекло́, рассекли́ (arch. forms: рассе́кла, рассе́кло, рассе́кли) (past), see **рассекý.**
РАССЕКИ́ (imp.), see **рассекý.**
РАССЕКРЕ́ТЬ (imp.), see **рассекречу.**
РАССЕКРЕ́ЧЕННЫЙ; рассекречен, —а, —о, —ы (ppp), see **рассекречу.**
РАССЕКРЕ́ЧУ, рассекретишь. P. **Рассекрети́ть** (acc.). I. **Рассекречивать.** 1. To declassify as secret (as documents, etc.). 2. To remove (s.o.) from the list of those having "secret" clearance.
РАССЕКУ́, рассечёшь, рассекут. P. **Рассе́чь** (acc.). I. **Рассека́ть.** 1. To cut, cleave. 2. To wound severely by cutting. 3. To dissect. 4. (fig.) To cut, cleave (as a ship cuts the waves). 5. (mil.) To cut to pieces, cut up (as the enemy's forces).
РАССЕ́ЛСЯ, рассе́лась (past). P. **Рассе́сться** (intr.). I. **Расса́живаться** (mean. 1 and 2), **расседа́ться** (mean. 3). 1. (1st and 2nd pers. sing. not used) To take seats, settle down. 2. To sprawl. 3. To settle, crack (as a wall). (Also see **расся́дусь.**)
РАССЕ́РЖЕННЫЙ; рассе́ржен, —а, —о, —ы (ppp), see **рассержý.**
РАССЕРЖУ́, рассе́рдишь. P. **Рассерди́ть** (acc.). I. **Серди́ть.** 1. To anger. 2. To irritate, annoy.
РАССЕЧЁННЫЙ; рассечён, —а́, —о́, —ы́ (ppp), see **рассекý.**
РАССЕ́ЧЕННЫЙ; рассе́чен, —а, —о, —ы (arch. forms) (ppp), see **рассекý.**
РАССЕЧЁШЬ, see **рассекý.**
РАССЕ́Ю, рассе́ешь. P. **Рассе́ять** (acc.). I. **Рассе́ивать.** 1. To disperse,

scatter. 2. To disseminate (as information, etc.). 3. (tech.) To diffract (e.g., light rays). 4. (agr.) To sow. 5. (fig.) To sow (dissension, etc.). 6. (fig.) To dispel, dissipate (e.g., gloom, doubt, etc.). 7. To divert, distract.

РАССЕ́ЯННЫЙ; рассе́ян, —а, —о, —ы (ppp), see рассе́ю.

РАССИДИ́СЬ (imp.), see рассижу́сь.

РАССИДИ́ШЬСЯ, see рассижу́сь.

РАССИДЯ́ТСЯ, see рассижу́сь.

РАССИЖУ́СЬ, рассиди́шься. Р. Рассиде́ться (intr.). I. Расси́живаться. To make o.s. comfortable, settle down (as in an armchair).

РАССКА́ЖЕШЬ, see расскажу́.

РАССКАЖИ́ (imp.), see расскажу́.

РАССКАЖУ́, расска́жешь. Р. Рассказа́ть (acc.). I. Расска́зывать. To tell, narrate, relate.

РАССКА́ЗАННЫЙ; расска́зан, —а, —о, —ы (ppp), see расскажу́.

РАССКА́ЧЕШЬСЯ, see расскачу́сь.

РАССКАЧИ́СЬ (imp.), see расскачу́сь.

РАССКАЧУ́СЬ, расска́чешься. Р. Расскака́ться (intr.). 1. To gallop at full speed. 2. To gallop in different directions.

РАССЛА́Б, рассла́бла (past). Р. Рассла́бнуть (intr.). To grow very weak, tired.

РАССЛА́БЛЕННЫЙ; рассла́блен, —а, —о, —ы (ppp), see рассла́блю.

РАССЛА́БЛЮ, рассла́бишь. Р. Рассла́бить (acc.). I. Расслабля́ть. To weaken.

РАССЛА́БЬ (imp.), see рассла́блю.

РАССЛА́ВЛЕННЫЙ; рассла́влен, —а, —о, —ы (ppp), see рассла́влю.

РАССЛА́ВЛЮ, рассла́вишь. Р. Рассла́вить (acc.). I. Расславля́ть. 1. To praise excessively. 2. To spread (e.g., rumors).

РАССЛА́ВЬ (imp.), see рассла́влю.

РАССЛЫ́ШАННЫЙ; расслы́шан, —а, —о, —ы (ppp), see расслы́шу.

РАССЛЫ́ШИШЬ, see расслы́шу.

РАССЛЫ́ШУ, расслы́шишь. Р. Расслы́шать (acc.). To make out, catch (what s.o. is saying).

РАССЛЫ́ШЬ (imp.), see расслы́шу.

РАССМЕЁШЬСЯ, see рассмею́сь.

РАССМЕ́ЙСЯ (imp.), see рассмею́сь.

РАССМЕЮ́СЬ, рассмеёшься. Р. Рас-

смея́ться (intr.). To burst out laughing.

РАССМО́ТРЕННЫЙ; рассмо́треп, —а, —о, —ы (ppp), see рассмотрю́.

РАССМОТРИ́ (imp.), see рассмотрю́.

РАССМО́ТРИШЬ, see рассмотрю́.

РАССМОТРЮ́, рассмо́тришь. Р. Рассмотре́ть (acc.). I. Рассма́тривать. 1. To examine, scrutinize. 2. To consider (e.g., a question). 3. To make out, discern, recognize.

РАССМО́ТРЯТ, see рассмотрю́.

РАССО́САННЫЙ; рассо́сан, —а, —о, —ы (ppp), see рассосу́.

РАССОСЁШЬ, see рассосу́.

РАССОСИ́ (imp.), see рассосу́.

РАССОСУ́, рассосёшь. Р. Рассоса́ть (acc.). I. Расса́сывать. 1. (med.) To resolve, cause to subside (e.g., a swelling). 2. To dissolve.

РАССО́ХСЯ, рассо́хлась (past). Р. Рассо́хнуться (intr.). I. Рассыха́ться. To crack (due to heat, or dryness).

РАССПРО́ШЕННЫЙ; расспро́шен, —а, —о, —ы (ppp), see расспрошу́.

РАССПРОШУ́, расспро́сишь. Р. Расспроси́ть (acc.). I. Расспра́шивать. 1. To question, interrogate (e.g., as a student with the objective of clearing up s.t.). 2. To question (s.o. about s.t.) (o + prep.).

РАССТАВА́ЙСЯ (imp.), see расстаю́сь.

РАССТАВА́ЯСЬ (adv. pres. part.), see расстаю́сь.

РАССТА́ВЛЕННЫЙ; расста́влен, —а, —о, —ы (ppp), see расста́влю.

РАССТА́ВЛЮ, расста́вишь. Р. Расста́вить (acc.). I. Расставля́ть. 1. To arrange, place, post. 2. To move apart, spread. 3. To let out (as a skirt).

РАССТА́ВЬ (imp.), see расста́влю.

РАССТАЁШЬСЯ, see расстаю́сь.

РАССТА́НЕШЬСЯ, see расста́нусь.

РАССТА́НУСЬ, расста́нешься. Р. Расста́ться (intr.) (с + inst.). I. Расстава́ться. 1. To part from (as friends). 2. To part with, let go (as possessions). 3. To renounce, repudiate.

РАССТА́НЬСЯ (imp.), see расста́нусь.

РАССТАЮ́СЬ, расстаёшься. I. Расстава́ться (intr.) (с + inst.). Р. Расста́ться. 1. To part from (as friends). 2. To part with, let go, (as possessions). 3. To renounce, repudiate.

РАССТЕ́ЛЕННЫЙ; расстле́н, —а, —о, —ы (ppp), see расстелю́.

РАССТЕ́ЛЕШЬ, see расстелю́.

РАССТЕЛИ́ (imp.), see расстелю́.

РАССТЕЛЮ́, расстéлешь. Р. Разостла́ть (acc.), расстели́ть. I. Расстила́ть. 1. To spread (as a carpet, tablecloth, etc.). 2. To spread, strew (as a layer of sand). 3. (fig.) To spread (as the sun spreads its rays).

РАССТРИ́Г, расстри́гла (past), see расстригу́.

РАССТРИГИ́ (imp.), see расстригу́.

РАССТРИГУ́, расстрижёшь, расстригу́т. Р. Расстри́чь (acc.). I. Расстрига́ть. To defrock (as a priest).

РАССТРИ́ЖЕННЫЙ; расстри́жен, —а, —о, —ы (ppp), see расстригу́.

РАССТРИЖЁШЬ, see расстригу́.

РАССТУПЛЮ́СЬ, расступишься. Р. Расступи́ться (intr.). I. Расступа́ться. 1. To step aside, part (of a crowd of people). 2. (fig.) To open wide (e.g., the earth opened wide, the waves parted). 3. (arch.) To be generous (as with money).

РАССУ́ЖЕННЫЙ; рассу́жен, —а, —о, —ы (ppp), see рассужу́.

РАССУЖУ́, рассу́дишь. Р. Рассуди́ть. I. Рассу́живать (mean. 1). 1. To judge (e.g., people, disputes, etc.) (acc.). 2. To decide, come to a conclusion (intr.).

РАССЫ́ПАННЫЙ; рассы́пан, а, —о, —ы (ppp), see рассы́плю.

РАССЫ́ПЛЕШЬ, see рассы́плю.

РАССЫ́ПЛЮ, рассы́плешь. Р. Рассы́пать (acc.). I. Рассыпа́ть. 1. To scatter, spill, strew (as grain, salt, etc.). 2. To pour (as salt, grain, etc., into bags). 3. (mil.) to disperse, distribute (as men on a firing line).

РА́ССЫПЬ (imp.), see рассы́плю.

РАССЯ́ДЕШЬСЯ, see расся́дусь.

РАССЯ́ДУСЬ, расся́дешься. Р. Рассе́сться (intr.). I. Расса́живаться (mean. 1 and 2), рассед́аться (mean. 3). 1. (3rd pers.) To take seats, settle down. 2. To sprawl. 3. To settle and crack (as a wall).

РАССЯ́ДЬСЯ (imp.), see расся́дусь.

РАСТА́ЕШЬ, see раста́ю.

РАСТА́Й, see раста́ю.

РАСТА́Ю, раста́ешь. Р. Раста́ять. I. Раста́ивать, та́ять (mean. 1, 2, 4, 5). 1. To melt, thaw (of snow, ice, etc.) (intr.). 2. To melt (of wax) (intr.). 3. It thawed, etc. (impers.) (intr.). 4. (fig.) To fade, dwindle, melt away (of one's strength, fog, a crowd, money, etc.) (intr.). 5. (fig.) To be thrilled, melt with emotion (from s.t.) (intr.) (от + gen.) 6. To melt (acc.).

РАСТЁКСЯ, растекла́сь (past), see растечёться.

РАСТЕКУ́ТСЯ (3rd pers. pl.), see растечёться

РАСТЁР, растёрла (past). Р. Растере́ть (acc.). I. Растира́ть. 1. To grind. 2. To rub, spread (s.t. on the surface of s.t.) (на + prep.). 3. To massage, rub (as one's arms). (Also see разотру́.)

РАСТЕРЕБЛЁННЫЙ; растереблён, —а́, —б, —ы́ (ppp), see растереблю́,

РАСТЕРЕБЛЮ́, растереби́шь. Р. Растереби́ть (acc.). 1. To rumple, dishevel. 2. To scratch raw (e.g., a spot on one's skin).

РАСТЕРЁВ and растёрши (adv. past, part.), see растёр and разотру́.

РАСТЁРТЫЙ, растёрт, —а, —о, —ы (ppp), see растёр and разотру́.

РАСТЁРШИ and растере́б (adv. past part.), see растёр and разотру́.

РАСТЕЧЁТЬСЯ, растеку́тся (3rd pers. only). Р. Расте́чься (intr.). I. Растека́ться. 1. To flow, spread, run (of liquids, etc.). 2. (fig.) to flow, spread (of crowds of people). 3. (fig.) to spread (as a smile spreads over one's face) (по + dat. of face).

РАСТЁШЬ, see расту́.

РАСТИ́¹ (imp.) and (inf.), see расту́.

РАСТИ́² (imp.). I. Расти́ть (acc.). 1. To rear, bring up (children). 2. To breed (animals). 3. To cultivate, grow (as crops, a beard, etc.). 4. To train (e.g., personnel). (Also see ращу́.)

РАСТОЛКИ́ (imp.), see растолку́.

РАСТОЛКЛА́ (past), see растоло́к.

РАСТОЛКУ́, растолчёшь, растолку́т. Р. Растоло́чь (acc.). I. Толо́чь. 1. To pound, crush, pulverize. 2. To grind.

РАСТОЛО́К, растолкла́ (past), see растолку́.

РАСТОЛЧЁННЫЙ; растолочён, —а́, —б, —ы́ (ppp), see растолку́.

РАСТОЛЧЁШЬ, see растолку́.

РАСТО́ПЛЕННЫЙ; расто́плен, —а, —о, —ы (ppp), see растоплю́.

РАСТОПЛЮ́, расто́пишь. Р. Растопи́ть (acc.). I. Раста́пливать. 1. To light (as a stove). 2. To melt.

РАСТО́ПТАННЫЙ; расто́птан, —а, —о, —ы (ppp), see растопчу́.

РАСТО́ПЧЕШЬ, see растопчу́.

РАСТОПЧИ́ (imp.), see растопчу́.

РАСТОПЧУ́, расто́пчешь. Р. Растопта́ть (acc.). I. Раста́птывать. 1. To trample, crush. 2. To wear out (as one's shoes).

РАСТО́РГ (and расто́ргнул), расто́ргла (past), Р. Расто́ргнуть (acc.). I. Расторга́ть. To annul, cancel, abrogate.

РАСТО́РГНУТЫЙ; расто́ргнут, —а, —о, —ы (ppp), see расто́рг.

РАСТО́РЖЕННЫЙ; расто́ржен, —а, —о, —ы (ppp), see расто́рг.

РАСТРА́ВЛЕННЫЙ; растра́влен, —а —о, —ы (ppp), see растравлю́.

РАСТРАВЛЮ́, растра́вишь. Р. Растрави́ть (acc.). I. Растравля́ть, растра́вливать.1.To irritate, exasperate, provoke. 2. To aggravate (as a wound, grief, etc.). 3. To etch. 4. To corrode, destroy by chemical action.

РАСТРА́ТЬ (imp.), see растра́чу.

РАСТРА́ЧЕННЫЙ; растра́чен, —а, —о, —ы (ppp), see растра́чу.

РАСТРА́ЧУ, растра́тишь. Р. Растра́тить (acc.). I. Растра́чивать. 1. (lit. and fig.) To squander, spend. 2. To embezzle.

РАСТРЁПАННЫЙ; растрёпан, —а, —о, —ы (ppp), see растреплю́.

РАСТРЕ́ПЛЕШЬ, see растреплю́.

РАСТРЕПЛИ́ (imp.), see растреплю́.

РАСТРЕПЛЮ́, растре́плешь. Р. Растрепа́ть (acc.). I. Растрёпывать. 1. To disarrange, rumple, dishevel. 2. To damage by mistreatment, fray, tatter (e.g., clothes, books, etc.). 3. To comb or card (e.g., wool, etc.).

РАСТРУБЛЮ́, раструби́шь. Р. Раструби́ть. To proclaim, trumpet (acc.) or (o + prep.).

РАСТРУ́ШЕННЫЙ; растру́шен, —а, —о, —ы (ppp), see раструшу́.

РАСТРУШУ́, раструси́шь. Р. Рас-

труси́ть (acc.). I. Растру́шивать. To spill, scatter, strew (e.g., grain).

РАСТРЯ́С, растрясла́ (past), see растрясу́.

РАСТРЯСЁННЫЙ; растрясён, —а́, —б, —ы́ (ppp), see растрясу́.

РАСТРЯСЁШЬ, see растрясу́.

РАСТРЯСИ́ (imp.), see растрясу́.

РАСТРЯСУ́, растрясёшь. Р. Растрясти́ (acc.). I. Растряса́ть, растря́сывать. 1. To strew, spread evenly. 2. To shake, jolt about (impers. + acc.). 3. To awaken by shaking. 4. To squander (as money).

РАСТУ́, растёшь. I. Расти́ (intr.). Р. Вы́расти (mean. 1 thru 4). 1. To grow (in size). 2. To grow up (of a child). 3. (fig.) To increase, grow. 4. To mature, improve, develop (as an artist). 5. To grow, exist (as bananas grow in the tropics).

РАСХА́ЕШЬ, see расха́ю.

РАСХА́Й (imp.), see расха́ю.

РАСХА́Ю, расха́ешь. Р. Расха́ять (acc.). I. Расха́ивать. 1. To denounce, discredit, 2. To criticize severely.

РАСХА́ЯННЫЙ; расха́ян, —а, —о, —ы (ppp), see расха́ю.

РАСХИ́ТЬ (imp.), see расхи́щу.

РАСХИ́ЩЕННЫЙ; расхи́щен, —а, —о, —ы (ppp), see расхи́щу.

РАСХИ́ЩУ, расхи́тишь. Р. Расхи́тить (acc.). I. Расхища́ть. To embezzle, misappropriate, plunder.

РАСХЛЁСТАННЫЙ; расхлёстан, —а, —о, —ы (ppp), see расхлещу́.

РАСХЛЁЩЕШЬ, see расхлещу́.

РАСХЛЕЩИ́ (imp.) see расхлещу́.

РАСХЛЕЩУ́, расхле́щешь. Р. Расхлеста́ть (acc.). I. Расхлёстывать. To wear out by lashing (as a whip, a switch).

РАСХЛОПО́ЧЕШЬСЯ, see расхлопочу́сь.

РАСХЛОПОЧИ́СЬ (imp.), see расхлопочу́сь.

РАСХЛОПОЧУ́СЬ, расхлопо́чешься. Р. Расхлопота́ться (intr.) To begin to busy oneself assiduously, begin to bustle about.

РАСХОЖУ́СЬ[1], расхо́дишься. I. Расходи́ться (intr.). Р. Разойти́сь. 1. To disperse, separate. 2. To be sold out. 3. To be out of print. 4. To be spent (as money). 5. To melt; dissolve. 6. To vanish, disappear. 7. To spread (as news). 8. To discontinue a relationship (part from, get a divorce from, etc.) (с + instr.). 9. (lit. and fig.) To separate (of roads, ways, etc.). 10. To differ from (s.o. in s.t.) (с + inst. + в + prep.). 11. To pick up speed. 12. To increase in intensity (e.g., rain). 13. To surpass, outdo oneself. 14. To pass without meeting (said of two or more people).

РАСХОЖУ́СЬ², расхо́дишься. Р. Расходи́ться (intr.). 1. To begin to walk up and down. 2. To loosen up (as one's stiffened muscles) by walking. 3. To lose self control, let o.s. go.

РАСХОЛОЖЁННЫЙ; Расхоложён, —а́, —о́, —ы́ (ppp), see расхоложу́.

РАСХОЛОЖУ́, расхолоди́шь. Р. Расхолоди́ть (acc.). I. Расхола́живать. (fig.) To cool, cause (s.o.) to lose interest (as poor players cause people to lose interest in a team).

РАСХОТИ́ (imp.), see расхочу́.

РАСХОТИ́М, расхоти́те, расхотя́т (pl. forms), see расхочу́.

РАСХОТЯ́Т, see расхочу́ and расхоти́м.

РАСХО́ЧЕШЬ, see расхочу́.

РАСХОЧУ́, расхо́чешь, расхо́чет (sing. forms). Р. Расхоте́ть (acc./gen.) or (+ inf.) To cease to want or desire (s.t., or to do s.t.).

РАСЦВЁЛ, расцвела́ (past), see расцвету́.

РАСЦВЕТЁШЬ, see расцвету́.

РАСЦВЕТИ́ (imp.), see расцвету́.

РАСЦВЕТУ́, расцветёшь. Р. Расцвести́ (intr.). I. Расцвета́ть. 1. To bloom, blossom. 2. (fig.) To prosper, flourish. 3. (fig.) To blossom (as one's face with a smile) (inst.).

РАСЦВЕ́ТШИЙ (pap), see расцвету́.

РАСЦВЕ́ЧЕННЫЙ; расцве́чен, —а, —о, —ы (ppp), see расцвечу́.

РАСЦВЕЧУ́, расцвети́шь. Р. Расцвети́ть (acc.). I. Расцве́чивать. 1. To paint or decorate with gay colors. 2. To decorate (e.g., with flags) (acc. + inst.).

РАСЦЕ́ПЛЕННЫЙ; расце́плен, —а, —о, —ы (ppp), see расцеплю́.

РАСЦЕПЛЮ́, расце́пишь. Р. Расцепи́ть (acc.). I. Расцепля́ть. 1. To unhook, uncouple, unlink (e.g., R. R. car). 2. To trip (e.g., an electrical

relay). 3. To release, disengage (e.g. a clutch).

РАСЧЁЛ, разочла́, разочло́, разочли́ (past). Р. Расче́сть (acc.). I. Рассчи́тывать. 1. To calculate, compute. 2. To figure out. 3. (tech.) To design. 4. To dismiss, pay off (s.o.). (Also see разочту́.) (For other idiomatic usages see unabridged dictionary.)

РАСЧЕ́РЧЕННЫЙ; расче́рчен, —а, —о, —ы (ppp), see расчерчу́.

РАСЧЕРЧУ́, расче́ртишь. Р. Расчерти́ть (acc.). I. Расче́рчивать. To rule or line (e.g., a sheet of paper).

РАСЧЁСАННЫЙ; расчёсан, —а, —о, —ы (ppp), see расчешу́.

РАСЧЁТШИЙ (pap), see расчёл and разочту́.

РАСЧЁШЕШЬ, see расчешу́.

РАСЧЕШИ́ (imp.), see расчешу́.

РАСЧЕШУ́, расчёшешь. Р. Расчеса́ть (acc.). I. Расчёсывать. 1. To comb (e.g., hair). 2. To card, comb (wool, etc.). 3. To scratch raw (e.g., a mosquito bite). 4. To smash, defeat, thrash.

РАСЧИ́СТИ (imp.), see расчи́щу.

РАСЧИ́СТЬ (imp.), see расчи́щу.

РАСЧИ́ЩЕННЫЙ; расчи́щен, —а, —о, —ы (ppp), see расчи́щу.

РАСЧИ́ЩУ, расчи́стишь. Р. Расчи́стить (acc.). I. Расчища́ть. To clear (as a road, a field, etc.).

РАСШЕ́Й (imp.). Р. Расши́ть (acc.). I. Расшива́ть. 1. To rip (as a seam), remove stitching. 2. To embroider. 3. (tech.) To point (smooth) (the mortared joints of brickwork, etc.). (Also see разошью́.)

РАСШИ́Б, расши́бла (past), see расшибу́.

РАСШИБЁШЬ, see расшибу́.

РАСШИБИ́ (imp.), see расшибу́.

РАСШИ́БЛЕННЫЙ; расши́блен, —а, —о, —ы (ppp), see расшибу́.

РАСШИБУ́, расшибёшь. Р. Расшиби́ть (acc.). I. Расшиба́ть. 1. To injure. 2. To smash or break to pieces.

РАСШИ́ТЫЙ; расши́т, —а, —о, —ы (ppp), see расше́й and разошью́.

РАСШУМИ́СЬ (imp.), see расшумлю́сь.

РАСШУМИ́ШЬСЯ, see расшумлю́сь.

РАСШУМЛЮ́СЬ, расшуми́шься. Р. Расшуме́ться (intr.). 1. To begin to make a lot of noise. 2. To begin to argue or quarrel loudly.

РАСШУМЯ́ТСЯ, see **расшумлю́сь.**

РАСЩЕМЛЁННЫЙ; расщемлён, —а́, —о́, —ы́ (ppp), see **расщемлю́.**

РАСЩЕМЛЮ́, расщеми́шь. P. Расщеми́ть (acc.). I. **Расщемля́ть.** To part, open (e.g., pincers, tongs; to open a clenched fist, etc.).

РАСЩЕПЛЁННЫЙ; расщеплён, —а́, —о́, —ы́ (ppp), see **расщеплю́.**

РАСЩЕПЛЮ́, расщепи́шь. P. Расщепи́ть (acc.). I. **Расщепля́ть.** 1. To split. 2. To splinter, break to pieces. 3. (phys.) To split, break down (e.g., atom, etc.). 4. (chem.) To break down, decompose.

РАСЩИ́ПАННЫЙ; расщи́пан, —а, —о, —ы (ppp), see **расщиплю́.**

РАСЩИ́ПЛЕШЬ, see **расщиплю́.**

РАСЩИ́ПЛЙ (imp.), see **расщиплю́.**

РАСЩИПЛЮ́, расщи́плешь. P. Расщипать (acc.). I. **Расщи́пывать.** To shred (as fibre).

РАЩЁННЫЙ; ращён, —а́, —о́, —ы́ (ppp), see **ращу́.**

РАЩУ́, расти́шь. I. **Расти́ть** (acc.). 1. To rear, bring up (children). 2. To breed (animals). 3. To cultivate, grow (as crops, a beard, etc.). 4. To train (e.g., personnel).

РВЁШЬ, see **рву.**

РВИ (imp.), see **рву.**

РВУ, рвёшь. I. **Рвать** (acc.). P. **Вы́рвать** (mean. 1 and 8). 1. To extract, pull out. 2. To snatch (s.t. from s.o., etc.). 3. To tear to pieces. 4. To pluck, pick (as flowers). 5. To break, blow up (with, explosives). 6. (fig.) To break, sever. 7. To pain intensely (e.g., one's head) (impers. + acc.). 8. To vomit (impers. + acc.).

РЕВЁШЬ, see **реву́.**

РЕВИ́ (imp.), see **реву́.**

РЕВУ́, ревёшь. I. **Реве́ть** (intr.). (lit. and fig.) To roar, bellow, howl (of animals, children, wind, etc.).

РЕГО́ЧЕШЬ, see **регочу́.**

РЕГОЧИ́ (imp.), see **регочу́.**

РЕГОЧУ́, рего́чешь. I. **Регота́ть** (intr.). To laugh loudly, boisterously.

РЕ́ЕШЬ, see **ре́ю.**

РЕ́ЖЕШЬ, see **ре́жу.**

РЕ́ЖУ, ре́жешь. I. **Ре́зать.** P. **Заре́зать** (mean. 5 and 6), **разре́зать**

(mean. 1, 2, 3), **сре́зать** (mean. 2, 10, 11). 1. To cut, cut to pieces (acc.). 2. To cut off (acc.). 3. (med.) to lance. 4. To cut (intr.). 5. To slaughter, kill (acc.). 6. To ruin, spoil (s.o. or s.t.) (acc.). 7. To engrave, carve (acc.). 8. (fig.) To cut (as wind cuts one's face, a ring cuts one's finger) (acc.). 9. (fig.) To irritate, grate, etc. (acc.). 10. (fig.) To cut (as a ball, in tennis) (acc.). 11. (fig.) To fail (s.o., as in an examination) (acc. + на + prep.). (For other uses see unabridged dictionary.)

РЕЖЬ (imp.), see **ре́жу.**

РЕ́ЗАННЫЙ, ре́зан, —а, —о, —ы (ppp), see **ре́жу.**

РЕЗВЛЮ́СЬ, резви́шься. I. **Резви́ться** (intr.). To frolic, gambol, romp.

РЕЙ (imp.), see **ре́ешь.**

РЕМИ́ЖУ, реми́зишь. I. **Реми́зить** (acc.). P. **Обреми́зить.** To set (as in a bridge game).

РЕМИ́ЗЬ (imp.), see **реми́жу.**

РЕ́Ю, ре́ешь. I. **Ре́ять** (intr.). 1. To soar, sail. 2. To hover, float.

РЖЁШЬ, see **ржу.**

РЖИ (imp.), see **ржу.**

РЖУ, ржёшь. I. **Ржать** (intr.). 1. To neigh (of horses). 2. (fig.) To neigh, emit a coarse laugh (of people).

РОДИ́ (imp.), see **рожу́.**

РО́ЕШЬ, see **ро́ю.**

РОЖДЁННЫЙ; рождён, —а́, —о́, —ы́ (ppp), see **рожу́.**

РОЖУ́, роди́шь. P. and I. Роди́ть. 1. To give birth to, bear (acc.). 2. To beget (acc.). 3. (fig.) To give rise to, produce, cause (acc.). 4. To bear, produce (of the soil, trees, etc.) (acc.) or (intr.).

РО́ЗДАЛ, раздала́, ро́здало, ро́здали (also **разда́л, раздала́, разда́ло, разда́ли**) (past), see **ро́зданный** and **раздам.**

РО́ЗДАННЫЙ; ро́здан, раздана́, ро́здано, ро́зданы. P. Разда́ть (acc.). I. **Раздава́ть.** 1. To distribute (e.g., supplies). 2. To stretch (e.g., shoes), widen, expand. (Also see **раздам.**)

РО́ЗНЯЛ, разняла́, ро́зняло, ро́зняли (also **разня́л, разняла́, разня́ло, разня́ли**) (past). P. **Разня́ть** (acc.). I. **Разнима́ть.** 1. To separate, part. 2. To tear apart. 3. To take apart, dismantle. 4. To dismember. (Also see разниму́.)

РО́ЗНЯТ, разнята́, ро́знято, ро́зняты (ppp short forms), see ро́знял, разня́тый, and разниму́.

РОЙ (imp.), see ро́ю.

РОКО́ЧЕШЬ, see рокочу́.

РОКОЧЙ (imp.), see рокочу́.

РОКОЧУ́, роко́чешь. I. Рокота́ть (intr.). 1. To emit, cause a muffled roar, rumble (of waves, thunder, voice, etc.). 2. To murmur.

РО́ПЩЕШЬ, see ропщу́.

РОПЩЙ (imp.), see ропщу́.

РОПЩУ́, ро́пщешь. I. Ропта́ть. 1. To grumble (about or at s.t. or s.o.) (на + acc.). 2. (arch.) To murmur (of a forest, etc.) (intr.).

РОС, росла́ (past). I. Расти́ (intr.). P. Вы́расти (mean. 1 thru 4). 1. To grow (in size). 2. To grow up (of a child). 3. (fig.) To grow, increase. 4. To mature, improve, develop, (as an artist). 5. To grow, exist (as bananas grow in the tropics). (Also see расту́.)

РО́СПИЛ, распила́, ро́спило, ро́спили (also распи́л, распила́, распи́ло, распи́ли) (past). P. Распи́ть (acc.). I. Распива́ть. To drink (s.t. with s.o.) (e.g., split a bottle) (also see разопью́).

РО́СПИТ, распита́, ро́спито, ро́спиты (ppp short forms of распи́тый), see ро́спил and разопью́.

РО́Ю, ро́ешь. I. Рыть (acc.). P. Вы́рыть (mean. 1, 2, 3), отры́ть (mean. 2 and 3). 1. To dig. 2. To dig out, up. 3. To excavate.

РУ́БЛЕННЫЙ; ру́блен, —а, —о, —ы (ppp), see рублю́.

РУБЛЮ́, ру́бишь. I. Руби́ть (acc.), сруби́ть (mean. 1, 4). P. Рубну́ть and рубану́ть (mean. 1, 2, 3, 5). 1. To cut down, fell. 2. To chop (e.g., firewood, a hole, etc.). 3. To chop, mince (as food). 4. To construct (as

a wooden barn). 5. To slash (as with a sword). 6. To speak (as the truth) (acc.), (bluntly) (intr.).

РУКОВОЖУ́, руководи́шь. I. Руководи́ть (inst.) and (arch.) (acc.). 1. To guide, lead. 2. To direct, manage.

РУКОПЛЕ́ЩЕШЬ, see рукоплещу́.

РУКОПЛЕЩЙ (imp.), see рукоплещу́.

РУКОПЛЕЩУ́, рукопле́щешь. I. Рукоплеска́ть (dat.). To applaud, clap.

РЫСКАЙ (imp.), see ры́щу.

РЫ́ТЫЙ; рыт, —а, —о, —ы (ppp), see ро́ю.

РЫЧА́Т, see рычу́.

РЫЧИ́ (imp.), see рычу́.

РЫЧИ́ШЬ, see рычу́.

РЫЧУ́, рычи́шь. I. Рыча́ть (intr.). To growl, snarl (of an animal or person).

РЫ́ЩЕШЬ, see ры́щу.

РЫ́ЩУ, ры́щешь (also ры́скаю, ры́скаешь). I. Ры́скать (intr.). 1. To rove, to scour (as wolves rove or scour the woods for prey). 2. (naut.) To yaw.

РЯ́ЖЕННЫЙ; ря́жен, —а, —о, —ы (ppp), see ряжу́[1] and [2].

РЯЖУ́[1], ря́дишь (arch.: ряди́шь). I. Ряди́ть (acc.). 1. To dress up (s.o.). 2. To disguise (s.o.) (as for a masquerade).

РЯЖУ́[2], ряди́шь (also ря́дишь). I. Ряди́ть (arch.) (acc.). P. Поряди́ть (mean. 1). 1. To hire (s.o.), having bargained (with him). 2. To control, govern, rule.

РЯЖУ́СЬ[1], ряди́шься (arch. ря́дишься). I. Ряди́ться (intr.). 1. To dress o.s. up (in s.t.) (в + acc.). 2. To disguise o.s. (as for a masquerade).

РЯЖУ́СЬ[2], ряди́шься (also ря́дишься). I. Ряди́ться (arch.). P. Поряди́ться. 1. To bargain (with s.o.) (с + inst.). 2. To accept a job (as), assume responsibility (of) (в + acc. pl.).

С

СА́ЖЕННЫЙ; са́жен, —а, —о, —ы (ppp), see **сажу́.**

САЖУ́, са́дишь. I. **Сади́ть** (acc.). P. **Посади́ть** (mean. 1 thru 6). 1. To plant (as flowers). 2. To seat (as guests). 3. To set down (as a plane on an airfield). 4. To put (as s.o. in prison). 5. To place (as bread in an oven). 6. To sew on (as a patch). 7. To strike with force (acc.) or (intr.). (For other usages see unabridged dictionary.)

САЖУ́СЬ, сади́шься. I. **Сади́ться** (intr.). P. **Сесть.** 1. To sit down (on: **на** + acc.) (at a table: **за** + acc.) (by: **у** + gen.) (in: **в** + acc.). 2. To sit down (to do s.t.) (+ inf.) or (**на/за** + acc.). 3. To board, take (e.g., a train) (**на** + acc.). 4. To get in a train, auto, etc. (**в** + acc.). 5. To alight (of a bird) (on: **на** + acc.). (in: **в** + acc.). 6. To land (of a plane). 7. To settle (on) (of dust or fog) (**на** + acc.). 8. To set (of the sun). 9. To spend time (in prison). 10. To shrink (of cloth). 11. To settle (of a building) etc.

СБА́ВЛЕННЫЙ; сба́влен, —а, —о, —ы (ppp), see **сба́влю.**

СБА́ВЛЮ, сба́вишь. P. **Сба́вить** (acc./gen.). I. **Сбавля́ть.** 1. To reduce, lower (e.g., a price, speed, one's voice, etc.). 2. To take away, deduct, subtract (from) (acc./gen. + **с** + gen.).

СБА́ВЬ (imp.), see **сба́влю.**

СБЕГИ́ (imp.), see **сбегу́.**

СБЕГУ́, сбежи́шь, сбегу́т. P. **Сбежа́ть** (intr.). I. **Сбега́ть.** 1. To run down (from) (**с** + gen.). 2. To run down (e.g., a slope) (**по** + dat.). 3. To run away (from) (**от** + gen.). 4. To fleet, flee, vanish (**с/из** + gen.).

СБЕЖИ́ШЬ, see **сбегу́.**

СБЕЙ (imp.). P. **Сбить** (acc.). I. **Сбива́ть.** 1. To knock down, off. 2. To divert (from direction of movement, course of action, etc.) (acc. +

с + gen.). 3. (fig.) To turn (as a conversation, thoughts, to s.t.) (acc. + **на** + acc.). 4. To put, knock together (as a box, building, etc.). 5. To whip, churn (e.g., cream, butter, mud in a road, etc.). 6. To lower (as a price, temperature, etc.). 7. To wear down (as the heel of a shoe). 8. To confuse (s.o.) (acc. + **с** + то́лку). (Also see **собью́.**) (For other usages see unabridged dictionary.)

СБЕРЁГ, сберегла́ (past), see **сберегу́.**

СБЕРЕГИ́ (imp.), see **сберегу́.**

СБЕРЕГУ́, сбережёшь, сберегу́т. P. **Сбере́чь** (acc.). I. **Сберега́ть, бере́чь** (mean. 1 and 2). 1. To preserve, protect (against) (acc. + **от** + gen.). 2. To take care of. 3. To save, lay up, put aside. 4. To save, (as time).

СБЕРЕЖЁННЫЙ; сбережён, —а́ —о́, —ы́ (ppp), see **сберегу́.**

СБЕРЕЖЁШЬ, see **сберегу́.**

СБИ́ТЫЙ; сби́т, —а, —о, —ы (ppp), see **сбей** and **собью́.**

СБЛИ́ЖЕННЫЙ; сбли́жен, —а, —о, —ы (ppp), see **сбли́жу.**

СБЛИ́ЖУ, сбли́зишь. P. **Сбли́зить** (acc.). I. **Сближа́ть.** 1. To bring together, draw together. 2. To bind (as friendship binds people). 3. To compare, connect (s.t. or s.o. with s.t. or s.o.) with respect to similarities (acc. + **с** + inst.).

СБЛИЗЬ (imp.), see **сбли́жу.**

СБРЕДЁТСЯ, сбреду́тся (1st and 2nd pers. sing. not used). P. **Сбрести́сь** (intr.). I. **Сбреда́ться.** To wander in, assemble or collect in one place (of a number of people).

СБРЕДИ́СЬ (imp.), see **сбредётся.**

СБРЕДУ́ТСЯ (3rd pers. pl.), see **сбредётся.**

СБРЕ́ДШИЙСЯ (pap), see **сбредётся.**

СБРЕ́ЕШЬ, see **сбре́ю.**

СБРЕЙ (imp.), see **сбре́ю.**

СБРЁЛСЯ, сбрела́сь (past), see **сбредётся.**

СБРЁХНУТЫЙ; сбрёхнут, —а, —о, —ы (ppp). Р. Сбрехну́ть (acc.) or (intr.). 1. To lie without design. 2. To talk nonsense.

СБРЕ́ШЕШЬ, see сбрешу́.

СБРЕШИ́ (imp.), see сбрешу́.

СБРЕШУ́, сбре́шешь. Р. Сбреха́ть (acc.) or (intr.). 1. To lie without design. 2. To talk nonsense.

СБРЕ́Ю, сбре́ешь. Р. Сбри́ть (acc.). I. Сбрива́ть. To shave off (e.g., a moustache).

СБРИ́ТЫЙ; сбри́т, —а, —о, —ы (ppp), see сбре́ю.

СБРОСЬ (imp.), see сбро́шу.

СБРО́ШЕННЫЙ; сбро́шен, —а, —о, —ы (ppp), see сбро́шу.

СБРО́ШУ, сбро́сишь. Р. Сбро́сить (acc.). I. Сбра́сывать. 1. To throw down. 2. To throw off (e.g., one's coat). 3. To pile up (many things in one place). 4. To dump (as goods, or stock on the market, water into a lake, etc.). 5. To discard (unwanted items, or cards in a game). 6. To reduce, throw off (weight).

СБУ́ДЕШЬ, see сбу́ду.

СБУ́ДУ, сбу́дешь. Р. Сбыть. I. Сбыва́ть. 1. To sell (s.t.), get rid of (acc.). 2. To get rid of (as an unwanted person) (acc.). 3. To subside (e.g., temperature, water level (intr.)).

СБУДЬ (imp.), see сбу́ду.

СБЫ́ТЫЙ; сбы́т, —а, —о, —ы (ppp), see сбу́ду.

СВЕДЁННЫЙ; сведён, —а́, —о́, —ы́ (ppp), see сведу́.

СВЕДЁШЬ, see сведу́.

СВЕДИ́ (imp.), see сведу́.

СВЕДУ́, сведёшь. Р. Свести́ (acc.). I. Своди́ть (mean. 1, 2, 3, 6, 7, 8). 1. To take down, help down. 2. To bring together. 3. To take away, remove. 4. To take somewhere. 5. To take there and back. 6. To reduce (s.t.) to (s.t.) (e.g., to nothing) (acc. + на + acc.); to turn (s.t.) into (s.t.) (e.g., into a farce) (acc. + к + dat.); to lead (s.t.) into (s.t.) (e.g., a conversation into s.t.) (acc. + на + acc.). 7. To cramp, distort (of cold, convulsions, etc.) (sometimes impers.). 8. To settle with (s.o.) (e.g., an account or score) (acc. of account + с + inst. of s.o.). (For other usages see unabridged dictionary.)

СВЕ́ДШИЙ (pap), see сведу́.

СВЕДЯ́ (adv. past part.), see сведу́.

СВЁЗ, свезла́ (past), see свезу́.

СВЕЗЁННЫЙ; свён, —а́, —о́, —ы́ (ppp), see свезу́.

СВЕЗЁШЬ, see свезу́.

СВЕЗИ́ (imp.), see свезу́.

СВЕЗУ́, сьезёшь. Р. Сьезти́ (acc.). I. Свози́ть (mean. 1 thru 3). 1. To bring together by vehicle. 2. To bring down by vehicle. 3. To take away by vehicle. 4. To take somewhere by vehicle. 5. To take there and back by vehicle.

СВЕЗЯ́ (adv. past part.), see свезу́.

СВЕЙ (imp.). Р. Свить (acc.). I. Вить, свива́ть. 1. To twist, spin (as a thread, rope, etc.). 2. To wind, coil. 3. To weave (as a wreath, a nest, etc.). (Also see совью.)

СВЕ́ЙСЯ (imp.). Р. Сви́ться (intr.). I. Свива́ться. 1. To roll up. 2. To coil (of a snake). (Also see совьюсь.)

СВЁЛ, свела́ (past), see сведу́.

СВЕРБИ́ (imp.), see сверби́т.

СВЕРБИ́Т, сербя́т (3rd pers. only). I. Свербе́ть (intr.). To itch.

СВЕРБЯ́Т (3rd pers. pl.), see сверби́т.

СВЕРГ (and све́ргнул), све́ргла (past). Р. Све́ргнуть (acc.). I. Сверга́ть. 1. (arch.) To throw down. 2. To overthrow (as a government).

СВЕ́РГНУТЫЙ; све́ргнут, —а, —о, —ы (ppp), see сверг.

СВЕ́РЖЕННЫЙ; све́ргжен, —а, —о, —ы (ppp), see сверг.

СВЕ́РЖУСЬ, све́рзишься. Р. Све́рзиться (intr.). To fall (as from a building, a horse, etc.).

СВЕ́РЗИСЬ (imp.), see све́ржусь.

СВЕСЬ (imp.), see све́шу.

СВЕЧУ́, све́тишь. I. Свети́ть (intr.). Р. Посвети́ть (mean. 2). 1. (lit. and fig.) To shine, give off light. 2. To light the way, throw light (for s.o.) (dat. of s.o.).

СВЕ́ШЕННЫЙ; све́шен, —а, —о, —ы (ppp), see све́шу.

СВЕ́ШУ, све́сишь. Р. Све́сить (acc.). I. Све́шивать (mean. 1). 1. To let down, lower, hang down. 2. To weigh (s.t.). 3. To weigh out (as a pound of salt).

СВИ́ДИШЬСЯ, see сви́жусь.

СВИ́ДЯТСЯ, see сви́жусь.

СВИЖУСЬ, сви́дишься. Р. Сви́деть-ся (intr.). I. **Ви́деться.** To see each other, meet.

СВИ́НЧЕННЫЙ; сви́нчен, —а, —о, —ы (ppp), see свинчу́.

СВИНЧУ́, сви́нтишь. Р. Свинти́ть (acc.). I. **Сви́нчивать.** 1. To screw together. 2. To unscrew. 3. To spoil (a thread) by screwing and un-screwing.

СВИСТИ́ (imp.), see свищу́[1] and [2].

СВИСТИ́ШЬ, see свищу́[1].

СВИСТЯ́ (adv. pres. part.), see свищу́[1] and [2].

СВИСТЯ́Т, see свищу́[1].

СВИ́ТЫЙ; свит, —а́, —о, —ы (ppp), see свей and совью́.

СВИ́ЩЕШЬ, see свищу́[2].

СВИЩИ́ (imp.) see свищу́[2].

СВИЩУ́[1], свисти́шь. I. **Свисте́ть.** 1. To whistle (of people, birds, bullets, wind, etc.) (intr.). 2. To whistle (e.g., a tune) (acc.). 3. To call by whistling (e.g., a dog) (acc.).

СВИЩУ́[2], сви́щешь. I. **Свиста́ть.** 1. To whistle (of people, birds, bullets, wind, etc.) (intr.). 2. To whistle (e.g., a tune) (acc.). 3. To call by whistling (e.g., a dog) (acc.). 4. To gush (e.g., blood from a wound) (intr.).

СВО́ЖЕННЫЙ; сво́жен, —а, —о, —ы (ppp), see свожу́[2] and [3].

СВОЖУ́[1], сво́дишь. I. Своди́ть (acc.). Р. Свести́. 1. To take down, help down. 2. To bring together. 3. To reduce (s.t.) to (s.t.), bring (s.t.) to (s.t.) (e.g., to nothing) (acc. + на + acc.); to turn (s.t.) into (s.t.) (e.g., a farce) (acc. + к + dat.); to lead (s.t.) into (s.t.) (e.g., a conversation into s.t.) (acc. + на + acc.). 4. To take away, remove. 5. To cramp, distort (of cold, convulsions, etc.) (sometimes impers.). 6. To settle with (s.o.) (e.g., an account or score) (acc. of account + c + inst. of s.o.). (For other usages see unabridged dictionary.)

СВОЖУ́[2], сво́дишь. Р. Своди́ть (acc.). To take there and back (as children to the theater).

СВОЖУ́[3], сво́зишь. Р. Свози́ть (acc.). 1. To take there and back by vehicle (as s.o. to the theater). 2. To bring (many, a number of) together by vehicle.

СВОЖУ́[4], сво́зишь. I. Свози́ть (acc.). Р. Свезти́. 1. To bring together by vehicle. 2. To bring down by vehicle. 3. To take away by vehicle.

СВОЛО́К, сволокла́ (past), see сво-локу́.

СВОЛОКИ́ (imp.), see сволоку́.

СВОЛОКУ́, сволочёшь, сволоку́т. Р. Своло́чь (acc.). I. Свола́кивать. 1. To drag away, drag somewhere. 2. To carry away, carry somewhere. 3. To take off (e.g., one's cap). 4. To drag together (a number of). 5. To steal, pilfer.

СВОЛОЧЁННЫЙ; сволочён, —а́, —о́, —ы́ (ppp), see сволоку́.

СВОЛОЧЁШЬ, see сволоку́.

СВОРО́ЧЕННЫЙ; своро́чен, —а, —о, —ы (ppp), see сворочу́.

СВОРОЧУ́, своро́тишь. Р. Свороти́ть. I. Свора́чивать. 1. To remove, dis-lodge, by turning or rolling (acc.). 2. To turn aside (e.g., a horse, etc.) (acc.). 3. To cause (s.o.) to change, renounce, abandon (e.g., an opinion, intentions, course of action, etc.) (acc. of s.o. + c + gen.). 4. To turn (e.g., a conversation to another subject) (acc. + на + acc.). 5. To turn (e.g., to the right, off a road, etc.) (intr.). 6. To dislocate, distort (a part of s.o.'s body) (acc. + dat.) (что + кому). 7. To throw down (s.t. from someplace) (acc. + c + gen.). 8. To do, make, build (s.t. large, difficult) (acc.).

СВЯ́ЖЕШЬ, see свяжу́.

СВЯЖИ́ (imp.), see свяжу́.

СВЯЖУ́, свя́жешь. Р. Связа́ть. I. Свя́зывать (mean. 1 thru 4), вяза́ть (mean. 1 and 5). 1. To tie, bind together (acc.). 2. (fig.) To bind (as by oath) (acc. + inst.). 3. To involve, entail, be closely associated (with s.o. or s.t.) (past part. + c + inst.). 4. To connect, link. (e.g., cities by telephone, one's fate with s.t., etc.) (acc. + c + inst.). 5. To knit, crochet (acc.).

СВЯ́ЗАННЫЙ; свя́зан, —а, —о, —ы (ppp), see свяжу́.

СВЯЧУ́, святи́шь. I. Святи́ть (acc.). Р. Освяти́ть. To consecrate, sanctify.

СГЛАДЬ (imp.), see сгла́жу[1].

СГЛА́ЖЕННЫЙ; сгла́жен, —а, —о, —ы (ppp), see сгла́жу[1] and [2].

СГЛА́ЖУ[1], сгла́дишь. Р. Сгла́дить (acc.). I. Сгла́живать. (lit. and fig.) To smooth out, over.

СГЛА́ЖУ[2], сгла́зишь. Р. Сгла́зить (acc.). To put the evil eye on (s.o.), bewitch.

СГЛА́ЗЬ (imp.), see сгла́жу[2].

СГЛО́ДАННЫЙ; сгло́дан, —а, —о, —ы (ppp), see сгложу́.

СГЛО́ЖЕШЬ, see сгложу́.

СГЛОЖИ́ (imp.) see сгложу́.

СГЛОЖУ́, сгло́жешь. Р. Сглода́ть (acc.). To eat by gnawing.

СГЛУПЛЮ́, сглупи́шь. Р. Сглупи́ть (intr.). I. Глупи́ть. To be foolish, act foolishly.

СГНИЁШЬ, see сгнию́.

СГНИЮ́, сгниёшь. Р. Сгнить (intr.). I. Гнить. 1. To rot, decompose, decay. 2. (fig.) To rot, decay.

СГОНИ́ (imp.), see сгоню́.

СГО́НИШЬ, see сгоню́.

СГОНЮ́, сго́нишь. Р. Согна́ть (acc.). I. Сгоня́ть. 1. To drive away (cattle, people, etc.). 2. To drive together into one place (cattle, people, etc.). 3. To get rid of (e.g., wrinkles, freckles, etc.). 4. (fig.) To drive away (sleep, gloom, etc.). 5. To float, raft (as logs down stream).

СГО́РБИ and сгорбь (imp.), see сго́рблю.

СГО́РБЛЕННЫЙ; сго́рблен, —а, —о, —ы (ppp), see сго́рблю.

СГО́РБЛЮ, сго́рбишь. Р. Сго́рбить (acc.). I. Го́рбить. To hunch, arch, bend (as one's back).

СГОРБЬ and сго́рби (imp.), see сго́рблю.

СГОРИ́ (imp.), see сгорю́.

СГОРИ́ШЬ, see сгорю́.

СГОРЮ́, сгори́шь. Р. Сгоре́ть (intr.). I. Сгора́ть, горе́ть (mean. 1, 6, 7, 8). 1. To burn. 2. To burn down/out/up. 3. To be burnt out (i.e., lose one's possessions in a fire). 4. To burn from overheating (e.g., pie crust). 5. To burn from excessive heat/sun (as crops, etc.). 6. (fig.) To burn (from emotion, shame, fever, etc.). 7. To rot (of damp hay, etc.). 8. To wear out (of shoes, etc.).

СГОРЯ́Т, see сгорю́.

СГРЁБ, сгребла́ (past), see сгребу́.

СГРЕБЁННЫЙ; сгребён, —а́, —о́, —ы́ (ppp), see сгребу́.

СГРЕБЁШЬ, see сгребу́.

СГРЕБИ́ (imp.), see сгребу́.

СГРЕБУ́, сгребёшь. Р. Сгрести́ (acc.). I. Сгреба́ть. 1. To rake up, off, away. 2. To shovel up, off, away. 3. To grasp, seize.

СГРУ́ЖЕННЫЙ; сгру́жен, —а, —о, —ы (ppp), see сгружу́.

СГРУЖЁННЫЙ; сгружён, —а́, —о́, —ы́ (ppp), see сгружу́.

СГРУЖУ́, сгру́зишь (also сгрузи́шь). Р. Сгрузи́ть (acc.). I. Сгружа́ть. 1. To unload. 2. To pile up, load (s.t.) on (s.t.) (acc. + на + acc.).

СГРЫ́З, сгры́зла (past), see сгрызу́.

СГРЫ́ЗЕННЫЙ; сгры́зен, —а, —о, —ы (ppp), see сгрызу́.

СГРЫЗЁШЬ, see сгрызу́.

СГРЫЗИ́ (imp.), see сгрызу́.

СГРЫЗУ́, сгрызёшь. Р. Сгрызть (acc.). I. Сгрыза́ть. 1. To eat up by gnawing or nibbling (as a bone, a loaf of sugar, etc.). 2. To spoil (s.t.) by chewing or gnawing. 3. (fig.) To gnaw (as one's conscience gnaws one).

СГУ́БЛЕННЫЙ; сгу́блен, —а, —о, —ы (ppp), see сгублю́.

СГУБЛЮ́, сгу́бишь. Р. Сгуби́ть (acc.). To ruin, destroy, spoil, waste.

СГУЩЁННЫЙ; сгущён, —а́, —о́, —ы́ (ppp), see сгущу́.

СГУЩУ́, сгусти́шь. Р. Сгусти́ть (acc.). I. Сгуща́ть. 1. To thicken. 2. To condense, concentrate. 3. To compress. 4. To coagulate, clot, curdle.

СДАВА́Й (imp.), see сдаю́.

СДАВА́Я (adv. pres. part.), see сдаю́.

СДА́ВЛЕННЫЙ; сда́влен, —а, —о, —ы (ppp), see сдавлю́.

СДАВЛЮ́, сда́вишь. Р. Сдави́ть (acc.). I. Сда́вливать. 1. To squeeze, press, compress. 2. To crush. 3. To contract. 4. To throttle.

СДАДИ́М, сдади́те, сдаду́т (pl. forms), see сдам.

СДАЁШЬ, see сдаю́.

СДАЙ (imp.), see сдам.

СДАМ, сдашь, сдаст (sing. forms). Р. Сдать. I. Сдава́ть. 1. To hand in, over (acc.). 2. To yield, give up, surrender (acc.). 3. To check (as luggage, etc.) (acc.). 4. To give (as change) (acc.). 5. To rent out, lease out (acc.). 6. To deal (as cards) (acc.).7. To pass (as an examination) (acc.). 8. To grow weak, weaken, grow worse (intr.).

СДАННЫЙ; сдан, —á, —ó, —ы́ (ppp), see сдам.

СДАСТ, see сдам.

СДАШЬ, see сдам.

СДАЮ, сдаёшь. I. Сдавáть. Р. Сдать. 1. To hand in, over (acc.). 2. To yield, give up, surrender (acc.). 3. To check (as luggage) (acc.). 4. To give (as change) (acc.). 5. To rent out, lease out (acc.). 6. To deal (as cards) (acc.). 7. To pass (as an examination) (acc.). 8. To grow weak, weaken, grow worse (intr.).

СДЕРЁШЬ, see сдеру́.

СДЕ́РЖАННЫЙ; сде́ржан, —а, —о, —ы (ppp), see сдержу́.

СДЕ́РЖАТ, see сдержу́.

СДЕРЖИ́ (imp.), see сдержу́.

СДЕ́РЖИШЬ, see сдержу́.

СДЕРЖУ́, сде́ржишь. Р. Сдержáть (acc.). I. Сде́рживать (mean. 1 thru 3). 1. (lit. and fig.) To hold back, restrain (e.g., horses, anger, etc.) 2. To support, sustain (e.g., a weight, pressure, etc.). 3. To deter. 4. (fig.) To keep (as one's word, promise, etc.).

СДЕРИ́ (imp.), see сдеру́.

СДЕРУ́, сдерёшь. Р. Содрáть (acc.). I. Сдирáть, драть. 1. To bark. 2. To strip, strip off. 3. To skin, flay. 4. To scrape. 5. To swindle (take s.t. from s.o. by cheating) (acc. + с + gen.).

СДОХ, сдóхла (past). Р. Сдóхнуть (intr.). I. Дóхнуть. To die (of animals).

СДУ́ЕШЬ, see сдую.

СДУ́Й (imp.), see сдую.

СДУ́ТЫЙ; сдут, —а, —о, —ы (ppp), see сдую.

СДУ́Ю, сду́ешь. Р. Сдуть (acc.). I. Сдувáть. 1. To blow away. 2. To blow together. 3. To copy, crib (e.g., an essay).

СЕЕШЬ, see сею.

СЕЙ (imp.), see сею.

СЕК, секлá (also сéкла, etc.) (past), see секу́.

СЕКИ́ (imp.), see секу́.

СЕКИ́СЬ (imp.), see секу́сь.

СЕ́КСЯ, секлáся (past), see секу́сь.

СЕКУ́, сечёшь, секу́т. I. Сечь. Р. Вы́сечь (mean. 1). 1. To flog, whip

(acc.). 2. To cut into pieces (as meat) (acc.). 3. To chop off, chop down (acc.). 4. To slash (as with a sabre) (acc.). 5. To hew, carve (as stone) (acc.). 6. To beat, lash (of rain, etc.) (acc.) or (intr.).

СЕКУ́СЬ, сечёшься, секу́тся. I. Сéчься (intr.). Р. Посéчься (mean. 1 and 2). 1. To split (of hair) (3rd pers. only). 2. To cut (of silk) (3rd pers. only). 3. (arch.) To fight (in battle).

СЕЛ, сéла (past). Р. Сесть (intr.). I. Садиться. 1. To sit down (on: на + acc.) (at a table: за + acc.) (by: у + gen.) (in: в + acc.). 2. To sit down (to do s.t.) (+ inf.) or (на/за + acc.). 3. To board, take (e.g., a train) (на + acc.). 4. To get in a train, auto, etc., (в + acc.). 5. To alight (of a bird) (on: на + acc.) (in: в + acc.). 6. To land (of a plane). 7. To settle (on) (of dust or fog) (на + acc.). 8. To set (of the sun). 9. To spend time (in prison). 10. To shrink (of cloth). 11. To settle (of a building, etc.). (Also see сáду.)

СЕРЖУ́, сéрдишь. I. Серди́ть (acc.). Р. Рассерди́ть. 1. To anger. 2. To irritate, annoy.

СЕ́ЧЕННЫЙ; сéчен, —а, —о, —ы (ppp), see секу́.

СЕЧЁШЬ, see секу́.

СЕЧЁШЬСЯ, see секу́сь.

СЕ́Ю, сéешь. I. Сéять. Р. Посéять (mean. 1). 1. (lit. and fig.) To sow, strew (acc.). 2. To sift (as flour) (acc.). 3. To fall gently (of light rain, snow, etc.) (intr.).

СЕ́ЯННЫЙ; сéян, —а, —о, —ы (ppp), see сéю.

СЖА́ТЫЙ¹; сжат, —а, —о, —ы (ppp). Р. Сжать (acc.). I. Сжимáть. 1. To squeeze, compress. 2. To grip. 3. To clench. 4. To shorten, compress (as an essay). (Also see сожму́.)

СЖА́ТЫЙ²; сжáт, —а, —о, —ы (ppp). Р. Сжать (acc.). I. Жать. To reap, cut. (Also see сожну́.)

СЖЁВАННЫЙ; сжёван, —а, —о, —ы (ppp), see сжую́.

СЖЁГ, сожглá (past). Р. Сжечь (acc.). I. Сжигáть, жечь (mean. 1 and 3). 1. To burn, burn up. 2. To spoil by burning, overheating (as a pie, a shirt while ironing, etc.). 3. To burn (as the sun burns one's face, a grain field, etc.). 4. (fig.) To consume (as anger consumes one). (Also see сожгу́.)

СЖИВЁШЬ, see сживу́.

СЖИВИ́ (imp.), see сживу́.

СЖИВУ́, сживёшь. Р. Сжить. I. Сжива́ть (acc.). 1. To force, drive (s.o.) out (of someplace) by creating unbearable conditions (e.g., force s.o. out of an apartment) (acc. + с + gen.). 2. (idiomatic usage) To worry s.o. to death (acc. + со + све́та).

СЖИ́ТЫЙ; сжит, —а́, —о, —ы (ppp), see сживу́.

СЖУЁШЬ, see сжую́.

СЖУЙ (imp.), see сжую́.

СЖУЮ́, сжуёшь. Р. Сжева́ть (acc.). To masticate and swallow.

СИДИ́ (imp.), see сижу́.

СИДИ́ШЬ, see сижу́.

СИДЯ́Т, see сижу́.

СИЖУ́, сиди́шь. I. Сиде́ть (intr.). 1. To sit (of a person or thing). 2. To be (as without money, etc.). 3. To spend time, be (somewhere, or doing something). 4. To fit (s.o.) (of clothing) (на + prep.). 5. (naut.) To draw water (of a ship) (в + prep. of water); sit in the water (в + prep.).

СИП (and си́пнул), си́пла (past). I. Си́пнуть (intr.). Р. Оси́пнуть. To become hoarse.

СИПИ́ (imp.), see сиплю́.

СИПИ́ШЬ, see сиплю́.

СИПЛЮ́, сипи́шь. I. Сипе́ть (intr.). 1. To make a hoarse sound (e.g., a fog horn). 2. To speak in a hoarse or husky voice.

СИПЯ́Т, see сиплю́.

СКА́ЖЕШЬ, see скажу́.

СКАЖИ́ (imp.), see скажу́.

СКАЖУ́, ска́жешь. Р. Сказа́ть. I. Говори́ть. 1. To say, tell, speak (acc.) or (о + prep.). 2. (arch.) To order (acc.) or (+ inf.). (For numerous idiomatic usages see unabridged dictionary.)

СКА́ЗАННЫЙ; ска́зан, —а, —о, —ы (ppp), see скажу́.

СКАПУ́СТИСЬ (imp.), see скапу́щусь.

СКАПУ́ТЬСЯ (imp.), see скапу́чусь.

СКАПУ́ЧУСЬ, скапу́тишься. Р. скапу́титься (intr.), To die, perish.

СКАПУ́ЩУСЬ, скапу́стишься. Р.

Скапу́ститься (intr.). To die, perish.

СКА́ЧЕННЫЙ; ска́чен, —а, —о, —ы (ppp), see скачу́[1].

СКА́ЧЕШЬ, see скачу́[2].

СКАЧИ́, see скачу́[2].

СКАЧУ́[1], ска́тишь. Р. Скати́ть (acc.). I. Ска́тывать, ска́чивать (mean. 2). 1. To roll or slide (s.t.) down. 2. To wash/rinse off (e.g., dishes).

СКАЧУ́[2], ска́чешь. I. Скака́ть (intr.). 1. To skip, jump, leap, hop. 2. To gallop. 3. To race, participate in races (of horses).

СКИПИ́СЬ (imp.), see скипи́тся.

СКИ́ЙТСЯ, скипя́тся. Р. Скипе́ться (intr.). I. Скипа́ться. To cake, form a solid mass, chunks, etc., as a result of heating or melting (as coal forms clinkers, melting snow forms ice, etc.).

СКИПЯ́ТСЯ (3rd pers. pl.), see скипи́тся.

СКИС, ски́сла (past). Р. Ски́снуть (intr.). I. Скиса́ть. 1. To sour, turn sour, curdle. 2. To become despondent, depressed.

СКЛЕПА́Й and склепи́ (imp.), see склеплю́.

СКЛЁПАННЫЙ; склёпан, —а, —о, —ы (ppp), see склеплю́.

СКЛЁПЛЕШЬ, see склеплю́.

СКЛЕПЛИ́ and склепа́й (imp.), see склеплю́.

СКЛЕПЛЮ́, скле́плешь, (also склепа́ю, склепа́ешь). Р. Склепа́ть (acc.). I. Склёпывать. To rivet.

СКЛИ́ЧЕШЬ, see скли́чу.

СКЛИ́ЧУ, скли́чешь. Р. Скли́кать (acc.). I. Склика́ть. 1. To call together (e.g., people, chickens, etc.). 2. To call (s.o.) loudly.

СКЛИЧЬ (imp.), see скли́чу.

СКО́ЛЕШЬ, see сколю́.

СКОЛИ́ (imp.), see сколю́.

СКО́ЛОТЫЙ; ско́лот, —а, —о, —ы (ppp), see сколю́.

СКОЛО́ЧЕННЫЙ; сколо́чен, —а, —о, —ы (ppp), see сколочу́.

СКОЛОЧУ́, сколо́тишь. Р. Сколоти́ть (acc.). I. Скола́чивать. 1. To knock or put together (e.g., a box, shack, etc.). 2. To knock off (e.g., boards from a building). 3. (fig.) To put together, scrape together (as a fortune).

СКОЛЬЖУ́, скользи́шь. I. Скользи́ть (intr.). Р. Скользну́ть. 1. To slide, slip, skid. 2. (lit. and fig.) To glide, float.

СКОЛЮ́, ско́лешь. Р. Сколо́ть (acc.). I. Ска́лывать. 1. To split off, chop off. 2. To pin together. 3. To transfer, copy (as design) by means of pin pricks.

СКОНФУ́ЖЕННЫЙ; сконфу́жен, —а, —о, —ы (ppp), see сконфу́жу.

СКОНФУ́ЖУ, сконфу́зишь. Р. Сконфу́зить (acc.). I. Конфу́зить. To disconcert, fluster.

СКОНФУ́ЗЬ (imp.), see сконфу́жу.

СКО́ПЛЕННЫЙ; ско́плен, —а, —о, —ы (ppp), see скоплю́[1].

СКОПЛЮ́[1], ско́пишь. Р. Скопи́ть (acc./gen.). I. Ска́пливать. 1. To store up, (as goods). 2. To save (as money). 3. To collect (e.g., antiques).

СКОПЛЮ́[2], скопи́шь. I. Скопи́ть (acc.). To castrate.

СКОРБИ́ (imp.), see скорблю́.

СКОРБИ́ШЬ, see скорблю́.

СКОРБЛЮ́, скорби́шь. I. Скорбе́ть (intr.). To grieve (about: о + prep.), (over: над + inst.), (for: за + acc.).

СКОРБЯ́Т, see скорблю́.

СКО́РМЛЕННЫЙ; ско́рмлен, —а, —о, —ы (ppp), see скормлю́.

СКОРМЛЮ́, ско́рмишь. Р. Скорми́ть (acc.). I. Ска́рмливать. To feed (s.t. to s.o. or s.t.) (acc. + dat.).

СКОРО́ЖЕННЫЙ; скоро́жен, —а, —о, —ы (ppp), see скорожу́.

СКОРОЖУ́, скороди́шь (and скоро́жу, скоро́дишь). Р. Скороди́ть (and скоро́дить) (acc.) or (intr.). To harrow.

СКОРО́МЛЮСЬ, скоро́мишься. I. Скоро́миться (intr.). Р. Оскоро́миться. To eat meat on days of fast.

СКОРО́МЬСЯ (imp.), see скоро́млюсь.

СКОШЁННЫЙ; скошён, —а́, —о́, —ы́ (ppp), see скошу́[2].

СКО́ШЕННЫЙ; ско́шен, —а, —о, —ы (ppp), see скошу́[1] and [2].

СКОШУ́[1], ско́сишь. Р. Скоси́ть (acc.). I. Коси́ть, ска́шивать. 1. To mow, cut. 2. (fig.) To mow down, cut down, kill.

СКОШУ́[2], скоси́шь. Р. Скоси́ть. I. Коси́ть, ска́шивать. 1. To cock, slant, make crooked, slope, bevel (acc.). 2. To squint, cock (e.g., one's eyes, etc.) (acc./inst.).

СКОЩЁННЫЙ; скощён, —а́, —о́, —ы́ (ppp), see скощу́.

СКОЩУ́, скости́шь. Р. Скости́ть (acc.). I. Ска́щивать. To knock off, deduct (s.t.) from (a price, account, etc.).

СКРАСЬ (imp.), see скра́шу.

СКРА́ШЕННЫЙ; скра́шен, —а, —о, —ы (ppp), see скра́шу.

СКРА́ШУ, скра́сишь. Р. Скра́сить (acc.). I. Скра́шивать. To make more pleasant or bearable, brighten (e.g., life, etc.).

СКРЁБ, скребла́ (past), see скребу́.

СКРЕБЁШЬ, see скребу́.

СКРЕБИ́ (imp.), see скребу́.

СКРЕБУ́, скребёшь. I. Скрести́ (acc.) or (intr.). 1. To scrape. 2. To claw, scratch. 3. To torment (of thoughts, etc.).

СКРЕЖЕЩА́ (adv. pres. part.), see скрежещу́.

СКРЕЖЕ́ЩЕШЬ, see скрежещу́.

СКРЕЖЕЩИ́ (imp.), see скрежещу́.

СКРЕЖЕЩУ́, скреже́щешь. I. Скрежета́ть (intr.). 1. To make a grinding noise (e.g., of an anchor chain, tractor, etc.). 2. To gnash, grit (as one's teeth) (inst.).

СКРЕПЛЁННЫЙ; скреплён, —а́, —о́, —ы́ (ppp), see скреплю́.

СКРЕПЛЮ́, скрепи́шь. Р. Скрепи́ть (acc.). I. Скрепля́ть. 1. To fasten firmly, make fast, fix. 2. To tie, clamp, bolt. 3. (lit. and fig.) To cement. 4. To authenticate, certify, ratify. 5. (arch.) To control o.s. (+ себя́).

СКРЕЩЁННЫЙ; скрещён, —а́, —о́, —ы́ (ppp), see скрещу́.

СКРЕЩУ́, скрести́шь. Р. Скрести́ть (acc.). I. Скре́щивать. 1. To cross (as one's arms, etc.). 2. To interbreed, or cross (as animals, plants, etc.) (acc. + с + inst.).

СКРИВЛЁННЫЙ; скривлён, —а́, —о́, —ы́ (ppp), see скривлю́.

СКРИВЛЮ́, скриви́шь. Р. Скриви́ть. I. Криви́ть. 1. To distort (as one's features, e.g., one's mouth by sneering) (acc.). 2. To bend, twist (acc.). 3. To act hypocritically (intr.) (+ inst of soul: душо́й).

СКРИПИ́ (imp.), see скриплю́.

СКРИПЙШЬ, see скриплю́.

СКРИПЛЮ́, скрипи́шь. I. Скрипе́ть (intr.). P. Проскрипе́ть, скри́пнуть (mean. 1 and 3). 1. To squeak, creak, grate, crunch. 2. (fig.) To barely get by (of a person in poor circumstances). 3. To gnash, grate (as one's teeth) (inst.).

СКРИПЯ́Т, see скриплю́.

СКРО́ЕШЬ, see скро́ю.

СКРОЙ (imp.), see скро́ю.

СКРО́Ю, скро́ешь. P. Скрыть (acc.). I. Скрыва́ть. (lit. and fig.) To hide, conceal.

СКРУ́ЧЕННЫЙ; скру́чен, —а, —о, —ы (ppp), see скручу́.

СКРУЧУ́, скру́тишь. P. Скрути́ть (acc.). I. Скру́чивать, крути́ть (mean. 1 thru 3). 1. To twist, spin (e.g., wool into yarn, hemp into rope, etc.). 2. To roll (e.g., a cigarette, a piece of paper, etc.). 3. To bind or pinion (as s.o.'s arms). 4. To force to obey. 5. To overcome (as illness overcomes one).

СКРЫ́ТЫЙ; скры́т, —а, —о, —ы (ppp), see скро́ю.

СКУ́ПЛЕННЫЙ; ску́плен, —а, —о, —ы (ppp), see скуплю́.

СКУПЛЮ́, ску́пишь. P. Скупи́ть (acc.). I. Скупа́ть. 1. To buy up. 2. corner the market (on s.t., as wheat) (acc. of wheat).

СКУПЛЮ́СЬ, скупи́шься. I. Скупи́ться (intr.). P. Поскупи́ться (mean. 2). 1. To be stingy, tight fisted. 2. To skimp (on s.t.), be sparing (of) (на + acc.).

СЛАБ, сла́бла (past). I. Сла́бнуть (intr.). P. Осла́бнуть. 1. To weaken, grow weak. 2. To relax, slacken (of tension, attention, etc.).

СЛА́ВЛЮ, сла́вишь. I. Сла́вить (acc.). P. Осла́вить (mean. 2 and 3). 1. To praise, honor. 2. To spread rumors about (s.o.). 3. To defame, give a bad name.

СЛАВОСЛО́ВЛЕННЫЙ; славосло́влен, —а, —о, —ы (ppp), see славосло́влю.

СЛАВЛОСЛО́ВЛЮ, славлосло́вишь. I. Славосло́вить (acc.). To eulogize.

СЛАВОСЛО́ВЬ (imp.), see славосло́влю.

СЛАВЬ (imp.), see сла́влю.

СЛАДЬ (imp.), see сла́жу¹.

СЛА́ЖЕННЫЙ; сла́жен, —а, —о, —ы (ppp), see сла́жу¹.

СЛА́ЖУ¹, сла́дишь. P. Сла́дить. I. Сла́живать. 1. To arrange, organize, put together (acc.). 2. To come to an agreement (with) (с + inst.). 3. To manage, cope (with) (с + inst.).

СЛА́ЖУ², сла́зишь. P. Сла́зить (intr.) 1. To go and get (s.t.) (за + inst.). 2. To reach into (as one's pocket with one's hand) (в + acc.). 3. To get down (from or out of) (e.g., a bus) (с + gen.).

СЛАЗЬ (imp.), see сла́жу².

СЛАЛ, сла́ла (past). I. Слать (acc.). To send (also see шлю).

СЛАЩЁННЫЙ; слащён, —а́, —о́, —ы́ (ppp), see слащу́.

СЛАЩУ́, сласти́шь. I. Сласти́ть. P. Посласти́ть (mean. 1). 1. To sweeten (acc.). 2. To have a sweet taste (intr.).

СЛЁГ, слегла́ (past). P. Слечь (intr.). 1. To take to one's bed (due to illness). 2. To bend down (of grain, grass, etc.). (Also see сля́гу.)

СЛЕЖУ́¹, следи́шь. I. Следи́ть. 1. To watch (s.t. moving) (acc., arch.) or (за + inst.). 2. (fig.) To follow (e.g., a conversation, trends, etc.) (за + inst.). 3. To look after (as children) (за + inst.). 4. To spy on, observe (за + inst.). 5. To track (as a bear) (acc.).

СЛЕЖУ́², следи́шь. I. Следи́ть (intr.). P. Наследи́ть. To leave dirty tracks (as on a floor with one's boots) (на + prep. of floor + inst. of boots).

СЛЕЗ, слёзла (past), see слёзу.

СЛЁЗЕШЬ, see слёзу.

СЛЁЗУ, слёзешь. P. Слезть (intr.). I. Слеза́ть. 1. To get down, dismount from (с + gen.). 2. To alight from, get off (с + gen.). 3. To descend (into: в + acc.), (from: с + gen.), (on: на + acc.). 4. To come off, peel off (of paint, etc.) (с + gen.).

СЛЕЗЬ (imp.), see слёзу.

СЛЕЙ (imp.). P. Слить. I. Слива́ть (mean. 1, 2, 3, 5). 1. To pour off (e.g., cream, etc.) (acc.). 2. To pour out (acc.). 3. To pour together, mix, combine (acc.). 4. (fig.) To fuse, blend, mix (acc.). 5. (arch.) To flow from, away, down, etc. (intr.). (Also see солью́.)

СЛЕП (and слёпнул), слепла (past). I.
Слёпнуть (intr.). P. Ослёпнуть.
(lit. and fig.) To become blind.

СЛЕПЛЕННЫЙ; слёплен, —а, —о,
—ы (ppp), see слеплю¹.

СЛЕПЛЮ¹, слёпишь. P. Слепить
(acc.). I. Слеплять, лепить (mean. 1
and 2). 1. To model, sculpture. 2. To
stick (together), make adhere. 3.
(fig.) To throw or put together
carelessly (e.g., a building, a novel,
etc.).

СЛЕПЛЮ², слепишь. I. Слепить
(acc.). 1. (arch.) To blind (s.o. or s.t.).
2. To tire, dazzle one's eyes (acc. of
eyes). 3. (fig.) To blind (as snow,
rain, mist gets in one's eyes, inter-
fering with vision) (acc. of eyes).

СЛЕПНУВШИЙ (pap), see слеп.

СЛЕПШИЙ (pap), see слеп.

СЛЕТИ (imp.), see слечу.

СЛЕТИШЬ, see слечу.

СЛЕТЯТ, see слечу.

СЛЕЧУ, слетишь. P. Слететь (intr.)
(с + gen.). I. Слетать. 1. (lit. and
fig.) To fly down (from). 2. (lit. and
fig.) To fly away, off. 3. To fall off,
fall from. 4. To vanish, disappear.

СЛИЖЕШЬ, see слижу.

СЛИЖИ (imp.), see слижу.

СЛИЖУ, слижешь. P. Слизать (acc.).
I. Слизывать. 1. To lick off (e.g., a
dish). 2. (fig.) To lick, eat away (as
flames lick a log).

СЛИЗАННЫЙ; слизан, —а, —о, —ы
(ppp), see слижу.

СЛИТЫЙ, слит, —á, —о, —ы (ppp),
see слей and солью.

СЛОМЛЕННЫЙ; слóмлен, —а, —о,
—ы (ppp), see сломлю.

СЛОМЛЮ, сломишь. P. Сломить
(acc.). I. Сламывать. 1. To break.
2. (fig.) To break (as the enemy's
resistance), to overcome. 3. To
demolish (e.g., a building).

СЛУПЛЕННЫЙ; слуплен, —а, —о,
—ы (ppp), see слуплю.

СЛУПЛЮ, слупишь. P. Слупить. I.
Лупить. 1. To peel, bark, strip
(acc.). 2. To overcharge, cheat
(intr.) or (acc. of amount of overcharge + с + gen. of pers.).

СЛЫВЁШЬ, see слыву.

СЛЫВУ, слывёшь. I. Слыть (intr.).
P. Прослыть (mean. 1). 1. To be

reputed to be, have a reputation as
(inst.) or (за + acc.). 2. To be
known as (e.g., by another name)
(inst.).

СЛЫШАННЫЙ; слышан, —а, —о,
—ы (ppp), see слышу.

СЛЫШАТ, see слышу.

СЛЫШИШЬ, see слышу.

СЛЫШУ, слышишь. I. Слышать. P.
Услышать (mean. 1, 3, 4, 5). 1. To
hear (acc.). 2. To hear (intr.). 3. To
hear (about) (о + prep.) (про +
acc.) or (+ что). 4. To scent (as a
dog scents an animal) (acc.). 5. To
catch, smell (e.g., the fragrance of
flowers) (acc.) (запах + gen. of
flowers). 6. To notice, feel, sense
(acc.) or (+ как) or (+ что).

СЛЮБЛЮСЬ, слюбишься. P. Слю-
биться (intr.). I. Слюбляться (mean.
1). 1. To fall in love (with) (с +
inst.). 2. (arch.) To please (s.o.) (dat.)
(same as понравиться).

СЛЮНЯВЛЮ, слюнявишь. I. Слюня-
вить (acc.). To wet with saliva.

СЛЮНЯВЬ (imp.), see слюнявлю.

СЛЯГ (imp.), see слягу.

СЛЯГУ, сляжешь, слягут. P. Слечь
(intr.). 1. To take to one's bed (due
to illness). 2. To bend down (of
grass, grain, etc.).

СЛЯЖЕШЬ, see слягу.

СМАЖЕШЬ, see смажу.

СМАЖУ, смажешь. P. Смазать (acc.).
I. Смазывать. 1. To grease, oil,
lubricate. 2. To smear. 3. To bribe.
4. To slur over (as a question), blur.
5. To spoil. 6. To strike hard.

СМАЖЬ (imp.), see смажу.

СМАЗАННЫЙ; смазан, —а, —о, —ы
(ppp), see смажу.

СМЕЁШЬСЯ, see смеюсь.

СМЕЙСЯ (imp.), see смеюсь.

СМЁЛ, смела (past), see смету.

СМЕЛЕШЬ, see смелю.

СМЕЛИ (imp.), see смелю.

СМЕЛЮ, смелешь. P. Смолоть. I.
Молоть. 1. To grind (as grain, etc.)
(acc.). 2. (fig.) To babble, talk
nonsense (intr.) or (acc.).

СМЕРДИ (imp.), see смержу.

СМЕРДИШЬ, see смержу.

СМЕРДЯТ, see смержу.

СМЕРЖУ, смердишь. I. Смердеть
(intr.). 1. To emit a stench, stink. 2.
To stink (of) (inst.).

СМЁРЗСЯ, смёрзлась. Р. Смёрзнуться (intr.). I. Смерзаться. 1. To freeze together. 2. To freeze.

СМЕРК (and смёркнул), смёркла (past). Р. Смёркнуть (intr.). I. Смеркать. 1. To grow dark. 2. (lit. and fig.) To grow dim, fade.

СМЕТАННЫЙ; смётан, —а, —о, —ы (ppp), see смечу.

СМЕТЁННЫЙ; сметён, —а, —о, —ы (ppp), see смету.

СМЕТЁШЬ, see смету.

СМЕТИ (imp.), see смету.

СМЕТУ, сметёшь. Р. Смести (acc.). I. Сметать. 1. (lit. and fig.) To sweep away. 2. To sweep up (into a pile).

СМЁТШИЙ (pap), see смету.

СМЕТЯ (adv. past part.), see смету.

СМЕЧЕШЬ, see смечу.

СМЕЧИ (imp.), see смечу.

СМЕЧУ, смечешь. Р. Сметать (acc.). I. Смётывать. 1. To pile, stack (e.g., hay, etc.). 2. To throw down, off.

СМЕШЕННЫЙ; смешен, —а, —о, —ы (ppp), see смешу.

СМЕШУ, смесишь. Р. Смесить (acc.). I. Месить. 1. To knead (as dough). 2. To puddle (as clay).

СМЕЩЁННЫЙ; смещён, —а, —о, —ы (ppp), see смещу.

СМЕЩУ, сместишь. Р. Сместить (acc.). I. Смещать. 1. To remove, discharge (as a person). 2. To displace, remove (s.t.). 3. To disrupt.

СМЕЮСЬ, смеёшься. I. Смеяться (intr.). 1. To laugh. 2. To laugh at, make fun of, ridicule (s.o. or s.t.) (над + inst.) or (arch.: dat.). 3. To joke (intr.).

СМОГ, смогла (past), see смогу.

СМОГУ, сможешь, смогут. Р. Смочь (intr.). I. Мочь. To be able (to do s.t.).

СМОЕШЬ, see смою.

СМОЖЕШЬ, see смогу.

СМОЙ (imp.), see смою.

СМОЛК (arch. смолкнул), смолкла (past). Р. Смолкнуть (intr.). I. Смолкать. 1. To cease (of sounds). 2. To become silent, cease talking etc. (of people).

СМОЛОТЫЙ; смолот, —а, о, —ы (ppp), see смелю.

СМОЛОЧЕННЫЙ; смолочен, —а, —о, —ы (ppp), see смолочу.

СМОЛОЧУ, смолотишь. Р. Смолотить (acc.). I. Молотить. To thresh.

СМОЛЧАТ, see смолчу.

СМОЛЧИ (imp.), see смолчу.

СМОЛЧИШЬ, see смолчу.

СМОЛЧУ, смолчишь. Р. Смолчать (intr.). To hold one's tongue, keep quiet.

СМОРОЖЕННЫЙ; сморожен, —а, —о, —ы (ppp), see сморожу.

СМОРОЖУ, сморозишь. Р. Сморозить (acc.). To say, blurt out (s.t. nonsensical, stupid).

СМОРОЗЬ (imp.), see сморожу.

СМОТРЕННЫЙ; смотрен, —а, —о, —ы (ppp), see смотрю.

СМОТРИ (imp.), see смотрю.

СМОТРИШЬ, see смотрю.

СМОТРЮ, смотришь. I. Смотреть. Р. Посмотреть (mean. 1, 2, 3, 4, 5, 9). 1. (lit. and fig.) To look (at) (на + acc.). 2. To look through (as a book) (acc.). 3. To look after (as a child) (за + inst.). 4. To examine (acc.). 5. To look through, into, out (as a window) (в + acc.). 6. To look, appear, (as young) (inst.). 7. To follow (s.o.'s) example (на + acc. of s.o.). 8. (fig.) To look into (as a window looks into a garden) (в + acc.). 9. To see, watch (as a play) (acc.).

СМОТРЯТ, see смотрю.

СМОЮ, смоешь. Р. Смыть (acc.). I. Смывать. 1. To wash, wash off, wash away. 2. (fig.) To wash away. 3. (fig.) To whitewash.

СМУЧУ, смутишь (arch. forms). Р. Смутить (acc.). I. Смущать. 1. To embarrass, confuse. 2. To disturb. 3. (arch.) To stir up, make turbid (as water). 4. (arch.) To stir up (the populace).

СМУЩЁННЫЙ; смущён, —а, —о, —ы (ppp), see смущу and смучу.

СМУЩУ, смутишь. Р. Смутить (acc.). I. Смущать. 1. To embarrass, confuse. 2. To disturb. 3. (arch.) To stir up, make turbid (as water). 4. (arch.) To stir up (e.g., the populace).

СМЫТЫЙ; смыт, —а, —о, —ы (ppp), see смою.

СМЯ́ТЫЙ; смят, —а, —о, —ы (ppp).
Р. Смять (acc.). I. Мять (mean. 1
thru 3). 1. To rumple, crumple. 2.
To trample. 3. To knead, work up,
(as clay, leather, etc.). 4. (fig.) To
crush (as an enemy, one's spirits,
etc.). (Also see сомну́.)

СНАБЖЁННЫЙ; снабжён, —а́, —о,
—ы́ (ppp), see снабжу́.

СНАБЖУ́, снабди́шь. Р. Снабди́ть
(acc.). I. Снабжа́ть. To supply,
furnish, provide (s.t. or s.o.) with
(s.t.) (acc. + inst.).

СНАРЯЖЁННЫЙ; снаряжён, —а́,
—о́, —ы́ (ppp), see снаряжу́.

СНАРЯЖУ́, снаряди́шь. Р. Снаря-
ди́ть (acc.). I. Снаряжа́ть. 1. To
equip (as an expedition). 2. To
supply (as goods, provisions, etc.).
3. To supply (s.o. or s.t. with s.t.)
(acc. + inst.). 4. (mil.) To charge,
load with explosives (as a bomb).
5. To send (s.o. someplace to do s.t.).

СНЁС, снесла́ (past), see снесу́.

СНЕСЁННЫЙ; снесён, —а́, —о́, —ы́
(ppp), see снесу́.

СНЕСЁШЬ, see снесу́.

СНЕСИ́ (imp.), see снесу́.

СНЕСУ́, снесёшь. Р. Снести́ (acc.). I.
Нести́ (mean. 7), сноси́ть (mean. 2
thru 6, 9). 1. To carry, take somewhere. 2. To carry away. 3. To carry
down. 4. To demolish. 5. To cut off
(s.o.'s head). 6. To bear, endure. 7.
To lay (as an egg). 8. To bring
together. 9. To discard (in a card
game).

СНЕСЯ́ (adv. past part.), see снесу́.

СНИ́ЖЕННЫЙ; сни́жен, —а, —о,
—ы (ppp), see снижу́.

СНИ́ЖЕШЬ, see снижу́.

СНИЖИ́ (imp.), see снижу́.

СНИ́ЖУ, сни́зишь. Р. Сни́зить. I.
Снижа́ть. 1. To lower (acc.). 2. To
lower, reduce, (e.g., quality, prices,
temperature, etc.) (acc.). 3. To lose
altitude, to descend (intr.).

СНИЖУ́, сни́жешь. Р. Сниза́ть (acc.).
To string (as beads).

СНИ́ЗАННЫЙ; сни́зан, —а, —о, —ы
(ppp), see снижу́.

СНИЗОЙДЁШЬ, see снизойду́.

СНИЗОЙДИ́ (imp.), see снизойду́.

СНИЗОЙДУ́, снизойдёшь. Р. Сни-
зойти́. I. Снисходи́ть. 1. To con-

descend, deign (to do s.t.) (+ inf.).
2. To concede to (as a request, etc.)
(к + dat.). 3. To consent to (as a
meeting, etc.) (до + gen.). 4. To be
magnanimous (intr.), magnanimous
to (к + dat.). 5. (arch.) To descend
(intr.). 6. (arch.) To descend (on),
envelope (на + acc.).

СНИЗОЙДЯ́ (adv. past part.), see
снизойду́.

СНИЗОШЕ́ДШИЙ (pap), see сни-
зойду́.

СНИЗОШЁЛ, снизошла́ (past), see
снизойду́.

СНИЗЬ (imp.), see снижу́.

СНИК, сни́кла (past). Р. Сни́кнуть
(intr.). I. Ни́кнуть (mean. 1 and 2).
1. (lit. and fig.) To droop, wilt. 2.
(lit. and fig.) To weaken. 3. To
become depressed.

СНИ́МЕШЬ, see сниму́.

СНИМИ́ (imp.), see сниму́.

СНИМУ́, сни́мешь. Р. Снять (acc.). I.
Снима́ть. 1. To take away, remove.
2. To take off, remove. 3. To abolish,
remove. 4. To take, obtain. 5. To
take (as a photograph). 6. To rent
(as a room). 7. To reap (as a harvest).
8. To cut (as playing cards). 9. To
make a copy of (acc. of copy + с +
gen.). (For detailed usages see
unabridged dictionary.)

СНИ́СКАННЫЙ; сни́скан, —а, —о,
—ы (ppp), see снищу́.

СНИСХОЖУ́, снисхо́дишь. I. Снисхо-
ди́ть (intr.). Р. Снизойти́. 1. To
condescend, deign (to do s.t.) (+
inf.). 2. To concede to (as a request,
etc.) (к + dat.). 3. To consent to
(as a meeting, etc.) (до + gen.). 4.
To be magnanimous, magnanimous
to (к + dat.). 5. (arch.) To descend.
6. (arch., fig.) To descend (on),
envelope (на + acc.).

СНИСШЕ́ДШИЙ (arch.) (pap), see
снизоше́дший and снизойду́.

СНИСШЁЛ (arch.; masc. sing) (past),
see снизошёл and снизойду́.

СНИ́ЩЕШЬ, see снищу́.

СНИЩИ́ (imp.), see снищу́.

СНИЩУ́, сни́щешь. Р. Сниска́ть
(acc.). I. Сни́скивать. To gain,
obtain, get, win.

СНО́ШЕННЫЙ; сно́шен, —а, —о,
—ы (ppp), see сношу́[2] and [3].

СНОШУ¹, сно́сишь. I. Сноси́ть (acc.). Р. Снести́. 1. To carry away. 2. To carry down. 3. To demolish. 4. To cut off (s.o.'s head). 5. To bear, endure. 6. To discard (in game of cards).

СНОШУ², сно́сишь. Р. Сноси́ть (acc.). I. Сна́шивать (mean. 2). 1. To take there and back. 2. To bring together.

СНОШУ³, сно́сишь. Р. Сноси́ть (acc.). I. Сна́шивать. To wear out (e.g., clothes).

СНЯ́ТЫЙ; снят, —а́, —о, —ы (ppp), see сниму́.

СОБЕРЁШЬ, see соберу́.

СОБЕРИ́ (imp.), see соберу́.

СОБЕРУ́, соберёшь. Р. Собра́ть. I. Собира́ть. 1. To collect (acc./gen.). 2. To gather (acc.). 3. To harvest (acc.). 4. To assemble (as a machine, a library, etc.) (acc.). 5. To equip (e.g., a person, an expedition, etc.) (acc.). 6. To convoke (as parliament) (acc.). 7. To set (the table) (на + acc.). 8. To clear (the table) (с + gen.). 9. To gather (e.g., dress at the waist) (acc. + в + prep.). 10. (fig.) To collect (one's strength, thoughts, etc.) (acc.).

СОБЛЮДЁННЫЙ; соблюдён, —а́, —о́, —ы́ (ppp), see соблюду́.

СОБЛЮДЁШЬ, see соблюду́.

СОБЛЮДИ́ (imp.), see соблюду́.

СОБЛЮДУ́, соблюдёшь. Р. Соблюсти́ (acc.). I. Соблюда́ть, блюсти́ (mean. 2 and 3). 1. To observe strictly (as customs, laws, etc.). 2. To preserve, keep, protect (as order, interests of the government, etc.). 3. To look at, observe.

СОБЛЮ́ДШИЙ (pap), see соблюду́.

СОБЛЮДЯ́ (adv. past part.), see соблюду́.

СОБЛЮ́Л, соблюла́ (past), see соблюду́.

СО́БРАННЫЙ; со́бран, —а́ (and —а), —о, —ы (ppp), see соберу́.

СОБЬЁШЬ, see собью́.

СОБЬЮ́, собьёшь. Р. Сбить (acc.). I. Сбива́ть. 1. To knock down, off (acc.). 2. To divert (from direction of movement, course of action, etc.) (acc. + с + gen.). 3. (fig.) To turn (as a conversation, one's thoughts to s.t.) (acc. + на + acc.). 4. To

put, knock together (as a box, building, etc.). 5. To whip, churn (e.g., cream, butter, mud in a road, etc.). 6. To lower (as a price, temperature, etc.). 7. To wear down (as the heel of a shoe). 8. To confuse (s.o.) (acc. + с + то́лку). (For other usages see unabridged dictionary.)

СО́ВЕСТИ (imp.), see со́вещу.

СО́ВЕСТИСЬ (imp.), see со́вещусь.

СО́ВЕЩУ, со́вестишь. I. Со́вестить (acc.). Р. Усо́вестить. To shame, make ashamed.

СО́ВЕЩУСЬ, со́вестишься. I. Со́веститься (intr.). Р. Посо́веститься. To be ashamed (of) (gen.) or (+ inf.).

СОВЛЁК, совлекла́ (past), see совлеку́.

СОВЛЕКИ́ (imp.), see совлеку́.

СОВЛЕКУ́, совлечёшь, совлеку́т. Р. Совле́чь (acc.). I. Совлека́ть. 1. To take off, remove (e.g., a coat, cover, etc.). 2. To induce (s.o. or s.t.) to leave or sever connections with (s.t.) (e.g., with the Communist Party, etc.) (acc. + с + gen.).

СОВЛЕЧЁННЫЙ; совлечён, —а́, —о́, —ы́ (ppp), see совлеку́.

СОВЛЕЧЁШЬ, see совлеку́.

СОВМЕЩЁННЫЙ; совмещён, —а́, —о́, —ы́ (ppp), see совмещу́.

СОВМЕЩУ́, совмести́шь. Р. Совмести́ть (acc.). I. Совмеща́ть. 1. To combine (s.t. with s.t.) (acc. + с + inst.). 2. To combine (as several qualities, features in s.o. or s.t.) (acc. + в + prep.). 3. (geom.) To superpose (e.g., two triangles).

СОВОКУПЛЁННЫЙ; совокуплён, —а́, —о́, —ы́ (ppp), see совокуплю́.

СОВОКУПЛЮ́, совокупи́шь. Р. Совокупи́ть (acc.). I. Совокупля́ть. To combine, join, unite.

СОВПАДЁТ, совпаду́т (3rd pers. only). Р. Совпа́сть (intr.) (с + inst.). I. Совпада́ть. 1. To coincide (with). 2. To conform (to). 3. To concur, agree (with). 4. To merge (with).

СОВПАДИ́ (imp.), see совпадёт.

СОВПАДУ́Т (3rd pers. pl.), see совпадёт.

СОВПА́Л, совпа́ла (past), see совпадёт.

СО́БРАННЫЙ; со́бран, —а́, (and —а) —о, —ы (ppp), see совру́.

СОВРАЩЁННЫЙ; совращён, —а́,
—о́, —ы́ (ppp), see совращу́.
СОВРАЩУ́, совратишь. Р. Совратить
(acc.). I. Совращать. 1. To lead
astray. 2. To seduce.
СОВРЁШЬ, see совру́.
СОВРИ́ (imp.), see совру́.
СОВРУ́, соврёшь. Р. Совра́ть (intr.).
I. Врать. 1. To lie, to tell lies. 2. To
chatter, talk nonsense. 3. To make
mistakes (in s.t., as in music, etc.)
(в + prep.).
СОВЬЁШЬ, see совью́.
СОВЬЁШЬСЯ, see совью́сь.
СОВЬЮ́, совьёшь. Р. Свить (acc.). I.
Вить, свива́ть. 1. To twist, spin,
(as a thread, rope, etc.). 2. To
weave (as a wreath, a nest). 3. To
wind, to coil.
СОВЬЮ́СЬ, совьёшься. Р. Сви́ться
(intr.). I. Свива́ться. 1. To roll up.
2. To coil (e.g., a snake).
СОГЛАШЁННЫЙ; соглашён, —а́,
—о́, —ы́ (ppp), see соглашу́.
СОГЛАШУ́, согласи́шь. Р. Согла-
си́ть (arch. and bookish) (acc.). I.
Соглаша́ть. 1. To reconcile (e.g.,
differences of opinion, etc.). 2. To
conciliate. 3. To persuade.
СОГЛАШУ́СЬ, согласи́шься. Р. Сог-
ласи́ться (intr.). I. Соглаша́ться.
1. To agree (to s.t.) (на + acc.) or
(to do s.t.) (+ inf.). 2. To agree
(with s.t. or s.o.) (с + inst.). 3. To
come to an agreement (on s.t.)
(на + prep.).
СО́ГНАННЫЙ; со́гнан, —а, —о, —ы
(ppp). Р. Согна́ть (acc.). I. Сгоня́ть.
1. To drive away (people, cattle, etc.).
2. To drive together into one place
(people, cattle, etc.). 3. To get rid of
(e.g., freckles, wrinkles, etc.). 4.
(fig.) To drive away (e.g., sleep,
gloom, etc.). 5. To float, raft (e.g.
logs down a river). (Also see
сгоню́.)
СОДЕ́ЕШЬ, see соде́ю.
СОДЕ́Й (imp.), see соде́ю.
СОДЕ́РЖАТ, see содержу́.
СОДЕ́РЖИ (imp.), see содержу́.
СОДЕ́РЖИШЬ, see содержу́.
СОДЕРЖУ́, соде́ржишь. I. Содержа́ть
(acc.). 1. To support, maintain (e.g.,
a family, an activity, etc.). 2. To
contain (e.g., as a bucket contains
water, ore, gold, etc.). 3. To keep

(e.g., under arrest, in order, at
pasture, etc.).
СОДЕ́Ю, соде́ешь. Р. Соде́ять (acc.).
To accomplish, commit, perform, do.
СОДЕ́ЯННЫЙ; соде́ян, —а, —о, —ы
(ppp), see соде́ю.
СО́ДРАННЫЙ; со́дран, —а (and
—а́), —о, —ы (ppp). Р. Содра́ть
(acc.). I. Сдира́ть, драть. 1. To bark.
2. To strip, strip off. 3. To skin, flay.
4. To scrape. 5. (fig.) To swindle
(take s.t. from s.o. by cheating)
(acc. + с + gen.). (Also see сдеру́.)
СОЖГИ́ (imp.). see сожгу́.
СОЖГЛА́, сожгло́, сожгли́ (past), see
сожгу́ and сжёг.
СОЖГУ́, сожжёшь, сожгу́т. Р. Сжечь
(acc.). I. Сжига́ть, жечь (mean. 1
and 3). 1. To burn, burn up. 2. To
spoil by burning, overheating (as a
pie, a shirt while ironing, etc.). 3. To
burn (as the sun burns one's face, a
grain field, etc.). 4. (fig.) To consume
(as anger consumes one).
СОЖЖЁННЫЙ; сожжён, —а́, —о́,
—ы́ (ppp), see сожгу́.
СОЖЖЁШЬ, see сожгу́.
СОЖМЁШЬ, see сожму́.
СОЖМИ́ (imp.), see сожму́.
СОЖМУ́, сожмёшь. Р. Сжать (acc.).
I. Сжима́ть. 1. To squeeze, compress.
2. To grip. 3. To clench. 4. (fig.) To
shorten, compress (as an essay).
СОЖНЁШЬ, see сожну́.
СОЖНИ́ (imp.), see сожну́.
СОЖНУ́, сожнёшь. Р. Сжать (acc.).
I. Жать. To reap, cut.
СО́ЖРАННЫЙ; со́жран, —а́ (and
—а), —о, —ы (ppp), see сожру́.
СОЖРЁШЬ, see сожру́.
СОЖРИ́ (imp.), see сожру́.
СОЖРУ́, сожрёшь. Р. Сожра́ть (acc.).
I. Жрать. To eat (s.t.) greedily, gorge,
devour.
СО́ЗВАННЫЙ; со́зван, —а́ (and —а),
—о, —ы (ppp), созову́.
СОЗДАВА́Й (imp.), see создаю́.
СОЗДАВА́Я (adv. pres. part.), see
создаю́.
СОЗДАДИ́М, создади́те, создаду́т (pl.
forms), see созда́м.
СОЗДАЁШЬ, see создаю́.
СОЗДА́Й (imp.), see созда́м.
СОЗДА́М, созда́шь, созда́ст (sing.
forms). Р. Созда́ть (acc.). I. Созда-
ва́ть, созида́ть (bookish). 1. To

create. 2. To originate. 3. To found, establish. 4. To form, build (e.g., as discipline builds character).

СОЗДАННЫЙ; создан, —á (and —a), —о, —ы (ppp), see создам.

СОЗДАСТ, see создам.

СОЗДАШЬ, see создам.

СОЗДАЮ, создаёшь. Р. Создавать (acc.). I. Создать. 1. To create. 2. To originate. 3. To found, establish. 4. To form, build (e.g., as discipline builds character).

СОЗНАВАЙ (imp.), see сознаю.

СОЗНАВАЯ (adv. pres. part.), see сознаю.

СОЗНАЕШЬ, see сознаю.

СОЗНАЮ, сознаёшь. I. Сознавать (acc.). Р. Сознать. 1. To realize, be conscious of. 2. To acknowledge, recognize.

СОЗОВЁШЬ, see созову.

СОЗОВИ (imp.), see созову.

СОЗОВУ, созовёшь. Р. Созвать (acc.). I. Созывать, сзывать (mean. 1 and 2). 1. To invite a number of (guests, people, etc.). 2. To summon a number of (e.g., subordinates). 3. To convene, convoke (e.g., a council, etc.).

СОЙДЁШЬ, see сойду.

СОЙДИ (imp.), see сойду.

СОЙДУ, сойдёшь. Р. Сойти (intr.). I. Сходить. 1. To descend, come down, get off (from) (с + gen.). 2. To leave (e.g., the road, rails, etc.) (с + gen.). 3. To come off (from) (as paint from a wall, etc.) (с + gen.). 4. To disappear (from) (as color from one's face, snow from a garden, etc.) (с + gen.). 5. (fig.) To descend (on) (e.g., quiet on a city) (на + acc.). 6. To turn out (e.g., all right, badly, etc.). 7. To be taken for (e.g., s.o. or s.t. else) (за + acc.). 8. To go mad (с + ума).

СОЙДЯ (adv. past part.), see сойду.

СОКРАЩЁННЫЙ; сокращён, —á, —о, —ы (ppp), see сокращу.

СОКРАЩУ, сократишь. Р. Сократить (acc.). I. Сокращать. 1. To shorten, abridge, abbreviate. 2. To curtail, reduce. 3. To discharge, dismiss. 4. To restrain, curb (e.g., s.o., etc.). 5. (math.) To cancel (as in calculation employing fractions).

СОКРОЕШЬ, see сокрою.

СОКРОЙ (imp.), see сокрою.

СОКРОЮ, сокроешь. Р. Сокрыть (arch.) (acc.). (lit. and fig.) To hide, conceal.

СОКРЫТЫЙ; сокрыт, —а, —о, —ы (ppp), see сокрою.

СОЛГАННЫЙ; солган, —á, —о, —ы (ppp), see солгу.

СОЛГИ (imp.), see солгу.

СОЛГУ, солжёшь, солгут. Р. Солгать. I. Лгать. 1. To tell lies (intr.). 2. (arch.) To slander (на + acc.).

СОЛЖЁШЬ, see солгу.

СОЛОЖЁННЫЙ; соложён, —á, —о, —ы (ppp), see соложу.

СОЛОЖУ, солодишь. I. Солодить (acc.). To malt (as barley).

СОЛЬЁШЬ, see солью.

СОЛЬЮ, сольёшь. Р. Слить. I. Сливать (mean. 1, 2, 3, 5). 1. To pour off (e.g., cream, etc.) (acc.). 2. To pour out (acc.). 3. To pour together, mix, combine (acc.). 4. (fig.) To fuse, blend, mix (acc.). 5. (arch.) To flow from, away, down, etc. (intr.).

СОМНЁШЬ, see сомну.

СОМНИ (imp.), see сомну.

СОМНУ, сомнёшь. Р. Смять (acc.). I. Мять (mean. 1 thru 3). 1. To rumple, crumple. 2. To trample. 3. To knead, work up (as clay, leather). 4. (fig.) To crush (as an enemy, one's spirits, etc.).

СООБРАЖЁННЫЙ; соображён, —á, —о, —ы (ppp), see соображу.

СООБРАЖУ, сообразишь. Р. Сообразить. I. Соображать. 1. To ponder, weigh, consider (acc.). 2. To understand, grasp (intr./acc.) or (+ что). 3. To contrive, devise (acc.) or (+ inf.).

СООРУЖЁННЫЙ; сооружён, —á, —о, —ы (ppp), see сооружу.

СООРУЖУ, соорудишь. Р. Соорудить (acc.). I. Сооружать. 1. To build, construct, erect, make. 2. To organize, arrange (usually humorously).

СООТНЁС, соотнесла (past), see соотнесу.

СООТНЕСЁННЫЙ; соотнесён, —á, —о, —ы (ppp), see соотнесу.

СООТНЕСЁШЬ, see соотнесу.

СООТНЕСИ (imp.), see соотнесу.

СООТНЕСУ́, соотнесёшь. Р. Со-отнести́ (acc.). I. Соотноси́ть. To correlate.

СООТНЕСЯ́ (adv. past part.), see соотнесу́.

СООТНОШУ́, соотно́сишь. I. Со-относи́ть (acc.). Р. Соотнести́. To correlate.

СОПЙ (imp.), see соплю́.

СОПИ́ШЬ, see соплю́.

СОПЛЮ́, сопи́шь. I. Сопе́ть (intr.). 1. To puff, breathe heavily. 2. To puff (as on a pipe) (inst.).

СОПОСТА́ВЛЕННЫЙ; сопоста́влен, —а, —о, —ы (ppp), see сопоста́влю.

СОПОСТА́ВЛЮ, сопоста́вишь. Р. Сопоста́вить (acc.). I. Сопоставля́ть. 1. To compare (e.g., literary works, methods, etc.). 2. To compare (with) (acc. + с + inst.).

СОПОСТА́ВЬ (imp.), see сопоста́влю.

СОПРЁШЬ, see сопру́.

СОПРЙ (imp.), see сопру́.

СОПРУ́, сопрёшь. Р. Спере́ть (acc.). I. Спира́ть (mean. 3 and 4). 1. To steal (take away). 2. To carry away, take away, pull away. 3. To compress, squeeze. 4. To take away (one's breath) (impers. + acc. of breath or chest).

СОПЬЁШЬСЯ, see сопью́сь.

СОПЬЮ́СЬ, сопьёшься. Р. Спи́ться (intr.). I. Спива́ться. To become a drunkard.

СОПЯ́Т, see соплю́.

СО́РВАННЫЙ; со́рван, —а, —о, —ы (ppp), see сорву́.

СОРВЁШЬ, see сорву́.

СОРВЙ (imp.), see сорву́.

СОРВУ́, сорвёшь. Р. Сорва́ть (acc.). I. Срыва́ть. 1. To pluck, pick. 2. To tear away, off, down. 3. To spoil, frustrate, wreck. 4. To vent (as anger on s.o., etc.) (acc. + на + prep.). 5. To extort, extract (as money from s.o.) (acc. + с + gen.).

СО́САННЫЙ; со́сан, —а, —о, —ы (ppp), see сосу́.

СОСЁШЬ, see сосу́.

СОСЙ (imp.), see сосу́.

СОСКРЁБ, соскребла́ (past), see соскребу́.

СОСКРЕБЁННЫЙ; соскребён, —а́, —о́, —ы́ (ppp), see соскребу́.

СОСКРЕБЁШЬ, see соскребу́.

СОСКРЕБЙ (imp.), see соскребу́.

СОСКРЕБУ́, соскребёшь. Р. Соскрести́ (acc.). I. Соскреба́ть. To scrape off, rasp off.

СО́СЛАННЫЙ; со́слан, —а, —о, —ы (ppp). Р. Сосла́ть (acc.). I. Ссыла́ть. 1. To exile, banish. 2. To deport. (Also see сошлю́.)

СОСЛЁЖЕННЫЙ; сосле́жен, —а, —о, —ы (ppp), see сослежу́.

СОСЛЕЖУ́, соследи́шь. Р. Соследи́ть (arch.) (acc.). I. Сосле́живать. To track down (a wild animal).

СОСТА́ВЛЕННЫЙ; соста́влен, —а, —о, —ы (ppp), see соста́влю.

СОСТА́ВЛЮ, соста́вишь. Р. Соста́вить (acc.). I. Составля́ть. 1. To place (all or many). 2. To place together. 3. To formulate (e.g., a plan, an answer, etc.). 4. To form (e.g., an organization, an opinion, etc.). 5. To compose (e.g., sentences, a poem, etc.). 6. To compile. 7. To constitute, comprise, amount to. 8. To create (e.g., a name, happiness, etc.).

СОСТА́ВЬ (imp.), see соста́влю.

СОСТОЙ́ШЬ, see состою́.

СОСТОЙ (imp.), see состою́.

СОСТОЮ́, состои́шь. I. Состоя́ть (intr.). 1. To consist of, be made up of, include (e.g., a building of 10 floors, etc.) (из + gen.). 2. To consist in (e.g., "understanding consists in knowledge") (в + prep.). 3. To be (e.g., a subscriber, a member of, etc.) (inst. + gen.). 4. To be attached to (e.g., a consulate) (при + prep.). 5. To hold, occupy (the post or position of) (в + prep. + gen.). 6. To be in some condition or position (e.g., under the supervision of s.o., etc.) (под + inst.). 7. To be (as in the service) (на + prep.). 8. To be (e.g., in an organization) (в + prep.).

СОСТОЯ́Т, see состою́.

СОСТРИ́Г, состри́гла (past), see состригу́.

СОСТРИГЙ (imp.), see состригу́.

СОСТРИГУ́, состижёшь, состригу́т. Р. Состри́чь (acc.). I. Состига́ть. To shear off, clip off.

СОСТРИ́ЖЕННЫЙ; состри́жен, —а, —о, —ы (ppp), see состригу́.

СОСТРИЖЁШЬ, see состригу́.

СОСУ́, сосёшь. I. Соса́ть (acc.). 1. To suck (a liquid). 2. To suck on (as candy). 3. To have a dull pain (e.g., as in one's stomach) (intr.) (impers. + в + prep.). 4. (fig.) To cause pain (e.g., as grief gnaws at one's heart) (acc. of heart).

СО́ТКАННЫЙ; со́ткан, —а, —о, —ы (ppp), see сотку́.

СОТКЁШЬ, see сотку́.

СОТКИ́ (imp.), see сотку́.

СОТКУ́, соткёшь. Р. Сотка́ть (acc.). I. Ткать (mean. 1 and 2). 1. To weave (e.g., cloth). 2. To spin (e.g., a web) (of a spider). 3. (fig.) To weave or spin.

СОТРЁШЬ, see сотру́.

СОТРИ́ (imp.), see сотру́.

СОТРУ́, сотрёшь. Р. Стере́ть (acc.). I. Стира́ть. 1. To wipe off, wipe clean (acc. + с + gen.). 2. To erase, rub out, obliterate. 3. To rub (sore) (as one's heel). 4. To abrade, erode. 5. To grind (e.g., s.t. to powder (acc. + в + acc.). 6. (fig.) To erase, obliterate, blot out, (e.g., s.t. from memory).

СОТРЯ́С, сотряла́ (past), see сотрясу́.

СОТРЯСЁ́ННЫЙ; сотрясён, —а́, —о́, —ы́ (ppp), see сотрясу́.

СОТРЯСЁ́ШЬ, see сотрясу́.

СОТРЯСИ́ (imp.), see сотрясу́.

СОТРЯСУ́, сотрясёшь. Р. Сотрясти́ (acc.). I. Сотряса́ть. 1. (lit. and fig.) To shake. 2. To rend (as the air).

СОХ, со́хла (past). I. Со́хнуть (intr.). Р. Вы́сохнуть, засо́хнуть, просо́хнуть (mean. 1). 1. To dry, become dry. 2. To wither (of flowers). 3. To waste away (of people).

СОЧЛА́, сочло́, сочли́ (past), see сочту́ and счёл.

СОЧТЁ́ННЫЙ; сочтён, —а́, —о́, —ы́ (ppp), see сочту́.

СОЧТЁШЬ, see сочту́.

СОЧТИ́ (imp.), see сочту́.

СОЧТУ́, сочтёшь. Р. Счесть. I. Счита́ть. 1. To count, compute, reckon (intr.) or (acc.). 2. To consider (e.g., s.o. or s.t. to be s.t.) (acc. + inst.) or (acc. + за + acc.). 3. To consider (that) (что). 4. To take (s.t.) into consideration (e.g., enemy strength) (acc.).

СОЧТЯ́ (adv. past part.), see сочту́.

СОШЕ́ДШИЙ (arch.: сше́дший) (pap), see сошёл and сойду́.

СОШЁЛ, сошла́ (past). Р. Сойти́ (intr.). I. Сходи́ть. 1. To descend, come down, get off (from) (с + gen.). 2. To leave (e.g., the road, rails, etc.) (с + gen.). 3. To come off (from) (as paint from a wall, etc.) (с + gen.). 4. To disappear (from) (as color from one's face, snow from a garden, etc.) (с + gen.). 5. (fig.) To descend (on) (e.g., quiet on a city) (на + acc.). 6. To turn out (e.g., all right, badly, etc.) (intr.). 7. To be taken for (e.g., s.o. or s.t. else) (за + acc.). 8. To go mad (с + ума́). (Also see сойду́.)

СОШЛА́, сошло́, сошли́ (past), see сошёл and сойду́.

СОШЛЁШЬ, see сошлю́.

СОШЛИ́[1] (past), see сошёл and сойду́.

СОШЛИ́[2] (imp.), see сошлю́.

СОШЛЮ́, сошлёшь. Р. Сосла́ть (acc.). I. Ссыла́ть. 1. To exile, banish. 2. To deport.

СОШЬЁШЬ, see сошью́.

СОШЬЮ́, сошьёшь. Р. Сшить (acc.). I. Шить (mean. 1), сшива́ть. 1. To sew, make (e.g., a coat). 2. To sew together. 3. To lace together. 4. (med.) To suture. 5. To join (e.g., planks, etc.). 6. To build, make (e.g., a boat, door, etc.).

СПАДЁШЬ, see спаду́.

СПАДИ́ (imp.), see спаду́.

СПАДУ́, спадёшь. Р. Спасть (intr.). I. Спада́ть. 1. To lose (weight) (с + те́ла) or (с + лица́) or (в + те́ле). 2. To lose (one's voice) (с + го́лоса). 3. To fall off (as a wheel from a vehicle), fall down (from) (as a jacket from one's shoulders) (с + gen.) (3rd pers. only). 4. To abate, subside, (e.g., wind, heat, etc.).

СПАЛ[1], спа́ла (past), see спаду́.

СПАЛ[2], спала́, спа́ло, спа́ли (past). I. Спать (intr.). (lit. and fig.) To sleep, be asleep (also see сплю).

СПАС, спасла́ (past), see спасу́.

СПАСЁ́ННЫЙ; спасён, —а́, —о́, —ы́ (ppp), see спасу́.

СПАСЁШЬ, see спасу́.

СПАСИ́ (imp.), see спасу́.

СПАСУ́, спасёшь. Р. Спасти́ (acc.). I. Спаса́ть. 1. To save, rescue. 2.

To save (the life of s.o.) (acc. + dat.) (кому).

СПЕЙСЯ (imp.). Р. **Спиться** (intr.). I. **Спиваться**. To become a drunkard (also see **сопьюсь**).

СПЁК, **спекла** (past), see **спеку**.

СПЕКИ (imp.), see **спеку**.

СПЕКИСЬ (imp.), see **спекусь**.

СПЁКСЯ, **спеклась** (past), see **спекусь** and **спечётся**.

СПЕКУ́, **спечёшь**, **спекут**. Р. **Спечь** (acc./gen.). To bake.

СПЕКУ́СЬ, **спечёшься**, **спекутся**. Р. **Спечься** (intr.). 1. To bake. 2. To become burned (as a person burns in the sun).

СПЕКУ́ТСЯ (3rd pers. pl.), see **спечётся** and **спекусь**.

СПЁР, **сперла** (past). Р. **Спереть** (acc.). I. **Спирать** (mean. 3 and 4). 1. To steal (take away). 2. To carry away, take away, pull away. 3. To compress, squeeze. 4. To take away (one's breath) (impers. + acc. of breath or chest). (Also see **сопру**.)

СПЁРТЫЙ; **спёрт**, —а, —о, —ы (ppp), see **спёр** and **сопру**.

СПЕ́ТЫЙ; **спет**, —а, —о, —ы (ppp). Р. **Спеть**. I. **Петь**. 1. To sing (intr.). 2. To sing (a song, a part, etc.) (acc.). (Also see **спою**.)

СПЕЧЁННЫЙ; **спечён**, —а, —о, —ы (ppp), see **спеку**.

СПЕЧЁТСЯ, **спекутся** (3rd pers. only). Р. **Спечься** (intr.). I. **Спекаться**. 1. To coagulate, clot (of blood). 2. To cake (of coal, clay, mud, etc.).

СПЕЧЁШЬ, see **спеку**.

СПЕЧЁШЬСЯ, see **спекусь**.

СПЕ́ШЕННЫЙ; **спешен**, —а, —о, —ы (ppp), see **спешу**.

СПЕШИ́ (imp.), see **спешу**.

СПЕ́ШУ, **спешишь**. Р. **Спешить** (acc.). I. **Спешивать**. To dismount, order to dismount (e.g., a cavalry troop).

СПЕШУ́, **спешишь**. I. **Спешить** (intr.). Р. **Поспешить** (mean. 1). 1. To hurry. 2. To be fast (of a watch).

СПЕШЬ (imp.), see **спешу**.

СПИ (imp.), see **сплю**.

СПИ́САННЫЙ; **списан**, —а, —о, —ы (ppp), see **спишу**.

СПИ́ШЕШЬ, see **спишу**.

СПИШИ́ (imp.), see **спишу**.

СПИШУ́, **спишешь**. Р. **Списать** (acc.).

I. **Списывать**. 1. To copy (write down). 2. To copy (from), (reproduce a drawing, etc.) (с + gen.). 3. To copy, to cheat, crib (s.t. from s.o.) (acc. + у + gen.). 4. To represent (as a character on the stage). 5. To write off (s.t.) (e.g., a debt). 6. (mil.) To transfer (s.o.).

СПИШЬ, see **сплю**.

СПЛА́ВЛЕННЫЙ; **сплавлен**, —а, —о, —ы (ppp), see **сплавлю**.

СПЛА́ВЛЮ, **сплавишь**. Р. **Сплавить** (acc.). I. **Сплавлять**. 1. To fuse, melt, alloy. 2. To float away/down, raft (as logs down a stream). 3. To get rid of (as s.o., s.t.).

СПЛАВЬ (imp.), see **сплавлю**.

СПЛЁЛ, **сплела** (past), see **сплету**.

СПЛЕТЁННЫЙ; **сплетён**, —а, —о, —ы (ppp), see **сплету**.

СПЛЕТЁШЬ, see **сплету**.

СПЛЕТИ́ (imp.), see **сплету**.

СПЛЕТУ́, **сплетёшь**. Р. **Сплести** (acc.). I. **Сплетать**, **плести** (mean. 1, 2, 5). 1. To braid. 2. To weave (e.g., a basket, etc.). 3. To interweave. 4. (fig.) To weave, interweave. 5. To concoct (a plot, intrigue, etc.). 6. To splice.

СПЛЁТШИЙ (pap), see **сплету**.

СПЛЕТЯ́ (adv. past part.), see **сплету**.

СПЛОЧЁННЫЙ; **сплочён**, —а, —о, —ы (ppp), see **сплочу**.

СПЛОЧУ́, **сплотишь**. Р. **Сплотить** (acc.). I. **Сплачивать**. 1. To join (as planks, in carpentry). 2. To close (as ranks, in marching). 3. To unite (e.g., the working people).

СПЛЫВЁШЬ, see **сплыву**.

СПЛЫВИ́ (imp.), see **сплыву**.

СПЛЫВУ́, **сплывёшь**. Р. **Сплыть** (intr.). I. **Сплывать**. 1. To float away down stream. 2. To overflow. 3. To run off, flow away.

СПЛЮ, **спишь**. I. **Спать** (intr.). (lit. and fig.) To sleep, to be asleep.

СПЛЯ́САННЫЙ; **сплясан**, —а, —о, —ы (ppp), see **спляшу**.

СПЛЯ́ШЕШЬ, see **спляшу**.

СПЛЯШИ́ (imp.), see **спляшу**.

СПЛЯШУ́, **спляшешь**. Р. **Сплясать** (acc.) or (intr.). I. **Плясать**. (lit. and fig.) To dance.

СПОДО́БЛЕННЫЙ; **сподоблен**, —а, —о, —ы (ppp), see **сподоблю**.

СПОДОБЛЮ, сподобишь. Р. Сподобить (arch.) (acc.) (often impers.). I. Сподоблять. 1. To favor (s.o. with s.t.) (acc. + inst.). 2. To grant (s.o.) the favor of (doing s.t.) (acc. + inf.).

СПОДОБЛЮСЬ, сподобишься. Р. Сподобиться (arch.) (gen.) or (+ inf.). I. Сподобляться. 1. To be considered worthy of. 2. To be favored with (used ironically or jokingly).

СПОДОБЬ (imp.), see сподоблю.

СПОДОБЬСЯ (imp.), see сподоблюсь.

СПОЁШЬ, see спою.

СПОЙ (imp.), see спою.

СПОЛЗ, сползла (past), see сползу.

СПОЛЗЁШЬ, see сползу.

СПОЛЗЙ (imp.), see сползу.

СПОЛЗУ, сползёшь. Р. Сползти (intr.) I. Сползать, спалзывать. 1. To slip down, creep down, slip off, slide down, work down (of things and people). 2. (fig.) To backslide, slip back (to), lapse (into) (к + dat.).

СПОРЕШЬ, see спорю.

СПОРЙ (imp.), see спорю.

СПОРОТЫЙ; спорот, —а, —о, —ы (ppp), see спорю.

СПОРЮ, спорешь. Р. Спороть (acc.). I. Спарывать. To rip off.

СПОХВАЧУСЬ, спохватишься. Р. Спохватиться (intr.). I. Спохватываться. To recollect suddenly, become suddenly aware (often with that, что).

СПОЮ, споёшь. Р. Спеть. I. Петь. 1. To sing (intr.). 2. To sing (a song or part, etc.) (acc.).

СПРАВЛЕННЫЙ; справлен, —а, —о, —ы (ppp), see справлю.

СПРАВЛЮ, справишь. Р. Справить (acc.). I. Справлять. 1. To celebrate (as an anniversary). 2. To do, accomplish (e.g., some work, business, etc.). 3. To buy. 4. To obtain. 5. To repair.

СПРАВЬ (imp.), see справлю.

СПРОВАДЬ (imp.), see спроважу.

СПРОВАЖЕННЫЙ; спроважен, —а, —о, —ы (ppp), see спроважу.

СПРОВАЖУ, спровадишь. Р. Спровадить (acc.). I. Спроваживать. 1. To escort or show (s.o.) out, send on one's way (as an unwanted guest). 2. To get rid of (s.o.).

СПРОШЕННЫЙ; спрошен, —а, —о, —ы (ppp), see спрошу.

СПРОШУ, спросишь. Р. Спросить.

I. Спрашивать. 1. To ask (intr.). 2. To ask (s.o.) about (s.o. or s.t.) (acc. + о + prep.). 3. To ask, request (s.t.) of (s.o.) (acc. + у + gen.). 4. To ask, inquire, about (s.o. or s.t.) (о + prep.). 5. To ask to see or talk to (s.o.) (acc.). 6. To ask for (s.t.) (acc./gen.). 7. To hold (s.o.) accountable for (s.t.) (c + gen. + за + acc.).

СПРЯГ, спрягла (past), see спрягу.

СПРЯГЙ (imp.), see спрягу.

СПРЯГУ, спряжёшь, спрягут. Р. Спрячь (acc.). I. Спрягать. To hitch together (e.g., horses).

СПРЯДЁННЫЙ; спрядён, —а, —о, —ы (ppp), see спряду.

СПРЯДЁШЬ, see спряду.

СПРЯДЙ (imp.), see спряду.

СПРЯДУ, спрядёшь. Р. Спрясть (acc.). I. Прясть. To spin (as yarn).

СПРЯЖЁННЫЙ; спряжён, —а, —о, —ы (ppp), see спрягу.

СПРЯЖЁШЬ, see спрягу.

СПРЯЛ, спряла (and спряла), спряло, спряли (past), see спряду.

СПРЯМЛЁННЫЙ; спрямлён, —а, —о, —ы (ppp), see спрямлю.

СПРЯМЛЮ, спрямишь. Р. Спрямить (acc.). I. Спрямлять. To straighten (s.t. crooked).

СПРЯТАННЫЙ; спрятан, —а, —о, —ы (ppp), see спрячу.

СПРЯЧЕШЬ, see спрячу.

СПРЯЧУ, спрячешь. Р. Спрятать (acc.). I. Прятать. 1. (lit. and fig.) To conceal, hide, secrete. 2. To put away.

СПРЯЧЬ (imp.), see спрячу.

СПУЩЕННЫЙ; спущен, —а, —о, —ы (ppp), see спущу.

СПУЩУ, спустишь. Р. Спустить (acc.). I. Спускать. 1. To let down, lower, put down (as a window, a flag, etc.). 2. To reduce, lower (as a price, water level, noise level). 3. To launch (as a boat). 4. To let loose, out, free, release. 5. To empty, drain, deflate. 6. To trip, release, trigger. 7. To lose (as weight). 8. To squander (as money). 9. To get rid of, sell off. 10. (typ.) To impose. (For other usages see unabridged dictionary.)

СПЯТ (3rd pers. pl.). I. Спать (intr.). (lit. and fig.) To sleep, be asleep (also see сплю).

СПЯТЬ (imp.), see спя́чу.
СПЯ́ЧУ, спя́тишь. Р. Спя́тить (intr.).
To go out of one's mind.
СРАЖЁННЫЙ; сражён, —а́, —о́, —ы́
(ppp), see сражу́.
СРАЖУ́, срази́шь. Р. Срази́ть (acc.).
I. Сража́ть. 1. To slay, kill. 2. To
strike down (of a bullet, etc.). 3. (fig.)
To strike (down) (of an illness).
4. (fig.) To overwhelm, shock, stagger.
СРАМЛЮ́, срами́шь. I. Срами́ть (acc.).
Р. Осрами́ть (mean. 1). 1. To put to
shame, shame. 2. To reproach, scold.
СРАСТЁШЬСЯ, see срасту́сь.
СРАСТИ́СЬ (imp.), see срасту́сь.
СРАСТУ́СЬ, срастёшься. Р. Срасти́сь
(intr.). I. Сраста́ться. 1. To knit,
grow together (of broken bones, etc.).
2. (bot.) To accrete. 3. (fig.) To grow
together, to become accustomed to,
become inseparable (of people) (с +
inst.).
СРАЩЁННЫЙ; сращён, —а́, —о́, —ы́
(ppp), see сращу́.
СРАЩУ́, срасти́шь. Р. Срасти́ть (acc.).
I. Сра́щивать. 1. (lit. and fig.) To
join. 2. To set (as a broken leg).
3. To splice.
СРЕ́ЖЕШЬ, see сре́жу.
СРЕ́ЖУ, сре́жешь. Р. Сре́зать (acc.).
I. Среза́ть, реза́ть (mean. 1, 5, 6).
1. To cut off. 2. (fig.) To cut down.
3. (fig.) To shock, stagger. 4. (fig.)
To cut short (e.g., s.o. who is talking).
5. (fig.) To cut (as a ball in tennis).
6. To fail (s.o.) (in an exam., etc.).
СРЕ́ЖЬ (imp.), see сре́жу.
СРЕ́ЗАННЫЙ; сре́зан, —а, —о, —ы
(ppp), see сре́жу.
СРО́ЕШЬ, see сро́ю.
СРОЙ (imp.), see сро́ю.
СРОСЛА́СЬ (past), see срасту́сь and
сро́сся.
СРО́ССЯ, сросла́сь (past), see срасту́сь.
СРО́Ю, сро́ешь. Р. Срыть (acc.). I.
Срыва́ть. 1. To raze (e.g., a structure).
2. To level (e.g., a mound).
СРУ́БЛЕННЫЙ; сру́блен, —а, —о,
—ы (ppp), see срублю́.
СРУБЛЮ́, сру́бишь. Р. Сруби́ть (acc.).
I. Сруба́ть (mean. 1 and 2), руби́ть
(mean. 1 and 3). 1. To fell, cut down.
2. To cut off, to chop off. 3. To con-
struct (with logs, trees, etc.) (e.g., a
barn, etc.).

СРЫ́ТЫЙ; сры́т, —а, —о, —ы (ppp),
see сро́ю.
ССА́ЖЕННЫЙ; сса́жен, —а, —о, —ы
(ppp), see ссажу́.
ССАЖУ́, сса́дишь. Р. Ссади́ть (acc.).
I. Сса́живать. 1. To help (s.o.) down.
2. To assist in alighting (as a passenger). 3. To drop or put ashore (a
passenger). 4. To scratch, abrade.
5. To knock down, bring down (with
a shot).
ССЕК, ссекла́ (and arch.: ссе́кла,
ссе́кло, etc.) (past), see ссеку́.
ССЕКИ́ (imp.), see ссеку́.
ССЕКУ́, ссечёшь, ссеку́т. Р. Ссечь
(acc.). I. Ссека́ть. To cut off.
ССЕЧЁННЫЙ; ссечён, —а́, —о́, —ы́
(ppp), see ссеку́.
ССЕ́ЧЕННЫЙ; ссе́чен, —а, —о, —ы
(arch.) (ppp), see ссеку́.
ССЕЧЁШЬ, see ссеку́.
ССО́САННЫЙ; ссо́сан, —а, —о, —ы
(ppp), see ссосу́.
ССОСЁШЬ, see ссосу́.
ССОСИ́ (imp.), see ссосу́.
ССОСУ́, ссосёшь. Р. Ссоса́ть. I. Сса́сы-
вать. 1. To suck all of (some liquid)
(acc.). 2. To suck and finish (as
candy, etc.) (acc./gen.). 3. To suck a
quantity of (e.g., milk) (acc.).
ССУ́ЖЕННЫЙ; ссу́жен, —а, —о, —ы
(ppp), see ссужу́.
ССУЖУ́, ссу́дишь. Р. Ссуди́ть (acc. +
inst.) or (dat. + acc.). I. Ссужа́ть.
To lend, loan (as s.o. money) (acc. of
pers. + inst. of money) or (dat. of
pers. + acc. of money).
ССЫ́ПАННЫЙ; ссы́пан, —а, —о, —ы
(ppp), see ссы́плю.
ССЫ́ПЛЕШЬ, see ссы́плю.
ССЫ́ПЛЮ, ссы́плешь. Р. Ссы́пать
(acc.). I. Ссыпа́ть. To pour (as sand,
grain, etc., in, into, on, s.t.).
ССЫПЬ (imp.), see ссы́плю.
СТАВА́Й (imp.), see стаёт.
СТАВА́Я (adv. pres. part.), see стаёт.
СТА́ВЛЕННЫЙ; ставлён, —а, —о,
—ы (ppp), see ста́влю.
СТА́ВЛЮ, ста́вишь. I. Ста́вить (acc.).
Р. Поста́вить. 1. (lit. and fig.) To
place, put, set. 2. To erect, raise,
install, mount. 3. To organize, regulate. 4. To produce, stage, put on (as
a play). 5. To raise, ask, put (e.g., a
problem, a question). 6. To conduct

(as an experiment). 7. To regard, value, consider (as s.t. the equal of s.t. else, etc.). 8. To bet, stake. (For other lit. and fig. meanings see unabridged dictionary.)

СТАВЬ (imp.), see **ставлю.**

СТАЕТ, стают (3rd pers. only). Р. **Стаять** (intr.). I. **Стаивать.** To melt away (of snow or ice).

СТАЁТ, стают. I. **Ставать** (arch.). 1. To become. 2. To be sufficient (impers. + gen.).

СТАЙ (imp.), see **стает.**

СТАНЕШЬ, see **стану.**

СТАНОВЛЮСЬ, становишься. I. **Становиться.** Р. **Стать.** 1. To stand (intr.). 2. To start (e.g., to work, or some activity) (к + dat.) also (на/в/за + acc.) and (у + gen.). 3. To be, exist (impers. + gen.) (e.g., a forest). 4. To become (e.g., a doctor) (inst.). 5. (lit. and fig.) To take up a position (intr.). (For other detailed idiomatic usages see unabridged dictionary.)

СТАНУ, станешь. Р. **Стать.** I. **Становиться** (mean. 1, 4, 5, 7, 13). 1. To stand (intr.). 2. To stand for (e.g., the right) (за + acc.), (the defense of) (на + acc. + gen.). 3. To start, begin (to do s.t.) (+ inf.). 4. To start (e.g., work or some activity) (к + dat.) (also (на/в/за + acc.) and (у + gen.). 5. To be, exist (impers. + gen.) (e.g., a forest). 6. To be sufficient (impers. + gen.). 7. To become (e.g., a doctor) (inst.). 8. To happen (e.g., to or with s.o.) (с + inst.). 9. To cost (e.g., s.o. $10) (inst. of s.o. + в + acc. of $10). 10. To die (gen. + не + impers.). 11. To arise (as a question) (intr.). 12. To stop (intr.). 13. (lit. and fig.) To take up a position (intr.). (For other detailed idiomatic usages see unabridged dictionary.)

СТАНЬ (imp.), see **стану.**

СТАЮТ (3rd pers. pl.), see **стает.**

СТАЮТ (3rd pers. pl.), see **стаёт.**

СТЁК, стекла (past), see **стечёт.**

СТЕКИ (imp.), see **стечёт.**

СТЕКУТ (3rd pers. pl.), see **стечёт.**

СТЕЛЕШЬ, see **стелю.**

СТЕЛИ (imp.), see **стелю.**

СТЕЛЮ, стелешь. I. **Стлать** and **стелить** (acc.). Р. **Постлать** (mean. 1, 2, 5), **постелить** (mean. 1, 2, 5), **настлать** (mean. 3, 4, 5), **настелить**

(mean. 3, 5). 1. To spread (as a tablecloth, etc.). 2. To make, spread (as a bed). 3. To lay (as a carpet). 4. To lay (as a floor). 5. To spread (as a layer of straw).

СТЁР, стёрла (past). Р. **Стереть** (acc.). I. **Стирать.** 1. To wipe off, wipe clean (acc. + с + gen.). 2. To erase, rub out, obliterate. 3. To rub (sore) (as one's heel). 4. To abrade, erode. 5. To grind (e.g., s.t. to powder) (acc. + в + acc.). 6. (fig.) To erase, blot out, obliterate (e.g., s.t. from memory). (Also see **сотру.**)

СТЕРЕВ and **стёрши** (adv. past part.), see **стёр** and **сотру.**

СТЕРЁГ, стерегла (past), see **стерегу.**

СТЕРЕГИ (imp.), see **стерегу.**

СТЕРЕГУ, стережёшь, стерегут. I. **Стеречь** (acc.). 1. To watch, guard. 2. To take care of, observe closely. 3. To be on the lookout for, watch for.

СТЕРЕЖЁШЬ, see **стерегу.**

СТЕРПИ (imp.), see **стерплю.**

СТЕРПИШЬ, see **стерплю.**

СТЕРПЛЮ, стерпишь. Р. **Стерпеть.** 1. To bear, endure (acc.). 2. To restrain oneself (intr.) (employed usually with the negative).

СТЕРПЯТ, see **стерплю.**

СТЁРТЫЙ; стёрт, —а, —о, —ы (ppp), see **стёр** and **сотру.**

СТЁРШИ and **стерёв** (adv. past part.), see **стёр** and **сотру.**

СТЁСАННЫЙ; стёсан, —а, —о, —ы (ppp), see **стешу.**

СТЕЧЁТ, стекут (3rd pers. only). Р. **Стечь** (intr.). I. **Стекать.** 1. To flow off/down, run off/down; drain off. 2. To trickle down, drip off.

СТЁШЕШЬ, see **стешу.**

СТЕШИ (imp.), see **стешу.**

СТЕШУ, стёшешь. Р. **Стесать** (acc.). I. **Стёсывать.** To hew off, plane off.

СТИХ, стихла (past). Р. **Стихнуть** (intr.). I. **Стихать.** 1. To cease (of noise, etc.). 2. To cease making noise (of people, birds, etc.). 3. To calm down, abate (of wind, etc.).

СТОЛКИ (imp.), see **столку.**

СТОЛКУ, столчёшь, столкут. Р. **Столочь** (acc.). To grind.

СТОЛОК, столкла (past), see **столку.**

СТОЛЧЁННЫЙ; столчён, —а, —о, —ы (ppp), see **столку.**

СТОЛЧЁШЬ, see столку́.

СТОНА́Я (adv. pres. part.), see стону́.

СТО́НЕШЬ, see стону́.

СТОНИ́ (imp.), see стону́.

СТОНУ́ (and стона́ю), сто́нешь. I.
Стона́ть. 1. (lit. and fig.) To groan,
moan (intr.) or (acc.). 2. To suffer,
languish (intr.).

СТО́ПЛЕННЫЙ; сто́плен, —а, —о,
—ы (ppp), see стоплю́.

СТОПЛЮ́, сто́пишь. Р. Стопи́ть
(acc.). I. Ста́пливать (mean. 1, 2).
1. To fuse. 2. To melt. 3. To heat
(e.g., a bath, a stove, etc.).

СТО́ПТАННЫЙ; сто́птан, —а, —о,
—ы (ppp), see стопчу́.

СТО́ПЧЕШЬ, see стопчу́.

СТОПЧИ́ (imp.), see стопчу́.

СТОПЧУ́, сто́пчешь. Р. Стопта́ть
(acc.). I. Ста́птывать. 1. To wear
down (at the heels) (shoes). 2. To
trample (as grass, etc.).

СТО́ЙШЬ, see стою́.

СТОЙ (imp.), see стою́.

СТОЮ́, стои́шь. I. Стоя́ть (intr.).
1. To stand (in a vertical position).
2. To stand, be located (as a glass in
a cupboard) (в + prep.), (a house on
a lot) (на + prep.), (a soldier at his
post) (на + prep.), (etc.). 3. To be
(of weather, frost, noise, etc.). 4. To
be (e.g., on an agenda) (на + prep.).
5. To stop, be at a standstill (of a
clock, a bus, work). 6. To stay, live
(e.g., in an apartment) (в + prep.).
7. (fig.) To stand up (for), uphold
(s.o. or s.t.) (за + acc.). 8. Halt!
(imp.: стой!). 9. To not stint (on),
not spare (не + стоя́ть + за + inst.).
(For other usages see unabridged
dictionary.)

СТОЯ́Т, see стою́.

СТРА́ВЛЕННЫЙ; стра́влен, —а, —о,
—ы (ppp), see стравлю́.

СТРАВЛЮ́, стра́вишь. Р. Стра́вить
(acc.). I. Стра́вливать. 1. To set on,
against (as one person against another,
one dog on another, etc.). 2. To clean,
pickle, etch. 3. To ruin, spoil (as a
field by allowing cattle to graze).
4. To use up (as hay, corn, for feed).
5. To waste, spend (e.g., money).
6. To poison (s.o. or s.t.). 7. (naut.)
To slack off. 8. To let out, let off (as
steam, to reduce pressure).

СТРА́ЖДЕШЬ, see стра́жду.

СТРА́ЖДИ (imp.), see стра́жду.

СТРА́ЖДУ, стра́ждешь (arch. and
bookish forms) (modern forms: стра-
да́ю, страда́ешь, etc.). I. Страда́ть
(intr.). Р. Пострада́ть (mean. 3, 4, 5).
1. To suffer (from an illness) (inst.).
2. To suffer (from some deficiency:
as a person from megalomania, a
book from turgid style, etc.) (inst.).
3. To suffer (e.g., from floods, drought
etc.) (of people, crops, etc.) (от +
gen.). 4. To suffer (for s.o. or s.t.) (за
+ acc.). 5. To suffer (because of s.o.
or s.t.) (из-за + gen.). 6. To pine for
(s.o. or s.t.) (по + dat./prep.). 7. To
suffer (e.g., of a person, as one's
memory, etc.).

СТРА́ЖДУЩИЙ (arch., bookish) (pres.
a.p.) (modern form: страда́ющий),
see стра́жду.

СТРЕКО́ЧЕШЬ, see стрекочу́.

СТРЕКОЧИ́ (imp.), see стрекочу́.

СТРЕКОЧУ́, стреко́чешь. I. Стреко-
та́ть (intr.). 1. To chirr, make a
chirring sound. 2. (fig.) To chatter
incessantly (of people).

СТРЕМЛЮ́, стреми́шь. I. Стреми́ть
(bookish) (acc.). (lit. and fig.) To
direct (s.t., a stream of water, one's
thoughts, etc.).

СТРИГ, стри́гла (past), see стригу́.

СТРИГИ́ (imp.), see стригу́.

СТРИГУ́, стрижёшь, стригу́т. I.
Стричь (acc.). Р. Остри́чь, обстри́чь.
1. To cut, clip, shear. 2. To give (s.o.)
a hair cut (acc. of person).

СТРИ́ЖЕННЫЙ; стри́жен, —а, —о,
—ы (ppp), see стригу́.

СТРИЖЁШЬ, see стригу́.

СТРУСЬ (imp.), see стру́шу.

СТРУ́ШЕННЫЙ; стру́шен, —а, —о,
—ы (ppp), see стружу́.

СТРУШУ́, струси́шь. Р. Струси́ть
(acc.). To pour out while shaking (as
sugar from a sack).

СТРУ́ШУ, стру́сишь. Р. Стру́сить
(intr.). I. Тру́сить. 1. To be afraid,
frightened. 2. To be afraid of (gen.)
or (пе́ред + inst.).

СТРЯС, стрясла́ (past), see стрясу́.

СТРЯСЁННЫЙ; стрясён, —а́, —о́,
—ы́ (ppp), see стрясу́.

СТРЯСЁШЬ, see стрясу́.

СТРЯСИ́ (imp.), see стрясу́.

СТРЯСУ́, стрясёшь. Р. Стрясти́ (acc.). I. Стряса́ть. To shake down.

СТУ́ЖЕННЫЙ; сту́жен, —а, —о, —ы (ppp), see стужу́.

СТУЖУ́, сту́дишь. I. Студи́ть (acc.). Р. Остуди́ть. 1. To cool. 2. To chill.

СТУПЛЮ́, сту́пишь. Р. Ступи́ть (intr.). I. Ступа́ть. 1. To step, take a step. 2. To enter. 3. To find o.s. (somewhere), set foot (on) (e.g., foreign soil) (на + acc.).

СТУЧА́Т, see стучу́.

СТУЧИ́ (imp.), see стучу́.

СТУЧИ́ШЬ, see стучу́.

СТУЧУ́, стучи́шь. I. Стуча́ть (intr.). Р. Постуча́ть (mean. 2). 1. To make a knocking noise, knock. 2. To knock (e.g., at the door) (в + acc.).

СТЫЖУ́, стыди́шь. I. Стыди́ть (acc.). Р. Пристыди́ть (mean. 1). 1. To make (s.o.) ashamed of himself. 2. To disgrace.

СТЫЛ, сты́ла (past), see сты́ну.

СТЫ́НЕШЬ, see сты́ну.

СТЫ́НУ, сты́нешь. I. Стыть and сты́нуть (intr.). Р. Осты́ть and осты́нуть (mean. 1 and 3). 1. To cool off, become cool. 2. (fig.) To chill, freeze (e.g., one's blood). 3. (fig.) To cool (down) (of one's interest, ardor, animation, etc.).

СТЫНЬ (imp.), see сты́ну.

СУГУ́БЛЮ, сугу́бишь. I. Сугу́бить (arch.) (acc.). To intensify, increase, multiply.

СУГУ́БЬ (imp.), see сугу́блю.

СУЕЧУ́СЬ, суети́шься. I. Суети́ться (intr.). To bustle about.

СУЁШЬ, see сую́.

СУЖДЁННЫЙ; сужде́н, —а́, —б, —ы́ (ppp), see сужу́ (mean. 6).

СУ́ЖЕННЫЙ; су́жен, —а, —о, —ы (ppp), see су́жу.

СУЖУ́, су́дишь. I. Суди́ть (mean. 1 thru 5). Р. Суди́ть (mean. 6). 1. To try (as a criminal) (acc.). 2. To referee, umpire (as a game) (acc.). 3. To judge, evaluate (s.o. or s.t.) (acc.). 4. To judge, think (intr.). 5. To form an opinion about (s.t. or s.o.) (о + prep.) or (по + dat.). 6. To be fated to (of a person) (impers. + dat. + inf.).

СУ́ЖУ, су́зишь. Р. Су́зить (acc.). I. Су́живать. 1. To narrow. 2. To

taper. 3. To lessen, limit. 4. (tech.) To throttle.

СУЗЬ (imp.), see су́жу.

СУЙ (imp.), see сую́.

СУМАСБРО́ДЬ (imp.), see сумасбро́жу.

СУМАСБРО́ЖУ, сумасбро́дишь. I. Сумасбро́дить (intr.). To behave rashly or whimsically.

СУ́ПЛЮ, су́пишь. I. Су́пить (acc.). Р. Насу́пить. To frown, knit one's brow (acc. of brow).

СУ́ПЬ (imp.), see су́плю.

СУРЬМЛЁННЫЙ; сурьмлён, —а́, —б, —ы́ (ppp), see сурьмлю́.

СУРЬМЛЮ́, сурьми́шь. I. Сурьми́ть (arch.) (acc.). Р. Насурьми́ть. To decorate, cover with antimony (used as a cosmetic and in pigments).

СУЮ́, суёшь. I. Сова́ть (acc.). Р. Су́нуть. To thrust, shove, poke (as one's hand in one's pocket, a fist in one's face, etc.).

СФАЛЬШИ́ВЛЮ, сфальши́вишь. Р. Сфальши́вить (intr.). I. Фальши́вить. 1. To dissemble, act hypocritically. 2. To sing or play off key.

СФАЛЬШИ́ВЬ (imp.), see сфальши́влю.

СХВА́ЧЕННЫЙ; схва́чен, —а, —о, —ы (ppp), see схвачу́.

СХВАЧУ́, схва́тишь. Р. Схвати́ть (acc.). I. Схва́тывать. 1. To grasp, seize, snatch. 2. To fasten together, bind. 3. To catch (as a cold, measles, etc.). 4. (fig.) To grasp (as a meaning). 5. To set, harden (as concrete, etc.) (impers. + acc.). 6. To note, describe.

СХЛОПО́ТАННЫЙ; схлопо́тан, —а, —о, —ы (ppp), see схлопочу́.

СХЛОПО́ЧЕШЬ, see схлопочу́.

СХЛОПОЧИ́ (imp.), see схлопочу́.

СХЛОПОЧУ́, схлопо́чешь. Р. Схлопота́ть. 1. To obtain (after some effort) (acc.). 2. To look after (s.t.), try to obtain (s.t.) (acc.) or (насчёт + gen.).

СХОЖУ́[1], схо́дишь. I. Сходи́ть (intr.). Р. Сойти́. 1. To descend, come down, get off (from) (с + gen.). 2. To leave (e.g., the road, rails, etc.) (с + gen.). 3. To come off (from) (as paint from a wall, etc.) (с + gen.). 4. To disappear (from) (as color from one's face, snow from a garden, etc.) (с + gen.). 5. (fig.) To descend (on) (e.g., quiet on a city) (на + acc.). 6. To turn out (e.g., all right, badly, etc.).

7. To be taken for (e.g., s.o. or s.t. else) (за + acc.). 8. To go mad (с + ума́).

СХОЖУ², схо́дишь. P. Сходи́ть (intr.). I. Ходи́ть (mean. 2). 1. To go (and do s.t.) and return. 2. To relieve o.s. (i.e., nature).

СЦЕ́ЖЕННЫЙ; сце́жен, —а, —о, —ы (ppp), see сцежу́.

СЦЕЖУ́, сце́дишь. P. Сцеди́ть (acc.). I. Сце́живать. To decant, draw off.

СЦЕ́ПЛЕННЫЙ; сце́плен, —а, —о, —ы (ppp), see сцеплю́.

СЦЕПЛЮ́, сце́пишь. P. Сцепи́ть (acc.). I. Сцепля́ть. 1. To couple, join together, hook up. 2. To mesh, engage, put in gear. 3. To clench (e.g., one's teeth, jaws).

СЧЁЛ, сочла́ (past). P. Счесть. I. Счита́ть. 1. To count, compute, reckon (intr.) or (acc.). 2. To consider (e.g., s.o. or s.t. to be s.t.) (acc. + inst.) or (acc. + за + acc.). 3. To consider (that) (что). 4. To take (s.t.) into consideration (e.g., enemy strength) (acc.). (Also see сочту́.)

СЧЁРЧЕННЫЙ; сче́рчен, —а, —о, —ы (ppp), see счерчу́.

СЧЕРЧУ́, сче́ртишь. P. Счерти́ть (acc.). I. Сче́рчивать. To copy (e.g., a sketch, drawing, etc.).

СЧЁСАННЫЙ; счёсан, —а, —о, —ы (ppp), see счешу́.

СЧЁТШИЙ (pap), see сочту́.

СЧЁШЕШЬ, see счешу́.

СЧЕШИ́ (imp.), see счешу́.

СЧЕШУ́, сче́шешь. P. Счеса́ть (acc.). I. Счёсывать. 1. To comb out (as hair). 2. To scratch off. 3. To card (wool, flax, etc.).

СЧИ́СТИ (imp.), see счи́щу.

СЧИСТЬ (imp.), see счи́щу.

СЧИ́ЩЕННЫЙ; счи́щен, —а, —о, —ы (ppp), see счи́щу.

СЧИ́ЩУ, счи́стишь. P. Счи́стить (acc.). I. Счища́ть. 1. To clear away, remove. 2. To clean off.

СШЕ́ДШИЙ (arch.) (also соше́дший) (pap). P. Сойти́ (intr.). I. Сходи́ть. 1. To descend (come down, get off (from) (с + gen.). 2. To leave (e.g., the road, rails, etc.) (с + gen.). 3. To come off (from) (as paint from a wall, etc.) (с + gen.). 4. To disappear (from) (as color from one's face, snow

from a garden, etc.) (с + gen.). 5. (fig.) To descend (on) (e.g., quiet on a city) (на + acc.). 6. To turn out (e.g., all right, badly, etc.). 7. To be taken for (e.g., s.o. or s.t. else (за + acc.). 8. To go mad (с + ума́). (Also see сойду́.)

СШЕЙ (imp.). P. Сшить (acc.). I. Шить (mean. 1 and 2), сшива́ть. 1. To sew, make (e.g., a coat). 2. To sew together. 3. To lace together. 4. (med.) To suture. 5. To join (e.g., planks, etc.). 6. To build, make (e.g., a boat, door, etc.). (Also see сошью́.)

СШИБ, сши́бла (past), see сшибу́.

СШИБЁШЬ, see сшибу́.

СШИБИ́ (imp.), see сшибу́.

СШИ́БЛЕННЫЙ; сши́блен, —а, —о, —ы (ppp), see сшибу́.

СШИБУ́, сшибёшь. P. Сшиби́ть (acc.). I. Сшиба́ть. 1. To knock down with a blow (e.g., off one's feet) (acc. + с + gen.). 2. To knock together (as billiard balls).

СШИ́ТЫЙ; сши́т, —а, —о, —ы (ppp), see сшей and сошью́.

С'Е́ДЕННЫЙ; с'е́ден, —а, —о, —ы (ppp), see с'ем.

С'Е́ДЕШЬ, see с'е́ду.

С'ЕДИ́М, с'еди́те, с'едя́т (pl. forms), see с'ем.

С'Е́ДУ, с'е́дешь. P. С'е́хать (intr.). I. С'езжа́ть. 1. To go or come down (from) (с + gen.). 2. To leave or move from (e.g., as a car leaves or turns off the highway, a person leaves an apartment) (с + gen.). 3. To shift, slip (as a tie, hat slips to one side). 4. (fig.) To shift (e.g., as a topic of discussion shifts from one thing to another) (с + gen. + на + acc.). 5. (fig.) To come down (from one price to a lower) (с + gen. + на + acc.).

С'ЕДЯ́Т, see с'еди́м and с'ем.

С'Е́ЗДИ (imp.), see с'е́зжу.

С'ЕЗЖА́Й (imp.), see с'е́ду.

С'Е́ЗЖУ, с'е́здишь. P. С'е́здить. 1. To go (somewhere) and return (by conveyance) (intr.). 2. To strike, hit (s.o.) (acc./dat.).

С'ЕЛ, с'е́ла (past), see с'ем.

С'ЕМ, с'ешь, с'ест (sing. forms). P. С'есть (acc.). I. Есть (mean. 1 thru 4), с'еда́ть. 1. (lit. and fig.) To eat (up). 2. To corrode (of chemical action). 3. To sting or burn (as one's eyes). 4. To exasperate, abuse, reproach. 5. To bear, endure, receive (as an insult). 6. To grind off, wear off (as teeth).

С’ЕСТ, see **с’ем**.

С’ЕШЬ[1] (2nd pers. sing.), see **с’ем**.

С’ЕШЬ[2] (imp.), see **с’ем**.

С’ЯЗВЛЮ, **с’язви́шь**. Р. **С’язви́ть** (intr.) or (acc.). I. **Язви́ть**. To speak sarcastically, caustically.

СЫ́ПЛЕШЬ, see **сы́плю**.

СЫ́ПЛЮ, **сы́плешь**. I. **Сы́пать**. 1. To strew, scatter (as sand, grain, etc.) (acc.). 2. To pour (as sand, grain, etc.) (acc.). 3. To throw about (as sand, etc.) (acc./inst.). 4. (fig.) To pour, rain (as shells on the enemy) (acc./inst.). 5. (fig.) To spout verbally (of a person) (e.g., data, witticisms, etc.) (acc./inst.). 6. To fall (of rain, snow, etc.) (intr.). 7. To lower, cast (a net into the water) (acc.).

СЫПЬ (imp.), see **сы́плю**.

СЫ́СКАННЫЙ; **сы́скан, —а, —о, —ы** (ppp), see **сыщу́**.

СЫ́ЩЕШЬ, see **сыщу́**.

СЫЩИ́ (imp.), see **сыщу́**.

СЫЩУ́, **сы́щешь**. Р. **Сыска́ть** (acc.). 1. To find. 2. To track down (as an animal).

СЭКОНО́МЛЕННЫЙ; **сэконо́млен, —а, —о, —ы** (ppp), see **сэконо́млю**.

СЭКОНО́МЛЮ, **сэконо́мишь**. Р. **Сэконо́мить** (acc.). I. **Эконо́мить**. To save (e.g., time, gasoline, etc.).

СЭКОНО́МЬ (imp.), see **сэконо́млю**.

СЯ́ДЕШЬ, see **ся́ду**.

СЯ́ДУ, **ся́дешь**. Р. **Сесть** (intr.). I. **Сади́ться**. 1. To sit down (on: **на** + acc.) (at a table: **за** + acc.) (by: **у** + gen.) (in: **в** + acc.). 2. To sit down (to do s.t.) (+ inf.) or (**на/за** + acc.). 3. To board, take (e.g., a train) (**на** + acc.). 4. To get in a train, auto, etc. (**в** + acc.). 5. To alight (of a bird) (on: **на** + acc.) (in: **в** + acc.). 6. To land (of a plane). 7. To settle (on) (of dust, fog) (**на** + acc.). 8. To set (of the sun). 9. To spend time (in prison). 10. To shrink (of cloth). 11. To settle (of a building, etc.).

СЯДЬ (imp.), see **ся́ду**.

T

ТА́ЕШЬ, see та́ю.

ТАЙ (imp.), see та́ю.

ТАРАНЧУ́, таранти́шь. I. Таранти́ть (intr.). To talk incessantly.

ТАРАХТИ́ (imp.), see тарахчу́.

ТАРАХТИ́ШЬ, see тарахчу́.

ТАРАХТЯ́Т, see тарахчу́.

ТАРАХЧУ́, тарахти́шь. I. Тарахте́ть. 1. To rattle, creak, crackle (intr.). 2. (fig.) To rattle on, talk incessantly (intr.) or (acc.).

ТА́Ю, та́ешь. I. Та́ять (intr.). P. Раста́ять (mean. 1, 4, 5). 1. Tom elt, thaw (of snow, ice, etc.). 2. To burn down (of a candle). 3. It is/was thawing (impers.). 4. (fig.) To fade, melt, dwindle (e.g., one's strength, fog, a crowd, money,). 5. (fig.) To be thrilled, melt with emotion, pleasure, etc. (from s.t.) (от + gen.). 6. To waste away (of a person).

ТВЕРЖЁННЫЙ; твержён, —а́, —о́, —ы́ (ppp), see твержу́.

ТВЕРЖУ́, тверди́шь. I. Тверди́ть (acc.). P. Вы́твердить (mean. 2), затверди́ть (mean. 2). 1. To reiterate, repeat again. 2. To learn by heart, by repetition.

ТЁК, текла́ (past), see течёт.

ТЕКИ́ (imp.), see течёт.

ТЕКУ́Т (3rd pers. pl.), see течёт.

ТЁР, тёрла (past). I. Тере́ть (acc.). 1. To rub (e.g., one's eyes, etc.). 2. To grate, shred (as vegetables, etc.). 3. To grind. 4. To chafe (of shoes, etc.). 5. To polish. (Also see тру.)

ТЕРЕБЛЁННЫЙ; тереблён, —а́, —о́, —ы́ (ppp), see тереблю́.

ТЕРЕБЛЮ́, тереби́шь. I. Тереби́ть (acc.). 1. To pluck, pull at, finger. 2. To rumple, tousle (e.g., hair, etc.). 3. (agr.) To pull up by the roots (e.g., flax). 4. (fig.) To pester.

ТЕРПИ́ (imp.), see терплю́.

ТЕ́РПИШЬ, see терплю́.

ТЕРПЛЮ́, те́рпишь. I. Терпе́ть. 1. To endure, tolerate, put up with (acc.). 2. To experience, suffer (as pain) (acc.). 3. To suffer (as from s.o. or s.t.) (intr.) (от + gen.). 4. In the expression, "there is no hurry:" вре́мя те́рпит.

ТЕ́РПЯТ, see терплю́.

ТЁРТЫЙ; тёрт, —а, —о, —ы (ppp), see тёр and тру.

ТЁСАННЫЙ; тёсан, —а, —о, —ы (ppp), see тешу́.

ТЕЧЁТ, теку́т (3rd pers. only). I. Течь (intr.). 1. (lit. and fig.) To flow, glide. 2. To leak (of a roof, pail, etc.). 3. (fig.) To go by, pass (of time, etc.).

ТЕ́ШЕШЬ, see тешу́.

ТЕШИ́ (imp.), see тешу́.

ТЕШУ́, те́шешь. I. Теса́ть. 1. To hew, cut (intr.) or (acc.). 2. To make, manufacture by cutting or hewing from logs, stone, etc. (e.g., a raft, gravestone, etc.) (acc.).

ТИХ, ти́хла (past). I. Ти́хнуть (intr.). 1. To quiet down. 2. To fall silent.

ТКА́ННЫЙ; ткан, —а́, —о, —ы (ppp), see тку.

ТКЁШЬ, see тку.

ТКИ (imp.), see тку.

ТКУ, ткёшь. I. Ткать (acc.) or (intr.). P. Сотка́ть. 1. To weave (as cloth). 2. To spin (as a spider web).

ТОЛКИ́ (imp.), see толку́.

ТОЛКЛА́ (past), see толо́к and толку́.

ТОЛКУ́, толчёшь, толку́т. I. Толо́чь (acc.). P. Истоло́чь, растоло́чь. 1. To pound, crush, pulverize. 2. To grind.

ТОЛО́К, толкла́ (past), see толку́.

ТОЛЧЁННЫЙ; толчён, —а́, —о́, —ы́ (ppp), see толку́.

ТОЛЧЁШЬ, see толку́.

ТОМЛЁННЫЙ; томлён, —а́, —о́, —ы́ (ppp), see томлю́.

ТОМЛЮ́, томи́шь. I. Томи́ть (acc.). P. Истоми́ть (mean. 1 and 2). 1. To weary, wear out. 2. To torment. 3. To stew, cook, braise. 4. To heat until malleable (of metal).

ТÓПЛЕННЫЙ; тóплен, —а, —о, —ы (ppp), see топлю́[1].

ТОПЛЮ́[1], то́пишь. I. Топи́ть (acc.). 1. To heat or warm. 2. To melt down (as wax). 3. To render (as lard from fat).

ТОПЛЮ́[2], то́пишь. I. Топи́ть (acc.). P. Потопи́ть, утопи́ть. 1. To sink. 2. To inundate, flood, submerge. 3. (lit. and fig.) To drown. 4. To ruin (as s.o., a business, etc.).

ТОПÓЧЕШЬ, see топочу́.

ТОПОЧИ́ (imp.), see топочу́.

ТОПОЧУ́, топóчешь. I. Топота́ть (intr.). To stamp (of people, horses) (intr.) or (inst. of shoes, feet, etc.).

ТÓПТАННЫЙ; тóптан, —а, —о, —ы (ppp), see топчу́.

ТÓПЧЕШЬ, see топчу́.

ТОПЧИ́ (imp.), see топчу́.

ТОПЧУ́, тóпчешь. I. Топта́ть (acc.). 1. To trample, tread. 2. To dirty, track (as a floor). 3. To flout, scorn, belittle. 4. To wear down at the heels. 5. To mate with (of fowl).

ТОРМОЖЁННЫЙ; тороможён, —а́, —ó, —ы́ (ppp), see торможу́.

ТОРМОЖУ́, тормози́шь. I. Тормози́ть. P. Затормози́ть. 1. To brake (as an auto) (acc.). 2. To put on the brakes, slow down, or stop (intr.). 3. To inhibit, impede, hamper (acc.).

ТОРОПЛЮ́, торóпишь. I. Торопи́ть. P. Поторопи́ть (mean. 1). 1. To hasten, hurry (s.o., s.t., some event etc.) (acc.). 2. To hurry (to do s.t.) (+ inf.). 3. To hurry, or hurry somewhere (intr.). 4. To hurry, press (e.g., s.o. for an answer) (acc. + с + inst.).

ТОРЧА́Т, see торчу́.

ТОРЧИ́ (imp.), see торчу́.

ТОРЧИ́ШЬ, see торчу́.

ТОРЧУ́, торчи́шь. I. Торча́ть (intr.). 1. To jut out, protrude, stick out. 2. (fig.) To stand out. 3. To stay, stick, "hang around," "hang out" (as at home).

ТРА́ВЛЕННЫЙ; тра́влен, —а, —о, —ы (ppp), see травлю́.

ТРАВЛЮ́, тра́вишь. I. Трави́ть (acc.). P. Вы́травить (mean. 1, 3, 5, 7, 10), затрави́ть (mean. 3 and 4), потрави́ть (mean. 7). 1. To exterminate (by poison). 2. To poison (e.g., to injure o.s. with alcohol). 3. To hunt

down (as game). 4. To persecute. 5. To etch. 6. To burn with acid. 7. To damage by trampling (as crops). 8. To feed (as grain, hay, to cattle) (acc. + dat.). 9. To spend or waste (as money). 10. (naut.) To slacken off, pay out.

ТРАТЬ (imp.), see тра́чу.

ТРА́ЧЕННЫЙ; тра́чен, —а, —о, —ы (ppp), see тра́чу.

ТРА́ЧУ, тра́тишь. I. Тра́тить (acc.). P. Истра́тить, потра́тить. 1. To spend, expend. 2. To waste.

ТРЕЗВЛЮ́, трезви́шь. I. Трезви́ть (intr.) or (acc.). (lit. and fig.) To sober.

ТРЁПАННЫЙ; трёпан, —а, —о, —ы (ppp), see треплю́.

ТРЕПÉЩЕШЬ, see трепещу́.

ТРЕПЕЩИ́ (imp.), see трепещу́.

ТРЕПЕЩУ́, трепéщешь. I. Трепета́ть (intr.). 1. (lit. and fig.) To tremble, quiver. 2. To palpitate. 3. To flicker, flutter.

ТРÉПЛЕШЬ, see треплю́.

ТРЕПЛИ́ (imp.), see треплю́.

ТРЕПЛЮ́, трéплешь. I. Трепа́ть (acc.). P. Истрепа́ть (mean. 3), потрепа́ть (mean. 1 thru 5). 1. To pull, tug. 2. To pester, bother. 3. To wear out, abuse (as clothing). 4. To blow, toss about (of wind, waves, etc.). 5. To pat (as s.o. on the back) (acc. + по + dat.). 6. To chatter (of people) (intr.) or (о + prep.) or (про + acc.). 7. To scutch.

ТРЁШЬ, see тру.

ТРЕЩА́Т, see трещу́.

ТРЕЩИ́ (imp.), see трещу́.

ТРЕЩИ́ШЬ, see трещу́.

ТРЕЩУ́, трещи́шь. I. Треща́ть (intr.). P. Протреща́ть (mean. 4 and 5). 1. To crack (of a noise). 2. To crackle. 3. To creak. 4. To chirp (of grasshoppers, crickets, etc.). 5. To chatter, talk incessantly. 6. (fig.) To crack, be on the point of collapse (of an army, defense, etc.). 7. To ache (of one's head, etc.).

ТРИ (imp.), see тру.

ТРУ, трёшь. I. Тере́ть (acc.). 1. To rub (e.g., one's eyes, etc.). 2. To grate, shred (as vegetables). 3. To grind. 4. To chafe (of shoes, etc.). 5. To polish.

ТРУБЛЮ, труби́шь. I. **Труби́ть.** Р. **Протруби́ть.** 1. To blow (into) (as into a trumpet) (в + acc.). 2. To blare, sound (as a trumpet) (intr.). 3. To sound (as retreat) (acc.). 4. To proclaim (о + prep.). 5. To work hard (as in an office) (в + acc.).

ТРУЖУ́СЬ, тру́дишься. I. **Труди́ться** (intr.). 1. To labor, toil. 2. To labor (over or at s.t.) (над + inst.). 3. To trouble o.s. (to do s.t.) (+ inf.).

ТРУСИ́ (imp.), see **трушу́**[1] and [2].

ТРУСЬ (imp.), see **тру́шу.**

ТРУШУ́[1]**, труси́шь.** I. **Труси́ть** (intr.). To go at an easy trot.

ТРУШУ́[2]**, труси́шь.** I. **Труси́ть** (acc.). Р. **Натруси́ть.** To scatter while shaking (as grain from a sack).

ТРУ́ШУ, тру́сишь. I. **Тру́сить** (intr.). Р. **Стру́сить.** 1. To be afraid, frightened. 2. To' be afraid of (gen.) or (пе́ред + inst.).

ТРЯС, трясла́ (past), see **трясу́.**

ТРЯСЁШЬ, see **трясу́.**

ТРЯСИ́ (imp.), see **трясу́.**

ТРЯСУ́, трясёшь. I. **Трясти́.** Р. **Вы́трясти** (mean. 2), **тряхну́ть** (mean. 1, 2, 3, 4). 1. To shake, jolt (acc.) or (intr.). 2. To shake out (e.g., a rug, crumbs, etc.) (acc.). 3. To shake (as one's head) (inst.). 4. To shake (as s.o.'s hand) (acc. of hand + dat. of s.o.). 5. To shake, shiver (e.g., from fear, cold, etc.) (acc. of person + impers. + от + gen. of fear etc.).

ТУЖУ́, тизи́шь. I. **Тузи́ть** (acc.). Р. **Оттузи́ть.** To pommel, thrash (as with one's fists).

ТУПЛЮ́, ту́пишь. I. **Тупи́ть** (acc.). Р. **Затупи́ть, иступи́ть.** To dull, blunt.

ТУХ, ту́хла (past). I. **Ту́хнуть** (intr.). Р. **Поту́хнуть** (mean. 1), **проту́хнуть** (mean. 2). 1. (lit. and fig.) To go out, die out, vanish, fade (e.g., of a fire, one's desire, etc.). 2. To spoil, decay.

ТЫКА́Й and **тычь** (imp.), see **ты́чу**[1] and [2].

ТЫКА́Я (adv. pres. part.), see **ты́чу**[1] and [2].

ТЫ́ЧА (adv. pres. part.), see **ты́чу**[1] and [2].

ТЫ́ЧЕШЬ see **ты́чу**[1] and [2].

ТЫ́ЧУ[1]**, ты́чешь** (also **ты́каю, ты́каешь**). I. **Ты́кать.** Р. **Ты́кнуть, ткнуть.** 1. To stick, push, shove (e.g., a stake in the ground, a key in the lock, etc.) (acc. + в + acc.) or (inst. + в + acc.). 2. To poke, prod (s.t./s.o. with s.t.) (в + acc. + inst.) or (acc. + в + acc.). 3. To send/ direct indiscriminately, force (e.g., all travelers into a 2nd class waiting room) (acc. + в + acc.). 4. (fig.) To push, insistently offer (s.t. to s.o.) (e.g., as a peddler pushes his wares on s.o.) (acc. + dat.). 5. To importunately call (s.t.) to (s.o.'s) attention (acc. + dat. of s.o.).

ТЫ́ЧУ[2]**, ты́чешь** (also **ты́каю, ты́каешь**). I. **Ты́кать** (acc.) or (intr.). To address s.o. in a familiar manner.

ТЫЧЬ and **ты́кай** (imp.), see **ты́чу**[1] and [2].

У

УБА́ВЛЕННЫЙ; уба́влен, —а, —о, —ы (ppp), see **уба́влю**.

УБА́ВЛЮ, уба́вишь. Р. **Уба́вить**. I. **Убавля́ть**. 1. To reduce, diminish, lower (e.g., price, speed, quantity) (acc./gen.). 2. To shorten (e.g., a sleeve) (acc.) or (в + prep.). 3. To reduce (lose weight) (intr.) (в + prep. of weight).

УБА́ВЬ (imp.), see **уба́влю**.

УБЕГИ́ (imp.), see **убегу́**.

УБЕГУ́, убежи́шь, убегу́т. Р. **Убежа́ть** (intr.). I. **Убега́ть**. 1. To run away, hurry away. 2. To escape. 3. To boil over, away (e.g., milk etc.).

УБЕЖДЁННЫЙ; убеждён, —а́, —о́, —ы́ (ppp). Р. **Убеди́ть** (acc.) (1st pers. sing. not used). I. **Убежда́ть**. 1. To convince (e.g., s.o. of s.t.) (acc. + в + prep.). 2. To convince (e.g., s.o. that...) (acc. + что). 3. To persuade (s.o. to do s.t.) (acc. + inf.) or (acc. + чтобы).

УБЕЖИ́ШЬ, see **убегу́**.

УБЕ́Й (imp.), see **убью́**.

УБЕРЁГ, убeregла́ (past), see **уберегу́**.

УБЕРЕГИ́ (imp.), see **уберегу́**.

УБЕРЕГУ́, убережёшь, уберегу́т. Р. **Убере́чь** (acc.). I. **Уберега́ть**. To protect, preserve (e.g., s.t. or s.o. from s.t. or s.o.) (acc.) or (acc. + от + gen.).

УБЕРЕЖЁННЫЙ; убережён, —а́, —о́, —ы́ (ppp), see **уберегу́**.

УБЕРЕЖЁШЬ, see **уберегу́**.

УБЕРЁШЬ, see **уберу́**.

УБЕРИ́ (imp.), see **уберу́**.

УБЕРУ́, уберёшь. Р. **Убра́ть** (acc.). I. **Убира́ть**. 1. To take away, put away, store, stow. 2. To clear (as dishes from the table) (acc. + со + стола́). 3. To remove. 4. To conceal. 5. (fig.) To put out of the way (kill). 6. To take up (e.g., a hem). 7. To eat up. 8. To harvest (e.g., grain). 9. To put in order, tidy up, clear. 10. To decorate, adorn, trim (with s.t.

(acc. + inst.). 11. (arch.) To dress (s.o.).

УБИЕ́ННЫЙ; убие́н, —а, —о, —ы (arch.) (ppp), see **убью́**.

УБИ́ТЫЙ; уби́т, —а, —о, —ы (ppp), see **убью́**.

УБОИ́ШЬСЯ, see **убою́сь**.

УБО́ЙСЯ (imp.), see **убою́сь**.

УБОЮ́СЬ, убои́шься. Р. **Убоя́ться** (arch.) (intr.), or (gen.). To be frightened (of s.t.) (now used humorously).

У́БРАННЫЙ; у́бран, —а́, (and —а), —о, —ы (ppp), see **уберу́**.

УБУ́ДЕШЬ, see **убу́ду**.

УБУ́ДУ, убу́дешь. Р. **Убы́ть** (intr.). I. **Убыва́ть**. 1. To decrease, diminish. 2. To subscribe, sink, fall (of water, etc.). 3. To wane (of the moon). 4. To leave, go away (of people).

УБУ́ДЬ (imp.), see **убу́ду**.

УБЬЁШЬ, see **убью́**.

УБЬЮ́, убьёшь. Р. **Уби́ть** (acc.). I. **Убива́ть**. 1. To kill, murder, assassinate. 2. (fig.) To kill (e.g., time, hope, ambition, etc.). 3. (fig.) To kill (in the sense of bringing to a state of despair) (e.g., the news killed him). 4. (fig.) To waste (as money, one's youth). 5. To cover (a surface with s.t.) (acc. + inst.). 6. To cover (as a king with an ace). 7. To pack (as a dirt floor).

УВЕДЁННЫЙ; уведён, —а́, —о́, —ы́ (ppp), see **уведу́**.

УВЕДЁШЬ, see **уведу́**.

УВЕДИ́ (imp.), see **уведу́**.

УВЕ́ДОМЛЕННЫЙ; уве́домлен, —а, —о, —ы (ppp), see **уве́домлю**.

УВЕ́ДОМЛЮ, уве́домишь. Р. **Уве́домить** (acc.). I. **Уведомля́ть**. To inform, notify, advise.

УВЕ́ДОМВ (imp.), see **уве́домлю**.

УВЕДУ́, уведёшь. Р. **Увести́** (acc.). I. **Уводи́ть**. 1. To take away, lead away. 2. (fig.) To lead away; divert (e.g., one's thoughts, attention, etc.). 3. (mil.) To withdraw (e.g., troops).

4. To steal, carry off. 5. (tech.) To drain off.

УВЕ́ДШИЙ (pap), see **уведу́.**

УВЕДЯ́ (adv. past part.), see **уведу́.**

УВЁЗ, увезла́ (past), see **увезу́.**

УВЕЗЁННЫЙ; увезён, —а́, —о́, —ы́ (ppp), see **увезу́.**

УВЕЗЁШЬ, see **увезу́.**

УВЕЗИ́ (imp.), see **увезу́.**

УВЕЗУ́, увезёшь. Р. **Увезти́** (acc.). I. **Увози́ть.** 1. To take away, carry away (s.o. or s.t. by conveyance). 2. To abduct, kidnap. 3. To steal.

УВЕЗЯ́ (adv. past part.), see **увезу́.**

УВЕ́Й (imp.), see **увью́.**

УВЁЛ, увела́ (past), see **уведу́.**

УВИ́ДЕННЫЙ; уви́ден, —а, —о, —ы (ppp), see **уви́жу.**

УВИ́ДИШЬ, see **уви́жу.**

УВИ́ДИШЬСЯ, see **уви́жусь.**

УВИ́ДЯТ, see **уви́жу.**

УВИ́ДЯТСЯ, see **уви́жусь.**

УВИ́ЖУ, уви́дишь. Р. **Уви́деть** (acc.) I. **Ви́деть.** 1. To see (s.o. or s.t.). 2. To realize, understand.

УВИ́ЖУСЬ, уви́дишься. Р. **Уви́-деться** (intr.). I. **Ви́деться.** 1. To see, meet each other. 2. To meet, see (s.o.) (с + inst.).

УВИ́ТЫЙ; уви́т, —а́, —о, —ы (ppp), see **увью́.**

УВЛЁК, увлекла́ (past), see **увлеку́.**

УВЛЕКИ́ (imp.), see **увлеку́.**

УВЛЕКУ́, увлечёшь, увлеку́т. Р. **Увле́чь** (acc.). I. **Увлека́ть.** 1. (lit. and fig.) To carry along, carry away. 2. To fascinate, captivate. 3. To allure, entice.

УВЛЕЧЁННЫЙ; увлечён, —а́, —о́, —ы́ (ppp), see **увлеку́.**

УВЛЕЧЁШЬ, see **увлеку́.**

УВО́ЖЕННЫЙ; уво́жен, —а, —о, —ы (ppp), see **увожу́³.**

УВОЖУ́¹, уво́дишь. I. **Уводи́ть** (acc.). Р. **Увести́.** 1. To take away, lead away. 2. (fig.) To lead away; divert (e.g., one's thoughts, attention, etc.). 3. (mil.) To withdraw (e.g., troops). 4. To steal, carry off. 5. (tech.) To drain off.

УВОЖУ́², уво́зишь. I. I. **Увози́ть** (acc.). Р. **Увезти́.** 1. To take away, carry away (s.o. or s.t. by convey-ance). 2. To abduct, kidnap. 3. To steal.

УВОЖУ́³, уво́зишь. Р. **Увози́ть** (acc.). To make, get (s.t.) very dirty (as one's shirt).

УВОЛО́К, уьолокла́ (past), see **уволо-ку́.**

УВОЛОКИ́ (imp.), see **уволоку́.**

УВОЛОКУ́, уволочёшь, уволоку́т. Р. **Уволо́чь** (acc.). I. **Уволáкивать.** 1. To drag away. 2. To steal.

УВОЛОЧЁННЫЙ; уволочён, —а́, —о́, —ы́ (ppp), see **уволоку́.**

УВОЛО́ЧЕННЫЙ; уволо́чен, —а, —о, —ы (ppp), see **уволоку́.**

УВОЛОЧЁШЬ, see **уволоку́.**

УВЬЁШЬ, see **увью́.**

УВЬЮ́, увьёшь. Р. **Уви́ть** (acc.). I. **Увива́ть.** 1. To entwine, wrap, wind (s.t. with s.t.) (acc. + inst.). 2. To wrap, wind (s.t. on or around s.t.) (as thread on a spool) (acc. + на + acc.).

УВЯ́ДШИЙ (and **увя́нувший**) (pap), see **увя́л.**

УВЯ́ЖЕШЬ, see **увяжу́.**

УВЯЖИ́ (imp.), see **увяжу́.**

УВЯЖУ́, увя́жешь. Р. **Увяза́ть** (acc.). I. **Увя́зывать.** 1. To wrap up, pack up. 2. To coordinate, link, bring into harmony (as s.t. with s.t.) (acc. + с + inst.).

УВЯ́З, увя́зла (past). Р. **Увя́знуть** (intr.) (в + prep.). I. **Увяза́ть, вя́з-нуть** (mean.). 1. To become stuck (as in the mud). 2. (fig.) To become entangled (in), become mired, sunk (e.g., in gloom, debt, etc.).

УВЯ́ЗАННЫЙ; увя́зан, —а, —о, —ы (ppp), see **увяжу́.**

УВЯЗНИ́ (imp.), see **увя́з.**

УВЯ́ЗНУВШИЙ (pap), see **увя́з.**

УВЯ́ЗШИЙ (pap), see **увя́з.**

УВЯ́Л, увя́ла (past). Р. **Увя́нуть** (intr.). I. **Вя́нуть.** (lit. and fig.) To fade, wither, droop.

УВЯ́НУВШИЙ (and **увя́дший**) (pap), see **увя́л.**

УВЯ́НЬ (imp.), see **увя́л.**

УГА́С, уга́сла (past). Р. **Уга́снуть** (intr.). I. **Угаса́ть, га́снуть** (mean. 1 and 2). 1. To go out (as a light, flame, etc.). 2. (lit. and fig.) To grow dim, fade, die out. 3. To die (of a person).

УГА́ШЕННЫЙ; уга́шен, —а, —о, —ы (ppp), see **угашу́.**

УГАШУ́, уга́сишь. Р. Угаси́ть (acc.). I. Угаша́ть. 1. To extinguish (e.g., a light, etc.). 2. (fig.) To stifle, suppress (e.g., one's feelings, emotions, thoughts, etc.).

УГЛУБЛЁННЫЙ; углублён, —а́, —о́, —ы́ (ppp), see углублю́.

УГЛУБЛЮ́, углуби́шь. Р. Углуби́ть (acc.). I. Углубля́ть. 1. (lit. and fig.) To deepen, extend (e.g., a hole, one's knowledge, etc.). 2. To drive deeper (e.g., piling, etc.).

УГЛЯДИ́ (imp.), see угляжу́.

УГЛЯДИ́ШЬ, see угляжу́.

УГЛЯДЯ́Т, see угляжу́.

УГЛЯЖУ́, угляди́шь. Р. Углядеть. 1. To see (acc.). 2. To look after, to take care of (3а + inst.).

У́ГНАННЫЙ; у́гнан, —а, —о, —ы (ppp), see угоню́.

УГНЕТЁННЫЙ; угнетён, —а́, —о́, —ы́ (ppp), see угнету́.

УГНЕТУ́, угнетёшь (future seldom used; past not used). Р. Угнести́ (acc.). I. Угнета́ть. 1. To oppress (as people). 2. To depress (as spirits).

УГОЖУ́, угоди́шь. Р. Угоди́ть. I. Угожда́ть (mean. 1). 1. To please, gratify (dat.) or (на + acc.). 2. To come across, stumble into, end up at, in, under (+ appropriate preposition + acc.). 3. To strike (as s.o. on the head) (dat. of s.o. + в + acc. of head). 4. To arrive in time (intr.).

УГОНИ́ (imp.), see угоню́.

УГО́НИШЬ, see угоню́.

УГОНЮ́, уго́нишь. Р. Угна́ть. I. Угоня́ть (mean. 1 thru 4). 1. To drive away, drive out (e.g., cattle etc.) (acc.). 2. To rustle, steal (e.g., cattle, etc.) (acc.). 3. To send away, drive out (of people, against their will) (acc.). 4. To transport rapidly, take somewhere rapidly (e.g., troops) (acc.). 5. (arch.) To ride or drive away rapidly (intr.).

УГО́НЯТ, see угоню́.

УГОРИ́ (imp.), see угорю́.

УГОРИ́ШЬ, see угорю́.

УГОРЮ́, угори́шь. Р. Угоре́ть (intr.). I. Угора́ть (mean. 1 and 3). 1. To be poisoned by carbon monoxide. 2. (fig.) To go out of one's mind. 3. To

diminish or shrink as result of burning or melting (3rd pers. only).

УГОРЯ́Т, see угорю́.

УГОТО́ВЛЕННЫЙ; угото́влен, —а, —о, —ы (ppp), see угото́влю.

УГОТО́ВЛЮ, угото́вишь. Р. Угото́вить (arch.) (acc.). I. Угота́вливать, уготовля́ть. To prepare.

УГОТО́ВЬ (imp.), see угото́влю.

УГОЩЁННЫЙ; угощён, —а́, —о́, —ы́ (ppp), see угощу́.

УГОЩУ́, угости́шь. Р. Угости́ть (acc.). I. Угоща́ть. To entertain, treat (as s.o. with a drink, dinner, etc.) (acc. + inst.).

УГРО́БЛЕННЫЙ; угро́блен, —а, —о, —ы (ppp), see угро́блю.

УГРО́БЛЮ, угро́бишь. Р. Угро́бить (acc.). 1. To kill. 2. To ruin, wreck (e.g., s.o., a business, etc.).

УГРО́БЬ (imp.), see угро́блю.

УДА́ВЛЕННЫЙ; уда́влен, —а, —о, —ы (ppp), see удавлю́.

УДАВЛЮ́, уда́вишь. Р. Удави́ть (acc.). I. Уда́вливать, дави́ть. To strangle (s.o. or s.t.).

УДАВЛЮ́СЬ, уда́вишься. Р. Удави́ться (intr.). I. Дави́ться. To hang o.s.

УДАДИ́МСЯ, удади́тесь, удаду́тся (pl. forms), see уда́мся.

УДАЁТСЯ, удаю́тся (3rd pers. only). I. Удава́ться (intr.). Р. Уда́ться. 1. To turn out well, be completed successfully. 2. To succeed in doing, manage to do (s.t.) (dat. + impers. + inf.).

УДА́ЙСЯ (imp.), see уда́мся.

УДА́МСЯ, уда́шься, уда́стся (sing. forms). Р. Уда́ться (intr.). I. Удава́ться (mean. 1 and 2). 1. To turn out well, be completed successfully. 2. To succeed in doing, manage to do s.t.) (dat. + impers. + inf.). 3. To turn out like, grow to be like (e.g., one's father) (в + acc.).

УДА́СТСЯ, see уда́мся.

УДА́ШЬСЯ, see уда́мся.

УДАЮ́ТСЯ (3rd pers. pl.), see удаётся.

УДЕРЁШЬ, see удеру́.

УДЕ́РЖАННЫЙ; уде́ржан, —а, —о, —ы (ppp), see удержу́.

УДЕ́РЖАТ, see удержу́.

УДЕРЖИ́ (imp.), see удержу́.

УДЕ́РЖИШЬ, see удержу́.

УДЕРЖУ́, уде́ржишь. Р. Удержа́ть (acc.). I. Уде́рживать. 1. To retain, hold. 2. To withhold (e.g., as s.t. from a sale, wages, etc.). 3. To suppress (as anger). 4. To hold back, keep, restrain. 5. To delay, detain. 6. To preserve.

УДЕРИ́ (imp.), see удеру́.

УДЕРУ́, удерёшь. Р. Удра́ть (intr.). I. Удира́ть. To take to one's heels, run away.

УДЕШЕВЛЁННЫЙ; удешевлён, —а́, б, и́ (ppp), see удешевлю́.

УДЕШЕВЛЮ́, удешеви́шь. Р. Удешеви́ть (acc.). I. Удешевля́ть. To reduce the price (of s.t.).

УДИВЛЁННЫЙ; удивлён, —а́, —б, —ы́ (ppp), see удивлю́.

УДИВЛЮ́, удиви́шь. Р. Удиви́ть (acc.). I. Удивля́ть. To astonish, amaze.

УЕ́ДЕШЬ, see уе́ду.

УЕ́ДУ, уе́дешь. Р. Уе́хать (intr.). I. Уезжа́ть. To leave, depart (for s.p.).

УЕ́ЗДИ (imp.), see уе́зжу.

УЕЗЖА́Й (imp.), see уе́ду.

УЕ́ЗЖЕННЫЙ; уе́зжен, —а, —о, —ы (ppp), see уе́зжу.

УЕ́ЗЖУ, уе́здишь. Р. Уе́здить (acc.). 1. To pack smooth, pack down (of traffic) (e.g., traffic packs a road surface). 2. To exhaust by riding or driving (as a horse).

УЖИВЁШЬСЯ, see уживу́сь.

УЖИВИ́СЬ (imp.), see уживу́сь.

УЖИВУ́СЬ, уживёшься. Р. Ужи́ться (intr.). I. Ужива́ться. 1. To get along with (c + inst.). 2. To become accustomed to living (somewhere).

УЖУ́, у́дишь. I. Уди́ть (acc.). To fish for, angle for, catch (using a fishing rod).

У́ЖУ, у́зишь. I. У́зить (acc.). 1. To make (too) tight, narrow. 2. To make appear (too) thin (e.g., as a dress makes a woman look too thin).

УЗНАВА́Й (imp.), see узнаю́.

УЗНАВА́Я (adv. pres. part.), see узнаю́.

УЗНАЁШЬ, see узнаю́.

УЗНАЮ́, узнаёшь. I. Узнава́ть. Р. Узна́ть. 1. To recognize, identify (acc.). 2. To learn, find out (about s.o. or s.t.) (acc.) or (о + prep.). 3. To know (e.g., s.o. or s.t.) (acc.).

У́ЗРЕННЫЙ; у́зрен, —а, —о, —ы (ppp), see узрю́.

УЗРИ́ (imp.), see узрю́.

У́ЗРИШЬ, see узрю́.

УЗРЮ́, у́зришь (and узри́шь). Р. Узре́ть (arch., poetic) (acc.). I. Зреть (mean. 1). 1. To see. 2. To discover, suspect, perceive (as deceit, etc.).

У́ЗРЯТ, see узрю́.

УЗЬ (imp.), see у́жу.

УЙДЁШЬ, see уйду́.

УЙДИ́ (imp.), see уйду́.

УЙДУ́, уйдёшь. Р. Уйти́ (intr.). I. Уходи́ть. 1. To leave, go away. 2. To quit, leave (as work, the stage, etc.) (с + gen.). 3. To escape, get away from (из/от + gen.). 4. (fig.) To pass, elapse (of time). 5. To be necessary (as cloth for a suit.) (на + acc.). 6. To go into (в + acc.). 7. To leak or boil away. 8. To be spent, consumed (on) (на + acc.). (For other usages see unabridged dictionary.)

УЙДЯ́ and уше́дши (adv. past part.), see уйду́.

УЙМЁШЬ, see уйму́.

УЙМИ́ (imp.), see уйму́.

УЙМУ́, уймёшь. Р. Уня́ть (acc.). I. Унима́ть. 1. To quiet, calm, soothe. 2. To restrain, suppress (as one's emotions, actions, etc.). 3. To stop (as the flow of blood, etc.).

УКА́ЖЕШЬ, see укажу́.

УКАЖИ́ (imp.), see укажу́.

УКАЖУ́, ука́жешь. Р. Указа́ть, I. Ука́зывать. 1. To point at (на + acc.). 2. To refer to, allude to (на + acc.). 3. To indicate, point out (acc.). 4. To explain (acc.), to explain (how) (как + inf.). 5. (arch.) to order (s.o. to do s.t.) (dat. + inf.).

УКА́ЗАННЫЙ; ука́зан, —а, —о, —ы (ppp), see укажу́.

УКА́ЧЕННЫЙ; ука́чен, —а, —о, —ы (ppp), see укачу́.

УКАЧУ́, ука́тишь. Р. Укати́ть. I. Ука́тывать. 1. To roll away (as a ball) (acc.). 2. To drive off (as in a car) (intr.). 3. To go away, leave, depart (e.g., for Europe, etc.) (intr.). 4. To run away (intr.).

УКО́ЛЕШЬ, see уколю́.

УКОЛИ́, see уколю́.

УКОЛОТЫЙ; уколот, —а, —о, —ы (ppp), see уколю́.

УКОЛОЧЕННЫЙ; уколо́чен, —а, —о, —ы (ppp), see уколочу́.

УКОЛОЧУ́, уколо́тишь. Р. Уколоти́ть (acc.). I. Укола́чивать. 1. To ram, tamp, compact (as earth). 2. To nail (a quantity of s.t. on s.t.). 3. To kill.

УКОЛЮ́, уко́лешь. Р. Уколо́ть (acc.). I. Ука́лывать. 1. To prick (e.g., with a pin). 2. To stick or stab. 3. (fig.) To prick, touch, wound (e.g., s.o.'s pride, etc.).

УКОРО́ЧЕННЫЙ; укоро́чен, —а, —о, —ы (ppp), see укорочу́.

УКОРОЧУ́, укороти́шь (arch.: укоро́тишь). Р. Укороти́ть (acc.). I. Укора́чивать. 1. To shorten, make shorter, physically (e.g., a coat, a belt, etc.). 2. To reduce, shorten (e.g., production time). 3. (fig.) To take (s.o.) down a peg.

УКО́ШЕННЫЙ; уко́шен, —а, —о, —ы (ppp), see укошу́.

УКОШУ́, уко́сишь. Р. Укоси́ть (acc.). To mow completely, finish mowing.

УКРА́ДЕННЫЙ; укра́ден, —а, —о, —ы (ppp), see украду́.

УКРАДЁШЬ, see украду́.

УКРАДИ́ (imp.), see украду́.

УКРАДУ́, украдёшь. Р. Укра́сть (acc.) or (intr.). I. Красть. To steal.

УКРА́Л, укра́ла (past), see украду́.

УКРА́СЬ (imp.), see укра́шу.

УКРА́ШЕННЫЙ; укра́шен, —а, —о, —ы (ppp), see укра́шу.

УКРА́ШУ, укра́сишь. Р. Укра́сить (acc.). I. Украша́ть. 1. To decorate, adorn. 2. To beautify. 3. To embellish (e.g., one's speech, etc.).

УКРЕПЛЁННЫЙ; укреплён, —а́, —о́, —ы́ (ppp), see укреплю́.

УКРЕПЛЮ́, укрепи́шь. Р. Укрепи́ть (acc.). I. Укрепля́ть. 1. (lit. and fig.) To strengthen. 2. To brace, reinforce. 3. To fortify. 4. To make healthier. 5. To fasten, fix.

УКРО́ЕШЬ, see укро́ю.

УКРО́Й (imp.), see укро́ю.

УКРОЩЁННЫЙ; укрощён, —а́, —о́, —ы́ (ppp), see укрощу́.

УКРОЩУ́, укроти́шь. Р. Укроти́ть (acc.). I. Укроща́ть. 1. To tame, subdue (e.g., animals, etc.). 2. To curb (passion, anger, etc.).

УКРО́Ю, укро́ешь. Р. Укры́ть (acc.). I. Укрыва́ть. 1. To cover. 2. (lit. and fig.) To screen, protect, shield. 3. To conceal, hide (s.o. or s.t. from s.o. or s.t.) (acc. + от + gen.).

УКРУ́ЧЕННЫЙ, укру́чен, —а, —о, —ы (ppp), see укручу́.

УКРУЧУ́, укру́тишь. Р. Укрути́ть (acc.). I. Укру́чивать. To wind around (s.t. with s.t.) (e.g., a chain around a log) (acc. of log + inst. of chain).

УКРЫ́ТЫЙ; укры́т, —а, —о, —ы (ppp), see укро́ю.

УКУ́ПЛЕННЫЙ; ку́плен, —а, —о, —ы (ppp), see укуплю́.

УКУПЛЮ́, ку́пишь. Р. Укупи́ть (acc.). To buy at a suitable price (usually used in the negative with the particle "не").

УКУ́ШЕННЫЙ; уку́шен, —а, —о, —ы (ppp), see укушу́.

УКУШУ́, уку́сишь. Р. Укуси́ть (acc.). 1. To bite. 2. To bite off. 3. To sting (of insects).

УЛА́ДЬ (imp.), see ула́жу.

УЛА́ЖЕННЫЙ; ула́жен, —а, —о, —ы (ppp), see ула́жу.

УЛА́ЖУ, ула́дишь. Р. Ула́дить (acc.). I. Ула́живать. 1. To settle (e.g., a controversial question, an affair, etc.). 2. To reconcile (e.g., differences). 3. To put in order (e.g., one's personal affairs, etc.). 4. To repair.

УЛЁГСЯ, улегла́сь (past). Р. Улёчься (intr.). I. Укла́дываться (mean. 1, 2, 3). 1. To lie down (as to sleep). 2. To lie in a normal position (e.g., bridge stringers, R.R. rails, etc.). 3. To settle (of dust). 4. To subside, abate (of wind, passions, etc.). (Also see уля́гусь.)

УЛЕЖА́Т, see улежу́.

УЛЕЖИ́ (imp.), see улежу́.

УЛЕЖИ́ШЬ, see улежу́.

УЛЕЖУ́, улежи́шь. Р. Улежа́ть (intr.). To lie (down) for a while.

УЛЁЗ, уле́зла (past), see уле́зу.

УЛЕ́ЗЕШЬ, see уле́зу.

УЛЕ́ЗУ, уле́зешь. Р. Уле́зть (intr.). I. Улеза́ть. To crawl away (on all fours).

УЛЕ́ЗЬ (imp.), see уле́зу.

УЛЕЙ (imp.), see улью.

УЛЕ́ПЛЕННЫЙ; уле́плен, —а, —о, —ы (ppp), see улеплю́.

УЛЕПЛЮ́, уле́пишь. Р. Улепи́ть (acc.). I. Улепля́ть. To cover an area completely by pasting or sticking (e.g., signs, notices on a wall, etc.).

УЛЕТИ́ (imp.), see улечу́.

УЛЕТИ́ШЬ, see улечу́.

УЛЕТЯ́Т, see улечу́.

УЛЕЧУ́, улети́шь. Р. Улете́ть (intr.). I. Улета́ть. 1. (lit. and fig.) To fly away. 2. (fig.) To disappear, pass rapidly (of time, hope, etc.).

УЛЕЩЁННЫЙ; улещён, —а́, —о́, —ы́ (ppp), see улещу́.

УЛЕЩУ́, улести́шь. Р. Улести́ть (acc.). I. Улеща́ть. To influence, win over (s.o.) through flattery or promises.

УЛИ́ТЫЙ; ули́т, —а́, —о, —ы (ppp), see улью́.

УЛИЦЕЗРИ́ (imp.), see улицезрю́.

УЛИЦЕЗРИ́ШЬ, see улицезрю́.

УЛИЦЕЗРЮ́, улицезри́шь. Р. Улицезре́ть (arch.) (acc.). I. Лицезре́ть. To contemplate, see (s.o. or s.t.) with one's own eyes.

УЛИЦЕЗРЯ́Т, see улицезрю́.

УЛО́ВЛЕННЫЙ; уло́влен, —а, —о, —ы (ppp), see уловлю́.

УЛОВЛЮ́, уло́вишь. Р. Улови́ть (acc.). I. Ула́вливать. 1. To grasp, understand, catch (by sight or sound) (e.g., a faint sound, a glance, etc.). 2. To sense (e.g., the meaning of s.t.). 3. (fig.) To seize (i.o., take advantage of) (e.g., the moment, opportunity, etc.). 4. (fig.) To catch, trap (e.g., s.o. in a lie). 5. To catch (physically), capture. 6. To discover (e.g., s.o. in the act).

УЛЬЁШЬ, see улью́.

УЛЬЮ́, ульёшь. Р. Ули́ть (acc.). I. Улива́ть. To pour over, inundate, drench, flood.

УЛЯ́ГСЯ (imp.), see уля́гусь.

УЛЯ́ГУСЬ, уля́жешься, уля́гутся. Р. Уле́чься (intr.). I. Укла́дываться (mean. 1, 2, 3). 1. To lie down (as to sleep). 2. To lie in a normal position (e.g., bridge stringers, R.R. rails, etc.). 3. To settle (of dust). 4. To subside, abate (of wind, anger, etc.).

УЛЯ́ЖЕШЬСЯ, see уля́гусь.

УМА́ЕШЬ, see ума́ю.

УМА́Й (imp.), see ума́ю.

УМАЩЁННЫЙ; умащён, —а́, —о́, —ы́ (ppp), see умащу́.

УМАЩУ́, умасти́шь. Р. Умасти́ть (acc.). I. Умаща́ть. To rub (s.o. or s.t.) with a fragrant ointment.

УМА́Ю, ума́ешь. Р. Ума́ять (acc.). To tire out, wear out, exhaust.

УМА́ЯННЫЙ; ума́ян, —а, —о, —ы (ppp), see ума́ю.

У́МЕР, умерла́, у́мерло, у́мерли (past), see умру́.

УМЕРЩВЛЁННЫЙ; умерщвлён, —а́, —о́, —ы́ (ppp), see умерщвлю́.

УМЕРЩВЛЮ́, умертви́шь. Р. Умертви́ть (acc.). I. Умерщвля́ть. 1. To kill. 2. (fig.) To destroy (e.g., one's soul, o.s., ambition, etc.).

УМЕЩЁННЫЙ; умещён, —а́, —о́, —ы́ (ppp), see умещу́.

УМЕЩУ́, умести́шь. Р. Умести́ть (acc.). I. Умеща́ть. To pack, place, find room for (as one's clothes in a travelling bag, books on a shelf, etc.).

УМНЁШЬ, see умну́.

УМНИ́ (imp.), see умну́.

УМНУ́, умнёшь. Р. Умя́ть (acc.). I. Умина́ть. 1. To knead. 2. To trample, tread down, compact (e.g., hay, snow, etc.). 3. To eat greedily, heartily.

УМО́ЕШЬ, see умо́ю.

УМО́Й (imp.), see умо́н.

УМО́ЛК (and arch. умо́лкнул), умо́лкла (past). Р. Умо́лкнуть (intr.). I. Умолка́ть. 1. To fall silent, to become silent. 2. To cease (of sounds, etc.). 3. (fig.) To vanish (of emotions, etc.).

УМОЛО́ЧЕННЫЙ; умоло́чен, —а, —о, —ы (ppp), see умолочу́.

УМОЛОЧУ́, умоло́тишь. Р. Умолоти́ть (acc.). I. Умола́чивать. To thresh (grain, etc.).

УМОЛЧА́Т, see умолчу́.

УМОЛЧИ́ (imp.), see умолчу́.

УМОЛЧИ́ШЬ, see умолчу́.

УМОЛЧУ́, умолчи́шь. Р. Умолча́ть (intr.). I. Ума́лчивать. To keep quiet (about s.t. or s.o.) (o + prep.).

УМО́Ю, умо́ешь. Р. Умы́ть (acc.). I. Умыва́ть. 1. To wash (the surface of s.t.) (e.g., one's hands, face, etc.). 2. (fig.) To wash (one's hands of s.t.) (acc. of hands).

УМРЁШЬ, see умру́.

УМРИ́ (imp.), see умру́.

УМРУ́, умрёшь. Р. Умере́ть (intr.). I. Умира́ть. 1. To die. 2. (fig.) To disappear, die out (e.g., old customs).

УМЧА́Т, see умчу́.

УМЧИ́ (imp.), see умчу́.

УМЧИ́ШЬ, see умчу́.

УМЧУ́, умчи́шь. Р. Умча́ть (acc.). To whirl, carry away rapidly (s.o. or s.t.) (of a horse, vehicle, wind, etc.).

УМЫ́ТЫЙ; умы́т, —а, —о, —ы (ppp), see умо́ю.

УМЯ́ТЫЙ; умя́т, —а, —о, —ы (ppp), see умну́.

УНАВО́ЖЕННЫЙ; унаво́жен, —а, —о, —ы (ppp), see унаво́жу.

УНАВО́ЖУ, унаво́зишь. Р. Унаво́зить (acc.). I. Унаво́живать, наво́зить (mean. 1). 1. To fertilize, manure. 2. To cover with dung (as horses cover a road or pasture with dung).

УНАВО́ЗЬ (imp.), see унаво́жу.

УНЁС, унесла́ (past), see унесу́.

УНЕСЁННЫЙ; унесён, —а́, —о́, —ы́ (ppp), see унесу́.

УНЕСЁШЬ, see унесу́.

УНЕСИ́ (imp.), see унесу́.

УНЕСУ́, унесёшь. Р. Унести́ (acc.). I. Уноси́ть. 1. (lit. and fig.) To carry away, carry off. 2. To steal.

УНЕСЯ́ (adv. past part.), see унесу́.

УНИ́ЖЕННЫЙ; уни́жен, —а, —о, —ы (ppp), see уни́жу.

УНИ́ЖЕШЬ, see унижу́.

УНИЖИ́ (imp.), see унижу́.

УНИ́ЖУ, уни́зишь. Р. Уни́зить (acc.). I. Унижа́ть. 1. To humiliate. 2. To humble. 3. To belittle, disparage.

УНИЖУ́, уни́жешь. Р. Униза́ть (acc. + inst.). I. Уни́зывать. To cover or stud (s.t. with s.t.) (e.g., a belt with beads, a hillside with pine trees, etc.).

УНИ́ЗАННЫЙ; уни́зан, —а, —о, —ы (ppp), see унижу́.

УНИ́ЗЬ (imp.), see унижу́.

УНОШУ́, уно́сишь. I. Уноси́ть (acc.). Р. Унести́. 1. (lit. and fig.) To carry away, carry off. 2. To steal.

УНЯ́ТЫЙ, уня́т, —а́, —о, —ы (ppp). Р. Уня́ть (acc.). I. Унима́ть. 1. To

quiet, calm, soothe. 2. To restrain, suppress (as one's emotions, actions, etc.). 3. To stop (e.g., the flow of blood etc.). (Also see уйму́.)

УПА́ВШИЙ and упа́дший (arch.) (pap), see упаду́.

УПАДЁШЬ, see упаду́.

УПАДИ́ (imp.), see упаду́.

УПАДУ́, упадёшь. Р. Упа́сть (intr.). I. Па́дать. 1. (lit. and fig.) To fall, drop. 2. To fall, hang down (of hair, etc.). 3. To diminish, decrease, decline. 4. (lit. and fig.) To fall on (на + acc.). (For other usages see unabridged dictionary.)

УПА́ДШИЙ (arch.) and упа́вший (pap), see упаду́.

УПА́Л, упа́ла (past), see упаду́.

УПА́С, упасла́ (past), see упасу́.

УПАСЁННЫЙ; упасён, —а́, —о́, —ы́ (ppp), see упасу́.

УПАСЁШЬ, see упасу́.

УПАСИ́ (imp.), see упасу́.

УПАСУ́, упасёшь. Р. Упасти́ (acc.). To save, preserve, protect.

УПЕ́ЙСЯ (imp.). Р. Упи́ться (intr.). I. Упива́ться. 1. To get drunk. 2. To get drunk on (s.t.) (inst.). 3. To enjoy (s.t.) thoroughly, to revel in (s.t.) (inst.). (Also see упью́сь.)

УПЁК, упекла́ (past), see упеку́.

УПЕКИ́ (imp.), see упеку́.

УПЕКУ́, упечёшь, упеку́т. Р. Упе́чь (acc.). I. Упека́ть. 1. To bake properly. 2. To send (s.o.) away against his will, banish. 3. To imprison.

УПЁР, упёрла (past), see упру́.

УПЕРЁВ and упёрши (adv. past part.), see упру́.

УПЁРТЫЙ; упёрт, —а, —о, —ы (ppp), see упру́.

УПЁРШИ and уперёв (adv. past part.), see упру́.

УПЕЧЁННЫЙ; упечён, —а́, —о́, —ы́ (ppp), see упеку́.

УПЕЧЁШЬ, see упеку́.

УПИ́САННЫЙ; упи́сан, —а, —о, —ы (ppp), see упишу́.

УПИ́ШЕШЬ, see упишу́.

УПИШИ́ (imp.), see упишу́.

УПИШУ́, упи́шешь. Р. Уписа́ть (acc.). I. Упи́сывать. 1. To fill (as a page, book, etc.) with writing. 2. To eat with zest.

УПЛА́ЧЕННЫЙ; упла́чен, —а, —о, —ы (ppp), see уплачу́.

УПЛАЧУ́, упла́тишь. Р. Уплати́ть. I. Упла́чивать, плати́ть. 1. To pay (as a debt) (acc.). 2. To pay for (s.t. with s.t.) (за + acc. + inst.).

УПЛЁЛ, уплела́ (past), see уплету́.

УПЛЕТЁННЫЙ; уплетён, —а́, —о́, —ы́ (ppp), see уплету́.

УПЛЕТЁШЬ, see уплету́.

УПЛЕТИ́ (imp.), see уплету́.

УПЛЕТУ́, уплетёшь. Р. Уплести́ (acc.). I. Уплета́ть. 1. To wind, wrap (s.t. with s.t.) (acc. + inst.) 2. To intertwine, interweave (s.t. with s.t.) (acc. + inst.). 3. To braid, plait (e.g., a rope). 4. To eat (s.t.) with gusto.

УПЛЁТШИЙ (pap), see уплету́.

УПЛЫВЁШЬ, see уплыву́.

УПЛЫВИ́ (imp.), see уплыву́.

УПЛЫВУ́, уплывёшь. Р. Уплы́ть (intr.). I. Уплыва́ть. 1. To swim away. 2. To sail, float away. 3. (fig.) To pass, go by, slip away (of time, money, etc.).

УПОДО́БЛЕННЫЙ; уподо́блен, —а, —о, —ы (ppp), see уподо́блю.

УПОДО́БЛЮ, уподо́бишь. Р. Уподо́бить (acc. + dat.). I. Уподобля́ть. To liken to (s.t.), to compare with (s.t.).

УПОДО́БЬ (imp.), see уподо́блю.

УПО́ЛЗ, уползла́ (past), see уползу́.

УПОЛЗЁШЬ, see уползу́.

УПОЛЗИ́ (imp.), see уползу́.

УПОЛЗУ́, уползёшь. Р. Уползти́ (intr.). I. Уполза́ть. 1. To crawl away, creep away. 2. To move away slowly (e.g., a train, a tank, etc.). 3. To slide, slip (as a cliff slips into the sea).

УПОТРЕБЛЁННЫЙ; употреблён, —а́, —о́, —ы́ (ppp), see употреблю́.

УПОТРЕБЛЮ́, употреби́шь. Р. Употреби́ть (acc.). I. Употребля́ть. To use, employ, apply.

УПРА́ВЛЮ, упра́вишь. Р. Упра́вить (inst.). I. Управля́ть. 1. To govern, rule. 2. To manage (e.g., a business, etc.). 3. To direct (e.g., an orchestra, a choir, etc.).

УПРА́ВЛЮСЬ, упра́вишься. Р. Упра́виться (intr.). I. Управля́ться. 1. To manage. 2. To finish (with s.t.) (с + inst.). 3. To cope or deal (with s.o. or s.t.) (с + inst.).

УПРА́ВЬ (imp.), see упра́влю.

УПРА́ВЬСЯ (imp.), see упра́влюсь.

УПРЕЖДЁННЫЙ; упреждён, —а́, —о́, —ы́ (ppp), see упрежу́.

УПРЕЖУ́, упреди́шь. Р. Упреди́ть (acc.). I. Упрежда́ть. 1. (arch.) To warn. 2. To forestall, prevent. 3. To anticipate. 4. To precede.

УПРЁШЬ, see упру́.

УПРИ́ (imp.), see упру́.

УПРО́ШЕННЫЙ; упро́шен, а, —о, —ы (ppp), see упрошу́.

УПРОШУ́, упро́сишь. Р. Упроси́ть (acc.). I. Упра́шивать (mean. 1). 1. To entreat, urge. 2. To persuade, prevail on.

УПРОЩЁННЫЙ; упрощён, —а́, —о́, —ы́ (ppp), see упрощу́.

УПРОЩУ́, упрости́шь. Р. Упрости́ть (acc.). I. Упроща́ть. 1. To simplify. 2. To oversimplify.

УПРУ́, упрёшь. Р. Упере́ть. I. Упира́ть. 1. To rest, prop, lean (s.t. on or against s.t.) (acc. + в + acc.). 2. (fig.) to rest (e.g., one's eyes, gaze on s.t.) (acc. + в + acc.) 3. To emphasize, stress (the meaning of s.t.) (e.g., a word) (на + acc.). 4. To go (somewhere) (intr.). 5. To steal, filch (acc.). 6. To carry away (acc.).

УПРЯ́МЛЮСЬ, упря́мишься, I. Упря́миться (intr.). To be obstinate, persist.

УПРЯ́МЬСЯ (imp.), see упря́млюсь.

УПРЯ́ТАННЫЙ; упря́тан, —а, —о, —ы (ppp), see упря́чу.

УПРЯ́ЧЕШЬ, see упря́чу.

УПРЯ́ЧУ, упря́чешь. Р. Упря́тать (acc.). I. Упря́тывать. 1. To hide, conceal. 2. To put away (as in prison).

УПРЯ́ЧЬ (imp.), see упря́чу.

УПУ́ЩЕННЫЙ; упу́щен, —а, —о, —ы (ppp), see упущу́.

УПУЩУ́, упу́стишь. Р. Упусти́ть (acc.). I. Упуска́ть. 1. To let go accidentally, let escape, let slip. 2. To miss, overlook (e.g., an opportunity, etc.).

УПЬЁШЬСЯ, see упью́сь.

УПЬЮ́СЬ, упьёшься. Р. Упи́ться (intr.). I. Упива́ться. 1. To get drunk. 2. To get drunk on (inst.). 3.

To enjoy (s.t.) thoroughly, to revel in (s.t.) (inst.).

УРАВНОВЕ́СЬ (imp.), see уравнове́шу.

УРАВНОВЕ́ШЕННЫЙ; уравнове́шен, —а, —о, —ы (ppp), see уравнове́шу.

УРАВНОВЕ́ШУ, уравнове́сишь. Р. Уравнове́сить (acc.). I. Уравнове́шивать. 1. To balance (e.g., scales, etc.). 2. (fig.) To balance, counterbalance, equalize (e.g., forces, losses and gains, etc.).

У́РВАННЫЙ; у́рван, —а, —о, —ы (ppp), see урву́.

УРВЁШЬ, see урву́.

УРВИ́ (imp.), see урву́.

УРВУ́, урвёшь. Р. Урва́ть (acc.). I. Урыва́ть. 1. To snatch, grab. 2. (fig.) To snatch, find (e.g., some time to do s.t.).

УРЕ́ЖЕШЬ, see уре́жу.

УРЕ́ЖУ, уре́жешь. Р. Уре́зать (acc.). I. Уре́зывать, уреза́ть. 1. To cut off, shorten. 2. To cut down, reduce (e.g., expenses, the length of an essay, etc.). 3. To curtail.

УРЕ́ЖЬ (imp.), see уре́жу.

УРЕ́ЗАННЫЙ; уре́зан, —а, —о, —ы (ppp), see уре́жу.

УРОЖДЁННЫЙ; урождён, —а́, —о́, —ы́ (ppp), see урожу́.

УРОЖУ́, уроди́шь. Р. Уроди́ть (acc.). I. Урожда́ть. 1. To bear (of the soil, plants, etc.). 2. To bear (of humans).

УРЧА́Т, see урчу́.

УРЧИ́ (imp.), see урчу́.

УРЧИ́ШЬ, see урчу́.

УРЧУ́, урчи́шь. I. Урча́ть (intr.). 1. To rumble, grumble (of a dog). 2. To rumble (of one's stomach, etc.) (impers.) or (impers. + в + prep.).

УРЯ́ЧЖЕННЫЙ; уря́жен, —а, —о, —ы (ppp), see уря́жу.

УРЯЖУ́, уря́дишь (and уряди́шь). Р. Уряди́ть. I. Уряжа́ть. 1. (arch.) To organize, put in order (acc.). 2. (arch.) To decide (acc.) or (+ inf.) 3. To dress up, adorn (acc.).

УСА́ЖЕННЫЙ; уса́жен, —а, —о, —ы (ppp), see усажу́.

УСАЖУ́, уса́дишь. Р. Усади́ть (acc.) I. Уса́живать. 1. To seat (e.g., s.o.). 2. To set (s.o. to doing s.t.) (e.g., to read a book) (acc. + за + acc.

of book) or (acc. + inf.). 3. To place, put (e.g., s.t. in the oven, s.o. in jail, etc.). 4. To plant (e.g., a garden with flowers (acc. + inst.). 5. To stud (with) (usually as ppp) (inst.). 6. (arch.) To spend.

УСЕ́ЕШЬ, see усе́ю.

УСЕ́Й (imp.), see усе́ю.

УСЕ́К, усекла́, усекло́, усекли́ (and arch.: усе́к, усе́кла, усе́кло, усе́кли) (past), see усеку́.

УСЕКИ́ (imp.), see усеку́.

УСЕКУ́, усечёшь, усеку́т. Р. Усе́чь (acc.). I. Усека́ть. 1. To truncate (as a cone). 2. To shorten (by cutting off).

УСЕ́ЛСЯ, усе́лась (past). Р. Усе́сться (intr.). I. Уса́живаться. 1. To take a seat. 2. To set to doing (s.t.) (e.g., reading a book) (за + acc. of book) or (+ inf.). 3. To take up residence, settle down. (Also see уся́дусь.)

УСЕЧЁННЫЙ; усечён, —а́, —о́, —ы́ (ppp) see усеку́.

УСЕ́ЧЕННЫЙ; усе́чен, —а, —о, —ы (arch.) (ppp), see усеку́.

УСЕЧЁШЬ, see усеку́.

УСЕ́Ю, усе́ешь. Р. Усе́ять (acc.). I. Усе́ивать. 1. To sow (e.g., a field with grain) (acc. + inst.). 2. To strew (s.t. with s.t.) (acc. + inst.). 3. To stud (e.g., stars stud the sky) (acc.).

УСЕ́ЯННЫЙ; усе́ян, —а, —о, —ы (ppp), see усе́ю.

УСИДИ́ (imp.), see усижу́.

УСИДИ́ШЬ, see усижу́.

УСИДЯ́Т, see усижу́.

УСИЖУ́, усиди́шь. Р. Усиде́ть. I. Уси́живать. 1. To keep one's seat, remain seated (intr.). 2. To stay, remain (intr.). 3. To sit and eat or drink much (of s.t.) (acc.). 4. To soil (as flies soil a surface) (acc.).

УСКА́ЧЕШЬ, see ускачу́.

УСКАЧИ́ (imp.), see ускачу́.

УСКАЧУ́, уска́чешь. Р. Ускака́ть (intr.). I. Уска́кивать. 1. To gallop off. 2. To bound off, skip off, hop off.

УСЛАЖДЁННЫЙ; услаждён, —а́, —о́, —ы́ (ppp), see услажу́.

УСЛАЖУ́, услади́шь. Р. Услади́ть (arch., poetic) (acc.). I. Услажда́ть. 1. To delight, charm (s.o. with s.t.) (acc. + inst.). 2. To brighten (e.g., s.o.'s life).

У́СЛАННЫЙ; у́слан, —а, —о, —ы (ppp). Р. Усла́ть (acc.). I. Усыла́ть. To send off, away (also see ушлю́).

УСЛАЩЁННЫЙ; услащён, —а́, —о́, —ы́ (ppp), see услащу́.

УСЛАЩУ́, усласти́шь. Р. Усласти́ть (arch.) (acc.). I. Услаща́ть. 1. To sweeten. 2. To flatter.

УСЛЁЖЕННЫЙ; услёжен, —а, —о, —ы (ppp), see услежу́.

УСЛЕЖУ́, уследи́шь. Р. Уследи́ть. I. Услёживать. 1. To look after (за + inst.). 2. To follow (e.g., the course of a discussion) (за + inst.). 3. To observe, note, detect (acc.) or (+ что).

УСЛО́ВЛЮСЬ, усло́вишься. Р. Усло́виться. I. Усло́вливаться, усла́вливаться. 1. To come to an agreement, agree, make arrangements (with: с + inst.), (about: о + prep.), (on: на + prep.). 2. To agree (to do) (+ inf.).

УСЛО́ВЬСЯ (imp.), see усло́влюсь.

УСЛЫ́ШАННЫЙ; услы́шан, —а, —о, —ы (ppp), see услы́шу[1] and [2].

УСЛЫ́ШАТ, see услы́шу[1] and [2].

УСЛЫ́ШИШЬ, see услы́шу[1] and [2].

УСЛЫ́ШУ[1], услы́шишь. Р. Услыха́ть. I. Слы́шать, слыха́ть (pres. tense not used). 1. To hear (acc.). 2. To hear (about) (о + prep.). (про + acc.) or (+ что). 3. To catch or smell (e.g., the fragrance of flowers) (acc.) (за́пах + gen. of flowers). 4. To scent (e.g., as a dog scents an animal) (acc.). 5. To notice, feel, sense (acc.) or (+ как) or (+ что).

УСЛЫ́ШУ[2], услы́шишь. Р. Услы́шать. I. Слы́шать. 1. To hear (acc.). 2. To hear (about) (о + prep.), (про + acc.) or (+ что). 3. To catch, smell (e.g., the fragrance of flowers) (acc.) (за́пах + gen. of flowers). 4. To scent (e.g., as a dog scents an animal) (acc.). 5. To notice, feel, sense (acc.) or (+ как) or (+ что).

УСЛЫ́ШЬ (imp.), see услы́шу[1] and [2].

УСМО́ТРЕННЫЙ; усмо́трен, —а, —о, —ы (ppp), see усмотрю́.

УСМОТРИ́ (imp.), see усмотрю́.

УСМО́ТРИШЬ, see усмотрю́.

УСМОТРЮ́, усмо́тришь. Р. Усмотре́ть. I. Усма́тривать. 1. To attend to, look after (за + inst.). 2. To

perceive, discover, detect (s.t. in s.o. or s.t.) (e.g., a trait in s.o., etc.) (acc. + в + prep.). 3. To observe, note (acc.).

УСМО́ТРЯТ, see усмотрю́.

УСНАЩЁННЫЙ; уснащён, —а́, —о́, —ы́ (ppp), see уснащу́.

УСНАЩУ́, уснасти́шь. Р. Уснасти́ть (acc. + inst.). I. Уснаща́ть. 1. To supply plentifully, provide (with s.t.). 2. (fig.) To garnish, lard, embellish (e.g., an article with statistical data, a speech with quotations, etc.).

УСО́ВЕСТИ (imp.), see усо́вещу.

УСО́ВЕЩЕННЫЙ; усо́вещен, —а, —о, —ы (ppp), see усо́вещу.

УСО́ВЕЩУ, усо́вестишь. Р. Усо́вестить (acc.). I. Усо́вещивать, со́вестить (mean. 1). 1. To shame, make ashamed. 2. To appeal to the conscience (of s.o.).

УСО́Х, усо́хла (past). Р. Усо́хнуть (intr.). I. Усыха́ть. (lit. and fig.) To dry up (of things and people).

УСТАВА́Й (imp.), see устаю́.

УСТАВА́Я (adv. pres. part.), see устаю́.

УСТА́ВЛЕННЫЙ; уста́влен, —а, —о, —ы (ppp), see уста́влю.

УСТА́ВЛЮ, уста́вишь. Р. Уста́вить (acc.). I. Уставля́ть (mean. 1, 2, 3). 1. To place, arrange. 2. To set, arrange, cover (e.g., a table with dishes, a shelf with books, etc.) (acc. + inst.). 3. To establish (e.g., standards, harmony, etc.). 4. To direct, point (s.t. at s.o. or s.t.) (acc. + на + acc.). 5. To stare at (acc. of eyes + на + acc.).

УСТА́ВЬ (imp.), see уста́влю.

УСТАЁШЬ, see устаю́.

УСТА́НЕШЬ, see уста́ну.

УСТАНО́ВЛЕННЫЙ; устано́влен, —а, —о, —ы (ppp), see установлю́.

УСТАНОВЛЮ́, устано́вишь. Р. Установи́ть (acc.). I. Устана́вливать. 1. To place. 2. To install, mount, erect (e.g., machinery, apparatus, etc.). 3. To adjust, regulate (e.g., machinery, a watch, etc.). 4. To establish (e.g., procedures, relations, order, etc.). 5. To ascertain, establish, determine (e.g., facts, truth, time, etc.). 6. To cover (with) (as a table with dishes) (acc. + inst.).

УСТА́НУ, уста́нешь. Р. Уста́ть (intr.). I. **Устава́ть.** 1. To get tired, tire. 2. To get tired, tire (of or from) (**от** + gen.) or (+ inf.).

УСТА́НЬ (imp.), see **уста́ну.**

УСТАЮ́, устаёшь. I. Устава́ть (intr.). Р. **Уста́ть.** 1. To get tired, tire. 2. To get tired, tire (of or from) (**от** + gen.) or (+ inf.).

УСТЕ́ЛЕННЫЙ; усте́лен, —а, —о, —ы (ppp), see **устелю́[1].**

УСТЕ́ЛЕШЬ, see **устелю́[1] and [2].**

УСТЕЛИ́ (imp.), see **устелю́[1] and [2].**

УСТЕЛЮ́[1], усте́лешь. Р. Устели́ть (acc. + inst.). I. **Устила́ть.** 1. To cover, strew, spread (e.g., the floor with a carpet, sawdust, etc.). 2. To pave (e.g., the street with bricks, etc.).

УСТЕЛЮ́[2], усте́лешь. Р. Устла́ть (acc. + inst.). I. **Устила́ть.** 1. To cover, strew, spread (e.g., the floor with a carpet, sawdust, etc.). 2. To pave (e.g., the street with bricks, etc.).

УСТЕРЁГ, устерегла́ (past), see **устерегу́.**

УСТЕРЕГИ́ (imp.), see **устерегу́.**

УСТЕРЕГУ́, устережёшь, устерегу́т. Р. Устере́чь (acc.). I. **Устерега́ть.** 1. To preserve, protect, guard. 2. To protect, preserve (from) (**от** + gen.). 3. (arch.) To watch for (e.g., a thief). 4. (arch.) To choose (as the time, moment, etc.).

УСТЕРЕЖЁННЫЙ; устережён, —а́, —о́, —ы́ (ppp), see **устерегу́.**

УСТЕРЕЖЁШЬ, see **устерегу́.**

У́СТЛАННЫЙ; у́стлан, —а, —о, —ы (ppp), see **устелю́[2].**

УСТОИ́ШЬ, see **устою́.**

УСТО́Й (imp.), see **устою́.**

УСТОЮ́, устои́шь. Р. Устоя́ть (intr.). I. **Уста́ивать.** 1. To keep one's feet, to stand. 2. (fig.) To stand one's ground. 3. To resist, stand up against (**про́тив** + gen.). 4. (fig.) To stand up (e.g., under attack, etc.) (**под** + inst.). 5. To stand up (e.g., in an argument) (**в** + prep.). 6. To withstand (e.g., blandishment, temptation, etc.) (**пе́ред** + inst.).

УСТОЯ́Т, see **устою́.**

УСТРЕМЛЁННЫЙ; устремлён, —а́, —о́, —ы́ (ppp), see **устремлю́.**

УСТРЕМЛЮ́, устреми́шь. Р. Устреми́ть (acc.). I. **Устремля́ть.** 1. To rush (e.g., as troops to the front) (acc. + **на** + acc.). 2. To direct (e.g., a gun, a search light at a tank, etc.) (acc. + **в** + acc.). 3. To direct (e.g., attention, effort, at s.t. or s.o.) (acc. + **на** + acc.). 4. To direct (e.g., one's thoughts toward s.t.) (acc. + **к** + dat.).

УСТУ́ПЛЕННЫЙ; усту́плен, —а, —о, —ы (ppp), see **уступлю́.**

УСТУПЛЮ́, усту́пишь. Р. Уступи́ть. I. **Уступа́ть.** 1. To give up, yield (s.t. to s.o.) (acc. + dat.). 2. To yield, give in (intr.). 3. To yield to, be inferior (to s.o. in s.t.) (dat. + **в** + prep.). 4. To come down in price (e.g., come down $5.00) (acc.). 5. To let (s.o.) have (s.t.), sell (s.t. to s.o.) (dat. of s.o. + acc. of s.t.).

УСТЫЖЁННЫЙ; устыжён, —а́, —о́, —ы́ (ppp), see **устыжу́.**

УСТЫЖУ́, устыди́шь. Р. Устыди́ть (acc.). I. **Устыжа́ть.** To shame, put to shame.

УСУГУБИ́ (imp.), see **усугублю́.**

УСУГУ́БЛЕННЫЙ; усугу́блен, —а, —о, —ы (ppp), see **усугу́блю.**

УСУГУБЛЁННЫЙ; усугублён, —а́, —о́, —ы́ (ppp), see **усугублю́.**

УСУГУ́БЛЮ, усугу́бишь. Р. Усугу́бить (acc.). I. **Усугубля́ть.** 1. To increase greatly, double or redouble (as one's efforts). 2. To aggravate, make worse.

УСУГУБЛЮ́, усугуби́шь. Р. Усугуби́ть (acc.). I. **Усугубля́ть.** 1. To increase greatly, double or redouble (as one's efforts). 2. To aggravate, make worse.

УСУГУ́БЬ (imp.), see **усугу́блю.**

УСЫНОВЛЁННЫЙ; усыновлён, —а́, —о́, —ы́ (ppp), see **усыновлю́.**

УСЫНОВЛЮ́, усынови́шь. Р. Усынови́ть (acc.). I. **Усыновля́ть.** To adopt (s.o.).

УСЫ́ПАННЫЙ; усы́пан, —а, —о, —ы (ppp), see **усы́плю.**

УСЫПЛЁННЫЙ, усыплён, —а́, —о́, —ы́ (ppp), see **усыплю́.**

УСЫ́ПЛЕШЬ, see **усы́плю.**

УСЫ́ПЛЮ, усы́плешь. Р. Усы́пать (acc.). I. **Усыпа́ть.** 1. To strew, litter, cover (e.g., the floor with sawdust, etc.) (acc. + inst.). 2. To strew, stud (e.g., the heavens with stars, etc.) (acc. + inst.).

УСЫПЛЮ, усыпишь. Р. **Усыпить** (acc.). I. **Усыплять**. 1. To put to sleep. 2. To anesthetize; hypnotize. 3. (fig.) To put to sleep (kill) (e.g., a sick animal). 4. To lull. 5. (fig.) To put to sleep (as with a boring tale).

УСЫПЬ (imp.), see **усыплю**.

УСЯДЕШЬСЯ, see **усядусь**.

УСЯДУСЬ, усядешься. Р. **Усесться** (intr.). I. **Усаживаться**. 1. To take a seat. 2. To set to doing (s.t.) (e.g., reading) (за + acc. of book) or (+ inf.). 3. To take up residence, settle down.

УСЯДЬСЯ (imp.), see **усядусь**.

УТВЕРЖДЁННЫЙ; утверждён, —а, —о, —ы (ppp), see **утвержу**.

УТВЕРЖУ́, утвердишь. Р. **Утвердить** (acc.). I. **Утверждать**. 1. To confirm, approve, ratify. 2. To consolidate, strengthen (e.g., democracy, etc.). 3. To assert, affirm. 4. To convince, assure (e.g., s.o. of s.t.) (acc. + в + prep.). 5. To allot, secure (s.t. to s.o.) (e.g., the rights of access to s.o., etc.) (acc. + за + inst. of s.o.). 6. (arch.) To mount (e.g., a machine on a base) (acc. + на + prep.).

УТЁК, утекла (past), see **утеку**.

УТЕКИ (imp.), see **утеку**.

УТЕКУ́, утечёшь, утекут. Р. **Утечь** (intr.). I. **Утекать**. 1. To flow away, escape (of fluids). 2. To pass, go by (as years, events). 3. To flee, run away, escape.

УТЁР, утёрла (past). Р. **Утереть** (acc.). I. **Утирать**. 1. To wipe dry, wipe clean. 2. To wipe away (e.g., tears, perspiration, etc.). (Also see **утру**.)

УТЕРЁВ and **утёрши** (adv. past part.), see **утёр** and **утру**.

УТЕРПИ (imp.), see **утерплю**.

УТЕРПИШЬ, see **утерплю**.

УТЕРПЛЮ, утерпишь. Р. **Утерпеть** (intr.). To restrain oneself.

УТЕРПЯТ, see **утерплю**.

УТЁРТЫЙ; утёрт, —а, —о, —ы (ppp), see **утёр** and **утру**.

УТЁРШИ and **утерёв** (adv. past part.), see **утёр** and **утру**.

УТЁСАННЫЙ; утёсан, —а, —о, —ы (ppp), see **утешу**.

УТЕЧЁШЬ, see **утеку**.

УТЕШЕШЬ, see **утешу**.

УТЕШИ (imp.), see **утешу**.

УТЕШУ́, утешешь. Р. **Утесать** (acc.). I. **Утёсывать**. To reduce the thickness by hewing, trimming (e.g., a board, a log, etc.).

УТИХ, утихла (past). Р. **Утихнуть** (intr.). I. **Утихать**. 1. To cease, die down (of sounds, noise, etc.). 2. To subside, abate (of natural phenomena, storms, pain, etc.). 3. To become calm, calm down, (of humans and animals). 4. To cease to cry, scream, etc. (of humans and animals).

УТИХШИЙ and **утихнувший** (pap), see **утих**.

УТКАННЫЙ; уткан, —а, —о, —ы (ppp), see **утку**.

УТКЁШЬ, see **утку**.

УТКИ (imp.), see **утку**.

УТКУ́, уткёшь. Р. **Уткать** (acc.). To interweave (e.g., a fabric with gold thread, creating a design) (acc. + inst. of gold).

УТОЛЩЁННЫЙ; утолщён, —а, —б, —ы (ppp), see **утолщу**.

УТОЛЩУ́, утолстишь. Р. **Утолстить** (acc.). I. **Утолщать**. To make thicker, thicken, (e.g., a cable, etc.).

УТОМЛЁННЫЙ; утомлён, —а, —б, —ы (ppp), see **утомлю**.

УТОМЛЮ́, утомишь. Р. **Утомить** (acc.). I. **Утомлять**. To weary, tire.

УТОПЛЕННЫЙ; утоплен, —а, —о, —ы (ppp), see **утоплю**.

УТОПЛЮ́, утопишь. Р. **Утопить** (acc.). I. **Топить** (mean. 1 thru 4), **утапливать** (mean. 5 and 6). 1. To sink. 2. To inundate, flood, submerge. 3. (lit. and fig.) To drown. 4. To ruin (e.g., a business, a person, etc.). 5. (tech.) To embed, countersink (as a rivet, etc.). 6. To heat (s.t.) in an oven.

УТОПТАННЫЙ; утоптан, —а, —о, —ы (ppp), see **утопчу**.

УТОПЧЕШЬ, see **утопчу**.

УТОПЧИ (imp.), see **утопчу**.

УТОПЧУ́, утопчешь. Р. **Утоптать** (acc.). I. **Утаптывать**. 1. To trample down. 2. To tramp, pack (as earth, etc.).

УТРА́ТЬ (imp.), see утра́чу.

УТРА́ЧЕННЫЙ; утра́чен, —а, —о, —ы (ppp), see утра́чу.

УТРА́ЧУ, утра́тишь. Р. Утра́тить (acc.). I. Утра́чивать. To lose (as one's health, color, friends, ability, etc.).

УТРЁШЬ, see утру́.

УТРИ́ (imp.), see утру́.

УТРУ́, утрёшь. Р. Утере́ть (acc.). I. Утира́ть. 1. To wipe dry, wipe clean. 2. To wipe away (e.g., tears, perspiration, etc.).

УТРУЖДЁННЫЙ; утруждён, —а́, —о́, —ы́ (ppp), see утружу́.

УТРУЖУ́, утруди́шь. Р. Утруди́ть (acc.). I. Утружда́ть. To trouble, bother, inconvenience.

УТРЯ́С, утрясла́ (past), see утрясу́.

УТРЯСЁННЫЙ; утрясён, —а́, —о́, —ы́ (ppp), see утрясу́.

УТРЯСЁШЬ, see утрясу́.

УТРЯСИ́ (imp.), see утрясу́.

УТРЯСУ́, утрясёшь. Р. Утрясти́ (acc.). I. Утряса́ть. 1. To shake down (e.g., a sack of nuts to reduce the volume). 2. To shake up (as a car or carriage on a rough road shakes up a person) (often impers.). 3. (fig.) To settle (e.g., a question, problem, affair, etc.).

УХВА́ЧЕННЫЙ; ухва́чен, —а, —о, —ы (ppp), see ухвачу́.

УХВАЧУ́, ухва́тишь. Р. Ухвати́ть (acc.). I. Ухва́тывать. 1. To grasp, seize. 2. (fig.) To seize (as s.o.'s property). 3. (fig.) To grasp, understand.

УХИ́ТЬ (imp.), see ухи́чу.

УХИ́ЧЕННЫЙ; ухи́чен, —а, —о, —ы (ppp), see ухи́чу.

УХИ́ЧУ, ухи́тишь. Р. Ухи́тить (arch.) (acc.). I. Ухи́чивать. To fix up (e.g., a house).

УХО́ЖЕННЫЙ; ухо́жен, —а, —о, —ы (ppp), see ухожу́[2].

УХОЖУ́[1], ухо́дишь. I. Уходи́ть (intr.). Р. Уйти́ (mean. 1 thru 8). 1. To leave, go away. 2. To quit, leave (as work, the stage, etc.) (с + gen.). 3. To escape, get away from (из/от + gen.). 4. (fig.) To pass, elapse (of time). 5. To be necessary (as cloth for a suit) (на + acc.). 6. To go into (в + acc.). 7. To leak or boil away.

8. To be spent, consumed (on) (на + acc.). 9. To lead (off/into) (of a road). (For other usages, see unabridged dictionary.)

УХОЖУ́[2], ухо́дишь. Р. Уходи́ть (acc.). 1. To tire, wear out. 2. (fig.) To destroy or ruin. 3. To eliminate, get rid of.

УЦЕ́ПЛЕННЫЙ; уце́плен, —а, —о, —ы (ppp), see уцеплю́.

УЦЕПЛЮ́, уце́пишь. Р. Уцепи́ть (acc.). I. Уцепля́ть. To grab, catch, seize, grasp.

УЧАЩЁННЫЙ; учащён, —а́, —о́, —ы́ (ppp), see учащу́.

УЧАЩУ́, участи́шь. Р. Участи́ть (acc.). I. Учаща́ть. To increase the frequency (e.g., of visits, vibration, etc.).

УЧЁЛ, учла́ (past), see учту́.

УЧЁТШИЙ (pap), see учту́.

УЧЛА́, учло́, учли́ (past), see учёл and учту́.

УЧНЁШЬ, see учну́.

УЧНИ́ (imp.), see учну́.

УЧНУ́, учнёшь. Р. Уча́ть. I. Учина́ть. 1. To begin (s.t.) (acc.). 2. To begin to do (s.t.) (+ inf.).

УЧРЕЖДЁННЫЙ; учреждён, —а́, —о́, —ы́ (ppp), see учрежу́.

УЧРЕЖУ́, учреди́шь. Р. Учреди́ть (acc.). I. Учрежда́ть. 1. To found, establish (e.g., a university). 2. To establish (e.g., a scholarship, a commission, controls, a position, etc.).

УЧТЁННЫЙ; учтён, —а́, —о́, —ы́ (ppp), see учту́.

УЧТЁШЬ, see учту́.

УЧТИ́ (imp.), see учту́.

УЧТУ́, учтёшь. Р. Уче́сть (acc.). I. Учи́тывать. 1. To count, inventory. 2. To take into consideration. 3. To discount (e.g., a promissory note, etc.).

УЧТЯ́ (adv. past part.), see учту́.

УЧУ́ЕШЬ, see учу́ю.

УЧУ́Й (imp.), see учу́ю.

УЧУ́Ю, учу́ешь. Р. Учу́ять (acc.). I. Учу́ивать. 1. To scent, pick up a scent, smell (e.g., as a dog smells a bear). 2. (fig.) To sense, smell (e.g., trouble).

УЧУ́ЯННЫЙ; учу́ян, —а, —о, —ы (ppp), see учу́ю.

УШЁДШИ and уйдя́ (adv. past part.),
see ушёл and уйду́.

УШЁДШИЙ (pap), see ушёл and
уйду́.

УШЕЙ (imp.), see ушью́.

УШЁЛ, ушла́ (past). Р. Уйти́ (intr.).
I. Уходи́ть. 1. To leave, go away.
2. To quit, leave (as work, the stage,
etc.) (с + gen.). 3. To escape, get
away from (из/от + gen.). 4. (fig.)
To pass, elapse (of time). 5. To be
necessary (as cloth for a suit) (на +
acc.). 6. To go into (в + acc.). 7. To
leak or boil away. 8. To be spent,
consumed (on) (на + acc.). (Also
see уйду́.) (For other usages see
unabridged dictionary.)

УШИ́Б, уши́бла (past), see ушибу́.

УШИБЁШЬ, see ушибу́.

УШИБИ́ (imp.), see ушибу́.

УШИ́БЛЕННЫЙ; уши́блен, —а, —о,
—ы (ppp), see ушибу́.

УШИБУ́, ушибёшь. Р. Ушиби́ть
(acc.). I. Ушиба́ть (mean. 1). 1. To
bruise, injure with a blow. 2. (fig.)
To shock, astound.

УШИ́ТЫЙ; уши́т, —а, —о, —ы
(ppp), see ушью́.

УШЛЁШЬ, see ушлю́.

УШЛИ́[1] (past pl.), see ушёл and
уйду́.

УШЛИ́[2] (imp.), see ушлю́.

УШЛЮ́, ушлёшь. Р. Усла́ть (acc.). I.
Усыла́ть. To send off, away.

УШЬЁШЬ, see ушью́.

УШЬЮ́, ушьёшь. Р. Уши́ть (acc.). I.
Ушива́ть. 1. To take in, narrow
(e.g., the waist of a dress). 2. To
shorten, take up (as a hem). 3. To
embroider. 4. To sew up (as a bale of
goods).

УЩЕМЛЁННЫЙ; ущемлён, —а́, —о́,
—ы́ (ppp), see ущемлю́.

УЩЕМЛЮ́, ущеми́шь. Р. Ущеми́ть
(acc.). I. Ущемля́ть. 1. To pinch,
jam (as one's hand). 2. (fig.) To
wound (as one's pride). 3. To
infringe (as one's rights, interests,
etc.). 4. (med.) To strangulate.

УЩЕРБЛЁННЫЙ; ущерблён, —а́,
—о́, —ы́ (ppp), see ущерблю́.

УЩЕРБЛЮ́, ущерби́шь. Р. Ущерби́ть
(acc.). I. Ущербля́ть. 1. To cause
(s.o.) damage, loss. 2. To restrict,
limit, (e.g., s.o.'s enjoyment of life,
etc.).

УЯЗВЛЁННЫЙ; уязвлён, —а́, —о́,
—ы́ (ppp), see уязвлю́.

УЯЗВЛЮ́, уязви́шь. Р. Уязви́ть
(acc.). I. Уязвля́ть. 1. (fig.) To
wound deeply, offend deeply. 2. To
wound, sting.

Ф

ФАЛЬШИ́ВЛЮ, фальши́вишь. I.
Фальши́вить (intr.). Р. **Сфальши́-**
вить. 1. To dissemble, act hypocritically. 2. To sing or play off
key.
ФАЛЬШИ́ВЬ (imp.), see **фальши́влю.**
ФИНЧУ́, финти́шь. I. Финти́ть (intr.).
1. To be cunning, devious, resort to
subterfuge. 2. To fawn (upon s.o.),
curry favor (with s.o.) (**пе́ред** +
inst.). 3. To carouse, make merry.
ФОРШУ́, форси́шь. I. Форси́ть (intr.).
1. To put on airs, show off, swagger.
2. To play the dandy, be a fop.
ФРАНЧУ́, франти́шь. I. Франти́ть

(intr.). To dress foppishly, dress
like a dandy.
ФУРЧА́Т, see **фурчу́.**
ФУРЧИ́ (imp.), see **фурчу́.**
ФУРЧИ́ШЬ, see **фурчу́.**
ФУРЧУ́, фурчи́шь. I. Фурча́ть (intr.).
To snort.
ФЫРЧА́Т, see **фырчу́.**
ФЫРЧИ́ (imp.), see **фырчу́.**
ФЫРЧИ́ШЬ, see **фырчу́.**
ФЫРЧУ́, фырчи́шь. I. Фырча́ть (intr.)
1. To snort (with indignation or
amusement) (of people). 2. To snort
(of animals). 3. (fig.) To snort (of
machines).

Х

ХА́ЕШЬ, see **ха́ю.**
ХА́Й (imp.), see **ха́ю.**
ХАМЛЮ́, хами́шь. I. Хами́ть (intr.).
To behave boorishly.
ХА́Ю, ха́ешь. I. Ха́ять (acc.). Р.
Оха́ять. To find fault with, abuse,
run down, discredit.
ХВА́ТИТ (3rd pers. only). Р. **Хвати́ть**
(gen.) (impers.). I. **Хвата́ть.** 1. To be
sufficient, suffice (e.g., he has sufficient money) (dat. + gen.) (**ему́** +
gen. of money). 2. To be adequate
(to s.t.) (e.g., he is adequate to the
job) (gen. of person + **на** + acc. of
job).
ХВА́ЧЕННЫЙ; хва́чен, —а, —о, —ы
(ppp), see **хвачу́.**
ХВАЧУ́, хва́тишь. Р. Хвати́ть. I.
Хвата́ть (mean. 1 only). 1. To seize,
snatch (acc.). 2. To drink or eat
(s.t.) rapidly (acc.) or (intr.). 3.
(lit. and fig.) To strike, damage,
injure (s.o./s.t.) (of paralysis, a
person, frost, etc.) (acc.). 4. To
experience, undergo (e.g., grief,
pain, etc.) (gen. of pain, etc.). 5.
(fig.) To go too far (intr.). 6; To do

or say (s.t.) unexpected, ill-advised,
rash (acc.). (For other usages see
unabridged dictionary.)
ХЛЁСТАННЫЙ; хлёстан, —а, —о,
—ы (ppp), see **хлещу́.**
ХЛЕ́ЩЕШЬ, see **хлещу́.**
ХЛЕЩИ́ (imp.), see **хлещу́.**
ХЛЕЩУ́, хле́щешь. I. Хлеста́ть. Р.
Хлестну́ть. 1. To whip, lash (acc.).
2. (fig.) To lash, beat (of rain, etc.)
(as rain beats against a window)
(intr.) (**в** + acc.). 3. To gush, rush,
pour (e.g., as water, blood, etc.)
(intr.). 4. To drink, guzzle, swill
(e.g., wine, etc.) (acc.). 5. To splash
(as water) (acc.).
ХЛОБЫ́ЩЕШЬ, see **хлобыщу́.**
ХЛОБЫЩИ́ (imp.), see **хлобыщу́.**
ХЛОБЫЩУ́, хлобы́щешь. I. Хлобы-
ста́ть. Р. Хлобыстну́ть. 1. (lit. and fig).
To beat, whip, lash (acc.). 2. To gush,
pour (of water blood, etc.) (intr.).
ХЛОПО́ЧЕШЬ, see **хлопочу́.**
ХЛОПОЧИ́ (imp.), see **хлопочу́.**
ХЛОПОЧУ́, хлопо́чешь. I. Хлопо-
та́ть (intr.). Р. **Похлопота́ть** (mean.

2, 3,). 1. To bustle about. 2. To solicit, try to obtain (s.t.) (e.g., a position) (o + prep.) or (+ что́бы). 3. To intercede for, try to help (s.o.) (за + acc.), (o + prep.).

ХЛЫ́ЩЕШЬ, see хлыщу́.

ХЛЫЩИ́ (imp.), see хлыщу́.

ХЛЫЩУ́, хлы́щешь. I. Хлыста́ть. Р. Хлыстну́ть. 1. To whip, lash (acc.). 2. (fig.) To lash, beat (of rain, etc.) (as rain beats against a window) (intr.) (в + acc.). 3. To gush, rush, pour (e.g., as water, blood, etc.) (intr.). 4. To drink, guzzle, swill (e.g., wine, etc.) (acc.). 5. To splash (as water) (acc.).

ХНЫ́КАЙ (imp.), see хны́чу.

ХНЫ́ЧЕШЬ, see хны́чу.

ХНЫ́ЧУ, хны́чешь (and хны́каю, хны́каешь). I. Хны́кать (intr.). 1. To snivel, whine. 2. To complain.

ХНЫЧЬ (imp.), see хны́чу.

ХОДИ́ (imp.), see хожу́.

ХОЖУ́, хо́дишь. I. Ходи́ть (intr.). 1. To go (in various usages). 2. To walk. 3. To attend, go to (e.g., school, lectures, the theatre, etc.). 4. To wear (e.g., a coat, glasses, etc.) (в + prep.). 5. To run, go, work (of timepieces, etc.). 6. To run (of busses, trains, etc.). 7. To look after, take care of (за + inst.). 8. To flow (of electric current). 9. To play (a card) (e.g., a heart) (inst.). (For numerous other idiomatic usages see unabridged dictionary.)

ХОЛОЖУ́, холоди́шь. I. Холоди́ть. Р. Нахолоди́ть (mean. 1). 1. To cool, chill, refrigerate (acc.). 2. To produce a cool sensation (e.g., of mint) (intr.)

(also impers.). 3. To numb (as fear numbs one's senses) (acc.).

ХОЛОЩЁННЫЙ; холощён, —а́, —о́, —ы́ (ppp), see холощу́.

ХОЛОЩУ́, холости́шь. I. Холости́ть (acc.). Р. Вы́холостить (mean. 1), охолости́ть. 1. To castrate, emasculate. 2. To geld.

ХОТИ́ (imp.), see хочу́.

ХОТИ́М, хоти́те, хотя́т (pl. forms), see хочу́.

ХОТЯ́Т, see хоти́м.

ХОХО́ЧЕШЬ, see хохочу́.

ХОХОЧИ́ (imp.), see хохочу́.

ХОХОЧУ́, хохо́чешь. I. Хохота́ть (int.). To laugh loudly.

ХО́ЧЕШЬ, see хочу́.

ХОЧУ́, хо́чешь, хо́чет (sing. forms). I. Хоте́ть (acc./gen.) or (+ inf.) Р. Захоте́ть. To want, wish, like, desire (s.t.) or (to do s.t.).

ХРАПИ́ (imp.), see храплю́.

ХРАПИ́ШЬ, see храплю́.

ХРАПЛЮ́, храпи́шь. I. Храпе́ть (intr.). 1. To snore (of persons). 2. To snort (of animals).

ХРАПЯ́Т, see храплю́.

ХРИПИ́ (imp.), see хриплю́.

ХРИПИ́ШЬ, see хриплю́.

ХРИПЛЮ́, хрипи́шь. I. Хрипе́ть. Р. Прохрипе́ть. 1. To wheeze (intr.). 2. To speak or sing in a hoarse voice (intr.) or (acc.).

ХРИПЯ́Т, see хриплю́.

ХРУСТИ́ (imp.), see хрущу́.

ХРУСТИ́ШЬ, see хрущу́.

ХРУЩУ́, хрусти́шь (usually 3rd pers.). I. Хрусте́ть (intr.). Р. Хру́стнуть. To make a crackling or crunching noise.

ХРУСТЯ́Т (3rd pers. pl.), see хрущу́.

Ц

ЦВЁЛ, цвела (past), see **цвету**.
ЦВЕТЁШЬ, see **цвету**.
ЦВЕТИ (imp.), see **цвету**.
ЦВЕТУ́, цветёшь. I. **Цвести** (intr.). 1. To bloom, flower (of plants, etc.). 2. (fig.) To be in bloom of youth/health (of a person). 3. (fig.) To develop, flourish (of a country). 4. To become overgrown with algae, water plants, etc. (of ponds, etc.). 5. To become mouldy. 6. To break out with, become covered with rash.
ЦВЕ́ТШИЙ (pap), see **цвету**.

ЦВЕЧУ́, цветишь. I. **Цветить** (acc.). To paint in gay colors.
ЦЕ́ЖЕННЫЙ; цежен, —а, —о, —ы (ppp), see **цежу**.
ЦЕЖУ́, це́дишь. I. **Цедить** (acc.). 1. To strain, filter. 2. To decant. 3. To speak (words) through one's teeth. 4. To sip.
ЦОКО́ЧЕШЬ, see **цокочу**.
ЦОКОЧИ (imp.), see **цокочу**.
ЦОКОЧУ́, цоко́чешь. I. **Цокотать** (intr.). 1. To chatter, click, clatter (of machinery, horses' hoofs, etc.). 2. To chatter continually (of peopl e.

Ч

ЧА́ЕШЬ, see **чаю**.
ЧАЖУ́, чади́шь. I. **Чадить** (intr.). P. **Начадить.** 1. To smoke (of a stove, etc.). 2. To fill with smoke (e.g., a room with tobacco smoke) (**на** + acc. of room + inst. of tobacco).
ЧАЙ (imp.), see **чаю**.
ЧАХ, ча́хла (past). I. **Ча́хнуть** (intr.). P. **Зача́хнуть.** 1. To wither (of plants). 2. To pine (of people).
ЧАЩУ́, частишь. I. **Частить.** 1. To do (s.t.) hurriedly, too rapidly (e.g., play the piano too rapidly) (**на** + acc.). 2. To speak hurriedly (intr.) or (acc.). 3. To visit (s.o.) often (**к** + dat.).
ЧА́Ю, ча́ешь, 1. Ча́ять, 1. To expect, hope for (gen.). 2. To expect to, to hope to (+ inf.). 3. To think, suppose, conclude (usually + that, **что**).
ЧЕ́РЧЕННЫЙ; че́рчен, —а, —о, —ы (ppp), see **черчу**.
ЧЕРЧУ́, че́ртишь. I. **Чертить**: P. **Начертить** (mean. 1). 1. To draw, describe, sketch, trace, design, plot (acc.) or (intr.). 2. To leave a trace

(as a ship leaves a wake on the surface of the ocean) (acc. of ocean). 3. (fig.) To trace, cut (as birds trace circles in the air) (acc. of circle).
ЧЕРЧУ́, че́ртишь. I. **Чертить** (arch.) (intr.) To misbehave.
ЧЁСАННЫЙ; чёсан, —а, —о, —ы (ppp), see **чешу**.
ЧЕ́ШЕШЬ, see **чешу**.
ЧЕШИ (imp.), see **чешу**.
ЧЕШУ́, че́шешь. I. **Чесать.** P. **Почесать** (mean. 1, 2, 3). 1. To scratch (to relieve itch) (acc.). 2. To comb (as hair) (acc.). 3. To comb or card (as flax) (acc.). 4. (Used in placé of another verb, understood, to express strong action or emotion, etc.) (e.g., "He danced the polka vigorously": **он чесал по́льку**) (acc.) or (intr.).
ЧЕЩУ́, честишь. I. **Честить** (acc.). 1. To revile, abuse. 2. (arch.) To honor (s.o.). 3. (arch.) To call, name (s.o. s.t.) (acc. + inst.).
ЧИСТИ (imp.), see **чищу**.
ЧИСТЬ (imp.), see **чищу**.
ЧИХВО́СТИ (imp.), see **чихво́щу**.

ЧИХВО́ЩУ, чихво́стишь. I. Чихво́-
стить (acc.). 1. To scold, abuse, rail
at. 2. To beat, flog.
ЧИ́ЩЕННЫЙ; чи́щен, —а, —о, —ы
(ppp), see **чи́щу.**
ЧИ́ЩУ, чи́стишь. I. Чи́стить (acc.).
P. **Вы́чистить** (mean. 1), **очи́стить**
(mean. 1 thru 4), **почи́стить** (mean.
1). 1. To clean. 2. To peel, shell. 3.
(fig.) To clean out. 4. To rob. 5. To
scold, rail at.
ЧТЁШЬ, see **чту.**[1]
ЧТИ (imp.), see **чту**[1] and [2].

ЧТУ[1]**, чтёшь. I. Честь** (arch.) (acc.).
1. To recognize, consider (e.g., s.o.
to be a scholar) (acc. + за + acc.
of scholar). 2. To read.
ЧТУ[2]**, чтишь, чтят** (and **чтут**). I.
Чтить (acc.). To honor, esteem,
respect, revere.
ЧТУТ (3rd pers. pl.), see **чту**[1] and [2].
ЧУ́ЕШЬ, see **чу́ю.**
ЧУЙ (imp.), see **чу́ю.**
ЧУ́Ю, чу́ешь. I. Чу́ять. 1. To scent,
smell (of an animal) (acc.). 2. To feel
(acc.). 3. (fig.) To feel, sense (s.t.)
(of a person) (acc.) or (**что**).

Ш

ШЕ́ДШИЙ (pap), see шёл and иду́.

ШЕЙ (imp.). I. Шить. Р. Сшить (mean. 2). 1. To sew, stitch (intr.). 2. To sew, make (e.g., a coat) (acc.). 3. To embroider (intr.) (e.g., with silk) (inst.). (Also see шью.)

ШЁЛ, шла (past). I. Идти́ (intr.). 1. To go (of a person, on foot). 2. To go (of a vehicle). 3. To start, leave (of a train, etc.). 4. To go, lead (of a road, etc.). 5. To take place, occur (of rain, snow, etc.). 6. To go on, proceed (of classes, discussions, etc.). 7. To play (as a motion picture). 8. To elapse, pass (of time). 9. To function (of a watch, etc.). 10. To become or suit (s.o.) (e.g., of clothes) (dat.). (Also see иду́.) (For other usages see unabridged dictionary.)

ШЕЛЕСТИ́ (imp.), see шелести́шь.

ШЕЛЕСТИ́ШЬ, шелести́т (1st pers. not used). I. Шелесте́ть (intr.). 1. To rustle (as leaves rustle). 2. To rustle (as wind rustles leaves) (inst. of leaves.)

ШЕЛЕСТЯ́Т (3rd pers. pl.), see шелести́шь.

ШЕПЕЛЯ́ВЛЮ, шепеля́вишь. I. Шепеля́вить (intr.). To lisp.

ШЕПЕЛЯ́ВЬ (imp.), see шепеля́влю.

ШЁ́ПЧЕШЬ, see шепчу́.

ШЕПЧИ́ (imp.), see шепчу́.

ШЕПЧУ́, шёпчешь. I. Шепта́ть. Р. Прошепта́ть (mean. 1). 1. (lit. and fig.) To whisper (acc.) or (intr.). 2. To whisper incantations (over s.t.) in the practice of witchcraft (на + acc.).

ШИПИ́ (imp.), see шиплю́.

ШИПИ́ШЬ, see шиплю́.

ШИПЛЮ́, шипи́шь. I. Шипе́ть. Р.

Прошипе́ть (mean. 1 and 3). 1. (lit. and fig.) To hiss (intr.) or (acc.). 2. To sizzle, sputter, effervesce (intr.). 3. To speak in a low, hissing voice (intr.) or (acc.).

ШИПЯ́Т, see шиплю́.

ШИ́ТЫЙ; шит, —а, —о, —ы (ppp), see шей and шью.

ШЛА, шло, шли (past), see шёл and иду́.

ШЛЁШЬ, see шлю.

ШЛИ¹ (past), see шла and иду́.

ШЛИ² (imp.), see шлю.

ШЛЮ, шлёшь. I. Слать (acc.). To send.

ШУМИ́ (imp.), see шумлю́.

ШУМИ́ШЬ, see шумлю́.

ШУМЛЮ́, шуми́шь. I. Шуме́ть (intr.). 1. To make noise. 2. To brawl, quarrel. 3. To make a fuss (over), to show uncalled for interest (in) (о + prep.). 4. To attract attention.

ШУМЯ́Т, see шумлю́.

ШУРША́Т, see шуршу́.

ШУРШИ́ (imp.), see шуршу́.

ШУРШИ́ШЬ, see шуршу́.

ШУРШУ́, шурши́шь. I. Шурша́ть (intr.). 1. To rustle. 2. To rustle (as one rustles the pages of a book) (inst. of pages).

ШУЧУ́, шу́тишь. I. Шути́ть (intr.). Р. Пошути́ть. 1. To joke (intr.). 2. To mock, deride (s.o.) (над + inst.). 3. To trifle (with) (с + inst.) or (inst.).

ШЬЁШЬ, see шью.

ШЬЮ, шьёшь. I. Шить. Р. Сшить (mean. 2). 1. To sew, stitch (intr.). 2. To sew, make (e.g., a coat) (acc.). 3. To embroider (intr.) (with silk, etc.) (inst.).

Щ

ЩАЖУ́, щади́шь. I. Щади́ть (acc.). Р. Пощади́ть. 1. To show compassion, pity for (s.o.). 2. To spare (s.o. or s.t.). 3. To spare (s.t. or s.o. from s.t.) (acc. + от + gen.).

ЩЕБЕ́ЧЕШЬ, see щебечу́.

ЩЕБЕЧИ́ (imp.), see щебечу́.

ЩЕБЕЧУ́, щебе́чешь. I. Щебета́ть (intr.). 1. To chirp or twitter (of birds). 2. (fig.) To chatter, prattle (of people).

ЩЕКО́ЧЕШЬ, see щекочу́[1].

ЩЕКОЧИ́ (imp.), see щекочу́[1].

ЩЕКОЧУ́[1], щеко́чешь. I. Щекота́ть. Р. Пощекота́ть (mean. 1 and 2). 1. (lit. and fig.) To tickle (acc.). 2. To have a tickling sensation (as in the throat) (intr.) (impers. + в + prep.). 3. To sing (of canaries, nightingales, etc.) (intr.).

ЩЕКОЧУ́[2], щеко́тишь. I. Щекоти́ть. 1. (lit. and fig.) To tickle (acc.). 2. To have a tickling sensation (as in the throat) (intr.) (impers. + в + prep.).

ЩЕПА́Й and щепли́ (imp.), see щеплю́.

ЩЕ́ПАННЫЙ; ще́пан, —а, —о, —ы (ppp), see щеплю́.

ЩЕПА́Я and щепля́ (adv. pres. part.), see щеплю́.

ЩЕ́ПЛЕШЬ, see щеплю́.

ЩЕПЛИ́ and щепа́й (imp.), see щеплю́.

ЩЕПЛЮ́, ще́плешь (and щепа́ю, щепа́ешь). 1. Щепа́ть (acc.). To chip, splinter.

ЩЕПЛЯ́ and щепа́я (adv. pres. part.), see щеплю́.

ЩИПА́Й and щипли́ (imp.), see щиплю́.

ЩИ́ПАННЫЙ; щи́пан, —а, —о, —ы (ppp), see щиплю́.

ЩИПА́Я and щипли́ (adv. pres. part.), see щиплю́.

ЩИ́ПЛЕШЬ, see щиплю́.

ЩИПЛИ́ and щипа́й (imp.), see щиплю́.

ЩИПЛЮ́, щи́плешь (also щипа́ю, щипа́ешь). I. Щипа́ть (acc.). Р. Общипа́ть (mean. 3), Ощипа́ть (mean. 3). 1. To pinch. 2. (fig.) To bite, burn, etc. (as pepper bites the tongue, smoke burns the eyes, etc.). 3. To pluck (grass, feathers, etc.). 4. To pluck (as strings of a guitar). 5. To nibble, browse, crop.

ЩИПЛЯ́ and щипа́я (adv. pres. part.), see щиплю́.

Э

ЭКОНО́МЛЮ, эконо́мишь. I. эконо́мить. Р. Сэконо́мить (mean. 1). 1. To save (e.g., time, gasoline, food, etc.) (acc.). 2. To use sparingly (acc.). 3. To save on, economize on (e.g., clothing, etc.) (на + prep.). (on housekeeping) (в + prep.). 4. To economize (intr.).
ЭКОНО́МЬ (imp.), see эконо́млю.

Ю

ЮЧУ́СЬ, юти́шься. I. Юти́ться (intr.). 1. To huddle (together). 2. To take shelter.

Я

Я́ВЛЕННЫЙ; я́влен, —а, —о, —ы (ppp.), see явлю́.
ЯВЛЮ́, Я́ВИШЬ. Р. Яви́ть (acc.). I. Явля́ть. To show, display, manifest.
ЯЗВЛЮ́, язви́шь. I. Язви́ть. Р. С'язви́ть (mean. 3). 1. (arch.) To sting, bite (acc.). 2. (arch.) To scold, abuse, (acc.). 3. To speak sarcastically, caustically (intr.).

APPENDIX

Listed in alphabetical order in the appendix are the infinitives whose finite forms appear as entries in the main body of the Dictionary. The order in which the finite forms follow their related infinitives is indicated below:

1. First person singular, second person singular, and where necessary, third person plural.

2. Imperative.

3. Past tense: masculine singular, and where necessary, feminine singular, neuter singular, and plural.

4. Present Active Participle.

5. Present passive participle.

6. Past active participle.

7. Past passive participle.

8. Adverbial participles (gerunds, present or past).

А

АЛКА́ТЬ I.; а́лчу, а́лчешь (also алка́ю, алка́ешь); а́лчи and алка́й; а́лча and алка́я.

Б

БАЛАМУ́ТИТЬ I.; баламу́чу, баламу́тишь; баламу́ть.

БА́ЯТЬ I.; ба́ю, ба́ешь; бай.

БЕЖА́ТЬ I.; бегу́, бежи́шь, бегу́т; беги́.

БЕЗОБРА́ЗИТЬ I.; безобра́жу, безобра́зишь; безобра́зь.

БЕРЕДИ́ТЬ Р.; бережу́, береди́шь.

БЕРЕ́ЧЬ I.; берегу́, бережёшь, берегу́т; береги́; берёг.

БЕСИ́ТЬ I.; бешу́, бе́сишь.

БЕСЧЕ́СТИТЬ I.; бесче́щу, бесче́стишь; бесче́сти.

БИТЬ I.; бью, бьёшь; бей; би́тый.

БЛА́ГОВЕСТИТЬ I.; бла́говещу, бла́говестишь; бла́говести.

БЛАГОСЛОВИ́ТЬ Р.; благословлю́, благослови́шь.

БЛЁКНУТЬ I.; блёк, блёкла.

БЛЕСТЕ́ТЬ[1] I.; блещу́[1], блести́шь; блести́.

БЛЕСТЕ́ТЬ[2] I.; блещу́[2], бле́щешь; блещи́.

БЛЕ́ЯТЬ I.; бле́ет, бле́ют; блей.

БЛУДИ́ТЬ[1] I.; блужу́[1], блуди́шь.

БЛУДИ́ТЬ[2] I.; блужу́[2], блу́дишь.

БЛЮСТИ́ I.; блюду́, блюдёшь; блюди́; блюл; блю́дший.

БОЛЕ́ТЬ[1] I.; боле́ю, боле́ешь.

БОЛЕ́ТЬ[2] I.; боли́т, боля́т.

БОРМОТА́ТЬ I.; бормочу́, бормо́чешь; бормочи́.

БОРОЗДИ́ТЬ I.; борозжу́, борозди́шь.

БОРО́ТЬСЯ I.; борю́сь, бо́решься; бори́сь.

БОЯ́ТЬСЯ I.; бою́сь, бои́шься; бо́йся.

БРАТЬ I.; беру́, берёшь; бери́.

БРЕ́ДИТЬ I.; бре́жу, бре́дишь; бредь.

БРЕНЧА́ТЬ I.; бренчу́, бренчи́шь; бренчи́.

БРЕСТИ́ I.; бреду́, бредёшь; бреди́; брёл; бре́дший.

БРЕХА́ТЬ I.; брешу́, бре́шешь; бреши́.

БРИТЬ I.; бре́ю, бре́ешь; брей; бри́тый.

БРОДИ́ТЬ I.; брожу́, бро́дишь.

БРО́СИТЬ Р.; бро́шу, бро́сишь; брось; бро́шенный.

БРЫ́ЗГАТЬ I.; бры́зжу, бры́зжешь; бры́зжи.

БРЮЗЖА́ТЬ I.; брюзжу́, брюзжи́шь; брюзжи́.

БУДИ́ТЬ I.; бужу́, бу́дишь.

БУРА́ВИТЬ I.; бура́влю, бура́вишь; бура́вь.

БУРЧА́ТЬ I.; бурчу́, бурчи́шь; бурчи́.

БУТИ́ТЬ I.; бучу́, бути́шь.

БУ́ХНУТЬ I.; бух, бу́хла.

БУ́ХНУТЬ Р.; бу́хнул, бу́хнула.

БЫТЬ I.; бу́ду, бу́дешь; будь; бу́дучи; есть (3rd pers. sing. pres. tense); (arch. суть, 3rd pers. pl. pres. tense)

В

ВА́КСИТЬ I.; ва́кшу, ва́ксишь; ва́кси.

ВБЕЖА́ТЬ Р.; вбегу́, вбежи́шь, вбегу́т; вбеги́.

ВБИТЬ Р.; вобью́, вобьёшь; вбей; вби́тый.

ВБРО́СИТЬ Р.; вбро́шу, вбро́сишь; вбро́сь; вбро́шенный.

ВВЕЗТИ Р.; ввезу́, ввезёшь; ввези́; ввёз; ввезённый.

ВВЕ́РГНУТЬ Р.; вверг, вве́ргла.

ВВЕСТИ́ Р.; введу́, введёшь; введи́; ввёл; вве́дший; введённый.

ВВИНТИ́ТЬ Р.; ввинчу́, ввинти́шь; вви́нченный.

ВВИТЬ Р.; вовью́, вовьёшь; ввей; вви́тый.

ВВОДИ́ТЬ I.; ввожу́[1], вво́дишь.

ВВОЗИ́ТЬ I.; ввожу́[2], вво́зишь.

ВВЯЗА́ТЬ Р.; ввяжу́, ввя́жешь; ввяжи́; ввя́занный.

ВГЛЯДЕ́ТЬСЯ Р.; вгляжу́сь, вгляди́шься; вгляди́сь.

ВГРЫ́ЗТЬСЯ Р.; вгрызу́сь, вгрызёшься; вгрызи́сь; вгры́зся.

ВДАВА́ТЬСЯ I.; вдаю́сь, вдаёшься; вдава́йся; вдава́ясь.

ВДАВИ́ТЬ Р.; вдавлю́, вда́вишь; вда́вленный.

ВДА́ТЬСЯ Р.; вда́мся, вда́шься, вда́стся, вдади́мся, вдади́тесь, вдаду́тся; вда́йся.

ВДЕТЬ Р.; вде́ну, вде́нешь; вдень; вде́тый.

ВДОЛБИ́ТЬ Р.; вдолблю́, вдолби́шь; вдолблённый.

ВДОХНОВИ́ТЬ Р.; вдохновлю́, вдохнови́шь; вдохновлённый.

ВДУТЬ Р.; вду́ю, вду́ешь; вдуй; вду́тый.

ВЕЗТИ́[1] I.; везёт.

ВЕЗТИ́[2] I.; везу́, везёшь; вези́; вёз.

ВЕЛЕ́ТЬ I. and Р.; велю́, вели́шь; вели́.

ВЕРЕДИ́ТЬ I.; вережу́, вереди́шь.

ВЕРЕЩА́ТЬ I.; верещу́, верещи́шь; верещи́.

ВЕРТЕ́ТЬ I.; верчу́, ве́ртишь; верти́; ве́рченный.

ВЕРХОВОДИ́ТЬ I.; верховожу́, верхово́дишь.

ВЕ́СИТЬ I.; ве́шу, ве́сишь; весь.

ВЕСТИ́ I.; веду́, ведёшь; веди́; вёл; ведо́мый; ве́дший.

ВЕ́ЯТЬ I.; ве́ю, ве́ешь; вей[1]; ве́янный.

ВЖИ́ТЬСЯ Р.; вживу́сь, вживёшься; вживи́сь.

ВЗБАЛАМУ́ТИТЬ Р.; взбаламу́чу, взбаламу́тишь; взбаламу́ть; взбаламу́ченный.

ВЗБЕЖА́ТЬ Р.; взбегу́, взбежи́шь, взбегу́т; взбеги́.

ВЗБЕСИ́ТЬ Р.; взбешу́, взбе́сишь; взбешённый.

ВЗБИТЬ Р.; взобью́, взобьёшь; взбей; взби́тый.

ВЗБОРОЗДИ́ТЬ Р.; взборозжу́, взборозди́шь; взборождённый.

ВЗБРЕСТИ́ Р.; взбреду́, взбредёшь; взбреди́; взбрёл; взбре́дший.

ВЗБУ́ХНУТЬ Р.; взбух, взбу́хла.

ВЗВЕ́СИТЬ Р.; взве́шу, взве́сишь; взвесь; взве́шенный.

ВЗВЕСТИ́ Р.; взведу́, взведёшь; взведи́; взвёл; взве́дший; взведённый.

ВЗВИНТИ́ТЬ Р.; взвинчу́, взвинти́шь; взви́нченный.

ВЗВИТЬ Р.; взовью́, взовьёшь; взвей; взви́тый.

ВЗВОДИ́ТЬ I.; взвожу́, взво́дишь.

ВЗВЫТЬ Р.; взво́ю, взво́ешь; взвой.

ВЗГРОМОЗДИ́ТЬ Р.; взгромозжу́, взгромозди́шь; взгромождённый.

ВЗДЕ́ТЬ Р.; взде́ну, взде́нешь; вздень; взде́тый.

ВЗДУТЬ Р.; взду́ю, взду́ешь; вздуй; взду́тый.

ВЗДЫ́БИТЬ Р.; взды́блю, взды́бишь; вздыбь; взды́бленный.

ВЗЛЕЛЕ́ЯТЬ Р.; взлеле́ю, взлеле́ешь; взлеле́й; взлеле́янный.

ВЗЛЕТЕ́ТЬ Р.; взлечу́, взлети́шь; взлети́.

ВЗЛОХМА́ТИТЬ Р.; взлохма́чу, взлохма́тишь; взлохма́ть; взлохма́ченный.

ВЗМЕСТИ́ Р.; взмету́, взметёшь; взмети́; взмёл; взмётший; взметённый; взмети́.

ВЗМЕТА́ТЬ Р.; взмечу́, взме́чешь; взмечи́; взмётанный.

ВЗМОСТИ́ТЬСЯ Р.; взмощу́сь, взмости́шься.

ВЗМУТИ́ТЬ Р.; взмучу́, взмути́шь (and взму́тишь); взму́ченный.

ВЗМЫТЬ Р.; взмо́ю, взмо́ешь; взмой.

ВЗОЙТИ́ Р.; взойду́, взойдёшь; взойди́; взошёл, взошла́; взоше́дший; взойдя́.

ВЗОРВА́ТЬ Р.; взорву́, взорвёшь; взорви́; взо́рванный.

ВЗРАСТИ́ТЬ Р.; взращу́, взрасти́шь; взращённый.

ВЗРЕВЕ́ТЬ Р.; взреву́, взревёшь; взреви́.

ВЗРЕ́ЗАТЬ Р.; взре́жу, взре́жешь; взрежь; взре́занный.

ВЗРЫТЬ Р.; взро́ю, взро́ешь; взрой; взры́тый.

ВЗ'Е́СТЬСЯ Р.; вз'е́мся, вз'е́шься[1], вз'е́стся, вз'еди́мся, вз'еди́тесь, вз'едя́тся; вз'е́шься[2] (imp.); вз'е́лся.

ВЗЫСКА́ТЬ Р.; взыщу́, взы́щешь; взыщи́; взы́сканный.

ВЗЯТЬ Р.; возьму́, взьмёшь; возьми́; взя́тый.

ВИ́ДЕТЬ I.; ви́жу, ви́дишь; ви́денный.

ВИ́ДЕТЬСЯ I.; ви́жусь, ви́дишься.

ВИЗЖА́ТЬ I.; визжу́, визжи́шь; визжи́.

ВИНТИ́ТЬ I.; винчу́, винти́шь.

ВИСЕ́ТЬ I.; вишу́, виси́шь; виси́.

ВИ́СНУТЬ I.; вис (and ви́снул), ви́сла.

ВИТЬ I.; вью, вьёшь; вей[2]; ви́тый.

ВКАТИ́ТЬ Р.; вкачу́, вка́тишь; вка́ченный.

ВКОЛОТИ́ТЬ Р.; вколочу́, вколо́тишь; вколо́ченный.

ВКОЛО́ТЬ Р.; вколю́, вко́лешь; вколи́; вко́лотый.

ВКРА́ПИТЬ Р.; вкра́плю, вкра́пишь; вкрапь; вкра́пленный.

ВКРАПИ́ТЬ Р.; вкраплю́, вкрапи́шь; вкраплённый.

ВКРА́СТЬСЯ Р.; вкраду́сь, вкрадёшься; вкради́сь; вкра́лся.

ВКРУТИ́ТЬ Р.; вкручу́, вкру́тишь; вкру́ченный.

ВКУСИ́ТЬ Р.; вкушу́, вку́сишь; вкушённый.

ВЛЕЗТЬ Р.; вле́зу, вле́зешь; влезь; влез.

ВЛЕПИ́ТЬ Р.; влеплю́, вле́пишь; вле́пленный.

ВЛЕТЕ́ТЬ Р.; влечу́, влети́шь; влети́.

ВЛЕЧЬ I.; влеку́, влечёшь, влеку́т; влеки́; влёк; влеко́мый.

ВЛЕЧЬ Р.; вля́гу, вля́жешь, вля́гут; вляг; влёг.

ВЛИТЬ Р.; волью́, вольёшь; влей; вли́тый.

ВЛОМИ́ТЬСЯ Р.; вломлю́сь, вло́мишься.

ВЛЮБИ́ТЬ Р.; влюблю́, влю́бишь.

ВМА́ЗАТЬ Р.; вма́жу, вма́жешь; вмажь; вма́занный.

ВМЁРЗНУТЬ Р.; вмёрз, вмёрзла.

ВМЕСИ́ТЬ Р.; вмешу́, вме́сишь; вме́шенный.

ВМЕСТИ́ Р.; вмету́, вметёшь; вмети́; вмёл; вмётший; вметённый.

ВМЕСТИ́ТЬ Р.; вмещу́, вмести́шь; вмещённый.

ВМЯТЬ Р.; вомну́, вомнёшь; вомни́; вмя́тый.

ВНЕСТИ́ Р.; внесу́, внесёшь; внеси́; внёс; внесённый.

ВНИ́КНУТЬ Р.; вник, вни́кла.

ВНИМА́ТЬ I.; (archaic and poetic forms) вне́млю, вне́млешь; внемли́ and вне́мли.

ВНОСИ́ТЬ I.; вношу́, вно́сишь.

ВОБРА́ТЬ Р.; вберу́, вберёшь; вбери́; во́бранный.

ВОВЛЕ́ЧЬ Р.; вовлеку́, вовлечёшь, вовлеку́т; вовлеки́; вовлёк; вовлечённый.

ВОГНА́ТЬ Р.; вгоню́, вго́нишь; вгони́; во́гнанный.

ВОДИ́ТЬ I.; вожу́[1], во́дишь.

ВОДРУЗИ́ТЬ Р.; водружу́, водрузи́шь; водружённый.

ВОЕВА́ТЬ I.; вою́ю, вою́ешь; вою́й.

ВОЗБУДИ́ТЬ Р.; возбужу́, возбуди́шь; возбуждённый.

ВОЗВЕСТИ́ Р.; возведу́, возведёшь; возведи́; возвёл; возве́дший; возведённый.

ВОЗВЕСТИ́ТЬ Р.; возвещу́, возвести́шь; возвещённый.

ВОЗВОДИ́ТЬ I.; возвожу́, возво́дишь.

ВОЗВРАТИ́ТЬ Р.; возвращу́, возврати́шь; возвращённый.

ВОЗВЫ́СИТЬ Р.; возвы́шу, возвы́сишь; возвы́сь; возвы́шенный.

ВОЗГЛА́ВИТЬ Р.; возгла́влю, возгла́вишь; возгла́вь; возгла́вленный.

ВОЗГЛАСИ́ТЬ Р.; возглашу́, возгласи́шь; возглашённый.

ВОЗГОРДИ́ТЬСЯ Р.; розгоржу́сь, возгорди́шься.

ВОЗГОРЕ́ТЬСЯ Р.; возгорю́сь, возгори́шься; возгори́сь.

ВОЗДАВА́ТЬ I.; воздаю́, воздаёшь; воздава́й; воздава́я.

ВОЗДА́ТЬ Р.; возда́м, возда́шь, возда́ст, воздади́м, воздади́те, воздаду́т; возда́й; во́зданный.

ВОЗДВИ́ГНУТЬ Р.; воздви́г, воздви́гла.

ВОЗДЕРЖА́ТЬСЯ Р.; воздержу́сь, воздержи́шься; воздержи́сь.

ВОЗДЕ́ТЬ Р.; возде́ну, возде́нешь; возде́нь; возде́тый.

ВОЗЖЕ́ЧЬ Р.; возжгу́, возжжёшь, возжгу́т; возжги́; возжёг, возжгла́; возжжённый.

ВОЗЗВА́ТЬ Р.; воззову́, воззовёшь; воззови́.

ВОЗИ́ТЬ I.; вожу́[2], во́зишь.

ВОЗЛЕЖА́ТЬ I.; возлежу́, возлежи́шь; возлежи́.

ВОЗЛЕ́ЧЬ Р.; возля́гу, возля́жешь, возля́гут; возля́г; возлёг.

ВОЗЛЮБИ́ТЬ Р.; возлюблю́, возлю́бишь; возлю́бленный.

ВОЗМЕСТИ́ТЬ Р.; возмещу́, возмести́шь; возмещённый.

ВОЗМУТИ́ТЬ Р.; возмущу́, возмути́шь; возмущённый.

ВОЗНАГРАДА́ТЬ Р.; вознагражу́, вознаградишь; вознаграждённый.

ВОЗНЕНАВИ́ДЕТЬ Р.; возненави́жу, возненави́дишь; возненави́дь.

ВОЗНЕСТИ́ Р.; вознесу́, вознесёшь; вознеси́; вознёс; вознесённый.

ВОЗНИ́КНУТЬ Р.; возни́к, возни́кла.

ВОЗНОСИ́ТЬ I.; возношу́, возно́сишь.

ВОЗОБНОВИ́ТЬ Р.; возобновлю́, возобнови́шь; возобновлённый.

ВОЗОПИ́ТЬ Р.; возоплю́, возопи́шь.

ВОЗОПИЯ́ТЬ Р.; возопию́, возопие́шь; возопий.

ВОЗРАЗИ́ТЬ Р.; возражу́, возрази́шь.

ВОЗРАСТИ́ Р.; возрасту́, возрастёшь; возрасти́ (imp.); возро́с.

ВОЗРОДИ́ТЬ Р.; возрожу́, возроди́шь; возрождённый.

ВОЗРОПТА́ТЬ Р.; возропщу́, возро́пщешь; возропщи́.

ВОЙТИ́ Р.; войду́, войдёшь; войди́; вошёл, вошла́; воше́дший; войда́.

ВОЛО́ЧЬ I.; волоку́, волочёшь, волоку́т; волоки́; воло́к; волоча́.

ВОМЧА́ТЬСЯ Р.; вомчу́сь, вомчи́шься; вомчи́сь.

ВОНЗИ́ТЬ Р.; вонжу́, вонзи́шь; вонзённый.

ВООБРАЗИ́ТЬ Р.; воображу́, вообрази́шь; воображённый.

ВООДУШЕВИ́ТЬ Р.; воодушевлю́, воодушеви́шь; воодушевлённый.

ВОПИ́ТЬ I.; воплю́, вопи́шь.

ВОПИЯ́ТЬ I.; вопию́, вопие́шь; вопий.

ВОПЛОТИ́ТЬ Р.; вомлощу́, воплоти́шь; воплощённый.

ВОПРОСИ́ТЬ Р.; вопрошу́, вопроси́шь; вопрошённый.

ВОРВА́ТЬСЯ Р.; ворву́сь, ворвёшься; ворви́сь.

ВОРОТИ́ТЬ Р.; ворочу́[1], воро́тишь.

ВОРОТИ́ТЬ I.; ворочу́[2], воро́тишь.

ВОРЧА́ТЬ I.; ворчу́, ворчи́шь; ворчи́.

ВОСКРЕСИ́ТЬ Р.; воскрешу́, воскреси́шь; воскрешённый.

ВОСКРЕ́СНУТЬ Р.; воскре́с, воскре́сла.

ВОСПЕ́ТЬ Р.; воспою́, воспоёшь; воспо́й; воспе́тый.

ВОСПРЕТИ́ТЬ Р.; воспрещу́, воспрети́шь; воспрещённый.

ВОСПРИНЯ́ТЬ Р.; восприму́, восприме́шь; восприми́; воспри́нятый.

ВОСПРОИЗВЕСТИ́ Р.; воспроизведу́, воспроизведёшь; воспроизведи́; воспроизвёл; воспроизве́дший; воспроизведённый; воспроизве́дши and воспроизведя́.

ВОСПРОИЗВОДИ́ТЬ I.; воспроизвожу́, воспроизво́дишь.

ВОСПРОТИ́ВИТЬСЯ Р.; воспроти́влюсь, воспроти́вишься; воспроти́вься.

ВОССЕ́СТЬ Р.; восся́ду, восся́дешь; восся́дь; воссе́л.

ВОССЛА́ВИТЬ Р.; воссла́влю, воссла́вишь; воссла́вь; воссла́вленный.

ВОССОЗДАВА́ТЬ I.; воссоздаю́, воссоздаёшь; воссоздава́й; воссоздава́я.

ВОССОЗДА́ТЬ Р.; воссозда́м, воссозда́шь, воссозда́ст, воссоздади́м, воссоздади́те, воссоздаду́т; воссозда́й; воссо́зданный.

ВОССТАВА́ТЬ I.; восстаю́, восстаёшь; восстава́й; восстава́я.

ВОССТА́ВИТЬ Р.; восста́влю, восста́вишь; восста́вь; восста́вленный.

ВОССТАНОВИ́ТЬ Р.; восстановлю́, восстано́вишь; восстано́вленный.

ВОССТА́ТЬ Р.; восста́ну, восста́нешь; восста́нь.

ВОСХИ́ТИТЬ Р.; восхи́щу, восхи́тишь; восхи́ть; восхи́щенный.

ВОСХИТИ́ТЬ Р.; восхищу́, восхити́шь; восхищённый.

ВОСХОДИ́ТЬ I.; восхожу́, восхо́дишь.

ВОТКА́ТЬ Р.; вотку́, воткёшь; вотки́; во́тканный.

ВПАСТЬ; впаду́, впадёшь; впади́; впал.

ВПИСА́ТЬ Р.; впишу́, впи́шешь; впиши́; впи́санный.

ВПИТЬСЯ Р.; вопьюсь, вопьёшься; впейся.

ВПЛЕСТИ Р.; вплету, вплетёшь; вплети; вплёл; вплётший; вплетённый.

ВПЛЫТЬ Р.; вплыву, вплывёшь; вплыви.

ВПОЛЗТИ Р.; вползу, вползёшь; вползи; вполз.

ВПРАВИТЬ Р.; вправлю, вправишь; вправь; вправленный.

ВПРЯЧЬ Р.; впрягу, впряжёшь, впрягут; впряги; впряг; впряжённый.

ВПУСТИТЬ Р.; впущу, впустишь; впущенный.

ВРАЗУМИТЬ Р.; вразумлю, вразумишь; вразумлённый.

ВРАСТИ Р.; врастёт, врастут; врос.

ВРАТЬ I., вру, врёшь; ври.

ВРЕДИТЬ I.; врежу, вредишь.

ВРЕЗАТЬ Р.; врежу, врежешь; врежь; врезанный.

ВРУБИТЬ Р.; врублю, врубишь; врубленный.

ВРЫТЬ Р.; врою, вроешь; врой; врытый.

ВСАДИТЬ Р.; всажу, всадишь; всаженный.

ВСКИПЕТЬ Р.; вскиплю, вскипишь; вскипи.

ВСКИПЯТИТЬ Р.; вскипячу, вскипятишь, вскипячённый.

ВСКОРМИТЬ Р.; вскормлю, вскормишь; вскормленный (and arch. вскормлённый).

ВСКРИЧАТЬ Р.; вскричу, вскричишь; вскричи.

ВСКРЫТЬ Р.; вскрою, вскроешь; вскрой; вскрытый.

ВСМОТРЕТЬСЯ Р.; всмотрюсь, всмотришься; всмотрись.

ВСОСАТЬ Р.; всосу, всосёшь; всоси; всосанный.

ВСПАХАТЬ Р.; вспашу, вспашешь; вспаши; вспаханный.

ВСПЛЫТЬ Р.; всплыву, всплывёшь; всплыви.

ВСПОРОТЬ Р.; вспорю, вспорешь; вспори; вспоротый.

ВСПУХНУТЬ Р.; вспух, вспухла.

ВСТАВАТЬ I.; встаю, встаёшь; вставай; вставая.

ВСТАВИТЬ Р.; вставлю, вставишь; вставь; вставленный.

ВСТАТЬ Р.; встану, встанешь; встань.

ВСТРЕТИТЬ Р.; встречу, встретишь; встреть; встреченный.

ВСТРЯТЬ Р.; встряну, встрянешь; встрянь.

ВСТУПИТЬ Р.; вступлю, вступишь.

ВСХОДИТЬ I.; всхожу, всходишь.

ВСЫПАТЬ Р.; всыплю, всыплешь; всыпь; всыпанный.

ВТЕРЕТЬ Р.; вотру, вотрёшь; вотри; втёр; втёртый; втерев and втёрши.

ВТЕСАТЬСЯ Р.; втешусь, втешешся; втешись.

ВТЕЧЬ Р.; втечёт, втекут; втёк.

ВТОПТАТЬ Р.; втопчу, втопчешь; втопчи; втоптанный.

ВТРАВИТЬ Р.; втравлю, втравишь; втравленный.

ВХОДИТЬ I.; вхожу, входишь.

ВЦЕПИТЬСЯ Р.; вцеплюсь, вцепишься.

ВШИТЬ Р.; вошью, вошьёшь; вшей; вшитый.

В'ЕСТЬСЯ Р.; в'емся, в'ешься[1], в'естся, в'едимся, в'едитесь, в'едятся; в'ешься[2] (imp.); в'елся.

В'ЕХАТЬ Р.; в'еду, в'едешь; в'езжай.

ВЫБЕЖАТЬ Р.; выбегу, выбежишь, выбегут; выбеги.

ВЫБИТЬ Р.; выбью, выбьешь; выбей; выбитый.

ВЫБРАТЬ Р.; выберу, выберешь; выбери; выбранный.

ВЫБРЕСТИ Р.; выбреду, выбредешь; выбреди; выбрел; выбредший.

ВЫБРИТЬ Р.; выбрею, выбреешь; выбрей; выбритый.

ВЫБРОСИТЬ Р.; выброшу, выбросишь; выбрось and выброси.

ВЫБЫТЬ Р.; выбуду, выбудешь; выбудь.

ВЫВЕЗТИ Р.; вывезу, вывезешь; вывези; вывез; вывезенный.

ВЫВЕРТЕТЬ Р.; выверчу, вывертишь; выверти; выверченный.

ВЫВЕСИТЬ Р.; вывешу, вывесишь; вывеси and вывесь; вывешенный.

ВЫВЕСТИ Р.; выведу, выведешь; выведи; вывел; выведший; выведенный.

ВЫВИНТИТЬ Р.; вывинчу, вывинтишь; вывинченный.

ВЫ́ВОДИТЬ Р.; вы́вожу[1], вы́водишь; вы́воженный.

ВЫВОДИ́ТЬ I.; вывожу́[1], выво́дишь.

ВЫ́ВОЗИТЬ Р.; вы́вожу[2], вы́возишь; вы́воженный.

ВЫВОЗИ́ТЬ I.; вывожу́[2], выво́зишь.

ВЫ́ВОЛОЧЬ Р.; вы́волоку, вы́волочешь, вы́волокут; вы́волоки; вы́волок; вы́волоченный.

ВЫ́ВОРОТИТЬ Р.; вы́ворочу, вы́воротишь.

ВЫ́ВЯЗАТЬ Р.; вы́вяжу, вы́вяжешь; вы́вяжи; вы́вязанный.

ВЫ́ГЛАДИТЬ Р.; вы́глажу, вы́гладишь; вы́гладь; вы́глаженный.

ВЫ́ГЛЯДЕТЬ I.; вы́гляжу[1], вы́глядишь; вы́гляди.

ВЫ́ГЛЯДЕТЬ Р.; вы́гляжу[2], вы́глядишь; вы́гляди.

ВЫ́ГНАТЬ Р.; вы́гоню, вы́гонишь; вы́гони; вы́гнанный.

ВЫ́ГНИТЬ Р.; вы́гниет, вы́гниют.

ВЫ́ГОРЕТЬ Р.; вы́горит, вы́горят.

ВЫ́ГОРОДИТЬ Р.; вы́горожу, вы́городишь; вы́гороженный.

ВЫ́ГРЕСТИ, Р.; вы́гребу, вы́гребешь; вы́греби; вы́греб; вы́гребенный.

ВЫ́ГРУЗИТЬ Р.; вы́гружу, вы́грузишь; вы́груженный.

ВЫ́ГРЫЗТЬ Р.; вы́грызу, вы́грызешь; вы́грызи; вы́грыз; вы́грызенный.

ВЫДАВА́ТЬ I.; выдаю́, выдаёшь; выдава́й; выдава́я.

ВЫ́ДАВИТЬ Р.; вы́давлю, вы́давишь; вы́давленный.

ВЫ́ДАТЬ Р.; вы́дам, вы́дашь, вы́даст, вы́дадим, вы́дадите, вы́дадут; вы́дай; вы́данный.

ВЫ́ДЕРЖАТЬ Р.; вы́держу, вы́держишь; вы́держи; вы́держанный.

ВЫ́ДОЛБИТЬ Р.; вы́долблю, вы́долбишь; вы́долбленный.

ВЫ́ДРАТЬ Р.; вы́деру, вы́дерешь; вы́дери; вы́дранный.

ВЫ́ДУБИТЬ Р.; вы́дублю, вы́дубишь; вы́дубленный.

ВЫ́ДУТЬ Р.; вы́дую, вы́дуешь; вы́дуй; вы́дутый.

ВЫ́ЕЗДИТЬ Р.; вы́езжу, вы́ездишь; вы́езженный.

ВЫ́ЕСТЬ Р.; вы́ем, вы́ешь[1], вы́ест, вы́едим, вы́едите, вы́едят; вы́ешь[2] (imp.); вы́ел; вы́еденный.

ВЫ́ЕХАТЬ Р.; вы́еду, вы́едешь; вы́езжай.

ВЫ́ЖАТЬ[1] Р.; вы́жму, вы́жмешь; вы́жми; вы́жатый[1].

ВЫ́ЖАТЬ[2] Р.; вы́жну, вы́жнешь; вы́жни; вы́жатый[2].

ВЫ́ЖДАТЬ Р.; вы́жду, вы́ждешь; вы́жди; вы́жданный.

ВЫ́ЖЕЧЬ Р.; вы́жгу, вы́жжешь, вы́жгут; вы́жги; вы́жег, вы́жгла; вы́жженный.

ВЫ́ЖИТЬ Р.; вы́живу, вы́живешь; вы́живи; вы́житый.

ВЫ́ЗВАТЬ Р.; вы́зову, вы́зовешь; вы́зови; вы́званный.

ВЫ́ЗОЛТИТЬ Р.; вы́золочу, вы́золотишь; вы́золоченный.

ВЫ́ЗЯБНУТЬ Р.; вы́зяб, вы́зябла.

ВЫ́ИСКАТЬ Р.; вы́ищу, вы́ищешь; вы́ищи; вы́исканный.

ВЫ́ЙТИ Р.; вы́йду, вы́йдешь; вы́йди; вы́шел, вы́шла; вы́шедший; вы́йдя.

ВЫ́КАЗАТЬ Р.; вы́кажу, вы́кажешь; вы́кажи; вы́казанный.

ВЫ́КАТИТЬ Р.; вы́качу, вы́катишь; вы́каченный.

ВЫ́КИПЕТЬ Р.; вы́кипит, вы́кипят.

ВЫ́КИПЯТИТЬ Р.; вы́кипячу, вы́кипятишь; вы́кипяченный.

ВЫ́КИСНУТЬ Р.; вы́кис, вы́кисла.

ВЫ́КОЛОТИТЬ Р.; вы́колочу, вы́колотишь; вы́колоченный.

ВЫ́КОЛОТЬ Р.; вы́колю, вы́колешь; вы́коли; вы́колотый.

ВЫ́КОРМИТЬ Р.; вы́кормлю, вы́кормишь; вы́кормленный.

ВЫ́КОСИТЬ Р.; вы́кошу, вы́косишь; вы́кошенный.

ВЫ́КРАСИТЬ Р.; вы́крашу, вы́красишь; вы́крась; вы́крашенный.

ВЫ́КРАСТЬ Р.; вы́краду, вы́крадешь; вы́кради; вы́крал; вы́краденный.

ВЫ́КРУТИТЬ Р.; вы́кручу, вы́крутишь; вы́крученный.

ВЫ́КУПИТЬ Р.; вы́куплю, вы́купишь; вы́купленный.

ВЫ́ЛЕЖАТЬ Р.; вы́лежу, вы́лежишь; вы́лежи.

ВЫ́ЛЕЗТИ Р.; вы́лезу, вы́лезешь; вы́лези and вы́лезь; вы́лез.

ВЫ́ЛЕЗТЬ Р.; вы́лезу, вы́лезешь; вы́лези and вы́лезь; вы́лез.

ВЫ́ЛЕПИТЬ Р.; вы́леплю, вы́лепишь; вы́лепленный.

ВЫ́ЛЕТЕТЬ Р.; вы́лечу, вы́летишь; вы́лети.

ВЫ́ЛИЗАТЬ Р.; вы́лижу, вы́лижешь; вы́лижи; вы́лизанный.

ВЫ́ЛИТЬ Р.; вы́лью, вы́льешь; вы́лей; вы́литый.

ВЫ́ЛОВИТЬ Р.; вы́ловлю, вы́ловишь; вы́ловленный.

ВЫ́ЛУДИТЬ Р.; вы́лужу, вы́лудишь; вы́луженный.

ВЫ́ЛУПИТЬ Р.; вы́луплю, вы́лупишь; вы́лупленный.

ВЫ́МАЗАТЬ Р.; вы́мажу, вы́мажешь; вы́мажи and вы́мажь; вы́мазанный.

ВЫ́МЕРЕТЬ Р.; вы́мрет, вы́мрут; вы́мри; вы́мер (1st and 2nd pers. sing. not used).

ВЫ́МЕРЗНУТЬ Р.; вы́мерз, вы́мерзла.

ВЫ́МЕСИТЬ Р.; вы́мешу, вы́месишь; вы́мешенный.

ВЫ́МЕСТИ Р.; вы́мету, вы́метешь; вы́мети; вы́мел; вы́метший; вы́метенный; вы́метя.

ВЫ́МЕСТИТЬ Р.; вы́мещу, вы́местишь; вы́мещенный.

ВЫ́МЕТАТЬ Р.; вы́мечу[1], вы́мечешь; вы́мечи; вы́меченный.

ВЫ́МЕТИТЬ Р.; вы́мечу[2], вы́метишь; вы́меть; вы́меченный.

ВЫ́МОКНУТЬ Р.; вы́мок, вы́мокла.

ВЫ́МОЛВИТЬ Р.; вы́молвлю, вы́молвишь; вы́молви; вы́молвленный.

ВЫ́МОРОЗИТЬ Р.; вы́морожу, вы́морозишь; вы́морозь; вы́мороженный.

ВЫ́МОСТИТЬ Р.; вы́мощу, вы́мостишь; вы́мощенный.

ВЫ́МЫТЬ Р.; вы́мою, вы́моешь; вы́мой; вы́мытый.

ВЫ́НЕСТИ Р.; вы́несу, вы́несешь; вы́неси; вы́нес; вы́несенный.

ВЫ́НОСИТЬ Р.; вы́ношу, вы́носишь; вы́ношенный.

ВЫНОСИ́ТЬ I.; выношу́, выноси́шь.

ВЫ́НУДИТЬ Р.; вы́нужу, вы́нудишь; вы́нужденный.

ВЫ́НУТЬ Р.; вынь (imp.); вы́нутый.

ВЫ́ПАСТЬ Р.; вы́паду, вы́падешь; вы́пади; вы́пал.

ВЫ́ПЕРЕТЬ Р.; вы́пру, вы́прешь; вы́при; вы́пер; вы́пертый.

ВЫ́ПЕТЬ Р.; вы́пою, вы́поешь; вы́пой; вы́петый.

ВЫ́ПЕЧЬ Р.; вы́пеку, вы́печешь, вы́пекут; вы́пеки; вы́пек; вы́печенный.

ВЫ́ПИСАТЬ Р.; вы́пишу, вы́пишешь; вы́пиши; вы́писанный.

ВЫ́ПИТЬ Р.; вы́пью, вы́пьешь; вы́пей; вы́питый.

ВЫ́ПЛАВИТЬ Р.; вы́плавлю, вы́плавишь; вы́плави and вы́плавь; вы́плавленный.

ВЫ́ПЛАКАТЬ Р.; вы́плачу[1], вы́плачешь; вы́плачь; вы́плаканный.

ВЫ́ПЛАТИТЬ Р.; вы́плачу[2], вы́платишь; вы́плаченный.

ВЫ́ПЛЕСКАТЬ Р.; вы́плещу, вы́плещешь; вы́плещи; вы́плесканный.

ВЫ́ПЛЕСТИ Р.; вы́плету, вы́плетешь; вы́плети; вы́плел; вы́плетший; вы́плетенный; вы́плетя.

ВЫ́ПЛЫТЬ Р.; вы́плыву, вы́плывешь; вы́плыви.

ВЫ́ПОЛЗТИ Р.; вы́ползу, вы́ползешь; вы́ползи; вы́полз.

ВЫ́ПОЛОСКАТЬ Р.; вы́полощу, вы́полощешь; вы́полощи; вы́полосканный.

ВЫ́ПОЛОТЬ Р.; вы́полю, вы́полешь; вы́поли; вы́полотый.

ВЫ́ПОРОТЬ[1] Р.; вы́порю[1], вы́порешь; вы́пори; вы́поротый.

ВЫ́ПОРОТЬ[2] Р.; вы́порю[2], вы́порешь; вы́пори; вы́поротый.

ВЫ́ПРАВИТЬ Р.; вы́правлю, вы́правишь; вы́правь; вы́правленный.

ВЫ́ПРОВОДИТЬ Р.; вы́провожу, вы́проводишь; вы́провоженный.

ВЫ́ПРОСИТЬ Р.; вы́прошу, вы́просишь; вы́прошенный.

ВЫ́ПРЯМИТЬ Р.; вы́прямлю, вы́прямишь; вы́прямленный.

ВЫ́ПРЯЧЬ Р.; вы́прягу, вы́пряжешь, вы́прягут; вы́пряги; вы́пряг; вы́пряженный.

ВЫ́ПУСТИТЬ Р.; вы́пущу, вы́пустишь; вы́пущенный.

ВЫ́ПЯТИТЬ Р.; вы́пячу, вы́пятишь; вы́пяченный.

ВЫ́РАЗИТЬ Р.; вы́ражу, вы́разишь; вы́раженный.

ВЫ́РАСТИ Р.; вы́расту, вы́растешь; вы́расти (imp.); вы́рос.

ВЫ́РАСТИТЬ P.; вы́ращу, вы́растишь; вы́расти; вы́ращенный.

ВЫ́РВАТЬ P.; вы́рву, вы́рвешь; вы́рви; вы́рванный.

ВЫ́РЕЗАТЬ P.; вы́режу, вы́режешь; вы́режи and вы́режь; вы́резанный.

ВЫ́РУБИТЬ P.; вы́рублю, вы́рубишь; вы́рубленный.

ВЫ́РЫТЬ P.; вы́рою, вы́роешь; вы́рой; вы́рытый.

ВЫ́РЯДИТЬ P.; вы́ряжу, вы́рядишь; вы́ряженный.

ВЫ́САДИТЬ P.; вы́сажу, вы́садишь; вы́саженный.

ВЫ́СВОБОДИТЬ P.; вы́свобожу, вы́свободишь; вы́свобожденный.

ВЫ́СЕЧЬ P.; вы́секу, вы́сечешь, вы́секут; вы́секи; вы́сек; вы́сеченный.

ВЫ́СЕЯТЬ P.; вы́сею, вы́сеешь; вы́сей; вы́сеянный.

ВЫ́СИДЕТЬ P.; вы́сижу, вы́сидишь; вы́сиди; вы́сиженный.

ВЫ́СКАЗАТЬ P.; вы́скажу, вы́скажешь; вы́скажи; вы́сказанный.

ВЫ́СКРЕСТИ P.; вы́скребу, вы́скребешь; вы́скреби; вы́скреб; вы́скребенный.

ВЫ́СЛАТЬ P.; вы́шлю, вы́шлешь; вы́шли²; вы́сланный.

ВЫ́СЛЕДИТЬ P.; вы́слежу, вы́следишь; вы́следженный.

ВЫ́СМЕЯТЬ P.; вы́смею, вы́смеешь; вы́смей; вы́смеянный.

ВЫ́СМОТРЕТЬ P.; вы́смотрю, вы́смотришь; вы́смотри; вы́смотренный.

ВЫ́СОСАТЬ P.; вы́сосу, вы́сосешь; вы́соси; вы́сосанный.

ВЫ́СОХНУТЬ P.; вы́сох, вы́сохла.

ВЫ́СПАТЬСЯ P.; вы́сплюсь, вы́спишься; вы́спись.

ВЫ́СПРОСИТЬ P.; вы́спрошу, вы́спросишь; вы́спрошенный.

ВЫ́СТАВИТЬ P.; вы́ставлю, вы́ставишь; вы́ставь; вы́ставленный.

ВЫ́СТЕЛИТЬ P.; вы́стелю, вы́стелешь; вы́стели; вы́стланный.

ВЫ́СТЛАТЬ P.; вы́стелю, вы́стелешь; вы́стели; вы́стланный.

ВЫ́СТОЯТЬ P.; вы́стою, вы́стоишь; вы́стои and вы́стой.

ВЫ́СТРИЧЬ P.; вы́стригу, вы́стрижешь, вы́стригут; вы́стриги; вы́стриг; вы́стриженный.

ВЫ́СТУДИТЬ P.; вы́стужу, вы́студишь; вы́стуженный.

ВЫ́СТУПИТЬ P.; вы́ступлю, вы́ступишь.

ВЫ́СУДИТЬ P.; вы́сужу, вы́судишь; вы́суженный.

ВЫ́СЫПАТЬ P.; вы́сыплю, вы́сыплешь; вы́сыпи and вы́сыпь; вы́сыпанный.

ВЫ́ТВЕРДИТЬ P.; вы́твержу, вы́твердишь; вы́твержденный.

ВЫ́ТЕРЕБИТЬ P.; вы́тереблю, вы́теребишь; вы́теребленный.

ВЫ́ТЕРЕТЬ P.; вы́тру, вы́трешь; вы́три; вы́тер; вы́тертый; вы́терев and вы́терши.

ВЫ́ТЕРПЕТЬ P.; вы́терплю, вы́терпишь; вы́терпи.

ВЫ́ТЕСАТЬ P.; вы́тешу, вы́тешешь; вы́теши; вы́тесанный.

ВЫ́ТЕЧЬ P.; вы́течет, вы́текут; вы́теки; вы́тек.

ВЫ́ТКАТЬ P.; вы́тку, вы́ткешь; вы́тки; вы́тканный.

ВЫ́ТОПИТЬ P.; вы́топлю, вы́топишь; вы́топленный.

ВЫ́ТОПТАТЬ P.; вы́топчу, вы́топчешь; вы́топчи; вы́топтанный.

ВЫ́ТРАВИТЬ P.; вы́травлю, вы́травишь; вы́травленный.

ВЫ́ТРЕЗВИТЬ P.; вы́трезвлю, вы́трезвишь; вы́трезвленный.

ВЫ́ТРУСИТЬ P.; вы́трушу, вы́трусишь; вы́трушенный.

ВЫ́ТРЯСТИ P.; вы́трясу, вы́трясешь; вы́тряси; вы́тряс; вы́трясенный.

ВЫ́ТЬ I.; во́ю, во́ешь; вой.

ВЫ́УДИТЬ P.; вы́ужу, вы́удишь; вы́уженный.

ВЫ́ХВАТИТЬ P.; вы́хвачу, вы́хватишь; вы́хваченный.

ВЫ́ХЛОПОТАТЬ P.; вы́хлопочу, вы́хлопочешь; вы́хлопочи; вы́хлопотанный.

ВЫХОДИ́ТЬ I.; выхожу́, выхо́дишь.

ВЫ́ХОДИТЬ P.; вы́хожу, вы́ходишь; вы́хоженный.

ВЫ́ХОЛОСТИТЬ P.; вы́холощу, вы́холостишь; вы́холощенный.

ВЫ́ЦВЕСТИ P.; вы́цветет, вы́цветут; вы́цвети; вы́цвел; вы́цветший.

ВЫ́ЦЕДИТЬ P.; вы́цежу, вы́цедишь; вы́цеженный.

ВЫ́ЧЕРТИТЬ P.; вы́черчу, вы́чертишь; вы́черченный.

ВЫ́ЧЕСАТЬ Р.; вы́чешу, вы́чешешь; вы́чеши; вы́чесанный.

ВЫ́ЧЕСТЬ Р.; вы́чту, вы́чтешь; вы́чти; вы́чел, вы́чла; вы́четший; вы́чтенный; вы́чтя.

ВЫ́ЧИСТИТЬ Р.; вы́чищу, вы́чистишь; вы́чисти and вы́чисть; вы́чищенный.

ВЫ́ШИБИТЬ Р.; вы́шибу, вы́шибешь; вы́шиби; вы́шиб; вы́шибленный.

ВЫ́ШИТЬ Р.; вы́шью, вы́шьешь; вы́шей; вы́шитый.

ВЫ́ШУТИТЬ Р.; вы́шучу, вы́шутишь; вы́шученный.

ВЫ́ЩЕРБИТЬ Р.; вы́щерблю, вы́щербишь; вы́щербленный.

ВЫ́ЩИПАТЬ Р.; вы́щиплю, вы́щиплешь; вы́щипли; вы́щипанный.

ВЫ́ЯВИТЬ Р.; вы́явлю, вы́явишь; вы́явленный.

ВЯЗА́ТЬ І.; вяжу́, вя́жешь; вяжи́; вя́занный.

ВЯ́ЗНУТЬ І.; вяз, вя́зла.

ВЯ́НУТЬ І.; вял, вя́ла; вя́нувший.

Г

ГА́ДИТЬ І.; га́жу, га́дишь; га́дь.

ГАЛДѢ́ТЬ І.; галди́шь, галдя́т; галди́ (1st pers. sing. not used).

ГАСИ́ТЬ І.; гашу́, га́сишь.

ГА́СНУТЬ І.; гас, га́сла.

ГАТИ́ТЬ І.; гачу́, гати́шь.

ГИ́БНУТЬ І.; гиб, ги́бла.

ГЛА́ДИТЬ І.; гла́жу, гла́дишь; гладь; гла́женный.

ГЛАСИ́ТЬ І.; глашу́, гласи́шь.

ГЛОДА́ТЬ І.; гложу́, гло́жешь; гложи́; гло́данный; гложа́ and глодая.

ГЛО́ХНУТЬ І.; глох, гло́хла.

ГЛУПИ́ТЬ І.; глуплю́, глупи́шь.

ГЛЯДѢ́ТЬ І.; гляжу́, гляди́шь; гляди́; гля́дючи, гля́дя and глядя́.

ГНАТЬ І.; гоню́, го́нишь; гони́.

ГНѢВИ́ТЬ І.; гневлю́, гневи́шь.

ГНЕСТИ́ І.; гнету́, гнетёшь; гнети́ (past tense not used).

ГНИТЬ І.; гнию́, гниёшь (no imperative).

ГНУСА́ВИТЬ І.; гнуса́влю, гнуса́вишь; гнуса́вь.

ГНУСИ́ТЬ І.; гнушу́, гнуси́шь.

ГОГОТА́ТЬ І.; гогочу́, гого́чешь; гогочи́.

ГОДИ́ТЬСЯ І.; гожу́сь, годи́шься; годи́сь.

ГОЛОСИ́ТЬ І.; голошу́, голоси́шь.

ГОЛУ́БИТЬ І.; голу́блю, голу́бишь; голу́бь.

ГО́РБИТЬ І.; го́рблю, го́рбишь; го́рби and горбь.

ГОРДИ́ТЬСЯ І.; горжу́сь, горди́шься.

ГОРѢ́ТЬ І.; горю́, гори́шь; гори́.

ГО́РКНУТЬ І.; горк, го́ркла.

ГОРОДИ́ТЬ І.; горожу́, горо́дишь (and городи́шь).

ГОСТИ́ТЬ І.; гощу́, гости́шь.

ГОТО́ВИТЬ І.; гото́влю, гото́вишь; гото́вь.

ГРА́БИТЬ І.; гра́блю, гра́бишь; грабь.

ГРАФИ́ТЬ І.; графлю́, графи́шь; графлённый.

ГРѢ́ЗИТЬ І.; грѣ́жу, грѣ́зишь; грѣзь.

ГРЕМѢ́ТЬ І.; гремлю́, греми́шь; греми́.

ГРЕСТИ́ І.; гребу́, гребёшь; греби́; грёб.

ГРОЗИ́ТЬ І.; грожу́, грози́шь.

ГРОМИ́ТЬ І.; громлю́, громи́шь.

ГРОМОЗДИ́ТЬ І.; громозжу́, громозди́шь.

ГРОХОТА́ТЬ І.; грохочу́[1], грохо́чешь; грохочи́.

ГРОХОТИ́ТЬ І.; грохочу́[2], грохоти́шь.

ГРУБИ́ТЬ І.; грублю́, груби́шь.

ГРУЗИ́ТЬ І.; гружу́, гру́зишь (and грузи́шь); гру́женный and гружённый.

ГРУСТИ́ТЬ І.; грущу́, грусти́шь.

ГРЫЗТЬ І.; грызу́, грызёшь; грызи́; грыз.

ГРЯСТИ́ І.; гряду́, грядёшь; гряди́ (inf. and past tense not used; 1st pers. seldom used).

ГУБИ́ТЬ І.; гублю́, гу́бишь.

ГУДѢ́ТЬ І.; гужу́, гуди́шь; гуди́.

Д

ДАВА́ТЬ I.; даю́, даёшь; дава́й; дава́я.

ДАВИ́ТЬ I.; давлю́, да́вишь; да́вленный.

ДАВИ́ТЬСЯ I.; давлю́сь, да́вишься.

ДАТЬ Р.; дам, дашь, даст, дади́м, дади́те, даду́т; дай; да́нный.

ДВИ́ГАТЬ I.; дви́жу, дви́жешь (also дви́гаю, дви́гаешь); дви́гай; дви́жимый; дви́гая.

ДЕРЖА́ТЬ I.; держу́, де́ржишь; держи́; де́ржанный.

ДЕТЬ Р.; де́ну, де́нешь; день.

ДЕ́ЯТЬСЯ I.; де́ется (3rd pers. only).

ДИВИ́ТЬ I.; дивлю́, диви́шь.

ДОБА́ВИТЬ Р.; доба́влю, доба́вишь; доба́вь; доба́вленный.

ДОБЕЖА́ТЬ Р.; добегу́, добежи́шь, добегу́т; добеги́.

ДОБИ́ТЬ Р.; добью́, добьёшь; добе́й; доби́тый.

ДОБРА́ТЬ Р.; доберу́, доберёшь; добери́; до́бранный.

ДОБРА́ТЬСЯ Р.; доберу́сь, доберёшься; добери́сь.

ДОБРЕСТИ́ Р.; добреду́, добредёшь; добреди́; добрёл; добре́дший; добредя́.

ДОБРО́СИТЬ Р.; добро́шу, добро́сишь; добро́сь; добро́шенный.

ДОБУДИ́ТЬСЯ Р.; добужу́сь, добу́дишься.

ДОБЫ́ТЬ Р.; добу́ду, добу́дешь; добу́дь; до́был; добы́тый.

ДОВЕЗТИ́ Р.; довезу́, довезёшь; довези́; довёз; довезённый; довезя́ and довёзши.

ДОВЕСТИ́ Р.; доведу́, доведёшь; доведи́; довёл; дове́дший; доведённый; доведя́ and дове́дши.

ДОВОДИ́ТЬ I.; довожу́[2], дово́дишь.

ДОВОЗИ́ТЬ I.; довожу́[1], дово́зишь.

ДОВОЛО́ЧЬ Р.; доволоку́, доволочёшь, доволоку́т; доволоки́; доволо́к.

ДОГЛЯДЕ́ТЬ Р.; догляжу́, догляди́шь; догляди́.

ДОГНА́ТЬ Р.; догоню́, дого́нишь; догони́; до́гнанный.

ДОГОРЕ́ТЬ Р.; догорю́, догори́шь; догори́.

ДОГРЕСТИ́ Р.; догребу́, догребёшь; догреби́; догрёб; догребённый.

ДОГРУЗИ́ТЬ Р.; догружу́, догру́зишь (and догрузи́шь); догру́женный and догружённый.

ДОДАВА́ТЬ I.; додаю́, додаёшь; додава́й; додава́я.

ДОДА́ТЬ Р.; дода́м, дода́шь, дода́ст, додади́м, додади́те, додаду́т; дода́й; до́данный.

ДОЕ́СТЬ Р.; дое́м, дое́шь[1], дое́ст, доеди́м, доеди́те, доедя́т; дое́шь[2] (imp.); дое́л; дое́денный.

ДОЕ́ХАТЬ Р.; дое́ду, дое́дешь; доезжа́й.

ДОЖДА́ТЬСЯ Р.; дождусь, дождёшься; дожди́сь.

ДОЖИ́ТЬ Р.; доживу́, доживёшь; доживи́; до́житый.

ДОЗВА́ТЬСЯ Р.; дозову́сь, дозовёшься; дозови́сь.

ДОИСКА́ТЬСЯ Р.; доищу́сь, дои́щешься; доищи́сь.

ДОЙТИ́ Р.; дойду́, дойдёшь; дойди́; дошёл, дошла́; доше́дший; дойдя́ and доше́дши.

ДОКАЗА́ТЬ Р.; докажу́, дока́жешь; докажи́; дока́занный.

ДОКАТИ́ТЬ Р.; докачу́, дока́тишь; дока́ченный.

ДОКРИЧА́ТЬСЯ Р.; докричу́сь, докричи́шься; докричи́сь.

ДОЛБИ́ТЬ I.; долблю́, долби́шь; долблённый.

ДОЛЕТЕ́ТЬ Р.; долечу́, долети́шь; долети́.

ДОЛИ́ТЬ Р.; долью́, дольёшь; доле́й; до́литый and доли́тый.

ДОМОЛОТИ́ТЬ Р.; домолочу́, домоло́тишь; домоло́ченный.

ДОМОЛО́ТЬ Р.; домелю́, доме́лешь; домели́; домо́лотый.

ДОМЧА́ТЬ Р.; домчу́, домчи́шь; домчи́.

ДОНЕСТИ́ Р.; донесу́, донесёшь; донеси́; донёс; донесённый; донеся́ and донёсши.

ДОНОСИ́ТЬ I.; доношу́[1], доно́сишь.

ДОНОСИ́ТЬ Р.; доношу́[2], доно́сишь; доно́шенный.

ДОНЯ́ТЬ Р.; дойму́, доймёшь; дойми́; до́нятый.

ДОПЕ́ЧЬ Р.; допеку́, допечёшь, допеку́т; допеки́; допёк; допечённый.

ДОПИСА́ТЬ Р.; допишу́, допи́шешь; допиши́; допи́санный.

ДОПИ́ТЬ Р.; допью́, допьёшь; допе́й; допи́тый.

ДОПЛАТИ́ТЬ Р.; доплачу́, допла́тишь; допла́ченный.

ДОПЛЕСТИ́СЬ Р.; доплету́сь, доплетёшься; доплети́сь; доплёлся; доплётшийся.

ДОПЛЫ́ТЬ Р.; доплыву́, доплывёшь; доплыви́.

ДОПРОСИ́ТЬ Р.; допрошу́, допро́сишь; допро́шенный.

ДОПУСТИ́ТЬ Р.; допущу́, допу́стишь; допу́щенный.

ДОРАСТИ́ Р.; дорасту́, дорастёшь; дорасти́ (imp.); доро́с.

ДОРВА́ТЬ Р.; дорву́, дорвёшь; дорви́; до́рванный.

ДОРВА́ТЬСЯ Р.; дорву́сь, дорвёшься.

ДОРЕ́ЗАТЬ Р.; доре́жу, доре́жешь; доре́жь; доре́занный.

ДОСАДИ́ТЬ[1] Р.; досажу́[1], досади́шь.

ДОСАДИ́ТЬ[2] Р.; досажу́[2], доса́дишь; доса́женный.

ДОСКАЗА́ТЬ Р.; доскажу́, доска́жешь; доскажи́; доска́занный.

ДОСКАКА́ТЬ Р.; доскачу́, доска́чешь; доскачи́.

ДОСЛА́ТЬ Р.; дошлю́, дошлёшь; дошли́[2]; до́сланный.

ДОСМОТРЕ́ТЬ Р.; досмотрю́, досмо́тришь; досмотри́; досмо́тренный.

ДОСПА́ТЬ Р.; досплю́, доспи́шь; доспи́.

ДОСТАВА́ТЬ I.; достаю́, достаёшь; доставай; доставая.

ДОСТА́ВИТЬ Р.; доста́влю, доста́вишь; доста́вь; доста́вленный.

ДОСТА́ТЬ Р.; доста́ну, доста́нешь; доста́нь.

ДОСТИ́ГНУТЬ Р.; дости́г, дости́гла; дости́гнутый.

ДОСТИ́ЧЬ Р.; дости́г, дости́гла; дости́гнутый.

ДОСТУЧА́ТЬСЯ Р.; достучу́сь, достучи́шься; достучи́сь.

ДОСЫПА́ТЬ Р.; досы́плю, досы́плешь; досы́пь; досы́панный.

ДО́ХНУТЬ I.; дох, до́хла.

ДОХОДИ́ТЬ I.; дохожу́, дохо́дишь.

ДОЧИ́СТИТЬ Р.; дочи́щу, дочи́стишь; дочи́сти and дочи́сть; дочи́щенный.

ДРАТЬ I.; деру́, дерёшь; дери́.

ДРА́ТЬСЯ I.; деру́сь, дерёшься; дери́сь.

ДРЕБЕЗЖА́ТЬ I.; дребезжи́т, дребезжа́т; дребезжи́.

ДРЕ́ЙФИТЬ I.; дре́йфлю, дре́йфишь; дре́йфь.

ДРЕМА́ТЬ I.; дремлю́, дре́млешь; дремли́.

ДРОБИ́ТЬ I.; дроблю́, дроби́шь; дроблённый.

ДРО́ГНУТЬ I.; дрог, дро́гла.

ДРО́ГНУТЬ Р.; дро́гнул, дро́гнула.

ДРОЖА́ТЬ I.; дрожу́, дрожи́шь; дрожи́.

ДРЫ́ХНУТЬ I.; дрых (and дры́хнул), дры́хла.

ДУБА́СИТЬ I.; дуба́шу, дуба́сишь; дуба́сь.

ДУБИ́ТЬ I.; дублю́, дуби́шь; ду́бленный.

ДУДЕ́ТЬ I.; дуди́шь, дудя́т; дуди́ (1st pers. sing. not used).

ДУТЬ I.; ду́ю, ду́ешь; дуй.

ДЫМИ́ТЬ I.; дымлю́, дыми́шь.

ДЫША́ТЬ I.; дышу́, ды́шишь; дыши́.

Е

ЕГОЗИ́ТЬ I.; егожу́, егози́шь.

Е́ЗДИТЬ I.; е́зжу, е́здишь.

ЕЛО́ЗИТЬ I.; ело́жу, ело́зишь; ело́зь.

ЕСТЬ I.; ем, ешь[1], ест, еди́м, еди́те, едя́т; ешь[2] (imp.); ел.

Е́ХАТЬ I.; е́ду, е́дешь; поезжа́й; е́дучи.

Ж

ЖА́ЖДАТЬ I.; жа́жду, жа́ждешь; жа́ждай and жа́жди.

ЖАТЬ[1] I.; жму, жмёшь; жми; жа́тый.

ЖАТЬ[2] I.; жну, жнёшь; жни; жа́тый.

ЖДАТЬ I.; жду, ждёшь; жди.

ЖЕВА́ТЬ I.; жую́, жуёшь; жуй; жёванный.

ЖЕЛТИ́ТЬ I.; желчу́, желти́шь.

ЖЕЧЬ I.; жгу, жжёшь, жгут; жги; жёг, жгла.

ЖИВИ́ТЬ I.; живлю́, живи́шь; живи́.

ЖИВОПИСА́ТЬ I. and Р.; живопису́ю, живопису́ешь; живопису́й.

ЖИТЬ I.; живу́, живёшь; живи́.

ЖРАТЬ I.; жру, жрёшь; жри.

ЖУЖЖА́ТЬ I.; жужжу́, жужжи́шь; жужжи́.

ЖУРЧА́ТЬ I.; журчи́т, журча́т (3rd pers. only); журчи́.

З

ЗАБА́ВИТЬ I. and Р.; заба́влю, заба́вишь; заба́вь.

ЗАБѢЖА́ТЬ Р.; забегу́, забежи́шь, забегу́т; забеги́.

ЗАБИ́ТЬ Р.; забью́, забьёшь; забе́й; заби́тый.

ЗАБЛЕСТѢ́ТЬ[1] Р.; заблещу́[1], заблести́шь; заблести́.

ЗАБЛЕСТѢ́ТЬ[2] Р.; заблещу́[2], забле́щешь; заблещи́.

ЗАБЛУДИ́ТЬСЯ Р.; заблужу́сь, заблу́дишься.

ЗАБОЛѢ́ТЬ[1] Р.; заболи́т, заболя́т.

ЗАБОЛѢ́ТЬ[2] Р.; заболѣ́ю, заболѣ́ешь; заболѣ́й.

ЗАБО́ТИТЬ I.; забо́чу, забо́тишь; забо́ть.

ЗАБРА́ТЬ Р.; заберу́, заберёшь; забери́; за́бранный.

ЗАБРѢ́ДИТЬ Р.; забрѣ́жу, забрѣ́дишь; забрѣ́дь.

ЗАБРЕСТИ́ Р.; забреду́, забредёшь; забреди́; забрёл; забрѣ́дший; забредя́ and забре́дши.

ЗАБРИ́ТЬ Р.; забрѣ́ю, забрѣ́ешь; забрѣ́й; забри́тый.

ЗАБРО́СИТЬ Р.; забро́шу, забро́сишь; забро́сь; забро́шенный.

ЗАБРЫ́ЗГАТЬ Р.; забры́зжу, забры́зжешь (also забры́згаю, забры́згаешь); забры́зжи.

ЗАБУТИ́ТЬ Р.; забучу́, забути́шь; забу́ченный.

ЗАБУ́ХНУТЬ Р.; забу́х, забу́хла.

ЗАБЫ́ТЬ Р.; забу́ду, забу́дешь; забу́дь; забы́тый.

ЗАВЕЗТИ́ Р.; завезу́, завезёшь; завези́; завёз; завезённый; завезя́ and завёзши.

ЗАВЕРТѢ́ТЬ Р.; заверчу́, заве́ртишь; заверти́; заве́рченный.

ЗАВѢ́СИТЬ Р.; завѣ́шу, завѣ́сишь; завѣ́сь; завѣ́шенный.

ЗАВЕСТИ́ Р.; заведу́, заведёшь; заведи́; завёл; заве́дший; заведённый; заведя́.

ЗАВѢ́ЯТЬ Р.; завѣ́ю, завѣ́ешь; завѣ́й[1]; завѣ́янный.

ЗАВИ́ДѢТЬ Р.; зави́жу, зави́дишь; зави́дев and зави́дя.

ЗАВИНТИ́ТЬ Р.; завинчу́, завинти́шь; зави́нченный.

ЗАВИ́СѢТЬ I.; зави́шу, зави́сишь.

ЗАВИ́ТЬ Р.; завью́, завьёшь; завѣ́й[2]; зави́тый.

ЗАВЛѢ́ЧЬ Р.; завлеку́, завлечёшь, завлеку́т; завлеки́; завлёк; завлечённый.

ЗАВОДИ́ТЬ I.; завожу́[1], заво́дишь.

ЗАВОЗИ́ТЬ I.; завожу́[2], заво́зишь.

ЗАВОЗИ́ТЬ Р.; завожу́[3], заво́зишь; заво́женный.

ЗАВОЛО́ЧЬ Р.; заволоку́, заволочёшь, заволоку́т; заволоки́; заволо́к; заволочённый.

ЗАВОПИ́ТЬ Р.; заволплю́, завопи́шь.

ЗАВОРОТИ́ТЬ Р.; заворочу́, заворо́тишь; заворо́ченный.

ЗАВРА́ТЬСЯ Р.; завру́сь, заврёшься; заври́сь.

ЗАВЫ́СИТЬ Р.; завы́шу, завы́сишь; завы́сь; завы́шенный.

ЗАВЫ́ТЬ Р.; заво́ю, заво́ешь; заво́й.

ЗАВЯЗА́ТЬ Р.; завяжу́, завя́жешь; завяжи́; завя́занный.

ЗАВЯ́ЗНУТЬ Р.; завя́з, завя́зла; завя́знувший; завя́знув.

ЗАВЯ́НУТЬ Р.; завя́л, завя́ла; завя́дший and завя́нувший.

ЗАГА́ДИТЬ Р.; зага́жу, зага́дишь; зага́дь; зага́женный.

ЗАГАСИ́ТЬ Р.; загашу́, зага́сишь; зага́шенный.

ЗАГА́СНУТЬ Р.; зага́с, зага́сла.

ЗАГАТИ́ТЬ Р.; загачу́, загати́шь; зага́ченный.

ЗАГЛА́ДИТЬ Р.; загла́жу, загла́дишь; загла́дь; загла́женный.

ЗАГЛО́ХНУТЬ Р.; загло́х, загло́хла.

ЗАГЛЯДѢ́ТЬСЯ Р.; загляжу́сь, загляди́шься; загляди́сь.

ЗАГНА́ТЬ P.; загоню́, заго́нишь; загони́; за́гнанный.

ЗАГНИ́ТЬ P.; загнию́, загниёшь.

ЗАГОРДИ́ТЬСЯ P.; загоржу́сь, загорди́шься.

ЗАГОРЕ́ТЬ P.; загорю́, загори́шь; загори́.

ЗАГОРОДИ́ТЬ P.; загорожу́, загоро́дишь (and загороди́шь); загоро́женный.

ЗАГОСТИ́ТЬСЯ P.; загощу́сь, загости́шься.

ЗАГОТО́ВИТЬ P.; загото́влю, загото́вишь; загото́вь; загото́вленный.

ЗАГРАДИ́ТЬ P.; загражу́, загради́шь; загражде́нный.

ЗАГРЕМЕ́ТЬ P.; загремлю́, загреми́шь; загреми́.

ЗАГРЕСТИ́ P.; загребу́, загребёшь; загреби́; загрёб; загребённый.

ЗАГРОМОЗДИ́ТЬ P.; загромозжу́, загромозди́шь; загромождённый.

ЗАГРУЗИ́ТЬ P.; загружу́, загру́зишь (and загрузи́шь); загру́женный and загружённый.

ЗАГРУСТИ́ТЬ P.; загрущу́, загрусти́шь.

ЗАГРЫ́ЗТЬ P;. загрызу́, загрызёшь; загрызи́; загры́з; загры́зенный.

ЗАГУБИ́ТЬ P.; загублю́, загу́бишь; загу́бленный.

ЗАГУСТИ́ТЬ P.; загущу́, загусти́шь; загущённый.

ЗАДАВА́ТЬ I.; задаю́, задаёшь; задава́й; задава́я.

ЗАДАВИ́ТЬ P.; задавлю́, зада́вишь; зада́вленный.

ЗАДА́ТЬ P.; зада́м, зада́шь, зада́ст, задади́м, задади́те, зададу́т; зада́й; за́данный.

ЗАДЕРЖА́ТЬ P.; задержу́, заде́ржишь; задержи́; заде́ржанный.

ЗАДЕ́ТЬ P.; заде́ну, заде́нешь; заде́нь; заде́тый.

ЗАДРА́ТЬ P.; задеру́, задерёшь; задери́; за́дранный.

ЗАДРЕМА́ТЬ P.; задремлю́, задре́млешь; задремли́.

ЗАДУ́ТЬ P.; заду́ю, заду́ешь; заду́й; заду́тый.

ЗАДЫМИ́ТЬ P.; задымлю́, задыми́шь; задымлённый.

ЗАЕ́ЗДИТЬ P.; зае́зжу, зае́здишь; зае́зди; зае́зженный.

ЗАЕ́СТЬ P.; зае́м, зае́шь[1], зае́ст,

заеди́м, заеди́те, заедя́т; зае́шь[2] (imp.); зае́л; зае́денный.

ЗАЕ́ХАТЬ P.; зае́ду, зае́дешь; заезжа́й.

ЗАЖА́ТЬ P.; зажму́, зажмёшь; зажми́; зажа́тый.

ЗАЖДА́ТЬСЯ P.; зажду́сь, заждёшься зажди́сь.

ЗАЖЕЛТИ́ТЬ P.; зажелчу́, зажелти́шь; зажелчённый.

ЗАЖЕ́ЧЬ P.; зажгу́, зажжёшь, зажгу́т; зажги́; зажёг, зажгла́; зажжённый.

ЗАЖИВИ́ТЬ P.; заживлю́, заживи́шь; заживи́; заживлённый.

ЗАЖИ́ТЬ P.; заживу́[1] and [2], заживёшь; заживи́.

ЗАЗВА́ТЬ P.; зазову́, зазовёшь; зазови́; за́званный.

ЗАЗВЕНЕ́ТЬ P.; зазвени́т, зазвеня́т (1st and 2nd pers. seldom used); зазвени́.

ЗАЗНАВА́ТЬСЯ I.; зазнаю́сь, зазнаёшься; зазнава́йся; зазнава́ясь.

ЗАЙТИ́ P.; зайду́, зайдёшь; зайди́; зашёл, зашла́; заше́дший; зайди́.

ЗАКАЗА́ТЬ P.; закажу́, зака́жешь; закажи́; зака́занный.

ЗАКАТИ́ТЬ P.; закачу́, зака́тишь; зака́ченный.

ЗАКВА́СИТЬ P.; заква́шу, заква́сишь; заква́сь; заква́шенный.

ЗАКИПЕ́ТЬ P.; закиплю́, закипи́шь; закипи́.

ЗАКИ́СНУТЬ P.; заки́с, заки́сла.

ЗАКЛЕЙМИ́ТЬ P.; заклеймлю́, заклейми́шь; заклеймённый.

ЗАКЛЯ́СТЬСЯ P.; закляну́сь, заклянёшься; закляни́сь; закля́лся.

ЗАКОЛОТИ́ТЬ P.; заколочу́, заколо́тишь; заколо́ченный.

ЗАКОЛО́ТЬ P.; заколю́, зако́лешь; заколи́; зако́лотый.

ЗАКОНОПА́ТИТЬ P.; законопа́чу, законопа́тишь; законопа́ть; законопа́ченный.

ЗАКО́НЧИТЬ P.; зако́нчу, зако́нчишь; зако́нчи; зако́нченный.

ЗАКОПТЕ́ТЬ P.; закопти́т, закоптя́т (3rd pers. only); закопти́.

ЗАКОПТИ́ТЬ P.; закопчу́, закопти́шь; закопти́; закопчённый.

ЗАКОРМИ́ТЬ P.; закормлю́, зако́рмишь; зако́рмленный.

ЗАКОСИ́ТЬ P.; закошу́, зако́сишь; зако́шенный.

ЗАКРА́СИТЬ Р.; закра́шу, закра́сишь; закра́сь; закра́шенный.

ЗАКРА́СТЬСЯ Р.; закраду́сь, закрадёшься; закради́сь; закра́лся.

ЗАКРЕПИ́ТЬ Р.; закреплю́, закрепи́шь; закреплённый.

ЗАКРЕПОСТИ́ТЬ Р.; закрепощу́, закрепости́шь; закрепощённый.

ЗАКРИЧА́ТЬ Р.; закричу́, закричи́шь; закричи́.

ЗАКРУТИ́ТЬ Р.; закручу́, закру́тишь; закру́ченный.

ЗАКРЫ́ТЬ Р.; закро́ю, закро́ешь; закро́й; закры́тый.

ЗАКУПИ́ТЬ Р.; закуплю́, заку́пишь; заку́пленный.

ЗАКУСИ́ТЬ Р.; закушу́, заку́сишь; заку́шенный.

ЗАЛА́ДИТЬ Р.; зала́жу, зала́дишь; зала́дь; зала́женный.

ЗАЛА́ЯТЬ Р.; зала́ю, зала́ешь; зала́й.

ЗАЛЕЖА́ТЬСЯ Р.; залежу́сь, залежи́шься; залежи́сь.

ЗАЛЕ́ЗТЬ Р.; зале́зу, зале́зешь; зале́зь; зале́з.

ЗАЛЕПИ́ТЬ Р.; залеплю́, зале́пишь; зале́пленный.

ЗАЛЕТЕ́ТЬ Р.; залечу́, залети́шь; залети́.

ЗАЛЕ́ЧЬ Р.; заля́гу, заля́жешь, заля́гут; заля́г; залёг.

ЗАЛИЗА́ТЬ Р.; залижу́, зали́жешь; залижи́; зали́занный.

ЗАЛИ́ТЬ Р.; залью́, зальёшь; зале́й; за́литый and зали́тый.

ЗАЛОМИ́ТЬ Р.; заломлю́, зало́мишь; зало́мленный.

ЗАМА́ЗАТЬ Р.; зама́жу, зама́жешь; зама́жь; зама́занный.

ЗАМАХА́ТЬ Р.; замашу́, зама́шешь (and замаха́ю, замаха́ешь); замаши́.

ЗАМА́ЯТЬСЯ Р.; зама́юсь, зама́ешься; зама́йся.

ЗАМЕРЕ́ТЬ Р.; замру́, замрёшь; замри́; за́мер.

ЗАМЁРЗНУТЬ Р.; замёрз, замёрзла.

ЗАМЕСИ́ТЬ Р.; замешу́, заме́сишь; заме́шенный.

ЗАМЕСТИ́ Р.; замету́, заметёшь; замети́; замёл; замётший; заметённый; замети́.

ЗАМЕСТИ́ТЬ Р.; замещу́, замести́шь; замещённый.

ЗАМЕТА́ТЬСЯ Р.; замечу́сь, заме́чешься; замечи́сь.

ЗАМЕ́ТИТЬ Р.; заме́чу, заме́тишь; заме́ть; заме́ченный.

ЗАМО́КНУТЬ Р.; замо́к, замо́кла.

ЗАМО́ЛВИТЬ Р.; замо́лвлю, замо́лвишь; замо́лви.

ЗАМО́ЛКНУТЬ Р.; замо́лк, замо́лкла.

ЗАМОЛЧА́ТЬ Р.; замолчу́[1] and [2] замолчи́шь; замолчи́.

ЗАМОРО́ЗИТЬ Р.; заморо́жу, заморо́зишь; заморо́зь; заморо́женный.

ЗАМОСТИ́ТЬ Р.; замощу́, замости́шь; замощённый.

ЗАМУТИ́ТЬ Р.; замучу́, замути́шь (and заму́тишь); замутнённый.

ЗАМЫ́ТЬ Р.; замо́ю, замо́ешь; замо́й; замы́тый.

ЗАМЯ́ТЬ Р.; замну́, замнёшь; замни́; замя́тый.

ЗАНАВЕ́СИТЬ Р.; занаве́шу, занаве́сишь; занаве́сь; занаве́шенный.

ЗАНЕМО́ЧЬ Р.; занемогу́, занемо́жешь, занемо́гут; занемоги́; занемо́г, занемогла́.

ЗАНЕСТИ́ Р.; занесу́, занесёшь; занеси́; занёс; занесённый; занеси́ and занеши́.

ЗАНИ́ЗИТЬ Р.; зани́жу, зани́зишь; зани́зь; зани́женный.

ЗАНОЗИ́ТЬ Р.; заножу́, занози́шь.

ЗАНОСИ́ТЬ I.; заношу́[1], зано́сишь.

ЗАНОСИ́ТЬ Р.; заношу́[2], зано́сишь; зано́шенный.

ЗАНЫ́ТЬ Р.; заною́, зано́ешь; зано́й.

ЗАНЯ́ТЬ Р.; займу́, займёшь; займи́; за́нятый.

ЗАПА́КОСТИТЬ Р.; запа́кощу, запа́костишь; запа́кости; запа́кощенный.

ЗАПАСТИ́ Р.; запасу́, запасёшь; запаси́; запа́с; запасённый.

ЗАПА́СТЬ Р.; западёт, западу́т; запади́; запа́л.

ЗАПАХА́ТЬ Р.; запашу́, запа́шешь; запаши́; запа́ханный.

ЗАПЕРЕ́ТЬ Р.; запру́, запрёшь; запри́; за́пер; за́пертый; заперёв (or за́перши).

ЗАПЕ́ТЬ Р.; запою́, запоёшь; запо́й; запе́тый.

ЗАПЕ́ЧЬ Р.; запеку́, запечёшь, запеку́т; запеки́; запёк; запечённый.

ЗАПИСА́ТЬ Р.; запишу́, запи́шешь; запиши́; запи́санный.

ЗАПИ́ТЬ Р.; запью́, запьёшь; запе́й; запи́тый.

ЗАПЛАТИТЬ P.; заплачу, заплатишь; заплаченный.

ЗАПЛЕСКАТЬ P.; заплещу, заплещешь (also заплескаю, заплескаешь); заплещи and заплескай; заплёсканный.

ЗАПЛЕСТИ P.; заплету, заплетёшь; заплети; заплёл; заплётший; заплетённый; заплетя.

ЗАПЛЫТЬ P.; заплыву, заплывёшь; заплыви.

ЗАПОЛЗТИ P.; заползу, заползёшь; заползи; заполз.

ЗАПОРОТЬ P.; запорю, запорешь; запори; запоротый.

ЗАПРАВИТЬ P.; заправлю, заправишь; заправь; заправленный.

ЗАПРЕТИТЬ P.; запрещу, запретишь; запрещённый.

ЗАПРЕЧЬ (arch.) P.; запрягу, запряжёшь, запрягут; запряги; запрягг; запряжённый.

ЗАПРИМЕТИТЬ P.; запримечу, заприметишь; заприметь; запримеченный.

ЗАПРОДАВАТЬ I.; запродаю, запродаёшь; запродавай; запродавая.

ЗАПРОДАТЬ P.; запродам, запродашь, запродаст, запродадим, запродадите, запродут; запродай; запроданный.

ЗАПРОПАСТИТЬСЯ P.; запропащусь, запропастишься.

ЗАПРОПАСТЬ P.; запропаду, запропадёшь; запропади; запропал.

ЗАПРОСИТЬ P.; запрошу, запросишь; запрошенный.

ЗАПРУДИТЬ P.; запружу, запрудишь (and запрудишь); запруженный and запружённый.

ЗАПРЯТАТЬ P.; запрячу, запрячешь; запрячь (imp.); запрятанный.

ЗАПРЯЧЬ P.; запрягу, запряжёшь, запрягут; запряги; запрягг; запряжённый.

ЗАПУСТИТЬ P.; запущу, запустишь; запущенный.

ЗАПЫХТЕТЬ P.; запыхчу, запыхтишь; запыхти.

ЗАРАЗИТЬ P.; заражу, заразишь; заражённый.

ЗАРАСТИ P.; зарасту, зарастёшь; зарасти (imp.); зарос.

ЗАРВАТЬСЯ P.; зарвусь, зарвёшься; зарвись.

ЗАРЕВЕТЬ P.; зареву, заревёшь; зареви.

ЗАРЕЗАТЬ P.; зарежу, зарежешь; зарежь; зарезанный.

ЗАРЕЧЬСЯ P.; зарекусь, заречёшься, зарекутся; зарекись; зарёкся.

ЗАРОДИТЬ P.; зарожу, зародишь; зарождённый.

ЗАРУБИТЬ P.; зарублю, зарубишь; зарубленный.

ЗАРЫТЬ P.; зарою, заробешь; зарой; зарытый.

ЗАРЫЧАТЬ P.; зарычу, зарычишь; зарычи.

ЗАРЯДИТЬ P.; заряжу, зарядишь (and зарядишь); заряжённый and заряженный.

ЗАСАДИТЬ P.; засажу, засадишь; засаженный.

ЗАСВЕТИТЬ P.; засвечу, засветишь; засвеченный.

ЗАСЕКРЕТИТЬ P.; засекречу, засекретишь; засекреть; засекреченный.

ЗАСЕСТЬ P.; засиду, засидешь; засидь; засел.

ЗАСЕЧЬ P.; засеку, засечёшь, засекут; засеки; засёк; засечённый and засеченный.

ЗАСИДЕТЬ P.; засидит, засидят; засиди; засиженный.

ЗАСИДЕТЬСЯ P.; засижусь, засидишься; засидись.

ЗАСКАКАТЬ P.; заскачу, заскачешь; заскачи.

ЗАСКОРУЗНУТЬ P.; заскоруз, заскорузла.

ЗАСКРЕЖЕТАТЬ P.; заскрежещу, заскрежещешь; заскрежещи.

ЗАСЛАТЬ P.; зашлю, зашлёшь; зашли[1]; засланный.

ЗАСЛЕДИТЬ P.; заслежу, заследишь; заслеженный.

ЗАСЛЫШАТЬ P.; заслышу, заслышишь; заслышь; заслышанный.

ЗАСМЕЯТЬ P.; засмею, засмеёшь; засмей; засмеянный.

ЗАСМОТРЕТЬСЯ P.; засмотрюсь, засмотришься; засмотрись.

ЗАСНЯТЬ P.; засниму, заснимешь; засними; заснятый.

ЗАСОВЕСТИТЬСЯ P.; засовещусь, засовеститься.

ЗАСОСАТЬ P.; засосу, засосёшь; засоси; засосанный.

ЗАСОХНУТЬ P.; засох, засохла.

ЗАСПА́ТЬ Р.; засплю́, заспи́шь; заспи́; за́спанный.

ЗАСПА́ТЬСЯ Р.; засплю́сь, заспи́шься; заспи́сь.

ЗАСРАМИ́ТЬ Р.; засрамлю́, засрами́шь; засрамлённый.

ЗАСТАВА́ТЬ I.; застаю́, застаёшь; застава́й; застава́я.

ЗАСТА́ВИТЬ Р.; заста́влю, заста́вишь; заста́вь; заста́вленный.

ЗАСТА́ТЬ Р.; заста́ну, заста́нешь; заста́нь.

ЗАСТЕЛИ́ТЬ Р.; застелю́, засте́лешь; застели́; засте́ленный.

ЗАСТИ́ГНУТЬ Р.; засти́гну, засти́гнешь; засти́гни; засти́г, засти́гла; засти́гнутый.

ЗА́СТИТЬ I.; за́щу, за́стишь; за́сти and засть.

ЗАСТИ́ЧЬ Р.; засти́гну, засти́гнешь; засти́гни; засти́г, засти́гла; засти́гнутый.

ЗАСТЛА́ТЬ Р.; застелю́, засте́лешь; застели́; за́стланный.

ЗАСТОЯ́ТЬСЯ Р.; застою́сь, засто́ишься; засто́йся.

ЗАСТРИ́ЧЬ Р.; застригу́, застрижёшь, застригу́т; застриги́; застри́г; застри́женный.

ЗАСТРЯ́ТЬ Р.; застря́ну, застря́нешь; застря́нь.

ЗАСТУДИ́ТЬ Р.; застужу́, засту́дишь; засту́женный.

ЗАСТУПИ́ТЬ Р.; заступлю́, засту́пишь.

ЗАСТУПИ́ТЬСЯ Р.; заступлю́сь, засту́пишься.

ЗАСТЫДИ́ТЬ Р.; застыжу́, застыди́шь; застыжённый.

ЗАСТЫ́ТЬ Р.; засты́ну, засты́нешь; засты́нь.

ЗАСУДИ́ТЬ Р.; засужу́, засу́дишь; засу́женный.

ЗАСЫПА́ТЬ Р.; засы́плю, засы́плешь; засы́пь; засы́панный.

ЗАТВЕРДИ́ТЬ Р.; затвержу́, затверди́шь; затвержённый and затве́рженный.

ЗАТЕРЕ́ТЬ Р.; затру́, затрёшь; затри́; затёр; затёртый; затере́в an затёрши.

ЗАТЕСА́ТЬ Р.; затешу́, зате́шешь; затеши́; затёсанный.

ЗАТЕ́ЧЬ Р.; затечёт, затеку́т; затёк.

ЗАТЕ́ЯТЬ Р.; зате́ю, зате́ешь; зате́й; зате́янный.

ЗАТКА́ТЬ Р.; затку́, заткёшь; затки́; за́тканный.

ЗАТОПИ́ТЬ Р.; затоплю́[1] and [2], зато́пишь; зато́пленный.

ЗАТОПТА́ТЬ Р.; затопчу́, зато́пчешь; затопчи́; зато́птанный.

ЗАТОРМОЗИ́ТЬ Р.; заторможу́, затормози́шь; заторможённый.

ЗАТОРОПИ́ТЬСЯ Р.; затороплю́сь, заторо́пишься.

ЗАТРАВИ́ТЬ Р.; затравлю́, затра́вишь; затра́вленный.

ЗАТРА́ТИТЬ Р.; затра́чу, затра́тишь; затра́ть; затра́ченный.

ЗАТРЕПА́ТЬ Р.; затреплю́, затре́плешь; затрепли́; затрёпанный.

ЗАТРЕПЕТА́ТЬ Р.; затрепещу́, затрепе́щешь; затрепещи́.

ЗАТРЯСТИ́ Р.; затрясу́, затрясёшь; затряси́; затря́с.

ЗАТУПИ́ТЬ Р.; затуплю́, зату́пишь; зату́пленный.

ЗАТУ́ХНУТЬ Р.; зату́х, зату́хла.

ЗАХА́ЯТЬ Р.; заха́ю, заха́ешь; заха́й; заха́янный.

ЗАХВАТИ́ТЬ Р.; захвачу́, захва́тишь; захва́ченный.

ЗАХЛЕСТА́ТЬ Р.; захлещу́, захле́щешь; захлещи́; захлёстанный.

ЗАХЛОПОТА́ТЬСЯ Р.; захлопочу́сь, захлопо́чешься; захлопочи́сь.

ЗАХОДИ́ТЬ Р.; захожу́[1], захо́дишь.

ЗАХОДИ́ТЬ I.; захожу́[2], захо́дишь.

ЗАХОТЕ́ТЬ Р.; захочу́, захо́чешь, захо́чет, захоти́м, захоти́те, захотя́т.

ЗАЦВЕСТИ́ Р.; зацвету́, зацветёшь; зацвети́; зацвёл; зацве́тший.

ЗАЦЕПИ́ТЬ Р.; зацеплю́, заце́пишь; заце́пленный.

ЗАЧАСТИ́ТЬ Р.; зачащу́, зачасти́шь.

ЗАЧА́ТЬ Р.; зачну́, зачнёшь; зачни́; зача́тый.

ЗАЧА́ХНУТЬ Р.; зача́х, зача́хла.

ЗАЧЕРТИ́ТЬ Р.; зачерчу́, заче́ртишь; заче́рченный.

ЗАЧЕСА́ТЬ Р.; зачешу́, заче́шешь; зачеши́; зачёсанный.

ЗАЧЕ́СТЬ Р.; зачту́, зачтёшь; зачти́; зачёл, зачла́; зачётший; зачтённый; зачтя́.

ЗАЧИ́СТИТЬ Р.; зачи́шу, зачи́стишь; зачи́сти and зачи́сть; зачи́щенный.

ЗАЧУ́ЯТЬ Р.; зачу́ю, зачу́ешь; зачу́й; зачу́янный.

ЗАШИБИТЬ Р.; зашибу́, зашибёшь; зашиби́; заши́б; заши́бленный.

ЗАШИТЬ Р.; зашью́, зашьёшь; зашей; заши́тый.

ЗАШУРШАТЬ Р.; зашуршу́, зашурши́шь; зашурши́.

ЗАЩЕКОТАТЬ Р.; защекочу́, защеко́чешь; защекочи́; защеко́ченный.

ЗАЩЕМИТЬ Р.; защемлю́, защеми́шь; защемлённый.

ЗАЩИПАТЬ Р.; защиплю́, защи́плешь; защипли́; защи́панный.

ЗАЩИТИТЬ Р.; защищу́, защити́шь; защищённый.

ЗАЯВИТЬ Р.; заявлю́, зая́вишь; зая́вленный.

ЗВАТЬ I.; зову́, зовёшь; зови́; зва́нный.

ЗВЕНЕТЬ I.; звеню́, звени́шь; звени́.

ЗВУЧАТЬ I.; звучу́, звучи́шь; звучи́.

ЗИЖДИТЬСЯ I.; зи́ждеться, зи́ждуться.

ЗЛОБИТЬСЯ I.; зло́блюсь, зло́бишься; зло́бься.

ЗЛОСЛОВИТЬ I.; злосло́влю, злосло́вишь; зло́словь.

ЗЛОУПОТРЕБИТЬ Р.; злоупотреблю́, злоупотреби́шь.

ЗНАКОМИТЬ I.; знако́млю, знако́мишь; знако́мь.

ЗОЛОТИТЬ I.; золочу́, золоти́шь; золочённый.

ЗРЕТЬ[1] I.; зрю, зришь; зри́мый.

ЗРЕТЬ[2] I.; зре́ю, зре́ешь (meaning: to ripen; not shown in body of text as conjugation is regular).

ЗУДЕТЬ[1] I.; зуди́т, зудя́т; зуди́.

ЗУДЕТЬ[2] I.; зужу́, зуди́шь; зуди́.

ЗУДИТЬ[1] I.; зуди́т, зудя́т; зуди́.

ЗУДИТЬ[2] I.; зужу́, зуди́шь; зуди́.

ЗЫБИТЬСЯ I.; зы́блется, зы́блются.

ЗЯБНУТЬ I.; зяб, зя́бла.

И

ИДТИ I.; иду́, идёшь; иди́; шёл, шла; ше́дший; и́дучи and идя́.

ИЗБАВИТЬ Р.; изба́влю, изба́вишь; изба́вь; изба́вленный.

ИЗБЕГНУТЬ Р.; избе́г (arch.: избе́гнул), избе́гла.

ИЗБЕЖАТЬ Р.; избегу́, избежи́шь, избегу́т; избеги́.

ИЗБИТЬ Р.; изобью́, изобьёшь; избей; изби́тый.

ИЗБОРОЗДИТЬ Р.; изборозжу́, изборозди́шь; изборождённый.

ИЗБРАТЬ Р.; изберу́, изберёшь; избери́; и́збранный.

ИЗБЫТЬ Р.; избу́ду, избу́дешь; избу́дь; избы́тый.

ИЗВЕРГНУТЬ Р.; изве́рг, изве́ргла; изве́рженный and узве́ргнутый.

ИЗВЕСТИ Р.; изведу́, изведёшь; изведи́; извёл; изве́дший; изведённый; изве́дши and изведя́.

ИЗВЕСТИТЬ Р.; извещу́, извести́шь; извещённый.

ИЗВИТЬ Р.; изовью́, изовьёшь; извей; изви́тый.

ИЗВЛЕЧЬ Р.; извлеку́, извлечёшь; извлеку́т; извлеки́; извлёк; извлечённый.

ИЗВОДИТЬ I.; извожу́[1], изво́дишь.

ИЗВОЗИТЬ Р.; извожу́[2], изво́зишь; изво́женный.

ИЗВРАТИТЬ Р.; извращу́,изврати́шь; извращённый.

ИЗГАДИТЬ Р.; изга́жу, изга́дишь; изга́дь; изга́женный.

ИЗГЛАДИТЬ Р.; изгла́жу, изгла́дишь; изгла́дь; изгла́женный.

ИЗГНАТЬ Р.; изгоню́, изго́нишь; изгони́; и́згнанный.

ИЗГОТОВИТЬ Р.; изгото́влю, изгото́вишь; изгото́вь; изгото́вленный.

ИЗГРЫЗТЬ Р.; изгрызу́, изгрызёшь; изгрызи́; изгры́з; изгры́зенный.

ИЗДАВАТЬ I.; издаю́, издаёшь; издава́й; издава́я.

ИЗДАТЬ Р.; изда́м, изда́шь, изда́ст, издади́м, издади́те, издаду́т; изда́й; и́зданный.

ИЗДЕРЖАТЬ Р.; издержу́, изде́ржишь; издержи́; изде́ржанный.

ИЗДОХНУТЬ Р.; издо́х, издо́хла.

ИЗЖИТЬ Р.; изживу́, изживёшь; изживи́; изжи́тый.

ИЗЗЯБНУТЬ Р.; иззя́б, иззя́бла.

ИЗЛАДИТЬ Р.; изла́жу[1], изла́дишь; изла́дь; изла́женный.

ИЗЛА́ЗИТЬ Р.; изла́жу², изла́зишь; изла́зь; изла́женный.

ИЗЛА́ЯТЬ Р.; изла́ю, изла́ешь; изла́й; изла́янный.

ИЗЛИ́ТЬ Р.; изолью́, изольёшь; излей; изли́тый.

ИЗЛОВИ́ТЬ Р.; изловлю́, изло́вишь; изло́вленный.

ИЗМА́ЗАТЬ Р.; изма́жу, изма́жешь; изма́жь; изма́занный.

ИЗМА́ЯТЬ Р.; изма́ю, изма́ешь; изма́й; изма́янный.

ИЗМО́КНУТЬ Р.; измо́к, измо́кла.

ИЗМЯ́ТЬ Р.; изомну́, изомнёшь; изомни́; изми́тый.

ИЗНЕМО́ЧЬ Р.; изнемогу́, изнемо́жешь изнемо́гут; изнемоги́; изнемо́г.

ИЗНОСИ́ТЬ Р.; изношу́, изно́сишь; изно́шенный.

ИЗНЫ́ТЬ Р.; изно́ю изно́ешь; изно́й.

ИЗОБИ́ДЕТЬ Р.; изоби́жу, изоби́дишь; изоби́дь; изоби́женный.

ИЗОБРАЗИ́ТЬ Р.; изображу́, изобрази́шь; изображённый.

ИЗОБРЕСТИ́ Р.; изобрету́, изобретёшь; изобрети́; изобрёл; изобре́тший; изобретённый; узобретя́.

ИЗОВРА́ТЬСЯ Р.; изоврусь, изоврёшься; изоврись.

ИЗОДРА́ТЬ Р.; издеру́, издерёшь; издери́; изо́дранный.

ИЗОЙТИ́ Р.; изойду́, изойдёшь; изойди́; изошёл, изошла́; изоше́дший; изойдя́.

ИЗОЛГА́ТЬСЯ Р.; изолгу́сь, изолжёшься; изолги́сь.

ИЗОРВА́ТЬ Р.; изорву́, изорвёшь; изорви́; изо́рванный.

ИЗРЕ́ЗАТЬ Р.; изре́жу, изре́жешь; изре́жь; изре́занный.

ИЗРЕ́ЧЬ Р.; изреку́, изречёшь, изреку́т; изреки́; изрёк; изре́кший; изречённый (arch.: изрече́нный).

ИЗРЕШЕТИ́ТЬ Р.; изрешечу́, изрешети́шь; изрешечённый and изреше́ченный.

ИЗРУБИ́ТЬ Р.; изрублю́, изру́бишь; изру́бленный.

ИЗРЫ́ТЬ Р.; изро́ю, изро́ешь; изро́й; изры́тый.

ИЗУКРА́СИТЬ Р.; изукра́шу, изукра́сишь; изукра́сь; изукра́шенный.

ИЗУМИ́ТЬ Р.; изумлю́, изуми́шь; изумлённый.

ИЗ’Е́ЗДИТЬ Р.; из’е́зжу, из’е́здишь; из’е́зди; из’е́зженный.

ИЗ’Е́СТЬ Р.; из’е́ст, из’е́дят; из’е́л; из’е́денный.

ИЗ’ЯВИ́ТЬ Р.; из’явлю́, из’я́вишь; из’я́вленный.

ИЗ’ЯЗВИ́ТЬ Р.; из’язвлю́, из’язви́шь; из’язвлённый.

ИЗ’Я́ТЬ Р.; изыму́, изы́мешь; изыми́; из’я́тый.

ИЗЫМА́ТЬ I.; из’е́млю, из’е́млешь (arch. forms) (modern forms: изыма́ю, изыма́ешь); из’е́мли (arch.).

ИЗЫСКА́ТЬ Р.; изыщу́, изы́щешь; изыщи́; изы́сканный.

ИМА́ТЬ I.; е́млю, е́млешь (arch. forms) (modern forms: има́ю, има́ешь); е́мли (arch.).

ИСКАЗИ́ТЬ Р.; искажу́, искази́шь; искажённый.

ИСКА́ТЬ I.; ищу́, и́щешь; ищи́; иско́мый; и́сканный.

ИСКОЛЕСИ́ТЬ Р.; исколешу́, исколеси́шь; исколешённый.

ИСКОЛОТИ́ТЬ Р.; исколочу́, иско́лотишь; исколо́ченный.

ИСКОЛО́ТЬ Р.; исколю́, иско́лешь; исколи́; иско́лотый.

ИСКРИВИ́ТЬ Р.; искривлю́, искриви́шь; искривлённый.

ИСКУПИ́ТЬ Р.; искуплю́, искупишь; иску́пленный.

ИСКУСИ́ТЬ Р.; искушу́, искуси́шь; искушённый.

ИСПА́КОСТИТЬ Р.; испа́кощу, испа́костишь; испа́кости; испа́кощенный.

ИСПЕ́ЧЬ Р.; испеку́, испечёшь, испеку́т; испеки́; испёк; испечённый.

ИСПИСА́ТЬ Р.; испишу́, испи́шешь; испиши́; испи́санный.

ИСПИ́ТЬ Р.; изопью́, изопьёшь; испе́й; испи́тый.

ИСПО́РТИТЬ Р.; испо́рчу, испо́ртишь; испо́рти and испо́рть; испо́рченный.

ИСПОХА́БИТЬ Р.; испоха́блю, испоха́бишь; испоха́бь; испоха́бленный.

ИСПРА́ВИТЬ Р.; испра́влю, испра́вишь; испра́вь; испра́вленный.

ИСПРОСИ́ТЬ Р.; испрошу́, испро́сишь; испро́шенный.

ИСПУСТИ́ТЬ Р.; испущу́, испу́стишь; испу́щенный.

ИССЕ́ЧЬ Р.; иссеку́, иссечёшь, иссеку́т; иссеки́; иссе́к; иссечённый and иссе́ченный.

ИССЛЕДИ́ТЬ Р.; исслежу́, исследи́шь; исслеженный.

ИССО́ХНУТЬ Р.; иссо́х, иссо́хла.

ИСТА́ЯТЬ Р.; иста́ю, иста́ешь; иста́й.

ИСТЕРЕ́ТЬ Р.; изотру́, изотрёшь; изотри́; истёр; истёртый; истере́в and истёрши.

ИСТЕ́ЧЬ Р.; истеку́, истечёшь; истеку́т; истеки́; истёк.

ИСТОЛО́ЧЬ Р.; истолку́, истолчёшь, истолку́т; истолки́; истоло́к; истолчённый.

ИСТОМИ́ТЬ Р.; истомлю́, истоми́шь; истомлённый.

ИСТОПИ́ТЬ Р.; истоплю́, исто́пишь; исто́пленный.

ИСТОПТА́ТЬ Р.; истопчу́, исто́пчешь; истопчи́; исто́птанный.

ИСТО́РГНУТЬ Р.; исто́рг, исто́ргла; исто́рженный and исто́ргнутый.

ИСТРА́ТИТЬ Р.; истра́чу, истра́тишь; истра́ть; истра́ченный.

ИСТРЕБИ́ТЬ Р.; истреблю́, истреби́шь; истреблённый.

ИСТРЕПА́ТЬ Р.; истреплю́, истре́плешь; истрепли́; истрёпанный.

ИСТУПИ́ТЬ Р.; иступлю́, исту́пишь; исту́пленный.

ИСХИ́ТИТЬ Р.; исхи́щу, исхи́тишь; исхи́ть; исхи́щенный.

ИСХЛСТА́ТЬ Р.; исхлещу́. исхле́щешь; исхлещи́; исхлёстанный.

ИСХЛОПОТА́ТЬ Р.; исхлопочу́, исхлопо́чешь; исхлопочи́; исхлопо́танный.

ИСХОДИ́ТЬ Р.; исхожу́[1], исхо́дишь; исхо́женный.

ИСХОДИ́ТЬ[1] І.; исхожу́[2], исхо́дишь.

ИСХОДИ́ТЬ[2] І.; исхожу́[3], исхо́дишь.

ИСЧА́ХНУТЬ Р.; исча́х, исуа́хла.

ИСЧЕРТИ́ТЬ Р.; исчерчу́, исче́ртишь; исче́рченный.

К

КА́ВЕРЗИТЬ І.; ка́вержу, ка́верзишь; ка́верзи.

КАДИ́ТЬ І.; кажу́[1], кади́шь.

КАЗА́ТЬ І.; кажу́[2], ка́жешь; кажи́.

КА́ПАТЬ І.; ка́плю, ка́плешь; ка́пай; ка́пая.

КАРТА́ВИТЬ І.; карта́влю, карта́вишь; карта́вь.

КАТИ́ТЬ І.; качу́, ка́тишь.

КА́ЯТЬСЯ І.; ка́юсь, ка́ешься; ка́йся.

КВА́СИТЬ І.; ква́шу, ква́сишь; квась; ква́шенный.

КВОХТА́ТЬ І.; кво́хчет, кво́хчут; квохчи́.

КИПЕ́ТЬ І.; киплю́, кипи́шь; кипи́.

КИПЯТИ́ТЬ І.; кипячу́, кипяти́шь; кипячённый.

КИ́СНУТЬ І.; кис, ки́сла.

КИШЕ́ТЬ І.; киши́т, киша́т; киши́.

КЛАСТЬ І.; кладу́, кладёшь; клади́; клал.

КЛЕВЕТА́ТЬ І.; клевещу́, клеве́щешь; клевещи́.

КЛЕЙМИ́ТЬ І.; клеймлю́, клейми́шь; клеймённый.

КЛЕКОТА́ТЬ І.; клеко́чет, клеко́чут.

КЛЕПА́ТЬ[1] І.; клеплю́[1], кле́плешь; клепли́.

КЛЕПА́ТЬ[2] І.; клеплю́[2], кле́плешь (also клепа́ю, клепа́ешь); клепа́й and клепли́; клёпанный.

КЛИ́КАТЬ І.; кли́чу, кли́чешь; кличь.

КЛОКОТА́ТЬ І.; клокочу́, клоко́чешь; клокочи́.

КЛОХТА́ТЬ І.; клохчу́, кло́хчешь; клохчи́.

КЛЯСТЬ І.; кляну́, клянёшь; кляни́; клял; кля́тый.

КЛЯ́СТЬСЯ І.; кляну́сь, клянёшься; кляни́сь; кля́лся.

КОЛЕБА́ТЬ І.; коле́блю, коле́блешь; коле́бли; коле́блемый.

КОЛЕСИ́ТЬ І.; колешу́, колеси́шь.

КОЛОТИ́ТЬ І.; колочу́, коло́тишь.

КОЛО́ТЬ І.; колю́, ко́лешь; коли́; ко́лотый.

КОЛЫХА́ТЬ І.; колы́шу, колы́шешь (also колыха́ю, колыха́ешь); колыха́й; колыха́я and колы́ша.

КОНОВО́ДИТЬ І.; коново́жу, коново́дишь; коново́дь.

КОНОПА́ТИТЬ І.; конопа́чу, конопа́тишь; конопа́ть, конопа́ченный.

КОНТУ́ЗИТЬ Р.; конту́жу, конту́зишь; конту́зь; конту́женный.
КОНФУ́ЗИТЬ I.; конфу́жу, конфу́зишь; конфу́зь.
КО́НЧИТЬ Р.; ко́нчу, ко́нчишь; ко́нчи; ко́нченный.
КОПИ́ТЬ I.; коплю́, ко́пишь.
КОПТЕ́ТЬ[1] I.; копти́т, коптя́т; копти́.
КОПТЕ́ТЬ[2] I.; копчу́[1], копти́шь; копти́.
КОПТИ́ТЬ I.; копчу́[2], копти́шь; копти́.
КОРМИ́ТЬ I.; кормлю́, ко́рмишь; ко́рмленный.
КОРО́БИТЬ I.; коро́блю, коро́бишь; коро́бь.
КОРПЕ́ТЬ I.; корплю́, корпи́шь; корпи́.
КОСИ́ТЬ[1] I.; кошу́[1], коси́шь.
КОСИ́ТЬ[2] I.; кошу́[2], ко́сишь; ко́шенный.
КОСИ́ТЬСЯ I.; кошу́сь, коси́шься.
КОСМА́ТИТЬ I.; косма́чу, косма́тишь; косма́ть.
КОСТИ́ТЬ I.; кощу́, кости́шь.
КРА́ПАТЬ I.; кра́плю, кра́плешь (also кра́паю, кра́паешь); кра́пли and кра́пай; кра́пленный.

КРА́СИТЬ I.; кра́шу, кра́сишь; крась; кра́шенный.
КРАСТЬ I.; краду́, крадёшь; кради́; крал; кра́денный.
КРЕПИ́ТЬ I.; креплю́, крепи́шь; креплённый.
КРЕ́ПНУТЬ I.; креп (and кре́пнул), кре́пла.
КРЕСТИ́ТЬ[1] I.; крещу́[1], кре́стишь; крещённый.
КРЕСТИ́ТЬ[2] I.; крещу́[2], кре́стишь; крещённый.
КРИВИ́ТЬ I.; кривлю́, криви́шь.
КРИЧА́ТЬ I.; кричу́, кричи́шь; кричи́.
КРОПИ́ТЬ I.; кроплю́, кропи́шь.
КРУТИ́ТЬ I.; кручу́, кру́тишь; кру́ченный.
КРЫТЬ I.; кро́ю, кро́ешь; крой; кры́тый.
КРЯХТЕ́ТЬ I.; кряхчу́, кряхти́шь; кряхти́.
КУДА́ХТАТЬ I.: куда́хчу, куда́хчешь; куда́хчи.
КУ́КСИТЬСЯ I.; ку́кшусь, ку́ксишься; ку́ксись.
КУМИ́ТЬСЯ I.; кумлю́сь, куми́шься.
КУПИ́ТЬ Р.; куплю́, ку́пишь; ку́пленный.
КУТИ́ТЬ I.; кучу́, ку́тишь.

Л

ЛА́ДИТЬ I.; ла́жу[1], ла́дишь; ладь.
ЛА́ЗИТЬ I.; ла́жу[2], ла́зишь; лазь.
ЛА́КОМИТЬ I.; ла́комлю, ла́комишь; ла́коми and ла́комь.
ЛА́КОМИТЬСЯ I.; ла́комлюсь, ла́комишься; ла́комись and ла́комься.
ЛА́ЯТЬ I.; ла́ю, ла́ешь; лай.
ЛГАТЬ I.; лгу, лжёшь, лгут; лги.
ЛЕБЕЗИ́ТЬ I.; лебежу́, лебези́шь.
ЛЕЖА́ТЬ I.; лежу́, лежи́шь; лежи́; лёжа.
ЛЕЗТЬ I.; ле́зу, ле́зешь; лезь; лез.
ЛЕЛЕ́ЯТЬ I.; леле́ю, леле́ешь; леле́й; леле́янный.
ЛЕПЕТА́ТЬ I.; лепечу́, лепе́чешь; лепечи́.
ЛЕПИ́ТЬ I.; леплю́, ле́пишь.
ЛЕТЕ́ТЬ I.; лечу́, лети́шь; лети́.
ЛЕЧЬ Р.; ля́гу, ля́жешь, ля́гут; ляг; лёг.
ЛИЗА́ТЬ I.; лижу́, ли́жешь; лижи́.

ЛИ́ПНУТЬ I.; лип (and ли́пнул), ли́пла.
ЛИТЬ I.; лью, льёшь; лей; ли́тый.
ЛИЦЕЗРЕ́ТЬ I.; лицезрю́, лицезри́шь; лицезри́.
ЛОВИ́ТЬ I.; ловлю́, ло́вишь; ло́вленный.
ЛОМИ́ТЬ I.; ломлю́, ло́мишь.
ЛОПА́ТИТЬ I.; лопа́чу, лопа́тишь; лопа́ть; лопа́ченный.
ЛОПОТА́ТЬ I.; лопочу́, лопо́чешь; лопочи́.
ЛОХМА́ТИТЬ I.; лохма́чу, лохма́тишь; лохма́ть.
ЛУДИ́ТЬ I.; лужу́, лу́дишь; лужённый.
ЛУКА́ВИТЬ I.; лука́влю, лука́вишь; лука́вь.
ЛУПИ́ТЬ I.; луплю́, лу́пишь; лу́пленный.
ЛЬСТИ́ТЬ I.; льщу, льсти́шь.
ЛЮБИ́ТЬ I.; люблю́, лю́бишь.

М

МА́ЗАТЬ[1] I.; ма́жу[1], ма́жешь; мажь; ма́занный.

МА́ЗАТЬ[2] I.; ма́жу[2], ма́жешь; мажь.

МАХА́ТЬ I.; машу́, ма́шешь (also маха́ю, маха́ешь); маши́; маха́я and маша́.

МА́ЯТЬСЯ I.; ма́юсь, ма́ешься; ма́йся.

МЕРЕ́ТЬ I.; мрёт, мрут; мри; мёр.

МЁРЗНУТЬ I.; мёрз (and мёрзнул), мёрзла.

МЕ́РКНУТЬ I.; мерк (and ме́ркнул), ме́ркла.

МЕРТВИ́ТЬ I.; мертвлю́, мертви́шь.

МЕСИ́ТЬ I.; мешу́, ме́сишь; ме́шенный.

МЕСТИ́ I.; мету́, метёшь; мети́; мёл; мётший; метённый.

МЕТА́ТЬ I.; мечу́, ме́чешь; мечи́.

МЕ́ТИТЬ[1] I.; ме́чу[1], ме́тишь; меть; ме́ченный.

МЕ́ТИТЬ[2] I.; ме́чу[2], ме́тишь; меть.

МО́КНУТЬ I.; мок (and мо́кнул), мо́кла.

МО́ЛВИТЬ Р.; мо́лвишь; мо́лви.

МОЛОДИ́ТЬ I.; моложу́, молоди́шь.

МОЛОТИ́ТЬ I.; молочу́, моло́тишь; моло́ченный.

МОЛО́ТЬ I.; мелю́, ме́лешь; мели́; мо́лотый.

МОЛЧА́ТЬ I.; молчу́, молчи́шь; молчи́.

МОРО́ЗИТЬ I.; моро́жу, моро́зишь; моро́женный.

МОСТИ́ТЬ I.; мощу́, мости́шь; мощённый.

МОЧЬ I.; могу́, мо́жешь, мо́гут; мог.

МСТИТЬ I.; мщу, мсти́шь.

МУРА́ВИТЬ I.; мура́влю, мура́вишь; мура́вь; мура́вленный.

МУТИ́ТЬ I.; мучу́, мути́шь (also му́тишь).

МЧАТЬ I.; мчу, мчишь; мчи.

МЫТЬ I.; мо́ю, мо́ешь; мой; мы́тый.

МЫЧА́ТЬ I.; мычу́, мычи́шь; мычи́.

МЯСТИ́СЬ I.; мяту́сь, мятёшься; мяти́сь (past tense not used).

МЯТЬ I.; мну, мнёшь; мни; мя́тый.

Н

НАБА́ВИТЬ Р.; наба́влю, наба́вишь; наба́вь; наба́вленный.

НАБАЛАМУ́ТИТЬ Р.; набаламу́чу, набаламу́тишь; набаламу́ть; набаламу́ченный.

НАБЕЖА́ТЬ Р.; набегу́, набежи́шь, набегу́т; набеги́.

НАБИ́ТЬ Р.; набью́, набьёшь; набе́й; наби́тый.

НАБЛЮСТИ́ Р.; наблюду́, наблюдёшь; наблюди́; наблю́л; наблю́дший; наблюдённый.

НАБОРМОТА́ТЬ Р.; набормочу́, набормо́чешь; набормочи́.

НАБРА́ТЬ Р.; наберу́, наберёшь; набери́; на́бранный.

НАБРЕСТИ́ Р.; набреду́, набредёшь; набреди́; набрёл; набре́дший.

НАБРО́СИТЬ Р.; набро́шу, набро́сишь; набро́сь; набро́шенный.

НАБУ́ХНУТЬ Р.; набу́х, набу́хла.

НАВА́КСИТЬ Р.; нава́кшу, нава́ксишь; нава́кси; нава́кшенный.

НАВЕЗТИ́ Р.; навезу́, навезёшь; навези́; навёз; навезённый.

НАВЕРТЕ́ТЬ Р.; наверчу́, наве́ртишь; наверти́; наве́рченный.

НАВЕ́СИТЬ Р.; наве́шу, наве́сишь; наве́сь; наве́шенный.

НАВЕСТИ́ Р.; наведу́, наведёшь; наведи́; навёл; наве́дший; наведённый; наведя́.

НАВЕСТИ́ТЬ Р.; навещу́, навести́шь; навещённый.

НАВЕ́ЯТЬ Р.; наве́ю, наве́ешь; наве́й[1]; наве́янный.

НАВИНТИ́ТЬ Р.; навинчу́, навинти́шь; нави́нченный.

НАВИ́СНУТЬ Р.; нави́с, нави́сла.

НАВИ́ТЬ Р.; навью́, навьёшь; наве́й[2]; нави́тый.

НАВЛЕ́ЧЬ Р.; навлеку́, навлечёшь,

303

навлеку́т; навлеки́; навлёк; навлечённый.

НАВОДИ́ТЬ I.; навожу́[1], наво́дишь.

НАВОЗИ́ТЬ Р.; навожу́[2], наво́зишь; наво́женный.

НАВОЗИ́ТЬ I.; навожу́[3], наво́зишь.

НАВО́ЗИТЬ I.; наво́жу, наво́зишь; наво́зь; наво́женный.

НАВОЛО́ЧЬ Р.; наволоку́, наволочёшь, наволоку́т; наволоки́; наволо́к; наволочённый.

НАВОРОТИ́ТЬ Р.; наворочу́, наворо́тишь; наворо́ченный.

НАВОРЧА́ТЬ Р.; наворчу́, наворчи́шь; наворчи́.

НАВРА́ТЬ Р.; навру́, наврёшь; наври́; на́вранный.

НАВРЕДИ́ТЬ Р.; наврежу́, навреди́шь.

НАВЫ́КНУТЬ Р.; навы́к, навы́кла.

НАВЯЗА́ТЬ Р.; навяжу́, навя́жешь; навяжи́; навя́занный.

НАВЯ́ЗНУТЬ Р.; навя́з, навя́зла.

НАГА́ДИТЬ Р.; нага́жу, нага́дишь; нага́дь; нага́женный.

НАГЛА́ДИТЬ Р.; нагла́жу, нагла́дишь; нагла́дь; нагла́женный.

НАГЛЯДЕ́ТЬСЯ Р.; нагляжу́сь, нагляди́шься; нагляди́сь.

НАГНА́ТЬ Р.; нагоню́, наго́нишь; нагони́; на́гнанный.

НАГНЕСТИ́ Р.; нагнету́, нагнетёшь; нагнети́; нагнетённый; нагнетя́ (past tense not used).

НАГОРЕ́ТЬ Р.; нагори́т, нагоря́т.

НАГОРОДИ́ТЬ Р.; нагорожу́, нагоро́дишь (and нагороди́шь); нагоро́женный.

НАГОТО́ВИТЬ Р.; нагото́влю, нагото́вишь; нагото́вь; нагото́вленный.

НАГРА́БИТЬ Р.; награ́блю, награ́бишь; награ́бь; награ́бленный.

НАГРАДИ́ТЬ Р.; награжу́, награди́шь; награждённый.

НАГРАФИ́ТЬ Р.; награфлю́, награфи́шь; награфлённый.

НАГРЕМЕ́ТЬ Р.; нагремлю́, нагреми́шь; нагреми́.

НАГРЕСТИ́ Р.; нагребу́, нагребёшь; нагреби́; нагрёб; нагребённый.

НАГРОМОЗДИ́ТЬ Р.; нагромозжу́, нагромозди́шь; нагромождённый.

НАГРУБИ́ТЬ Р.; нагрублю́, нагруби́шь.

НАГРУЗИ́ТЬ Р.; нагружу́, нагру́зишь (also нагрузи́шь); нагру́женный and нагружённый.

НАГРЫ́ЗТЬ Р.; нагрызу́, нагрызёшь; нагрызи́; нагры́з; нагры́зенный.

НАДАВИ́ТЬ Р.; надавлю́, нада́вишь; нада́вленный.

НАДБА́ВИТЬ Р.; надба́влю, надба́вишь; надба́вь; надба́вленный.

НАДБИ́ТЬ Р.; надобью́, надобьёшь; надбе́й; надби́тый.

НАДВЯЗА́ТЬ Р.; надвяжу́, надвя́жешь; надвяжи́; надвя́занный.

НАДДАВА́ТЬ I.; наддаю́, наддаёшь; наддава́й; наддава́я.

НАДДА́ТЬ Р.; надда́м, надда́шь, надда́ст, наддади́м, наддади́те, наддаду́т; надда́й; на́дданный.

НАДЕ́ТЬ Р.; наде́ну, наде́нешь; наде́нь; наде́тый.

НАДЕ́ЯТЬСЯ I.; наде́юсь. наде́ешься; наде́йся.

НАДИВИ́ТЬСЯ Р.; надивлю́сь, надиви́шься.

НАДКОЛО́ТЬ Р.; надколю́, надко́лешь; надколи́; надко́лотый.

НАДКУСИ́ТЬ Р.; надкушу́, надку́сишь; надку́шенный.

НАДЛЕЖА́ТЬ I.; надлежи́т; надлежа́ло (infinitive not used).

НАДЛОМИ́ТЬ Р.; надпомлю́, надло́мишь; надло́мленный.

НАДОЕ́СТЬ Р.; надое́м, надое́шь, надое́ст, надоеди́м, надоеди́те, надоедя́т; надое́л (no imperative).

НАДОРВА́ТЬ Р.; надорву́, надорвёшь; надорви́; надо́рванный.

НАДПИСА́ТЬ I.; надпишу́, надпи́шешь; надпиши́; надпи́санный.

НАДПОРО́ТЬ Р.; надпорю́, надпо́решь; надпори́; надпо́ротый.

НАДРА́ТЬ Р.; надеру́, надерёшь; надери́; на́дранный.

НАДРЕ́ЗАТЬ Р.; надре́жу, надре́жешь; надре́жь; надре́занный.

НАДРУБИ́ТЬ Р.; надрублю́, надру́бишь; надру́бленный.

НАДСАДИ́ТЬ Р.; надсажу́, надса́дишь; надса́женный.

НАДСЕ́ЧЬ Р.; надсеку́, надсечёшь, надсеку́т; надсеки́; надсе́к; надсечённый.

НАДСТА́ВИТЬ Р.; надста́влю, надста́вишь; надста́вь; надста́вленный.

НАДУ́ТЬ Р.; наду́ю, наду́ешь; наду́й; наду́тый.

НАДШИ́ТЬ Р.; надошью́, надошьёшь; надшей; надши́тый.

НАДЫМИ́ТЬ Р.; надымлю́, надыми́шь.

НАДЫША́ТЬ Р.; надышу́, нады́шишь; надыши́.

НАЕ́ЗДИТЬ Р.; нае́зжу, нае́здишь; нае́зди; нае́зженный.

НАЕ́СТЬ Р.; нае́м, нае́шь[1], нае́ст, наеди́м, наеди́те, наедя́т; нае́шь[2] (imp.); нае́л; нае́денный.

НАЕ́ХАТЬ Р.; нае́ду, нае́дешь; наезжа́й.

НАЖА́ТЬ[1] Р.; нажму́, нажмёшь; нажми́; нажа́тый.

НАЖА́ТЬ[2] Р.; нажну́, нажнёшь; нажни́; нажа́тый.

НАЖЕ́ЧЬ Р.; нажгу́, нажжёшь, нажгу́т; нажги́; нажёг, нажгла́; нажжённый.

НАЖИВИ́ТЬ Р.; наживлю́, наживи́шь; наживи́; наживлённый.

НАЖИ́ТЬ Р.; наживу́, наживёшь; наживи́; на́житый and нажи́тый.

НАЗВА́ТЬ Р.; назову́, назовёшь; назови́; на́званный.

НАЙТИ́ Р.; найду́, найдёшь; найди́; нашёл, нашла́; наше́дший; на́йденный; найдя́ and наше́дши.

НАКА́ВЕРЗИТЬ Р.; нака́вержу, нака́верзишь; нака́верзи.

НАКАЗА́ТЬ Р.; накажу́, нака́жешь; накажи́; нака́занный.

НАКА́ПАТЬ Р.; нака́плю, нака́плешь (arch. forms) (modern forms: нака́паю, нака́паешь); нака́пай; нака́панный.

НАКАТИ́ТЬ Р.; накачу́, нака́тишь; кака́ченный.

НАКВА́СИТЬ Р.; наква́шу, наква́сишь; наква́сь; наква́шенный.

НАКИПЕ́ТЬ Р.; напипи́т, накипя́т.

НАКИПЯТИ́ТЬ Р.; накипячу́, накипяти́шь; накипячённый.

НАКЛЕВЕТА́ТЬ Р.; наклевещу́, наклеве́щешь; наклевещи́.

НАКЛЕПА́ТЬ[1] Р.; наклеплю́[1], накле́плешь; наклепли́.

НАКЛЕПА́ТЬ[2] Р.; наклеплю́[2], накле́плешь (also наклепа́ю, наклепа́ешь; наклепа́й); наклепли́; накле́панный.

НАКЛИ́КАТЬ Р.; накли́чу, накли́чешь; накли́чь; накли́канный.

НАКОЛОТИ́ТЬ Р.; наколочу́, наколо́тишь; наколо́ченный.

НАКОЛО́ТЬ Р.; наколю́, нако́лешь; наколи́; нако́лотый.

НАКОПИ́ТЬ Р.; накоплю́, нако́пишь; нако́пленный.

НАКОПТИ́ТЬ Р.; накопчу́, накопти́шь; накопчённый.

НАКОРМИ́ТЬ Р.; накормлю́, нако́рмишь; нако́рмленный.

НАКОСИ́ТЬ Р.; накошу́, нако́сишь; нако́шенный.

НАКРА́СИТЬ Р.; накра́шу, накра́сишь; накра́сь; накра́шенный.

НАКРА́СТЬ Р.; накраду́, накрадёшь; накради́; накра́л; накра́денный; накра́в and накрадя́.

НАКРИЧА́ТЬ Р.; накричу́, накричи́шь; накричи́.

НАКРУТИ́ТЬ Р.; накручу́, накру́тишь; накру́ченный.

НАКРЫ́ТЬ Р.; накро́ю, накро́ешь; накро́й; накры́тый.

НАКУПИ́ТЬ Р.; накуплю́, наку́пишь; наку́пленный.

НАЛА́ДИТЬ Р.; нала́жу, нала́дишь; нала́дь; нала́женный.

НАЛГА́ТЬ Р.; налгу́, налжёшь, налгу́т; налги́.

НАЛЕЖА́ТЬ Р.; належу́, належи́шь; належи́; налёжанный.

НАЛЕ́ЗТЬ Р.; нале́зет, нале́зут; нале́з.

НАЛЕПИ́ТЬ Р.; налеплю́, нале́пишь; нале́пленный.

НАЛЕТЕ́ТЬ Р.; налечу́, налети́шь; налети́.

НАЛЕ́ЧЬ Р.; наля́гу, наля́жешь, наля́гут; наля́г; налёг.

НАЛИЗА́ТЬСЯ Р.; налижу́сь, налижешься; налижи́сь.

НАЛИ́ТЬ Р.; налью́, нальёшь; налей; на́литый and нали́тый.

НАЛОВИ́ТЬ Р.; наловлю́, нало́вишь; нало́вленный.

НАМАГНИ́ТИТЬ Р.; намагни́чу, намагни́тишь; намагни́ть; намагни́ченный.

НАМА́ЗАТЬ Р.; нама́жу, нама́жешь; нама́жь; нама́занный.

НАМА́ЯТЬСЯ Р.; нама́юсь, нама́ешься; нама́йся.

НАМЁРЗНУТЬ Р.; намёрз, намёрзла.

НАМЕСИ́ТЬ Р.; намешу́, наме́сишь; наме́шенный.

НАМЕСТИ́ Р.; намету́, наметёшь; намети́; намёл; намётший; наметённый; намета́.

НАМЕТА́ТЬ Р.; намечу́, наме́чешь; намечи́; намётанный.

НАМЕ́ТИТЬ Р.; наме́чу, наме́тишь; наме́ть; наме́ченный.

НАМО́КНУТЬ Р.; намо́к, намо́кла.

НАМОЛОТИ́ТЬ Р.; намолочу́, намоло́тишь; намоло́ченный.

НАМОЛО́ТЬ Р.; намелю́, наме́лешь; намели́; намо́лотый.

НАМОСТИ́ТЬ Р.; намощу́, намости́шь; намощённый.

НАМУТИ́ТЬ Р.; намучу́, намути́шь (and наму́тишь).

НАМЫ́ТЬ Р.; намо́ю, намо́ешь; намо́й; намы́тый.

НАМЯ́ТЬ Р.; намну́, намнёшь; намни́; намя́тый.

НАНЕСТИ́ Р.; нанесу́, нанесёшь; нанеси́; нанёс; нанесённый; нанеся́.

НАНИЗА́ТЬ Р.; нанижу́, нани́жешь; нанижи́; нани́занный.

НАНОСИ́ТЬ I.; наношу́[1], нано́сишь.

НАНОСИ́ТЬ Р.; наношу́[2], нано́сишь; нано́шенный.

НАНЯ́ТЬ Р.; найму́, наймёшь; найми́; на́нятый.

НАОРА́ТЬ Р.; наору́, наорёшь; наори́.

НАПА́КОСТИТЬ Р.; напа́кощу, напа́костишь; напа́кости; напа́кощенный.

НАПАСТИ́ Р.; напасу́, напасёшь; напаси́; напа́с; напасённый.

НАПА́СТЬ Р.; нападу́, нападёшь; напади́; напа́л.

НАПАХА́ТЬ Р.; напашу́, напа́шешь; напаши́; напа́ханный.

НАПЕРЕ́ТЬ Р.; напру́, напрёшь; напри́; напёр; напере́в and напёрши.

НАПЕ́ТЬ Р.; напою́, напоёшь; напо́й; напе́тый.

НАПЕ́ЧЬ Р.; напеку́, напечёшь; напеку́т; напеки́; напёк; напечённый.

НАПИСА́ТЬ Р.; напишу́, напи́шешь; напиши́; напи́санный.

НАПИ́ТЬСЯ Р.; напью́сь, напьёшься; напе́йся.

НАПЛА́КАТЬ Р.; напла́чу, напла́чешь; напла́чь; напла́канный.

НАПЛЕСКА́ТЬ Р.; наплещу́, наплещешь; наплещи́; наплёсканный.

НАПЛЕСТИ́ Р.; наплету́, наплетёшь; наплети́; наплёл; наплётший; наплетённый; наплета́

НАПЛОДИ́ТЬ Р.; напложу́, наплоди́шь; напложённый.

НАПЛЫ́ТЬ Р.; наплыву́, наплывёшь; наплыви́.

НАПОЛЗТИ́ Р.; наползу́, наползёшь; наползи́; напо́лз.

НАПОМА́ДИТЬ Р.; напома́жу, напома́дишь; напома́дь; напома́женный.

НАПОРО́ТЬ Р.; напорю́, напо́решь; напори́; напо́ротый.

НАПО́РТИТЬ Р.; напо́рчу, напо́ртишь; напо́рти and напо́рть; напо́рченный.

НАПРА́ВИТЬ Р.; напра́влю, напра́вишь; напра́вь; напра́вленный.

НАПРОКА́ЗИТЬ Р.; напрока́жу, напрока́зишь; напрока́зь.

НАПРОСИ́ТЬСЯ Р.; напрошу́сь, напро́сишься.

НАПРЯ́ЧЬ Р.; напрягу́, напряжёшь; напрягу́т; напряги́; напря́г; напряжённый.

НАПУСТИ́ТЬ Р.; напущу́, напу́стишь; напу́щенный.

НАРАСТИ́ Р.; нарастёт, нараст́ут; наро́с.

НАРАСТИ́ТЬ Р.; наращу́, нарасти́шь; наращённый.

НАРВА́ТЬ[1] Р.; нарвёт, нарву́т.

НАРВА́ТЬ[2] Р.; нарву́, нарвёшь; нарви́; на́рванный.

НАРЕ́ЗАТЬ Р.; наре́жу, наре́жешь; наре́жь; наре́занный.

НАРЕ́ЧЬ Р.; нареку́, наречёшь, нареку́т; нареки́; нарёк; наречённый and наре́ченный.

НАРОДИ́ТЬ Р.; нарожу́, народи́шь; нарождённый.

НАРУБИ́ТЬ Р.; нарублю́, нару́бишь; нару́бленный.

НАРЫ́ТЬ Р.; наро́ю, наро́ешь; наро́й; нары́тый.

НАРЯДИ́ТЬ[1] Р.; наряжу́[1], наря́дишь (and наряди́шь); наря́женный.

НАРЯДИ́ТЬ[2] Р.; наряжу́[2], наряди́шь; наряжённый.

НАСАДИ́ТЬ Р.; насажу́, наса́дишь; наса́женный.

НАСЕ́СТЬ Р.; нася́ду, нася́дешь; нася́дь; насе́л.

НАСЕ́ЧЬ Р.; насеку́, насечёшь, насеку́т; насеки́; насёк; насечённый.

НАСЕ́ЯТЬ Р.; насе́ю, насе́ешь; насе́й; насе́янный.

НАСИДЕ́ТЬ Р.; насижу́, насиди́шь; насиди́; наси́женный.

НАСКАЗА́ТЬ Р.; наскажу́, наска́жешь; наскажи́; наска́занный.

НАСКАКА́ТЬ Р.; наскачу́, наска́чешь; наскачи́.

НАСКРЕСТИ́ Р.; наскребу́, наскрёшь; наскреби́; наскрёб; наскребённый.

НАСЛАДИ́ТЬСЯ Р.; наслажу́сь, насладишься.

НАСЛАСТИ́ТЬ Р.; наслащу́, насласти́шь; наслащённый.

НАСЛА́ТЬ Р.; нашлю́, нашлёшь; нашли́[1]; на́сланный.

НАСЛЕДИ́ТЬ Р.; наслежу́, наследи́шь; наслеженный.

НАСМЕЯ́ТЬСЯ Р.; насмею́сь, насмеёшься; насме́йся.

НАСМОТРЕ́ТЬ Р.; насмотрю́, насмо́тришь; насмотри́; насмо́тренный.

НАСОСА́ТЬ Р.; насосу́, насосёшь; насоси́; насо́санный.

НАСТАВА́ТЬ I.; настаёт, настаю́т; настава́й.

НАСТА́ВИТЬ Р.; наста́влю, наста́вишь; наста́вь; наста́вленный.

НАСТА́ТЬ Р.; наста́нет, наста́нут; наста́нь.

НАСТЕЛИ́ТЬ Р.; настелю́, насте́лешь; настели́; насте́ленный.

НАСТИ́ГНУТЬ Р.; насти́гну, насти́гнешь; насти́гни; насти́г; насти́гнутый.

НАСТИ́ЧЬ Р.; насти́гну, насти́гнешь; насти́гни; насти́г; насти́гнутый.

НАСТЛА́ТЬ Р.; настелю́, насте́лешь; настели́; на́стланный.

НАСТОЯ́ТЬ Р.; настою́, настои́шь; настои́; настоя́нный.

НАСТРИ́ЧЬ Р.; настригу́, настри́жешь; настригу́т; настриги́; настри́г; настри́женный.

НАСТУДИ́ТЬ Р.; настужу́, насту́дишь; насту́женный.

НАСТУПИ́ТЬ Р.; наступлю́, насту́пишь.

НАСТЫ́НУТЬ Р.; насты́ну, насты́нешь; насты́нь; насты́л.

НАСТЫ́ТЬ Р.; насты́ну, насты́нешь; насты́нь; насты́л.

НАСУ́ПИТЬ Р.; насу́плю, насу́пишь; насу́пь; насу́пленный.

НАСУРЬМИ́ТЬ Р.; насурьмлю́, насурьми́шь; насурьмлённый.

НАСЫ́ПАТЬ Р.; насы́плю, насы́плешь; насы́пь; насы́панный.

НАСЫ́ТИТЬ Р.; насы́щу, насы́тишь; насы́ть; насы́щенный.

НАТА́ЯТЬ Р.; ната́ю, ната́ешь; ната́й; ната́янный.

НАТЕРЕБИ́ТЬ Р.; натереблю́, натереби́шь; натереблённый.

НАТЕРЕ́ТЬ Р.; натру́, натрёшь; натри́; натёр; натёртый; натерев and натёрши.

НАТЕРПЕ́ТЬСЯ Р.; натерплю́сь, натерпишься; натерпи́сь.

НАТЕСА́ТЬ Р.; натешу́, нате́шешь; натеши́; натёсанный.

НАТЕ́ЧЬ Р.; натечёт, натеку́т; натёк.

НАТКА́ТЬ Р.; натку́, наткёшь; натки́; на́тканный.

НАТОЛО́ЧЬ Р.; натолку́, натолчёшь, натолку́т; натолки́; натоло́к; натолчённый.

НАТОПИ́ТЬ Р.; натоплю́, нато́пишь; нато́пленный.

НАТОПТА́ТЬ Р., натопчу́, нато́пчешь; натопчи́; нато́птанный.

НАТРА́ВИТЬ Р.; натравлю́, натра́вишь; натра́вленный.

НАТРУБИ́ТЬ Р.; натрублю́, натруби́шь.

НАТРУДИ́ТЬ Р.; натружу́, натруди́шь (and натру́дишь); натружённый and натру́женный.

НАТРУСИ́ТЬ Р.; натрушу́, натруси́шь; натру́шенный.

НАТРЯСТИ́ Р.; натрясу́, натрясёшь; натряси́; натря́с; натрясённый.

НАУДИ́ТЬ Р.; наужу́, нау́дишь; нау́женный.

НАУСТИ́ТЬ Р.; наущу́, наусти́шь; наущённый.

НАХАМИ́ТЬ Р.; нахамлю́, нахами́шь.

НАХЛЕСТА́ТЬ Р.; нахлещу́, нахле́щешь; нахлещи́; нахлёстанный.

НАХОДИ́ТЬ I.; нахожу́, нахо́дишь.

НАХОЛОДИ́ТЬ Р.; нахоложу́, нахолоди́шь; нахоложённый.

НАХОХОТА́ТЬСЯ Р.; нахохочу́сь, нахохо́чешься; нахохочи́сь.

НАЦЕДИ́ТЬ Р.; нацежу́, наце́дишь; наце́женный.

НАЦЕПИ́ТЬ Р.; нацеплю́, наце́пишь; наце́пленный.

НАЧАДИ́ТЬ Р.; начажу́, начади́шь.

НАЧА́ТЬ Р.; начну́, начнёшь; начни́; на́чатый.

НАЧЕРТИ́ТЬ P.; начерчу́, наче́ртишь; наче́рченный.
НАЧЕСА́ТЬ P.; начешу́, наче́шешь; начеши́; начёсанный.
НАЧЕ́СТЬ P.; начту́, начтёшь; начёл, начла́; начётший; начтённый.
НАЧИ́СТИТЬ P.; начи́щу, начи́стишь; начи́сти and начи́сть; начи́щенный.
НАШЕПТА́ТЬ P.; нашепчу́, нашеп-чешь; нашепчи́; нашёптанный.
НАШИ́ТЬ P.; нашью́, нашьёшь; нашей; наши́тый.
НАШУМЕ́ТЬ P.; нашумлю́, нашуми́шь; нашуми́.
НАЩЕПА́ТЬ P.; нащеплю́, наще́плешь; нащепли́; наще́панный.
НАЩИПА́ТЬ P.; нащиплю́, нащи́плешь; нащипли́; нащи́панный.
НАЭКОНО́МИТЬ P.; наэконо́млю, наэконо́мишь; наэконо́мь; наэконо́мленный.
НЕБРЕ́ЧЬ I.; небрегу́, небрежёшь, небрегу́т; небреги́; небрёг.
НЕВЗВИ́ДЕТЬ P.; невзви́жу, невзви́дишь.
НЕВЗЛЮБИ́ТЬ P.; невзлюблю́, невзлю́бишь.
НЕДОБРА́ТЬ P.; недоберу́, недобе-рёшь; недобери́; недо́бранный.
НЕДОВЕ́СИТЬ P.; недове́шу, недове́сишь; недове́сь; недове́шенный.
НЕДОГЛЯДЕ́ТЬ P.; неголяжу́, неголяди́шь; неголяди́.
НЕДОПЛАТИ́ТЬ P.; недоплачу́, недопла́тишь; недопла́ченный.
НЕДОСКАЗА́ТЬ P.; недоскажу́, недоска́жешь; недоскажи́; недоска́занный.
НЕДОСЛА́ТЬ P.; недошолю́, недошлёшь; недошли́; недо́сланный.
НЕДОСЛЫ́ШАТЬ P.; недослы́шу, недослы́шишь; недослы́шанный.

НЕДОСМОТРЕ́ТЬ P.; недосмотрю́, недосмо́тришь; недосмотри́; недосмо́тренный.
НЕДОСПА́ТЬ P.; недосплю́, недоспи́шь; недоспи́.
НЕДОСТАВА́ТЬ I.; недостаёт (impers.).
НЕДОСТА́ТЬ P.; недоста́нет (impers.).
НЕЙТИ́ I.; нейду́, нейдёшь (used in place of не идти́).
НЕНАВИ́ДЕТЬ P.; ненави́жу, ненави́дишь; ненави́дь.
НЕСТИ́ I.; несу́, несёшь; неси́; нёс; несо́мый.
НИЗА́ТЬ I.; нижу́, ни́жешь; нижи́.
НИЗВЕСТИ́ P.; низведу́, низведёшь; низведи́; низвёл; низве́дший; низведённый; низведя́ and низве́дши.
НИЗВОДИ́ТЬ I.; низвожу́, низво́дишь.
НИЗОЙТИ́ P.; низойду́, низойдёшь; низойди́; нисшёл, низошла́; нисше́дший; низойдя́ and нисше́дши.
НИ́КНУТЬ I.; ник, ни́кла.
НИСПА́СТЬ P.; ниспадёт, ниспаду́т; ниспади́; ниспа́л.
НИСПОСЛА́ТЬ P.; ниспошлю́, ниспошлёшь; ниспошли́; ниспо́сланный.
НИСПРОВЕ́РГНУТЬ P.; ниспрове́рг (and ниспрове́ргнул), ниспрове́ргла; ниспрове́ргнутый and ниспрове́рженный.
НИСХОДИ́ТЬ I.; нисхожу́, нисхо́дишь.
НИШКНУ́ТЬ P.; нишкни́ (imperative only).
НОРОВИ́ТЬ I.; норовлю́, норови́шь.
НОСИ́ТЬ I.; ношу́, но́сишь; но́шеный.
НРА́ВИТЬСЯ I.; нра́влюсь, нра́вишься; нра́вься.
НУ́ДИТЬ I.; ну́жу, ну́дишь; нудь.
НЫТЬ I.; но́ю, но́ешь; ной.

O

ОБАНКРО́ТИТЬСЯ P.; обанкро́чусь, обанкро́тишься; обанкро́ться.
ОБАНКРУ́ТИТЬСЯ P.; обанкру́чусь, обанкру́тишься; обанкру́ться.
ОБВЕРТЕ́ТЬ P.; обверчу́, обве́ртишь; обверти́; обве́рченный.
ОБВЕ́СИТЬ P.; обве́шу, обве́сишь; обве́сь; обве́шенный.

ОБВЕСТИ́ P.; обведу́, обведёшь; обведи́; обвёл; обве́дший; обведённый; обве́дши and обведя́.
ОБВЕ́ЯТЬ P.; обве́ю, обве́ешь; обве́й[2]; обве́янный.
ОБВИ́СНУТЬ P.; обви́с, обви́сла.
ОБВИ́ТЬ P.; обовью́, обовьёшь; обве́й[1]; обви́тый.

ОБВОДИ́ТЬ I.; обвожу́, обво́дишь.

ОБВОЛО́ЧЬ Р.; обволочёт, обволоку́т; обволо́к; обволоки́; обволочённый.

ОБВЫ́КНУТЬ Р.; обвы́к, обвы́кла.

ОБВЯЗА́ТЬ Р.; обвяжу́, обвя́жешь; обвяжи́; обвя́занный.

ОБГЛОДА́ТЬ Р.; обгложу́, обгло́жешь; обгложи́; обгло́данный.

ОБГОРЕ́ТЬ Р.; обгорю́, обгори́шь; обгори́.

ОБГРЫ́ЗТЬ Р.; обгрызу́, обгрызёшь; обгрызи́; обгры́з; обгры́зенный.

ОБДАВА́ТЬ I.; обдаю, обдаёшь; обдава́й; обдава́я.

ОБДА́ТЬ Р.; обда́м, обда́шь, обда́ст, обдади́м, обдади́те, обдаду́т; обда́й; о́бданный.

ОБДУ́ТЬ Р.; обду́ю, обду́ешь; обду́й; обду́тый.

ОБЕЖА́ТЬ Р.; обегу́, обежи́шь, обегу́т; обеги́.

ОБЕЗВО́ДИТЬ Р.; обезво́жу, обезво́дишь; обезво́дь; обезво́женный.

ОБЕЗВРЕ́ДИТЬ Р.; обезвре́жу, обезвре́дишь; обезвре́дь; обезвре́женный.

ОБЕЗГЛА́ВИТЬ Р.; обезгла́влю, обезгла́вишь; обезгла́вь; обезгла́вленный.

ОБЕЗЗАРА́ЗИТЬ Р.; обеззара́жу, обеззара́зишь; обеззара́зь; обеззара́женный.

ОБЕЗОБРА́ЗИТЬ Р.; обезобра́жу, обезобра́зишь; обезобра́зь; обезобра́женный.

ОБЕЗОПА́СИТЬ Р.; обезопа́шу, обезопа́сишь; обезопа́сь; обезопа́сенный.

ОБЕРЕ́ЧЬ Р.; оберегу́, обережёшь, оберегу́т; обереги́; оберёг; обережённый.

ОБЕСКРО́ВИТЬ Р.; обескро́влю, обескро́вишь; обескро́вь; обескро́вленный.

ОБЕСПЛО́ДИТЬ Р.; обеспло́жу, обеспло́дишь; обеспло́дь; обеспло́женный.

ОБЕССЛА́ВИТЬ Р.; обессла́влю, обессла́виыь; обессла́вь; обессла́вленный.

ОБЕССМЕ́РТИТЬ Р.; обессме́рчу, обессме́ртишь; обессме́рть; обессме́рченный.

ОБЕССУ́ДИТЬ Р.; обессу́дь, обессу́дьте (imperative) (used with не).

ОБЕСЦВЕ́ТИТЬ Р.; обесцве́чу, обесцве́тишь; обесцве́ть; обесцве́ченный.

ОБЕСЧЕ́СТИТЬ Р.; обесче́щу, обесче́стишь; обесче́сти; обесче́щенный.

ОБЖА́ТЬ[1] Р.; обожму́, обожмёшь; обожми́; обжа́тый[1].

ОБЖА́ТЬ[2] Р.; обожну́, обожнёшь обожни́; обжа́тый[2].

ОБЖЕ́ЧЬ Р.; обожгу́, обожжёшь, обожгу́т; обожги́; обжёг, обожгла́; обожжённый.

ОБЖИ́ТЬ Р.; обживу́, обживёшь; обживи́; обжито́й and обжи́тый.

ОБЗАВЕСТИ́ Р.; обзаведу́, обзаведёшь; обзаведи́; обзавёл; обзаве́дший; обзаведя́.

ОБЗАВОДИ́ТЬ I.; обзавожу́, обзаво́дишь.

ОБИ́ДЕТЬ Р.; оби́жу, оби́дишь; оби́дь; оби́женный.

ОБИ́ТЬ Р. обобью́, обобьёшь; обе́й; оби́тый.

ОБКОЛО́ТЬ Р.; обколю́, обко́лешь; обколи́; обко́лотый.

ОБКОРМИ́ТЬ Р.; обкормлю́, обко́рмишь; обко́рмленный.

ОБКОСИ́ТЬ Р.; обкошу́, обко́сишь; обко́шенный.

ОБЛАГОРО́ДИТЬ Р.; облагоро́жу, облагоро́дишь; облагоро́дь; облагоро́женный.

ОБЛА́ДИТЬ Р.; обла́жу[1], обла́дишь; обла́дь; обла́женный.

ОБЛА́ЗИТЬ Р.; обла́жу[2], обла́зишь; обла́зь.

ОБЛА́ПИТЬ Р.; обла́плю, обла́пишь; обла́пь; обла́пленный.

ОБЛА́ЯТЬ Р.; обла́ю, обла́ешь; обла́й; обла́янный.

ОБЛЕ́ЗТЬ[1] Р.; обле́зет, обле́зут; обле́зь; обле́з.

ОБЛЕ́ЗТЬ[2] Р.; обле́зу, обле́зешь; обле́зь; обле́з.

ОБЛЕПИ́ТЬ Р.; облеплю́, обле́пишь; обле́пленный.

ОБЛЕТЕ́ТЬ Р.; облечу́, облети́шь; облети́.

ОБЛЕ́ЧЬ[1] Р.; облеку́, облечёшь, облеку́т; облеки́; облёк; облечённый.

ОБЛЕ́ЧЬ[2] Р.; обля́жет, обля́гут; облёг.

ОБЛИЗА́ТЬ Р.; оближу́, обли́жешь; оближи́; обли́занный.

ОБЛИ́ПНУТЬ Р.; обли́п, обли́пла.

ОБЛИ́ТЬ Р.; оболью́, обольёшь; обле́й; обли́тый and о́блитый and облито́й.

ОБЛОКОТИ́ТЬ Р.; облокочу́, облоко́тишь (and облокоти́шь); облоко́ченный.

ОБЛОМИ́ТЬ Р.; обломлю́, обло́мишь; обло́мленный.

ОБЛУПИ́ТЬ Р.; облуплю́, облу́пишь; облу́пленный.

ОБМА́ЗАТЬ Р.; обма́жу, обма́жешь; обма́жь; обма́занный.

ОБМЕРЕ́ТЬ Р.; обомру́, обомрёшь; обомри́; о́бмер; обмере́в.

ОБМЁРЗНУТЬ Р.; обмёрз, обмёрзла.

ОБМЕСТИ́ Р.; обмету́, обметёшь; обмети́; обмёл; обмётший; обметённый; обметя́.

ОБМЕТА́ТЬ Р.; обмечу́, обме́чешь; обмечи́; обмётанный.

ОБМО́ЛВИТЬСЯ Р.; обмо́лвлюсь, обмо́лвишься; обмо́лвись and обмо́лвься.

ОБМОЛОТИ́ТЬ Р.; обмолочу́, обмоло́тишь; обмоло́ченный.

ОБМОРО́ЗИТЬ Р.; обморо́жу, обморо́зишь; обморо́зь; обморо́женный.

ОБМЫ́ТЬ Р.; обмо́ю, обмо́ешь; обмо́й; обмы́тый.

ОБМЯ́КНУТЬ Р.; обмя́к, обмя́кла.

ОБМЯ́ТЬ Р.; обомну́, обомнёшь; обомни́; обмя́тый.

ОБНЕСТИ́ Р.; обнесу́, обнесёшь; обнеси́; обнёс; обнесённый; обнеся́ and обнёсши.

ОБНОВИ́ТЬ Р.; обновлю́, обнови́шь; обновлённый.

ОБНОСИ́ТЬ I.; обношу́[1], обно́сишь.

ОБНОСИ́ТЬ Р.; обношу́[2], обно́сишь; обно́шенный.

ОБНЯ́ТЬ Р.; обниму́, обни́мешь; обними́; обня́тый; (also обойму́, обоймёшь; обойми́; о́бнятый).

ОБОБРА́ТЬ Р.; оберу́, оберёшь; обери́; обо́бранный.

ОБОБЩЕСТВИ́ТЬ Р.; обобществлю́, обобществи́шь; обобществлённый.

ОБОГАТИ́ТЬ Р.; обогащу́, обогати́шь; обогащённый.

ОБОГНА́ТЬ Р.; обгоню́, обго́нишь; обгони́; обо́гнанный.

ОБОДРА́ТЬ Р.; обдеру́, обдерёшь; обдери́; обо́дранный.

ОБОЖДА́ТЬ Р.; обожду́, обождёшь; обожди́.

ОБОЖЕСТВИ́ТЬ Р.; обожествлю́, обожестви́шь; обожествлённый.

ОБОЗВА́ТЬ Р.; обзову́, обзовёшь; обзови́; обо́званный.

ОБОЗНАВА́ТЬСЯ I.; обознаю́сь, обознаёшься; обознава́йся; обознава́ясь.

ОБОЗРЕ́ТЬ Р.; обозрю́, обозри́шь; обозри́.

ОБОЙТИ́ Р.; обойду́, обойдёшь; обойди́; обошёл, обошла́; обоше́дший; обойдённый; обойдя́ and обоше́дши.

ОБОКРА́СТЬ Р.; обкраду́, обкрадёшь; обкради́; обкра́л; обкра́денный and обокра́денный.

ОБОЛГА́ТЬ Р.; оболгу́, оболжёшь; оболгу́т; оболги́; обо́лганный.

ОБОЛЬСТИ́ТЬ Р.; обольщу́, обольсти́шь; обольщённый.

ОБОРВА́ТЬ Р.; оборву́, оборвёшь; оборви́; обо́рванный.

ОБОРОТИ́ТЬ Р.; оборочу́, оборо́тишь; оборо́ченный.

ОБОСО́БИТЬ Р.; обосо́блю, обосо́бишь; обосо́бь; обосо́бленный.

ОБРАЗУ́МИТЬ Р.; образу́млю, образу́мишь; образу́мь; образу́мленный.

ОБРА́МИТЬ Р.; обра́млю, обра́мишь; обра́мь; обра́мленный.

ОБРАМИ́ТЬ Р.; обрамлю́, обрами́шь; обрамлённый.

ОБРАСТИ́ Р.; обрасту́, обрастёшь; обрасти́ (imp.); обро́с.

ОБРАТИ́ТЬ Р.; обращу́, обрати́шь; обращённый.

ОБРЕ́ЗАТЬ Р.; обре́жу, обре́жешь; обре́жь; обре́занный.

ОБРЕМИ́ЗИТЬ Р.; обреми́жу, обреми́зишь; обреми́зь; обреми́зенный.

ОБРЕСТИ́ Р.; обрету́, обретёшь; обрети́; обрёл; обре́тший; обретённый; обретя́ and обре́тши.

ОБРЕ́ЧЬ Р.; обреку́, обречёшь; обреку́т; обреки́; обрёк; обречённый.

ОБРЕШЕ́ТИТЬ Р.; обрешечу́, обреше́тишь; обреше́ть; обреше́ченный.

ОБРИ́ТЬ Р.; обре́ю, обре́ешь; обре́й; обри́тый.

ОБРУБИ́ТЬ Р.; обрублю́, обру́бишь; обру́бленный.

ОБРЮ́ЗГНУТЬ Р.; обрю́зг, обрю́згла.

ОБРЯДИ́ТЬ Р.; обряжу́, обря́дишь (and обряди́шь); обря́женный.

ОБСАДИ́ТЬ Р.; обсажу́, обса́дишь; обса́женный.

ОБСЕ́СТЬ Р.; обса́дет, обса́дем, обса́-
дете, обса́дут (1st and 2nd pers.
sing. not used); обса́дьте; обсе́л.

ОБСЕ́ЧЬ Р.; обсеку́, обсечёшь, обсе-
ку́т; обсеки́; обсе́к; обсечённый.

ОБСКАКА́ТЬ Р.; обскачу́, обска́чешь;
обскачи́; обска́канный.

ОБСМОТРЕ́ТЬ Р.; обсмотрю́, обсмо́-
тришь; обсмотри́; обсмо́тренный.

ОБСОСА́ТЬ Р.; обсосу́, обсосёшь;
обсоси́; обсо́санный.

ОБСО́ХНУТЬ Р.; обсо́х, обсо́хла.

ОБСТА́ВИТЬ Р.; обста́влю, обста́-
вишь; обста́вь; обста́вленный.

ОБСТРИ́ЧЬ Р.; обстригу́, обстрижёшь; обстригу́т; обстриги́; об-
стри́г; обстри́женный.

ОБСТУПИ́ТЬ Р.; обступлю́, обсту́-
пишь; обсту́пленный.

ОБСУДИ́ТЬ Р.; обсужу́, обсу́дишь;
обсуждённый.

ОБСЫПА́ТЬ Р.; обсы́плю, обсы́-
плешь; обсы́пь; обсы́панный.

ОБТА́ЯТЬ Р.; обта́ет, обта́ют; обта́й.

ОБТЕРЕ́ТЬ Р.; оботру́, оботрёшь;
оботри́; обтёр; обтёртый; обтерёв
and обтёрши.

ОБТЕРПЕ́ТЬСЯ Р.; обтерплю́сь, обте́-
рпишься; обтерпи́сь.

ОБТЕСА́ТЬ Р.; обтешу́, обте́шешь;
обтеши́; обтёсанный.

ОБТЕ́ЧЬ Р.; обтечёт, обтеку́т; об-
теки́; обтёк.

ОБТРЕПА́ТЬ Р.; обтреплю́, обтре́-
плешь; обтрепли́; обтрёпанный.

ОБУ́ЗИТЬ Р.; обу́жу, обу́зишь; обу́-
зь; обу́женный.

ОБУ́ТЬ Р.; обу́ю, обу́ешь; обу́й;
обу́тый.

ОБХВАТИ́ТЬ Р.; обхвачу́, об-
хва́тишь; обхва́ченный.

ОБХОДИ́ТЬ Р.; обхожу́[1], обхо́дишь;
обхо́женный.

ОБХОДИ́ТЬ I.; обхожу́[2], обхо́дишь.

ОБХОХОТА́ТЬСЯ Р.; обхохочу́сь, об-
хохо́чешься; обхохочи́сь.

ОБЧЕ́СТЬ Р.; обочту́, обочтёшь;
обочти́; обчёл, обочла́; обочтя́.

ОБЧИ́СТИТЬ Р.; обчи́щу, обчи́стишь;
обчи́сти and обчи́сть; обчи́щенный.

ОБШИ́ТЬ Р.; обошью́, обошьёшь;
обше́й; обши́тый.

ОБЩИПА́ТЬ Р.; общиплю́, общи́-
плешь; общипли́; общи́панный.

ОБ'Е́ЗДИТЬ Р.; об'е́зжу, об'е́здишь;
об'е́зди; об'е́зженный.

ОБ'Е́СТЬ Р.; об'е́м, об'е́шь[1], об'е́ст,
об'еди́м, об'еди́те, об'едя́т; об'е́шь[2]
(imp.); об'е́л; об'е́денный.

ОБ'Е́ХАТЬ Р.; об'е́ду, об'е́дешь;
об'езжа́й.

ОБ'ЯВИ́ТЬ Р.; об'явлю́, об'я́вишь;
об'я́вленный.

ОБ'Я́ТЬ Р.; обойму́, обоймёшь;
обойми́; об'я́тый (arch. forms:
обыму́, обы́мешь; обыми́; об'я́тый).

ОБЫ́КНУТЬ Р.; обы́к, обы́кла.

ОБЫМА́ТЬ I.; об'е́млю, об'е́млешь
(arch. and bookish forms); (modern
forms: обыма́ю, обыма́ешь);
об'е́мли.

ОБЫСКА́ТЬ Р.; обыщу́, обы́щешь;
обыщи́; обы́сканный.

ОБЮРОКРА́ТИТЬ Р.; обюрокра́чу,
обюрокра́тишь; обюрокра́ть; обю-
рокра́ченный.

ОБЯЗА́ТЬ Р.; обяжу́, обя́жешь; об-
яжи́.

ОВЕЩЕСТВИ́ТЬ Р.; овеществлю́,
овеществи́шь; овеществлённый.

ОВЕ́ЯТЬ I.; ове́ю, ове́ешь; ове́й;
ове́янный.

ОГЛА́ДИТЬ Р.; огла́жу, огла́дишь;
огла́дь; огла́женный.

ОГЛАСИ́ТЬ Р.; оглашу́, огласи́шь;
оглашённый.

ОГЛО́ХНУТЬ Р.; огло́х, огло́хла.

ОГЛУПИ́ТЬ Р.; оглуплю́, оглупи́шь;
оглуплённый.

ОГЛЯДЕ́ТЬ Р.; огляжу́, огляди́шь;
огляди́.

ОГОРОДИ́ТЬ Р.; огорожу́, огоро́дишь
(and огороди́шь); огоро́женный.

ОГРА́БИТЬ Р.; огра́блю, огра́бишь;
огра́бь; огра́бленный.

ОГРАДИ́ТЬ Р.; огражу́, огради́шь;
ограждённый.

ОГРЕСТИ́ Р.; обребу́, огребёшь; ог-
реби́; огрёб; огребённый.

ОГРУ́ЗНУТЬ Р.; огру́з, огру́зла.

ОДЕРЖА́ТЬ Р.; одержу́, оде́ржишь;
одержи́; оде́ржанный.

ОДЕ́ТЬ Р.; оде́ну, оде́нешь; оде́нь;
оде́тый.

ОДУШЕВИ́ТЬ Р.; одушевлю́, оду-
шеви́шь; одушевлённый.

ОЖЕ́ЧЬ Р.; ожгу́, ожжёшь, ожгу́т;
ожги́; ожёг, ожгла́; ожжённый.

ОЖИВИ́ТЬ Р.; оживлю́, оживи́шв;
оживи́; оживлённый.

ОЖИ́ТЬ Р.; оживу́, оживёшь; оживи́.

ОЗАБОТИТЬ Р.; озабочу, озаботишь; озаботь; озабоченный.

ОЗАГЛАВИТЬ Р.; озаглавлю, озаглавишь; озаглавь; озаглавленный.

ОЗДОРОВИТЬ Р.; оздоровлю, оздоровишь; оздоровлённый.

ОЗЛОБИТЬ Р.; озлоблю, озлобишь; озлобь; озлобленный.

ОЗНАКОМИТЬ Р.; ознакомлю, ознакомишь; ознакомь; ознакомленный.

ОЗНОБИТЬ Р.; озноблю, ознобишь; озноблённый.

ОЗОЛОТИТЬ Р.; озолочу, озолотишь; озолочённый.

ОЗЯБНУТЬ Р.; озяб, озябла.

ОКАЗАТЬ Р.; окажу, окажешь; окажи; оказанный.

ОКАЙМИТЬ Р.; окаймлю, окаймишь; окаймлённый.

ОКАТИТЬ Р.; окачу, окатишь; окаченный.

ОКОЛОТИТЬ Р.; околочу, околотишь; околоченный.

ОКОЛОТЬ Р.; околю, околешь; околи; околотый.

ОКОНФУЗИТЬ Р.; оконфужу, оконфузишь; оконфузь; оконфуженный.

ОКОРМИТЬ Р.; окормлю, окормишь; окормленный.

ОКОРОТИТЬ Р.; окорочу, окоротишь; окороченный.

ОКОСИТЬ Р.; окошу, окосишь; окошенный.

ОКРАСИТЬ Р.; окрашу, окрасишь; окрась; окрашенный.

ОКРЕПНУТЬ Р.; окреп, окрепла.

ОКРЕСТИТЬ Р.; окрещу, окрестишь; окрещённый.

ОКРОВАВИТЬ Р.; окровавлю, окровавишь; окровавь; окровавленный.

ОКРОПИТЬ Р.; окроплю, окропишь; окроплённый.

ОКРУТИТЬ Р.; окручу, окрутишь; окрученный.

ОКУПИТЬ Р.; окуплю, окупишь; окупленный.

ОКУРГУЗИТЬ Р.; окургужу, окургузишь; окургузь; окургуженный.

ОМЕРТВИТЬ Р.; омертвлю, омертвишь; омертвлённый.

ОМОЛОДИТЬ Р.; омоложу, омолодишь; омоложённый.

ОМЫТЬ Р.; омою, омоешь; омой; омытый.

ОПАЛУБИТЬ Р.; опалублю, опалубишь; опалубь; опалубленный.

ОПАСТЬ Р.; опаду, опадёшь; опади; опал.

ОПАХАТЬ Р.; опашу, опашешь; опаши; опаханный.

ОПЕРЕДИТЬ Р.; опережу, опередишь; опережённый.

ОПЕРЕТЬ Р.; обопру, обопрёшь; обопри; опёр; опёртый; оперев and опёрши.

ОПИСАТЬ Р.; опишу, опишешь; опиши; описанный.

ОПИТЬ Р.; обопью, обопьёшь; опей.

ОПЛАКАТЬ Р.; оплачу, оплачешь; оплачь; оплаканный.

ОПЛАТИ́Ь Р.; оплачу, оплатишь; оплаченный.

ОПЛЕСТИ Р.; оплету, оплетёшь; оплети; оплёл; оплётший; оплетённый; оплетя and оплётши.

ОПЛЫТЬ Р.; оплыву, оплывёшь; оплыви; оплытый.

ОПОВЕСТИТЬ Р.; оповещу, оповестишь; оповещённый.

ОПОЗНАВАТЬ I.; опознаю, опознаёшь; опознавай; опознавая.

ОПОЛЗТИ Р.; оползу, оползёшь; оползи; ополз.

ОПОЛОСКАТЬ Р.; ополощу, ополощешь; ополощи; ополосканный.

ОПОСТЫНУТЬ Р.; опостыну, опостынешь; опостынь.

ОПОСТЫТЬ Р.; опостыну, опостынешь; опостынь.

ОПОЧИТЬ Р.; опочию, опочиешь; опочий.

ОПОЯСАТЬ Р.; опояшу, опояшешь; опояшь; опоясанный.

ОПРАВИТЬ Р.; оправлю, оправишь; оправь; оправленный.

ОПРОСИТЬ Р.; опрошу, опросишь; опрошенный.

ОПРОСТИТЬСЯ Р.; опрощусь, опростишься.

ОПУСТИТЬ Р.; опущу, опустишь; опущенный.

ОПУХНУТЬ Р.; опух, опухла.

ОРАТЬ[1] I.; ору, орёшь; ори; ораный.

ОРАТЬ[2] I.; орю, орёшь; ори; ораный.

ОРОСИТЬ Р.; орошу, оросишь; орошённый.

ОСАДИТЬ[1] Р.; осажу[1], осадишь; осаждённый.

ОСАДИТЬ[2] Р.; осажу[2], осадишь; осаждённый.

ОСАДИТЬ³ Р.; осажу³, оса́дишь; оса́женный.

ОСВЕ́ДОМИТЬ Р.; осве́домлю, осве́домишь; осве́домь; осведомлённый.

ОСВЕТИ́ТЬ Р.; освещу́, освети́шь; освещённый.

ОСВИСТА́ТЬ Р.; освищу́, осви́щешь; освищи́; осви́станный.

ОСВОБОДИ́ТЬ Р.; освобожу́, освободи́шь; освобождённый.

ОСВЯТИ́ТЬ Р.; освящу́, освяти́шь; освящённый.

ОСЕРДИ́ТЬСЯ Р.; осержу́сь, осе́рдишься.

ОСЕ́СТЬ Р.; оса́ду, оса́дешь; оса́дь; осёл.

ОСЕ́ЧЬСЯ Р.; осеку́сь, осечёшься, осеку́ться; осеки́сь; осёкся.

ОСИ́ПНУТЬ Р.; оси́п, оси́пла.

ОСКЛА́БИТЬСЯ Р.; оскла́блюсь, оскла́бишься; оскла́бься.

ОСКОПИ́ТЬ Р.; оскоплю́, оскопи́шь; оскоплённый.

ОСКОРБИ́ТЬ Р.; оскорблю́, оскорби́шь; оскорблённый.

ОСКОРО́МИТЬСЯ Р.; оскоро́млюсь, оскоро́мишься; оскоро́мься.

ОСЛА́БИТЬ Р.; осла́блю, осла́бишь; осла́бь; осла́бленный.

ОСЛА́БНУТЬ Р.; осла́б, осла́бла.

ОСЛА́ВИТЬ Р.; осла́влю, осла́вишь; осла́вь; осла́вленный.

ОСЛЕПИ́ТЬ Р.; ослеплю́, ослепи́шь; ослеплённый.

ОСЛЕ́ПНУТЬ Р.; ослеп, осле́пла.

ОСЛИ́ЗНУТЬ Р.; осли́з, осли́зла.

ОСЛЫ́ШАТЬСЯ Р.; ослы́шусь, ослы́шишься.

ОСМЕЯ́ТЬ Р.; осмею́, осмеёшь; осмей; осмеянный.

ОСМОТРЕ́ТЬ Р.; осмотрю́, осмо́тришь; осмотри́; осмо́тренный.

ОСНАСТИ́ТЬ Р.; оснащу́, оснасти́шь; оснащённый.

ОСОЗНАВА́ТЬ I.; осознаю́, осознаёшь; осознава́й; осознава́я.

ОСРАМИ́ТЬ Р.; осрамлю́, осрами́шь; осрамлённый.

ОСТАВА́ТЬСЯ I.; остаю́сь, остаёшься; остава́йся; остава́ясь.

ОСТА́ВИТЬ Р.; оста́влю, оста́вишь; оста́вь; оста́вленный.

ОСТАНОВИ́ТЬ Р.; остановлю́, остано́вишь; остано́вленный.

ОСТА́ТЬСЯ Р.; оста́нусь, оста́нешься; оста́нься.

ОСТЕРЕ́ЧЬ Р.; остерегу́, остережёшь, остерегу́т; остереги́; остерёг; остережённый.

ОСТРИ́ЧЬ Р.; остригу́, острижёшь, остригу́т; остриги́; остри́г; острижженный.

ОСТРОСЛО́ВИТЬ I.; остросло́влю, острослó́вишь; острослó́вь.

ОСТУДИ́ТЬ Р.; остужу́, осту́дишь; осту́женный.

ОСТУПИ́ТЬСЯ Р.; оступлю́сь, осту́пишься.

ОСТЫ́НУТЬ Р.; осты́ну, осты́нешь; осты́нь.

ОСТЫ́ТЬ Р.; осты́ну, осты́нешь; осты́нь.

ОСУДИ́ТЬ Р.; осужу́, осу́дишь; осуждённый.

ОСУЩЕСТВИ́ТЬ Р.; осуществлю́, осуществи́шь; осуществлённый.

ОСЧАСТЛИ́ВИТЬ Р.; осчастли́влю, осчастли́вишь; осчастли́вь; осчастли́вленный.

ОСЫ́ПАТЬ Р.; осы́плю, осы́плешь; осы́пь; осы́панный.

ОТБА́ВИТЬ Р.; отба́влю, отба́вишь; отба́вь; отба́вленный.

ОТБЕЖА́ТЬ Р.; отбегу́, отбежи́шь, отбегу́т; отбеги́.

ОТБИ́ТЬ Р.; отобью́, отобьёшь; отбе́й; отби́тый.

ОТБЛАГОВЕ́СТИТЬ Р.; отбла́говещу, отбла́говестишь; отбла́говести.

ОТБОМБИ́ТЬСЯ Р.; отбомблю́сь, отбомби́шься.

ОТБРИ́ТЬ Р.; отбре́ю, отбре́ешь; отбре́й; отбри́тый.

ОТБРО́СИТЬ Р.; отбро́шу, отбро́сишь; отбро́сь; отбро́шенный.

ОТБЫ́ТЬ Р.; отбу́ду, отбу́дешь; отбу́дь.

ОТВА́ДИТЬ Р.; отва́жу, отва́дишь; отва́дь; отва́женный.

ОТВЕЗТИ́ Р.; отвезу́, отвезёшь; отвези́; отвёз; отвезённый; отвезя́.

ОТВЕ́РГНУТЬ Р.; отве́рг, отве́ргла (arch. отве́ргнул, отве́ргнула); отве́ргнутый (and arch. отве́рженный).

ОТВЕРТЕ́ТЬ Р.; отверчу́, отве́ртишь; отверти́; отве́рченный.

ОТВЕ́СИТЬ Р.; отве́шу, отве́сишь; отве́сь; отве́шенный.

ОТВЕСТИ́ Р.; отведу́, отведёшь; отведи́; отвёл; отве́дший; отведённый; отведя́.

ОТВЕТВИ́ТЬ Р.; ответвлю́, ответ-
ви́шь; ответвлённый.

ОТВЕ́ТИТЬ Р.; отве́чу, отве́тишь;
отве́ть; отве́ченный.

ОТВИНТИ́ТЬ Р.; отвинчу́, отвин-
ти́шь; отви́нченный.

ОТВИСЕ́ТЬСЯ Р.; отвиси́тья; отви-
ся́тся.

ОТВИ́СНУТЬ Р.; отви́с, отви́сла.

ОТВЛЕ́ЧЬ Р.; отвлеку́, отвлечёшь,
отвлеку́т; отвлеки́; отвлёк; отвлечённый.

ОТВОДИ́ТЬ I.; отвожу́[1], отво́дишь.

ОТВОЗИ́ТЬ I.; отвожу́[2], отво́зишь.

ОТВОЗИ́ТЬ Р.; отвожу́[3], отво́зишь;
отво́женный.

ОТВОЛО́ЧЬ Р.; отволоку́, отволочёшь, отволоку́т; отволоки́; отво-
ло́к; отволочённый.

ОТВОРОТИ́ТЬ Р.; отворочу́, отворо́-
тишь; отворо́ченный.

ОТВРАТИ́ТЬ Р.; отвращу́, отвра-
ти́шь; отвращённый.

ОТВЫ́КНУТЬ Р.; отвы́к, отвы́кла.

ОТВЯЗА́ТЬ Р.; отвяжу́, отвя́жешь;
отвяжи́; отвя́занный.

ОТГЛА́ДИТЬ Р.; отгла́жу, отгла́-
дишь; отгла́дь; отгла́женный.

ОТГНИ́ТЬ Р.; отгниёт, отгнию́т.

ОТГОРЕ́ТЬ Р.; отгори́т, отгоря́т;
отгори́.

ОТГОРОДИ́ТЬ Р.; отгорожу́, отгоро́-
дишь (and отгороди́шь); отгоро́-
женный.

ОТГОСТИ́ТЬ Р.; отгощу́, отгости́шь.

ОТГРЕМЕ́ТЬ Р.; отгреми́т, отгремя́т;
отгреми́.

ОТГРЕСТИ́ Р.; отгребу́, отгребёшь;
отгреби́; отгрёб; отгребённый; от-
гребя́.

ОТГРУЗИ́ТЬ Р.; отгружу́, отгру́зишь
(and отгрузи́шь); отгру́женный and
отгружённый.

ОТГРЫ́ЗТЬ Р.; отгрызу́, отгрызёшь;
отгрызи́; отгры́з; отгры́зенный.

ОТДАВА́ТЬ I.; отдаю́, отдаёшь; отда-
ва́й; отдава́я.

ОТДАВИ́ТЬ Р.; отдавлю́, отда́вишь;
отда́вленный.

ОТДА́ТЬ Р.; отда́м, отда́шь, отда́ст,
отдади́м, отдади́те, отдаду́т; отда́й;
о́тданный.

ОТДУБА́СИТЬ Р.; отдуба́шу, отду-
ба́сишь; отдуба́сь; отдуба́шенный.

ОТДУ́ТЬ Р.; отду́ю, отду́ешь; отду́й;
отду́тый.

ОТДЫША́ТЬСЯ Р.; отдышу́сь, отды-
ши́шься; отдыши́сь.

ОТЕРЕ́ТЬ Р.; отру́, отрёшь; отри́;
отёр; отёртый; отере́в and отёрши.

ОТЕСА́ТЬ Р.; отешу́, оте́шешь; от-
еши́; отёсанный.

ОТЕ́ЧЬ Р.; отеку́, отечёшь, отеку́т;
отеки́; отёк.

ОТЖА́ТЬ[1] Р.; отожму́, отожмёшь;
отожми́; отжа́тый.

ОТЖА́ТЬ[2] Р.; отожну́, отожнёшь;
отожни́; отжа́тый.

ОТЖЕ́ЧЬ Р.; отожгу́, отожжёшь,
отожгу́т; отожги́; отжёг; отожгла́;
отожжённый.

ОТЖИ́ТЬ Р.; отживу́, отживёшь;
отживи́; о́тжитый and отжи́тый.

ОТКАЗА́ТЬ Р.; откажу́, отка́жешь;
откажи́; отка́занный.

ОТКАТИ́ТЬ Р.; откачу́, отка́тишь;
отка́ченный.

ОТКОЛОТИ́ТЬ Р.; отколочу́, отколо́-
тишь; отколо́ченный.

ОТКОЛО́ТЬ Р. отколю́, отко́лешь;
отколи́; отко́лотый.

ОТКОРМИ́ТЬ Р.; откормлю́, отко́р-
мишь; отко́рмленный.

ОТКРЕПИ́ТЬ Р.; откреплю́, откре-
пи́шь; откр't;plённый.

ОТКРУТИ́ТЬ Р.; откручу́, откру́-
тишь; откру́ченный.

ОТКРЫ́ТЬ Р.; откро́ю, откро́ешь;
откро́й; откры́тый.

ОТКУПИ́ТЬ Р.; откуплю́, отку́пишь;
отку́пленный.

ОТКУСИ́ТЬ Р.; откушу́, отку́сишь;
отку́шенный.

ОТЛЕЖА́ТЬ Р.; отлежу́, отлежи́шь;
отлежи́; отлёжанный.

ОТЛЕПИ́ТЬ Р.; отлеплю́, отле́пишь;
отле́пленный.

ОТЛЕТЕ́ТЬ Р.; отлечу́, отлети́шь;
отлети́.

ОТЛЕ́ЧЬ Р.; отля́гу, отля́жешь,
отля́гут; отля́г; отлёг.

ОТЛИ́ПНУТЬ Р.; отли́п, отли́пла.

ОТЛИ́ТЬ Р.; отолью́, отольёшь;
отле́й; отли́тый.

ОТЛОВИ́ТЬ Р.; отловлю́, отло́вишь;
отло́вленный.

ОТЛОМИ́ТЬ Р.; отломлю́, отло́мишь;
отло́мленный.

ОТЛУПИ́ТЬ Р.; отлуплю́, отлу́пишь;
отлу́пленный.

ОТМАХА́ТЬ Р.; отмашу́, отма́шешь,

(also отмаха́ю, отмаха́ешь) отмаши́
and отмаха́й; отма́ханный.

ОТМЕРЕ́ТЬ Р.; отомрёт, отомру́т;
отомри́; о́тмер; отмере́в and отме́р-
ши.

ОТМЁРЗНУТЬ Р.; отмёрз, отмёрзла.

ОТМЕСТИ́ Р.; отмету́, отметёшь;
отмети́; отмёл; отмётший; отметённый; отмета́.

ОТМЕ́ТИТЬ Р.; отме́чу, отме́тишь;
отме́ть; отме́ченный.

ОТМО́КНУТЬ Р.; отмо́к, отмо́кла.

ОТМОЛОТИ́ТЬ Р.; отмолочу́, отмоло́-
тишь; отмоло́ченный.

ОТМОЛО́ТЬ Р.; отмелю́, отме́лешь;
отмели́; отмо́лотый.

ОТМОЛЧА́ТЬСЯ Р.; отмолчу́сь, от-
молчи́шься; отмолчи́сь.

ОТМОРО́ЗИТЬ Р.; отморо́жу, отморо́-
зишь; отморо́зь; отморо́женный.

ОТМСТИ́ТЬ Р.; отмщу́, отмсти́шь;
отмщённый.

ОТМЫ́ТЬ Р.; отмо́ю, отмо́ешь; отмо́й;
отмы́тый.

ОТМЯ́КНУТЬ Р.; отмя́к, отмя́кла.

ОТНЕСТИ́ Р.; отнесу́, отнесёшь;
отнеси́; отнёс; отнесённый; отнеся́.

ОТНОСИ́ТЬ Р.; отношу́[1], отно́сишь;
отно́шенный.

ОТНОСИ́ТЬ I.; отношу́[2], отно́сишь.

ОТНЯ́ТЬ Р.; отниму́, отни́мешь;
отними́; о́тнятый.

ОТОБРАЗИ́ТЬ Р.; отображу́, отобра-
зи́шь; отображённый.

ОТОБРА́ТЬ Р.; отберу́, отберёшь;
отбери́; ото́бранный.

ОТОГНА́ТЬ Р.; отгоню́, отго́нишь;
отгони́; ото́гнанный.

ОТОДРА́ТЬ Р.; отдеру́, отдерёшь;
отдери́; ото́дранный.

ОТОЖДЕСТВИ́ТЬ Р.; отождествлю́,
отождестви́шь; отождествлённый.

ОТОЖЕСТВИ́ТЬ Р.; отожествлю́, ото-
жестви́шь; отожествлённый.

ОТОЗВА́ТЬ Р.; отзову́, отзовёшь;
отзови́; ото́званный.

ОТОЙТИ́ Р.; отойду́, отойдёшь; отой-
ди́; отошёл, отошла́; отоше́дший;
отойдя́.

ОТОМСТИ́ТЬ Р.; отомщу́, отомсти́шь;
отомщённый.

ОТОПИ́ТЬ Р.; отоплю́, ото́пишь;
ото́пленный.

ОТОРВА́ТЬ Р.; оторву́, оторвёшь;
оторви́; ото́рванный.

ОТОСЛА́ТЬ Р.; отошлю́, отошлёшь;
отошли́[2]; ото́сланный.

ОТОСПА́ТЬСЯ Р.; отоспю́сь, ото-
спи́шься; отоспи́сь.

ОТПА́СТЬ Р.; отпаду́, отпадёшь;
отпади́; отпа́л; отпа́вший (and
arch.: отпа́дший).

ОТПАХА́ТЬ Р.; отпашу́, отпа́шешь;
отпаши́; отпа́ханный.

ОТПЕРЕ́ТЬ Р.; отопру́, отопрёшь;
отопри́; о́тпер; о́тпертый; отпере́в
and отпе́рши.

ОТПЕ́ТЬ Р.; отпою, отпоёшь; отпо́й;
отпе́тый.

ОТПИСА́ТЬ Р.; отпишу́, отпи́шешь;
отпиши́; отпи́санный.

ОТПИ́ТЬ Р.; отопью, отопьёшь;
отпе́й; отпи́тый.

ОТПЛАТИ́ТЬ Р.; отплачу́, отпла́-
тишь; отпла́ченный.

ОТПЛЕСТИ́ Р.; отплету́, отплетёшь;
отплети́; отплёл; отплётший; отплетённый; отплетя́ and отплётши.

ОТПЛЫ́ТЬ Р.; отплыву́, отплывёшь; отплыви́; отплыва́.

ОТПЛЯСА́ТЬ Р.; отпляшу́, отпля́-
шешь; отпляши́; отпля́санный.

ОТПОЛЗТИ́ Р.; отползу́, отползёшь;
отползи́; отпо́лз.

ОТПОРО́ТЬ Р.; отпорю́, отпо́решь;
отпори́; отпо́ротый.

ОТПРА́ВИТЬ Р.; отпра́влю, отпра́-
вишь; отпра́вь; отпра́вленный.

ОТПРОСИ́ТЬСЯ Р.; отпрошу́еь, от-
про́сишься.

ОТПРЯ́ЧЬ Р.; отпрягу́, отпряжёшь,
отпрягу́т; отпряги́; отпря́г; отпряжённый.

ОТПУСТИ́ТЬ Р.; отпущу́, отпу́с-
тишь; отпу́щенный.

ОТРА́ВИТЬ Р.; отравлю́, отра́вишь;
отра́вленный.

ОТРАЗИ́ТЬ Р.; отражу́, отрази́шь;
отражённый.

ОТРАСТИ́ Р.; отрастёт, отрасту́т;
отрасти́ (imp.); отро́с.

ОТРАСТИ́ТЬ Р.; отращу́, отрасти́шь;
отращённый.

ОТРЕ́ЗАТЬ Р.; отре́жу, отре́жешь;
отре́жь; отре́занный.

ОТРЕЗВИ́ТЬ Р.; отрезвлю́, отре-
зви́шь; отрезвлённый.

ОТРЕПА́ТЬ Р.; отреплю́, отре́плешь;
отрепли́; отрёпанный.

ОТРЕ́ЧЬСЯ Р.; отреку́сь, отречёшься, отреку́тся; отреки́сь; отрёкся.

ОТРУБИ́ТЬ Р.; отрублю́, отру́бишь; отру́бленный.

ОТРЫ́ТЬ Р.; отро́ю, отро́ешь; отро́й; отры́тый.

ОТРЯДИ́ТЬ Р.; отряжу́, отряди́шь; отряжённый.

ОТРЯСТИ́ Р.; отрясу́, отрясёшь; отряси́; отря́с; отрясённый.

ОТСАДИ́ТЬ Р.; отсажу́, отса́дишь; отса́женный.

ОТСЕ́СТЬ Р.; отся́ду, отся́дешь; отся́дь; отсе́л.

ОТСЕ́ЧЬ Р.; отсеку́, отсечёшь; отсеку́т; отсеки́; отсе́к; отсечённый.

ОТСЕ́ЯТЬ Р.; отсе́ю, отсе́ешь; отсе́й; отсе́янный.

ОТСИДЕ́ТЬ Р.; отсижу́, отсиди́шь; отсиди́; отси́женный.

ОТСКАКА́ТЬ Р.; отскачу́, отска́чешь; отскачи́.

ОТСКРЕСТИ́ Р.; отскребу́, отскребёшь; отскреби́; отскрёб; отскребённый.

ОТСОСА́ТЬ Р.; отсосу́, отсосёшь; отсоси́; отсо́санный.

ОТСО́ХНУТЬ Р.; отсо́х, отсо́хла.

ОТСТАВА́ТЬ I.; отстаю́, отстаёшь; отставай; отставая.

ОТСТА́ВИТЬ Р.; отста́влю, отста́вишь; отста́вь; отста́вленный.

ОТСТА́ТЬ Р.; отста́ну, отста́нешь; отста́нь.

ОТСТОЯ́ТЬ Р.; отстою́[1], отстои́шь; отстой; отсто́янный.

ОТСТОЯ́ТЬ I.; отстою́[2], отстои́шь.

ОТСТРИ́ЧЬ Р.; отстригу́, отстрижёшь; отстригу́т; отстриги́; отстри́г; отстри́женный.

ОТСТУПИ́ТЬ Р.; отступлю́, отсту́пишь; отступи́в and отступя́.

ОТСУДИ́ТЬ Р.; отсужу́, отсу́дишь; отсу́женный.

ОТСЫПА́ТЬ Р.; отсы́плю, отсы́плешь; отсы́пь; отсы́панный.

ОТТА́ЯТЬ Р.; отта́ю, отта́ешь; отта́й; отта́янный.

ОТТЕРЕ́ТЬ Р.; ототру́, ототрёшь; ототри́; оттёр; оттёртый; оттере́в and оттёрши.

ОТТЕСА́ТЬ Р.; оттешу́, оттѐшешь; оттеши́; оттёсанный.

ОТТЕ́ЧЬ Р.; оттечёт, оттеку́т; оттёк.

ОТТОПТА́ТЬ Р.; оттопчу́, отто́пчешь; оттопчи́; отто́птанный.

ОТТО́РГНУТЬ Р.; отто́рг, отто́ргла; отто́ргнутый (and arch. отто́рженный).

ОТТРЕПА́ТЬ Р.; оттреплю́, оттре́плешь; оттрепли́; оттрёпанный.

ОТТРЯСТИ́ Р.; оттрясу́, оттрясёшь; оттряси́; оттря́с; оттрясённый.

ОТТУЗИ́ТЬ Р.; оттужу́, оттузи́шь.

ОТХЛЕСТА́ТЬ Р.; отхлещу́, отхлѐщешь; отхлещи́; отхлёстанный.

ОТХОДИ́ТЬ I.; отхожу́[1], отхо́дишь.

ОТХОДИ́ТЬ Р.; отхожу́[2], отхо́дишь; отхо́женный.

ОТЦВЕСТИ́ Р.; отцвету́, отцветёшь; отцвети́; отцвёл; отцве́тший; отцвета́.

ОТЦЕДИ́ТЬ Р.; отцежу́, отце́дишь; отце́женный.

ОТЦЕПИ́ТЬ Р.; отцеплю́, отце́пишь; отце́пленный.

ОТЧА́ЯТЬСЯ Р.; отча́юсь, отча́ешься; отча́йся.

ОТЧИ́СТИТЬ Р.; отчи́щу, отчи́стишь; отчи́сти and отчи́сть; отчи́щенный.

ОТЧУДИ́ТЬ Р.; отчужу́, отчуди́шь; отчуждённый.

ОТШИБИ́ТЬ Р.; отшибу́, отшибёшь; отшиби́; отши́б; отши́бленный.

ОТШИ́ТЬ Р.; отошью́, отошьёшь; отшей; отши́тый.

ОТШУМЕ́ТЬ Р.; отшумлю́, отшуми́шь; отшуми́.

ОТШУТИ́ТЬСЯ Р.; отшучу́сь, отшу́тишься.

ОТЩЕПИ́ТЬ Р.; отщеплю́, отще́пишь; отщеплённый.

ОТЩИПА́ТЬ Р.; отщиплю́, отщи́плешь; отщипли́; отщи́панный.

ОТЕ́ЗДИТЬ Р.; от'е́зжу, от'е́здишь; от'е́зди.

ОТ'Е́СТЬ Р.; от'е́м, от'е́шь[1], от'е́ст, от'еди́м, от'еди́те, от'едя́т; от'е́шь[2] (imp.); от'е́л; от'е́денный.

ОТ'Е́ХАТЬ Р.; от'е́ду, от'е́дешь; от'езжа́й.

ОТ'Я́ТЬ Р.; отыму́, оты́мешь; отыми́; от'я́тый.

ОТЫСКА́ТЬ Р.; отыщу́, оты́щешь; отыщи́; оты́сканный.

ОТЯГОТИ́ТЬ Р.; отягощу́, отяготи́шь; отягощённый.

ОФО́РМИТЬ Р.; офо́рмлю, офо́рмишь; офо́рми; офо́рмленный.

ОХА́ЯТЬ Р.; оха́ю, оха́ешь; оха́й; оха́янный.

ОХВАТИ́ТЬ Р.; охвачу́, охва́тишь; охва́ченный.

ОХЛАДИ́ТЬ Р.; охлажу́, охлади́шь; охлаждённый.

ОХОЛОДИ́ТЬ Р.; охоложу́, охолоди́шь.

ОХОЛОСТИ́ТЬ Р.; охолощу́, охолости́шь; охолощённый.

ОХО́ТИТЬСЯ I.; охо́чусь, охо́тишься; охо́ться.

ОХРИ́ПНУТЬ Р.; охри́п, охри́пла.

ОЦЕПИ́ТЬ Р.; оцеплю́, оце́пишь; оце́пленный.

ОЧЕРТИ́ТЬ Р.; очерчу́, оче́ртишь; оче́рченный.

ОЧЕСА́ТЬ Р.; очешу́, оче́шешь; очеши́; очёсанный.

ОЧИ́СТИТЬ Р.; очи́щу, очи́стишь; очи́сти and очи́сть; очи́щенный.

ОШЕЛОМИ́ТЬ Р.; ошеломлю́, ошеломи́шь; ошеломлённый.

ОШИБИ́ТЬСЯ Р.; ошибу́сь, ошибёшься; ошиби́сь; оши́бся.

ОЩИПА́ТЬ Р.; ощиплю́, ощи́плешь; ощипли́; ощи́панный.

ОЩУТИ́ТЬ Р.; ощущу́, ощути́шь; ощущённый.

П

ПА́КОСТИТЬ I.; па́кощу, па́костишь; па́кости.

ПАСКУ́ДИТЬ I.; паскужу́, паску́дишь; паску́дь.

ПАСТИ́ I.; пасу́, пасёшь; паси́; пас.

ПАСТЬ Р.; паду́, падёшь; пади́; пал; па́вший (and arch. па́дший).

ПАХА́ТЬ I.; пашу́, па́шешь; паши́; па́ханный.

ПА́ХНУТЬ I.; пах, па́хла.

ПЕРЕБЕЖА́ТЬ Р.; перебегу́, перебежи́шь, перебегу́т; перебеги́.

ПЕРЕБЕСИ́ТЬСЯ Р.; перебешу́сь, перебе́сишься.

ПЕРЕБИ́ТЬ Р.; перебью́, перебьёшь; перебе́й; переби́тый.

ПЕРЕБОЛЕ́ТЬ[1] Р.; переболи́т, переболя́т.

ПЕРЕБОЛЕ́ТЬ[2] Р.; переболе́ю, переболе́ешь (this verb is regular; does not appear in text).

ПЕРЕБОРО́ТЬ Р.; переборю́, перебо́решь; перебори́.

ПЕРЕБРА́ТЬ Р.; переберу́, переберёшь; перебери́; перебранный.

ПЕРЕБРО́СИТЬ Р.; переброшу, перебро́сишь; перебро́сь; перебро́шенный.

ПЕРЕВЕЗТИ́ Р.; перевезу́, перевезёшь; перевези́; перевёз; перевезённый; перевезя́.

ПЕРЕВЕРТЕ́ТЬ Р.; переверчу́, переве́ртишь; переверти́; переве́рченный.

ПЕРЕВЕ́СИТЬ Р.; переве́шу, переве́сишь; переве́сь; переве́шенный.

ПЕРЕВЕСТИ́ Р.; переведу́, переведёшь; переведи́; перевёл; переве́дший; переведённый; переве́дши and переведя́.

ПЕРЕВИНТИ́ТЬ Р.; перевинчу́, перевинти́шь; переви́нченный.

ПЕРЕВИ́ТЬ Р.; перевью́, перевьёшь; переве́й; переви́тый (and перевито́й).

ПЕРЕВОДИ́ТЬ I.; перевожу́[1], перево́дишь.

ПЕРЕВОЗИ́ТЬ I.; перевожу́[2], перево́зишь.

ПЕРЕВОЛО́ЧЬ Р.; переволоку́, переволочешь, переволоку́т; переволоки́; переволо́к; переволо́ченный and переволочённый; переволо́кши and переволоча́.

ПЕРЕВОПЛОТИ́ТЬ Р.; перевоплощу́, перевоплоти́шь; перевоплощённый.

ПЕРЕВОРОТИ́ТЬ Р.; переворочу́, переворо́тишь; перевороченный.

ПЕРЕВРА́ТЬ Р.; перевру́, переврёшь; переври́; переврранный.

ПЕРЕВЫ́БРАТЬ Р.; перевы́беру, перевы́берешь; перевы́бери; перевы́бранный.

ПЕРЕВЯЗА́ТЬ Р.; перевяжу́, перевя́жешь; перевяжи́; перевя́занный.

ПЕРЕГЛА́ДИТЬ Р.; перегла́жу, перегла́дишь; перегла́дь; перегла́женный.

ПЕРЕГЛЯДЕ́ТЬ Р.; перегляжу́, перегляди́шь; перегляди́.

ПЕРЕГНА́ТЬ Р.; перегоню́, перего́нишь; перегони́; пере́гнанный.

ПЕРЕГНИ́ТЬ Р.; перегниёт, перегниёт.

ПЕРЕГОДИ́ТЬ Р.; перегожу́, перого-
ди́шь.

ПЕРЕГОРЕ́ТЬ Р.; перегори́т, пере-
горя́т; перегори́.

ПЕРЕГОРОДИ́ТЬ Р.; перегорожу́,
перегоро́дишь (and перегороди́шь);
перегоро́женный.

ПЕРЕГРУЗИ́ТЬ Р.; перегружу́, пере-
гру́зишь (and перегрузи́шь); пере-
гру́женный and перегружённый.

ПЕРЕГРЫ́ЗТЬ Р.; перегрызу́, перегрызёшь; перегрызи́; перегры́з;
перегры́зенный.

ПЕРЕДАВА́ТЬ I.; передаю́, передаёшь; передава́й; передава́я.

ПЕРЕДА́ТЬ Р.; переда́м, переда́шь,
переда́ст, передади́м, передади́те,
передаду́т; переда́й; пе́реданный.

ПЕРЕДЕРЖА́ТЬ Р.; передержу́, пере-
де́ржишь; передержи́; переде́ржан-
ный.

ПЕРЕДОПРОСИ́ТЬ Р.; передопрошу́,
передопро́сишь; передопро́шенный.

ПЕРЕДО́ХНУТЬ Р.; передо́х, пере-
до́хла.

ПЕРЕДРА́ТЬ Р.; передеру́, передерёшь; передери́; передра́нный.

ПЕРЕДРА́ТЬСЯ Р.; передеру́сь, передерёшься; передери́сь.

ПЕРЕДРЕМА́ТЬ Р.; передремлю́,
передре́млешь; передремли́.

ПЕРЕЕ́СТЬ Р.; перее́м, перее́шь[1],
перее́ст, перееди́м, перееди́те, пере-
едя́т; перее́шь[2] (imp.); перее́л;
перее́денный.

ПЕРЕЕ́ХАТЬ Р.; перее́ду, перее́дешь;
переезжа́й.

ПЕРЕЖДА́ТЬ Р.; пережду́, переждёшь; пережди́.

ПЕРЕЖЕ́ЧЬ Р.; пережгу́, пережжёшь, пережгу́т; пережги́; пережёг, пережгла́; пережжённый.

ПЕРЕЖИ́ТЬ Р.; переживу́, переживёшь; переживи́; пе́режитый and
пережи́тый.

ПЕРЕЗАБЫ́ТЬ Р.; перезабу́ду, пере-
забу́дешь; перезабу́дь; перезабы́-
тый.

ПЕРЕЗАРАЗИ́ТЬ Р.; перезаражу́,
перезарази́шь; перезаражённый.

ПЕРЕЗАРЯДИ́ТЬ Р.; перезаряжу́,
перезаряди́шь (and перезаря́дишь);
перезаряжённый and перезаря́-
женный.

ПЕРЕЗНАКО́МИТЬ Р.; перезнако́-
млю, перезнако́мишь; перезана-
ко́мь; перезнако́мленный.

ПЕРЕЗЯ́БНУТЬ Р.; перезя́б, пере-
зя́бла.

ПЕРЕИЗБРА́ТЬ Р.; переизберу́, переизберёшь; переизбери́; переи́з-
бранный.

ПЕРЕИЗДАВА́ТЬ I.; переиздаю́,
переиздаёшь; переиздава́й; пере-
издава́я.

ПЕРЕИЗДА́ТЬ Р.; переизда́м, переиз-
да́шь, переизда́ст, переиздади́м,
переиздади́те, переиздаду́т; пере-
изда́й; переи́зданный.

ПЕРЕЙТИ́ Р.; перейду́, перейдёшь;
перейди́; перешёл, перешла́; пере-
ше́дший; перейдённый; перейдя́.

ПЕРЕКАТИ́ТЬ Р.; перекачу́, пере-
ка́тишь; перека́ченный.

ПЕРЕКИПЕ́ТЬ Р.; перекиплю́, пере-
кипи́шь; перекипи́.

ПЕРЕКИПЯТИ́ТЬ Р.; перекипячу́,
перекипяти́шь; перекипячённый.

ПЕРЕКОЛОТИ́ТЬ Р.; переколочу́,
переколо́тишь; переколо́ченный.

ПЕРЕКОЛО́ТЬ Р.; переколю́, пере-
ко́лешь; переколи́; переко́лотый.

ПЕРЕКОРМИ́ТЬ Р.; перекормлю́, пе-
реко́рмишь; переко́рмленный.

ПЕРЕКОСИ́ТЬ[1] Р.; перекошу́[1], пере-
коси́шь; переко́шенный and перекошённый.

ПЕРЕКОСИ́ТЬ[2] Р.; перекошу́[2], пере-
ко́сишь; переко́шенный.

ПЕРЕКРА́СИТЬ Р.; перекра́шу, пере-
кра́сишь; перекра́сь; перекра́шен-
ный.

ПЕРЕКРЕСТИ́ТЬ Р.; перекрещу́, пе-
рекре́стишь; перекрещённый.

ПЕРЕКРИЧА́ТЬ Р.; перекричу́, пере-
кричи́шь; перекричи́.

ПЕРЕКРУТИ́ТЬ Р.; перекручу́, пере-
кру́тишь; перекру́ченный.

ПЕРЕКРЫ́ТЬ Р.; перекро́ю, пере-
кро́ешь; перекро́й; перекры́тый.

ПЕРЕКУПИ́ТЬ Р.; перекуплю́, пере-
ку́пишь; переку́пленный.

ПЕРЕКУСИ́ТЬ Р.; перекушу́, пере-
ку́сишь; переку́шенный.

ПЕРЕЛЕЖА́ТЬ Р.; перележу́, пере-
лежи́шь; перележи́.

ПЕРЕЛЕ́ЗТЬ Р.; переле́зу, пере-
ле́зешь; переле́зь; переле́з.

ПЕРЕЛЕТЕ́ТЬ Р.; перелечу́, пере-
лети́шь; перелети́.

ПЕРЕЛЕ́ЧЬ Р.; переля́гу, переля́жешь, переля́гут; переля́г; перелёг.

ПЕРЕЛИ́ТЬ Р.; перелью́, перельёшь; переле́й; перели́тый.

ПЕРЕЛОВИ́ТЬ Р.; переловлю́, перело́вишь; перело́вленный.

ПЕРЕЛОМИ́ТЬ Р.; переломлю́, перело́мишь; перело́мленный.

ПЕРЕЛОПА́ТИТЬ Р.; перелопа́чу, перелопа́тишь; перелопа́ть; перелопа́ченный.

ПЕРЕМА́ЗАТЬ Р.; перема́жу, перема́жешь; перема́жь; перема́занный.

ПЕРЕМЕРЕ́ТЬ Р.; перемрёт, перемрём, перемрёте, перемру́т (1st and 2nd pers. sing. not used); перемри́; пе́ремер.

ПЕРЕМЁРЗНУТЬ Р.; перемёрз, перемёрзла.

ПЕРЕМЕСИ́ТЬ Р.; перемешу́, переме́сишь; переме́шенный.

ПЕРЕМЕСТИ́, перемету́, переметёшь; перемети́; перемёл; перемётший; переметённый; перемета́.

ПЕРЕМЕСТИ́ТЬ Р.; перемещу́, переме́стишь; перемещённый.

ПЕРЕМЕ́ТИТЬ Р.; переме́чу, переме́тишь; переме́ть; переме́ченный.

ПЕРЕМО́ЛВИТЬ Р.; перемо́лвлю, перемо́лвишь; перемо́лви; перемо́лвленный.

ПЕРЕМОЛО́ТЬ Р.; перемелю́, переме́лешь; перемели́; перемо́лотый.

ПЕРЕМОРО́ЗИТЬ Р.; переморо́жу, переморо́зишь; переморо́зь; переморо́женный.

ПЕРЕМОСТИ́ТЬ Р.; перемощу́, перемости́шь; перемощённый.

ПЕРЕМО́ЧЬ Р.; перемогу́, перемо́жешь, перемо́гут; перемоги́; перемо́г.

ПЕРЕМЫ́ТЬ Р.; перемо́ю, перемо́ешь; перемо́й; перемы́тый.

ПЕРЕНАПРЯ́ЧЬ Р.; перенапрягу́, перенапряжёшь, перенапрягу́т; перенапряги́; перенапря́г; перенапряжённый.

ПЕРЕНАСЫ́ТИТЬ Р.; перенасы́щу, перенасы́тишь; перенасы́ть; перенасы́щенный.

ПЕРЕНЕСТИ́ Р.; перенесу́, перенесёшь; перенеси́; перенёс; перенесённый; перенеся́.

ПЕРЕНОСИ́ТЬ I.; переношу́[1], перено́сишь.

ПЕРЕНОСИ́ТЬ Р.; переношу́[2], перено́сишь; перено́шенный.

ПЕРЕНЯ́ТЬ Р.; перейму́, переймёшь; перейми́; пе́ренятый.

ПЕРЕОБУ́ТЬ Р.; переобу́ю, переобу́ешь; переобу́й; переобу́тый.

ПЕРЕОДЕ́ТЬ Р.; переоде́ну, переоде́нешь; переоде́нь; переоде́тый.

ПЕРЕОСНАСТИ́ТЬ Р.; переоснащу́, переоснасти́шь; переоснащённый.

ПЕРЕПА́КОСТИТЬ Р.; перепа́кощу, перепа́костишь; перепа́кости; перепа́кощенный.

ПЕРЕПА́СТЬ Р.; перепадёт, перепаду́т; перепа́л.

ПЕРЕПАХА́ТЬ Р.; перепашу́, перепа́шешь; перепаши́; перепа́ханный.

ПЕРЕПЕ́ЧЬ Р.; перепеку́, перепечёшь, перепеку́т; перепеки́; перепёк; перепечённый.

ПЕРЕПИСА́ТЬ Р.; перепишу́, перепи́шешь; перепиши́; перепи́санный.

ПЕРЕПИ́ТЬ Р.; перепью́, перепьёшь; перепе́й.

ПЕРЕПЛА́ВИТЬ Р.; перепла́влю, перепла́вишь; перепла́вь; перепла́вленный.

ПЕРЕПЛАТИ́ТЬ Р.; переплачу́, перепла́тишь; перепла́ченный.

ПЕРЕПЛЕСТИ́ Р.; переплету́, переплетёшь; переплети́; переплёл; переплётший; переплетённый; переплетя́.

ПЕРЕПЛЫ́ТЬ Р.; переплыву́, переплывёшь; переплыви́.

ПЕРЕПОЛЗТИ́ Р.; переползу́, переползёшь; переползи́; перепо́лз.

ПЕРЕПОЛО́ТЬ Р.; переполю́, перепо́лешь перепо́ли перепо́лотый.

ПЕРЕПО́РТИТЬ Р.; перепо́рчу, перепо́ртишь; перепо́рти and перепо́рть; перепо́рченный.

ПЕРЕПОЯ́САТЬ Р.; перепоя́шу, перепоя́шешь; перепоя́шь; перепоя́санный.

ПЕРЕПРА́ВИТЬ Р.; перепра́влю, перепра́вишь; перепра́вь; перепра́вленный.

ПЕРЕПРОДАВА́ТЬ I.; перепродаю́, перепродаёшь; перепродава́й; перепродава́я.

ПЕРЕПРОДА́ТЬ Р.; перепрода́м, перепрода́шь, перепрода́ст, перепродади́м, перепродади́те, перепродаду́т; перепрода́й; перепро́данный.

ПЕРЕПРУДИ́ТЬ Р.; перепружу́, перепру́дишь; перепру́женный.

ПЕРЕПРЯ́ЧЬ Р.; перепрягу́, перепряжёшь, перепрягу́т; перепряги́; перепря́г; перепряжённый.

ПЕРЕРАСТИ́ Р.; перерасту́, перерастёшь; перерасти́ (imp.); переро́с.

ПЕРЕРВА́ТЬ Р.; перерву́, перервёшь; перерви́; переро́рванный.

ПЕРЕРЕ́ЗАТЬ Р.; перере́жу, перере́жешь; перере́жь; перере́занный.

ПЕРЕРОДИ́ТЬ Р.; перерожу́, переродишь; перерождённый.

ПЕРЕРУБИ́ТЬ Р.; перерублю́, перерубишь; переру́бленный.

ПЕРЕРЫ́ТЬ Р.; переро́ю, переро́ешь; переро́й; перерытый.

ПЕРЕРЯДИ́ТЬ Р.; переряжу́, переря́дишь (and перерядишь); переря́женный.

ПЕРЕСАДИ́ТЬ Р.; пересажу́, переса́дишь; переса́женный.

ПЕРЕСДАВА́ТЬ I.; пересдаю́, пересдаёшь; пересдава́й; пересдава́я.

ПЕРЕСДА́ТЬ Р.; пересда́м, пересда́шь, пересда́ст, пересдади́м, пересдади́те, пересдаду́т; пересда́й; пересда́нный.

ПЕРЕСЕ́СТЬ Р.; переся́ду, переся́дешь; переся́дь; пересе́л.

ПЕРЕСЕ́ЧЬ Р.; пересеку́, пересечёшь, пересеку́т; пересеки́; пересе́к; пересечённый; пересе́ченный.

ПЕРЕСИДЕ́ТЬ Р.; пересижу́, пересидишь; пересиди́; переси́женный.

ПЕРЕСКАЗА́ТЬ Р.; перескажу́, переска́жешь; перескажи́; переска́занный.

ПЕРЕСЛАСТИ́ТЬ Р.; переслащу́, пересласти́шь; переслащённый.

ПЕРЕСЛА́ТЬ Р.; перешлю́, перешлёшь; перешли́[2], пере́сланный.

ПЕРЕСМОТРЕ́ТЬ Р.; пересмотрю́, пересмо́тришь; пересмотри́; пересмо́тренный.

ПЕРЕСНЯ́ТЬ Р.; пересниму́, пересни́мешь; пересними́; пересня́тый.

ПЕРЕСОЗДАВА́ТЬ I.; пересоздаю́, пересоздаёшь; пересоздава́й; пересоздава́я.

ПЕРЕСОЗДА́ТЬ Р.; пересозда́м, пересозда́шь, пересозда́ст, пересозда-

дим; пересоздади́те, пересоздаду́т; пересозда́й; пересо́зданный.

ПЕРЕСО́ХНУТЬ Р.; пересо́х, пересо́хла.

ПЕРЕСПА́ТЬ Р.; пересплю́, переспи́шь; переспи́; пере́спанный.

ПЕРЕСПРОСИ́ТЬ Р.; переспрошу́, переспро́сишь; переспро́шенный.

ПЕРЕСТАВА́ТЬ I.; перестаю́, перестаёшь; перестава́й; перестава́я.

ПЕРЕСТА́ВИТЬ Р.; переста́влю, переста́вишь; переста́вь; переста́вленный.

ПЕРЕСТА́ТЬ Р.; переста́ну, переста́нешь; переста́нь.

ПЕРЕСТЕЛИ́ТЬ Р.; перестелю́, пересте́лешь; перестели́; пересте́ленный.

ПЕРЕСТЛА́ТЬ Р.; перестелю́, пересте́лишь; перестели́; пере́стланный.

ПЕРЕСТОЯ́ТЬ Р.; перестою́, перестои́шь; перестой.

ПЕРЕСТУПИ́ТЬ Р.; переступлю́, переступишь; переступленный.

ПЕРЕСЫ́ПАТЬ Р.; пересы́плю, пересы́плешь; пересы́пь; пересы́панный.

ПЕРЕСЫ́ТИТЬ Р.; пересы́щу, пересы́тишь; пересы́ть; пересы́щенный.

ПЕРЕТЕРЕ́ТЬ Р.; перетру́, перетрёшь; перетри́; перетёр; перетёртый; перетере́в and перетёрши.

ПЕРЕТЕРПЕ́ТЬ Р.; перетерплю́, перетерпишь; перетерпи́.

ПЕРЕТОПИ́ТЬ Р.; перетоплю́[1,2,3], перето́пишь; перето́пленный.

ПЕРЕТРУСИ́ТЬ Р.; перетрушу́, перетруси́шь; перетру́шенный.

ПЕРЕТРУ́СИТЬ Р.; перетру́шу, перетру́сишь; перетру́сь.

ПЕРЕТРЯСТИ́ Р.; перетрясу́, перетрясёшь; перетряси́; перетря́с; перетрясённый.

ПЕРЕ́ТЬ I.; пру, прёшь; при; пёр.

ПЕРЕУПРЯ́МИТЬ Р.; переупря́млю, переупря́мишь; переупря́мь.

ПЕРЕУСТУПИ́ТЬ Р.; переуступлю́, переусту́пишь; переусту́пленный.

ПЕРЕУТОМИ́ТЬ Р.; переутомлю́, переутоми́шь; переутомлённый.

ПЕРЕУЧЕ́СТЬ Р.; переучту́, переучтёшь; переучти́; переучёл; переучла́; переучтённый; переучтя́.

ПЕРЕХВАТИ́ТЬ Р.; перехвачу́, перехва́тишь; перехва́ченный.

ПЕРЕХОДИ́ТЬ I.; перехожу́, перехо́дишь.

ПЕРЕЧЕРТИ́ТЬ Р.; перечерчу́, перече́ртишь; перече́рченный.

ПЕРЕЧЕСА́ТЬ Р.; перечешу́, перече́шешь; перечеши́; перечёсанный.

ПЕРЕЧЕ́СТЬ Р.; перечту́[1] and [2], перечтёшь; перечти́; перечёл, перечла́; перечётший; перечтённый; перечтя́.

ПЕРЕШИБИ́ТЬ Р.; перешибу́, перешибёшь; перешиби́; переши́б; переши́бленный.

ПЕРЕШИ́ТЬ Р.; перешью́, перешьёшь; перешей; переши́тый.

ПЕСТРЕ́ТЬ I.; пестри́т, пестра́т; пестри́.

ПЕТЬ I.; пою́, поёшь; пой; пе́тый.

ПЕЧЬ I.; пеку́, печёшь, пеку́т; пеки́; пёк; печённый.

ПИСА́ТЬ I.; пишу́, пи́шешь; пиши́; пи́санный.

ПИТЬ I.; пью, пьёшь; пей; пи́тый.

ПИЩА́ТЬ I.; пищу́, пищи́шь; пищи́.

ПЛА́ВИТЬ I.; пла́влю, пла́вишь; плавь; пла́вленный.

ПЛА́КАТЬ I.; пла́чу, пла́чешь; плачь.

ПЛАТИ́ТЬ I.; плачу́, пла́тишь; пла́ченный.

ПЛЕСКА́ТЬ I.; плещу́, пле́щешь; плещи́; плеска́я and плеща́.

ПЛЕСТИ́ I.; плету́, плетёшь; плети́; плёл; плётший; плетённый.

ПЛЕСТИ́СЬ I.; плету́сь, плетёшься; плети́сь; плёлся, плела́сь; плётшийся.

ПЛОДИ́ТЬ I.; пложу́, плоди́шь.

ПЛЫТЬ I.; плыву́, плывёшь; плыви́.

ПЛЯСА́ТЬ I.; пляшу́, пля́шешь; пляши́.

ПОБЕЖА́ТЬ Р.; побегу́, побежи́шь, побегу́т; побеги́.

ПОБЕРЕ́ЧЬ Р.; поберегу́, побережёшь, поберегу́т; побереги́; поберёг; побережённый.

ПОБИ́ТЬ Р.; побью́, побьёшь; побе́й; поби́тый.

ПОБЛЁКНУТЬ Р.; поблёк, поблёкла.

ПОБОРО́ТЬ Р.; поборю́, побо́решь; побори́.

ПОБОЯ́ТЬСЯ Р.; побою́сь, побои́шься; побо́йся.

ПОБРА́ТЬ Р.; поберу́, поберёшь; побери́; по́бранный.

ПОБРЕСТИ́ Р.; побреду́, побредёшь; побреди́; побрёл; побре́дший.

ПОБРИ́ТЬ Р.; побре́ю, побре́ешь; побре́й; побри́тый.

ПОБРОДИ́ТЬ Р.; поброжу́, побро́дишь.

ПОБУДИ́ТЬ[1] Р.; побужу́[1], побу́дишь; побу́женный.

ПОБУДИ́ТЬ[2] Р.; побужу́[2], побуди́шь (and побу́дишь); побуждённый.

ПОБЫ́ТЬ Р.; побу́ду, побу́дешь; побу́дь.

ПОВА́ДИТЬСЯ Р.; пова́жусь, пова́дишься; пова́дься.

ПОВЕЗТИ́ Р.; повезу́, повезёшь; повези́; повёз; повезённый; повезя́.

ПОВЕ́РГНУТЬ Р.; пове́рг (and пове́ргнул), пове́ргла; пове́ргнутый and пове́рженный.

ПОВЕ́СИТЬ Р.; пове́шу, пове́сишь; пове́сь; пове́шенный.

ПОВЕСТИ́ Р.; поведу́[1] and [2], поведёшь; поведи́; повёл; пове́дший; поведённый; поведя́.

ПОВЕ́ЯТЬ Р.; пове́ет, пове́ют; пове́й.

ПОВИСЕ́ТЬ Р.; повишу́, повиси́шь; повиси́.

ПОВИ́СНУТЬ Р.; пови́с (and пови́снул), пови́сла.

ПОВЛЕ́ЧЬ Р.; повлеку́, повлечёшь, повлеку́т; повлеки́; повлёк; повлечённый.

ПОВОДИ́ТЬ I.; повожу́[1], пово́дишь.

ПОВОДИ́ТЬ Р.; повожу́[2], пово́дишь; пово́женный.

ПОВОЗИ́ТЬ Р.; повожу́[3], пово́зишь; пово́женный.

ПОВОЛО́ЧЬ Р.; поволоку́, поволочёшь, поволоку́т; поволоки́; поволо́к; поволочённый.

ПОВОРОТИ́ТЬ Р.; поворочу́, поворо́тишь; поворо́ченный.

ПОВРЕДИ́ТЬ Р.; поврежу́, повреди́шь; повреждённый.

ПОВЫ́СИТЬ Р.; повы́шу, повы́сишь; повы́сь; повы́шенный.

ПОВЯЗА́ТЬ Р.; повяжу́, повя́жешь; повяжи́; повя́занный.

ПОВЯ́НУТЬ Р.; повя́л, повя́ла; повя́дший and повя́нувший.

ПОГАСИ́ТЬ Р.; погашу́, пога́сишь; пога́шенный.

ПОГА́СНУТЬ Р.; пога́с, пога́сла.

ПОГИ́БНУТЬ Р.; поги́б, поги́бла.

ПОГЛА́ДИТЬ Р.; погла́жу, погла́дишь; погла́дь; погла́женный.

ПОГЛОТИ́ТЬ Р.; поглощу́, погло-
ти́шь; поглощённый.
ПОГЛЯДЕ́ТЬ Р.; погляжу́, погля-
ди́шь; погляди́.
ПОГНА́ТЬ Р.; погоню́, пого́нишь;
погони́; по́гнанный.
ПОГНИ́ТЬ Р.; погниёт, погнию́т.
ПОГОДИ́ТЬ Р.; погожу́, погоди́шь.
ПОГОРЕ́ТЬ Р.; погорю́, погори́шь;
погори́.
ПОГРЕСТИ́ Р.; погребу́, погребёшь;
погреби́; погрёб; погребённый.
ПОГРОЗИ́ТЬ Р.; погрожу́, погрози́шь.
ПОГРУЗИ́ТЬ Р.; погружу́[1], погру́-
зишь (and погрузи́шь); погру́-
женный and погружённый.
ПОГРУЗИ́ТЬ Р.; погружу́[2], погру-
зи́шь; погружённый.
ПОГРЯ́ЗНУТЬ Р.; погря́з, погря́зла.
ПОГУБИ́ТЬ Р.; погублю́, погу́бишь;
погу́бленный.
ПОДАВА́ТЬ I.; подаю́, подаёшь;
подава́й; подава́я.
ПОДАВИ́ТЬ Р.; подавлю́, пода́вишь;
пода́вленный.
ПОДАВИ́ТЬСЯ Р.; подавлю́сь, по-
да́вишься.
ПОДА́ТЬ Р.; пода́м, пода́шь, пода́ст,
подади́м, подади́те, подаду́т; по-
да́й; по́данный.
ПОДБА́ВИТЬ Р.; подба́влю, подба́-
вишь; подба́вь; подба́вленный.
ПОДБЕЖА́ТЬ Р.; подбегу́, подбе-
жи́шь, подбегу́т; подбеги́.
ПОДБИ́ТЬ Р.; подобью́, подобьёшь;
подбе́й; подби́тый.
ПОДБРИ́ТЬ Р.; подбре́ю, подбре́ешь;
подбре́й; подбри́тый.
ПОДБРО́СИТЬ Р.; подбро́шу, под-
бро́сишь; подбро́сь; подбро́шен-
ный.
ПОДВЕЗТИ́ Р.; подвезу́, подвезёшь;
подвези́; подвёз; подвезённый; под-
веза́.
ПОДВЕ́РГНУТЬ Р.; подве́рг (and
arch. подве́ргнул), подве́ргла; под-
ве́ргнутый (and arch. подве́р-
женный).
ПОДВЕ́СИТЬ Р.; подве́шу, подве́-
сишь; подве́сь; подве́шенный.
ПОДВЕСТИ́ Р.; подведу́, подведёшь;
подведи́; подвёл; подве́дший; подведённый; подведя́.
ПОДВИНТИ́ТЬ Р.; подвинчу́, под-
винти́шь; подви́нченный.

ПОДВИ́ТЬ Р.; подовью́, подовьёшь;
подве́й; подви́тый.
ПОДВОДИ́ТЬ I.; подвожу́[1], подво́-
дишь.
ПОДВОЗИ́ТЬ I.; подвожу́[2], подво́-
зишь.
ПОДВЫ́ПИТЬ Р.; подвы́пью, под-
вы́пьешь; подвы́пей.
ПОДВЯЗА́ТЬ Р.; подвяжу́, подвя́-
жешь; подвяжи́; подвя́занный.
ПОДГА́ДИТЬ Р.; подга́жу, подга́-
дишь; подга́дь.
ПОДГЛЯДЕ́ТЬ Р.; подгляжу́, под-
гляди́шь; подгляди́.
ПОДГНИ́ТЬ Р.; подгниёт, подгнию́т.
ПОДГОРЕ́ТЬ Р.; подгори́т, подгоря́т;
подгори́.
ПОДГОТО́ВИТЬ Р.; подгото́влю, под-
гото́вишь; подгото́вь; подгото́-
вленный.
ПОДГРЕСТИ́ Р.; подгребу́, подгребёшь; подгреби́; подгрёб; под-
гребённый.
ПОДГРУЗИ́ТЬ Р.; подгружу́, под-
гру́зишь (and подгрузи́шь); под-
гру́женный and подгружённый.
ПОДДАВА́ТЬ I.; поддаю́, поддаёшь;
поддава́й; поддава́я.
ПОДДА́ТЬ Р.; подда́м, подда́шь,
подда́ст, поддади́м, поддади́те, под-
даду́т; подда́й; по́дданный.
ПОДДЕРЖА́ТЬ Р.; поддержу́, под-
де́ржишь; поддержи́; подде́ржан-
ный.
ПОДДЕ́ТЬ Р.; подде́ну, подде́нешь;
подде́нь; подде́тый.
ПОДЕРЖА́ТЬ Р.; подержу́, поде́р-
жишь; подержи́; поде́ржанный.
ПОДЖА́ТЬ Р.; подожму́, подожмёшь;
подожми́; поджа́тый.
ПОДЖЕ́ЧЬ Р.; подожгу́, подожжёшь, подожгу́т; подожги́; поджёг, подожгла́; подожжённый.
ПОДЖИ́ТЬ Р.; поджмвёт, подживу́т;
поживи́.
ПОДЗАБЫ́ТЬ Р.; подзабу́ду, под-
забу́дешь; подзабу́дь; подзабы́тый.
ПОДЗАКУСИ́ТЬ Р.; подзакушу́, под-
заку́сишь.
ПОДЗУДИ́ТЬ Р.; подзужу́, подзу́-
дишь; подзу́женный.
ПОДИВИ́ТЬ Р.; подивлю́, подиви́шь.
ПОДКАТИ́ТЬ Р.; подкачу́, подка́-
тишь; подка́ченный.
ПОДКОЛО́ТЬ Р.; подколю́, под-
ко́лешь; подколи́; подко́лотый.

ПОДКОРМИТЬ Р.; подкормлю, подкормишь; подкормленный.

ПОДКОСИТЬ Р.; подкошу, подкосишь; подкошенный.

ПОДКРАСИТЬ Р.; подкрашу, подкрасишь; подкрась; подкрашенный.

ПОДКРАСТЬСЯ Р.; подкрадусь, подкрадёшься; подкрадись; подкрался.

ПОДКРЕПИТЬ Р.; подкреплю, подкрепишь; подкреплённый.

ПОДКУЗЬМИТЬ Р.; подкузьмлю, подкузьмишь.

ПОДКУПИТЬ Р.; подкуплю, подкупишь; подкупленный.

ПОДЛАДИТЬ Р.; подлажу, подладишь; подладь; подлаженный.

ПОДЛАДИТЬСЯ Р.; подлажусь, подладишься; подладься.

ПОДЛЕЖАТЬ I.; подлежу, подлежишь; подлежи.

ПОДЛЕЗТЬ Р.; подлезу, подлезешь; подлезь; подлез (past).

ПОДЛЕТЕТЬ Р.; подлечу, подлетишь; подлети.

ПОДЛИЗАТЬ Р.; порлижу, подлижешь; подлижи; подлизанный.

ПОДЛИЗАТЬСЯ Р.; подлижусь, подлижешься; подлижись.

ПОДЛИТЬ Р.; подолью, подольёшь; подлей; подлитый and подлитый.

ПОДЛОМИТЬ Р.; подломлю, подломишь; подломленный.

ПОДМАЗАТЬ Р.; подмажу, подмажешь; подмажь; подмазанный.

ПОДМЁРЗНУТЬ Р.; подмёрз, подмёрзла.

ПОДМЕСИТЬ Р.; подмешу, подмесишь; подмешенный.

ПОДМЕСТИ Р.; подмету, подметёшь; подмети; подмёл; подмётший; подметённый; подметя.

ПОДМЕТИТЬ Р.; подмечу, подметишь; подметь; подмеченный.

ПОДМОКНУТЬ Р.; подмок, подмокла.

ПОДМЫТЬ Р.; подмою, подмоешь; подмой; подмытый.

ПОДМЯТЬ Р.; подомну, подомнёшь; подомни; подмятый.

ПОДНАЖАТЬ Р.; поднажму, поднажмёшь; поднажми.

ПОДНЕСТИ Р.; поднесу, поднесёшь; поднеси; поднёс; поднесённый; поднеся.

ПОДНОВИТЬ Р.; подновлю, подновишь; подновлённый.

ПОДНОСИТЬ I.; подношу, подносишь.

ПОДНЯТЬ Р.; подниму, поднимешь; подними; поднятый.

ПОДОБРАТЬ Р.; подберу, подберёшь; подбери; подобранный.

ПОДОГНАТЬ Р.; подгоню, подгонишь; подгони; подогнанный.

ПОДОЖДАТЬ Р.; подожду, подождёшь; подожди.

ПОДОЗВАТЬ Р.; подзову, подзовёшь; подзови; подозванный.

ПОДОЙТИ Р.; подойду, подойдёшь; подошёл, подошла; подошедший; подойдя.

ПОДОЛЬСТИТЬСЯ Р.; подольщусь, подольстишься.

ПОДОРВАТЬ Р.; подорву, подорвёшь; подорви; подорванный.

ПОДОСЛАТЬ Р.; подошлю, подошлёшь; подошли[2]; подосланный.

ПОДОСТЛАТЬ Р.; подстелю, подстелешь; подстели; подостланный.

ПОДОХНУТЬ Р.; подох, подохла.

ПОДПАСТЬ Р.; подпаду, подпадёшь; подпади; подпал.

ПОДПЕРЕТЬ Р.; подопру, подопрёшь; подопри; подпёр; подпёртый; подперев and подпёрши.

ПОДПИСАТЬ Р.; подпишу, подпишешь; подпиши; подписанный.

ПОДПЛЫТЬ Р.; подплыву, подплывёшь; подплыви.

ПОДПОЛЗТИ Р.; подползу, подползёшь; подползи; подполз.

ПОДПОРОТЬ Р.; подпорю, подпорешь; подпори; подпоротый.

ПОДПОЯСАТЬ Р.; подпояшу, подпояшешь; подпояшь; подпоясанный.

ПОДПРАВИТЬ Р.; подправлю, подправишь; подправь; подправленный.

ПОДПУСТИТЬ Р.; подпущу, подпустишь; подпущенный.

ПОДРАСТИ Р.; подрасту, подрастёшь; подрасти (imp.); подрос.

ПОДРАСТИТЬ Р.; подращу, подрастишь; подращённый.

ПОДРАТЬСЯ Р.; подерусь, подерёшься; подерись.

ПОДРЕЗАТЬ Р.; подрежу, подрежешь; подрежь; подрезанный.

ПОДРЕМА́ТЬ Р.; подремлю́, подре́млешь; подремли́.

ПОДРУБИ́ТЬ Р.; подрублю́, подру́бишь; подру́бленный.

ПОДРЫ́ТЬ Р.; подро́ю, подро́ешь; подро́й; подры́тый.

ПОДРЯДИ́ТЬ Р.; подряжу́, подряди́шь; подряжённый and подря́женный.

ПОДСАДИ́ТЬ Р.; подсажу́, подса́дишь; подса́женный.

ПОДСВЕТИ́ТЬ Р.; подсвечу́, подсве́тишь; подсве́ченный.

ПОДСЕ́СТЬ Р.; подся́ду, подся́дешь; подся́дь; подсе́л.

ПОДСЕ́ЧЬ Р.; подсеку́, подсечёшь; подсеку́т; подсеки́; подсе́к; подсечённый.

ПОДСЕ́ЯТЬ Р.; подсе́ю, подсе́ешь; подсе́й; подсе́янный.

ПОДСИДЕ́ТЬ Р.; подсижу́, подсиди́шь; подсиди́; подси́женный.

ПОДСКАЗА́ТЬ Р.; подскажу́, подска́жешь; подскажи́; подска́занный.

ПОДСКАКА́ТЬ Р.; подскачу́, подска́чешь; подскачи́.

ПОДСКОБЛИ́ТЬ Р.; подскоблю́, подско́блишь (and подскобли́шь); подско́бленный.

ПОДСКРЕСТИ́ Р.; подскребу́, подскребёшь; подскреби́; подскрёб; подскребённый.

ПОДСЛАСТИ́ТЬ Р.; подслащу́, подсласти́шь; подслащённый.

ПОДСМОТРЕ́ТЬ Р.; подсмотрю́, подсмо́тришь; подсмотри́; подсмо́тренный.

ПОДСОБИ́ТЬ Р.; подсоблю́, подсоби́шь.

ПОДСО́ХНУТЬ Р.; подсо́х, подсо́хла.

ПОДСТА́ВИТЬ Р.; подста́влю, подста́вишь; подста́вь; подста́вленный.

ПОДСТЕЛИ́ТЬ Р.; подстелю́, подсте́лешь; подстели́; подсте́ленный.

ПОДСТЕРЕ́ЧЬ Р.; подстерегу́, подстережёшь, подстерегу́т; подстереги́; подстерёг; подстережённый.

ПОДСТРИ́ЧЬ Р.; подстригу́, подстрижёшь, подстригу́т; подстриги́; подстри́г; подстри́женный.

ПОДСТУПИ́ТЬ Р.; подступлю́, подсту́пишь.

ПОДСЫ́ПАТЬ Р.; подсы́плю, подсы́плешь; подсы́пь; подсы́панный.

ПОДТА́ЯТЬ Р.; подта́ет, подта́ют.

ПОДТВЕРДИ́ТЬ Р.; подтвержу́, подтверди́шь; подтверждённый.

ПОДТЕРЕ́ТЬ Р.; подотру́, подотрёшь; подотри́; подтёр; подтёртый; подтере́в and подтёрши.

ПОДТЕ́ЧЬ Р.; подтечёт, подтеку́т; подтеки́; подтёк.

ПОДТОПИ́ТЬ Р.; подтоплю́, подто́пишь; подто́пленный.

ПОДУ́ТЬ Р.; поду́ю, поду́ешь; поду́й.

ПОДХВАТИ́ТЬ Р.; подхвачу́, подхва́тишь; подхва́ченный.

ПОДХОДИ́ТЬ I.; подхожу́, подхо́дишь.

ПОДЦЕПИ́ТЬ Р.; подцеплю́, подце́пишь; подце́пленный.

ПОДЧИ́СТИТЬ Р.; подчи́щу, подчи́стишь; подчи́сти and подчи́сть; подчи́щенный.

ПОДШИБИ́ТЬ Р.; подшибу́, подшибёшь; подшиби́; подши́б; подши́бленный.

ПОДШИ́ТЬ Р.; подошью́, подошьёшь; подшей; подши́тый.

ПОДШУТИ́ТЬ Р.; подшучу́, подшу́тишь.

ПОД’Е́СТЬ Р.; под’е́м, под’е́шь[1], под’е́ст, под’еди́м, под’еди́те, под’едя́т; под’е́шь[2] (imp.); под’е́л; под’е́денный.

ПОД’Е́ХАТЬ Р.; под’е́ду, под’е́дешь; под’езжа́й.

ПОД’Я́ТЬ Р.; подыму́, поды́мешь; подыми́; под’я́тый.

ПОДЫМА́ТЬ I.; под’е́млю, под’е́млешь (arch. forms); (modern forms: подыма́ю, подыма́ешь); под’е́мли.

ПОДЫСКА́ТЬ Р.; подыщу́, поды́щешь; подыщи́; поды́сканный.

ПОДЫША́ТЬ Р.; подышу́, поды́шишь; подыши́.

ПОЕ́ЗДИТЬ Р.; пое́зжу, пое́здишь; пое́зди.

ПОЕ́СТЬ Р.; пое́м, пое́шь[1], пое́ст, поеди́м, поеди́те, поедя́т; пое́шь[2] (imp.); пое́л, пое́денный.

ПОЕ́ХАТЬ Р.; пое́ду, пое́дешь; поезжа́й.

ПОЖА́ТЬ[1] Р.; пожму́, пожмёшь; пожми́; пожа́тый.

ПОЖА́ТЬ[2] Р.; пожну́, пожнёшь; пожни́; пожа́тый.

ПОЖДА́ТЬ Р.; пожду́, пождёшь; пожди́.

ПОЖÉЧЬ Р.; пожгý, пожжёшь, по-
жгýт; пожги́; пожёг, пожгла́; пожжённый.

ПОЖИВИ́ТЬСЯ Р.; поживлю́сь, по-
живи́шься.

ПОЖИ́ТЬ Р.; поживý, поживёшь;
поживи́.

ПОЖРÁТЬ Р.; пожрý, пожрёшь;
пожри́; пóжранный.

ПОЗАБÁВИТЬ Р.; позабáвлю; по-
забáвишь; позабáвь; позабáвлен-
ный.

ПОЗАБЫ́ТЬ Р.; позабýду, позабý-
дешь; позабýдь; позабы́тый.

ПОЗВÁТЬ Р.; позовý, позовёшь;
позови́; пóзванный.

ПОЗДРÁВИТЬ Р.; поздрáвлю, по-
здрáвишь; поздрáвь; поздрáвлен-
ный.

ПОЗЛАТИ́ТЬ Р.; позлащý, по-
злати́шь; позлащённый.

ПОЗНАВÁТЬ I.; познаю́, познаёшь;
познавáй; познавáя.

ПОЗНАКÓМИТЬ Р.; познакóмлю,
познакóмишь; познакóмь; позна-
кóмленный.

ПОЗОЛОТИ́ТЬ Р.; позолочý, позо-
лоти́шь; позолóченный.

ПОИСКÁТЬ Р.; поищý, пои́щешь;
поищи́.

ПОЙТИ́ Р.; пойдý, пойдёшь; пойди́;
пошёл, пошла́; поше́дший; пойдя́
and поше́дши.

ПОКАЗÁТЬ Р.; покажý, покáжешь;
покажи́; покáзанный.

ПОКАТИ́ТЬ Р.; покачý, покáтишь;
покáченный.

ПОКÁЯТЬСЯ Р.; покáюсь, покá-
ешься; покáйся.

ПОКЛИ́КАТЬ Р.; покли́чу, покли́-
чешь; покли́чь.

ПОКЛЯ́СТЬСЯ Р.; поклянýсь, поклянёшься; поклянись; покля́лся.

ПОКОЛЕБÁТЬ Р.; поколéблю, по-
колéблешь; поколéбли; поколéб-
ленный.

ПОКОЛОТИ́ТЬ Р.; поколочý, по-
колóтишь; поколóченный.

ПОКОРМИ́ТЬ Р.; покормлю́, по-
кóрмишь; покóрмленный.

ПОКОРÓБИТЬ Р.; покорóблю, по-
корóбишь; покорóбь; покорóблен-
ный.

ПОКОСИ́ТЬ[1] Р.; покошý[1], покоси́шь;
покóшенный.

ПОКОСИ́ТЬ[2] Р.; покошý[2], покóсишь;
покóшенный.

ПОКОСИ́ТЬСЯ Р.; покошýсь, поко-
си́шься.

ПОКРÁПАТЬ Р.; покрáплю, по-
крáплешь (also покрáпаю, покрá-
паешь); покрáпли and покрáпай.

ПОКРÁСИТЬ Р.; покрáшу, покрá-
сишь; покрáсь; покрáшенный.

ПОКРÁСТЬ Р.; покрадý, покрадёшь;
покради́; покрáл; покрáденный.

ПОКРИВИ́ТЬ Р.; покривлю́, по-
криви́шь; покривлённый.

ПОКРИЧÁТЬ Р.; покричý, по-
кричи́шь; покричи́.

ПОКРЫ́ТЬ Р.; покрóю, покрóешь;
покрóй; покры́тый.

ПОКУМИ́ТЬСЯ Р.; покумлю́сь, по-
куми́шься.

ПОКУСИ́ТЬСЯ Р.; покушýсь, по-
куси́шься.

ПОЛÁДИТЬ Р.; полáжу[1], полáдишь;
полáдь.

ПОЛÁЗИТЬ Р.; полáжу[2], полáзишь;
полáзь.

ПОЛÁКОМИТЬ Р.; полáкомлю, по-
лáкомишь; полáкоми and полá-
комь.

ПОЛÁКОМИТЬСЯ Р.; полáкомлюсь,
полáкомишься; полáкомись and
полáкомься.

ПОЛЕЖÁТЬ Р.; полежý, полежи́шь;
полежи́.

ПОЛÉЗТЬ Р.; полéзу, полéзешь;
полезáй and полéзь; полéз.

ПОЛЕТÉТЬ Р.; полечý, полети́шь;
полети́.

ПОЛÉЧЬ Р.; поля́жет (3rd pers. sing.;
1st and 2nd pers. sing. not used);
поля́жем, поля́жете, поля́гут; по-
ля́гте (pl. imp.); полёг.

ПОЛЗТИ́ I.; ползý, ползёшь; ползи́;
полз.

ПОЛИЗÁТЬ Р.; полижý, поли́жешь;
полижи́; поли́занный.

ПОЛИ́ТЬ Р.; полью́, польёшь;
полéй; пóлитый and поли́тый.

ПОЛОСКÁТЬ I.; полощý, полóщешь;
полощи́; полóсканный.

ПОЛÓТЬ I.; полю́, пóлешь; поли́;
пóлотый.

ПОЛУДИ́ТЬ Р.; полужý, полу́дишь;
полу́женный.

ПОЛУЛЕЖÁТЬ I.; полулежý, по-
лулежи́шь; полулежи́; полулёжа.

ПОЛУЛЕЧЬ Р.; полуля́гу, полуля́жешь, полуля́гут; полуля́г; полулёг.

ПОЛЬСТИТЬ Р.; польщу́, польсти́шь.

ПОЛЮБИТЬ Р.; полюблю́, полю́бишь.

ПОМА́ДИТЬ I.; пома́жу[1], пома́дишь; пома́дь.

ПОМА́ЗАТЬ Р.; пома́жу[2], пома́жешь; пома́жь; пома́занный.

ПОМАХА́ТЬ Р.; помашу́, пома́шешь; помаши́.

ПОМЕРЕ́ТЬ Р.; помру́, помрёшь; помри́; по́мер.

ПОМЁРЗНУТЬ Р.; помёрз, помёрзла.

ПОМЕ́РКНУТЬ Р.; поме́рк (and arch. поме́ркнул); поме́ркла.

ПОМЕСТИ́ТЬ Р.; помещу́, помести́шь; помещённый.

ПОМЕ́ТИТЬ Р.; поме́чу, поме́тишь; поме́ть; поме́ченный.

ПОМО́ЛВИТЬ Р.; помо́лвлю, помо́лвишь; помо́лви; помо́лвленный.

ПОМОЛЧА́ТЬ Р.; помолчу́, помолчи́шь; помолчи́.

ПОМОРО́ЗИТЬ Р.; поморо́жу, поморо́зишь; поморо́зь; поморо́женный.

ПОМО́ЧЬ Р.; помогу́, помо́жешь, помо́гут; помоги́; помо́г.

ПОМУТИ́ТЬ Р.; помучу́, помути́шь (and помути́шь); помутнённый.

ПОМЧА́ТЬ Р.; помчу́, помчи́шь; помчи́.

ПОМЫ́ТЬ Р.; помо́ю, помо́ешь; помо́й; помы́тый.

ПОМНЯ́ТЬ Р.; помню́, помнёшь; помни́; помя́тый.

ПОНАДЕ́ЯТЬСЯ Р.; понаде́юсь, понаде́ешься; понаде́йся.

ПОНА́ДОБИТЬСЯ Р.; пона́доблюсь, пона́добишься; пона́добись.

ПОНАЕ́ХАТЬ Р.; понае́дет, понае́дем, понае́дете, помае́дут (1st and 2nd pers. sing. not used).

ПОНЕСТИ́ Р.; понесу́, понесёшь; понеси́; понёс; понесённый; понеся́.

ПОНИ́ЗИТЬ Р.; пони́жу, пони́зишь; пони́зь; пони́женный.

ПОНИ́КНУТЬ Р.; пони́к, пони́кла.

ПОНОСИ́ТЬ Р.; поношу́[1], поно́сишь; поно́шенный.

ПОНОСИ́ТЬ I.; поношу́[2], поно́сишь.

ПОНУ́ДИТЬ Р.; понужу́, пону́дишь; пону́дь; понуждённый.

ПОНЯ́ТЬ Р.; пойму́, поймёшь; пойми́; по́нятый.

ПООБЖИ́ТЬСЯ Р.; пообживу́сь, пообживёшься; пообживи́сь.

ПООБНОСИ́ТЬСЯ Р.; пообношу́сь, пообно́сишься; пообноси́сь.

ПОПА́СТЬ Р.; попаду́, попадёшь; попади́; попа́л.

ПОПЕРЕ́ТЬ Р.; попру́[1], попрёшь; попри́; попёр; попёртый.

ПОПИСА́ТЬ Р.; попишу́, попи́шешь; попиши́.

ПОПИ́ТЬ Р.; попью́, попьёшь; попе́й; по́пито.

ПОПЛА́КАТЬ Р.; попла́чу, попла́чешь; попла́чь.

ПОПЛАТИ́ТЬСЯ Р.; поплачу́сь, попла́тишься; поплати́сь.

ПОПЛЕСТИ́СЬ Р.; поплету́сь, поплетёшься; поплети́сь; поплёлся.

ПОПЛЫ́ТЬ Р.; поплыву́, поплывёшь; поплыви́.

ПОПЛЯСА́ТЬ Р.; попляшу́, попля́шешь; попляши́.

ПОПОЛЗТИ́ Р.; поползу́, поползёшь; поползи́; попо́лз.

ПОПОЛОСКА́ТЬ Р.; пополощу́, пополо́щешь; пополощи́.

ПОПРА́ВИТЬ Р.; попра́влю, попра́вишь; попра́вь; попра́вленный.

ПОПРА́ТЬ Р.; попру́[2], попрёшь; попри́; по́пранный.

ПОПРОСИ́ТЬ Р.; попрошу́, попро́сишь; попро́шенный.

ПОПРЯ́ТАТЬ Р.; попря́чу, попря́чешь; попря́чь; попря́танный.

ПОПУСТИ́ТЬ Р.; попущу́, попу́стишь; попу́щенный.

ПОПЯ́ТИТЬ Р.; попя́чу, попя́тишь; попя́ть; попя́ченный.

ПОПЯ́ТИТЬСЯ Р.; попя́чусь, попя́тишься; попя́ться.

ПОРАБОТИ́ТЬ Р.; порабощу́, поработи́шь; порабощённый.

ПОРАЗИ́ТЬ Р.; поражу́, порази́шь; поражённый.

ПОРАСТИ́ Р.; порасту́, порастёшь; порасти́ (imp.); поро́с.

ПОРВА́ТЬ Р.; порву́, порвёшь; порви́; по́рванный.

ПОРЕ́ЗАТЬ Р.; поре́жу, поре́жешь; поре́жь; поре́занный.

ПОРОДИ́ТЬ Р.; порожу́, породи́шь; порождённый.

ПОРО́ТЬ[1] I.; порю́[1], по́решь; пори́; по́ротый.

ПОРО́ТЬ² I.; порю́², по́решь; пори́; по́ротый.

ПО́РТИТЬ I.; по́рчу, по́ртишь; по́рти and порть; по́рченный.

ПОРУБИ́ТЬ Р.; порублю́, пору́бишь; пору́убленный.

ПОРЫ́ТЬСЯ Р.; поро́юсь, поро́ешься; поро́йся.

ПОРЯДИ́ТЬ Р.; поряжу́, поряди́шь (and поря́дишь); поря́женный.

ПОРЯДИ́ТЬСЯ Р.; поряжу́сь, поряди́шься (and поря́дишься).

ПОСАДИ́ТЬ Р.; посажу́, поса́дишь; поса́женный.

ПОСВЕТИ́ТЬ Р.; посвечу́, посве́тишь.

ПОСВИСТА́ТЬ Р.; посвищу́¹, посви́щешь; посвищи́.

ПОСВИСТЕ́ТЬ Р.; посвищу́², посвисти́шь; посвисти́.

ПОСВЯТИ́ТЬ Р.; посвящу́, посвяти́шь; посвящённый.

ПОСЕТИ́ТЬ Р.; посещу́, посети́шь; посещённый.

ПОСЕ́ЧЬ Р.; посеку́, посечёшь, посеку́т; посеки́; посе́к; посечённый and посе́ченный.

ПОСЕ́ЧЬСЯ Р.; посечётся, посеку́тся.

ПОСЕ́ЯТЬ Р.; посе́ю, посе́ешь; посе́й; посе́янный.

ПОСИДЕ́ТЬ Р.; посижу́, посиди́шь; посиди́.

ПОСКАКА́ТЬ Р.; поскачу́, поска́чешь; поскачи́.

ПОСКРИПЕ́ТЬ Р.; поскриплю́, поскрипи́шь; поскрипи́.

ПОСКУПИ́ТЬСЯ Р.; поскуплю́сь, поскупи́шься.

ПОСЛАСТИ́ТЬ Р.; послащу́, посласти́шь; послащённый.

ПОСЛА́ТЬ Р.; пошлю́, пошлёшь; пошли́²; по́сланный.

ПОСЛЕДИ́ТЬ Р.; послежу́, последи́шь.

ПОСЛЫ́ШАТЬ Р.; послы́шу, послы́шишь; послы́шь; послы́шанный.

ПОСМОТРЕ́ТЬ Р.; посмотрю́, посмо́тришь; посмотри́; посмо́тренный.

ПОСОБИ́ТЬ Р.; пособлю́, пособи́шь.

ПОСОВЕ́СТИТЬСЯ Р.; посо́вещусь, посо́вестишься; посо́вестись.

ПОСО́ХНУТЬ Р.; посо́х, посо́хла.

ПОСПА́СТЬ Р.; поспаду́, поспадёшь; поспади́; поспа́л¹, поспа́ла.

ПОСПА́ТЬ Р.; посплю́, поспи́шь; поспи́; поспа́л², поспала́, поспа́ло, поспа́ли.

ПОСРАМИ́ТЬ Р.; посрамлю́, посрами́шь; посрамлённый.

ПОСТА́ВИТЬ¹ Р.; поста́влю¹, поста́вишь; поста́вь; поста́вленный.

ПОСТА́ВИТЬ² Р.; поста́влю², поста́вишь; поста́вь; поста́вленный.

ПОСТАНОВИ́ТЬ Р.; постановлю́, постано́вишь; постано́вленный.

ПОСТЕЛИ́ТЬ Р.; постелю́, посте́лешь; постели́; посте́ленный.

ПОСТИ́ГНУТЬ Р.; пости́гну, пости́гнешь; пости́гни; пости́г (and arch. пости́гнул), пости́гла; пости́гнутый.

ПОСТИ́ТЬСЯ I.; пощу́сь, пости́шься.

ПОСТИ́ЧЬ Р.; пости́гну, пости́гнешь; пости́гни; пости́г (and arch. пости́гнул), пости́гла; пости́гнутый.

ПОСТЛА́ТЬ Р.; постелю́, посте́лешь; постели́; по́стланный.

ПОСТОЯ́ТЬ Р.; постою́, постои́шь; посто́й.

ПОСТРИ́ЧЬ Р.; постригу́, постри-жёшь, постригу́т; постриги́; постри́г; постри́женный.

ПОСТУПИ́ТЬ Р.; поступлю́, посту́пишь.

ПОСТУЧА́ТЬ Р.; постучу́, постучи́шь; постучи́.

ПОСТЫДИ́ТЬ Р.; постыжу́, постыди́шь; постыжённый.

ПОСУДИ́ТЬ Р.; посужу́, посу́дишь; посуди́.

ПОСЫ́ПАТЬ Р.; посы́плю, посы́плешь; посы́пь; посы́панный.

ПОТЕРЕ́ТЬ Р.; потру́, потрёшь; потри́; потёр; потёртый; потере́в and поте́рши.

ПОТЕРПЕ́ТЬ Р.; потерплю́, поте́рпишь; потерпи́.

ПОТЕ́ЧЬ Р.; потечёт, потеку́т; потёк.

ПОТОПИ́ТЬ Р.; потоплю́, пото́пишь; пото́пленный.

ПОТОПТА́ТЬ Р.; потопчу́, пото́пчешь; потопчи́; пото́птанный.

ПОТОРОПИ́ТЬ Р.; потороплю́, поторо́пишь; поторо́пленный.

ПОТРАВИ́ТЬ Р.; потравлю́, потра́вишь; потра́вленный.

ПОТРА́ТИТЬ Р.; потра́чу, потра́тишь; потра́ть; потра́ченный.

ПОТРА́ФИТЬ Р.; потра́флю, потра́фишь; потра́фь.

ПОТРЕБИ́ТЬ Р.; потреблю́, потреби́шь; потреблённый.

ПОТРЕПА́ТЬ Р.; потреплю́, потре́плешь; потрепли́; потрёпанный.

ПОТРЕЩА́ТЬ Р.; потрещу́, потрещи́шь; потрещи́.

ПОТРУДИ́ТЬСЯ Р.; потружу́сь, потру́дишься; потруди́сь.

ПОТРЯСТИ́ Р.; потрясу́, потрясёшь; потряси́; потрясённый.

ПОТУ́ПИТЬ Р.; поту́плю, поту́пишь; поту́пь; поту́пленный.

ПОТУ́ХНУТЬ Р.; поту́х, поту́хла.

ПОХИ́ТИТЬ Р.; похи́щу, похи́тишь; похи́ть; похи́щенный.

ПОХЛОПОТА́ТЬ Р.; похлопочу́, похлопо́чешь; похлопочи́.

ПОХОДИ́ТЬ I.; похожу́[1], похо́дишь.

ПОХОДИ́ТЬ Р.; похожу́[2], похо́дишь.

ПОХОХОТА́ТЬ Р.; похохочу́, похохо́чешь; похохочи́.

ПОЧА́ТЬ Р.; почну́, почнёшь; почни́; по́чатый and поча́тый.

ПОЧЕСА́ТЬ Р.; почешу́, поче́шешь; почеши́; почёсанный.

ПОЧЕ́СТЬ Р.; почту́[1], почтёшь; почти́; почёл, почла́; почётший; почтённый; почти́.

ПОЧИ́СТИТЬ Р.; почи́щу, почи́стишь; почи́сти and почи́сть; почи́щенный.

ПОЧИ́ТЬ Р.; почи́ю, почи́ешь; почи́й.

ПОЧТИ́ТЬ Р.; почту́[2], почти́шь; почту́т and почтя́т; почти́; почтённый.

ПОЧУ́ЯТЬ Р.; почу́ю, почу́ешь; почу́й; почу́янный.

ПОШИ́ТЬ Р.; пошью́, пошьёшь; поше́й; поши́тый.

ПОШУМЕ́ТЬ Р.; пошумлю́, пошуми́шь; пошуми́.

ПОШУТИ́ТЬ Р.; пошучу́, пошу́тишь.

ПОЩАДИ́ТЬ Р.; пощажу́, пощади́шь; пощажённый.

ПОЩЕКОТА́ТЬ Р.; пощекочу́, пощеко́чешь; пощекочи́.

ПОЩИПА́ТЬ Р.; пощиплю́, пощи́плешь; пощипли́; пощи́панный.

ПОЯВИ́ТЬСЯ Р.; появлю́сь, поя́вишься.

ПРА́ВИТЬ I.; пра́влю, пра́вишь; пра́вь; пра́вленный.

ПРЕВЗОЙТИ́ Р.; превзойду́, превзойдёшь; превзойди́; превзошёл, превзошла́; превзоше́дший; превзойдённый; превзойдя́.

ПРЕВОЗВЫ́СИТЬ Р.; превозвы́шу, превозвы́сишь; превозвы́сь; превозвы́шенный.

ПРЕВОЗМО́ЧЬ Р.; превозмогу́, превозмо́жешь, превозмо́гут; превозмоги́; превозмо́г.

ПРЕВОЗНЕСТИ́ Р.; превознесу́, превознесёшь; превознеси́; превознёс; превознесённый; превознеся́.

ПРЕВОЗНОСИ́ТЬ I.; превозношу́, превозно́сишь.

ПРЕВОСХОДИ́ТЬ I.; превосхожу́, превосхо́дишь.

ПРЕВРАТИ́ТЬ Р.; превращу́, преврати́шь; превращённый.

ПРЕВЫ́СИТЬ Р.; превы́шу, превы́сишь; превы́сь; превы́шенный.

ПРЕГРАДИ́ТЬ Р.; прегражу́, прегради́шь; преграждённый.

ПРЕДАВА́ТЬ I.; предаю́, предаёшь; предава́й; предава́я.

ПРЕДА́ТЬ Р.; преда́м, преда́шь, преда́ст, предади́м, предади́те, предаду́т; преда́й; пре́данный.

ПРЕДВИ́ДЕТЬ I.; предви́жу, предви́дишь; предви́денный.

ПРЕДВКУСИ́ТЬ Р.; предвкушу́, предвку́сишь; предвкушённый.

ПРЕДВОЗВЕСТИ́ТЬ Р.; предвозвещу́, предвозвести́шь; предвозвещённый.

ПРЕДВОСХИ́ТИТЬ Р.; предвосхи́щу (and предвосхищу́), предвосхи́тишь; предвосхи́щенный.

ПРЕДОСТА́ВИТЬ Р.; предоста́влю, предоста́вишь; предоста́вь; предоста́вленный.

ПРЕДОСТЕРЕ́ЧЬ Р.; предостерегу́, предостережёшь, предостерегу́т; предостереги́; предостерёг; предостережённый.

ПРЕДОТВРАТИ́ТЬ Р.; предотвращу́, предотврати́шь; предотвращённый.

ПРЕДПИСА́ТЬ Р.: предпишу́, предпи́шешь; предпиши́; предпи́санный.

ПРЕДПОСЛА́ТЬ Р.; предпошлю́, предпошлёшь; предпошли́; предпо́сланный.

ПРЕДПОЧЕ́СТЬ Р.; предпочту́, предпочтёшь; предпочти́; предпочёл, предпочла́; предпочётший; предпочтённый; предпочти́.

ПРЕДПРИНЯ́ТЬ Р.; предприму́, предпри́мешь; предприми́; предпри́нятый.

ПРЕДРЕ́ЧЬ Р.; предреку́, предречёшь, предреку́т; предреки́;
предрёк; предречённый.
ПРЕДСКАЗА́ТЬ Р.; прдскажу́,
предска́жешь; предскажи́; предска-
занный.
ПРЕДСТАВА́ТЬ I.; предстаю́, предстаёшь; представа́й; представа́я.
ПРЕДСТА́ВИТЬ Р.; предста́влю,
предста́вишь; предста́вь; предста́-
вленный.
ПРЕДСТА́ТЬ Р.; предста́ну, пред-
ста́нешь; предста́нь.
ПРЕДСТОЯ́ТЬ I.; предстою́, пред-
стои́шь; прдстой.
ПРЕДУБЕДИ́ТЬ Р.; предубеди́шь;
предубеждённый (1st pers. not
used).
ПРЕДУВЕ́ДОМИТЬ Р.; предуве́-
домлю, предуве́домишь; предуве́-
домь; предуве́домленный.
ПРЕДУПРЕДИ́ТЬ Р.; предупрежу́,
предупреди́шь; предупреждённый.
ПРЕДУСМОТРЕ́ТЬ Р.; предусмотрю́,
предусмо́тришь; предусмотри́;
предусмо́тренный.
ПРЕД'ЯВИ́ТЬ Р.; пред'явлю́, пред'-
я́вишь; пред'яви́; пред'я́вленный.
ПРЕЗРЕ́ТЬ Р.; презрю́, презри́шь;
презри́; презре́нный and пре́зрен-
ный.
ПРЕКОСЛО́ВИТЬ I.; прекосло́влю,
прекосло́вишь; прекосло́вь.
ПРЕКРАТИ́ТЬ Р.; прекращу́, прекра-
ти́шь; прекращённый.
ПРЕЛОМИ́ТЬ Р.; преломлю́, прело́-
мишь; преломлённый.
ПРЕЛЬСТИ́ТЬ Р.; прельщу́, прель-
сти́шь; прельщённый.
ПРЕНЕБРЕ́ЧЬ Р.; пренебрегу́, пренебрежёшь, пренебрегу́т; прене-
бреги́; пренебрёг; пренебрежённый.
ПРЕОБРАЗИ́ТЬ Р.; преоражу́, пре-
образи́шь; преображённый.
ПРЕПОДАВА́ТЬ I.; преподаю́, преподаёшь; преподава́й; преподава́я.
ПРЕПОДА́ТЬ Р.; препода́м, препо-
да́шь, препода́ст, преподади́м, пре-
подади́те, преподаду́т; препода́й;
препо́данный.
ПРЕПОДНЕСТИ́ Р.; преподнесу́, преподнесёшь; преподнеси́; преподн-
нёс; преподнесённый; преподнеся́.
ПРЕПОДНОСИ́ТЬ I.; преподношу́,
преподно́сишь.

ПРЕПОЯ́САТЬ Р.; препоя́шу, пре-
поя́шешь; препоя́шь; препоя́сан-
ный.
ПРЕПРОВОДИ́ТЬ Р.; препровожу́,
препроводи́шь; препровождённый.
ПРЕРВА́ТЬ Р.; прерву́, прервёшь;
прерви́; пре́рванный.
ПРЕСЕ́ЧЬ Р.; пресеку́, пресечёшь,
пресеку́т; пресеки́; пресе́к; пресечённый.
ПРЕСТА́ВИТЬСЯ Р.; преста́влюсь,
преста́вишься; преста́вься.
ПРЕСТУПИ́ТЬ Р.; преступлю́, пре-
сту́пишь; престу́пленный.
ПРЕСЫ́ТИТЬ Р.; пресы́щу, пресы́-
тишь; пресы́ть; пресы́щенный.
ПРЕТЕРПЕ́ТЬ Р.; претерплю́, пре-
те́рпишь; претерпи́; претерпе́нный
and прете́рпенный.
ПРИБА́ВИТЬ Р.; приба́влю, приба́-
вишь; приба́вь; приба́вленный.
ПРИБЕ́ГНУТЬ Р.; прибе́г (and
прибе́гнул), прибе́гла.
ПРИБЕЖА́ТЬ Р.; прибегу́, прибе-
жи́шь, прибегу́т; прибеги́.
ПРИБЕРЕ́ЧЬ Р.; приберегу́, прибережёшь, приберегу́т; прибереги́;
приберёг; прибережённый.
ПРИБИ́ТЬ Р.; прибью́, прибьёшь;
прибе́й; приби́тый.
ПРИБЛИ́ЗИТЬ Р.; прибли́жу, при-
бли́зишь; прибли́зь; прибли́женный.
ПРИБРА́ТЬ Р.; приберу́, приберёшь;
прибери́; при́бранный.
ПРИБРЕСТИ́ Р.; прибреду́, прибредёшь; прибреди́; прибрёл; при-
бре́дший; прибредя́.
ПРИБЫ́ТЬ Р.; прибу́ду, прибу́дешь;
прибу́дь.
ПРИВА́ДИТЬ Р.; прива́жу, прива́-
дишь; прива́дь; прива́женный.
ПРИВЕЗТИ́ Р.; привезу́, привезёшь;
привези́; привёз; привезённый;
привезя́.
ПРИВЕРТЕ́ТЬ Р.; приверчу́, при-
ве́ртишь; приверти́; приве́рченный.
ПРИВЕ́СИТЬ Р.; приве́шу, приве́-
сишь; приве́сь; приве́шенный.
ПРИВЕСТИ́ Р.; приведу́, приведёшь;
приведи́; привёл; приве́дший;
приведённый; приведя́.
ПРИВИ́ДЕТЬСЯ Р.; приви́жусь,
приви́дишься.
ПРИВИНТИ́ТЬ Р.; привинчу́, при-
винти́шь; приви́нченный.

ПРИВИ́ТЬ Р.; привью́, привьёшь; приве́й; приви́тый (and привито́й).

ПРИВЛЕ́ЧЬ Р.; привлеку́, привлечёшь, привлеку́т; привлеки́; привлёк; привлечённый.

ПРИВНЕСТИ́ Р.; привнесу́, привнесёшь; привнеси́; привнёс; привнесённый; привнеся́.

ПРИВНОСИ́ТЬ I.; привношу́, привно́сишь.

ПРИВОДИ́ТЬ I.; привожу́[2], приво́дишь.

ПРИВОЗИ́ТЬ I.; привожу́[1], приво́зишь.

ПРИВОЛО́ЧЬ Р.; приволоку́, приволочёшь, приволоку́т; приволоки́; приволо́к; приволочённый and приволо́ченный; приволоча́.

ПРИВРА́ТЬ Р.; привру́, привре́шь; приври́; при́вранный.

ПРИВСТАВА́ТЬ I.; привстаю́, привстаёшь; привстава́й; привстава́я.

ПРИВСТА́ТЬ Р.; привста́ну, привста́нешь; привста́нь.

ПРИВЫ́КНУТЬ Р.; привы́к, привы́кла.

ПРИВЯЗА́ТЬ Р.; привяжу́, привя́жешь; привяжи́; привя́занный.

ПРИГВОЗДИ́ТЬ Р.; пригвозжу́, пригвозди́шь; пригвождённый.

ПРИГЛА́ДИТЬ Р.; пригла́жу, пригла́дишь; пригла́дь; пригла́женный.

ПРИГЛАСИ́ТЬ Р.; приглашу́, пригласи́шь; приглашённый.

ПРИГЛЯДЕ́ТЬ Р.; пригляжу́, пригляди́шь; пригляди́.

ПРИГНА́ТЬ Р.; пригоню́, приго́нишь; пригони́; при́гнанный.

ПРИГОДИ́ТЬСЯ Р.; пригожу́сь, пригоди́шься.

ПРИГОЛУ́БИТЬ Р.; приголу́блю, приголу́бишь; приголу́бь; приголу́бленный.

ПРИГОРЕ́ТЬ Р.; пригори́т, пригоря́т; пригори́.

ПРИГОТО́ВИТЬ Р.; пригото́влю, пригото́вишь; пригото́вь; пригото́вленный.

ПРИГРЕСТИ́ Р.; пригребу́, пригребёшь; пригреби́; пригрёб; пригребённый.

ПРИГРОЗИ́ТЬ Р.; пригрожу́, пригрози́шь.

ПРИГУ́БИТЬ Р.; пригу́блю, пригу́бишь; пригу́бь; пригу́бленный.

ПРИДАВА́ТЬ I.; придаю́, придаёшь; придава́й; придава́я.

ПРИДАВИ́ТЬ Р.; придавлю́, прида́вишь; прида́вленный.

ПРИДА́ТЬ Р.; прида́м, прида́шь, прида́ст, придади́м, придади́те; придаду́т; прида́й; при́данный.

ПРИДЕРЖА́ТЬ Р.; придержу́, приде́ржишь; придержи́; приде́ржанный.

ПРИДРА́ТЬСЯ Р.; придеру́сь, придерёшься; придери́сь.

ПРИЕ́СТЬ Р.; прие́м, прие́шь[1], прие́ст, приеди́м, приеди́те, приедя́т; прие́шь[2] (imp.); прие́л, прие́денный.

ПРИЕ́СТЬСЯ Р.; прие́стся, приедя́тся; прие́лся.

ПРИЕ́ХАТЬ Р.; прие́ду, прие́дешь; приезжа́й.

ПРИЖА́ТЬ Р.; прижму́, прижмёшь; прижми́; прижа́тый.

ПРИЖЕ́ЧЬ Р.; прижгу́, прижжёшь, прижгу́т; прижги́; прижёг, прижгла́; прижжённый.

ПРИЖИ́ТЬ Р.; приживу́, приживёшь; приживи́; прижи́тый (also прижито́й) and при́житый.

ПРИЖИ́ТЬСЯ Р.; приживу́сь, приживёшься; приживи́сь.

ПРИЗАНЯ́ТЬ Р.; призайму́, призаймёшь; призайми́; приза́нятый.

ПРИЗВА́ТЬ Р.; призову́, призовёшь; призови́; при́званный.

ПРИЗНАВА́ТЬ I.; признаю́, признаёшь; признава́й; признава́я.

ПРИЗРЕ́ТЬ Р.; призрю́, при́зришь (and призри́шь); призри́; при́зренный.

ПРИИСКА́ТЬ Р.; приищу́, прии́щешь; приищи́; прии́сканный.

ПРИЙТИ́ Р.; приду́, придёшь; приди́; пришёл, пришла́; прише́дший; придя́.

ПРИКАЗА́ТЬ Р.; прикажу́, прика́жешь; прикажи́; прика́занный.

ПРИКАТИ́ТЬ Р.; прикачу́, прика́тишь; прика́ченный.

ПРИКИПЕ́ТЬ Р.; прикипи́т, прикипя́т; прикипи́.

ПРИКОЛОТИ́ТЬ Р.; приколочу́, приколо́тишь; приколо́ченный.

ПРИКОЛО́ТЬ Р.; приколю́, прико́лешь; приколи́; прико́лотый.

ПРИКОПИ́ТЬ Р.; прикоплю́, прико́пишь; прико́пленный.

ПРИКОРМИ́ТЬ Р.; прикормлю́, прико́рмишь; прико́рмленный.

ПРИКРА́СИТЬ Р.; прикра́шу, прикра́сишь; прикра́сь; прикра́шенный.

ПРИКРЕПИ́ТЬ Р.; прикреплю́, прикрепи́шь; прикреплённый.

ПРИКРУТИ́ТЬ Р.; прикручу́, прикру́тишь; прикру́ченный.

ПРИКРЫ́ТЬ Р.; прикро́ю, прикро́ешь; прикро́й; прикры́тый.

ПРИКУПИ́ТЬ Р.; прикуплю́,прику́пишь; прику́пленный.

ПРИКУСИ́ТЬ Р.; прикушу́, прику́сишь; прику́шенный.

ПРИЛА́ДИТЬ Р.; прила́жу, прила́дишь; прила́дь; прила́женный.

ПРИЛЕЖА́ТЬ I.; прилежу́, прилежи́шь; прилежи́.

ПРИЛЕПИ́ТЬ Р.; прилеплю́, приле́пишь; приле́пленный.

ПРИЛЕТЕ́ТЬ Р.; прилечу́, прилети́шь; прилети́.

ПРИЛЕ́ЧЬ Р.; приля́гу, приля́жешь, приля́гут; приля́г; прилёг.

ПРИЛИЗА́ТЬ Р.; прилижу́, прили́жешь; прилижи́; прили́занный.

ПРИЛИ́ПНУТЬ Р.; прили́п, прили́пла.

ПРИЛИ́ТЬ Р.; прилью́, прильёшь; приле́й; прили́тый.

ПРИМА́ЗТЬСЯ Р.; прима́жусь, прима́жешься; прима́жься.

ПРИМЁРЗНУТЬ Р.; примёрз, примёрзла.

ПРИМЕ́ТИТЬ Р.; примечу́, приме́тишь; приме́ть; приме́ченный.

ПРИМО́ЛКНУТЬ Р.; примо́лк, примо́лкла.

ПРИМОСТИ́ТЬ Р.; примощу́, мости́шь; примощённый.

ПРИМЧА́ТЬСЯ Р.; примчу́сь, примчи́шься; примчи́сь.

ПРИМЯ́ТЬ Р.; примну́, примнёшь; примни́; примя́тый.

ПРИНАДЛЕЖА́ТЬ I.; принадлежу́, принадлежи́шь; принадлежи́.

ПРИНАЛЕ́ЧЬ Р.; приналя́гу, приналя́жешь, приналя́гут; приналя́г; приналёг.

ПРИНАРЯДИ́ТЬ Р.; принаряжу́, принаря́дишь (and принаряди́шь); принаря́женный.

ПРИНЕСТИ́ Р.; принесу́, принесёшь; принеси́; принёс; принесённый; принеся́.

ПРИНИ́ЗИТЬ Р.; прини́жу, прини́зишь; прини́зь; прини́женный.

ПРИНИ́КНУТЬ Р.; прини́к, прини́кла.

ПРИНОРОВИ́ТЬ Р.; приноровлю́, принорови́шь; приноро́вленный.

ПРИНОСИ́ТЬ I.; приношу́, прино́сишь.

ПРИНУ́ДИТЬ Р.; прину́жу, прину́дишь; прину́дь; принуждённый.

ПРИНЯ́ТЬ Р.; приму́, при́мешь; прими́; при́нятый.

ПРИОБРЕСТИ́ Р.; приобрету́, приобретёшь; приобрети́; приобрёл; приобре́тший and приобрёвший; приобретённый; приобре́тши and приобретя́.

ПРИОДЕ́ТЬ Р.; приоде́ну, приоде́нешь; приоде́нь; приоде́тый.

ПРИОСТАНОВИ́ТЬ Р.; приостановлю́, приостано́вишь; приостано́вленный.

ПРИОТКРЫ́ТЬ Р.; приоткро́ю, приоткро́ешь; приоткро́й; приоткры́тый.

ПРИОХО́ТИТЬ Р.; приохо́чу, приохо́тишь; приохо́ть; приохо́ченный.

ПРИПАСТИ́ Р.; припасу́, припасёшь; припаси́; припа́с; припасённый.

ПРИПА́СТЬ Р.; припаду́, припадёшь; припади́; припа́л; припа́вший (and arch.: припа́дший).

ПРИПЕРЕ́ТЬ Р.; припру́, припрёшь; припри́; припёр; припёртый; припере́в and припёрши.

ПРИПИСА́ТЬ Р.; припишу́, припи́шешь; припиши́; припи́санный.

ПРИПЛАТИ́ТЬ Р.; приплачу́, припла́тишь; припла́ченный.

ПРИПЛЕСТИ́ Р.; приплету́, приплетёшь; приплети́; приплёл; приплётший; приплетённый; приплетя́.

ПРИПОДНЯ́ТЬ Р.; приподниму́, приподни́мешь (also приподыму́, приподы́мешь); приподними́ (also приподыми́); припо́днятый.

ПРИПОЛЗТИ́ Р.; приползу́, приползёшь; приползи́; припо́лз.

ПРИПРА́ВИТЬ Р.; припра́влю, припра́вишь; припра́вь; припра́вленный.

ПРИПРОСИ́ТЬ Р.; припрошу́, припро́сишь; припро́шенный.

ПРИПРЯ́СТЬ Р.; припряду́, припрядёшь; припряди́; припря́л; припрядённый.

ПРИПРЯ́ТАТЬ Р.; припря́чу, припря́чешь; припря́чь[1] (imp.); припря́танный.

ПРИПРЯ́ЧЬ Р.; припрягу́, припряжёшь, припрягу́т; припряги́; припря́г; припряжённый.

ПРИПУСТИ́ТЬ Р.; припущу́, припу́стишь; припу́щенный.

ПРИПУ́ХНУТЬ Р.; припу́х, припу́хла.

ПРИРАСТИ́ Р.; прирасту́, прирастёшь; прирасти́ (imp.); приро́с.

ПРИРЕ́ЗАТЬ Р.; прире́жу, прире́жешь; прире́жь; прире́занный.

ПРИСЕ́СТЬ Р.; прися́ду, прися́дешь; прися́дь; присе́л.

ПРИСКАКА́ТЬ Р.; прискачу́, приска́чешь; прискачи́.

ПРИСЛА́ТЬ Р.; пришлю́, пришлёшь; пришли́[2] (imp.); при́сланный.

ПРИСМОТРЕ́ТЬ Р.; присмотрю́, присмо́тришь; присмотри́; присмо́тренный.

ПРИСОВОКУПИ́ТЬ Р.; присовокуплю́, присовокупи́шь; присовокуплённый.

ПРИСОСА́ТЬСЯ Р.; присосу́сь, присосёшься; присоси́сь.

ПРИСОСЕ́ДИТЬСЯ Р.; присосе́жусь, присосе́дишься; присосе́дься.

ПРИСО́ХНУТЬ Р.; присо́х, присо́хла.

ПРИСПОСО́БИТЬ Р.; приспосо́блю, приспосо́бишь; приспосо́бь; приспосо́бленный.

ПРИСПУСТИ́ТЬ Р.; приспущу́, приспу́стишь; приспу́щенный.

ПРИСТАВА́ТЬ I.; пристаю́, пристаёшь; пристава́й; пристава́я.

ПРИСТА́ВИТЬ Р.; приста́влю, приста́вишь; приста́вь; приста́вленный.

ПРИСТА́ТЬ Р.; приста́ну, приста́нешь; приста́нь.

ПРИСТРАСТИ́ТЬ Р.; пристращу́, пристрасти́шь; пристращённый.

ПРИСТУПИ́ТЬ Р.; приступлю́, присту́пишь.

ПРИСТЫДИ́ТЬ Р.; пристыжу́, пристыди́шь; пристыжённый.

ПРИСУДИ́ТЬ Р.; присужу́, прису́дишь; присуждённый.

ПРИСЫ́ПАТЬ Р.; присы́плю, присы́плешь; присы́пь; присы́панный.

ПРИТЕРЕ́ТЬ Р.; притру́, притрёшь; притри́; притёр; притёртый; притере́в and притёрши.

ПРИТЕРПЕ́ТЬСЯ Р.; притерплю́сь, притерпишься; притерпи́сь.

ПРИТЕСА́ТЬ Р.; притешу́, прите́шешь; притеши́; притёсанный.

ПРИТЕ́ЧЬ Р.; притечёт, притеку́т; притёк; притёкший and прите́кший.

ПРИТИ́ХНУТЬ Р.; прити́х, прити́хла.

ПРИТОМИ́ТЬ Р.; притомлю́, притоми́шь; притомлённый.

ПРИТОПТА́ТЬ Р.; притопчу́, прито́пчешь; притопчи́; прито́птанный.

ПРИТОРМОЗИ́ТЬ Р.; приторможу́, притормози́шь; приторможённый.

ПРИТУПИ́ТЬ Р.; притуплю́, приту́пишь; приту́пленный and притуплённый.

ПРИТУ́ХНУТЬ Р.; приту́х, приту́хла.

ПРИУГОТО́ВИТЬ Р.; приугото́влю, приугото́вишь; приугото́вь; приугото́вленный.

ПРИУКРА́СИТЬ Р.; приукра́шу, приукра́сишь; приукра́сь; приукра́шенный.

ПРИУМО́ЛКНУТЬ Р.; приумо́лк, приумо́лкла.

ПРИУНЫ́ТЬ Р.; приуно́ю, приуно́ешь; приуно́й.

ПРИУСТА́ТЬ Р.; приуста́ну, приуста́нешь; приуста́нь.

ПРИУТИ́ХНУТЬ Р.; приути́х, приути́хла.

ПРИХВАТИ́ТЬ Р.; прихвачу́, прихва́тишь; прихва́ченный.

ПРИХОДИ́ТЬ I.; прихожу́, прихо́дишь.

ПРИЦЕПИ́ТЬ Р.; прицеплю́, прице́пишь; прице́пленный.

ПРИЧАСТИ́ТЬ Р.; причащу́, прича́стишь; причащённый.

ПРИЧЕСА́ТЬ Р.; причешу́, приче́шешь; причеши́; причёсанный.

ПРИЧЕ́СТЬ Р.; причту́, причтёшь; причти́; причёл, причла́; приче́тший; причтённый; причтя́.

ПРИШИБИ́ТЬ Р.; пришибу́, пришибёшь; пришиби́; пришиб; приши́бленный.

ПРИШИ́ТЬ Р.; пришью́, пришьёшь; прише́й; приши́тый.

ПРИЩЕМИ́ТЬ Р.; прищемлю́, прищеми́шь; прищемлённый.

ПРИЩЕПИ́ТЬ Р.; прищеплю́, прище́пишь; прищеплённый.

ПРИЮТИТЬ Р.; приючу́, приюти́шь.

ПРОБАСИТЬ Р.; пробашу́, проба́сишь.

ПРОБЕЖА́ТЬ Р.; пробегу́, пробежи́шь, пробегу́т; пробеги́.

ПРОБИ́ТЬ Р.; пробью, пробьёшь; пробе́й; проби́тый.

ПРОБОЛЕ́ТЬ[1] Р.; проболе́ю, проболе́ешь; проболе́й.

ПРОБОЛЕ́ТЬ[2] Р.; проболи́т, проболя́т.

ПРОБОРМОТА́ТЬ Р.; пробормочу́, пробормо́чешь; пробормочи́.

ПРОБРА́ТЬ Р.; проберу́, проберёшь; пробери́; про́бранный.

ПРОБРИ́ТЬ Р.; пробре́ю, пробре́ешь; пробре́й; пробри́тый.

ПРОБРОДИ́ТЬ Р.; проброжу́, пробро́дишь.

ПРОБРО́СИТЬ Р.; пробро́шу, пробро́сишь; пробро́сь; пробро́шенный.

ПРОБУДИ́ТЬ Р.; пробужу́, пробу́дишь (and пробуди́шь); пробуждённый.

ПРОБУРА́ВИТЬ Р.; пробура́влю, пробура́вишь; пробура́вь; пробура́вленный.

ПРОБУРЧА́ТЬ Р.; пробурчу́, пробурчи́шь; пробурчи́.

ПРОБЫ́ТЬ Р.; пробу́ду, пробу́дешь; пробу́дь.

ПРОВЕЗТИ́ Р.; провезу́, провезёшь; провези́; провёз; провезённый; провезя́.

ПРОВЕРТЕ́ТЬ Р.; проверчу́, прове́ртишь; проверти́; прове́рченный.

ПРОВЕ́СИТЬ Р.; прове́шу, прове́сишь; прове́сь; прове́шенный.

ПРОВЕСТИ́ Р.; проведу́, проведёшь; проведи́; провёл; прове́дший; проведённый; проведя́.

ПРОВЕ́ЯТЬ Р.; прове́ю, прове́ешь; прове́й; прове́янный.

ПРОВИ́ДЕТЬ I.; прови́жу, прови́дишь; прови́дь.

ПРОВИ́СНУТЬ Р.; прови́с, прови́сла.

ПРОВОДИ́ТЬ I.; провожу́[1], прово́дишь.

ПРОВОДИ́ТЬ Р.; провожу́[2], прово́дишь.

ПРОВОЗВЕСТИ́ТЬ Р.; провозвещу́, провозвести́шь; провозвещённый.

ПРОВОЗГЛАСИ́ТЬ Р.; провозглашу́, провозгласи́шь; провозглашённый.

ПРОВОЗИ́ТЬ I.; провожу́[3], прово́зишь.

ПРОВОЗИ́ТЬ Р.; провожу́[4], прово́зишь.

ПРОВОЛО́ЧЬ Р.; проволоку́, проволочёшь, проволоку́т; проволоки́; проволо́к; проволочённый and проволо́ченный.

ПРОВОРЧА́ТЬ Р.; проворчу́, проворчи́шь; проворчи́.

ПРОВРА́ТЬСЯ Р.; проврусь, проврёшься; проври́сь.

ПРОГЛА́ДИТЬ Р.; прогла́жу, прогла́дишь; прогла́дь; прогла́женный.

ПРОГЛОТИ́ТЬ Р.; проглочу́, прогло́тишь; прогло́ченный.

ПРОГЛЯДЕ́ТЬ Р.; прогляжу́, прогляди́шь; прогляди́.

ПРОГНА́ТЬ Р.; прогоню, прого́нишь; прогони́; про́гнанный.

ПРОГНЕВИ́ТЬ Р.; прогневлю́, прогневи́шь; прогневлённый.

ПРОГНИ́ТЬ Р.; прогниёт, прогнию́т.

ПРОГОРЕ́ТЬ Р.; прогорю́, прогори́шь; прогори́.

ПРОГО́РКНУТЬ Р.; прого́рк, прого́ркла.

ПРОГОСТИ́ТЬ Р.; прогощу́, прогости́шь.

ПРОГРЕМЕ́ТЬ Р.; прогремлю́, прогреми́шь; прогреми́.

ПРОГРЕСТИ́ Р.; прогребу́, прогребёшь; прогреби́; прогрёб; прогребённый.

ПРОГРОХОТА́ТЬ Р.; прогрохочу́[1], прогрохо́чешь; прогрохочи́.

ПРОГРОХОТИ́ТЬ Р.; прогрохочу́[2], про́грохоти́шь.

ПРОГРЫ́ЗТЬ Р.; прогрызу́, прогрызёшь; прогрызи́; прогры́з; прогры́зенный.

ПРОГУДЕ́ТЬ Р.; прогужу́, прогуди́шь; прогуди́.

ПРОДАВА́ТЬ I.; продаю́, продаёшь; продава́й; продава́я.

ПРОДАВИ́ТЬ Р.; продавлю́, прода́вишь; прода́вленный.

ПРОДА́ТЬ Р.; прода́м, прода́шь, прода́ст, продади́м, продади́те, продаду́т; прода́й; про́данный.

ПРОДЕРЖА́ТЬ Р.; продержу́, проде́ржишь; продержи́; прпде́ржанный.

ПРОДЕ́ТЬ Р.; проде́ну, проде́нешь; проде́нь; проде́тый.

ПРОДЕШЕВИ́ТЬ P.; продешевлю́, продешеви́шь; продешевлённый.

ПРОДОЛБИ́ТЬ P.; продолблю́, продолби́шь; продолблённый.

ПРОДРА́ТЬ P.; продеру́, продерёшь; продери́; про́дранный.

ПРОДУ́ТЬ P.; проду́ю, проду́ешь; проду́й; проду́тый.

ПРОДЫРЯ́ВИТЬ P.; продыря́влю, продыря́вишь; продыря́вь; продыря́вленный.

ПРОДЫША́ТЬ P.; продышу́, продышишь; продыши́.

ПРОДЫША́ТЬСЯ P.; продышу́сь, проды́шишься; продыши́сь.

ПРОЕ́ЗДИТЬ P.; прое́зжу, прое́здишь; прое́зди; прое́зженный.

ПРОЕ́СТЬ P.; прое́м, прое́шь², прое́ст, проеди́м, проеди́те, проедя́т; прое́шь¹ (imp.); прое́л; прое́денный.

ПРОЕ́ХАТЬ P.; прое́ду, прое́дешь; проезжа́й.

ПРОЖДА́ТЬ P.; прожду́, прождёшь; прожди́; про́жданный.

ПРОЖЕВА́ТЬ P.; прожую́, прожуёшь; прожуй; прожёванный.

ПРОЖЕ́ЧЬ P.; прожгу́, прожжёшь, прожгу́т; прожги́; прожёг, прожгла́; прожжённый.

ПРОЖИ́ТЬ P.; проживу́, проживёшь; проживи́; про́житый and прожи́тый.

ПРОЖУЖЖА́ТЬ P.; прожужжу́, прожужжи́шь; прожужжи́.

ПРОЗВА́ТЬ P.; прозову́, прозовёшь; прозови́; про́званный.

ПРОЗВЕНЕ́ТЬ P.; прозвени́т, прозвеня́т; прозвени́.

ПРОЗВУЧА́ТЬ P.; прозвучи́т, прозвуча́т; прозвучи́.

ПРОЗРЕ́ТЬ P.; прозрю́, прозри́шь (also прозре́ю, прозре́ешь); прозри́.

ПРОЗЯ́БНУТЬ P.; прозя́б, прозя́бла.

ПРОИЗВЕСТИ́ P.; произведёшь; произведи́; произвёл; произве́дший; произведённый; произведя́.

ПРОИЗВОДИ́ТЬ I.; произвожу́, произво́дишь.

ПРОИЗНЕСТИ́ P.; произнесу́, произнесёшь; произнеси́; произнёс; произнесённый; произнеся́.

ПРОИЗНОСИ́ТЬ I.; произношу́, произно́сишь.

ПРОИЗОЙТИ́ P.; произойдёт, произойду́т; произошёл, произошла́;
происше́дший; произойдя́ and произше́дши.

ПРОИЗРАСТИ́ P.; произрастёт, произрасту́т; произрасти́ (imp.); произро́с.

ПРОИСТЕ́ЧЬ P.; проистечёт, проистеку́т; проистёк, проистекла́.

ПРОИСХОДИ́ТЬ I.; происхожу́, происхо́дишь.

ПРОЙТИ́ P.; пройду́, пройдёшь; пройди́; прошёл, прошла́; проше́дший; про́йденный and пройдённый; пройдя́.

ПРОЙТИ́СЬ P.; пройду́сь, пройдёшься; пройди́сь; прошёлся, прошла́сь; проше́дшийся; пройдя́сь.

ПРОКА́ЗИТЬ I.; прока́жу, прока́зишь; прока́зь.

ПРОКАТИ́ТЬ P.; прокачу́, прока́тишь; прока́ченный.

ПРОКВА́СИТЬ P.; проква́шу, проква́сь; проква́шенный.

ПРОКИПЕ́ТЬ P.; прокипи́т, прокипя́т; прокипи́.

ПРОКИПЯТИ́ТЬ P.; прокипячу́, прокипяти́шь; прокипячённый.

ПРОКИ́СНУТЬ P.; проки́с, проки́сла.

ПРОКЛЯ́СТЬ P.; прокляну́, проклянёшь; прокляни́; про́клял; про́клятый.

ПРОКОЛО́ТЬ P.; проколю́, проко́лешь; проколи́; проко́лотый.

ПРОКОНОПА́ТИТЬ P.; проконопа́чу, проконопа́тишь; проконопа́ть; проконопа́ченный.

ПРОКОПТИ́ТЬ P.; прокопчу́, прокопти́шь; прокопчённый.

ПРОКОРМИ́ТЬ P.; прокормлю́, проко́рмишь; проко́рмленный.

ПРОКОСИ́ТЬ P.; прокошу́, проко́сишь; проко́шенный.

ПРОКРА́СИТЬ P.; прокра́шу, прокра́сишь; прокра́сь; прокра́шенный.

ПРОКРА́СТЬСЯ P.; прокраду́сь, прокрадёшься; прокради́сь; прокра́лся.

ПРОКРИЧА́ТЬ P.; прокричу́, прокричи́шь; прокричи́.

ПРОКУСИ́ТЬ P.; прокушу́, проку́сишь; проку́шенный.

ПРОКУТИ́ТЬ P.; прокучу́, проку́тишь; проку́ченный.

ПРОЛА́ЯТЬ P.; прола́ю, прола́ешь; прола́й.

ПРОЛЕЖА́ТЬ P.; пролежу́, пролежи́шь; пролежи́; пролёжанный.

ПРОЛѢЗТЬ Р.; пролѣзу, пролѣзешь; пролѣз; пролѣз.

ПРОЛЕТѢТЬ Р.; пролечу, пролети́шь; пролети́.

ПРОЛѢЧЬ Р.; проля́жет, проля́гут; пролёг.

ПРОЛИ́ТЬ Р.; пролью, прольёшь; проле́й; про́литый and проли́тый.

ПРОЛОМИ́ТЬ Р.; проломлю, проло́мишь; проло́мленный.

ПРОМА́ЗАТЬ Р.; прома́жу, прома́жешь; прома́жь; прома́занный.

ПРОМЁРЗНУТЬ Р.; промёрз, промёрзла.

ПРОМЕСИ́ТЬ Р.; промешу́, проме́сишь; проме́шенный.

ПРОМЕСТИ́ Р.; промету́, прометёшь; промети́; промёл; промётший; прометённый; прометя́.

ПРОМО́КНУТЬ Р.; промо́к, промо́кла.

ПРОМО́ЛВИТЬ Р.; промо́лвлю, промо́лвишь; промо́лви; промо́лвленный.

ПРОМОЛОТИ́ТЬ Р.; · промолочу́, промоло́тишь; промолоти́; промоло́ченный.

ПРОМОЛО́ТЬ Р.; промелю́, проме́лешь; промели́; промо́лотый.

ПРОМОЛЧА́ТЬ Р.; промолчу́, промолчи́шь; промолчи́.

ПРОМОРО́ЗИТЬ Р.; проморо́жу, проморо́зишь; проморо́зь; проморо́женный.

ПРОМЧА́ТЬСЯ Р.; промчу́сь, промчи́шься; промчи́сь.

ПРОМЫ́ТЬ Р.; промо́ю, промо́ешь; промо́й; промы́тый.

ПРОМЯ́ТЬ Р.; промну́, промнёшь; промни́; промя́тый.

ПРОНЕСТИ́ Р.; пронесу́, пронесёшь; пронеси́; пронёс; пронесённый; пронеся́.

ПРОНЕСТИ́СЬ Р.; пронесу́сь, пронесёшься; пронеси́сь; пронёсся, пронесла́сь (past); пронеси́сь.

ПРОНЗИ́ТЬ Р.; пронжу́, пронзи́шь; пронзённый.

ПРОНИЗА́ТЬ Р.; пронижу́, прони́жешь; пронижи́; прони́занный.

ПРОНИ́КНУТЬ Р.; проник, проникла.

ПРОНОСИ́ТЬ Р.; проношу́[1], проно́сишь; проно́шенный.

ПРОНОСИ́ТЬ I.; проношу́[2], проно́сишь.

ПРОНОСИ́ТЬСЯ I.; проношу́сь, проно́сишься.

ПРОНЯ́ТЬ Р.; пройму́, проймёшь; пройми́; про́нятый.

ПРОПА́СТЬ Р.; пропаду́, пропадёшь; пропади́; пропа́л.

ПРОПАХА́ТЬ Р.; пропашу́, пропа́шешь; пропаши́; пропа́ханный.

ПРОПА́ХНУТЬ Р.; пропа́х, пропа́хла.

ПРОПЕ́ТЬ Р.; пропою, пропоёшь; пропо́й; пропе́тый.

ПРОПЕ́ЧЬ Р.; пропеку́, пропечёшь, пропеку́т; пропеки́; пропёк; пропечённый.

ПРОПИСА́ТЬ Р.; пропишу́, пропи́шешь; пропиши́; пропи́санный.

ПРОПИ́ТЬ Р.; пропью, пропьёшь; пропе́й; про́питый and пропи́тый.

ПРОПИЩА́ТЬ Р.; пропищу́, пропищи́шь; пропищи́.

ПРОПЛА́КАТЬ Р.; пропла́чу, пропла́чешь; пропла́чь.

ПРОПЛЕСТИ́СЬ Р.; проплету́сь, проплетёшься; проплети́сь; проплёлся, проплела́сь.

ПРОПЛЫ́ТЬ Р.; проплыву́, проплывёшь; проплыви́.

ПРОПОЛЗТИ́ Р.; проползу́, проползёшь; проползи́; пропо́лз.

ПРОПОЛОСКА́ТЬ Р.; прополощу́, прополо́щешь; прополощи́; прополо́сканный.

ПРОПОЛО́ТЬ Р.; прополю́, прополешь; прополи́; прополотый.

ПРОПОРО́ТЬ Р.; пропорю́, пропо́решь; пропори́; пропо́ротый.

ПРОПУСТИ́ТЬ Р.; пропущу́, пропу́стишь; пропу́щенный.

ПРОРАСТИ́ Р.; прорастёт, прорасту́т; проро́с.

ПРОРАСТИ́ТЬ Р.; проращу́, прорасти́шь; проращённый.

ПРОРВА́ТЬ Р.; прорву́, прорвёшь; прорви́; про́рванный.

ПРОРЕДИ́ТЬ Р.; прорежу́, прореди́шь; прорежённый.

ПРОРЕ́ЗАТЬ Р.; проре́жу, проре́жешь; проре́жь; проре́занный.

ПРОРУБИ́ТЬ Р.; прорублю́, прору́бишь; прору́бленный.

ПРОРЫ́ТЬ Р.; проро́ю, проро́ешь; проро́й; проры́тый.

ПРОСАДИ́ТЬ Р.; просажу́, проса́дишь; проса́женный.

ПРОСВЕТИ́ТЬ[1] Р.; просвечу́, просве́тишь; просве́ченный.

ПРОСВЕТИТЬ² Р.; просвещу, просветишь; просвещённый.

ПРОСВИСТАТЬ Р.; просвищу¹, просвищешь; просвищи; просвистанный.

ПРОСВИСТЕТЬ Р.; просвищу², просвистишь; просвисти.

ПРОСЕЧЬ Р.; просеку, просечёшь, просекут; просеки; просек; просечённый.

ПРОСЕЯТЬ Р.; просею, просеешь; просей; просеянный.

ПРОСИДЕТЬ Р.; просижу, просидишь; просиди; просиженный.

ПРОСИТЬ I.; прошу, просишь; прошенный.

ПРОСКАКАТЬ Р.; проскачу, проскачешь; проскачи.

ПРОСКРЕСТИ Р.; проскребу, проскребёшь; проскреби; проскрёб; проскребённый.

ПРОСКРИПЕТЬ Р.; проскриплю, проскрипишь; проскрипи.

ПРОСЛАВИТЬ Р.; прославлю, прославишь; прославь; прославленный.

ПРОСЛЕДИТЬ Р.; прослежу, проследишь; прослеженный.

ПРОСЛЕЗИТЬСЯ Р.; прослежусь, прослезишься.

ПРОСЛЫТЬ Р.; прослыву, прослывёшь; прослыви.

ПРОСЛЫШАТЬ Р.; прослышу, прослышишь; прослышь.

ПРОСМОТРЕТЬ Р.; просмотрю, просмотришь; просмотри; просмотренный.

ПРОСОСАТЬ Р.; прососу, прососёшь; прососи; прососанный.

ПРОСОХНУТЬ Р.; просох, просохла.

ПРОСПАТЬ Р.; просплю, проспишь; проспи.

ПРОСТАВИТЬ Р.; проставлю, проставишь; проставь; проставленный

ПРОСТЕРЕТЬ Р.; простру, прострёшь; простри; простёр; простёртый; простерев and простёрши.

ПРОСТИТЬ Р.; прощу, простишь; прости, простите (imp.); прощённый.

ПРОСТОНАТЬ Р.; простону (and простонаю), простонешь; простони.

ПРОСТОЯТЬ Р.; простою, простоишь; простой.

ПРОСТРИЧЬ Р.; простригу, прострижёшь; простригут; простриги; простриг; простриженный.

ПРОСТУДИТЬ Р.; простужу, простудишь; простуженный.

ПРОСТЫНУТЬ Р.; простыну, простынешь; простынь.

ПРОСТЫТЬ Р.; простыну, простынешь; простынь.

ПРОСЫПАТЬ Р.; просыплю, просыплешь; просыпь; просыпанный.

ПРОТЕРЕТЬ Р.; протру, протрёшь; протри; протёр; протёртый; протерев and протёрши.

ПРОТЕРПЕТЬ Р.; протерплю, протерпишь; протерпи.

ПРОТЕСАТЬ Р.; протешу, протешешь; протеши; протёсанный.

ПРОТЕЧЬ Р.; протечёт, протекут; протеки; протёк.

ПРОТИВИТЬСЯ Р.; противлюсь, противишься; противься.

ПРОТИВОПОСТАВИТЬ Р.; противопоставлю, противопоставишь; противопоставленный.

ПРОТИВОСТОЯТЬ I.; противостою, противостоишь; противостой.

ПРОТКАТЬ Р.; протку, проткёшь; протки; протканный.

ПРОТОПИТЬ Р.; протоплю, протопишь; протопленный.

ПРОТОПТАТЬ Р.; протопчу, протопчешь; протопчи; протоптанный.

ПРОТРАВИТЬ Р.; протравлю, протравишь; протравленный.

ПРОТРЕЗВИТЬ Р.; протрезвлю, протрезвишь; протрезвлённый.

ПРОТРЕЩАТЬ Р.; протрещу, протрещишь; протрещи.

ПРОТРУБИТЬ Р.; протрублю, протрубишь.

ПРОТРУСИТЬ Р.; протрушу, протрусишь.

ПРОТУХНУТЬ Р.; протух, протухла.

ПРОХВАТИТЬ Р.; прохвачу, прохватишь; прохваченный.

ПРОХЛАДИТЬСЯ Р.; прохлажусь, прохладишься.

ПРОХОДИТЬ I.; прохожу¹, проходишь.

ПРОХОДИТЬ Р.; прохожу², проходишь.

ПРОХРИПЕТЬ Р.; прохриплю, прохрипишь; прохрипи.

ПРОЦВЕСТИ Р.; процвету, процветёшь; процвети; процвёл; процветший.

ПРОЦЕДИТЬ Р.; процежу, процедишь; процеженный.

ПРОЧЕРТИТЬ Р.; прочерчу́, проче́р-
тишь; проче́рченный.
ПРОЧЕСАТЬ Р.; прочешу́, прочёшешь; прочё́санный.
ПРОЧЕСТЬ Р.; прочту́, прочтёшь;
прочти́; прочёл, прочла́; прочётший;
прочтённый; прочта́.
ПРОЧИСТИТЬ Р.; прочи́щу, прочи́-
стишь; прочи́сти and прочи́сть
(imp.); прочи́щенный.
ПРОШЕПТАТЬ Р.; прошепчу́, про-
ше́пчешь; прочепчи́; прошёптанный.
ПРОШИБИТЬ Р.; прошибу́, прошиб-
бёшь; прошиб; прошиблённый.
ПРОШИПЕТЬ Р.; прошиплю́, про-
шипи́шь; прошипи́.
ПРОШИТЬ Р.; прошью́, прошьёшь;
проше́й; проши́тый.
ПРОШЛЯ́ПИТЬ Р.; прошля́плю, про-
шля́пишь; прошля́пь.
ПРОШТРАФИТЬСЯ Р.; проштра́-
флюсь, проштра́фишься; про-
штра́фься.

ПРОШУМЕТЬ Р.; прошумлю́, прошу-
ми́шь; прошуми́.
ПРОЯВИТЬ Р.; проявлю́, проя́вишь;
проя́вленный.
ПРУДИТЬ I.; пружу́, пру́дишь (and
пруди́шь).
ПРЯСТЬ I.; пряду́, прядёшь; пряди́;
прял; пря́денный.
ПРЯ́ТАТЬ I.; пря́чу, пря́чешь;
прячь.
ПУСТИТЬ Р.; пущу́, пу́стишь; пу́-
щенный.
ПУСТОСЛО́ВИТЬ I.; пустосло́влю,
пустосло́вишь; пустосло́вь.
ПУ́ХНУТЬ Р.; пух (and пу́хнул),
пу́хла.
ПЫ́ХАТЬ I.; пы́ху, пы́шешь (also
пы́хаю, пы́хаешь); пышь; пы́шу-
щий (pres. a.p.).
ПЫХТЕ́ТЬ I.; пыхчу́, пыхти́шь;
пыхти́.
ПЯ́ТИТЬ I.; пя́чу, пя́тишь; пять.
ПЯ́ТИТЬСЯ I.; пя́чусь, пя́тишься;
пя́ться.

Р

РАЗБА́ВИТЬ Р.; разба́влю, разба́-
вишь; разба́вь; разба́вленный.
РАЗБЕЖА́ТЬСЯ Р.; разбегу́сь, раз-
бежи́шься, разбегу́тся; разбеги́сь.
РАЗБЕРЕДИ́ТЬ Р.; разбережу́, раз-
береди́шь; разбережённый.
РАЗБИ́ТЬ Р.; разобью́, разобьёшь;
разбе́й; разби́тый.
РАЗБОЛЕ́ТЬСЯ[1] Р.; разболо́юсь, раз-
боле́ешься; разболе́йся.
РАЗБОЛЕ́ТЬСЯ[2] Р.; разболи́тся, раз-
боля́тся.
РАЗБОМБИ́ТЬ Р.; разбомблю́, раз-
бомби́шь; разбомблённый.
РАЗБРЕСТИ́СЬ Р.; разбредётся, разбредёмся, разбредётесь, разбреду́тся
(1st and 2nd pers. sing. not used);
разбреди́тесь; разбрёлся, разбре-
ла́сь; разбре́дшийся; разбредя́сь.
РАЗБРО́СИТЬ Р.; разбро́шу, разбро́-
сишь; разбро́сь; разбро́шенный.
РАЗБРЫ́ЗГАТЬ Р.; разбры́зжу, раз-
бры́зжешь (also разбры́згаю, раз-
бры́згаешь); разбры́зжи; разбры́-
зганный.

РАЗБРЮЖА́ТЬСЯ Р.; разбрюзжу́сь,
разбрюзжи́шься; разбрюзжи́сь.
РАЗБУДИ́ТЬ Р.; разбужу́, разбу́дишь;
разбу́женный.
РАЗБУ́ХПУТЬ Р.; разбу́х, разбу́хла.
РАЗВЕЗТИ́ Р.; развезу́, развезёшь;
развези́; развёз; развезённый; раз-
везя́.
РАЗВЕРЕДИ́ТЬ Р.; развережу́, раз-
вереди́шь; развережённый.
РАЗВЕ́РЗНУТЬ Р.; разве́рз (and
разве́рзнул), разве́рзла; разве́рстый
(ppp).
РАЗВЕРТЕ́ТЬ Р.; разверчу́, разве́р-
тишь; разверти́; разве́рченный.
РАЗВЕ́СИТЬ Р.; разве́шу, разве́сишь;
разве́сь; разве́шенный.
РАЗВЕСТИ́ Р.; разведу́, разведёшь;
разведи́; развёл; разве́дший; разведённый; разведя́.
РАЗВЕТВИ́ТЬ Р.; разветвлю́, развет-
ви́шь; разветвлённый.
РАЗВЕ́ЯТЬ Р.; разве́ю, разве́ешь;
разве́й[1]; разве́янный.
РАЗВИНТИ́ТЬ Р.; развинчу́, развин-
ти́шь; разви́нченный.

РАЗВИ́ТЬ Р.; разовью́, разовьёшь; разве́й[2]; разви́тый (and развито́й).

РАЗВЛЕ́ЧЬ Р.; развлеку́, развлечёшь, развлеку́т; развлеки́; развлёк; развлечённый.

РАЗВОДИ́ТЬ I.; развожу́[1], разво́дишь.

РАЗВОЗИ́ТЬ I.; развожу́[2], разво́зишь.

РАЗВОРОТИ́ТЬ Р.; разворочу́, разворо́тишь; разворо́ченный.

РАЗВОРЧА́ТЬСЯ Р.; разворчу́сь, разворчи́шься; разворчи́сь.

РАЗВРАТИ́ТЬ Р.; развращу́, разврати́шь; развращённый.

РАЗВЯЗА́ТЬ Р.; развяжу́, развя́жешь; развяжи́; развя́занный.

РАЗГЛА́ДИТЬ Р.; разгла́жу, разгла́дишь; разгла́дь; разгла́женный.

РАЗГЛАСИ́ТЬ Р.; разглашу́, разгласи́шь; разглашённый.

РАЗГЛЯДЕ́ТЬ Р.; разгляжу́, разгляди́шь; разгляди́.

РАЗГОРЕ́ТЬСЯ Р.; разгорю́сь, разгори́шься; разгори́сь.

РАЗГОРОДИ́ТЬ Р.; разгорожу́, разгоро́дишь (and разгороди́шь); разгоро́женный.

РАЗГРА́БИТЬ Р.; разгра́блю, разгра́бишь; разгра́бь; разгра́бленный.

РАЗГРАФИ́ТЬ Р.; разграфлю́, разграфи́шь; разграфлённый.

РАЗГРЕСТИ́ Р.; разгребу́, разгребёшь; разгреби́; разгрёб; разгребённый.

РАЗГРОМИ́ТЬ Р.; разгромлю́, разгроми́шь; разгро́мленный and разгромлённый.

РАЗГРУЗИ́ТЬ Р.; разгружу́, разгру́зишь (and разгрузи́шь); разгру́женный and разгружённый.

РАЗГРЫ́ЗТЬ Р.; разгрызу́, разгрызёшь; разгрызи́; разгры́з; разгры́зенный.

РАЗДАВА́ТЬ I.; раздаю́, раздаёшь; раздава́й; раздава́я.

РАЗДАВИ́ТЬ Р.; раздавлю́, разда́вишь; разда́вленный.

РАЗДА́ТЬ Р.; разда́м, разда́шь, разда́ст, раздади́м, раздади́те, раздаду́т; разда́й; past forms: ро́здал (and разда́л), раздала́, ро́здало (and разда́ло), ро́здали (and разда́ли); ppp: ро́зданный, ро́здан, раздана́, ро́здано, ро́зданы.

РАЗДЕ́ТЬ Р.; разде́ну, разде́нешь; разде́нь; разде́тый.

РАЗДОБЫ́ТЬ Р.; раздобу́ду, раздобу́дешь; раздобу́дь; раздобы́тый.

РАЗДОЛБИ́ТЬ Р.; раздолблю́, раздолби́шь; раздолблённый.

РАЗДРОБИ́ТЬ Р.; раздроблю́, раздроби́шь; раздро́бленный and раздроблённый.

РАЗДУ́ТЬ Р.; разду́ю, разду́ешь; разду́й; разду́тый.

РАЗЖА́ЛОБИТЬ Р.; разжа́лоблю, разжа́лобишь; разжа́лобь; разжа́лобленный.

РАЗЖА́ТЬ Р.; разожму́, разожмёшь; разожми́; разжа́тый.

РАЗЖЕВА́ТЬ Р.; разжую́, разжуёшь; разжуй; разжёванный.

РАЗЖЕ́ЧЬ Р.; разожгу́, разожжёшь; разожгу́т; разожги́; разжёг, разожгла́; разожжённый.

РАЗЖИДИ́ТЬ Р.; разжижу́, разжиди́шь; разжижённый.

РАЗЖИ́ТЬСЯ Р.; разживу́сь, разживёшься; разживи́сь.

РАЗЗНАКО́МИТЬ Р.; раззнако́млю, раззнако́мишь; раззнако́мь; раззнако́мленный.

РАЗЗУДЕ́ТЬСЯ Р.; раззуди́тся, раззудя́тся; раззуди́сь.

РАЗЗУДИ́ТЬ Р.; раззужу́, раззуди́шь; раззу́женный.

РАЗИ́ТЬ I.; ражу́, рази́шь.

РАЗЛА́ДИТЬ Р.; разла́жу, разла́дишь; разла́дь; разла́женный.

РАЗЛА́КОМИТЬ Р.; разла́комлю, разла́комишь; разла́комь; разла́комленный.

РАЗЛЕЖА́ТЬСЯ Р.; разлежу́сь, разлежи́шься; разлежи́сь.

РАЗЛЕ́ЗТЬСЯ Р.; разле́зется, разле́зутся; разле́зься; разле́зся.

РАЗЛЕПИ́ТЬ Р.; разлеплю́, разле́пишь; разле́пленный.

РАЗЛЕТЕ́ТЬСЯ Р.; разлечу́сь, разлети́шься; разлети́сь.

РАЗЛЕ́ЧЬСЯ Р.; разля́гусь, разля́жешься, разля́гутся; разля́гся (imp.); разлёгся, разлегла́сь.

РАЗЛИ́ТЬ Р.; разолью́, разольёшь; разле́й; разли́тый.

РАЗЛОМИ́ТЬ Р.; разломлю́, разло́мишь; разло́мленный.

РАЗЛЮБИ́ТЬ Р.; разлюблю́, разлю́бишь; разлю́бленный.

РАЗМА́ЗАТЬ Р.; разма́жу, разма́жешь; разма́жь; разма́занный.

РАЗМАХА́ТЬСЯ Р.; размашу́сь, размашешься (and размаха́юсь, размаха́ешься); размашись.
РАЗМА́ЯТЬ Р.; размаю, размаешь; размай; размаянный.
РАЗМЕСИ́ТЬ Р.; размешу́, разме́сишь; разме́шенный.
РАЗМЕСТИ́ Р.; размету́, разметёшь; размети́; размёл; размётший; разметённый; разметя́.
РАЗМЕСТИ́ТЬ Р.; размещу́, размести́шь; размещённый.
РАЗМЕТА́ТЬ Р.; размечу́, разме́чешь; размечи́; размётанный.
РАЗМЕ́ТИТЬ Р.; разме́чу, разме́тишь; разме́ть; разме́ченный.
РАЗМО́КНУТЬ Р.; размо́к, размо́кла.
РАЗМОЛО́ТЬ Р.; размелю́, разме́лешь; размели́; размо́лотый.
РАЗМЫ́ТЬ Р.; размо́ю, размо́ешь; размо́й; размы́тый.
РАЗМЯ́КНУТЬ Р.; размя́к, размя́кла.
РАЗМЯ́ТЬ Р.; разомну́, разомнёшь; разомни́; размя́тый.
РАЗНЕМО́ЧЬСЯ Р.; разнемогу́сь, разнемо́жешься; разнемо́гутся; разнемоги́сь; разнемо́гся, разнемогла́сь.
РАЗНЕСТИ́ Р.; разнесу́, разнесёшь; разнеси́; разнёс; разнесённый; разнеся́.
РАЗНООБРА́ЗИТЬ I.; разнообра́жу, разнообра́зишь; разнообра́зь.
РАЗНОСИ́ТЬ I.; разношу́[1], разно́сишь
РАЗНОСИ́ТЬ Р.; разношу́[2], разно́сишь; разно́шенный.
РАЗНЯ́ТЬ Р.; разниму́, разни́мешь; разними́; past forms: разня́л (and ро́знял) разняла́, разня́ло (and ро́зняло), разня́ли (and ро́зняли); ppp: разня́тый, разня́т (and arch. ро́знят) разнята́, разня́то (and arch. ро́знято), разня́ты (and arch. ро́зняты).
РАЗОБИ́ДЕТЬ Р.; разоби́жу, разоби́дешь; разоби́дь; разоби́женный.
РАЗОБРА́ТЬ Р.; разберу́, разберёшь; разбери́; разо́бранный.
РАЗОГНА́ТЬ Р.; разгоню́, разго́нишь; разгони́; разо́гнанный.
РАЗОДЕ́ТЬ Р.; разоде́ну, разоде́нешь; разоде́нь; разоде́тый.
РАЗОДРА́ТЬ Р.; раздеру́, раздерёшь; раздери́; разо́дранный.
РАЗОЙТИ́СЬ Р.; разойду́сь, разой-

дёшься; разойди́сь; разошёлся, разошла́сь; разоше́дшийся; разойди́сь (and arch. разоше́дшись).
РАЗОРВА́ТЬ Р.; разорву́, разорвёшь; разорви́; разо́рванный.
РАЗОСЛА́ТЬ Р.; разошлю́, разошлёшь; разошли́; разо́сланный.
РАЗОСПА́ТЬСЯ Р.; разосплю́сь, разоспи́шься; разоспи́сь.
РАЗОСТЛА́ТЬ Р.; расстелю́, расстелешь; расстели́; разо́стланный.
РАЗОТКА́ТЬ Р.; разотку́, разоткёшь; разотки́; разо́тканный.
РАЗОХО́ТИТЬ Р.; разохо́чу, разохо́тишь; разохо́ть; разохо́ченный.
РАЗРАЗИ́ТЬСЯ Р.; разражу́сь, разрази́шься.
РАЗРАСТИ́СЬ Р.; разрастётся, разрасту́тся; разрасти́сь (imp.); разро́сся, разросла́сь.
РАЗРЕВЕ́ТЬСЯ Р.; разреву́сь, разревёшься; разреви́сь.
РАЗРЕДИ́ТЬ Р.; разрежу́, разреди́шь; разрежённый.
РАЗРЕ́ЗАТЬ Р.; разре́жу, разре́жешь; разре́жь; разре́занный.
РАЗРОДИ́ТЬСЯ Р.; разрожу́сь, разроди́шься.
РАЗРУБИ́ТЬ Р.; разрублю́, разру́бишь; разру́бленный.
РАЗРЫ́ТЬ Р.; разро́ю, разро́ешь; разро́й; разры́тый.
РАЗРЯДИ́ТЬ Р.; разряжу́, разря́дишь (and разряди́шь); разря́женный, разряжённый.
РАЗУБЕДИ́ТЬ Р.; разубежу́, разубеди́шь; разубеждённый.
РАЗУКРА́СИТЬ Р.; разукра́шу, разукра́сишь; разукра́сь; разукра́шенный.
РАЗУ́ТЬ Р.; разу́ю, разу́ешь; разу́й; разу́тый.
РАЗ’Е́ЗДИТЬ Р.; разъе́зжу, разъе́здишь; разъе́зди; разъе́зженный.
РАЗ’Е́ЗДИТЬСЯ Р.; разъе́зжусь, разъе́здишься; разъе́здись.
РАЗ’Е́СТЬ Р.; разъе́ст, разъедя́т; разъе́л; разъе́денный.
РАЗ’Е́СТЬСЯ Р.; разъе́мся, разъе́шься[1], разъе́стся, разъеди́мся, разъеди́тесь, разъедя́тся; разъе́шься[2] (imp.); разъе́лся.
РАЗ’Е́ХАТЬСЯ Р.; разъе́дусь, разъе́дешься; разъезжа́йся.
РАЗ’Я́ТЬ Р.; разыму́, разы́мешь;

разыми́; раз'я́л; разя́тый (Note: past and infinitive are archaic).

РАЗЫСКА́ТЬ Р.; разыщу́, разы́щешь; разыщи́; разы́сканный.

РАСКАТИ́ТЬ Р.; разкачу́, раска́тишь; раска́ченный.

РАСКВА́СИТЬ Р.; расква́шу, расква́сишь; расква́сь; расква́шенный.

РАСКИ́СНУТЬ Р.; раски́с, раски́сла.

РАСКОЛОТИ́ТЬ Р.; расколочу́, расколо́тишь; расколо́ченный.

РАСКОЛО́ТЬ Р.; расколю́, раско́лешь; расколи́; раско́лотый.

РАСКОРМИ́ТЬ Р.; раскормлю́, раско́рмишь; раско́рмленный.

РАСКОСИ́ТЬ Р.; раскошу́, раскоси́шь; раскошённый and раско́шенный.

РАСКРА́СИТЬ Р.; раскра́шу, раскра́сишь; раскра́сь; раскра́шенный.

РАСКРА́СТЬ Р.; раскраду́, раскрадёшь; раскради́; раскра́л; раскра́денный.

РАСКРЕПИ́ТЬ Р.; раскреплю́, раскрепи́шь; раскреплённый.

РАСКРЕПОСТИ́ТЬ Р.; раскрепощу́, раскрепости́шь; раскрепощённый.

РАСКРИЧА́ТЬСЯ Р.; раскричу́сь, раскричи́шься; раскричи́сь.

РАСКРО́ЙТЬ Р.; раскро́ю, раскро́йшь; раскро́й; раскро́енный.

РАСКРУТИ́ТЬ Р.; раскручу́, раскру́тишь; раскру́ченный.

РАСКРЫ́ТЬ Р.; раскро́ю, раскро́ешь; раскро́й; раскры́тый.

РАСКУСИ́ТЬ Р.; раскушу́, раску́сишь; раску́шенный.

РАСКУТИ́ТЬСЯ Р.; раскучу́сь, раску́тишься.

РАСПА́СТЬСЯ Р.; распадётся, распаду́тся; распади́сь; распа́лся.

РАСПАХА́ТЬ Р.; распашу́, распа́шешь; распаши́; распа́ханный.

РАСПЕРЕ́ТЬ Р.; разопру́, разопрёшь; разопри́; рапёр; распёртый.

РАСПЕ́ТЬ Р.; распою́, распоёшь; распо́й; распе́тый.

РАСПЕ́ЧЬ Р.; распеку́, распечёшь, распеку́т; распеки́; распёк; распечённый

РАСПИСА́ТЬ Р.; распишу́, распи́шешь; распиши́; распи́санный.

РАСПИ́ТЬ Р.; разопью́, разопьёшь; распе́й; past forms: распи́л (and ро́спил), распила́, распи́ло (and ро́спило), распи́ли (and ро́спили); ppp: распи́тый; распи́т (and ро́спит)

распита́, распи́то (and ро́спито), распи́ты (and ро́спиты).

РАСПЛА́ВИТЬ Р.; распла́влю, распла́вишь; распла́вь; распла́вленный.

РАСПЛАТИ́ТЬСЯ Р.; расплачу́сь, распла́тишься.

РАСПЛЕСКА́ТЬ Р.; расплещу́, распле́щешь; расплещи́; расплёсканный.

РАСПЛЕСТИ́ Р.; расплету́, расплетёшь; расплети́; расплёл; расплётший; расплетённый; расплетя́.

РАСПЛОДИ́ТЬ Р.; распложу́, распложу́, расплоди́шь; распложённый.

РАСПЛЫ́ТЬСЯ Р.; расплыву́сь, расплывёшься; расплыви́сь.

РАСПОЛЗТИ́СЬ Р.; расползу́сь, расползёшься; расползи́сь; распо́лзся, располза́сь.

РАСПОРО́ТЬ Р.; распорю́, распо́решь; распори́; распо́ротый.

РАСПОРЯДИ́ТЬСЯ Р.; распоряжу́сь, распоряди́шься; распоряди́сь.

РАСПОЯ́САТЬ Р.; распоя́шу, распоя́шешь; распоя́шь; распоя́санный.

РАСПРА́ВИТЬ Р.; распра́влю, распра́вишь; распра́вь; распра́вленный.

РАСПРА́ВИТЬСЯ Р.; распра́влюсь, распра́вишься; распра́вься.

РАСПРОДАВА́ТЬ I.; распродаю́, распродаёшь; распродава́й; распродава́я.

РАСПРОДА́ТЬ Р.; распрода́м, распрода́шь, распрода́ст, распродади́м, распродади́те, распродаду́т; распрода́й; распро́данный.

РАСПРОСТЕРЕ́ТЬ Р.; распростру́, распрострёшь (future seldom used); распростри́; распростёр; распростёртый; распростерёв and распростёрши.

РАСПРОСТИ́ТЬСЯ Р.; распрощу́сь, распрости́шься.

РАСПРЯМИ́ТЬ Р.; распрямлю́, распрями́шь; распрямлённый.

РАСПРЯ́ЧЬ Р.; распрягу́, распряжёшь, распрягу́т; распряги́, распря́г; распряжённый.

РАСПУСТИ́ТЬ Р.; распущу́, распу́стишь; распу́щенный.

РАСПУ́ХНУТЬ Р.; распу́х, распу́хла.

РАСПЯ́ТЬ Р.; распну́, распнёшь; распни́; распя́тый.

РАССАДИ́ТЬ Р.; рассажу́, расса́дишь; расса́женный.

РАССВЕСТИ́ Р.; рассветёт; рассвело́ (3rd pers. sing., impers.).

РАССЕКРЕ́ТИТЬ Р.; рассекре́чу, рассекре́тишь; рассекре́ть; рассекре́ченный.

РАССЕРДИ́ТЬ Р.; рассержу́, рассе́рдишь; рассе́рженный.

РАССЕ́СТЬСЯ Р.; расса́дусь, расса́дешься; расса́дься; рассе́лся.

РАССЕ́ЧЬ Р.; рассеку́, рассечёшь, рассеку́т; рассеки́; рассе́к; рассечённый (arch.: рассе́ченный).

РАССЕ́ЯТЬ Р.; рассе́ю, рассе́ешь; рассе́й; рассе́янный.

РАССИДЕ́ТЬСЯ Р.; рассижу́сь, рассиди́шься; рассиди́сь.

РАССКАЗА́ТЬ Р.; расскажу́, расска́жешь; расскажи́; расска́занный.

РАССКАКА́ТЬСЯ Р.; расскачу́сь, расска́чешься; расскачи́сь.

РАССЛА́БИТЬ Р.; рассла́блю, рассла́бишь; рассла́бь; рассла́бленный.

РАССЛА́БНУТЬ Р.; рассла́б, рассла́бла.

РАССЛА́ВИТЬ Р.; рассла́влю, рассла́вишь; рассла́вь; рассла́вленный.

РАССЛЫ́ШАТЬ Р.; расслы́шу, расслы́шишь; расслы́шь; расслы́шанный.

РАССМЕЯ́ТЬСЯ Р.; рассмею́сь, рассмеёшься; рассме́йся.

РАССМОТРЕ́ТЬ Р.; рассмотрю́, рассмо́тришь; рассмотри́; рассмо́тренный.

РАССОСА́ТЬ Р.; рассосу́, рассосёшь; рассоси́; рассо́санный.

РАССО́ХНУТЬСЯ Р.; рассо́хся, рассо́хлась.

РАССПРОСИ́ТЬ Р.; расспрошу́, расспро́сишь; расспро́шенный.

РАССТАВА́ТЬСЯ I.; расстаю́сь, расстаёшься; расставайся; расстава́ясь.

РАССТА́ВИТЬ Р.; расста́влю, расста́вишь; расста́вь; расста́вленный.

РАССТА́ТЬСЯ Р.; расста́нусь, расста́нешься; расста́нься.

РАССТЕЛИ́ТЬ Р.; расстелю́, рассте́лешь; расстели́; рассте́ленный.

РАССТРИ́ЧЬ Р.; расстригу́, расстрижёшь, расстригу́т; расстриги́; расстри́г; расстри́женный.

РАССТУПИ́ТЬСЯ Р.; расступлю́сь, расступишься.

РАССУДИ́ТЬ Р.; рассужу́, рассу́дишь; рассу́женный.

РАССЫ́ПАТЬ Р.; рассы́плю, рассы́плешь; рассы́пь; рассы́панный.

РАСТА́ЯТЬ Р.; раста́ю, раста́ешь; раста́й.

РАСТЕРЕБИ́ТЬ Р.; растереблю́, растереби́шь; растереблённый.

РАСТЕРЕ́ТЬ Р.; разотру́, разотрёшь; разотри́; растёр, растёртый; растере́в and растёрши.

РАСТЕ́ЧЬСЯ Р.; растечётся, растеку́тся; растёкся.

РАСТИ́ I.; расту́, растёшь; расти́[1] (imp.); рос.

РАСТИ́ТЬ I.; ращу́, расти́шь; расти́[2] (imp.); ращённый.

РАСТОЛО́ЧЬ Р.; растолку́, растолчёшь, растолку́т; растолки́; растоло́к, растолкла́; растолчённый.

РАСТОПИ́ТЬ Р.; растоплю́, расто́пишь; расто́пленный.

РАСТОПТА́ТЬ Р.; растопчу́, расто́пчешь; растопчи́; расто́птанный.

РАСТО́РГНУТЬ Р.; расто́рг (and расто́ргнул), расто́ргла; расто́ргнутый and расто́рженный.

РАСТРА́ВИТЬ Р.; растравлю́, растра́вишь; растра́вленный.

РАСТРА́ТИТЬ Р.; растра́чу, растра́тишь; растра́ть; растра́ченный.

РАСТРЕПА́ТЬ Р.; растреплю́, растре́плешь; растрепли́; растрёпанный.

РАСТРУБИ́ТЬ Р.; раструблю́, раструби́шь.

РАСТРУСИ́ТЬ Р.; раструшу́, раструси́шь; раструшенный.

РАСТРЯСТИ́ Р.; растрясу́, растрясёшь; растряси́; растря́с; растрясённый.

РАСХА́ЯТЬ Р.; расха́ю, расха́ешь; расха́й; расха́янный.

РАСХИ́ТИТЬ Р.; расхи́щу, расхи́тишь; расхи́ть; расхи́щенный.

РАСХЛЕСТА́ТЬ Р.; расхлещу́, расхле́щешь; расхлещи́; расхлёстанный.

РАСХЛОПОТА́ТЬСЯ Р.; расхлопочу́сь, расхлопо́чешься; расхлопочи́сь.

РАСХОДИ́ТЬСЯ I.; расхожу́сь[1], расхо́дишься.

РАСХОДИ́ТЬСЯ Р.; расхожу́сь[2], расхо́дишься.

РАСХОЛОДИ́ТЬ Р.; расхоложу́, расхолоди́шь; расхоложённый.

РАСХОТЕ́ТЬ Р.; расхочу́, расхо́чешь, расхо́чет, расхоти́м, расхоти́те, расхотя́т; расхоти́.

РАСЦВЕСТИ́ Р.; расцвету́, расцветёшь; расцвети́; расцвёл; расцве́тший.

РАСЦВЕТИ́ТЬ Р.; расцвечу́, расцвети́шь; расцве́ченный.

РАСЦЕПИ́ТЬ Р.; расцеплю́, расце́пишь; расце́пленный.

РАСЧЕРТИ́ТЬ Р.; расчерчу́, расче́ртишь; расче́рченный.

РАСЧЕСА́ТЬ Р.; расчешу́, расче́шешь; расчеши́; расчёсанный.

РАСЧЕ́СТЬ Р.; разочту́, разочтёшь; разочти́; расчёл, разочла́; расчётший; разочтённый; разочтя́.

РАСЧИ́СТИТЬ Р.; расчи́щу, расчи́стишь; расчи́сти and расчи́сть; расчи́щенный.

РАСШИБИ́ТЬ Р.; расшибу́, расшибёшь; расшиби́; расши́б; расши́бленный.

РАСШИ́ТЬ Р.; разошью́, разошьёшь; расше́й; расши́тый

РАСШУМЕ́ТЬСЯ Р.; расшумлю́сь, расшуми́ься; расшуми́сь.

РАСЩЕМИ́ТЬ Р.; расщемлю́, расщеми́шь; расщемлённый.

РАСЩЕПИ́ТЬ Р.; расщеплю́, расщепи́шь; расщеплённый.

РАСЩИПА́ТЬ Р.; расщиплю́, расщи́плешь; расщипли́; расщи́панный.

РВАТЬ I.; рву, рвёшь; рви.

РЕВЕ́ТЬ I.; реву, ревёшь; реви́.

РЕГОТА́ТЬ I.; регочу́, regó́чешь; регочи́.

РЕ́ЗАТЬ I.; ре́жу, ре́жешь; режь; ре́занный.

РЕЗВИ́ТЬСЯ I.; резвлю́сь, резви́шься.

РЕМИ́ЗИТЬ I.; реми́жу, реми́зишь; реми́зь.

РЕ́ЯТЬ I.; ре́ю, ре́ешь; рей.

РЖАТЬ I.; ржу, ржёшь; ржи.

РОДИ́ТЬ Р. and I.; рожу́, роди́шь; роди́; рождённый.

РОКОТА́ТЬ I.; рокочу́, роко́чешь; рокочи́.

РОПТА́ТЬ I.; ропщу́, ро́пщешь; ропщи́.

РУБИ́ТЬ I.; рублю́, ру́бишь; ру́бленный.

РУКОВОДИ́ТЬ I.; руковожу́, руководи́шь.

РУКОПЛЕСКА́ТЬ I.; рукоплещу́, рукоплещешь; рукоплещи́.

РЫ́СКАТЬ I.; ры́щу, ры́щешь (also ры́скаю, ры́скаю, ры́скаешь); ры́скай.

РЫТЬ I.; ро́ю, ро́ешь; рой; ры́тый.

РЫЧА́ТЬ I.; рычу́, рычи́шь; рычи́.

РЯДИ́ТЬ[1] I.; ряжу́[1], ря́дишь (arch.: ряди́шь); ря́женный.

РЯДИ́ТЬ[2] I. (arch.); ряжу́[2], ряди́шь (also ря́дишь); ря́женный.

РЯДИ́ТЬСЯ[1] I.; ряжу́сь[1], ря́дишься (arch.: ряди́шься).

РЯДИ́ТЬСЯ[2] I. (arch.); ряжу́сь[2], ряди́шься (also ря́дишься).

С

САДИ́ТЬ I.; сажу́, са́дишь; са́женный.

САДИ́ТЬСЯ I.; сажу́сь, сади́шься.

СБА́ВИТЬ Р.; сба́влю, сба́вишь; сбавь; сба́вленный.

СБЕЖА́ТЬ Р.; сбегу́, сбежи́шь, сбегу́т; сбеги́.

СБЕРЕ́ЧЬ Р.; сберегу́, сбережёшь, сберегу́т; сбереги́; сберёг; сбережённый.

СБИТЬ Р.; собью́, собьёшь; сбей; сби́тый.

СБЛИ́ЗИТЬ Р.; сбли́жу, сбли́зишь; сблизь; сбли́женный.

СБРЕСТИ́СЬ Р.; сбредётся, сбреду́тся (1st and 2nd pers. sing. not used); сбреди́сь; сбрёлся; сбрёдшийся.

СБРЕХА́ТЬ Р.; сбрешу́, сбре́шешь; сбреши́.

СБРЕХНУ́ТЬ Р.: сбрёхнутый; сбрёхнут, —а, —о, —ы.

СБРИТЬ Р.; сбре́ю, сбре́ешь; сбрей; сбри́тый.

СБРО́СИТЬ Р.; сбро́шу, сбро́сишь; сбрось; сбро́шенный.

СБЫТЬ Р.; сбу́ду, сбу́дешь; сбудь; сбы́тый.

СВЕЗТИ́ Р.; свезу́, свезёшь; свези́; свёз; свезённый; свезя́.

СВЕРБЕ́ТЬ I.; сверби́т, сверба́т; сверби́.

СВЕ́РГНУТЬ Р.; сверг (and све́ргнул), све́ргла; све́ргнутый and све́рженный.

СВЕ́РЗИТЬСЯ Р.; све́ржусь, све́рзишься; све́рзись.

СВЕ́СИТЬ Р.; све́шу, све́сишь; свесь; све́шенный.

СВЕСТИ́ Р.; сведу́, сведёшь; сведи́; свёл; све́дший; сведённый; сведя́.

СВЕТИ́ТЬ I.; свечу́, све́тишь.

СВИ́ДЕТЬСЯ Р.; свижу́сь, сви́дишься.

СВИНТИ́ТЬ Р.; свинчу́, свинти́шь; сви́нченный.

СВИСТА́ТЬ I.; свищу́[2], сви́щешь; свисти́ and свищи́; свиста́.

СВИСТЕ́ТЬ I.; свищу́[1], свисти́шь; свисти́; свиста́.

СВИТЬ Р.; совью́, совьёшь; свей; сви́тый.

СВИ́ТЬСЯ Р.; совью́сь, совьёшься; све́йся.

СВОДИ́ТЬ I.; свожу́[1], сво́дишь.

СВОДИ́ТЬ Р.; свожу́[2], сво́дишь; сво́женный.

СВОЗИ́ТЬ Р.; свожу́[3], сво́зишь; сво́женный.

СВОЗИ́ТЬ I.; свожу́[4], сво́зишь.

СВОЛО́ЧЬ Р.; сволоку́, сволочёшь, сволоку́т; сволоки́; своло́к; сволочённый.

СВОРОТИ́ТЬ Р.; сворочу́, своро́тишь; своро́ченный.

СВЯЗА́ТЬ Р.; свяжу́, свя́жешь; свяжи́; свя́занный.

СВЯТИ́ТЬ I.; свячу́, святи́шь.

СГЛА́ДИТЬ Р.; сгла́жу[1], сгла́дишь; сгладь; сгла́женный.

СГЛА́ЗИТЬ Р.; сгла́жу[2], сгла́зишь; сглазь; сгла́женный.

СГЛОДА́ТЬ Р.; сгложу́, сгло́жешь; сгложи́; сгло́данный.

СГЛУПИ́ТЬ Р.; сглуплю́, сглупи́шь.

СГНИ́ТЬ Р.; сгнию́, сгниёшь.

СГО́РБИТЬ Р.; сго́рблю, сго́рбишь; сго́рби and сгорбь; сго́рбленный.

СГОРЕ́ТЬ Р.; сгорю́, сгори́шь; сгори́.

СГРЕСТИ́ Р.; сгребу́, сгребёшь; сгреби́; сгрёб; сгребённый.

СГРУЗИ́ТЬ Р.; сгружу́, сгру́зишь (also сгрузи́шь); сгру́женный and сгружённый.

СГРЫЗТЬ Р.; сгрызу́, сгрызёшь; сгрызи́; сгрыз; сгры́зенный.

СГУБИ́ТЬ Р.; сгублю́, сгу́бишь сгу́бленный.

СГУСТИ́ТЬ Р.; сгущу́, сгусти́шь; сгущённый.

СДАВА́ТЬ I.; сдаю́, сдаёшь; сдава́й; сдава́я.

СДАВИ́ТЬ Р.; сдавлю́, сда́вишь; сда́вленный.

СДАТЬ Р.: сдам, сдашь, сдаст, сдади́м, сдади́те, сдаду́т; сдай; сда́нный.

СДЕРЖА́ТЬ Р.; сдержу́, сде́ржишь; сдержи́; сде́ржанный.

СДО́ХНУТЬ Р.; сдох, сдо́хла.

СДУТЬ Р.; сду́ю, сду́ешь; сдуй; сду́тый.

СЕРДИ́ТЬ I.; сержу́, се́рдишь.

СЕСТЬ Р.; ся́ду, ся́дешь; сядь; сел.

СЕЧЬ I.; секу́, сечёшь, секу́т; секи́; сек; сечённый.

СЕ́ЧЬСЯ I.; секу́сь, сечёшься, секу́тся; секи́сь; се́кся.

СЕ́ЯТЬ I.; се́ю, се́ешь; сей; се́янный.

СЖАТЬ[1] Р.; сожму́, сожмёшь; сожми́; сжа́тый[1].

СЖАТЬ[2] Р.; сожну́, сожнёшь; сожни́; сжа́тый[2].

СЖЕВА́ТЬ Р.; сжую́, сжуёшь; сжуй; сжёванный.

СЖЕЧЬ Р.; сожгу́, сожжёшь, сожгу́т; сожги́; сжёг, сожгла́; сожжённый.

СЖИТЬ Р.; сживу́, сживёшь; сживи́; сжи́тый.

СИДЕ́ТЬ I.; сижу́, сиди́шь; сиди́.

СИПЕ́ТЬ I.; сиплю́, сипи́шь; сипи́.

СИ́ПНУТЬ I.; сип (and си́пнул), си́пла.

СКАЗА́ТЬ Р.; скажу́, ска́жешь; скажи́; ска́занный.

СКАКА́ТЬ I.; скачу́[2], ска́чешь; скачи́.

СКАПУ́СТИТЬСЯ Р.; скапу́щусь, скапу́стишься; скапу́стись.

СКАПУ́ТИТЬСЯ Р.; скапу́чусь, скапу́тишься; скапу́ться.

СКАТИ́ТЬ Р.; скачу́[1], ска́тишь; ска́ченный.

СКИПЕ́ТЬСЯ Р.; скипи́тся, скипя́тся; скипи́сь.

СКИ́СНУТЬ Р.; скис, ски́сла.

СКЛЕПА́ТЬ Р.: склеплю́ скле́плешь, (and склепа́ю, склепа́ешь); склепа́й and склепли́; склёпанный.

СКЛИ́КАТЬ Р.: скличу́, скли́чешь; скличь.

СКОЛОТИТЬ P.; сколочу́, сколо́-
тишь; сколо́ченный.

СКОЛО́ТЬ P.; сколю́, ско́лешь; сколи́;
ско́лотый.

СКОЛЬЗИ́ТЬ I.; скольжу́, скользи́шь.

СКОНФУ́ЗИТЬ P.; сконфу́жу, скон-
фу́зишь; сконфу́зь; сконфу́жен-
ный.

СКОПИ́ТЬ P.; скоплю́[1], ско́пишь;
ско́пленный.

СКОПИ́ТЬ I.; скоплю́[2], скопи́шь.

СКОРБЕ́ТЬ I.; скорблю́, скорби́шь;
скорби́.

СКОРМИ́ТЬ P.; скормлю́, ско́рмишь;
ско́рмленный.

СКОРОДИ́ТЬ (and скороди́ть) P.;
скорожу́, скороди́шь (and скоро́жу,
скоро́дишь); скоро́женный.

СКОРО́МИТЬСЯ I.; скоро́млюсь, ско-
ро́мишься; скоро́мься.

СКОСИ́ТЬ[1] P.; скошу́[1], ско́сишь;
ско́шенный.

СКОСИ́ТЬ[2] P.; скошу́[2], скоси́шь;
ско́шенный and скошённый.

СКОСТИ́ТЬ P.; скощу́, скости́шь;
скощённый.

СКРА́СИТЬ P.; скра́шу, скра́сишь;
скрась; скра́шенный.

СКРЕЖЕТА́ТЬ I.; скрежещу́, скре-
же́щешь; скрежещи́; скрежеща́.

СКРЕПИ́ТЬ P.; скреплю́, скрепи́шь;
скреплённый.

СКРЕСТИ́ I.; скребу́, скребёшь;
скреби́; скрёб; скребённый.

СКРЕСТИ́ТЬ P.; скрещу́, скрести́шь;
скрещённый.

СКРИВИ́ТЬ P.; скривлю́, скриви́шь;
скривлённый.

СКРИПЕ́ТЬ I.; скриплю́ скрипи́шь;
скрипи́.

СКРУТИ́ТЬ P.; скручу́, скру́тишь;
скру́ченный.

СКРЫ́ТЬ P.; скро́ю, скро́ешь; скрой;
скры́тый.

СКУПИ́ТЬ P.; скуплю́, ску́пишь;
ску́пленный.

СКУПИ́ТЬСЯ I.; скуплю́сь, ску-
пи́шься.

СЛА́БНУТЬ I.; слаб, сла́бла.

СЛА́ВИТЬ I.; сла́влю, сла́вишь;
славь.

СЛАВОСЛО́ВИТЬ I.; славосло́влю,
славосло́вишь; славосло́вь; славо-
сло́вленный.

СЛА́ДИТЬ P.; сла́жу[1], сла́дишь;
сладь; сла́женный.

СЛА́ЗИТЬ P.; сла́жу[2], сла́зишь; слазь.

СРАСТИ́ТЬ I.; слащу́, сласти́шь;
слащённый.

СЛАТЬ I.; шлю, шлёшь; шли[2] (imp.).

СЛЕДИ́ТЬ I.; слежу́[1] and [2], следи́шь.

СЛЕЗТЬ P.; слёзу, слёзешь; слезь;
слез.

СЛЕПИ́ТЬ P.; слеплю́[1], сле́пишь;
сле́пленный.

СЛЕПИ́ТЬ I.; слеплю́[2], слепи́шь.

СЛЕ́ПНУТЬ I.; слеп (and сле́пнул),
слепла; сле́пнувший and сле́пший.

СЛЕТЕ́ТЬ P.; слечу́, слети́шь; слети́.

СЛЕЧЬ P.; сля́гу, сля́жешь, сля́гут;
сля́г; слёг.

СЛИЗА́ТЬ P.; слижу́, сли́жешь;
слижи́; сли́занный.

СЛИТЬ P.; солью́, сольёшь; слей;
сли́тый.

СЛОМИ́ТЬ P.; сломлю́, сло́мишь;
сло́мленный.

СЛУПИ́ТЬ P.; слуплю́, слу́пишь;
слу́пленный.

СЛЫ́ТЬ I.; слыву́, слывёшь.

СЛЫ́ШАТЬ I.; слы́шу, слы́шишь.

СЛЮБИ́ТЬСЯ P.: слюблю́сь, слюбишься.

СЛЮНЯ́ВИТЬ I.; слюня́влю, слюня́-
вишь; слюня́в.

СМА́ЗАТЬ P.; сма́жу, сма́жешь;
смажь; сма́занный.

СМЕРДЕ́ТЬ I.: смержу́, смерди́шь;
смерди́.

СМЁРЗНУТЬСЯ P.; смёрзся, смёрзлась.

СМЁРКНУТЬ P.; смерк (and смёркнул), смёркла.

СМЕСИ́ТЬ P.; смешу́, сме́сишь; сме́-
шенный.

СМЕСТИ́ P.; смету́, сметёшь; смети́;
смёл; смётший; сметённый; смета́.

СМЕСТИ́ТЬ P.; смещу́, смести́шь;
смещённый.

СМЕТА́ТЬ P.; смечу́, сме́чешь; смечи́;
смётанный.

СМЕЯ́ТЬСЯ I.; смею́сь, смеёшься;
смейся.

СМО́ЛКНУТЬ P.: смолк (and arch.
смо́лкнул), смо́лкла.

СМОЛОТИ́ТЬ P.; смолочу́, смоло́-
тишь; смоло́ченный.

СМОЛО́ТЬ P.; смелю́, сме́лешь;
смели́; смо́лотый.

СМОЛЧА́ТЬ P.; смолчу́, смолчи́шь;
смолчи́.

СМОРО́ЗИТЬ Р.; сморо́жу, сморо́зишь; сморо́зь; сморо́женный.

СМОТРЕ́ТЬ I.; смотрю́, смо́тришь; смотри́; смо́тренный.

СМОЧЬ Р.; смогу́, смо́жешь, смо́гут; смог, смогла́.

СМУТИ́ТЬ Р.; смучу́, сму́тишь (arch. forms): modern forms: смущу́, смути́шь; смущённый.

СМЫТЬ Р.; смо́ю, смо́ешь; смой; смы́тый.

СМЯТЬ Р.; сомну́, сомнёшь; сомни́; смя́тый.

СНАБДИ́ТЬ Р.; снабжу́, снабди́шь; снабжённый.

СНАРЯДИ́ТЬ Р.; снаряжу́, снаряди́шь; снаряжённый.

СНЕСТИ́ Р.; снесу́, снесёшь; снеси́; снёс; снесённый; снеся́.

СНИЗА́ТЬ Р.; снижу́, сни́жешь; снижи́; сни́занный.

СНИ́ЗИТЬ Р.; сни́жу, сни́жишь; снизь; сни́женный.

СНИЗОЙТИ́ Р.: снизойду́, снизойдёшь; снизойди́; снизошёл (arch.: снисшёл), снизошла́; снизоше́дший (and arch.: снисше́дший); снизойдя́.

СНИ́КНУТЬ Р.; сник, сни́кла.

СНИСКА́ТЬ Р.; снищу́, сни́щешь; снищи́; сни́сканный.

СНИСХОДИ́ТЬ I.; снисхожу́, снисхо́дишь.

СНОСИ́ТЬ I.; сношу́[1], сно́сишь.

СНОСИ́ТЬ[1] Р.; сношу́[2], сно́сишь; сно́шенный.

СНОСИ́ТЬ[2] Р.; сношу́[3], сно́сишь; сно́шенный.

СНЯТЬ Р.; сниму́, сни́мешь; сними́; сня́тый.

СОБЛЮСТИ́ Р.; соблюду́, соблюдёшь; соблюди́; соблю́л; соблю́дший; соблюдённый; соблюдя́.

СОБРА́ТЬ Р.; соберу́, соберёшь; собери́; со́бранный.

СОВА́ТЬ I.; сую́, суёшь; суй.

СО́ВЕСТИТЬ I.; со́вещу, со́вестишь; со́вести.

СО́ВЕСТИТЬСЯ I.; со́вещусь, со́вестишься; со́вестись.

СОВЛЕ́ЧЬ Р.; совлеку́, совлечёшь, совлеку́т; совлеки́; совлёк; совлечённый.

СОВМЕСТИ́ТЬ Р.; совмещу́, совмести́шь; совмещённый.

СОВОКУПИ́ТЬ Р.; совокуплю́, совокупи́шь; совокуплённый.

СОВПА́СТЬ Р.; совпадёт, совпаду́т; совпади́; совпа́л.

СОВРАТИ́ТЬ Р.; совращу́, соврати́шь; совращённый.

СОВРА́ТЬ Р.; совру́, соврёшь; соври́; со́вранный.

СОГЛАСИ́ТЬ Р.; соглашу́, согласи́шь; соглашённый.

СОГЛАСИ́ТЬСЯ Р.; соглашу́сь, согласи́шься.

СОГНА́ТЬ Р.; сгоню́, сго́нишь; сгони́; со́гнанный.

СОДЕРЖА́ТЬ I.; содержу́, соде́ржишь; содержи́.

СОДЕ́ЯТЬ Р.; соде́ю, соде́ешь; соде́й; соде́янный.

СОДРА́ТЬ Р.; сдеру́, сдерёшь; сдери́; со́дранный.

СОЖРА́ТЬ Р.; сожру́, сожрёшь; сожри́; со́жранный.

СОЗВА́ТЬ Р.; созову́, созовёшь; созови́; со́званный.

СОЗДАВА́ТЬ I.; создаю́, создаёшь; создава́й; создава́я.

СОЗДА́ТЬ Р.; созда́м, созда́шь, созда́ст, создади́м, создади́те, создаду́т; созда́й; со́зданный.

СОЗНАВА́ТЬ I.; сознаю́, сознаёшь; сознава́й; сознава́я.

СОЙТИ́ Р.; сойду́, сойдёшь; сойди́; сошёл, сошла́; соше́дший (and arch.: сше́дший); сойдя́.

СОКРАТИ́ТЬ Р.; сокращу́, сократи́шь; сокращённый.

СОКРЫ́ТЬ Р.; сокро́ю, сокро́ешь; сокро́й; сокры́тый.

СОЛГА́ТЬ Р.; солгу́, солжёшь, солгу́т; солги́; со́лганный.

СОЛОДИ́ТЬ I.; соложу́, солоди́шь; соложённый.

СООБРАЗИ́ТЬ Р.; соображу́, сообрази́шь; соображённый.

СООРУДИ́ТЬ Р.; сооружу́, сооруди́шь; сооружённый.

СООТНЕСТИ́ Р.; соотнесу́, соотнесёшь; соотнеси́; соотнёс; соотнесённый; соотнеся́.

СООТНОСИ́ТЬ I.; соотношу́, соотно́сишь.

СОПЕ́ТЬ I.; соплю́, сопи́шь; сопи́.

СОПОСТА́ВИТЬ Р.; сопоста́влю, сопоста́вишь; сопоста́вь; сопоста́вленный.

СОРВА́ТЬ Р.; сорву́, сорвёшь; сорви́; со́рванный.

СОСА́ТЬ I.; сосу́, сосёшь; соси́; со́санный.

СОСКРЕСТИ́ Р.; соскребу́, соскребёшь; соскреби́; соскрёб; соскребённый.

СОСЛА́ТЬ Р.; сошлю́, сошлёшь; сошли́[2] (imp.); со́сланный.

СОСЛЕДИ́ТЬ Р.; сослежу́, соследи́шь; сосле́женный.

СОСТА́ВИТЬ Р.; соста́влю, соста́вишь; соста́вь; соста́вленный.

СОСТОЯ́ТЬ I.; состою́, состои́шь; состо́й.

СОСТРИ́ЧЬ Р.; состригу́, сострижёшь, состригу́т; состриги́; состри́г; состри́женный.

СОТКА́ТЬ Р.; сотку́, соткёшь; сотки́; со́тканный.

СОТРЯСТИ́ Р.; сотрясу́, сотрясёшь; сотряси́; сотря́с; сотрясённый.

СО́ХНУТЬ I.; сох, со́хла.

СПАСТИ́ Р.; спасу́, спасёшь; спаси́; спас; спасённый.

СПАСТЬ Р.; спаду́, спадёшь; спади́; спал[1], спа́ла.

СПАТЬ I.; сплю, спишь; спи; спал[2], спала́, спа́ло, спа́ли.

СПЕРЕ́ТЬ Р.; сопру́, сопрёшь; сопри́; спёр; спёртый.

СПЕТЬ Р.; спою́, споёшь; спой; спе́тый.

СПЕЧЬ Р.; спеку́, спечёшь, спеку́т; спеки́; спёк; спечённый.

СПЕ́ЧЬСЯ[1] Р.; спеку́сь, спечёшься, спеку́тся; спеки́сь; спёкся.

СПЕ́ЧЬСЯ[2] Р.; спечётся, спеку́тся; спёкся.

СПЕШИ́ТЬ Р.; спе́шу, спе́шишь; спешь; спе́шенный.

СПЕШИ́ТЬ I.; спешу́, спеши́шь; спеши́.

СПИСА́ТЬ Р.; спишу́, спи́шешь; спиши́; спи́санный.

СПИ́ТЬСЯ Р.; сопью́сь, сопьёшься; спе́йся.

СПЛА́ВИТЬ Р.; спла́влю, спла́вишь; сплавь; спла́вленный.

СПЛЕСТИ́ Р.; сплету́, сплетёшь; сплети́; сплёл; сплётший; сплетённый; сплетя́.

СПЛОТИ́ТЬ Р.; сплочу́, сплоти́шь; сплочённый.

СПЛЫ́ТЬ Р.; сплыву́, сплывёшь; сплыви́.

СПЛЯСА́ТЬ Р.; спляшу́, спля́шешь; спляши́; спля́санный.

СПОДО́БИТЬ Р.; сподо́блю, сподо́бишь; сподо́бь; сподо́бленный.

СПОДО́БИТЬСЯ Р.; сподо́блюсь, сподо́бишься; сподо́бься.

СПОЛЗТИ́ Р.; сползу́, сползёшь; сползи́; сполз.

СПОРО́ТЬ Р.; спорю́, спо́решь; спори́; спо́ротый.

СПОХВАТИ́ТЬСЯ Р.; спохвачу́сь, спохва́тишься.

СПРА́ВИТЬ Р.; спра́влю, спра́вишь; справь; спра́вленный.

СПРОВА́ДИТЬ Р.; спрова́жу, спрова́дишь; спрова́дь; спрова́женный.

СПРОСИ́ТЬ Р.; спрошу́, спро́сишь; спро́шенный.

СПРЯМИ́ТЬ Р.; спрямлю́, спрями́шь; спрямлённый.

СПРЯСТЬ Р.; спряду́, спрядёшь; спряди́; спрял; спрядённый.

СПРЯ́ТАТЬ Р.; спря́чу, спря́чешь; спрячь (imp.); спря́танный.

СПРЯЧЬ Р.; спрягу́, спряжёшь, спрягу́т; спряги́; спряг; спряжённый.

СПУСТИ́ТЬ Р.; спущу́, спу́стишь; спу́щенный.

СПЯ́ТИТЬ Р.; спя́чу, спя́тишь; спять.

СРАЗИ́ТЬ Р.; сражу́, срази́шь; сражённый.

СРАМИ́ТЬ I.; срамлю́, срами́шь.

СРАСТИ́СЬ Р.; срасту́сь, срастёшься; срасти́сь (imp.); сро́сся, срослась́.

СРАСТИ́ТЬ Р.; сращу́, срасти́шь; сращённый.

СРЕ́ЗАТЬ Р.; сре́жу, сре́жешь; срежь; сре́занный.

СРУБИ́ТЬ Р.; срублю́, сру́бишь; сру́бленный.

СРЫ́ТЬ Р.; сро́ю, сро́ешь; срой; сры́тый.

ССАДИ́ТЬ Р.; ссажу́, сса́дишь; сса́женный.

ССЕ́ЧЬ Р.; ссеку́, ссечёшь, ссеку́т; ссеки́; ссек; ссечённый (arch.: ссе́ченный).

ССОСА́ТЬ Р.; ссосу́, ссосёшь; ссоси́; ссо́санный.

ССУДИ́ТЬ Р.; ссужу́, ссу́дишь; ссу́женный.

ССЫ́ПАТЬ Р.; ссы́плю, ссы́плешь; ссыпь; ссы́панный.

СТАВА́ТЬ I. (arch.); стаёт, стаю́т; става́й; става́я.

СТА́ВИТЬ I.; ста́влю, ста́вишь; ставь; ста́вленный.

СТАНОВИ́ТЬСЯ I.; становлю́сь, стано́вишься.

СТАТЬ Р.; ста́ну, ста́нешь; стань.

СТА́ЯТЬ Р.; ста́ет, ста́ют; стай.

СТЕЛИ́ТЬ I.; стелю́, сте́лешь; стели́.

СТЕРЕ́ТЬ Р.; сотру́, сотрёшь; сотри́; стёр; стёртый; стере́в and стёрши.

СТЕРЕ́ЧЬ I.; стерегу́, стережёшь, стерегу́т; стереги́; стерёг.

СТЕРПЕ́ТЬ Р.; стерплю́, сте́рпишь; стерпи́.

СТЕСА́ТЬ Р.; стешу́, сте́шешь; стеши́; стёсанный.

СТЕЧЬ Р.; стечёт, стеку́т; стеки́; стёк.

СТИ́ХНУТЬ Р.; стих, сти́хла.

СТЛАТЬ I.; стелю́, сте́лешь; стели́.

СТОЛО́ЧЬ Р.; столку́, столчёшь, столку́т; столки́; столо́к, столкла́; столчённый.

СТОНА́ТЬ I.; стону́ (and стона́ю), сто́нешь; стони́; стона́я.

СТОПИ́ТЬ Р.; стоплю́, сто́пишь; сто́пленный.

СТОПТА́ТЬ Р.; стопчу́, сто́пчешь; стопчи́; сто́птанный.

СТОЯ́ТЬ I.; стою́, стои́шь; стой.

СТРА́ВИТЬ Р.; стравлю́, стра́вишь; стра́вленный.

СТРАДА́ТЬ I.; стра́жду, стра́ждешь (arch. and bookish); modern forms: страда́ю, страда́ешь; стра́жди (arch.); стра́ждущий (arch. form pres. a.p.); modern form pres. a.p.: страда́ющий.

СТРЕКОТА́ТЬ I.; стрекочу́, стреко́чешь; стрекочи́.

СТРЕМИ́ТЬ I. (bookish); стремлю́, стреми́шь.

СТРИЧЬ I.; стригу́, стрижёшь, стригу́т; стриги́; стриг; стри́женный.

СТРУСИ́ТЬ Р.; струшу́, струси́шь; стру́шенный.

СТРУ́СИТЬ Р.; стру́шу, стру́сишь; струсь.

СТРЯСТИ́ Р.; стрясу́, стрясёшь; стряси́; стряс; стрясённый.

СТУДИ́ТЬ I.; стужу́, сту́дишь; сту́женный.

СТУПИ́ТЬ Р.; ступлю́, сту́пишь.

СТУЧА́ТЬ I.; стучу́, стучи́шь; стучи́.

СТЫДИ́ТЬ I.; стыжу́, стыди́шь.

СТЫ́НУТЬ I.; сты́ну, сты́нешь; стынь; стыл, сты́ла.

СТЫТЬ I.; сты́ну, сты́нешь; стынь; стыл, сты́ла.

СУГУ́БИТЬ I.; сугу́блю, сугу́бишь; сугу́бь.

СУДИ́ТЬ I. and Р.; сужу́, су́дишь; суждённый.

СУЕТИ́ТЬСЯ I.; суечу́сь, суети́шься.

СУ́ЗИТЬ Р.; су́жу, су́зишь; сузь; су́женный.

СУМАСБРО́ДИТЬ I.; сумасбро́жу, сумасбро́дишь; сумасбро́дь.

СУ́ПИТЬ I.; су́плю, су́пишь; супь.

СУРЬМИ́ТЬ I.; сурьмлю́, сурьми́шь; сурьмлённый.

СФАЛЬШИ́ВИТЬ Р.; сфальши́влю, сфальши́вишь; сфальши́вь.

СХВАТИ́ТЬ Р.; схвачу́, сва́хтишь; схва́ченный.

СХЛОПОТА́ТЬ Р.; схлопочу́, схло́почешь; схлопочи́; схлопо́танный.

СХОДИ́ТЬ I.; схожу́[1], схо́дишь.

СХОДИ́ТЬ Р.; схожу́[2], схо́дишь.

СЦЕДИ́ТЬ Р.; сцежу́, сце́дишь; сце́женный.

СЦЕПИ́ТЬ Р.; сцеплю́, сце́пишь; сце́пленный.

СЧЕРТИ́ТЬ Р.; счерчу́, сче́ртишь; сче́рченный.

СЧЕСА́ТЬ Р.; счешу́, сче́шешь; счеши́; счёсанный.

СЧЕСТЬ Р.; сочту́, сочтёшь; сочти́; счёл, сочла́; счётший; сочтённый; сочтя́.

СЧИ́СТИТЬ Р.; счи́щу, счи́стишь; счи́сти and счисть; счи́щенный.

СШИБИ́ТЬ Р.; сшибу́, сшибёшь; сшиби́; сшиб; сши́бленный.

СШИТЬ Р.; сошью́, сошьёшь; сшей; сши́тый.

С'Е́ЗДИТЬ Р.; с'е́зжу, с'е́здишь; с'е́зди.

С'ЕСТЬ Р.; с'ем, с'ешь[1], с'ест, с'еди́м, с'еди́те, с'едя́т; с'ешь[2] (imp.); с'ел; с'е́денный.

С'Е́ХАТЬ Р.; с'е́ду, с'е́дешь; с'езжа́й.

С'ЯЗВИ́ТЬ Р.; с'язвлю́, с'язви́шь.

СЫ́ПАТЬ I.; сы́плю, сы́плешь; сыпь.

СЫСКА́ТЬ Р.; сыщу́, сы́щешь; сыщи́; сы́сканный.

СЭКОНО́МИТЬ Р.; сэконо́млю, сэконо́мишь; сэконо́мь; сэконо́мленный.

Т

ТАРАНТИ́ТЬ I.; таранчу́, таранти́шь.
ТАРАХТЕ́ТЬ I.; тарахчу́, тарахти́шь; тарахти́.
ТА́ЯТЬ I.; та́ю, та́ешь; тай.
ТВЕРДИ́ТЬ I.; твержу́, тверди́шь; твержённый.
ТЕРЕБИ́ТЬ I.; тереблю́, тереби́шь; тереблённый.
ТЕРЕ́ТЬ I.; тру́, трёшь; три; тёр; тёртый.
ТЕРПЕ́ТЬ I.; терплю́, те́рпишь; терпи́.
ТЕСА́ТЬ I.; тешу́, те́шешь; теши́; тёсанный.
ТЕЧЬ I.; течёт, теку́т; теки́; тёк.
ТИ́ХНУТЬ I.; тих, ти́хла.
ТКАТЬ I.; тку, ткёшь; тки; тка́нный.
ТОЛО́ЧЬ I.; толку́, толчёшь, толку́т; толки́; толо́к, толкла́; толчённый.
ТОМИ́ТЬ I.; томлю́, томи́шь; томлённый.
ТОПИ́ТЬ[1] I.; топлю́[1], то́пишь; то́пленный.
ТОПИ́ТЬ[2] I.; топлю́[2], то́пишь.
ТОПОТА́ТЬ I.; топочу́, топо́чешь; топочи́.
ТОПТА́ТЬ I.; топчу́, то́пчешь; топчи́; то́птанный.
ТОРМОЗИ́ТЬ I.; тормозу́, тормози́шь; торможённый.
ТОРОПИ́ТЬ I.; тороплю́, торо́пишь.

ТОРЧА́ТЬ I.; торчу́, торчи́шь; торчи́
ТРАВИ́ТЬ I.; травлю́, тра́вишь; тра́вленный.
ТРА́ТИТЬ I.; тра́чу, тра́тишь; трать; тра́ченный.
ТРЕЗВИ́ТЬ I.; трезвлю́, трезви́шь.
ТРЕПА́ТЬ I.; треплю́, тре́плешь; трепли́; трёпанный.
ТРЕПЕТА́ТЬ I.; трепещу́, трепе́щешь; трепещи́.
ТРЕЩА́ТЬ I.; трещу́, трещи́шь; трещи́.
ТРУБИ́ТЬ I.; трублю́, труби́шь.
ТРУДИ́ТЬСЯ I.; тружу́сь, тру́дишься.
ТРУСИ́ТЬ[1] I.; трушу́[1], труси́шь; труси́.
ТРУСИ́ТЬ[2] I.; трушу́[2], труси́шь; труси́.
ТРУ́СИТЬ I.; тру́шу, тру́сишь; трусь.
ТРЯСТИ́ I.; трясу́, трясёшь; тряси́; тряс.
ТУЗИ́ТЬ I.; тужу́, тузи́шь.
ТУПИ́ТЬ I.; туплю́, ту́пишь.
ТУ́ХНУТЬ I.; тух, ту́хла.
ТЫ́КАТЬ[1] I.; ты́чу[1], ты́чешь (also ты́каю, ты́каешь); тычь (and ты́кай); ты́ча (and ты́кая).
ТЫ́КАТЬ[2] I.; ты́чу[2], ты́чешь (also ты́каю, ты́каешь); тычь (and ты́кай); ты́ча (and ты́кая).

У

УБА́ВИТЬ Р.; уба́влю, уба́вишь; уба́вь; уба́вленный.
УБЕДИ́ТЬ Р.; (1st pers. sing. not used); убеждённый.
УБЕЖА́ТЬ Р.; убегу́, убежи́шь, убегу́т; убеги́.
УБЕРЕ́ЧЬ Р.; уберегу́, убережёшь, уберегу́т; убереги́; уберёг; убережённый.
УБИ́ТЬ Р.; убью́, убьёшь; убе́й; уби́тый (and arch. убие́нный).
УБОЯ́ТЬСЯ Р.; убою́сь, убои́шься; убо́йся.
УБРА́ТЬ Р.; уберу́, уберёшь; убери́; у́бранный.

УБЫ́ТЬ Р.; убу́ду, убу́дешь; убу́дь.
УВЕ́ДОМИТЬ Р.; уве́домлю, уве́домишь; уве́домь; уве́домленный.
УВЕЗТИ́ Р.; увезу́, увезёшь; увези́; увёз; увезённый; увезя́.
УВЕСТИ́ Р.; уведу́, уведёшь; уведи́; увёл; уве́дший; уведённый; уведя́.
УВИ́ДЕТЬ Р.; уви́жу, уви́дишь; уви́денный.
УВИ́ДЕТЬСЯ Р.; уви́жусь, уви́дишься.
УВИ́ТЬ Р.; увью́, увьёшь; уве́й; уви́тый.
УВЛЕ́ЧЬ Р.; увлеку́, увлечёшь, увлеку́т; увлеки́; увлёк; увлечённый.

348

УВОДИТЬ I.; увожу[1], уводишь.

УВОЗИТЬ I.; увожу[2], возишь.

УВОЗИТЬ Р.; увожу[3], увозишь; увоженный.

УВОЛОЧЬ Р.; уволоку, уволочёшь, уволокут; уволоки; уволок; уволочённый and уволоченный.

УВЯЗАТЬ Р.; увяжу, увяжешь; увяжи; увязанный.

УВЯЗНУТЬ Р.; увяз, увязла; увязни; увязнувший and увязший.

УВЯНУТЬ Р.; увял, увяла; увянь; увядший and увянувший.

УГАСИТЬ Р.; угашу, угасишь; угашенный.

УГАСНУТЬ Р.; угас, угасла.

УГЛУБИТЬ Р.; углублю, углубишь; углублённый.

УГЛЯДЕТЬ Р.; угляжу, углядишь; угляди.

УГНАТЬ Р.; угоню, угонишь; угони; угнанный.

УГНЕСТИ Р.; угнету, угнетёшь (future seldom used; past not used); угнетённый.

УГОДИТЬ Р.; угожу, угодишь.

УГОРЕТЬ Р.; угорю, угоришь; угори.

УГОСТИТЬ Р.; угощу, угостишь; угощённый.

УГОТОВИТЬ Р.; уготовлю, угуто́вишь; уготовь; уготовленный.

УГРОБИТЬ Р.; угроблю, угробишь; угробь; угробленный.

УДАВАТЬСЯ I.; удаётся, удаются.

УДАВИТЬ Р.; удавлю, удавишь; удавленный.

УДАТЬСЯ Р.; удамся, удашься, удастся, удадимся, удадитесь, удадутся; удайся.

УДЕРЖАТЬ Р.; удержу, удержишь; удержи; удержанный.

УДЕШЕВИТЬ Р.; удешевлю, удешевишь; удешевлённый.

УДИВИТЬ Р.; удивлю, удивишь; удивлённый.

УДИТЬ I.; ужу, удишь.

УДРАТЬ Р.; удеру, удерёшь; удери.

УЕЗДИТЬ Р.; уезжу, уездишь; уезди; уезженный.

УЕХАТЬ Р.; уеду, уедешь; уезжай.

УЖИТЬСЯ Р.; уживусь, уживёшься; уживись.

УЗИТЬ I.; ужу, узишь; узь.

УЗНАВАТЬ I.; узнаю, узнаёшь; узнавай; узнавая.

УЗРЕТЬ Р.; узрю узришь (and узришь); узри; узренный.

УЙТИ Р.; уйду, уйдёшь; уйди; ушёл, ушла; ушедший; уйдя and ушедши.

УКАЗАТЬ Р.; укажу, укажешь; укажи; указанный.

УКАТИТЬ Р.; укачу, укатишь; укаченный.

УКОЛОТИТЬ Р.; уколочу, уколотишь; уколоченный.

УКОЛОТЬ Р.; уколю, уколешь; уколи; уколотый.

УКОРОТИТЬ Р.; укорочу, укоротишь (and arch. укоротишь); укороченный.

УКОСИТЬ Р.; укошу, укосишь; укошенный.

УКРАСИТЬ Р.; украшу, украсишь; укрась; украшенный.

УКРАСТЬ Р.; украду, украдёшь; укради; украл; украденный.

УКРЕПИТЬ Р.; укреплю, укрепишь; укреплённый.

УКРОТИТЬ Р.; укрощу, укротишь; укрощённый.

УКРУТИТЬ Р.; укручу, укрутишь; укрученный.

УКРЫТЬ Р.; укрою, укроешь; укрой; укрытый.

УКУПИТЬ Р.; укуплю, укупишь; укупленный.

УКУСИТЬ Р.; укушу, укусишь; укушенный.

УЛАДИТЬ Р.; улажу, уладишь; уладь; улаженный.

УЛЕЖАТЬ Р.; улежу, улежишь; улежи.

УЛЕЗТЬ Р.; улезу, улезешь; улезь; улез.

УЛЕПИТЬ Р.; улеплю, улепишь; улепленный.

УЛЕСТИТЬ Р.; улещу, улестишь; улещённый.

УЛЕТЕТЬ Р.; улечу, улетишь; улети.

УЛЕЧЬСЯ Р.; улягусь, уляжешься, улягутся; улягся; улёгся, углеглась.

УЛИТЬ Р.; улью, ульёшь; улей; улитый.

УЛИЦЕЗРЕТЬ Р.; улицезрю, улицезришь; улицезри.

УЛОВИТЬ Р.; уловлю, уловишь; уловленный.

УМАСТИТЬ Р.; умащу, умастишь; умащённый.

УМАЯТЬ Р.; умаю, умаешь; умай; умаянный.

УМЕРЕ́ТЬ Р.; умру́, умрёшь; умри́; у́мер.

УМЕРТВИ́ТЬ Р.; умерщвлю́, умертви́шь; умерщвлённый.

УМЕСТИ́ТЬ Р.; умещу́, умести́шь; умещённый.

УМО́ЛКНУТЬ Р.; умо́лк (and arch. умо́лкнул), умо́лкла.

УМОЛОТИ́ТЬ Р.; умолочу́, умоло́тишь; умоло́ченный.

УМОЛЧА́ТЬ Р.; умолчу́, умолчи́шь; умолчи́.

УМЧА́ТЬ Р.; умчу́, умчи́шь; умчи́.

УМЫ́ТЬ Р.; умо́ю, умо́ешь; умо́й; умы́тый.

УМЯ́ТЬ Р.; умну́, умнёшь; умни́; умя́тый.

УНАВО́ЗИТЬ Р.; унаво́жу, унаво́зишь; унаво́зь; унаво́женный.

УНЕСТИ́ Р.; унесу́, унесёшь; унеси́; унёс; унесённый; унеся́.

УНИЗА́ТЬ Р.; унижу́, уни́жешь; унижи́; уни́занный.

УНИ́ЗИТЬ Р.; уни́жу, уни́зишь; уни́зь; уни́женный.

УНОСИ́ТЬ I.; уношу́, уно́сишь.

УНЯ́ТЬ Р.; уйму́, уймёшь; уйми́; уня́тый.

УПАСТИ́ Р.; упасу́, упасёшь; упаси́; упа́с; упасённый.

УПА́СТЬ Р.; упаду́, упадёшь; упади́; упа́л; упа́вший (and arch. упа́дший).

УПЕРЕ́ТЬ Р.; упру́, упрёшь; упри́; упёр; упёртый; упере́в and упёрши.

УПЕ́ЧЬ Р.; упеку́, упечёшь, упеку́т; упеки́; упёк; упечённый.

УПИСА́ТЬ Р.; упишу́, упи́шешь; упиши́; упи́санный.

УПИ́ТЬСЯ Р.; упью́сь, упьёшься; упе́йся.

УПЛАТИ́ТЬ Р.; уплачу́, упла́тишь; упла́ченный.

УПЛЕСТИ́ Р.; уплету́, уплетёшь; уплети́; уплёл; уплётший; уплетённый.

УПЛЫ́ТЬ Р.; уплыву́, уплывёшь; уплыви́.

УПОДО́БИТЬ Р.; уподо́блю, уподо́бишь; уподо́бь; уподо́бленный.

УПОЛЗТИ́ Р.; уползу́, уползёшь; уползи́; упо́лз.

УПОТРЕБИ́ТЬ Р.; употреблю́, употреби́шь; употреблённый.

УПРА́ВИТЬ Р.; упра́влю, упра́вишь; упра́вь.

УПРА́ВИТЬСЯ Р.; упра́влюсь, упра́вишься; упра́вься.

УПРЕДИ́ТЬ Р.; упрежу́, упреди́шь; упреждённый.

УПРОСИ́ТЬ Р.; упрошу́, упро́сишь; упро́шенный.

УПРОСТИ́ТЬ Р.; упрощу́, упрости́шь; упрощённый.

УПРЯ́МИТЬСЯ I.; упря́млюсь, уппря́мишься; упря́мься.

УПРЯ́ТАТЬ Р.; упря́чу, упря́чешь; упря́чь; упря́танный.

УПУСТИ́ТЬ Р.; упущу́, упу́стишь; упу́щенный.

УРАВНОВЕ́СИТЬ Р.; уравнове́шу, уравнове́сишь; уравнове́сь; уравнове́шенный.

УРВА́ТЬ Р.; урву́, урвёшь; урви́; у́рванный.

УРЕ́ЗАТЬ Р.; уре́жу, уре́жешь; уре́жь; уре́занный.

УРОДИ́ТЬ Р.; урожу́, уроди́шь; урождённый.

УРЧА́ТЬ I.; урчу́, урчи́шь; урчи́.

УРЯДИ́ТЬ Р.; уряжу́, уря́дишь (and уряди́шь); уря́женный.

УСАДИ́ТЬ Р.; усажу́, уса́дишь; уса́женный.

УСЕ́СТЬСЯ Р.; уся́дусь, уся́дешься; уся́дься; усе́лся.

УСЕ́ЧЬ Р.; усеку́, усечёшь, усеку́т; усеки́; усе́к; усечённый (and arch. усе́ченный).

УСЕ́ЯТЬ Р.; усе́ю, усе́ешь; усе́й; усе́янный.

УСИДЕ́ТЬ Р.; усижу́, усиди́шь; усиди́.

УСКАКА́ТЬ Р.; ускачу́, уска́чешь; ускачи́.

УСЛАДИ́ТЬ Р.; услажу́, услади́шь; услаждённый.

УСЛАСТИ́ТЬ Р.; услащу́, усласти́шь; услащённый.

УСЛА́ТЬ Р.; ушлю́, ушлёшь; ушли́[2] (imp.); у́сланный.

УСЛЕДИ́ТЬ Р.; услежу́, уследи́шь; услеженный.

УСЛО́ВИТЬСЯ Р.; усло́влюсь, усло́вишься; усло́вься.

УСЛЫХА́ТЬ Р.; услы́шу[1], услы́шишь; услы́шь; услы́шанный.

УСЛЫ́ШАТЬ Р.; услы́шу[2], услы́шишь; услы́шь; услы́шанный.

УСМОТРЕ́ТЬ Р.; усмотрю́, усмо́тришь; усмотри́; усмо́тренный.

УСНАСТИТЬ Р.; уснащу́, уснасти́шь; уснащённый.
УСОВЕСТИТЬ Р.; усо́вещу, усове́стишь; усо́вестить; усо́вещенный.
УСОХНУТЬ Р.; усо́х, усо́хла.
УСТАВА́ТЬ I.; устаю́, устаёшь; устава́й; устава́я.
УСТА́ВИТЬ Р.; уста́влю, уста́вишь; уста́вь; уста́вленный.
УСТАНОВИ́ТЬ Р.; установлю́, устано́вишь; устано́вленный.
УСТА́ТЬ Р.; уста́ну, уста́нешь; уста́нь.
УСТЕЛИ́ТЬ Р.; устелю́[1], усте́лешь; устели́; усте́ленный.
УСТЕРЕ́ЧЬ Р.; устерегу́, устережёшь, устерегу́т; устереги́; устерёг; устережённый.
УСТЛА́ТЬ Р.; устелю́[2], усте́лешь; устели́; у́стланный.
УСТОЯ́ТЬ Р.; устою́, устои́шь; устои́.
УСТРЕМИ́ТЬ Р.; устремлю́, устреми́шь; устремлённый.
УСТУПИ́ТЬ Р.; уступлю́, усту́пишь; усту́пленный.
УСТЫДИ́ТЬ Р.; устыжу́, устыди́шь; устыжённый.
УСУГУ́БИТЬ Р.; усугу́блю, усугу́бишь; усугу́бь; усугу́бленный.
УСУГУБИ́ТЬ Р.; усугублю́, усугуби́шь; усугуби́; усугублённый.
УСЫНОВИ́ТЬ Р.; усыновлю́, усынови́шь; усыновлённый.
УСЫ́ПАТЬ Р.; усы́плю, усы́плешь; усы́пь; усы́панный.
УСЫПИ́ТЬ Р.; усыплю́, усыпи́шь; усыплённый.
УТВЕРДИ́ТЬ Р.; утвержу́, утверди́шь; утверждённый.
УТЕРЕ́ТЬ Р.; утру́, утрёшь; утри́; утёр; утёртый; утере́в and утёрши.
УТЕРПЕ́ТЬ Р.; утерплю́, уте́рпишь; утерпи́.
УТЕСА́ТЬ Р.; утешу́, уте́шешь; утеши́; утёсанный.
УТЕ́ЧЬ Р.; утеку́, утечёшь, утеку́т; утеки́; утёк.

УТИ́ХНУТЬ Р.; ути́х, ути́хла; ути́хший and ути́хнувший.
УТКА́ТЬ Р.; утку́, уткёшь; утки́; у́тканный.
УТОЛСТИ́ТЬ Р.; утолщу́, утолсти́шь; утолщённый.
УТОМИ́ТЬ Р.; утомлю́, утоми́шь; утомлённый.
УТОПИ́ТЬ Р.; утоплю́, уто́пишь; уто́пленный.
УТОПТА́ТЬ Р.; утопчу́, уто́пчешь; утопчи́; уто́птанный.
УТРА́ТИТЬ Р.; утра́чу, утра́тишь; утра́ть; утра́ченный.
УТРУДИ́ТЬ Р.; утружу́, утруди́шь; утружённый.
УТРЯСТИ́ Р.; утрясу́, утрясёшь; утряси́; утря́с; утрясённый.
УХВАТИ́ТЬ Р.; ухвачу́, ухва́тишь; ухва́ченный.
УХИ́ТИТЬ Р.; ухи́чу, ухи́тишь; ухи́ть; ухи́ченный.
УХОДИ́ТЬ I.; ухожу́[1], ухо́дишь.
УХОДИ́ТЬ Р.; ухожу́[2], ухо́дишь; ухо́женный.
УЦЕПИ́ТЬ Р.; уцеплю́, уце́пишь; уце́пленный.
УЧАСТИ́ТЬ Р.; учащу́, участи́шь; учащённый.
УЧА́ТЬ Р.; учну́, учнёшь; учни́.
УЧЕ́СТЬ Р.; учту́, учтёшь; учти́; учёл, учла́; учётший; учтённый; учтя́.
УЧРЕДИ́ТЬ Р.; учережу́, учреди́шь; учреждённый.
УЧУ́ЯТЬ Р.; учу́ю, учу́ешь; учу́й; учу́янный.
УШИБИ́ТЬ Р.; ушибу́, ушибёшь; ушиби́; ушиб; уши́бленный.
УШИ́ТЬ Р.; ушью́, ушьёшь; ушей; уши́тый.
УЩЕМИ́ТЬ Р.; ущемлю́, ущеми́шь; ущемлённый.
УЩЕРБИ́ТЬ Р.; ущерблю́, ущерби́шь; ущерблённый.
УЯЗВИ́ТЬ Р.; уязвлю́, уязви́шь; уязвлённый.

Ф

ФАЛЬШИ́ВИТЬ I.; фальши́влю, фальши́вишь; фальши́вь.
ФИНТИ́ТЬ I.; финчу́, финти́шь.
ФОРСИ́ТЬ I.; форшу́, форси́шь.

ФРАНТИ́ТЬ I.; франчу́, франти́шь.
ФУРЧА́ТЬ I.; фурчу́, фурчи́шь; фурчи́.
ФЫРЧА́ТЬ I.; фырчу́, фырчи́шь; фырчи́.

Х

ХАМИ́ТЬ I.; хамлю́, хами́шь.
ХА́ЯТЬ I.; ха́ю, ха́ешь; хай.
ХВАТИ́ТЬ Р.; хвачу́, хва́тишь; хва́-ченный.
ХЛЕСТА́ТЬ I.; хлещу́, хле́щешь; хлещи́; хлёстанный.
ХЛОБЫСТА́ТЬ I.; хлобыщу́, хлобы́-щешь; хлобыщи́.
ХЛОПОТА́ТЬ I.; хлопочу́, хлопо́чешь; хлопочи́.
ХЛЫСТА́ТЬ I.; хлыщу́, хлы́щешь; хлыщи́.
ХНЫ́КАТЬ I.; хны́чу, хны́чешь (also хны́каю, хны́каешь); хны́кай and хнычь.

ХОДИ́ТЬ I.; хожу́, хо́дишь.
ХОЛОДИ́ТЬ I.; холожу́, холоди́шь.
ХОЛОСТИ́ТЬ I.; холощу́, холости́шь; холощённый.
ХОТЕ́ТЬ I.; хочу́, хо́чешь, хо́чет, хоти́м, хоти́те, хотя́т; хоти́.
ХОХОТА́ТЬ I.; хохочу́, хохо́чешь; хохочи́.
ХРАПЕ́ТЬ I.; храплю́, храпи́шь; храпи́.
ХРИПЕ́ТЬ I.; хриплю́, хрипи́шь; хрипи́.
ХРУСТЕ́ТЬ I.; хрущу́, хрусти́шь; хрусти́.

Ц

ЦВЕСТИ́ I.; цвету́, цветёшь; цвети́; цвёл; цве́тший.
ЦВЕТИ́ТЬ I.; цвечу́, цвети́шь.

ЦЕДИ́ТЬ I.; цежу́, це́дишь; це́женный.
ЦОКОТА́ТЬ I.; цокочу́, цоко́чешь; цокочи́.

Ч

ЧАДИ́ТЬ I.; чажу́, чади́шь.
ЧАСТИ́ТЬ I.; чащу́, части́шь.
ЧА́ХНУТЬ I.; чах, ча́хла.
ЧА́ЯТЬ I.; ча́ю, ча́ешь; чай.
ЧЕРТИ́ТЬ[1] I.; черчу́, че́ртишь; че́р-ченный.
ЧЕРТИ́ТЬ[2] I.; черчу́, черти́шь.
ЧЕСА́ТЬ I.; чешу́, че́шешь; чеши́; чёсанный.

ЧЕСТИ́ТЬ I.; чещу́, чести́шь.
ЧЕСТЬ I.; чту[1], чтёшь; чти.
ЧИ́СТИТЬ I.; чи́щу, чи́стишь; чи́сти and чисть; чи́щенный.
ЧИХВО́СТИТЬ I.; чихво́щу, чихво́с-тишь; чихво́сти.
ЧТИТЬ I.; чту[2], чтишь, чтят (and чтут); чти.
ЧУ́ЯТЬ I.; чу́ю, чу́ешь; чуй.

Ш

ШЕЛЕСТЕ́ТЬ I.; шелести́шь, ше-лести́т (1st pers. sing. not used); шелести́.
ШЕПЕЛЯ́ВИТЬ I.; шепеля́влю, ше-пеля́вишь; шепеля́вь.
ШЕПТА́ТЬ I.; шепчу́, ше́пчешь; шепчи́.

ШИПЕ́ТЬ I.; шиплю́, шипи́шь; шипи́.
ШИТЬ I.; шью, шьёшь; шей; ши́тый.
ШУМЕ́ТЬ I.; шумлю́, шуми́шь; шуми́.
ШУРША́ТЬ I.; шуршу́, шурши́шь; шурши́.
ШУТИ́ТЬ I.; шучу́, шу́тишь.

Щ

ЩАДИ́ТЬ I.; щажу́, щади́шь.

ЩЕБЕТА́ТЬ I.; щебечу́, щебе́чешь; щебечи́.

ЩЕКОТА́ТЬ I.; щекочу́[1], щеко́чешь; щекочи́.

ЩЕКОТИ́ТЬ I.; щекочу́[2], щеко́тишь.

ЩЕПА́ТЬ I.; щеплю́, ще́плешь (and щепа́ю, щепа́ешь); щепли́ (and щепа́й); ще́панный; щепля́ (and щепа́я).

ЩИПА́ТЬ I.; щиплю́, щи́плешь (and щипа́ю, щипа́ешь); щипли́ (and щипа́й); щи́панный; щипля́ (and щипа́я).

Э

ЭКОНО́МИТЬ I.; эконо́млю, эконо́мишь; эконо́мь.

Ю

ЮТИ́ТЬСЯ I.; ючу́сь, юти́шься.

Я

ЯВИ́ТЬ Р.; явлю́, я́вишь; я́вленный.

ЯЗВИ́ТЬ I.; язвлю́, язви́шь.

353